The Sporting News

PRO FOOTBALL GUIDE

1 9 9 5   E D I T I O N

Editors/Pro Football Guide
CRAIG CARTER
DAVE SLOAN

—— PUBLISHING CO. ——

Francis P. Pandolfi, Chairman; **Nicholas H. Niles,** President and Chief Executive Officer; **Francis X. Farrell,** Senior Vice President, Publisher; **John D. Rawlings,** Senior Vice President, Editorial Director; **John Kastberg,** Vice President, General Manager; **Kathy Kinkeade,** Vice President, Production; **Mike Nahrstedt,** Managing Editor; **Mike Huguenin,** Assistant Managing Editor; **Joe Hoppel,** Senior Editor; **Tom Dienhart and Dave Sloan,** Associate Editors; **Craig Carter,** Statistical Editor; **George Puro and Kyle Veltrop,** Assistant Editors; **Graham Boain, Jay Davis and Robb McSorley,** Editorial Assistant; **Fred Barnes,** Director of Graphics; **Angie Blackwell,** Art Director; **Steve Levin,** Photo Editor; **Gary Brinker,** Director, Information Systems; **Bob Parajon,** Prepress Director; **Patrick Koliebol,** Network Manager; **Terry Shea,** Database Analyst; **Marilyn Kasal,** Production Manager; **Mike Bruner,** Graphics Network Manager; **Michael Behrens,** Macintosh Production Artist; **Vern Kasal,** Composing Room Supervisor.

A Times Mirror
Company

CONTENTS

ON THE COVER: San Francisco wide receiver Jerry Rice had a monstrous 1994 season. He led the NFL with 1,499 yards receiving, passed Jim Brown on the career touchdowns list (finishing with 139) and helped the 49ers win their record fifth Super Bowl title. (Photo by Stephen Dunn/Allsport)

Spine photo of Emmitt Smith by Doug DeVoe/The Sporting News.

NFL week-by-week and postseason highlights written by Tom Dienhart, Mike Huguenin and Dave Sloan of THE SPORTING NEWS.

NFL statistics compiled by Elias Sports Bureau, New York.

ISBN: 0-89204-525-6 (perfect-bound)
       0-89204-527-2 (comb-bound)

10 9 8 7 6 5 4 3 2 1

1995 SEASON

NFL directory

Team information

Schedule

College draft

Playoff plan

NFL DIRECTORY

COMMISSIONER'S OFFICE

Address
410 Park Avenue
New York, NY 10022
Phone
212-758-1500
212-826-3454 (FAX)
Commissioner
Paul Tagliabue
President
Neil Austrian
Executive vice president and league counsel
Jay Moyer
V.P. of communications and gov't affairs
Joe Browne
Vice president of business development
Roger Goodell
V.P. of broadcasting and productions
Val Pinchbeck Jr.
Chief financial officer
Tom Spock
Executive director of special events
Jim Steeg
Vice president-internal audit
Tom Sullivan

Exec. V.P. for labor rel./chairman NFLMC
Harold Henderson
Vice president/general counsel
Dennis Curran
V.P. for operations and compliance
Peter Ruocco
Dir. of player personnel/football operations
Joel Bussert
Director of player programs
Lem Burnham
Director of communications
Greg Aiello
Director of international public relations
Pete Abitante
Director of information, AFC
Leslie Hammond
Director of information, NFC
Reggie Roberts
Director of broadcasting services
Dick Maxwell
Director of broadcasting research
Joe Ferreira
Asst. dir. of broadcasting/productions
Nancy Behar

Dir. club relations/stadium operations
Joe Ellis
Dir. of game operations/league secretary
Jan Van Duser
Director of football development
Gene Washington
Assistant director of game operations
Tim Davey
Director of administration
John Buzzeo
Comptroller
Joe Siclare
Director of officiating
Jerry Seeman
Assistant director of officiating
Jack Reader
Supervisors of officials
Leo Miles
Ron DeSouza
Director of security
Warren Welsh
Assistant director of security
Charles Jackson Jr.

OTHER ORGANIZATIONS

NFL MANAGEMENT COUNCIL
Address
410 Park Avenue, 7th Floor
New York, NY 10022
Phone
212-758-1500
212-759-6367 (FAX)
Exec. V.P. for labor rel./chairman NFLMC
Harold Henderson
Vice president and general counsel
Dennis Curran
Director of labor relations
Lal Heneghan
Labor relations counsel
Belinda Lerner
Rapheal Prevot
V.P. of operations and compliance
Peter Ruocco
Director of compliance
Bill Duffy
Director of labor operations
Peter Hadhazy
Director of player programs
Lem Burnham
Director of player personnel
Joel Bussert

PRO FOOTBALL HALL OF FAME
Address
2121 George Halas Drive, N.W.
Canton, OH 44708
Phone
216-456-8207
216-456-8175 (FAX)
Executive director
Pete Elliott
Vice president/public relations
Don R. Smith
Vice president/operations
John W. Bankert

NFL ALUMNI ASSOCIATION
Address
6550 N. Federal Highway
Suite 400
Ft. Lauderdale, FL 33308-1400
Phone
305-492-1220
305-492-8297 (FAX)
Executive director/CEO
Frank Krauser
Vice president/alumni relations
To be announced
Chairman of the board
Donny Anderson
Director of public relations
Remy Mackowski

NFL PROPERTIES
Address
410 Park Avenue
New York, NY 10022
Phone
212-838-0660
212-758-4239 (FAX)
Interim chief operating officer
Sara Levinson
V.P., world wide retail licensing
Jim Connelly
V.P., development/special events
Don Garber
V.P., marketing/sales
Jim Schwebel

NFL PLAYERS ASSOCIATION
Address
2021 L Street, N.W.
Washington, DC 20036
Phone
202-463-2200
202-857-0380 (FAX)
Executive director
Gene Upshaw
Assistant executive director
Doug Allen
Dir. P.R. and NFLPA retired players org.
Frank Woschitz
General counsel
Richard Berthelsen
Director of communications
Carl Francis

NFL FILMS, INC.
Address
330 Fellowship Road
Mt. Laurel, NJ 08054
Phone
609-778-1600
609-722-6779 (FAX)
President
Steve Sabol

PRO FOOTBALL WRITERS OF AMERICA
President
Len Pasquarelli, Atlanta Journal-Constitution
First vice president
Steve Schoenfeld, Arizona Republic
Second vice president
John Clayton, Tacoma Morning News Tribune
Secretary/treasurer
Howard Balzer

ARIZONA CARDINALS
NFC EASTERN DIVISION

1994 REVIEW

RESULTS

Sept.	4—at L.A. Rams	L	12-14
Sept.	11—N.Y. GIANTS	L	17-20
Sept.	18—at Cleveland	L	0-32
Sept.	25—Open date		
Oct.	2—MINNESOTA	W	17-7
Oct.	9—at Dallas	L	3-38
Oct.	16—at Was. (OT)	W	19-16
Oct.	23—DALLAS	L	21-28
Oct.	30—PITTSBURGH (OT)	W	20-17
Nov.	6—at Philadelphia	L	7-17
Nov.	13—at N.Y. Giants	W	10-9
Nov.	20—PHILADELPHIA	W	12-6
Nov.	27—CHICAGO (OT)	L	16-19
Dec.	4—at Houston	W	30-12
Dec.	11—WASHINGTON	W	17-15
Dec.	18—CINCINNATI	W	28-7
Dec.	24—at Atlanta	L	6-10

RECORDS/RANKINGS

1994 regular-season record: 8-8 (3rd in NFC East); 4-4 in division; 5-7 in conference; 5-3 at home; 3-5 on road.
Team record last five years: 28-52 (.350, ranks 24th in league in that span).
1994 team rankings:

	No.	NFC	NFL
Total offense	*287.9	13	25
Rushing offense	*97.5	7	17
Passing offense	*190.4	12	22
Scoring offense	235	14	27
Total defense	*275.5	2	3
Rushing defense	*85.6	4	4
Passing defense	*189.9	2	4
Scoring defense	267	2	4
Takeaways	36	1	4
Giveaways	29	9	14
Turnover differential	7	T4	T8
Sacks	35	7	13
Sacks allowed	34	9	16

*Yards per game.

TEAM LEADERS

Scoring (kicking): Greg Davis, 77 pts. (17/17 PATs, 20/26 FGs).
Scoring (touchdowns): Larry Centers, 42 pts. (5 rushing, 2 receiving).
Passing: Jay Schroeder, 1,510 yds. (238 att., 133 comp., 55.9%, 4 TDs, 7 int.).
Rushing: Ron Moore, 780 yds. (232 att., 3.4 avg., 4 TDs).
Receptions: Larry Centers, 77 (647 yds., 8.4 avg., 2 TDs).
Interceptions: Aeneas Williams, 9 (89 yds., 0 TDs).
Sacks: Eric Swann, 7.0.
Punting: Jeff Feagles, 40.8 avg. (98 punts, 3,997 yds., 0 blocked).
Punt returns: Patrick Robinson, 7.0 avg. (41 att., 285 yds., 0 TDs).
Kickoff returns: Chuck Levy, 19.7 avg. (26 att., 513 yds., 0 TDs).

1995 SEASON

CLUB DIRECTORY

President
William V. Bidwill
Head coach
Buddy Ryan
General manager
Joe Woolley
Vice president
Larry Wilson
Vice president
William Bidwill Jr.
Vice president, sales
John Shean
Secretary and general counsel
Thomas J. Guilfoil
Treasurer/chief financial officer
Charley Schlegel
Director/marketing
Joe Castor
Ticket manager
Steve Bomar
Director/community affairs
Adele Harris
Director/public relations
Paul Jensen
Media coordinator
Greg Gladysiewski
Dir./Hispanic market dev.
Gina Quintana
Director/college scouting
Bo Bolinger
Director/pro scouting
Keith Kidd
Scouts
Jerry Hardaway
Leland Kendall
Bob Mazie
Cole Proctor

Head coach
Buddy Ryan
Assistant coaches
Dave Atkins (off. coordinator)
Matt Cavanaugh (quarterbacks)
Rex Ryan (linebackers)
Ronnie Jones (def. coordinator)
George Martinez (running backs)
Dan Neal (offensive line)
Ted Plumb (receivers/tight ends)
Al Roberts (special teams)
Bob Rogucki (strength and conditioning)
Jim Stanley (defensive line)
Rob Ryan (defensive backs)

Head trainer
John Omohundro
Assistant trainers
Jim Shearer
Jeff Herndon
Orthopedist
Russell Chick
Internist
Wayne Kuhl
Equipment manager
Mark Ahlemeier
Assistant equipment manager
Steve Christensen
Video director
Benny Greenberg

SCHEDULE

Sept.	3—at Washington	4:00
Sept.	10—PHILADELPHIA	5:00
Sept.	17—at Detroit	1:00
Sept.	24—at Dallas	3:00
Oct.	1—KANSAS CITY	1:00
Oct.	8—at N.Y. Giants	4:00
Oct.	15—WASHINGTON	1:00
Oct.	22—Open date	
Oct.	29—SEATTLE	2:00
Nov.	5—at Denver	2:00
Nov.	12—MINNESOTA	2:00
Nov.	19—at Carolina	1:00
Nov.	26—ATLANTA	2:00
Nov.	30—N.Y. GIANTS (Thur.)	6:00
Dec.	9—at San Diego (Sat.)	1:00
Dec.	17—at Philadelphia	1:00
Dec.	25—DALLAS (Mon.)	7:00

All times are for home team.
All games Sunday unless noted.

DRAFT CHOICES

Frank Sanders, WR, Auburn (second round/47th pick overall).
Stoney Case, QB, New Mexico (3/80).
Cedric Davis, DB, Tenn. State (5/150).
Lance Scott, C, Utah (5/165).
Tito Paul, DB, Ohio State (5/167).
Anthony Bridges, DB, North Texas (6/205).
Billy Williams, WR, Tennessee (7/212).
Wesley Leasy, LB, Miss. State (7/224).
Chad Eaton, DT, Washington St. (7/241).

1995 SEASON

TRAINING CAMP ROSTER

No.	QUARTERBACKS	Ht./Wt.	Born	NFL Exp.	College	How acq.	'94 Games GP/GS
7	Bonds, John	6-4/230	12-6-70	1	Northern Arizona	FA/95	0/0
16	Buck, Mike	6-3/227	4-22-67	4	Maine	FA/95	0/0
15	Case, Stoney	6-2/206	7-7-72	R	New Mexico	D3/95	—
17	Krieg, Dave	6-1/202	10-20-58	16	Milton College (Wis.)	FA/95	*14/7
	RUNNING BACKS						
37	Centers, Larry	5-11/215	6-1-68	6	Stephen F. Austin State	D5/90	16/5
26	Dunson, Walter	5-8/173	10-24-70	1	Middle Tennessee State	FA/95	0/0
49	Gant, Eric (FB)	6-2/245	10-13-70	1	Grambling State	FA/95	0/0
32	Gray, Oscar (FB)	6-1/265	9-25-72	R	Arkansas	FA/95	—
23	Hearst, Garrison	5-11/215	1-4-71	3	Georgia	D1/93	8/0
22	Higgs, Mark	5-7/199	4-11-66	8	Kentucky	FA/94	*11/1
	Levy, Chuck	6-0/197	1-7-72	R	Arizona	D2/94	—
33	Rivers, Terrance	5-9/183	2-10-72	R	The Citadel	FA/95	—
31	Terry, Ryan	5-11/203	9-20-71	R	Iowa	FA/95	—
	RECEIVERS						
83	Edwards, Anthony	5-10/190	5-26-66	6	New Mexico Highlands	FA/91	0/0
86	Fann, Chad (TE)	6-3/250	6-7-70	3	Florida A&M	FA/93	16/9
87	Frazier, Lamont (TE)	6-2/245	3-23-72	R	Missouri	FA/95	—
89	Gaines, Wendall (TE/DT)	6-4/293	1-17-72	2	Oklahoma State	FA/94	0/0
18	Howard, Ed	6-4/195	1-14-73	R	Rice	FA/95	—
82	Knox, Kevin	6-3/195	1-30-71	1	Florida State	FA/94	2/0
4	Levy, Chuck (KR)	6-0/197	1-7-72	2	Arizona	D2/94	11/0
48	McBride, Oscar (TE)	6-5/266	7-23-72	R	Notre Dame	FA/95	—
85	Moore, Rob	6-3/205	9-27-68	6	Syracuse	T-NYJ/95	*16/16
80	Reeves, Bryan (KR)	5-11/195	7-10-70	2	Nevada	FA/94	14/0
44	Samuels, Terry (TE)	6-2/254	9-27-70	2	Kentucky	D6/94	16/6
81	Sanders, Frank	6-1/202	2-17-73	R	Auburn	D2/95	—
12	Turner, Cornelius	6-0/176	1-4-72	R	Mississippi Valley State	FA/95	—
84	Williams, Billy (KR)	5-11/175	6-7-71	R	Tennessee	D7/95	—
	OFFENSIVE LINEMEN						
69	Askin, Mark (T)	6-4/295	8-1-71	R	Kentucky	FA/95	—
74	Booth, Blayne (T)	6-4/259	5-27-70	R	Texas-El Paso	FA/95	—
62	Coleman, Ben (T)	6-6/335	5-18-71	3	Wake Forest	D2/93	15/13
79	Cunningham, Ed (C)	6-3/285	8-17-69	4	Washington	D3/92	16/16
76	Davidson, Will (G/T)	6-4/298	1-26-72	R	Baylor	FA/95	—
65	Dye, Ernest (G)	6-6/325	7-15-71	3	South Carolina	D1/93	16/16
72	Gentry, Mike (G)	6-0/269	....	R	Eastern Kentucky	FA/95	—
66	Hardy, Sam (G)	6-2/280	8-7-72	R	Carson-Newman (Tenn.)	FA/95	—
61	Jones, Todd (C)	6-3/295	7-3-67	3	Henderson State (Ark.)	FA/95	0/0
67	Love, Duval (G)	6-3/288	6-24-63	11	UCLA	FA/95	*16/16
75	Meyer, Pat	6-0/274	4-4-72	R	Colorado State	FA/95	—
60	Redmon, Anthony (G)	6-4/308	4-6-71	2	Auburn	D5/94	6/5
70	Scott, Lance (C)	6-3/285	2-15-72	R	Utah	D5/95	—
71	Tharpe, Larry (T)	6-4/299	11-19-70	4	Tennessee State	FA/95	0/0
	DEFENSIVE LINEMEN						
63	Bankston, Michael	6-3/280	3-12-70	4	Sam Houston State	D4/92	16/16
73	Barrie, Sebastian (E)	6-2/280	5-26-70	3	Liberty (Va.)	FA/94	10/0
78	Brown, Chad (E)	6-7/265	7-9-71	3	Mississippi	D8/93	8/2
76	Drake, Jerry (E)	6-4/292	7-9-69	R	Hastings College (Neb.)	FA/95	—
93	Dunbar, Karl (E)	6-4/275	5-18-67	4	Louisiana State	FA/95	4/0
90	Eaton, Chad (T)	6-4/292	4-6-72	R	Washington State	D7/95	—
92	England, Eric (E)	6-2/283	3-25-71	2	Texas A&M	D3/94	11/1
97	Hooks, Bryan (E)	6-3/286	9-15-70	1	Arizona State	FA/95	0/0
74	Lopez, Justin	6-4/300	....	R	Pittsburgh	FA/95	—
96	Simmons, Clyde (E)	6-6/280	8-4-64	10	Western Carolina	FA/94	16/16
98	Swann, Eric (T)	6-5/295	8-16-70	5	Wake Technical (N.C.)	D1/91	16/16
94	Wilson, Bernard	6-2/295	8-17-70	2	Tennessee State	W-TB/94	*14/12
	LINEBACKERS						
54	Hardy, Darryl	6-2/230	11-22-68	1	Tennessee	FA/95	0/0
39	Harper, Jermaine	6-1/235	....	R	Northeast Oklahoma	FA/95	—
58	Hill, Eric	6-2/255	11-14-66	7	Louisiana State	D1/89	16/15
56	Irving, Terry	6-0/224	7-3-71	2	McNeese State	D4/94	16/0
53	Jax, Garth	6-2/250	9-16-63	10	Florida State	PlanB/89	16/0
59	Joyner, Seth	6-2/235	11-18-64	10	Texas-El Paso	FA/94	16/16
57	Kirk, Randy	6-2/231	12-27-64	8	San Diego State	FA/94	16/0
52	Leasy, Wesley	6-2/234	9-7-71	R	Mississippi State	D7/95	—
50	Merritt, David	6-1/237	9-8-71	3	North Carolina State	FA/93	16/0
95	Miller, Jamir	6-4/242	11-19-73	2	UCLA	D1/94	16/0
51	Shanks, Simon	6-1/215	10-16-71	R	Coahoma J.C. (Miss.)	FA/95	—

No.	DEFENSIVE BACKS	Ht./Wt.	Born	NFL Exp.	College	How acq.	'94 Games GP/GS
41	Bowens, Larry	6-0/166	8-10-72	R	Mississippi Valley State	FA/95	—
46	Alexander, Brent (S)	5-10/184	7-10-70	2	Tennessee State	FA/94	16/7
36	Bridges, Anthony (CB)	5-9/181	1-1-73	R	North Texas	D6/95	—
25	Brooks, Carlos	6-0/200	5-8-71	R	Bowling Green State	FA/94	—
38	Burke, Patrick (CB)	5-11/180	11-6-68	1	Fresno City J.C.	FA/95	0/0
21	Davis, Cedric (CB)	5-9/170	9-7-72	R	Tennessee State	D5/95	—
20	Gillock, Mike	5-10/175	5-20-72	R	Indianapolis	FA/95	—
34	Hoage, Terry (S)	6-2/201	4-11-62	12	Georgia	FA/94	16/16
24	Hunter, Patrick (CB)	5-11/186	10-24-64	10	Nevada	FA/95	*5/5
42	Lassiter, Kwamie	5-11/180	12-3-69	R	Kansas	FA/95	—
29	Lynch, Lorenzo (S)	5-11/200	4-6-63	9	Sacramento State	PlanB/90	15/15
45	McGhee, Eric	6-0/193	7-21-72	R	South Carolina State	FA/95	—
27	Paul, Tito	6-0/195	5-24-72	R	Ohio State	D5/95	—
47	West, Frank	5-10/170	3-21-72	R	Illinois State	FA/95	—
35	Williams, Aeneas (CB)	5-10/190	1-29-68	5	Southern	D3/90	16/16
	SPECIALISTS						
13	Caflisch, Andy (P)	6-2/190	8-7-70	R	Wisconsin-Stout	FA/95	—
5	Davis, Greg (K)	6-0/205	10-29-65	8	The Citadel	PlanB/91	14/0
10	Feagles, Jeff (P)	6-1/205	3-7-66	8	Miami (Fla.)	FA/94	16/0
6	Maston, Richard (K)	5-11/195	6-2-72	R	Temple	FA/95	—

*Higgs played 5 games with Dolphins and 6 games with Cardinals in '94; Hunter played 5 games with Seahawks; Krieg played 14 games with Lions; Love played 16 games with Steelers; Moore played 16 games with Jets; Wilson played 1 game with Buccaneers and 13 games with Cardinals.

Also played with Cardinals in '94: QB Steve Beuerlein (9 games); DE Michael Brandon (1); WR Gary Clark (15); T Rick Cunningham (11); CB Herschel Currie (1); S Odie Harris (13); FB Frank Harvey (2); FB Brian Henesey (3); WR Randal Hill (14); LB Wilber Marshall (15); RB Fred McAfee (7); DE Keith McCants (8); QB Jim McMahon (2); RB Ronald Moore (16); CB Chris Oldham (11); K Todd Peterson (2); WR Ricky Proehl (16); WR Patrick Robinson (15); QB Jay Schroeder (9); T Luis Sharpe (11); C Mark Tucker (16); TE Derek Ware (15); S Andre Waters (12); CB James Williams (15); G Joe Wolf (7); RB Barry Word (1).

Abbreviations: D1—draft pick, first round; SupD2—supplemental draft pick, second round; W-Den—waivers acquisition from Denver; T-Sea—trade acquisition from Seattle; PlanB—Plan B free-agent acquisition; FA—free-agent acquisition (other than Plan B).

MISCELLANEOUS TEAM DATA

Stadium (capacity, surface):
Sun Devil Stadium
(73,521, grass)

Business address:
P.O. Box 888
Phoenix, AZ 85001-0888

Business phone:
602-379-0101

Ticket Information:
602-379-0102

Team colors:
Cardinal red, black and white

Flagship radio station:
KESZ, 99.9 FM

Training site:
Northern Arizona University
Flagstaff, Ariz.
602-379-0101

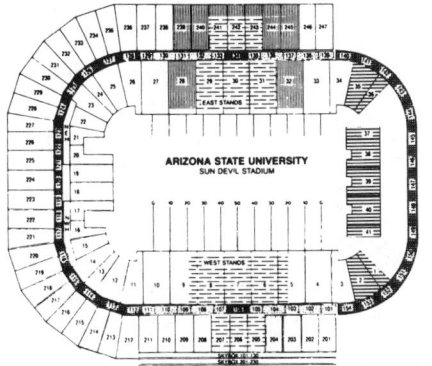

ATLANTA FALCONS
NFC WESTERN DIVISION

1994 REVIEW

RESULTS

Sept. 4—at Detroit (OT)	L	28-31
Sept. 11—L.A. RAMS	W	31-13
Sept. 18—KANSAS CITY	L	10-30
Sept. 25—at Washington	W	27-20
Oct. 2—at L.A. Rams	W	8-5
Oct. 9—TAMPA BAY	W	34-13
Oct. 16—SAN FRANCISCO	L	3-42
Oct. 23—at L.A. Raiders	L	17-30
Oct. 30—Open date		
Nov. 6—SAN DIEGO	W	10-9
Nov. 13—at New Orleans	L	32-33
Nov. 20—at Denver	L	28-32
Nov. 27—PHILADELPHIA	W	28-21
Dec. 4—at San Francisco	L	14-50
Dec. 11—NEW ORLEANS	L	20-29
Dec. 18—at G. Bay (Milw.)	L	17-21
Dec. 24—ARIZONA	W	10-6

RECORDS/RANKINGS

1994 regular-season record: 7-9 (T2nd in NFC West); 2-4 in division; 6-6 in conference; 5-3 at home; 2-6 on road.
Team record last five years: 34-46 (.425, ranks T19th in league in that span).

1994 team rankings:	No.	NFC	NFL
Total offense	*335.1	3	7
Rushing offense	*78.1	14	28
Passing offense	*257.0	3	5
Scoring offense	317	8	15
Total defense	*364.3	14	27
Rushing defense	*105.8	7	14
Passing defense	*258.5	14	27
Scoring defense	385	12	24
Takeaways	33	T5	T8
Giveaways	36	13	24
Turnover differential	-3	11	T18
Sacks	32	8	14
Sacks allowed	37	12	19

   *Yards per game.

TEAM LEADERS

Scoring (kicking): Norm Johnson, 95 pts. (32/32 PATs, 21/25 FGs).
Scoring (touchdowns): Terance Mathis, 70 pts. (11 receiving, 2 2-pt. conv.).
Passing: Jeff George, 3,734 yds. (524 att., 322 comp., 61.5%, 23 TDs, 18 int.).
Rushing: Craig Heyward, 779 yds. (183 att., 4.3 avg., 7 TDs).
Receptions: Terance Mathis, 111 (1,342 yds., 12.1 avg., 11 TDs).
Interceptions: D.J. Johnson, 5 (0 yds., 0 TDs).
Sacks: Chuck Smith, 11.0.
Punting: Harold Alexander, 39.9 avg. (71 punts, 2,836 yds., 0 blocked).
Punt returns: Clarence Verdin, 4.9 avg. (23 att., 113 yds., 0 TDs).
Kickoff returns: Clarence Verdin, 23.3 avg. (44 att., 1,026 yds., 0 TDs).

1995 SEASON

CLUB DIRECTORY

Chairman of the board
   Rankin M. Smith Sr.
President
   Taylor Smith
Special assistant to president
   Jerry Rhea
Vice president and chief financial officer
   Jim Hay
Administrative assistant
   Kevin Anthony
Vice president of player personnel
   Ken Herock
Director of administration
   Rob Jackson
Marketing representatives
   Todd Marble
   John O. Knox
   Trisha Williamson
Director of public relations
   Charlie Taylor
Assistant director of public relations
   Frank Kleha
Public relations assistant
   Gary Glenn
Director of community relations
   Carol Breeding
Coordinator of player programs
   Billy "White Shoes" Johnson
Director of ticket operations
   Jack Ragsdale
Asst. director of ticket operations
   Mike Jennings
Vault manager
   Thomas Meunier
Administrative assistants/player personnel
   Danny Mock
   LaDonna Jones
Scouts
   Bill Baker
   Scott Campbell
   Dick Corrick
   Elbert Dubenion
   Bill Groman

Head coach:
   June Jones
Assistant coaches
   Keith Armstrong (defense)
   Mouse Davis (quarterbacks)
   Frank Gansz (assistant head coach/special teams)
   Joe Haering (def. coordinator)
   Milt Jackson (assistant head coach/wide receivers)
   Tim Jorgensen (strength and conditioning)
   Bill Kollar (defensive line)
   Bob Palcic (offensive line)
   Rod Rust (defense)
   Ollie Wilson (running backs)

Director of pro personnel
   Chuck Connor
Director of player development
   Tommy Nobis
Controller
   Wallace Norman
Accounting
   Carolyn Cathey
Tax advisor
   Hamilton Childree
Trainer
   Ron Medlin
Team doctors
   Dr. Charles Harrison
   Dr. John Garrett
Equipment manager
   Craig Camponozzi
Sr. equip. dir./gameday op. coord.
   Horace Daniel
Video director
   Tom Atcheson

SCHEDULE

Sept. 3—CAROLINA	1:00
Sept. 10—at San Francisco	1:00
Sept. 17—at New Orleans	12:00
Sept. 24—N.Y. JETS	4:00
Oct. 1—NEW ENGLAND	1:00
Oct. 8—Open date	
Oct. 12—at St. Louis (Thur.)	7:00
Oct. 22—at Tampa Bay	1:00
Oct. 29—DALLAS	1:00
Nov. 5—DETROIT	1:00
Nov. 12—at Buffalo	1:00
Nov. 19—ST. LOUIS	1:00
Nov. 26—at Arizona	2:00
Dec. 3—at Miami	1:00
Dec. 10—NEW ORLEANS	1:00
Dec. 17—at Carolina	1:00
Dec. 24—SAN FRANCISCO	1:00

   All times are for home team.
   All games Sunday unless noted.

DRAFT CHOICES

Devin Bush, DB, Florida State (first round/26th pick overall).
Ronald Davis, DB, Tennessee (2/41).
Lorenzo Styles, LB, Ohio State (3/77).
Roell Preston, WR, Mississippi (5/145).
Travis Hall, DT, Brigham Young (6/181).
John Burrough, DE, Wyoming (7/245).

TRAINING CAMP ROSTER

No.	QUARTERBACKS	Ht./Wt.	Born	NFL Exp.	College	How acq.	'94 Games GP/GS
1	George, Jeff	6-4/210	12-8-67	6	Illinois	T-Ind/94	16/16
3	Hebert, Bobby	6-4/215	8-19-60	10	Northwestern State	FA/93	8/0
8	Jones, Preston	6-3/223	7-3-70	1	Georgia	FA/95	0/0
7	Klein, Perry	6-2/218	3-25-71	2	C.W. Post (N.Y.)	D4/94	2/0
	RUNNING BACKS						
32	Anderson, Jamal	5-10/240	3-6-72	2	Utah	D7/94	3/0
34	Heyward, Craig (FB)	5-11/265	9-26-66	8	Pittsburgh	FA/94	16/11
	RECEIVERS						
89	Birden, J.J.	5-9/170	6-16-65	6	Oregon	FA/90	*13/13
19	Dixon, Corey	5-7/155	2-16-72	1	Nebraska	FA/94	0/0
87	Emanuel, Bert	5-10/175	10-27-70	2	Rice	D2/94	16/16
82	Harris, Leonard	5-8/162	11-27-60	10	Texas Tech	FA/94	8/2
88	LeBel, Harper (TE)	6-4/255	7-14-63	7	Colorado State	PlanB/91	0/0
80	Lewis, Nate (KR)	5-11/198	10-19-66	6	Oregon Tech	FA/95	*13/0
86	Lyons, Mitch (TE)	6-4/265	5-13-70	3	Michigan State	D6/93	7/2
81	Mathis, Terance (KR)	5-10/180	6-7-67	6	New Mexico	FA/94	16/16
21	Metcalf, Eric (KR)	5-10/190	1-23-68	7	Texas	FA/95	*16/8
85	Preston, Roell	5-10/187	6-23-72	R	Mississippi	D5/95	—
15	Rogers, Joe	5-7/161	5-23-71	1	Texas Southern	FA/94	0/0
83	Sanders, Ricky	5-11/180	8-30-62	10	Southwest Texas State	FA/94	14/12
84	Spencer, Darryl	5-8/172	3-21-70	2	Miami (Fla.)	FA/94	8/0
	OFFENSIVE LINEMEN						
65	Fortin, Roman (G/C)	6-5/295	2-26-67	4	San Diego State	PlanB/92	16/16
75	Kennedy, Lincoln (G/T)	6-6/350	2-12-71	3	Washington	D1/93	16/2
94	Norman, Todd (T)	6-5/300	9-11-71	1	Notre Dame	FA/95	0/0
64	Pahukoa, Jeff (G/T)	6-2/298	2-9-69	5	Washington	FA/95	0/0
62	Richards, Dave (G)	6-5/310	4-11-66	8	UCLA	FA/94	15/15
	Selby, Rob (G)	6-3/286	10-11-67	5	Auburn	FA/95	*2/0
61	Tobeck, Robbie (C)	6-4/287	3-6-70	2	Washington State	FA/93	5/0
70	Whitfield, Bob (T)	6-5/300	10-18-71	4	Stanford	D1a/92	16/16
72	Zandofsky, Mike (C/G)	6-2/305	11-30-65	7	Washington	FA/94	16/16
	DEFENSIVE LINEMEN						
68	Agee, Mel	6-5/298	11-22-68	5	Illinois	FA/92	16/6
73	Anderson, Dunstan (E)	6-4/254	12-31-70	2	Tulsa	FA/94	1/0
92	Archambeau, Lester (E)	6-5/275	6-27-67	6	Stanford	T-GB/93	16/12
96	Brewer, George (T)	6-5/295	6-11-69	1	Savannah State	FA/95	0/0
91	Burrough, John	6-5/265	5-17-72	R	Wyoming	D7/95	—
56	Doleman, Chris (E)	6-5/275	10-16-61	11	Pittsburgh	T-Min/94	14/7
54	Donahue, Mitch (E)	6-3/247	2-4-68	5	Wyoming	FA/95	*3/0
67	Gardner, Moe (NT)	6-2/265	8-10-68	5	Illinois	D4/91	16/16
98	Hall, Travis	6-5/278	8-3-72	R	Brigham Young	D6/95	—
95	Holt, Pierce	6-4/275	1-1-62	9	Angelo State (Tex.)	FA/93	12/12
69	Williams, Thomas (E)	6-3/274	12-19-70	1	Wyoming	FA/94	0/0
	LINEBACKERS						
50	George, Ron	6-2/225	3-20-70	3	Stanford	D5/93	16/9
53	Gordon, Dwayne	6-1/240	11-2-69	3	New Hampshire	FA/93	16/0
57	Matthews, Clay	6-2/245	3-15-56	18	Southern California	FA/94	15/15
55	Miller, Maurice	6-3/220	9-6-69	1	Wake Forest	FA/95	0/0
90	Smith, Chuck (E)	6-2/257	12-21-69	4	Tennessee	D2/92	15/10
59	Styles, Lorenzo	6-1/244	1-31-74	R	Ohio State	D3/95	—
99	Talley, Darryl	6-4/235	7-10-60	13	West Virginia	FA/95	*16/16
52	Tippins, Ken	6-1/235	7-22-66	7	Middle Tennessee State	FA/90	16/7
58	Tuggle, Jessie	5-11/230	2-14-65	9	Valdosta (Ga.) State	FA/87	16/16
	DEFENSIVE BACKS						
42	Bush, Devin (S)	5-11/208	7-3-73	R	Florida State	D1/95	—
28	Davis, Ronald (CB)	5-10/190	2-24-72	R	Tennessee	D2/95	—
20	Edwards, Brad (S)	6-2/207	3-22-66	8	South Carolina	FA/94	4/0
33	Evans, Bobby (S)	6-2/200	12-2-67	1	Southern Arkansas	FA/95	0/0
47	Harper, Roger (S)	6-2/223	10-26-70	3	Ohio State	D2/93	10/10
39	Jack, Eric (CB)	5-10/177	4-19-72	2	New Mexico	FA/94	16/0
44	Johnson, D.J. (CB)	6-0/190	7-14-66	7	Kentucky	FA/95	*16/0
38	Miano, Rich (S)	6-1/200	9-3-62	11	Hawaii	FA/95	16/0
22	Montgomery, Alton (S)	6-0/205	6-16-68	6	Houston	T-Den/93	2/1
26	Phillips, Anthony (CB)	6-2/207	10-5-70	2	Texas A&M-Kingsville	D3/94	5/0
36	Ross, Kevin (S)	5-9/185	1-16-62	12	Temple	FA/94	16/16
37	Shelley, Elbert (CB)	5-11/190	12-24-64	9	Arkansas State	D11/87	16/0
24	Taylor, Terry (CB)	5-10/185	7-18-61	11	Southern Illinois	FA/95	*5/3
45	Walker, Darnell (CB)	5-8/168	1-17-70	3	Oklahoma	D7/93	16/5
46	Washington, Charles (S)	6-1/214	10-8-66	7	Cameron (Okla.)	FA/93	16/1

No.	SPECIALISTS	Ht./Wt.	Born	NFL Exp.	College	How acq.	'94 Games GP/GS
9	Johnson, Norm (K) 6-2/203		5-31-60	14	UCLA	FA/91	16/0
4	Stryzinski, Dan (P) 6-2/200		5-15-65	6	Indiana	FA/95	*16/0
2	Tyner, Scott (P) 6-1/189		4-11-72	2	Oklahoma State	FA/94	6/0

*Birden played 13 games with Chiefs in '94; Donahue played 3 games with Broncos; Lewis played 13 games with Bears; Metcalf played 16 games with Browns; Miano played 16 games with Eagles; Selby played 2 games with Eagles; Stryzinski played 16 games with Buccaneers; Talley played 16 games with Bills; Taylor played 5 games with Seahawks.

Also played with Falcons in '94: P Harold Alexander (15 games); S Scott Case (15); CB Vinnie Clark (11); T Irv Eatman (4); LB Darryl Ford (15); DT Bill Goldberg (5); T Mike Kenn (15); S Brett Maxie (4); WR David Mims (2); RB Erric Pegram (13); WR Andre Rison (15); G Jim Ritcher (2); RB Tony Smith (4); WR Clarence Verdin (12).

Abbreviations: D1—draft pick, first round; SupD2—supplemental draft pick, second round; W-Den—waivers acquisition from Denver; T-Sea—trade acquisition from Seattle; PlanB—Plan B free-agent acquisition; FA—free-agent acquisition (other than Plan B).

MISCELLANEOUS TEAM DATA

Stadium (capacity, surface):
Georgia Dome
(71,280, artificial)
Business address:
Atlanta Falcons Complex
2745 Burnett Road
Suwanee, Ga. 30174
Business phone:
404-945-1111
Ticket information:
404-223-8000
Team colors:
Black, red, silver and white
Flagship radio station:
WZGC, 92.9 FM
Training site:
Atlanta Falcons Complex
Suwanee, Ga.
404-945-1111

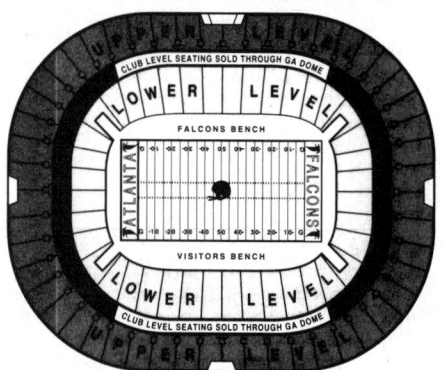

BUFFALO BILLS
AFC EASTERN DIVISION

1994 REVIEW

RESULTS

Sept. 4—N.Y. JETS	L	3-23
Sept. 11—at New England	W	38-35
Sept. 18—at Houston	W	15-7
Sept. 26—DENVER	W	27-20
Oct. 2—at Chicago	L	13-20
Oct. 9—MIAMI	W	21-11
Oct. 16—INDIANAPOLIS	L	17-27
Oct. 23—Open date		
Oct. 30—KANSAS CITY	W	44-10
Nov. 6—at N.Y. Jets	L	17-22
Nov. 14—at Pittsburgh	L	10-23
Nov. 20—GREEN BAY	W	29-20
Nov. 24—at Detroit	L	21-35
Dec. 4—at Miami	W	42-31
Dec. 11—MINNESOTA	L	17-21
Dec. 18—NEW ENGLAND	L	17-41
Dec. 24—at Indianapolis	L	9-10

RECORDS/RANKINGS

1994 regular-season record: 7-9 (4th in AFC East); 3-5 in division; 6-6 in conference; 4-4 at home; 3-5 on road.
Team record last five years: 56-24 (.700, ranks 2nd in league in that span).

1994 team rankings:	No.	AFC	NFL
Total offense	*327.8	5	10
Rushing offense	*114.4	5	8
Passing offense	*213.3	5	10
Scoring offense	340	T5	T11
Total defense	*323.4	8	17
Rushing defense	*94.7	4	8
Passing defense	*228.8	11	23
Scoring defense	356	12	22
Takeaways	28	T9	T18
Giveaways	34	10	T21
Turnover differential	-6	12	24
Sacks	25	13	26
Sacks allowed	41	10	22

*Yards per game.

TEAM LEADERS

Scoring (kicking): Steve Christie, 110 pts. (38/38 PATs, 24/28 FGs).
Scoring (touchdowns): Thurman Thomas, 54 pts. (7 rushing, 2 receiving).
Passing: Jim Kelly, 3,114 yds. (448 att., 285 comp., 63.6%, 22 TDs, 17 int.).
Rushing: Thurman Thomas, 1,093 yds. (287 att., 3.8 avg., 7 TDs).
Receptions: Andre Reed, 90 (1,303 yds., 14.5 avg., 8 TDs).
Interceptions: Matt Darby, 4 (20 yds., 0 TDs).
Sacks: Bruce Smith, 10.0.
Punting: Chris Mohr, 41.8 avg. (67 punts, 2,799 yds., 0 blocked).
Punt returns: Jeff Burris, 10.4 avg. (32 att., 332 yds., 0 TDs).
Kickoff returns: Yonel Jourdain, 22.3 avg. (27 att., 601 yds., 0 TDs).

1995 SEASON

CLUB DIRECTORY

President
Ralph C. Wilson Jr.
Exec. vice president/general manager
John Butler
Corporate vice president
Linda Bogdan
Treasurer
Jeffrey C. Littmann
Dir. of admin./ticket sales
Jerry Foran
Asst. general manager/business operations
Bill Munson
Director of business operations
Jim Overdorf
Controller
Frank Wojnicki
Director of merchandising
Christy Wilson Hofmann
Director of player/alumni relations
Jerry Butler
Director of marketing and sales
John Livsey
Dir. of public/community relations
Denny Lynch
Director of media relations
Scott Berchtold
Ticket director
June Foran
Video director
Henry Kunttu
Director of stadium operations
George Koch
Director of security
Bill Bambach
Stadium operations supervisor
Pete Riedy
Director of pro personnel
A.J. Smith
Director of player personnel
Dwight Adams

SCHEDULE

Sept. 3—at Denver	6:00
Sept. 10—CAROLINA	1:00
Sept. 17—INDIANAPOLIS	1:00
Sept. 24—Open date	
Oct. 2—at Cleveland (Mon.)	9:00
Oct. 8—N.Y. JETS	1:00
Oct. 15—SEATTLE	1:00
Oct. 23—at New Eng. (Mon.)	9:00
Oct. 29—at Miami	4:00
Nov. 5—at Indianapolis	1:00
Nov. 12—ATLANTA	1:00
Nov. 19—at N.Y. Jets	4:00
Nov. 26—NEW ENGLAND	1:00
Dec. 3—at San Francisco	5:00
Dec. 10—at St. Louis	12:00
Dec. 17—MIAMI	1:00
Dec. 24—HOUSTON	1:00

All times are for home team.
All games Sunday unless noted.

Vice president/head coach:
Marv Levy
Assistant coaches
Elijah Pitts (assistant head coach/running backs)
Tom Bresnahan (offensive coordinator/offensive line)
Ted Cottrell (linebackers)
Charlie Joiner (receivers)
Rusty Jones (strength & conditioning)
Don Lawrence (offensive quality control/tight ends)
Chuck Lester (def. quality control/admin. asst. to head coach)
Wade Phillips (def. coordinator)
Bruce DeHaven (special teams)
Dick Roach (defensive backs)
Dan Sekanovich (defensive line)
Jim Shofner (quarterbacks)

Scouts
Tom Beck
Doug Majeski
Buddy Nix
Bob Ryan
Chink Sengel
Dave G. Smith
Dave W. Smith
Head trainer
Ed Abramoski
Assistant trainers
Bud Carpenter
Bill Ford
Equipment manager
Dave Hojnowski
Asst. equipment manager
Woody Ribbeck

DRAFT CHOICES

Ruben Brown, G, Pittsburgh (first round/14th pick overall).
Todd Collins, QB, Michigan (2/45).
Marlon Kerner, DB, Ohio State (3/76).
Damien Covington, LB, N.C. State (3/96).
Ken Irvin, DB, Memphis (4/109).
Justin Armour, WR, Stanford (4/113).
Tony Cline, TE, Stanford (4/131).
John Holecek, LB, Illinois (5/144).
Shannon Clavelle, DE, Colorado (6/185).
Tom Nutten, C, Western Michigan (7/221).
Darick Holmes, RB, Portland State (7/244).

BUFFALO BILLS

1995 SEASON

BUFFALO BILLS

TRAINING CAMP ROSTER

No.	QUARTERBACKS	Ht./Wt.	Born	NFL Exp.	College	How acq.	'94 Games GP/GS
15	Collins, Todd	6-4/224	11-5-71	R	Michigan	D2/95	—
12	Kelly, Jim	6-3/226	2-14-60	10	Miami (Fla.)	D1/83	14/14
11	Strom, Rick	6-2/197	3-11-65	7	Georgia Tech	FA/94	0/0
10	Van Pelt, Alex	6-1/219	5-1-70	2	Pittsburgh	FA/94	0/0
	RUNNING BACKS						
45	Bender, Carey	5-8/185	1-28-72	R	Coe College (Ia.)	FA/95	—
49	Foster, Che' (FB)	6-2/240	1-16-73	R	Michigan	FA/95	—
35	Gardner, Carwell (FB)	6-2/244	11-27-66	6	Louisville	D2/90	16/7
44	Holmes, Darick	6-0/226	7-1-71	R	Portland State	D7b/95	—
26	Humphrey, Bobby	6-1/201	10-11-66	5	Alabama	FA/95	0/0
30	Jourdain, Yonel (KR)	5-11/204	4-20-71	2	Southern Illinois	FA/93	9/0
34	Thomas, Thurman	5-10/198	5-16-66	8	Oklahoma State	D2/88	15/15
33	Tindale, Tim	5-10/220	4-15-71	1	Western Ontario	FA/94	0/0
21	Turner, Nate	6-1/255	5-28-69	3	Nebraska	D6/92	13/0
	RECEIVERS						
42	Anderson, Jason	6-0/175	9-11-71	R	Eastern Washington	FA/95	—
19	Armour, Justin	6-4/221	1-1-73	R	Stanford	D4/95	—
81	Brooks, Bucky (KR)	6-0/190	1-22-71	2	North Carolina	D2/94	3/0
88	Cline, Tony (TE)	6-4/251	11-24-71	R	Stanford	D4/95	—
87	Coons, Robert (TE)	6-5/249	9-18-69	1	Pittsburgh	FA/95	0/0
85	Copeland, Russell (KR)	6-0/200	11-4-71	3	Memphis	D4/93	15/4
16	Evans, Randall	5-11/190	10-26-70	R	St. Augustine's (N.C.)	FA/95	—
17	Green, Eric	5-10/170	4-7-71	1	Illinois Benedictine	FA/95	0/0
19	Hill, Adrian	6-2/180	10-14-72	R	North Carolina State	FA/95	—
84	Johnson, Lonnie (TE)	6-3/230	2-14-71	2	Florida State	D2/94	10/1
86	Ofodile, A.J. (TE)	6-7/260	10-9-73	1	Missouri	D5/94	0/0
83	Reed, Andre	6-2/190	1-29-64	11	Kutztown (Pa.) State	D4/85	16/16
89	Tasker, Steve	5-9/181	4-10-62	11	Northwestern	W-Hou/86	14/0
82	Thomas, Damon	6-2/215	12-15-70	2	Wayne (Neb.) State	FA/94	3/0
18	Williams, Tyrone	6-5/220	3-26-70	3	Western Ontario	FA/95	0/0
	OFFENSIVE LINEMEN						
79	Brown, Ruben (T)	6-3/304	2-13-02	R	Pittsburgh	D1/95	—
62	Devlin, Mike (C/G)	6-1/293	11-16-69	3	Iowa	D5/93	16/0
70	Fina, John	6-4/285	3-11-69	4	Arizona	D1/92	12/12
76	Hoyem, Steve (T)	6-7/287	11-12-70	2	Stanford	FA/94	6/0
67	Hull, Kent (C)	6-5/284	1-13-61	9	Mississippi State	FA/86	16/16
68	Lacina, Corbin	6-4/297	11-2-70	3	Augustana (S.D.)	D6/93	11/10
63	Lingner, Adam (C)	6-4/268	11-2-60	13	Illinois	PlanB/89	16/0
72	Louchiey, Corey (T)	6-7/305	10-10-71	1	South Carolina	D3/94	0/0
64	Nutten, Tom (C/G)	6-4/276	6-8-71	R	Western Michigan	D7a/95	—
60	Ostroski, Jerry (G)	6-4/310	7-12-70	2	Tulsa	FA/93	4/3
74	Parker, Glenn (G/T)	6-5/305	4-22-66	6	Arizona	D3/90	16/16
71	Sheldon, Michael (G)	6-4/278	6-8-73	R	Grand Valley St. (Mich.)	FA/95	—
	DEFENSIVE LINEMEN						
93	Clavelle, Shannon (E)	6-2/283	12-12-73	R	Colorado	D6/95	—
98	Counts, Eric (NT)	6-2/275	1-11-72	R	North Carolina State	FA/95	—
90	Hansen, Phil (E)	6-5/278	5-20-68	5	North Dakota State	D2/91	16/16
77	Jeffcoat, Jim (E)	6-5/280	4-1-61	13	Arizona State	FA/95	*16/0
99	Patton, James	6-3/287	1-5-70	3	Texas	D2/92	11/0
75	Philion, Ed (T)	6-2/273	3-27-70	2	Ferris State (Mich.).	FA/94	4/0
94	Pike, Mark (E)	6-4/272	12-27-63	9	Georgia Tech	D7/86	16/0
78	Smith, Bruce (E)	6-4/273	6-18-63	11	Virginia Tech	D1/85	15/15
92	Washington, Ted (NT)	6-4/315	4-13-68	5	Louisville	FA/95	*15/15
	LINEBACKERS						
97	Bennett, Cornelius	6-2/238	8-25-66	9	Alabama	T-Ind/87	16/16
96	Brown, Monty	6-0/228	4-13-70	3	Ferris State (Mich.)	FA/93	3/0
57	Covington, Damien	5-11/236	12-4-72	R	North Carolina State	D3b/95	—
54	Damas, Herve	6-0/235	2-16-72	R	Hofstra	FA/95	—
53	Harvey, Steve	6-3/230	4-21-71	R	Kansas	FA/95	—
52	Holecek, John	6-2/238	5-7-72	R	Illinois	D5/95	—
55	Maddox, Mark	6-1/233	3-23-68	5	Northern Michigan	D9/91	15/14
95	Paup, Bryce	6-5/247	2-29-68	6	Northern Iowa	FA/95	*16/16
58	Perry, Marlo	6-4/250	8-25-72	2	Jackson State	D3/94	2/0
59	Rogers, Sam	6-3/245	5-30-70	2	Colorado	D2/94	14/0
50	White, David	6-2/235	2-27-70	2	Nebraska	FA/95	0/0
	DEFENSIVE BACKS						
22	Burris, Jeff	6-0/204	6-7-72	2	Notre Dame	D1/94	16/0
43	Darby, Matt (S)	6-1/200	11-19-68	4	UCLA	D5/92	16/16

No.	DEFENSIVE BACKS	Ht./Wt.	Born	NFL Exp.	College	How acq.	'94 Games GP/GS
41	Evans, Greg (S)	6-1/217	6-28-71	1	Texas Christian	FA/94	0/0
36	Glass, Myron (CB)	5-8/170	1-10-73	R	Northern Iowa	FA/95	—
47	Hendricks, Michael	6-0/190	2-24-73	R	Texas A&M	FA/95	—
27	Irvin, Ken (CB)	5-10/182	7-11-72	R	Memphis	D4/95	—
39	Johnson, Filmel	5-10/187	12-24-70	1	Illinois	D7/94	0/0
20	Jones, Henry (S)	5-11/197	12-29-67	5	Illinois	D1/91	16/16
46	Kerner, Marlon (CB)	5-10/187	3-18-73	R	Ohio State	D3/95	—
29	Lang, Le-Lo (CB)	5-11/185	1-23-67	5	Washington	FA/95	0/0
25	Quinn, Terry (S)	6-0/200	1-15-70	R	Louisville	FA/95	—
24	Schulz, Kurt (S)	6-1/208	12-12-68	4	Eastern Washington	D7/92	16/0
28	Smith, Thomas (CB)	5-11/188	12-5-70	3	North Carolina	D1/93	16/16
	SPECIALISTS						
2	Christie, Steve (K)	6-0/185	11-13-67	6	William & Mary	PlanB/92	16/0
1	Kratz, Steve (K)	6-2/185	12-16-70	1	Kutztown (Pa.)	FA/95	0/0
9	Mohr, Chris (P)	6-5/215	5-11-66	6	Alabama	FA/91	16/0

*Jeffcoat played 16 games with Cowboys in '94; Paup played 16 games with Packers; Washington played 15 games with Broncos.

Also played with Bills in '94: DE Oliver Barnett (16 games); WR Don Beebe (13); WR Bill Brooks (16); T Jerry Crafts (16); RB Kenneth Davis (16); G John Davis (16); S Mike Dumas (14); LB Keith Goganious (16); DB Jerome Henderson (12); NT Mike Lodish (15); TE Vince Marrow (10); TE Pete Metzelaars (16); LB Marvcus Patton (16); QB Frank Reich (16); LB Darryl Talley (16); CB Mickey Washington (16); NT Jeff Wright (12).

Abbreviations: D1—draft pick, first round; SupD2—supplemental draft pick, second round; W-Den—waivers acquisition from Denver; T-Sea—trade acquisition from Seattle; PlanB—Plan B free-agent acquisition; FA—free-agent acquisition (other than Plan B).

MISCELLANEOUS TEAM DATA

Stadium (capacity, surface):
Rich Stadium
(80,091, artificial)
Business address:
One Bills Drive
Orchard Park, N.Y. 14127
Business phone:
716-648-1800
Ticket information:
716-649-0015
Team colors:
Royal blue, scarlet and white
Flagship radio station:
WBEN, 930 AM
Training site:
Fredonia State University
Fredonia, N.Y.
716-648-1800

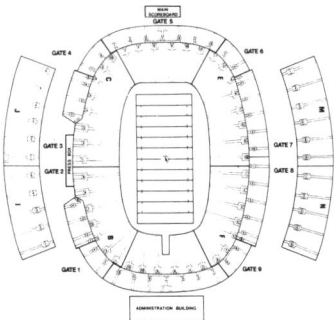

CAROLINA PANTHERS
NFC WESTERN DIVISION

1995 SEASON

SCHEDULE

Sept. 3	—at Atlanta	1:00
Sept. 10	—at Buffalo	1:00
Sept. 17	—ST. LOUIS	1:00
Sept. 24	—Open date	
Oct. 1	—TAMPA BAY	1:00
Oct. 8	—at Chicago	12:00
Oct. 15	—N.Y. JETS	4:00
Oct. 22	—NEW ORLEANS	1:00
Oct. 29	—at New England	1:00
Nov. 5	—at San Francisco	1:00
Nov. 12	—at St. Louis	12:00
Nov. 19	—ARIZONA	1:00
Nov. 26	—at New Orleans	7:00
Dec. 3	—INDIANAPOLIS	1:00
Dec. 10	—SAN FRANCISCO	1:00
Dec. 17	—ATLANTA	1:00
Dec. 24	—at Washington	4:00

All times are for home team.
All games Sunday unless noted.

DRAFT CHOICES

Kerry Collins, QB, Penn State (first round/fifth pick overall).
Tyrone Poole, DB, Fort Valley (Ga.) State (1/22).
Blake Brockermeyer, T, Texas (1/29).
Shawn King, DE, Northeast Louisiana (2/36).
Frank Garcia, C, Washington (4/132).
Mike Senters, WR, Northwestern (5/135).
Andrew Peterson, T, Washington (5/171).
Steve Strahan, DT, Baylor (6/188).
Jerry Colquitt, QB, Tennessee (6/191).
Chad Cota, DB, Oregon (7/209).
Michael Reed, DB, Boston College (7/249).

CLUB DIRECTORY

Owner & founder
Jerry Richardson
President
Mike McCormack
General manager
Bill Polian
Assistant general manager
Joe Mack
Dir. of business operations
Mark Richardson
Dir. of stadium operations
Jon Richardson
Chief financial officer
Dave Olsen
General counsel
Richard Thigpen Jr.
Asst. dir. of business operations
Charles Waddell
Director of sales
Phil Youtsey
Director of communications
Charlie Dayton
Dir. of community & player relations
Donnie Shell
Dir. of football administration
Steve Champlin
Dir. of football security
Ed Stillwell
Director of facilities
Tom Fellows
Director of player personnel
Dom Anile
Pro scout
Chris Polian
Regional scouts
Jack Bushofsky
Ralph Hawkins
Area scouts
Hal Athon
Edwin Bailey

Head coach
Dom Capers
Assistant coaches
Vic Fangio (def. coordinator)
Joe Pendry (off. coordinator)
Don Breaux (tight ends)
George Catavolos (def. backs)
Billy Davis (outside linebackers)
Cary Godette (defensive line)
Chick Harris (running backs)
Jim McNally (offensive line)
Chip Morton (strength & condi-
tioning)
Brad Seely (special teams)
John Shoop (quality control/
offense)
Kevin Steele (linebackers)
Richard Williamson (wide re-
ceivers)

Boyd Dowler
Bob Guarini
Gary Petercuskie
Scouting assistant
Steve Hinshaw
Head groundskeeper
Michal Martin
Equipment manager
Jackie Miles
Video director
Dave Sutherby
Head trainer
John Kasik
Assitant trainer
Al Shuford
Orthopedist
Dr. Don D'Alessandro

CAROLINA PANTHERS

1995 SEASON

CAROLINA PANTHERS

TRAINING CAMP ROSTER

No.	QUARTERBACKS	Ht./Wt.	Born	NFL Exp.	College	How acq.	'94 Games GP/GS
12	Collins, Kerry	6-5/240	12-30-72	R	Penn State	D1a/95	—
7	Colquitt, Jerry	6-4/208	6-28-72	R	Tennessee	D6b/95	—
14	Reich, Frank	6-4/210	12-4-61	11	Maryland	FA/95	*16/2
10	Trudeau, Jack	6-3/227	9-9-62	10	Illinois	ED/95	*5/2
	RUNNING BACKS						
23	Baldwin, Randy (KR)	5-10/216	8-19-67	5	Mississippi	FA/95	*16/0
26	Brewer, Dewell (KR)	5-8/199	5-22-70	2	Oklahoma	ED/95	*16/0
44	Christian, Bob	5-10/225	11-14-68	3	Northwestern	ED/95	*12/0
43	Cuthbert, Randy	6-2/224	1-16-70	3	Duke	FA/95	*1/0
	Foster, Barry	5-10/218	12-8-68	6	Arkansas	T-Pit/95	*11/10
34	Fuller, Eddie	5-9/198	6-22-68	5	Louisiana State	FA/95	0/0
35	Garrett, Judd	6-1/214	6-25-67	1	Princeton	FA/95	0/0
33	Griffith, Howard (FB)	6-0/226	11-17-67	3	Illinois	ED/95	*16/10
32	Lassic, Derrick	5-10/188	1-26-70	3	Alabama	ED/95	0/0
31	O'Neal, Brian	6-0/233	2-25-70	2	Penn State	ED/95	*14/0
28	Smith, Tony (KR)	6-1/212	6-29-70	3	Southern Mississippi	FA/95	*4/0
	RECEIVERS						
82	Beebe, Don	5-11/183	12-18-64	7	Chadron (Neb.) State	FA/95	*13/11
11	Buchanan, Richard	5-10/178	5-8-69	3	Northwestern	ED/95	*3/0
48	Campbell, Matthew (TE)	6-4/257	7-14-72	1	South Carolina	FA/95	0/0
83	Carrier, Mark	6-0/185	10-28-65	9	Nicholls State (La.)	ED/95	*16/6
18	Clifton, Greg	6-0/178	2-6-68	1	Johnson C. Smith (N.C.)	FA/95	0/0
19	Frazier, Daryl	6-1/181	1-23-71	1	Florida	FA/95	0/0
86	Green, Willie	6-4/188	4-2-66	6	Mississippi	FA/95	*5/0
84	Guliford, Eric	5-8/165	10-25-69	3	Arizona State	ED/95	*7/1
80	Hawkins, Steve	6-5/210	3-16-71	2	Western Michigan	ED/95	*7/0
89	Haws, Kurt (TE)	6-5/248	9-25-69	2	Utah	ED/95	*6/0
87	Marrow, Vince (TE)	6-3/251	8-17-68	2	Toledo	ED/95	*10/0
88	Metzelaars, Pete (TE)	6-7/254	5-24-60	14	Wabash (Ind.)	FA/95	*16/16
81	Mims, David	5-8/191	7-7-70	2	Baylor	ED/95	*2/2
15	Ryans, Larry	5-11/182	7-28-71	2	Clemson	ED/95	0/0
47	Senters, Mike	5-11/173	12-14-71	R	Northwestern	D5a/95	—
	Stone, Dwight	6-0/180	1-28-64	9	Middle Tennessee State	FA/95	*15/1
85	Tillman, Lawyer	6-5/230	5-20-66	6	Auburn	FA/95	0/0
5	Wiggins, Brian	5-11/183	6-14-68	1	Texas Southern	FA/95	0/0
	OFFENSIVE LINEMEN						
77	Boatswain, Harry (T)	6-4/295	6-26-69	5	New Haven (Conn.)	ED/95	*13/4
68	Brockermeyer, Blake (T)	6-4/305	4-11-73	R	Texas	D1c/95	—
73	Carlson, Leomiti (G)	6-3/380	1-10-71	1	San Diego State	FA/95	0/0
52	Elliott, Matt (C/G)	6-3/294	10-1-68	2	Michigan	FA/95	0/0
70	Farkas, Kevin (T)	6-9/375	2-4-71	1	Appalachian State	FA/95	0/0
79	Finn, Mike (T)	6-5/275	9-26-67	3	Arkansas-Pine Bluff	FA/95	0/0
65	Garcia, Frank (C)	6-1/290	1-28-72	R	Washington	D4/95	—
74	Graham, Derrick (T)	6-4/315	3-18-67	6	Appalachian State	FA/95	*16/11
78	Martin, Emerson (G)	6-2/297	5-6-70	1	Hampton (Va.)	FA/95	0/0
76	Moore, Darryl (G)	6-3/293	1-27-69	4	Texas-El Paso	FA/95	0/0
60	Peterson, Andrew (T)	6-5/310	6-11-72	R	Washington	D5b/95	—
63	Rodenhauser, Mark (C)	6-5/280	6-1-61	8	Illinois State	ED/95	*16/0
72	Rollins, Baron (G)	6-4/335	7-23-70	2	Louisiana Tech	ED/95	0/0
64	Whitley, Curtis (C/G)	6-1/288	5-10-69	4	Clemson	ED/95	*12/2
	DEFENSIVE LINEMEN						
97	Fields, Jeff (NT)	6-3/320	7-3-67	1	Arkansas State	FA/95	0/0
93	Fox, Mike (E)	6-6/288	8-5-67	6	West Virginia	FA/95	*16/16
96	King, Shawn (E)	6-3/280	6-24-72	R	Northeast Louisiana	D2/95	—
71	Kragen, Greg (NT)	6-3/265	3-4-62	11	Utah State	ED/95	*16/2
92	Price, Shawn (E)	6-5/260	3-28-70	3	Pacific	ED/95	*6/0
90	Rodgers, Tyrone (T)	6-3/276	4-27-69	4	Washington	ED/95	*5/0
94	Strahan, Steve (NT)	6-1/298	10-29-72	R	Baylor	D6a/95	—
91	Teeter, Mike (T)	6-3/272	10-4-67	4	Michigan	ED/95	*14/0
75	Thomas, Mark (E)	6-5/273	5-6-69	4	North Carolina State	ED/95	*9/0
98	Williams, Gerald (E)	6-3/293	9-8-63	10	Auburn	FA/95	*11/11
	LINEBACKERS						
54	Bailey, Carlton	6-3/235	12-15-64	8	North Carolina	FA/95	*16/11
53	Butcher, Paul	6-0/240	11-8-63	9	Wayne State (Mich.)	ED/95	*13/0
56	Conner, Darion	6-2/242	9-28-67	6	Jackson State	FA/95	*16/13
57	Lathon, Lamar	6-3/252	12-23-67	6	Houston	FA/95	*16/15
51	Mills, Sam	5-9/225	6-3-59	10	Montclair (N.J.) State	FA/95	*16/16
55	Powell, Andre	6-1/235	6-5-69	3	Penn State	ED/95	*1/0

No.	LINEBACKERS	Ht./Wt.	Born	NFL Exp.	College	How acq.	'94 Games GP/GS
95	Scott, Patrick	6-4/241	6-4-71	2	South Carolina State	FA/95	0/0
58	Sims, William	6-3/265	12-30-70	2	Southwestern Louisiana	ED/95	*8/0
50	Stams, Frank	6-2/240	7-17-66	7	Notre Dame	FA/95	*16/15
	DEFENSIVE BACKS						
40	Brabham, Cary	6-0/195	8-11-70	2	Southern Methodist	ED/95	*7/0
41	Cota, Chad (S)	6-1/188	8-13-71	R	Oregon	D7a/95	—
36	Foggie, Fred	6-0/200	6-10-69	4	Minnesota	ED/95	*3/0
24	Haller, Alan (CB)	5-11/186	8-9-70	3	Michigan State	FA/95	0/0
29	Lofton, Steve (CB)	5-9/185	11-26-68	4	Texas A&M	FA/95	0/0
39	Maxie, Brett (S)	6-2/194	1-13-62	11	Texas Southern	FA/95	*4/2
25	McDowell, Bubba (S)	6-1/198	11-4-66	7	Miami (Fla.)	FA/95	*9/3
22	McKyer, Tim (CB)	6-0/178	9-5-63	10	Texas-Arlington	ED/95	*16/2
38	Poole, Tyrone (CB/KR)	5-8/185	2-3-72	R	Fort Valley (Ga.) State	D1/95	—
45	Reed, Mike (CB)	5-9/177	8-16-72	R	Boston College	D7b/95	—
21	Smith, Rod (CB)	5-11/187	3-12-70	4	Notre Dame	ED/95	*16/7
20	Williams, James (CB)	5-10/190	3-30-67	6	Fresno State	FA/95	*15/7
	SPECIALISTS						
6	Barnhardt, Tommy (P)	6-2/207	6-11-63	9	North Carolina	FA/95	*16/0
4	Kasay, John (K)	5-10/189	10-27-69	5	Georgia	FA/95	*16/0
30	Turner, Vernon (KR)	5-8/185	1-6-67	5	Carson-Newman (Tenn.)	FA/95	*12/1

*Bailey played 16 games with Giants in '94; Baldwin played 16 games with Browns; Barnhardt played 16 games with Saints; Beebe played 13 games with Bills; Boatswain played 13 games with 49ers; Brabham played 7 games with Raiders; Brewer played 16 games with Colts; Buchanan played 3 games with Rams; Butcher played 13 games with Colts; Carrier played 16 games with Browns; Christian played 16 games with Bears; Conner played 16 games with Saints; Cuthbert played 1 game with Steelers; Foggie played 3 games with Vikings; Foster played 11 games with Steelers; Fox played 16 games with Giants; Graham played 16 games with Chiefs; Green played 5 games with Buccaneers; Griffith played 16 games with Rams; Guliford played 7 games with Vikings; Hawkins played 7 games with Patriots; Haws played 6 games with Redskins; Kasay played 16 games with Seahawks; Kragen played 16 games with Chiefs; Lathon played 16 games with Oilers; Marrow played 10 games with Bills; Maxie played 4 games with Falcons; McDowell played 9 games with Oilers; McKyer played 16 games with Steelers; Metzelaars played 16 games with Bills; Mills played 16 games with Saints; Mims played 2 games with Falcons; O'Neal played 14 games with Eagles; Powell played 1 game with Giants; Price played 6 games with Buccaneers; Reich played 16 games with Bills; Rodenhauser played 16 games with Lions; Rodgers played 5 games with Seahawks; Sims played 8 games with Vikings; R. Smith played 16 games with Patriots; T. Smith played 4 games with Falcons; Stams played 16 games with Browns; Stone played 15 games with Steelers; Teeter played 14 games with Oilers; Thomas played 9 games with 49ers; Trudeau played 5 games with Jets; Turner played 12 games with Buccaneers; Whitley played 12 games with Chargers; G. Williams played 11 games with Steelers; J. Williams played 15 games with Cardinals.

Abbreviations: ED—expansion draft pick; D1—draft pick, first round; SupD2—supplemental draft pick, second round; W-Den—waivers acquisition from Denver; T-Sea—trade acquisition from Seattle; PlanB—Plan B free-agent acquisition; FA—free-agent acquisition (other than Plan B).

MISCELLANEOUS TEAM DATA

Stadium (capacity, surface):
Clemson Memorial Stadium
(81,473, grass)
Business address:
227 W. Trade St., Suite 1600
Charlotte, NC 28202
Business phone:
704-358-7000
Ticket information:
704-358-7800
Team colors:
Blue, black and silver
Flagship radio station:
WBT-1110 AM
Training site:
Wofford College
Spartanburg, S.C.
704-358-7000

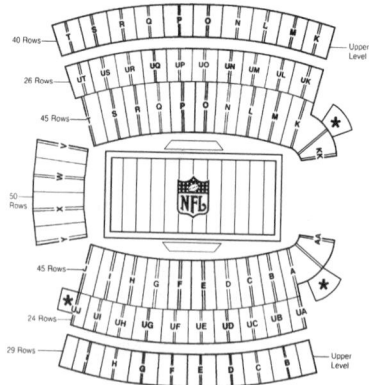

Clemson Memorial Stadium

CHICAGO BEARS
NFC CENTRAL DIVISION

1994 REVIEW

RESULTS

Sept. 4—TAMPA BAY	W	21-9	
Sept. 12—at Philadelphia	L	22-30	
Sept. 18—MINNESOTA	L	14-42	
Sept. 25—at N.Y. Jets	W	19-7	
Oct. 2—BUFFALO	W	20-13	
Oct. 9—NEW ORLEANS	W	17-7	
Oct. 16—Open date			
Oct. 23—at Detroit	L	16-21	
Oct. 31—GREEN BAY	L	6-33	
Nov. 6—at Tampa Bay	W	20-6	
Nov. 13—at Miami	W	17-14	
Nov. 20—DETROIT	W	20-10	
Nov. 27—at Arizona (OT)	W	19-16	
Dec. 1—at Minnesota (OT)	L	27-33	
Dec. 11—at Green Bay	L	3-40	
Dec. 18—L.A. RAMS	W	27-13	
Dec. 24—NEW ENGLAND	L	3-13	

RECORDS/RANKINGS

1994 regular-season record: 9-7 (T2nd in NFC Central); 3-5 in division; 6-6 in conference; 5-3 at home; 4-4 on road.
Team record last five years: 43-37 (.538, ranks 13th in league in that span).

1994 team rankings:	No.	NFC	NFL
Total offense	*292.4	12	23
Rushing offense	*99.3	6	15
Passing offense	*193.2	11	21
Scoring offense	271	12	24
Total defense	*313.1	8	13
Rushing defense	*120.1	12	24
Passing defense	*192.9	3	5
Scoring defense	307	6	10
Takeaways	22	12	25
Giveaways	26	T7	T9
Turnover differential	-4	12	T20
Sacks	28	T9	T21
Sacks allowed	25	4	8

*Yards per game.

TEAM LEADERS

Scoring (kicking): Kevin Butler, 87 pts. (24/24 PATs, 21/29 FGs).
Scoring (touchdowns): Lewis Tillman, 42 pts. (7 rushing).
Passing: Steve Walsh, 2,078 yds. (343 att., 208 comp., 60.6%, 10 TDs, 8 int.).
Rushing: Lewis Tillman, 899 yds. (275 att., 3.3 avg., 7 TDs).
Receptions: Jeffrey Graham, 68 (944 yds., 13.9 avg., 4 TDs).
Interceptions: Donnell Woolford, 5 (30 yds., 0 TDs).
Sacks: Trace Armstrong, 7.5.
Punting: Chris Gardocki, 37.8 avg. (76 punts, 2,871 yds., 0 blocked).
Punt returns: Jeffrey Graham, 9.3 avg. (15 att., 140 yds., 1 TD).
Kickoff returns: Nate Lewis, 25.0 avg. (35 att., 874 yds., 0 TDs).

1995 SEASON

CLUB DIRECTORY

Chairman of the board
Edward W. McCaskey
President and chief executive officer
Michael B. McCaskey
Vice president
Timothy E. McCaskey
Secretary
Virginia H. McCaskey
Vice president of operations
Ted Phillips
Director/administration
Tim LeFevour
Director/marketing and communications
Ken Valdiserri
Manager of promotions and special events
John Bostrom
Manager of sales
Jack Trompeter
Director/public relations
Bryan Harlan
Assistant director/public relations
Doug Green
Ticket manager
George McCaskey
Assistant ticket manager
Betty Swanson
Director of college scouting
Rod Graves
Pro scout
Mike McCartney
Regional scouts
Charlie Mackey
Bobby Riggle
Jeff Shiver
Gary Smith

SCHEDULE

Sept. 3—MINNESOTA	3:00	
Sept. 11—GREEN BAY (Mon.)	8:00	
Sept. 17—at Tampa Bay	4:00	
Sept. 24—at St. Louis	12:00	
Oct. 1—Open date		
Oct. 8—CAROLINA	12:00	
Oct. 15—at Jacksonville	1:00	
Oct. 22—HOUSTON	12:00	
Oct. 30—at Minnesota (Mon.)	8:00	
Nov. 5—PITTSBURGH	3:00	
Nov. 12—at Green Bay	12:00	
Nov. 19—DETROIT	12:00	
Nov. 26—at N.Y. Giants	1:00	
Dec. 4—at Detroit (Mon.)	9:00	
Dec. 10—at Cincinnati	1:00	
Dec. 17—TAMPA BAY	12:00	
Dec. 24—PHILADELPHIA	12:00	

All times are for home team.
All games Sunday unless noted.

Head coach:
Dave Wannstedt
Assistant coaches
Danny Abramowicz (special teams)
Clarence Brooks (defensive line)
Ivan Fears (wide receivers)
Carlos Mainord (defensive assistant)
Dave McGinnis (linebackers)
Willie Peete (running backs)
Mike Shula (tight ends)
Bob Slowik (defensive coordinator/defensive backs)
Ron Turner (offensive coordinator/quarterbacks)
Tony Wise (assistant head coach/offensive line)

Head trainer
Fred Caito
Strength coordinator
Clyde Emrich
Physical development coordinator
Russ Riederer
Equipment manager
Gary Haeger
Assistant equipment manager
Tony Medlin
Director of video services
Dean Pope
Assistant video director
Mark Bienvenu

DRAFT CHOICES

Rashaan Salaam, RB, Colorado (first round/21st pick overall).
Patrick Riley, DT, Miami (Fla.). (2/52).
Todd Sauerbrun, P, West Virginia (2/56).
Sean Harris, LB, Arizona (3/83).
Evan Pilgrim, G, Brigham Young (3/87).
Jack Jackson, WR, Florida (4/116).
Kenny Gales, DB, Wisconsin (6/193).
Carl Reeves, DE, N.C. State (6/198).
Jamal Cox, LB, Georgia Tech (7/229).

1995 SEASON

TRAINING CAMP ROSTER

No.	QUARTERBACKS	Ht./Wt.	Born	NFL Exp.	College	How acq.	'94 Games GP/GS
12	Kramer, Erik	6-1/200	11-6-64	6	North Carolina State	FA/94	6/5
9	Matthews, Shane	6-3/196	6-1-70	3	Florida	FA/93	0/0
4	Walsh, Steve	6-3/200	12-1-66	7	Miami (Fla.)	FA/94	12/11
	RUNNING BACKS						
30	Carter, Tony (FB)	5-11/216	8-23-72	2	Minnesota	FA/95	14/0
43	Cobb, Trevor	5-9/209	11-20-70	3	Rice	FA/94	1/0
22	Green, Robert	5-8/212	9-10-70	4	William & Mary	W-Was/93	15/0
29	Harris, Raymont	6-0/225	12-23-70	2	Ohio State	D4/94	16/11
25	Johnson, Anthony (FB)	6-0/222	10-25-67	6	Notre Dame	FA/95	*15/0
31	Salaam, Rashaan	6-1/228	10-8-74	R	Colorado	D1/95	—
33	Thompson, Darrell	6-1/217	11-23-67	6	Minnesota	FA/95	*8/0
27	Tillman, Lewis	6-0/204	4-16-66	7	Jackson State	FA/94	16/15
	RECEIVERS						
15	Bownes, Fabien	5-11/180	2-29-72	R	Western Illinois	FA/95	—
80	Conway, Curtis (KR)	6-0/193	3-13-71	3	Southern California	D1/93	13/12
84	Gedney, Chris (TE)	6-5/265	8-9-70	3	Syracuse	D3/93	7/7
81	Graham, Jeff	6-2/196	2-14-69	5	Ohio State	T-Pit/94	16/15
82	Jackson, Jack	5-8/171	11-11-72	R	Florida	D4/95	—
85	Jennings, Keith (TE)	6-4/270	5-19-66	6	Clemson	FA/91	9/1
88	McMurtry, Greg	6-2/210	10-15-67	6	Michigan	FA/94	9/4
87	McNerney, Pat (TE)	6-3/258	1-3-71	R	Weber State	FA/95	—
83	Obee, Terry	5-10/189	6-15-68	3	Oregon	FA/93	0/0
18	Primus, Greg	5-11/190	10-20-70	2	Colorado State	FA/94	3/1
19	Shedd, Kenny (KR)	5-9/171	2-14-71	2	Northern Iowa	FA/94	0/0
86	Timpson, Michael	5-10/180	6-6-67	7	Penn State	FA/95	*15/14
89	Wetnight, Ryan (TE)	6-2/235	11-5-70	3	Stanford	FA/93	11/0
	OFFENSIVE LINEMEN						
72	Adams, Scott	6-5/293	9-28-66	4	Georgia	FA/95	*11/0
70	Auzenne, Troy (T)	6-7/300	6-26-69	4	California	D2/92	11/3
63	Burger, Todd (G)	6-3/296	3-20-70	2	Penn State	FA/93	4/0
67	Fontenot, Jerry (C)	6-3/285	11-21-66	7	Texas A&M	D3/89	16/16
53	Greeley, Bucky (C)	6-2/276	7-30-72	R	Penn State	FA/95	—
64	Heck, Andy (T)	6-6/296	1-1-67	7	Notre Dame	FA/94	14/14
73	Kmet, Frank (G)	6-3/294	3-13-70	1	Purdue	FA/93	0/0
58	Leeuwenburg, Jay (G/C)	6-3/290	6-18-69	4	Colorado	W-KC/92	16/16
	Lewis, Tim (T)	6-4/300	4-24-71	R	Northern Illinois	FA/95	—
	Lumelski, Zev (T)	6-8/304	4-14-72	R	Miami (Fla.)	FA/95	—
75	Perry, Todd (G)	6-5/310	11-28-70	3	Kentucky	D4a/93	15/4
65	Pilgrim, Evan (G)	6-4/298	8-14-72	R	Brigham Young	D3/95	—
	Polk, Octus (G)	6-3/354	9-17-71	R	Stephen F. Austin State	FA/95	—
76	Spears, Marcus (G/T)	6-4/300	9-28-71	2	Northwestern State	D2/94	0/0
71	Williams, James (T)	6-7/335	3-29-68	5	Cheyney (Pa.)	FA/91	16/15
	DEFENSIVE LINEMEN						
93	Collier, Ervin (T)	6-3/287	5-12-71	1	Florida A&M	FA/94	0/0
99	Flanigan, Jim (T)	6-2/280	8-27-71	2	Notre Dame	D3/94	14/0
96	Fontenot, Albert (E)	6-4/272	9-17-70	3	Baylor	D4c/93	16/8
74	Hawkins, Garland (E)	6-3/253	2-19-70	2	Syracuse	FA/94	16/0
	Krichbaum, Mark (T)	6-5/283	8-8-72	R	Virginia	FA/95	0/0
68	Reeves, Carl (E)	6-4/241	12-17-71	R	North Carolina State	D6b/95	—
95	Riley, Patrick (E)	6-5/278	3-8-72	R	Miami (Fla.)	D2/95	—
98	Simpson, Carl (T)	6-2/285	4-18-70	4	Florida State	D2/93	15/8
90	Spellman, Alonzo (E)	6-4/285	9-27-71	4	Ohio State	D1/92	16/16
94	Thierry, John (E)	6-4/260	9-4-71	2	Alcorn State	D1/94	16/1
	Tobias, Michael (T)	6-1/282	4-29-71	R	Southern Mississippi	FA/95	—
97	Zorich, Chris (T)	6-1/277	3-13-69	5	Notre Dame	D2/91	16/16
	LINEBACKERS						
91	Baker, Myron	6-1/228	1-6-71	3	Louisiana Tech	D4b/93	16/3
52	Bass, Robert	6-1/239	11-10-70	2	Miami (Fla.)	FA/94	0/0
59	Cain, Joe	6-1/237	6-11-65	7	Oregon Tech	FA/93	16/15
62	Cox, Jamal	6-1/239	1-21-72	R	Georgia Tech	D7/95	—
54	Cox, Ron	6-2/235	2-27-68	6	Fresno State	D2b/90	15/3
	Gavin, Lauren	6-1/229	8-5-75	R	Jackson State	FA/95	—
57	Harris, Sean	6-3/244	2-25-72	R	Arizona	D3/95	—
60	Ireland, Darwin	5-11/240	5-26-71	2	Arkansas	FA/94	2/0
92	Minter, Barry	6-2/239	1-28-70	3	Tulsa	T-Dal/93	13/1
55	Smith, Vinson	6-2/247	7-3-65	9	East Carolina	T-Dal/93	12/10
	DEFENSIVE BACKS						
35	Burton, James (CB)	5-9/181	4-22-71	2	Fresno State	FA/94	13/1

— 18 —

No.	DEFENSIVE BACKS	Ht./Wt.	Born	NFL Exp.	College	How acq.	'94 Games GP/GS
20	Carrier, Mark (S)	6-1/190	4-28-68	6	Southern California	D1/90	16/15
23	Carter, Marty (S)	6-1/200	12-17-69	5	Middle Tennessee State	FA/95	*16/14
47	Crumpton, Robert (S)	6-0/191	2-14-72	R	Illinois	FA/95	—
37	Eilers, Pat (S)	5-11/197	9-3-66	5	Notre Dame	FA/95	*16/0
46	Forbes, Marlon (CB)	6-1/202	12-25-71	R	Penn State	FA/95	—
48	Gales, Kenny (CB)	5-11/173	4-1-72	R	Wisconsin	D6a/95	—
32	Joseph, Dwayne (CB)	5-9/188	6-2-72	2	Syracuse	FA/94	0/0
39	Lincoln, Jeremy (CB)	5-10/180	4-7-69	4	Tennessee	D3/92	15/14
26	Mangum, John (S)	5-10/192	3-16-67	6	Alabama	D7/90	16/3
36	Marshall, Anthony (S)	6-1/205	9-16-70	2	Louisiana State	FA/94	3/0
24	Miniefield, Kevin (S)	5-9/180	3-2-70	3	Arizona State	FA/93	12/0
44	Walker, Cedric (S)	6-0/205	2-16-71	1	Stephen F. Austin State	FA/94	0/0
21	Woolford, Donnell (CB)	5-9/188	1-6-66	7	Clemson	D1a/89	16/16
	SPECIALISTS						
6	Butler, Kevin (K)	6-1/205	7-24-62	11	Georgia	D4/85	15/0
10	Kaplan, Scott (K)	6-0/195	2-17-70	1	Pittsburgh	FA/95	0/0
16	Sauerbrun, Todd (P)	5-10/206	1-20-71	R	West Virginia	D2/95	

*Adams played 11 games with Saints in '94; M. Carter played 16 games with Buccaneers; Eilers played 16 games with Redskins; Johnson played 15 games with Jets; Thompson played 8 games with Packers; Timpson played 15 games with Patriots.

Also played with Bears in '94: DE Trace Armstrong (15 games); G Mark Bortz (12); RB Bob Christian (12); TE Marv Cook (16); CB Maurice Douglass (16); DT Tory Epps (5); P/K Chris Gardocki (16); S Shaun Gayle (16); RB Merril Hoge (5); CB Keshon Johnson (6); LB Dante Jones (15); WR Nate Lewis (13); G Tom Myslinski (4); WR Tom Waddle (9); RB Tim Worley (5).

Abbreviations: D1—draft pick, first round; SupD2—supplemental draft pick, second round; W-Den—waivers acquisition from Denver; T-Sea—trade acquisition from Seattle; PlanB—Plan B free-agent acquisition; FA—free-agent acquisition (other than Plan B).

MISCELLANEOUS TEAM DATA

Stadium (capacity, surface):
Soldier Field (66,944, grass)

Business address:
Halas Hall
250 N. Washington Road
Lake Forest, IL 60045

Business phone:
708-295-6600

Ticket information:
708-615-2327

Team colors:
Navy blue, orange and white

Flagship radio station:
WGN, 720 AM

Training site:
University of Wisconsin-
Platteville
Platteville, Wis.
608-342-1201

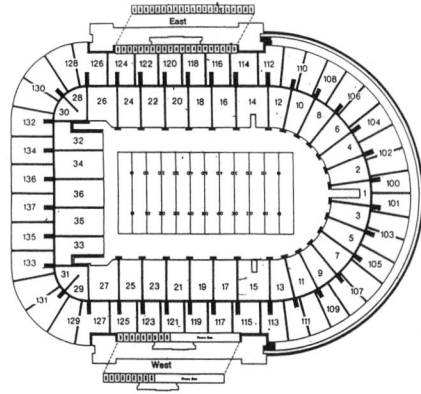

CINCINNATI BENGALS
AFC CENTRAL DIVISION

1994 REVIEW

RESULTS

Sept. 4—CLEVELAND	L	20-28
Sept. 11—at San Diego	L	10-27
Sept. 18—NEW ENGLAND	L	28-31
Sept. 25—at Houston	L	13-20
Oct. 2—MIAMI	L	7-23
Oct. 9—Open date		
Oct. 16—at Pittsburgh	L	10-14
Oct. 23—at Cleveland	L	13-37
Oct. 30—DALLAS	L	20-23
Nov. 6—at Seattle (OT)	W	20-17
Nov. 13—HOUSTON	W	34-31
Nov. 20—INDIANAPOLIS	L	13-17
Nov. 27—at Denver	L	13-15
Dec. 4—PITTSBURGH	L	15-38
Dec. 11—at N.Y. Giants	L	20-27
Dec. 18—at Arizona	L	7-28
Dec. 24—PHILADELPHIA	W	33-30

RECORDS/RANKINGS

1994 regular-season record: 3-13 (3rd in AFC Central); 1-5 in division; 2-10 in conference; 2-6 at home; 1-7 on road.
Team record last five years: 23-57 (.288, ranks T27th in league in that span).

1994 team rankings:

	No.	AFC	NFL
Total offense	*299.5	9	18
Rushing offense	*97.3	11	18
Passing offense	*202.3	8	18
Scoring offense	276	12	23
Total defense	*322.1	7	15
Rushing defense	*119.1	12	23
Passing defense	*203.0	4	9
Scoring defense	406	14	26
Takeaways	18	14	28
Giveaways	41	13	27
Turnover differential	-23	14	28
Sacks	31	T7	T15
Sacks allowed	44	11	23

*Yards per game.

TEAM LEADERS

Scoring (kicking): Doug Pelfrey, 108 pts. (24/25 PATs, 28/33 FGs).
Scoring (touchdowns): Carl Pickens, 66 pts. (11 receiving).
Passing: Jeff Blake, 2,154 yds. (306 att., 156 comp., 51.0%, 14 TDs, 9 int.).
Rushing: Derrick Fenner, 468 yds. (141 att., 3.3 avg., 1 TD).
Receptions: Carl Pickens, 71 (1,127 yds., 15.9 avg., 11 TDs).
Interceptions: Louis Oliver, 3 (36 yds., 0 TDs).
Sacks: Alfred Williams, 9.5.
Punting: Lee Johnson, 43.8 avg. (79 punts, 3,461 yds., 1 blocked).
Punt returns: Corey Sawyer, 11.8 avg. (26 att., 307 yds., 1 TD).
Kickoff returns: Eric Ball, 21.8 avg. (42 att., 915 yds., 0 TDs).

1995 SEASON

CLUB DIRECTORY

Chairman of the board
Austin E. Knowlton
President/general manager
Mike Brown
Vice president
John Sawyer
Corporate secretary/counsel
Katie Brown Blackburn
Director/player personnel
Pete Brown
Scouting/asst. sec.-treasurer
Paul H. Brown
Business manager
Bill Connelly
Scouting/personnel
Jim Lippincott
Director/public relations
Jack Brennan
Ticket manager
Paul Kelly
Accountants
Jay Reis
Bill Scanlon
Consultants
John Murdough
Bill Johnson
Security
Howard Whitson
Scouts
Earl Biederman
Frank Smouse
Frank Uible

Head coach
Dave Shula
Assistant coaches
Paul Alexander (offensive line)
Jim Anderson (running backs)
Ken Anderson (quarterbacks)
Bruce Coslet (off. coordinator)
Bobby DePaul (defensive line)
John Garrett (off. asst./wide rec.)
Tim Krumrie (def. assistant)
Ron Meeks (defensive backfield)
Joe Pascale (linebackers)
Larry Peccatiello (def. coord.)
Joe Wessel (special teams)
Kim Wood (strength)

Team physicians
Robert Heidt Jr.
Walter Timperman
Michael Welch
Trainer
Paul Sparling
Assistant trainer
Rob Recker
Equipment manager
Tom Gray
Video director
Al Davis
Video assistant
Dave Slyby
Ben Gals coordinator
Charlotte Jacobs

SCHEDULE

Sept. 3—at Indianapolis	12:00
Sept. 10—JACKSONVILLE	4:00
Sept. 17—at Seattle	1:00
Sept. 24—HOUSTON	4:00
Oct. 1—MIAMI	1:00
Oct. 8—at Tampa Bay	1:00
Oct. 15—Open date	
Oct. 19—at Pittsburgh (Thur.)	8:00
Oct. 29—CLEVELAND	1:00
Nov. 5—LOS ANGELES	4:00
Nov. 12—at Houston	12:00
Nov. 19—PITTSBURGH	1:00
Nov. 26—at Jacksonville	1:00
Dec. 3—at Green Bay	12:00
Dec. 10—CHICAGO	1:00
Dec. 17—at Cleveland	1:00
Dec. 24—MINNESOTA	1:00

All times are for home team.
All games Sunday unless noted.

DRAFT CHOICES

Ki-Jana Carter, RB, Penn State (first round/first pick overall).
Melvin Tuten, T, Syracuse (3/69).
Sam Shade, DB, Alabama (4/102).
David Dunn, WR, Fresno State (5/139).
Ryan Grigson, T, Purdue (6/175).
John Walsh, QB, Brigham Young (7/213).

TRAINING CAMP ROSTER

No.	QUARTERBACKS	Ht./Wt.	Born	NFL Exp.	College	How acq.	'94 Games GP/GS
16	Ballard, Jim	6-3/223	4-16-72	1	Mount Union (O.)	FA/94	0/0
8	Blake, Jeff	6-0/202	12-4-70	4	East Carolina	W-NYJ/94	10/9
7	Klingler, David	6-2/205	2-17-69	4	Houston	D1/92	10/7
10	Walsh, John	6-4/215	12-12-72	R	Brigham Young	D7/95	—
4	Wilhelm, Erik	6-3/217	11-16-65	6	Oregon State	FA/93	1/0
	RUNNING BACKS						
21	Bieniemy, Eric	5-7/198	8-15-69	5	Colorado	FA/95	*16/0
38	Burns, Jason	5-7/195	11-27-72	R	Wisconsin	FA/95	—
32	Carter, Ki-Jana	5-10/227	9-12-73	R	Penn State	D1/95	—
46	Cothran, Jeff (FB)	6-1/249	6-28-71	2	Ohio State	D3/94	14/4
20	Dickerson, Bryan	6-1/260	3-22-72	R	Eastern Kentucky	FA/95	—
28	Green, Harold	6-2/222	1-29-68	6	South Carolina	D2/90	14/11
36	Joseph, James	6-2/222	10-28-67	5	Auburn	FA/95	*14/5
	RECEIVERS						
18	Bailey, Thomas	6-0/196	12-6-71	R	Auburn	FA/95	—
80	Dunn, David (KR)	6-3/210	6-10-72	R	Fresno State	D5/95	—
83	Frisch, David (TE)	6-7/260	6-22-70	3	Colorado State	FA/93	16/0
19	Hill, Jeff (KR)	5-11/178	9-24-72	2	Purdue	FA/94	1/0
85	McGee, Tim	5-10/183	8-7-64	10	Tennessee	FA/94	14/1
82	McGee, Tony (TE)	6-3/246	4-21-71	3	Michigan	D2/93	16/16
81	Pickens, Carl	6-2/206	3-23-70	4	Tennessee	D2/92	15/15
89	Query, Jeff	6-0/165	3-7-67	7	Millikin (Ill.)	W-Hou/92	10/4
16	Rhodes, David	6-1/200	3-15-72	R	Central Florida	FA/95	—
17	Rowlett, J.J.	6-2/215	10-15-72	R	Texas-El Paso	FA/95	—
87	Sadowski, Troy (TE)	6-5/250	12-8-65	6	Georgia	FA/94	15/1
86	Scott, Darnay (KR)	6-1/180	7-7-72	2	San Diego State	D2/94	16/12
88	Ware, Derek (TE)	6-2/255	9-17-67	4	Central Oklahoma	W-Ari/94	*15/12
	OFFENSIVE LINEMEN						
74	Braham, Rich (T)	6-4/290	11-6-70	2	West Virginia	W-Ari/94	3/0
65	Brilz, Darrick (G)	6-3/287	2-14-64	9	Oregon State	FA/94	15/15
75	Brown, Anthony (T)	6-5/310	11-6-72	R	Utah	FA/95	—
72	Brumfield, Scott (T)	6-8/320	8-19-70	3	Brigham Young	FA/93	2/0
68	Cadigan, Dave (G)	6-4/285	4-6-65	8	Southern California	FA/94	13/13
78	Forsythe, Ray (G)	6-3/310	2-13-72	R	Central Florida	FA/95	—
62	Grigson, Ryan (T)	6-6/290	2-23-72	R	Purdue	D6/95	—
66	Jones, Dan (T)	6-7/298	7-22-70	3	Maine	FA/93	14/0
71	Joseph, Sherrard (T)	6-5/304	7-27-72	R	Connecticut	FA/95	—
64	Kozerski, Bruce (G)	6-4/287	4-2-62	12	Holy Cross	D9/84	16/16
60	Moore, Eric (G)	6-5/290	1-21-65	8	Indiana	FA/94	6/6
76	Pollard, Trent (T)	6-4/304	11-20-72	2	Eastern Washington	D5/94	8/0
77	Sargent, Kevin (T)	6-6/284	3-31-69	4	Eastern Washington	FA/92	15/15
59	Truitt, Greg (C)	6-0/235	12-8-65	2	Penn State	FA/94	16/0
61	Tuten, Melvin (T)	6-6/305	11-11-71	R	Syracuse	D3/95	—
63	Walter, Joe (T)	6-7/292	6-18-63	11	Texas Tech	D7/85	0/0
	DEFENSIVE LINEMEN						
92	Copeland, John (E)	6-3/286	9-20-70	3	Alabama	D1/93	12/12
96	Flores, Mike (E)	6-3/256	12-1-66	5	Louisville	FA/95	*15/2
93	Parten, Ty (E)	6-4/272	10-13-69	3	Arizona	D3a/93	14/4
95	Rucker, Keith (T)	6-4/340	11-20-68	4	Ohio Wesleyan	FA/94	16/14
70	Smith, Artie (E)	6-4/285	5-15-70	3	Louisiana Tech	W-SF/94	*9/0
79	Stallings, Ramondo (E)	6-7/285	11-21-71	2	San Diego State	D7/94	6/0
97	Stewart, Vince (T)	6-4/295	5-7-72	R	Penn State	FA/95	—
99	Wilkinson, Dan (T)	6-5/313	3-13-73	2	Ohio State	D1/94	16/14
94	Williams, Alfred (E)	6-6/265	11-6-68	5	Colorado	D1/91	16/16
67	von Oelhoffen, Kimo (T)	6-4/300	1-30-71	2	Boise State	D6/94	7/0
	LINEBACKERS						
54	Braxton, David	6-2/240	5-25-65	6	Wake Forest	FA/90	9/0
	Collins, Andre	6-1/231	5-4-68	6	Penn State	FA/95	*16/16
90	Collins, Gerald	6-2/250	2-13-71	R	Vanderbilt	FA/95	—
50	Francis, James	6-5/252	8-4-68	6	Baylor	D1/90	16/16
55	Hollinquest, Lamont	6-3/245	10-24-70	3	Southern California	W-Was/94	*14/0
57	Jefferson, Kevin	6-2/232	1-14-74	2	Lehigh	FA/94	6/0
56	McDonald, Ricardo	6-2/235	11-8-69	4	Pittsburgh	D4/92	13/13
52	Shine, Steven	6-6/232	11-28-70	1	Northwestern	D3/94	0/0
51	Tovar, Steve	6-3/244	4-25-70	3	Ohio State	D3/93	16/16
91	Wallerstedt, Brett	6-1/240	11-24-70	3	Arizona State	W-Den/94	10/0
49	Yurkiewicz, Rich	6-3/235	5-2-73	R	Kent	FA/95	—
	DEFENSIVE BACKS						
43	Brim, Mike (CB)	6-0/192	1-23-66	8	Virginia Union	FA/93	16/16

No.	DEFENSIVE BACKS	Ht./Wt.	Born	NFL Exp.	College	How acq.	'94 Games GP/GS
45	Hardy, Adrian (CB/KR)	5-11/194	8-16-70	3	Northwestern State	W-SF/94	*16/0
25	Jones, Rod (CB)	6-0/185	3-31-64	10	Southern Methodist	T-TB/90	16/16
24	Jones, Roger (CB)	5-9/175	4-22-69	5	Tennessee State	W-TB/94	16/0
23	Sawyer, Corey (CB)	5-11/171	10-4-71	2	Florida State	D4/94	15/0
35	Shade, Sam (S)	6-1/191	6-14-73	R	Alabama	D4/95	—
30	Shelling, Chris (CB)	5-10/180	11-3-72	R	Auburn	FA/95	—
22	Toomer, Donald (CB)	6-1/192	8-10-72	R	Utah State	FA/95	—
27	Walker, Bracey (S)	5-10/200	10-28-70	2	North Carolina	W-KC/94	*9/0
37	Wheeler, Leonard (CB)	5-11/189	1-15-69	4	Troy (Ala.) State	D3/92	0/0
31	Williams, Darryl (S)	6-0/191	1-7-70	4	Miami (Fla.)	D1a/92	16/16
	SPECIALISTS						
5	Culley, Blair (K)	6-1/190	11-29-68	R	Oklahoma	FA/95	—
11	Johnson, Lee (P/K)	6-2/200	11-27-61	11	Brigham Young	W-Cle/88	16/0
9	Pelfrey, Doug (K)	5-11/185	9-25-70	3	Kentucky	D8/93	16/0

*Bieniemy played 16 games with Chargers in '94; Collins played 16 games with Redskins; Flores played 15 games with Eagles; Hardy played 2 games with 49ers and 14 games with Bengals; Hollinquest played 14 games with Redskins; Joseph played 14 games with Eagles; Smith played 2 games with 49ers and 7 games with Bengals; Walker played 2 games with Chiefs and 7 games with Bengals; Ware played 15 games with Cardinals.

Also played with Bengals in '94: RB Eric Ball (16 games); RB Steve Broussard (13); T Mark Dennis (7); CB Forey Duckett (2); RB Derrick Fenner (16); DE Mike Frier (1); QB Donald Hollas (2); LB John Johnson (5); NT Tim Krumrie (16); LB Kanavis McGhee (1); T Ken Moyer (16); S Louis Oliver (12); LB Eric Shaw (3); WR Milt Stegall (1); LB Santo Stephens (14); S Fernandus Vinson (16).

Abbreviations: D1—draft pick, first round; SupD2—supplemental draft pick, second round; W-Den—waivers acquisition from Denver; T-Sea—trade acquisition from Seattle; PlanB—Plan B free-agent acquisition; FA—free-agent acquisition (other than Plan B).

MISCELLANEOUS TEAM DATA

Stadium (capacity, surface):
Riverfront Stadium
(60,389, artificial)
Business address:
200 Riverfront Stadium
Cincinnati, OH 45202
Business phone:
513-621-3550
Ticket information:
513-621-3550
Team colors:
Black, orange and white
Flagship radio station:
WCKY, 550 AM
Training site:
Wilmington College
Wilmington, O.

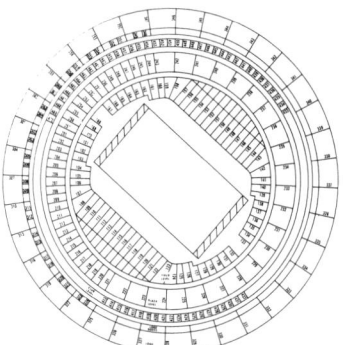

CLEVELAND BROWNS
AFC CENTRAL DIVISION

1994 REVIEW

RESULTS

Sept. 4—at Cincinnati	W	28-20
Sept. 11—PITTSBURGH	L	10-17
Sept. 18—ARIZONA	W	32-0
Sept. 25—at Indianapolis	W	21-14
Oct. 2—N.Y. JETS	W	27-7
Oct. 9—Open date		
Oct. 13—at Houston	W	11-8
Oct. 23—CINCINNATI	W	37-13
Oct. 30—at Denver	L	14-26
Nov. 6—NEW ENGLAND	W	13-6
Nov. 13—at Philadelphia	W	26-7
Nov. 20—at Kansas City	L	13-20
Nov. 27—HOUSTON	W	34-10
Dec. 4—N.Y. GIANTS	L	13-16
Dec. 10—at Dallas	W	19-14
Dec. 18—at Pittsburgh	L	7-17
Dec. 24—SEATTLE	W	35-9

RECORDS/RANKINGS

1994 regular-season record: 11-5 (2nd in AFC Central); 4-2 in division; 8-4 in conference; 6-2 at home; 5-3 on road.
Team record last five years: 34-46 (.425, ranks T19th in league in that span).

1994 team rankings:	No.	AFC	NFL
Total offense	*302.0	8	16
Rushing offense	*103.6	9	14
Passing offense	*198.4	9	19
Scoring offense	340	T5	T11
Total defense	*301.6	2	7
Rushing defense	*104.3	7	13
Passing defense	*197.3	3	7
Scoring defense	204	1	1
Takeaways	31	T6	T13
Giveaways	35	11	23
Turnover differential	-4	9	T20
Sacks	38	T5	T7
Sacks allowed	14	1	1

*Yards per game.

TEAM LEADERS

Scoring (kicking): Matt Stover, 110 pts. (32/32 PATs, 26/28 FGs).
Scoring (touchdowns): Leroy Hoard, 54 pts. (5 rushing, 4 receiving).
Passing: Vinny Testaverde, 2,575 yds. (376 att., 207 comp., 55.1%, 16 TDs, 18 int.).
Rushing: Leroy Hoard, 890 yds. (209 att., 4.3 avg., 5 TDs).
Receptions: Derrick Alexander, 48 (828 yds., 17.3 avg., 2 TDs).
Interceptions: Eric Turner, 9 (199 yds., 1 TD).
Sacks: Rob Burnett, 10.0.
Punting: Tom Tupa, 40.1 avg. (80 punts, 3,211 yds., 0 blocked).
Punt returns: Eric Metcalf, 9.9 avg. (35 att., 348 yds., 2 TDs).
Kickoff returns: Randy Baldwin, 26.9 avg. (28 att., 753 yds., 1 TD).

1995 SEASON

CLUB DIRECTORY

Owner/president
Arthur B. Modell
Executive V.P./legal and administration
Jim Bailey
Assistant to the president
David O. Modell
Treasurer
Mike Srsen
Vice president/public relations
Kevin Byrne
Assistant director/public relations
Francine Lubera
Director/operations and information
Bob Eller
Player relations and media services
Dino Lucarelli
Director/marketing
Gary Gottfried
Assistant director/marketing
John Cicero
Ticket director
Bill Breit
Player personnel director
Michael Lombardi
Pro personnel director
Ozzie Newsome
Area scouts
Tom Dimitroff
Ron Marciniak
Terry McDonough
Ernie Plank
Ellis Rainsberger
Bill Shunkwiler
Phil Savage
Lionel Vital

SCHEDULE

Sept. 3—at New England	1:00
Sept. 10—TAMPA BAY	1:00
Sept. 17—at Houston	12:00
Sept. 24—KANSAS CITY	4:00
Oct. 2—BUFFALO (Mon.)	9:00
Oct. 8—at Detroit	4:00
Oct. 15—Open date	
Oct. 22—JACKSONVILLE	1:00
Oct. 29—at Cincinnati	1:00
Nov. 5—HOUSTON	1:00
Nov. 13—at Pittsburgh (Mon.)	9:00
Nov. 19—GREEN BAY	1:00
Nov. 26—PITTSBURGH	4:00
Dec. 3—at San Diego	1:00
Dec. 9—at Minnesota (Sat.)	11:30
Dec. 17—CINCINNATI	1:00
Dec. 24—at Jacksonville	1:00

All times are for home team.
All games Sunday unless noted.

Head coach:
Bill Belichick
Assistant coaches
Ernie Adams (special assignment)
Jim Bates (def. assignment)
Jacob Burney (defensive line)
Steve Crosby (off. coordinator)
Kirk Ferentz (offensive line)
Pat Hill (tight ends/off. line)
Scott O'Brien (special teams)
Mike Sheppard (receivers)
Jerry Simmons (strength and conditioning)
John Settle (off. assistant)
Rick Venturi (def. coordinator)

Facilities manager
Charlie Cusick
Head trainer
Bill Tessendorf
Assistant trainers
Mark Smith
Lloyd Givan
Team physician
John Bergfeld
Equipment manager
Ed Carroll
Equipment assistants
J.J. Miller
William Sheridan Jr.
Video director
John Wuehrmann

DRAFT CHOICES

Craig Powell, LB, Ohio State (first round/30th pick overall).
Eric Zeier, QB, Georgia (3/84).
Mike Frederick, DE, Virginia (3/94).
Tau Pupua, DL, Weber State (5/136).
Mike Miller, WR, Notre Dame (5/147).
A.C. Tellison, WR, Miami (Fla.) (7/231).

1995 SEASON

TRAINING CAMP ROSTER

No.	QUARTERBACKS	Ht./Wt.	Born	NFL Exp.	College	How acq.	'94 Games GP/GS
8	Goebel, Brad	6-3/214	10-13-67	5	Baylor	FA/93	1/0
4	Schade, Tim	6-5/228	9-3-71	R	Minnesota	FA/95	—
12	Testaverde, Vinny	6-5/215	11-13-63	9	Miami (Fla.)	FA/93	14/13
10	Zeier, Eric	6-0/205	9-6-72	R	Georgia	D3/95	—
	RUNNING BACKS						
21	Byner, Earnest	5-10/215	9-15-62	12	East Carolina	FA/94	16/1
39	Harvey, Frank (FB)	6-0/245	1-19-71	2	Georgia	FA/94	*2/0
33	Hoard, Leroy	5-11/225	5-15-68	6	Michigan	D2/90	16/12
23	Hunter, Ernest	5-8/201	12-21-70	R	Southeast Oklahoma State	FA/95	—
22	Powers, Ricky	6-0/213	11-30-70	1	Michigan	FA/94	0/0
30	Smith, Avrom	5-10/191	3-13-72	R	New Hampshire	FA/95	—
35	Strait, Robert (FB)	6-1/230	11-14-69	1	Baylor	FA/95	0/0
44	Vardell, Tommy (FB)	6-2/230	2-20-69	4	Stanford	D1/92	5/5
34	White, Lorenzo	5-11/222	4-12-66	8	Michigan State	FA/95	*15/8
	RECEIVERS						
85	Alexander, Derrick	6-2/195	11-6-71	2	Michigan	D1b/94	14/12
	Bishop, Harold (TE)	6-4/254	4-8-70	2	Louisiana State	T-TB/95	*6/0
17	Cates, Toby	6-1/194	3-3-72	R	South Carolina	FA/95	—
47	DeLong, Greg (TE)	6-4/245	4-3-73	R	North Carolina	FA/95	—
16	Ethridge, Ray	5-10/180	9-11-68	3	Pasadena (Calif.) City College	FA/95	0/0
48	Hartley, Frank (TE)	6-2/268	12-15-67	2	Illinois	FA/95	10/5
81	Jackson, Michael	6-4/195	4-12-69	5	Southern Mississippi	D6/91	9/7
88	Kinchen, Brian (TE)	6-2/240	8-6-65	8	Louisiana State	FA/91	16/11
87	McCardell, Keenan	6-1/175	1-6-70	4	UNLV	FA/94	13/3
89	Miller, Mike (KR)	5-7/160	6-9-72	R	Notre Dame	D5/95	—
86	Reeves, Walter (TE)	6-4/270	12-16-65	7	Auburn	FA/94	5/5
80	Rison, Andre	6-1/188	3-18-67	7	Michigan State	FA/95	*15/14
18	Senior, Mike	6-1/195	1-4-72	R	Nevada	FA/95	—
84	Smith, Rico	6-0/185	1-14-69	4	Colorado	D6a/92	5/4
83	Tellison, A.C.	6-3/208	9-5-71	R	Miami (Fla.)	D7/95	—
	OFFENSIVE LINEMEN						
70	Arvie, Herman (T)	6-4/305	10-12-70	3	Grambling State	FA/95	16/1
71	Bedosky, Mike (G)	6-4/290	2-13-71	2	Missouri	W-Atl/94	0/0
77	Brown, Orlando (T)	6-7/325	12-12-70	3	South Carolina State	FA/93	14/8
72	Dahl, Bob (G)	6-5/310	11-5-68	3	Notre Dame	FA/92	15/15
60	Devries, Jed	6-5/282	1-6-71	1	Utah State	FA/94	0/0
61	Everitt, Steve (C)	6-5/290	8-21-70	3	Michigan	D1/93	15/15
	Isaia, Sale	6-5/315	6-13-72	R	UCLA	FA/95	—
66	Jones, Tony (T)	6-5/295	5-24-66	8	Western Carolina	FA/88	16/16
67	Neujahr, Quentin	6-4/285	1-30-71	1	Kansas State	FA/94	0/0
	Poumele, Pulu	6-3/300	1-31-72	R	Arizona	FA/95	—
79	Schad, Mike (G)	6-5/290	10-2-63	10	Queen's University, Canada	FA/94	0/0
	Smigiel, Joe	6-4/305	12-31-71	R	Arizona	FA/95	—
62	Williams, Gene (T/G)	6-2/305	10-14-68	5	Iowa State	T-Mia/93	15/9
63	Williams, Wally (C)	6-2/300	2-19-71	3	Florida A&M	FA/93	11/7
	DEFENSIVE LINEMEN						
97	Bandison, Romeo (T)	6-5/290	2-12-71	2	Oregon	D3/94	0/0
90	Burnett, Rob (E)	6-4/280	8-27-67	6	Syracuse	D5/90	16/16
91	Dixon, Ronnie	6-3/292	5-10-71	2	Cincinnati	FA/95	0/0
	Fleming, Joe	6-3/291	12-5-71	R	New Hampshire	FA/95	—
78	Footman, Dan (E)	6-5/290	1-13-69	3	Florida State	D2/93	16/2
	Fortune, Elliott	6-4/275	5-28-74	R	Georgia Tech	FA/95	—
94	Frederick, Mike (E)	6-5/280	8-6-72	R	Virginia	D3b/95	—
73	Goad, Tim (NT)	6-3/280	2-28-66	8	North Carolina	FA/95	*13/13
96	Johnson, Bill	6-4/290	12-9-68	4	Michigan State	D3a/92	14/13
68	Johnson, Mario (T)	6-3/288	1-30-70	3	Missouri	FA/95	0/0
95	Lyle, Rick	6-5/275	2-26-71	2	Missouri	FA/94	3/0
98	Pleasant, Anthony (E)	6-5/280	1-27-68	6	Tennessee State	D3/90	14/14
92	Pupua, Tau	6-5/290	8-24-71	R	Weber State	D5/95	—
75	Sagapolutele, Pio	6-6/297	11-28-69	5	San Diego State	D4/91	11/0
74	Webster, Larry (T)	6-5/288	1-18-69	4	Maryland	FA/95	*16/7
	LINEBACKERS						
58	Banks, Carl	6-4/235	8-29-62	11	Michigan State	FA/94	16/15
56	Caldwell, Mike	6-2/235	8-31-71	3	Middle Tennessee State	D3/93	16/1
51	Dixon, Gerald	6-3/250	6-20-69	4	South Carolina	D3b/92	16/0
53	Hickson, Don	6-2/238	7-13-72	R	Georgia Tech	FA/95	—
55	Hill, Travis	6-2/240	10-3-69	3	Nebraska	D7/93	14/0
52	Johnson, Pepper	6-3/248	6-29-64	10	Ohio State	FA/93	16/16

No.	LINEBACKERS	Ht./Wt.	Born	NFL Exp.	College	How acq.	'94 Games GP/GS
99	McKenzie, Rich	6-2/240	4-15-71	1	Penn State	D6/93	0/0
50	Neal, Randy	6-3/236	12-29-72	R	Virginia	FA/95	—
59	Powell, Craig	6-4/230	11-13-71	R	Ohio State	D1/95	—
49	Royal, Andre	6-2/220	12-1-72	R	Alabama	FA/95	—
54	Sutter, Eddie	6-3/235	10-3-69	3	Northwestern	W-NE/93	16/0
5	Thomas, Marquise	6-3/255	5-25-71	R	Mississippi	FA/95	—
	DEFENSIVE BACKS						
43	Adams, Vashon	5-10/196	9-12-73	R	Eastern Michigan	FA/95	—
36	Booth, Issac	6-3/190	5-23-71	2	California	D5/94	16/1
15	Brady, Donny	6-2/195	11-24-73	R	Wisconsin	FA/95	—
26	Cecil, Chuck (S)	6-0/185	11-8-64	7	Arizona	FA/95	0/0
28	Griffin, Don (CB)	6-0/176	3-17-64	10	Middle Tennessee State	FA/94	15/15
31	Hairston, Stacey (CB)	5-9/185	8-16-67	3	Ohio Northern	FA/93	15/0
25	Hall, Dana (S)	6-2/206	7-8-69	4	Washington	FA/95	*16/4
41	Jacobs, Tim (CB)	5-10/185	4-5-70	3	Delaware	FA/93	9/1
38	Langham, Antonio (CB)	6-0/180	7-31-72	2	Alabama	D1a/94	16/16
27	Moore, Stevon (S)	5-11/210	2-9-67	7	Mississippi	PlanB/92	16/16
42	Riddick, Louis (S)	6-2/215	3-15-69	4	Pittsburgh	FA/93	16/0
20	Thomas, Johnny (CB)	5-9/191	8-3-64	7	Baylor	FA/95	*16/0
37	Thompson, Bennie (S)	6-0/214	2-10-63	6	Grambling State	FA/94	16/0
29	Turner, Eric (S)	6-1/207	9-20-68	5	UCLA	D1/91	16/16
40	Williams, Mike	6-3/201	7-7-71	R	Alabama State	FA/95	—
	SPECIALISTS						
3	Stover, Matt (K)	5-11/178	1-27-68	6	Louisiana Tech	PlanB/91	16/0
7	Tupa, Tom (P)	6-4/230	2-6-66	7	Ohio State	FA/94	16/0

*Bishop played 6 games with Buccaneers in '94; Goad played 13 games with Patriots; Hall played 16 games with 49ers; Harvey played 2 games with Cardinals; Rison played 15 games with Falcons; Thomas played 16 games with Redskins; Webster played 16 games with Dolphins; White played 15 games with Oilers.

Also played with Browns in '94: RB Randy Baldwin (16 games); WR Mark Carrier (16); G Doug Dawson (12); DT James Jones (16); TE Tom McLemore (2); RB Eric Metcalf (16); WR Patrick Newman (1); DT Michael Dean Perry (15); QB Mark Rypien (6); S Del Speer (8); LB Frank Stams (16).

Abbreviations: D1—draft pick, first round; SupD2—supplemental draft pick, second round; W-Den—waivers acquisition from Denver; T-Sea—trade acquisition from Seattle; PlanB—Plan B free-agent acquisition; FA—free-agent acquisition (other than Plan B).

MISCELLANEOUS TEAM DATA

Stadium (capacity, surface):
Cleveland Stadium
(78,512, grass)
Business address:
80 First Avenue
Berea, OH 44017-0679
Business phone:
216-891-5000
Ticket information:
216-696-3800
Team colors:
Seal brown, orange and white
Flagship radio stations:
WDOK, 102.1 FM; WKNR 1220 AM
Training site:
Berea Complex
Berea, O.
216-891-5000

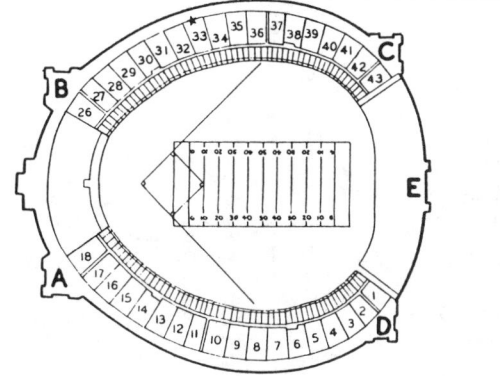

DALLAS COWBOYS
NFC EASTERN DIVISION

1994 REVIEW

RESULTS

Sept.	4—at Pittsburgh	W	26-9
Sept.	11—HOUSTON	W	20-17
Sept.	19—DETROIT (OT)	L	17-20
Sept.	25—Open date		
Oct.	2—at Washington	W	34-7
Oct.	9—ARIZONA	W	38-3
Oct.	16—PHILADELPHIA	W	24-13
Oct.	23—at Arizona	W	28-21
Oct.	30—at Cincinnati	W	23-20
Nov.	7—N.Y. GIANTS	W	38-10
Nov.	13—at San Francisco	L	14-21
Nov.	20—WASHINGTON	W	31-7
Nov.	24—GREEN BAY	W	42-31
Dec.	4—at Philadelphia	W	31-19
Dec.	10—CLEVELAND	L	14-19
Dec.	19—at New Orleans	W	24-16
Dec.	24—at N.Y. Giants	L	10-15

RECORDS/RANKINGS

1994 regular-season record: 12-4 (1st in NFC East); 7-1 in division; 9-3 in conference; 6-2 at home; 6-2 on road.
Team record last five years: 55-25 (.688), ranks 3rd in league in that span).

1994 team rankings:

	No.	NFC	NFL
Total offense	*332.6	4	8
Rushing offense	*122.1	2	5
Passing offense	*210.5	7	T12
Scoring offense	414	2	2
Total defense	*269.6	1	1
Rushing defense	*97.6	5	10
Passing defense	*172.0	1	1
Scoring defense	248	1	3
Takeaways	31	T8	T13
Giveaways	24	T3	T5
Turnover differential	7	T4	T8
Sacks	47	1	2
Sacks allowed	20	1	4

*Yards per game.

TEAM LEADERS

Scoring (kicking): Chris Boniol, 114 pts. (48/48 PATs, 22/29 FGs).
Scoring (touchdowns): Emmitt Smith, 132 pts. (21 rushing, 1 receiving).
Passing: Troy Aikman, 2,676 yds. (361 att., 233 comp., 64.5%, 13 TDs, 12 int.).
Rushing: Emmitt Smith, 1,484 yds. (368 att., 4.0 avg., 21 TDs).
Receptions: Michael Irvin, 79 (1,241 yds., 15.7 avg., 6 TDs).
Interceptions: Darren Woodson, 5 (140 yds., 1 TD).
Sacks: Charles Haley, 12.5.
Punting: John Jett, 41.9 avg. (70 punts, 2,935 yds., 0 blocked).
Punt returns: Kevin Williams, 8.9 avg. (39 att., 349 yds., 1 TD).
Kickoff returns: Kevin Williams, 26.7 avg. (43 att., 1,148 yds., 1 TD).

1995 SEASON

CLUB DIRECTORY

President/general manager
  Jerry Jones
Vice presidents
  Stephen Jones
  Mike McCoy
  George Hays
Treasurer
  Jack Dixon
Director of public relations
  Rich Dalrymple
Assistant director of public relations
  Brett Daniels
Ticket manager
  Carol Padgett
Director of college scouting
  Larry Lacewell
Scouts
  Tom Ciskowski
  Jim Garrett
  Walter Juliff
  Bobby Marks
  Walt Yowarsky
Head trainer
  Kevin O'Neill
Assistant trainer
  Jim Maurer
Physicians
  Robert Vandermeer
  John Baker
  J.R. Zamorano

Head coach
  Barry Switzer
Assistant coaches
  Ernie Zampese (offensive coordinator)
  Hubbard Alexander (wide receivers)
  Joe Avezzano (special teams)
  John Blake (defensive line)
  Joe Brodsky (running backs)
  Dave Campo (def. coordinator)
  Jim Eddy (defensive assistant)
  Robert Ford (tight ends)
  Steve Hoffman (kickers/quality control)
  Hudson Houck (offensive line)
  Mike Woicik (strength and conditioning)
  Mike Zimmer (defensive backs)

Equipment/practice fields manager
  Buck Buchanan
Video director
  Robert Blackwell
Director of operations
  Bruce Mays

SCHEDULE

Sept.	4—at N.Y. Giants (Mon.)	9:00
Sept.	10—DENVER	3:00
Sept.	17—at Minnesota	7:00
Sept.	24—ARIZONA	3:00
Oct.	1—at Washington	1:00
Oct.	8—GREEN BAY	12:00
Oct.	15—at San Diego	1:00
Oct.	22—Open date	
Oct.	29—at Atlanta	1:00
Nov.	6—PHILADELPHIA (Mon.)	8:00
Nov.	12—SAN FRANCISCO	3:00
Nov.	19—at Los Angeles	1:00
Nov.	23—KAN. CITY (Thanks.)	3:00
Dec.	3—WASHINGTON	3:00
Dec.	10—at Philadelphia	1:00
Dec.	17—N.Y. GIANTS	3:00
Dec.	25—at Arizona (Mon.)	7:00

All times are for home team.
All games Sunday unless noted.

DRAFT CHOICES

Sherman Williams, RB, Alabama (second round/46th pick overall).
Kendell Watkins, TE, Miss. State (2/59).
Shane Hannah, G, Michigan State (2/63).
Charlie Williams, DB, Bowling Green State (3/92).
Eric Bjornson, WR, Washington (4/110).
Alundis Brice, DB, Mississippi (4/129).
Linc Harden, LB, Oklahoma State (4/130).
Edward Hervey, WR, Southern Cal (5/166).
Dana Howard, LB, Illinois (5/168).
Oscar Sturgis, DE, North Carolina (7/236).

TRAINING CAMP ROSTER

No.	QUARTERBACKS	Ht./Wt.	Born	NFL Exp.	College	How acq.	'94 Games GP/GS
8	Aikman, Troy	6-4/228	11-21-66	7	UCLA	D1/89	14/14
17	Garrett, Jason	6-2/195	3-28-66	3	Princeton	FA/93	2/1
9	Semptimphelter, Scott	6-2/199	5-15-72	R	Lehigh	FA/95	—
	Wilson, Wade	6-3/206	2-1-59	15	East Texas State	FA/95	*4/0
	RUNNING BACKS						
44	Coleman, Lincoln	6-1/239	8-12-69	3	Baylor	FA/94	11/0
35	Graham, Roger	5-10/212	11-8-72	R	New Haven	FA/95	—
33	Johnson, Curtis	5-9/204	11-11-71	R	North Carolina	FA/95	—
48	Johnston, Daryl (FB)	6-2/242	2-10-66	7	Syracuse	D2/89	16/16
38	Lang, David	5-11/213	3-28-68	5	Northern Arizona	FA/95	*13/0
41	McClenton, Michael (FB)	5-11/252	12-9-69	R	North Carolina	FA/95	—
45	McGuire, Stephen	5-11/215	11-20-69	1	Miami (Fla.)	FA/95	0/0
36	Ross, Dominique	6-0/203	1-12-72	R	Valdosta (Ga.) State	FA/95	—
22	Smith, Emmitt	5-9/209	5-15-69	6	Florida	D1/90	15/15
29	Williams, Germaine (FB)	5-10/228	2-4-71	1	Louisiana State	FA/95	0/0
20	Williams, Sherman	5-8/190	8-13-73	R	Alabama	D2/95	—
	RECEIVERS						
86	Bjornson, Eric (TE)	6-4/215	12-15-71	R	Washington	D4/95	—
4	Davis, Billy	6-1/199	7-6-72	R	Pittsburgh	FA/95	—
87	Davis, John (TE)	6-4/257	5-14-73	1	Emporia (Kan.) State	FA/95	0/0
82	Fleming, Cory	6-1/216	3-19-71	2	Tennessee	FA/94	2/0
1	Gadsden, Oronde	6-3/218	8-20-71	R	Winston-Salem State	FA/95	—
2	Goosby, Michael	6-3/207	10-15-70	R	North Texas	FA/95	—
3	Harris, Rodney	6-5/207	12-1-71	R	Kansas	FA/95	—
81	Hervey, Edward	6-3/179	5-4-73	R	Southern California	D5a/95	—
88	Irvin, Michael	6-2/205	3-5-66	8	Miami (Fla.)	D1/88	16/16
49	McGrath, Ryan (TE)	6-5/255	8-23-72	R	SW Louisiana	FA/95	—
84	Novacek, Jay (TE)	6-4/234	10-24-62	11	Wyoming	PlanB/90	16/14
6	Thomas, Jeff	6-0/192	1-13-72	R	Georgia	FA/95	—
83	Watkins, Kendell (TE)	6-1/305	3-8-73	R	Mississippi State	D2/95	—
85	Williams, Kevin (KR)	5-9/195	1-25-71	3	Miami (Fla.)	D2/93	15/2
	OFFENSIVE LINEMEN						
73	Allen, Larry (T)	6-3/325	11-27-71	2	Sonoma State (Calif.)	D2/94	16/10
53	Donaldson, Ray (C)	6-3/300	5-18-58	16	Georgia	FA/95	*16/16
60	Gruttadauria, Mike (C)	6-3/273	12-6-72	R	Central Florida	FA/95	—
63	Hannah, Shane (G)	6-5/345	10-21-71	R	Michigan State	D2/95	—
69	Hegamin, George (T)	6-7/338	2-14-73	2	North Carolina State	D3/94	2/0
70	Hellestrae, Dale (G/C)	6-5/286	7-11-62	11	Southern Methodist	T-Rai/90	16/0
75	Hmielewski, Jim (T)	6-5/314	2-13-72	R	Kansas State	FA/95	—
62	Jones, John (G)	6-1/309	12-8-72	R	Kansas	FA/95	—
61	Newton, Nate (G)	6-3/320	12-20-61	10	Florida A&M	FA/86	16/16
76	Reynolds, Jerry (T)	6-6/315	4-2-70	2	UNLV	FA/94	0/0
65	Stone, Ron (T/G)	6-5/309	7-20-71	3	Boston College	D4/93	16/0
72	Tagoai, Mu (G)	6-3/305	4-10-72	R	Arizona	FA/95	—
71	Tuinei, Mark (T)	6-5/305	3-31-60	13	Hawaii	FA/83	15/15
66	Vaughn, DeMario (T)	6-5/283	3-21-72	R	Arizona State	FA/95	—
79	Williams, Erik (T)	6-6/322	9-7-68	5	Central State (O.)	D3/91	7/7
	DEFENSIVE LINEMEN						
97	Batiste, Michael (T)	6-3/295	12-24-70	1	Tulane	FA/95	0/0
96	Carver, Shante (E)	6-5/242	2-12-71	2	Arizona State	D1/94	10/0
74	Dickson, Wayne (E)	6-3/265	11-27-67	1	Oklahoma	FA/95	0/0
93	Edwards, Demetrius (T)	6-3/287	3-25-72	R	Fresno State	FA/95	—
92	Evans, Josh (T)	6-2/283	9-6-72	R	Alabama-Birmingham	FA/95	—
94	Haley, Charles (E)	6-5/255	1-6-64	10	James Madison	T-SF/92	16/16
95	Hennings, Chad (T)	6-6/288	10-20-65	4	Air Force	D11/88	16/0
78	Lett, Leon	6-6/288	10-12-68	5	Emporia (Kan.) State	D7/91	16/16
67	Maryland, Russell (T)	6-1/279	3-22-69	5	Miami (Fla.)	D1/91	16/16
99	McCormack, Hurvin (T)	6-5/274	4-6-72	2	Indiana	FA/94	4/0
90	Sturgis, Oscar (E)	6-5/280	1-12-71	R	North Carolina	D7/95	—
92	Tolbert, Tony (E)	6-6/263	12-29-67	7	Texas-El Paso	D4/89	16/16
	LINEBACKERS						
56	Barnes, Reggie	6-1/240	10-23-69	2	Oklahoma	FA/95	0/0
54	Coger, Freddie	6-2/248	2-9-70	R	Georgia Tech	FA/95	—
58	Edwards, Dixon	6-1/225	3-25-68	5	Michigan State	D2/91	16/15
57	Harden, Linc	6-3/238	4-9-72	R	Oklahoma State	D4/95	—
50	Howard, Dana	6-0/238	2-25-72	R	Illinois	D5b/95	—
55	Jones, Robert	6-2/237	9-27-69	4	East Carolina	D1/92	16/16
98	Myles, Godfrey	6-1/242	9-22-68	5	Florida	D3/91	15/0

No.	LINEBACKERS	Ht./Wt.	Born	NFL Exp.	College	How acq.	'94 Games GP/GS
52	Schwantz, Jim	6-2/232	1-23-70	2	Purdue	T-Chi/94	7/0
59	Smith, Darrin	6-1/230	4-15-70	3	Miami (Fla.)	D2/93	16/16
DEFENSIVE BACKS							
39	Anderson, John (S)	5-10/186	11-30-71	R	Oklahoma	FA/95	—
40	Bates, Bill (S)	6-1/210	6-6-61	13	Tennessee	FA/83	15/0
21	Brice, Alundis (CB)	5-10/178	5-1-70	R	Mississippi	D4b/95	—
24	Brown, Larry (CB)	5-11/186	11-30-69	5	Texas Christian	D12/91	15/15
23	Fields, Floyd (S)	6-1/200	1-7-69	4	Arizona State	FA/95	0/0
47	Holmes, Clayton (CB/KR)	5-10/181	8-23-69	4	Carson-Newman (Tenn.)	D3/92	16/1
27	Houston, Artis (CB)	5-7/179	11-29-72	R	California	FA/95	—
31	Marion, Brock (S)	5-11/189	6-11-70	3	Nevada	D7/93	14/1
26	Smith, Kevin (CB)	5-11/184	4-7-70	4	Texas A&M	D1/92	16/16
30	Studstill, Darren (S)	6-1/186	8-9-70	1	West Virginia	D6/94	1/0
25	Tremble, Greg (S)	5-11/188	4-16-72	1	Georgia	FA/95	0/0
42	Williams, Charlie (S)	6-0/190	2-2-72	R	Bowling Green State	D3/95	—
28	Woodson, Darren (S)	6-1/215	4-25-69	4	Arizona State	D2/92	16/16
SPECIALISTS							
10	Baker, Jon (K)	6-1/170	8-13-72	R	Arizona State	FA/95	—
18	Boniol, Chris (K)	5-11/159	12-9-71	2	Louisiana Tech	FA/94	16/0
19	Jett, John (P)	6-0/194	11-11-68	3	East Carolina	FA/93	16/0
13	McCord, Paul (P)	6-6/229	9-23-71	R	Western Maryland	FA/95	—

*Donaldson played 16 games with Seahawks in '94; Lang played 13 games with Rams; Wilson played 4 games with Saints.

Also played with Cowboys in '94: RB Tommie Agee (15 games); LB Darrick Brownlow (16); S Joe Fishback (12); TE Scott Galbraith (16); S Kenneth Gant (16); WR Alvin Harper (16); DE Jim Jeffcoat (16); G Derek Kennard (16); QB Rodney Peete (7); RB Blair Thomas (2); CB Dave Thomas (16); LB/DE Matt Vanderbeek (12); S James Washington (16); FB Robert Wilson (2).

Abbreviations: D1—draft pick, first round; SupD2—supplemental draft pick, second round; W-Den—waivers acquisition from Denver; T-Sea—trade acquisition from Seattle; PlanB—Plan B free-agent acquisition; FA—free-agent acquisition (other than Plan B).

MISCELLANEOUS TEAM DATA

Stadium (capacity, surface):
Texas Stadium
(65,024, artificial)
Business address:
One Cowboys Parkway
Irving, TX 75063
Business phone:
214-556-9900
Ticket information:
214-579-5000
Team colors:
Royal blue, metallic silver blue
and white
Flagship radio station:
KVIL, 103.7 FM
Training site:
St. Edward's University
Austin, Tex.
214-556-9900

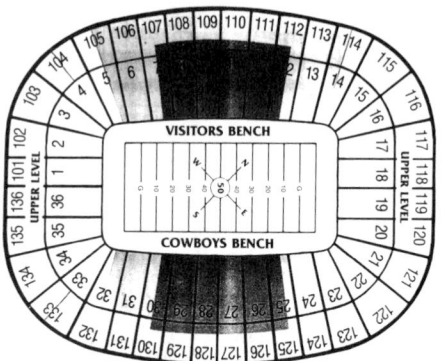

DENVER BRONCOS
AFC WESTERN DIVISION

RESULTS

Sept.	4—SAN DIEGO	L	34-37
Sept.	11—at N.Y. Jets (OT)	L	22-25
Sept.	18—L.A. RAIDERS	L	16-48
Sept.	26—at Buffalo	L	20-27
Oct.	2—Open date		
Oct.	9—at Seattle	W	16-9
Oct.	17—KANSAS CITY	L	28-31
Oct.	23—at San Diego	W	20-15
Oct.	30—CLEVELAND	W	26-14
Nov.	6—at L.A. Rams	L	21-27
Nov.	13—SEATTLE	W	17-10
Nov.	20—ATLANTA	W	32-28
Nov.	27—CINCINNATI	W	15-13
Dec.	4—at Kan. City (OT)	W	20-17
Dec.	11—at L.A. Raiders	L	13-23
Dec.	17—at San Francisco	L	19-42
Dec.	24—NEW ORLEANS	L	28-30

RECORDS/RANKINGS

1994 regular-season record: 7-9 (4th in AFC West); 4-4 in division; 6-6 in conference; 4-4 at home; 3-5 on road.
Team record last five years: 41-39 (.513, ranks 15th in league in that span).
1994 team rankings:

	No.	AFC	NFL
Total offense	*342.9	4	6
Rushing offense	*91.9	13	23
Passing offense	*251.1	3	6
Scoring offense	347	4	10
Total defense	*369.2	14	28
Rushing defense	*109.5	9	17
Passing defense	*259.7	14	28
Scoring defense	396	13	25
Takeaways	26	T11	T20
Giveaways	31	T7	T16
Turnover differential	-5	T10	T22
Sacks	23	14	27
Sacks allowed	55	13	27

*Yards per game.

TEAM LEADERS

Scoring (kicking): Jason Elam, 119 pts. (29/29 PATs, 30/37 FGs).
Scoring (touchdowns): Leonard Russell, 54 pts. (9 rushing).
Passing: John Elway, 3,490 yds. (494 att., 307 comp., 62.1%, 16 TDs, 10 int.).
Rushing: Leonard Russell, 620 yds. (190 att., 3.3 avg., 9 TDs).
Receptions: Shannon Sharpe, 87 (1,010 yds., 11.6 avg., 4 TDs).
Interceptions: Ray Crockett, 2 (6 yds., 0 TDs); Randy Hilliard, 2 (8 yds., 0 TDs); Rondell Jones, 2 (9 yds., 0 TDs).
Sacks: Simon Fletcher, 7.0.
Punting: Tom Rouen, 42.9 avg. (76 punts, 3,258 yds., 0 blocked).
Punt returns: Glyn Milburn, 9.2 avg. (41 att., 379 yds., 0 TDs).
Kickoff returns: Butler By'Not'e, 22.7 avg. (24 att., 545 yds., 0 TDs).

CLUB DIRECTORY

President/chief executive officer
Pat Bowlen
General manager
John Beake
Special assistant to the president
Bob Hampe
Dir./football op. and player personnel
Bob Ferguson
Controller
Alex Rohr
Dir. of ticket operations/bus. dev.
Rick Nichols
Stadium operations manager
Gail Stuckey
Director of operations
Bill Harpole
Director of media relations
Jim Saccomano
Director of marketing
Rosemary Hanratty
Asst. to the g.m./community relations
Fred Fleming
Dir. of player relations
Bill Thompson
Community relations coordinator
Steve Sewell
Asst. director of player personnel
Cornell Green
Director of college scouting
Jeff Smith
Scouts
Scott DiStefano
Jack Elway
Dave Gettleman
Charlie Lee
Ted Sundquist

SCHEDULE

Sept.	3—BUFFALO	6:00
Sept.	10—at Dallas	3:00
Sept.	17—WASHINGTON	2:00
Sept.	24—at San Diego	1:00
Oct.	1—at Seattle	1:00
Oct.	8—at New England	8:00
Oct.	16—LOS ANGELES (Mon.)	7:00
Oct.	22—KANSAS CITY	2:00
Oct.	29—Open date	
Nov.	5—ARIZONA	2:00
Nov.	12—at Philadelphia	8:00
Nov.	19—SAN DIEGO	2:00
Nov.	26—at Houston	3:00
Dec.	3—JACKSONVILLE	2:00
Dec.	10—SEATTLE	2:00
Dec.	17—at Kansas City	3:00
Dec.	24—at Los Angeles	1:00

All times are for home team.
All games Sunday unless noted.

Head coach
Mike Shanahan
Assistant coaches
Frank Bush (linebackers)
Alex Gibbs (assistant head coach/offensive line)
Gary Kubiak (offensive coordinator/quarterbacks)
Greg Robinson (def. coord.)
Barney Chavous (def. assistant)
Rick Dennison (off. assistant)
Ed Donatell (defensive backs)
George Dyer (defensive line)
Mike Heimerdinger (wide receivers)
Brian Pariani (tight ends)
Al Reynolds (def. assistant)
Richard Smith (special teams)
Bobby Turner (running backs)
Rich Tuten (strength and conditioning)

Head trainer
Steve Antonopulos
Assistant trainers
James Collins
Jim Keller
Physician
Richard Hawkins
Equipment manager
Doug West
Director/video operations
Kent Erickson

DRAFT CHOICES

Jamie Brown, T, Florida A&M (fourth round/121st pick overall).
Ken Brown, LB, Virginia Tech (4/124).
Phil Yeboah-Kodie, LB, Penn State (5/146).
Fritz Fequiere, G, Iowa (6/182).
Terrell Davis, RB, Georgia (6/196).
Steve Russ, LB, Air Force (7/218).
Byron Chamberlain, WR, Wayne (Neb.) State (7/222).

TRAINING CAMP ROSTER

No.	QUARTERBACKS	Ht./Wt.	Born	NFL Exp.	College	How acq.	'94 Games GP/GS
7	Elway, John	6-3/215	6-28-60	13	Stanford	T-Bal/83	14/14
10	McCoy, Mike	6-2/204	4-1-72	R	Utah	FA/95	—
17	Millen, Hugh	6-5/216	11-22-63	10	Washington	FA/94	5/2
14	Musgrave, Bill	6-2/205	11-11-67	5	Oregon	FA/91	0/0
	RUNNING BACKS						
33	Bernstine, Rod	6-3/238	2-8-65	9	Texas A&M	FA/93	3/3
20	Canley, Sheldon	5-9/195	4-19-68	2	San Jose State	FA/95	0/0
43	Clark, Derrick	6-1/235	5-4-71	2	Evangel (Mo.)	FA/94	16/4
29	Craver, Aaron	6-0/220	12-18-68	5	Fresno State	FA/95	*8/0
30	Davis, Terrell	5-11/200	10-28-72	R	Georgia	D6b/95	—
35	Ivlow, John (FB)	5-1/210	1-26-70	2	Colorado State	FA/95	0/0
22	Milburn, Glyn (KR)	5-8/177	2-19-71	3	Stanford	D2/93	16/3
36	Miles, Ostell	6-0/227	8-6-71	3	Houston	FA/95	0/0
38	Rivers, Reggie	6-1/215	2-22-68	5	Southwest Texas State	FA/91	16/1
41	Strother, Deon	5-11/213	4-12-72	2	Southern California	FA/94	2/0
	RECEIVERS						
85	Bonner, Melvin	6-3/207	2-18-70	3	Baylor	D6/93	0/0
86	Campbell, Jeff	5-8/167	3-26-68	6	Colorado	FA/94	16/1
89	Carswell, Dwayne (TE)	6-3/261	1-18-72	2	Liberty	FA/94	4/0
15	Chamberlain, Byron	6-1/225	10-17-71	R	Wayne (Neb.) State	D7/95	—
88	Evans, Jerry (TE)	6-4/250	9-28-68	3	Toledo	FA/93	16/11
82	Johnson, Vance	5-11/185	3-13-63	10	Arizona	FA/95	0/0
80	Kimbrough, Tony	6-2/192	9-17-70	3	Jackson State	D7b/93	12/0
87	McCaffrey, Ed	6-5/215	8-17-68	5	Stanford	FA/95	*16/0
83	Miller, Anthony	5-11/190	4-15-65	8	Tennessee	FA/94	16/15
81	Pritchard, Mike	5-10/190	10-26-69	5	Colorado	T-Atl/94	3/0
84	Sharpe, Shannon (TE)	6-2/230	6-26-68	6	Savannah (Ga.) State	D7/90	15/13
45	Wainright, Frank (TE)	6-3/245	10-10-67	4	Northern Colorado	FA/95	0/0
	OFFENSIVE LINEMEN						
70	Brown, Jamie (T)	6-8/300	4-24-72	R	Florida A&M	D4/95	—
60	Burch, Joe (C)	6-2/280	8-8-71	2	Texas Southern	FA/94	0/0
64	Fequiere, Fritz (G)	6-2/289	1-31-72	R	Iowa	D6a/95	—
75	Habib, Brian (G)	6-7/292	12-2-64	7	Washington	FA/93	16/16
79	Johnson, Chuck (T)	6-3/290	5-22-69	2	Texas	FA/95	0/0
72	Kartz, Keith (C)	6-4/270	5-5-63	9	California	FA/87	0/0
62	Lewis, Bill (C)	6-6/290	7-12-63	10	Nebraska	FA/95	0/0
68	McElroy, Reggie (T)	6-6/290	3-4-60	12	West Texas State	FA/95	*10/0
61	Meeks, Bob (C)	6-2/279	5-28-69	4	Auburn	D10/92	0/0
66	Nalen, Tom	6-2/280	5-13-71	2	Boston College	D7c/94	7/1
69	Schlereth, Mark (G)	6-3/278	1-25-66	7	Idaho	FA/95	*16/6
74	Schultz, Bill (G/T)	6-5/305	5-1-67	6	Southern California	FA/95	0/0
76	Thompson, Broderick (T)	6-5/295	8-14-60	10	Kansas	FA/95	*14/14
65	Zimmerman, Gary (T)	6-6/294	12-13-61	10	Oregon	T-Min/93	16/16
	DEFENSIVE LINEMEN						
99	Dronett, Shane (E)	6-6/275	1-12-71	4	Texas	D2/92	16/15
96	Hasselbach, Harold	6-6/280	9-22-67	3	Washington	FA/94	16/9
93	Jones, James (T)	6-2/290	2-6-69	5	Northern Iowa	FA/95	*16/5
97	Lodish, Mike (NT)	6-3/280	8-11-67	6	UCLA	FA/95	*15/5
91	Oshodin, Willie (E)	6-4/265	9-16-69	4	Villanova	FA/92	13/0
95	Perry, Michael Dean (T)	6-1/285	8-27-65	7	Clemson	FA/95	*15/14
94	Robinson, Jeff (E)	6-4/265	2-20-70	3	Idaho	D4/93	16/0
98	Tanuvasa, Maa (T)	6-2/277	11-6-70	1	Hawaii	FA/95	0/0
90	Williams, Dan (E)	6-4/290	12-15-69	3	Toledo	D1/93	12/7
	LINEBACKERS						
57	Aldridge, Allen	6-1/245	5-30-72	2	Houston	D2/94	16/2
58	Alexander, Elijah	6-2/230	8-8-70	4	Kansas State	W-TB/93	16/16
55	Brown, Ken	6-1/235	5-5-71	R	Virginia Tech	D4b/95	—
56	Burns, Keith	6-2/235	5-16-72	2	Oklahoma State	D7a/94	11/1
73	Fletcher, Simon	6-5/240	2-18-62	11	Houston	D2b/85	16/16
54	Hager, Britt	6-1/225	2-20-66	7	Texas	FA/95	*16/5
50	Jacobs, Ray	6-2/244	8-18-72	2	North Carolina	FA/94	16/0
77	Mecklenburg, Karl	6-3/235	9-1-60	12	Minnesota	D12/83	16/15
92	Wyman, David	6-2/248	3-31-64	9	Stanford	FA/93	4/0
51	Yeboah-Kodie, Phil	6-2/220	1-22-71	R	Penn State	D5/95	—
	DEFENSIVE BACKS						
27	Atwater, Steve (S)	6-3/217	10-28-66	7	Arkansas	D1/89	14/14
23	Bradford, Ronnie (CB)	5-10/188	10-1-70	3	Colorado	FA/93	12/0
34	Braxton, Tyrone (CB)	5-11/185	12-17-64	9	North Dakota State	FA/95	*16/0

No.	DEFENSIVE BACKS	Ht./Wt.	Born	NFL Exp.	College	How acq.	'94 Games GP/GS
28	By'not'e, Butler (CB/KR)	5-9/190	9-29-72	2	Ohio State	D7/94	9/0
39	Crockett, Ray (CB)	5-10/185	1-5-67	7	Baylor	FA/94	14/14
24	Fuller, Randy (CB)	5-9/173	6-2-70	2	Tennessee State	D4/94	10/1
40	Hall, Darryl (S)	6-2/210	8-1-66	3	Washington	FA/93	16/3
37	Hauck, Tim (S)	5-10/185	12-20-66	6	Montana	FA/95	*13/3
21	Hilliard, Randy (CB)	5-11/165	2-6-67	6	Northwestern (La.) State	FA/94	15/6
31	Jones, Rondell (S)	6-2/210	5-7-71	3	North Carolina	D3a/93	16/3
49	Smith, Dennis (S)	6-3/200	2-3-59	14	Southern California	D1/81	12/12
26	Thomas, Eric (CB)	5-11/184	9-11-64	9	Tulane	FA/95	*1/0
48	Washington, Lionel (CB)	6-0/185	10-21-60	13	Tulane	FA/95	*11/7
	SPECIALISTS						
1	Elam, Jason (K)	5-11/192	3-8-70	3	Hawaii	D3/93	16/0
16	Rouen, Tom (P)	6-3/215	6-9-68	3	Colorado	FA/93	16/0

*Braxton played 16 games with Dolphins in '94; Craver played 8 games with Dolphins; Hager played 16 games with Eagles; Hauck played 13 games with Packers; Jones played 16 games with Browns; Lodish played 15 games with Bills; McCaffrey played 16 games with 49ers; McElroy played 10 games with Vikings; Perry played 15 games with Browns; Schlereth played 16 games with Redskins; Thomas played 1 game with Jets; Thompson played 14 games with Eagles; Washington played 11 games with Raiders.

Also played with Broncos in '94: LB Mike Croel (13 games); LB Mitch Donahue (3); T Russell Freeman (13); LB Richard Harvey (16); T Ken Lanier (4); T Don Maggs (9); G Jon Melander (15); WR Derek Russell (12); RB Leonard Russell (14); LB Glenell Sanders (1); T Kirk Scrafford (16); CB Ben Smith (14); WR Charles Swann (13); WR Cedric Tillman (16); NT Ted Washington (15); C/G Dave Widell (16).

Abbreviations: D1—draft pick, first round; SupD2—supplemental draft pick, second round; W-Den—waivers acquisition from Denver; T-Sea—trade acquisition from Seattle; PlanB—Plan B free-agent acquisition; FA—free-agent acquisition (other than Plan B).

MISCELLANEOUS TEAM DATA

Stadium (capacity, surface):
Mile High Stadium
(76,273, grass)
Business address:
13655 Broncos Parkway
Englewood, CO 80112
Business phone:
303-649-9000
Ticket information:
303-433-7466
Team colors:
Orange, royal blue and white
Flagship radio station:
KOA, 850 AM
Training site:
University of Northern Colorado
Greeley, Colo.
303-623-5212

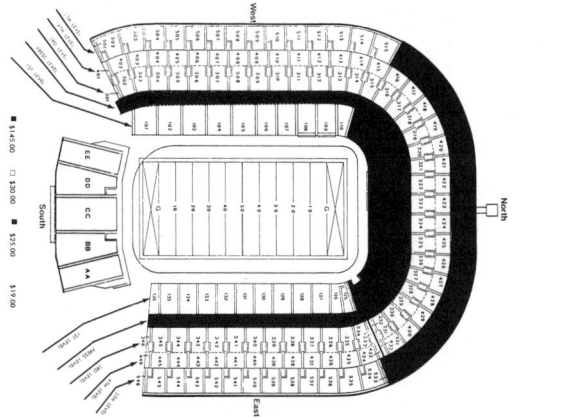

DETROIT LIONS
NFC CENTRAL DIVISION

1994 REVIEW

RESULTS

Sept. 4—ATLANTA (OT)	W	31-28
Sept. 11—at Minnesota	L	3-10
Sept. 19—at Dallas (OT)	W	20-17
Sept. 25—NEW ENGLAND	L	17-23
Oct. 2—at Tampa Bay	L	14-24
Oct. 9—SAN FRANCISCO	L	21-27
Oct. 16—Open date		
Oct. 23—CHICAGO	W	21-16
Oct. 30—at N.Y. Giants (OT)	W	28-25
Nov. 6—at G. Bay (Milw.)	L	30-38
Nov. 13—TAMPA BAY	W	14-9
Nov. 20—at Chicago	L	10-20
Nov. 24—BUFFALO	W	35-21
Dec. 4—GREEN BAY	W	34-31
Dec. 10—at N.Y. Jets	W	18-7
Dec. 17—MINNESOTA	W	41-19
Dec. 25—at Miami	L	20-27

RECORDS/RANKINGS

1994 regular-season record: 9-7 (T2nd in NFC Central); 4-4 in division; 7-5 in conference; 6-2 at home; 3-5 on road. **Team record last five years:** 42-38 (.525, ranks 14th in league in that span).

1994 team rankings:	No.	NFC	NFL
Total offense	*312.6	8	15
Rushing offense	*130.0	1	3
Passing offense	*182.6	13	24
Scoring offense	357	4	6
Total defense	*337.8	11	24
Rushing defense	*116.2	11	22
Passing defense	*221.6	10	19
Scoring defense	342	9	19
Takeaways	23	T10	T23
Giveaways	24	T3	T5
Turnover differential	-1	T8	T15
Sacks	28	T9	T21
Sacks allowed	26	5	9

*Yards per game.

TEAM LEADERS

Scoring (kicking): Jason Hanson, 93 pts. (39/40 PATs, 18/27 FGs).
Scoring (touchdowns): Herman Moore, 66 pts. (11 receiving).
Passing: Scott Mitchell, 1,456 yds. (246 att., 119 comp., 48.4%, 10 TDs, 11 int.).
Rushing: Barry Sanders, 1,883 yds. (331 att., 5.7 avg., 7 TDs).
Receptions: Herman Moore, 72 (1,173 yds., 16.3 avg., 11 TDs).
Interceptions: Robert Massey, 4 (25 yds., 0 TDs).
Sacks: Broderick Thomas, 7.0.
Punting: Greg Montgomery, 44.2 avg. (63 punts, 2,782 yds., 1 blocked).
Punt returns: Mel Gray, 11.1 avg. (21 att., 233 yds., 0 TDs).
Kickoff returns: Mel Gray, 28.4 avg. (45 att., 1,276 yds., 3 TDs).

1995 SEASON

CLUB DIRECTORY

Owner/president
William Clay Ford
Vice-chairman
William Clay Ford Jr.
Exec. V.P./chief operating officer
Chuck Schmidt
V.P. of administration/communications
Bill Keenist
V.P.-general counsel
David Potts
Secretary
David Hempstead
Controller
Tom Lesnau
Director/marketing
Steve Harms
Director/community relations and charities
Tim Pendell
Director of media relations
Mike Murray
Media relations assistant
James Petrylka
Director/sales and ticket operations
Fred Otto
Assistant ticket manager
Mark Graham
Director/player personnel
Ron Hughes
Director/pro scouting
Kevin Colbert
Dir. of player programs/pro scouting asst.
Larry Lee
Scouts
Milt Davis
Dirk Dierking
Tom Dimitroff
Scott McEwen
Jim Owens
Rick Spielman
Head athletic trainer
Kent Falb

Head coach:
Wayne Fontes
Assistant coaches
Paul Boudreau (offensive line)
Don Clemons (outside linebackers)
John Fontes (defensive backs)
Mo Forte (running backs)
Bert Hill (strength coach/defensive assistant)
Steve Kazor (tight ends/H-backs)
Greg Landry (quarterbacks)
Dave Levy (assistant head coach)
Tom Moore (off. coord.)
Frank Novak (special teams)
Herb Paterra (def. coord.)
Charlie Sanders (receivers)
John Teerlinck (assistant head coach/defense)
Howard Tippett (linebackers)

Assistant athletic trainers
Joe Recknagel
Robert Thomas
Physicians
Keith Burch
David Collon
Groundskeeper
George Karas
Equipment manager
Dan Jaroshewich
Assistant equipment manager
Mark Glenn
Video director
Steve Hermans

SCHEDULE

Sept. 3—at Pittsburgh	1:00
Sept. 10—at Minnesota	12:00
Sept. 17—ARIZONA	1:00
Sept. 25—SAN FRAN. (Mon.)	9:00
Oct. 1—Open date	
Oct. 8—CLEVELAND	4:00
Oct. 15—at Green Bay	12:00
Oct. 22—at Washington	1:00
Oct. 29—GREEN BAY	1:00
Nov. 5—at Atlanta	1:00
Nov. 12—TAMPA BAY	1:00
Nov. 19—at Chicago	12:00
Nov. 23—MINNESOTA (Thanks.)	12:30
Dec. 4—CHICAGO (Mon.)	9:00
Dec. 10—at Houston	12:00
Dec. 17—JACKSONVILLE	1:00
Dec. 23—at Tampa Bay (Sat.)	4:00

All times are for home team.
All games Sunday unless noted.

DRAFT CHOICES

Luther Elliss, DT, Utah (first round/20th pick overall).
David Sloan, TE, New Mexico (3/70).
Stephen Boyd, LB, Boston College (5/141).
Kez McCorvey, WR, Florida State (5/156).
Ronald Cherry, T, McNeese St. (5/163).
Kevin Hickman, TE, Navy (6/186).
Cory Schlesinger, RB, Nebraska (6/192).
Hessley Hempstead, G, Kansas (7/228).

TRAINING CAMP ROSTER

No.	QUARTERBACKS	Ht./Wt.	Born	NFL Exp.	College	How acq.	'94 Games GP/GS
16	Hollas, Donald	6-3/215	11-22-67	4	Rice	FA/95	*2/0
1	Majkowski, Don	6-3/208	2-25-64	9	Virginia	FA/95	*9/6
19	Mitchell, Scott	6-6/230	1-2-68	6	Utah	FA/94	9/9
13	Torretta, Gino	6-2/215	8-10-70	3	Miami (Fla.)	FA/94	0/0
	RUNNING BACKS						
26	Lynch, Eric	5-10/224	5-16-70	3	Grand Valley State (Mich.)	FA/92	12/3
34	Rivers, Ron	5-8/205	11-13-71	1	Fresno State	FA/94	0/0
20	Sanders, Barry	5-8/203	7-16-68	7	Oklahoma State	D1/89	16/16
30	Schlesinger, Cory (FB)	6-0/230	6-23-72	R	Nebraska	D6/95	—
23	Williams, Earnest	5-11/185	7-29-72	R	Fort Hayes State (Kan.)	FA/95	—
	RECEIVERS						
15	Boyd, Tommy	6-0/195	12-21-71	R	Toledo	FA/95	—
18	Coleman, Mill	5-9/175	6-19-72	R	Michigan State	FA/95	—
14	Dixson, Kevin	5-8/166	3-14-72	R	Illinois State	FA/95	—
89	Hall, Ron (TE)	6-4/245	3-15-64	9	Hawaii	FA/94	13/10
46	Hickman, Kevin (TE)	6-4/258	8-20-71	R	Navy	D6/95	—
82	Holman, Rodney (TE)	6-3/238	4-20-60	14	Tulane	FA/93	15/7
83	Matthews, Aubrey	5-7/165	9-15-62	10	Delta State (Miss.)	FA/90	14/3
41	McCorvey, Kez	6-0/180	1-23-72	R	Florida State	D5/95	—
84	Moore, Herman	6-3/210	10-20-69	5	Virginia	D1/91	16/16
87	Morton, Johnnie (KR)	6-0/190	10-7-71	2	Southern California	D1/94	14/0
80	Perriman, Brett	5-9/180	10-10-65	8	Miami (Fla.)	T-NO/91	16/14
86	Sloan, David (TE)	6-6/254	6-8-72	R	New Mexico	D3/95	—
44	Woodley, Richard	5-9/180	1-13-72	1	Texas Christian	FA/95	0/0
	OFFENSIVE LINEMEN						
75	Brown, Lomas (T)	6-4/275	3-30-63	11	Florida	D1/85	16/16
68	Burton, Leonard (C)	6-3/275	6-18-64	9	South Carolina	FA/94	0/0
72	Cherry, Ronald (T)	6-4/300	4-15-72	R	McNeese State	D5/95	—
77	Compton, Mike (C)	6-6/297	9-18-70	3	West Virginia	D3/93	2/0
76	Conover, Scott (T)	6-4/285	9-27-68	5	Purdue	D5/91	11/0
53	Glover, Kevin (C)	6-2/282	6-17-63	11	Maryland	D2/85	16/16
79	Hatfield, Mark (T)	6-6/305	8-21-70	R	Bishop's, Canada	FA/95	—
66	Hempstead, Hessley (G)	6-1/295	1-29-72	R	Kansas	D7/95	—
70	Jones, Jeff (T)	6-6/310	5-30-72	R	Northeastern	FA/95	—
73	Lutz, David (G/T)	6-6/305	12-20-59	13	Georgia Tech	FA/93	16/16
71	Moss, Zefross (T)	6-6/324	8-17-66	7	Alabama State	FA/95	*11/11
74	Nonhoff, Randy (G)	6-5/305	10-12-70	R	California	FA/95	—
62	Semple, Tony (G)	6-4/286	12-20-70	2	Memphis	D5/94	0/0
67	Widell, Doug (G)	6-4/280	9-23-66	7	Boston College	FA/94	16/16
	DEFENSIVE LINEMEN						
96	Bonham, Shane	6-4/260	10-18-70	2	Tennessee	D3/94	15/1
94	Elliss, Luther (E)	6-5/291	3-22-73	R	Utah	D1/95	—
61	Heinrich, Josh (E)	6-7/260	5-13-72	R	Northeastern	FA/95	—
90	Owens, Dan (E)	6-3/280	3-16-67	6	Southern California	D2/90	16/8
91	Porcher, Robert (E)	6-3/283	7-30-69	3	South Carolina State	D1/92	15/15
98	Thomas, Henry	6-2/277	1-12-65	9	Louisiana State	FA/95	*16/16
95	Wells, Mike (E)	6-3/287	1-6-71	2	Iowa	D4/94	4/0
	LINEBACKERS						
48	Beer, Thomas	6-1/237	3-27-69	2	Wayne State (Mich.)	D7/94	9/0
50	Boyd, Stephen	6-0/247	8-22-72	R	Boston College	D5/95	—
99	Hayworth, Tracy	6-3/260	12-18-67	6	Tennessee	D7/90	9/1
59	Johnson, Mike	6-1/230	11-26-62	9	Virginia Tech	FA/94	16/16
52	Kowalkowski, Scott	6-2/228	8-23-68	4	Notre Dame	FA/94	16/0
55	London, Antonio	6-2/234	4-14-71	3	Alabama	D3/93	16/0
51	Major, Darryl	6-1/240	12-24-72	R	Missouri	FA/95	—
59	Scroggins, Tracy (E)	6-2/255	9-11-69	4	Tulsa	D2/92	16/9
	Smith, Willie	6-1/225	2-13-73	R	Penn State	FA/95	—
54	Spielman, Chris	6-0/247	10-11-65	8	Ohio State	D2/88	16/16
64	Wilson, James	6-3/253	1-10-70	1	Tennessee	FA/94	0/0
	DEFENSIVE BACKS						
21	Bevill, Bryce (CB)	5-9/185	7-27-72	R	Syracuse	FA/95	—
36	Blades, Bennie (S)	6-1/221	9-3-66	8	Miami (Fla.)	D1/88	16/16
27	Borgella, Jocelyn (CB)	5-10/180	8-26-71	2	Cincinnati	D6/94	4/0
32	Clay, Willie (S)	5-9/184	9-5-70	3	Georgia Tech	D8/92	16/16
25	Jeffries, Greg (CB)	5-9/184	10-16-71	3	Virginia	D6/93	16/1
39	Malone, Van (S)	5-11/186	7-1-70	2	Texas	D2/94	16/0
40	Massey, Robert (CB)	5-11/195	2-17-67	8	North Carolina Central	FA/94	16/15
47	McNeil, Ryan (CB)	6-2/192	10-4-70	3	Miami (Fla.)	D2/93	14/13

No.	DEFENSIVE BACKS	Ht./Wt.	Born	NFL Exp.	College	How acq.	'94 Games GP/GS
	Raymond, Corey (CB)	5-11/185	7-28-69	4	Louisiana State	T-Jac/95	*16/12
28	Rice, Ron (S)	6-1/206	11-9-72	R	Eastern Michigan	FA/95	—
29	Vanhorse, Sean (CB)	5-10/180	7-22-68	6	Howard	FA/95	*16/1
	SPECIALISTS						
5	Alexander, Harold (P)	6-2/224	10-20-70	3	Appalachian State	T-Atl/95	*15/0
4	Hanson, Jason (K)	5-11/183	6-17-70	4	Washington State	D2/92	16/0
2	Pooler, Kyle (K)	5-11/202	5-29-72	R	Missouri	FA/95	—
3	Royals, Mark (P)	6-5/215	6-22-64	6	Appalachian State	FA/95	*16/0

*Alexander played 15 games with Falcons in '94; Hollas played 2 games with Bengals; Majkowski played 9 games with Colts; Moss played 11 games with Colts; Raymond played 16 games with Giants; Royals played 16 games with Steelers; Thomas played 16 games with Vikings; Vanhorse played 16 games with Chargers.

Also played with Lions in '94: G Shawn Bouwens (16 games); WR Anthony Carter (4); S Harry Colon (16); WR/KR Mel Gray (16); TE Ty Hallock (15); LB Victor Jones (16); QB Dave Krieg (14); CB Milton Mack (16); P Greg Montgomery (16); RB Derrick Moore (16); DE Kelvin Pritchett (16); C Mark Rodenhauser (16); DB Marc Spindler (9); LB Pat Swilling (16); LB Broderick Thomas (16).

Abbreviations: D1—draft pick, first round; SupD2—supplemental draft pick, second round; W-Den—waivers acquisition from Denver; T-Sea—trade acquisition from Seattle; PlanB—Plan B free-agent acquisition; FA—free-agent acquisition (other than Plan B).

MISCELLANEOUS TEAM DATA

Stadium (capacity, surface):
Pontiac Silverdome
(80,368, artificial)
Business address:
1200 Featherstone Road
Pontiac, MI 48342
Business phone:
810-335-4131
Ticket information:
810-335-4151
Team colors:
Honolulu blue and silver
Flagship radio station:
WWJ, 950 AM
Training site:
Pontiac Silverdome
Pontiac, Mich.
810-335-4131

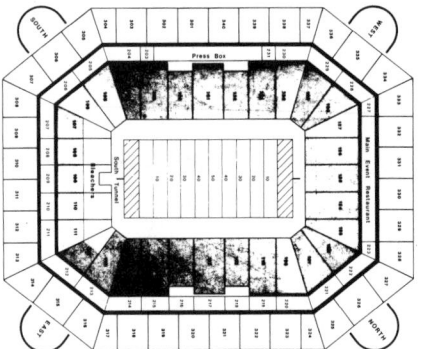

GREEN BAY PACKERS
NFC CENTRAL DIVISION

1994 REVIEW

RESULTS

Sept.	4—MINNESOTA	W	16-10
Sept.	11—MIAMI (Milw.)	L	14-24
Sept.	18—at Philadelphia	L	7-13
Sept.	25—TAMPA BAY	W	30-3
Oct.	2—at New England	L	16-17
Oct.	9—L.A. RAMS	W	24-17
Oct.	16—Open date		
Oct.	20—at Minnesota (OT)	L	10-13
Oct.	31—at Chicago	W	33-6
Nov.	6—DETROIT (Milw.)	W	38-30
Nov.	13—N.Y. JETS	W	17-10
Nov.	20—at Buffalo	L	20-29
Nov.	24—at Dallas	L	31-42
Dec.	4—at Detroit	L	31-34
Dec.	11—CHICAGO	W	40-3
Dec.	18—ATLANTA (Milw.)	W	21-17
Dec.	24—at Tampa Bay	W	34-19

RECORDS/RANKINGS

1994 regular-season record: 9-7 (T2nd in NFC Central); 6-2 in division; 8-4 in conference; 7-1 at home; 2-6 on road.
Team record last five years: 37-43 (.463, ranks 18th in league in that span).

1994 team rankings:	No.	NFC	NFL
Total offense	*332.3	5	9
Rushing offense	*96.4	8	19
Passing offense	*235.8	5	9
Scoring offense	382	3	4
Total defense	*297.8	5	6
Rushing defense	*85.2	3	3
Passing defense	*212.6	8	15
Scoring defense	287	3	5
Takeaways	33	T5	T8
Giveaways	22	1	2
Turnover differential	11	T1	T3
Sacks	37	4	10
Sacks allowed	33	8	15

*Yards per game.

TEAM LEADERS

Scoring (kicking): Chris Jacke, 98 pts. (41/43 PATs, 19/26 FGs).
Scoring (touchdowns): Sterling Sharpe, 108 pts. (18 receiving).
Passing: Brett Favre, 3,882 yds. (582 att., 363 comp., 62.4%, 33 TDs, 14 int.).
Rushing: Edgar Bennett, 623 yds. (178 att., 3.5 avg., 5 TDs).
Receptions: Sterling Sharpe, 94 (1,119 yds., 11.9 avg., 18 TDs).
Interceptions: Terrell Buckley, 5 (38 yds., 0 TDs).
Sacks: Sean Jones, 10.5.
Punting: Craig Hentrich, 41.4 avg. (81 punts, 3,351 yds., 0 blocked).
Punt returns: Robert Brooks, 8.8 avg. (40 att., 352 yds., 1 TD).
Kickoff returns: Corey Harris, 21.3 avg. (29 att., 618 yds., 0 TDs).

1995 SEASON

CLUB DIRECTORY

President/chief executive officer
Robert E. Harlan
Vice president
John Fabry
Secretary
Peter M. Platten III
Treasurer
John R. Underwood
Executive V.P./general manager
Ron Wolf
Executive assistant to president
Phil Pionek
Chief financial officer
Mike Reinfeldt
General legal counsel
Lance Lopes
Corporate security officer
Jerry Parins
Controller
Vicki Vannieuwenhoven
Exec. dir./public relations and marketing
Lee Remmel
Director/marketing
Jeff Cieply
Asst. directors/public relations
Jeff Blumb
Mack Schiefelbeiw
Ticket director/Green Bay
Mark Wagner
Director/pro personnel
Ted Thompson
Director/college scouting
John Math
College scouts
John (Red) Cochran
John Dorsey
Dave Hanner
Shaun Herock
Scott McLoughan
George Streeter
Ray Wietecha
Head trainer
Pepper Burruss

Head coach
Mike Holmgren
Assistant coaches
Larry Brooks (defensive line)
Nolan Cromwell (special teams)
Gil Haskell (wide receivers)
Johnny Holland (defensive assistant/quality control)
Kent Johnston (strength/conditioning)
Sherman Lewis (off. coord.)
Jim Lind (linebackers)
Tom Lovat (offensive line)
Steve Mariucci (quarterbacks)
Marty Mornhinweg (offensive assistant/quality control)
Andy Reid (tight ends/offensive assistant)
Fritz Shurmur (def. coord.)
Harry Sydney (off. backs)
Bob Valesente (def. secondary)

Assistant trainers
Kurt Fielding
Sam Ramsden
Physicians
Patrick McKenzie
John Gray
Buildings supervisor
Ted Eisenreich
Fields supervisor
Todd Edlebeck
Equipment manager
Gordon Batty
Assistant equipment managers
Bryan Nehring
Tom Bakken
Video director
Al Treml

SCHEDULE

Sept.	3—ST. LOUIS	12:00
Sept.	11—at Chicago (Mon.)	8:00
Sept.	17—at N.Y. GIANTS	12:00
Sept.	24—at Jacksonville	8:00
Oct.	1—Open date	
Oct.	8—at Dallas	12:00
Oct.	15—DETROIT	12:00
Oct.	22—MINNESOTA	12:00
Oct.	29—at Detroit	1:00
Nov.	5—at Minnesota	12:00
Nov.	12—CHICAGO	12:00
Nov.	19—at Cleveland	1:00
Nov.	26—TAMPA BAY	12:00
Dec.	3—CINCINNATI	12:00
Dec.	10—at Tampa Bay	8:00
Dec.	16—at New Orleans (Sat.)	3:00
Dec.	24—PITTSBURGH	12:00

All times are for home team.
All games Sunday unless noted.

DRAFT CHOICES

Craig Newsome, DB, Arizona State (first round/32nd pick overall).
Darius Holland, DT, Colorado (3/65).
William Henderson, FB, N. Carolina (3/66).
Brian Williams, LB, Southern Cal (3/73).
Antonio Freeman, WR, Virginia Tech (3/90).
Jeff Miller, T, Mississippi (4/117).
Jay Barker, QB, Alabama (5/160).
Travis Jervey, RB, The Citadel (5/170).
Charlie Simmons, WR, Georgia Tech (6/173).
Adam Timmerman, G, S. Dakota St. (7/230).

TRAINING CAMP ROSTER

No.	QUARTERBACKS	Ht./Wt.	Born	NFL Exp.	College	How acq.	'94 Games GP/GS
7	Barker, Jay	6-2/215	7-20-72	R	Alabama	D5/95	—
11	Detmer, Ty	6-0/186	10-30-67	4	Brigham Young	D9/92	0/0
4	Favre, Brett	6-2/222	10-10-69	5	Southern Mississippi	T-Atl/92	16/16
12	Rubley, T.J.	6-3/205	11-29-68	4	Tulsa	FA/95	0/0
	RUNNING BACKS						
40	Becton, Lee	5-11/194	2-11-73	R	Notre Dame	FA/95	—
34	Bennett, Edgar (FB)	6-0/224	2-15-69	4	Florida State	D4/92	16/15
28	Chaffey, Pat	6-1/225	4-19-67	4	Oregon State	PlanB/92	0/0
30	Henderson, William (FB)	6-1/245	2-19-71	R	North Carolina	D3/95	—
32	Jervey, Travis	5-11/219	5-5-72	R	The Citadel	D5/95	—
42	Johnson, LeShon	5-11/200	1-15-71	2	Northern Illinois	D3/94	12/0
25	Levens, Dorsey	6-1/235	5-21-70	2	Georgia Tech	D5/94	14/0
38	Satterfield, Brian (FB)	6-0/215	12-22-69	1	North Alabama	FA/95	0/0
27	Saunders, Mike	5-11/212	10-3-69	1	Iowa	FA/95	0/0
24	White, Russell	5-11/220	12-15-70	2	California	FA/95	0/0
	RECEIVERS						
48	Bartrum, Michael (TE)	6-4/243	6-23-70	2	Marshall	FA/93	0/0
87	Brooks, Robert (KR)	6-0/175	6-23-70	4	South Carolina	D3/92	16/16
89	Chmura, Mark (TE)	6-5/245	2-22-69	4	Boston College	D6/92	14/4
86	Freeman, Antonio	6-0/185	5-27-72	R	Virginia Tech	D3/95	—
82	Ingram, Mark	5-11/194	8-23-65	9	Michigan State	T-Mia/95	*15/13
88	Jackson, Keith (TE)	6-2/258	4-19-65	8	Oklahoma	T-Mia/95	*16/16
80	Jordan, Charles (KR)	5-10/175	10-9-69	3	Long Beach City College	T-Rai/94	10/0
16	Lamb, Brad	5-10/175	10-7-67	4	Anderson (Ind.)	FA/95	0/0
85	Mickens, Terry	6-0/200	2-21-71	2	Florida A&M	D5/94	12/0
81	Morgan, Anthony	6-1/195	11-15-67	5	Tennessee	W-Chi/93	16/0
19	Schroeder, Bill	6-1/195	1-9-71	2	Wisconsin-La Crosse	D6/94	0/0
20	Simmons, Charlie	6-3/215	8-25-72	R	Georgia Tech	D6/95	—
18	Stegall, Milt	6-0/185	1-25-70	4	Miami of Ohio	FA/95	*1/0
49	Thomason, Jeff (TE)	6-4/233	12-30-69	3	Oregon	FA/92	0/0
83	Wilner, Jeff (TE)	6-4/250	12-31-71	2	Wesleyan (Conn.)	FA/94	11/1
	OFFENSIVE LINEMEN						
61	Bollinger, Brian (G)	6-5/290	11-21-68	4	North Carolina	FA/95	*7/0
71	Brown, Gary (T)	6-4/290	6-25-71	2	Georgia Tech	D5/94	1/0
77	Crafts, Jerry (T)	6-6/350	1-6-68	4	Louisville	FA/95	*16/7
72	Dotson, Earl (T)	6-3/310	12-17-70	3	Texas A&I	D3/93	4/0
76	Galbreath, Harry (G)	6-1/285	1-1-65	8	Tennessee	FA/93	16/16
70	Hope, Charles (G/C)	6-3/303	3-12-70	2	Central State (O.)	FA/94	6/0
67	Hutchins, Paul (T)	6-4/335	2-11-70	3	Western Michigan	D6/93	16/2
65	Miller, Jeff (T)	6-3/300	11-23-72	R	Mississippi	D4/95	—
73	Robbins, Tootie (T)	6-5/315	6-2-58	13	East Carolina	FA/93	0/0
75	Ruettgers, Ken (T)	6-6/290	8-20-62	10	Southern California	D1/85	16/16
73	Taylor, Aaron (G)	6-4/300	11-14-72	2	Notre Dame	D1/94	0/0
63	Timmerman, Adam (G)	6-4/289	8-14-71	R	South Dakota State	D7/95	—
74	Wagner, Keith (T)	6-4/300	1-22-70	1	Abilene Christian	FA/95	0/0
52	Winters, Frank (C/G)	6-3/290	1-23-64	9	Western Illinois	PlanB/92	16/16
	DEFENSIVE LINEMEN						
99	Brock, Randy (E)	6-6/265	11-20-71	R	Brigham Young	FA/95	—
93	Brown, Gilbert (T)	6-2/330	2-22-71	3	Kansas	W-Min/93	13/1
78	Fagan, Tommy (E)	6-5/265	3-26-71	1	Northeast Louisiana	FA/95	0/0
90	Holland, Darius (T)	6-4/303	11-10-73	R	Colorado	D3/95	—
96	Jones, Sean (E)	6-7/275	12-19-62	12	Northeastern	FA/94	16/16
64	Jurkovic, John (NT)	6-2/290	8-18-67	4	Eastern Illinois	FA/91	16/15
94	Kuberski, Robert (E)	6-4/295	4-5-71	1	Navy	D7/93	0/0
97	LaBounty, Matt (E)	6-3/268	1-3-69	3	Oregon	W-SF/93	0/0
92	White, Reggie (E)	6-5/295	12-19-61	11	Tennessee	FA/93	16/15
98	Wilkins, Gabe (E)	6-4/300	9-1-71	2	Gardner-Webb (N.C.)	D4/94	15/0
68	Wilson, Oscar (T)	6-2/290	12-6-70	R	Cal State-Northridge	FA/95	—
	LINEBACKERS						
51	Alipate, Tuineau	6-2/245	8-21-67	2	Washington State	FA/95	*8/0
54	Carter, Bernard	6-3/237	8-22-71	2	East Carolina	D6/94	0/0
69	Goheen, Justin	6-2/239	8-16-73	R	Notre Dame	FA/95	—
49	Hamilton, Ruffin	6-1/230	3-2-71	2	Tulane	D6/94	5/0
41	Hampton, Andre	6-0/227	6-4-71	R	Valdosta (Ga.) State	FA/95	—
91	Harris, Bernardo	6-2/238	10-15-71	1	North Carolina	FA/95	0/0
53	Koonce, George	6-1/240	10-15-68	4	East Carolina	FA/92	16/16
59	Simmons, Wayne	6-2/245	12-15-69	3	Clemson	D1/93	12/1
55	Strickland, Fred	6-2/250	8-15-66	8	Purdue	FA/93	16/14

No.	LINEBACKERS	Ht./Wt.	Born	NFL Exp.	College	How acq.	'94 Games GP/GS
50	Williams, Brian	6-1/238	12-17-72	R	Southern California	D3/95	—
95	Williams, Jerrol	6-4/240	7-5-67	7	Purdue	FA/95	*6/0
56	Willis, James	6-1/238	9-2-72	3	Auburn	D5/93	12/0
	DEFENSIVE BACKS						
44	Bergman, Jeff (S)	6-0/186	2-24-73	R	Northern Arizona	FA/95	—
36	Butler, LeRoy (S)	6-0/193	7-19-68	6	Florida State	D2/90	13/13
45	Crawford, Keith (CB)	6-2/188	11-21-70	2	Howard Payne (Tex.)	FA/94	0/0
29	Dixon, Rickey (S)	5-11/188	12-26-66	7	Oklahoma	T-Cin/93	0/0
43	Dorsett, Matthew (CB)	5-11/188	8-23-73	R	Southern	FA/95	—
33	Evans, Doug (CB)	6-0/188	5-13-70	3	Louisiana Tech	D6/93	16/15
47	Henley, Stephen (S)	6-0/220	8-30-71	R	Mankato State	FA/95	—
26	Hogan, Chauncey (CB)	6-1/180	2-24-72	1	Southern	FA/95	0/0
46	Holt, Reggie (S)	5-11/202	2-18-71	1	Wisconsin	FA/95	0/0
22	McGill, Lenny (CB)	6-1/194	5-31-71	2	Arizona State	FA/94	6/0
21	Newsome, Craig (CB)	5-11/185	8-10-71	R	Arizona State	D1/95	—
39	Prior, Mike (S)	6-0/215	11-14-63	10	Illinois State	FA/93	16/0
31	Teague, George (S)	6-1/190	2-18-71	3	Alabama	D1/93	16/16
23	Walker, Sammy (CB)	5-11/200	1-20-69	5	Texas Tech	FA/93	0/0
	SPECIALISTS						
9	Borgognone, Dirk (K)	6-2/225	1-9-68	1	Pacific	FA/95	0/0
17	Hentrich, Craig (P)	6-3/200	5-18-71	2	Notre Dame	FA/93	16/0
13	Jacke, Chris (K)	6-0/200	3-12-66	7	Texas-El Paso	D6/89	16/0
6	Nedney, Joe (K)	6-5/205	3-22-73	R	San Jose State	FA/95	—

*Alipate played 8 games with Jets in '94; Bollinger played 7 games with 49ers; Crafts played 16 games with Bills; Ingram played 15 games with Dolphins; Jackson played 16 games with Dolphins; Stegall played 1 game with Bengals; J. Williams played 6 games with Chiefs.

Also played with Packers in '94: DE Matt Brock (5 games); QB Mark Brunell (2); RB Reggie Cobb (16); DE Don Davey (16); CB Forey Duckett (3); C Jamie Dukes (6); CB Corey Harris (16); S Tim Hauck (13); TE Reggie Johnson (9); CB Keshon Johnson (7); WR Ron Lewis (6); G Guy McIntyre (10); DT Steve McMichael (16); CB Roland Mitchell (1); LB Bryce Paup (16); WR Sterling Sharpe (16); T Joe Sims (15); RB Darrell Thompson (8); TE Ed West (14); LB Mark Williams (16); RB Marcus Wilson (12), S Ray Wilson (3).

Abbreviations: D1—draft pick, first round; SupD2—supplemental draft pick, second round; W-Den—waivers acquisition from Denver; T-Sea—trade acquisition from Seattle; PlanB—Plan B free-agent acquisition; FA—free-agent acquisition (other than Plan B).

MISCELLANEOUS TEAM DATA

Stadium (capacity, surface):
Lambeau Field
(59,543, grass)
Business address:
P.O. Box 10628
Green Bay, WI 54307-0628
Business phone:
414-496-5700
Ticket Information:
414-496-5719
Team colors:
Hunter green, gold and white
Flagship radio station:
WTMJ, 620 AM
Training site:
St. Norbert College
West DePere, Wis.
414-496-5700

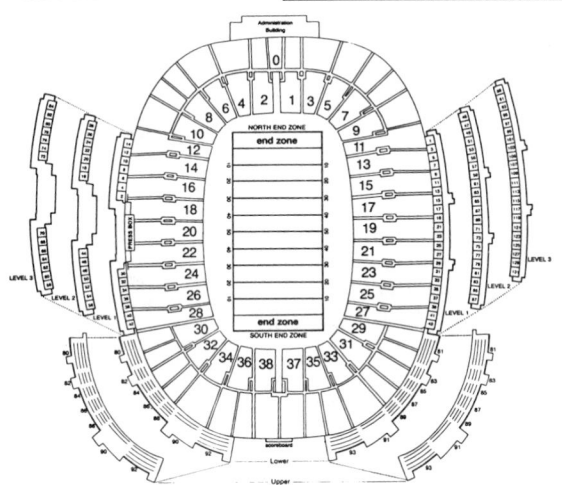

HOUSTON OILERS
AFC CENTRAL DIVISION

1994 REVIEW

RESULTS

Date		Result	
Sept.	4—at Indianapolis	L	21-45
Sept.	11—at Dallas	L	17-20
Sept.	18—BUFFALO	L	7-15
Sept.	25—CINCINNATI	W	20-13
Oct.	3—at Pittsburgh	L	14-30
Oct.	9—Open date		
Oct.	13—CLEVELAND	L	8-11
Oct.	24—at Philadelphia	L	6-21
Oct.	30—at L.A. Raiders	L	14-17
Nov.	6—PITTSBURGH (OT)	L	9-12
Nov.	13—at Cincinnati	L	31-34
Nov.	21—N.Y. GIANTS	L	10-13
Nov.	27—at Cleveland	L	10-34
Dec.	4—ARIZONA	L	12-30
Dec.	11—SEATTLE	L	14-16
Dec.	18—at Kansas City	L	9-31
Dec.	24—N.Y. JETS	W	24-10

RECORDS/RANKINGS

1994 regular-season record: 2-14 (4th in AFC Central); 1-5 in division; 2-10 in conference; 2-6 at home; 0-8 on road.
Team record last five years: 44-36 (.550, ranks T11th in league in that span).

1994 team rankings:	No.	AFC	NFL
Total offense	*280.1	13	26
Rushing offense	*105.1	7	12
Passing offense	*174.9	12	25
Scoring offense	226	14	28
Total defense	*307.2	3	9
Rushing defense	*132.5	14	28
Passing defense	*174.7	14	2
Scoring defense	352	11	21
Takeaways	26	T11	T20
Giveaways	42	14	28
Turnover differential	-16	13	26
Sacks	31	T7	T15
Sacks allowed	65	14	28

*Yards per game.

TEAM LEADERS

Scoring (kicking): Al Del Greco, 66 pts. (18/18 PATs, 16/20 FGs).
Scoring (touchdowns): Haywood Jeffires, 42 pts. (6 receiving, 3 2-pt. conv.).
Passing: Billy Joe Tolliver, 1,287 yds. (240 att., 121 comp., 50.4%, 6 TDs, 7 int.).
Rushing: Lorenzo White, 757 yds. (191 att., 4.0 avg., 3 TDs).
Receptions: Webster Slaughter, 68 (846 yds., 12.4 avg., 2 TDs); Haywood Jeffires, 68 (783 yds., 11.5 avg., 6 TDs).
Interceptions: Darryll Lewis, 5 (57 yds., 0 TDs).
Sacks: Lamar Lathon, 8.5.
Punting: Rich Camarillo, 42.9 avg. (96 punts, 4,115 yds., 0 blocked).
Punt returns: Ernest Givins, 5.7 avg. (37 att., 210 yds., 1 TD).
Kickoff returns: Todd McNair, 20.9 avg. (23 att., 481 yds., 0 TDs.)

1995 SEASON

CLUB DIRECTORY

Owner/president
K.S. "Bud" Adams Jr.
Executive vice president/general manager
Floyd Reese
Executive vice president/administration
Mike McClure
Executive vice president/finance
Scott Thompson
Executive assistant to president
Thomas S. Smith
V.P./player personnel and scouting
Mike Holovak
Vice president/legal counsel
Steve Underwood
Sr. v.p./broadcasting and marketing
Don MacLachlan
Director of pro personnel
Rich Snead
Director/business operations
Lewis Mangum
Dir. of media relations and services
Dave Pearson
Dir. of public and community relations
Rod St. Clair
Controller
Jackie Curley
Director of accounting services
Marilan Logan
Director/ticket admin. and services
Mike Mullis
Director/security
Grady Sessums
Director/player relations
Willie Alexander
Asst. dir. of media rel. and services
Bob Schranz

SCHEDULE

Date		Time
Sept.	3—at Jacksonville	1:00
Sept.	10—PITTSBURGH	12:00
Sept.	17—CLEVELAND	12:00
Sept.	24—at Cincinnati	4:00
Oct.	1—JACKSONVILLE	3:00
Oct.	8—at Minnesota	12:00
Oct.	15—Open date	
Oct.	22—at Chicago	12:00
Oct.	29—TAMPA BAY	3:00
Nov.	5—at Cleveland	1:00
Nov.	12—CINCINNATI	12:00
Nov.	19—at Kansas City	7:00
Nov.	26—DENVER	3:00
Dec.	3—at Pittsburgh	1:00
Dec.	10—DETROIT	12:00
Dec.	17—N.Y. JETS	12:00
Dec.	24—at Buffalo	1:00

All times are for home team.
All games Sunday unless noted.

Head coach
Jeff Fisher
Assistant coaches
Larry Beightol (offensive line)
Dick Coury (offensive assistant)
Rex Norris (defensive line)
Rod Perry (defensive backs)
Russ Purnell (special teams)
Jerry Rhome (off. coordinator)
Steve Sidwell (def. coordinator)
Sherman Smith (running backs)
Les Steckel (wide receivers/tight ends)
Steve Watterson (strength and rehabilitation)
Gregg Williams (linebackers)

Scouts
Ray Biggs
C.O. Brocato
Glenn Cumbee
Dub Fesperman
Head trainer
Brad Brown
Equipment manager
Dan Murray
Videotape coordinator
Ken Sparacino
Physicians
Tom Cain
Robert Fain Sr.
Robert Fain Jr.
James Muntz

DRAFT CHOICES

Steve McNair, QB, Alcorn State (first round/third pick overall).
Anthony Cook, DT, S. Carolina St. (2/35).
Chris Sanders, WR, Ohio State (3/67).
Rodney Thomas, RB, Texas A&M (3/89).
Torey Hunter, DB, Washington St. (3/95).
Michael Roan, TE, Wisconsin (4/101).
Gary Walker, DE, Auburn (5/159).
Hicham El-Mashtoub, C, Arizona (6/174).
C.J. Richardson, DB, Miami (Fla.) (7/211).

TRAINING CAMP ROSTER

No.	QUARTERBACKS	Ht./Wt.	Born	NFL Exp.	College	How acq.	'94 Games GP/GS
14	Carlson, Cody	6-3/202	11-5-63	9	Baylor	D3/87	5/5
17	Chandler, Chris	6-4/225	10-12-65	8	Washington	FA/95	*12/6
9	McNair, Steve	6-2/224	2-14-73	R	Alcorn State	D1/95	—
7	Richardson, Bucky	6-1/228	2-7-69	4	Texas A&M	D8/92	7/4
10	Williamson, Lee	6-4/206	8-10-68	2	Presbyterian (S.C.)	FA/94	0/0
	RUNNING BACKS						
33	Brown, Gary	5-11/233	7-1-69	5	Penn State	D8/91	12/8
27	Jackson, Sean	6-1/222	2-6-71	1	Florida State	D4/94	0/0
40	Lundy, Dennis	5-9/190	7-6-72	R	Northwestern	FA/95	—
20	Thomas, Rodney	5-10/213	3-30-73	R	Texas A&M	D3/95	—
	RECEIVERS						
89	Brown, Reggie	6-1/195	5-5-70	3	Alabama State	FA/93	4/0
85	Carter, Pat (TE)	6-4/258	8-1-66	8	Florida State	FA/94	16/13
82	Hannah, Travis (KR)	5-7/161	1-31-70	3	Southern California	D4/93	9/0
80	Jeffires, Haywood	6-2/201	12-12-64	9	North Carolina State	D1b/87	16/16
49	Lewis, Rod (TE)	6-5/254	6-9-71	2	Arizona	D5/94	3/1
95	Mills, John Henry (TE)	6-0/222	10-31-69	3	Wake Forest	D5/93	16/1
19	Neal, Keith	6-2/183	7-26-71	R	Idaho	FA/95	—
46	Roan, Michael (TE)	6-3/251	8-29-72	R	Wisconsin	D4/95	—
	Russell, Derek	6-0/179	6-22-69	4	Arkansas	FA/95	*12/12
18	Sanders, Chris	6-0/184	5-8-72	R	Ohio State	D3/95	—
83	Seabron, Malcolm	6-0/194	12-29-72	2	Fresno State	D3/94	13/0
84	Slaughter, Webster	6-1/175	10-19-64	10	San Diego State	FA/92	16/12
88	Wellman, Gary	5-9/173	8-9-67	4	Southern California	D5/91	8/0
	OFFENSIVE LINEMEN						
77	Donnalley, Kevin (T/G)	6-5/305	6-10-68	5	North Carolina	D3/91	13/11
60	El-Mashtoub, Hicham (C)	6-2/288	5-11-72	R	Arizona	D6/95	—
55	Flannery, John (G/C)	6-3/304	1-13-69	5	Syracuse	D2/91	16/16
72	Hopkins, Brad (T)	6-3/306	9-5-70	3	Illinois	D1/93	16/15
66	Hunt, Purvis (G)	6-4/378	11-25-70	R	Mississippi State	FA/95	—
74	Matthews, Bruce (C/G)	6-5/298	8-8-61	13	Southern California	D1/83	16/16
64	Norgard, Erik (C/G)	6-1/282	11-4-65	7	Colorado	FA/90	16/7
67	Reid, Jim (T)	6-6/306	2-13-71	1	Virginia	D5/94	0/0
62	Sharkey, Neal (G)	6-2/297	6-27-72	R	Northwestern State	FA/95	—
53	Stepnoski, Mark (C)	6-2/269	1-20-67	7	Pittsburgh	FA/95	*16/16
73	Williams, David (T)	6-5/292	6-21-66	7	Florida	D1/89	16/16
	DEFENSIVE LINEMEN						
79	Childress, Ray (T)	6-6/272	10-20-62	11	Texas A&M	D1/85	16/16
78	Cook, Anthony	6-3/293	5-30-72	R	South Carolina State	D2/95	—
90	Davidson, Kenny (E)	6-5/288	8-17-67	6	Louisiana State	FA/94	16/16
92	Ford, Henry (E)	6-3/284	10-30-71	2	Arkansas	D1/94	11/0
91	Lewis, Scotty (E)	6-3/266	12-30-71	R	Baylor	FA/95	—
94	Montgomery, Glenn (T)	6-0/282	3-31-67	7	Houston	D5/89	14/14
93	Nunley, Jeremy (E)	6-5/278	9-19-71	2	Alabama	D2/94	12/0
96	Walker, Gary (E)	6-2/285	2-28-73	R	Auburn	D5/95	—
	LINEBACKERS						
56	Barrow, Micheal	6-1/236	4-19-70	3	Miami (Fla.)	D2/93	16/16
59	Bowden, Joe	5-11/230	2-25-70	4	Oklahoma	D5/92	14/1
51	Hall, Lemanski	6-0/229	11-24-70	1	Alabama	D7/94	0/0
58	Logan, James	6-2/210	12-6-72	R	Memphis	FA/95	—
50	Robinson, Eddie	6-1/245	4-13-70	4	Alabama State	D2/92	15/15
54	Smith, Al	6-1/244	11-26-64	9	Utah State	D6/87	16/16
52	Wortham, Barron	5-11/244	11-1-69	2	Texas-El Paso	D6/94	16/1
	DEFENSIVE BACKS						
22	Barnes, Tomur (CB)	5-10/188	9-8-70	2	North Texas	FA/94	1/0
23	Bishop, Blaine (S)	5-9/197	7-24-70	3	Ball State	D8/93	16/13
28	Dishman, Cris (CB)	6-0/188	8-13-65	8	Purdue	D5/88	16/16
36	Hunter, Torey (CB)	5-9/176	2-10-72	R	Washington State	D3/95	—
24	Jackson, Steve (CB)	5-8/182	4-8-69	5	Purdue	D3/91	11/0
29	Lewis, Darryll (CB)	5-9/183	12-16-68	5	Arizona	D2/91	16/15
30	Richardson, C.J. (S)	5-10/209	6-10-72	R	Miami (Fla.)	D7/95	—
31	Robertson, Marcus (S)	5-11/197	10-2-69	5	Iowa State	D4/91	16/16
	SPECIALISTS						
16	Camarillo, Rich (P)	5-11/202	11-29-59	15	Washington	FA/94	16/0
3	Del Greco, Al (K)	5-10/202	3-2-62	12	Auburn	FA/91	16/0
21	Gray, Mel (KR)	5-9/171	3-16-61	10	Purdue	FA/95	*16/0

*Chandler played 12 games with Rams in '94; Gray played 16 games with Lions; Russell played 12 games with Broncos; Stepnoski played 16 games with Cowboys.

Also played with Oilers in '94: WR Pat Coleman (10 games); CB Michael Davis (16); LB Brett Faryniarz (16); WR Ernest Givins (16); LB Lamar Lathon (16); LB Le'Shai Maston (5); De Keith McCants (4); S Bubba McDowell (9); RB Todd McNair (16); S Bo Orlando (16); DE Mike Teeter (14); T Stan Thomas (16); RB Spencer Tillman (16); QB Billy Joe Tolliver (10); RB Lorenzo White (15).

Abbreviations: D1—draft pick, first round; SupD2—supplemental draft pick, second round; W-Den—waivers acquisition from Denver; T-Sea—trade acquisition from Seattle; PlanB—Plan B free-agent acquisition; FA—free-agent acquisition (other than Plan B).

MISCELLANEOUS TEAM DATA

Stadium (capacity, surface):
Astrodome
(59,984, artificial)
Business address:
6910 Fannin Street
Lower Level
Houston, TX 77030
Business phone:
713-797-9111
Ticket Information:
713-797-1000
Team colors:
Columbia blue, scarlet and white
Flagship radio station:
KTRH, 740 AM
Training site:
Trinity University
San Antonio, Tex.
713-797-9111

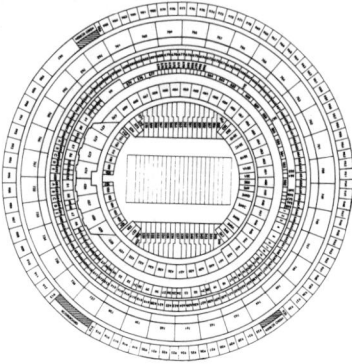

INDIANAPOLIS COLTS
AFC EASTERN DIVISION

1994 REVIEW

RESULTS

Sept. 4—HOUSTON	W	45-21
Sept. 11—at Tampa Bay	L	10-24
Sept. 18—at Pittsburgh	L	21-31
Sept. 25—CLEVELAND	L	14-21
Oct. 2—SEATTLE	W	17-15
Oct. 9—at N.Y. Jets	L	6-16
Oct. 16—at Buffalo	W	27-17
Oct. 23—WASHINGTON	L	27-41
Oct. 30—N.Y. JETS	W	28-25
Nov. 6—at Miami	L	21-22
Nov. 13—Open date		
Nov. 20—at Cincinnati	W	17-13
Nov. 27—NEW ENGLAND	L	10-12
Dec. 4—at Seattle	W	31-19
Dec. 11—at New England	L	13-28
Dec. 18—MIAMI	W	10-6
Dec. 24—BUFFALO	W	10-9

RECORDS/RANKINGS

1994 regular-season record: 8-8 (3rd in AFC East); 4-4 in division; 8-6 in conference; 5-3 at home; 3-5 on road.
Team record last five years: 29-51 (.363, ranks 23rd in league in that span).

1994 team rankings:	No.	AFC	NFL
Total offense	*275.8	14	27
Rushing offense	*128.8	3	4
Passing offense	*147.1	14	28
Scoring offense	307	9	18
Total defense	*332.8	11	20
Rushing defense	*102.9	6	12
Passing defense	*229.9	12	24
Scoring defense	320	T6	T14
Takeaways	28	T9	T18
Giveaways	31	T7	T16
Turnover differential	-3	8	T18
Sacks	29	T9	T17
Sacks allowed	28	T5	T10

*Yards per game.

TEAM LEADERS

Scoring (kicking): Dean Biasucci, 85 pts. (37/37 PATs, 16/24 FGs).
Scoring (touchdowns): Marshall Faulk, 72 pts. (11 rushing, 1 receiving).
Passing: Jim Harbaugh, 1,440 yds. (202 att., 125 comp., 61.9%, 9 TDs, 6 int.).
Rushing: Marshall Faulk, 1,282 yds. (314 att., 4.1 avg., 11 TDs).
Receptions: Marshall Faulk, 52 (522 yds., 10.0 avg., 1 TD); Floyd Turner, 52 (593 yds., 11.4 avg., 6 TDs).
Interceptions: Ray Buchanan, 8 (221 yds., 3 TDs).
Sacks: Tony Bennett, 9.0.
Punting: Rohn Stark, 42.4 avg. (73 punts, 3,092 yds., 1 blocked).
Punt returns: Dewell Brewer, 8.1 avg. (42 att., 339 yds., 1 TD).
Kickoff returns: Ronald Humphrey, 22.4 avg. (35 att., 783 yds., 1 TD).

1995 SEASON

CLUB DIRECTORY

President and treasurer
Robert Irsay
Vice president and general manager
James Irsay
V.p. and director of football operations
Bill Tobin
Vice president and general counsel
Michael G. Chernoff
Assistant general manager
Bob Terpening
Controller
Kurt Humphrey
Director/operations
Pete Ward
Director/public relations
Craig Kelley
Assistant director/public relations
Todd Stewart
Ticket manager
Larry Hall
Purchasing administrator
David Filar
Administrative assistant
Nicole Kucharski
Director of pro player personnel
Clyde Powers
Director of college player personnel
George Boone
College scouts
Mike Butler
John Goeller
Don Joyce
Paul Roell
William Scherer
Ron Toman

Head coach
Ted Marchibroda
Assistant coaches
Tom Batta (tight ends/quality control)
Greg Blache (defensive line)
Ron Blackledge (offensive line)
Fred Bruney (def. assistant)
Gene Huey (running backs)
Lindy Infante (off. coord.)
Jim Johnson (linebackers)
Hank Kuhlmann (special teams)
Jimmy Robinson (receivers)
Pat Thomas (secondary)
Vince Tobin (def. coordinator)
Tom Zupancic (strength and conditioning)

Head trainer
Hunter Smith
Assistant trainer
Dave Hammer
Team physician/orthopedic surgeon
K. Donald Shelbourne
Orthopedic surgeon
Arthur C. Rettig
Equipment manager
Jon Scott
Assistant equipment manager
Mike Mays
Video director
Marty Heckscher

SCHEDULE

Sept. 3—CINCINNATI	12:00	
Sept. 10—at N.Y. Jets	4:00	
Sept. 17—at Buffalo	1:00	
Sept. 24—Open date		
Oct. 1—ST. LOUIS	12:00	
Oct. 8—at Miami	4:00	
Oct. 15—SAN FRANCISCO	12:00	
Oct. 22—at Los Angeles	1:00	
Oct. 29—N.Y. JETS	1:00	
Nov. 5—BUFFALO	1:00	
Nov. 12—at New Orleans	12:00	
Nov. 19—at New England	1:00	
Nov. 26—MIAMI	1:00	
Dec. 3—at Carolina	1:00	
Dec. 10—at Jacksonville	1:00	
Dec. 17—SAN DIEGO	4:00	
Dec. 23—NEW ENGLAND (Sat.)	8:00	

All times are for home team.
All games Sunday unless noted.

DRAFT CHOICES

Ellis Johnson, DT, Florida (first round/ 15th pick overall).
Ken Dilger, TE, Illinois (2/48).
Zack Crockett, FB, Florida State (3/79).
Ray McElroy, DB, Eastern Illinois (4/114).
Derek West, T, Colorado (5/149).
Brian Gelzheiser, LB, Penn State (6/187).
Jessie Cox, LB, Texas Southern (7/223).

1995 SEASON

TRAINING CAMP ROSTER

No.	QUARTERBACKS	Ht./Wt.	Born	NFL Exp.	College	How acq.	'94 Games GP/GS
7	Erickson, Craig	6-2/215	5-17-69	4	Miami (Fla.)	T-TB/95	*15/15
12	Harbaugh, Jim	6-3/215	12-23-63	9	Michigan	FA/94	12/9
11	Justin, Paul	6-4/202	5-19-68	1	Arizona State	FA/94	0/0
18	Nagle, Browning	6-3/225	4-29-68	5	Louisville	FA/94	1/1
	RUNNING BACKS						
32	Crockett, Zack (FB)	6-2/244	12-2-72	R	Florida State	D3/95	—
28	Faulk, Marshall	5-10/200	2-26-73	2	San Diego State	D1a/94	16/16
46	Harris, Lamar (TE)	6-2/255	5-19-72	R	Arizona	FA/95	—
25	Humphrey, Ronald (KR)	5-10/211	3-3-69	2	Mississippi Valley State	D8/92	15/0
26	Johnson, Eric	5-10/200	6-7-71	R	Central Michigan	FA/95	—
42	Potts, Roosevelt	6-0/245	1-8-71	3	Northeast Louisiana	D2/93	16/15
21	Warren, Lamont	5-11/194	1-4-73	2	Colorado	D6/94	11/0
	RECEIVERS						
8	Anderson, Phil	5-11/190	5-20-72	R	Delaware State	FA/95	—
84	Anderson, Willie	6-0/175	3-7-65	8	UCLA	FA/95	*16/16
81	Arbuckle, Charles (TE)	6-3/248	9-13-68	5	UCLA	FA/92	7/1
80	Bailey, Aaron	5-10/184	10-24-71	2	Louisville	FA/94	13/0
83	Banta, Bradford (TE)	6-6/255	12-14-70	2	Southern California	D4/94	16/0
2	Bronson, Ben	5-10/165	9-9-72	R	Baylor	FA/95	—
87	Dawkins, Sean	6-4/210	2-3-71	3	California	D1/93	16/16
44	Dilger, Ken (TE)	6-5/249	2-2-71	R	Illinois	D2/95	—
16	Hill, Aubrey	5-11/169	2-2-72	R	Florida	FA/95	—
6	Jones, Tyronne	5-8/165	9-12-71	R	Grambling State	FA/95	—
1	Marshall, Marvin	5-10/175	6-21-72	R	South Carolina State	FA/95	—
47	McLemore, Tom (TE)	6-5/250	3-14-70	3	Southern	FA/95	*2/1
48	Pollard, Marcus (TE)	6-4/248	2-8-72	R	Bradley	FA/95	—
15	Smith, Terry	6-0/200	4-20-71	R	Clemson	FA/95	—
86	Stablein, Brian	6-1/191	4-14-70	2	Ohio State	FA/93	0/0
88	Turner, Floyd	5-11/198	5-29-66	7	Northwestern State	FA/94	16/16
85	West, Ed (TE)	6-1/259	8-2-61	12	Auburn	FA/95	*14/12
	OFFENSIVE LINEMEN						
53	Conway, Duane (C)	6-2/288	8-24-72	R	Eastern Illinois	FA/95	—
69	Dixon, Randy (G)	6-3/305	3-12-65	9	Pittsburgh	D4/87	14/14
66	Duggins, Brent (T)	6-4/288	1-19-72	R	Southern Mississippi	FA/95	—
64	Patrick, Garin	6-3/265	8-31-71	R	Louisville	FA/95	—
	Hardin, Steve (G)	6-7/310	12-30-71	R	Oregon	FA/95	—
63	Lowdermilk, Kirk (C)	6-4/280	4-10-63	11	Ohio State	FA/93	16/16
65	Mahlum, Eric (G)	6-4/285	12-6-70	2	California	D2/94	16/2
74	Mathews, Jason (T)	6-5/284	2-9-71	2	Texas A&M	D3/94	10/0
76	Smith, Warner (G)	6-2/291	3-30-73	R	Arizona	FA/95	—
79	Staysniak, Joe (G)	6-4/302	12-8-66	5	Ohio State	FA/92	16/16
71	Vickers, Kipp	6-2/288	8-27-69	2	Miami (Fla.)	FA/93	0/0
72	West, Derek (T)	6-8/298	3-28-72	R	Colorado	D5/95	—
67	Wolford, Will (T)	6-5/300	5-18-64	10	Vanderbilt	FA/93	16/16
	DEFENSIVE LINEMEN						
	Berry, Mike (T)	6-4/268	2-13-69	R	Valdosta State	FA/95	—
66	Copher, Chad (T)	6-7/265	12-1-71	R	Illinois	FA/95	—
90	Emtman, Steve	6-4/300	4-16-70	4	Washington	D1/92	4/0
62	Johnson, Ellis (T)	6-2/290	10-30-73	R	Florida	D1/95	—
61	McCoy, Tony (NT)	6-0/279	6-10-69	4	Florida	D4/92	15/15
98	Siragusa, Tony (NT)	6-3/315	5-14-67	6	Pittsburgh	FA/90	16/16
95	Whittington, Bernard (E)	6-6/257	7-20-71	2	Indiana	FA/94	13/8
	LINEBACKERS						
51	Alberts, Trev	6-4/243	8-8-70	2	Nebraska	D1b/94	5/0
56	Bennett, Tony	6-2/243	7-1-67	6	Mississippi	FA/94	16/15
55	Coryatt, Quentin	6-3/250	8-1-70	4	Texas A&M	D1/92	16/16
50	Cox, Jessie	6-2/222	9-8-71	R	Texas Southern	D7/95	—
99	Gelzheiser, Brian	6-1/235	2-12-72	R	Penn State	D6/95	—
59	Grant, Stephen	6-0/242	12-23-69	4	West Virginia	D10/92	16/12
54	Herrod, Jeff	6-0/249	7-29-66	8	Mississippi	D9/88	15/15
57	McDonald, Devon	6-4/248	11-8-69	3	Notre Dame	D4/93	16/3
97	Radecic, Scott	6-3/240	6-14-62	12	Penn State	W-Buf/90	16/1
52	Ratigan, Brian	6-4/241	12-27-70	2	Notre Dame	FA/93	14/0
58	Sanders, Glen	6-1/240	11-4-66	3	Louisiana Tech	FA/95	*1/0
96	Wilmot, Trevor	6-2/220	10-30-72	R	Indiana	FA/95	—
	DEFENSIVE BACKS						
33	Ambrose, Ashley	5-10/185	9-17-70	4	Mississippi Valley State	D2/92	16/4
29	Belser, Jason	5-9/187	5-28-70	4	Oklahoma	D8/92	13/12

No.	DEFENSIVE BACKS	Ht./Wt.	Born	NFL Exp.	College	How acq.	'94 Games GP/GS
20	Biggens, Wilbert	5-8/187	12-24-72	R	Texas A&M	FA/95	—
34	Buchanan, Ray	5-9/193	9-29-71	3	Louisville	D3/93	16/16
35	Clarks, Conrad	5-10/212	4-21-69	R	Northeast Louisiana	FA/95	—
39	Covington, John	6-0/198	4-22-72	2	Notre Dame	D5/94	3/0
31	Craft, Douglas	6-0/190	7-23-68	1	Southern	FA/95	0/0
38	Daniel, Eugene	5-11/188	5-4-61	12	Louisiana State	D8/84	16/15
30	Gray, Derwin	5-11/198	4-9-71	3	Brigham Young	D4/93	16/2
23	Humphries, Leonard	5-9/180	6-19-70	2	Penn State	FA/94	13/0
41	Jaunich, Mike	6-0/217	2-16-73	R	South Dakota State	FA/95	—
40	McElroy, Ray (CB/KR)	5-11/188	7-31-72	R	Eastern Illinois	D4/95	—
37	Smith, Carl	6-0/199	3-12-73	R	Virginia	FA/95	—
36	Watts, Damon	5-10/173	4-8-72	2	Indiana	FA/94	16/8
	SPECIALISTS						
3	Cofer, Mike (K)	6-1/195	2-19-64	8	North Carolina State	FA/95	0/0
17	Gardocki, Chris (P)	6-1/196	2-7-70	5	Clemson	FA/95	*16/0

*Anderson played 16 games with Rams in '94; Erickson played 15 games with Buccaneers; Gardocki played 16 games with Bears; McLemore played 2 games with Browns; Sanders played 1 game with Broncos; West played 14 games with Packers.

Also played with Colts in '94: WR Shannon Baker (4); PK Dean Biasucci (16); RB/PR Dewell Brewer (16); LB Paul Butcher (13); TE Kerry Cash (16); TE Carlos Ethredge (9); T Cecil Gray (16); DE Jon Hand (5); NT Garry Howe (1); WR Mark Jackson (12); QB Don Majkowski (9); T Zefross Moss (11); DE Al Noga (4); LB Freddie Joe Nunn (11); DB Robert O'Neal (2); DL Tom Sims (16); P Rohn Stark (16); DB David Tate (16); RB Ed Toner (9).

Abbreviations: D1—draft pick, first round; SupD2—supplemental draft pick, second round; W-Den—waivers acquisition from Denver; T-Sea—trade acquisition from Seattle; PlanB—Plan B free-agent acquisition; FA—free-agent acquisition (other than Plan B).

MISCELLANEOUS TEAM DATA

Stadium (capacity, surface):
RCA Dome (60,127, artificial)

Business address:
P.O. Box 535000
Indianapolis, IN 46253

Business phone:
317-297-2658

Ticket information:
317-297-7000

Team colors:
Royal blue and white

Flagship radio station:
WIBC, 1070 AM/WNAP, 93.1 FM

Training site:
Anderson University
Anderson, Ind.
317-297-2658

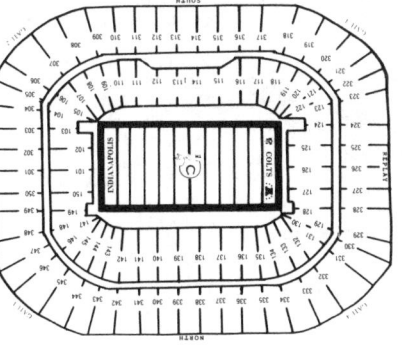

JACKSONVILLE JAGUARS
AFC CENTRAL DIVISION

1995 SEASON

SCHEDULE

Sept. 3—HOUSTON	1:00
Sept. 10—at Cincinnati	4:00
Sept. 17—at N.Y. Jets	4:00
Sept. 24—GREEN BAY	8:00
Oct. 1—at Houston	3:00
Oct. 8—PITTSBURGH	1:00
Oct. 15—CHICAGO	1:00
Oct. 22—at Cleveland	1:00
Oct. 29—at Pittsburgh	1:00
Nov. 5—Open date	
Nov. 12—SEATTLE	1:00
Nov. 19—at Tampa Bay	1:00
Nov. 26—CINCINNATI	1:00
Dec. 3—at Denver	2:00
Dec. 10—INDIANAPOLIS	1:00
Dec. 17—at Detroit	1:00
Dec. 24—CLEVELAND	1:00

All times are for home team.
All games Sunday unless noted.

DRAFT CHOICES

Tony Boselli, T, Southern California (first round/second pick overall).
James Stewart, RB, Tennessee (1/19).
Brian DeMarco, T, Michigan State (2/40).
Bryan Schwartz, LB, Augustana (S.D.) (2/64).
Chris Hudson, DB, Colorado (3/71).
Rob Johnson, QB, Southern Cal (4/99).
Mike Thompson, DT, Wisconsin (4/123).
Ryan Christopherson, FB, Wyoming (5/169).
Marcus Price, T, Louisiana State (6/172).
Curtis Marsh, WR, Utah (7/219).

CLUB DIRECTORY

Chairman & CEO
Wayne Weaver
President & COO
David Seldin
V.P./football operations
Michael Huyghue
General counsel
Paul Vance
Senior v.p./marketing
Dan Connell
V.P./ticket operations
Judy Seldin
V.P./broadcast & creative services
Peter Scheurmier
Exec. director of communications
Dan Edwards
Exec. director of administration
John Jones
Director of pro personnel
Ron Hill
Director of college scouting
Rick Reiprish
Director of finance
David Blasic
Dir. of special events & promotions
Ann Carroll
Dir. of corporate sponsorship
David Rowan
Director of facilities
Jeff Cannon
Director of computer services
Bruce Swindell

Head coach
Tom Coughlin
Assistant coaches
Joe Baker (asst. special teams)
Pete Carmichael (wide receivers)
Randy Edsall (secondary)
Kevin Gilbride (off. coord.)
Jerald Ingram (running backs)
Dick Jauron (def. coordinator)
Mike Maser (offensive line)
Nick Nicolau (tight ends)
Jerry Palmieri (strength & conditioning)
Larry Pasquale (special teams coordinator)
John Pease (defensive line)
Lucious Selmon (outside linebackers)
Steve Szabo (inside linebackers)

Director of player programs
Paul Lankford
Head athletic trainer
Mike Ryan
Video director
Mike Perkins
Equipment manager
Bob Monica

TRAINING CAMP ROSTER

No.	QUARTERBACKS	Ht./Wt.	Born	NFL Exp.	College	How acq.	'94 Games GP/GS
7	Beuerlein, Steve	6-3/210	3-7-65	8	Notre Dame	ED/95	*9/7
8	Brunell, Mark	6-1/208	9-17-70	2	Washington	T-GB/95	*2/0
10	Johnson, Rob	6-3/220	3-18-73	R	Southern California	D4/95	—
11	Ware, Andre	6-2/220	7-31-68	5	Houston	FA/95	0/0
	RUNNING BACKS						
32	Brown, Leon	5-10/190	5-16-70	1	Eastern Kentucky	FA/95	0/0
42	Christopherson, Ryan (FB)	5-11/238	7-26-72	R	Wyoming	D5/95	—
34	Cobb, Reggie	6-0/215	7-7-68	6	Tennessee	ED/95	*16/13
23	Jordan, Randy	5-10/208	6-6-70	1	North Carolina	FA/94	0/0
35	Maston, Le'Shai	6-1/232	10-7-70	3	Baylor	ED/95	*5/1
22	McNabb, Dexter (FB)	6-2/245	7-9-69	3	Florida	FA/94	0/0
31	Royster, Mazio	6-1/200	8-3-70	4	Southern California	ED/95	*14/1
33	Stewart, James	6-1/222	12-27-71	R	Tennessee	D1/95	—
	RECEIVERS						
83	Baker, Shannon	5-10/190	7-20-71	2	Florida State	FA/94	*4/0
5	Bech, Brett	6-1/184	8-20-71	R	Louisiana State	FA/95	—
86	Brown, Derek (TE)	6-6/260	3-31-70	4	Notre Dame	ED/95	*13/0
89	Davenport, Charles	6-3/216	11-22-68	4	North Carolina State	ED/95	*7/0
88	Etheredge, Carlos (TE)	6-5/259	8-10-70	2	Miami (Fla.)	FA/94	*9/0
	Givins, Ernest	5-9/178	9-3-64	10	Louisville	FA/95	*16/16
48	Griffith, Rich (TE)	6-5/252	7-31-69	2	Arizona	FA/95	0/0
15	Hall, Matt	6-4/215	9-22-72	R	Murray State	FA/95	—
	Hallock, Ty (TE)	6-3/249	4-30-71	3	Michigan State	T-Det/95	*15/10
6	Harris, Willie	6-2/196	11-8-70	1	Mississippi State	FA/95	0/0
81	Howard, Desmond	5-9/180	5-15-70	4	Michigan	ED/95	*16/15
80	Jackson, Willie	6-1/205	8-16-71	1	Florida	ED/95	0/0
40	Laro, Gordon (TE)	6-3/257	4-17-72	R	Boston College	FA/95	—
3	Marsh, Curtis	6-1/212	11-24-70	R	Utah	D7/95	—
85	Morton, John	6-0/185	9-24-69	1	Western Michigan	FA/95	0/0
49	Schorp, Greg (TE)	6-3/242	9-6-71	1	Texas A&M	FA/95	0/0
82	Smith, Jimmy	6-1/205	2-9-69	3	Jackson State	FA/95	0/0
87	Tillman, Cedric	6-2/204	7-22-70	4	Alcorn State	ED/95	*16/4
	OFFENSIVE LINEMEN						
71	Boselli, Tony (T)	6-7/323	4-17-72	R	Southern California	D1a/95	—
66	Bouwens, Shawn (G)	6-4/290	5-25-68	5	Nebraska Wesleyan	FA/95	*16/16
60	Colins, Ron (G/T)	6-5/289	9-30-71	1	Fresno State	FA/95	0/0
69	Chung, Eugene (G)	6-4/295	6-14-69	4	Virginia Tech	ED/95	*3/0
73	DeMarco, Brian (T)	6-5/314	4-9-72	R	Michigan State	D2/95	—
	Dausin, Chris (C)	6-5/285	12-18-69	1	Texas A&M	FA/95	0/0
78	Dillard, Ivory (G/T)	6-3/299	8-15-71	1	Florida A&M	FA/95	0/0
68	Huntington, Greg (G)	6-3/295	9-22-70	2	Penn State	FA/944	0/0
	Moore, Andrew (T)	6-5/300	12-22-72	R	Somona State	FA/95	—
50	Myslinski, Tom (G)	6-2/289	12-7-68	4	Tennessee	ED/95	*4/0
67	Novak, Jeff (T)	6-5/295	7-27-67	2	Southwest Texas State	ED/95	*6/0
63	Price, Marcus (T)	6-5/303	3-3-72	2	Louisiana State	D6/95	—
	Shaw, Rickie (T)	6-5/305	12-26-69	2	North Carolina	FA/94	0/0
76	Siever, Paul (G)	6-6/294	8-10-69	3	Penn State	FA/94	0/0
75	Tucker, Mark (C/G)	6-3/290	4-29-68	3	Southern California	ED/95	*16/3
79	Widell, Dave (C/G)	6-6/292	5-14-65	8	Boston College	FA/95	*16/16
	DEFENSIVE LINEMEN						
	Brown, Kendall (E)	6-3/267	9-12-71	R	Louisville	FA/95	—
92	Davey, Don (T)	6-4/270	4-8-68	5	Wisconsin	FA/95	*16/2
96	Duff, John (E)	6-7/250	7-31-67	3	New Mexico	ED/95	*4/0
77	Floyd, Gonzalo (E)	6-3/260	9-2-71	1	Texas-El Paso	FA/95	0/0
91	Frase, Paul (T/E)	6-5/260	5-5-65	8	Syracuse	ED/95	*16/5
62	Hall, Ray (T)	6-4/267	3-2-71	1	Washington State	FA/95	0/0
56	Lageman, Jeff (E)	6-5/266	7-18-67	7	Virginia	FA/95	*16/16
93	Logan, Ernie (E)	6-4/280	5-18-68	4	East Carolina	FA/94	0/0
98	Mayfield, Corey (T)	6-3/290	2-25-70	2	Oklahoma	FA/95	0/0
94	Pritchett, Kelvin (T)	6-2/281	10-24-69	5	Mississippi	FA/95	*16/15
	Simmons, Jason (E)	6-5/250	12-20-70	1	Ohio State	FA/94	0/0
99	Smeenge, Joel (E)	6-5/250	4-1-68	6	Western Michigan	FA/95	*16/2
61	Sutton, Ricky (T)	6-2/281	4-27-71	2	Auburn	FA/94	0/0
65	Thompson, Mike (T)	6-3/276	12-22-72	R	Wisconsin	D4/95	—
70	Williams, Chris (T)	6-3/281	8-8-70	1	Hampton (Va.)	FA/94	0/0
	LINEBACKERS						
52	Boyer, Brant	6-0/237	6-27-71	2	Arizona	ED/95	*14/0
95	Carthen, Jason	6-3/255	11-16-70	2	Ohio University	FA/94	*1/0

No.	LINEBACKERS	Ht./Wt.	Born	NFL Exp.	College	How acq.	'94 Games GP/GS
59	Clark, Reggie	6-2/225	10-17-67	2	North Carolina	FA/95	*5/0
58	Freeman, Reggie	6-2/233	5-8-70	2	Florida State	FA/94	0/0
54	Goganious, Keith	6-2/239	12-7-68	4	Penn State	ED/95	*16/1
45	Mason, Andy	6-2/228	8-31-71	1	Washington	FA/94	0/0
57	McCoy, Ryan	6-2/237	3-13-72	1	Houston	FA/95	0/0
44	McManus, Tom	6-2/240	7-30-70	1	Boston College	FA/95	0/0
	Meinert, Ben	6-3/245	11-10-72	R	NE Oklahoma State	FA/95	—
	Schwartz, Bryan	6-3/256	12-5-71	R	Augustana (S.D.)	D2/95	—
	Smalley, Rod	6-4/235	12-8-71	R	UCLA	FA/95	—
53	Stephens, Santo	6-4/232	6-16-69	3	Temple	ED/95	*14/3
90	Williams, James	6-0/230	10-10-68	6	Mississippi State	ED/95	*16/7
51	Williams, Mark	6-3/240	5-17-71	2	Ohio State	ED/95	*16/0
	DEFENSIVE BACKS						
36	Boykin, Deral (S)	5-11/196	9-2-70	3	Louisville	FA/94	*12/0
29	Carrington, Darren (S)	6-2/200	10-10-66	7	Northern Arizona	ED/95	*16/16
27	Clark, Vinnie (CB)	6-0/192	1-22-69	5	Ohio State	FA/95	*16/15
24	Colon, Harry (S)	6-0/203	2-14-69	5	Missouri	ED/95	*16/0
30	Davis, Michael (CB)	6-1/192	1-14-72	2	Cincinnati	ED/95	*16/0
38	Dumas, Mike (S)	5-11/181	3-18-69	5	Indiana	FA/95	*14/0
26	Green, Rogerick (CB)	6-0/184	12-15-69	4	Kansas State	ED/95	*11/0
28	Grow, Monty (S)	6-3/214	9-4-71	2	Florida	ED/95	*15/0
20	Henderson, Othello (S)	6-0/192	8-23-72	3	UCLA	ED/95	*16/0
19	Hudson, Chris (S)	5-9/195	10-6-71	R	Colorado	D3/95	—
80	Jackson, Al (CB)	6-0/182	9-7-71	2	Georgia	ED/95	*11/0
18	Johnson, Tommy (CB)	5-10/180	12-5-71	R	Alabama	FA/95	—
46	Mills, Vidal (SS)	5-11/190	7-21-72	1	Bethune-Cookman	FA/95	0/0
43	Robinson, Frank (CB)	5-11/180	1-11-69	3	Boise State	ED/95	0/0
37	Simmons, Marcello (CB)	6-1/180	8-8-71	2	Southern Methodist	FA/94	0/0
41	Thomas, Dave (CB)	6-2/205	8-25-68	3	Tennessee	ED/95	*16/0
25	Washington, Mickey (CB)	5-9/191	7-8-68	5	Texas A&M	FA/95	*16/16
	SPECIALISTS						
4	Barker, Bryan (P)	6-1/187	6-28-64	6	Santa Clara	FA/95	*11/0
9	Sisson, Scott (K)	6-0/197	7-21-71	2	Georgia Tech	FA/95	0/0
1	Stoft, Jason (P)	6-0/185	6-19-72	R	Houston	FA/95	—

*Baker played 4 games with Colts in '94; Barker played 11 games with Eagles; Beuerlein played 9 games with Cardinals; Bouwens played 16 games with Lions; Boyer played 14 games with Dolphins; Boykin played 12 games with Redskins; D. Brown played 13 games with Giants; Brunell played 2 games with Packers; Carthen played 1 game with Patriots; Chung played 3 games with Patriots; R. Clark played 5 games with Steelers; V. Clark played 11 games with Falcons and 5 with Saints; Carrington played 16 games with Chargers; Cobb played 16 games with Packers; Colon played 16 games with Lions; Davenport played 7 games with Steelers; Davey played 16 games with Packers; Davis played 16 games with Oilers; Duff played 4 games with Raiders; Dumas played 14 games with Bills; Etheredge played 9 games with Colts; Frase played 16 games with Giants; Givins played 16 games with Oilers; Goganious played 16 games with Bills; Green played 11 games with Buccaneers; Grow played 15 games with Chiefs; Hallock played 15 games with Lions; Henderson played 16 games with Saints; Howard played 16 games with Redskins; A. Jackson played 11 games with Eagles; Lageman played 16 games with Jets; Maston played 5 games with Oilers; Myslinski played 4 games with Bears; Novak played 6 games with Dolphins; Pritchett played 16 games with Lions; Royster played 14 games with Buccaneers; Smeenge played 16 games with Saints; Stephens played 16 games with Bengals; Thomas played 16 games with Cowboys; Tillman played 16 games with Broncos; Tucker played 16 games with Cardinals; Washington played 16 games with Bills; Widell played 16 games with Broncos; J. Williams played 16 games with Saints; M. Williams played 16 games with Packers.

Abbreviations: ED—expansion draft pick; D1—draft pick, first round; SupD2—supplemental draft pick, second round; W-Den—waivers acquisition from Denver; T-Sea—trade acquisition from Seattle; PlanB—Plan B free-agent acquisition; FA—free-agent acquisition (other than Plan B).

MISCELLANEOUS TEAM DATA

Stadium (capacity, surface):
To be announced
(73,000, grass)

Business address:
One Stadium Place
Jacksonville, FL 32202

Business phone:
904-633-6000

Ticket information:
904-633-2000

Team colors:
Teal, black and gold

Flagship radio station:
To be announced

Training site:
U. of Wisconsin-Stevens Point
Stevens Point, Wis.
904-633-6000

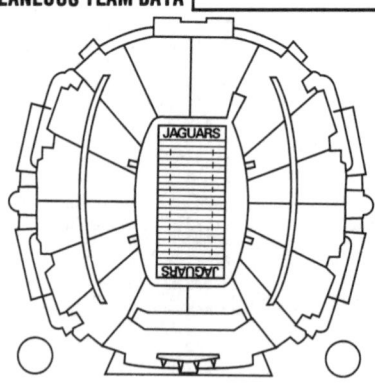

KANSAS CITY CHIEFS
AFC WESTERN DIVISION

1994 REVIEW

RESULTS

Sept. 4—at New Orleans	W	30-17
Sept. 11—SAN FRANCISCO	W	24-17
Sept. 18—at Atlanta	W	30-10
Sept. 25—L.A. RAMS	L	0-16
Oct. 2—Open date		
Oct. 9—at San Diego	L	6-20
Oct. 17—at Denver	W	31-28
Oct. 23—SEATTLE	W	38-23
Oct. 30—at Buffalo	L	10-44
Nov. 6—L.A. RAIDERS	W	13-3
Nov. 13—SAN DIEGO	L	13-14
Nov. 20—CLEVELAND	W	20-13
Nov. 27—at Seattle	L	9-10
Dec. 4—DENVER (OT)	L	17-20
Dec. 12—at Miami	L	28-45
Dec. 18—HOUSTON	W	31-9
Dec. 24—at L.A. Raiders	W	19-9

RECORDS/RANKINGS

1994 regular-season record: 9-7 (T2nd in AFC West); 4-4 in division; 6-6 in conference; 5-3 at home; 4-4 on road.
Team record last five years: 51-29 (.638), ranks 4th in league in that span).

1994 team rankings:	No.	AFC	NFL
Total offense	*355.8	3	5
Rushing offense	*108.3	6	11
Passing offense	*247.5	4	7
Scoring offense	319	7	14
Total defense	*312.5	5	12
Rushing defense	*108.4	8	16
Passing defense	*204.1	5	10
Scoring defense	298	3	7
Takeaways	38	T2	T2
Giveaways	26	3	T9
Turnover differential	12	2	2
Sacks	39	T3	T5
Sacks allowed	19	3	3

*Yards per game.

TEAM LEADERS

Scoring (kicking): Lin Elliott, 105 pts. (30/30 PATs, 25/30 FGs).
Scoring (touchdowns): Marcus Allen, 44 pts. (7 rushing, 1 2-pt. conv.).
Passing: Joe Montana, 3,283 yds. (493 att., 299 comp., 60.6%, 16 TDs, 9 int.).
Rushing: Marcus Allen, 709 yds. (189 att., 3.8 avg., 7 TDs).
Receptions: Kimble Anders, 67 (525 yds., 7.8 avg., 1 TD).
Interceptions: Charles Mincy, 3 (49 yds., 0 TDs).
Sacks: Neil Smith, 11.5.
Punting: Louie Aguiar, 42.1 avg. (85 punts, 3,582 yds., 0 blocked).
Punt returns: Danan Hughes, 7.1 avg. (27 att., 192 yds., 0 TDs).
Kickoff returns: Ron Dickerson, 22.5 avg. (21 att., 472 yds., 0 TDs).

1995 SEASON

CLUB DIRECTORY

Founder
Lamar Hunt
Chairman of the board
Jack Steadman
President/G.M./chief executive officer
Carl Peterson
Executive vice president/COO
Tim Connolly
Assistant general manager
Dennis Thum
Secretary/legal
Jim Seigfried
Treasurer and director/finance
Dale Young
V.P./sales and marketing
Dennis Watley
Director/operations
Jeff Klein
Director/development
Ken Blume
Director/promotions
Phil Thomas
Director/public relations
Bob Moore
Assistant director/public relations
Jim Carr
Community relations manager
Brenda Sniezek
Vice president/Player personnel
Lynn Stiles
Director of pro scouting
Mark Hatley
Director of college scouting
Terry Bradway
Scouts
Bill Baker
Chuck Cook
Roger Jackson
Fred Schubach

Head coach
Marty Schottenheimer
Assistant coaches
Russ Ball (assistant strength and conditioning)
John Bunting (linebackers)
Gunther Cunningham (def. coordinator)
Jim Erkenbeck (tight ends)
Paul Hackett (off. coord.)
Carl Hairston (def. line)
Woodrow Lowe (def. & special teams assistant)
Michael McCarthy (quarterbacks)
Jimmy Raye (running backs)
Dave Redding (strength and conditioning)
Al Saunders (assistant head coach/receivers)
Kurt Schottenheimer (defensive backs)
Art Shell (offensive line)
Mike Stock (special teams)
Darvin Wallis (quality control/defense)

Trainer
Dave Kendall
Assistant trainer
Bud Epps
Physicians
Jon Browne
Ray Baker
Chris Barnthouse
Equipment manager
Mike Davidson
Video coordinator
Mike Dennis

SCHEDULE

Sept. 3—at Seattle	1:00
Sept. 10—N.Y. GIANTS	12:00
Sept. 17—LOS ANGELES	12:00
Sept. 24—at Cleveland	4:00
Oct. 1—at Arizona	1:00
Oct. 9—SAN DIEGO (Mon.)	8:00
Oct. 15—NEW ENGLAND	12:00
Oct. 22—at Denver	2:00
Oct. 29—Open date	
Nov. 5—WASHINGTON	12:00
Nov. 12—at San Diego	1:00
Nov. 19—HOUSTON	7:00
Nov. 23—at Dallas (Thanks.)	3:00
Dec. 3—at Los Angeles	1:00
Dec. 11—at Miami (Mon.)	9:00
Dec. 17—DENVER	3:00
Dec. 24—SEATTLE	12:00

All times are for home team.
All games Sunday unless noted.

DRAFT CHOICES

Trezelle Jenkins, T, Michigan (first round/31st pick overall).
Tamarick Vanover, WR, Florida St. (3/81).
Troy Dumas, LB, Nebraska (3/97).
Steve Stenstrom, QB, Stanford (4/134).
Mike Pelton, DT, Auburn (5/155).
Jerrott Willard, LB, California (5/164).
Bryan Proby, DT, Arizona State (6/202).
Tom Barndt, C, Pittsburgh (6/207).

1995 SEASON

TRAINING CAMP ROSTER

No.	QUARTERBACKS	Ht./Wt.	Born	NFL Exp.	College	How acq.	'94 Games GP/GS
14	Blundin, Matt	6-6/233	3-7-69	4	Virginia	D2/92	1/0
13	Bono, Steve	6-4/215	5-11-62	11	UCLA	T-SF/94	7/2
12	Gannon, Rich	6-3/208	12-20-65	8	Delaware	FA/95	0/0
15	Matthews, Steve	6-3/209	10-13-70	1	Memphis	D7a/94	0/0
18	Stenstrom, Steve	6-2/200	12-23-71	R	Stanford	D4/95	—
	RUNNING BACKS						
32	Allen, Marcus	6-2/210	3-26-60	14	Southern California	FA/93	13/13
38	Anders, Kimble (FB)	5-11/230	9-10-66	5	Houston	FA/91	16/13
30	Bennett, Donnell (FB)	6-0/241	9-14-72	2	Miami (Fla.)	D2/94	15/0
23	Dickerson, Ron (KR)	6-0/225	8-31-71	3	Arkansas	FA/93	9/0
29	Hill, Greg	5-11/205	2-23-72	2	Texas A&M	D1/94	16/1
46	Jones, Victor (FB)	5-8/223	12-5-67	6	Louisiana State	FA/95	*11/0
39	Richardson, Terry	6-0/204	10-8-71	1	Syracuse	FA/95	0/0
49	Richardson, Tony	6-1/224	12-17-71	1	Auburn	FA/95	0/0
26	Smith, J.J.	6-0/207	10-14-72	R	Kansas State	FA/95	—
21	Vaughn, Jon (KR)	5-9/203	3-12-70	5	Michigan	FA/94	*12/0
45	Washington, Michael (FB)	6-0/266	1-3-72	R	Missouri	FA/95	—
	RECEIVERS						
85	Bailey, Victor	6-2/198	7-3-70	3	Missouri	T-Phi/95	*16/0
82	Barnett, Tim	6-1/200	4-19-68	4	Jackson State	D3/91	0/0
4	Carroll, Wesley	6-2/183	9-6-67	4	Miami (Fla.)	FA/95	0/0
89	Cash, Keith (TE)	6-4/248	8-7-69	5	Texas	PlanB/92	6/5
84	Davis, Willie	6-0/181	10-10-67	4	Central Arkansas	FA/92	14/13
80	Dawson, Lake	6-1/204	1-2-72	2	Notre Dame	D3a/94	12/6
6	DeGraffenreid, Allen	6-2/210	5-1-70	1	Ohio State	FA/94	0/0
87	Greene, Tracy (TE)	6-5/282	11-5-72	2	Grambling State	D7b/94	7/2
9	Houston, Harrison	5-9/180	1-26-72	1	Florida	FA/95	0/0
83	Hughes, Danan (KR)	6-2/205	12-11-70	3	Iowa	D7/93	16/0
88	LaChapelle, Sean	6-3/205	7-29-70	2	UCLA	FA/95	0/0
81	Penn, Chris (KR)	6-0/198	4-20-71	2	Tulsa	D3b/94	8/0
	Scott, Sean (KR)	6-3/204	5-23-73	R	Pittsburg (Kan.) State	FA/95	—
47	Stowers, Tommie (TE)	6-3/240	11-18-66	4	Missouri	FA/94	1/0
	Tate, Willy (TE)	6-3/240	8-7-72	R	Oregon	FA/95	—
17	Vanover, Tamarick (KR)	5-11/213	2-25-74	R	Florida State	D3/95	—
82	Walker, Derrick (TE)	6-0/244	6-23-67	6	Michigan	FA/94	15/11
	Williams, Robert (TE)	6-3/240	2-1-72	R	Valdosta (Ga.) State	FA/95	—
	OFFENSIVE LINEMEN						
76	Alt, John (T)	6-8/307	5-30-62	12	Iowa	D1/84	13/13
71	Barndt, Tom (C)	6-3/290	3-14-72	R	Pittsburgh	D6b/95	—
69	Criswell, Jeff (T)	6-7/291	3-7-64	9	Graceland College (Ia.)	FA/95	*15/15
	Florine, Ron (T)	6-6/297	9-27-71	R	Central Missouri State	FA/95	—
61	Grunhard, Tim (C)	6-2/299	5-17-68	6	Notre Dame	D2/90	16/16
74	Jenkins, Trezelle (T)	6-7/322	3-13-73	R	Michigan	D1/95	—
65	Knapp, Lindsay (G/T)	6-6/290	2-25-70	3	Notre Dame	D5/93	2/0
60	Pay, Garry (C)	6-4/285	1-20-68	1	Brigham Young	FA/95	0/0
68	Shields, Will (G)	6-3/300	9-15-71	3	Nebraska	D3/93	16/16
66	Siglar, Ricky (T/G)	6-7/307	6-14-66	4	San Jose State	FA/93	16/8
79	Szott, David (G)	6-4/290	12-12-67	6	Penn State	D7/90	16/16
73	Valerio, Joe (T/C)	6-5/295	2-11-69	5	Pennsylvania	D2/91	16/1
72	Villa, Danny (T/G)	6-5/308	9-21-64	9	Arizona State	FA/93	14/0
62	Ware, David (T/G)	6-5/290	2-21-70	3	Virginia	FA/95	0/0
	DEFENSIVE LINEMEN						
	Bonds, Byron (T)	6-3/290	4-21-72	1	Southern Methodist	FA/95	0/0
99	Booker, Vaughn (E)	6-5/283	2-24-68	2	Cincinnati	FA/94	13/0
77	McDaniels, Pellom (E)	6-3/275	2-21-68	3	Oregon State	FA/93	12/3
92	Mickell, Darren (T)	6-4/284	8-3-70	4	Florida	D2/92	16/13
64	Pelton, Mike (T)	6-2/284	12-31-71	R	Auburn	D5a/95	—
75	Phillips, Joe (T)	6-5/300	7-15-63	10	Southern Methodist	FA/92	16/16
67	Proby, Bryan (T)	6-5/283	11-30-71	R	Arizona State	D6a/95	—
97	Saleaumua, Dan (T)	6-0/300	11-25-64	9	Arizona State	PlanB/89	14/14
90	Smith, Neil (E)	6-4/273	4-10-66	8	Nebraska	D1/88	14/13
98	Waldrop, Rob (T)	6-1/276	12-1-71	2	Arizona	D5/94	3/0
	LINEBACKERS						
58	Ale, Arnold	6-2/234	6-17-70	2	UCLA	FA/94	2/0
	Childs, Ron	5-11/212	9-18-71	R	Washington State	FA/95	—
50	Davis, Anthony	6-0/231	3-7-69	3	Utah	FA/94	5/0
96	Dumas, Troy	6-3/233	9-30-72	R	Nebraska	D3b/95	—
59	Fields, Jaime	5-11/236	8-28-70	3	Washington	D4/93	11/2

No.	LINEBACKERS	Ht./Wt.	Born	NFL Exp.	College	How acq.	'94 Games GP/GS
53	Hamilton, Rick	6-2/241	4-19-70	3	Central Florida	FA/94	*3/0
57	Jamison, George	6-1/235	9-30-62	10	Cincinnati	FA/94	13/12
93	Johnson, John	6-3/247	5-8-68	5	Clemson	FA/95	*5/0
51	Manusky, Greg	6-1/233	8-12-66	8	Colgate	FA/94	16/2
52	Rogers, Tracy	6-2/241	8-13-67	6	Fresno State	FA/90	14/3
91	Shaw, Eric	6-3/247	9-17-71	4	Louisiana Tech	FA/95	*3/0
54	Simien, Tracy	6-1/250	5-21-67	5	Texas Christian	FA/91	15/15
58	Thomas, Derrick	6-3/247	1-1-67	7	Alabama	D1/89	16/15
94	Traylor, Keith	6-2/295	9-3-69	3	Central Oklahoma	FA/95	0/0
95	Willard, Jerrott	6-1/233	7-11-72	R	California	D5b/95	—
55	Woolfork, Ronnie	6-3/254	12-21-70	1	Colorado	FA/94	0/0
	DEFENSIVE BACKS						
44	Anderson, Darren (CB)	5-10/180	1-11-69	3	Toledo	FA/94	15/1
34	Carter, Dale (CB)	6-1/188	11-28-69	4	Tennessee	D1/92	16/16
22	Carter, Perry (CB)	5-11/194	8-15-71	1	Southern Mississippi	FA/94	0/0
25	Collins, Mark (CB)	5-10/198	1-16-64	10	Cal State Fullerton	FA/94	14/13
31	Crocker, Sean	5-9/191	6-14-71	1	North Carolina	FA/95	0/0
41	Fulcher, David (S)	6-3/238	9-28-64	9	Arizona State	FA/95	0/0
40	Hasty, James (CB)	6-0/201	5-23-65	8	Washington State	FA/95	*16/16
42	Lott, Ronnie (S)	6-1/203	5-8-59	15	Southern California	FA/95	*15/15
43	Reece, John (CB)	6-0/203	1-24-71	1	Nebraska	FA/95	0/0
24	Terry, Doug (S)	5-11/204	12-12-69	4	Kansas	FA/92	10/1
48	Washington, Brian (S)	6-1/210	9-10-65	7	Nebraska	FA/95	*15/15
26	Watson, Tim (S)	6-1/215	8-13-70	3	Howard	FA/93	1/0
35	White, William (S)	5-10/200	2-19-66	8	Ohio State	T-Det/94	15/14
	SPECIALISTS						
5	Aguiar, Louie (K)	6-2/222	6-30-66	5	Utah State	FA/94	16/0
2	Elliott, Lin (K)	6-0/182	11-11-68	4	Texas Tech	FA/94	16/0
20	Layton, Gary (P)	6-1/205	9-28-72	R	Miami of Ohio	FA/95	—

*Bailey played 16 games with Eagles in '94; Criswell played 15 games with Jets; Hamilton played 1 game with Redskins and 2 games with Chiefs; Hasty played 16 games with Jets; Johnson played 5 games with Bengals; Jones played 10 games with Steelers and 1 game with Chiefs; Lott played 15 games with Jets; Shaw played 3 games with Bengals; Vaughn played 9 games with Seahawks and 3 games with Chiefs; Washington played 15 games with Jets.

Also played with Chiefs in '94: WR J.J. Birden (13 games); S Matt Gay (2); T Derrick Graham (16); S Monty Grow (15); TE Jimmie Johnson (7); NT Greg Kragen (16); WR Eric Martin (10); S Charles Mincy (16); QB Joe Montana (14); CB Jay Taylor (16); S Bracey Walker (2); S David Whitmore (12); LB Jerrol Williams (6); WR Mike Young (2).

Abbreviations: D1—draft pick, first round; SupD2—supplemental draft pick, second round; W-Den—waivers acquisition from Denver; T-Sea—trade acquisition from Seattle; PlanB—Plan B free-agent acquisition; FA—free-agent acquisition (other than Plan B).

MISCELLANEOUS TEAM DATA

Stadium (capacity, surface):
Arrowhead Stadium
(77,872, grass)
Business address:
One Arrowhead Drive
Kansas City, MO 64129
Business phone:
816-924-9300
Ticket information:
816-924-9400
Team colors:
Red, gold and white
Flagship radio station:
KCFX, 101.1 FM
Training site:
U. of Wisconsin-River Falls
River Falls, Wis.
715-425-4580

LOS ANGELES RAIDERS
AFC WESTERN DIVISION

1994 REVIEW

RESULTS

Sept.	5—at San Francisco	L	14-44
Sept.	11—SEATTLE	L	9-38
Sept.	18—at Denver	W	48-16
Sept.	25—SAN DIEGO	L	24-26
Oct.	2—Open date		
Oct.	9—at New England	W	21-17
Oct.	16—at Miami (OT)	L	17-20
Oct.	23—ATLANTA	W	30-17
Oct.	30—HOUSTON	W	17-14
Nov.	6—at Kansas City	L	3-13
Nov.	13—at L.A. Rams	W	20-17
Nov.	20—NEW ORLEANS	W	24-19
Nov.	27—PITTSBURGH	L	3-21
Dec.	5—at San Diego	W	24-17
Dec.	11—DENVER	W	23-13
Dec.	18—at Seattle	W	17-16
Dec.	24—KANSAS CITY	L	9-19

RECORDS/RANKINGS

1994 regular-season record: 9-7 (T2nd in AFC West); 4-4 in division; 6-6 in conference; 4-4 at home; 5-3 on road.
Team record last five years: 47-33 (.588, ranks T7th in league in that span).

1994 team rankings:	No.	AFC	NFL
Total offense	*298.7	10	19
Rushing offense	*94.5	12	21
Passing offense	*204.2	7	16
Scoring offense	303	10	19
Total defense	*308.9	4	10
Rushing defense	*96.4	5	9
Passing defense	*212.5	7	14
Scoring defense	327	T9	T17
Takeaways	25	13	22
Giveaways	30	6	15
Turnover differential	-5	T10	T22
Sacks	38	T5	T7
Sacks allowed	50	12	26

*Yards per game.

TEAM LEADERS

Scoring (kicking): Jeff Jaeger, 97 pts. (31/31 PATs, 22/28 FGs).
Scoring (touchdowns): Tim Brown, 54 pts. (9 receiving).
Passing: Jeff Hostetler, 3,334 yds. (455 att., 263 comp., 57.8%, 20 TDs, 16 int.).
Rushing: Harvey Williams, 983 yds. (282 att., 3.5 avg., 4 TDs).
Receptions: Tim Brown, 89 (1,309 yds., 14.7 avg., 9 TDs).
Interceptions: Terry McDaniel, 7 (103 yds., 2 TD).
Sacks: Chester McGlockton, 9.5.
Punting: Jeff Gossett, 43.9 avg. (77 punts, 3,377 yds., 0 blocked).
Punt returns: Tim Brown, 12.2 avg. (40 att., 487 yds., 0 TDs).
Kickoff returns: Rocket Ismail, 21.5 avg. (43 att., 923 yds., 0 TDs).

1995 SEASON

CLUB DIRECTORY

President of the general partner
Al Davis
Executive assistant
Al LoCasale
Pro personnel
George Karras
Senior assistant
Bruce Allen
Senior administrator
Morris Bradshaw
Administrative assistants
Mario Perez
Marc McKinney
Business manager
John Novak
Finance
Tom Blanda
Legal affairs
Jeff Birren
Amy Trask
Senior executive
John Herrera
Community relations
Gil Lafferty-Hernandez
Ticket manager
Peter Eiges
Admin. assistant to head coach
Mark Arteaga
Head trainer
H. Rod Martin
Trainer
Jonathan Jones
Strength and conditioning
Garrett Giemont
Player personnel
Angelo Coia
Dan Conners

Head coach
Mike White
Assistant coaches
Fred Biletnikoff (quality control-offense)
Willie Brown (director of squad development)
Joe Bugel (assistant head coach-offense)
Jim Fassel (quarterbacks)
John Fox (defense)
John Guy (def. assistant)
Bishop Harris (running backs)
Bill Meyers (tight ends)
Floyd Peters (defensive line)
Steve Shafer (defensive backs)
Kevin Spencer (special teams)
Fred Whittingham (linebackers)
Mike Wilson (wide receivers)

Bruce Kebric
Jon Kingdon
Mickey Marvin
Kent McCloughan
Building and grounds
Ken Irons
Equipment manager
Richard Romanski
Equipment assistant
Bob Romanski
Video coordinators
Dave Nash
Jim Otten
John Otten

SCHEDULE

Sept.	3—SAN DIEGO	1:00
Sept.	10—at Washington	1:00
Sept.	17—at Kansas City	12:00
Sept.	24—PHILADELPHIA	1:00
Oct.	1—at N.Y. Jets	8:00
Oct.	8—SEATTLE	1:00
Oct.	16—at Denver (Mon.)	7:00
Oct.	22—INDIANAPOLIS	1:00
Oct.	29—Open date	
Nov.	5—at Cincinnati	4:00
Nov.	12—at N.Y. Giants	1:00
Nov.	19—DALLAS	1:00
Nov.	27—at San Diego (Mon.)	6:00
Dec.	3—KANSAS CITY	1:00
Dec.	10—PITTSBURGH	1:00
Dec.	17—at Seattle	5:00
Dec.	24—DENVER	1:00

All times are for home team.
All games Sunday unless noted.

DRAFT CHOICES

Napoleon Kaufman, RB, Washington (first round/18th pick overall).
Barret Robbins, C, Texas Christian (2/49).
Joe Aska, RB, Central St. (Okla.) (3/86).
Mike Morton, LB, North Carolina (4/118).
Matt Dyson, LB, Michigan (5/138).
Jeff Kysar, T, Arizona State (5/154).
Eli Herring, T, Brigham Young (6/190).

TRAINING CAMP ROSTER

No.	QUARTERBACKS	Ht./Wt.	Born	NFL Exp.	College	How acq.	'94 Games GP/GS
11	Evans, Vince	6-2/215	6-14-55	16	Southern California	FA/90	9/0
12	Hobert, Billy Joe	6-3/225	1-8-71	3	Washington	D3/93	0/0
15	Hostetler, Jeff	6-3/220	4-22-61	12	West Virginia	FA/93	16/16
	RUNNING BACKS						
	Aska, Joe	5-11/230	7-14-72	R	Central Oklahoma	D3/95	—
49	Bender, Wes	5-10/230	8-2-70	2	Southern California	FA/94	9/0
44	Fenner, Derrick	6-3/230	4-6-67	7	Gardner-Webb (N.C.)	FA/95	*16/13
27	Jones, Calvin	5-11/205	11-27-70	2	Nebraska	D3/94	7/0
	Kaufman, Napoleon (KR)	5-9/185	6-7-73	R	Washington	D1/95	—
21	Montgomery, Tyrone	6-0/190	8-3-70	3	Mississippi	FA/93	6/6
28	Robinson, Greg	5-10/205	8-7-69	3	Northeast Louisiana	D8/93	0/0
22	Williams, Harvey	6-2/215	4-22-67	5	Louisiana State	FA/94	16/10
	RECEIVERS						
89	Bobo, Phillip	5-11/185	12-6-71	1	Washington State	FA/95	0/0
81	Brown, Tim (KR)	6-0/195	7-22-66	8	Notre Dame	D1/88	16/16
	Cash, Kerry (TE)	6-4/245	8-7-69	5	Texas	FA/95	*16/16
87	Glover, Andrew (TE)	6-6/245	8-12-67	5	Grambling State	D10/91	16/16
1	Hobbs, Daryl	6-2/180	5-23-68	3	Pacific	FA/93	10/0
86	Ismail, Rocket (KR)	5-11/175	11-18-69	3	Notre Dame	D4/91	16/0
82	Jett, James	5-10/165	12-28-70	3	West Virginia	FA/93	16/1
84	Jones, Hassan	6-0/200	7-2-64	9	Florida State	FA/95	0/0
39	Smith, Kevin (TE/FB)	6-4/255	7-25-69	3	UCLA	D7/92	3/0
	OFFENSIVE LINEMEN						
66	Gogan, Kevin (G/T)	6-7/320	11-2-64	9	Washington	FA/94	16/16
	Gray, Cecil (T)	6-4/305	2-16-68	6	North Carolina	FA/95	*16/5
64	Jenkins, Robert (T)	6-5/285	12-30-63	9	UCLA	FA/94	10/4
	Kysar, Jeff (T)	6-7/320	6-14-72	R	Arizona State	D5/95	—
73	McCullough, Russ (T)	6-10/315	10-31-68	1	Missouri	FA/95	0/0
72	Mosebar, Don (C)	6-6/295	9-11-61	13	Southern California	D1/83	16/16
71	Perry, Gerald (T)	6-6/290	11-12-64	8	Southern	FA/92	12/12
	Robbins, Barret (C)	6-3/310	8-26-73	R	Texas Christian	D2/95	—
78	Skrepenak, Greg (T)	6-6/310	1-31-70	3	Michigan	D2/92	12/10
77	Stephens, Rich (G)	6-7/310	1-1-65	3	Tulsa	FA/92	0/0
61	Stubbins, Willie (T)	6-5/290	5-23-67	1	Texas Southern	FA/95	0/0
67	Turk, Dan (C)	6-4/290	6-25-62	11	Wisconsin	FA/89	16/0
68	Wilkerson, Bruce (T)	6-5/295	7-28-64	9	Tennessee	D2/87	11/6
76	Wisniewski, Steve (G)	6-4/285	4-7-67	7	Penn State	D2/89	16/16
	DEFENSIVE LINEMEN						
90	Baker, Jon (T)	6-7/280	3-6-68	1	Pittsburgh	FA/95	0/0
93	Ball, Jerry (T)	6-1/315	12-15-64	9	Southern Methodist	T-Det/93	16/14
56	Bruce, Aundray (E)	6-5/260	4-30-66	8	Auburn	PlanB/92	16/0
70	Davis, Scott (E)	6-7/285	7-8-65	6	Illinois	FA/94	14/1
55	Folston, James (E)	6-3/235	8-14-71	2	Northeast Louisiana	D2/94	7/0
74	Harrison, Nolan (T)	6-5/285	1-25-69	5	Indiana	D6/91	16/16
91	McGlockton, Chester (T)	6-4/310	9-16-69	4	Clemson	D1/92	16/16
95	Robbins, Austin (T)	6-6/290	3-1-71	2	North Carolina	D4/94	2/0
94	Smith, Anthony (E)	6-3/265	6-28-67	6	Arizona	D1/90	16/16
56	Swilling, Pat (E)	6-3/245	10-25-64	10	Georgia Tech	FA/95	*16/7
96	White, Alberto (E)	6-3/245	4-8-71	2	Texas Southern	D10/92	8/0
	LINEBACKERS						
54	Biekert, Greg	6-2/240	3-14-69	3	Colorado	D7/93	16/14
	Dyson, Matt	6-4/275	8-1-72	R	Michigan	D5/95	—
53	Fredrickson, Rob	6-4/240	5-13-71	2	Michigan State	D1/94	16/12
57	Holmberg, Rob	6-3/230	5-6-71	2	Penn State	D7/94	16/0
52	Jones, Mike	6-1/230	4-15-69	5	Missouri	FA/91	16/1
	Morton, Mike	6-4/230	3-28-72	R	North Carolina	D4/95	—
51	Wallace, Aaron	6-3/245	4-17-67	6	Texas A&M	D2/90	16/5
	DEFENSIVE BACKS						
33	Anderson, Eddie (S)	6-1/210	7-22-63	10	Fort Valley (Ga.) State	FA/87	14/14
29	Bates, Patrick (S)	6-3/215	11-27-70	3	Texas A&M	D1/93	16/9
20	Hoskins, Derrick (S)	6-2/200	11-14-70	4	Southern Mississippi	D5/92	15/9
25	Land, Dan (CB)	6-0/195	7-3-65	8	Albany (Ga.) State	FA/89	16/0
29	Lewis, Albert (CB)	6-2/195	10-6-60	13	Grambling State	FA/94	14/9
36	McDaniel, Terry (CB)	5-10/180	2-8-65	8	Tennessee	D1/88	16/16
48	Mustafaa, Najee (CB)	6-1/190	6-20-64	8	Georgia Tech	FA/95	0/0
39	Pickens, Bruce (CB)	5-11/190	5-9-68	5	Nebraska	FA/95	0/0
37	Trapp, James (CB)	6-0/180	12-28-69	3	Clemson	D3/93	16/2

No.	SPECIALISTS	Ht./Wt.	Born	NFL Exp.	College	How acq.	'94 Games GP/GS
7	Gossett, Jeff (P)	6-2/190	1-25-57	14	Eastern Illinois	T-Hou/88	16/0
18	Jaeger, Jeff (K)	5-11/190	11-26-64	9	Washington	PlanB/89	16/0

*Cash played 16 games with Colts in '94; Fenner played 16 games with Bengals; Gray played 16 games with Colts; Swilling played 16 games with Lions.

Also played with Raiders in '94: DB Cary Brabham (7 games); RB Jarrod Bunch (3); TE John Duff (4); CB Donald Frank (16); RB Napoleon McCallum (1); OL Max Montoya (13); LB Winston Moss (16); FB Tom Rathman (16); CB Lionel Washington (11); TE Jamie Williams (16); WR Alexander Wright (16).

Abbreviations: D1—draft pick, first round; SupD2—supplemental draft pick, second round; W-Den—waivers acquisition from Denver; T-Sea—trade acquisition from Seattle; PlanB—Plan B free-agent acquisition; FA—free-agent acquisition (other than Plan B).

MISCELLANEOUS TEAM DATA

Stadium (capacity, surface):
Los Angeles Memorial Coliseum
(67,800, grass)

Business address:
332 Center Street
El Segundo, CA 90245

Business phone:
310-322-3451

Ticket information:
310-322-5901

Team colors:
Silver and black

Flagship radio station:
KLSX, 97.1 FM

Training site:
El Segundo, Calif.
310-322-3451

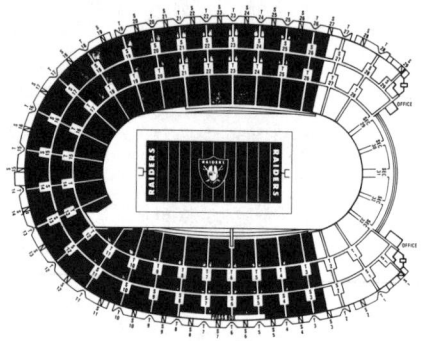

MIAMI DOLPHINS
AFC EASTERN DIVISION

1994 REVIEW

RESULTS

Sept. 4—NEW ENGLAND	W	39-35
Sept. 11—at G. Bay (Milw.)	W	24-14
Sept. 18—N.Y. JETS	W	28-14
Sept. 25—at Minnesota	L	35-38
Oct. 2—at Cincinnati	W	23-7
Oct. 9—at Buffalo	L	11-21
Oct. 16—L.A. RAIDERS (OT)	W	20-17
Oct. 23—Open date		
Oct. 30—at New England	W	23-3
Nov. 6—INDIANAPOLIS	W	22-21
Nov. 13—CHICAGO	L	14-17
Nov. 20—at Pittsburgh (OT)	L	13-16
Nov. 27—at N.Y. Jets	W	28-24
Dec. 4—BUFFALO	L	31-42
Dec. 12—KANSAS CITY	W	45-28
Dec. 18—at Indianapolis	L	6-10
Dec. 25—DETROIT	W	27-20

RECORDS/RANKINGS

1994 regular-season record: 10-6 (1st in AFC East); 5-3 in division; 8-4 in conference; 6-2 at home; 4-4 on road.
Team record last five years: 50-30 (.625, ranks 5th in league in that span).

1994 team rankings:	No.	AFC	NFL
Total offense	*379.9	1	1
Rushing offense	*103.6	8	13
Passing offense	*276.3	2	2
Scoring offense	389	1	3
Total defense	*326.5	10	19
Rushing defense	*89.4	2	6
Passing defense	*237.1	13	25
Scoring defense	327	T9	T17
Takeaways	32	T4	T10
Giveaways	32	9	T19
Turnover differential	0	7	T13
Sacks	29	T9	T17
Sacks allowed	18	2	2

*Yards per game.

TEAM LEADERS

Scoring (kicking): Pete Stoyanovich, 107 pts. (35/35 PATs, 24/31 FGs).
Scoring (touchdowns): Irving Fryar, 46 pts. (7 receiving, 2 2-pt. conv.).
Passing: Dan Marino, 4,453 yds. (615 att., 385 comp., 62.6%, 30 TDs, 17 int.).
Rushing: Bernie Parmalee, 868 yds. (216 att., 4.0 avg., 6 TDs).
Receptions: Irving Fryar, 73 (1,270 yds., 17.4 avg., 7 TDs).
Interceptions: Troy Vincent, 5 (113 yds., 1 TD).
Sacks: Jeff Cross, 9.5.
Punting: Jim Arnold, 39.3 avg. (46 punts, 1,810 yds., 0 blocked).
Punt returns: O.J. McDuffie, 7.1 avg. (32 att., 228 yds., 0 TDs).
Kickoff returns: O.J. McDuffie, 21.3 avg. (36 att., 767 yds., 0 TDs).

1995 SEASON

CLUB DIRECTORY

Owner/president
H. Wayne Huizenga
Exec. vice president/general manager
Eddie J. Jones
Vice president/administration
Bryan Wiedmeier
Vice president/finance
Jill R. Strafaci
Ticket director
Bill Galante
Director/media relations
Harvey Greene
Coordinator/media relations
Mike Hanson
Director/publications
Scott Stone
Director/community relations
Maraleen (Fudge) Browne
Director/player personnel
Tom Heckert
Director/scouting
Tom Braatz
Scouts
Joe Bushofsky
Mike Cartwright
Ron Labadie
Jere Stripling
Bobby Williams
Trainer
Ryan Vermillion

SCHEDULE

Sept. 3—N.Y. JETS		4:00
Sept. 10—at New England		1:00
Sept. 18—PITTSBURGH (Mon.)		9:00
Sept. 24—Open date		
Oct. 1—at Cincinnati		1:00
Oct. 8—INDIANAPOLIS		4:00
Oct. 15—at New Orleans		3:00
Oct. 22—at N.Y. Jets		1:00
Oct. 29—BUFFALO		4:00
Nov. 5—at San Diego		5:00
Nov. 12—NEW ENGLAND		1:00
Nov. 20—SAN FRAN. (Mon.)		9:00
Nov. 26—at Indianapolis		1:00
Dec. 3—ATLANTA		1:00
Dec. 11—KANSAS CITY (Mon.)		9:00
Dec. 17—at Buffalo		1:00
Dec. 24—at St. Louis		3:00

All times are for home team.
All games Sunday unless noted.

Vice president/head coach
Don Shula
Assistant coaches
Monte Clark (offensive line)
Joel Collier (staff assistant)
John Gamble (strength)
Joe Greene (defensive line)
George Hill (linebackers)
Rich McGeorge (asst. off. line)
Tony Nathan (offensive backs)
Tom Olivadotti (defense)
Mel Phillips (defensive backs)
Larry Seiple (receivers)
Gary Stevens (offense/quarterbacks)
Junior Wade (conditioning)
Mike Westhoff (special teams)

Assistant trainers
Britt Brown
Troy Mauer
Physician
Daniel Kanell
Equipment manager
Tony Egues
Video manager
Dave Hack

DRAFT CHOICES

Billy Milner, T, Houston (first round/25th pick overall).
Andrew Greene, G, Indiana (2/53).
Pete Mitchell, TE, Boston College (4/122).
Norman Hand, DT, Mississippi (5/158).
Jeff Kopp, LB, Southern Cal (6/194).
Corey Swinson, DT, Hampton (Va.) (7/233).
Shannon Myers, WR, Lenoir-Rhyne (N.C.) (7/246).

1995 SEASON

TRAINING CAMP ROSTER

No.	QUARTERBACKS	Ht./Wt.	Born	NFL Exp.	College	How acq.	'94 Games GP/GS
9	Bonner, Sherdrick	6-5/225	10-19-68	R	Cal State-Northridge	FA/95	—
19	Kosar, Bernie	6-5/214	11-25-63	11	Miami (Fla.)	FA/94	2/0
13	Marino, Dan	6-4/224	9-15-61	13	Pittsburgh	D1/83	16/16
11	McGwire, Dan	6-8/240	12-18-67	5	San Diego State	FA/94	*7/3

RUNNING BACKS

No.		Ht./Wt.	Born	NFL Exp.	College	How acq.	GP/GS
41	Byars, Keith (FB)	6-1/255	10-14-63	10	Ohio State	FA/94	9/9
	Carter, Ontiwaun	5-10/177	7-3-72	R	Arizona	FA/95	—
21	Dar Dar, Kirby	5-9/183	3-27-72	R	Syracuse	FA/95	—
36	Davis, Michael (FB)	5-11/230	7-7-71	R	Mississippi State	FA/95	—
43	Kirby, Terry	6-1/218	1-20-70	3	Virginia	D3/93	4/4
44	Lynch, Tarrant (FB)	5-11/226	1-28-72	R	Alabama	FA/95	—
48	McClinton, Lee (FB)	5-11/252	8-2-72	R	New Hampshire	FA/95	—
	Moss, Brent	5-9/205	1-30-72	R	Wisconsin	FA/95	—
30	Parmalee, Bernie	5-11/196	9-16-67	4	Ball State	FA/92	15/10
40	Spikes, Irving (KR)	5-8/206	12-21-70	2	Northeast Louisiana	FA/94	12/1
49	Wilson, Robert (FB)	6-0/255	1-13-69	3	Texas A&M	FA/94	*4/0

RECEIVERS

No.		Ht./Wt.	Born	NFL Exp.	College	How acq.	GP/GS
	Clark, Gary	5-9/175	5-1-62	10	James Madison	FA/94	*15/2
80	Fryar, Irving	6-0/200	9-28-62	12	Nebraska	T-NE/93	16/16
16	Gatewood, Randy	6-0/180	1-31-73	R	UNLV	FA/95	—
86	Green, Eric (TE)	6-5/280	6-22-67	6	Liberty	FA/95	—
89	Hill, Randal	5-10/180	9-21-69	5	Miami (Fla.)	FA/95	*15/14
15	Johnson, Demeris	6-0/182	8-26-69	1	Western Illinois	FA/95	*14/14
81	McDuffie, O.J. (KR)	5-10/188	12-2-69	3	Penn State	D1/93	0/0
83	Miller, Scott	5-11/185	10-20-68	5	UCLA	FA/94	15/3
82	Mitchell, Pete (TE)	6-2/243	10-9-71	R	Boston College	D4/95	9/0
18	Myers, Shannon	6-0/171	6-16-73	R	Lenoir-Rhyne (N.C.)	D7/95	—
84	Pl`nansky, Joe (TE)	6-4/250	10-21-71	R	Chadron (Neb.) State	FA/95	—
2	Rashad-Amir, Robert	6-3/188	11-11-68	1	Florida State	FA/95	0/0
3	Thornton, Burt	6-1/202	1-30-72	R	Purdue	FA/95	—
1	Whittemore, Mark	5-9/170	4-18-73	R	Central Florida	FA/95	—
87	Williams, Mike	5-11/190	10-9-66	5	Northeastern	FA/91	15/0
85	Williams, Ronnie (TE)	6-3/258	1-19-66	3	Oklahoma State	FA/93	14/0

OFFENSIVE LINEMEN

No.		Ht./Wt.	Born	NFL Exp.	College	How acq.	GP/GS
71	Albright, Ethan (T)	6-5/292	5-1-71	1	North Carolina	FA/95	0/0
77	Brothen, Kevin (G/C)	6-1/293	11-16-69	2	Vanderbilt	FA/94	0/0
75	Dittman, Seth (T)	6-7/273	7-23-72	R	Stanford	FA/95	—
62	Gray, Chris (G)	6-4/292	6-19-70	3	Auburn	D5/93	16/2
68	Greene, Andrew (G)	6-3/304	9-24-69	R	Indiana	D2/95	—
67	Hack, Dave (G)	6-6/285	4-22-72	R	Maryland	FA/95	—
73	Heller, Ron (T)	6-6/290	8-25-62	12	Penn State	FA/93	16/16
63	James, Jason (C)	6-4/302	12-15-71	R	Fresno State	FA/95	—
76	Milner, Billy (T)	6-5/293	6-21-72	R	Houston	D1/95	—
66	Needham, Gary (G)	6-3/352	8-28-67	1	Eastern Washington	FA/95	0/0
61	Ruddy, Tim (C)	6-3/290	4-27-72	2	Notre Dame	D2/94	16/0
69	Sims, Keith (G)	6-3/309	6-17-67	6	Iowa State	D2/90	16/16
78	Webb, Richmond (T)	6-6/303	1-11-67	6	Texas A&M	D1/90	16/16

DEFENSIVE LINEMEN

No.		Ht./Wt.	Born	NFL Exp.	College	How acq.	GP/GS
92	Armstrong, Trace (E)	6-4/260	10-5-65	7	Florida	T-Chi/95	*15/15
95	Bowens, Tim (T)	6-4/310	2-7-73	2	Mississippi	D1/94	16/15
98	Caesar, Mark (NT)	6-2/295	1-12-70	1	Miami (Fla.)	FA/95	0/0
90	Coleman, Marco (E)	6-3/260	12-18-69	4	Georgia Tech	D1/92	16/16
91	Cross, Jeff (E)	6-4/280	3-25-66	8	Missouri	D9/88	13/10
93	Gaines, William (T)	6-5/294	6-20-71	2	Florida	D5/94	7/0
96	Hand, Norman (T)	6-3/329	9-4-72	R	Mississippi	D5/95	—
74	Hawthorne, Ed (NT)	6-1/305	7-30-70	R	Minnesota	FA/95	—
97	Jackson, Tyoka (E)	6-2/266	11-22-71	1	Penn State	FA/94	1/0
99	Klingbeil, Chuck (NT)	6-1/288	11-2-65	5	Northern Michigan	FA/91	16/15
72	Perkins, Steve (E)	6-2/250	12-21-71	R	West Virginia	FA/95	—
64	Swinson, Corey (T)	6-5/334	12-15-69	R	Hampton (Va.) Institute	D7/95	—

LINEBACKERS

No.		Ht./Wt.	Born	NFL Exp.	College	How acq.	GP/GS
53	Beavers, Aubrey	6-3/231	8-30-71	2	Oklahoma	D2/94	16/10
54	Bullough, Chuck	6-1/238	3-3-69	3	Michigan State	FA/93	1/1
47	Cooper, Travis	6-2/242	12-16-73	R	Central Florida	FA/95	—
51	Cox, Bryan	6-4/248	2-17-68	5	Western Illinois	D5/91	16/16
59	Dotson, Dewayne	6-1/256	6-10-71	1	Mississippi	FA/94	0/0
57	Foxx, Dion	6-3/250	6-11-71	2	James Madison	FA/94	16/0
50	Hollier, Dwight	6-2/250	4-21-69	4	North Carolina	D4/92	11/7

No.	LINEBACKERS	Ht./Wt.	Born	NFL Exp.	College	How acq.	'94 Games GP/GS
52	Kopp, Jeff	6-3/243	7-8-71	R	Southern California	D6/95	—
46	Meredith, John	6-2/246	9-30-72	R	Hampton Institute	FA/95	—
55	Singleton, Chris	6-2/246	2-20-67	6	Arizona	FA/93	11/11
	DEFENSIVE BACKS						
28	Atkins, Gene (S)	5-11/201	11-22-64	9	Florida A&M	FA/94	15/15
37	Brown, J.B. (CB)	6-0/191	1-5-67	7	Maryland	D12/89	16/16
27	Buckley, Terrell (CB)	5-9/176	6-7-71	4	Florida State	T-GB/95	*16/16
45	Crawford, Melvin (S)	5-11/176	2-18-73	R	Hampton Institute	FA/95	—
24	Glenn, Maurice (S)	6-1/184	10-7-73	R	Richmond	FA/95	—
31	Hill, Sean (CB)	5-10/179	8-14-71	2	Montana State	D7/94	16/1
38	Jackson, Calvin (CB)	5-9/185	10-28-72	1	Auburn	FA/95	2/0
20	Johnson, Deon (S)	6-0/214	9-25-71	R	Michigan	FA/95	—
25	Johnson, Pat (S)	6-1/204	6-10-72	1	Purdue	FA/95	0/0
22	Kennedy, Larry (S)	5-10/190	7-28-71	R	Florida	FA/95	—
26	Nelson, Chico (S)	6-0/198	12-25-69	1	Tennessee	FA/95	0/0
	Oliver, Louis (S)	6-2/224	3-9-66	7	Florida	FA/95	*12/12
33	Seigler, Dexter (CB)	5-9/179	1-11-72	1	Miami (Fla.)	FA/95	0/0
29	Smith, Frankie (CB)	5-9/182	10-8-68	3	Baylor	FA/93	13/2
34	Smith, Kwane (CB)	5-9/172	1-1-71	1	West Virginia	FA/95	0/0
35	Stewart, Michael (S)	5-11/202	7-12-65	9	Fresno State	FA/94	16/16
23	Vincent, Troy (CB)	6-0/184	6-8-70	4	Wisconsin	D1/92	13/12
	SPECIALISTS						
5	Bender, Jason (P)	6-2/212	8-14-71	R	Georgia Tech	FA/95	—
4	Fayak, Craig (K)	6-1/188	7-22-72	1	Penn State	FA/95	0/0
17	Kidd, John (P)	6-3/214	8-22-61	12	Northwestern	FA/94	*6/0
10	Stoyanovich, Pete (K)	5-11/195	4-28-67	7	Indiana	D8/89	16/0

*Armstrong played 15 games with Bears in '94; Buckley played 16 games with Packers; Clark played 15 games with Cardinals; Green played 15 games with Steelers; Hill played 14 games with Cardinals; Kidd played 2 games with Chargers and 4 with Dolphins; McGwire played 7 games with Seahawks; Oliver played 12 games with Bengals; Wilson played 2 games with Cowboys and 2 with Dolphins.

Also played with Dolphins in '94: P Jim Arnold (12); TE Greg Baty (16); LB Brant Boyer (14); CB Tyrone Braxton (16); RB Aaron Craver (8); C Jeff Dellenbach (16); RB Cleveland Gary (2); S Chris Green (16); RB Mark Higgs (5); G Houston Hoover (3); WR Mark Ingram (15); T Tim Irwin (5); TE Keith Jackson (16); CB Darrell Malone (5); T Jeff Novak (6); CB Muhammad Oliver (13); CB David Pool (1); FB James Saxon (16); LB Jesse Solomon (6); DT Craig Veasey (12); DT Larry Webster (16); G Bert Webster (16).

Abbreviations: D1—draft pick, first round; SupD2—supplemental draft pick, second round; W-Den—waivers acquisition from Denver; T-Sea—trade acquisition from Seattle; PlanB—Plan B free-agent acquisition; FA—free-agent acquisition (other than Plan B).

MISCELLANEOUS TEAM DATA

Stadium (capacity, surface):
Joe Robbie Stadium
(74,916, grass)
Business address:
7500 S.W. 30th St.
Davie, FL 33314
Business phone:
305-452-7010
Ticket information:
305-620-2578
Team colors:
Aqua, coral and white
Flagship radio station:
WIOD, 610 AM
Training site:
Nova University
Miami, Fla.
305-452-7000

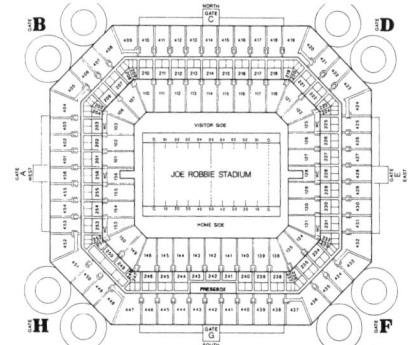

MINNESOTA VIKINGS
NFC CENTRAL DIVISION

1994 REVIEW

RESULTS

Sept. 4—at Green Bay	L	10-16
Sept. 11—DETROIT	W	10-3
Sept. 18—at Chicago	W	42-14
Sept. 25—MIAMI	W	38-35
Oct. 2—at Arizona	L	7-17
Oct. 10—at N.Y. Giants	W	27-10
Oct. 16—Open date		
Oct. 20—GREEN BAY (OT)	W	13-10
Oct. 30—at Tampa Bay	W	36-13
Nov. 6—NEW ORLEANS	W	21-20
Nov. 13—at New Eng. (OT)	L	20-26
Nov. 20—N.Y. JETS	L	21-31
Nov. 27—TAMPA BAY (OT)	L	17-20
Dec. 1—CHICAGO (OT)	W	33-27
Dec. 11—at Buffalo	W	21-17
Dec. 17—at Detroit	L	19-41
Dec. 26—SAN FRANCISCO	W	21-14

RECORDS/RANKINGS

1994 regular-season record: 10-6 (1st in NFC Central); 5-3 in division; 8-4 in conference; 6-2 at home; 4-4 on road.
Team record last five years: 44-36 (.550, ranks T11th in league in that span).

1994 team rankings:	No.	NFC	NFL
Total offense	*365.5	2	3
Rushing offense	*95.3	9	20
Passing offense	*270.3	1	3
Scoring offense	356	5	7
Total defense	*296.4	4	5
Rushing defense	*68.1	1	1
Passing defense	*228.3	12	21
Scoring defense	314	8	13
Takeaways	34	4	7
Giveaways	34	12	T21
Turnover differential	0	7	T13
Sacks	36	T5	T11
Sacks allowed	31	7	14

*Yards per game.

TEAM LEADERS

Scoring (kicking): Fuad Reveiz, 132 pts. (30/30 PATs, 34/39 FGs).
Scoring (touchdowns): Terry Allen, 50 pts. (8 rushing, 1 2-pt. conv.).
Passing: Warren Moon, 4,264 yds. (601 att., 371 comp., 61.7%, 18 TDs, 19 int.).
Rushing: Terry Allen, 1,031 yds. (255 att., 4.0 avg., 8 TDs).
Receptions: Cris Carter, 122 (1,256 yds., 10.3 avg., 7 TDs).
Interceptions: Vencie Glenn, 4 (55 yds., 0 TDs); Anthony Parker, 4 (99 yds., 2 TDs).
Sacks: John Randle, 13.5.
Punting: Mike Saxon, 42.9 avg. (77 punts, 3,301 yds., 0 blocked).
Punt returns: David Palmer, 6.4 avg. (30 att., 193 yds., 0 TDs).
Kickoff returns: Qadry Ismail, 23.1 avg. (35 att., 807 yds., 0 TDs).

1995 SEASON

CLUB DIRECTORY

Chairman of the board
John C. Skoglund
President/chief executive officer
Roger Headrick
V.P., administration/team operations
Jeff Diamond
V.P., player personnel
Frank Gilliam
V.P., marketing/bus. dev.
Stew Widdess
Assistant general manager, college scouting
Jerry Reichow
Assistant general manager, pro personnel
Paul Wiggin
Director of finance
Nick Valentine
Director of research and development
Mike Eayrs
Director of marketing
Kernal Buhler
Director of public relations
David Pelletier
Public relations assistants
Debra Pruitt
Bob Hagan
Director of security
Steve Rollins
Player personnel coordinator
Scott Studwell
Assistant head scout
Don Deisch
Regional scouts
Conrad Cardano
John Carson

Head coach
Dennis Green
Assistant coaches
Brian Billick (off. coord.)
Tony Dungy (def. coordinator)
Chris Foerster (tight ends/offensive line assistant)
Carl Hargrave (running backs)
Foge Fazio (inside linebackers)
Chip Myers (receivers)
Keith Rowen (offensive line)
Richard Solomon (secondary)
John Levra (defensive line)
Steve Wetzel (strength and conditioning)
Ray Sherman (quarterbacks)
Mark Asanovich (strength and conditioning assistant)
Gary Zauner (special teams)

Area scouts
John Fitzpatrick
Murray Warmath
Director of team operations
Breck Spinner
Equipment manager
Dennis Ryan
Medical director
Dr. David Fischer
Trainer
Fred Zamberletti
Assistant trainer
Chuck Barta

SCHEDULE

Sept. 3—at Chicago	3:00
Sept. 10—DETROIT	12:00
Sept. 17—DALLAS	7:00
Sept. 24—at Pittsburgh	1:00
Oct. 1—Open date	
Oct. 8—HOUSTON	12:00
Oct. 15—at Tampa Bay	1:00
Oct. 22—at Green Bay	12:00
Oct. 30—CHICAGO (Mon.)	8:00
Nov. 5—GREEN BAY	12:00
Nov. 12—at Arizona	2:00
Nov. 19—NEW ORLEANS	3:00
Nov. 23—at Detroit (Thanks.)	12:30
Dec. 3—TAMPA BAY	12:00
Dec. 9—CLEVELAND (Sat.)	11:30
Dec. 18—at San Fran. (Mon.)	6:00
Dec. 24—at Cincinnati	1:00

All times are for home team.
All games Sunday unless noted.

DRAFT CHOICES

Derrick Alexander, DE, Florida State (first round/11th pick overall).
Korey Stringer, T, Ohio State (1/24).
Orlanda Thomas, DB, Southwestern (La.) (2/42).
Corey Fuller, DB, Florida State (2/55).
Chad May, QB, Kansas State (4/111).
James Stewart, RB, Miami (Fla.) (5/157).
John Solomon, LB, Sam Houston State (6/189).
Jose White, LB, Howard (7/232).
Jason Fisk, DT, Stanford (7/243).

TRAINING CAMP ROSTER

No.	QUARTERBACKS	Ht./Wt.	Born	NFL Exp.	College	How acq.	'94 Games GP/GS
11	Burmiester, Paul	6-3/215	3-10-71	R	Iowa	FA/95	—
14	Johnson, Brad	6-5/220	9-13-68	4	Florida State	D9/92	4/0
5	May, Chad	6-1/219	9-28-71	R	Kansas State	D4/95	—
1	Moon, Warren	6-3/219	11-18-56	12	Washington	T-Hou/94	15/15
	RUNNING BACKS						
29	Evans, Chuck	6-1/232	4-16-67	3	Clark-Atlanta	D11/92	14/0
31	Graham, Scottie	5-9/217	3-28-69	3	Ohio State	FA/93	16/0
32	Lee, Amp	5-11/198	10-1-71	4	Florida State	FA/94	13/0
22	Palmer, David	5-8/167	11-19-72	2	Alabama	D2/94	13/1
40	Parnell, Charles	6-1/235	1-12-72	R	Arizona State	FA/95	—
30	Phillips, Bobby	5-9/194	12-8-69	R	Virginia Union	FA/95	—
26	Smith, Robert (KR)	6-0/197	3-4-72	3	Ohio State	D1/93	14/0
41	Staten, Robert	5-11/240	1-23-69	1	Jackson State	FA/95	0/0
28	Stewart, James	6-2/245	12-8-71	R	Miami (Fla.)	D5/95	—
	RECEIVERS						
80	Carter, Cris	6-3/202	11-25-65	9	Ohio State	W-Phi/90	16/16
87	Cooper, Adrian (TE)	6-5/268	4-27-68	5	Oklahoma	T-Pit/94	12/11
84	Cunningham, Jimmy	5-8/150	1-1-73	R	Howard	FA/95	—
18	Denson, Rafael	5-8/177	3-28-72	R	Oklahoma State	FA/95	—
46	Gerak, John (TE)	6-3/284	1-6-70	3	Penn State	D3a/93	13/3
82	Ismail, Qadry (KR)	6-0/191	11-8-70	3	Syracuse	D2/93	16/3
89	Jordan, Andrew (TE)	6-4/262	6-21-72	2	Western Carolina	D6/94	16/12
86	Reed, Jake	6-3/217	9-28-67	5	Grambling State	D3/91	16/16
81	Walsh, Chris	6-1/193	12-12-68	3	Stanford	FA/94	10/0
	OFFENSIVE LINEMEN						
63	Alex, Keith (G)	6-4/307	6-9-69	2	Texas A&M	FA/95	0/0
62	Christy, Jeff (C)	6-3/290	2-3-69	3	Pittsburgh	FA/93	16/16
67	Cunningham, Rick (T)	6-6/307	1-4-67	5	Texas A&M	FA/95	*11/10
75	Dafney, Bernard (G/T)	6-5/329	11-1-89	4	Tennessee	FA/92	16/16
71	Dixon, David (G/T)	6-5/354	1-5-69	2	Arizona State	FA/94	1/0
78	Hinton, Chris (G)	6-4/300	7-31-61	13	Northwestern	FA/94	16/16
61	Lindsay, Everett (G/C)	6-4/301	9-18-70	3	Mississippi	D5/93	0/0
64	McDaniel, Randall (G)	6-3/274	12-19-64	8	Arizona State	D1/88	16/16
68	Morris, Mike (C)	6-5/277	2-22-61	9	Northeast Missouri State	FA/91	16/0
74	Nelson, Royce	6-4/315	8-9-70	2	Nicholls State	FA/95	0/0
65	Ruether, Mike (C)	6-4/286	9-20-62	10	Texas	FA/94	0/0
73	Steussie, Todd (T)	6-6/304	12-1-70	2	California	D1b/94	16/16
77	Stringer, Korey (T)	6-4/332	5-8-74	R	Ohio State	D1b/95	—
	DEFENSIVE LINEMEN						
90	Alexander, Derrick (E)	6-4/276	11-3-73	R	Florida State	D1a/95	—
92	Barker, Roy (E)	6-4/286	2-14-69	4	North Carolina	D4/92	16/15
96	Boudreaux, Frank (T)	6-5/263	6-20-70	2	Northwestern	FA/95	0/0
72	Fisk, Jason (T)	6-3/286	9-4-72	R	Stanford	D7b/95	—
99	Harris, James (E)	6-6/255	5-13-68	3	Temple	FA/92	16/16
91	Harrison, Martin (E)	6-5/240	9-20-67	5	Washington	FA/94	13/0
76	O'Brien, Joe (T)	6-2/248	11-6-72	R	Boise State	FA/95	—
93	Randle, John (T)	6-1/272	12-12-67	6	Texas A&I	FA/90	16/16
94	Sims, Tom (T)	6-2/291	4-18-67	6	Pittsburgh	FA/95	*16/1
95	Smith, Fernando (E)	6-6/276	8-2-71	2	Jackson State	D2b/94	7/0
98	Tuaolo, Esera (T)	6-2/263	7-11-68	5	Oregon State	FA/92	16/0
79	Washington, Keith (E)	6-4/252	12-18-73	R	UNLV	FA/95	—
	LINEBACKERS						
56	Bercich, Pete	6-1/236	12-23-71	1	Notre Dame	D7/94	0/0
50	Brady, Jeff	6-1/238	11-9-68	5	Kentucky	FA/95	*16/0
52	Brown, Richard	6-3/240	9-21-65	7	San Diego State	FA/94	3/0
55	Del Rio, Jack	6-4/246	4-4-63	11	Southern California	PlanB/92	16/16
53	Jones, Don	6-0/232	3-26-69	3	Washington	FA/94	0/0
57	Mackey, Earl	6-0/224	5-25-73	R	Southern	FA/95	—
58	McDaniel, Ed	5-11/231	2-23-69	4	Clemson	D5/92	16/16
59	Sheppard, Ashley	6-3/240	1-21-69	3	Clemson	D4/93	7/0
54	Solomon, John	6-3/233	11-10-73	R	Sam Houston State	D6/95	—
51	Thomas, Broderick	6-4/242	2-20-67	7	Nebraska	FA/95	*16/16
97	White, Jose	6-3/261	2-2-73	R	Howard	D7a/95	—
	DEFENSIVE BACKS						
42	Barnett, Harlon (S)	5-11/200	1-2-67	6	Michigan State	FA/95	*16/16
36	Boyd, Malik (CB)	5-10/176	11-5-70	2	Southern	FA/94	16/1
37	Frank, Donald (CB)	6-0/192	10-24-65	6	Winston-Salem State	FA/95	*16/0
27	Fuller, Corey (CB)	5-10/197	5-11-71	R	Florida State	D2/95	—

No.	DEFENSIVE BACKS	Ht./Wt.	Born	NFL Exp.	College	How acq.	'94 Games GP/GS
24	Griffith, Robert (S)	5-11/189	11-30-70	2	San Diego State	Fa/94	15/0
23	Hammonds, Shelly (CB)	5-10/182	2-13-71	1	Penn State	D5/94	0/0
25	Jackson, Alfred (CB)	6-0/185	7-10-67	5	San Diego State	FA/95	0/0
35	Johnson, Chris (S)	6-0/205	8-7-71	1	San Diego State	FA/95	0/0
33	Mincy, Charles (S)	5-11/197	12-16-69	5	Washington	FA/95	*16/7
43	Thomas, Orlando (S)	6-1/209	10-21-72	R	Southwestern Louisiana	D2/95	—
20	Washington, Dewayne (CB)	5-11/189	12-27-72	2	North Carolina State	D1a/94	16/16
	SPECIALISTS						
8	Buffaloe, Jeff (P)	6-1/194	9-18-70	1	Memphis	FA/95	0/0
3	Kirchoff, Jay (K)	6-4/198	5-28-70	1	Arizona	FA/95	0/0
7	Reveiz, Fuad (K)	5-11/227	2-24-63	11	Tennessee	FA/93	16/0
4	Saxon, Mike (P)	6-3/205	7-10-62	11	San Diego State	FA/94	16/0

*Barnett played 16 games with Patriots in '94; Brady played 16 games with Buccaneers; Cunningham played 11 games with Cardinals; Frank played 16 games with Raiders; Mincy played 16 games with Chiefs; Sims played 16 games with Colts; Thomas played 16 games with Lions.

Also played with Vikings in '94: LB Bobby Abrams (16); RB Terry Allen (16); C/G Frank Cornish (7); CB Brian Davis (9); LB Dave Garnett (9); S Vencie Glenn (16); WR Eric Guliford (7); DE Robert Harris (11); LB Carlos Jenkins (16); TE Steve Jordan (4); T Reggie McElroy (10); DB Lamar McGriggs (16); DE Roosevelt Nix (2); TE Brent Novoselsky (12); CB Anthony Parker (15); QB Sean Salisbury (1); S Todd Scott (15); LB William Sims (8); DT Henry Thomas (16).

Abbreviations: D1—draft pick, first round; SupD2—supplemental draft pick, second round; W-Den—waivers acquisition from Denver; T-Sea—trade acquisition from Seattle; PlanB—Plan B free-agent acquisition; FA—free-agent acquisition (other than Plan B).

MISCELLANEOUS TEAM DATA

Stadium (capacity, surface):
Metrodome (64,035, artificial)
Business address:
9520 Viking Drive
Eden Prairie, MN 55344
Business phone:
612-828-6500
Ticket information:
612-333-8828
Team colors:
Purple, gold and white
Flagship radio station:
KFAN, 1130 AM
Training site:
Mankato State University
Mankato, Minn.
612-828-6500

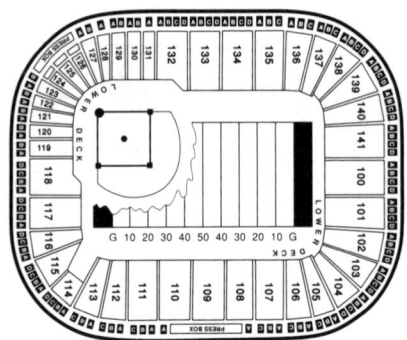

NEW ENGLAND PATRIOTS
AFC EASTERN DIVISION

1994 REVIEW

RESULTS

Sept.	4—at Miami	L	35-39
Sept.	11—BUFFALO	L	35-38
Sept.	18—at Cincinnati	W	31-28
Sept.	25—at Detroit	W	23-17
Oct.	2—GREEN BAY	W	17-16
Oct.	9—L.A. RAIDERS	L	17-21
Oct.	16—at N.Y. Jets	L	17-24
Oct.	23—Open date		
Oct.	30—MIAMI	L	3-23
Nov.	6—at Cleveland	L	6-13
Nov.	13—MINNESOTA (OT)	W	26-20
Nov.	20—SAN DIEGO	W	23-17
Nov.	27—at Indianapolis	W	12-10
Dec.	4—N.Y. JETS	W	24-13
Dec.	11—INDIANAPOLIS	W	28-13
Dec.	18—at Buffalo	W	41-17
Dec.	24—at Chicago	W	13-3

RECORDS/RANKINGS

1994 regular-season record: 10-6 (2nd in AFC East); 4-4 in division; 6-6 in conference; 5-3 at home; 5-3 on road.
Team record last five years: 24-56 (.300, ranks 26th in league in that span).

1994 team rankings:	No.	AFC	NFL
Total offense	*361.0	2	4
Rushing offense	*83.3	14	27
Passing offense	*277.8	1	1
Scoring offense	351	3	8
Total defense	*325.4	9	18
Rushing defense	*110.0	10	19
Passing defense	*215.4	8	16
Scoring defense	312	5	12
Takeaways	40	1	1
Giveaways	38	12	25
Turnover differential	2	T5	T11
Sacks	39	T3	T5
Sacks allowed	22	4	6

*Yards per game.

TEAM LEADERS

Scoring (kicking): Matt Bahr, 117 pts. (36/36 PATs, 27/34 FGs).
Scoring (touchdowns): Marion Butts, 48 pts. (8 rushing).
Passing: Drew Bledsoe, 4,555 yds. (691 att., 400 comp., 57.9%, 25 TDs, 27 int.).
Rushing: Marion Butts, 703 yds. (243 att., 2.9 avg., 8 TDs).
Receptions: Ben Coates, 96 (1,174 yds., 12.2 avg., 7 TDs).
Interceptions: Maurice Hurst, 7 (68 yds., 0 TDs).
Sacks: Chris Slade, 9.5.
Punting: Pat O'Neill, 41.2 avg. (69 punts, 2,841 yds., 0 blocked).
Punt returns: Troy Brown, 8.4 avg. (24 att., 202 yds., 0 TDs).
Kickoff returns: Ray Crittenden, 19.2 avg. (24 att., 460 yds., 0 TDs).

1995 SEASON

CLUB DIRECTORY

President and chief executive officer
Robert K. Kraft
Vice president/owner's representative
Jonathan A. Kraft
Vice president, business operations
Andrew Wasynczuk
Vice president, finance
James Hausmann
Vice president, event management
Brian O'Donovan
Director of corporate media sales
Daniel A. Kraft
Director of public and community relations
Donald Lowery
Director of media relations
Stacey James
Director of player resources
Andre Tippett
Controller
Virginia Widman
Director of player personnel
Bobby Grier
Director of college scouting
Charles Armey
Director of data processing
Peg Myers
Director of ticketing
Ken Sternfeld
Director of sales
Mitch Hardin

SCHEDULE

Sept.	3—CLEVELAND	1:00
Sept.	10—MIAMI	1:00
Sept.	17—at San Francisco	1:00
Sept.	24—Open date	
Oct.	1—at Atlanta	1:00
Oct.	8—DENVER	8:00
Oct.	15—at Kansas City	12:00
Oct.	23—BUFFALO (Mon.)	9:00
Oct.	29—CAROLINA	1:00
Nov.	5—at N.Y. Jets	1:00
Nov.	12—at Miami	1:00
Nov.	19—INDIANAPOLIS	1:00
Nov.	26—at Buffalo	1:00
Dec.	3—NEW ORLEANS	1:00
Dec.	10—N.Y. JETS	1:00
Dec.	16—at Pittsburgh (Sat.)	12:30
Dec.	23—at Indianapolis (Sat.)	8:00

All times are for home team.
All games Sunday unless noted.

Head coach
Bill Parcells
Assistant coaches
Maurice Carthon (fullbacks and special teams)
Romeo Crennel (defensive line)
Al Groh (defensive coordinator)
Fred Hoaglin (offensive line)
Chris Palmer (wide receivers)
Johnny Parker (strength and conditioning)
Ray Perkins (off. coord.)
Mike Pope (tight ends)
Dante Scarnecchia (linebackers/defense)
Mike Sweatman (special teams)
Bob Trott (defensive backs)
Charlie Weis (running backs)

Building services superintendent
Bernie Reinhart
Head trainer
Ron O'Neil
Equipment manager
Don Brocher
Video director
Ken Deininger

DRAFT CHOICES

Ty Law, DB, Michigan (first round/23rd pick overall).
Ted Johnson, LB, Colorado (2/57).
Curtis Martin, RB, Pittsburgh (3/74).
Jimmy Hitchcock, DB, N. Carolina (3/88).
Dave Wohlabaugh, C, Syracuse (4/112).
Dino Philyaw, RB, Oregon (6/195).
Carlos Yancy, DB, Georgia (7/234).

1995 SEASON

TRAINING CAMP ROSTER

No.	QUARTERBACKS	Ht./Wt.	Born	NFL Exp.	College	How acq.	'94 Games GP/GS
11	Bledsoe, Drew	6-5/233	2-14-72	3	Washington State	D1/93	16/16
7	Walker, Jay	6-3/232	1-24-72	1	Howard	D7/94	0/0
16	Zolak, Scott	6-5/222	12-13-67	5	Maryland	D4/91	16/0
	RUNNING BACKS						
26	Croom, Corey (KR)	5-11/208	5-22-71	3	Ball State	FA/93	16/0
33	Gash, Sam (FB)	5-11/224	3-7-69	4	Penn State	D8/92	13/6
34	Grant, Rupert (FB)	6-1/233	11-5-73	R	Howard	FA/95	—
31	Green, David	5-11/193	4-18-72	R	Boston College	FA/95	—
35	Legette, Burnie (FB)	6-1/243	12-5-70	3	Michigan	FA/93	3/0
39	Martin, Curtis	5-11/197	5-1-73	R	Pittsburgh	D3/95	—
22	Meggett, Dave (KR)	5-7/195	4-30-66	7	Towson State	FA/95	*16/3
32	Philyaw, Dino	5-10/192	10-30-70	R	Oregon	D6/95	—
	RECEIVERS						
19	Adams, Daniel	6-0/185	1-16-72	R	Houston	FA/95	—
49	Alford, Eric (TE)	6-1/232	8-12-72	R	Nebraska	FA/95	—
18	Andrews, David	6-2/174	11-11-71	R	Angelo State (Tex.)	FA/95	—
82	Brisby, Vincent	6-2/188	1-25-71	3	Northeast Louisiana	D2/93	14/11
86	Brown, Troy (KR)	5-9/190	7-2-71	3	Marshall	D8/93	9/0
17	Bullard, Kendricke	6-1/170	4-30-72	R	Arkansas State	FA/95	—
85	Burke, John (TE)	6-3/255	9-7-71	2	Virginia Tech	D4/94	16/6
87	Coates, Ben (TE)	6-5/245	8-16-69	5	Livingstone College (N.C.)	D5/91	16/16
81	Crittenden, Ray (KR)	6-1/188	3-1-70	3	Virginia Tech	FA/93	16/2
84	Ellis, Elbert	6-5/216	6-23-69	2	Pittsburgh	FA/95	0/0
88	Francisco, Paul (TE)	6-6/236	10-14-69	1	Boston University	FA/95	0/0
10	Graham, Hason	5-10/176	3-21-71	R	Georgia	FA/95	—
12	Henry, Mario	6-1/187	9-14-71	1	Rutgers	FA/95	0/0
19	Lee, Kevin	6-1/194	1-1-71	1	Alabama	D2/94	0/0
18	Moore, Will	6-2/180	2-21-70	1	Texas Southern	FA/95	0/0
48	President, Andre (TE)	6-3/255	6-16-71	R	Angelo State (Tex.)	FA/95	—
	OFFENSIVE LINEMEN						
78	Armstrong, Bruce (T)	6-4/284	9-7-65	9	Louisville	D1/87	16/16
65	Arthur, Mike (C)	6-3/280	5-7-68	5	Texas A&M	W-Cin/93	12/11
64	Dellenbach, Jeff (C)	6-6/300	2-14-63	11	Wisconsin	FA/95	*16/16
67	Gisler, Mike (G/C)	6-4/300	8-26-69	3	Houston	FA/93	15/5
77	Harlow, Pat (T)	6-6/290	3-16-69	5	Southern California	D1/91	16/16
61	Kratch, Bob (G)	6-3/288	1-6-66	7	Iowa	FA/94	16/16
69	Landry, Greg (G)	6-4/295	8-5-72	R	Boston College	FA/95	—
68	Lane, Max (T)	6-6/295	2-22-71	2	Navy	D6/94	14/0
70	Moore, Brandon (T)	6-6/295	6-21-70	3	Duke	FA/93	4/0
71	Rucci, Todd (G)	6-5/291	7-14-70	3	Penn State	D2/93	13/10
72	Suarez, Mike (T)	6-5/290	3-6-72	R	Illinois	FA/95	—
74	Skene, Doug (G)	6-6/295	6-17-70	3	Michigan	FA/93	6/6
62	Tylski, Rich (C)	6-4/289	2-27-71	1	Utah State	FA/95	0/0
66	Wohlabaugh, Dave (C/G)	6-3/304	4-13-72	R	Syracuse	D4/95	—
	DEFENSIVE LINEMEN						
98	Barnett, Troy (E)	6-4/280	5-24-71	2	North Carolina	FA/94	14/0
76	Gaines, Stephen (T)	6-2/314	9-28-72	R	Texas Tech	FA/95	—
76	Gregory, James (E)	6-3/310	7-26-71	1	Alabama	FA/95	0/0
92	Hand, Jon (E)	6-7/310	11-13-63	10	Alabama	FA/95	*5/3
60	Holcomb, Sean (E)	6-3/250	3-9-71	R	Texas A&I-Kingsville	FA/95	—
97	Jones, Aaron (E)	6-5/267	12-18-66	8	Eastern Kentucky	FA/93	16/0
96	Jones, Mike (E)	6-4/295	8-25-69	5	North Carolina State	FA/94	16/16
93	Pitts, Mike (T)	6-5/277	9-25-60	13	Alabama	FA/93	16/16
75	Ray, Leonard (E)	6-3/297	1-21-69	1	Louisville	FA/95	0/0
94	Roberts, Tim (E)	6-6/318	4-14-69	4	Southern Mississippi	FA/95	*12/2
63	Stanley, Buster (NT)	6-2/286	5-14-70	2	Michigan	FA/94	7/0
90	Walker, Bruce (E)	6-4/325	7-18-72	1	UCLA	FA/94	0/0
90	White, Reggie	6-4/300	3-22-70	4	North Carolina A&T	FA/95	*11/0
	LINEBACKERS						
50	Abrams, Bobby	6-3/230	4-12-67	6	Michigan	FA/95	*16/0
51	Bowden, Andre	6-3/240	4-4-68	1	Fayetteville (N.C.) State	FA/95	0/0
59	Brown, Vincent	6-2/245	1-9-65	8	Mississippi Valley State	D2/88	16/16
54	Collins, Todd	6-2/242	5-27-70	4	Carson-Newman (Tenn.)	D3/92	7/7
99	DeOssie, Steve	6-2/248	11-22-62	12	Boston College	FA/94	16/0
52	Johnson, Ted	6-2/240	12-4-72	R	Colorado	D2/95	—
55	McGinest, Willie	6-5/252	12-11-71	2	Southern California	D1/94	16/7
58	Moore, Marty	6-1/244	3-19-71	2	Kentucky	D7/94	16/4
46	Parker, Jeff	6-0/252	7-9-71	R	Albany State	FA/95	—

No.	LINEBACKERS	Ht./Wt.	Born	NFL Exp.	College	How acq.	'94 Games GP/GS
95	Sabb, Dwayne	6-4/248	10-9-69	4	New Hampshire	D5/92	16/8
53	Slade, Chris	6-4/232	1-30-71	3	Virginia	D2/93	16/16
47	Wright, Byron	6-4/245	3-24-72	R	Texas Tech	FA/95	—
	DEFENSIVE BACKS						
30	Brown, Corwin (S)	6-1/200	4-25-70	3	Michigan	D4/93	16/0
41	Cade, Eddie (S)	6-0/206	8-4-73	R	Arizona State	FA/95	—
45	Catanho, Alcides	6-3/216	1-20-72	R	Rutgers	FA/95	—
29	Guyton, Myron (S)	6-1/205	8-26-67	7	Eastern Kentucky	FA/94	16/16
38	Hitchcock, Jimmy (CB)	5-10/188	11-9-71	R	North Carolina	D3/95	—
37	Hurst, Maurice (CB)	5-10/185	9-17-67	7	Southern (La.)	D4/89	16/16
24	Law, Ty (CB)	6-0/201	2-10-74	R	Michigan	D1/95	—
43	Lewis, Vernon (CB)	5-10/192	10-27-70	3	Pittsburgh	FA/93	11/0
42	Provo, Dwayne	5-9/180	....	R	St. Mary's, Canada	FA/95	—
23	Ray, Terry (S)	6-1/205	10-12-69	4	Oklahoma	W-Atl/93	16/0
21	Reynolds, Ricky (CB)	5-11/190	1-19-65	9	Washington State	FA/94	15/10
25	Whigham, Larry (S)	6-2/202	6-23-72	2	Northeast Louisiana	FA/94	12/0
28	White, Brian (S)	6-0/190	4-21-73	R	Dartmouth	FA/95	—
40	Yancy, Carlos (CB)	6-2/190	6-26-70	R	Georgia	D7/95	—
	SPECIALISTS						
3	Bahr, Matt (K)	5-10/175	7-6-56	17	Penn State	FA/93	16/0
5	O'Neill, Pat (P)	6-1/200	2-9-71	2	Syracuse	D5/94	16/0

*Abrams played 16 games with Vikings in '94; Dellenbach played 16 games with Dolphins; Hand played 5 games with Colts; Meggett played 16 games with Giants; Roberts played 12 games with Oilers; White played 11 games with Chargers.

Also played with Patriots in '94: DT Ray Agnew (11 games); S Harlon Barnett (16); LB David Bavaro (9); RB Marion Butts (16); LB Jason Carthen (1); G Eugene Chung (3); NT Tim Goad (13); WR Ronnie Harris (1); WR Steve Hawkins (7); CB Rod Smith (16); RB Blair Thomas (4); RB Leroy Thompson (16); WR Michael Timpson (15); FB Kevin Turner (16); CB Darryl Wren (8).

Abbreviations: D1—draft pick, first round; SupD2—supplemental draft pick, second round; W-Den—waivers acquisition from Denver; T-Sea—trade acquisition from Seattle; PlanB—Plan B free-agent acquisition; FA—free-agent acquisition (other than Plan B).

MISCELLANEOUS TEAM DATA

Stadium (capacity, surface):
Foxboro Stadium
(60,326, grass)
Business address:
60 Washington St.
Foxboro, MA 02035
Business phone:
508-543-8200
Ticket information:
508-543-1776
Team colors:
Silver, blue and red
Flagship radio station:
WBCN, 104.1 FM
Training site:
Bryant College
Smithfield, R.I.
508-543-8200

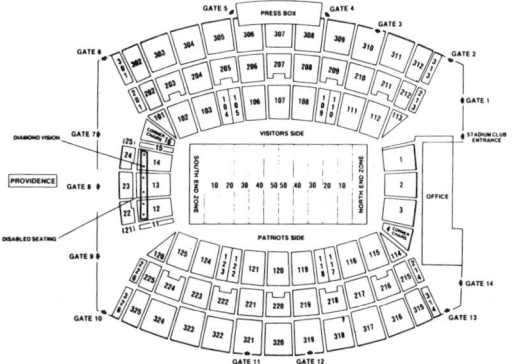

NEW ORLEANS SAINTS
NFC WESTERN DIVISION

1994 REVIEW

RESULTS

Sept. 4—KANSAS CITY	L	17-30
Sept. 11—WASHINGTON	L	24-38
Sept. 18—at Tampa Bay	W	9-7
Sept. 25—at San Francisco	L	13-24
Oct. 2—N.Y. GIANTS	W	27-22
Oct. 9—at Chicago	L	7-17
Oct. 16—SAN DIEGO	L	22-36
Oct. 23—L.A. RAMS	W	37-34
Oct. 30—Open date		
Nov. 6—at Minnesota	L	20-21
Nov. 13—ATLANTA	W	33-32
Nov. 20—at L.A. Raiders	L	19-24
Nov. 28—SAN FRANCISCO	L	14-35
Dec. 4—at L.A. Rams	W	31-15
Dec. 11—at Atlanta	W	29-20
Dec. 19—DALLAS	L	16-24
Dec. 24—at Denver	W	30-28

RECORDS/RANKINGS

1994 regular-season record: 7-9 (T2nd in NFC West); 4-2 in division; 6-6 in conference; 3-5 at home; 4-4 on road.
Team record last five years: 46-34 (.575, ranks T9th in league in that span).

1994 team rankings:	No.	NFC	NFL
Total offense	*323.9	6	12
Rushing offense	*83.5	13	26
Passing offense	*240.4	4	8
Scoring offense	348	6	9
Total defense	*348.1	12	25
Rushing defense	*109.9	9	18
Passing defense	*238.2	13	26
Scoring defense	407	13	27
Takeaways	31	T8	T13
Giveaways	32	11	T19
Turnover differential	-1	T8	T15
Sacks	36	T5	T11
Sacks allowed	24	3	7

*Yards per game.

TEAM LEADERS

Scoring (kicking): Morten Andersen, 116 pts. (32/32 PATs, 28/39 FGs).
Scoring (touchdowns): Mario Bates, 36 pts. (6 rushing).
Passing: Jim Everett, 3,855 yds. (540 att., 346 comp., 64.1%, 22 TDs, 18 int.).
Rushing: Mario Bates, 579 yds. (151 att., 3.8 avg., 6 TDs).
Receptions: Quinn Early, 82 (894 yds., 10.9 avg., 4 TDs).
Interceptions: Jimmy Spencer, 5 (24 yds., 0 TDs).
Sacks: Darion Conner, 10.5.
Punting: Tommy Barnhardt, 43.6 avg. (67 punts, 2,920 yds., 0 blocked).
Punt returns: Tyrone Hughes, 6.8 avg. (21 att., 143 yds., 0 TDs).
Kickoff returns: Tyrone Hughes, 24.7 avg. (63 att., 1,556 yds., 2 TDs).

1995 SEASON

CLUB DIRECTORY

Owner
Tom Benson
Executive vice president/administration
Jim Miller
Treasurer
Bruce Broussard
Comptroller
Charleen Sharpe
Vice president/marketing
Greg Suit
Director of corporate sales
Bill Ferrante
Director of ticket sales
Sandy King
Ticket office supervisor
Judy Chavis
Director/media relations
Rusty Kasmiersky
Assistant director/media relations
Neal Gulkis
Dir. travel/entertainment/special projects
Barra L. Birrcher
Director/community relations
Chanel Lagarde
Vice president football operations
Bill Kuharich
Administrative coordinator
Austin Dejan
Director of pro personnel
Chet Franklin
Director of college scouting
Bruce Lemmerman
Scouts
Bill Baker
Hamp Cook
Hokie Gajan
Tom Marino
Carmen Piccone

Vice president/head coach
Jim Mora
Assistant coaches
Jim Haslett (linebackers)
Larry Kennan (tight ends)
Monte Kiffin (defensive coord.)
Joe Marciano (special teams)
John Matsko (offensive line)
Jim L. Mora (defensive backs)
Wayne Nunnely (defensive line)
Russell Paternostro (strength and conditioning)
Jim Skipper (running backs)
Carl Smith (offensive coordinator/quarterbacks)
Steve Trimble (defensive asst.)
Steve Walters (wide receivers)

Trainer
Dean Kleinschmidt
Asst. trainer/dir. of rehabilitation
Kevin Mangum
Physicians
Charles L. Brown
Terry Habig
Lee Moss
Grounds superintendent
Lester Vallet Jr.
Facilities manager
Luke Jenkins
Equipment manager
Dan Simmons
Assistant equipment manager
Glennon "Silky" Powell
Director of videotape
Albert Aucoin

SCHEDULE

Sept. 3—SAN FRANCISCO	12:00
Sept. 10—at St. Louis	12:00
Sept. 17—at ATLANTA	12:00
Sept. 24—at N.Y. Giants	1:00
Oct. 1—PHILADELPHIA	12:00
Oct. 8—Open date	
Oct. 15—MIAMI	3:00
Oct. 22—at Carolina	1:00
Oct. 29—at San Francisco	1:00
Nov. 5—ST. LOUIS	12:00
Nov. 12—INDIANAPOLIS	12:00
Nov. 19—at Minnesota	3:00
Nov. 26—CAROLINA	7:00
Dec. 3—at New England	1:00
Dec. 10—at Atlanta	1:00
Dec. 16—GREEN BAY (Sat.)	3:00
Dec. 24—at N.Y. Jets	1:00

All times are for home team.
All games Sunday unless noted.

DRAFT CHOICES

Mark Fields, LB, Washington State (first round/13th pick overall).
Ray Zellars, FB, Notre Dame (2/44).
Mike Verstegen, T, Wisconsin (3/75).
Dameian Jeffries, DE, Alabama (4/108).
William Strong, DB, N.C. State (5/148).
Lee DeRamus, WR, Wisconsin (6/184).
Travis Davis, DB, Notre Dame (7/242).

TRAINING CAMP ROSTER

No.	QUARTERBACKS	Ht./Wt.	Born	NFL Exp.	College	How acq.	'94 Games GP/GS
17	Everett, Jim	6-5/212	1-3-63	10	Purdue	T-Ram/94	16/16
14	Hodson, Tom	6-3/195	1-28-67	4	Louisiana State	FA/95	0/0
13	Nussmeier, Doug	6-3/211	12-11-70	2	Idaho	D4/94	0/0
3	Rosenbach, Timm	6-1/215	10-27-66	4	Washington State	FA/95	0/0
	RUNNING BACKS						
24	Bates, Mario	6-1/217	1-16-73	2	Arizona State	D2/94	11/7
20	Brown, Derek	5-9/197	4-15-71	3	Nebraska	D4b/93	16/9
28	Dawkins, Ralph	5-8/195	10-20-70	1	Louisville	FA/95	0/0
32	Dunbar, Vaughn	5-10/204	9-4-68	4	Indiana	D1/92	8/0
25	Muster, Brad (FB)	6-4/235	4-11-65	8	Stanford	FA/93	7/1
22	Neal, Lorenzo (FB)	5-11/240	12-27-70	3	Fresno State	D4a/93	16/7
36	Ned, Derrick (FB)	6-1/220	1-5-69	3	Grambling State	FA/92	16/1
34	Zellars, Ray (FB)	5-11/221	3-25-73	R	Notre Dame	D2/95	—
	RECEIVERS						
86	Botkin, Kirk (TE)	6-3/245	3-19-71	1	Arkansas	FA/94	3/0
87	DeRamus, Lee	6-0/191	8-24-72	R	Wisconsin	D6/95	—
89	Early, Quinn	6-0/190	4-13-65	8	Iowa	PlanB/91	16/13
81	Haynes, Michael	6-0/184	12-24-65	8	Northern Arizona	FA/94	16/16
12	Henry, Adam	6-1/184	4-27-72	1	McNeese State	FA/95	0/0
80	Johnson, Tyrone	5-11/184	9-4-71	2	Western State (Colo.)	FA/94	1/0
19	Jones, Terrance	6-1/210	6-18-66	1	Tulane	FA/95	0/0
49	Kramer, Kyle (TE)	6-5/230	2-11-72	R	Oklahoma	FA/95	—
16	Latson, Lawann	5-8/170	3-11-71	1	Northwestern State	FA/95	0/0
88	Mitchell, Derrell (KR)	5-9/190	9-16-71	2	Texas Tech	D6/94	14/0
15	Moore, Travis	6-0/187	8-5-70	1	Ball State	FA/95	0/0
84	Rhem, Steve	6-2/212	11-9-71	2	Rowan (N.J.)	FA/94	7/0
83	Small, Torrance	6-3/201	9-6-70	4	Alcorn State	D5/92	16/0
82	Smith, Irv (TE)	6-3/246	10-13-71	3	Notre Dame	D1/93	16/16
85	Walls, Wesley (TE)	6-5/250	2-26-66	7	Mississippi	FA/94	15/7
	OFFENSIVE LINEMEN						
64	Bravy, Brian (G)	6-4/332	4-27-95	R	Georgia Tech	FA/95	—
71	Cooper, Richard (T)	6-5/290	11-1-64	6	Tennessee	FA/89	14/14
72	Dombrowski, Jim (G/T)	6-5/300	10-19-63	10	Virginia	D1/86	16/16
61	Durnim, Paul (C)	6-3/265	7-26-72	R	McNeese State	FA/95	—
69	Goo, Kendall (G)	6-6/286	2-5-72	R	Hawaii	FA/95	—
68	Kline, Alan (T)	6-5/277	5-25-71	1	Ohio State	FA/95	0/0
67	McCollum, Andy (C/G)	6-4/270	6-6-70	2	Toledo	FA/94	0/0
60	Novitsky, Craig (G)	6-5/295	5-12-71	2	UCLA	D5b/94	9/1
63	Palermo, Mike (T)	6-5/290	10-10-70	R	Gannon (Pa.)	FA/95	—
70	Port, Chris (G/T)	6-5/295	11-2-67	5	Duke	D12/90	16/16
77	Roaf, Willie (T)	6-5/300	4-18-70	3	Louisiana Tech	D1/93	16/16
78	Roth, Tom (C/G)	6-5/285	9-19-68	2	Southern Illinois	FA/94	0/0
62	Uhlenhake, Jeff (C)	6-3/284	1-28-66	7	Ohio State	FA/94	16/15
66	Verstegen, Mike	6-6/311	10-24-71	R	Wisconsin	D3/95	—
65	Williams, Willie (T)	6-6/295	8-6-67	4	Louisiana State	FA/94	16/5
	DEFENSIVE LINEMEN						
92	Benson, Mitchell (T)	6-4/300	5-30-67	4	Texas Christian	FA/95	0/0
74	Carroll, Herman (E)	6-4/265	6-20-71	2	Mississippi State	D5a/94	4/0
75	Dyet, Brian (E)	6-5/260	12-12-70	1	Colorado	FA/95	0/0
79	Epps, Tory (T)	6-1/280	5-28-67	6	Memphis	FA/95	*5/0
73	Farrell, Derrick (E)	6-5/290	1-10-72	R	Louisiana State	FA/95	—
91	Goff, Robert (E/NT)	6-3/280	10-2-65	8	Auburn	T-TB/90	16/0
98	Hanna, Jim (T)	6-4/275	8-10-71	2	Louisville	FA/94	7/0
95	Ingram, Kelvin (T)	6-5/276	10-25-70	R	Oklahoma State	FA/95	—
96	Jeffries, Dameian (E)	6-4/277	5-7-73	R	Alabama	D4/95	—
94	Johnson, Joe (E)	6-4/285	7-11-72	2	Louisville	D1/94	15/14
93	Martin, Wayne (E)	6-5/275	10-26-65	7	Arkansas	D1/89	16/16
90	Stanley, Isreal (T)	6-3/260	4-21-70	1	Arizona State	FA/95	0/0
99	Tuatagaloa, Natu (E)	6-4/275	5-25-66	6	California	FA/95	0/0
	LINEBACKERS						
50	Bavaro, David	6-1/237	3-27-67	4	Syracuse	FA/95	*9/5
56	Dixon, Ernest	6-1/250	10-17-71	2	South Carolina	FA/94	15/1
55	Fields, Mark	6-2/244	11-9-72	R	Washington State	D1/95	—
52	Harvey, Richard	6-1/242	9-11-66	6	Tulane	FA/95	*16/1
59	Porter, Rufus	6-1/230	5-18-65	8	Southern	FA/95	*16/15
58	Roberson, James	6-3/244	5-3-71	R	Florida State	FA/95	—
54	Tubbs, Winfred	6-4/250	9-24-70	2	Texas	D3/94	13/7
97	Turnbull, Renaldo	6-4/250	1-5-66	6	West Virginia	D1/90	16/16

No.	DEFENSIVE BACKS	Ht./Wt.	Born	NFL Exp.	College	How acq.	'94 Games GP/GS
21	Allen, Eric (CB)	5-10/180	11-22-65	8	Arizona State	FA/95	*16/16
26	Buck, Vince (CB)	6-0/198	1-12-68	6	Central State (O.)	D2/90	16/16
45	Byrd, Israel (CB)	5-11/184	2-1-71	1	Utah State	FA/94	3/0
47	Davis, Travis (S)	6-0/200	1-10-73	R	Notre Dame	D7/95	—
40	Fuller, James (S)	5-11/208	8-5-69	3	Portland State	FA/95	0/0
29	Gaines, Kevin (CB)	6-0/181	8-7-71	R	Louisville	FA/95	—
30	Gunn, Lance (S)	6-3/222	1-9-70	2	Texas	FA/95	0/0
33	Hughes, Tyrone (CB/KR)	5-9/175	1-14-70	3	Nebraska	D5/93	15/5
27	Jones, Selwyn (CB)	6-0/185	5-13-70	4	Colorado State	W-Cle/94	5/1
43	Legette, Tyrone (CB)	5-9/177	2-15-70	4	Nebraska	D3/92	15/2
46	Lumpkin, Sean (S)	6-0/206	1-4-70	4	Minnesota	D4b/92	16/15
44	McCleskey, J.J. (S)	5-7/177	4-10-70	2	Tennessee	FA/94	13/0
35	Pahukoa, Shane (S)	6-2/202	11-25-70	R	Washington	FA/95	—
37	Spencer, Jimmy (CB)	5-9/180	3-29-69	4	Florida	FA/92	16/16
41	Strong, William (CB)	5-10/191	11-3-71	R	North Carolina State	D5/95	—
	SPECIALISTS						
7	Andersen, Morten (K)	6-2/221	8-19-60	14	Michigan State	D4/82	16/0
9	Blanchard, Cary (K)	6-1/225	11-5-68	3	Oklahoma State	FA/95	0/0
4	Nesbitt, Mike (P)	6-2/180	2-3-71	1	New Mexico	FA/95	0/0
10	Wilmsmeyer, Klaus (P)	6-1/210	12-4-67	4	Louisville	FA/95	*16/0

*Allen played 16 games with Eagles in '94; Bavaro played 9 games with Patriots; Epps played 5 games with Bears; Harvey played 16 games with Broncos; Porter played 16 games with Seahawks; Wilmsmeyer played 16 games with 49ers.

Also played with Saints in '94: G/T Scott Adams (11); P Tommy Barnhardt (16); CB Vinnie Clark (5); CB Darion Conner (16); S Othello Henderson (16); CB Reginald Jones (1); CB Carl Lee (12); DE Wayne Martin (16); DE/NT Les Miller (8); LB Sam Mills (16); DE Joel Smeenge (16); LB Mike Stonebreaker (2); DE Frank Warren (16); LB James Williams (16); S Ray Wilson (3); QB Wade Wilson (4); LB DeMond Winston (3).

Abbreviations: D1—draft pick, first round; SupD2—supplemental draft pick, second round; W-Den—waivers acquisition from Denver; T-Sea—trade acquisition from Seattle; PlanB—Plan B free-agent acquisition; FA—free-agent acquisition (other than Plan B).

MISCELLANEOUS TEAM DATA

Stadium (capacity, surface):
Louisiana Superdome
(69,065, artificial)

Business address:
6928 Saints Drive
Metairie, LA 70003

Business phone:
504-733-0255

Ticket information:
504-522-2600

Team colors:
Old gold, black and white

Flagship radio station:
WWL (870 AM)

Training site:
U. of Wisconsin-La Crosse
La Crosse, Wis.
608-789-4550

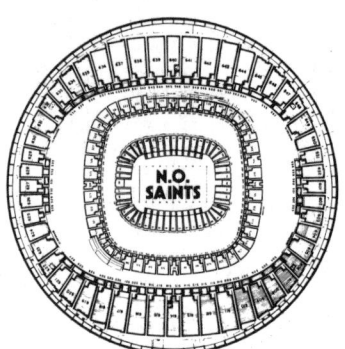

NEW YORK GIANTS
NFC EASTERN DIVISION

1994 REVIEW

RESULTS

Sept. 4—PHILADELPHIA	W	28-23
Sept. 11—at Arizona	W	20-17
Sept. 18—WASHINGTON	W	31-23
Sept. 25—Open date		
Oct. 2—at New Orleans	L	22-27
Oct. 10—MINNESOTA	L	10-27
Oct. 16—at L.A. Rams	L	10-17
Oct. 23—PITTSBURGH	L	6-10
Oct. 30—DETROIT (OT)	L	25-28
Nov. 7—at Dallas	L	10-38
Nov. 13—ARIZONA	L	9-10
Nov. 21—at Houston	W	13-10
Nov. 27—at Washington	W	21-19
Dec. 4—at Cleveland	W	16-13
Dec. 11—CINCINNATI	W	27-20
Dec. 18—at Philadelphia	W	16-13
Dec. 24—DALLAS	W	15-10

RECORDS/RANKINGS

1994 regular-season record: 9-7 (2nd in NFC East); 6-2 in division; 6-6 in conference; 4-4 at home; 5-3 on road.
Team record last five years: 47-33 (.588, ranks T7th in league in that span).

1994 team rankings:

	No.	NFC	NFL
Total offense	*263.5	14	28
Rushing offense	*109.6	5	10
Passing offense	*160.1	14	27
Scoring offense	279	11	22
Total defense	*309.4	7	11
Rushing defense	*108.0	8	15
Passing defense	*201.4	5	8
Scoring defense	305	5	8
Takeaways	32	7	T10
Giveaways	25	6	8
Turnover differential	7	T4	T8
Sacks	26	T12	T24
Sacks allowed	46	13	24

*Yards per game.

TEAM LEADERS

Scoring (kicking): David Treadwell, 55 pts. (22/23 PATs, 11/17 FGs).
Scoring (touchdowns): Rodney Hampton, 38 pts. (6 rushing, 1 2 pt. conv.).
Passing: Dave Brown, 2,536 yds. (350 att., 201 comp., 57.4%, 12 TDs, 16 int.).
Rushing: Rodney Hampton, 1,075 yds. (327 att., 3.3 avg., 6 TDs).
Receptions: Mike Sherrard, 53 (825 yds., 15.6 avg., 6 TDs).
Interceptions: John Booty, 3 (95 yds., 0 TDs); Phillippi Sparks, 3 (4 yds., 0 TDs).
Sacks: Keith Hamilton, 6.5; Erik Howard, 6.5.
Punting: Mike Horan, 41.4 avg. (85 punts, 3,521 yds., 2 blocked).
Punt returns: Dave Meggett, 12.4 avg. (26 att., 323 yds., 2 TDs).
Kickoff returns: Thomas Lewis, 19.6 avg. (26 att., 509 yds., 0 TDs).

1995 SEASON

CLUB DIRECTORY

President/co-CEO
Wellington T. Mara
Chairman/co-CEO
Preston Robert Tisch
Exec. V.P./general counsel
John K. Mara
Vice president/general manager
George Young
Treasurer
Jonathan Tisch
Assistant general manager
Ernie Accorsi
Assistant to the general manager
Harry Hulmes
Controller
John Pasquali
Assistant controller
Christine Procops
Director/player personnel
Tom Boisture
Director/administration
Tom Power
Director/marketing
Rusty Hawley
Director/promotion
Francis X. Mara
Ticket manager
John Gorman
Director/pro personnel
Tim Rooney
Assistant director/player personnel
Rick Donohue
Director/research and development
Raymond J. Walsh Jr.
Director/college scouting
Jerry Shay
Director/computer services
Jon Berger
Director/public relations
Pat Hanlon
Assistant director/public relations
Aaron Salkin
Assistant director/marketing
Bill Smith
Manager of creative services
Doug Murphy

SCHEDULE

Sept. 4—DALLAS (Mon.)		9:00
Sept. 10—at Kansas City		12:00
Sept. 17—at Green Bay		12:00
Sept. 24—NEW ORLEANS		1:00
Oct. 1—at San Francisco		1:00
Oct. 8—ARIZONA		4:00
Oct. 15—PHILADELPHIA		1:00
Oct. 22—Open date		
Oct. 29—at Washington		8:00
Nov. 5—at Seattle		1:00
Nov. 12—LOS ANGELES		1:00
Nov. 19—at Philadelphia		1:00
Nov. 26—CHICAGO		1:00
Nov. 30—at Arizona (Thur.)		6:00
Dec. 10—WASHINGTON		4:00
Dec. 17—at Dallas		3:00
Dec. 23—SAN DIEGO (Sat.)		12:30

All times are for home team.
All games Sunday unless noted.

Head coach
Dan Reeves
Assistant coaches
Don Blackmon (linebackers)
Dave Brazil (defensive quality control)
James Daniel (tight ends)
Steve DeBerg (quarterbacks)
Joe DeCamillis (special teams)
Kerry Goode (assistant strength and conditioning/offensive quality control)
George Henshaw (off. coord.)
Earl Leggett (defensive line)
Pete Managurian (off. line)
Al Miller (strength and conditioning)
Mike Nolan (def. coordinator)
Dick Rehbein (wide receivers)
George Sefcik (running backs)
Zaven Yaralian (def. backs)

Scouts
Rosey Brown
John Crea
Jeremiah Davis
Greg Gabriel
Ken Kavanaugh
Jerry Reese
Steve Verderosa
Head trainer
Ronnie Barnes
Assistant trainers
Michael Colello
Steve Kennelly
Team physician
Russell Warren
Locker room manager
Ed Wagner
Equipment manager
Ed Wagner Jr.
Video director
Tony Ceglio

DRAFT CHOICES

Tyrone Wheatley, RB, Michigan (first round/17th pick overall).
Scott Gragg, T, Montana (2/54).
Rodney Young, DB, Louisiana State (3/85).
Rob Zatechka, G, Nebraska (4/128).
Ben Talley, LB, Tennessee (4/133).
Roderick Mullen, DB, Grambling State (5/153).
Jamal Duff, DE, San Diego State (6/204).
Charles Way, RB, Virginia (6/206).
Bryne Diehl, P, Alabama (7/225).

1995 SEASON

TRAINING CAMP ROSTER

No.	QUARTERBACKS	Ht./Wt.	Born	NFL Exp.	College	How acq.	'94 Games GP/GS
17	Brown, Dave	6-5/225	2-25-70	4	Duke	SupD1/92	15/15
10	Graham, Kent	6-5/236	11-1-68	4	Ohio State	D8/92	13/1
8	White, Stan	6-2/202	8-14-71	2	Auburn	FA/95	0/0
	RUNNING BACKS						
45	Downs, Gary	6-0/212	6-28-71	2	North Carolina State	D3/94	14/0
20	Elias, Keith	5-9/191	2-3-72	2	Princeton	FA/94	2/0
27	Hampton, Rodney	5-11/230	4-3-69	6	Georgia	D1/90	14/13
44	Rasheed, Kenyon (FB)	5-10/235	8-23-70	3	Oklahoma	FA/93	16/7
34	Walker, Herschel (KR)	6-1/225	3-3-62	10	Georgia	FA/95	*16/14
30	Way, Charles (FB)	6-0/236	12-27-72	R	Virginia	D6b/95	—
28	Wheatley, Tyrone	6-0/227	1-19-72	R	Michigan	D1/95	—
	RECEIVERS						
80	Calloway, Chris	5-10/185	3-29-68	6	Michigan	PlanB/92	16/14
87	Cross, Howard (TE)	6-5/258	8-8-67	7	Alabama	D6/89	16/16
82	Douglas, Omar	5-10/170	6-3-72	2	Minnesota	FA/94	6/0
89	Harrell, Gary	5-7/170	1-23-72	1	Howard	FA/95	0/0
85	Kozlowski, Brian (TE)	6-3/250	10-4-70	2	Connecticut	FA/94	16/2
81	Lewis, Thomas (KR)	6-1/185	1-10-72	2	Indiana	D1/94	9/0
83	Marshall, Arthur (KR)	5-11/178	4-29-69	4	Georgia	T-Den/94	16/0
84	Pierce, Aaron (TE)	6-5/248	9-6-69	4	Washington	D3/92	16/11
88	Sherrard, Mike	6-2/187	6-21-63	10	UCLA	FA/93	16/14
	OFFENSIVE LINEMEN						
78	Bishop, Greg (T)	6-5/295	5-2-71	3	Pacific	D4/93	16/1
62	Davis, Scott (G)	6-3/289	1-29-70	3	Iowa	D6/93	15/4
76	Elliott, John (T)	6-7/308	4-1-65	8	Michigan	D2/88	16/15
74	Gragg, Scott (T)	6-8/316	2-28-72	R	Montana	D2/95	—
63	Reese, Darren (G)	6-4/285	10-25-70	2	Ohio University	FA/95	0/0
72	Riesenberg, Doug (T)	6-5/280	7-22-65	9	California	D6a/87	16/16
67	Schreiber, Adam (C)	6-4/290	2-20-62	12	Texas	FA/94	16/2
61	Smith, Lance (G)	6-3/290	1-1-63	11	Louisiana State	FA/94	13/13
59	Williams, Brian (C/G)	6-5/300	6-8-66	7	Minnesota	D1/89	14/14
68	Winrow, Jason (G)	6-4/321	1-16-71	2	Ohio State	D6/94	0/0
73	Zatechka, Rob (G)	6-4/307	12-1-71	R	Nebraska	D4/95	—
	DEFENSIVE LINEMEN						
93	Agnew, Ray (T)	6-3/295	12-9-67	6	North Carolina State	FA/95	*11/3
77	Bratzke, Chad (E)	6-4/262	9-15-71	2	Eastern Kentucky	D5/94	2/0
71	Dillard, Stacey (T)	6-5/292	9-17-68	4	Oklahoma	D6/92	16/0
96	Duff, Jamal (E)	6-7/259	3-11-72	R	San Diego State	D6a/95	—
75	Hamilton, Keith (E)	6-6/290	5-25-71	4	Pittsburgh	D4/92	15/15
97	Harris, Robert (E)	6-4/290	6-13-69	4	Southern	FA/95	*11/1
99	Maumalanga, Chris (T)	6-2/288	12-15-71	2	Kansas	D4/94	7/0
91	Rudolph, Coleman (E/T)	6-4/270	10-22-70	3	Georgia Tech	W-NYJ/94	12/2
92	Strahan, Michael (E)	6-4/270	11-21-71	3	Texas Southern	D2/93	15/15
	LINEBACKERS						
98	Armstead, Jessie	6-1/228	10-26-70	3	Miami (Fla.)	D8/93	16/0
94	Brooks, Michael	6-1/235	3-2-64	9	Louisiana State	FA/93	16/16
55	Buckley, Marcus	6-3/235	2-3-71	3	Texas A&M	D3/93	16/1
51	Croel, Mike	6-3/240	6-6-69	5	Nebraska	FA/95	*13/12
52	Davis, Mitch	6-3/238	7-7-71	1	Georgia	FA/95	0/0
53	Lawrence, Tyler	6-4/248	9-7-70	1	North Carolina State	FA/95	0/0
57	Miller, Corey	6-2/255	10-25-68	5	South Carolina	D6/91	15/13
58	Shufelt, Pete	6-3/240	10-28-69	2	Texas-El Paso	FA/94	5/0
54	Talley, Ben	6-3/248	7-14-72	R	Tennessee	D4/95	—
90	Widmer, Corey	6-3/250	12-25-68	4	Montana State	D7/92	16/5
	DEFENSIVE BACKS						
21	Beamon, Willie (CB)	5-11/175	6-14-70	3	Northern Iowa	FA/93	15/0
37	Campbell, Jesse (S)	6-1/215	4-11-69	5	North Carolina State	FA/92	14/10
43	Douglass, Maurice (S)	5-11/203	2-12-64	10	Kentucky	FA/95	*16/4
25	Glenn, Vencie (S)	6-0/189	10-26-64	10	Indiana State	T-Min/95	*16/16
39	Mullen, Roderick (S)	6-1/204	12-5-72	R	Grambling State	D5/95	—
23	Randolph, Thomas (CB)	5-9/176	10-5-70	2	Kansas State	D2a/94	16/10
31	Sehorn, Jason (S)	6-2/212	4-15-71	2	Southern California	D2b/94	8/0
22	Sparks, Phillippi (CB)	5-11/190	4-15-69	4	Arizona State	D2/92	11/11
29	Wooten, Tito (S)	6-0/181	12-12-71	2	Northeast Louisiana	D4/94	16/2
47	Young, Rodney (S)	6-1/206	1-25-73	R	Louisiana State	D3/95	—
	SPECIALISTS						
3	Daluiso, Brad (K)	6-2/215	12-31-67	5	UCLA	FA/93	16/0
5	Diehl, Bryne (P)	6-1/220	12-20-71	R	Alabama	D7/95	—
2	Horan, Mike (P)	5-11/188	2-1-59	12	Long Beach State	FA/93	16/0

*Agnew played 11 games with Patriots in '94; Croel played 13 games with Broncos; Douglass played 16 games with Bears; Glenn played 16 games with Vikings; Harris played 11 games with Vikings; Walker played 16 games with Eagles.

Also played with Giants in '94: LB Carlton Bailey (16 games); S John Booty (16); TE Derek Brown (13); DE Mike Fox (16); DT Erik Howard (16); CB Mark Jackson (2); LB Andre Powell (1); CB Corey Raymond (16); G William Roberts (16); K David Treadwell (13); S Jarvis Williams (13).

Abbreviations: D1—draft pick, first round; SupD2—supplemental draft pick, second round; W-Den—waivers acquisition from Denver; T-Sea—trade acquisition from Seattle; PlanB—Plan B free-agent acquisition; FA—free-agent acquisition (other than Plan B).

MISCELLANEOUS TEAM DATA

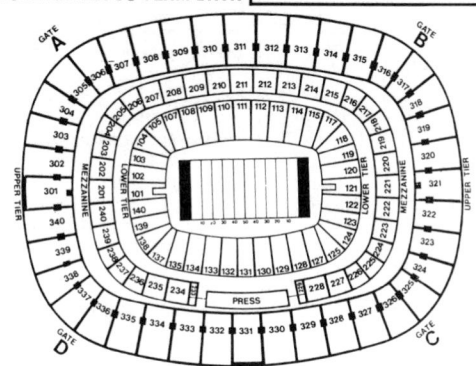

Stadium (capacity, surface):
Giants Stadium
(78,148, artificial)
Business address:
East Rutherford, NJ 07073
Business phone:
201-935-8111
Ticket information:
201-935-8222
Team colors:
Blue, white and red
Flagship radio station:
WOR, 710 AM
Training site:
Fairleigh Dickinson U.-Madison
Madison, N.J.
201-935-8111

NEW YORK JETS
AFC EASTERN DIVISION

1994 REVIEW

RESULTS

Sept. 4—at Buffalo	W	23-3	
Sept. 11—DENVER (OT)	W	25-22	
Sept. 18—at Miami	L	14-28	
Sept. 25—CHICAGO	L	7-19	
Oct. 2—at Cleveland	L	7-27	
Oct. 9—INDIANAPOLIS	W	16-6	
Oct. 16—NEW ENGLAND	W	24-17	
Oct. 23—Open date			
Oct. 30—at Indianapolis	L	25-28	
Nov. 6—BUFFALO	W	22-17	
Nov. 13—at Green Bay	L	10-17	
Nov. 20—at Minnesota	W	31-21	
Nov. 27—MIAMI	L	24-28	
Dec. 4—at New England	L	13-24	
Dec. 10—DETROIT	L	7-18	
Dec. 18—SAN DIEGO	L	6-21	
Dec. 24—at Houston	L	10-24	

RECORDS/RANKINGS

1994 regular-season record: 6-10 (5th in AFC East); 4-4 in division; 5-7 in conference; 4-4 at home; 2-6 on road.
Team record last five years: 32-48 (.400), ranks 21st in league in that span).

1994 team rankings:

	No.	AFC	NFL
Total offense	*293.9	11	22
Rushing offense	*97.9	10	16
Passing offense	*196.1	10	20
Scoring offense	264	13	25
Total defense	*333.6	12	22
Rushing defense	*113.1	11	21
Passing defense	*220.6	9	18
Scoring defense	320	T6	T14
Takeaways	38	T2	T2
Giveaways	28	T4	T12
Turnover differential	10	3	5
Sacks	29	T9	T17
Sacks allowed	28	T5	T10

*Yards per game.

TEAM LEADERS

Scoring (kicking): Nick Lowery, 86 pts. (26/27 PATs, 20/23 FGs).
Scoring (touchdowns): Rob Moore, 40 pts. (6 receiving, 2 2-pt. conv.).
Passing: Boomer Esiason, 2,782 yds. (440 att., 255 comp., 58.0%, 17 TDs, 13 int.).
Rushing: Johnny Johnson, 931 yds. (240 att., 3.9 avg., 3 TDs).
Receptions: Rob Moore, 78 (1,010 yds., 12.9 avg., 6 TDs).
Interceptions: Marcus Turner, 5 (155 yds., 1 TD).
Sacks: Jeff Lageman, 6.5.
Punting: Brian Hansen, 42.1 avg. (84 punts, 3,534 yds., 0 blocked).
Punt returns: Cliff Hicks, 9.0 avg. (38 att., 342 yds., 0 TDs).
Kickoff returns: Aaron Glenn, 21.6 avg. (27 att., 582 yds., 0 TDs).

1995 SEASON

CLUB DIRECTORY

Chairman of the board
Leon Hess
President
Steve Gutman
Vice president/general manager
Dick Steinberg
Assistant general manager
James Harris
Treasurer & chief financial officer
Mike Gerstle
Controller
Mike Minarczyk
Director/public relations
Frank Ramos
Asst. director/public relations
Brooks Thomas
Public relations assistants
Ken Ilchuk
Sharon Czark
Community affairs manager
Doug Miller
Executive director of business operations
Bob Parente
Marketing manager
Beth Conroy
Director of ticket operations
John Buschhorn
Asst. dir. of ticket operations
Gerry Parravano
Director/operations
Mike Kensil
Travel coordinator
Kevin Coyle
Director/player personnel
Dick Haley
Pro personnel director
Jim Royer
Dir. of player administration
Pat Kirwan

Head coach
Rich Kotite
Assistant coaches
Zeke Bratkowski (offensive co-ordinator/quarterbacks)
Chip Falivene (asst. to head coach)
Tom Gamble (defensive assistant/quality control)
Peter Giunta (defensive backs)
Ray Hamilton (defensive line)
Richard Mann (receivers/tight ends)
Bill Muir (offensive line)
Ken Rose (special teams)
Jim Vechiarella (defensive co-ordinator/linebackers)
Jim Williams (strength & conditioning)
Richard Wood (running backs)

Scouts
Joe Collins
Don Grammer
Sid Hall
Jesse Kay
Marv Sunderland
Head trainer
Bob Reese
Assistant trainers
Joe Patten
Darryl Conway
Equipment manager
Bill Hampton
Groundskeeper
Bob Hansen
Video director
Jim Pons

SCHEDULE

Sept. 3—at Miami	4:00	
Sept. 10—INDIANAPOLIS	4:00	
Sept. 17—JACKSONVILLE	4:00	
Sept. 24—at Atlanta	4:00	
Oct. 1—LOS ANGELES	8:00	
Oct. 8—at Buffalo	1:00	
Oct. 15—at Carolina	4:00	
Oct. 22—MIAMI	1:00	
Oct. 29—at Indianapolis	1:00	
Nov. 5—NEW ENGLAND	1:00	
Nov. 12—Open date		
Nov. 19—BUFFALO	4:00	
Nov. 26—at Seattle	1:00	
Dec. 3—ST. LOUIS	1:00	
Dec. 10—at New England	1:00	
Dec. 17—at Houston	12:00	
Dec. 24—NEW ORLEANS	1:00	

All times are for home team.
All games Sunday unless noted.

DRAFT CHOICES

Kyle Brady, TE, Penn State (first round/ninth pick overall).
Hugh Douglas, DE, Central State (Ohio) (1/16).
Matt O'Dwyer, G, Northwestern (2/33).
Melvin Hayes, T, Mississippi State (4/106).
Tyrone Davis, WR, Virginia (4/107).
Carl Greenwood, DB, UCLA (5/142).
Eddie Mason, LB, North Carolina (6/178).
Curtis Ceaser, WR, Grambling St. (7/217).

TRAINING CAMP ROSTER

No.	QUARTERBACKS	Ht./Wt.	Born	NFL Exp.	College	How acq.	'94 Games GP/GS
6	Brister, Bubby	6-3/207	8-15-62	10	Northeast Louisiana	FA/95	*7/2
7	Esiason, Boomer	6-5/224	4-17-61	12	Maryland	T-Cin/93	15/14
4	Foley, Glenn	6-2/210	10-10-70	2	Boston College	D7/94	1/0
14	Sacca, John	6-2/203	12-12-71	R	Eastern Kentucky	FA/95	—

RUNNING BACKS

No.		Ht./Wt.	Born	NFL Exp.	College	How acq.	'94 Games GP/GS
20	Anderson, Richie	6-2/225	9-13-71	3	Penn State	D6/93	13/5
30	Baxter, Brad	6-1/235	5-5-67	6	Alabama State	FA/89	15/9
35	Carter, Dexter (KR)	5-9/175	9-15-67	6	Florida State	FA/95	*16/0
39	Johnson, Johnny	6-3/220	6-11-68	6	San Jose State	T-Pho/93	16/14
32	Lester, Fredrick (FB)	6-0/245	8-1-71	1	Alabama A&M	D6/94	0/0
36	Marsh, Erik	5-10/195	5-2-73	R	Lafayette	FA/95	—
44	May, Sheriden (FB)	6-0/215	8-10-73	R	Idaho	FA/95	—
33	Moore, Ronald	5-10/225	11-26-70	3	Pittsburg (Kan.) State	T-Ari/95	*16/16
29	Murrell, Adrian	5-11/214	10-16-70	3	West Virginia	D5/93	10/1

RECEIVERS

No.		Ht./Wt.	Born	NFL Exp.	College	How acq.	'94 Games GP/GS
18	Allen, Alan	6-1/186	8-9-71	R	Idaho	FA/95	—
88	Anderson, Stevie	6-5/215	5-12-70	2	Grambling State	FA/93	10/0
16	Askew, Chad	6-4/200	1-27-72	R	Pittsburgh	FA/95	—
47	Ball, Lavar (TE)	6-5/254	10-23-68	1	Cal-State Los Angeles	FA/95	0/0
84	Baxter, Fred (TE)	6-3/260	6-14-71	3	Auburn	D5/93	11/1
81	Brady, Kyle (TE)	6-6/260	1-14-72	R	Penn State	D1/95	—
46	Burke, Paul (TE)	6-3/250	2-16-69	R	Idaho	FA/95	—
17	Ceaser, Curtis	6-2/190	8-11-72	R	Grambling State	D7/95	—
3	Chrebet, Wayne	5-10/180	8-14-73	R	Hofstra	FA/95	—
83	Davis, Tyrone	6-4/229	6-30-72	R	Virginia	D4/95	—
15	Garlick, Tom	5-11/187	9-22-71	R	Fordham	FA/95	—
86	Mitchell, Johnny (TE)	6-3/241	1-20-71	4	Nebraska	D1/92	16/14
89	Parker, Orlando (KR)	5-11/195	3-7-72	2	Troy (Ala.) State	D4/94	2/0
19	Sallee, Brian	6-2/194	5-12-72	R	Missouri	FA/95	—
87	Yarborough, Ryan	6-2/195	4-26-71	2	Wyoming	D2/94	13/0

OFFENSIVE LINEMEN

No.		Ht./Wt.	Born	NFL Exp.	College	How acq.	'94 Games GP/GS
65	Baczek, Todd (G)	6-3/297	2-1-72	R	Northwestern	FA/95	—
76	Brown, James (T)	6-6/335	1-3-70	3	Virginia State	W-Ind/92	16/6
69	Cronin, Colin (G)	6-6/285	10-15-71	R	Michigan State	FA/95	—
52	Dixon, Cal (C/G)	6-4/302	10-11-69	4	Florida	D5/92	15/0
62	Duffy, Roger (G/C)	6-3/294	7-16-67	6	Penn State	D8/90	16/14
79	Hayes, Melvin	6-6/329	4-28-73	R	Mississippi State	D4/95	—
64	Jerich, Mike (T)	6-5/295	7-10-72	R	Stanford	FA/95	—
60	Lamb, Marc (C)	6-5/292	5-4-72	R	Montana	FA/95	—
75	Malamala, Siupeli (G/T)	6-5/315	1-15-69	4	Washington	D3/92	12/10
67	McIver, Everett (G)	6-6/315	8-5-70	2	Elizabeth (N.C.) City State	FA/93	4/0
70	O'Dwyer, Matt (G)	6-5/308	9-1-72	R	Northwestern	D2/95	—
61	Thompson, Brian (C)	6-2/290	9-28-73	R	Wayne State (Neb.)	FA/95	—
77	Willig, Matt (T)	6-8/317	1-21-69	3	Southern California	FA/92	16/3
72	Wisdom, Terrance (G)	6-4/300	12-4-71	1	Syracuse	FA/95	0/0

DEFENSIVE LINEMEN

No.		Ht./Wt.	Born	NFL Exp.	College	How acq.	'94 Games GP/GS
91	Bazile, Wilky (T)	6-3/280	11-12-71	R	Syracuse	FA/95	—
78	Benfatti, Lou (T)	6-4/278	3-9-71	2	Penn State	D3/94	7/0
94	Brock, Matt (E)	6-5/280	1-14-66	7	Oregon	FA/95	*5/0
92	Casillas, Tony (T)	6-3/278	10-26-63	9	Oklahoma	FA/94	12/11
96	Connealy, Terry (T)	6-5/278	6-10-72	R	Nebraska	FA/95	—
99	Douglas, Hugh (E)	6-2/265	8-23-71	R	Central State (O.)	D1/95	—
66	Evans, Donald (E/T)	6-2/282	3-14-64	8	Winston-Salem State	FA/94	16/16
74	Howard, Erik (T/E)	6-4/275	11-12-64	10	Washington State	FA/95	*16/16
95	Oglesby, Alfred (T)	6-4/290	1-27-67	5	Houston	FA/94	15/1
97	Washington, Marvin (E)	6-6/280	10-22-65	7	Idaho	D6/89	15/15

LINEBACKERS

No.		Ht./Wt.	Born	NFL Exp.	College	How acq.	'94 Games GP/GS
98	Barber, Kurt	6-4/249	1-5-69	4	Southern California	D2/92	15/0
50	Cadrez, Glenn	6-3/245	1-2-70	4	Houston	D6/92	16/0
48	Cascadden, Chad	6-1/225	5-14-72	R	Wisconsin	FA/95	—
59	Clifton, Kyle	6-4/236	8-23-62	12	Texas Christian	D3/84	16/5
49	Davis, Don	6-1/239	12-17-72	R	Kansas	FA/95	—
55	Houston, Bobby	6-2/245	10-26-67	5	North Carolina State	PlanB/91	16/16
54	Jones, Marvin	6-2/249	6-28-72	3	Florida State	D1/93	15/11
58	Knutson, Jon	6-3/249	5-31-73	R	Colorado	FA/95	—
57	Lewis, Mo	6-3/250	10-21-69	5	Georgia	D3/91	16/16
51	Mason, Eddie	6-0/230	1-9-72	R	North Carolina	D6/95	—

No.	DEFENSIVE BACKS	Ht./Wt.	Born	NFL Exp.	College	How acq.	'94 Games GP/GS
31	Glenn, Aaron (CB/KR)	5-9/185	9-16-72	2	Texas A&M	D1/94	15/15
21	Green, Victor (CB)	5-9/195	12-8-69	3	Akron	FA/93	16/0
22	Greenwood, Carl (CB)	5-11/186	3-11-72	R	UCLA	D5/95	—
25	Jones, Gary (S)	6-1/217	11-30-67	6	Texas A&M	FA/95	*14/0
43	Joseph, Vance	6-0/202	9-20-72	R	Colorado	FA/95	—
37	Prior, Anthony	5-11/185	3-27-70	3	Washington State	FA/93	13/0
40	Rhodes, Elton	6-1/196	5-22-72	R	Central Oklahoma State	FA/95	—
38	Scott, Todd (S)	5-10/207	1-23-68	5	Southwestern Louisiana	FA/95	*15/15
26	Seapker, Jason (S)	6-3/193	11-28-71	R	Northeastern	FA/95	—
45	Smith, Otis (CB)	5-11/190	10-22-65	6	Missouri	FA/95	*16/2
27	Terrell, Pat (S)	6-2/210	3-18-68	6	Notre Dame	FA/94	16/2
23	Turner, Marcus (CB/S)	6-0/190	1-13-66	7	UCLA	PlanB/92	16/1
	SPECIALISTS						
5	Conley, Sean (K)	6-0/192	2-1-70	R	Pittsburgh	FA/95	—
11	Hansen, Brian (P)	6-4/215	10-26-60	11	Sioux Falls (S.D) College	FA/94	16/0
8	Lowery, Nick (K)	6-4/215	5-27-56	16	Dartmouth	FA/94	16/0

*Brister played 7 games with Eagles in '94; Brock played 5 games with Packers; Carter played 16 games with 49ers; Howard played 16 games with Giants; G. Jones played 14 games with Steelers; Moore played 16 games with Cardinals; Scott played 15 games with Vikings; Smith played 16 games with Eagles.

Also played with Jets in '94: LB Tuineau Alipate (8); WR Rob Carpenter (3); T Jeff Criswell (15); DT/DE Paul Frase (16); DT Mark Gunn (3); CB James Hasty (16); DB/PR Clifford Hicks (16); FB Anthony Johnson (15); DE Jeff Lageman (16); S Ronnie Lott (15); WR Rob Moore (16); DT Bill Pickel (11); C Jim Sweeney (16); LB Eric Thomas (1); QB Jack Trudeau (5); S Brian Washington (15); G Dwayne White (16).

Abbreviations: D1—draft pick, first round; SupD2—supplemental draft pick, second round; W-Den—waivers acquisition from Denver; T-Sea—trade acquisition from Seattle; PlanB—Plan B free-agent acquisition; FA—free-agent acquisition (other than Plan B).

Stadium (capacity, surface):
Giants Stadium
(77,716, artificial)
Business address:
1000 Fulton Avenue
Hempstead, NY 11550
Business phone:
516-538-6600
Ticket information:
516-538-7200
Team colors:
Kelly green, white with black trim
Flagship radio station:
WFAN, 660 AM
Training site:
Hofstra University
Hempstead, N.Y.
516-538-6600

MISCELLANEOUS TEAM DATA

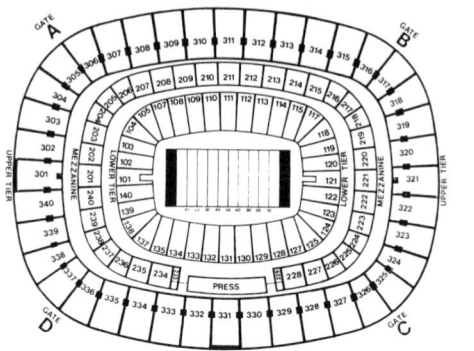

PHILADELPHIA EAGLES
NFC EASTERN DIVISION

1994 REVIEW

RESULTS

Sept.	4—at N.Y. Giants	L	23-28
Sept.	12—CHICAGO	W	30-22
Sept.	18—GREEN BAY	W	13-7
Sept.	25—Open date		
Oct.	2—at San Francisco	W	40-8
Oct.	9—WASHINGTON	W	21-17
Oct.	16—at Dallas	L	13-24
Oct.	24—HOUSTON	W	21-6
Oct.	30—at Washington	W	31-29
Nov.	6—ARIZONA	W	17-7
Nov.	13—CLEVELAND	L	7-26
Nov.	20—at Arizona	L	6-12
Nov.	27—at Atlanta	L	21-28
Dec.	4—DALLAS	L	19-31
Dec.	11—at Pittsburgh	L	3-14
Dec.	18—N.Y. GIANTS	L	13-16
Dec.	24—at Cincinnati	L	30-33

RECORDS/RANKINGS

1994 regular-season record: 7-9 (4th in NFC East); 3-5 in division; 6-6 in conference; 5-3 at home; 2-6 on road.
Team record last five years: 46-34 (.575, ranks T9th in league in that span).
1994 team rankings:

	No.	NFC	NFL
Total offense	*320.3	7	14
Rushing offense	*110.1	4	9
Passing offense	*210.3	8	14
Scoring offense	308	9	17
Total defense	*294.4	3	4
Rushing defense	*101.0	6	11
Passing defense	*193.4	4	6
Scoring defense	308	7	11
Takeaways	35	T2	T5
Giveaways	26	T7	T9
Turnover differential	9	3	T6
Sacks	42	2	4
Sacks allowed	48	14	25

*Yards per game.

TEAM LEADERS

Scoring (kicking): Eddie Murray, 96 pts. (33/33 PATs, 21/25 FGs).
Scoring (touchdowns): Herschel Walker, 48 pts. (5 rushing, 2 receiving, 1 kickoff return).
Passing: Randall Cunningham, 3,229 yds. (490 att., 265 comp., 54.1%, 16 TDs, 13 int.).
Rushing: Herschel Walker, 528 yds. (113 att., 4.7 avg., 5 TDs).
Receptions: Fred Barnett, 78 (1,127 yds., 14.4 avg., 5 TDs).
Interceptions: Greg Jackson, 6 (86 yds., 1 TD).
Sacks: William Fuller, 9.5.
Punting: Bryan Barker, 40.8 avg. (66 punts, 2,696 yds., 0 blocked).
Punt returns: Jeff Sydner, 13.2 avg. (36 att., 475 yds., 2 TDs).
Kickoff returns: Herschel Walker, 27.7 avg. (21 att., 581 yds., 1 TD).

1995 SEASON

CLUB DIRECTORY

Owner
Jeffrey Lurie
V.P.-bus. dev. and broadcasting
Jeffrey Auerbach
Vice president
Joe Banner
V.P./chief financial officer
Mimi Box
V.P.-player personnel
John Wooten
Director of football administration
Bob Ackles
Director of pro personnel
Chuck Banker
Asst. to president/general counsel
Bob Wallace
Assistant to president
George Azar
Director of marketing/sponsorships
Karen Levine
Director of corporate sales
Scott O'Neil
Director of penthouse suites
Debbie Santore
Director of public relations
Ron Howard
Asst. dir. of public relations
Michael Gilbert
Dir. of alumni rel./traveling sec.
Jim Gallagher
Director of administration
Vicki Chatley
Ticket manager
Leo Carlin

SCHEDULE

Sept.	3—TAMPA BAY	1:00
Sept.	10—at Arizona	5:00
Sept.	17—SAN DIEGO	1:00
Sept.	24—at Los Angeles	1:00
Oct.	1—at New Orleans	12:00
Oct.	8—WASHINGTON	1:00
Oct.	15—at N.Y. Giants	1:00
Oct.	22—Open date	
Oct.	29—ST. LOUIS	1:00
Nov.	6—at Dallas (Mon.)	8:00
Nov.	12—DENVER	8:00
Nov.	19—N.Y. GIANTS	1:00
Nov.	26—at Washington	1:00
Dec.	3—at Seattle	1:00
Dec.	10—DALLAS	1:00
Dec.	17—ARIZONA	1:00
Dec.	24—at Chicago	12:00

All times are for home team.
All games Sunday unless noted.

Head coach:
Ray Rhodes
Assistant coaches
Bill Callahan (offensive line)
Gerald Carr (wide receivers)
Juan Castillo (off. assistant)
Jon Gruden (off. coordinator)
Dick Jamieson (running backs)
Chuck Knox Jr. (def. assistant)
Danny Smith (special teams)
Emmitt Thomas (def. coord.)
Mike Trgovac (defensive line)
Joe Vitt (linebackers)
Ted Williams (tight ends)
Mike Wolf (strength and conditioning)

Asst. dir. of penthouse sales
Ken Iman
Dir. of penthouse operations
Christiana Noyalas
Trainer
Otho Davis
Assistant trainer
David Price
Equipment manager
Rusty Sweeney
Video director
Mike Dougherty

DRAFT CHOICES

Mike Mamula, DE, Boston College (first round/seventh pick overall).
Bobby Taylor, DB, Notre Dame (2/50).
Barrett Brooks, T, Kansas State (2/58).
Greg Jefferson, DE, Central Florida (3/72).
Chris T. Jones, WR, Miami (Fla.) (3/78).
Dave Barr, QB, California (4/119).
Fred McCrary, FB, Miss. State (6/208).
Kevin Boule, RB, Mississippi State (7/210).
Howard Smothers, T, Bethune-Cookman (7/248).

PHILADELPHIA EAGLES

1995 SEASON

TRAINING CAMP ROSTER

No.	QUARTERBACKS	Ht./Wt.	Born	NFL Exp.	College	How acq.	'94 Games GP/GS
16	Barr, Dave	6-3/210	5-9-72	R	California	D4/94	—
12	Cunningham, Randall	6-4/205	3-27-63	11	UNLV	D2/85	14/14
11	Fielder, Jay	6-1/215	12-29-71	2	Dartmouth	FA/95	0/0
9	Peete, Rodney	6-0/193	3-16-66	7	Southern California	FA/95	*7/1
	RUNNING BACKS						
35	Bouie, Kevin	6-1/228	8-18-71	R	Mississippi State	D7/95	—
30	Garner, Charlie	5-9/181	2-13-72	2	Tennessee	D2/94	10/8
45	Hebron, Vaughn	5-8/196	10-7-70	3	Virginia Tech	FA/93	16/2
37	Henesey, Brian (FB)	5-10/215	12-10-69	2	Bucknell	FA/95	*3/0
33	Marshall, Malcolm (FB)	6-1/246	8-29-72	R	North Carolina	FA/95	—
41	McCrary, Fred (FB)	6-0/210	9-19-72	R	Mississippi State	D6/95	—
34	Turner, Kevin (FB)	6-1/230	6-12-69	4	Alabama	FA/95	*16/9
32	Watters, Ricky	6-1/212	4-7-69	5	Notre Dame	FA/95	*16/16
31	Wills, Shawn	5-10/185	6-22-70	R	UCLA	FA/95	—
20	Witherspoon, Derrick	5-10/197	2-14-71	1	Clemson	FA/95	0/0
	RECEIVERS						
86	Barnett, Fred	6-0/199	6-17-66	6	Arkansas State	D3/90	16/16
88	Burnett, Bryce (TE)	6-2/235	3-9-69	1	San Jose State	FA/95	0/0
83	Ford, Bernard	5-9/169	2-27-66	3	Central Florida	FA/95	0/0
19	George, Chris	5-10/188	11-27-71	R	Glenville State (W.Va.)	FA/95	—
87	Johnson, Maurice (TE)	6-2/243	1-9-67	5	Temple	FA/90	16/10
80	Johnson, Reggie (TE)	6-2/256	1-27-68	5	Florida State	FA/95	*9/2
82	Jones, Chris T.	6-3/210	8-7-71	R	Miami (Fla.)	D3/95	—
13	Jones, Kendrick	5-8/185	12-1-72	R	Tennessee	FA/95	—
81	Kearney, Jay	6-1/195	9-29-71	1	West Virginia	FA/94	0/0
18	Lewis, Ron	5-11/192	3-25-68	6	Florida State	FA/95	*6/1
	Mundy, Aaron (TE)	6-5/252	12-9-71	1	Virginia	FA/95	0/0
7	Solomon, Freddie (KR)	5-10/180	8-15-72	R	South Carolina State	FA/95	—
85	Sydner, Jeff (KR)	5-6/170	11-11-69	4	Hawaii	D6/92	16/0
89	Williams, Calvin	5-11/190	3-3-67	6	Purdue	D5/90	16/14
	OFFENSIVE LINEMEN						
72	Alexander, David (C)	6-3/275	7-28-64	9	Tulsa	D5/87	16/16
76	Brooks, Barrett (T)	6-4/305	5-5-72	R	Kansas State	D2/95	—
67	Canter, Andy (T)	6-4/279	6-18-72	R	Ohio University	FA/95	—
78	Davis, Antone (T)	6-4/325	2-28-67	5	Tennessee	D1/91	16/14
	Drake, Troy (T)	6-6/268	5-15-72	R	Indiana	FA/95	—
73	Holmes, Lester (G)	6-3/301	9-27-69	3	Jackson State	D1/93	16/16
66	Hudson, John (G/C)	6-2/275	1-29-68	6	Auburn	D11/90	16/0
62	McKenzie, Raleigh (G/C)	6-2/277	2-8-63	11	Tennessee	FA/95	*16/16
65	O'Brien, Chris (T)	6-5/291	8-23-72	R	Central Michigan	FA/95	—
63	Panos, Joe (G/C)	6-2/296	1-24-71	2	Wisconsin	D3/94	16/2
69	Prinbow, Kerry (T)	6-5/290	7-30-72	R	Montana	FA/95	—
	Rudolph, Joe (G)	6-1/282	7-21-72	R	Wisconsin	FA/95	—
68	Sims, Joe (T)	6-3/310	3-1-69	5	Nebraska	FA/92	*15/14
77	Smothers, Howard (T)	6-3/285	11-16-73	R	Bethune-Cookman	D7/95	—
74	Williams, Bernard (T)	6-8/317	7-18-72	2	Georgia	D1/94	16/16
	DEFENSIVE LINEMEN						
	Baskin, Thomas (T)	6-0/288	12-9-72	R	Texas	FA/95	—
71	Brown, Curt (T)	6-5/260	4-5-70	1	North Carolina	FA/95	0/0
95	Chalenski, Mike	6-5/288	1-28-70	3	UCLA	FA/93	0/0
96	Fuller, William (E)	6-3/274	3-8-62	10	North Carolina	FA/94	16/16
97	Gunn, Mark	6-4/279	7-24-68	4	Pittsburgh	FA/95	0/0
91	Hall, Rhett (T)	6-2/260	12-5-68	3	California	FA/95	*12/2
79	Harmon, Andy (T)	6-4/265	4-6-69	5	Kent	D6/91	16/16
98	Jefferson, Greg (E)	6-3/256	8-31-71	R	Central Florida	D3/95	—
59	Jeter, Tommy (T)	6-5/282	9-20-69	4	Texas	D3/92	14/0
94	Mamula, Mike (E)	6-4/248	8-14-73	R	Boston College	D1/95	—
93	Owens, Gerald (T)	6-2/283	7-29-69	R	Florida State	FA/95	—
	Renfro, Leonard (T)	6-2/291	6-29-70	3	Colorado	D1/93	9/0
	Stubbs, Daniel (E)	6-4/264	1-3-65	7	Miami (Fla.)	FA/95	0/0
	LINEBACKERS						
39	Allen, Andre	6-0/215	6-24-73	R	Northern Iowa	FA/95	—
55	Dillon, Jerry	6-3/221	9-17-69	1	East Carolina	FA/95	0/0
54	Gouveia, Kurt	6-1/233	9-14-64	9	Brigham Young	FA/95	*14/1
50	Lee, Reginald	6-2/241	11-27-73	R	Youngstown State	FA/95	—
43	Lillibridge, Marc	6-1/232	2-18-72	R	Iowa State	FA/95	—
49	Nau, Jeremy	6-4/233	1-28-72	R	Notre Dame	FA/95	—
58	Oden, Derrick	5-11/230	9-29-70	3	Alabama	D6/93	11/0

No.	LINEBACKERS	Ht./Wt.	Born	NFL Exp.	College	How acq.	'94 Games GP/GS
53	Romanowski, Bill	6-4/231	4-2-66	8	Boston College	T-SF/94	16/15
46	Sneathen, Bob	6-1/224	5-22-71	R	Rutgers	FA/95	—
51	Thomas, William	6-2/218	8-13-68	5	Texas A&M	D4/91	16/16
57	Woodard, Marc	6-0/234	2-21-70	2	Mississippi State	FA/93	16/0
	DEFENSIVE BACKS						
24	Barlow, Corey (CB)	5-9/182	11-1-70	3	Auburn	D5/92	0/0
25	Ellis, Jamal (CB)	5-10/192	6-21-72	R	Duke	FA/95	—
23	Frazier, Derrick (CB)	5-10/178	4-29-70	3	Texas A&M	D3/93	12/0
22	Goodwin, Marvin (S)	6-0/199	9-21-72	2	UCLA	D5/94	0/0
26	Henderson, Jerome (CB)	5-10/189	8-8-69	4	Clemson	FA/95	*12/0
47	Jackson, Greg (S)	6-1/210	8-20-66	7	Louisiana State	FA/94	16/16
2	Johnson, George (CB)	5-10/186	8-22-72	R	Bowling Green State	FA/95	—
29	McMillian, Mark (CB)	5-7/162	4-29-70	4	Alabama	D10/92	16/16
42	Reid, Mike (S)	6-1/218	11-24-70	3	North Carolina State	D3/93	3/0
21	Taylor, Bobby	6-3/208	12-28-73	R	Notre Dame	D2/95	—
48	Wilburn, Barry (CB)	6-2/190	12-9-63	7	Mississippi	FA/95	0/0
27	Zomalt, Eric (S)	5-11/197	8-9-72	2	California	D3/94	12/0
36	Zordich, Michael (S)	6-1/201	10-12-63	9	Penn State	FA/94	16/16
	SPECIALISTS						
17	Beckley, Jeff (P/K)	6-1/195	2-8-71	R	Boston College	FA/95	—
4	Hutton, Tom (P/K)	6-1/186	7-8-72	R	Tennessee	FA/95	—
3	Murray, Eddie (K)	5-11/195	8-29-56	16	Tulane	FA/94	16/0
14	Wilkins, Jeff (K)	6-1/180	4-19-72	2	Youngstown State	FA/94	6/0

*Gouveia played 14 games for Redskins in '94; Hall played 12 games for 49ers; Henderson played 12 games for Bills; Henesey played 3 games for Cardinals; R. Johnson played 9 games for Packers; Lewis played 6 games for Packers; McKenzie played 16 games for Redskins; Peete played 7 games for Cowboys; Sims played 15 games for Packers; Turner played 16 games for Patriots; Watters played 16 games for 49ers.

Also played with Eagles in '94: CB Eric Allen (16); WR Victor Bailey (16); P Bryan Barker (11); TE Mark Bavaro (12); P Mitch Berger (5); QB Bubby Brister (7); LB Byron Evans (10); DE Mike Flores (15); DE Burt Grossman (14); LB Britt Hager (16); CB Al Jackson (11); LB Vaughan Johnson (4); RB James Joseph (14); G Tom McHale (13); S Rich Miano (16); RB Brian O'Neal (14); DT William Perry (16); LB Ken Rose (16); G Rob Selby (2); CB Otis Smith (16); T Broderick Thompson (14); DE Greg Townsend (16); RB/KR Herschel Walker (16).

Abbreviations: D1—draft pick, first round; SupD2—supplemental draft pick, second round; W-Den—waivers acquisition from Denver; T-Sea—trade acquisition from Seattle; PlanB—Plan B free-agent acquisition; FA—free-agent acquisition (other than Plan B).

MISCELLANEOUS TEAM DATA

Stadium (capacity, surface):
Veterans Stadium
(64,889, artificial)
Business address:
3501 South Broad Street
Philadelphia, PA 19148
Business phone:
215-463-2500
Ticket information:
215-463-5500
Team colors:
Kelly green, silver and white
Flagship radio station:
WYSP, 94.1 FM
Training site:
West Chester University
West Chester, Pa.
215-463-2500

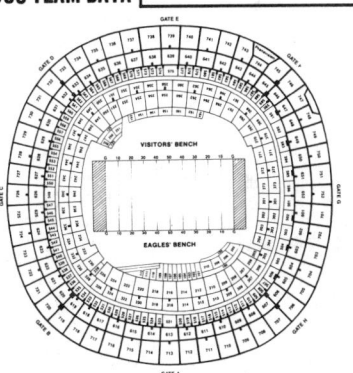

PITTSBURGH STEELERS
AFC CENTRAL DIVISION

1994 REVIEW

RESULTS

Sept. 4—DALLAS	L	9-26	
Sept. 11—at Cleveland	W	17-10	
Sept. 18—INDIANAPOLIS	W	31-21	
Sept. 25—at Seattle	L	13-30	
Oct. 3—HOUSTON	W	30-14	
Oct. 10—Open date			
Oct. 16—CINCINNATI	W	14-10	
Oct. 23—at N.Y. Giants	W	10-6	
Oct. 30—at Arizona (OT)	L	17-20	
Nov. 6—at Houston (OT)	W	12-9	
Nov. 14—BUFFALO	W	23-10	
Nov. 20—MIAMI (OT)	W	16-13	
Nov. 27—at L.A. Raiders	W	21-3	
Dec. 4—at Cincinnati	W	38-15	
Dec. 11—PHILADELPHIA	W	14-3	
Dec. 18—CLEVELAND	W	17-7	
Dec. 24—at San Diego	L	34-37	

RECORDS/RANKINGS

1994 regular-season record: 12-4 (1st in AFC Central); 6-0 in division; 10-2 in conference; 7-1 at home; 5-3 on road.
Team record last five years: 48-32 (.600, ranks 6th in league in that span).

1994 team rankings:

	No.	AFC	NFL
Total offense	*321.5	7	13
Rushing offense	*136.3	1	1
Passing offense	*185.3	11	23
Scoring offense	316	8	16
Total defense	*270.4	1	2
Rushing defense	*90.8	3	7
Passing defense	*179.6	2	3
Scoring defense	234	2	2
Takeaways	31	T6	T13
Giveaways	17	1	1
Turnover differential	14	1	1
Sacks	55	1	1
Sacks allowed	39	8	20

*Yards per game.

TEAM LEADERS

Scoring (kicking): Gary Anderson, 104 pts. (32/32 PATs, 24/29 FGs).
Scoring (touchdowns): Bam Morris 42 pts. (7 rushing).
Passing: Neil O'Donnell, 2,443 yds. (370 att., 212 comp., 57.3%, 13 TDs, 9 int.).
Rushing: Barry Foster, 851 yds. (216 att., 3.9 avg., 5 TDs).
Receptions: John L. Williams, 51 (378 yds., 7.4 avg., 2 TDs).
Interceptions: Darren Perry, 7 (112 yds., 0 TDs).
Sacks: Kevin Greene, 14.0.
Punting: Mark Royals, 39.7 avg. (97 punts, 3,849 yds., 0 blocked).
Punt returns: Rod Woodson, 8.2 avg. (39 att., 319 yds., 0 TDs).
Kickoff returns: Rod Woodson, 24.3 avg. (15 att., 365 yds., 0 TDs).

1995 SEASON

CLUB DIRECTORY

President
Daniel M. Rooney
Vice presidents
John R. McGinley
Arthur J. Rooney Jr.
Secretary and counsel
Arthur J. Rooney II
Administration advisor
Charles H. Noll
Director of communications
Joe Gordon
Assistant controllers
Dan Ferens
Jim Ellenberger
Ticket sales manager
Geraldine Glenn
Director of football operations
Tom Donahoe
Player relations
Anthony Griggs
Media relations director
Rob Boulware
Director of pro personnel
Tom Modrak
College scouting coordinator
Charles Bailey
College scouts
Phil Kriedler
Bob Lane
Max McCartney
Bob Schmitz

SCHEDULE

Sept. 3—DETROIT	1:00
Sept. 10—at Houston	12:00
Sept. 18—at Miami (Mon.)	9:00
Sept. 24—MINNESOTA	1:00
Oct. 1—SAN DIEGO	4:00
Oct. 8—at Jacksonville	1:00
Oct. 15—Open date	
Oct. 19—CINCINNATI (Thur.)	8:00
Oct. 29—JACKSONVILLE	1:00
Nov. 5—at Chicago	3:00
Nov. 13—CLEVELAND (Mon.)	9:00
Nov. 19—at Cincinnati	1:00
Nov. 26—at Cleveland	4:00
Dec. 3—HOUSTON	1:00
Dec. 10—at Los Angeles	1:00
Dec. 16—NEW ENG. (Sat.)	12:30
Dec. 24—at Green Bay	12:00

All times are for home team.
All games Sunday unless noted.

Head coach
Bill Cowher
Assistant coaches
Bobby April (special teams)
Dick LeBeau (def. coordinator)
Ron Erhardt (off. coordinator)
Chan Gailey (wide receivers)
Dick Hoak (running backs)
Pat Hodgson (tight ends)
Tim Lewis (defensive backs)
Marvin Lewis (linebackers)
John Mitchell (defensive line)
Kent Stephenson (offensive line)

Trainers
John Norwig
Rick Burkholder
Physicians
James P. Bradley
Richard Rydze
Abraham J. Twerski
Anthony P. Yates
Equipment manager
Anthony Parisi
Field manager
Rodgers Freyvogel
Video director
Bob McCartney
Video assistant
Pat Dolan
Photographer
Mike Fabus

DRAFT CHOICES

Mark Bruener, TE, Washington (first round/27th pick overall).
Kordell Stewart, QB, Colorado (2/60).
Brenden Stai, G, Nebraska (3/91).
Oliver Gibson, DE, Notre Dame (4/120).
Donta Jones, LB, Nebraska (4/125).
Lethon Flowers, DB, Georgia Tech (5/151).
Lance Brown, DB, Indiana (5/161).
Barron Miles, DB, Nebraska (6/199).
Henry Bailey, WR, UNLV (7/235).
Cole Ford, K, Southern California (7/247).

TRAINING CAMP ROSTER

No.	QUARTERBACKS	Ht./Wt.	Born	NFL Exp.	College	How acq.	'94 Games GP/GS
16	Miller, Jim	6-2/226	2-9-71	2	Michigan State	D6/94	0/0
14	O'Donnell, Neil	6-3/230	7-3-66	6	Maryland	D3/90	14/14
10	Stewart, Kordell	6-1/212	10-16-72	R	Colorado	D2/95	—
18	Tomczak, Mike	6-1/207	10-23-62	11	Ohio State	FA/93	6/2
	RUNNING BACKS						
43	Avery, Steve	6-2/233	8-18-66	2	Northern Michigan	FA/93	14/1
35	Coleman, LaMonte (FB)	5-10/227	6-24-71	R	Slippery Rock	FA/95	—
23	Daigle, Anthony	5-10/203	4-5-70	1	Fresno State	FA/94	1/0
25	McAfee, Fred	5-10/192	6-20-68	5	Mississippi College	FA/94	*13/0
33	Morris, Bam	6-0/235	1-13-72	2	Texas Tech	D3/94	15/6
9	Pegram, Erric	5-10/195	1-7-69	5	North Texas	FA/95	*13/5
44	Toner, Ed (FB)	6-0/245	3-22-68	4	Boston College	FA/95	*9/0
22	Williams, John L. (FB)	5-11/231	11-23-64	10	Florida	FA/94	15/12
	RECEIVERS						
19	Bailey, Henry (KR)	5-8/176	2-28-73	R	UNLV	D7/95	—
80	Barnes, Johnnie	6-1/185	7-21-68	4	Hampton (Va.)	FA/95	*11/0
46	Bruener, Mark (TE)	6-4/250	9-16-72	R	Washington	D1/95	—
17	Grant, Doug	5-8/171	2-7-68	R	Savannah (Ga.) State	FA/95	—
88	Hastings, Andre (KR)	6-0/190	11-7-70	3	Georgia	D3/93	16/8
85	Hayes, Jonathan (TE)	6-5/248	8-11-62	11	Iowa	FA/94	16/6
83	Holliday, Corey	6-2/208	1-31-71	1	North Carolina	FA/95	0/0
81	Johnson, Charles	6-0/189	1-3-72	2	Colorado	D1/94	16/9
87	Keith, Craig (TE)	6-3/264	4-27-71	3	Lenoir-Rhyne (N.C.)	D7/93	16/1
2	Mays, Damon	5-9/170	5-20-68	1	Missouri	FA/95	0/0
89	Mills, Ernie	5-11/192	10-28-68	5	Florida	D3/91	15/6
84	Rasby, Walter (TE)	6-3/247	9-7-72	2	Wake Forest	FA/94	2/0
82	Thigpen, Yancey	6-1/208	8-15-69	4	Winston-Salem State	FA/92	15/6
48	Thompson, Craig (TE)	6-2/244	1-13-69	3	North Carolina A&T	FA/95	0/0
	OFFENSIVE LINEMEN						
63	Dawson, Dermontti (C)	6-2/286	6-17-65	8	Kentucky	D2/88	16/16
60	Gammon, Kendall (C)	6-4/288	10-23-68	4	Pittsburg (Kan.) State	D11/92	16/0
71	Greene, Tirrell (G)	6-2/305	5-15-72	R	Miami (Fla.)	FA/95	—
61	Ingrassia, Anthony (T)	6-2/313	5-28-72	R	Florida	FA/95	—
65	Jackson, John (T)	6-6/297	1-4-65	8	Eastern Kentucky	D10/88	16/16
62	Kalis, Todd (G)	6-6/296	5-10-65	8	Arizona State	FA/94	11/11
64	Newberry, Tom (G)	6-2/285	12-20-62	10	Wisconsin-La Crosse	FA/95	*15/14
66	Palelei, Siulagi (G)	6-3/320	10-15-70	3	UNLV	D5/93	0/0
79	Parrish, James (T)	6-6/320	5-19-68	1	Temple	FA/95	0/0
72	Searcy, Leon (T)	6-3/304	12-21-69	4	Miami (Fla.)	D1/92	16/16
61	Simpson, Tim (G/C)	6-2/284	3-5-69	2	Illinois	FA/93	4/0
69	Solomon, Ariel (C/G)	6-5/290	7-16-68	5	Colorado	D10/91	16/0
68	Stai, Brenden (G)	6-4/305	3-30-72	R	Nebraska	D3/95	—
73	Strzelczyk, Justin (T/G)	6-6/295	8-18-68	6	Maine	D11/90	16/5
	DEFENSIVE LINEMEN						
61	Black, Greg (T)	6-4/306	9-14-73	R	North Carolina	FA/95	—
96	Buckner, Brentson (E)	6-2/305	9-30-71	2	Clemson	D2/94	13/5
98	Esters, Jeff (NT)	6-2/300	7-6-69	1	Pittsburgh	FA/95	—
78	Faumui, Ta'ase	6-3/278	3-19-71	2	Hawaii	D4/94	5/0
74	Gibson, Oliver (T)	6-2/283	3-15-72	R	Notre Dame	D4/95	—
76	Henry, Kevin (E)	6-4/270	10-23-68	3	Mississippi State	D4/93	16/5
76	Holden, Germaine (E)	6-3/268	1-17-73	R	Notre Dame	FA/95	—
97	Seals, Ray (E)	6-3/309	6-17-65	8	None	FA/94	13/11
93	Steed, Joel (NT)	6-2/295	2-17-69	4	Colorado	D3/92	16/16
90	Zgonina, Jeff (T)	6-1/287	5-24-70	3	Purdue	D7/93	16/0
	LINEBACKERS						
94	Brown, Chad	6-2/236	7-12-70	3	Colorado	D2/93	16/16
92	Gildon, Jason	6-3/237	7-31-72	2	Oklahoma State	D3/94	16/1
91	Greene, Kevin	6-3/247	7-31-62	11	Auburn	FA/93	16/16
54	Jones, Donta	6-2/226	8-27-72	R	Nebraska	D4/95	—
99	Kirkland, Levon	6-1/252	2-17-69	4	Clemson	D2/92	16/15
95	Lloyd, Greg	6-2/226	5-26-65	9	Fort Valley (Ga.) State	D6/87	15/15
56	Mack, Rico	6-4/242	2-22-71	3	Appalachian State	FA/93	0/0
55	Olsavsky, Jerry	6-1/221	3-29-67	7	Pittsburgh	D10/89	1/0
57	Ravotti, Eric	6-3/254	3-16-71	2	Penn State	D6/94	2/0
51	Robinson, Ed	6-0/228	12-7-70	2	Florida	FA/94	16/0
	DEFENSIVE BACKS						
40	Bell, Myron (S)	5-11/203	9-15-71	2	Michigan State	D5/94	15/0
45	Brown, Lance (S)	6-0/200	2-2-72	R	Indiana	D5/95	—

No.	DEFENSIVE BACKS	Ht./Wt.	Born	NFL Exp.	College	How acq.	'94 Games GP/GS
47	Ellis, Joey	5-8/194	4-6-73	R	Texas	FA/95	—
21	Figures, Deon (CB)	6-0/203	1-10-70	3	Colorado	D1/93	16/15
41	Flowers, Lethon (CB)	6-0/202	1-14-73	R	Georgia Tech	D5/95	—
37	Lake, Carnell (S)	6-1/210	7-15-67	7	UCLA	D2/89	16/16
	Mays, Alvoid (CB)	5-9/172	7-10-66	6	West Virginia	FA/95	*2/0
49	Miles, Barron (CB)	5-8/165	1-1-72	R	Nebraska	D6/95	—
24	Oldham, Chris (CB)	5-9/183	10-26-68	4	Oregon	FA/95	*11/1
36	Patillo, Tim	5-10/179	5-24-72	R	Ohio State	FA/95	—
39	Perry, Darren (S)	5-11/196	12-29-68	4	Penn State	D8/92	16/16
27	Williams, Willie (CB)	5-9/185	12-26-70	3	Western Carolina	D6/93	16/1
26	Woodson, Rod (CB/KR)	6-0/200	3-10-65	9	Purdue	D1/87	15/15
	SPECIALISTS						
1	Anderson, Gary (K)	5-11/179	7-16-59	14	Syracuse	W-Buf/82	16/0
4	Ford, Cole (K)	6-2/195	12-31-72	R	Southern California	D7/95	—
3	Stark, Rohn (P)	6-3/203	5-4-59	14	Florida State	FA/95	*16/0
5	Stewart, Ty (K)	5-11/194	9-13-71	R	Iowa State	FA/95	—

*Barnes played 11 games with Chargers in '94; Mays played 2 games with Redskins; McAfee played 7 games with Cardinals and 6 with Steelers; Newberry played 15 games with Rams; Oldham played 11 games with Cardinals; Pegram played 13 games with Falcons; Stark played 16 games with Colts; Toner played 9 games with Colts.

Also played with Steelers in '94: LB Reggie Clark (5); RB Randy Cuthbert (1); WR Charles Davenport (7); DB Fred Foggie (3); RB Barry Foster (11); TE Eric Green (15); WR John Jackson (16); FB Victor Jones (14); S Gary Jones (14); G Duval Love (16); CB Tim McKyer (16); P Mark Royals (16); WR Dwight Stone (15); DE Gerald Williams (11).

Abbreviations: D1—draft pick, first round; SupD2—supplemental draft pick, second round; W-Den—waivers acquisition from Denver; T-Sea—trade acquisition from Seattle; PlanB—Plan B free-agent acquisition; FA—free-agent acquisition (other than Plan B).

MISCELLANEOUS TEAM DATA

Stadium (capacity, surface):
  Three Rivers Stadium
    (59,600, artificial)
Business address:
  300 Stadium Circle
  Pittsburgh, PA 15212
Business phone:
  412-323-1200
Ticket information:
  412-323-1200
Team colors:
  Black and gold
Flagship radio station:
  WTAE, 1250 AM
Training site:
  St. Vincent College
  Latrobe, Pa.
  412-539-8515

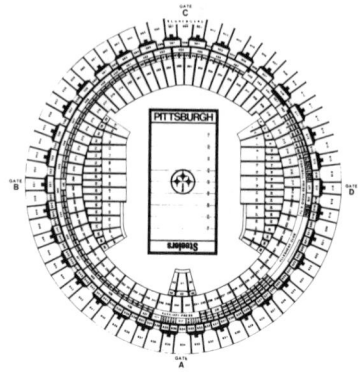

ST. LOUIS RAMS
NFC WESTERN DIVISION

1994 REVIEW

RESULTS

Sept. 4—ARIZONA	W	14-12
Sept. 11—at Atlanta	L	13-31
Sept. 18—SAN FRANCISCO	L	19-34
Sept. 25—at Kansas City	W	16-0
Oct. 2—ATLANTA	L	5-8
Oct. 9—at Green Bay	L	17-24
Oct. 16—N.Y. GIANTS	W	17-10
Oct. 23—at New Orleans	L	34-37
Oct. 30—Open date		
Nov. 6—DENVER	W	27-21
Nov. 13—L.A. RAIDERS	L	17-20
Nov. 20—at San Francisco	L	27-31
Nov. 27—at San Diego	L	17-31
Dec. 4—NEW ORLEANS	L	15-31
Dec. 11—at Tampa Bay	L	14-24
Dec. 18—at Chicago	L	13-27
Dec. 24—WASHINGTON	L	21-24

RECORDS/RANKINGS

1994 regular-season record: 4-12 (4th in NFC West); 0-6 in division; 2-10 in conference; 3-5 at home; 1-7 on road.
Team record last five years: 23-57 (.288, ranks T27th in league in that span).

1994 team rankings:	No.	NFC	NFL
Total offense	*296.7	11	21
Rushing offense	*86.8	12	25
Passing offense	*209.9	9	15
Scoring offense	286	10	21
Total defense	*323.1	9	16
Rushing defense	*111.3	10	20
Passing defense	*211.8	7	12
Scoring defense	365	11	23
Takeaways	20	14	27
Giveaways	31	10	T16
Turnover differential	-11	13	25
Sacks	26	T12	T24
Sacks allowed	35	T10	T17

*Yards per game.

TEAM LEADERS

Scoring (kicking): Tony Zendejas, 82 pts. (28/28 PATs, 18/23 FGs).
Scoring (touchdowns): Troy Drayton, 36 pts. (6 receiving).
Passing: Chris Miller, 2,104 yds. (317 att., 173 comp., 54.6%, 16 TDs, 14 int.).
Rushing: Jerome Bettis, 1,025 yds. (319 att., 3.2 avg., 3 TDs).
Receptions: Johnny Bailey, 58 (516 yds., 8.9 avg., 0 TDs).
Interceptions: Darryl Henley, 3 (46 yds., 0 TDs); Marquez Pope, 3 (66 yds., 0 TDs).
Sacks: Robert Young, 6.5.
Punting: Sean Landeta, 44.8 avg. (78 punts, 3,494 yds., 0 blocked).
Punt returns: Todd Kinchen, 9.9 avg. (16 att., 158 yds., 0 TDs).
Kickoff returns: Todd Kinchen, 24.3 avg. (21 att., 510 yds., 0 TDs).

1995 SEASON

CLUB DIRECTORY

Owner/chairman
Georgia Frontiere
President
John Shaw
Senior vice president
Jay Zygmunt
V.P./football operations
Steve Ortmayer
V.P./media and community relations
Marshall Klein
Ticket manager
Don Nims
Director of operations
John Oswald
Director/public relations
Rick Smith
Asst. director/public relations
Tony Wyllie
Director/player relations
Paul (Tank) Younger
Director/player personnel
John Becker
Entertainment coordinator
Tom Guthrie
Director/suite sales
Pete Donovan
Scouts
Lawrence McCutcheon
David Razzano
Pete Russell
Harley Sewell
Frank Trump
Trainers
Jim Anderson
Assistant trainer
Dake Walden

Head coach
Rich Brooks
Assistant coaches
Nick Aliotti (safeties)
Steve Brown (defensive assistant/quality control)
Chris Clausen (strength and conditioning)
Steve Greatwood (asst. offensive line/tight ends)
Mike Martz (receivers)
Don "Deek" Pollard (def. line)
Dan Radakovich (off. line)
John Ramsdell (offensive assistant/quality control)
Jack Reilly (offensive coordinator/quarterbacks)
Johnny Roland (asst. head coach/running backs)
Dick Selcer (linebackers)
Wayne Sevier (special teams)
Willie Shaw (defensive coordinator/cornerbacks)

Physician
Clarence Shields
Senior equipment manager
Don Hewitt
Equipment manager
Todd Hewitt
Video director
Mickey Dukich

SCHEDULE

Sept. 3—at Green Bay	12:00
Sept. 10—NEW ORLEANS	12:00
Sept. 17—at Carolina	1:00
Sept. 24—CHICAGO	12:00
Oct. 1—at Indianapolis	12:00
Oct. 8—Open date	
Oct. 12—ATLANTA (Thur.)	7:00
Oct. 22—SAN FRANCISCO	3:00
Oct. 29—at Philadelphia	1:00
Nov. 5—at New Orleans	12:00
Nov. 12—CAROLINA	12:00
Nov. 19—at Atlanta	1:00
Nov. 26—at San Francisco	1:00
Dec. 3—at N.Y. Jets	1:00
Dec. 10—BUFFALO	12:00
Dec. 17—WASHINGTON	12:00
Dec. 24—MIAMI	3:00

All times are for home team.
All games Sunday unless noted.

DRAFT CHOICES

Kevin Carter, DE, Florida (first round/sixth pick overall).
Zach Wiegert, T, Nebraska (2/38).
Jesse James, G, Mississippi State (2/62).
Steve McLaughlin, K, Arizona (3/82).
Lovell Pinkney, TE, Texas (4/115).
Mike Scurlock, DB, Arizona (5/140).
Gerald McBurrows, DB, Kansas (7/214).
Herman O'Berry, DB, Oregon (7/220).
Bronzell Miller, DE, Utah (7/239).
Johnny Thomas, WR, Arizona St. (7/240).

1995 SEASON

TRAINING CAMP ROSTER

No.	QUARTERBACKS	Ht./Wt.	Born	NFL Exp.	College	How acq.	'94 Games GP/GS
8	Maddox, Tommy	6-4/205	9-2-71	4	UCLA	T-Den/94	5/0
9	Martin, Jamie	6-2/215	2-8-70	2	Weber State	FA/94	0/0
12	Miller, Chris	6-2/212	8-9-65	9	Oregon	FA/94	13/10
4	Morris, Cree	6-7/230	12-17-70	R	St. Mary's (Calif.)	FA/95	—
	Rypien, Mark	6-4/234	10-2-62	9	Washington State	FA/95	*6/3
	RUNNING BACKS						
21	Bailey, Johnny (KR)	5-8/180	3-17-67	6	Texas A&I	FA/94	14/0
36	Bettis, Jerome	5-11/243	2-16-72	3	Notre Dame	D1/93	16/16
33	Bostic, James	5-11/230	3-13-72	2	Auburn	D3/94	0/0
43	Gary, Cleveland	6-0/226	5-4-66	7	Miami (Fla.)	FA/95	*2/0
34	Lester, Tim (FB)	5-9/215	6-15-68	4	Eastern Kentucky	D10/92	14/4
	Russell, Leonard	6-2/235	11-17-69	5	Arizona State	FA/95	*14/13
	RECEIVERS						
83	Brady, Rickey (TE)	6-4/246	11-19-70	1	Oklahoma	D6/94	1/0
88	Brantley, Chris (KR)	5-10/180	12-12-70	2	Rutgers	D4/94	15/0
45	Brooks, Steve (TE)	6-5/245	6-2-71	1	Occidental (Calif.)	FA/95	0/0
80	Bruce, Isaac	6-0/178	11-10-72	2	Memphis	D2/94	12/0
	Cook, Marv (TE)	6-4/234	2-4-66	7	Iowa	FA/95	*16/8
84	Drayton, Troy (TE)	6-3/255	6-29-70	3	Penn State	D2/93	16/16
86	Hester, Jessie	5-11/175	1-21-63	10	Florida State	FA/94	16/15
49	Jackson, Yonnie (TE)	6-2/260	2-28-71	1	Southern California	FA/95	0/0
81	Kinchen, Todd (KR)	5-11/187	1-7-69	4	Louisiana State	D3/92	13/0
17	Pinkney, Lovell (TE)	6-4/248	8-18-72	R	Texas	D4/95	—
48	Price, Jim (TE)	6-4/247	10-2-66	4	Stanford	FA/95	0/0
82	Ross, Jermaine	5-11/192	4-27-71	1	Purdue	FA/94	4/0
18	Thomas, Johnny	5-10/173	12-15-71	R	Arizona State	D7/95	—
89	Wright, Alexander	6-0/195	7-19-67	6	Auburn	FA/95	*16/15
	OFFENSIVE LINEMEN						
77	Ashmore, Darryl (T)	6-7/300	11-1-69	4	Northwestern	D7/92	11/3
71	Belin, Chuck (G)	6-2/312	10-27-70	3	Wisconsin	D5/93	14/6
61	Brostek, Bern (C)	6-3/300	9-11-66	6	Washington	D1/90	10/10
67	Edwards, Ron (T)	6-5/311	9-18-71	2	North Carolina A&T	D6/94	0/0
70	Gandy, Wayne (T)	6-4/289	2-10-71	2	Auburn	D1/94	16/9
79	Goeas, Leo (G/T)	6-4/300	8-15-66	6	Hawaii	T-SD/93	13/13
69	James, Jesse	6-4/318	9-16-71	R	Mississippi State	D2b/95	—
72	Jones, Clarence (T)	6-6/280	5-6-68	5	Maryland	FA/94	16/16
64	Loneker, Keith (G)	6-3/330	6-21-71	3	Kansas	FA/93	2/2
62	Patterson, Roosevelt (G)	6-3/310	7-12-70	1	Alabama	FA/94	0/0
78	Slater, Jackie (T)	6-4/285	5-27-54	20	Jackson State	D3/76	12/7
68	White, Dwayne (G)	6-2/315	2-10-67	6	Alcorn State	FA/95	*16/16
73	Wiegert, Zach (T)	6-4/311	8-16-72	R	Nebraska	D2a/95	—
63	Zeno, Lance (G)	6-4/279	4-15-67	3	UCLA	FA/95	0/0
	DEFENSIVE LINEMEN						
93	Carter, Kevin (E)	6-5/274	9-21-73	R	Florida	D1/95	—
75	Farr, D'Marco (T)	6-1/270	6-9-71	2	Washington	FA/94	10/3
90	Gilbert, Sean (T)	6-4/315	4-10-70	4	Pittsburgh	D1/92	14/14
94	Jones, Ernest (E)	6-2/270	4-1-71	2	Oregon	D3/94	0/0
98	Jones, Jimmie (T)	6-4/276	1-9-66	6	Miami (Fla.)	FA/94	14/14
91	McCants, Keith (E)	6-3/265	4-19-68	6	Alabama	FA/95	12/2
99	Miller, Bronzell (E)	6-3/247	10-12-71	R	Utah	D7/95	—
95	Ottis, Brad (E)	6-4/272	8-2-72	2	Wayne State (Neb.)	D2/94	13/0
97	Robinson, Gerald (E)	6-3/280	5-4-63	8	Auburn	PlanB/91	13/0
92	Rocker, David (T)	6-4/267	3-12-69	5	Auburn	FA/91	11/1
60	Stokes, Fred (E)	6-3/274	3-14-64	9	Georgia Southern	FA/93	16/15
96	Williams, Jay (E)	6-3/266	10-13-71	1	Wake Forest	FA/94	—
76	Young, Robert (E)	6-6/273	1-29-69	5	Mississippi State	D5/91	16/16
	LINEBACKERS						
56	Conlan, Shane	6-3/235	3-4-64	9	Penn State	FA/93	15/15
57	Homco, Thomas	6-0/245	1-8-70	3	Northwestern	FA/92	15/0
51	Jenkins, Carlos	6-3/217	7-12-68	5	Michigan State	FA/95	*16/16
52	Kelly, Joe	6-2/235	12-11-64	10	Washington	FA/94	16/14
58	Phifer, Roman	6-2/230	3-5-68	5	UCLA	D2/91	16/15
59	Rolling, Henry	6-2/225	9-8-65	9	Nevada	FA/93	9/2
	DEFENSIVE BACKS						
28	Bailey, Robert (CB)	5-9/176	9-3-68	5	Miami (Fla.)	D4/91	16/2
29	Davis, Dexter (CB)	5-10/184	3-20-70	5	Clemson	FA/93	4/0
46	Dorn, Torin (CB)	6-0/190	2-29-68	5	North Carolina	FA/95	0/0
31	Israel, Steve (CB)	5-11/186	3-16-69	4	Pittsburgh	D2/92	10/2

No.	DEFENSIVE BACKS	Ht./Wt.	Born	NFL Exp.	College	How acq.	'94 Games GP/GS
25	Kors, R.J. (S)	6-0/200	6-27-66	4	Long Beach State	FA/95	0/0
41	Lyght, Todd (CB)	6-0/186	2-9-69	5	Notre Dame	D1/91	16/16
35	Lyle, Keith (S)	6-2/204	4-17-72	2	Virginia	D3/94	16/0
23	McBurrows, Gerald	5-11/188	10-7-73	R	Kansas	D7/95	—
26	Newman, Anthony (S)	6-0/199	11-21-65	8	Oregon	D2/88	16/14
24	O'Berry, Herman (CB)	5-9/195	7-11-71	R	Oregon	D7/95	—
27	Parker, Anthony (CB)	5-10/181	2-11-66	6	Arizona State	FA/95	*15/15
22	Scurlock, Mike	5-10/197	2-26-72	R	Arizona	D5/95	—
32	Wright, Toby (S)	5-11/203	11-19-70	2	Nebraska	D2/94	16/2
	SPECIALISTS						
5	Landeta, Sean (P)	6-0/210	1-6-62	11	Towson State	FA/93	16/0
3	McLaughlin, Steve (K)	6-0/167	10-2-71	R	Arizona	D3/95	—
11	Zendejas, Tony (K)	5-8/165	5-15-60	11	Nevada	PlanB/91	16/0

*Cook played 16 games with Bears in '94; Gary played 2 games with Dolphins; Jenkins played 16 games with Vikings; Parker played 15 games with Vikings; Russell played 14 games with Broncos; Rypien played 6 games with Browns; White played 16 games with Jets; Wright played 16 games with Raiders.

Also played with Rams in '94: WR Willie Anderson (16); WR Richard Buchanan (3); C Blair Bush (16); QB Chris Chandler (12); LB Brett Collins (2); C Brad Fichtel (1); RB Howard Griffith (16); CB Wymon Henderson (15); CB Darryl Henley (15); RB David Lang (13); LB Chris Martin (14); TE Ron Middleton (16); G Tom Newberry (15); DB Marquez Pope (16).

Abbreviations: D1—draft pick, first round; SupD2—supplemental draft pick, second round; W-Den—waivers acquisition from Denver; T-Sea—trade acquisition from Seattle; PlanB—Plan B free-agent acquisition; FA—free-agent acquisition (other than Plan B).

MISCELLANEOUS TEAM DATA

Stadium (capacity, surface):
Busch Stadium (artificial)
New domed facility (artificial)
Business address:
To be announced
Business phone:
To be announced
Ticket information:
To be announced
Team colors:
Royal blue, gold and white
Flagship radio station:
KSD, 550 AM
Training site:
Mathews-Dickey Boys Club
St. Louis

NOTE: A stadium diagram was not available at deadline. The Rams will play their first few games at Busch Stadium before moving into an indoor facility that is expected to be completed near the end of October.

SAN DIEGO CHARGERS
AFC WESTERN DIVISION

1994 REVIEW

RESULTS

Sept. 4—at Denver	W	37-34
Sept. 11—CINCINNATI	W	27-10
Sept. 18—at Seattle	W	24-10
Sept. 25—at L.A. Raiders	W	26-24
Oct. 2—Open date		
Oct. 9—KANSAS CITY	W	20-6
Oct. 16—at New Orleans	W	36-22
Oct. 23—DENVER	L	15-20
Oct. 30—SEATTLE	W	35-15
Nov. 6—at Atlanta	L	9-10
Nov. 13—at Kansas City	W	14-13
Nov. 20—at New England	L	17-23
Nov. 27—L.A. RAMS	W	31-17
Dec. 5—L.A. RAIDERS	L	17-24
Dec. 11—SAN FRANCISCO	L	15-38
Dec. 18—at N.Y. Jets	W	21-6
Dec. 24—PITTSBURGH	W	37-34

RECORDS/RANKINGS

1994 regular-season record: 11-5 (1st in AFC West); 6-2 in division; 9-3 in conference; 5-3 at home; 6-2 on road.
Team record last five years: 40-40 (.500), ranks T 16th in league in that span).
1994 team rankings:

	No.	AFC	NFL
Total offense	*326.3	6	11
Rushing offense	*115.8	4	7
Passing offense	*210.5	6	T 12
Scoring offense	381	2	5
Total defense	*316.4	6	14
Rushing defense	*87.8	1	5
Passing defense	*228.6	10	22
Scoring defense	306	4	9
Takeaways	32	T4	T 10
Giveaways	23	2	T3
Turnover differential	9	4	T6
Sacks	43	2	3
Sacks allowed	29	7	12

*Yards per game.

TEAM LEADERS

Scoring (kicking): John Carney, 135 pts. (33/33 PATs, 34/38 FGs).
Scoring (touchdowns): Natrone Means, 72 pts. (12 rushing).
Passing: Stan Humphries, 3,209 yds. (453 att., 264 comp., 58.3%, 17 TDs, 12 int.).
Rushing: Natrone Means, 1,350 yds. (343 att., 3.9 avg., 12 TDs).
Receptions: Ronnie Harmon, 58 (615 yds., 10.6 avg., 1 TD).
Interceptions: Darrien Gordon, 4 (32 yds., 0 TDs); Stanley Richard, 4 (224 yds., 2 TDs).
Sacks: Leslie O'Neal, 12.5.
Punting: Bryan Wagner, 41.6 avg. (65 punts, 2,705 yds., 0 blocked).
Punt returns: Darrien Gordon, 13.2 avg. (36 att., 475 yds., 2 TDs).
Kickoff returns: Andre Coleman, 26.4 avg. (49 att., 1,293 yds., 2 TDs).

1995 SEASON

CLUB DIRECTORY

Chairman of the board
Alex G. Spanos
President/vice chairman
Dean A. Spanos
General manager
Bobby Beathard
Assistant to general manager
Dick Daniels
Business manager
John Hinek
Director/marketing
Richard V. Israel
Director/ticket operations
Ron Tuck
Vice president/finance
Jeremiah T. Murphy
Chief financial officer
Jeanne Bonk
Director/public relations
Bill Johnston
Asst. director, public relations
David Neville
Marketing manager
Paul Restelli
Ticket marketing manager
Sean O'Connor
Director/player personnel
Billy Devaney
Director/pro personnel
Rudy Feldman
Director/security
Dick Lewis
Coordinator/football operations
Marty Hurney

SCHEDULE

Sept. 3—at Los Angeles	1:00	
Sept. 10—SEATTLE	1:00	
Sept. 17—at Philadelphia	1:00	
Sept. 24—DENVER	1:00	
Oct. 1—at Pittsburgh	4:00	
Oct. 9—at Kansas City (Mon.)	8:00	
Oct. 15—DALLAS	1:00	
Oct. 22—at Seattle	1:00	
Oct. 29—Open date		
Nov. 5—MIAMI	5:00	
Nov. 12—KANSAS CITY	1:00	
Nov. 19—at Denver	2:00	
Nov. 27—LOS ANGELES (Mon.)	6:00	
Dec. 3—CLEVELAND	1:00	
Dec. 9—ARIZONA (Sat.)	1:00	
Dec. 17—at Indianapolis	4:00	
Dec. 23—at N.Y. Giants (Sat.)	12:30	

All times are for home team.
All games Sunday unless noted.

CLUB DIRECTORY (continued)

Head coach:
Bobby Ross
Assistant coaches
Dave Adolph (defensive coordinator)
Greg Brown (secondary)
Sylvester Croom (offensive backs)
John Dunn (strength and conditioning)
Frank Falks (tight ends/H-backs)
Ralph Friedgen (offensive coordinator)
John Hastings (strength and conditioning assistant)
Stan Kwan (offense and special teams assistant)
Dale Lindsey (linebackers)
Carl Mauck (offensive line)
John Misciagna (quality control)
Dennis Murphy (defensive line)
Kevin O'Dea (defense assistant)
Dwain Painter (quarterbacks/passing game coordinator)
Chuck Priefer (special teams)
Jerry Sullivan (wide receivers)

Trainer
Keoki Kamau
Equipment manager
Sid Brooks
Director/video operations
Gene B. Leff

DRAFT CHOICES

Terrance Shaw, DB, Stephen F. Austin St. (second round/34th pick overall).
Terrell Fletcher, RB, Wisconsin (2/51).
Jimmy Oliver, WR, Texas Christian (2/61).
Don Sasa, DT, Washington State (3/93).
Preston Harrison, LB, Ohio State (3/98).
Chris Cowart, LB, Florida State (4/100).
Aaron Hayden, RB, Tennessee (4/104).
'OMar Ellison, WR, Florida State (5/162).
Troy Sienkiewicz, G, New Mexico State (6/177).
Brandon Harrison, WR, Howard Payne (Tex.) (6/183).
Craig Whelihan, QB, Pacific (6/197).
Tony Berti, T, Colorado (6/200).
Mark Montreuil, DB, Concordia (Canada) (7/237).

TRAINING CAMP ROSTER

No.	QUARTERBACKS	Ht./Wt.	Born	NFL Exp.	College	How acq.	'94 Games GP/GS
11	Brohm, Jeff	6-1/200	4-24-71	2	Louisville	FA/95	0/0
13	Gilbert, Gale	6-3/209	12-20-61	10	California	FA/94	15/1
12	Humphries, Stan	6-2/223	4-14-65	8	Northeast Louisiana	T-Was/92	15/15
5	Whelihan, Craig	6-5/204	4-15-71	R	Pacific	D6c/95	—
	RUNNING BACKS						
42	Brown, Charlie	5-9/200	10-22-71	R	Utah	FA/95	—
22	Culver, Rodney	5-9/224	12-23-69	4	Notre Dame	W-Ind/94	3/0
41	Fletcher, Terrell	5-8/196	9-14-73	R	Wisconsin	D2/95	—
33	Harmon, Ronnie	5-11/207	5-7-64	10	Iowa	PlanB/90	16/0
24	Hayden, Aaron	6-0/218	4-13-73	R	Tennessee	D4/95	—
47	Kahl, Kent	6-1/217	9-21-71	R	Iowa	FA/95	—
20	Means, Natrone	5-10/245	4-26-72	3	North Carolina	D2/93	16/16
35	Vinson, Tony	6-1/229	3-13-71	1	Towson State	FA/95	0/0
	RECEIVERS						
83	Coleman, Andre (KR)	5-9/165	1-18-71	2	Kansas State	D3a/94	13/0
15	Ellison, 'OMar	6-0/200	10-8-71	R	Florida State	D5/95	—
16	Harrison, Brandon	5-10/181	9-10-71	R	Howard Payne (Tex.)	D6b/95	—
80	Jefferson, Shawn	5-11/180	2-22-69	5	Central Florida	T-Hou/91	16/16
46	Harrell, Maurice (TE)	6-4/245	4-10-72	R	Georgia	FA/95	—
84	Laing, Aaron (TE)	6-3/264	7-19-71	2	New Mexico State	D5a/94	5/1
81	Martin, Tony	6-0/181	9-5-65	6	Mesa State (Colo.)	T-Mia/94	16/1
88	May, Deems (TE)	6-4/263	3-6-69	4	North Carolina	D7/92	5/2
89	Mitchell, Shannon (TE)	6-2/245	3-28-72	2	Georgia	FA/94	16/6
85	Oliver, Jimmy	5-10/173	1-30-73	R	Texas Christian	D2/95	—
86	Pupunu, Alfred (TE)	6-2/265	10-17-69	4	Weber State	W-KC/92	13/10
82	Seay, Mark	6-0/175	4-11-67	4	Long Beach State	W-SF/93	16/14
10	Thymes, Derrick	5-11/180	1-14-72	R	Louisiana State	FA/95	—
17	Watkins, Michael	5-9/173	12-28-71	R	Northeast Louisiana	FA/95	—
87	Young, Duane (TE)	6-1/270	5-29-68	5	Michigan State	D5/91	14/14
	OFFENSIVE LINEMEN						
61	Bertl, Tony (T)	6-5/287	6-21-72	R	Colorado	D6d/95	—
67	Brock, Stan (T)	6-6/295	6-8-58	16	Colorado	FA/95	0/0
62	Cavil, Ben (G)	6-2/310	1-31-72	R	Oklahoma	FA/95	—
68	Cocozzo, Joe (G)	6-4/300	8-7-70	3	Michigan	D3/93	13/13
73	Davis, Isaac (G)	6-3/320	4-8-72	2	Arkansas	D2/94	13/2
60	Engel, Greg (C)	6-3/285	1-18-71	2	Illinois	FA/95	0/0
66	Greene, Earnest (T)	6-5/308	2-25-71	1	Savannah (Ga.) State	FA/95	0/0
53	Hall, Courtney (C)	6-2/281	8-26-68	7	Rice	D2a/89	15/15
74	Jonassen, Eric (T/G)	6-5/310	8-16-68	4	Bloomsburg (Pa.)	D5c/92	16/0
77	Moten, Eric (G/T)	6-2/306	4-11-68	5	Michigan State	D2/91	0/0
70	Parker, Vaughn (G/T)	6-3/296	6-5-71	2	UCLA	D2b/94	6/0
65	Sienkiewicz, Troy (T)	6-4/300	5-27-72	R	New Mexico State	D6a/95	—
64	Slovacek, Gerald (C)	6-1/282	6-26-72	R	New Mexico State	FA/95	—
72	Swayne, Harry (T)	6-5/295	2-2-65	9	Rutgers	PlanB/91	16/16
75	Vander Poel, Mark (T)	6-7/303	3-5-68	5	Colorado	FA/95	0/0
	DEFENSIVE LINEMEN						
69	Campbell, David (T)	6-0/280	1-16-73	R	Oklahoma	FA/95	—
93	Davis, Reuben (T)	6-5/320	5-7-65	8	North Carolina	FA/94	16/16
76	Edwards, Vernon (E)	6-4/255	6-23-72	R	Southern Methodist	FA/95	—
95	Huzzie, Tracy (T)	6-4/300	5-24-70	R	Georgia	FA/95	—
99	Johnson, Raylee (E)	6-3/265	6-1-70	3	Arkansas	D4a/93	15/0
98	Lee, Shawn (T)	6-2/300	10-24-66	8	North Alabama	FA/92	15/15
94	Mims, Chris (E)	6-5/290	9-29-70	4	Tennessee	D1/92	16/16
91	O'Neal, Leslie (E)	6-4/265	5-7-64	10	Oklahoma State	D1a/86	16/16
90	Parker, Riddick (T)	6-3/274	11-20-72	R	North Carolina	FA/95	—
97	Parrella, John (T)	6-3/290	11-22-69	3	Nebraska	FA/94	13/1
96	Sasa, Don (T)	6-3/286	9-16-72	R	Washington State	D3/95	—
78	Simon, Damon (E)	6-5/251	6-16-70	R	Missouri	FA/95	—
79	Thomas, Cornell (E)	6-3/270	11-11-72	2	West Georgia	FA/94	0/0
	LINEBACKERS						
96	Beehn, Zane	6-4/252	9-28-71	R	Kentucky	D7/94	—
50	Binn, Dave	6-3/240	2-6-72	2	California	FA/94	16/0
58	Bush, Lewis	6-2/245	12-2-69	3	Washington State	D4b/93	16/0
54	Cowart, Chris	6-2/232	6-14-71	R	Florida State	D4/95	—
57	Gibson, Dennis	6-2/240	2-8-64	9	Iowa State	FA/94	16/15
92	Griggs, David	6-3/250	2-5-67	7	Virginia	FA/94	16/15
51	Harrison, Preston	6-4/243	9-14-71	R	Ohio State	D3/95	—
56	Krein, Darren	6-4/272	7-7-71	1	Miami (Fla.)	D5c/94	0/0

SAN DIEGO CHARGERS 1995 SEASON SAN DIEGO CHARGERS

No.	LINEBACKERS	Ht./Wt.	Born	NFL Exp.	College	How acq.	'94 Games GP/GS
52	Proctor, Basil	6-3/243	10-6-67	1	West Virginia	FA/95	0/0
55	Seau, Junior	6-3/250	1-19-69	6	Southern California	D1/90	16/16
59	Young, Glen	6-3/235	5-2-69	1	Syracuse	FA/94	0/0
	DEFENSIVE BACKS						
25	Allred, Brian (CB)	5-10/180	3-16-69	2	Sacramento State	FA/95	0/0
44	Castle, Eric (S)	6-3/212	3-15-70	3	Oregon	D6/93	16/1
31	Clark, Willie (CB)	5-10/186	1-6-72	2	Notre Dame	D3b/94	6/0
23	Gayle, Shaun (S)	5-11/202	3-8-62	12	Ohio State	FA/95	*16/16
21	Gordon, Darrien (CB)	5-11/182	11-14-70	3	Stanford	D1/93	16/16
28	Harper, Dwayne (CB)	5-11/175	3-29-66	8	South Carolina State	FA/94	16/16
37	Harrison, Rodney (S)	6-0/201	12-15-72	2	Western Illinois	D5b/94	15/0
38	Hendrix, David (S)	6-1/213	5-29-72	R	Georgia Tech	FA/95	—
36	Holland, Melvin (S)	6-2/180	9-2-72	R	Florida State	FA/95	—
48	Montgomery, Bill (S)	6-0/186	12-23-70	R	Georgia	FA/95	—
40	Montreuil, Mark (CB)	6-2/200	12-29-71	R	Concordia, Canada	D7/95	—
26	Orlando, Bo (S)	5-10/180	4-3-66	6	West Virginia	FA/95	*16/0
27	Pool, David (CB)	5-9/184	12-20-66	5	Carson-Newman	FA/95	*1/0
35	Shaw, Terrance (CB)	5-11/189	11-11-73	R	Stephen F. Austin State	D2/95	—
	SPECIALISTS						
4	Araguz, Leo (P)	6-0/185	1-18-70	1	Stephen F. Austin State	FA/95	0/0
2	Bennett, Darren (P)	6-5/235	1-9-65	1	None	FA/95	0/0
3	Carney, John (K)	5-11/170	4-20-64	7	Notre Dame	FA/90	16/0

*Gayle played 16 games with Bears in '94; Orlando played 16 games with Oilers; Pool played 1 game with Dolphins.

Also played with Chargers in '94: WR Johnnie Barnes (11); RB Eric Bieniemy (16); S Darren Carrington (16); RB Steve Hendrickson (16); P John Kidd (2); G Joe Milinichik (16); DE/NT Les Miller (4); LB Doug Miller (15); S Stanley Richard (16); CB Sean Vanhorse (16); P Bryan Wagner (14); DT Reggie White (11); G/T Curtis Whitley (12); DL Blaise Winter (2); S Lonnie Young (12).

Abbreviations: D1—draft pick, first round; SupD2—supplemental draft pick, second round; W-Den—waivers acquisition from Denver; T-Sea—trade acquisition from Seattle; PlanB—Plan B free-agent acquisition; FA—free-agent acquisition (other than Plan B).

MISCELLANEOUS TEAM DATA

Stadium (capacity, surface):
San Diego Jack Murphy Stadium
(60,794, grass)
Business address:
P.O. Box 609609
San Diego, CA 92160-9609
Business phone:
619-280-2111
Ticket information:
619-280-2121; 619-563-8281
Team colors:
Navy blue, white and gold
Flagship radio station:
XTRA, 690 AM
Training site:
UC San Diego
La Jolla, Calif.
619-280-2111

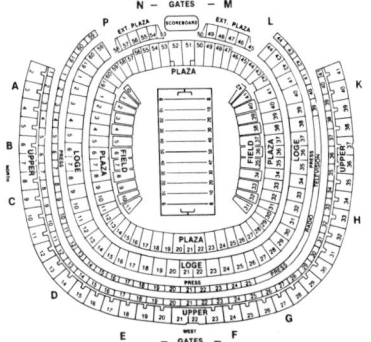

SAN FRANCISCO 49ERS
NFC WESTERN DIVISION

RESULTS

Sept. 5—L.A. RAIDERS	W	44-14
Sept. 11—at Kansas City	L	17-24
Sept. 18—at L.A. Rams	W	34-19
Sept. 25—NEW ORLEANS	W	24-13
Oct. 2—PHILADELPHIA	L	8-40
Oct. 9—at Detroit	W	27-21
Oct. 16—at Atlanta	W	42-3
Oct. 23—TAMPA BAY	W	41-16
Oct. 30—Open date		
Nov. 6—at Washington	W	37-22
Nov. 13—DALLAS	W	21-14
Nov. 20—L.A. RAMS	W	31-27
Nov. 28—at New Orleans	W	35-14
Dec. 4—ATLANTA	W	50-14
Dec. 11—at San Diego	W	38-15
Dec. 17—DENVER	W	42-19
Dec. 26—at Minnesota	L	14-21

RECORDS/RANKINGS

1994 regular-season record: 13-3 (1st in NFC West); 6-0 in division; 10-2 in conference; 7-1 at home; 6-2 on road.
Team record last five years: 61-19 (.763, ranks 1st in league in that span).
1994 team rankings:

	No.	NFC	NFL
Total offense	*378.8	1	2
Rushing offense	*118.6	3	6
Passing offense	*260.2	2	4
Scoring offense	505	1	1
Total defense	*302.4	6	8
Rushing defense	*83.6	2	2
Passing defense	*218.8	9	17
Scoring defense	296	4	6
Takeaways	35	T2	T5
Giveaways	24	T3	T5
Turnover differential	11	T1	T3
Sacks	38	3	T7
Sacks allowed	35	T10	T17

*Yards per game.

TEAM LEADERS

Scoring (kicking): Doug O'Brien, 105 pts. (60/62 PATs, 15/20 FGs).
Scoring (touchdowns): Jerry Rice, 92 pts. (2 rushing, 13 receiving, 1 2-pt. conv.).
Passing: Steve Young, 3,969 yds. (461 att., 324 comp., 70.3%, 35 TDs, 10 int.).
Rushing: Ricky Watters, 877 yds. (239 att., 3.7 avg., 6 TDs).
Receptions: Jerry Rice, 112 (1,499 yds., 13.4 avg., 13 TDs).
Interceptions: Merton Hanks, 7 (93 yds., 0 TDs).
Sacks: Dana Stubblefield, 8.5.
Punting: Klaus Wilmsmeyer, 41.4 avg. (54 punts, 2,235 yds., 0 blocked).
Punt returns: Dexter Carter, 8.4 avg. (38 att., 321 yds., 0 TDs).
Kickoff returns: Dexter Carter, 23.0 avg. (48 att., 1,105 yds., 1 TD).

CLUB DIRECTORY

Owner
Edward J. DeBartolo Jr.
President
Carmen Policy
Vice president/football operations
Dwight Clark
Assistant to the president
John McVay
V.P./business operations and CFO
Keith Simon
Director of football personnel
Vinny Cerrato
Marketing/promotions director
Laurie Albrecht
Controller
Melrene Frear
Director of public/community relations
Rodney Knox
Assistant director of public relations
Dave Rahn
Communications coordinator
Ron Juanso
Public relations assistants
Darla Maeda
Cynthia Turner
Pro personnel administration
Allan Webb
Scouts
Jim Abrams
John Brunner
Mike Faulkiner
Jim Gruden
Oscar Lofton
Ben Parks Jr.
Billy Wilson
Trainer
Lindsy McLean
Assistant trainers
Ray Tufts
Scottie Patton

SCHEDULE

Sept. 3—at New Orleans	12:00
Sept. 10—ATLANTA	1:00
Sept. 17—NEW ENGLAND	1:00
Sept. 25—at Detroit (Mon.)	9:00
Oct. 1—N.Y. GIANTS	1:00
Oct. 8—Open date	
Oct. 15—at Indianapolis	12:00
Oct. 22—at St. Louis	3:00
Oct. 29—NEW ORLEANS	1:00
Nov. 5—CAROLINA	1:00
Nov. 12—at Dallas	3:00
Nov. 20—at Miami (Mon.)	9:00
Nov. 26—ST. LOUIS	1:00
Dec. 3—BUFFALO	5:00
Dec. 10—at Carolina	1:00
Dec. 18—MINNESOTA (Mon.)	6:00
Dec. 24—at Atlanta	1:00

All times are for home team.
All games Sunday unless noted.

Head coach
George Seifert
Assistant coaches
Jerry Attaway (physical development)
Michael Barnes (asst. strength and conditioning)
Dwaine Board (defensive line)
Pete Carroll (def. coord.)
Tom Holmoe (defensive backs)
Carl Jackson (running backs)
Larry Kirksey (receivers)
Alan Lowry (special teams)
John Marshall (linebackers)
Bobb McKittrick (offensive line)
Bill McPherson (assistant head coach)
Mike Solari (tight ends/offensive line assistant)
Marc Trestman (offensive coordinator/quarterbacks)

Physicians
Michael Dillingham
James B. Klint
Stadium operations coordinator
Jim Wyatt
Equipment manager
Bronco Hinek
Assistant equipment manager
Ted Walsh
Director/video operations
Robert Yanagi

DRAFT CHOICES

J.J. Stokes, WR, UCLA (first round/10th pick overall).
Tim Hanshaw, TE, Brigham Young (4/127).
Antonio Armstrong, DE, Texas A&M (6/201).
Herb Coleman, DE, Trinity (Ill.) (7/238).

TRAINING CAMP ROSTER

No.	QUARTERBACKS	Ht./Wt.	Born	NFL Exp.	College	How acq.	'94 Games GP/GS
14	Cook, Wayne	6-4/215	4-13-71	R	UCLA	FA/95	—
11	Gagliano, Bob	6-3/205	9-5-58	7	Utah State	FA/95	0/0
18	Grbac, Elvis	6-5/232	8-13-70	3	Michigan	D8/93	11/0
8	Young, Steve	6-2/205	10-11-61	11	Brigham Young	T-TB/87	16/16

RUNNING BACKS

No.		Ht./Wt.	Born	NFL Exp.	College	How acq.	'94 Games GP/GS
40	Floyd, William (FB)	6-1/242	2-17-72	2	Florida State	D1/94	16/11
20	Loville, Derek (KR)	5-10/205	7-4-68	4	Oregon	FA/94	14/0
29	Lynn, Anthony	6-3/230	12-21-68	2	Texas Tech	FA/95	0/0
32	Mills, Troy	6-0/212	7-1-66	1	Sacramento State	FA/95	0/0
	Moore, Derrick	6-1/227	10-13-67	4	Northeastern Oklahoma State	T-Det/95	*16/0
27	Walker, Adam	6-1/210	6-7-68	3	Pittsburgh	FA/94	8/0
28	Wilburn, Terry	5-10/212	5-30-72	R	UT Chattanooga	FA/95	—
38	Willis, Jamal	6-2/218	12-12-72	R	Brigham Young	FA/95	—

RECEIVERS

No.		Ht./Wt.	Born	NFL Exp.	College	How acq.	'94 Games GP/GS
48	Allen, Brian (TE)	6-4/240	9-18-70	R	UCLA	FA/95	—
89	Browning, Alfonso	6-2/203	7-27-72	1	Kentucky	FA/95	0/0
81	Caldwell, Mike	6-2/200	3-28-71	1	California	FA/95	0/0
86	Carolan, Brett (TE)	6-3/241	3-10-71	2	Washington State	FA/94	4/0
15	Cook, Mike	6-5/205	3-20-71	1	Stanford	FA/95	0/0
84	Jones, Brent (TE)	6-4/230	2-12-63	9	Santa Clara	FA/87	15/15
13	Orlando, Mark	6-0/184	10-23-72	R	Towson State	FA/95	—
85	Popson, Ted (TE)	6-4/250	9-10-66	2	Portland State	FA/93	16/1
80	Rice, Jerry	6-2/200	10-13-62	11	Mississippi Valley State	D1/85	16/16
10	Rowe, Patrick	6-1/195	2-17-69	3	San Diego State	FA/95	0/0
88	Singleton, Nate	5-11/190	7-5-68	4	Grambling State	FA/93	16/1
83	Stokes, J.J.	6-4/217	10-6-72	R	UCLA	D1/95	—
82	Taylor, John	6-1/185	3-31-62	10	Delaware State	D3/86	15/15

OFFENSIVE LINEMEN

No.		Ht./Wt.	Born	NFL Exp.	College	How acq.	'94 Games GP/GS
60	Adams, Theo (G)	6-5/300	4-24-66	3	Hawaii	FA/95	0/0
79	Barton, Harris (T)	6-4/286	4-19-64	9	North Carolina	D1/87	9/9
	Childs, Jason (T)	6-4/292	1-6-69	2	North Dakota	FA/95	0/0
67	Dalman, Chris (G/C)	6-3/285	3-15-70	3	Stanford	D6/93	16/4
63	Deese, Derrick (G)	6-3/270	5-17-70	4	Southern California	FA/94	16/15
59	Gordon, Steve (C)	6-4/290	4-14-69	2	California	FA/95	0/0
77	Hanshaw, Tim (G)	6-5/300	4-27-70	R	Brigham Young	D4/95	—
69	Milstead, Rod (G)	6-2/290	11-10-69	4	Delaware State	FA/95	5/0
66	Oates, Bart (C)	6-4/275	12-16-58	11	Brigham Young	FA/94	16/15
	Pollack, Frank (G/T)	6-5/285	11-5-67	4	Northern Arizona	FA/94	12/4
61	Sapolu, Jesse (G)	6-4/278	3-10-61	13	Hawaii	D11/83	13/13
76	Scrafford, Kirk (T/G)	6-6/275	3-16-67	6	Montana	FA/95	*16/7
74	Wallace, Steve (T)	6-5/280	12-27-64	10	Auburn	D4/86	15/15

DEFENSIVE LINEMEN

No.		Ht./Wt.	Born	NFL Exp.	College	How acq.	'94 Games GP/GS
56	Armstrong, Antonio (E)	6-1/234	10-15-73	R	Texas A&M	D6/95	—
72	Barnett, Oliver	6-3/285	4-9-66	6	Georgia State	FA/95	*16/2
96	Brown, Dennis (E)	6-4/290	11-6-67	6	Washington	D2/90	16/14
90	Bryant, Junior (E)	6-4/275	1-16-71	1	Notre Dame	FA/95	0/0
95	Coleman, Herb (E)	6-4/285	9-4-71	R	Trinity College (Ill.)	D7/95	—
91	Collins, Shane (E)	6-3/267	4-11-69	4	Arizona State	T-Was/95	*7/0
52	Fountaine, Jamal (E)	6-3/240	1-25-71	1	Washington	FA/95	0/0
63	Hawkins, Barry (T)	6-4/295	5-17-71	R	West Virginia	FA/95	—
	Holland, Troy (E)	6-6/270	2-23-67	R	Navy	FA/95	—
58	Kelly, Todd (E)	6-2/259	11-27-70	3	Tennessee	D1/93	11/1
	Kuehl, Randy (T)	6-4/280	1-18-72	R	Virginia	FA/95	—
	Shepherd, Chris (E)	6-4/274	7-9-71	R	Boise State	FA/95	—
94	Stubblefield, Dana (T)	6-2/302	11-14-70	3	Kansas	D1/93	14/14
71	Wahler, Jim (T)	6-4/280	7-29-66	6	UCLA	FA/95	0/0
	Whiteside, Willie (E)	6-3/231	1-26-73	R	Auburn	FA/95	—
97	Young, Bryant (T)	6-2/276	1-27-72	2	Notre Dame	D1/94	16/16

LINEBACKERS

No.		Ht./Wt.	Born	NFL Exp.	College	How acq.	'94 Games GP/GS
	Crawford, Darrel	6-2/250	12-28-69	1	Auburn	FA/95	0/0
98	Goss, Antonio	6-4/228	8-11-66	6	North Carolina	FA/94	16/1
65	Hairston, Jason	6-2/242	7-17-71	R	UC Davis	FA/95	—
93	Jordan, Darin	6-2/245	12-4-64	5	Northeastern	FA/91	0/0
55	Mitchell, Kevin	6-1/260	1-1-71	2	Syracuse	D2/94	16/0
51	Norton, Ken	6-2/241	9-29-66	8	UCLA	FA/94	16/16
53	Peterson, Tony	6-0/223	1-23-72	2	Notre Dame	D5/94	15/0
50	Plummer, Gary	6-2/247	1-26-60	10	California	FA/94	16/16
62	Thompson, Chris	6-4/260	6-17-69	1	Bowie State (Md.)	FA/95	0/0

No.	LINEBACKERS	Ht./Wt.	Born	NFL Exp.	College	How acq.	'94 Games GP/GS
92	Wilson, Troy (E)	6-4/250	11-22-70	3	Pittsburg (Kan.) State	D7/93	11/0
54	Woodall, Lee	6-0/220	10-31-69	2	West Chester (Pa.)	D6/94	15/13
	DEFENSIVE BACKS						
24	Calloway, Dominic (CB)	6-1/184	4-24-72	1	Memphis	FA/95	0/0
25	Davis, Eric (CB)	5-11/178	1-26-68	6	Jacksonville (Ala.) State	D2/90	16/16
33	Dodge, Dedrick (S)	6-2/184	6-14-67	4	Florida State	FA/95	15/0
22	Drakeford, Tyronne (CB)	5-9/185	6-21-71	2	Virginia Tech	D2/94	13/0
36	Hanks, Merton (CB)	6-2/185	3-12-68	5	Iowa	D5/91	16/16
47	Hicks, Clifford (S/CB)	5-9/190	8-18-64	8	Oregon	FA/95	*16/0
30	Kellogg, Jackie (CB)	6-1/188	3-29-71	1	Eastern Washington	FA/95	0/0
46	McDonald, Tim (S)	6-2/215	1-6-65	9	Southern California	FA/93	16/16
28	Peoples, Sam	6-1/175	1-14-71	R	Portland State	FA/95	—
	Pieri, Damon (S)	6-0/186	9-25-70	1	San Diego State	FA/95	0/0
23	Pope, Marquez (S/CB)	5-11/193	10-29-70	4	Fresno State	FA/95	*16/16
26	Richardson, Moses (CB)	6-1/178	11-22-70	1	Indiana	FA/95	0/0
45	Williams, Michael (CB)	5-10/185	5-28-70	1	UCLA	FA/95	0/0
	SPECIALISTS						
4	Brien, Doug (K)	5-11/177	11-24-70	2	California	D3/94	16/0
6	Colley, Rob (P)	6-2/220	6-9-72	R	Virginia Tech	FA/95	—
5	Sieler, Tom (K)	6-5/205	2-11-72	R	Nebraska	FA/95	—
3	Thompson, Tommy (P)	5-10/192	4-27-72	1	Oregon	FA/95	0/0

*Barnett played 16 games with Bills in '94; Collins played 7 games with Redskins; Hicks played 16 games with Jets; Moore played 16 games with Lions; Pope played 16 games with Rams; Scrafford played 16 games with Broncos.

Also played with 49ers in '94: T Harry Boatswain (13); G Brian Bollinger (7); RB Dexter Carter (16); CB Toi Cook (16); DE Richard Dent (2); DT Rhett Hall (12); S Dana Hall (16); CB Adrian Hardy (2); DE Tim Harris (5); LB Rickey Jackson (16); RB Marc Logan (10); DE Charles Mann (14); WR Ed McCaffrey (16); LB Kevin Mitchell (16); LB Tony Peterson (15); DB Deion Sanders (14); DT Artie Smith (2); G/C Ralph Tamm (1); DE Mark Thomas (9); RB Ricky Watters (16); P Klaus Wilmsmeyer (16).

Abbreviations: D1—draft pick, first round; SupD2—supplemental draft pick, second round; W-Den—waivers acquisition from Denver; T-Sea—trade acquisition from Seattle; PlanB—Plan B free-agent acquisition; FA—free-agent acquisition (other than Plan B).

MISCELLANEOUS TEAM DATA

Stadium (capacity, surface):
Candlestick Park
(69,497, grass)
Business address:
4949 Centennial Blvd.
Santa Clara, CA 95054-1229
Business phone:
408-562-4949
Ticket information:
415-468-2249
Team colors:
Forty Niners gold and scarlet
Flagship radio station:
KGO, 810 AM
Training site:
Sierra Community College
Rocklin, Calif.
916-624-8241

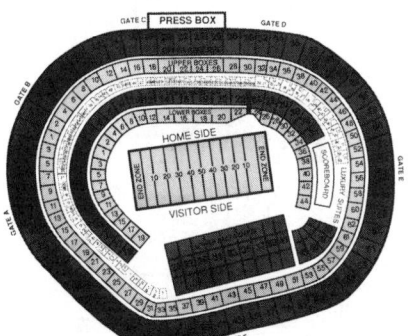

SEATTLE SEAHAWKS
AFC WESTERN DIVISION

RESULTS

Sept. 4	—at Washington	W	28-7
Sept. 11	—at L.A. Raiders	W	38-9
Sept. 18	—SAN DIEGO	L	10-24
Sept. 25	—PITTSBURGH	W	30-13
Oct. 2	—at Indianapolis	L	15-17
Oct. 9	—DENVER	L	9-16
Oct. 16	—Open date		
Oct. 23	—at Kansas City	L	23-38
Oct. 30	—at San Diego	L	15-35
Nov. 6	—CINCINNATI (OT)	L	17-20
Nov. 13	—at Denver	L	10-17
Nov. 20	—TAMPA BAY	W	22-21
Nov. 27	—KANSAS CITY	W	10-9
Dec. 4	—INDIANAPOLIS	L	19-31
Dec. 11	—at Houston	W	16-14
Dec. 18	—L.A. RAIDERS	L	16-17
Dec. 24	—at Cleveland	L	9-35

RECORDS/RANKINGS

1994 regular-season record: 6-10 (5th in AFC West); 2-6 in division; 4-10 in conference; 3-5 at home; 3-5 on road.
Team record last five years: 30-50 (.375, ranks 22nd in league in that span).

1994 team rankings:	No.	AFC	NFL
Total offense	*290.8	12	24
Rushing offense	*130.3	2	2
Passing offense	*160.5	13	26
Scoring offense	287	11	20
Total defense	*334.3	13	23
Rushing defense	*122.0	13	25
Passing defense	*212.3	6	13
Scoring defense	323	8	16
Takeaways	30	8	17
Giveaways	28	T4	T12
Turnover differential	2	T5	T11
Sacks	29	T9	T17
Sacks allowed	40	9	21

*Yards per game.

TEAM LEADERS

Scoring (kicking): John Kasay, 85 pts. (25/26 PATs, 20/24 FGs).
Scoring (touchdowns): Chris Warren 68 pts., (9 rushing, 2 receiving, 1 2-pt. conv.).
Passing: Rick Mirer, 2,151 yds. (381 att., 195 comp., 51.2%, 11 TDs, 7 int.).
Rushing: Chris Warren, 1,545 yds. (333 att., 4.6 avg., 9 TDs).
Receptions: Brian Blades, 81 (1,086 yds., 13.4 avg., 4 TDs).
Interceptions: Patrick Hunter, 3 (85 yds., 0 TDs); Orlando Watters, 3 (39 yds., 1 TD); Terry Wooden, 3 (78 yds., 1 TD).
Sacks: Mike Sinclair, 4.5.
Punting: Rick Tuten, 42.9 avg. (91 punts, 3,905 yds., 0 blocked).
Punt returns: Kelvin Martin, 8.5 avg. (33 att., 280 yds., 0 TDs).
Kickoff returns: Michael Bates, 19.5 avg. (26 att., 508 yds., 0 TDs).

CLUB DIRECTORY

Owner
Ken Behring
President
David Behring
Executive vice president/finance
Mickey Loomis
V.P./public relations/administration
Gary Wright
Publicity director
Dave Neubert
Community services director
Sandy Gregory
Sales and marketing director
Reggie McKenzie
Admin. assistant/public relations
Charlotte Kores
Player personnel director
Mike Allman
Assistant player personnel director
Rick Thompson
Pro personnel director
Randy Mueller
College personnel director
Phil Neri
Eastern supervisor
Rick Reiprish
Scouts
Warren Harper
Derrick Jensen
Doug Kretz
Dave Nusz
Ticket director
James Nagaoka
Head trainer
Jim Whitesel
Assistant trainer
Todd Sperber

SCHEDULE

Sept. 3	—KANSAS CITY	1:00
Sept. 10	—at San Diego	1:00
Sept. 17	—CINCINNATI	1:00
Sept. 24	—Open date	
Oct. 1	—DENVER	1:00
Oct. 8	—at Los Angeles	1:00
Oct. 15	—at Buffalo	1:00
Oct. 22	—SAN DIEGO	1:00
Oct. 29	—at Arizona	2:00
Nov. 5	—N.Y. GIANTS	1:00
Nov. 12	—at Jacksonville	1:00
Nov. 19	—at Washington	1:00
Nov. 26	—N.Y. JETS	1:00
Dec. 3	—PHILADELPHIA	1:00
Dec. 10	—at Denver	2:00
Dec. 17	—LOS ANGELES	5:00
Dec. 24	—at Kansas City	12:00

All times are for home team.
All games Sunday unless noted.

CLUB DIRECTORY

Head coach
Dennis Erickson
Assistant coaches
Dave Arnold (special teams)
Tommy Brasher (def. line)
Bob Bratkowski (offensive co-ordinator/wide receivers)
Dave Brown (defensive coach)
Tom Catlin (quality control)
Dana LeDuc (strength and conditioning)
Arnie Matsumoto (staff asst.)
Greg McMackin (def. coord.)
Howard Mudd (offensive line)
Mike Murphy (linebackers)
Rich Olson (quarterbacks)
Willy Robinson (def. backs)
Clarence Shelmon (running backs)
Gregg Smith (asst. head coach/tight ends)

Physicians
Kevin Auld
Pierce Scranton
James Trombold
Equipment manager
Terry Sinclair
Assistant equipment manager
Howard Baus
Video director
Thom Fermstad
Video projects director
Mike Wacker

DRAFT CHOICES

Joey Galloway, WR, Ohio State (first round/eighth pick overall).
Christian Fauria, TE, Colorado (2/39).
Jason Kyle, LB, Arizona State (4/126).
Henry McMillian, DT, Florida (6/180).
Eddie Goines, WR, North Carolina State (6/203).
Keif Bryant, DE, Rutgers (7/216).

TRAINING CAMP ROSTER

No.	QUARTERBACKS	Ht./Wt.	Born	NFL Exp.	College	How acq.	'94 Games GP/GS
17	Friesz, John	6-4/220	5-19-67	6	Idaho	FA/95	*16/4
18	Gelbaugh, Stan	6-3/215	12-4-62	8	Maryland	PlanB/92	1/0
3	Mirer, Rick	6-2/211	3-19-70	3	Notre Dame	D1/93	13/13
16	Pickens, Joe	6-3/221	2-11-72	R	Duke	FA/95	—
	RUNNING BACKS						
32	Anderson, Kelvin	5-8/198	2-4-72	R	Southeast Missouri State	FA/95	—
33	Baldwin, Robert (FB)	6-0/230	9-1-72	R	Duke	FA/95	—
22	Bryant, Beno (KR)	5-9/170	1-1-71	1	Washington	FA/94	2/0
46	Dye, Tyree	6-0/210	11-19-72	R	Ferris State	FA/95	—
43	Johnson, Tracy (FB)	6-0/242	11-29-66	7	Clemson	PlanB/92	16/10
44	Shelman, Anthony	6-3/214	6-21-71	R	Louisville	FA/95	—
36	Smith, Lamar	5-11/224	11-29-70	2	Houston	D3/94	2/0
35	Smith, Steve (FB)	6-1/242	8-30-64	9	Penn State	FA/94	16/0
38	Strong, Mack (FB)	6-0/222	9-11-71	2	Georgia	FA/93	8/1
42	Warren, Chris	6-2/225	1-24-67	6	Ferrum (Va.)	D4/90	16/15
	RECEIVERS						
81	Bates, Michael	5-10/196	12-19-69	3	Arizona	D6/92	15/0
89	Blades, Brian	5-11/186	7-24-65	8	Miami (Fla.)	D2/88	16/16
48	Crumpler, Carlester (TE)	6-6/255	9-5-71	2	East Carolina	D7/94	9/4
85	Fauria, Christian (TE)	6-4/245	9-22-71	R	Colorado	D2/95	—
84	Galloway, Joey (KR)	5-11/188	11-20-71	R	Ohio State	D1/95	—
10	Goines, Eddie	6-0/186	8-16-72	R	North Carolina State	D6/95	—
87	Green, Paul (TE)	6-3/230	10-8-66	4	Southern California	FA/92	16/11
11	Harris, Ronnie	5-11/180	6-4-70	1	Oregon	FA/94	*2/0
83	Junkin, Trey (TE)	6-2/241	1-23-61	13	Louisiana Tech	FA/90	16/0
49	McKeehan, James (TE)	6-3/250	8-9-73	R	Texas A&M	FA/95	—
19	McKnight, James	6-0/186	6-17-72	1	Liberty	FA/94	2/0
82	Proehl, Ricky	6-0/190	3-7-68	6	Wake Forest	T-Ari/95	*16/16
86	Thomas, Robb	5-11/175	3-29-66	7	Oregon State	FA/92	16/1
88	Warren, Terrence (KR)	6-1/205	8-2-69	3	Hampton (Va.)	D5/93	14/0
15	Woods, Manley	6-2/169	7-28-72	R	New Mexico	FA/95	—
	OFFENSIVE LINEMEN						
62	Arial, Mills (T)	6-3/288	5-17-73	R	Davidson	FA/95	—
74	Atkins, James (G)	6-6/303	1-28-70	2	Southwestern Louisiana	FA/93	4/2
75	Ballard, Howard (T)	6-6/332	11-3-63	8	Alabama A&M	FA/94	16/16
69	Blackshear, Jeff (G)	6-6/323	3-29-69	3	Northeast Louisiana	D8/93	16/16
54	Heath, Bryan (C)	6-2/288	7-17-72	R	Virginia	FA/95	—
76	Hitchcock, Bill (G)	6-6/306	8-26-65	5	Purdue	D8/90	5/5
77	Joyce, Matt (G)	6-7/283	3-30-72	1	Richmond	FA/95	0/0
65	Kegarise, Mike (G)	6-5/300	6-19-70	2	Edinboro (Pa.)	FA/94	0/0
78	Keim, Mike (T)	6-7/302	11-12-65	4	Brigham Young	FA/92	16/0
52	Mawae, Kevin (G)	6-4/288	1-23-71	2	Louisiana State	D2/94	14/11
71	Moody, Mike (T)	6-7/305	5-6-69	1	Southern California	FA/94	0/0
61	Pollack, Kris (G)	6-4/290	12-21-71	R	Southern California	FA/95	—
73	Roberts, Ray (T)	6-6/308	6-3-69	4	Virginia	D1/92	14/14
53	Sweeney, Jim (C)	6-4/284	8-8-62	12	Pittsburgh	FA/95	*16/16
56	Tofflemire, Joe (C)	6-2/277	7-7-65	7	Arizona	D2/89	1/0
63	Willis, Donald (G)	6-3/330	7-15-73	R	North Carolina A&T	FA/95	—
	DEFENSIVE LINEMEN						
98	Adams, Sam (T)	6-3/285	6-13-73	2	Texas A&M	D1/94	12/7
97	Allen, Ernest (T)	6-2/289	3-11-73	R	Cincinnati	FA/95	—
68	Bryant, Keif	6-4/275	3-12-73	R	Rutgers	D7/95	—
67	Edwards, Antonio (E)	6-3/271	3-10-70	3	Valdosta (Ga.) State	D8/93	15/14
64	Hamilton, Bobby (E)	6-4/269	7-1-71	2	Southern Mississippi	FA/94	0/0
96	Kennedy, Cortez (T)	6-3/293	8-23-68	6	Miami (Fla.)	D1/90	16/16
99	McCrary, Michael (E)	6-4/267	7-7-70	3	Wake Forest	D7/93	16/0
92	McMillian, Henry (T)	6-3/275	10-17-71	R	Florida	D6/95	—
94	Patterson, DeWayne (E)	6-0/257	6-15-72	R	Washington State	FA/95	—
70	Sinclair, Michael (E)	6-4/271	1-31-68	5	Eastern New Mexico	D6/91	12/2
91	Werner, Matt (T)	6-3/262	6-14-71	2	UCLA	FA/94	0/0
93	Williams, Brent (E)	6-4/283	10-23-64	10	Toledo	FA/94	10/9
	LINEBACKERS						
60	Barber, Michael	6-1/247	11-9-71	R	Clemson	FA/95	—
50	Bickett, Duane	6-5/245	12-1-62	11	Southern California	FA/94	7/1
51	Brandon, David	6-4/240	2-9-65	9	Memphis State	FA/93	13/0
57	Kyle, Jason	6-3/240	5-12-72	R	Arizona State	D4/95	—
55	Moss, Winston	6-3/245	12-24-65	9	Miami (Fla.)	FA/95	*16/15
58	Spitulski, Bob	6-3/246	9-10-69	4	Central Florida	D3/92	16/1

— 87 —

No.	LINEBACKERS	Ht./Wt.	Born	NFL Exp.	College	How acq.	'94 Games GP/GS
59	Stowe, Tyronne	6-2/250	5-30-65	9	Rutgers	FA/95	*16/15
95	Wells, Dean	6-3/242	7-20-70	3	Kentucky	D4/93	15/0
90	Wooden, Terry	6-3/239	1-14-67	6	Syracuse	D2/90	16/15
	DEFENSIVE BACKS						
20	Bellamy, Jay (S)	5-11/193	7-8-72	2	Rutgers	FA/94	3/0
25	Blackmon, Robert (S)	6-0/203	5-12-67	6	Baylor	D2/90	15/15
39	Bledsoe, Jerrick (CB)	5-10/180	7-1-72	R	Texas Southern	FA/95	—
29	Brown, Tony (CB)	5-9/183	5-15-70	4	Fresno State	FA/94	13/5
27	Covington, Tony (S)	5-11/193	12-26-67	5	Virginia	FA/95	*14/2
23	Duckett, Forey (CB)	6-3/195	2-5-70	3	Nevada	FA/94	*7/0
26	Gray, Carlton (CB)	6-0/196	6-26-71	3	UCLA	D2/93	11/11
30	Harris, Corey (CB)	5-11/190	10-25-69	4	Vanderbilt	FA/95	*16/2
47	Jackson, Kirby (CB)	5-10/176	2-2-65	9	Mississippi State	FA/94	0/0
34	Lambert, Dion (S)	6-1/190	2-12-69	3	UCLA	FA/94	1/1
37	Odomes, Nate (CB)	5-10/188	8-25-65	9	Wisconsin	FA/94	0/0
41	Robinson, Eugene (S)	6-0/195	5-28-63	11	Colgate	FA/85	14/14
21	Robinson, Rafael (S)	5-11/195	6-19-69	4	Wisconsin	FA/92	16/1
28	Speer, Del (S)	6-0/200	2-1-70	3	Florida	FA/94	*9/0
31	Watters, Orlando (CB)	5-11/173	10-26-71	2	Arkansas	FA/94	16/8
24	Wilson, Chad (CB)	5-11/178	5-23-72	R	Miami (Fla.)	FA/95	—
	SPECIALISTS						
6	Davis, Judd (K)	6-1/186	8-28-71	R	Florida	FA/95	—
2	Peterson, Todd (K)	5-10/175	2-4-70	1	Georgia	FA/95	*2/0
14	Tuten, Rick (P)	6-2/218	1-5-65	7	Florida State	FA/91	16/0

*Covington played 14 games with Buccaneers in '94; Duckett played 2 games with Bengals, 3 with Packers and 2 with Seahawks; Friesz played 16 games with Redskins; C. Harris played 16 games with Packers; R. Harris played 1 game with Patriots and 1 with Seahawks; Moss played 16 games with Raiders; Peterson played 2 games with Cardinals; Proehl played 16 games with Cardinals; Speer played 8 games with Browns and 1 game with Seahawks; Stowe played 16 games with Redskins; Sweeney played 16 games with Jets.

Also played with Seahawks in '94: C Ray Donaldson (16); DE Mike Frier (3); CB Patrick Hunter (5); PK John Kasay (16); WR Kelvin Martin (16); S Dave McCloughan (13); QB Dan McGwire (7); DT Joe Nash (16); LB Rufus Porter (16); DT Tyrone Rodgers (5); DE Michael Sinclair (12); LB Rod Stephens (16); CB Terry Taylor (5); KR/RB Jon Vaughn (9).

Abbreviations: D1—draft pick, first round; SupD2—supplemental draft pick, second round; W-Den—waivers acquisition from Denver; T-Sea—trade acquisition from Seattle; PlanB—Plan B free-agent acquisition; FA—free-agent acquisition (other than Plan B).

MISCELLANEOUS TEAM DATA

Stadium (capacity, surface):
Kingdome (66,400, artificial)
Business address:
11220 N.E. 53rd Street
Kirkland, WA 98033
Business phone:
206-827-9777
Ticket information:
206-827-9766
Team colors:
Blue, green and silver
Flagship radio station:
KIRO, 710 AM
Training site:
Seahawks Headquarters
Kirkland, Wash.
206-827-9777

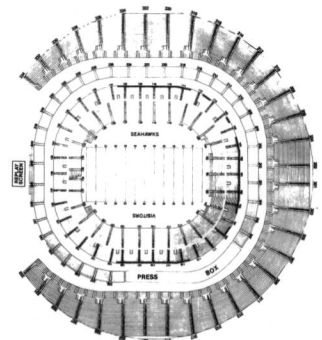

TAMPA BAY BUCCANEERS
NFC CENTRAL DIVISION

1994 REVIEW

RESULTS

Sept. 4—at Chicago	L	9-21
Sept. 11—INDIANAPOLIS	W	24-10
Sept. 18—NEW ORLEANS	L	7-9
Sept. 25—at Green Bay	L	3-30
Oct. 2—DETROIT	W	24-14
Oct. 9—at Atlanta	L	13-34
Oct. 16—Open date		
Oct. 23—at San Francisco	L	16-41
Oct. 30—MINNESOTA	L	13-36
Nov. 6—CHICAGO	L	6-20
Nov. 13—at Detroit	L	9-14
Nov. 20—at Seattle	L	21-22
Nov. 27—at Minnesota (OT)	W	20-17
Dec. 4—WASHINGTON	W	26-21
Dec. 11—L.A. RAMS	W	24-14
Dec. 18—at Washington	W	17-14
Dec. 24—GREEN BAY	L	19-34

RECORDS/RANKINGS

1994 regular-season record: 6-10 (5th in NFC Central); 2-6 in division; 5-9 in conference; 4-4 at home; 2-6 on road.
Team record last five years: 25-55 (.313, ranks 25th in league in that span).

1994 team rankings:

	No.	NFC	NFL
Total offense	*297.1	10	20
Rushing offense	*93.1	10	22
Passing offense	*204.1	10	17
Scoring offense	251	13	26
Total defense	*333.5	10	21
Rushing defense	*122.8	10	26
Passing defense	*210.8	6	11
Scoring defense	351	10	20
Takeaways	21	13	26
Giveaways	23	2	T3
Turnover differential	-2	10	17
Sacks	20	14	28
Sacks allowed	30	6	13

*Yards per game.

TEAM LEADERS

Scoring (kicking): Michael Husted, 89 pts. (20/20 PATs, 23/35 FGs).
Scoring (touchdowns): Errict Rhett, 44 pts. (7 rushing).
Passing: Craig Erickson, 2,919 yds. (399 att., 225 comp., 56.4%, 16 TDs, 10 int.).
Rushing: Errict Rhett, 1,011 yds. (284 att., 3.6 avg., 7 TDs).
Receptions: Lawrence Dawsey, 46 (673 yds., 14.6 avg., 1 TD).
Interceptions: Martin Mayhew, 2 (4 yds., 0 TDs); Hardy Nickerson, 2 (9 yds., 0 TDs).
Sacks: Brad Culpepper, 4.0.
Punting: Dan Stryzinski, 38.9 avg. (72 punts, 2,800 yds., 0 blocked).
Punt returns: Vernon Turner, 10.4 avg. (21 att., 218 yds., 1 TD).
Kickoff returns: Vernon Turner, 20.6 avg. (43 att., 886 yds., 0 TDs).

1995 SEASON

CLUB DIRECTORY

Owner
Malcolm Glazer
General manager
Richard McKay
Director/ticket sales and operations
Rick Odioso
Asst. director/ticket operations
Lori Grimm
Director/public relations
Chip Namias
Assistant director/public relations
Scott Smith
Public relations assistant
Nelson Luis
Director/corporate sales and broadcasting
Jim Overton
Controller
Patrick Smith
Director/sales and advertising
Paul Sickmon
Asst. dir./sales and advertising
Jayne Portnoy
Asst. dir./sales and fundraising
Sherry Gruden
Director/player personnel
Jerry Angelo
Director/college scouting
Tim Ruskell
College personnel scouts
Mike Ackerley
Brian Gardner
Ruston Webster
Mike Yowarsky

SCHEDULE

Sept. 3—at Philadelphia	1:00
Sept. 10—at Cleveland	1:00
Sept. 17—CHICAGO	4:00
Sept. 24—WASHINGTON	1:00
Oct. 1—at Carolina	1:00
Oct. 8—CINCINNATI	1:00
Oct. 15—MINNESOTA	1:00
Oct. 22—ATLANTA	1:00
Oct. 29—at Houston	3:00
Nov. 5—Open date	
Nov. 12—at Detroit	1:00
Nov. 19—JACKSONVILLE	1:00
Nov. 26—at Green Bay	12:00
Dec. 3—at Minnesota	12:00
Dec. 10—GREEN BAY	8:00
Dec. 17—at Chicago	12:00
Dec. 23—DETROIT (Sat.)	4:00

All times are for home team.
All games Sunday unless noted.

Head coach/director of football operations
Sam Wyche
Assistant coaches
Rusty Tillman (def. coord.)
Maxie Baughan (linebackers)
Tom Pratt (defensive line)
Ken Clarke (defensive line)
Johnnie Lynn (defensive backs)
David Culley (receivers)
Kippy Brown (running backs)
Turk Schonert (quarterbacks)
Bob Wylie (offensive line)
George Stewart (special teams)
Mike Mularkey (tight ends)
Brad Roll (strength/conditioning)

Pro personnel assistant
John Idzik
Trainer
Chris Smith
Assistant trainer
Joe Joe Petrone
Team physicians
Joseph Diaco
William Carson
Equipment manager
Frank Pupello
Video director
Dave Levy
Assistant video director
Pat Brazil

DRAFT CHOICES

Warren Sapp, DT, Miami (Fla.) (first round/12th pick overall).
Derrick Brooks, LB, Florida State (1/28).
Melvin Johnson, DB, Kentucky (2/43).
Jerry Wilson, DB, Southern (4/105).
Clifton Abraham, DB, Florida State (5/143).
Wardell Rouse, LB, Clemson (6/179).
Steve Ingram, G, Maryland (7/215).
Jeffrey Rodgers, DE, Texas A&M-Kingsville (7/227).

1995 SEASON

TRAINING CAMP ROSTER

No.	QUARTERBACKS	Ht./Wt.	Born	NFL Exp.	College	How acq.	'94 Games GP/GS
12	Dilfer, Trent	6-4/235	3-13-72	2	Fresno State	D1/94	5/2
10	Holcomb, Kelly	6-2/202	7-9-73	R	Middle Tennessee State	FA/95	—
17	Philcox, Todd	6-4/225	9-25-66	5	Syracuse	PlanB/91	0/0
11	Weldon, Casey	6-1/206	2-3-69	4	Florida State	FA/93	2/0
4	Willis, Peter Tom	6-2/204	1-4-67	5	Florida State	FA/95	0/0
	RUNNING BACKS						
41	Edmonds, Bobby Joe (KR)	5-11/186	9-26-64	5	Arkansas	FA/95	0/0
37	Ellison, Jerry	5-10/194	12-20-71	1	UT Chattanooga	FA/95	0/0
43	Harris, Rudy (FB)	6-1/257	9-18-71	3	Clemson	D4a/93	8/0
33	McDowell, Anthony (FB)	5-11/240	11-12-68	4	Texas Tech	D8/92	14/11
31	McMillon, Tiger	5-8/185	2-26-72	R	Florida State	FA/95	—
32	Rhett, Errict	5-11/211	12-11-70	2	Florida	D2/94	16/8
46	Workman, Vince	5-10/205	5-9-68	7	Ohio State	FA/93	15/8
	RECEIVERS						
86	Armstrong, Tyji (TE)	6-4/262	10-3-70	4	Mississippi	D3b/92	16/9
88	Copeland, Horace	6-2/198	1-2-71	2	Miami (Fla.)	D4B/93	16/2
18	Davis, Tyree	5-9/175	9-23-70	1	Central Arkansas	D7/93	0/0
80	Dawsey, Lawrence	6-0/192	11-16-67	5	Florida State	D3/91	10/5
82	Harper, Alvin	6-3/208	7-6-68	5	Tennessee	FA/95	*16/14
81	Harris, Jackie (TE)	6-4/248	1-4-68	6	Northeast Louisiana	FA/94	9/9
85	Hawkins, Courtney	5-9/183	12-12-69	4	Michigan State	D2/92	13/12
83	Moore, Dave (TE)	6-2/248	11-11-69	3	Pittsburgh	FA/92	15/5
49	Saunders, Cedric (TE)	6-3/240	9-30-72	1	Ohio State	FA/94	0/0
87	Thomas, Lamar	6-1/163	2-12-70	3	Miami (Fla.)	D3a/93	11/0
19	Verdin, Clarence (KR)	5-8/162	6-14-63	10	Southwestern Louisiana	FA/95	*12/0
17	Ware, Moses	6-4/191	8-12-73	R	North Carolina	FA/95	—
16	Willis, Dan	6-3/205	....	R	Southeastern Oklahoma State	FA/95	—
84	Wilson, Charles	5-10/185	7-1-68	5	Memphis	FA/92	14/7
	OFFENSIVE LINEMEN						
62	Beckles, Ian (G)	6-1/304	7-20-67	6	Indiana	D5/90	16/16
64	Cosby, Carlos (G)	6-2/306	8-19-72	R	Jackson State	FA/95	—
68	Crisman, Joel (G)	6-5/300	2-3-71	R	Southern California	FA/95	—
76	Dill, Scott (T/G)	6-5/295	4-5-66	8	Memphis	FA/90	16/16
74	Gruber, Paul (T)	6-5/296	2-24-65	8	Wisconsin	D1/88	16/16
65	Ingram, Stephen (T/G)	6-4/311	5-8-71	R	Maryland	D7a/95	—
79	Love, Sean (G)	6-3/300	9-6-68	3	Penn State	W-Buf/93	6/0
61	Mayberry, Tony (C)	6-4/292	12-8-67	6	Wake Forest	D4/90	16/16
70	McRae, Charles (T/G)	6-7/306	9-16-68	5	Tennessee	D1/91	15/10
69	Pierson, Pete (T)	6-5/295	2-4-71	1	Washington	D5/94	0/0
60	Pyne, Jim (C)	6-2/282	11-23-71	R	Virginia Tech	D7/94	—
67	Sullivan, Mike	6-3/292	12-22-67	4	Miami (Fla.)	FA/92	16/1
	DEFENSIVE LINEMEN						
72	Ahanotu, Chidi (E/T)	6-2/288	10-11-70	3	California	D6/93	16/16
73	Culpepper, Brad (T)	6-1/270	5-8-69	4	Florida	W-Min/94	16/15
75	Curry, Eric (E)	6-5/270	2-3-70	3	Alabama	D1/93	15/14
71	Dotson, Santana (E/T)	6-5/276	12-19-69	4	Baylor	D5b/92	16/9
92	Faulkner, Jeff (E)	6-4/305	4-4-64	5	Southern	FA/95	0/0
96	Hammonds, Juan (E)	6-3/260	3-5-72	R	Michigan State	FA/95	—
90	Jones, Milton (E)	6-5/270	3-24-71	R	Central State (O.)	FA/95	—
94	McIntosh, Toddrick (E/T)	6-3/277	1-22-72	2	Florida State	W-Dal/94	4/0
95	Powe, Keith (E)	6-3/265	6-5-69	2	Texas-El Paso	FA/94	5/0
78	Rodgers, Jeffrey (E)	6-3/273	6-10-73	R	Texas A&M-Kingsville	D7b/95	—
99	Sapp, Warren (T)	6-1/281	12-19-72	R	Miami (Fla.)	D1/95	—
98	Spindler, Marc (E/T)	6-5/290	11-28-69	6	Pittsburgh	FA/95	*9/8
77	Wheeler, Mark (T)	6-2/285	4-1-70	4	Texas A&M	D3a/92	15/8
	LINEBACKERS						
53	Brady, Ed	6-2/238	6-17-62	12	Illinois	FA/92	16/0
55	Brooks, Derrick	6-0/229	4-18-73	R	Florida State	D1b/95	—
93	DuBose, Demetrius	6-1/240	3-23-71	3	Notre Dame	D2/93	16/1
59	Harris, Dwayne	6-2/227	12-13-72	R	Nebraska	FA/95	—
58	Jones, Tim	6-1/239	11-15-71	R	Clemson	FA/95	—
51	Marts, Lonnie	6-1/236	11-10-68	6	Tulane	FA/94	16/14
57	Mock, Kerry	6-1/232	8-17-73	R	North Carolina	FA/95	—
56	Nickerson, Hardy	6-2/228	9-1-65	9	California	FA/93	14/14
52	Rouse, Wardell	6-2/231	6-9-72	R	Clemson	D6/95	—
54	Stephens, Darnell	5-11/253	1-29-73	R	Clemson	FA/95	—
97	Washington, Rodney	6-2/235	....	R	Southeastern Oklahoma State	FA/95	—

No.	DEFENSIVE BACKS	Ht./Wt.	Born	NFL Exp.	College	How acq.	'94 Games GP/GS
26	Abraham, Clifton (CB)	5-9/184	12-9-71	R	Florida State	D5/95	—
	Booty, John (S)	6-0/180	10-9-65	8	Texas Christian	FA/95	*16/9
23	Bouie, Tony (S)	5-10/187	8-7-72	R	Arizona	FA/95	—
28	Buckley, Curtis (S)	6-0/191	9-25-70	3	East Texas State	FA/93	13/0
27	Bussey, Barney (S)	6-0/215	5-20-62	10	South Carolina State	FA/93	16/15
39	Dimry, Charles (CB)	6-0/176	1-31-66	8	UNLV	FA/94	16/16
22	Everett, Thomas (S)	5-9/190	11-21-64	9	Baylor	T-Dal/94	15/15
29	Gant, Kenneth (S)	5-11/189	4-18-67	6	Albany (Ga.) State	FA/95	*16/0
25	Johnson, Melvin (S)	6-0/195	4-15-72	R	Kentucky	D2/95	—
47	Lynch, John (S)	6-2/216	9-25-71	3	Stanford	D3b/93	16/0
35	Mayhew, Martin (CB)	5-8/178	10-8-65	8	Florida State	FA/93	16/16
21	McGruder, Mike (CB)	5-10/182	5-6-64	6	Kent	FA/94	15/3
45	Stargell, Tony (CB)	5-11/186	8-7-66	6	Tennessee State	FA/94	10/2
24	Wilson, Jerry (CB)	5-10/184	7-17-73	R	Southern	D4/95	—
	SPECIALISTS						
2	Duvic, Tim (K)	5-10/170	1-2-72	R	Dayton	FA/95	—
3	Edge, Shayne (P)	5-11/173	8-21-71	R	Florida	FA/95	—
5	Husted, Michael (K)	6-0/188	6-16-70	3	Virginia	FA/93	16/0
1	Roby, Reggie (P)	6-2/258	7-30-61	13	Iowa	FA/95	*16/0

*Booty played 16 games with Giants in '94; Gant played 16 games with Cowboys; Harper played 16 games with Cowboys; Roby played 16 games with Redskins; Spindler played 9 games with Lions; Verdin played 12 games with Falcons.

Also played with Buccaneers in '94: TE Harold Bishop (6 games); LB Jeff Brady (16); S Marty Carter (16); S Tony Covington (14); DT Santana Dotson (16); CB Rogerick Green (11); WR Willie Green (5); DB Jeff Hunter (1); T Tim Irwin (8); DT Shawn Price (6); RB Mazio Royster (14); P Dan Stryzinski (16); KR/WR Vernon Turner (12); DT Bernard Wilson (1); DE/DT Karl Wilson (15).

Abbreviations: D1—draft pick, first round; SupD2—supplemental draft pick, second round; W-Den—waivers acquisition from Denver; T-Sea—trade acquisition from Seattle; PlanB—Plan B free-agent acquisition; FA—free-agent acquisition (other than Plan B).

MISCELLANEOUS TEAM DATA

Stadium (capacity, surface):
Tampa Stadium (74,301, grass)
Business address:
One Buccaneer Place
Tampa, FL 33607
Business phone:
813-870-2700
Ticket information:
813-870-2700
Team colors:
Florida orange, white and red
Flagship radio station:
WQYK, 99.5 FM
Training site:
University of Tampa
Tampa, Fla.
813-253-6215

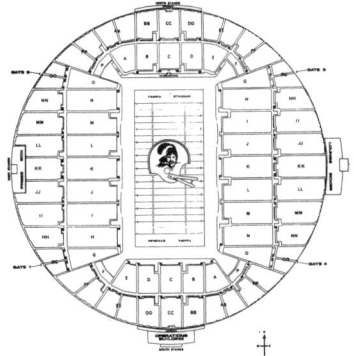

WASHINGTON REDSKINS
NFC EASTERN DIVISION

1994 REVIEW

RESULTS

Sept. 4—SEATTLE	L	7-28
Sept. 11—at New Orleans	W	38-24
Sept. 18—at N.Y. Giants	L	23-31
Sept. 25—ATLANTA	L	20-27
Oct. 2—DALLAS	L	7-34
Oct. 9—at Philadelphia	L	17-21
Oct. 16—ARIZONA (OT)	L	16-19
Oct. 23—at Indianapolis	W	41-27
Oct. 30—PHILADELPHIA	L	29-31
Nov. 6—SAN FRANCISCO	L	22-37
Nov. 13—Open date		
Nov. 20—at Dallas	L	7-31
Nov. 27—N.Y. GIANTS	L	19-21
Dec. 4—at Tampa Bay	L	21-26
Dec. 11—at Arizona	L	15-17
Dec. 18—TAMPA BAY	L	14-17
Dec. 24—at L.A. Rams	W	24-21

RECORDS/RANKINGS

1994 regular-season record: 3-13 (5th in NFC East); 0-8 in division; 2-12 in conference; 0-8 at home; 3-5 on road.
Team record last five years: 40-40 (.500), ranks T16th in league in that span).
1994 team rankings:

	No.	NFC	NFL
Total offense	*299.6	9	17
Rushing offense	*88.4	11	24
Passing offense	*211.1	6	11
Scoring offense	320	7	13
Total defense	*350.6	13	26
Rushing defense	*123.4	14	27
Passing defense	*227.1	11	20
Scoring defense	412	14	28
Takeaways	23	T10	T23
Giveaways	40	14	26
Turnover differential	-17	14	27
Sacks	28	T9	T21
Sacks allowed	21	2	5

*Yards per game.

TEAM LEADERS

Scoring (kicking): Chip Lohmiller, 90 pts. (30/32 PATs, 20/28 FGs).
Scoring (touchdowns): Henry Ellard, 36 pts. (6 receiving).
Passing: Heath Shuler, 1,658 yds. (265 att., 120 comp., 45.3%, 10 TDs, 12 int.).
Rushing: Ricky Ervins, 650 yds. (185 att., 3.5 avg., 3 TDs).
Receptions: Henry Ellard, 74 (1,397 yds., 18.9 avg., 6 TDs).
Interceptions: Andre Collins, 4 (150 yds., 2 TDs).
Sacks: Ken Harvey, 13.5.
Punting: Reggie Roby, 44.4 avg. (82 punts, 3,639 yds., 0 blocked).
Punt returns: Brian Mitchell, 14.1 avg. (32 att., 452 yds., 2 TDs).
Kickoff returns: Brian Mitchell, 25.5 avg. (58 att., 1,478 yds., 0 TDs).

1995 SEASON

CLUB DIRECTORY

Chairman of the board/CEO
Jack Kent Cooke
Executive vice president
John Kent Cooke
Secretary
Stuart Haney
Controller
Greg Dillon
General manager
Charley Casserly
Assistant general manager
Bobby Mitchell
Director of communications
Rick Vaughn
Dir. of stadium operations and club promotions
John Kent Cooke Jr.
Director of media relations
Mike McCall
Director of information
Chris Helein
Asst. promotions/advertising director
John Wagner
Ticket manager
Jeff Ritter
Director of player personnel
Kirk Mee
Director of college scouting
George Saimes
Scouting administrator
Scott Cohen
Scouts
Gene Bates
Larry Bryan
Mike Hagen
Mel Kaufman
Mike MacCagnan
Miller McCalmon
Joe Mendes

SCHEDULE

Sept. 3—ARIZONA	4:00
Sept. 10—LOS ANGELES	1:00
Sept. 17—at Denver	2:00
Sept. 24—at Tampa Bay	1:00
Oct. 1—DALLAS	1:00
Oct. 8—at Philadelphia	1:00
Oct. 15—at Arizona	1:00
Oct. 22—DETROIT	1:00
Oct. 29—N.Y. GIANTS	8:00
Nov. 5—at Kansas City	12:00
Nov. 12—Open date	
Nov. 19—SEATTLE	1:00
Nov. 26—PHILADELPHIA	1:00
Dec. 3—at Dallas	3:00
Dec. 10—at N.Y. Giants	4:00
Dec. 17—at St. Louis	12:00
Dec. 24—CAROLINA	4:00

All times are for home team.
All games Sunday unless noted.

Head coach
Norv Turner
Assistant coaches
Jason Arapoff (conditioning director)
Cam Cameron (quarterbacks)
Russ Grimm (tight ends)
Mike Haluchak (linebackers)
Jim Hanifan (offensive line)
Tom Hayes (def. backs)
Ray Horton (secondary assistant)
Bobby Jackson (running backs)
Bob Karmelowicz (def. line)
Ron Lynn (def. coord.)
Dan Riley (strength)
Terry Robiskie (wide receivers)
Pete Rodriguez (special teams)

Head trainer
Bubba Tyer
Assistant trainers
Al Bellamy
Kevin Bastin
Equipment manager
Jay Brunetti
Assistant equipment manager
Jeff Parsons
Director of video
Donnie Schoenmann
Asst. director of video
Hugh McPhilips
Video analyst
Mike Bean

DRAFT CHOICES

Michael Westbrook, WR, Colorado (first round/fourth pick overall).
Cory Raymer, C, Wisconsin (2/37).
Darryl Pounds, CB, Nicholls State (3/68).
Larry Jones, RB, Miami (Fla.) (4/103).
Jamie Asher, TE, Louisville (5/137).
Rich Owens, DE, Lehigh (5/152).
Brian Thure, T, California (6/176).
Scott Turner, DB, Illinois (7/226).

TRAINING CAMP ROSTER

No.	QUARTERBACKS	Ht./Wt.	Born	NFL Exp.	College	How acq.	'94 Games GP/GS
12	Frerotte, Gus	6-2/221	7-31-71	2	Tulsa	D7/94	4/4
10	Green, Trent	6-3/212	7-9-70	2	Indiana	FA/95	0/0
16	Roberts, John	6-3/190	6-20-72	R	Northern Colorado	FA/95	—
5	Shuler, Heath	6-2/221	12-31-71	2	Tennessee	D1/94	11/8
	RUNNING BACKS						
36	Bell, William	5-11/212	7-22-71	2	Georgia Tech	FA/94	7/0
40	Brooks, Reggie	5-8/211	1-19-71	3	Notre Dame	D2/93	13/5
32	Frasier, Joe (FB)	6-0/212	4-13-72	R	Auburn	FA/95	—
22	Jones, Larry (FB)	6-0/244	2-16-71	R	Miami (Fla.)	D4/95	—
20	Logan, Marc	6-0/212	5-9-65	8	Kentucky	FA/95	*10/5
30	Mitchell, Brian (FB/KR)	5-10/221	8-18-68	6	Southwestern Louisiana	D5/90	16/7
39	Rush, Tyrone	5-11/201	2-5-71	2	North Alabama	FA/94	5/0
34	Smith, Cedric (FB)	5-10/237	5-27-68	4	Florida	FA/94	14/8
48	Thompson, Ernie (FB)	6-0/260	10-25-69	3	Indiana	FA/95	0/0
	RECEIVERS						
46	Asher, Jamie (TE)	6-3/243	10-31-72	R	Louisville	D5a/95	—
	Bell, Coleman (TE)	6-2/243	4-22-70	1	Miami (Fla.)	FA/95	0/0
85	Ellard, Henry	5-11/185	7-21-61	13	Fresno State	FA/94	16/16
88	Jenkins, James (TE)	6-2/241	8-17-67	5	Rutgers	FA/91	16/3
18	Jones, Reggie	6-0/175	5-5-71	R	Louisiana State	FA/95	—
80	Newman, Patrick	6-0/209	9-10-68	5	Utah State	FA/95	*1/0
86	Shepherd, Leslie	5-11/189	11-3-69	2	Temple	FA/94	3/0
19	Thomas, Doug	5-11/178	9-18-69	3	Clemson	FA/95	0/0
84	Truitt, Olanda	6-0/186	1-4-71	3	Mississippi State	FA/94	9/0
82	Westbrook, Michael	6-3/215	7-7-72	R	Colorado	D1/95	—
83	Winans, Tydus	5-11/180	7-26-72	2	Fresno State	D3a/94	15/0
89	Wycheck, Frank (TE)	6-3/247	10-14-71	3	Maryland	D6b/93	9/1
	OFFENSIVE LINEMEN						
67	Brown, Ray (T)	6-5/312	12-12-62	10	Arkansas State	PlanB/89	16/16
60	Dammann, Ken (G)	6-5/285	1-17-72	R	Rutgers	FA/95	—
55	Fichtel, Brad (C)	6-2/285	3-10-70	3	Eastern Illinois	FA/95	*1/0
63	Gesek, John (G/C)	6-5/282	2-18-63	9	Sacramento State	FA/94	15/12
73	Henson, Don (T)	6-5/297	1-30-71	1	Sam Houston State	FA/94	0/0
77	Johnson, Tre' (T)	6-2/338	8-30-71	2	Temple	D2/94	14/1
62	Kalaniuvalu, Alai (G)	6-3/302	10-23-71	1	Oregon State	FA/94	0/0
79	Lachey, Jim (T)	6-6/294	6-4-63	11	Ohio State	T-Rai/88	13/13
64	Matich, Trevor (C)	6-4/297	10-9-61	11	Brigham Young	FA/94	16/0
68	Patton, Joe (G)	6-5/288	1-5-72	2	Alabama A&M	D3b/94	2/0
52	Raymer, Cory (C)	6-2/293	3-3-73	R	Wisconsin	D2/95	—
76	Simmons, Ed (T)	6-5/325	12-31-63	9	Eastern Washington	D6/87	16/16
61	Smith, Vernice (G)	6-3/298	10-24-65	7	Florida A&M	FA/95	4/0
74	Thure, Brian (T)	6-5/300	9-3-73	R	California	D6/95	—
	DEFENSIVE LINEMEN						
95	Abrams, Anthony (T)	6-4/298	2-16-71	1	Clark Atlanta	FA/94	0/0
93	Boutte, Marc (T)	6-4/311	7-25-69	4	Louisiana State	W-Ram/94	9/3
69	Burrest, Damon (T)	6-3/311	10-11-71	R	New Mexico	FA/95	—
78	Johnson, Tim (T)	6-3/286	1-29-65	9	Penn State	T-Pit/90	14/13
75	Mahone, Elic (E)	6-4/260	3-7-72	R	Southern California	FA/95	—
72	Mills, Lamar (T)	6-5/307	1-26-71	2	Indiana	FA/94	13/4
92	Nottage, Dexter (E)	6-4/290	11-14-70	2	Florida A&M	D6/94	15/1
96	Owens, Rich (E)	6-6/255	5-22-72	R	Lehigh	D5b/95	—
97	Palmer, Sterling (E)	6-5/277	2-4-71	3	Florida State	D4/93	16/16
71	Talanoa, Ken (E)	6-4/271	12-14-72	R	Arizona State	FA/95	—
94	Wilson, Bobby (T)	6-2/307	3-4-68	5	Michigan State	D1/91	9/9
98	Woods, Tony (E)	6-4/282	9-11-65	9	Pittsburgh	FA/94	15/15
	LINEBACKERS						
58	Alexander, Patrice	6-1/255	10-23-72	R	Southwestern Louisiana	FA/95	—
56	Anderson, Erick	6-1/240	10-7-68	4	Michigan	FA/94	2/0
50	Brownlow, Darrick	6-0/260	12-28-68	5	Illinois	FA/95	*16/0
90	Dubose, Craig	6-2/255	8-30-71	R	Clark (Ala.)	FA/95	—
57	Harvey, Ken	6-2/245	5-6-65	8	California	FA/94	16/16
59	Killian, P.J.	6-2/240	5-19-71	1	Virginia	FA/95	0/0
53	Patton, Marvcus	6-2/240	5-1-67	6	UCLA	FA/95	*16/16
99	Stephens, Rod	6-1/237	6-14-66	7	Georgia Tech	FA/95	*16/16
91	Vanderbeek, Matt	6-3/243	8-16-67	7	Michigan State	FA/95	*12/0
	DEFENSIVE BACKS						
25	Carter, Tom (CB)	6-0/181	9-5-72	3	Notre Dame	D1/93	16/16
29	Dillard, Barry	5-10/176	2-14-73	R	Memphis	FA/95	—

No.	DEFENSIVE BACKS	Ht./Wt.	Born	NFL Exp.	College	How acq.	'94 Games GP/GS
26	Grant, Alan (CB)	5-10/187	10-1-66	6	Stanford	FA/94	13/0
28	Green, Darrell (CB)	5-8/180	2-15-60	13	Texas A&I	D1/83	16/16
38	Morrison, Darryl (CB)	5-11/200	5-19-71	2	Arizona	D6a/93	16/16
41	Oliver, Muhammad (CB)	5-11/185	3-12-69	4	Oregon	FA/95	*13/2
31	Pounds, Darryl (CB)	5-10/177	7-21-72	R	Nicholls State (La.)	D3/95	—
24	Richard, Stanley (S)	6-2/197	10-21-67	5	Texas	FA/95	*16/16
23	Savage, Sebastian (S)	5-10/187	12-12-69	1	North Carolina State	FA/94	1/0
27	Taylor, Keith (S)	5-11/212	12-21-64	7	Illinois	FA/94	1/1
21	Turner, Scott (CB)	5-10/178	2-26-72	R	Illinois	D7/95	—
37	Washington, James (S)	6-1/209	1-10-65	8	UCLA	FA/95	*16/16
	SPECIALISTS						
4	Blanton, Scott (K)	6-2/233	7-1-73	R	Oklahoma	FA/95	—
8	Lohmiller, Chip (K)	6-3/215	7-16-66	8	Minnesota	D2/88	16/0
6	Sullivan, Kent (P)	6-0/202	5-15-64	3	California Lutheran	FA/95	0/0
1	Turk, Matt (P)	6-5/230	6-16-68	1	Wisconsin-Whitewater	FA/95	0/0
13	Videtich, Steve (K)	6-1/200	11-4-71	R	North Carolina State	FA/95	—

*Brownlow played 16 games with Cowboys in '94; Fichtel played 1 game with Rams; Logan played 10 games with 49ers; Newman played 1 game with Browns; Oliver played 13 games with Dolphins; Patton played 16 games with Bills; Richard played 16 games with Chargers; Stephens played 16 games with Seahawks; Vanderbeek played 12 games with Cowboys; Washington played 16 games with Cowboys.

Also played with Redskins in '94: S Martin Bayless (16); S Deral Boykin (12); LB Monte Coleman (16); LB Andre Collins (16); DE Shane Collins (7); S Pat Eilers (16); RB Ricky Ervins (16); QB John Friesz (16); LB Kurt Gouveia (14); LB Rick Hamilton (1); TE Kurt Haws (6); LB Lamont Hollinquest (14); TE Ethan Horton (16); WR Desmond Howard (16); CB A.J. Johnson (11); CB Alvoid Mays (2); C/G Raleigh McKenzie (16); CB Brian Mitchell (16); G Joe Patton (2); P Reggie Roby (16); G Mark Schlereth (16); LB Tyronne Stowe (16); CB Johnny Thomas (16).

Abbreviations: D1—draft pick, first round; SupD2—supplemental draft pick, second round; W-Den—waivers acquisition from Denver; T-Sea—trade acquisition from Seattle; PlanB—Plan B free-agent acquisition; FA—free-agent acquisition (other than Plan B).

MISCELLANEOUS TEAM DATA

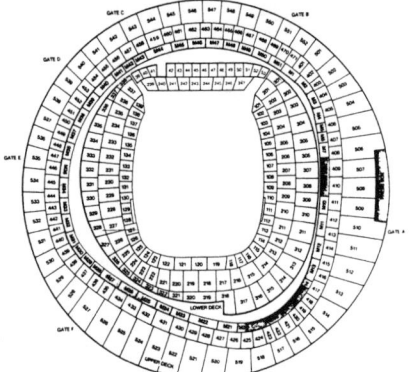

Stadium (capacity, surface):
Robert F. Kennedy Memorial
Stadium (56,454, grass)

Business address:
P.O. Box 17247
Dulles International Airport
Washington, D.C. 20041

Business phone:
703-478-8900

Ticket information:
202-546-2222

Team colors:
Burgundy and gold

Flagship radio station:
WJFK, 106.7 FM

Training site:
To be announced

SCHEDULE

(All times are Eastern)

WEEK 1

SATURDAY, JULY 29

Buffalo at Dallas	9:00
San Francisco at Denver	9:00
Carolina vs. Jacksonville at Canton, O.*	2:30

*Hall of Fame Game.

WEEK 2

FRIDAY, AUGUST 4

Detroit at New England	7:00
Jacksonville at Miami	7:00
Cincinnati at Indianapolis	7:30
Pittsburgh at Buffalo	7:30
Carolina at Chicago	8:30

SATURDAY, AUGUST 5

New Orleans vs. Green Bay at Madison, Wis.	1:00
Atlanta at Philadelphia	7:30
N.Y. Jets at Tampa Bay	7:30
Arizona at Houston	8:00
Washington at Kansas City	8:00
Los Angeles at Dallas	9:00
St. Louis at Seattle	10:00
Denver vs. San Francisco at Tokyo	10:00

SUNDAY, AUGUST 6

N.Y. Giants at Cleveland	4:00

MONDAY, AUGUST 7

Minnesota at San Diego	8:00

WEEK 3

THURSDAY, AUGUST 10

Jacksonville at Detroit	7:30

FRIDAY, AUGUST 11

Miami at Atlanta	7:30
Tampa Bay at Cincinnati	7:30
New Orleans at N.Y. Giants	8:00
Kansas City at Arizona	10:30

SATURDAY, AUGUST 12

Denver at Carolina	7:30
Houston vs. Washington at Knoxville, Tenn.	8:00
Buffalo vs. Dallas at Toronto	8:00
Minnesota at New England	8:00
N.Y. Jets vs. Philadelphia at Jackson, Miss.	9:00
Indianapolis at Seattle	10:00
St. Louis at Los Angeles	TBA

SUNDAY, AUGUST 13

Green Bay at Pittsburgh	1:00
San Francisco at San Diego	8:00

MONDAY, AUGUST 14

Chicago at Cleveland	8:00

WEEK 4

THURSDAY, AUGUST 17

Cincinnati at Detroit	7:30
New England at Phildelphia	8:00

FRIDAY, AUGUST 18

St. Louis at Jacksonville	7:00
Los Angeles at Minnesota	8:00

SATURDAY, AUGUST 19

Indianapolis at Green Bay	1:00
Cleveland at Atlanta	7:00
Washington at Miami	7:00
Pittsburgh at Tampa Bay	7:30
Buffalo at Kansas City	8:00
Carolina at San Francisco	8:00
N.Y. Jets at N.Y. Giants	8:00
San Diego at Houston	8:30

SUNDAY, AUGUST 20

Seattle at New Orleans	1:00
Arizona at Chicago	8:00

MONDAY, AUGUST 21

Dallas at Denver	8:00

WEEK 5

THURSDAY, AUGUST 24

Chicago at Indianapolis	7:30
Philadelphia at Pittsburgh	8:00

FRIDAY, AUGUST 25

Washington at Green Bay	7:00
Denver at Jacksonville	7:00
Atlanta at Buffalo	7:30
N.Y. Jets at Cincinnati	7:30
Detroit at New Orleans	8:00
Miami vs. Tampa Bay at Orlando, Fla.	8:00
New England vs. Los Angeles	9:00
St. Louis at San Diego	10:30
Cleveland at Arizona	10:30

SATURDAY, AUGUST 26

Kansas City at Minnesota	1:30
N.Y. Giants at Carolina	4:00
Dallas vs. Houston at San Antonio	8:00
Seattle at San Francisco	8:00

(All times local)

WEEK 1

SUNDAY, SEPTEMBER 3

Cincinnati at Indianapolis	12:00
Cleveland at New England	1:00
Houston at Jacksonville	1:00
Carolina at Atlanta	1:00
San Francisco at New Orleans	12:00
Tampa Bay at Philadelphia	1:00
St. Louis at Green Bay	12:00
Detroit at Pittsburgh	1:00
N.Y. Jets at Miami	4:00
San Diego at Los Angeles	1:00
Kansas City at Seattle	1:00
Arizona at Washington	4:00
Minnesota at Chicago	3:00
Buffalo at Denver	6:00

MONDAY, SEPTEMBER 4

Dallas at N.Y. Giants 9:00

WEEK 2

SUNDAY, SEPTEMBER 10

Miami at New England	1:00
Los Angeles at Washington	1:00
Pittsburgh at Houston	12:00
New Orleans at St. Louis	12:00
Detroit at Minnesota	12:00
Carolina at Buffalo	1:00
N.Y. Giants at Kansas City	12:00
Tampa Bay at Cleveland	1:00
Denver at Dallas	3:00
Indianapolis at N.Y. Jets	4:00
Seattle at San Diego	1:00
Jacksonville at Cincinnati	4:00
Atlanta at San Francisco	1:00
Philadelphia at Arizona	5:00

MONDAY, SEPTEMBER 11

Green Bay at Chicago................................... 8:00

WEEK 3

SUNDAY, SEPTEMBER 17

San Diego at Philadelphia	1:00
Indianapolis at Buffalo	1:00
Los Angeles at Kansas City	12:00
Cleveland at Houston	12:00
St. Louis at Carolina	1:00
Atlanta at New Orleans	12:00
Arizona at Detroit	1:00
N.Y. Giants at Green Bay	12:00
New England at San Francisco	1:00
Cincinnati at Seattle	1:00
Jacksonville at N.Y. Jets	4:00
Washington at Denver	2:00
Chicago at Tampa Bay	4:00
Dallas at Minnesota	7:00

MONDAY, SEPTEMBER 18

Pittsburgh at Miami 9:00

WEEK 4

SUNDAY, SEPTEMBER 24

Chicago at St. Louis	12:00
New Orleans at N.Y. Giants.........................	1:00
Washington at Tampa Bay	1:00
Minnesota at Pittsburgh	1:00
N.Y. Jets at Atlanta	4:00
Denver at San Diego	1:00
Houston at Cincinnati	4:00
Kansas City at Cleveland	4:00
Arizona at Dallas	3:00
Philadelphia at Los Angeles	1:00
Green Bay at Jacksonville	8:00

MONDAY, SEPTEMBER 25

San Francisco at Detroit 9:00

Open date: Buffalo, Carolina, Indianapolis, Miami, New England, Seattle

WEEK 5

SUNDAY, OCTOBER 1

New England at Atlanta	1:00
Miami at Cincinnati	1:00
Tampa Bay at Carolina	1:00
Philadelphia at New Orleans	12:00
Dallas at Washington	1:00
St. Louis at Indianapolis	12:00
Kansas City at Arizona	1:00
Jacksonville at Houston	3:00
Denver at Seattle	1:00

San Diego at Pittsburgh...............................	4:00
N.Y. Giants at San Francisco.......................	1:00
Los Angeles at N.Y. Jets	8:00

MONDAY, OCTOBER 2

Buffalo at Cleveland 9:00

Open date: Chicago, Detroit, Green Bay, Minnesota

WEEK 6

SUNDAY, OCTOBER 8

Cincinnati at Tampa Bay	1:00
N.Y. Jets at Buffalo......................................	1:00
Pittsburgh at Jacksonville	1:00
Green Bay at Dallas	12:00
Washington at Philadelphia	1:00
Carolina at Chicago	12:00
Houston at Minnesota	12:00
Cleveland at Detroit	4:00
Indianapolis at Miami	4:00
Seattle at Los Angeles	1:00
Arizona at N.Y. Giants	4:00
Denver at New England................................	8:00

MONDAY, OCTOBER 9

San Diego at Kansas City.............................. 8:00

Open date: Atlanta, New Orleans, St. Louis, San Francisco

WEEK 7

THURSDAY, OCTOBER 12

Atlanta at St. Louis 7:00

SUNDAY, OCTOBER 15

Seattle at Buffalo...	1:00
New England at Kansas City	12:00
Philadelphia at N.Y. Giants	1:00
Detroit at Green Bay	12:00
Minnesota at Tampa Bay	1:00
San Francisco at Indianapolis	12:00
Chicago at Jacksonville	1:00
Miami at New Orleans	3:00
N.Y. Jets at Carolina	4:00
Washington at Arizona	1:00
Dallas at San Diego	1:00

MONDAY, OCTOBER 16

Los Angeles at Denver 7:00

Open date: Cincinnati, Cleveland, Houston, Pittsburgh

WEEK 8

THURSDAY, OCTOBER 19

Cincinnati at Pittsburgh................................. 8:00

SUNDAY, OCTOBER 22

Houston at Chicago	12:00
Miami at N.Y. Jets	1:00
Jacksonville at Cleveland	1:00
New Orleans at Carolina	1:00
Detroit at Washington	1:00
Minnesota at Green Bay	12:00
Atlanta at Tampa Bay	1:00
Kansas City at Denver	2:00
Indianapolis at Los Angeles.........................	1:00
San Diego at Seattle	1:00
San Francisco at St. Louis	3:00

MONDAY, OCTOBER 23

Buffalo at New England 9:00

Open date: Arizona, Dallas, N.Y. Giants, Philadelphia

WEEK 9

SUNDAY, OCTOBER 29

Jacksonville at Pittsburgh.............................	1:00
N.Y. Jets at Indianapolis	1:00
Cleveland at Cincinnati	1:00

Dallas at Atlanta 1:00
St. Louis at Philadelphia 1:00
Green Bay at Detroit 1:00
Carolina at New England 1:00
Buffalo at Miami 4:00
Seattle at Arizona 2:00
New Orleans at San Francisco 1:00
Tampa Bay at Houston 3:00
N.Y. Giants at Washington 8:00

MONDAY, OCTOBER 30

Chicago at Minnesota 8:00

Open date: Denver, Kansas City, Los Angeles, San Diego

WEEK 10

SUNDAY, NOVEMBER 5

Buffalo at Indianapolis 1:00
New England at N.Y. Jets 1:00
Houston at Cleveland 1:00
Detroit at Atlanta 1:00
St. Louis at New Orleans 12:00
Green Bay at Minnesota 12:00
Washington at Kansas City 12:00
Pittsburgh at Chicago 3:00
Los Angeles at Cincinnati 4:00
Carolina at San Francisco 1:00
Arizona at Denver 2:00
N.Y. Giants at Seattle 1:00
Miami at San Diego 5:00

MONDAY, NOVEMBER 6

Philadelphia at Dallas 8:00

Open date: Jacksonville, Tampa Bay

WEEK 11

SUNDAY, NOVEMBER 12

Indianapolis at New Orleans 12:00
Los Angeles at N.Y. Giants 1:00
Atlanta at Buffalo 1:00
New England at Miami 1:00
Cincinnati at Houston 12:00
Seattle at Jacksonville 1:00
Carolina at St. Louis 12:00
Tampa Bay at Detroit 1:00
Chicago at Green Bay 12:00
Kansas City at San Diego 1:00
San Francisco at Dallas 3:00
Minnesota at Arizona 2:00
Denver at Philadelphia 8:00

MONDAY, NOVEMBER 13

Cleveland at Pittsburgh 9:00

Open date: N.Y. Jets, Washington

WEEK 12

SUNDAY, NOVEMBER 19

Seattle at Washington 1:00
Jacksonville at Tampa Bay 1:00
Indianapolis at New England 1:00
Pittsburgh at Cincinnati 1:00
St. Louis at Atlanta 1:00
Arizona at Carolina 1:00
N.Y. Giants at Philadelphia 1:00
Detroit at Chicago 12:00
Green Bay at Cleveland 1:00
San Diego at Denver 2:00
Buffalo at N.Y. Jets 4:00
Dallas at Los Angeles 1:00
New Orleans at Minnesota 3:00
Houston at Kansas City 7:00

MONDAY, NOVEMBER 20

San Francisco at Miami 9:00

WEEK 13

THURSDAY, NOVEMBER 23

Minnesota at Detroit 12:30
Kansas City at Dallas 3:00

SUNDAY, NOVEMBER 26

Miami at Indianapolis 1:00
New England at Buffalo 1:00
Cincinnati at Jacksonville 1:00
Chicago at N.Y. Giants 1:00
Philadelphia at Washington 1:00
Tampa Bay at Green Bay 12:00
Denver at Houston 3:00
N.Y. Jets at Seattle 1:00
Pittsburgh at Cleveland 4:00
St. Louis at San Francisco 1:00
Atlanta at Arizona 2:00
Carolina at New Orleans 7:00

MONDAY, NOVEMBER 27

Los Angeles at San Diego 6:00

WEEK 14

THURSDAY, NOVEMBER 30

N.Y. Giants at Arizona 6:00

SUNDAY, DECEMBER 3

Indianapolis at Carolina 1:00
Cincinnati at Green Bay 12:00
Houston at Pittsburgh 1:00
Atlanta at Miami 1:00
New Orleans at New England 1:00
St. Louis at N.Y. Jets 1:00
Tampa Bay at Minnesota 12:00
Jacksonville at Denver 2:00
Kansas City at Los Angeles 1:00
Cleveland at San Diego 1:00
Washington at Dallas 3:00
Philadelphia at Seattle 1:00
Buffalo at San Francisco 5:00

MONDAY, DECEMBER 4

Chicago at Detroit 9:00

WEEK 15

SATURDAY, DECEMBER 9

Cleveland at Minnesota 11:30
Arizona at San Diego 1:00

SUNDAY, DECEMBER 10

Buffalo at St. Louis 12:00
N.Y. Jets at New England 1:00
Indianapolis at Jacksonville 1:00
New Orleans at Atlanta 1:00
San Francisco at Carolina 1:00
Dallas at Philadelphia 1:00
Chicago at Cincinnati 1:00
Detroit at Houston 12:00
Seattle at Denver 2:00
Pittsburgh at Los Angeles 1:00
Washington at N.Y. Giants 4:00
Green Bay at Tampa Bay 8:00

MONDAY, DECEMBER 11

Kansas City at Miami 9:00

WEEK 16

SATURDAY, DECEMBER 16

New England at Pittsburgh 12:30
Green Bay at New Orleans 3:00

SUNDAY, DECEMBER 17

Jacksonville at Detroit 1:00
Miami at Buffalo 1:00
Cincinnati at Cleveland 1:00

N.Y. Jets at Houston	12:00
Atlanta at Carolina	1:00
Arizona at Philadelphia	1:00
Tampa Bay at Chicago	12:00
Washington at St. Louis	12:00
Denver at Kansas City	3:00
San Diego at Indianapolis	4:00
N.Y. Giants at Dallas	3:00
Los Angeles at Seattle	5:00

MONDAY, DECEMBER 18

Minnesota at San Francisco	6:00

WEEK 17

SATURDAY, DECEMBER 23

San Diego at N.Y. Giants	12:30

Detroit at Tampa Bay	4:00
New England at Indianapolis	8:00

SUNDAY, DECEMBER 24

Pittsburgh at Green Bay	12:00
Houston at Buffalo	1:00
Seattle at Kansas City	12:00
Cleveland at Jacksonville	1:00
San Francisco at Atlanta	1:00
Philadelphia at Chicago	12:00
New Orleans at N.Y. Jets	1:00
Minnesota at Cincinnati	1:00
Carolina at Washington	4:00
Denver at Los Angeles	1:00
Miami at St. Louis	3:00

MONDAY, DECEMBER 25

Dallas at Arizona	7:00

NATIONALLY TELEVISED GAMES

(All times local)

REGULAR SEASON

Sun. Sept. 3—Minnesota at Chicago (3:00, FOX)
Buffalo at Denver (6:00, TNT)
Mon. Sept. 4—Dallas at N.Y. Giants (9:00, ABC)
Sun. Sept. 10—Denver at Dallas (3:00, NBC)
Philadelphia at Arizona (5:00, TNT)
Mon. Sept. 11—Green Bay at Chicago (8:00, ABC)
Sun. Sept. 17—New England at San Francisco (1:00, NBC)
Dallas at Minnesota (7:00, TNT)
Mon. Sept. 18—Pittsburgh at Miami (9:00, ABC)
Sun. Sept. 24—San Francisco at Detroit (9:00, ABC)
Green Bay at Jacksonville (8:00, TNT)
Mon. Sept. 25—San Francisco at Detroit (9:00, ABC)
Sun. Oct. 1—San Diego at Pittsburgh (4:00, NBC)
Los Angeles at N.Y. Jets (8:00, TNT)
Mon. Oct. 2—Buffalo at Cleveland (9:00, ABC)
Sun. Oct. 8—Indianapolis at Miami (4:00, NBC)
Denver at New England (8:00, TNT)
Mon. Oct. 9—San Diego at Kansas City (9:00, ABC)
Thur. Oct. 12—Atlanta at St. Louis (7:00, TNT)
Sun. Oct. 15—Dallas at San Diego (1:00, FOX)
Mon. Oct. 16—Los Angeles at Denver (9:00, ABC)
Thur. Oct. 19—Cincinnati at Pittsburgh (8:00, TNT)
Sun. Oct. 22—Kansas City at Denver (2:00, NBC)
Mon. Oct. 23—Buffalo at New England (9:00, ABC)
Sun. Oct. 29—New Orleans at San Francisco (1:00, FOX)
N.Y. Giants at Washington (8:00, TNT)
Mon. Oct. 30—Chicago at Minnesota (8:00, ABC)
Sun. Nov. 5—Pittsburgh at Chicago (3:00, FOX)
Miami at San Diego (5:00, ESPN)
Mon. Nov. 6—Philadelphia at Dallas (8:00, ABC)
Sun. Nov. 12—San Francisco at Dallas (3:00, FOX)
Denver at Philadelphia (8:00, ESPN)
Mon. Nov. 13—Cleveland at Pittsburgh (9:00, ABC)
Sun. Nov. 19—Dallas at Los Angeles (1:00, FOX)
Houston at Kansas City (7:00, ESPN)

Mon. Nov. 20—San Francisco at Miami (9:00, ABC)
Thur. Nov. 23—Minnesota at Detroit (12:30, FOX)
Kansas City at Dallas (3:00, NBC)
Sun. Nov. 26—Pittsburgh at Cleveland (4:00, NBC)
Carolina at New Orleans (7:00, ESPN)
Mon. Nov. 27—Los Angeles at San Diego (6:00, ABC)
Thur. Nov. 30—N.Y. Giants at Arizona (6:00, ESPN)
Sun. Dec. 3—Washington at Dallas (3:00, FOX)
Buffalo at Cleveland (5:00, ESPN)
Mon. Dec. 4—Chicago at Detroit (9:00, ABC)
Sat. Dec. 9—Cleveland at Minnesota (11:30, NBC)
Arizona at San Diego (1:00, FOX)
Sun. Dec. 10—Pittsburgh at Los Angeles (1:00, NBC)
Green Bay at Tampa Bay (8:00, ESPN)
Mon. Dec. 11—Kansas City at Miami (9:00, ABC)
Sat. Dec. 16—New England at Pittsburgh (12:30, NBC)
Green Bay at New Orleans (3:00, FOX)
Sun. Dec. 17—N.Y. Giants at Dallas (3:00, FOX)
Los Angeles at Seattle (5:00, ESPN)
Mon. Dec. 18—Minnesota at San Francisco (6:00, ABC)
Sat. Dec. 23—San Diego at N.Y. Giants (12:30, NBC)
Detroit at Tampa Bay (4:00, FOX)
New England at Indianapolis (8:00, ESPN)
Sun. Dec. 24—Denver at Los Angeles (1:00, NBC)
Mon. Dec. 25—Dallas at Arizona (7:00, ABC)

POSTSEASON

Sat. Dec. 30—AFC, NFC wild-card playoffs (ABC)
Sun. Dec. 31—AFC, NFC wild-card playoffs (NBC, FOX)
Sat. Jan. 6—AFC, NFC divisional playoffs (NBC, FOX)
Sun. Jan. 7—AFC, NFC divisional playoffs (NBC, FOX)
Sun. Jan. 14—AFC, NFC championship games (NBC, FOX)
Sun. Jan. 28—Super Bowl XXX at Sun Devil Stadium,
Tempe, Ariz. (NBC)
Sun. Feb. 4—Pro Bowl at Honolulu (ABC)

INTERCONFERENCE GAMES

(All times local)

Sun. Sept. 3—Detroit at Pittsburgh ... 1:00
Sun. Sept. 10—Los Angeles at Washington ... 1:00
Carolina at Buffalo ... 1:00
N.Y. Giants at Kansas City ... 12:00
Tampa Bay at Cleveland ... 1:00
Denver at Dallas ... 3:00
Sun. Sept. 17—San Diego at Philadelphia ... 1:00
New England at San Francisco ... 1:00
Washington at Denver ... 2:00
Sun. Sept. 24—Minnesota at Pittsburgh ... 1:00
N.Y. Jets at Atlanta ... 4:00

Philadelphia at Los Angeles ... 1:00
Green Bay at Jacksonville ... 8:00
Sun. Oct. 1—New England at Atlanta ... 1:00
St. Louis at Indianapolis ... 12:00
Kansas City at Arizona ... 1:00
Sun. Oct. 8—Cincinnati at Tampa Bay ... 1:00
Houston at Minnesota ... 12:00
Cleveland at Detroit ... 4:00
Sun. Oct. 15—San Francisco at Indianapolis ... 12:00
Chicago at Jacksonville ... 1:00
Miami at New Orleans ... 3:00

		N.Y. Jets at Carolina	4:00
		Dallas at San Diego	1:00
Sun.	Oct.	22—Houston at Chicago	12:00
Sun.	Oct.	29—Carolina at New England	1:00
		Seattle at Arizona	2:00
		Tampa Bay at Houston	3:00
Sun.	Nov.	5—Washington at Kansas City	12:00
		Pittsburgh at Chicago	3:00
Sun.	Nov.	5—Arizona at Denver	2:00
		N.Y. Giants at Seattle	1:00
Sun.	Nov.	12—Indianapolis at New Orleans	12:00
		Los Angeles at N.Y. Giants	1:00
		Atlanta at Buffalo	1:00
		Denver at Philadelphia	8:00
Sun.	Nov.	19—Seattle at Washington	1:00
		Jacksonville at Tampa Bay	1:00
		Green Bay at Cleveland	1:00
		Dallas at Los Angeles	1:00
Mon.	Nov.	20—San Francisco at Miami	9:00
Thur.	Nov.	23—Kansas City at Dallas	3:00
Sun.	Dec.	3—Indianapolis at Carolina	1:00
		Cincinnati at Green Bay	12:00
		Atlanta at Miami	1:00
		New Orleans at New England	1:00
		St. Louis at N.Y. Jets	1:00
		Philadelphia at Seattle	1:00
		Buffalo at San Francisco	5:00
Sat.	Dec.	9—Cleveland at Minnesota	11:30
		Arizona at San Diego	1:00
Sun.	Dec.	10—Buffalo at St. Louis	12:00
		Chicago at Cincinnati	1:00
		Detroit at Houston	12:00
Sun.	Dec.	17—Jacksonville at Detroit	1:00
Sat.	Dec.	23—San Diego at N.Y. Giants	12:30
Sun.	Dec.	24—Pittsburgh at Green Bay	12:00
		New Orleans at N.Y. Jets	1:00
		Minnesota at Cincinnati	1:00
		Miami at St. Louis	3:00

COLLEGE DRAFT

ROUND-BY-ROUND SELECTIONS

FIRST ROUND

Team		Player selected	Pos.	College	Draft pick origination
1.	Cincinnati	Ki-Jana Carter	RB	Penn State	From Carolina
2.	Jacksonville	Tony Boselli	T	Southern California	
3.	Houston	Steve McNair	QB	Alcorn State	
4.	Washington	Michael Westbrook	WR	Colorado	
5.	Carolina	Kerry Collins	QB	Penn State	From Cincinnati
6.	St. Louis	Kevin Carter	DE	Florida	
7.	Philadelphia	Mike Mamula	DE	Boston College	From Tampa Bay
8.	Seattle	Joey Galloway	WR	Ohio State	
9.	N.Y. Jets	Kyle Brady	TE	Penn State	
10.	San Francisco	J.J. Stokes	WR	UCLA	From Atlanta through Cleveland
11.	Minnesota	Derrick Alexander	DE	Florida State	From Denver through Atlanta
12.	Tampa Bay	Warren Sapp	DT	Miami (Fla.)	From Philadelphia
13.	New Orleans	Mark Fields	LB	Washington State	
14.	Buffalo	Ruben Brown	G	Pittsburgh	
15.	Indianapolis	Ellis Johnson	DT	Florida	
16.	N.Y. Jets	Hugh Douglas	DE	Central State (O.)	From Arizona
17.	N.Y. Giants	Tyrone Wheatley	RB	Michigan	
18.	Los Angeles	Napoleon Kaufman	RB	Washington	
19.	Jacksonville	James Stewart	RB	Tennessee	From Kansas City
20.	Detroit	Luther Elliss	DT	Utah	
21.	Chicago	Rashaan Salaam	RB	Colorado	
22.	Carolina	Tyrone Poole	DB	Fort Valley (Ga.) State	From Green Bay
23.	New England	Ty Law	DB	Michigan	
24.	Minnesota	Korey Stringer	T	Ohio State	
25.	Miami	Billy Milner	T	Houston	
26.	Atlanta	Devin Bush	DB	Florida State	From Cleveland
27.	Pittsburgh	Mark Bruener	TE	Washington	
28.	Tampa Bay	Derrick Brooks	LB	Florida State	From Dallas
29.	Carolina	Blake Brockermeyer	T	Texas	From San Diego
30.	Cleveland	Craig Powell	LB	Ohio State	From San Francisco
31.	Kansas City	Trezelle Jenkins	T	Michigan	From Jacksonville
32.	Green Bay	Craig Newsome	DB	Arizona State	From Carolina

SECOND ROUND

Team		Player selected	Pos.	College	Draft pick origination
1.	N.Y. Jets	Matt O'Dwyer	G	Northwestern	From Jacksonville
2.	San Diego	Terrance Shaw	DB	Stephen F. Austin State	From Carolina
3.	Houston	Anthony Cook	DT	South Carolina State	
4.	Carolina	Shawn King	DE	Northeast Louisiana	From Cincinnati
5.	Washington	Cory Raymer	C	Wisconsin	
6.	St. Louis	Zach Wiegert	T	Nebraska	
7.	Seattle	Christian Fauria	TE	Colorado	
8.	Jacksonville	Brian DeMarco	T	Michigan State	From N.Y. Jets
9.	Atlanta	Ronald Davis	DB	Tennessee	From Tampa Bay through Dallas
10.	Minnesota	Orlanda Thomas	DB	Southwestern (La.)	From Denver
11.	Tampa Bay	Melvin Johnson	DB	Kentucky	From Philadelphia
12.	New Orleans	Ray Zellars	FB	Notre Dame	
13.	Buffalo	Todd Collins	QB	Michigan	
14.	Dallas	Sherman Williams	RB	Alabama	From Atlanta
15.	Arizona	Frank Sanders	WR	Auburn	
16.	Indianapolis	Ken Dilger	TE	Illinois	
17.	Los Angeles	Barret Robbins	C	Texas Christian	
18.	Philadelphia	Bobby Taylor	DB	Notre Dame	From Kansas City
19.	San Diego	Terrell Fletcher	RB	Wisconsin	From Detroit
20.	Chicago	Patrick Riley	DT	Miami (Fla.)	
21.	Miami	Andrew Greene	G	Indiana	From Green Bay
22.	N.Y. Giants	Scott Gragg	T	Montana	
23.	Minnesota	Corey Fuller	DB	Florida State	
24.	Chicago	Todd Sauerbrun	P	West Virginia	From Miami
25.	New England	Ted Johnson	LB	Colorado	
26.	Philadelphia	Barrett Brooks	T	Kansas State	From Cleveland
27.	Dallas	Kendell Watkins	TE	Mississippi State	
28.	Pittsburgh	Kordell Stewart	QB	Colorado	
29.	San Diego	Jimmy Oliver	WR	Texas Christian	
30.	St. Louis	Jesse James	G	Mississippi State	From San Francisco

Team	Player selected	Pos.	College	Draft pick origination
31. Dallas	Shane Hannah	G	Michigan State	From Philadelphia through Tampa Bay
Carolina forfeited selection.				
32. Jacksonville	Bryan Schwartz	LB	Augustana (S.D.)	

THIRD ROUND

Team	Player selected	Pos.	College	Draft pick origination
1. Green Bay	Darius Holland	DT	Colorado	From Carolina
2. Green Bay	William Henderson	FB	North Carolina	From Jacksonville
3. Houston	Chris Sanders	WR	Ohio State	
4. Washington	Darryl Pounds	CB	Nicholls State	
5. Cincinnati	Melvin Tuten	T	Syracuse	
6. Detroit	David Sloan	TE	New Mexico	From St. Louis
7. Jacksonville	Chris Hudson	DB	Colorado	From N.Y. Jets
8. Philadelphia	Greg Jefferson	DE	Central Florida	From Tampa Bay
9. Green Bay	Brian Williams	LB	Southern California	From Seattle
10. New England	Curtis Martin	RB	Pittsburgh	From Philadelphia
11. New Orleans	Mike Verstegen	T	Wisconsin	
12. Buffalo	Marlon Kerner	DB	Ohio State	
13. Atlanta	Lorenzo Styles	LB	Ohio State	
14. Philadelphia	Chris T. Jones	WR	Miami (Fla.)	From Denver
15. Indianapolis	Zack Crockett	FB	Florida State	
16. Arizona	Stoney Case	QB	New Mexico	
17. Kansas City	Tamarick Vanover	WR	Florida State	
18. St. Louis	Steve McLaughlin	K	Arizona	From Detroit
19. Chicago	Sean Harris	LB	Arizona	
20. Cleveland	Eric Zeier	QB	Georgia	From Green Bay
21. N.Y. Giants	Rodney Young	DB	Louisiana State	
22. Los Angeles	Joe Aska	RB	Central State (Okla.)	
23. Chicago	Evan Pilgrim	G	Brigham Young	From Miami
24. New England	Jimmy Hitchcock	DB	North Carolina	
25. Houston	Rodney Thomas	RB	Texas A&M	From Minnesota
26. Green Bay	Antonio Freeman	WR	Virginia Tech	From Cleveland
27. Pittsburgh	Brenden Stai	G	Nebraska	
28. Dallas	Charlie Williams	DB	Bowling Green State	
29. San Diego	Don Sasa	DT	Washington State	
30. Cleveland	Mike Frederick	DE	Virginia	From San Francisco
31. Houston*	Torey Hunter	DB	Washington State	
32. Buffalo*	Damien Covington	LB	North Carolina State	
33. Kansas City	Troy Dumas	LB	Nebraska	From Jacksonville
34. San Diego	Preston Harrison	LB	Ohio State	From Carolina

FOURTH ROUND

Team	Player selected	Pos.	College	Draft pick origination
1. Jacksonville	Rob Johnson	QB	Southern California	
2. San Diego	Chris Cowart	LB	Florida State	From Carolina
3. Houston	Michael Roan	TE	Wisconsin	
4. Cincinnati	Sam Shade	DB	Alabama	
5. Washington	Larry Jones	RB	Miami (Fla.)	
6. San Diego	Aaron Hayden	RB	Tennessee	From St. Louis
7. Tampa Bay	Jerry Wilson	DB	Southern	
8. N.Y. Jets	Melvin Hayes	T	Mississippi State	From Seattle through Arizona
9. N.Y. Jets	Tyrone Davis	WR	Virginia	
10. New Orleans	Dameian Jeffries	DE	Alabama	
11. Buffalo	Ken Irvin	DB	Memphis	
12. Dallas	Eric Bjornson	WR	Washington	From Atlanta
13. Minnesota	Chad May	QB	Kansas State	From Denver
14. New England	Dave Wohlabaugh	C	Syracuse	From Philadelphia through Kansas City
15. Buffalo	Justin Armour	WR	Stanford	From Arizona
16. Indianapolis	Ray McElroy	DB	Eastern Illinois	
17. St. Louis	Lovell Pinkney	TE	Texas	From Detroit
18. Chicago	Jack Jackson	WR	Florida	
19. Green Bay	Jeff Miller	T	Mississippi	
N.Y. Giants exercised selection in supplemental draft.				
20. Los Angeles	Mike Morton	LB	North Carolina	
21. Philadelphia	Dave Barr	QB	California	From K.C. through S.F. and Cle.
22. Pittsburgh	Oliver Gibson	DE	Notre Dame	From New England
23. Denver	Jamie Brown	T	Florida A&M	From Minnesota
24. Miami	Pete Mitchell	TE	Boston College	
25. Jacksonville	Mike Thompson	DT	Wisconsin	From Cleveland
26. Denver	Ken Brown	LB	Virginia Tech	From Dallas through St. Louis
27. Pittsburgh	Donta Jones	LB	Nebraska	
28. Seattle	Jason Kyle	LB	Arizona State	From San Diego
29. San Francisco	Tim Hanshaw	TE	Brigham Young	

Team	Player selected	Pos.	College	Draft pick origination
30. N.Y. Giants*	Rob Zatechka	G	Nebraska	
31. Dallas*	Alundis Brice	DB	Mississippi	
32. Dallas*	Linc Harden	LB	Oklahoma State	
33. Buffalo*	Tony Cline	TE	Stanford	
34. Carolina	Frank Garcia	C	Washington	
35. N.Y. Giants*	Ben Talley	LB	Tennessee	
36. Kansas City	Steve Stenstrom	QB	Stanford	From Jacksonville

FIFTH ROUND

Team	Player selected	Pos.	College	Draft pick origination
1. Carolina	Mike Senters	WR	Northwestern	
2. Cleveland	Tau Pupua	DL	Weber State	From Jacksonville
3. Washington	Jamie Asher	TE	Louisville	From Houston
4. Los Angeles	Matt Dyson	LB	Michigan	From Washington
5. Cincinnati	David Dunn	WR	Fresno State	
6. St. Louis	Mike Scurlock	DB	Arizona	
7. Detroit	Stephen Boyd	LB	Boston College	From Seattle
8. N.Y. Jets	Carl Greenwood	DB	UCLA	
9. Tampa Bay	Clifton Abraham	DB	Florida State	
10. Buffalo	John Holecek	LB	Illinois	
11. Atlanta	Roell Preston	WR	Mississippi	
12. Denver	Phil Yeboah-Kodie	LB	Penn State	
13. Cleveland	Mike Miller	WR	Notre Dame	From Philadelphia
14. New Orleans	William Strong	DB	North Carolina State	
15. Indianapolis	Derek West	T	Colorado	
16. Arizona	Cedric Davis	DB	Tennessee State	
17. Pittsburgh	Lethon Flowers	DB	Georgia Tech	From Chicago
18. Washington	Rich Owens	DE	Lehigh	From Green Bay through Los Angeles
19. N.Y. Giants	Roderick Mullen	DB	Grambling State	
20. Los Angeles	Jeff Kysar	T	Arizona State	
21. Kansas City	Mike Pelton	DT	Auburn	
22. Detroit	Kez McCorvey	WR	Florida State	
23. Minnesota	James Stewart	RB	Miami (Fla.)	
24. Miami	Norman Hand	DT	Mississippi	
25. Houston	Gary Walker	DE	Auburn	From New England
26. Green Bay	Jay Barker	QB	Alabama	From Cleveland
27. Pittsburgh	Lance Brown	DB	Indiana	
Dallas exercised selection in supplemental draft.				
28. San Diego	'OMar Ellison	WR	Florida State	
29. Detroit	Ronald Cherry	T	McNeese State	From San Francisco
30. Kansas City*	Jerrott Willard	LB	California	
31. Arizona*	Lance Scott	C	Utah	
32. Dallas*	Edward Hervey	WR	Southern California	
33. Arizona*	Tito Paul	DB	Ohio State	
34. Dallas*	Dana Howard	LB	Illinois	
35. Jacksonville	Ryan Christopherson	FB	Wyoming	From Philadelphia
36. Green Bay	Travis Jervey	RB	The Citadel	From Jacksonville
37. Carolina	Andrew Peterson	T	Washington	

SIXTH ROUND

Team	Player selected	Pos.	College	Draft pick origination
1. Jacksonville	Marcus Price	T	Louisiana State	
2. Green Bay	Charlie Simmons	WR	Georgia Tech	From Carolina
3. Houston	Hicham El-Mashtoub	C	Arizona	
4. Cincinnati	Ryan Grigson	T	Purdue	
5. Washington	Brian Thure	T	California	
6. San Diego	Troy Sienkiewicz	G	New Mexico State	From St. Louis
7. N.Y. Jets	Eddie Mason	LB	North Carolina	
8. Tampa Bay	Wardell Rouse	LB	Clemson	
9. Seattle	Henry McMillian	DT	Florida	
10. Atlanta	Travis Hall	DT	Brigham Young	
11. Denver	Fritz Fequiere	G	Iowa	
12. San Diego	Brandon Harrison	WR	Howard Payne (Tex.)	From Philadelphia
13. New Orleans	Lee DeRamus	WR	Wisconsin	
14. Buffalo	Shannon Clavelle	DE	Colorado	
15. Detroit	Kevin Hickman	TE	Navy	From Arizona
16. Indianapolis	Brian Gelzheiser	LB	Penn State	
17. Carolina	Steve Strahan	DT	Baylor	From Green Bay
18. Minnesota	John Solomon	LB	Sam Houston State	From N.Y. Giants
19. Los Angeles	Eli Herring	T	Brigham Young	
20. Carolina	Jerry Colquitt	QB	Tennessee	From Kansas City
21. Detroit	Cory Schlesinger	RB	Nebraska	
22. Chicago	Kenny Gales	DB	Wisconsin	

Team	Player selected	Pos.	College	Draft pick origination
23. Miami	Jeff Kopp	LB	Southern California	
24. New England	Dino Philyaw	RB	Oregon	
25. Denver	Terrell Davis	RB	Georgia	From Minnesota
26. San Diego	Craig Whelihan	QB	Pacific	From Cleveland
27. Chicago	Carl Reeves	DE	North Carolina State	From Dallas
28. Pittsburgh	Barron Miles	DB	Nebraska	
29. San Diego	Tony Berti	T	Colorado	
30. San Francisco	Antonio Armstrong	DE	Texas A&M	
31. Kansas City*	Bryan Proby	DT	Arizona State	
32. Seattle*	Eddie Goines	WR	North Carolina State	
33. N.Y. Giants*	Jamal Duff	DE	San Diego State	
34. Arizona*	Anthony Bridges	DB	North Texas	
35. N.Y. Giants*	Charles Way	RB	Virginia	
36. Kansas City*	Tom Barndt	C	Pittsburgh	
Carolina forfeited selection.				
37. Philadelphia	Fred McCrary	FB	Mississippi State	From Jacksonville

SEVENTH ROUND

Team	Player selected	Pos.	College	Draft pick origination
1. Carolina	Chad Cota	DB	Oregon	
2. Philadelphia	Kevin Bouie	RB	Mississippi State	From Jacksonville
3. Houston	C.J. Richardson	DB	Miami (Fla.)	
4. Arizona	Billy Williams	WR	Tennessee	From Washington
5. Cincinnati	John Walsh	QB	Brigham Young	
6. St. Louis	Gerald McBurrows	DB	Kansas	
7. Tampa Bay	Steve Ingram	G	Maryland	
8. Seattle	Keif Bryant	DE	Rutgers	
9. N.Y. Jets	Curtis Ceaser	WR	Grambling State	
10. Denver	Steve Russ	LB	Air Force	
11. Jacksonville	Curtis Marsh	WR	Utah	From Philadelphia
12. St. Louis	Herman O'Berry	DB	Oregon	From New Orleans
13. Buffalo	Tom Nutten	C	Western Michigan	
14. Denver	Byron Chamberlain	WR	Wayne (Neb.) State	From Atlanta
15. Indianapolis	Jessie Cox	LB	Texas Southern	
16. Arizona	Wesley Leasy	LB	Mississippi State	
17. N.Y. Giants	Bryne Diehl	P	Alabama	
18. Washington	Scott Turner	DB	Illinois	From Los Angeles
19. Tampa Bay	Jeffrey Rodgers	DE	Texas A&M-Kingsville	From Kansas City
20. Detroit	Hessley Hempstead	G	Kansas	
21. Chicago	Jamal Cox	LB	Georgia Tech	
22. Green Bay	Adam Timmerman	G	South Dakota State	
23. Cleveland	A.C. Tellison	WR	Miami (Fla.)	From New England
24. Minnesota	Jose White	LB	Howard	
25. Miami	Corey Swinson	DT	Hampton (Va.)	
26. New England	Carlos Yancy	DB	Georgia	From Cleveland
27. Pittsburgh	Henry Bailey	WR	UNLV	
28. Dallas	Oscar Sturgis	DE	North Carolina	
29. San Diego	Mark Montreuil	DB	Concordia (Canada)	
30. San Francisco	Herb Coleman	DE	Trinity (Ill.)	
31. St. Louis*	Bronzell Miller	DE	Utah	
32. St. Louis*	Johnny Thomas	WR	Arizona State	
33. Arizona*	Chad Eaton	DT	Washington State	
34. New Orleans*	Travis Davis	DB	Notre Dame	
35. Minnesota*	Jason Fisk	DT	Stanford	
36. Buffalo*	Darick Holmes	RB	Portland State	
37. Atlanta*	John Burrough	DE	Wyoming	
38. Miami*	Shannon Myers	WR	Lenoir-Rhyne (N.C.)	
39. Pittsburgh*	Cole Ford	K	Southern California	
40. Philadelphia	Howard Smothers	T	Bethune-Cookman	From Jacksonville
41. Carolina	Michael Reed	DB	Boston College	

*Pick awarded to team as compensation for loss of a free agent.

PLAYOFF PLAN

DIVISION TIES

TWO CLUBS

1. Head-to-head (best won-lost-tied percentage in games between the clubs).
2. Best won-lost-tied percentage in games played within the division.
3. Best won-lost-tied percentage in games played within the conference.
4. Best won-lost-tied percentage in common games, if applicable.
5. Best net points in division games.
6. Best net points in all games.
7. Strength of schedule.
8. Best net touchdowns in all games.
9. Coin toss.

THREE OR MORE CLUBS

(Note: If two clubs remain tied after other clubs are eliminated during any step, tie-breaker reverts to step 1 of two-club format.)

1. Head-to-head (best won-lost-tied percentage in games among the clubs).
2. Best won-lost-tied percentage in games played within the division.
3. Best won-lost-tied percentage in games played within the conference.
4. Best won-lost-tied percentage in common games.
5. Best net points in division games.
6. Best net points in all games.
7. Strength of schedule.
8. Best net touchdowns in all games.
9. Coin toss.

WILD-CARD TIES

If necessary to break ties to determine the three wild-card clubs from each conference, the following steps will be taken:

1. If all the tied clubs are from the same division, apply division tie-breaker.
2. If the tied clubs are from different divisions, apply the steps listed below.
3. When the first wild-card team has been identified, the procedure is repeated to name the second wild card (i.e., eliminate all but the highest-ranked club in each division prior to proceeding to step 2), and repeated a third time, if necessary, to identify the third wild card. In situations where three or more teams from the same division are involved in the procedure, the original seeding of the teams remains the same for subsequent applications of the tie-breaker if the top-ranked team in that division qualifies for a wild-card berth.

TWO CLUBS

1. Head-to-head, if applicable.
2. Best won-lost-tied percentage in games played within the conference.
3. Best won-lost-tied percentage in common games, minimum of four.
4. Best average net points in conference games.
5. Best net points in all games.
6. Strength of schedule.
7. Best net touchdowns in all games.
8. Coin toss.

THREE OR MORE CLUBS

(Note: If two clubs remain tied after other clubs are eliminated, tie-breaker reverts to step 1 of two-club format.)

1. Apply division tie-breaker to eliminate all but highest-ranked club in each division prior to proceeding to step 1. The original seeding within a division upon application of the division tie-breaker remains the same for all subsequent applications of the procedure that are necessary to identify the three wild-card participants.
2. Head-to-head sweep (applicable only if one club has defeated each of the others or one club has lost to each of the others).
3. Best won-lost-tied percentage in games played within the conference.
4. Best won-lost-tied percentage in common games, minimum of four.
5. Best average net points in conference games.
6. Best net points in all games.
7. Strength of schedule.
8. Best net touchdowns in all games.
9. Coin toss.

1994 REVIEW

Year in review

Final standings

Weeks 1 through 17

Wild-card games

Divisional playoffs

Conference championships

Super Bowl XXIX

Pro Bowl

Player participation

Attendance

Trades

YEAR IN REVIEW

THE TOP STORIES OF THE PAST YEAR

By VITO STELLINO

The NFL celebrated its past and took a bold step into the future during its 75th season in 1994.

While the league outfitted its teams in "throwback" uniforms and named an all-time team, it also implemented a salary cap tied to free agency that raised player salaries and still gave owners a ceiling on player expenses.

It also began an era in which teams have to learn how to structure contracts to stay under the cap and still be competitive on the field.

The San Francisco 49ers became a trendsetter when they rebuilt their defense with free agents such as Deion Sanders, Ken Norton, Rickey Jackson and Gary Plummer while remaining under the cap. As a result, they dethroned the Dallas Cowboys to become the NFL's first five-time Super Bowl champ.

The league also ushered in an era of free agency for franchises when the Los Angeles Rams abandoned the nation's second-largest market for a lucrative deal in St. Louis that virtually guarantees them more than $20 million in profits per season.

The owners rejected the move in March 1995 before approving it less than a month later when the Rams agreed to give them a bigger share of their financial windfall. It also sent a message to cities with inadequate stadiums: The price of an NFL franchise in the 21st century will be steep, and a modern stadium with luxury boxes and club seats will be necessary.

The league has come a long way since 1920, when George Halas and a few of his buddies gathered in a Hupmobile showroom in Canton, Ohio, to form the American Professional Football Conference. It changed its name to the National Football League in 1922. The membership fee was $100, but nobody paid it. Franchises now are going for close to $200 million.

The founding fathers never dreamed the league would one day become the nation's most popular sport, featuring Super Sundays, radio helmets and premium-seat licenses.

The NFL is the only sports league that can regularly draw big national TV ratings for regular-season games in prime time. Monday Night Football, a fixture on ABC since 1970, was the fifth highest-rated prime time show of the 1994-95 television season. Sitcoms and made-for-TV movies come and go, but MNF, which celebrated its 25th season in 1994, seems destined to remain popular for years to come.

While it was celebrating its milestones, the league also was looking ahead. It started NFL Season Ticket, a subscription service available for satellite TV dish owners. The league is expected to sign up more customers as the new 18-inch dishes become more popular.

The NFL even entered the brave new world of interactive media by creating an Internet site (http:/nflhome.com) for information on the draft.

Another NFL venture, an all-European six-team World League, suffered some growing pains. An earlier World League with U.S. teams folded after only two seasons, but the European version was a joint venture between the league and Rupert Murdoch's Fox/News Corporation. First-year attendance was disappointing, but the NFL supposedly is committed for four years.

On the field, the Dallas Cowboys discovered something that hasn't changed in 75 years: Winning three NFL titles in a row is hard. It has been done only twice in league history, both times by the Green Bay Packers, who turned the trick in 1929-30-31 (before there was a championship game) and in 1965-66-67 (the latter two climaxing in the first two Super Bowls).

Dallas lost in the NFC title game to the 49ers, who went on to carve out a place in NFL history by becoming the first team to win the Super Bowl five times. San Francisco's 49-26 rout of the San Diego Chargers in Super Bowl XXIX marked the NFC's 11th consecutive Super Bowl victory.

The most significant aspect of the 1994 season, however, may have been that it was played in its entirety. While baseball and hockey were hit by bitter work stoppages that shortened their seasons and the NBA played without a labor contract, the NFL enjoyed the second year of a seven-year deal that gives the players free agency and the owners a salary cap.

After enduring strikes in 1974, 1982 and 1987 and a war with the USFL in the mid-1980s, these are the best of times for the NFL.

The drive for five

A subplot to the 1994 season was the race to see which team would become the first to win five Super Bowls.

Three clubs—San Francisco, Dallas and Pittsburgh—had won four, and all three advanced to their conference title game.

The Steelers were stunned, 17-13, by the upstart Chargers in the AFC title game. It would be San Diego's first appearance in the Super Bowl, but it probably didn't matter which team represented the AFC in Miami. Once San Francisco beat Dallas for the NFC crown (dubbed "The Real Super Bowl" by many people), the 49ers knew the Super Bowl would be nothing more than a coronation. They were favored by 18 points—the biggest spread in the game's history—and covered easily as Steve Young threw a record six touchdown passes.

Even though his team was heavily favored, it still was an emotional victory for 49ers Owner Edward J. DeBartolo, Jr. As he accepted the gleaming Vince Lombardi Trophy from Commissioner Paul Tagliabue, he choked up and said, "This is a very, very important victory. This one's for dad." His father, shopping-center magnate Edward J. DeBartolo Sr., had died a few weeks earlier.

49ers President Carmen Policy had called the Super Bowl anticlimactic after the NFC title game but retracted those comments in the euphoria of the Super Bowl victory.

"If somebody would serve me a plate that was loaded with my words, I'd eat them," he said. "As a practical matter, I will say this: The feeling after the Dallas game was truly euphoric. But to suggest that the culmination of the season would be anticlimactic would be irresponsible. . . . Tonight we have closure, tonight we have fulfillment."

The 49ers' triumph was a victory for a team that handled the salary cap more shrewdly than any other. The cap was supposed to handicap free-spending clubs like San Francisco, but that's not how it worked.

When Sanders rejected better offers to sign with the 49ers because he wanted to win a Super Bowl, some teams thought San Francisco had to be cheating. The league checked the 49ers' books and found nothing.

The 49ers simply had succeeded again.

Nice guys finish first

The 1994 season was a triumph for two of the NFL's truly nice guys—San Francisco Coach George Seifert and quarterback Steve Young, who finally emerged from the huge shadows cast by Bill Walsh and Joe Montana, respectively.

Seifert won 50 games faster than any coach in NFL history, and the 49ers advanced to the NFC title game four times in his first five years and won the Super Bowl in his first season on the job (1989). But Seifert also presided over three title-game losses and had failed—at least in the minds of impatient 49ers fans—to r⌐et the standard set by Walsh.

When the 49ers, hit by numerous injuries on the offensive line, struggled to a 3-2 start (including a stunning 40-8 loss to Philadelphia), a San Francisco radio station polled its listeners about whether Seifert should be replaced by former Dallas coach Jimmy Johnson. Eighty-five percent of the respondents said yes, and there was speculation all season that Seifert would be fired if the 49ers did not win the Super Bowl. After the 49ers did win, Seifert got a two-year contract extension.

For Seifert, coaching the 49ers isn't just a job, it's a dream come true. He is a San Francisco na-

tive who went to high school across from old Kezar Stadium and was an usher there in the days of Y.A. Tittle.

"I have a love affair with this place. It's my home," he said. "It's unique that you can be the coach of your team."

Young, meanwhile, just wanted acceptance. Despite winning four NFL passing titles and a pair of MVP awards in his first four years as the 49ers' No. 1 quarterback, he still hadn't been accepted by the team's fans. His crime? He hadn't won a Super Bowl, something Montana did four times. 49ers followers weren't too pleased, either, after Montana, who had moved on to Kansas City, outdueled Young in the Chiefs' 24-17 victory over the 49ers in the second week of the season.

"Maybe the student still has something to learn from the master," Young said afterward.

Young went on to become a master himself, gradually winning over fans in the 49ers' playoff run. After the NFC title-game victory over the Cowboys at Candlestick Park, fans serenaded him with chants of "Steve, Steve, Steve!" as he held the ball over his head.

Two weeks later, Young cradled the Super Bowl trophy in his arms like a baby. An analytical sort who has a law degree from BYU, Young said he had no regrets about a football career that included stops in the old USFL, two ill-fated seasons in Tampa Bay and years of trying to live up to the Montana legend in San Francisco.

"A lot of the teammates that I had are still friends to this day," he said. "In 10 years, I'll have the ring, but I'll have the relationships and that will be more important."

Close, but no threepeat

Once again, injuries and turnovers proved to be the undoing of a team attempting to win its third consecutive Super Bowl.

In 1976, the Pittsburgh Steelers went into the AFC title game against the Oakland Raiders with both of their starting running backs, Franco Harris and Rocky Bleier, and their kicker, Roy Gerela, out with injuries. They lost, 24-7. In 1990, the 49ers had a 13-12 lead and possession late in the NFC title game against the Giants before Roger Craig fumbled and Lawrence Taylor recovered to set up Matt Bahr's game-winning field goal in a 15-13 New York win.

The Cowboys faced similar woes in 1994. They lost the league's best offensive tackle, Erik Williams, when he sustained a knee injury in a car accident October 23. Then, on December 19, Emmitt Smith pulled a hamstring in a game against the Saints and never regained his form the rest of the year.

In addition, quarterback Troy Aikman sprained his thumb two days before a big game at San Francisco on November 13. The 49ers intercepted Aikman three times and beat the Cowboys, 21-14, in a contest that ultimately decided home-field advantage in the playoffs. In the NFC title game, the Cowboys committed three turnovers in the first seven minutes to fall into a 21-0 hole and wound up losing, 38-28.

Another factor in the Cowboys' demise was the clash of egos between owner Jerry Jones and coach Jimmy Johnson that resulted in Jones paying Johnson $2 million to leave the team in March 1994. Jones replaced Johnson with former Oklahoma coach Barry Switzer, who'd been away from the game five years. The rookie coach took a crucial penalty in the NFC title game when he bumped an official while complaining that there should have been an interference call against Sanders as Dallas was attempting to cut into the 49ers' lead in the fourth quarter. The penalty pushed the Cowboys into a third-and-25 situation from their 42; they gave up the ball two plays later and didn't score again.

Switzer ranted about the condition of the field at Candlestick Park and the officiating after the game. Johnson, who took potshots at Switzer and Jones much of the season as an analyst for Fox and HBO, noted after the Cowboys' loss that he never was penalized in his coaching career.

The 'other' conference

Although the AFC, the NFL's version of the Washington Generals, lost in the Super Bowl for the 11th straight year, it did manage to produce a new champion for the first time in five seasons.

The Buffalo Bills, who in January 1994 became the first team to lose four consecutive Super Bowls, didn't get a chance to lose a fifth. Victimized by age and free agency, the Bills struggled through a 7-9 season and didn't qualify for postseason play.

San Diego replaced Buffalo as conference champion. With Stan Humphries passing for 3,209 yards, the Chargers started the season 6-0, won the AFC West with an 11-5 mark, then won back-to-back playoff games in nail-biting fashion. They beat the Miami Dolphins, 22-21, when Pete Stoyvanich missed a 48-yard field-goal attempt with a second left, and beat the Steelers in the AFC title game, 17-13, when linebacker Dennis Gibson batted away a Neil O'Donnell pass to Barry Foster on fourth down from the Steelers' 3 with 1:08 left.

It was a devastating loss for the Steelers, who had home-field advantage for the second time in Bill Cowher's three years as coach—and again failed to advance to the Super Bowl.

Miami's loss was just as frustrating for Don Shula, who had hoped to become the first coach to win the Super Bowl in his home stadium. Although Shula is the winningest coach in NFL history, he hasn't gotten Miami to the Super Bowl since the 1984 season and hasn't won it since the 1973 season.

The architects of San Diego's success were General Manager Bobby Beathard and Coach Bobby Ross. Beathard rebuilt the team after taking over in 1990; he hired Ross, then a successful college coach at Georgia Tech, two years later.

Ups and downs

Of the 12 teams that made the playoffs in 1993, seven returned in '94. Five of six NFC playoff teams made it back, with Chicago replacing the New York Giants. In the AFC, only Pittsburgh and Kansas City returned to postseason play. San Diego, Miami, Cleveland and New England replaced Buffalo, Houston, the Los Angeles Raiders and Denver.

The team that made the most dramatic turnaround was the Patriots, who went from 5-11 in 1993 to 10-6 and earned a wild-card berth. Coach Bill Parcells, who won a pair of Super Bowls with the Giants, may be building another Super Bowl contender. His quarterback, Drew Bledsoe, led the NFL in passing attempts (691), completions (400) and yardage (4,555) last year.

The team that suffered the biggest collapse was the Houston Oilers, who plummeted from 12-4 to 2-14. Management's decision to trade high-salaried veteran quarterback Warren Moon and go with younger, cheaper Cody Carlson backfired, costing Coach Jack Pardee his job. Pardee was fired after Houston started 1-9; his replacement, defensive coordinator Jeff Fisher, didn't fare much better. The Oilers went 1-5 under Fisher, who nonetheless retained the job for 1995.

Coaching merry-go-round

Pardee wasn't the only coach to get pink-slipped in 1994, although he was the only one to be fired during the season. Wade Phillips (Denver), Pete Carroll (New York Jets), Art Shell (Los Angeles Raiders), Tom Flores (Seattle), Chuck Knox (Los Angeles Rams) and Rich Kotite (Philadelphia) all were let go after the season.

Carroll's firing was the most surprising, coming after only one year. Even more surprising was Jets Owner Leon Hess' decision to hire Kotite to replace him. The Eagles lost their final seven games of 1994 under Kotite, but Hess was familiar with him from Kotite's days as a Jets assistant.

The San Francisco 49ers lost both their coordinators to coaching jobs, which isn't surprising for a Super Bowl winner. Offensive coordinator Mike Shanahan was hired by Denver. Ray Rhodes, a defensive mastermind, was hired by Philadelphia. Eagles Owner Jeff Lurie toyed with the idea of bringing back Dick Vermeil, who popularized the term "burnout" when he quit as Eagles coach in 1982. Vermeil was interested, but the two sides couldn't reach agreement.

The other new coaches are NFL first-timers: Dennis Erickson in Seattle, Mike White in Los Angeles and Rich Brooks in St. Louis. White was a Raiders assistant who moved up, while Erickson

(Miami) and Brooks (Oregon) left college jobs for the NFL.

Including expansion coaches Tom Coughlin (Jacksonville) and Dom Capers (Carolina), eight of the NFL's 30 teams will have new coaches.

NFL hot on TV

The NFL had a new look on TV in 1994 as CBS's 38-year association with the NFL ended and the Fox Network's began. Fox outbid CBS for the right to televise NFC games.

Fox, which estimates it will lose $350 million on its four-year, $1.58 billion deal, got a 12.1 rating in its initial NFL season. That was a 6 percent drop from that posted by CBS in 1993, mainly because many of Fox's affiliates are weaker UHF (above channel 13) stations.

The AFC package on NBC topped the NFC package for the first time since 1975. The AFC finished with a 12.5 rating, an 11 percent increase over the year before. The NFC package usually wins the ratings derby because it has more of the nation's bigger markets, but Fox's signal problems and a number of exciting AFC games gave NBC the edge. (Incidentally, NBC is paying $178 million less than Fox each year.)

Despite all that, Fox was pleased. The network feels pro football gives it more visibility and Fox thinks its ratings will improve because it is gaining 12 affiliates (eight from CBS) that are VHF stations (channels 2-13) in a $500 million deal with New World Communications.

Monday Night Football was the fifth highest-rated prime time show (17.8) in 1994. It increased one rating point over 1993 and helped give ABC its first overall prime time ratings victory in 15 years.

The cable packages on ESPN and TNT were popular, too. NFL games grabbed 18 of the top 20 spots on cable last year, and a Detroit-at-Miami game on Christmas night earned a 14.2 rating on ESPN, the highest of all cable shows in 1994.

Movin' East

The Rams, who started the westward migration of sports teams when they moved from Cleveland to Los Angeles in 1946, got formal approval to move to St. Louis in April 1995.

The owners, who initially rejected the move by a 21-3 margin in March (with six abstentions), voted to approve it (by a 23-6-1 margin) after the Rams offered to pay the league at least $46 million—a $17 million share of premium-seat license fees generated in St. Louis and a $29 million relocation fee. When the owners first rejected the proposal, the Rams were offering about $25 million.

The Rams agreed to pay up to $12.5 million toward a rebate to Fox if NFC ratings go down in the Los Angeles area. The Rams also will forego about $13 million in expansion fees if the league expands in the next 10 years and Southern California isn't awarded a team.

Despite the fact that nothing changed from March to April except the amount of money the Rams agreed to pay, Tagliabue insisted money wasn't a major issue in the voting reversal.

"It did not come down to a money deal. That's a completely erroneous implication. The money involved here was insignificant," he said. "It's a sign of the times that the NFL considers $46 million to be insignificant."

The Rams' move rendered the league's moving "guidelines" virtually meaningless. In effect, the owners said the Rams didn't meet them, but approved the move anyway.

"The NFL's got some mighty tall explaining to do as to how violations of their own relocation policy suddenly became acceptable," bellowed player agent Leigh Steinberg, who led an effort to keep the Rams in Los Angeles.

The explanation, however, was simple. The Rams, St. Louis and the state of Missouri threatened to file lawsuits against the league unless the move was approved. The Rams also threatened to move to St. Louis without league approval and dare the NFL to stop them.

Tagliabue decided he wanted peace in his time. He had misjudged the resolve of Rams Owner Georgia Frontiere, whom Tagliabue thought would back down or sell the team when the owners rejected the move the first time.

Instead, she was ready to go to court.

"I wouldn't say the Rams qualified (to move)," said Oilers Owner Bud Adams, chairman of the league's finance committee. "But business-wise, we voted them in because it's a good deal for them and a good deal for St. Louis."

It's not a good deal, it's a great one. In the 30-year lease, the Rams get all revenues from tickets except 15 percent of the club seat and luxury box revenue. They will pay only $250,000 a year in rent and half of game-day expenses. They get $13 million in relocation expenses, $12.5 million for a training facility and $30 million to pay off their stadium bonds in Anaheim. St. Louis even pays the Rams' insurance fees. On top of that, St. Louis also agreed to re-modernize the stadium in the future if it falls below the top 25 percent of NFL stadiums.

The hard (?) cap

When the NFL's so-called "hard" salary cap of $34.6 million a team was implemented in 1994, several teams cut high-priced veterans to meet it. The decision of the NFL Players Association to agree to a cap in a tradeoff for free agency was criticized.

But the cap isn't as hard as it appears. Since signing bonuses are pro-rated to future years, 18 clubs actually spent more than $34.6 million on player salaries in 1994. The Washington Redskins, who had to count only $625,000 of Heath Shuler's $5 million signing bonus toward their 1994 cap, actually had a payroll of $46.9 million (highest in the league) last season.

In 1992, the last year before free agency was instituted, the clubs spent $779 million on player salaries. That figure jumped to $1.097 billion in 1993 (an uncapped year) and dipped only slightly to $1.001 billion in 1994.

With the cap increasing to $37.1 million in 1995, salaries are expected to rise again. Of the 217 unrestricted free agents who signed by May 1, 1995, average salaries jumped from $499,999 to $849,176. For the 137 players who changed clubs, the average salary jumped from $527,361 to $926,796.

The biggest deal was a five-year, $17.028 million contract Andre Rison signed with the Cleveland Browns that made him the highest-paid wide receiver in the game.

Among other big deals were the five-year, $15 million contracts that Michael Irvin and Tony Tolbert signed with Dallas; Alvin Harper's four-year, $10.6 million deal with Tampa Bay; Mark Stepnoski's four-year, $9.2 million contract with Houston; Eric Green's six-year, $12 million deal with Miami; and Ricky Watters' three-year, $6.9 million deal with Philadelphia.

Building from scratch

The Carolina Panthers and Jacksonville Jaguars took different approaches in stocking their rosters in the expansion draft.

The Panthers, choosing to go with younger, cheaper players, spent $9.35 million on the 35 players they selected February 15. The Jaguars spent $15.5 million on 31 players, gambling that highly paid underachievers like Desmond Howard and Derek Brown, both former first-round picks, can turn their careers around.

Rule changes

The NFL, which refused to adopt the two-point conversion when it merged with the AFL in 1970, finally installed it nearly a quarter-century later. The strategy proved successful roughly half the time (59 of 116 during regular-season play), and it didn't seem to matter, statistically at least, whether a run or a pass was tried. The league's 28 teams were successful on 37 of 74 passing attempts and 22 of 42 runs.

Another major change was the moving of kickoffs from the 35- to the 30-yard line. The extra 5 yards gave kick returners more room to run, enabling New Orleans' Tyrone Hughes (1,556) and Washington's Brian Mitchell (1,478) to break the record for most kickoff return yards in a season.

Record-setters

Speaking of records, Jerry Rice broke Jim Brown's all-time touchdown mark of 126 when he scored three touchdowns in the 49ers' first game of the season, a 44-14 rout of the Los Angeles Raiders. Rice finished the season with 139 touchdowns in 156 regular-season games.

Art Monk, who was released by the New York Jets at the end of the season, caught a pass in all 16 games to break Steve Largent's mark of catching at least one pass in 177 consecutive games. Monk finished the season at 180.

Minnesota's Cris Carter caught 122 passes to break Sterling Sharpe's year-old, single-season record for receptions (112). San Francisco's Steve Young finished with a passer rating of 112.8 to break Joe Montana's single-season record of 112.4 set in 1989.

Big bucks for Bucs

The only team sold during the year was the Tampa Bay Buccaneers, who were purchased from the estate of Hugh Culverhouse by the Florida-based Malcolm Glazer family. The Glazers paid $175 million, but that will increase to $192 million if Tampa Stadium is renovated and $210 million if the Glazers move the club. The Glazers are committed to keeping the Bucs in Tampa for only two years because of what is perceived as an inadequate stadium.

Confidentiality?

Owners and players agreed to a new drug program in 1994, the cornerstones of which are testing, discipline, treatment and confidentiality.

But the league is having problems with the last part. Not only did information leak out last year, but some of it was inaccurate.

Just days before the draft, the New York Times reported that University of Miami defensive tackle Warren Sapp had tested positive for marijuana and cocaine at the NFL scouting combine. It also reported that Miami running back James Stewart tested positive for marijuana. The NFL said Sapp didn't test positive for cocaine and that Stewart didn't test positive for any substance. Stewart is suing the Times.

Meanwhile, the league did a background check and informed clubs right before the draft that Sapp allegedly failed at least seven drug tests at Miami. The information spread like wildfire the night before the draft.

Sapp, who had been considered a top-five pick, fell to 12th because of the reports. Sapp acknowledged testing positive twice—including once at the combine. In the aftermath of the Sapp affair, league and union officials were looking at ways to keep test results confidential in the future.

Although no players were suspended for drug or alcohol abuse in 1994, one player, Frank Wycheck of the Washington Redskins, was suspended for four games after testing positive for steroid use. Wycheck said he got the steroids in his system accidentally while putting the compound DMSO on a thigh bruise.

Rough year for refs

The '94 season was not a good one for NFL officials, who blew so many calls in high-profile games that there were proposals to restore instant replay.

The most obvious gaffes came in the Miami-San Diego playoff game, when the officials awarded Natrone Means a touchdown even though he failed to break the plane of the end zone. Later, they took a touchdown away from Chargers receiver Shawn Jefferson even though he clearly had both feet in bounds after catching a pass in the end zone.

Tagliabue, sensing fans' displeasure, proposed using instant replay with mobile sideline monitors so the referee on the field could reverse calls.

But there were so many problems with instant replay a few years ago that it died an ignominious death. NFL officials will be under the microscope more than ever in 1995, and if they don't have a better year, there'll be more calls for the return of instant replay.

Tragedy

Mike Frier, a 25-year-old defensive lineman for the Seattle Seahawks, was paralyzed from the waist down in a car crash December 1. Frier was a passenger in a car driven by teammate Lamar Smith that crashed into a utility pole near Seahawks headquarters in Kirkland, Wash. Neither Smith, who was charged with vehicular assault, nor teammate Chris Warren, another passenger in the car, was seriously injured.

Frier believes he will one day walk again.

"I believe in miracles," he said. "If I walk again, that's a miracle. I'll prove to everybody who said I couldn't walk and I'll prove to myself that I can walk. It'll take some time, but I'll get there."

Hall of Fame

The Pro Football Hall of Fame's Class of 1995 included Seattle wide receiver Steve Largent, Tampa Bay defensive end Lee Roy Selmon, San Diego tight end Kellen Winslow, the late Henry Jordan, a defensive tackle on Green Bay's championship teams of the 1960s, and the late Jim Finks, a former NFL quarterback and also a long-time executive with Minnesota, Chicago and New Orleans.

Largent and Selmon became the first players from the Seahawks and Buccaneers—NFL expansion brethren in 1976—to make the Hall of Fame. Largent's election to the Hall came about 11 weeks after his election to the U.S. House of Representatives from Oklahoma's 1st Congressional district.

Retirements

Joe Montana, the best quarterback of his time and arguably the best of all-time, was the most prominent player to announce his retirement after the 1994 season.

A four-time Super Bowl winner with the 49ers, Montana made his announcement at a gala ceremony in San Francisco on April 18 even though he spent his final two years with Kansas City. He invited many of his former teammates and coaches to the ceremony but declined to invite Young, the man who replaced him with the 49ers.

Phil Simms, who sat out the 1994 season after being waived by the New York Giants, officially retired to take a job with NBC after considering an offer from the Cleveland Browns.

Among other players to announce their retirements were defensive linemen Mike Golic, Frank Warren and Bill Pickel.

FINAL STANDINGS

FINAL NFL STANDINGS

AMERICAN FOOTBALL CONFERENCE

EASTERN DIVISION

	W	L	T	Pct.	Pts.	Opp.	Home	Away	Vs. AFC	Vs. NFC	Vs. AFC East
*Miami	10	6	0	.625	389	327	6-2	4-4	8-4	2-2	5-3
†New England	10	6	0	.625	351	312	5-3	5-3	6-6	4-0	4-4
Indianapolis	8	8	0	.500	307	320	5-3	3-5	8-6	0-2	4-4
Buffalo	7	9	0	.438	340	356	4-4	3-5	6-6	1-3	3-5
N.Y. Jets	6	10	0	.375	264	320	4-4	2-6	5-7	1-3	4-4

CENTRAL DIVISION

	W	L	T	Pct.	Pts.	Opp.	Home	Away	Vs. AFC	Vs. NFC	Vs. AFC Central
*Pittsburgh	12	4	0	.750	316	234	7-1	5-3	10-2	2-2	6-0
†Cleveland	11	5	0	.688	340	204	6-2	5-3	8-4	3-1	4-2
Cincinnati	3	13	0	.188	276	406	2-6	1-7	2-10	1-3	1-5
Houston	2	14	0	.125	226	352	2-6	0-8	2-10	0-4	1-5

WESTERN DIVISION

	W	L	T	Pct.	Pts.	Opp.	Home	Away	Vs. AFC	Vs. NFC	Vs. AFC West
*San Diego	11	5	0	.688	381	306	5-3	6-2	9-3	2-2	6-2
†Kansas City	9	7	0	.563	319	298	5-3	4-4	6-6	3-1	4-4
L.A. Raiders	9	7	0	.563	303	327	4-4	5-3	6-6	3-1	4-4
Denver	7	9	0	.438	347	396	4-4	3-5	6-6	1-3	4-4
Seattle	6	10	0	.375	287	323	3-5	3-5	4-10	2-0	2-6

*Division champion. †Wild-card team.

NATIONAL FOOTBALL CONFERENCE

EASTERN DIVISION

	W	L	T	Pct.	Pts.	Opp.	Home	Away	Vs. AFC	Vs. NFC	Vs. NFC East
*Dallas	12	4	0	.750	414	248	6-2	6-2	3-1	9-3	7-1
N.Y. Giants	9	7	0	.563	279	305	4-4	5-3	3-1	6-6	6-2
Arizona	8	8	0	.500	235	267	5-3	3-5	3-1	5-7	4-4
Philadelphia	7	9	0	.438	308	308	5-3	2-6	1-3	6-6	3-5
Washington	3	13	0	.188	320	412	0-8	3-5	1-1	2-12	0-8

CENTRAL DIVISION

	W	L	T	Pct.	Pts.	Opp.	Home	Away	Vs. AFC	Vs. NFC	Vs. NFC Central
*Minnesota	10	6	0	.625	356	314	6-2	4-4	2-2	8-4	5-3
†Detroit	9	7	0	.563	357	342	6-2	3-5	2-2	7-5	4-4
†Green Bay	9	7	0	.563	382	287	7-1	2-6	1-3	8-4	6-2
†Chicago	9	7	0	.563	271	307	5-3	4-4	3-1	6-6	3-5
Tampa Bay	6	10	0	.375	251	351	4-4	2-6	1-1	5-9	2-6

WESTERN DIVISION

	W	L	T	Pct.	Pts.	Opp.	Home	Away	Vs. AFC	Vs. NFC	Vs. NFC West
*San Francisco	13	3	0	.813	505	296	7-1	6-2	3-1	10-2	6-0
New Orleans	7	9	0	.438	348	407	3-5	4-4	1-3	6-6	4-2
Atlanta	7	9	0	.438	313	389	5-3	2-6	1-3	6-6	2-4
L.A. Rams	4	12	0	.250	286	365	3-5	1-7	2-2	2-10	0-6

*Division champion. †Wild-card team.

AFC PLAYOFFS

AFC wild card: Miami 27, Kansas City 17
Cleveland 20, New England 13
AFC semifinals: Pittsburgh 29, Cleveland 9
San Diego 22, Miami 21
AFC championship: San Diego 17, Pittsburgh 13

NFC PLAYOFFS

NFC wild card: Green Bay 16, Detroit 12
Chicago 35, Minnesota 18
NFC semifinals: San Francisco 44, Chicago 15
Dallas 35, Green Bay 9
NFC championship: San Francisco 38, Dallas 28

SUPER BOWL

San Francisco 49, San Diego 26

WEEK 1

RESULTS

Chicago 21, Tampa Bay 9
Cleveland 28, Cincinnati 20
Dallas 26, Pittsburgh 9
Detroit 31, Atlanta 28 (OT)
Green Bay 16, Minnesota 10
Indianapolis 45, Houston 21
Kansas City 30, New Orleans 17
L.A. Rams 14, Arizona 12
Miami 39, New England 35
N.Y. Giants 28, Philadelphia 23
N.Y. Jets 23, Buffalo 3
San Diego 37, Denver 34
Seattle 28, Washington 7
San Francisco 44, L.A. Raiders 14

STANDINGS

AFC EAST	W	L	T	Pct.
Indianapolis	0	1	0	1.000
Miami	1	0	0	1.000
N.Y. Jets	1	0	0	1.000
Buffalo	0	1	0	.000
New England	0	1	0	.000

AFC CENTRAL	W	L	T	Pct.
Cleveland	1	0	0	1.000
Cincinnati	0	1	0	.000
Houston	0	1	0	.000
Pittsburgh	0	1	0	.000

AFC WEST	W	L	T	Pct.
Kansas City	1	0	0	1.000
San Diego	1	0	0	1.000
Seattle	1	0	0	1.000
L.A. Raiders	0	1	0	.000
Denver	0	1	0	.000

NFC EAST	W	L	T	Pct.
Dallas	1	0	0	1.000
N.Y. Giants	1	0	0	1.000
Arizona	0	1	0	.000
Philadelphia	0	1	0	.000
Washington	0	1	0	.000

NFC CENTRAL	W	L	T	Pct.
Chicago	1	0	0	1.000
Detroit	1	0	0	1.000
Green Bay	1	0	0	1.000
Minnesota	0	1	0	.000
Tampa Bay	0	1	0	.000

NFC WEST	W	L	T	Pct.
L.A. Rams	1	0	0	1.000
San Francisco	1	0	0	1.000
Atlanta	0	1	0	.000
New Orleans	0	1	0	.000

HIGHLIGHTS

Hero of the week: Miami quarterback Dan Marino, who threw five touchdown passes in leading the Dolphins to a 39-35 come-from-behind victory over New England. Marino, who was playing in his first regular season game since tearing his right Achilles tendon in a game 11 months earlier, clinched the win with a 35-yard scoring pass to Irving Fryar on fourth and 5 with 3:19 left.

Goat of the week: Arizona quarterback Steve Beuerlein, who struggled in a 14-12 loss to the Los Angeles Rams. Beuerlein completed fewer than half his pass attempts, had two picked off and repeatedly underthrew and overthrew open receivers.

Sub(s) of the week: Although they weren't substitutes in the strictest sense, Erik Kramer, Lewis Tillman and Jeff Graham played pivotal roles in Chicago's 21-9 win over Tampa Bay. In making their first starts for the Bears at quarterback, running back and wide receiver, respectively, the trio led a new-look Chicago offense (seven new starters) that rolled up 270 total yards.

Comeback of the week: Detroit nipped Atlanta, 31-28, on Jason Hanson's 37-yard field goal 5:14 into overtime after tying the game on Scott Mitchell's 15-yard touchdown pass to Anthony Carter with 30 seconds left in regulation.

Blowout of the week: San Francisco destroyed the Los Angeles Raiders, 44-14, in a Monday night game that some observers had touted as an early-season Super Bowl preview. If so, the Raiders had their work cut out for them. Jerry Rice scored three times to become the NFL's all-time touchdown leader (127).

Nail-biter of the week: San Diego upended Denver, 37-34, behind three Stan Humphries touchdown passes and a bizarre fumble recovery by Junior Seau in the waning moments. The Broncos, who led 24-6 in the second quarter, seemed on the verge of retaking the lead after driving to the Chargers' 3-yard line with 35 seconds left. But the ball slipped out of quarterback John Elway's hand as he rolled to his right, and a surprised Seau sealed the win for San Diego by plucking the loose ball out of mid-air.

Hit of the week: By Rams linebacker Joe Kelly, who ripped the ball from the arms of Cardinals running back Larry Centers, forcing an airborne fumble that flew six yards downfield before being caught by Todd Lyght, who scampered 74 yards for the game's first touchdown.

Oddity of the week: Eric Metcalf and Thurman Thomas, two of the NFL's premier offensive weapons, combined for four rushing yards on 14 attempts.

Top rusher: Emmitt Smith carried 31 times for 171 yards and one touchdown in Dallas' 26-9 victory over Pittsburgh.

Top passer: Marino threw for 473 yards against the Patriots, the second-highest total of his career.

Top receiver: Fryar caught five of Marino's passes for 211 yards and three touchdowns.

Notes: Cleveland became the first NFL team since the 1977 Detroit Lions to return both a kickoff and a punt for touchdowns in the same game. Randy Baldwin (85-yard kickoff return) and Eric Metcalf (92-yard punt return) turned the trick in the Browns' 28-20 victory over Cincinnati.... The Colts set a team record for most points in a season-opener in a 45-21 win over Houston. Rookie Marshall Faulk, the second overall pick in the 1994 draft, rushed for 143 yards and three touchdowns in his NFL debut. All six Indianapolis touchdowns were scored by players not on the '93 roster.... Drew Bledsoe threw for a club-record 421 yards in the Patriots' loss to Miami.... Tom Flores and Marty Schottenheimer, former teammates in the old American Football League, each won the 100th game of his NFL coaching career in Week 1.... Washington's 28-7 loss to Seattle was the Redskins' worst in a home opener in 28 years. Their only score came on a 27-yard pass from John Friesz to Desmond Howard. It was the first NFL touchdown reception for Howard, who was playing in the 33rd game of his career.... Joe Montana improved his Superdome record to 10-0 and his record against the Saints to 15-2 in Kansas City's 30-17 win over New Orleans. . . . Offensive tackle Jackie Slater started his 19th season with the Rams, tying Jim Marshall's NFL record for most years of service with one team. Marshall, a defensive end, played with Minnesota from 1961-79. . . . There were more empty seats (36,039) than filled ones (32,969) at Anaheim Stadium for the Rams' home opener against Arizona. By contrast, a record crowd of 68,032 filled Candlestick Park for the 49ers' opener against the Raiders.

Quote of the week: First-year Cardinals Coach Buddy Ryan, on his team's inability to beat the Rams: "It looked to me like they were trying to die, but we couldn't kill them."

GAME SUMMARIES

BROWNS 28, BENGALS 20
Sunday, September 4

Cleveland	11	14	0	3—28
Cincinnati	0	10	3	7—20

First Quarter
Cle—FG Stover 19, 8:00.
Cle—Hoard 11 pass from Testaverde (Tupa run), 13:38.
Second Quarter
Cin—Fenner 1 run (Pelfrey kick), 5:28.
Cle—Baldwin 85 kickoff return (Stover kick), 5:47.
Cle—Metcalf 92 punt return (Stover kick), 8:28.
Cin—FG Pelfrey 38, 14:49.
Third Quarter
Cin—FG Pelfrey 49, 11:33.
Fourth Quarter
Cle—FG Stover 22, 3:54.
Cin—Scott 24 pass from Klingler (Pelfrey kick), 5:51.

TEAM STATISTICS

	Cleveland	Cincinnati
First downs	16	23
Rushes-yards	27-107	30-118
Passing	149	213
Punt returns-yards	4-115	1-17
Kickoff returns-yards	4-147	6-126
Interception returns-yards	2-0	2-82
Comp.-att.-int.	14-24-2	27-43-2
Sacked-yards lost	0-0	2-11
Punts-average	5-40	5-44
Fumbles-lost	2-0	1-0
Penalties-yards	4-44	6-40
Time of possession	25:37	34:23
Attendance—52,778.		

INDIVIDUAL STATISTICS
RUSHING—Cleveland, Hoard 16-92, Vardell 2-8, Baldwin 1-5, Testaverde 1-2, Metcalf 7-0. Cincinnati, Broussard 6-48, Fenner 13-41, Klingler 4-25, Green 7-4.
PASSING—Cleveland, Testaverde 14-24-2-149. Cincinnati, Klingler 27-43-2-224.
RECEIVING—Cleveland, Vardell 4-22, Jackson 3-45, Carrier 3-33, Metcalf 2-27, Hoard 1-11, Reeves 1-11. Cincinnati, Fenner 7-60, Broussard 6-35, Green 5-35, Scott 3-50, To. McGee 2-12, Query 1-14, Ti. McGee 1-10, Pickens 1-6, Sadowski 1-2.
MISSED FIELD GOAL ATTEMPTS—None.
INTERCEPTIONS—Cleveland, Griffin 1-0, Langham 1-0. Cincinnati, Grim 1-49, D. Williams 1-33.
KICKOFF RETURNS—Cleveland, Baldwin 2-113, Hoard 1-10, Metcalf 1-24. Cincinnati, Scott 6-126.
PUNT RETURNS—Cleveland, Metcalf 4-115. Cincinnati, Sawyer 1-17.
SACKS—Cleveland, Banks 1, Burnett 1.

CHIEFS 30, SAINTS 17
Sunday, September 4

Kansas City	7	10	3	10—30
New Orleans	0	3	7	7—17

First Quarter
K.C.—Davis 13 pass from Montana (Elliott kick), 10:44.
Second Quarter
K.C.—Allen 1 run (Elliott kick), 1:46.
N.O.—FG Andersen 48, 6:33.
K.C.—FG Elliott 24, 14:02.
Third Quarter
N.O.—Walls 12 pass from Everett (Andersen kick), 9:50.
K.C.—FG Elliott 22, 11:42.
Fourth Quarter
K.C.—Cash 2 pass from Montana (Elliott kick), 1:48.
K.C.—FG Elliott 27, 7:58.
N.O.—Brown 14 pass from Everett (Andersen kick), 11:00.

TEAM STATISTICS

	Kansas City	New Orleans
First downs	28	22
Rushes-yards	43-152	11-37
Passing	308	312
Punt returns-yards	1-8	0-0
Kickoff returns-yards	1-18	7-168
Interception returns-yards	2-41	0-0
Comp.-att.-int.	24-33-0	26-37-2
Sacked-yards lost	1-7	1-14
Punts-average	1-35	3-40
Fumbles-lost	1-0	2-2
Penalties-yards	8-52	7-44
Time of possession	37:03	22:57
Attendance—69,362.		

INDIVIDUAL STATISTICS
RUSHING—Kansas City, Allen 17-82, Hill 16-51, Anders 5-15, Bennett 2-6, Dickerson 1-0, Montana 2-(minus 2). New Orleans, Brown 9-35, Bates 2-2.
PASSING—Kansas City, Montana 24-33-0-315. New Orleans, Everett 26-37-2-326.
RECEIVING—Kansas City, Davis 7-109, Cash 5-53, Anders 5-49, Dawson 3-70, Allen 3-16, Birden 1-18. New Orleans, Early 8-101, Haynes 5-71, Brown 4-57, Small 4-43, Walls 3-44, I. Smith 1-6, Neal 1-4.
MISSED FIELD GOAL ATTEMPTS—New Orleans, Andersen 52. Kansas City, Elliott 26.
INTERCEPTIONS—Kansas City, Smith 1-41, Taylor 1-0.
KICKOFF RETURNS—Kansas City, Dickerson 1-18. New Orleans, Hughes 6-142, Bates 1-26.
PUNT RETURNS—Kansas City, Hughes 1-8.
SACKS—Kansas City, Smith 1. New Orleans, Conner 1.

COLTS 45, OILERS 21
Sunday, September 4

Houston	0	0	0	21—21
Indianapolis	7	28	7	3—45

First Quarter
Ind—Faulk 1 run (Biasucci kick), 12:56.
Second Quarter
Ind—Bennett 75 fumble recovery (Biasucci kick), 1:11.
Ind—Turner 4 pass from Harbaugh (Biasucci kick), 8:28.
Ind—Turner 9 pass from Harbaugh (Biasucci kick), 11:44.
Ind—Faulk 2 run (Biasucci kick), 13:42.
Third Quarter
Ind—Faulk 11 run (Biasucci kick), 10:01.
Fourth Quarter
Hou—Carter 2 pass from Richardson (Brown pass from Richardson), :05.
Ind—FG Biasucci 42, 4:08.
Hou—Jeffires 16 pass from Richardson (pass failed), 8:03.
Hou—Jeffires 15 pass from Richardson (Del Greco kick), 15:00.

TEAM STATISTICS

	Houston	Indianapolis
First downs	26	19
Rushes-yards	14-79	37-182
Passing	295	106
Punt returns-yards	1-9	2-31
Kickoff returns-yards	8-141	1-27
Interception returns-yards	1-0	1-22
Comp.-att.-int.	30-57-1	10-13-1
Sacked-yards lost	4-37	2-6
Punts-average	5-46	2-47
Fumbles-lost	2-2	2-2
Penalties-yards	13-104	11-67
Time of possession	28:00	32:00
Attendance—47,372.		

INDIVIDUAL STATISTICS

RUSHING—Houston, Brown 10-39, Richardson 3-36, Carlson 1-4. Indianapolis, Faulk 23-143, Potts 6-24, Toner 1-11, Warren 7-4.

PASSING—Houston, Richardson 19-35-0-203, Carlson 11-22-1-129. Indianapolis, Harbaugh 9-12-1-105, Majkowski 1-1-0-7.

RECEIVING—Houston, Slaughter 9-77, Jeffires 8-99, Brown 4-34, Givins 3-65, Hannah 3-27, Coleman 2-31, Carter 1-2. Indianapolis, Turner 3-29, Cash 3-27, Dawkins 2-18, Faulk 1-31, Bailey 1-7.

MISSED FIELD GOAL ATTEMPTS—Houston, Del Greco 55.

INTERCEPTIONS—Houston, Dishman 1-0. Indianapolis, Buchanan 1-22.

KICKOFF RETURNS—Houston, Hannah 4-77, Mills 3-55, Teeter 1-9. Indianapolis, Brewer 1-27.

PUNT RETURNS—Houston, Hannah 1-9. Indianapolis, Brewer 2-31.

SACKS—Houston, Davidson 1, Montgomery 1. Indianapolis, Bennett 1, Coryatt 1, Herrod 1, McCoy 1.

BEARS 21, BUCCANEERS 9

Sunday, September 4

Tampa Bay	0	3	6	0— 9
Chicago	7	7	0	7—21

First Quarter
Chi—Gedney 10 pass from Kramer (Butler kick), 3:34.
Second Quarter
T.B.—FG Husted 31, 9:45.
Chi—Tillman 1 run (Butler kick), 14:03.
Third Quarter
T.B.—FG Husted 49, 4:34.
T.B.—FG Husted 30, 11:56.
Fourth Quarter
Chi—Gedney 37 pass from Kramer (Butler kick), 9:25.

TEAM STATISTICS

	Tampa Bay	Chicago
First downs	17	17
Rushes-yards	30-123	25-66
Passing	181	204
Punt returns-yards	4-15	1-7
Kickoff returns-yards	4-58	4-77
Interception returns-yards	0-0	0-0
Comp.-att.-int.	18-32-0	18-25-0
Sacked-yards lost	3-16	2-8
Punts-average	5-37	6-41
Fumbles-lost	0-0	0-0
Penalties-yards	6-72	6-45
Time of possession	33:27	26:33
Attendance—61,844.		

INDIVIDUAL STATISTICS

RUSHING—Tampa Bay, Workman 15-81, Rhett 11-49, Erickson 1-1, McDowell 2-(minus 5), R. Harris 1-(minus 3). Chicago, Tillman 19-62, Hoge 3-5, Kramer 3-(minus 1).

PASSING—Tampa Bay, Erickson 18-32-0-197. Chicago, Kramer 18-25-0-212.

RECEIVING—Tampa Bay, McDowell 4-42, Green 3-53, Wilson 3-53, J. Harris 3-20, Workman 2-16, R. Harris 2-11, Copeland 1-2. Chicago, Hoge 4-18, Graham 3-58, Conway 3-25, Gedney 2-47, Green 2-25, Tillman 2-23, Waddle 2-16.

MISSED FIELD GOAL ATTEMPTS—Tampa Bay, Husted 54.

INTERCEPTIONS—None.

KICKOFF RETURNS—Tampa Bay, Turner 4-58. Chicago, Lewis 3-59, Harris 1-18.

PUNT RETURNS—Tampa Bay, Turner 4-15. Chicago, Lewis 1-7.

SACKS—Tampa Bay, Wheeler 1, Curry ½, K. Wilson ½. Chicago, Armstrong 2, Spellman 1.

GIANTS 28, EAGLES 23

Sunday, September 4

Philadelphia	0	10	3	10—23
N.Y. Giants	14	7	7	0—28

First Quarter
N.Y.—Hampton 1 run (Treadwell kick), 11:15.
N.Y.—Meggett 68 punt return (Treadwell kick), 13:54.
Second Quarter
Phi—FG Murray 21, 1:16.
N.Y.—Calloway 51 pass from Da. Brown (Treadwell kick), 3:51.
Phi—Bavaro 3 pass from Cunningham (Murray kick), 14:21.
Third Quarter
Phi—FG Murray 39, 3:11.
N.Y.—Meggett 26 run (Treadwell kick), 10:55.

Fourth Quarter
Phi—FG Murray 36, 2:51.
Phi—Williams 10 pass from Cunningham (Murray kick), 13:41.

TEAM STATISTICS

	Philadelphia	N.Y. Giants
First downs	20	15
Rushes-yards	25-78	34-141
Passing	317	149
Punt returns-yards	3-10	2-68
Kickoff returns-yards	4-95	4-74
Interception returns-yards	1-(-3)	0-0
Comp.-att.-int.	20-39-0	10-20-1
Sacked-yards lost	5-27	3-22
Punts-average	6-42	6-40
Fumbles-lost	1-1	2-1
Penalties-yards	9-70	4-26
Time of possession	29:59	30:01
Attendance—76,130.		

INDIVIDUAL STATISTICS

RUSHING—Philadelphia, Cunningham 5-35, Hebron 10-24, Walker 7-16, Joseph 3-3. New York, Hampton 21-85, Meggett 2-31, Calloway 1-20, Rasheed 3-6, Marshall 1-6, Da. Brown 5-3, Sherrard 1-(minus 10).

PASSING—Philadelphia, Cunningham 20-39-0-344. New York, Da. Brown 10-20-1-171.

RECEIVING—Philadelphia, C. Williams 5-76, Barnett 4-61, Joseph 4-43, Bailey 3-44, Walker 1-93, Johnson 1-22, Bavaro 1-3, Hebron 1-2. New York, Calloway 3-74, Sherrard 3-58, Cross 1-20, Marshall 1-10, Lewis 1-8, Meggett 1-1.

MISSED FIELD GOAL ATTEMPTS—None.

INTERCEPTIONS—Philadelphia, McMillian 1-(minus 3).

KICKOFF RETURNS—Philadelphia, Sydner 4-95. New York, Meggett 3-52, Lewis 1-22.

PUNT RETURNS—Philadelphia, Sydner 3-10. New York, Meggett 2-68.

SACKS—Philadelphia, Fuller 1, Grossman 1, Harmon 1. New York, Howard 2, Strahan 1½, Hamilton 1, Dillard ½.

LIONS 31, FALCONS 28

Sunday, September 4

Atlanta	0	7	7	14	0—28
Detroit	7	0	7	14	3—31

First Quarter
Det—D. Moore 1 run (Hanson kick), 3:55.
Second Quarter
Atl—Pegram 1 run (Johnson kick), 7:26.
Third Quarter
Det—H. Moore 4 pass from Mitchell (Hanson kick), 3:58.
Atl—Rison 2 pass from J. George (Johnson kick), 11:10.
Fourth Quarter
Det—Carter 9 pass from Mitchell (Hanson kick), 2:47.
Atl—Rison 69 pass from J. George (Johnson kick), 3:12.
Atl—Mathis 15 pass from J. George (Johnson kick), 11:03.
Det—Carter 15 pass from Mitchell (Hanson kick), 14:30.
Overtime
Det—FG Hanson 37, 5:14.

TEAM STATISTICS

	Atlanta	Detroit
First downs	22	21
Rushes-yards	28-118	31-149
Passing	271	203
Punt returns-yards	4-50	3-41
Kickoff returns-yards	6-152	5-107
Interception returns-yards	1-13	0-0
Comp.-att.-int.	29-37-0	16-31-1
Sacked-yards lost	2-10	0-0
Punts-average	6-47	5-49
Fumbles-lost	0-0	0-0
Penalties-yards	10-90	5-40
Time of possession	36:04	29:10
Attendance—60,740.		

INDIVIDUAL STATISTICS

RUSHING—Atlanta, Pegram 23-93, Heyward 2-12, J. George 2-11, Emanuel 1-2. Detroit, Sanders 27-120, D. Moore 2-13, Perriman 1-11, Mitchell 1-5.

PASSING—Atlanta, J. George 29-37-0-281. Detroit, Mitchell 16-31-1-203.

RECEIVING—Atlanta, Rison 14-193, Mathis 8-63, Emanuel 3-13, Pegram 3-6, Mims 1-6. Detroit, H. Moore 6-84, Carter 5-61, Perriman 2-35, Sanders 2-7, Holman 1-16.

MISSED FIELD GOAL ATTEMPTS—Atlanta, Johnson 52.
INTERCEPTIONS—Atlanta, Ross 1-10, Walker 0-3.
KICKOFF RETURNS—Atlanta, T. Smith 5-115, Montgomery 1-37. Detroit, Gray 3-74, D. Moore 2-33.
PUNT RETURNS—Atlanta, T. Smith 4-50. Detroit, Gray 2-29, Clay 1-12.
SACKS—Detroit, Hayworth 1, Pritchett 1.

PACKERS 16, VIKINGS 10

Sunday, September 4

Minnesota	0	0	3	7—	10
Green Bay	3	10	0	3—	16

First Quarter
G.B.—FG Jacke 25, 7:31.

Second Quarter
G.B.—Sharpe 14 pass from Favre (Jacke kick), 5:57.
G.B.—FG Jacke 39, 14:55.

Third Quarter
Min—FG Reveiz 28, 10:58.

Fourth Quarter
Min—Harris 17 fumble return (Reveiz kick), 1:31.
G.B.—FG Jacke 49, 7:17.

TEAM STATISTICS

	Minnesota	Green Bay
First downs	12	15
Rushes-yards	17-48	26-94
Passing	146	170
Punt returns-yards	5-37	4-20
Kickoff returns-yards	5-95	2-19
Interception returns-yards	0-0	3-34
Comp.-att.-int.	20-37-3	22-36-0
Sacked-yards lost	3-20	3-15
Punts-average	7-36	8-40
Fumbles-lost	2-0	1-1
Penalties-yards	9-66	8-60
Time of possession	26:11	33:49

Attendence—59,487.

INDIVIDUAL STATISTICS

RUSHING—Minnesota, Allen 11-33, Lee 4-13, Moon 2-2. Green Bay, Bennett 16-51, Cobb 9-35, Sharpe 1-8.
PASSING—Minnesota, Moon 20-37-3-166. Green Bay, Favre 22-36-0-185.
RECEIVING—Minnesota, Carter 5-35, Reed 4-42, Jordan 4-23, Ismail 2-31, Cooper 2-20, Lee 2-7, Allen 1-8. Green Bay, Sharpe 7-53, Bennett 4-39, Brooks 4-35, West 3-40, Cobb 3-9, Lewis 1-9.
MISSED FIELD GOAL ATTEMPTS—None.
INTERCEPTIONS—Green Bay, Teague 2-17, Willis 1-17.
KICKOFF RETURNS—Minnesota, Ismail 2-69, Lee 2-16, Novoselsky 1-10. Green Bay, Harris 2-19.
PUNT RETURNS—Minnesota, Palmer 5-37. Green Bay, Brooks 4-20.
SACKS—Minnesota, Randle 1, Thomas 1, Team 1. Green Bay, Jones 1, Paup 1, White 1.

SEAHAWKS 28, REDSKINS 7

Sunday, September 4

Seattle	7	14	7	0—	28
Washington	7	0	0	0—	7

First Quarter
Was—Howard 27 pass from Friesz (Lohmiller kick), 3:54.
Sea—Warren 12 run (Kasay kick), 8:07.

Second Quarter
Sea—Wooden 69 interception return (Kasay kick), 4:53.
Sea—Blades 5 pass from Mirer (Kasay kick), 14:49.

Third Quarter
Sea—Warren 4 run (Kasay kick), 11:14.

TEAM STATISTICS

	Seattle	Washington
First downs	23	17
Rushes-yards	38-184	19-42
Passing	176	216
Punt returns-yards	4-43	2-13
Kickoff returns-yards	1-23	5-94
Interception returns-yards	2-69	0-0
Comp.-att.-int.	17-28-0	20-40-2
Sacked-yards lost	1-7	2-8
Punts-average	8-33	7-43
Fumbles-lost	2-0	2-1
Penalties-yards	6-53	5-34
Time of possession	33:14	26:46

Attendance—56,454.

INDIVIDUAL STATISTICS

RUSHING—Seattle, Warren 22-100, Vaughn 8-58, S. Smith 3-20, Mirer 4-14, Blades 1-(minus-8). Washington, Brooks 12-31, Mitchell 4-18, Shuler 1-(minus-1), Ervins 2-(minus-6).
PASSING—Seattle, Mirer 17-28-0-183. Washington, Friesz 17-32-2-210, Shuler 3-8-0-14.
RECEIVING—Seattle, Blades 5-43, Martin 4-59, Warren 3-42, Green 2-14, S. Smith 1-13, Edmunds 1-6, T. Johnson 1-6. Washington, Ellard 7-105, Ervins 4-35, Brooks 3-12, Wycheck 2-14, Mitchell 2-13, Howard 1-27, Horton 1-18.
MISSED FIELD GOAL ATTEMPTS—Washington, Lohmiller 34.
INTERCEPTIONS—Seattle, Gray 1-0, Wooden 1-69.
KICKOFF RETURNS—Seattle, Bates 1-23. Washington, Mitchell 4-77, Ervins 1-17.
PUNT RETURNS—Seattle, Martin 4-43. Washington, Mitchell 2-13.
SACKS—Seattle, Kennedy 1, Williams 1. Washington, Woods 1.

JETS 23, BILLS 3

Sunday, September 4

N.Y. Jets	0	17	3	3—	23
Buffalo	3	0	0	0—	3

First Quarter
Buf—FG Christie 27, 5:19.

Second Quarter
N.Y.—R. Anderson 1 run (Lowery kick), :04.
N.Y.—Johnson 9 run (Lowery kick), 13:24.
N.Y.—FG Lowery 27, 14:55.

Third Quarter
N.Y.—FG Lowery 42, 5:50.

Fourth Quarter
N.Y.—FG Lowery 22, 9:52.

TEAM STATISTICS

	N.Y. Jets	Buffalo
First downs	17	13
Rushes-yards	41-116	13-43
Passing	214	173
Punt returns-yards	4-39	2-20
Kickoff returns-yards	2-33	6-100
Interception returns-yards	2-29	1-0
Comp.-att.-int.	14-28-1	22-38-2
Sacked-yards lost	0-0	3-22
Punts-average	4-39	4-40
Fumbles-lost	2-0	1-1
Penalties-yards	5-30	5-40
Time of possession	37:12	22:48

Attendance—79,460.

INDIVIDUAL STATISTICS

RUSHING—New York, Johnson 25-75, Murrell 10-28, Baxter 2-8, R. Anderson 3-5, Esiason 1-0. Buffalo, Gardner 4-33, Thomas 7-5, K. Davis 1-4, Kelly 1-1.
PASSING—New York, Esiason 14-28-1-214. Buffalo, Kelly 20-36-2-179, Reich 2-2-0-16.
RECEIVING—New York, Moore 5-83, Johnson 4-33, Mitchell 2-74, Thornton 2-19, Monk 1-5. Buffalo, Reed 6-77, Thomas 6-30, Metzelaars 4-32, Beebe 3-38, Gardner 2-14, Copeland 1-4.
MISSED FIELD GOAL ATTEMPTS—None.
INTERCEPTIONS—New York, Turner 1-30, M. Washington 1-(minus 1). Buffalo, Darby 1-0.
KICKOFF RETURNS—New York, Murrell 2-33. Buffalo, Beebe 5-98, Tasker 1-2.
PUNT RETURNS—New York, Hicks 4-39. Buffalo, Burris 2-20.
SACKS—New York, M. Washington 2, Barber 1.

RAMS 14, CARDINALS 12

Sunday, September 4

Arizona	0	6	6	0—	12
L.A. Rams	7	0	7	0—	14

First Quarter
L.A.—Lyght 74 fumble return (Zendejas kick), 7:54.

Second Quarter
Ari—FG Davis 37, 9:15.
Ari—FG Davis 34, 13:20.

Third Quarter
L.A.—Bettis 1 run (Zendejas kick), 3:04.
Ari—Centers 3 pass from Beuerlein (pass failed), 13:17.

TEAM STATISTICS

	Arizona	L.A. Rams
First downs	23	9
Rushes-yards	32-102	22-50
Passing	128	102
Punt returns-yards	5-50	3-25
Kickoff returns-yards	3-67	4-76
Interception returns-yards	1-0	2-1
Comp.-att.-int.	18-40-2	6-16-1
Sacked-yards lost	4-30	5-29
Punts-average	6-37	6-45
Fumbles-lost	1-1	3-1
Penalties-yards	6-84	10-77
Time of possession	38:22	21:38

Attendance—32,969.

INDIVIDUAL STATISTICS

RUSHING—Arizona, R. Moore 13-65, Centers 15-29, Beuerlein 4-8. Los Angeles, Bettis 21-52, Miller 1-(minus 2).

PASSING—Arizona, Beuerlein 18-40-2-158. Los Angeles, Miller 6-16-1-131.

RECEIVING—Arizona, R. Hill 5-46, Clark 4-55, Proehl 4-22, Ware 3-18, Centers 2-17. Los Angeles, J. Bailey 2-42, Hester 2-27, Anderson 1-44, Buchanan 1-18.

MISSED FIELD GOAL ATTEMPTS—Los Angeles, Zendejas 43.

INTERCEPTIONS—Arizona, J. Williams 1-0. Los Angeles, Lyle 1-1, Pope 1-0.

KICKOFF RETURNS—Arizona, Robinson 3-67. Los Angeles, Lang 4-76.

PUNT RETURNS—Arizona, Robinson 5-50. Los Angeles, J. Bailey 3-25.

SACKS—Arizona, Simmons 2, Bankston 1, Miller 1, Team 1. Los Angeles, Young 2, J. Jones 1, Rocker ½, Stokes ½.

DOLPHINS 39, PATRIOTS 35

Sunday, September 4

New England	7	7	14	7—35
Miami	0	10	15	14—39

First Quarter
N.E.—Turner 1 run (Bahr kick), 10:16.
Second Quarter
Mia—Ingram 64 pass from Marino (Stoyanovich kick), 12:45.
N.E.—Coates 16 pass from Bledsoe (Bahr kick), 14:35.
Mia—FG Stoyanovich 42, 15:00.
Third Quarter
N.E.—Coates 63 pass from Bledsoe (Bahr kick), 2:27.
Mia—Jackson 26 pass from Marino (Kirby run), 6:47.
N.E.—Timpson 5 pass from Bledsoe (Bahr kick), 10:33.
Mia—Fryar 54 pass from Marino (Stoyanovich kick), 11:51.
Fourth Quarter
Mia—Fryar 50 pass from Marino (Stoyanovich kick), 1:00.
N.E.—Crittenden 23 pass from Bledsoe (Bahr kick), 4:48.
Mia—Fryar 35 pass from Marino (Stoyanovich kick), 11:41.

TEAM STATISTICS

	New England	Miami
First downs	25	21
Rushes-yards	24-54	23-69
Passing	418	456
Punt returns-yards	4-28	2-21
Kickoff returns-yards	5-96	6-121
Interception returns-yards	1-5	2-17
Comp.-att.-int.	32-51-2	23-42-1
Sacked-yards lost	1-3	2-17
Punts-average	5-36	5-41
Fumbles-lost	2-1	2-2
Penalties-yards	5-62	8-65
Time of possession	32:42	27:18

Attendance—69,613.

INDIVIDUAL STATISTICS

RUSHING—New England, Butts 15-25, Thompson 6-22, Timpson 1-4, Turner 2-3. Miami, Kirby 19-56, Marino 2-8, Spikes 1-5, Dellenbach 1-0.

PASSING—New England, Bledsoe 32-51-2-421. Miami, Marino 23-42-1-473.

RECEIVING—New England, Coates 8-161, Turner 7-61, Timpson 6-69, Brisby 5-66, Thompson 5-41, Crittenden 1-23. Miami, Kirby 7-61, Fryar 5-211, Ingram 3-87, Miller 3-55, Jackson 2-29, Byars 2-9, McDuffie 1-21.

MISSED FIELD GOAL ATTEMPTS—None.

INTERCEPTIONS—New England, Sabb 1-5. Miami, Atkins 1-5, Vincent 1-12.

KICKOFF RETURNS—New England, Crittenden 4-76, Croom 1-20. Miami, McDuffie 3-69, Spikes 2-39, Miller 1-13.

PUNT RETURNS—New England, Crittenden 4-28. Miami, McDuffie 1-8, Miller 1-13.

SACKS—New England, Slade 1, Sabb ½, Smith ½. Miami, Cox 1.

COWBOYS 26, STEELERS 9

Sunday, September 4

Dallas	3	13	0	10—26
Pittsburgh	0	3	0	6— 9

First Quarter
Dal—FG Boniol 40, 12:00.
Second Quarter
Dal—FG Boniol 31, 3:52.
Pit—FG Anderson 41, 7:51.
Dal—Johnston 2 pass from Aikman (Boniol kick), 13:45.
Dal—FG Boniol 21, 15:00.
Fourth Quarter
Dal—FG Boniol 32, 2:25.
Pit—O'Donnell 2 run (pass failed), 6:41.
Dal—Smith 2 run (Boniol kick), 11:12.

TEAM STATISTICS

	Dallas	Pittsburgh
First downs	26	14
Rushes-yards	41-197	17-55
Passing	245	71
Punt returns-yards	2-5	1-18
Kickoff returns-yards	3-60	6-131
Interception returns-yards	0-0	1-42
Comp.-att.-int.	21-32-1	13-26-0
Sacked-yards lost	0-0	9-56
Punts-average	1-35	5-34
Fumbles-lost	0-0	0-0
Penalties-yards	6-31	2-17
Time of possession	35:55	24:05

Attendance—60,156.

INDIVIDUAL STATISTICS

RUSHING—Dallas, Smith 31-171, Johnston 6-21, Coleman 1-8, Aikman 3-(minus 3). Pittsburgh, Foster 14-44, O'Donnell 2-7, Stone 1-4.

PASSING—Dallas, Aikman 21-32-1-245. Pittsburgh, O'Donnell 13-26-0-127.

RECEIVING—Dallas, Irvin 8-139, Novacek 6-53, Smith 3-3, Johnston 2-9, Harper 1-37, K. Williams 1-4. Pittsburgh, Hastings 2-30, Green 2-24, C. Johnson 2-21, Foster 2-7, Thigpen 1-21, Mills 1-12, Hayes 1-9, J.L. Williams 1-2, Stone 1-1.

MISSED FIELD GOAL ATTEMPTS—None.

INTERCEPTIONS—Pittsburgh, Perry 1-42.

KICKOFF RETURNS—Dallas, K. Williams 3-60. Pittsburgh, Woodson 3-61, Johnson 1-29, Stone 1-18, Thigpen 1-23.

PUNT RETURNS—Dallas, K. Williams 2-5. Pittsburgh, Woodson 1-18.

SACKS—Dallas, Haley 4, Jeffcoat 3, Bates 1, Hennings 1.

CHARGERS 37, BRONCOS 34

Sunday, September 4

San Diego	6	21	3	7—37
Denver	17	7	3	7—34

First Quarter
Den—Pritchard 50 pass from Elway (Elam kick), 2:39.
Den—L. Russell 22 run (Elam kick), 7:15.
Den—FG Elam 25, 10:34.
S.D.—Pupunu 22 pass from Humphries (run failed), 14:35.
Second Quarter
Den—Milburn 8 pass from Elway (Elam kick), 3:35.
S.D.—Jefferson 47 pass from Humphries (Carney kick), 5:47.
S.D.—Seay 29 pass from Humphries (pass failed), 7:32.
S.D.—Richard 99 interception return (Harmon run), 15:00.
Third Quarter
Den—FG Elam 42, 5:28.
S.D.—FG Carney 27, 8:59.
Fourth Quarter
Den—Sharpe 5 pass from Elway (Elam kick), :53.
S.D.—Means 1 run (Carney kick), 11:59.

TEAM STATISTICS

	San Diego	Denver
First downs	19	30
Rushes-yards	34-138	18-129
Passing	232	341
Punt returns-yards	1-8	0-0
Kickoff returns-yards	5-102	5-99
Interception returns-yards	2-99	0-0

	San Diego	Denver
Comp.-att.-int.	12-22-0	36-46-2
Sacked-yards lost	0-0	4-30
Punts-average	3-38	1-59
Fumbles-lost	1-1	1-1
Penalties-yards	9-87	6-63
Time of possession	27:30	32:30
Attendance—74,032.		

INDIVIDUAL STATISTICS

RUSHING—San Diego, Means 22-96, Bieniemy 5-16, Jefferson 1-14, Harmon 2-13, Humphries 4-(minus 1). Denver, L. Russell 8-70, Bernstine 8-55, Clark 1-3, Elway 1-1.

PASSING—San Diego, Humphries 12-22-0-232. Denver, Elway 36-46-2-371.

RECEIVING—San Diego, Jefferson 3-79, Means 3-27, Pupunu 2-47, Harmon 2-25, Seay 1-29, Bieniemy 1-25. Denver, Sharpe 9-97, Bernstine 8-67, Pritchard 5-119, Milburn 5-20, L. Russell 3-20, D. Russell 2-19, Clark 2-15, Miller 2-14.

MISSED FIELD GOAL ATTEMPTS—None.

INTERCEPTIONS—San Diego, Richard 1-99, Carrington 1-0.

KICKOFF RETURNS—San Diego, Coleman 4-92, Martin 1-10. Denver, D. Russell 4-83, Swann 1-16.

PUNT RETURNS—San Diego, Gordon 1-8.

SACKS—San Diego, Seau 1½, Mims 1, Team 1, Lee ½.

49ERS 44, RAIDERS 14

Monday, September 5

L.A. Raiders	0	14	0	0—14
San Francisco	14	9	0	21—44

First Quarter
S.F.—Rice 69 pass from Young (Brien kick), 6:20.
S.F.—B. Jones 15 pass from Young (Brien kick), 12:35.

Second Quarter
L.A.—Brown 7 pass from Hostetler (Jaeger kick), 5:16.
S.F.—Watters 1 run (kick failed), 9:56.
L.A.—McCallum 1 run (Jaeger kick), 11:53.
S.F.—FG Brien 33, 14:57.

Fourth Quarter
S.F.—B. Jones 8 pass from Young (Brien kick), 0:05.
S.F.—Rice 23 run (Brien kick), 2:55.
S.F.—Rice 38 pass from Young (Brien kick), 10:55.

TEAM STATISTICS

	L.A. Raiders	San Francisco
First downs	12	24
Rushes-yards	20-34	36-156
Passing	147	292
Punt returns-yards	0-0	2-22
Kickoff returns-yards	6-140	3-62
Interception returns-yards	1-11	1-(-4)
Comp.-att.-int.	19-33-1	19-32-1
Sacked-yards lost	5-49	2-16
Punts-average	5-47	3-29
Fumbles-lost	2-1	0-0
Penalties-yards	6-40	4-20
Time of possession	26:33	33:27
Attendance—68,032.		

INDIVIDUAL STATISTICS

RUSHING—Los Angeles, Rathman 4-12, H. Williams 4-8, McCallum 3-5, Evans 2-4, Montgomery 6-4, Hostetler 1-1. San Francisco, Watters 18-37, Young 5-51, Rice 1-23, Logan 7-31, Floyd 2-8, Carter 1-7, Walker 1-0, Grbac 1-(minus 1).

PASSING—Los Angeles, Hostetler 17-28-1-168, Evans 2-5-0-28. San Francisco, Young 19-32-1-308.

RECEIVING—Los Angeles, T. Brown 5-42, Jett 3-39, Ismail 4-70, Glover 2-17, Rathman 2-9, Hobbs 1-12, H. Williams 1-7, Montgomery 1-0. San Francisco, Rice 7-169, Watters 5-55, B. Jones 4-59, Taylor 1-17, McCaffrey 1-7, Logan 1-1.

MISSED FIELD GOAL ATTEMPTS—Los Angeles, Jaeger 42. San Francisco, Brien 41.

INTERCEPTIONS—Los Angeles, Biekert 1-11. San Francisco, D. Brown 1-(minus 4).

KICKOFF RETURNS—Los Angeles, Ismail 3-84, H. Williams 3-56. San Francisco, Carter 2-56, Singleton 1-6.

PUNT RETURNS—San Francisco, Carter 2-22.

SACKS—Los Angeles, McGlockton 1, Ball 1. San Francisco, Dent 1, Stubblefield 1, B. Young 1, Jackson 1, Thomas 1.

WEEK 2

RESULTS

Atlanta 31, L.A. Rams 13
Buffalo 38, New England 35
Dallas 20, Houston 17
Kansas City 24, San Francisco 17
Miami 24, Green Bay 14
Minnesota 10, Detroit 3
N.Y. Giants 20, Arizona 17
N.Y. Jets 25, Denver 22 (OT)
Pittsburgh 17, Cleveland 10
San Diego 27, Cincinnati 10
Seattle 38, L.A. Raiders 9
Tampa Bay 24, Indianapolis 10
Washington 38, New Orleans 24
Philadelphia 30, Chicago 22

STANDINGS

AFC EAST

	W	L	T	Pct.
Miami	2	0	0	1.000
N.Y. Jets	2	0	0	1.000
Buffalo	1	1	0	.500
Indianapolis	1	1	0	.500
New England	0	2	0	.000

AFC CENTRAL

	W	L	T	Pct.
Cleveland	1	1	0	.500
Pittsburgh	1	1	0	.500
Cincinnati	0	2	0	.000
Houston	0	2	0	.000

AFC WEST

	W	L	T	Pct.
Kansas City	2	0	0	1.000
San Diego	2	0	0	1.000
Seattle	2	0	0	1.000
Denver	0	2	0	.000
L.A. Raiders	0	2	0	.000

NFC EAST

	W	L	T	Pct.
Dallas	2	0	0	1.000
N.Y. Giants	2	0	0	1.000
Philadelphia	1	1	0	.500
Washington	1	1	0	.500
Arizona	0	2	0	.000

NFC CENTRAL

	W	L	T	Pct.
Chicago	1	1	0	.500
Detroit	1	1	0	.500
Green Bay	1	1	0	.500
Minnesota	1	1	0	.500
Tampa Bay	1	1	0	.500

NFC WEST

	W	L	T	Pct.
Atlanta	1	1	0	.500
L.A. Rams	1	1	0	.500
San Francisco	1	1	0	.500
New Orleans	0	2	0	.000

HIGHLIGHTS

Hero of the week: Washington's Brian Mitchell, who returned five kicks for 225 yards in the Redskins' 38-24 victory over New Orleans. Mitchell ran a punt back 74 yards for a touchdown in the first quarter and returned the second-half kickoff 86 yards to set up a touchdown.

Goat of the week: Cleveland quarterback Vinny Testaverde, who threw four interceptions in the Browns' 17-10 loss to Pittsburgh. Testaverde also overthrew Derrick Alexander on what would have been a game-tying touchdown in the final minute.

Sub of the week: Houston quarterback Bucky Richardson, who did an admirable job subbing for the injured Cody Carlson in the Oilers' 20-17 loss at Dallas. In his first NFL start, the former Texas A&M star threw for 242 yards and ran seven times for 37 yards, twice for first downs.

Comeback of the week: The New York Jets beat Denver, 25-22, on a 39-yard field goal by Nick Lowery at 3:57 of overtime. The Jets appeared to be in control when Boomer Esiason and Rob Moore connected for a 35-yard touchdown pass and a two-point conversion pass with 4:15 left in regulation, but the Broncos tied it when Jason Elam kicked a 29-yard field goal with 1:46 left.

Blowout of the week: Seattle forced four Raiders turnovers and scored points after each in a 38-9 rout of its AFC West rivals. Seattle's Rick Mirer threw three touchdown passes in a span of 10:03 after interceptions of Jeff Hostetler passes. Eight Seahawks caught at least one pass, and the Raiders failed to score on an offensive touchdown.

Nail-biter of the week: Buffalo beat New England, 38-35, on Steve Christie's 32-yard field goal with 52 seconds left. Jim Kelly drove the Bills 42 yards on their final possession.

Hit of the week: By Kansas City linebacker Derrick Thomas, who sacked San Francisco quarterback Steve Young in the end zone for a safety to give the Chiefs momentum in a game they went on to win, 24-17. Thomas, who had two other sacks in the game, beat right tackle Harry Boatswain for the

safety that cut the Niners' lead to 14-9.

Oddity of the week: In 1993, the Giants failed to rush for 100 yards in only two games—both against the Cardinals. In their first game of 1994 against the Cards, now coached by the defensive-minded Buddy Ryan, the Giants rushed for 118.

Top rusher: Natrone Means carried 21 times for 107 yards and one touchdown in San Diego's 27-10 win over Cincinnati.

Top passer: Drew Bledsoe completed 26 of 42 passes for 380 yards and three touchdowns in New England's loss to Buffalo.

Top receiver: Willie Anderson caught five passes for 154 yards and one touchdown in the Rams' 31-13 loss at Atlanta.

Notes: The Green Bay Packers ran the ball only seven times in their 24-14 loss to Miami. In the 75-year history of the NFL, only the Chicago Cardinals (six times in an October 29, 1933, game against the Boston Redskins) had fewer.... Nearly 400 media credentials were issued for the San Francisco-Kansas City game, which pitted former 49ers star Joe Montana against his old team and QB successor, Steve Young.... Detroit's Barry Sanders (16 yards vs. Minnesota) was held to his lowest rushing total since a 10-yard effort against New Orleans in 1990.... The Tampa Bay Buccaneers had their smallest crowd ever for a home opener (36,631).... Marshall Faulk (104 yards against the Bucs) became the first Colts rookie to rush for 100 yards in each of his first two games since Alan Ameche did it in 1955.... Miami remained unbeaten against Green Bay (8-0) in regular-season play. The Dolphins are the only team the Packers have never beaten. ... John Friesz's four touchdown passes for Washington in Week 2 were as many as any Redskins quarterback (Mark Rypien, Cary Conklin, Rich Gannon) threw in the entire 1993 season.... The Eagles snapped a seven-game losing streak against Chicago but still trailed, 25-5-1, in the all-time series (including playoffs).... Denver

— 119 —

lost its fourth consecutive overtime game.

Quote of the week: Tampa Bay safety Thomas Everett, on Faulk: "Trying to catch him is like trying to catch a deer."

GAME SUMMARIES

FALCONS 31, RAMS 13

Sunday, September 11

L.A. Rams	0	7	0	6—13
Atlanta	14	3	7	7—31

First Quarter
Atl—Mathis 2 pass from J. George (N. Johnson kick), 7:02.
Atl—Rison 16 pass from J. George (N. Johnson kick), 12:46.
Second Quarter
L.A.—Bruce 34 pass from Miller (Zendejas kick), 13:42.
Atl—FG N. Johnson 48, 15:00.
Third Quarter
Atl—Walker 44 interception return (N. Johnson kick), 12:36.
Fourth Quarter
Atl—Rison 16 pass from J. George (N. Johnson kick), 3:39.
L.A.—W. Anderson 41 pass from Chandler (pass failed), 10:53.

TEAM STATISTICS

	L.A. Rams	Atlanta
First downs	20	24
Rushes-yards	29-140	24-124
Passing	281	304
Punt returns-yards	2-10	1-4
Kickoff returns-yards	4-80	3-57
Interception returns-yards	1-7	3-44
Comp.-att.-int.	19-37-3	30-42-1
Sacked-yards lost	2-24	0-0
Punts-average	3-46	3-43
Fumbles-lost	1-1	1-1
Penalties-yards	9-65	5-25
Time of possession	29:17	30:43

Attendance—55,378.

INDIVIDUAL STATISTICS
RUSHING—Los Angeles, Bettis 24-102, Lang 1-17, Miller 1-12, Chandler 2-8, J. Bailey 1-1. Atlanta, Heyward 9-68, Pegram 11-45, J. George 2-13, Hebert 2-(minus 2).
PASSING—Los Angeles, Miller 10-20-3-187, Chandler 9-17-0-118. Atlanta, J. George 29-38-0-287, Hebert 1-3-0-17, Emanuel 0-1-1-0.
RECEIVING—Los Angeles, W. Anderson 5-154, Buchanan 5-48, Bruce 2-37, Bettis 2-22, J. Bailey 2-21, Lang 2-17, Hester 1-6. Atlanta, Rison 12-123, Mathis 6-79, Emanuel 4-46, Pegram 4-20, Mims 2-8, Harris 1-17, Spencer 1-11.
MISSED FIELD GOAL ATTEMPTS—None.
INTERCEPTIONS—Los Angeles, Phifer 1-7. Atlanta, D. Johnson 2-0, Walker 1-44.
KICKOFF RETURNS—Los Angeles, Brantley 2-39, J. Bailey 1-27, Lang 1-14. Atlanta, T. Smith 2-36, Montgomery 1-21.
PUNT RETURNS—Los Angeles, J. Bailey 1-3, Brantley 1-7. Atlanta, T. Smith 1-4.
SACKS—Atlanta, C. Smith 1, Walker 1.

STEELERS 17, BROWNS 10

Sunday, September 11

Pittsburgh	0	14	0	3—17
Cleveland	7	3	0	0—10

First Quarter
Cle—Reeves 1 pass from Testaverde (Stover kick), 8:10.
Second Quarter
Cle—FG Stover 23, 3:39.
Pit—Thigpen 31 pass from O'Donnell (Anderson kick), 5:35.
Pit—Foster 1 run (Anderson kick), 13:38.
Fourth Quarter
Pit—FG Anderson 25, :36.

TEAM STATISTICS

	Pittsburgh	Cleveland
First downs	17	18
Rushes-yards	38-116	19-81
Passing	199	197
Punt returns-yards	0-0	1-0
Kickoff returns-yards	2-72	4-138
Interception returns-yards	4-50	0-0
Comp.-att.-int.	15-25-0	19-38-4
Sacked-yards lost	0-0	2-14
Punts-average	6-34	3-40
Fumbles-lost	0-0	1-1
Penalties-yards	15-115	5-40
Time of possession	30:47	29:13

Attendance—77,774.

INDIVIDUAL STATISTICS
RUSHING—Pittsburgh, Foster 31-84, O'Donnell 4-15, Williams 2-13, Morris 1-4. Cleveland, Metcalf 9-43, Hoard 5-15, Baldwin 3-13, Vardell 2-10.
PASSING—Pittsburgh, O'Donnell 15-25-0-199. Cleveland, Testaverde 19-37-4-211, Jackson 0-1-0-0.
RECEIVING—Pittsburgh, Johnson 5-72, Williams 3-31, Foster 3-26, Thigpen 2-47, Green 2-23. Cleveland, Vardell 4-36, Metcalf 3-45, Jackson 3-37, Carrier 3-35, Alexander 2-32, Reeves 2-23, Kinchen 1-4, Hoard 1-(minus 1).
MISSED FIELD GOAL ATTEMPTS—Pittsburgh, Anderson 46. Cleveland, Stover 32.
INTERCEPTIONS—Pittsburgh, Perry 3-30, Woodson 1-20.
KICKOFF RETURNS—Pittsburgh, Woodson 2-72. Cleveland, Baldwin 3-123, Kinchen 1-15.
PUNT RETURNS—Cleveland, Metcalf 1-0.
SACKS—Pittsburgh, Greene 1, Seals 1.

CHIEFS 24, 49ERS 17

Sunday, September 11

San Francisco	0	14	0	3—17
Kansas City	7	2	15	0—24

First Quarter
K.C.—Valerio 1 pass from Montana (Elliott kick), 5:44.
Second Quarter
S.F.—Jones 5 pass from Young (Brien kick), :03.
S.F.—Logan 1 run (Brien kick), 6:59.
K.C.—Safety, Thomas tackled Young in the end zone, 12:48.
Third Quarter
K.C.—Cash 8 pass from Montana (Birden pass from Montana), 6:17.
K.C.—Allen 4 run (Elliott kick), 10:01.
Fourth Quarter
S.F.—FG Brien 19, 9:26.

TEAM STATISTICS

	San Francisco	Kansas City
First downs	23	18
Rushes-yards	26-110	32-98
Passing	271	194
Punt returns-yards	2-40	2-47
Kickoff returns-yards	4-104	4-96
Interception returns-yards	0-0	2-31
Comp.-att.-int.	24-34-2	19-31-0
Sacked-yards lost	4-17	1-9
Punts-average	2-55	7-46
Fumbles-lost	2-2	1-0
Penalties-yards	9-73	6-70
Time of possession	31:29	28:31

Attendance—79,907.

INDIVIDUAL STATISTICS
RUSHING—San Francisco, Watters 14-59, Young 5-20, D. Carter 1-18, Logan 5-16, J. Taylor 1-(minus 3). Kansas City, Allen 20-69, Hill 4-12, Anders 4-8, Montana 3-6, Bennett 1-3.
PASSING—San Francisco, Young 24-34-2-288. Kansas City, Montana 19-31-0-203.
RECEIVING—San Francisco, B. Jones 6-69, Watters 6-64, Rice 5-78, J. Taylor 3-45, Logan 3-22, Singleton 1-10. Kansas City, Anders 7-35, W. Davis 4-59, Cash 3-36, Allen 2-45, Birden 1-25, Walker 1-2, Valerio 1-1.
MISSED FIELD GOAL ATTEMPTS—San Francisco, Brien 43.
INTERCEPTIONS—Kansas City, Mincey 1-31, White 1-0.
KICKOFF RETURNS—San Francisco, Carter 4-104. Kansas City, Dickerson 3-78, Hughes 1-18.
PUNT RETURNS—San Francisco, Carter 2-40. Kansas City, Hughes 2-47.
SACKS—San Francisco, Dent 1. Kansas City, Thomas 3, Collins 1.

BUCCANEERS 24, COLTS 10

Sunday, September 11

Indianapolis	0	3	7	0—10
Tampa Bay	7	3	7	7—24

First Quarter
T.B.—Wilson 50 pass from Erickson (Husted kick), 9:54.
Second Quarter
Ind—FG Biasucci 26, 5:37.
T.B.—FG Husted 47, 15:00.
Third Quarter
T.B.—Harris 48 pass from Erickson (Husted kick), 5:17.
Ind—Potts 8 run (Biasucci kick), 11:18.
Fourth Quarter
T.B.—Hawkins 3 pass from Erickson (Husted kick), 8:14.

TEAM STATISTICS

	Indianapolis	Tampa Bay
First downs	20	13
Rushes-yards	39-163	24-54
Passing	201	313
Punt returns-yards	3-6	1-8
Kickoff returns-yards	3-60	3-41
Interception returns-yards	0-0	1-0
Comp.-att.-int.	19-24-1	19-24-0
Sacked-yards lost	1-5	0-0
Punts-average	5-49	5-40
Fumbles-lost	1-0	0-0
Penalties-yards	4-23	6-45
Time of possession	34:27	25:33

Attendance—36,631.

INDIVIDUAL STATISTICS
RUSHING—Indianapolis, Faulk 18-104, Potts 9-30, Harbaugh 5-22, Humphrey 5-16, Warren 1-3, Turner 1-(minus 12). Tampa Bay, Rhett 13-36, Workman 5-13, McDowell 2-3, Erickson 4-2.

PASSING—Indianapolis, Harbaugh 19-24-1-206. Tampa Bay, Erickson 19-24-0-313.

RECEIVING—Indianapolis, Faulk 7-82, Dawkins 3-49, Turner 3-37, Baker 2-15, Cash 2-15, Warren 1-5, Potts 1-3. Tampa Bay, Harris 4-96, Hawkins 4-72, Rhett 3-4, Armstrong 2-30, W. Green 2-28, McDowell 2-8, Wilson 1-50, Armstrong 1-25.

MISSED FIELD GOAL ATTEMPTS—None.
INTERCEPTIONS—Tampa Bay, Mayhew 1-0.
KICKOFF RETURNS—Indianapolis, Brewer 2-35, Humphrey 1-25. Tampa Bay, Turner 2-29, Culpepper 1-12.
PUNT RETURNS—Indianapolis, Brewer 3-6. Tampa Bay, Turner 1-8.
SACKS—Tampa Bay, Culpepper 1.

VIKINGS 10, LIONS 3
Sunday, September 11

Detroit	0	0	0	3— 3
Minnesota	3	7	0	0—10

First Quarter
Min—FG Reveiz 36, 13:12.
Second Quarter
Min—Ismail 30 pass from Moon (Reveiz kick), 5:08.
Fourth Quarter
Det—FG Hanson 24, 6:44.

TEAM STATISTICS

	Detroit	Minnesota
First downs	13	14
Rushes-yards	15-37	30-86
Passing	175	203
Punt returns-yards	5-66	6-23
Kickoff returns-yards	3-77	2-51
Interception returns-yards	1-0	1-0
Comp.-att.-int.	18-41-1	22-35-1
Sacked-yards lost	6-37	2-18
Punts-average	7-47	8-49
Fumbles-lost	3-2	5-2
Penalties-yards	9-70	7-77
Time of possession	25:16	34:44

Attendance—57,349.

INDIVIDUAL STATISTICS
RUSHING—Detroit, Sanders 12-16, Perriman 1-12, Mitchell 1-7, D. Moore 1-2. Minnesota, Allen 12-41, Graham 12-36, Smith 1-7, Evans 1-3, Moon 3-2, Lee 1-(minus 3).

PASSING—Detroit, Mitchell 18-40-1-212, Perriman 0-1-0-0. Minnesota, Moon 22-35-1-221.

RECEIVING—Detroit, H. Moore 5-97, Sanders 4-22, Matthews 3-35, Hall 3-22, Carter 1-18, Hallock 1-14, Perriman 1-4. Minnesota, Carter 6-49, Reed 4-42, Smith 4-23, Ismail 2-34, Cooper 2-30, Jordan 2-22, Lee 2-21.

MISSED FIELD GOAL ATTEMPTS—Detroit, Hanson 42, 46. Minnesota, Reveiz 47.

INTERCEPTIONS—Detroit, Massey 1-0. Minnesota, Parker 1-0.
KICKOFF RETURNS—Detroit, Gray 2-57, Malone 1-20. Minnesota, Ismail 2-51.
PUNT RETURNS—Detroit, Gray 5-66. Minnesota, Palmer 6-23.
SACKS—Detroit, Thomas 2. Minnesota, Barker 2, J. Harris 2, Randle 2.

DOLPHINS 24, PACKERS 14
Sunday, September 11

Miami	3	14	7	0—24
Green Bay	0	0	0	14—14

First Quarter
Mia—FG Stoyanovich 48, 12:05.
Second Quarter
Mia—Jackson 3 pass from Marino (Stoyanovich kick), 9:17.
Mia—Byars 3 pass from Marino (Stoyanovich kick), 14:33.
Third Quarter
Mia—Kirby 6 run (Stoyanovich kick), 7:11.
Fourth Quarter
G.B.—West 2 pass from Favre (pass failed), 8:33.
G.B.—Sharpe 9 pass from Favre (West pass from Favre), 13:38.

TEAM STATISTICS

	Miami	Green Bay
First downs	20	23
Rushes-yards	34-146	7-38
Passing	162	345
Punt returns-yards	0-0	3-12
Kickoff returns-yards	1-17	4-71
Interception returns-yards	1-7	0-00
Comp.-att.-int.	17-25-0	31-51-1
Sacked-yards lost	2-15	4-17
Punts-average	4-38	2-39
Fumbles-lost	2-0	1-1
Penalties-yards	5-58	5-47
Time of possession	36:08	23:52

Attendance—55,011.

INDIVIDUAL STATISTICS
RUSHING—Miami, Spikes 13-70, Kirby 17-64, Byars 3-13, Marino 1-(minus 1). Green Bay, Cobb 4-28, Bennett 2-9, Johnson 1-1.

PASSING—Miami, Marino 17-25-0-177. Green Bay, Favre 31-51-1-362.

RECEIVING—Miami, Ingram 7-72, Kirby 3-48, Fryar 3-37, Byars 2-13, Jackson 2-7. Green Bay, Bennett 10-78, West 5-51, Sharpe 5-48, Wilner 3-20, Morgan 2-49, Brooks 2-31, Cobb 2-26, Johnson 1-33, Lewis 1-26.

MISSED FIELD GOAL ATTEMPTS—Green Bay, Jacke 46.
INTERCEPTIONS—Miami, Veasey 1-7.
KICKOFF RETURNS—Miami, Spikes 1-17. Green Bay, Harris 3-57, Wilson 1-14.
PUNT RETURNS—Green Bay, Brooks 3-12.
SACKS—Miami, Cross 2, Singleton 1, Team 1. Green Bay, Butler 1, Jones 1.

BILLS 38, PATRIOTS 35
Sunday, September 11

Buffalo	14	14	0	10—38
New England	7	7	7	14—35

First Quarter
Buf—Reed 37 pass from Kelly (Christie kick), 2:22.
Buf—Thomas 4 pass from Kelly (Christie kick), 8:02.
N.E.—Coates 18 pass from Bledsoe (Bahr kick), 14:53.
Second Quarter
Buf—Bi. Brooks 12 pass from Kelly (Christie kick), 2:56.
N.E.—Coates 5 pass from Bledsoe (Bahr kick), 12:02.
Buf—Beebe 14 pass from Kelly (Christie kick), 13:47.
Third Quarter
N.E.—Butts 19 run (Bahr kick), 2:27.
Fourth Quarter
Buf—Lodish fumble recovery in the end zone (Christie kick), :53.
N.E.—Timpson 21 pass from Bledsoe (Bahr kick), 5:43.
N.E.—Butts 6 run (Bahr kick), 10:38.
Buf—FG Christie 32, 14:08.

TEAM STATISTICS

	Buffalo	New England
First downs	25	26
Rushes-yards	38-144	25-96
Passing	322	371
Punt returns-yards	2-1	2-26

	Buffalo	New England
Kickoff returns-yards	3-74	7-154
Interception returns-yards	2-0	3-19
Comp.-att.-int.	25-41-3	26-42-2
Sacked-yards lost	2-6	2-9
Punts-average	6-46	5-34
Fumbles-lost	4-1	4-3
Penalties-yards	7-39	4-36
Time of possession	30:06	29:54

Attendance—60,274.

INDIVIDUAL STATISTICS

RUSHING—Buffalo, Thomas 26-106, Davis 6-21, Kelly 4-11, Reed 1-5, Gardner 1-1. New England, Butts 18-82, Turner 4-11, Bledsoe 2-2, Thompson 1-1.

PASSING—Buffalo, Kelly 25-41-3-328. New England, Bledsoe 26-42-2-380.

RECEIVING—Buffalo, Reed 7-142, Bi. Brooks 7-91, Marrow 4-30, Thomas 4-22, Beebe 3-43. New England, Coates 9-124, Timpson 5-101, Turner 4-44, Brisby 3-42, Crittenden 2-41, Thompson 2-13, Butts 1-15.

MISSED FIELD GOAL ATTEMPTS—None.

INTERCEPTIONS—Buffalo, M. Patton 1-0, B. Smith 1-0. New England, V. Brown 1-6, Guyton 1-15, Hurst 1-(minus 2).

KICKOFF RETURNS—Buffalo, Copeland 2-57, Beebe 1-17. New England, Croom 5-90, Crittenden 1-36, Timpson 1-18.

PUNT RETURNS—Buffalo, Burris 2-0. New England, Crittenden 2-26.

SACKS—Buffalo, Bennett 1, B. Smith ½, Washington ½. New England, Sabb 1, McGinest ½, Slade ½.

REDSKINS 38, SAINTS 24

Sunday, September 11

Washington	14	0	14	10—38
New Orleans	3	0	6	15—24

First Quarter
N.O.—FG Andersen 29, 6:51.
Was—Ellard 14 pass from Friesz (Lohmiller kick), 10:05.
Was—Mitchell 74 punt return (Lohmiller kick), 11:28.

Third Quarter
Was—Smith 1 pass from Friesz (Lohmiller kick), 3:37.
N.O.—Haynes 17 pass from Everett (pass failed), 7:09.
Was—Ellard 41 pass from Friesz (Lohmiller kick), 11:12.

Fourth Quarter
Was—FG Lohmiller 31, 2:12.
Was—Howard 31 pass from Friesz (Lohmiller kick), 8:25.
N.O.—Small 4 pass from Everett (Small pass from Everett), 10:19.
N.O.—Muster 3 run (Andersen kick), 12:55.

TEAM STATISTICS

	Washington	New Orleans
First downs	22	27
Rushes-yards	46-153	15-28
Passing	190	380
Punt returns-yards	2-87	1-0
Kickoff returns-yards	3-138	6-183
Interception returns-yards	1-16	0-0
Comp.-att.-int.	15-22-0	33-49-1
Sacked-yards lost	1-5	1-8
Punts-average	2-46	4-40
Fumbles-lost	2-1	3-2
Penalties-yards	6-28	5-29
Time of possession	33:34	26:26

Attendance—58,049.

INDIVIDUAL STATISTICS

RUSHING—Washington, Brooks 32-92, Ervins 6-33, Mitchell 7-27, Friesz 1-1. New Orleans, Brown 9-17, Bates 4-9, Muster 1-3, Neal 1-(minus 1).

PASSING—Washington, Friesz 15-22-0-195. New Orleans, Everett 31-46-1-376, Wilson 2-3-0-12.

RECEIVING—Washington, Ervins 4-28, Ellard 3-72, Horton 3-35, Howard 2-37, Brooks 1-16, Jenkins 1-6, C. Smith 1-1. New Orleans, Haynes 6-87, Early 5-83, Small 5-59, Muster 5-50, Brown 5-30, I. Smith 4-39, Walls 3-40.

MISSED FIELD GOAL ATTEMPTS—New Orleans, Andersen 53.

INTERCEPTIONS—Washington, Carter 1-16.

KICKOFF RETURNS—Washington, Mitchell 3-138. New Orleans, Hughes 6-183.

PUNT RETURNS—Washington, Mitchell 2-87. New Orleans, Legette 1-0.

SACKS—Washington, Harvey ½, Wilson ½. New Orleans, Turnbull 1.

CHARGERS 27, BENGALS 10

Sunday, September 11

Cincinnati	3	0	0	7—10
San Diego	3	10	7	7—27

First Quarter
S.D.—FG Carney 38, 4:54.
Cin—FG Pelfrey 19, 9:44.

Second Quarter
S.D.—Means 3 run (Carney kick), :16.
S.D.—FG Carney 20, 9:48.

Third Quarter
S.D.—Seay 49 pass from Humphries (Carney kick), 14:34.

Fourth Quarter
Cin—Green 5 pass from Klingler (Pelfrey kick), 3:01.
S.D.—Seay 4 pass from Humphries (Carney kick), 11:44.

TEAM STATISTICS

	Cincinnati	San Diego
First downs	17	21
Rushes-yards	22-113	35-166
Passing	165	299
Punt returns-yards	0-0	1-11
Kickoff returns-yards	6-110	3-63
Interception returns-yards	0-0	1-6
Comp.-att.-int.	21-34-1	18-29-0
Sacked-yards lost	2-15	0-0
Punts-average	5-50	4-33
Fumbles-lost	4-2	0-0
Penalties-yards	4-18	5-53
Time of possession	26:16	33:44

Attendance—53,217.

INDIVIDUAL STATISTICS

RUSHING—Cincinnati, Scott 3-42, Green 5-34, Fenner 7-33, Broussard 4-11, Klingler 2-11, Ti. McGee 1-(minus 18). San Diego, Means 21-107, Bieniemy 9-48, Humphries 1-8, Martin 1-4, Harmon 2-1, Gilbert 1-(minus 2).

PASSING—Cincinnati, Klingler 21-34-1-180. San Diego, Humphries 18-29-0-299.

RECEIVING—Cincinnati, Green 5-18, Pickens 4-45, Fenner 4-13, Scott 3-31, To. McGee 2-42, Query 1-12, Sadowski 1-11, Broussard 1-8. San Diego, Seay 8-119, Jefferson 4-64, Martin 1-61, Young 1-18, Means 1-16, Harmon 1-8, Bieniemy 1-7, Barnes 1-6.

MISSED FIELD GOAL ATTEMPTS—None.

INTERCEPTIONS—San Diego, Vanhorse 1-6.

KICKOFF RETURNS—Cincinnati, Ball 6-110. San Diego, Martin 2-45, Mitchell 1-18.

PUNT RETURNS—San Diego, Gordon 1-11.

SACKS—San Diego, Mims 1, Johnson ½, O'Neal ½.

JETS 25, BRONCOS 22

Sunday, September 11

Denver	0	13	6	3	0—22
N.Y. Jets	7	7	0	8	3—25

First Quarter
N.Y.—Lewis 67 interception return (Lowery kick), 10:44.

Second Quarter
Den—Miller 40 pass from Elway (Elam kick), 2:50.
Den—FG Elam 42, 7:51.
N.Y.—F. Baxter 1 pass from Esiason (Lowery kick), 11:33.
Den—FG Elam 21, 14:59.

Third Quarter
Den—L. Russell 3 run (pass failed), 5:56.

Fourth Quarter
N.Y.—Moore 35 pass from Esiason (Moore pass from Esiason), 10:45.
Den—FG Elam 29, 13:14.

Overtime
N.Y.—FG Lowery 39, 3:57.

TEAM STATISTICS

	Denver	N.Y. Jets
First downs	22	19
Rushes-yards	24-85	21-79
Passing	316	287
Punt returns-yards	2-28	2-30
Kickoff returns-yards	4-72	7-108
Interception returns-yards	2-9	1-67
Comp.-att.-int.	29-42-1	26-37-2
Sacked-yards lost	1-3	1-10

	Denver	N.Y. Jets
Punts-average	4-41	5-37
Fumbles-lost	0-0	1-0
Penalties-yards	4-35	4-31
Time of possession	31:57	32:00
Attendance—73,436.		

INDIVIDUAL STATISTICS

RUSHING—Denver, L. Russell 12-36, Bernstine 6-35, Clark 3-10, Elway 1-2, Milburn 1-2, Rivers 1-0. New York, J. Johnson 17-67, Esiason 4-12.

PASSING—Denver, Elway 29-42-1-319. New York, Esiason 26-37-2-297.

RECEIVING—Denver, Pritchard 9-100, Miller 6-105, Milburn 5-26, D. Russell 3-45, L. Russell 3-14, Tillman 2-26, Bernstine 1-3. New York, Moore 9-147, Monk 4-52, Mitchell 4-41, J. Johnson 3-27, R. Anderson 3-22, S. Anderson 1-5, A. Johnson 1-2, F. Baxter 1-1.

MISSED FIELD GOAL ATTEMPTS—None.

INTERCEPTIONS—Denver, Jones 2-9. New York, Lewis 1-67.

KICKOFF RETURNS—Denver, By'not'e 3-66, Evans 1-6. New York, Murrell 5-83, R. Anderson 2-25.

PUNT RETURNS—Denver, Milburn 2-28. New York, Hicks 2-30.

SACKS—Denver, Mecklenburg ½, T. Washington ½. New York, Oglesby ½, M. Washington ½.

COWBOYS 20, OILERS 17
Sunday, September 11

Houston	3	7	0	7—17
Dallas	7	6	7	0—20

First Quarter
Dal—E. Smith 1 run (Boniol kick), 7:29.
Hou—FG Del Greco 41, 13:06.

Second Quarter
Dal—FG Boniol 45, 2:38.
Hou—G. Brown 3 run (Del Greco kick), 6:41.
Dal—FG Boniol 29, 15:00.

Third Quarter
Dal—Harper 53 pass from Aikman (Boniol kick), 12:14.

Fourth Quarter
Hou—G. Brown 2 run (Del Greco kick), 10:53.

TEAM STATISTICS

	Houston	Dallas
First downs	20	18
Rushes-yards	28-137	34-115
Passing	208	225
Punt returns-yards	3-18	5-46
Kickoff returns-yards	4-81	3-62
Interception returns-yards	1-38	2-4
Comp.-att.-int.	20-42-2	14-25-1
Sacked-yards lost	4-34	3-3
Punts-average	6-43	7-43
Fumbles-lost	2-0	1-0
Penalties-yards	8-78	5-50
Time of possession	30:08	29:52
Attendance—64,402.		

INDIVIDUAL STATISTICS

RUSHING—Houston, G. Brown 20-93, Richardson 7-37, White 1-7. Dallas, E. Smith 27-90, Johnson 4-17, Aikman 3-8.

PASSING—Houston, Richardson 20-42-2-242. Dallas, Aikman 14-25-1-228.

RECEIVING—Houston, Jeffires 6-103, Coleman 6-58, Givins 4-57, G. Brown 4-24. Dallas, Novacek 4-45, Harper 3-109, Irvin 3-35, E. Smith 3-24, Johnston 1-15.

MISSED FIELD GOAL ATTEMPTS—None.

INTERCEPTIONS—Houston, Dishman 1-38. Dallas, Haley 1-1, Woodson 1-3.

KICKOFF RETURNS—Houston, Mills 2-34, White 2-47. Dallas, Holmes 1-21, Marion 1-21, K. Williams 1-20.

PUNT RETURNS—Houston, Givins 2-5, Hannah 2-13. Dallas, Holmes 3-36, K. Williams 2-10.

SACKS—Houston, Childress 1, Davidson 1, Lathon 1. Dallas, Haley 1½, Hennings 1, Jeffcoat 1, Maryland 1, Tolbert ½.

SEAHAWKS 38, RAIDERS 9
Sunday, September 11

Seattle	7	3	14	14—38
L.A. Raiders	3	0	0	6—9

First Quarter
Sea—C. Warren 4 run (Kasay kick), 4:55.
L.A.—FG Jaeger 26, 12:56.

Second Quarter
Sea—FG Kasay 33, 7:29.

Third Quarter
Sea—Blades 5 pass from Mirer (Kasay kick), 9:13.
Sea—M. Bates 40 pass from Mirer (Kasay kick), 14:03.

Fourth Quarter
Sea—C. Warren 38 pass from Mirer (Kasay kick), 4:16.
L.A.—McDaniel 41 fumble return (pass failed), 8:22.
Sea—Johnson 2 run (Kasay kick) 12:28.

TEAM STATISTICS

	Seattle	L.A. Raiders
First downs	22	20
Rushes-yards	38-97	14-99
Passing	235	198
Punt returns-yards	1-8	2-29
Kickoff returns-yards	2-32	6-103
Interception returns-yards	3-41	0-0
Comp.-att.-int.	19-25-0	21-42-3
Sacked-yards lost	1-7	4-33
Punts-average	4-43	3-43
Fumbles-lost	2-1	2-1
Penalties-yards	9-60	13-85
Time of possession	35:05	24:55
Attendance—47,319.		

INDIVIDUAL STATISTICS

RUSHING—Seattle, C. Warren 21-62, Vaughn 7-20, Mirer 4-14, S. Smith 3-10, Johnson 1-2, McGwire 1-0, M. Bates 1-(minus 11). Los Angeles, H. Williams 5-30, Hostetler 3-29, Evans 1-23, Montgomery 3-11, Rathman 1-2, Ismail 1-2.

PASSING—Seattle, Mirer 19-25-0-242. Los Angeles, Hostetler 17-36-3-181, Evans 4-6-0-50.

RECEIVING—Seattle, Martin 5-52, Blades 4-45, C. Warren 3-51, Edmunds 2-8, Green 2-6, M. Bates 1-40, S. Smith 1-23, Johnson 1-17. Los Angeles, Ismail 6-77, Brown 6-61, Wright 2-24, Glover 2-21, H. Williams 2-20, Jett 1-14, Hobbs 1-7, Montgomery 1-7.

MISSED FIELD GOAL ATTEMPTS—Los Angeles, Jaeger 38.

INTERCEPTIONS—Seattle, Hunter 1-34, Spitulski 1-7, Wooden 1-0.

KICKOFF RETURNS—Seattle, M. Bates 1-16, Vaughn 1-16. Los Angeles, Ismail 4-73, H. Williams 2-30.

PUNT RETURNS—Seattle, Martin 1-8. Los Angeles, Brown 2-29.

SACKS—Seattle, Stephens 2, Kennedy 1, Sinclair 1. Los Angeles, A. Smith 1.

GIANTS 20, CARDINALS 17
Sunday, September 11

N.Y. Giants	6	14	0	0—20
Arizona	3	7	0	7—17

First Quarter
N.Y.—Cross 1 pass from Da. Brown (kick failed), 3:05.
Ari—FG Davis 21, 13:12.

Second Quarter
Ari—McAfee 2 run (Davis kick), :03.
N.Y.—Hampton 3 run (Treadwell kick), 6:07.
N.Y.—Cross 1 pass from Da. Brown (Treadwell kick), 14:45.

Fourth Quarter
Ari—Moore 2 pass from McMahon (Davis kick), 4:08.

TEAM STATISTICS

	N.Y. Giants	Arizona
First downs	19	11
Rushes-yards	41-118	16-39
Passing	88	135
Punt returns-yards	3-18	0-0
Kickoff returns-yards	4-81	2-49
Interception returns-yards	2-4	1-23
Comp.-att.-int.	11-17-1	14-27-2
Sacked-yards lost	4-31	3-23
Punts-average	6-25	5-46
Fumbles-lost	1-1	2-1
Penalties-yards	8-60	10-150
Time of possession	35:15	24:45
Attendance—60,066.		

INDIVIDUAL STATISTICS

RUSHING—New York, Meggett 15-44, Hampton 17-39, Da. Brown 6-31, Elias 2-4, Rasheed 1-0. Arizona, Moore 10-25, Centers 2-18, McMahon 2-1, McAfee 2-(minus 5).

PASSING—New York, Da. Brown 11-17-1-119. Arizona, Beuerlein 10-22-1-108, McMahon 4-5-1-50.

RECEIVING—New York, Rasheed 3-47, Calloway 2-26, Meggett 2-17, Cross 2-2, Sherrard 1-21, Pierce 1-6. Arizona, R. Hill 5-62, Moore 3-16, Centers 2-23, Ware 1-33, Reeves 1-15, P. Robinson 1-5, McAfee 1-4.

MISSED FIELD GOAL ATTEMPTS—None.

INTERCEPTIONS—New York, Sparks 2-4. Arizona, Lynch 1-23.

KICKOFF RETURNS—New York, Lewis 4-81. Arizona, McAfee 2-49.

PUNT RETURNS—New York, Meggett 3-18.

SACKS—New York, Hamilton 2, Brooks 1. Arizona, Bankston 2½, Joyner 1½.

EAGLES 30, BEARS 22

Monday, September 12

Chicago	0	0	0	22—22
Philadelphia	7	17	6	0—30

First Quarter

Phi—C. Williams 9 pass from Cunningham (Murray kick), 11:41.

Second Quarter

Phi—C. Williams 14 pass from Cunningham (Murray kick), 2:54.
Phi—M. Johnson 7 pass from Cunningham (Murray kick), 6:59.
Phi—FG Murray 41, 14:58.

Third Quarter

Phi—FG Murray 29, 5:17.
Phi—FG Murray 33, 12:19.

Fourth Quarter

Chi—Conway 22 pass from Kramer (Butler kick), 2:45.
Chi—Conway 85 pass from Kramer (Conway pass from Kramer), 9:07.
Chi—Cook 16 pass from Kramer (Butler kick), 11:25.

TEAM STATISTICS

	Chicago	Philadelphia
First downs	13	24
Rushes-yards	11-37	38-106
Passing	275	310
Punt returns-yards	1-0	3-51
Kickoff returns-yards	6-117	4-50
Interception returns-yards	0-0	1-31
Comp.-att.-int.	18-31-1	24-36-0
Sacked-yards lost	3-14	1-1
Punts-average	6-37	4-31
Fumbles-lost	2-0	1-0
Penalties-yards	5-40	8-69
Time of possession	21:03	38:57
Attendance—64,890.		

INDIVIDUAL STATISTICS

RUSHING—Chicago, Tillman 7-22, Hoge 2-15, Kramer 1-0, Worley 1-0. Philadelphia, Walker 19-72, Joseph 11-24, Hebron 2-7, Cunningham 6-3.

PASSING—Chicago, Kramer 18-31-1-289. Philadelphia, Cunningham 24-36-0-311.

RECEIVING—Chicago, Conway 7-148, Cook 3-58, Graham 3-29, Tillman 2-16, Christian 1-21, Hoge 1-9, Worley 1-8. Philadelphia, Barnett 8-102, C. Williams 6-85, Joseph 4-43, Walker 3-36, Hebron 1-26, Bailey 1-12, M. Johnson 1-7.

MISSED FIELD GOAL ATTEMPTS—None.

INTERCEPTIONS—Philadelphia, G. Jackson 1-31.

KICKOFF RETURNS—Chicago, Conway 5-103, Flanigan 1-14. Philadelphia, Sydner 3-50, Zordich 1-0.

PUNT RETURNS—Chicago, Waddle 1-0. Philadelphia, Sydner 3-51.

SACKS—Chicago, Team 1. Philadelphia, Fuller 2, Grossman 1.

WEEK 3

RESULTS

Buffalo 15, Houston 7
Cleveland 32, Arizona 0
Kansas City 30, Atlanta 10
L.A. Raiders 48, Denver 16
Miami 28, N.Y. Jets 14
Minnesota 42, Chicago 14
N.Y. Giants 31, Washington 23
New England 31, Cincinnati 28
New Orleans 9, Tampa Bay 7
Philadelphia 13, Green Bay 7
Pittsburgh 31, Indianapolis 21
San Diego 24, Seattle 10
San Francisco 34, L.A. Rams 19
Detroit 20, Dallas 17 (OT)

STANDINGS

AFC EAST	W	L	T	Pct.	AFC CENTRAL	W	L	T	Pct.	AFC WEST	W	L	T	Pct.
Miami	3	0	0	1.000	Cleveland	2	1	0	.667	Kansas City	3	0	0	1.000
Buffalo	2	1	0	.667	Pittsburgh	2	1	0	.667	San Diego	3	0	0	1.000
N.Y. Jets	2	1	0	.667	Cincinnati	0	3	0	.000	Seattle	2	1	0	.667
Indianapolis	1	2	0	.333	Houston	0	3	0	.000	L.A. Raiders	1	2	0	.333
New England	1	2	0	.333						Denver	0	3	0	.000

NFC EAST	W	L	T	Pct.	NFC CENTRAL	W	L	T	Pct.	NFC WEST	W	L	T	Pct.
N.Y. Giants	3	0	0	1.000	Detroit	2	1	0	.667	San Francisco	2	1	0	.667
Dallas	2	1	0	.667	Minnesota	2	1	0	.667	Atlanta	1	2	0	.333
Philadelphia	2	1	0	.667	Chicago	1	2	0	.333	L.A. Rams	1	2	0	.333
Washington	1	2	0	.333	Green Bay	1	2	0	.333	New Orleans	1	2	0	.333
Arizona	0	3	0	.000	Tampa Bay	1	2	0	.333					

HIGHLIGHTS

Hero of the week: San Francisco quarterback Steve Young, who completed 31 of 39 passes for 355 yards and two touchdowns in the 49ers' 34-19 victory over the Rams. Young, who also ran for two touchdowns, completed his first 10 passes.

Goat of the week: Houston left tackle Bruce Matthews, who yielded four sacks to Bruce Smith in the Oilers' 15-7 loss to Buffalo. Matthews, a perennial Pro Bowl center/guard, was making his first start at left tackle in eight years.

Sub of the week: Giants running back Dave Meggett, who ran for two touchdowns and threw for another in New York's 31-23 victory over Washington. Meggett, subbing for the injured Rodney Hampton, took part in 31 of New York's 55 offensive plays.

Comeback of the week: Detroit beat Dallas, 20-17, on Jason Hanson's 44-yard field goal with 27 seconds left in overtime. The Cowboys, who lost for the first time in 10 games, trailed most of the contest before tying it on Emmitt Smith's 6-yard touchdown run with 4:09 left in regulation.

Blowout of the week: Minnesota rolled up 464 yards in total offense and another 112 on kick returns in its 42-14 rout of Chicago. The Vikings never punted and scored on their first four possessions of the second half. Minnesota's 42 points were the most it has scored in 66 games against the Bears.

Nail-biter of the week: New England beat Cincinnati, 31-28, behind Drew Bledsoe's club-record 365 yards passing.

Hit of the week: By Philadelphia defensive back Otis Smith, who stopped Green Bay's Edgar Bennett for no gain on a fourth-and-5 swing pass from the 6-yard line with 1:50 to play to seal the Eagles' 13-7 victory.

Oddity of the week: Meggett's touchdown pass was the third of his six-year NFL career. All have come against the Redskins.

Top rusher: Barry Sanders carried a career-high 40 times for 194 yards in Detroit's win over Dallas.

Top passer: John Friesz completed 32 of 50 passes for 381 yards and two touchdowns in the Redskins' loss to the Giants.

Top receiver: Henry Ellard caught 10 of Friesz's passes for 197 yards and one touchdown.

Notes: Denver's 48-16 loss to the Raiders was the Broncos' worst at home since 1968, which also was the last time they started a season 0-3. John Elway had an interception returned for a touchdown for the third consecutive week.... Stan Humphries and Tony Martin hooked up on a 99-yard touchdown pass against Seattle to tie an NFL record. There have been seven 99-yard passing plays in NFL history, the last coming in 1985 (Philadelphia's Ron Jaworski to Mike Quick).... Cleveland's 32-0 victory over Arizona handed Buddy Ryan his first shutout defeat as an NFL coach. The Browns preserved the shutout by stopping the Cardinals on the 2-yard line with one second left.... Steve Christie kicked five field goals for Buffalo's only points in its victory over Houston.... Week 3 marked the first of many Throwback Weekends during the 1994 season, when NFL teams wore replica uniforms from past eras. For example, the Bears wore uniforms from the 1925 season, the Steelers 1933, the Lions 1935, the Eagles 1948, the Colts 1958 and the Cowboys 1960.... The Seahawks were forced to move their game against San Diego to the University of Washington's Husky Stadium because the Kingdome was closed for ceiling and roof repairs. The game attracted a crowd of 65,536, the largest in team history.... Ellard became the 10th receiver in NFL history to eclipse the 10,000-yard mark. Buffalo's Andre Reed became the 13th player with 600 receptions.... Kansas City was 3-0 for the first time since 1966.... Atlanta's Jeff George had a string of 279 passes without an interception (third-longest in NFL history) snapped by Chiefs cornerback Dale Carter.... Bledsoe set a Patriots record with his fourth consecutive 300-yard passing game.... Dallas' Leon Lett blocked two field-goal attempts (57 and 51 yards) against the Lions.

Quote of the week: Martin, on his 99-yard touchdown reception: "I didn't realize I was tying a record. I was just trying to get into the end zone. The more I ran, the further away it seemed to be."

GAME SUMMARIES

STEELERS 31, COLTS 21
Sunday, September 18

Indianapolis	7	7	7	0—21
Pittsburgh	0	17	0	14—31

First Quarter
Ind—Humphrey 95 kickoff return (Biasucci kick), :16.
Second Quarter
Ind—Coryatt 78 fumble return (Biasucci kick), 1:25.
Pit—Green 27 pass from O'Donnell (Anderson kick), 5:02.
Pit—Foster 29 run (Anderson kick), 9:49.
Pit—FG Anderson 46, 15:00.
Third Quarter
Ind—Dawkins 19 pass from Harbaugh (Biasucci kick), 8:57.
Fourth Quarter
Pit—J.L Williams 8 pass from O'Donnell (Anderson kick), 3:52.
Pit—Morris 1 run (Anderson kick), 12:32.

TEAM STATISTICS

	Indianapolis	Pittsburgh
First downs	10	32
Rushes-yards	19-73	45-261
Passing	106	239
Punt returns-yards	2-7	5-40
Kickoff returns-yards	5-194	4-109
Interception returns-yards	1-8	1-0
Comp.-att.-int.	9-20-1	22-35-1
Sacked-yards lost	3-14	2-15
Punts-average	6-43	3-36
Fumbles-lost	1-0	1-1
Penalties-yards	7-55	4-40
Time of possession	20:29	39:31
Attendance—54,040.		

INDIVIDUAL STATISTICS
RUSHING—Indianapolis, Faulk 15-61, Harbaugh 2-10, Potts 2-2. Pittsburgh, Foster 31-179, Morris 10-56, J.L. Williams 2-26, O'Donnell 1-4, Johnson 1-(minus 4).
PASSING—Indianapolis, Harbaugh 9-20-1-120. Pittsburgh, O'Donnell 22-35-1-254.
RECEIVING—Indianapolis, Dawkins 5-78, Humphrey 1-12, Faulk 1-11, Cash 1-10, Potts 1-9. Pittsburgh, J.L. Williams 6-45, Green 4-60, Foster 3-13, Morris 2-55, Hastings 2-28, Thigpen 2-23, Johnson 2-20, Stone 1-10.
MISSED FIELD GOAL ATTEMPTS—None.
INTERCEPTIONS—Indianapolis, Ambrose 1-8. Pittsburgh, Henry 1-0.
KICKOFF RETURNS—Indianapolis, Humphrey 3-139, Brewer 2-55. Pittsburgh, Woodson 3-88, Morris 1-21.
PUNT RETURNS—Indianapolis, Brewer 2-7. Pittsburgh, Woodson 5-40.
SACKS—Indianapolis, Bennett 2. Pittsburgh, Lloyd 1, Greene 1, Kirkland 1.

BILLS 15, OILERS 7
Sunday, September 18

Buffalo	0	9	3	3—15
Houston	0	0	0	7— 7

Second Quarter
Buf—FG Christie 37, :03.
Buf—FG Christie 42, 2:36.
Buf—FG Christie 48, 13:23.
Third Quarter
Buf—FG Christie 29, 6:34.
Fourth Quarter
Buf—FG Christie 48, 5:11.
Hou—Coleman 22 pass from Richardson (Del Greco kick), 11:09.

TEAM STATISTICS

	Buffalo	Houston
First downs	17	13
Rushes-yards	34-115	27-97
Passing	183	159
Punt returns-yards	3-45	2-38
Kickoff returns-yards	2-65	6-136
Interception returns-yards	1-0	1-0
Comp.-att.-int.	18-28-1	11-24-1
Sacked-yards lost	1-7	5-34
Punts-average	4-39	5-46
Fumbles-lost	0-0	4-2
Penalties-yards	5-40	8-51
Time of possession	32:44	27:16
Attendance—55,424.		

INDIVIDUAL STATISTICS
RUSHING—Buffalo, Thomas 28-112, Gardner 3-7, Kelly 3-(minus 4). Houston, Brown 22-75, Richardson 5-22.
PASSING—Buffalo, Kelly 18-28-1-190. Houston, Richardson 11-24-1-193.
RECEIVING—Buffalo, Reed 6-89, Beebe 4-36, Metzelaars 3-16, Brooks 2-33, Thomas 2-19, Davis 1-(minus 3). Houston, Slaughter 4-110, Jeffires 3-22, Brown 2-26, Coleman 1-22, Givins 1-13.
MISSED FIELD GOAL ATTEMPTS—None.
INTERCEPTIONS—Buffalo, Darby 1-0. Houston, Jackson 1-0.
KICKOFF RETURNS—Buffalo, Beebe 2-65. Houston, White 5-102, Mills 1-34.
PUNT RETURNS—Buffalo, Burris 3-45. Houston, Givins 1-31, Hannah 1-7.
SACKS—Buffalo, B. Smith 4, Barnett 1. Houston, Montgomery 1.

BROWNS 32, CARDINALS 0
Sunday, September 18

Arizona	0	0	0	0— 0
Cleveland	0	3	15	14—32

Second Quarter
Cle—FG Stover 32, 1:31.
Third Quarter
Cle—Testaverde 1 run (Stover kick), 4:33.
Cle—Vardell 16 pass from Testaverde (Tupa run), 11:52.
Fourth Quarter
Cle—Alexander 81 pass from Testaverde (Stover kick), 6:19.
Cle—Turner 93 interception return (Stover kick), 13:00.

TEAM STATISTICS

	Arizona	Cleveland
First downs	21	17
Rushes-yards	17-63	27-79
Passing	255	243
Punt returns-yards	1-1	2-23
Kickoff returns-yards	6-93	1-20
Interception returns-yards	1-0	3-103
Comp.-att.-int.	26-58-3	17-27-1
Sacked-yards lost	2-14	1-5
Punts-average	7-40	5-37
Fumbles-lost	1-0	3-1
Penalties-yards	7-66	8-50
Time of possession	28:20	31:40
Attendance—62,818.		

INDIVIDUAL STATISTICS
RUSHING—Arizona, McMahon 4-31, Schroeder 1-16, Centers 6-11, Moore 6-5. Cleveland, Byner 8-24, Hoard 8-22, Vardell 6-22, Testaverde 3-12, Metcalf 2-(minus 1).
PASSING—Arizona, McMahon 19-38-2-169, Schroeder 7-20-1-100. Cleveland, Testaverde 17-27-1-248.
RECEIVING—Arizona, Centers 8-62, Proehl 4-40, Levy 4-35, Ware 3-18, B. Reeves 2-57, Hill 2-30, Clark 2-18, Moore 1-9. Cleveland, Alexander 6-136, Vardell 3-28, W. Reeves 3-27, Metcalf 2-9, Carrier 1-25, Byner 1-12, Smith 1-11.
MISSED FIELD GOAL ATTEMPTS—Arizona, Davis 49, 58.
INTERCEPTIONS—Arizona, A. Williams 1-0. Cleveland, Turner 2-101, Langham 1-2.
KICKOFF RETURNS—Arizona, Levy 6-93. Cleveland, Hoard 1-20.
PUNT RETURNS—Arizona, B. Reeves 1-1. Cleveland, Metcalf 3-23.
SACKS—Arizona, Swann 1. Cleveland, P. Johnson 1, Stams 1.

EAGLES 13, PACKERS 7
Sunday, September 18

Green Bay	7	0	0	0— 7
Philadelphia	0	3	10	0—13

First Quarter
G.B.—Cobb 37 pass from Favre (Jacke kick), 14:55.
Second Quarter
Phi—FG Murray 26, 14:59.

Third Quarter
Phi—Cunningham 1 run (Murray kick), 3:54.
Phi—FG Murray 26, 8:32.

TEAM STATISTICS

	Green Bay	Philadelphia
First downs	13	20
Rushes-yards	14-37	28-91
Passing	238	182
Punt returns-yards	5-50	1-11
Kickoff returns-yards	2-38	2-40
Interception returns-yards	1-0	2-6
Comp.-att.-int.	24-45-2	20-43-1
Sacked-yards lost	6-42	3-22
Punts-average	6-38	7-40
Fumbles-lost	2-1	1-0
Penalties-yards	8-67	8-61
Time of possession	26:17	33:43

Attendance—63,922.

INDIVIDUAL STATISTICS

RUSHING—Green Bay, Bennett 7-15, Cobb 4-8, Favre 1-8, Jordan 1-5, L. Johnson 1-1. Philadelphia, Hebron 5-28, Cunningham 7-26, Walker 8-16, Joseph 7-16, C. Williams 1-5.

PASSING—Green Bay, Favre 24-45-2-280. Philadelphia, Cunningham 20-43-1-204.

RECEIVING—Green Bay, Bennett 7-44, Sharpe 6-108, Brooks 4-22, Cobb 3-38, Morgan 2-16, L. Johnson 1-33, Lewis 1-19. Philadelphia, Joseph 6-37, Barnett 5-68, Walker 3-14, C. Williams 2-43, M. Johnson 2-18, Bailey 1-12, Bavaro 1-12.

MISSED FIELD GOAL ATTEMPTS—None.

INTERCEPTIONS—Green Bay, Buckley 1-0. Philadelphia, B. Evans 1-6, Zordich 1-0.

KICKOFF RETURNS—Green Bay, C. Harris 2-38. Philadelphia, Hebron 1-29, Sydner 1-11.

PUNT RETURNS—Green Bay, Brooks 5-50. Philadelphia, Sydner 1-11.

SACKS—Green Bay, G. Brown 1, McMichael ½, Davey ½. Philadelphia, Romanowski 1½, Thomas 1, Harmon 1, Fuller 1, Grossman 1, B. Evans ½.

VIKINGS 42, BEARS 14
Sunday, September 18

Minnesota	0	10	18	14—42
Chicago	0	0	0	14—14

Second Quarter
Min—Allen 12 run (Reveiz kick), 2:16.
Min—FG Reveiz 43, 11:27.

Third Quarter
Min—FG Reveiz 24, 3:00.
Min—Reed 18 pass from Moon (Reveiz kick), 3:17.
Min—Washington 81 interception return (Carter pass from Moon), 8:35.

Fourth Quarter
Min—Allen 1 run (Reveiz kick), 2:39.
Chi—Worley 1 run (pass failed), 5:42.
Min—Smith 14 run (Reveiz kick), 8:30.
Chi—Waddle 8 pass from Kramer (Graham pass from Kramer), 11:14.

TEAM STATISTICS

	Minnesota	Chicago
First downs	28	19
Rushes-yards	36-212	14-60
Passing	252	244
Punt returns-yards	0-0	0-0
Kickoff returns-yards	3-31	8-146
Interception returns-yards	1-81	1-18
Comp.-att.-int.	25-32-1	27-35-1
Sacked-yards lost	0-0	3-17
Punts-average	0-0	4-32
Fumbles-lost	3-1	1-1
Penalties-yards	4-22	4-20
Time of possession	34:08	25:52

Attendance—61,073.

INDIVIDUAL STATISTICS

RUSHING—Minnesota, Allen 22-159, Smith 6-35, Graham 6-14, Moon 2-4. Chicago, Tillman 10-44, Harris 2-16, Worley 1-1, Kramer 1-(minus 1).

PASSING—Minnesota, Moon 22-29-1-236, Johnson 3-3-0-16. Chicago, Kramer 27-35-1-261.

RECEIVING—Minnesota, Carter 9-86, Reed 7-90, Palmer 2-18, Smith 2-10, Cooper 1-21, Jordan 1-18, Novoselsky 1-4, Allen 1-3,

Evans 1-2. Chicago, Waddle 8-82, Graham 5-51, Gedney 4-43, Hoge 3-14, Harris 3-13, Cook 2-39, Conway 2-19.

MISSED FIELD GOAL ATTEMPTS—Chicago, Butler 54.

INTERCEPTIONS—Minnesota, Washington 1-81. Chicago, Douglass 1-18.

KICKOFF RETURNS—Minnesota, Ismail 1-21, Walsh 1-6, Evans 1-4. Chicago, Conway 4-92, Worley 3-54, Thierry 1-0.

PUNT RETURNS—None.

SACKS—Minnesota, Del Rio 1, Thomas 1, Randle ½, Harris ½.

SAINTS 9, BUCCANEERS 7
Sunday, September 18

New Orleans	6	3	0	0—9
Tampa Bay	0	7	0	0—7

First Quarter
N.O.—FG Andersen 43, 8:07.
N.O.—FG Andersen 31, 10:44.

Second Quarter
T.B.—J. Harris 10 pass from Erickson (Husted kick), 10:59.
N.O.—FG Andersen 43, 14:45.

TEAM STATISTICS

	New Orleans	Tampa Bay
First downs	12	16
Rushes-yards	23-57	26-85
Passing	176	147
Punt returns-yards	0-0	3-28
Kickoff returns-yards	2-38	2-33
Interception returns-yards	0-0	0-0
Comp.-att.-int.	19-31-0	17-32-0
Sacked-yards lost	0-0	5-29
Punts-average	6-40	6-36
Fumbles-lost	1-0	3-1
Penalties-yards	7-46	6-45
Time of possession	27:43	32:17

Attendance—45,522.

INDIVIDUAL STATISTICS

RUSHING—New Orleans, Brown 16-31, Ned 5-28, W. Wilson 1-0, Everett 1-(minus 2). Tampa Bay, Rhett 15-34, Workman 8-32, Erickson 2-16, R. Harris 1-3.

PASSING—New Orleans, Everett 10-19-0-108, W. Wilson 9-12-0-68. Tampa Bay, Erickson 17-32-0-176.

RECEIVING—New Orleans, Ned 5-38, Early 4-50, Brown 4-34, Walls 3-35, Haynes 2-13, Muster 1-6. Tampa Bay, W. Green 3-53, J. Harris 3-34, Armstrong 2-37, C. Wilson 2-19, Hawkins 2-18, Workman 2-5, Copeland 1-9, Rhett 1-5, Royster 1-(minus 4).

MISSED FIELD GOAL ATTEMPTS—Tampa Bay, Husted 54.

INTERCEPTIONS—None.

KICKOFF RETURNS—New Orleans, Hughes 2-38. Tampa Bay, Green 2-33.

PUNT RETURNS—Tampa Bay, Turner 3-28.

SACKS—New Orleans, Conner 3, Martin 1, Warren 1.

PATRIOTS 31, BENGALS 28
Sunday, September 18

New England	7	6	12	6—31
Cincinnati	6	7	7	8—28

First Quarter
Cin—Broussard 37 run (kick failed), 4:44.
N.E.—Butts 3 run (Bahr kick), 10:29.

Second Quarter
N.E.—FG Bahr 43, 2:09.
N.E.—FG Bahr 24, 11:10.
Cin—Pickens 7 pass from Klingler (Pelfrey kick), 13:41.

Third Quarter
N.E.—FG Bahr 28, 2:12.
N.E.—FG Bahr 35, 5:58.
Cin—Broussard 8 run (Pelfrey kick), 9:27.
N.E.—Timpson 34 pass from Bledsoe (pass failed), 12:50.

Fourth Quarter
N.E.—Butts 1 run (pass failed), 4:05.
Cin—Pickens 4 pass from Klingler (Broussard run), 13:47.

TEAM STATISTICS

	New England	Cincinnati
First downs	28	21
Rushes-yards	36-82	20-99
Passing	365	219
Punt returns-yards	2-12	0-0

	New England	Cincinnati
Kickoff returns-yards	4-45	8-177
Interception returns-yards	0-0	2-20
Comp.-att.-int.	30-50-2	21-29-0
Sacked-yards lost	0-0	7-47
Punts-average	1-50	3-46
Fumbles-lost	1-0	2-2
Penalties-yards	5-32	4-30
Time of possession	36:09	23:51

Attendance—46,640.

INDIVIDUAL STATISTICS

RUSHING—New England, Butts 25-72, Thompson 3-8, Turner 3-6, Bledsoe 5-(minus 4). Cincinnati, Broussard 6-53, Fenner 6-21, Green 6-15, Klingler 2-10.

PASSING—New England, Bledsoe 30-50-2-365. Cincinnati, Klingler 21-29-0-266.

RECEIVING—New England, Timpson 10-125, Coates 8-108, Turner 5-54, Brisby 3-47, Butts 2-9, Crittenden 1-11, Thompson 1-11. Cincinnati, To. McGee 5-56, Pickens 4-78, Fenner 4-35, Query 2-17, Broussard 2-15, Scott 1-56, Tl. McGee 1-10, Green 1-5, Klingler 1-(minus 6).

MISSED FIELD GOAL ATTEMPTS—None.

INTERCEPTIONS—Cincinnati, D. Williams 1-12, Oliver 1-8.

KICKOFF RETURNS—New England, Crittenden 2-38, Thomas 1-8, Guyton 1-(minus 1). Cincinnati, Scott 7-176, Shaw 1-1.

PUNT RETURNS—New England, Crittenden 2-12.

SACKS—New England, Barnett 2, Goad 1, Pitts 1, Sabb 1, Jones 1, McGinest 1.

DOLPHINS 28, JETS 14

Sunday, September 18

N.Y. Jets	0	0	7	7	—14
Miami	14	0	7	7	—28

First Quarter

Mia—Kirby 1 run (Stoyanovich kick), 1:17.
Mia—Byars 11 pass from Marino (Stoyanovich kick), 14:18.

Third Quarter

N.Y.—R. Anderson 27 pass from Esiason (Lowery kick), 4:08.
Mia—Fryar 2 lateral from Jackson (Stoyanovich kick), 6:08.

Fourth Quarter

Mia—Parmalee 5 run (Stoyanovich kick), 7:05.
N.Y.—J. Johnson 2 pass from Esiason (Lowery kick), 9:52.

TEAM STATISTICS

	N.Y. Jets	Miami
First downs	18	26
Rushes-yards	17-59	36-155
Passing	284	289
Punt returns-yards	0-0	2-(-3)
Kickoff returns-yards	4-82	2-61
Interception returns-yards	1-0	4-32
Comp.-att.-int.	22-37-4	23-31-1
Sacked-yards lost	1-9	0-0
Punts-average	4-51	2-31
Fumbles-lost	1-0	1-1
Penalties-yards	4-26	2-25
Time of possession	25:44	34:16

Attendance—68,192.

INDIVIDUAL STATISTICS

RUSHING—New York, J. Johnson 14-50, Murrrell 3-9. Miami, Kirby 15-100, Parmalee 10-37, Byars 5-18, Higgs 3-5, Marino 1-(minus 2), Saxon 2-(minus 3).

PASSING—New York, Esiason 22-37-4-293. Miami, Marino 23-31-1-289.

RECEIVING—New York, J. Johnson 5-46, Mitchell 4-71, Monk 4-43, Moore 3-43, S. Anderson 2-30, Murrell 2-37, R. Anderson 1-27, Thornton 1-8. Miami, Byars 7-73, Jackson 6-100, Fryar 3-42, Kirby 3-35, Ingram 3-28, Miller 1-11.

MISSED FIELD GOAL ATTEMPTS—Miami, Stoyanovich 63, 37.

INTERCEPTIONS—New York, Lewis 1-0. Miami, Brown 1-32, Beavers 1-0, Malone 1-0, Stewart 1-0.

KICKOFF RETURNS—New York, Murrell 2-52, Hicks 2-30. Miami, McDuffie 2-61, Ingram 1-0.

PUNT RETURNS—Miami, McDuffie 2-(minus 3).

SACKS—Miami, Cross 1.

CHARGERS 24, SEAHAWKS 10

Sunday, September 18

San Diego	0	10	14	0	—24
Seattle	0	3	0	7	—10

Second Quarter

Sea—FG Kasay 39, 2:00.
S.D.—FG Carney 36, 7:49.
S.D.—Means 1 run (Carney kick), 14:41.

Third Quarter

S.D.—Richard 73 interception return (Carney kick), 8:32.
S.D.—Martin 99 pass from Humphries (Carney kick), 13:05.

Fourth Quarter

Sea—Warren 11 run (Kasay kick), 5:11.

TEAM STATISTICS

	San Diego	Seattle
First downs	18	23
Rushes-yards	33-95	24-59
Passing	262	163
Punt returns-yards	1-3	0-0
Kickoff returns-yards	3-78	5-81
Interception returns-yards	1-73	1-51
Comp.-att.-int.	19-30-1	20-36-1
Sacked-yards lost	2-11	6-35
Punts-average	3-39	4-35
Fumbles-lost	1-1	1-1
Penalties-yards	14-105	3-35
Time of possession	32:52	27:08

Attendance—65,536.

INDIVIDUAL STATISTICS

RUSHING—San Diego, Means 24-86, Bieniemy 8-9, Humphries 1-0. Seattle, C. Warren 14-55, Mirer 4-18, S. Smith 3-2, Vaughn 3-(minus 16).

PASSING—San Diego, Humphries 19-29-0-262, T. Martin 0-1-1-0. Seattle, Mirer 20-36-1-163.

RECEIVING—San Diego, T. Martin 6-152, Harmon 5-44, Means 4-26, Jefferson 3-31, Pupunu 1-9. Seattle, Blades 8-66, K. Martin 4-40, C. Warren 3-15, Green 2-9, T. Johnson 1-15, Bates 1-12, Edmunds 1-6.

MISSED FIELD GOAL ATTEMPTS—San Diego, Carney 48.

INTERCEPTIONS—San Diego, Richard 1-73. Seattle, Hunter 1-51.

KICKOFF RETURNS—San Diego, Martin 2-56, Harmon 1-22. Seattle, Bates 3-49, Vaughn 1-18, Edmunds 1-14.

PUNT RETURNS—San Diego, Gordon 1-3.

SACKS—San Diego, O'Neal 3, Seau 1, Lee 1, Johnson 1. Seattle, B. Williams 1, Nash 1.

GIANTS 31, REDSKINS 23

Sunday, September 18

Washington	3	17	0	3	—23
N.Y. Giants	10	7	7	7	—31

First Quarter

N.Y.—Meggett 2 run (Treadwell kick), 4:38.
Was—FG Lohmiller 25, 9:09.
N.Y.—FG Treadwell 34, 12:41.

Second Quarter

Was—Ellard 3 pass from Friesz (Lohmiller kick), 5:18.
Was—FG Lohmiller 41, 7:38.
N.Y.—Sherrard 30 pass from Da. Brown (Treadwell kick), 10:46.
Was—Horton 4 pass from Friesz (Lohmiller kick), 13:52.

Third Quarter

N.Y.—Pierce 16 pass from Meggett (Treadwell kick), 3:20.

Fourth Quarter

Was—FG Lohmiller 35, 1:52.
N.Y.—Meggett 1 run (Treadwell kick), 7:51.

TEAM STATISTICS

	Washington	N.Y. Giants
First downs	24	20
Rushes-yards	21-80	33-109
Passing	376	228
Punt returns-yards	2-14	1-4
Kickoff returns-yards	3-73	5-100
Interception returns-yards	0-0	2-42
Comp.-att.-int.	32-50-2	15-20-0
Sacked-yards lost	1-5	2-9
Punts-average	1-42	3-44
Fumbles-lost	0-0	2-0
Penalties-yards	10-86	4-35
Time of possession	32:09	27:51

Attendance—77,298.

INDIVIDUAL STATISTICS

RUSHING—Washington, Brooks 13-57, Ervins 6-19, Mitchell 2-4. New York, Meggett 26-82, Da. Brown 4-17, Downs 2-7, Rasheed 1-3.

PASSING—Washington, Friesz 32-50-381-2. New York, Da. Brown 14-19-221-0, Meggett 1-1-16-0.

RECEIVING—Washington, Ellard 10-197, Ervins 8-56, Howard 4-56, Mitchell 3-22, Horton 3-16, Winans 2-22, Brooks 2-12. New York, Meggett 4-52, Sherrard 3-71, Calloway 3-51, Pierce 2-45, Rasheed 1-9, Cross 1-5, Marshall 1-4.

MISSED FIELD GOAL ATTEMPTS—Washington, Lohmiller 23.

INTERCEPTIONS—New York, Booty 1-36, Miller 1-6.

KICKOFF RETURNS—Washington, Mitchell 3-73. New York, Marshall 3-65, Lewis 2-35.

PUNT RETURNS—Washington, Mitchell 2-14. New York, Lewis 1-4.

SACKS—Washington, Harvey 1½, Woods ½. New York, Widmer 1.

RAIDERS 48, BRONCOS 16

Sunday, September 18

L.A. Raiders	21	7	10	10—48
Denver	3	0	13	0—16

First Quarter

L.A.—H. Williams 2 run (Jaeger kick), 4:19.
Den—FG Elam 43, 9:25.
L.A.—Montgomery 65 pass from Hostetler (Jaeger kick), 10:22.
L.A.—Brown 43 pass from Hostetler (Jaeger kick), 14:45.

Second Quarter

L.A.—Glover 7 pass from Hostetler (Jaeger kick), 4:44.

Third Quarter

Den—L. Russell 1 run (run failed), 2:12.
L.A.—H. Williams 5 pass from Hostetler (Jaeger kick), 5:41.
Den—L. Russell 4 run (Elam kick), 7:21.
L.A.—FG Jaeger 42, 12:03.

Fourth Quarter

L.A.—FG Jaeger 33, 1:24.
L.A.—McDaniel 15 interception return (Jaeger kick), 5:52.

TEAM STATISTICS

	L.A. Raiders	Denver
First downs	20	21
Rushes-yards	30-102	17-69
Passing	322	223
Punt returns-yards	2-23	1-(-1)
Kickoff returns-yards	3-70	5-119
Interception returns-yards	1-15	0-0
Comp.-att.-int.	21-34-0	25-50-1
Sacked-yards lost	2-16	4-29
Punts-average	5-51	4-40
Fumbles-lost	1-1	2-2
Penalties-yards	10-118	10-76
Time of possession	33:47	26:13
Attendance—75,764.		

INDIVIDUAL STATISTICS

RUSHING—Los Angeles, Montgomery 13-53, H. Williams 13-28, Rathman 3-19, K. Smith 1-2. Denver, L. Russell 8-22, Elway 2-22, Clark 3-14, Milburn 4-11.

PASSING—Los Angeles, Hostetler 21-33-0-338, Evans 0-1-0-0. Denver, Elway 14-33-1-151, Millen 11-17-0-101.

RECEIVING—Los Angeles, Brown 7-136, Glover 4-47, Montgomery 3-93, Rathman 3-29, Hobbs 1-14, K. Smith 1-8, Ismail 1-6, H. Williams 1-5. Denver, Milburn 9-85, Pritchard 5-52, L. Russell 3-5, D. Russell 2-40, Miller 2-26, Tillman 2-22, Evans 1-13, Clark 1-9.

MISSED FIELD GOAL ATTEMPTS—None.

INTERCEPTIONS—Los Angeles, McDaniel 1-15.

KICKOFF RETURNS—Los Angeles, Williams 2-46, Ismail 1-24. Denver, By'not'e 3-77, D. Russell 1-22, Clark 1-20.

PUNT RETURNS—Los Angeles, Brown 2-23. Denver, Milburn 1-(minus 1).

SACKS—Los Angeles, Anderson 2, Harrison 1, McGlockton 1. Denver, Alexander 1, Mecklenburg 1.

49ERS 34, RAMS 19

Sunday, September 18

San Francisco	10	7	3	14—34
L.A. Rams	7	3	0	9—19

First Quarter

S.F.—Taylor 3 pass from Young (Brien kick), 4:34.
L.A.—Drayton 4 pass from Miller (Zendejas kick), 8:55.
S.F.—FG Brien 33, 11:36.

Second Quarter

L.A.—FG Zendejas 25, 2:59.
S.F.—Young 1 run (Brien kick), 15:00.

Third Quarter

S.F.—FG Brien 47, 10:48.

Fourth Quarter

S.F.—Rice 1 pass from Young (Brien kick), 2:22.
L.A.—FG Zendejas 35, 6:00.
S.F.—Young 1 run (Brien kick), 11:32.
L.A.—Bettis 2 run (pass failed), 13:04.

TEAM STATISTICS

	San Francisco	L.A. Rams
First downs	28	22
Rushes-yards	30-105	24-115
Passing	349	163
Punt returns-yards	3-18	5-11
Kickoff returns-yards	4-106	5-104
Interception returns-yards	0-0	0-0
Comp.-att.-int.	31-39-0	17-34-0
Sacked-yards lost	2-6	1-10
Punts-average	3-47	5-44
Fumbles-lost	2-1	1-1
Penalties-yards	14-177	9-65
Time of possession	34:05	25:55
Attendance—56,479.		

INDIVIDUAL STATISTICS

RUSHING—San Francisco, Watters 18-56, Young 5-23, Loville 2-13, Rice 1-13, Logan 1-3, Floyd 1-(minus 1), Grbac 2-(minus 2). Los Angeles, Bettis 21-104, Miller 1-9, Bailey 1-3, Lester 1-(minus 1).

PASSING—San Francisco, Young 31-39-0-355. Los Angeles, Miller 8-19-0-86, Chandler 9-15-0-87.

RECEIVING—San Francisco, Rice 11-147, Taylor 7-103, B. Jones 6-60, Logan 4-27, Watters 3-18. Los Angeles, Bailey 5-33, J. Hester 4-58, Drayton 3-30, Bruce 2-24, Griffith 2-22, Brantley 1-6.

MISSED FIELD GOAL ATTEMPTS—None.

INTERCEPTIONS—None.

KICKOFF RETURNS—San Francisco, Carter 3-87, Loville 1-19. Los Angeles, Brantley 4-90, Lang 1-14.

PUNT RETURNS—San Francisco, Carter 3-18. Los Angeles, Brantley 2-11.

SACKS—San Francisco, Stubblefield 1. Los Angeles, Young 2.

CHIEFS 30, FALCONS 10

Sunday, September 18

Kansas City	7	3	7	13—30
Atlanta	0	0	3	7—10

First Quarter

K.C.—Birden 13 pass from Montana (Elliott kick), 4:57.

Second Quarter

K.C.—FG Elliott 48, 3:27.

Third Quarter

K.C.—Bennett 3 run (Elliott kick), 6:19.
Atl—FG N. Johnson 33, 11:50.

Fourth Quarter

K.C.—FG Elliott 19, :39.
K.C.—FG Elliott 45, 4:07.
Atl—Rison 25 pass from J. George (N. Johnson kick), 6:27.
K.C.—Birden 34 pass from Montana (Elliott kick), 8:43.

TEAM STATISTICS

	Kansas City	Atlanta
First downs	22	21
Rushes-yards	23-66	19-100
Passing	361	284
Punt returns-yards	3-30	0-0
Kickoff returns-yards	3-75	6-121
Interception returns-yards	2-45	2-2
Comp.-att.-int.	28-39-2	29-45-2
Sacked-yards lost	0-0	3-15
Punts-average	2-36	3-47
Fumbles-lost	2-2	4-4
Penalties-yards	14-99	10-77
Time of possession	31:06	28:54
Attendance—67,357.		

INDIVIDUAL STATISTICS

RUSHING—Kansas City, Hill 8-28, Anders 3-14, Allen 8-11, Bennett 2-7, Montana 2-6. Atlanta, Pegram 14-74, Heyward 3-16, J. George 1-8, Emanuel 1-2.

PASSING—Kansas City, Montana 28-39-2-361. Atlanta, J. George 29-45-2-299.

RECEIVING—Kansas City, Birden 7-99, Cash 7-73, Davis 6-78, Allen 3-22, Dawson 2-52, Walker 1-21, Hill 1-11, Anders 1-5. Atlanta, Mathis 13-123, Sanders 9-72, Rison 3-72, Pegram 2-0, Emanuel 1-19, Heyward 1-13.

MISSED FIELD GOAL ATTEMPTS—Atlanta, N. Johnson 50.

INTERCEPTIONS—Kansas City, Carter 1-24, Grow 1-21. Atlanta, Clark 1-2, D. Johnson 1-0.

KICKOFF RETURNS—Kansas City, Penn 2-56, Anders 1-19. Atlanta, T. Smith 6-121.

PUNT RETURNS—Kansas City, Hughes 3-30.

SACKS—Kansas City, Thomas 1, N. Smith 1, Saleaumua ½, Phillips ½.

LIONS 20, COWBOYS 17

Monday, September 19

Detroit	3	7	7	0	3—20
Dallas	7	0	3	7	0—17

First Quarter

Dal—Harper 17 pass from Aikman (Boniol kick), 5:49.

Det—FG Hanson 32, 11:53.

Second Quarter

Det—Perriman 25 pass from Mitchell (Hanson kick), 13:05.

Third Quarter

Det—H. Moore 9 pass from Mitchell (Hanson kick), 5:16.

Dal—FG Boniol 19, 14:16.

Fourth Quarter

Dal—E. Smith 6 run (Boniol kick), 10:51.

Overtime

Det—FG Hanson 44, 14:33.

TEAM STATISTICS

	Detroit	Dallas
First downs	22	25
Rushes-yards	47-206	34-162
Passing	173	209
Punt returns-yards	2-20	2-19
Kickoff returns-yards	4-96	3-68
Interception returns-yards	0-0	0-0
Comp.-att.-int.	13-27-0	26-39-0
Sacked-yards lost	1-1	2-14
Punts-average	4-40	4-47
Fumbles-lost	0-0	4-3
Penalties-yards	7-37	3-20
Time of possession	37:46	36:47
Attendance—64,102.		

INDIVIDUAL STATISTICS

RUSHING—Detroit, Sanders 40-194, D. Moore 5-9, Mitchell 2-3. Dallas, E. Smith 29-143, Johnston 4-10, Aikman 1-9.

PASSING—Detroit, Mitchell 13-27-0-174. Dallas, Aikman 26-39-0-223.

RECEIVING—Detroit, H. Moore 6-81, Perriman 5-66, Matthews 2-27. Dallas, E. Smith 7-49, Johnston 6-47, Novacek 5-41, Irvin 3-47, Harper 2-28, Coleman 1-7, Galbraith 1-7, Kennard 1-(minus 3).

MISSED FIELD GOAL ATTEMPTS—Detroit, Hanson 51, 57, 51.

INTERCEPTIONS—None.

KICKOFF RETURNS—Detroit, Gray 3-59, D. Moore 1-11, Morton 0-26. Dallas, Holmes 3-68.

PUNT RETURNS—Detroit, Gray 2-20. Dallas, Holmes 2-19.

SACKS—Detroit, Thomas 1, Swilling 1. Dallas, D. Smith 1.

WEEK 4

Atlanta 27, Washington 20
Chicago 19, N.Y. Jets 7
Cleveland 21, Indianapolis 14
Green Bay 30, Tampa Bay 3
Houston 20, Cincinnati 13
L.A. Rams 16, Kansas City 0
Minnesota 38, Miami 35
New England 23, Detroit 17
San Diego 26, L.A. Raiders 24
San Francisco 24, New Orleans 13
Seattle 30, Pittsburgh 13
Buffalo 27, Denver 20
    Open date: Arizona, Dallas, N.Y. Giants,
Philadelphia

STANDINGS

AFC EAST	W	L	T	Pct.
Miami	3	1	0	.750
Buffalo	3	1	0	.750
New England	2	2	0	.500
N.Y. Jets	2	2	0	.500
Indianapolis	1	3	0	.250

AFC CENTRAL	W	L	T	Pct.
Cleveland	3	1	0	.750
Pittsburgh	2	2	0	.500
Houston	1	3	0	.250
Cincinnati	0	4	0	.000

AFC WEST	W	L	T	Pct.
San Diego	4	0	0	1.000
Kansas City	3	1	0	.750
Seattle	3	1	0	.750
L.A. Raiders	1	3	0	.250
Denver	0	4	0	.000

NFC EAST	W	L	T	Pct.
N.Y. Giants	3	0	0	1.000
Dallas	2	1	0	.667
Philadelphia	2	1	0	.667
Washington	1	3	0	.250
Arizona	0	3	0	.000

NFC CENTRAL	W	L	T	Pct.
Minnesota	3	1	0	.750
Chicago	2	2	0	.500
Detroit	2	2	0	.500
Green Bay	2	2	0	.500
Tampa Bay	1	3	0	.250

NFC WEST	W	L	T	Pct.
San Francisco	3	1	0	.750
Atlanta	2	2	0	.500
L.A. Rams	2	2	0	.500
New Orleans	1	3	0	.250

HIGHLIGHTS

Hero of the week: Minnesota quarterback Warren Moon, who completed 26 of 37 passes for 326 yards and three touchdowns in the Vikings' 38-35 victory over Miami. Nine players caught passes from Moon, who was not intercepted.

Goat of the week: Denver quarterback John Elway, whose late-game miscue cost the Broncos a possible victory for the second time in four weeks. Elway, who fumbled when the ball slipped out of his hand while he was attempting to pass in the final minute of a Week 1 loss to San Diego, this time wildly overthrew Cedric Tillman in the Buffalo end zone on fourth down with 21 seconds left in a game the Broncos lost, 27-20.

Sub of the week: Seattle defensive back Orlando Watters, an undrafted rookie free agent making his first NFL start in place of injured Patrick Hunter, picked off a Neil O'Donnell pass with 4:15 left and returned it 35 yards for a touchdown in the Seahawks' 30-13 victory over Pittsburgh.

Comeback of the week: San Diego beat the Los Angeles Raiders, 26-24, on John Carney's 33-yard field goal with two seconds left. Lionel Washington had given the Raiders a 24-23 lead when he returned an interception of a Stan Humphries pass 31 yards for a touchdown with 7:01 left, but Humphries proceeded to guide the Chargers 65 yards in 14 plays to set up Carney's game-winner.

Blowout of the week: Green Bay beat Tampa Bay, 30-3, in a Battle of the Bays that became a rout. The Packers, with Brett Favre throwing three touchdown passes, rolled up 401 total yards, didn't commit a turnover and didn't allow a sack.

Nail-biter of the week: Minnesota's victory over Miami came after the Vikings blew a 28-0 second-quarter lead and had to rally to win. The Dolphins scored 28 consecutive points to tie it before the Vikes scored 10 points midway through the fourth quarter to retake the lead.

Hit of the week: By Seattle free safety Eugene Robinson, who stopped Barry Foster on fourth-and-goal at the 1-yard line after the Steelers, trailing 20-6, took the second-half kickoff, drove 68 yards in 13 plays and were on the verge of cutting the Seahawks' lead.

Oddity of the week: Kansas City's 16-0 loss at Arrowhead Stadium to the Rams was the Chiefs' first shutout loss at home since October 20, 1985, when they lost to the Rams, 16-0.

Top rusher: Jerome Bettis carried 35 times for 132 yards in the Rams' victory over Kansas City.

Top passer: Dan Marino completed 29 of 54 passes for 431 yards and three touchdowns in Miami's loss to Minnesota.

Top receiver: Henry Ellard caught six passes for 162 yards and one touchdown in Washington's 27-20 loss to Atlanta.

Notes: Joe Montana suffered the first shutout loss of his NFL career in the Chiefs' loss to the Rams. It was Montana's 204th NFL game, including playoffs. . . . The Falcons won at Washington's RFK Stadium for the first time in 11 tries. . . . Chris Jacke kicked three field goals against Tampa Bay to surpass Chester Marcol (122-120) as the Packers' all-time field-goal leader. . . . For the first time since 1983, the Vikings had a quarterback throw for 300 yards (Warren Moon), a running back run for 100 yards (Terry Allen) and a receiver catch passes for 100 yards (Jake Reed) in the same game. . . . Johnny Johnson had a 90-yard non-touchdown run in the New York Jets' loss to Chicago. Jeremy Lincoln caught Johnson at the Bears' 7-yard line, and the Jets failed to score. . . . Jim Harbaugh had a 41-yard run against the Browns, the longest by a Colts quarterback since 1953. . . . Chargers center Courtney Hall (biceps injury) had an 83-game starting streak end against the Raiders. . . . Houston, which was 0-3 before the game, beat Cincinnati for the 10th consecutive time at the Astrodome.

Quote of the week: Oilers defensive end Ray Childress, on the victory over the winless Bengals: "If we'd have lost this game, we couldn't have gone to our cars until it was dark."

GAME SUMMARIES
RAMS 16, CHIEFS 0
Sunday, September 25

L.A. Rams	13	0	3	0—16
Kansas City	0	0	0	0— 0

First Quarter
L.A.—FG Zendejas 29, 10:20.
L.A.—Anderson 72 pass from Chandler (Zendejas kick), 12:09.
L.A.—FG Zendejas 23, 13:43.
Third Quarter
L.A.—FG Zendejas 28, 11:09.

TEAM STATISTICS

	L.A. Rams	Kansas City
First downs	17	17
Rushes-yards	42-155	21-76
Passing	202	166
Punt returns-yards	4-27	3-26
Kickoff returns-yards	1-23	5-94
Interception returns-yards	3-15	0-0
Comp.-att.-int.	13-21-0	18-37-3
Sacked-yards lost	1-5	1-9
Punts-average	4-53	4-47
Fumbles-lost	1-0	1-0
Penalties-yards	9-75	6-30
Time of possession	34:07	25:53

Attendance—78,184.

INDIVIDUAL STATISTICS
RUSHING—Los Angeles, Bettis 35-132, Chandler 5-11, Anderson 1-11, Lang 1-1. Kansas City, Allen 15-59, Anders 3-14, Hill 1-3, Bennett 1-0, Montana 1-0.
PASSING—Los Angeles, Chandler 13-21-0-207. Kansas City, Montana 18-37-3-175.
RECEIVING—Los Angeles, Hester 3-52, Drayton 3-20, Anderson 2-83, Bettis 2-16, Bailey 2-16, Bruce 1-12. Kansas City, Davis 5-74, Anders 4-28, Birden 3-39, Cash 2-11, Allen 2-6, Hughes 1-9, Walker 1-8.
MISSED FIELD GOAL ATTEMPTS—None.
INTERCEPTIONS—Los Angeles, Lyle 1-0, Phifer 1-0, Pope 1-15.
KICKOFF RETURNS—Los Angeles, Lang 1-23. Kansas City, Penn 4-84, Booker 1-10.
PUNT RETURNS—Los Angeles, J. Bailey 3-25, Lyght 1-2. Kansas City, Hughes 3-26.
SACKS—Los Angeles, Gilbert 1. Kansas City, Team 1.

BROWNS 21, COLTS 14
Sunday, September 25

Cleveland	7	7	0	7—21
Indianapolis	7	0	7	0—14

First Quarter
Cle—Metcalf 57 pass from Testaverde (Stover kick), 1:48.
Ind—Faulk 1 run (Biasucci kick) 4:36.
Second Quarter
Cle—Metcalf 15 pass from Testaverde (Stover kick), 14:32.
Third Quarter
Ind—Potts 13 pass from Harbaugh (Biasucci kick), 9:39.
Fourth Quarter
Cle—Hoard 65 pass from Testaverde (Stover kick), 13:03.

TEAM STATISTICS

	Cleveland	Indianapolis
First downs	18	18
Rushes-yards	31-119	33-146
Passing	257	189
Punt returns-yards	3-13	3-5
Kickoff returns-yards	3-81	4-54
Interception returns-yards	1-10	1-0
Comp.-att.-int.	16-28-1	16-26-1
Sacked-yards lost	1-9	1-5
Punts-average	8-40	7-46
Fumbles-lost	0-0	1-1
Penalties-yards	10-89	10-112
Time of possession	31:02	28:58

Attendance—55,821.

INDIVIDUAL STATISTICS
RUSHING—Cleveland, Metcalf 8-42, Hoard 10-34, Byner 7-24, Alexander 1-11, Vardell 5-8. Indianapolis, Harbaugh 4-63, Faulk 22-61, Potts 3-9, Humphrey 3-8, Turner 1-5.
PASSING—Cleveland, Testaverde 16-28-1-266. Indianapolis, Harbaugh 16-26-1-194.
RECEIVING—Cleveland, Metcalf 5-74, Vardell 5-51, Hoard 2-88, Alexander 2-27, McCardell 1-18, Carrier 1-8. Indianapolis, Potts 6-87, Faulk 4-27, Gash 2-42, Turner 2-14, Dawkins 1-18, Etheredge 1-6.
MISSED FIELD GOAL ATTEMPTS—Indianapolis, Biasucci 46.
INTERCEPTIONS—Cleveland, Turner 1-10. Indianapolis, Watts 1-0.
KICKOFF RETURNS—Cleveland, Baldwin 3-81. Indianapolis, Humphrey 2-44, Brewer 1-18, Ratigan 1-0.
PUNT RETURNS—Cleveland, Metcalf 3-13. Indianapolis, Brewer 3-5.
SACKS—Cleveland, Footman 1. Indianapolis, Bennett 1.

PACKERS 30, BUCCANEERS 3
Sunday, September 25

Tampa Bay	0	0	3	0— 3
Green Bay	0	13	10	7—30

Second Quarter
G.B.—FG Jacke 21, 2:47.
G.B.—Bennett 9 pass from Favre (Jacke kick), 7:24.
G.B.—FG Jacke 20, 14:47.
Third Quarter
G.B.—FG Jacke 22, 8:02.
T.B.—FG Husted 24, 10:48.
G.B.—West 20 pass from Favre (Jacke kick), 14:57.
Fourth Quarter
G.B.—Sharpe 3 pass from Favre (Jacke kick), 12:35.

TEAM STATISTICS

	Tampa Bay	Green Bay
First downs	15	24
Rushes-yards	17-54	34-95
Passing	177	306
Punt returns-yards	0-0	2-8
Kickoff returns-yards	5-86	2-64
Interception returns-yards	0-0	1-16
Comp.-att.-int.	12-30-1	30-39-0
Sacked-yards lost	4-20	0-0
Punts-average	2-45	2-40
Fumbles-lost	2-2	0-0
Penalties-yards	2-20	4-22
Time of possession	21:28	38:32

Attendance—58,551.

INDIVIDUAL STATISTICS
RUSHING—Tampa Bay, Workman 8-21, Rhett 7-21, Dilfer 2-12. Green Bay, Cobb 12-46, Bennett 7-26, Johnson 10-21, Favre 3-4, Thompson 2-(minus 2).
PASSING—Tampa Bay, Erickson 7-20-1-124, Dilfer 5-10-0-73. Green Bay, Favre 30-39-0-306.
RECEIVING—Tampa Bay, Hawkins 5-61, Harris 2-48, Wilson 2-41, Copeland 1-26, Green 1-16, Rhett 1-5. Green Bay, Bennett 8-37, Johnson 6-84, Sharpe 5-43, Cobb 3-51, West 3-51, Brooks 3-29, Lewis 1-9, Wilner 1-2.
MISSED FIELD GOAL ATTEMPTS—None.
INTERCEPTIONS—Green Bay, McGill 1-16.
KICKOFF RETURNS—Tampa Bay, Turner 4-75, Moore 1-11. Green Bay, Jordan 2-64.
PUNT RETURNS—Green Bay, Brooks 2-8.
SACKS—Green Bay, Paup 2, Jones 1, White 1.

VIKINGS 38, DOLPHINS 35
Sunday, September 25

Miami	0	6	15	14—35
Minnesota	14	14	0	10—38

First Quarter
Min—Carter 2 pass from Moon (Reveiz kick), 7:17.
Min—Allen 8 run (Reveiz kick), 13:18.
Second Quarter
Min—Carter 44 pass from Moon (Reveiz kick), 9:09.
Min—Carter 8 pass from Moon (Reveiz kick), 14:36.
Mia—McDuffie 26 pass from Marino (run failed), 14:58.
Third Quarter
Mia—Baty 3 pass from Marino (Fryar pass from Marino), 4:37.
Mia—Jackson 25 pass from Marino (Stoyanovich kick), 14:20.
Fourth Quarter
Mia—Parmalee 10 run (Stoyanovich kick), 4:26.
Min—Graham 3 run (Reveiz kick), 7:35.
Min—FG Reveiz 38, 11:23.
Mia—Byars 1 run (Stoyanovich kick), 13:56.

TEAM STATISTICS

	Miami	Minnesota
First downs	27	24
Rushes-yards	19-47	31-147
Passing	426	311
Punt returns-yards	5-79	1-6
Kickoff returns-yards	6-101	5-90
Interception returns-yards	0-0	3-6
Comp.-att.-int.	29-54-3	26-37-0
Sacked-yards lost	1-5	2-15
Punts-average	2-43	5-49
Fumbles-lost	1-0	1-0
Penalties-yards	2-18	10-77
Time of possession	26:37	33:23

Attendance—64,035.

INDIVIDUAL STATISTICS

RUSHING—Miami, Parmalee 6-22, Byars 3-14, Kirby 9-13, Marino 1-(minus 2). Minnesota, Allen 15-113, Graham 8-28, Lee 1-5, Smith 3-4, Palmer 1-1, Moon 3-(minus 4).

PASSING—Miami, Marino 29-54-3-431. Minnesota, Moon 26-37-0-326.

RECEIVING—Miami, Byars 10-79, Fryar 6-160, Jackson 3-62, Ingram 3-36, McDuffie 2-38, M. Williams 2-34, Kirby 1-10, Parmalee 1-9, Baty 1-3. Minnesota, Reed 9-127, Carter 7-81, Allen 3-16, Ismail 2-44, Palmer 1-39, Cooper 1-7, Lee 1-7, Jordan 1-3, Smith 1-2.

MISSED FIELD GOALS—Miami, Stoyanovich 40. Minnesota, Reveiz 52.

INTERCEPTIONS—Minnesota, Del Rio 2-5, McGriggs 1-1.

KICKOFF RETURNS—Miami, McDuffie 4-101, Parmalee 1-0, Solomon 1-0, M. Williams 1-0. Minnesota, Ismail 2-57, R. Smith 2-33, Novoselsky 1-0.

PUNT RETURNS—Miami, McDuffie 5-79. Minnesota, Palmer 1-6.

SACKS—Miami, Bowens 1, Coleman 1. Minnesota, R. Harris 1.

FALCONS 27, REDSKINS 20
Sunday, September 25

Atlanta	7	0	17	3—27
Washington	0	13	0	7—20

First Quarter
Atl—Mathis 4 pass from George (Johnson kick), 6:05.
Second Quarter
Was—Brooks 2 run (Lohmiller kick), :57.
Was—Ellard 73 pass from Friesz (kick failed), 7:15.
Third Quarter
Atl—Emanuel 31 pass from George (Johnson kick), 6:21.
Atl—FG Johnson 30, 11:31.
Atl—Heyward 1 run (Johnson kick), 14:53.
Fourth Quarter
Atl—FG Johnson 22, 1:44.
Was—Ervins 3 run (Lohmiller kick), 13:07.

TEAM STATISTICS

	Atlanta	Washington
First downs	19	18
Rushes-yards	28-71	14-44
Passing	238	310
Punt returns-yards	3-21	3-42
Kickoff returns-yards	3-61	5-57
Interception returns-yards	4-47	1-34
Comp.-att.-int.	22-35-1	27-45-4
Sacked-yards lost	6-32	1-13
Punts-average	7-40	5-46
Fumbles-lost	3-0	1-1
Penalties-yards	6-40	8-88
Time of possession	35:30	24:30

Attendance—53,238.

INDIVIDUAL STATISTICS

RUSHING—Atlanta, Pegram 12-29, Heyward 7-23, George 9-19. Washington, Brooks 10-27, Ervins 3-13, Shuler 1-4.

PASSING—Atlanta, George 22-35-1-270. Washington, Friesz 17-29-3-230, Shuler 10-16-1-93.

RECEIVING—Atlanta, Mathis 9-92, Rison 4-74, Emanuel 4-64, Pegram 3-19, Heyward 1-15, Sanders 1-6. Washington, Ervins 9-51, Ellard 6-162, Mitchell 6-57, Brooks 3-11, Jenkins 2-17, Howard 1-25.

MISSED FIELD GOAL ATTEMPTS—Washington, Lohmiller 47.

INTERCEPTIONS—Atlanta, Case 1-0, Clark 1-22, D. Johnson 1-0, Walker 1-2. Washington, A. Collins 1-34.

KICKOFF RETURNS—Atlanta, T. Smith 3-61. Washington, Mitchell 3-47, Haws 1-10.

PUNT RETURNS—Atlanta, T. Smith 3-21. Washington, Mitchell 3-42.

SACKS—Atlanta, C. Smith 1. Washington, Harvey 2, Marshall 1, Nottage 1, Wilson 1, Woods 1.

49ERS 24, SAINTS 13
Sunday, September 25

New Orleans	3	10	0	0—13
San Francisco	3	7	7	7—24

First Quarter
S.F.—FG Brien 43, 2:31.
N.O.—FG Andersen 22, 10:48.
Second Quarter
S.F.—Rice 28 pass from Young (Brien kick), 1:17.
N.O.—Smith 17 pass from Everett (Andersen kick), 12:29.
N.O.—FG Andersen 26, 14:22.
Third Quarter
S.F.—Rice 6 pass from Young (Brien kick), 11:15.
Fourth Quarter
S.F.—Sanders 74 interception return (Brien kick), 14:28.

TEAM STATISTICS

	New Orleans	San Francisco
First downs	17	18
Rushes-yards	19-49	19-74
Passing	291	225
Punt returns-yards	5-50	4-17
Kickoff returns-yards	5-70	4-77
Interception returns-yards	2-9	2-74
Comp.-att.-int.	31-55-2	25-39-2
Sacked-yards lost	0-0	5-22
Punts-average	7-45	7-30
Fumbles-lost	0-0	0-0
Penalties-yards	5-34	4-33
Time of possession	32:26	27:34

Attendance—63,971.

INDIVIDUAL STATISTICS

RUSHING—New Orleans, Barnhardt 1-21, Haynes 1-13, Everett 1-5, Ned 5-5, Neal 3-4, Brown 8-1. San Francisco, Watters 15-49, Logan 3-25, Floyd 1-0.

PASSING—New Orleans, Everett 31-55-2-291. San Francisco, Young 25-39-2-247.

RECEIVING—New Orleans, Early 8-79, Haynes 7-81, Walls 6-36, Ned 4-20, Smith 3-33, Brown 2-33, Small 1-0. San Francisco, Watters 8-54, Rice 5-63, Jones 4-37, Logan 4-36, Taylor 3-52, Singleton 1-5.

MISSED FIELD GOAL ATTEMPTS—New Orleans, Ander-sen 50. San Francisco, Brien 55.

INTERCEPTIONS—New Orleans, Buck 1-0, J. Williams 1-9. San Francisco, Hanks 1-0, Sanders 1-74.

KICKOFF RETURNS—New Orleans, Hughes 4-61, Ned 1-9. San Francisco, Carter 4-77.

PUNT RETURNS—New Orleans, Hughes 5-50. San Francisco, Carter 4-17.

SACKS—New Orleans, Conner 2, Martin 2, Buck 1.

PATRIOTS 23, LIONS 17
Sunday, September 25

New England	3	14	3	3—23
Detroit	0	7	7	3—17

First Quarter
N.E.—FG Bahr 20, 9:08.
Second Quarter
N.E.—Butts 5 run (Bahr kick), 5:13.
Det—Sanders 35 run (Hanson kick), 8:40.
N.E.—Coates 7 pass from Bledsoe (Bahr kick), 14:33.
Third Quarter
N.E.—FG Bahr 28, 5:33.
Det—Sanders 39 run (Hanson kick), 8:18.
Fourth Quarter
N.E.—FG Bahr 21, 2:04.
Det—FG Hanson 27, 9:21.

TEAM STATISTICS

	New England	Detroit
First downs	21	15
Rushes-yards	37-108	22-159
Passing	245	183
Punt returns-yards	1-11	2-18
Kickoff returns-yards	3-77	4-103
Interception returns-yards	2-23	0-0
Comp.-att.-int.	21-33-0	14-29-2
Sacked-yards lost	1-6	1-6
Punts-average	4-54	4-35
Fumbles-lost	1-0	1-0

	New England	Detroit
Penalties-yards	8-56	9-55
Time of possession	34:48	25:12
Attendance—59,618.		

INDIVIDUAL STATISTICS

RUSHING—New England, Butts 18-54, Thompson 10-37, Turner 3-12, Gash 1-3, Bledsoe 5-2. Detroit, Sanders 18-131, Perriman 1-25, Mitchell 2-3, D. Moore 1-0.

PASSING—New England, Bledsoe 21-33-0-251. Detroit, Mitchell 14-29-2-189.

RECEIVING—New England, Turner 6-64, Coates 4-49, Gash 4-32, Brisby 3-67, Timpson 2-26, Thompson 1-9, Butts 1-4. Detroit, H. Moore 5-92, Matthews 3-40, Hallock 2-22, Sanders 2-14, Perriman 1-12, Holman 1-9.

MISSED FIELD GOAL ATTEMPTS—None.

INTERCEPTIONS—New England, Guyton 1-3, Hurst 1-20.

KICKOFF RETURNS—New England, Crittenden 3-77. Detroit, Gray 4-103.

PUNT RETURNS—New England, Crittenden 1-11. Detroit, Gray 2-18.

SACKS—New England, Slade 1. Detroit, Johnson 1.

OILERS 20, BENGALS 13

Sunday, September 25

Cincinnati	0	0	3	10—13
Houston	7	10	3	0—20

First Quarter

Hou—G. Brown 20 pass from Carlson (Del Greco kick), 9:14.

Second Quarter

Hou—G. Brown 1 run (Del Greco kick), 6:34.

Hou—FG Del Greco 45, 15:00.

Third Quarter

Cin—FG Pelfrey 21, 6:22.

Hou—FG Del Greco 24, 11:27.

Fourth Quarter

Cin—Sawyer 82 punt return (Pelfrey kick), 3:03.

Cin—FG Pelfrey 49, 8:15.

TEAM STATISTICS

	Cincinnati	Houston
First downs	13	19
Rushes-yards	22-102	42-148
Passing	74	193
Punt returns-yards	2-81	5-25
Kickoff returns-yards	4-88	3-64
Interception returns-yards	2-32	3-62
Comp.-att.-int.	10-30-3	12-34-2
Sacked-yards lost	7-41	3-18
Punts-average	6-37	7-42
Fumbles-lost	1-1	4-2
Penalties-yards	2-10	14-106
Time of possession	21:23	38:37
Attendance—44,253.		

INDIVIDUAL STATISTICS

RUSHING—Cincinnati, Broussard 11-65, Fenner 9-34, Green 1-4, Ball 1-(minus 1). Houston, G. Brown 19-87, White 15-42, Carlson 6-14, Tillman 1-3, Coleman 1-2.

PASSING—Cincinnati, Klingler 10-30-3-115. Houston, Carlson 12-33-2-211, Camarillo 0-1-0-0.

RECEIVING—Cincinnati, Scott 4-64, McGee 3-29, Pickens 1-14, Broussard 1-4, Fenner 1-4. Houston, Coleman 4-112, Givins 3-31, G. Brown 2-37, Slaughter 2-22, Jeffires 1-9.

MISSED FIELD GOAL ATTEMPTS—None.

INTERCEPTIONS—Cincinnati, Brim 1-23, Oliver 1-9. Houston, Bishop 1-21, Dishman 1-0, Robertson 1-41.

KICKOFF RETURNS—Cincinnati, Ball 4-88. Houston, Bishop 1-7, Hannah 1-39, White 1-18.

PUNT RETURNS—Cincinnati, Sawyer 2-81. Houston, Hannah 3-19, Givins 2-6.

SACKS—Cincinnati, A. Williams 2, Copeland 1. Houston, Davidson 2, Lathon 2, Bishop 1, Childress 1, A. Smith 1.

CHARGERS 26, RAIDERS 24

Sunday, September 25

San Diego	10	10	3	3—26
L.A. Raiders	0	3	14	7—24

First Quarter

S.D.—Gordon 90 punt return (Carney kick), 2:52.

S.D.—FG Carney 38, 9:05.

Second Quarter

S.D.—Means 1 run (Carney kick), 1:23.

L.A.—FG Jaeger 43, 5:24.

S.D.—FG Carney 24, 10:32.

Third Quarter

S.D.—FG Carney 27, 5:06.

L.A.—Hostetler 1 run (Jaeger kick), 8:02.

L.A.—Ismail 24 pass from Hostetler (Jaeger kick), 11:05.

Fourth Quarter

L.A.—Washington 31 interception return (Jaeger kick), 7:59.

S.D.—FG Carney 33, 14:58.

TEAM STATISTICS

	San Diego	L.A. Raiders
First downs	17	15
Rushes-yards	31-84	20-59
Passing	179	220
Punt returns-yards	3-95	1-12
Kickoff returns-yards	5-131	7-201
Interception returns-yards	0-0	2-31
Comp.-att.-int.	18-26-2	15-26-0
Sacked-yards lost	2-12	3-11
Punts-average	1-39	3-50
Fumbles-lost	1-0	2-1
Penalties-yards	2-20	7-80
Time of possession	33:30	26:30
Attendance—55,385.		

INDIVIDUAL STATISTICS

RUSHING—San Diego, Means 21-52, Bieniemy 5-21, Humphries 4-7, Jefferson 1-4. Los Angeles, H. Williams 11-24, Rathman 2-13, Ismail 1-11, Hostetler 2-6, Montgomery 4-5.

PASSING—San Diego, Humphries 18-26-2-191. Los Angeles, Hostetler 14-25-0-230, Evans 1-1-0-1.

RECEIVING—San Diego, Harmon 6-74, Seay 5-59, Means 3-20, May 2-22, Martin 1-11, D. Young 1-5. Los Angeles, H. Williams 5-48, Brown 4-88, Ismail 2-43, Jett 1-27, Hobbs 1-11, Montgomery 1-9, Glover 1-5.

MISSED FIELD GOAL ATTEMPTS—None.

INTERCEPTIONS—Los Angeles, McDaniel 1-0, Washington 1-31.

KICKOFF RETURNS—San Diego, Coleman 4-106, Harmon 1-25. Los Angeles, Ismail 3-59, Wright 3-121, H. Williams 1-21.

PUNT RETURNS—San Diego, Gordon 3-95. Los Angeles, Brown 1-12.

SACKS—San Diego, Seau 2, Lee 1. Los Angeles, Ball 1, Moss 1.

SEAHAWKS 30, STEELERS 13

Sunday, September 25

Pittsburgh	3	3	0	7—13
Seattle	7	13	0	10—30

First Quarter

Sea—Warren 3 run (Kasay kick), 2:38.

Pit—FG Anderson 31, 8:57.

Second Quarter

Sea—FG Kasay 31, 5:14.

Sea—Junkin 1 pass from Mirer (Kasay kick), 8:40.

Sea—FG Kasay 40, 14:14.

Pit—FG Anderson 38, 15:00.

Fourth Quarter

Sea—Watters 35 interception return (Kasay kick), 10:45.

Pit—C. Johnson 36 pass from O'Donnell (Anderson kick), 11:43.

Sea—FG Kasay 31, 13:54.

TEAM STATISTICS

	Pittsburgh	Seattle
First downs	29	20
Rushes-yards	30-131	35-145
Passing	321	152
Punt returns-yards	1-4	2-21
Kickoff returns-yards	7-170	2-44
Interception returns-yards	1-0	4-92
Comp.-att.-int.	24-46-4	14-24-1
Sacked-yards lost	0-0	2-14
Punts-average	4-35	5-48
Fumbles-lost	0-0	1-0
Penalties-yards	9-61	4-46
Time of possession	32:01	27:59
Attendance—59,637.		

INDIVIDUAL STATISTICS

RUSHING—Pittsburgh, Foster 21-96, Morris 3-14, J. Williams 5-13, O'Donnell 1-8. Seattle, C. Warren 26-126, T. Johnson 5-16, S. Smith 1-3, Mirer 1-1, L. Smith 2-(minus 1).

PASSING—Pittsburgh, O'Donnell 21-43-4-282, Tomczak 3-3-0-39.

Seattle, Mirer 14-24-1-166.

RECEIVING—Pittsburgh, C. Johnson 7-99, J. Williams 6-71, E. Green 5-67, Thigpen 3-35, Mills 2-42, Foster 1-7. Seattle, Martin 5-47, Blades 4-97, C. Warren 3-14, Edmunds 1-7, Junkin 1-1.

MISSED FIELD GOAL ATTEMPTS—None.

INTERCEPTIONS—Pittsburgh, Perry 1-0. Seattle, Watters 1-35, Porter 1-33, Blackmon 1-24, Robinson 1-0.

KICKOFF RETURNS—Pittsburgh, Morris 3-93, Woodson 3-53, Johnson 1-24. Seattle, Warren 1-30, Bates 1-14.

PUNT RETURNS—Pittsburgh, Woodson 1-4. Seattle, Martin 2-21.

SACKS—Pittsburgh, Brown 1, Greene 1.

BEARS 19, JETS 7
Sunday, September 25

Chicago	0	10	3	6— 19
N.Y. Jets	7	0	0	0— 7

First Quarter

N.Y.—J. Johnson 5 run (Lowery kick), 5:00.

Second Quarter

Chi—Tillman 2 run (Butler kick), 1:55.

Chi—FG Butler 44, 13:05.

Third Quarter

Chi—FG Butler 30, 9:33.

Fourth Quarter

Chi—Tillman 2 run (pass failed), 2:53.

TEAM STATISTICS

	Chicago	N.Y. Jets
First downs	17	17
Rushes-yards	40-104	18-164
Passing	122	161
Punt returns-yards	2-8	3-12
Kickoff returns-yards	2-71	5-100
Interception returns-yards	1-31	0-0
Comp.-att.-int.	14-24-0	16-32-1
Sacked-yards lost	4-21	4-19
Punts-average	5-41	4-39
Fumbles-lost	0-0	5-2
Penalties-yards	3-25	4-28
Time of possession	36:25	23:35

Attendance—70,806.

INDIVIDUAL STATISTICS

RUSHING—Chicago, Tillman 32-96, Worley 2-6, Christian 1-4, Walsh 5-(minus 2). New York, J. Johnson 12-126, B. Baxter 4-15, Trudeau 1-15, Esiason 1-8.

PASSING—Chicago, Walsh 14-24-0-143. New York, Esiason 11-20-0-112, Trudeau 5-12-1-68.

RECEIVING—Chicago, Hoge 4-34, Conway 3-35, Waddle 2-32, Graham 2-19, R. Green 1-10, Tillman 1-7, Cook 1-6. New York, Mitchell 4-65, J. Johnson 4-30, Moore 3-33, Monk 2-23, S. Anderson 2-22, Murrell 1-7.

MISSED FIELD GOAL ATTEMPTS—Chicago, Butler 42. New York, Lowery 47, 41.

INTERCEPTIONS—Chicago, Spellman 1-31.

KICKOFF RETURNS—Chicago, Lewis 2-71. New York, Murrell 4-82, R. Anderson 1-18.

PUNT RETURNS—Chicago, Waddle 2-8. New York, Hicks 3-12.

SACKS—Chicago, V. Smith 1, A. Fontenot 1, Zorich 1, Spellman 1. New York, Lageman 2½, Houston 1, M. Jones ½.

BILLS 27, BRONCOS 20
Monday, September 26

Denver	0	7	10	3—20
Buffalo	3	14	7	3—27

First Quarter

Buf—FG Christie 36, 10:32.

Second Quarter

Den—Miller 11 pass from Elway (Elam kick), 1:18.

Buf—Thomas 16 run (Christie kick), 13:06.

Buf—Thomas 27 run (Christie kick), 14:42.

Third Quarter

Buf—Gardner 3 run (Christie kick), 1:42.

Den—L. Russell 2 run (Elam kick), 5:24.

Den—FG Elam 28, 13:05.

Fourth Quarter

Buf—FG Christie 28, 3:39.

Den—FG Elam 43, 7:39.

TEAM STATISTICS

	Denver	Buffalo
First downs	21	19
Rushes-yards	23-77	35-149
Passing	260	166
Punt returns-yards	2-32	2-11
Kickoff returns-yards	5-104	5-67
Interception returns-yards	1-4	1-27
Comp.-att.-int.	26-46-1	16-26-1
Sacked-yards lost	4-20	2-12
Punts-average	2-50	4-33
Fumbles-lost	1-1	1-0
Penalties-yards	10-77	8-51
Time of possession	33:20	26:40

Attendance—75,373.

INDIVIDUAL STATISTICS

RUSHING—Denver, Elway 5-37, L. Russell 12-31, Milburn 2-6, Clark 1-2, Bernstine 3-1. Buffalo, Thomas 17-103, K. Davis 15-45, Gardner 1-3, Kelly 2-(minus 2).

PASSING—Denver, Elway 26-46-1-280. Buffalo, Kelly 16-26-1-178.

RECEIVING—Denver, L. Russell 10-68, Sharpe 4-90, Rivers 4-37, Milburn 4-30, Tillman 2-38, Miller 2-17. Buffalo, Reed 5-83, Beebe 4-39, K. Davis 3-20, Bill Brooks 2-17, Thomas 1-13, Metzelaars 1-6.

MISSED FIELD GOAL ATTEMPTS—Denver, Elam 41.

INTERCEPTIONS—Denver, Fletcher 1-4. Buffalo, M. Washington 1-27.

KICKOFF RETURNS—Denver, Milburn 5-104. Buffalo, Bu. Brooks 4-51, Beebe 1-16.

PUNT RETURNS—Denver, Milburn 2-32. Buffalo, Burris 2-11.

SACKS—Denver, Fletcher 2. Buffalo, Bennett 2, Br. Smith 1, Hansen 1.

WEEK 5

RESULTS

Arizona 17, Minnesota 7
Atlanta 8, L.A. Rams 5
Chicago 20, Buffalo 13
Cleveland 27, N.Y. Jets 7
Dallas 34, Washington 7
Indianapolis 17, Seattle 15
Miami 23, Cincinnati 7
New England 17, Green Bay 16
New Orleans 27, N.Y. Giants 22
Philadelphia 40, San Francisco 8
Tampa Bay 24, Detroit 14
Pittsburgh 30, Houston 14
    Open date: Denver, Kansas City, L.A.
Raiders, San Diego

STANDINGS

AFC EAST	W	L	T	Pct.
Miami	4	1	0	.800
Buffalo	3	2	0	.600
New England	3	2	0	.600
N.Y. Jets	2	3	0	.400
Indianapolis	2	3	0	.400

AFC CENTRAL	W	L	T	Pct.
Cleveland	4	1	0	.800
Pittsburgh	3	2	0	.600
Houston	1	4	0	.200
Cincinnati	0	5	0	.000

AFC WEST	W	L	T	Pct.
San Diego	4	0	0	1.000
Kansas City	3	1	0	.750
Seattle	3	2	0	.600
L.A. Raiders	1	3	0	.250
Denver	0	4	0	.000

NFC EAST	W	L	T	Pct.
Dallas	3	1	0	.750
N.Y. Giants	3	1	0	.750
Philadelphia	3	1	0	.750
Arizona	1	3	0	.250
Washington	1	4	0	.200

NFC CENTRAL	W	L	T	Pct.
Chicago	3	2	0	.600
Minnesota	3	2	0	.600
Detroit	2	3	0	.400
Green Bay	2	3	0	.400
Tampa Bay	2	3	0	.400

NFC WEST	W	L	T	Pct.
Atlanta	3	2	0	.600
San Francisco	3	2	0	.600
L.A. Rams	2	3	0	.400
New Orleans	2	3	0	.400

HIGHLIGHTS

Hero of the week: Philadelphia running back Charlie Garner, who rushed for 111 yards on 16 carries and scored two touchdowns in the Eagles' 40-8 rout of San Francisco. Garner, a rookie who had been sidelined with a fractured rib, was making his first NFL start.

Goat of the week: New York Giants wide receiver Chris Calloway, who was flagged for unsportsmanlike conduct after catching a 42-yard pass to the Saints' 3 with 11 minutes left and the Giants trailing 27-13. Calloway spiked the ball near fallen defensive back Carl Lee, whom he beat on the play, and New York eventually was forced to punt. The Giants went on to lose, 27-22.

Sub of the week: Atlanta quarterback Bobby Hebert, who entered after Jeff George sustained a concussion late in the third quarter, completed seven of nine passes for 79 yards and ran once for eight yards in an 89-yard drive that ended in his throwing for the game-winning touchdown, a 13-yard pass to Ricky Sanders with 3:14 left.

Comeback of the week: Chicago scored 10 points in the fourth quarter to beat Buffalo, 20-13. Steve Walsh completed 19 of 28 passes and scored the game-winning touchdown on a one-yard run with 11:25 left.

Blowout of the week: Dallas scored on five of its first six possessions en route to a 34-7 rout of Washington. It hardly mattered that Emmitt Smith, whose two touchdown runs helped the Cowboys to a commanding 31-0 halftime lead, sat out the second half because of a sore hamstring. The Redskins, in rookie quarterback Heath Shuler's first NFL start, mustered only 110 total yards, 14 in the first half.

Nail-biter of the week: Thanks to Packers mistakes in the final minutes, New England nipped visiting Green Bay, 17-16, on Matt Bahr's 33-yard field goal with four seconds left. After Reggie Cobb scored on a one-yard run with 1:14 to play, Green Bay botched the extra point when holder Craig Hentrich couldn't handle a low snap from Frank Winters, preventing Chris Jacke from getting a kick away. Then, on the ensuing kickoff, Jacke booted the ball out of bounds, giving the Patriots possession on their 40 with 1:04 left. Drew Bledsoe drove the Patriots 45 yards in 11 plays to set up Bahr's winning kick.

Hit of the week: By Indianapolis nose tackle Tony Siragusa, who sacked Seattle quarterback Rick Mirer on a fourth-down play after the Seahawks, trailing by two points with five minutes left, had driven to the Colts' 33.

Oddity of the week: For the first time in their 18-year history, the Tampa Bay Buccaneers returned a punt or a kickoff for a touchdown. Vernon Turner (80 yards against Detroit) did the honors on the 705th punt return in Bucs' history and the 1,320th punt by a Tampa Bay opponent.

Top rusher: Barry Sanders rushed for 166 yards on 20 carries in Detroit's 24-14 loss to Tampa Bay.

Top passer: Warren Moon completed 29 of 47 passes for 355 yards and one touchdown in Minnesota's 17-7 loss to Arizona.

Top receiver: Cris Carter caught 14 of Moon's passes for 167 yards.

Notes: San Francisco's 40-8 loss to Philadelphia was its worst in George Seifert's six years as coach and the 49ers' worst since a 49-3 shellacking by the Giants in an NFC playoff game on January 4, 1987. Quarterback Steve Young, taking a beating behind a patchwork offensive line missing three starters, was benched with the 49ers trailing 33-8 in the third period. . . . Indianapolis defensive tackle Steve Emtman played in his first game since tearing two ligaments and a tendon in his right knee in a game against Dallas on October 10, 1993. Emtman was in for 20 plays against Seattle and dumped running back Chris Warren for a 5-yard loss on his first play. . . . Sterling Sharpe caught nine passes against New England to surpass James Lofton (533-530) as the Packers' all-time leading receiver. . . . Cleveland was 4-1 for the first time since 1979, but it is worth noting that the Browns' four victims (the Bengals, Cardinals, Colts and Jets) entered Week 5 with a cumulative record of 3-12.... The Miami-Cincinnati game marked the first time in major pro sports history that a father and son coached against each another. Don Shula's Dolphins beat Dave Shula's Bengals, 23-7, and Cincinnati didn't help the younger Shula's cause by committing turnovers on all five of its second-half possessions.... Detroit's Jason Hanson had been successful on 44 consecutive field-goal attempts inside 42 yards before missing a 26-yarder against Tampa Bay.

Quote of the week: Rams Coach Chuck Knox, on seldom-used quarterback Tommy Maddox, whom Knox was forced to play after injuries sidelined Chris Miller and Chris Chandler: "He played about like you would think somebody would play who hasn't played."

GAME SUMMARIES

BROWNS 27, JETS 7

Sunday, October 2

N.Y. Jets	0	0	0	7 — 7	
Cleveland	7	17	3	0 — 27	

First Quarter
Cle—Metcalf 37 run (Stover kick), 14:10.
Second Quarter
Cle—FG Stover 23, 4:19.
Cle—Byner 1 run (Stover kick), 12:08.
Cle—Hoard 18 run (Stover kick), 13:55.
Third Quarter
Cle—FG Stover 45, 10:02.
Fourth Quarter
N.Y.—Moore 24 pass from Trudeau (Lowery kick), 8:05.

TEAM STATISTICS

	N.Y. Jets	Cleveland
First downs	19	18
Rushes-yards	19-72	26-117
Passing	274	246
Punt returns-yards	5-25	2-1
Kickoff returns-yards	5-101	1-20
Interception returns-yards	0-0	2-33
Comp.-att.-int.	28-46-2	21-36-0
Sacked-yards lost	2-14	1-11
Punts-average	8-39	7-49
Fumbles-lost	1-1	1-0
Penalties-yards	6-56	4-25
Time of possession	31:49	28:11
Attendance—76,188.		

INDIVIDUAL STATISTICS
RUSHING—New York, J. Johnson 12-34, Murrell 4-28, Baxter 2-8, Trudeau 1-2. Cleveland, Metcalf 5-44, Hoard 6-30, Alexander 1-25, Byner 9-15, Testaverde 5-3.
PASSING—New York, Trudeau 28-46-2-288. Cleveland, Testaverde 21-36-0-257.
RECEIVING—New York, Monk 6-55, Mitchell 5-79, R. Moore 5-78, J. Johnson 3-15, A. Johnson 2-16, Yarborough 2-16, Baxter 2-11, Anderson 2-7, Murrell 1-11. Cleveland, Alexander 7-105, Hoard 6-40, Metcalf 4-32, R. Smith 1-50, Kinchen 1-14, McCardell 1-13, Byner 1-3.
MISSED FIELD GOAL ATTEMPTS—None.
INTERCEPTIONS—Cleveland, Turner 1-32, Jacobs 1-1.
KICKOFF RETURNS—New York, Prior 5-101. Cleveland, Metcalf 1-2.
PUNT RETURNS—New York, Hicks 3-17, A. Johnson 2-8. Cleveland, Metcalf 2-1.
SACKS—New York, Houston 1. Cleveland, Turner 1, Burnett 1.

COLTS 17, SEAHAWKS 15

Sunday, October 2

Seattle	5	3	0	7 — 15	
Indianapolis	10	0	7	0 — 17	

First Quarter
Sea—FG Kasay 42, 2:52.
Ind—FG Biasucci 45, 7:32.
Sea—Safety, Harbaugh intentionally grounded ball in the end zone, 9:42.
Ind—Faulk 5 run (Biasucci kick), 13:39.
Second Quarter
Sea—FG Kasay 45, 14:48.
Third Quarter
Ind—Faulk 1 run (Biasucci kick), 9:11.
Fourth Quarter
Sea—Martin 30 pass from Mirer (Kasay kick), :38.

TEAM STATISTICS

	Seattle	Indianapolis
First downs	17	13
Rushes-yards	25-102	34-119
Passing	149	159
Punt returns-yards	3-10	3-14
Kickoff returns-yards	5-99	4-56
Interception returns-yards	0-0	1-0
Comp.-att.-int.	20-36-1	15-26-0
Sacked-yards lost	5-37	3-22
Punts-average	4-50	5-32
Fumbles-lost	1-1	1-1
Penalties-yards	8-35	8-48
Time of possession	27:28	32:32
Attendance—49,876.		

INDIVIDUAL STATISTICS
RUSHING—Seattle, C. Warren 23-81, Mirer 2-21. Indianapolis, Faulk 26-90, Potts 3-20, Harbaugh 4-11, Humphrey 1- (minus 2).
PASSING—Seattle, Mirer 20-36-1-186. Indianapolis, Harbaugh 15-26-0-181.
RECEIVING—Seattle, Martin 8-104, Blades 7-71, Warren 4-0, Bates 1-11. Indianapolis, Dawkins 5-99, Faulk 4-23, Potts 3-25, Turner 2-30, Cash 1-4.
MISSED FIELD GOAL ATTEMPTS—Seattle, Kasay 43.
INTERCEPTIONS—Indianapolis, Daniel 1-0.
KICKOFF RETURNS—Seattle, T. Warren 3-58, Bates 1-27, Martin 1-14. Indianapolis, Brewer 2-26, Humphrey 1-21, Etheredge 1-9.
PUNT RETURNS—Seattle, Martin 2-10, Bates 1-0. Indianapolis, Brewer 3-14.
SACKS—Seattle, Edwards 1, E. Robinson 1, McCrary 1. Indianapolis, Bennett 1½, Buchanan 1, Emtman 1, Siragusa 1, Noga ½.

COWBOYS 34, REDSKINS 7

Sunday, October 2

Dallas	7	24	3	0 — 34	
Washington	0	0	7	0 — 7	

First Quarter
Dal—E. Smith 4 run (Boniol kick), 6:10.
Second Quarter
Dal—E. Smith 6 run (Boniol kick), :03.
Dal—FG Boniol 28, 4:38.
Dal—Novacek 3 pass from Aikman (Boniol kick), 10:48.
Dal—Coleman 7 run (Boniol kick), 13:50.
Third Quarter
Dal—FG Boniol 47, 8:29.
Was—Wycheck 8 pass from Shuler (Lohmiller kick), 13:42.

TEAM STATISTICS

	Dallas	Washington
First downs	26	12
Rushes-yards	46-142	18-28
Passing	181	82
Punt returns-yards	5-57	1-58
Kickoff returns-yards	2-48	7-150
Interception returns-yards	1-4	1-2
Comp.-att.-int.	20-28-1	11-30-1
Sacked-yards lost	0-0	2-14
Punts-average	4-43	6-45
Fumbles-lost	1-0	4-3
Penalties-yards	9-95	8-85
Time of possession	40:01	19:59
Attendance—55,394.		

INDIVIDUAL STATISTICS
RUSHING—Dallas, Coleman 22-74, E. Smith 16-48, Johnston 3-17, Agee 2-3, Aikman 3-0. Washington, Mitchell 2-10, Ervins 7-9, Brooks 5-5, Shuler 4-4.
PASSING—Dallas, Aikman 20-28-1-181. Washington, Shuler 11-30-1-96.

RECEIVING—Dallas, Irvin 5-49, Johnston 5-43, Williams 3-23, Novacek 2-8, Coleman 2-7, E. Smith 2-5, Harper 1-46. Washington, Ellard 3-51, Winans 2-19, Mitchell 2-11, Ervins 2-5, Wycheck 1-8, Horton 1-2.
MISSED FIELD GOAL ATTEMPTS—None.
INTERCEPTIONS—Dallas, J. Washington 1-1, Holmes 0-3. Washington, Carter 1-2.
KICKOFF RETURNS—Dallas, K. Williams 2-48. Washington, Mitchell 6-130, Wycheck 1-20.
PUNT RETURNS—Dallas, K. Williams 5-57. Washington, Mitchell 1-58.
SACKS—Dallas, D. Smith 2.

BUCCANEERS 24, LIONS 14
Sunday, October 2

Detroit	0	14	0	0	—14
Tampa Bay	10	7	7	0	—24

First Quarter
T.B.—FG Husted 23, 8:15.
T.B.—Turner 80 punt return (Husted kick), 10:12.
Second Quarter
T.B.—Wilson 35 pass from Erickson (Husted kick), :59.
Det—Mitchell 5 run (Hanson kick), 5:49.
Det—D. Moore 5 run (Hanson kick), 10:24.
Third Quarter
T.B.—Rhett 1 run (Husted kick), 8:59.

TEAM STATISTICS

	Detroit	Tampa Bay
First downs	17	16
Rushes-yards	24-196	38-119
Passing	125	115
Punt returns-yards	0-0	3-92
Kickoff returns-yards	4-100	3-51
Interception returns-yards	0-0	0-0
Comp.-att.-int.	13-30-0	10-20-0
Sacked-yards lost	1-5	1-7
Punts-average	5-36	4-44
Fumbles-lost	1-1	1-0
Penalties-yards	12-66	11-75
Time of possession	25:04	34:56
Attendance—38,012.		

INDIVIDUAL STATISTICS

RUSHING—Detroit, Sanders 20-166, Perriman 2-20, Mitchell 1-5, D. Moore 1-5. Tampa Bay, Rhett 20-62, Workman 6-31, Turner 3-15, McDowell 3-12, Erickson 3-0, Royster 3-(minus 1).
PASSING—Detroit, Mitchell 13-30-0-130. Tampa Bay, Erickson 10-20-0-122.
RECEIVING—Detroit, Perriman 7-67, H. Moore 3-44, Sanders 2-10, Holman 1-9. Tampa Bay, Wilson 4-58, Copeland 1-19, Harris 1-14, Moore 1-13, Hawkins 1-9, Rhett 1-5, Armstrong 1-4.
MISSED FIELD GOAL ATTEMPTS—Detroit, Hanson 26. Tampa Bay, Husted 55.
INTERCEPTIONS—None.
KICKOFF RETURNS—Detroit, Gray 4-100. Tampa Bay, Turner 1-19, Culpepper 1-18, Buckley 1-14.
PUNT RETURNS—Tampa Bay, Turner 3-92.
SACKS—Detroit, Swilling 1. Tampa Bay, K. Wilson 1.

PATRIOTS 17, PACKERS 16
Sunday, October 2

Green Bay	3	7	0	6	—16
New England	0	0	7	10	—17

First Quarter
G.B.—FG Jacke 27, 8:58.
Second Quarter
G.B.—Sharpe 11 pass from Favre (Jacke kick), 8:20.
Third Quarter
N.E.—Brisby 10 pass from Bledsoe (Bahr kick), 11:45.
Fourth Quarter
N.E.—Brisby 37 pass from Bledsoe (Bahr kick), 1:27.
G.B.—Cobb 1 run (kick failed), 13:46.
N.E.—FG Bahr 33, 14:56.

TEAM STATISTICS

	Green Bay	New England
First downs	20	21
Rushes-yards	27-100	17-48
Passing	264	312
Punt returns-yards	7-34	7-63
Kickoff returns-yards	4-62	2-41

	Green Bay	New England
Interception returns-yards	1-7	2-14
Comp.-att.-int.	25-47-2	29-53-1
Sacked-yards lost	4-30	2-22
Punts-average	9-40	8-42
Fumbles-lost	2-0	1-1
Penalties-yards	8-69	3-15
Time of possession	33:33	26:27
Attendance—57,522.		

INDIVIDUAL STATISTICS

RUSHING—Green Bay, Cobb 16-68, Favre 2-12, Bennett 5-11, L. Johnson 4-9. New England, Thompson 5-21, Butts 7-10, Bledsoe 2-9, Thomas 2-5, Turner 1-3.
PASSING—Green Bay, Favre 25-47-2-294. New England, Bledsoe 29-53-1-334.
RECEIVING—Green Bay, Sharpe 9-132, Bennett 4-22, Brooks 3-35, Cobb 3-10, Lewis 2-42, Morgan 2-31, West 2-22. New England, Brisby 6-117, Coates 6-87, Thompson 5-39, Turner 4-31, Timpson 4-29, Crittenden 3-25, Thomas 1-6.
MISSED FIELD GOAL ATTEMPTS—New England, Bahr 48, 32.
INTERCEPTIONS—Green Bay, Strickland 1-7. New England, R. Smith 1-10, V. Brown 1-4.
KICKOFF RETURNS—Green Bay, Harris 1-33, Levens 1-15, J. Jurkovic 1-14, Jordan 1-0. New England, Crittenden 2-41.
PUNT RETURNS—Green Bay, Brooks 7-34. New England, Crittenden 7-63.
SACKS—Green Bay, Paup 1, White 1. New England, Slade 2½, Goad 1, M. Jones ½.

SAINTS 27, GIANTS 22
Sunday, October 2

N.Y. Giants	3	10	0	9	—22
New Orleans	3	14	3	7	—27

First Quarter
N.Y.—FG Treadwell 41, 9:01.
N.O.—FG Andersen 29, 14:39.
Second Quarter
N.Y.—Sherrard 10 pass from Da. Brown (Treadwell kick), 7:10.
N.Y.—FG Treadwell 32, 9:53.
N.O.—Early 4 pass from Everett (Andersen kick), 13:04.
N.O.—James Williams 33 interception return (Andersen kick), 14:00.
Third Quarter
N.O.—FG Andersen 32, 4:23.
Fourth Quarter
N.O.—Derek Brown 3 run (Andersen kick), 1:25.
N.Y.—FG Treadwell 35, 6:58.
N.Y.—Sherrard 3 pass from Da. Brown (run failed), 12:56.

TEAM STATISTICS

	N.Y. Giants	New Orleans
First downs	11	15
Rushes-yards	21-50	28-67
Passing	152	247
Punt returns-yards	4-60	2-28
Kickoff returns-yards	4-86	4-98
Interception returns-yards	1-34	2-33
Comp.-att.-int.	20-35-2	20-30-1
Sacked-yards lost	7-28	1-2
Punts-average	6-49	6-45
Fumbles-lost	2-0	2-2
Penalties-yards	4-30	5-49
Time of possession	29:16	30:44
Attendance—55,076.		

INDIVIDUAL STATISTICS

RUSHING—New York, Meggett 16-40, Rasheed 2-7, Marshall 1-2, Da. Brown 2-1. New Orleans, Derek Brown 22-64, Neal 1-5, Ned 1-3, Everett 4-(minus 5).
PASSING—New York, Da. Brown 20-35-2-180. New Orleans, Everett 20-30-1-249.
RECEIVING—New York, Sherrard 6-48, Meggett 5-35, Cross 3-66, Calloway 3-18, Pierce 2-10, Marshall 1-3. New Orleans, Smith 6-42, Early 3-43, Haynes 2-68, Walls 2-37, Ned 2-21, Small 2-21, Derek Brown 2-10, W. Williams 1-7.
MISSED FIELD GOAL ATTEMPTS—None.
INTERCEPTIONS—New York, Booty 1-34. New Orleans, Williams 1-33, Spencer 1-0.
KICKOFF RETURNS—New York, Lewis 4-86. New Orleans, Hughes 4-98.
PUNT RETURNS—New York, Lewis 4-60. New Orleans, Hughes 2-28.
SACKS—New York, Hamilton 1. New Orleans, Martin 2, Conner 2, Johnson 1, Legette 1, Mills 1.

FALCONS 8, RAMS 5

Sunday, October 2

Atlanta	0	0	0	8— 8
L.A. Rams	0	2	3	0— 5

Second Quarter
L.A.—Safety, Gilbert tackled George in the end zone, 8:27.
Third Quarter
L.A.—FG Zendejas 28, 8:58.
Fourth Quarter
Atl—Sanders 13 pass from Hebert (Mathis pass from Hebert), 11:46.

TEAM STATISTICS

	Atlanta	L.A. Rams
First downs	23	16
Rushes-yards	22-81	32-126
Passing	285	120
Punt returns-yards	2-6	2-26
Kickoff returns-yards	2-40	3-65
Interception returns-yards	2-16	1-51
Comp.-att.-int.	26-39-1	13-25-2
Sacked-yards lost	5-27	1-8
Punts-average	5-38	6-39
Fumbles-lost	2-0	1-0
Penalties-yards	7-42	6-41
Time of possession	28:58	31:02
Attendance—34,599.		

INDIVIDUAL STATISTICS

RUSHING—Atlanta, Pegram 13-45, Heyward 6-28, Hebert 2-7, George 1-1. Los Angeles, Bettis 29-117, Lang 2-8, Maddox 1-1.
PASSING—Atlanta, George 16-25-1-190, Hebert 10-14-0-122. Los Angeles, Chandler 6-10-0-42, Maddox 7-15-2-86.
RECEIVING—Atlanta, Emanuel 6-86, Sanders 6-58, Mathis 4-50, Rison 4-34, Lyons 3-29, Heyward 2-27, Pegram 1-28. Los Angeles, Bailey 5-54, Anderson 3-32, Hester 2-16, Bruce 1-16, Bettis 1-6, Drayton 1-4.
MISSED FIELD GOAL ATTEMPTS—Atlanta, N. Johnson 51.
INTERCEPTIONS—Atlanta, Ross 1-16, D. Johnson 1-0. Los Angeles, Pope 1-1.
KICKOFF RETURNS—Atlanta, Pegram 1-25, Verdin 1-15. Los Angeles, J. Bailey 2-44, Brantley 1-21.
PUNT RETURNS—Atlanta, Verdin 2-6. Los Angeles, J. Bailey 2-26.
SACKS—Atlanta, Geathers 1. Los Angeles, Conlan 1, Gilbert 1, Young 1, Phifer 1, Farr 1.

BEARS 20, BILLS 13

Sunday, October 2

Buffalo	3	3	7	0—13
Chicago	0	7	3	10—20

First Quarter
Buf—FG Christie 28, 7:34.
Second Quarter
Chi—Gedney 13 pass from Walsh (Butler kick), 6:20.
Buf—FG Christie 30, 14:39.
Third Quarter
Chi—FG Butler 50, 3:37.
Buf—Metzelaars 15 pass from Kelly (Christie kick), 4:51.
Fourth Quarter
Chi—Walsh 1 run (Butler kick), 3:35.
Chi—FG Butler 20, 11:52.

TEAM STATISTICS

	Buffalo	Chicago
First downs	13	17
Rushes-yards	22-105	42-111
Passing	99	150
Punt returns-yards	2-57	1-12
Kickoff returns-yards	5-85	4-81
Interception returns-yards	1-0	2-5
Comp.-att.-int.	19-33-2	19-28-1
Sacked-yards lost	2-17	2-10
Punts-average	6-45	5-37
Fumbles-lost	1-1	0-0
Penalties-yards	10-60	3-30
Time of possession	20:35	39:25
Attendance—62,406.		

INDIVIDUAL STATISTICS

RUSHING—Buffalo, K. Davis 18-78, Kelly 2-19, Gardner 2-8. Chicago, Tillman 19-48, Harris 11-45, Conway 1-9, Worley 4-8, Hoge 1-4, Green 1-1, Walsh 5-(minus 4).

PASSING—Buffalo, Kelly 19-33-2-116. Chicago, Walsh 19-28-1-160.
RECEIVING—Buffalo, K. Davis 7-23, Metzelaars 3-25, Reed 3-25, Bl. Brooks 3-21, Beebe 2-14, Copeland 1-8. Chicago, Graham 5-63, Conway 4-38, Harris 4-16, Gedney 2-19, Cook 2-13, Waddle 1-7, Hoge 1-4.
MISSED FIELD GOAL ATTEMPTS—None.
INTERCEPTIONS—Buffalo, Washington 1-0. Chicago, Lincoln 1-5, Woolford 1-0.
KICKOFF RETURNS—Buffalo, Copeland 3-53, Jourdain 2-32. Chicago, Lewis 3-69, Flanigan 1-12.
PUNT RETURNS—Buffalo, Burris 2-57. Chicago, Conway 1-12.
SACKS—Buffalo, Smith 1½, Bennett ½. Chicago, Armstrong 1, Spellman 1.

EAGLES 40, 49ERS 8

Sunday, October 2

Philadelphia	14	16	3	7—40
San Francisco	0	8	0	0— 8

First Quarter
Phi—Garner 1 run (Murray kick), 6:23.
Phi—Garner 28 run (Murray kick), 6:45.
Second Quarter
Phi—Safety, Fuller tackled Young in the end zone, :44.
Phi—Bailey 28 pass from Cunningham (Murray kick), 3:06.
S.F.—Young 1 run (Jones pass from Young), 10:35.
Phi—Walker 2 run (Murray kick), 13:45.
Third Quarter
Phi—FG Murray 36, 9:33.
Fourth Quarter
Phi—Bavaro 18 pass from Cunningham (Murray kick), 2:56.

TEAM STATISTICS

	Philadelphia	San Francisco
First downs	26	11
Rushes-yards	41-191	18-60
Passing	246	129
Punt returns-yards	1-17	1-6
Kickoff returns-yards	3-63	7-118
Interception returns-yards	2-11	0-0
Comp.-att.-int.	20-29-0	15-31-2
Sacked-yards lost	0-0	3-22
Punts-average	3-40	4-38
Fumbles-lost	0-0	2-1
Penalties-yards	10-75	4-41
Time of possession	39:16	20:44
Attendance—64,771.		

INDIVIDUAL STATISTICS

RUSHING—Philadelphia, Garner 16-111, Hebron 10-39, Walker 5-20, Cunningham 6-14, Joseph 4-7. San Francisco, Watters 7-22, Floyd 5-19, Loville 2-13, Young 3-5, Taylor 1-1.
PASSING—Philadelphia, Cunningham 20-29-0-246. San Francisco, Young 11-23-2-99, Grbac 4-8-0-52.
RECEIVING—Philadelphia, C. Williams 9-122, Bavaro 3-38, Hebron 2-12, Walker 2-8, Bailey 1-28, Garner 1-28, Barnett 1-5, Johnson 1-5. San Francisco, Rice 6-66, Singleton 2-31, Jones 2-14, Logan 2-6, Watters 1-14, Popson 1-13, Floyd 1-7.
MISSED FIELD GOAL ATTEMPTS—None.
INTERCEPTIONS—Philadelphia, Allen 1-11, Harmon 1-0.
KICKOFF RETURNS—Philadelphia, Sydner 3-63. San Francisco, Carter 5-86, Singleton 1-17, Loville 1-15.
PUNT RETURNS—Philadelphia, Sydner 2-17. San Francisco, Carter 1-6.
SACKS—Philadelphia, Fuller 1, Grossman 1, Townsend 1.

CARDINALS 17, VIKINGS 7

Sunday, October 2

Minnesota	0	7	0	0— 7
Arizona	7	0	0	10—17

First Quarter
Ari—Ware 4 pass from Schroeder (Davis kick), 9:21.
Second Quarter
Min—Reed 15 pass from Moon (Reveiz kick), 5:35.
Fourth Quarter
Ari—FG Davis 46, :51.
Ari—Centers 6 run (Davis kick), 4:02.

TEAM STATISTICS

	Minnesota	Arizona
First downs	19	22
Rushes-yards	13-18	30-109
Passing	340	200

	Minnesota	Arizona
Punt returns-yards	1-12	2-15
Kickoff returns-yards	4-116	2-58
Interception returns-yards	1-15	2-34
Comp.-att.-int.	29-47-2	20-36-1
Sacked-yards lost	1-15	2-21
Punts-average	3-49	5-40
Fumbles-lost	3-2	1-1
Penalties-yards	8-60	11-79
Time of possession	27:21	32:39
Attendance—67,950.		

INDIVIDUAL STATISTICS

RUSHING—Minnesota, Allen 12-18, Saxon 1-0. Arizona, Moore 23-82, Centers 5-16, Schroeder 2-11.

PASSING—Minnesota, Moon 29-47-2-355. Arizona, Schroeder 20-36-1-221.

RECEIVING—Minnesota, Carter 14-167, Reed 7-66, Cooper 3-60, Jordan 2-23, Allen 1-23, Palmer 1-13, Novoselsky 1-3. Arizona, Centers 9-66, Reeves 3-37, Ware 3-25, Proehl 2-29, Hill 1-45, Clark 1-16, Moore 1-3.

MISSED FIELD GOAL ATTEMPTS—Minnesota, Reveiz 30, 47. Arizona, Davis 39.

INTERCEPTIONS—Minnesota, Glenn 1-15. Arizona, Williams 1-21, Joyner 1-0, Marshall 0-13.

KICKOFF RETURNS—Minnesota, Ismail 4-116. Arizona, Robinson 2-58.

PUNT RETURNS—Minnesota, Palmer 1-12. Arizona, Robinson 2-15.

SACKS—Minnesota, McDaniel 1, Randle 1. Arizona, E. Hill 1.

DOLPHINS 23, BENGALS 7
Sunday, October 2

Miami	0	10	7	6—23
Cincinnati	7	0	0	0— 7

First Quarter
Cin—Scott 51 pass from Klingler (Pelfrey kick), 1:32.
Second Quarter
Mia—FG Stoyanovich 28, :09.
Mia—Byars 11 pass from Marino (Stoyanovich kick), 13:46.
Third Quarter
Mia—Ingram 4 pass from Marino (Stoyanovich kick), 6:30.
Fourth Quarter
Mia—FG Stoyanovich 27, 9:02.
Mia—FG Stoyanovich 32, 12:19.

TEAM STATISTICS

	Miami	Cincinnati
First downs	21	14
Rushes-yards	37-141	17-62
Passing	204	184
Punt returns-yards	1-4	4-40
Kickoff returns-yards	2-44	6-137
Interception returns-yards	3-41	0-0
Comp.-att.-int.	26-35-0	16-30-3
Sacked-yards lost	0-0	1-4
Punts-average	5-39	4-40
Fumbles-lost	0-0	2-2
Penalties-yards	7-70	5-28
Time of possession	38:37	21:23
Attendance—55,056.		

INDIVIDUAL STATISTICS

RUSHING—Miami, Parmalee 18-73, Higgs 11-46, Saxon 2-13, McDuffie 1-12, Marino 4-(minus 2), Byars 1-(minus 1). Cincinnati, Fenner

4-19, Broussard 6-16, Klingler 2-16, Scott 2-14, Green 3-(minus 3).

PASSING—Miami, Marino 26-35-0-204. Cincinnati, Klingler 16-30-3-188.

RECEIVING—Miami, Fryar 8-89, Byars 6-54, Ingram 5-22, Jackson 3-35, Parmalee 3-(minus 2), M. Williams 1-6. Cincinnati, Broussard 7-43, Scott 2-62, Pickens 2-39, To. McGee 2-23, Ti. McGee 1-15, Fenner 1-4, Sadowski 1-2.

MISSED FIELD GOAL ATTEMPTS—Cincinnati, Pelfrey 47.

INTERCEPTIONS—Miami, Brown 1-38, Braxton 1-3, Beavers 1-0.

KICKOFF RETURNS—Miami, McDuffie 2-44. Cincinnati, Green 2-52, Ball 2-45, Scott 2-40.

PUNT RETURNS—Miami, McDuffie 1-4. Cincinnati, Sawyer 4-40.

SACKS—Miami, Coleman 1.

STEELERS 30, OILERS 14
Monday, October 3

Houston	0	0	0	14—14
Pittsburgh	20	3	0	7—30

First Quarter
Pit—FG Anderson 42, 4:51.
Pit—FG Anderson 25, 8:22.
Pit—E. Green 3 pass from O'Donnell (Anderson kick), 9:18.
Pit—Foster 1 run (Anderson kick), 13:11.
Second Quarter
Pit—FG Anderson 22, 11:17.
Fourth Quarter
Pit—B. Morris 2 run (Anderson kick), 5:13.
Hou—Givins 76 pass from Richardson (Del Greco kick), 5:49.
Hou—Jeffires 2 pass from Richardson (Del Greco kick), 14:55.

TEAM STATISTICS

	Houston	Pittsburgh
First downs	14	21
Rushes-yards	19-67	44-215
Passing	221	164
Punt returns-yards	0-0	5-28
Kickoff returns-yards	7-97	2-8
Interception returns-yards	0-0	0-0
Comp.-att.-int.	17-32-0	10-18-0
Sacked-yards lost	6-27	1-3
Punts-average	8-44	5-41
Fumbles-lost	5-2	0-0
Penalties-yards	5-48	6-45
Time of possession	24:28	35:32
Attendance—57,274.		

INDIVIDUAL STATISTICS

RUSHING—Houston, White 14-39, Richardson 4-28, Matthews 1-0. Pittsburgh, Foster 21-115, B. Morris 17-70, J.L. Williams 3-16, C. Johnson 1-7, Avery 1-5, O'Donnell 1-2.

PASSING—Houston, Carlson 3-7-0-18, Richardson 14-25-0-230. Pittsburgh, O'Donnell 9-17-0-154, Tomczak 1-1-0-13.

RECEIVING—Houston, Jeffires 6-77, Coleman 4-47, Slaughter 3-32, Givins 2-82, White 2-10. Pittsburgh, E. Green 3-35, Thigpen 2-25, J.L. Williams 2-14, Hastings 1-46, Mills 1-43, Foster 1-4.

MISSED FIELD GOAL ATTEMPTS—Houston, Del Greco 48.

INTERCEPTIONS—None.

KICKOFF RETURNS—Houston, Mills 4-63, Tillman 3-37. Pittsburgh, Woodson 1-18, Stone 1-(minus 10).

PUNT RETURNS—Pittsburgh, Woodson 5-28.

SACKS—Houston, Lathon 1. Pittsburgh, Greene 2, G. Williams 1½, Lloyd 1, Steed 1, Brown ½.

WEEK 6

Atlanta 34, Tampa Bay 13
Buffalo 21, Miami 11
Chicago 17, New Orleans 7
Dallas 38, Arizona 3
Denver 16, Seattle 9
Green Bay 24, L.A. Rams 17
L.A. Raiders 21, New England 17
N.Y. Jets 16, Indianapolis 6
Philadelphia 21, Washington 17
San Diego 20, Kansas City 6
San Francisco 27, Detroit 21
Minnesota 27, N.Y. Giants 10
 Open date: Cincinnati, Cleveland, Houston, Pittsburgh

STANDINGS

AFC EAST

	W	L	T	Pct.
Buffalo	4	2	0	.667
Miami	4	2	0	.667
New England	3	3	0	.500
N.Y. Jets	3	3	0	.500
Indianapolis	2	4	0	.333

AFC CENTRAL

	W	L	T	Pct.
Cleveland	4	1	0	.800
Pittsburgh	3	2	0	.600
Houston	1	4	0	.200
Cincinnati	0	5	0	.000

AFC WEST

	W	L	T	Pct.
San Diego	5	0	0	1.000
Kansas City	3	2	0	.600
Seattle	3	3	0	.500
L.A. Raiders	2	3	0	.400
Denver	1	4	0	.200

NFC EAST

	W	L	T	Pct.
Dallas	4	1	0	.800
Philadelphia	4	1	0	.800
N.Y. Giants	3	2	0	.600
Arizona	1	4	0	.200
Washington	1	5	0	.167

NFC CENTRAL

	W	L	T	Pct.
Chicago	4	2	0	.667
Minnesota	4	2	0	.667
Green Bay	3	3	0	.500
Detroit	2	4	0	.333
Tampa Bay	2	4	0	.333

NFC WEST

	W	L	T	Pct.
Atlanta	4	2	0	.667
San Francisco	4	2	0	.667
L.A. Rams	2	4	0	.333
New Orleans	2	4	0	.333

HIGHLIGHTS

Hero of the week: Los Angeles Raiders cornerback Terry McDaniel, who had three interceptions in a 21-17 victory over New England. McDaniel returned one interception 14 yards for a touchdown and set up the game-winning touchdown with another. He also had two tackles and three assists.

Goat of the week: New York Giants quarterback Dave Brown, who had an interception returned for a touchdown for the second straight game. This time, Brown threw an ill-advised pass on the fourth play of the third quarter that Anthony Parker returned 44 yards for a Minnesota touchdown. The game was tied at the time of the interception, and the Vikings went on to win 27-10.

Sub of the week: San Francisco fullback William Floyd, a rookie from Florida State, scored two touchdowns and caught five passes in the 49ers' 27-21 victory over Detroit. Floyd, who replaced Marc Logan in the starting lineup, was making his first NFL start.

Comeback of the week: Green Bay scored 21 consecutive points in the second half to upend the Los Angeles Rams, 24-17. Robert Brooks' 85-yard punt return for a touchdown tied it midway through the third quarter, and the Packers' defense held the Rams without a first down in the time it took Green Bay to score its three touchdowns.

Blowout of the week: Dallas crushed Arizona, 38-3, in the most lopsided game between the teams since 1973. The Cowboys' top-rated defense intercepted three Jay Schroeder passes in the first half—all resulting in touchdowns—and the Cardinals didn't take a snap in Dallas territory until 4:15 remained in the third quarter.

Nail-biter of the week: Rookie cornerback Lenny McGill sealed the Packers' victory over the Rams by intercepting a Chris Miller pass in the end zone with a minute left.

Hit of the week: By Buffalo's Mark Pike, who knocked the ball loose from Miami punt returner O.J. McDuffie late in the third period of a game the Bills led, 7-3. Bucky Brooks recovered for Buffalo on Miami's 26, and Thurman Thomas scored the Bills' second touchdown on the next play.

Oddity of the week: Buffalo's victory over Miami marked the first time the home team won in the past seven meetings between the two teams.

Top rusher: Natrone Means carried 19 times for a career-high 125 yards and one touchdown in San Diego's 20-6 victory over Kansas City.

Top passer: Drew Bledsoe completed 23 of 55 passes for 321 yards and two touchdowns in New England's loss to the Raiders.

Top receiver: Michael Irvin caught eight passes for 136 yards and one touchdown in Dallas' rout of Arizona.

Notes: After six weeks, San Diego was the league's only unbeaten team and Cincinnati its only winless one.... The Chargers snapped an eight-game regular-season losing streak against Kansas City.... Because of a college game played in a downpour at Soldier Field the night before, the field conditions for the Saints-Bears game were awful. Workers spread sand on the muddy field to enhance the players' traction, but it probably made things worse.... Denver won for the first time in seven games.... Dan Marino's 46.5 completion percentage against Buffalo (20 of 43) was his lowest in five years.... The Jets beat the Colts at home for the first time since 1988.... Cardinals Coach Buddy Ryan had won seven consecutive games against Dallas before the Cowboys' romp in Week 6.... The Raiders and Patriots combined to turn the ball over five times on six consecutive possessions.... Joe Montana matched his career high with 37 completions in Kansas City's loss at San Diego. His 55 attempts were the third-highest total of his career. Despite those numbers, the Chiefs went three-plays-and-punt on five of their 11 possessions.... Bears wide receiver Jeff Graham caught the second touchdown pass of his NFL career against New Orleans. His previous touchdown catch came 103 receptions earlier, in

1992 when he was with the Steelers. . . . The New York Giants retired former linebacking great Lawrence Taylor's No. 56 at halftime of their Monday night game against Minnesota. Taylor, who was voted to a record 10 consecutive Pro Bowls from his rookie season of 1981 through 1990, became the eighth Giant to have his number retired.

Quote of the week: Dallas Coach Barry Switzer, after his team's easy win over Arizona: "Sometimes you eat the bear and sometimes the bear eats you. Today, we ate the bear."

GAME SUMMARIES

JETS 16, COLTS 6

Sunday, October 9

Indianapolis	3	3	0	0— 6
N.Y. Jets	0	6	0	10—16

First Quarter
Ind—FG Biasucci 37, 7:26.
Second Quarter
N.Y.—FG Lowery 27, 2:06.
Ind—FG Biasucci 44, 9:52.
N.Y.—FG Lowery 42, 14:05.
Fourth Quarter
N.Y.—FG Lowery 37, 8:37.
N.Y.—Mitchell 1 pass from Esiason (Lowery kick), 12:34.

TEAM STATISTICS

	Indianapolis	N.Y. Jets
First downs	10	14
Rushes-yards	29-141	41-150
Passing	90	100
Punt returns-yards	2-20	3-22
Kickoff returns-yards	5-94	3-62
Interception returns-yards	1-1	0-0
Comp.-att.-int.	12-21-0	13-29-1
Sacked-yards lost	1-5	1-8
Punts-average	5-44	5-42
Fumbles-lost	5-4	0-0
Penalties-yards	4-25	7-45
Time of possession	25:51	34:09
Attendance—66,244.		

INDIVIDUAL STATISTICS
RUSHING—Indianapolis, Faulk 20-93, Harbaugh 7-44, Potts 1-3, Humphrey 1-1. New York, J. Johnson 21-74, Murrell 10-65, B. Baxter 4-11, Esiason 5-0, Trudeau 1-0.
PASSING—Indianapolis, Harbaugh 12-21-0-95. New York, Trudeau 4-10-1-30, Esiason 9-19-0-78.
RECEIVING—Indianapolis, Faulk 4-26, Turner 4-22, Dawkins 2-30, Potts 2-17. New York, Moore 5-46, J. Johnson 2-15, B. Baxter 2-2, Monk 1-23, Murrell 1-12, S. Anderson 1-9, Mitchell 1-1.
MISSED FIELD GOAL ATTEMPTS—Indianapolis, Biasucci 35.
INTERCEPTIONS—Indianapolis, Humphries 1-1.
KICKOFF RETURNS—Indianapolis, Humphrey 4-79, Brewer 1-15. New York, Prior 2-44, Murrell 1-18.
PUNT RETURNS—Indianapolis, Brewer 2-20. New York, Hicks 3-22.
SACKS—Indianapolis, Bennett 1. New York, Casillas ½, Lewis ½.

49ERS 27, LIONS 21

Sunday, October 9

San Francisco	0	14	7	6—27
Detroit	7	7	0	7—21

First Quarter
Det—Perriman 33 pass from Mitchell (Hanson kick), 7:20.
Second Quarter
Det—Sanders 9 run (Hanson kick), 3:18.
S.F.—Floyd 1 run (Brien kick), 5:36.
S.F.—Watters 4 run (Brien kick), 12:43.
Third Quarter
S.F.—Floyd 1 run (Brien kick), 1:58.
Fourth Quarter
S.F.—Singleton 5 pass from Young (kick failed), 5:48.
Det—Moore 26 pass from Mitchell (Hanson kick), 11:34.

TEAM STATISTICS

	San Francisco	Detroit
First downs	20	21
Rushes-yards	32-90	25-98
Passing	143	242
Punt returns-yards	2-25	2-24
Kickoff returns-yards	4-98	5-151
Interception returns-yards	1-38	0-0
Comp.-att.-int.	19-26-0	18-27-1
Sacked-yards lost	2-9	2-4
Punts-average	4-55	3-52
Fumbles-lost	1-0	4-1
Penalties-yards	10-70	12-101
Time of possession	31:25	28:35
Attendance—77,340.		

INDIVIDUAL STATISTICS
RUSHING—San Francisco, Watters 16-42, Floyd 8-35, Logan 3-16, Young 4-0, Rice 1-(minus 3). Detroit, Sanders 22-95, Perriman 1-6, Mitchell 2-(minus 3).
PASSING—San Francisco, Young 19-25-0-152, Grbac 0-1-0-0. Detroit, Mitchell 18-27-1-246.
RECEIVING—San Francisco, Floyd 5-43, Rice 5-36, Jones 2-29, Taylor 2-13, Watters 2-13, Singleton 2-10, McCaffrey 1-8. Detroit, Perriman 5-78, Holman 4-41, H. Moore 3-65, Sanders 3-16, Matthews 2-33, Hall 1-13.
MISSED FIELD GOAL ATTEMPTS—Detroit, Hanson 52.
INTERCEPTIONS—San Francisco, Hanks 1-38.
KICKOFF RETURNS—San Francisco, Carter 4-98. Detroit, Gray 5-151.
PUNT RETURNS—San Francisco, Carter 2-25. Detroit, Gray 2-24.
SACKS—San Francisco, Jackson 1, Kelly 1. Detroit, Pritchett 1, Thomas 1.

BILLS 21, DOLPHINS 11

Sunday, October 9

Miami	3	0	0	8—11
Buffalo	0	7	7	7—21

First Quarter
Mia—FG Stoyanovich 40, 4:01.
Second Quarter
Buf—Thomas 1 run (Christie kick), 5:01.
Third Quarter
Buf—Thomas 26 run (Christie kick), 14:40.
Fourth Quarter
Buf—K. Davis 5 run (Christie kick), 7:51.
Mia—McDuffie 3 pass from Marino (Jackson pass from Marino), 10:55.

TEAM STATISTICS

	Miami	Buffalo
First downs	19	25
Rushes-yards	19-114	48-214
Passing	212	130
Punt returns-yards	4-16	3-34
Kickoff returns-yards	4-50	3-57
Interception returns-yards	1-11	0-0
Comp.-att.-int.	20-43-0	13-22-1
Sacked-yards lost	0-0	0-0
Punts-average	6-42	5-37
Fumbles-lost	1-1	2-1
Penalties-yards	12-94	6-40
Time of possession	23:17	36:43
Attendance—79,491.		

INDIVIDUAL STATISTICS
RUSHING—Miami, Parmalee 15-91, Higgs 2-15, Byars 2-8. Buffalo, Thomas 31-125, K. Davis 7-35, Reed 1-19, Gardner 6-18, Kelly 3-17.
PASSING—Miami, Marino 20-43-0-212. Buffalo, Kelly 13-22-1-130.
RECEIVING—Miami, Byars 7-35, Fryar 4-58, Jackson 4-52, Ingram 2-24, McDuffie 2-21, Williams 1-22. Buffalo, Reed 7-82, Metzelaars 2-15, K. Davis 1-12, Beebe 1-11, Bl. Brooks 1-9, Thomas 1-1.
MISSED FIELD GOAL ATTEMPTS—Miami, Stoyanovich 37.
INTERCEPTIONS—Miami, Stewart 1-11.
KICKOFF RETURNS—Miami, McDuffie 2-26, M. Williams 1-9, R. Williams 1-15. Buffalo, Bu. Brooks 2-47, Copeland 1-10.
PUNT RETURNS—Miami, McDuffie 4-16. Buffalo, Burris 3-34.
SACKS—None.

PACKERS 24, RAMS 17

Sunday, October 9

L.A. Rams	7	10	0	0—17
Green Bay	3	0	14	7—24

First Quarter
L.A.—Drayton 2 pass from Miller (Zendejas kick), 5:43.
G.B.—FG Jacke 25, 14:33.
Second Quarter
L.A.—Drayton 4 pass from Miller (Zendejas kick), 2:56.
L.A.—FG Zendejas 37, 8:55.
Third Quarter
G.B.—Sharpe 8 pass from Favre (Jacke kick), 6:02.
G.B.—Brooks 85 punt return (Jacke kick), 7:18.
Fourth Quarter
G.B.—Bennett 1 run (Jacke kick), 2:54.

TEAM STATISTICS

	L.A. Rams	Green Bay
First downs	13	21
Rushes-yards	24-64	29-84
Passing	147	208
Punt returns-yards	3-24	6-141
Kickoff returns-yards	5-93	3-50
Interception returns-yards	1-20	1-0
Comp.-att.-int.	18-29-1	25-41-1
Sacked-yards lost	3-19	2-14
Punts-average	8-42	6-39
Fumbles-lost	4-1	2-1
Penalties-yards	5-35	4-64
Time of possession	27:29	32:31

Attendance—58,911.

INDIVIDUAL STATISTICS
RUSHING—Los Angeles, Bettis 22-65, Miller 2-(minus 1). Green Bay, Cobb 11-37, Bennett 12-28, Favre 5-18, Johnson 1-1.
PASSING—Los Angeles, Miller 18-29-1-166. Green Bay, Favre 25-41-1-222.
RECEIVING—Los Angeles, Anderson 4-73, Drayton 4-20, Hester 3-22, J. Bailey 3-14, Bruce 2-21, Bettis 1-10, Kinchen 1-6. Green Bay, Sharpe 7-62, Bennett 6-39, West 4-53, Brooks 3-40, Cobb 3-29, Lewis 1-3, Johnson 1-(minus 4).
MISSED FIELD GOAL ATTEMPTS—Green Bay, Jacke 49.
INTERCEPTIONS—Los Angeles, Henley 1-20. Green Bay, McGill 1-0.
KICKOFF RETURNS—Los Angeles, J. Bailey 3-48, Kinchen 1-37, Lester 1-8. Green Bay, Harris 3-50.
PUNT RETURNS—Los Angeles, J. Bailey 3-24. Green Bay, Brooks 4-122, Prior 2-19.
SACKS—Los Angeles, Kelly 1, Robinson 1. Green Bay, White 2, Jones 1.

BEARS 17, SAINTS 7
Sunday, October 9

New Orleans	0	7	0	0—	7
Chicago	0	0	10	7—	17

Second Quarter
N.O.—Early 18 pass from Everett (Andersen kick), 11:23.
Third Quarter
Chi—FG Butler 46, 3:21.
Chi—Graham 21 pass from Walsh (Butler kick), 12:36.
Fourth Quarter
Chi—Tillman 25 run (Butler kick), 12:29.

TEAM STATISTICS

	New Orleans	Chicago
First downs	17	16
Rushes-yards	25-107	32-131
Passing	209	174
Punt returns-yards	1-1	1-8
Kickoff returns-yards	4-66	2-16
Interception returns-yards	0-0	1-33
Comp.-att.-int.	22-40-1	16-26-0
Sacked-yards lost	0-0	0-0
Punts-average	2-50	3-37
Fumbles-lost	1-1	1-1
Penalties-yards	1-10	6-45
Time of possession	29:03	30:57

Attendance—63,822.

INDIVIDUAL STATISTICS
RUSHING—New Orleans, Neal 14-63, Brown 8-25, Everett 3-19. Chicago, Tillman 23-100, Harris 7-28, Worley 1-2, Green 1-1.
PASSING—New Orleans, Everett 22-39-1-209, Barnhardt 0-1-0-0. Chicago, Walsh 16-26-0-174.
RECEIVING—New Orleans, Haynes 8-84, Brown 4-34, Smith 4-32, Early 3-44, Walls 3-15. Chicago, Tillman 5-38, Graham 3-61, Gedney 3-30, Harris 3-18, Cook 1-18, Green 1-9.
MISSED FIELD GOAL ATTEMPTS—New Orleans, Andersen 50, 36. Chicago, Butler 36.

INTERCEPTIONS—Chicago, Gayle 1-33.
KICKOFF RETURNS—New Orleans, Hughes 4-66. Chicago, Lewis 1-18, Worley 1-(minus 2).
PUNT RETURNS—New Orleans, Hughes 1-1. Chicago, Conway 1-8.
SACKS—None.

FALCONS 34, BUCCANEERS 13
Sunday, October 9

Tampa Bay	0	3	0	10—	13
Atlanta	14	10	3	7—	34

First Quarter
Atl—Heyward 1 run (N. Johnson kick), 5:01.
Atl—Rison 36 pass from J. George (N. Johnson kick), 13:47.
Second Quarter
Atl—FG N. Johnson 27, 3:01.
Atl—Heyward 5 run (N. Johnson kick), 13:56.
T.B.—FG Husted 35, 15:00.
Third Quarter
Atl—FG N. Johnson 29, 6:01.
Fourth Quarter
T.B.—J. Harris 11 pass from Erickson (Husted kick), :49.
Atl—Mathis 32 pass from J. George (N. Johnson kick), 8:32.
T.B.—FG Husted 38, 15:00.

TEAM STATISTICS

	Tampa Bay	Atlanta
First downs	19	20
Rushes-yards	16-32	23-85
Passing	288	271
Punt returns-yards	2-8	3-7
Kickoff returns-yards	7-151	1-21
Interception returns-yards	2-26	3-95
Comp.-att.-int.	30-47-3	24-36-2
Sacked-yards lost	5-23	2-4
Punts-average	6-36	3-36
Fumbles-lost	2-0	2-1
Penalties-yards	4-52	5-45
Time of possession	32:06	27:54

Attendance—52,633.

INDIVIDUAL STATISTICS
RUSHING—Tampa Bay, Erickson 3-20, Rhett 6-14, Workman 7-(minus 2). Atlanta, Heyward 18-87, J. George 2-1, Alexander 1-0, Pegram 2-(minus 3).
PASSING—Tampa Bay, Erickson 18-30-0-172, Dilfer 6-11-3-81, Weldon 6-6-0-58. Atlanta, J. George 23-35-2-269, Hebert 1-1-0-6.
RECEIVING—Tampa Bay, J. Harris 6-58, Rhett 5-40, L. Thomas 4-59, McDowell 4-27, Royster 3-16, Hawkins 2-40, C. Wilson 2-34, Copeland 2-22, Armstrong 2-15. Atlanta, Rison 7-77, Sanders 6-72, Mathis 6-71, Heyward 3-37, Emanuel 2-18.
MISSED FIELD GOALS—None.
INTERCEPTIONS—Tampa Bay, Dimry 1-0, Everett 1-26. Atlanta, Clark 2-95, Ross 1-0.
KICKOFF RETURNS—Tampa Bay, Turner 7-151. Atlanta, Verdin 1-21.
PUNT RETURNS—Tampa Bay, Turner 2-8. Atlanta, Verdin 3-7.
SACKS—Tampa Bay, K. Wilson 1, Bussey ½, Curry ½. Atlanta, Doleman 1, Geathers 1, Goldberg 1, Matthews 1, C. Smith 1.

BRONCOS 16, SEAHAWKS 9
Sunday, October 9

Denver	3	7	6	0—	16
Seattle	0	3	3	3—	9

First Quarter
Den—FG Elam 26, 11:10.
Second Quarter
Sea—FG Kasay 37, 10:59.
Den—Elway 2 run (Elam kick), 14:17.
Third Quarter
Sea—FG Kasay 36, 5:58.
Den—FG Elam 33, 10:46.
Den—FG Elam 37, 11:52.
Fourth Quarter
Sea—FG Kasay 42, 5:37.

TEAM STATISTICS

	Denver	Seattle
First downs	19	16
Rushes-yards	44-150	20-94
Passing	128	244
Punt returns-yards	3-18	3-26

	Denver	Seattle
Kickoff returns-yards	4-81	5-83
Interception returns-yards	2-32	0-0
Comp.-att.-int.	15-29-0	19-39-2
Sacked-yards lost	2-18	0-0
Punts-average	6-44	4-49
Fumbles-lost	3-0	3-3
Penalties-yards	3-35	8-46
Time of possession	34:10	25:50

Attendance—63,872.

INDIVIDUAL STATISTICS

RUSHING—Denver, L. Russell 24-103, Rivers 10-24, Milburn 4-15, Campbell 1-6, Clark 1-4, Elway 4-(minus 2). Seattle, C. Warren 18-80, Mirer 1-11, S. Smith 1-3.

PASSING—Denver, Elway 15-29-0 146. Seattle, Mirer 19-39-2-244.

RECEIVING—Denver, Sharpe 7-87, Milburn 4-31, Evans 2-18, L. Russell 2-10. Seattle, Blades 6-90, C. Warren 6-41, Martin 3-37, Bates 1-39, S. Smith 1-25, Edmunds 1-8, Johnson 1-4.

MISSED FIELD GOAL ATTEMPTS—Denver, Elam 43.

INTERCEPTIONS—Denver, Atwater 1-24, Hilliard 1-8.

KICKOFF RETURNS—Denver, By'not'e 4-81. Seattle, Vaughn 3-50, Bates 2-33.

PUNT RETURNS—Denver, Milburn 3-18. Seattle, Martin 3-26.

SACKS—Seattle, Adams 1, Spitulski 1.

CHARGERS 20, CHIEFS 6

Sunday, October 9

Kansas City	0	3	0	3—	6
San Diego	3	10	0	7—	20

First Quarter
S.D.—FG Carney 23, 9:36.

Second Quarter
K.C.—FG Elliott 25, 5:14.
S.D.—FG Carney 32, 8:14.
S.D.—Means 9 run (Carney kick), 12:04.

Fourth Quarter
K.C.—FG Elliott 25, 1:48.
S.D.—Seay 5 pass from Humphries (Carney kick), 7:13.

TEAM STATISTICS

	Kansas City	San Diego
First downs	20	18
Rushes-yards	18-64	30-151
Passing	295	171
Punt returns-yards	4-17	3-34
Kickoff returns-yards	3-54	3-56
Interception returns-yards	0-0	1-23
Comp.-att.-int.	37-55-1	16-25-0
Sacked-yards lost	2-15	0-0
Punts-average	5-45	5-42
Fumbles-lost	1-1	1-1
Penalties-yards	8-49	1-05
Time of possession	30:35	29:25

Attendance—62,923.

INDIVIDUAL STATISTICS

RUSHING—Kansas City, Hill 5-45, Allen 10-17, Anders 3-2. San Diego, Means 19-125, Bieniemy 8-22, Humphries 2-5, Harmon 1-(minus 1).

PASSING—Kansas City, Montana 37-55-1-310. San Diego, Humphries 16-25-0-171.

RECEIVING—Kansas City, Allen 9-83, Birden 7-72, Anders 7-46, Walker 5-49, W. Davis 3-19, Hill 3-17, Cash 2-19, Penn 1-5. San Diego, Seay 6-38, Means 3-21, Jefferson 2-28, D. Young 2-27, Martin 1-48, Pupunu 1-5, Harmon 1-4.

MISSED FIELD GOAL ATTEMPTS—None.

INTERCEPTIONS—San Diego, Gordon 1-23.

KICKOFF RETURNS—Kansas City, Penn 3-54. San Diego, Martin 3-56.

PUNT RETURNS—Kansas City, Hughes 3-17, Carter 1-0. San Diego, Gordon 3-34.

SACKS—San Diego, Mims 1, L. Young 1.

COWBOYS 38, CARDINALS 3

Sunday, October 9

Arizona	0	0	3	0—	3
Dallas	21	7	10	0—	38

First Quarter
Dal—Johnston 2 pass from Aikman (Boniol kick), 6:38.
Dal—E. Smith 3 run (Boniol kick), 10:33.
Dal—E. Smith 1 run (Boniol kick), 14:22.

Second Quarter
Dal—Irvin 12 pass from Aikman (Boniol kick), 6:25.

Third Quarter
Dal—FG Boniol 19, 8:10.
Ari—FG Davis 42, 11:27.
Dal—K. Williams 87 kickoff return (Boniol kick), 11:44.

TEAM STATISTICS

	Arizona	Dallas
First downs	10	22
Rushes-yards	18-53	36-86
Passing	159	273
Punt returns-yards	1-0	2-11
Kickoff returns-yards	6-94	2-111
Interception returns-yards	0-0	5-31
Comp.-att.-int.	15-34-5	19-28-0
Sacked-yards lost	1-1	0-0
Punts-average	5-41	5-40
Fumbles-lost	0-0	2-0
Penalties-yards	10-92	5-35
Time of possession	24:45	35:15

Attendance—64,518.

INDIVIDUAL STATISTICS

RUSHING—Arizona, R. Moore 9-28, Centers 8-20, Beuerlein 1-5. Dallas, Coleman 20-57, E. Smith 9-22, Johnston 1-3, K. Williams 1-2, Peete 1-0, Wilson 1-(minus 1), Agee 2-(minus 2).

PASSING—Arizona, Schroeder 4-8-3-25, Beuerlein 11-26-2-135. Dallas, Aikman 16-22-0-231, Peete 3-6-0-42.

RECEIVING—Arizona, Clark 4-51, R. Hill 4-46, Proehl 3-38, Centers 2-13, Ware 1-10, R. Moore 1-2. Dallas, Irvin 8-136, Coleman 4-28, Novacek 3-38, Harper 2-58, E. Smith 1-11, Johnston 1-2.

MISSED FIELD GOAL ATTEMPTS—Dallas, Boniol 41.

INTERCEPTIONS—Dallas, Brown 2-14, Woodson 2-17, Washington 1-0.

KICKOFF RETURNS—Arizona, Robinson 5-75, McAfee 1-19. Dallas, K. Williams 2-111.

PUNT RETURNS—Arizona, Robinson 1-0. Dallas, K. Williams 2-11.

SACKS—Dallas, Jeffcoat 1.

RAIDERS 21, PATRIOTS 17

Sunday, October 9

L.A. Raiders	0	14	7	0—	21
New England	0	17	0	0—	17

Second Quarter
N.E.—FG Bahr 24, 2:02.
L.A.—McDaniel 14 interception return (Jaeger kick), 4:02.
N.E.—Turner 7 pass from Bledsoe (Bahr kick), 8:51.
N.E.—Thompson 3 pass from Bledsoe (Bahr kick), 13:05.
L.A.—H. Williams 27 pass from Hostetler (Jaeger kick), 14:18.

Third Quarter
L.A.—Hostetler 3 run (Jaeger kick), 5:26.

TEAM STATISTICS

	L.A. Raiders	New England
First downs	14	25
Rushes-yards	27-86	29-54
Passing	242	305
Punt returns-yards	3-60	2-15
Kickoff returns-yards	2-36	4-55
Interception returns-yards	3-44	3-1
Comp.-att.-int.	17-31-3	23-55-3
Sacked-yards lost	1-8	3-16
Punts-average	5-41	6-44
Fumbles-lost	1-1	2-1
Penalties-yards	11-70	7-63
Time of possession	25:42	34:18

Attendance—59,889.

INDIVIDUAL STATISTICS

RUSHING—Los Angeles, H. Williams 17-65, Rathman 4-13, Montgomery 3-7, Hostetler 3-1. New England, Thompson 11-19, Butts 10-15, Turner 4-11, Bledsoe 4-9.

PASSING—Los Angeles, Hostetler 17-31-3-250. New England, Bledsoe 23-55-3-321.

RECEIVING—Los Angeles, Glover 5-46, H. Williams 3-41, Rathman 3-23, T. Brown 2-46, Wright 2-42, Ismail 1-38, Montgomery 1-14. New England, Coates 9-123, Thompson 7-73, Brisby 3-56, Turner 3-45, Crittenden 1-24.

MISSED FIELD GOAL ATTEMPTS—None.

INTERCEPTIONS—Los Angeles, McDaniel 3-44. New England, Sabb 1-1, Hurst 1-0, Smith 1-0.

KICKOFF RETURNS—Los Angeles, Ismail 2-36. New England, Crittenden 2-39, Croom 1-16.

PUNT RETURNS—Los Angeles, T. Brown 3-60. New England, Crittenden 2-15.

SACKS—Los Angeles, A. Smith 2, Fredrickson 1. New England, Hurst 1.

EAGLES 21, REDSKINS 17
Sunday, October 9

Washington	0	6	11	0—17
Philadelphia	7	0	7	7—21

First Quarter
Phi—Cunningham 20 run (Murray kick), 12:20.
Second Quarter
Was—Winans 27 pass from Shuler (kick failed), 14:55.
Third Quarter
Was—Winans 41 pass from Shuler (Howard pass from Shuler), 8:14.
Phi—Barnett 49 pass from Cunningham (Murray kick), 11:06.
Was—FG Lohmiller 47, 12:13.
Fourth Quarter
Phi—Walker 2 run (Murray kick), 5:02.

TEAM STATISTICS

	Washington	Philadelphia
First downs	12	26
Rushes-yards	16-55	44-193
Passing	171	238
Punt returns-yards	1-4	3-18
Kickoff returns-yards	4-178	4-84
Interception returns-yards	2-3	1-0
Comp.-att.-int.	10-27-1	22-39-2
Sacked-yards lost	2-15	3-23
Punts-average	7-42	5-35
Fumbles-lost	2-1	1-0
Penalties-yards	3-20	8-97
Time of possession	16:49	43:11
Attendance—63,947.		

INDIVIDUAL STATISTICS

RUSHING—Washington, Ervins 12-42, Shuler 2-16, C. Smith 1-2, Ellard 1-(minus 5). Philadelphia, Garner 28-122, Joseph 6-30, Cunningham 6-23, Walker 4-18.

PASSING—Washington, Shuler 10-27-1-186. Philadelphia, Cunningham 22-39-2-261.

RECEIVING—Washington, Ervins 3-9, Winans 2-68, Howard 2-46, Ellard 2-43, Horton 1-20. Philadelphia, Walker 7-53, Barnett 4-90, C. Williams 3-52, M. Johnson 3-15, Bavaro 2-25, Garner 2-13, Joseph 1-13.

MISSED FIELD GOAL ATTEMPTS—None.

INTERCEPTIONS—Washington, Collins 1-3, Green 1-0. Philadelphia, Jackson 1-0.

KICKOFF RETURNS—Washington, Mitchell 3-135, Wycheck 1-43. Philadelphia, Sydner 3-71, Hebron 1-13.

PUNT RETURNS—Washington, Mitchell 1-4. Philadelphia, Sydner 3-18.

SACKS—Washington, Harvey 1, Wilson 1, Woods 1. Philadelphia, Romanowski 1, Fuller 1.

VIKINGS 27, GIANTS 10
Monday, October 10

Minnesota	3	7	14	3—27
N.Y. Giants	0	10	0	0—10

First Quarter
Min—FG Reveiz 44, 11:18.
Second Quarter
N.Y.—FG Treadwell 22, 1:24.
Min—Allen 1 run (Reveiz kick), 9:29.
N.Y.—D. Brown 3 run (Treadwell kick), 14:53.
Third Quarter
Min—Parker 44 interception return (Reveiz kick), 1:44.
Min—Carter 20 pass from Moon (Reveiz kick), 12:12.
Fourth Quarter
Min—FG Reveiz 24, 1:40.

TEAM STATISTICS

	Minnesota	N.Y. Giants
First downs	25	16
Rushes-yards	36-103	18-37
Passing	292	203
Punt returns-yards	2-7	1-11
Kickoff returns-yards	0-0	7-145
Interception returns-yards	3-67	1-0
Comp.-att.-int.	23-34-1	19-36-3
Sacked-yards lost	1-7	4-23
Punts-average	2-39	6-35
Fumbles-lost	3-1	0-0
Penalties-yards	8-50	4-36
Time of possession	35:30	24:30
Attendance—77,294.		

INDIVIDUAL STATISTICS

RUSHING—Minnesota, Allen 21-75, R. Smith 5-17, S. Graham 4-12, Moon 4-1, B. Johnson 2-(minus 2). New York, Hampton 13-27, D. Brown 3-14, Meggett 1-(minus 2), Rasheed 1-(minus 2).

PASSING—Minnesota, Moon 23-34-1-299. New York, D. Brown 19-36-3-226.

RECEIVING—Minnesota, Ismail 7-117, Allen 4-53, Carter 4-50, Reed 4-37, Jordan 3-36, Cooper 1-6. New York, Sherrard 4-49, Marshall 4-35, Calloway 3-48, Meggett 3-23, Lewis 2-33, Cross 2-28, Downs 1-10.

MISSED FIELD GOAL ATTEMPTS—Minnesota, Reveiz 53.

INTERCEPTIONS—Minnesota, Parker 1-44, Boyd 1-15, Glenn 1-8. New York, Williams 1-0.

KICKOFF RETURNS—New York, Lewis 5-108, Meggett 2-37.

PUNT RETURNS—Minnesota, Palmer 2-7. New York, Meggett 1-11.

SACKS—Minnesota, Randle 2, Thomas 1, Glenn 1. New York, Fox 1.

WEEK 7

RESULTS

Cleveland 11, Houston 8
Arizona 19, Washington 16 (OT)
Dallas 24, Philadelphia 13
Indianapolis 27, Buffalo 17
L.A. Rams 17, N.Y. Giants 10
Miami 20, L.A. Raiders 17 (OT)
N.Y. Jets 24, New England 17
Pittsburgh 14, Cincinnati 10
San Diego 36, New Orleans 22
San Francisco 42, Atlanta 3
Kansas City 31, Denver 28
　Open date: Chicago, Detroit, Green Bay,
Minnesota, Seattle, Tampa Bay

STANDINGS

AFC EAST	W	L	T	Pct.
Miami	5	2	0	.714
Buffalo	4	3	0	.571
N.Y. Jets	4	3	0	.571
Indianapolis	3	4	0	.429
New England	3	4	0	.429

AFC CENTRAL	W	L	T	Pct.
Cleveland	5	1	0	.833
Pittsburgh	4	2	0	.667
Houston	1	5	0	.167
Cincinnati	0	6	0	.000

AFC WEST	W	L	T	Pct.
San Diego	6	0	0	1.000
Kansas City	4	2	0	.667
Seattle	3	3	0	.500
L.A. Raiders	2	4	0	.333
Denver	1	5	0	.167

NFC EAST	W	L	T	Pct.
Dallas	5	1	0	.833
Philadelphia	4	2	0	.667
N.Y. Giants	3	3	0	.500
Arizona	2	4	0	.333
Washington	1	6	0	.143

NFC CENTRAL	W	L	T	Pct.
Chicago	4	2	0	.667
Minnesota	4	2	0	.667
Green Bay	3	3	0	.500
Detroit	2	4	0	.333
Tampa Bay	2	4	0	.333

NFC WEST	W	L	T	Pct.
San Francisco	5	2	0	.714
Atlanta	4	3	0	.571
L.A. Rams	3	4	0	.429
New Orleans	2	5	0	.286

HIGHLIGHTS

Hero of the week: Miami running back Bernie Parmalee, who rushed 30 times for 150 yards in the Dolphins' 20-17 overtime victory against the Raiders. Parmalee carried five times for 45 yards in overtime to set up Pete Stoyanovich's game-winning field goal, and he also made three tackles—two on special teams and one after an interception.

Goat of the week: Philadelphia quarterback Randall Cunningham, who was sacked four times and threw four interceptions in the Eagles' 24-13 loss to Dallas. Kenny Gant's interception of Cunningham set up the Cowboys' second touchdown, and Darren Woodson's 26-yard interception return set up Dallas' third touchdown.

Sub of the week: Pittsburgh running back Bam Morris, a rookie from Texas Tech, carried 21 times for 82 yards in the Steelers' 14-10 victory over Cincinnati. Morris replaced starter Barry Foster after Foster sprained his right knee on the second play of the game.

Comeback of the week: Arizona nipped Washington, 19-16, on Todd Peterson's 29-yard field goal at 10:04 of overtime. The Cardinals tied it at 16 on Steve Beuerlein's 5-yard touchdown pass to Ricky Proehl with 19 seconds left. Peterson's winning kick came one play after Terry Hoage returned an interception 23 yards to the Redskins' 12.

Blowout of the week: San Francisco had little trouble disposing of Atlanta, 42-3. The 49ers forced six turnovers (two of which they returned for touchdowns) and quarterback Steve Young completed all but one of his 16 pass attempts in 2½ quarters of play. Young threw four touchdown passes and no interceptions.

Nail-biter of the week: Kansas City edged Denver, 31-28, on Joe Montana's 5-yard touchdown pass to Willie Davis with eight seconds left. Montana completed seven of eight passes on the game-winning drive after John Elway gave the Broncos a 28-24 lead on a 4-yard scoring run with 1:29 left.

Hit of the week: By Parmalee, whose jarring tackle of Rocket Ismail in the first half knocked the Raiders' big-play kick returner out of the game.

Oddity of the week: The Raiders scored a defensive touchdown for the fifth consecutive game.

Top rusher: Parmalee was awarded two game balls for his performance against the Raiders, a first for a player coached by Don Shula.

Top passer: Montana was 34 of 54 for 393 yards and three touchdowns against Denver.

Top receiver: Sean Dawkins caught six passes for 105 yards in Indianapolis' 27-17 victory over Buffalo.

Notes: A fight broke out between 49ers cornerback Deion Sanders and Falcons wide receiver Andre Rison in the San Francisco-Atlanta game. Sanders, a three-time Pro Bowler with the Falcons from 1989-93, was making his first appearance in Atlanta since signing a free-agent contract with San Francisco in September. . . . Chargers running back Natrone Means, who ran for 120 yards and three touchdowns against the Saints, had two other touchdowns called back because of penalties. . . . Kansas City's first touchdown against Denver ended a touchdown drought of 149:20 that spanned parts of 11 quarters over 29 days. The Chiefs' victory was their first in Denver since 1982. . . . Dallas rolled up 137 yards of offense in the second quarter against Philadelphia after getting zero yards in the first quarter. . . . How bad are the Bengals? The Steelers beat them for the seventh consecutive time despite allowing eight sacks, committing nine penalties and giving up a touchdown on a fake field goal. . . . The Colts' victory was their first at Buffalo in a non-strike game since 1980. In defeat, Jim Kelly threw for 286 yards to pass Joe Ferguson (27,820-27,590) as the Bills' all-time passing leader. . . . The Raiders-Dolphins game included a shouting match between Raiders Coach Art Shell and quarterback Jeff Hostetler, who was benched for two series late in the first half. . . . Darrell Green intercepted two passes against Arizona to surpass Brig Owens

(37-36) as the Redskins' career interceptions leader.... Morten Andersen missed two field goal attempts against San Diego to extend his streak of missed field goals to four (over two games), a first for the 13-year NFL veteran.

Quote of the week: Rams defensive tackle D'Marco Farr, an undrafted free agent who made his first NFL start in Week 7: "I'm 6-1, but all that means is I can't look over the bathroom stall."

GAME SUMMARIES

BROWNS 11, OILERS 8

Thursday, October 13

Cleveland	0	11	0	0—11
Houston	0	0	0	8— 8

Second Quarter
Cle—Carrier 25 pass from Testaverde (Tupa run), 6:39.
Cle—FG Stover 35, 15:00.
Fourth Quarter
Hou—White 5 pass from Tolliver (Jeffires pass from Tolliver), 14:32.

TEAM STATISTICS

	Cleveland	Houston
First downs	12	20
Rushes-yards	24-64	24-106
Passing	196	199
Punt returns-yards	2-0	3-16
Kickoff returns-yards	1-13	2-42
Interception returns-yards	1-4	2-27
Comp.-att.-int.	15-25-2	22-40-1
Sacked-yards lost	0-0	5-30
Punts-average	5-39	6-39
Fumbles-lost	0-0	1-1
Penalties-yards	6-50	11-75
Time of possession	27:36	32:24
Attendance—50,364.		

INDIVIDUAL STATISTICS

RUSHING—Cleveland, Byner 11-25, Metcalf 8-23, Hoard 2-10, Baldwin 2-7, Testaverde 1-(minus 1). Houston, White 19-58, Richardson 4-45, Tolliver 1-3.

PASSING—Cleveland, Testaverde 15-25-2-196. Houston, Richardson 13-23-0-114, Tolliver 9-17-1-115.

RECEIVING—Cleveland, Carrier 4-60, Metcalf 3-48, Hoard 3-40, Alexander 3-28, Byner 1-15, Kinchen 1-5. Houston, White 7-86, Jeffires 5-60, Slaughter 4-35, Givins 3-27, Coleman 2-20, Carter 1-1.

MISSED FIELD GOAL ATTEMPTS—Cleveland, Stover 50. Houston, Del Greco 29.

INTERCEPTIONS—Cleveland, Booth 1-4. Houston, D. Lewis 2-27.

KICKOFF RETURNS—Cleveland, Baldwin 1-13. Houston, Mills 2-32.

PUNT RETURNS—Cleveland, Metcalf 2-0. Houston, Givins 2-6, Coleman 1-10.

SACKS—Cleveland, Burnett 2, J. Jones 1, Pleasant 1, Griffin ½, P. Johnson ½.

COLTS 27, BILLS 17

Sunday, October 16

Indianapolis	3	7	7	10—27
Buffalo	7	3	0	7—17

First Quarter
Buf—K. Davis 13 run (Christie kick), 3:51.
Ind—FG Biasucci 43, 8:27.
Second Quarter
Ind—Turner 6 pass from Harbaugh (Biasucci kick), 7:29.
Buf—FG Christie 23, 14:39.
Third Quarter
Ind—Cash 10 pass from Harbaugh (Biasucci kick), 8:27.
Fourth Quarter
Ind—Turner 19 pass from Majkowski (Biasucci kick), 6:46.
Ind—FG Biasucci 33, 8:36.
Buf—Thomas 2 pass from Kelly (Christie kick), 11:14.

TEAM STATISTICS

	Indianapolis	Buffalo
First downs	20	22
Rushes-yards	37-94	22-79
Passing	231	250

	Indianapolis	Buffalo
Punt returns-yards	1-18	1-11
Kickoff returns-yards	3-43	4-51
Interception returns-yards	0-0	0-0
Comp.-att.-int.	20-24-0	25-34-0
Sacked-yards lost	0-0	4-36
Punts-average	2-40	3-41
Fumbles-lost	0-0	3-2
Penalties-yards	4-30	3-15
Time of possession	35:08	24:52
Attendance—79,404.		

INDIVIDUAL STATISTICS

RUSHING—Indianapolis, Faulk 26-64, Potts 5-23, Harbaugh 3-5, Humphrey 2-3, Majkowski 1-(minus 1). Buffalo, Thomas 14-51, K. Davis 4-16, Kelly 1-7, Gardner 3-5.

PASSING—Indianapolis, Harbaugh 18-22-0-206, Maj-kowski 2-2-0-25. Buffalo, Kelly 25-34-0-286.

RECEIVING—Indianapolis, Dawkins 6-105, Turner 4-45, Potts 4-28, Faulk 2-22, Cash 2-16, Jackson 1-12, Humphrey 1-3. Buffalo, Reed 6-88, Thomas 6-60, Brooks 4-36, Metzelaars 3-36, Gardner 2-25, Beebe 2-23, Copeland 2-18.

MISSED FIELD GOAL ATTEMPTS—None.

INTERCEPTIONS—None.

KICKOFF RETURNS—Indianapolis, Humphrey 2-24, Brewer 1-19. Buffalo, Beebe 3-34, Copeland 1-17.

PUNT RETURNS—Indianapolis, Brewer 1-18. Buffalo, Copeland 1-11.

SACKS—Indianapolis, Bennett 2, McCoy 1, McDonald 1.

STEELERS 14, BENGALS 10

Sunday, October 16

Cincinnati	0	0	7	3—10
Pittsburgh	0	14	0	0—14

Second Quarter
Pit—J.L. Williams 13 pass from O'Donnell (Anderson kick), 11:13.
Pit—Mills 14 pass from O'Donnell (Anderson kick), 14:18.
Third Quarter
Cin—Cothran 7 pass from Johnson (Pelfrey kick), 4:03.
Fourth Quarter
Cin—FG Pelfrey 47, 6:12.

TEAM STATISTICS

	Cincinnati	Pittsburgh
First downs	11	16
Rushes-yards	33-106	30-114
Passing	135	129
Punt returns-yards	4-37	5-64
Kickoff returns-yards	3-40	2-53
Interception returns-yards	0-0	1-0
Comp.-att.-int.	17-31-1	15-22-0
Sacked-yards lost	2-15	8-61
Punts-average	7-47	9-46
Fumbles-lost	1-1	5-1
Penalties-yards	5-39	9-65
Time of possession	28:28	31:32
Attendance—55,353.		

INDIVIDUAL STATISTICS

RUSHING—Cincinnati, Broussard 12-52, Fenner 10-36, Klingler 6-15, H. Green 4-6, Scott 1-(minus 3). Pittsburgh, Morris 21-82, Mills 1-17, O'Donnell 4-10, J.L. Williams 3-8, Foster 1-(minus 3).

PASSING—Cincinnati, Klingler 16-29-0-143, Johnson 1-1-0-7, Hollas 0-1-1-0. Pittsburgh, O'Donnell 15-22-0-190.

RECEIVING—Cincinnati, Scott 4-69, Broussard 4-8, Pickens 3-34, Fenner 2-10, Ti. McGee 1-16, Cothran 1-7, Sadowski 1-5, To. McGee 1-1. Pittsburgh, E. Green 6-80, J.L. Williams 4-39, Morris 2-21, Johnson 1-25, Mills 1-14, Hayes 1-11.

MISSED FIELD GOAL ATTEMPTS—None.

INTERCEPTIONS—Pittsburgh, Kirkland 1-0.

KICKOFF RETURNS—Cincinnati, Ball 3-40. Pittsburgh, Stone 1-26, Woodson 1-27.

PUNT RETURNS—Cincinnati, Sawyer 4-37. Pittsburgh, Woodson 5-64.

SACKS—Cincinnati, A. Williams 4, Francis 1, McDonald 1, Tovar 1, D. Williams 1. Pittsburgh, Buckner 1, Lloyd 1.

49ERS 42, FALCONS 3

Sunday, October 16

San Francisco	14	14	14	0—42
Atlanta	0	3	0	0— 3

First Quarter
S.F.—Watters 10 pass from Young (Brien kick), 5:46.
S.F.—McDonald 49 fumble return (Brien kick), 7:11.

Second Quarter
S.F.—Rice 1 pass from Young (Brien kick), :04.
Atl—FG N. Johnson 34, 5:16.
S.F.—D. Sanders 93 interception return (Brien kick), 13:28.
Third Quarter
S.F.—B. Jones 7 pass from Young (Brien kick), 1:10.
S.F.—Watters 4 pass from Young (Brien kick), 5:25.

TEAM STATISTICS

	San Francisco	Atlanta
First downs	16	17
Rushes-yards	35-101	18-62
Passing	180	192
Punt returns-yards	1-26	1-7
Kickoff returns-yards	2-51	6-163
Interception returns-yards	4-115	0-0
Comp.-att.-int.	16-19-0	25-37-4
Sacked-yards lost	1-5	6-40
Punts-average	2-46	1-57
Fumbles-lost	0-0	3-2
Penalties-yards	8-65	6-47
Time of possession	29:00	31:00
Attendance—67,298.		

INDIVIDUAL STATISTICS

RUSHING—San Francisco, Watters 10-53, Floyd 11-20, Loville 9-20, Logan 4-9, Young 1-(minus 1). Atlanta, Heyward 13-33, Pegram 2-20, J. George 2-9, Hebert 1-0.

PASSING—San Francisco, Young 15-16-0-143, Grbac 1-3-0-42. Atlanta, J. George 19-27-2-177, Hebert 6-10-2-55.

RECEIVING—San Francisco, Rice 6-65, Watters 5-33, Taylor 3-38, Singleton 1-42, B. Jones 1-7. Atlanta, Emanuel 9-91, Mathis 5-64, Heyward 5-39, Rison 5-32, R. Sanders 1-6.

MISSED FIELD GOAL ATTEMPTS—Atlanta, N. Johnson 52.

INTERCEPTIONS—San Francisco, D. Hall 2-0, Hanks 1-22, D. Sanders 1-93.

KICKOFF RETURNS—San Francisco, Carter 2-51. Atlanta, Verdin 4-113, Pegram 2-50.

PUNT RETURNS—San Francisco, Carter 1-26. Atlanta, Verdin 1-7.

SACKS—San Francisco, Stubblefield 2, Wilson 2, B. Young 2. Atlanta, C. Smith 1.

JETS 24, PATRIOTS 17

Sunday, October 16

New England	0	7	0	10	17
N.Y. Jets	7	14	0	3	24

First Quarter
N.Y.—B. Baxter 1 run (Lowery kick), 7:45.
Second Quarter
N.E.—Crittenden 3 pass from Bledsoe (Bahr kick), 6:11.
N.Y.—B. Baxter 2 run (Lowery kick), 13:03.
N.Y.—Mitchell 4 pass from Esiason (Lowery kick), 14:34.
Fourth Quarter
N.E.—Thomas 4 run (Bahr kick), 5:40.
N.Y.—FG Lowery 37, 13:24.
N.E.—FG Bahr 40, 14:37.

TEAM STATISTICS

	New England	N.Y. Jets
First downs	19	17
Rushes-yards	30-104	37-172
Passing	220	70
Punt returns-yards	3-26	2-25
Kickoff returns-yards	5-57	2-44
Interception returns-yards	0-0	1-(-3)
Comp.-att.-int.	22-41-1	12-17-0
Sacked-yards lost	3-22	6-37
Punts-average	2-36	6-45
Fumbles-lost	3-3	4-2
Penalties-yards	1-5	10-65
Time of possession	27:22	32:38
Attendance—71,123.		

INDIVIDUAL STATISTICS

RUSHING—New England, Thomas 14-63, Butts 9-28, Thompson 4-7, Bledsoe 3-6. New York, J. Johnson 21-122, B. Baxter 12-38, Murrell 2-8, A. Johnson 1-5, Esiason 1-(minus 1).

PASSING—New England, Bledsoe 22-41-1-242. New York, Esiason 12-17-0-107.

RECEIVING—New England, Coates 7-92, Crittenden 6-74, Thompson 4-13, Brisby 2-38, Harris 1-11, Thomas 1-9, Turner 1-5. New York, J. Johnson 4-35, Mitchell 3-27, Monk 2-30, Moore 1-11, Yarborough 1-3, B. Baxter 1-1.

MISSED FIELD GOAL ATTEMPTS—New England, O'Neill 47. New York, Lowery 32.

INTERCEPTIONS—New York, B. Washington 1-(minus 3).

KICKOFF RETURNS—New England, Crittenden 2-19, Thomas 2-32, Burke 1-6. New York, Prior 2-44.

PUNT RETURNS—New England, Harris 3-26. New York, Hicks 2-25.

SACKS—New England, V. Brown 1½, Goad 1, A. Jones 1, Reynolds 1, Sabb 1, M. Jones ½. New York, Hasty 1, Houston 1, Lott 1.

DOLPHINS 20, RAIDERS 17

Sunday, October 16

L.A. Raiders	10	0	7	0	0 — 17
Miami	0	7	3	7	3 — 20

First Quarter
L.A.—FG Jaeger 19, 10:04.
L.A.—Smith 25 fumble return (Jaeger kick), 10:53.
Second Quarter
Mia—Jackson 15 pass from Marino (Stoyanovich kick), 10:05.
Third Quarter
Mia—FG Stoyanovich 21, 6:45.
L.A.—Brown 7 pass from Hostetler (Jaeger kick), 10:17.
Fourth Quarter
Mia—Byars 18 pass from Marino (Stoyanovich kick), 2:39.
Overtime
Mia—FG Stoyanovich 29, 5:46.

TEAM STATISTICS

	L.A. Raiders	Miami
First downs	12	19
Rushes-yards	29-124	38-169
Passing	86	175
Punt returns-yards	3-15	3-12
Kickoff returns-yards	4-91	4-77
Interception returns-yards	1-8	0-0
Comp.-att.-int.	9-27-0	17-37-1
Sacked-yards lost	4-17	2-11
Punts-average	9-38	6-45
Fumbles-lost	1-1	3-2
Penalties-yards	6-49	3-20
Time of possession	28:36	37:10
Attendance—69,380.		

INDIVIDUAL STATISTICS

RUSHING—Los Angeles, H. Williams 16-72, Hostetler 4-20, Montgomery 7-17, Rathman 2-15. Miami, Parmalee 30-150, McDuffie 1-8, Byars 3-7, Higgs 3-2, Marino 1-2.

PASSING—Los Angeles, Hostetler 8-23-0-95, Evans 1-4-0-8. Miami, Marino 17-37-1-186.

RECEIVING—Los Angeles, T. Brown 6-86, Hobbs 1-8, Glover 1-6, Montgomery 1-3. Miami, Byars 5-69, M. Williams 3-36, Ingram 2-23, K. Jackson 2-23, Fryar 2-17, McDuffie 2-10, Baty 1-8.

MISSED FIELD GOAL ATTEMPTS—None.

INTERCEPTIONS—Los Angeles, Frank 1-8.

KICKOFF RETURNS—Los Angeles, Ismail 2-38, Wright 2-53. Miami, McDuffie 4-77.

PUNT RETURNS—Los Angeles, Brown 3-14. Miami, McDuffie 3-12.

SACKS—Los Angeles, Harrison 2. Miami, Atkins 1, Coleman 1, Cross 1, Cox ½, Veasey ½.

CARDINALS 19, REDSKINS 16

Sunday, October 16

Arizona	0	3	0	13	3 — 19
Washington	0	14	0	2	0 — 16

Second Quarter
Was—Mitchell 46 pass from Shuler (Lohmiller kick), 1:47.
Was—Green 27 interception return (Lohmiller kick), 13:51.
Ari—FG Peterson 35, 14:55.
Fourth Quarter
Ari—Moore 10 run (conversion failed), 4:12.
Was—Safety, Feagles stepped out of the end zone, 10:03.
Ari—Proehl 5 pass from Beuerlein (Peterson kick), 14:41.
Overtime
Ari—FG Peterson 29, 10:04.

TEAM STATISTICS

	Arizona	Washington
First downs	19	11
Rushes-yards	48-151	29-85
Passing	173	149
Punt returns-yards	4-47	2-8

	Arizona	Washington
Kickoff returns-yards	2-35	5-89
Interception returns-yards	5-85	3-72
Comp.-att.-int.	16-34-3	11-32-5
Sacked-yards lost	3-21	1-9
Punts-average	8-46	10-45
Fumbles-lost	2-0	0-0
Penalties-yards	9-70	7-61
Time of possession	41:10	28:54
Attendance—50,019.		

INDIVIDUAL STATISTICS

RUSHING—Arizona, R. Moore 28-118, Centers 8-26, Hearst 6-7, Beuerlein 4-6, Levy 1-(minus 2), Feagles 1-(minus 4). Washington, Ervins 20-57, Mitchell 6-16, Shuler 3-12.

PASSING—Arizona, Beuerlein 16-34-3-194. Washington, Shuler 11-32-5-158.

RECEIVING—Arizona, Centers 6-66, Proehl 5-63, Clark 3-36, Hill 2-29. Washington, Mitchell 3-65, Ellard 3-50, Smith 2-19, Ervins 2-4, Wycheck 1-20.

MISSED FIELD GOAL ATTEMPTS—Arizona, Peterson 43, 45. Washington, Lohmiller 51.

INTERCEPTIONS—Arizona, A. Williams 2-43, J. Williams 2-19, Hoage 1-23. Washington, Green 2-32, Carter 1-40.

KICKOFF RETURNS—Arizona, Levy 2-35. Washington, Mitchell 4-81, Wycheck 1-8.

PUNT RETURNS—Arizona, Robinson 4-47. Washington, Mitchell 2-8.

SACKS—Arizona, Bankston 1. Washington, Harvey 2, Woods 1.

CHARGERS 36, SAINTS 22

Sunday, October 16

San Diego	14	13	6	3—36
New Orleans	0	7	7	8—22

First Quarter
S.D.—Means 16 run (Carney kick), 5:56.
S.D.—Means 8 run (Carney kick), 14:37.

Second Quarter
S.D.—FG Carney 49, 3:05.
S.D.—Means 1 run (Carney kick), 4:14.
N.O.—Early 18 pass from Everett (Andersen kick), 6:50.
S.D.—FG Carney 31, 14:00.

Third Quarter
S.D.—FG Carney 29, 1:14.
N.O.—Smith 1 pass from Everett (Andersen kick), 4:35.
S.D.—FG Carney 29, 12:29.

Fourth Quarter
N.O.—Neal 1 run (Walls pass from Everett), 5:21.
S.D.—FG Carney 28, 11:21.

TEAM STATISTICS

	San Diego	New Orleans
First downs	25	24
Rushes-yards	40-198	18-104
Passing	180	176
Punt returns-yards	2-8	1-1
Kickoff returns-yards	4-103	8-196
Interception returns-yards	0-0	0-0
Comp.-att.-int.	17-29-0	24-35-0
Sacked-yards lost	1-6	3-30
Punts-average	2-44	3-45
Fumbles-lost	0-0	2-2
Penalties-yards	8-92	4-77
Time of possession	34:06	25:54
Attendance—50,565.		

INDIVIDUAL STATISTICS

RUSHING—San Diego, Means 26-120, Bieniemy 8-53, Harmon 4-27, Humphries 2-(minus 2). New Orleans, Brown 13-81, Haynes 1-15, Early 1-8, Neal 3-0.

PASSING—San Diego, Humphries 17-29-0-186. New Orleans, Everett 24-35-0-206.

RECEIVING—San Diego, T. Martin 5-51, Harmon 4-34, Young 3-41, Jefferson 2-30, Pupunu 2-20, Means 1-10. New Orleans, Haynes 7-51, Early 6-58, Brown 5-29, Small 3-48, Walls 2-19, Smith 1-1.

MISSED FIELD GOAL ATTEMPTS—New Orleans, Andersen 54, 38.

INTERCEPTIONS—None.

KICKOFF RETURNS—San Diego, Coleman 3-90, Harmon 1-13. New Orleans, Hughes 8-196.

PUNT RETURNS—San Diego, Gordon 2-8. New Orleans, Hughes 1-1.

SACKS—San Diego, Mims 2, Lee 1. New Orleans, W. Martin 1.

RAMS 17, GIANTS 10

Sunday, October 16

N.Y. Giants	7	3	0	0—10
L.A. Rams	14	3	0	0—17

First Quarter
L.A.—Bruce 19 pass from Miller (Zendejas kick), 4:19.
N.Y.—Hampton 27 run (Treadwell kick), 10:29.
L.A.—Drayton 12 pass from Miller (Zendejas kick), 13:52.

Second Quarter
N.Y.—FG Treadwell 24, 5:16.
L.A.—FG Zendejas 22, 11:38.

TEAM STATISTICS

	N.Y. Giants	L.A. Rams
First downs	14	18
Rushes-yards	31-121	36-105
Passing	161	169
Punt returns-yards	4-57	2-8
Kickoff returns-yards	3-47	2-51
Interception returns-yards	1-0	2-55
Comp.-att.-int.	15-27-2	13-26-1
Sacked-yards lost	1-4	3-28
Punts-average	6-45	6-47
Fumbles-lost	0-0	0-0
Penalties-yards	7-60	4-35
Time of possession	29:18	30:42
Attendance—40,474.		

INDIVIDUAL STATISTICS

RUSHING—New York, Hampton 27-112, Downs 2-4, Meggett 1-3, Brown 1-2. Los Angeles, Bettis 30-88, Miller 5-13, Hester 1-4.

PASSING—New York, Brown 15-27-2-165. Los Angeles, Miller 13-26-1-197.

RECEIVING—New York, Cross 5-47, Sherrard 4-66, Calloway 3-34, Hampton 1-7, Meggett 1-6, Lewis 1-5. Los Angeles, Bettis 3-62, Drayton 3-39, Kinchen 2-29, Griffith 2-20, Bruce 1-19, Anderson 1-16, Hester 1-12.

MISSED FIELD GOAL ATTEMPTS—None.

INTERCEPTIONS—New York, Miller 1-0. Los Angeles, Kelly 1-31, Newman 1-24.

KICKOFF RETURNS—New York, Lewis 2-26, Meggett 1-21. Los Angeles, Kinchen 2-51.

PUNT RETURNS—New York, Meggett 4-57. Los Angeles, J. Bailey 2-8.

SACKS—New York, Beamon 1, Hamilton 1, Strahan 1. Los Angeles, Phifer ½, Stokes ½.

COWBOYS 24, EAGLES 13

Sunday, October 16

Philadelphia	7	0	0	6—13
Dallas	0	14	7	3—24

First Quarter
Phi—Walker 32 pass from Cunningham (Murray kick), 9:31.

Second Quarter
Dal—E. Smith 2 run (Boniol kick), 13:11.
Dal—Harper 16 pass from Aikman (Boniol kick), 13:52.

Third Quarter
Dal—Novacek 14 pass from Aikman (Boniol kick), 6:20.

Fourth Quarter
Dal—FG Boniol 37, 2:17.
Phi—Joseph 34 run (run failed), 9:33.

TEAM STATISTICS

	Philadelphia	Dallas
First downs	18	19
Rushes-yards	24-124	35-113
Passing	170	153
Punt returns-yards	3-50	0-0
Kickoff returns-yards	5-93	2-20
Interception returns-yards	1-0	4-51
Comp.-att.-int.	17-34-4	12-23-1
Sacked-yards lost	4-28	2-3
Punts-average	5-52	5-40
Fumbles-lost	1-1	1-0
Penalties-yards	12-78	7-96
Time of possession	28:00	32:00
Attendance—64,703.		

INDIVIDUAL STATISTICS

RUSHING—Philadelphia, Garner 17-57, Joseph 4-52, Cunningham 2-12, Hebron 1-3. Dallas, E. Smith 26-106, Coleman 3-4, Johnston 1-3, K. Williams 1-3, Aikman 4-(minus 3).

PASSING—Philadelphia, Cunningham 17-34-4-198. Dallas, Aikman 12-23-1-156.

RECEIVING—Philadelphia, Walker 5-56, Barnett 3-33, C. Williams 2-48, Bavaro 2-21, Joseph 2-11, Hebron 1-13, Bailey 1-12, Johnson 1-4. Dallas, Harper 4-52, Novacek 3-30, Irvin 2-33, Galbraith 1-15, Johnston 1-15, K. Williams 1-11.

MISSED FIELD GOAL ATTEMPTS—None.

INTERCEPTIONS—Philadelphia, G. Jackson 1-0. Dallas, Brown 1-0, Gant 1-0, Washington 1-25, Woodson 1-26.

KICKOFF RETURNS—Philadelphia, Hebron 3-66, Sydner 2-27. Dallas, Marion 1-18, K. Williams 1-2.

PUNT RETURNS—Philadelphia, Sydner 3-50.

SACKS—Philadelphia, Fuller 1, Harmon 1. Dallas, Hennings 2, Jeffcoat 1, D. Smith 1.

CHIEFS 31, BRONCOS 28

Monday, October 17

Kansas City	0	14	7	10—31
Denver	0	14	7	7—28

Second Quarter
Den—L. Russell 12 run (Elam kick), :44.
K.C.—Allen 7 run (Elliott kick), 8:03.
Den—Miller 27 pass from Elway (Elam kick), 11:25.
K.C.—Birden 6 pass from Montana (Elliott kick), 13:48.

Third Quarter
K.C.—Valerio 4 pass from Montana (Elliott kick), 4:58.
Den—Evans 20 pass from Elway (Elam kick), 14:38.

Fourth Quarter
K.C.—FG Elliott 19, 10:52.
Den—Elway 4 run (Elam kick), 13:31.
K.C.—Davis 5 pass from Montana (Elliott kick), 14:52.

TEAM STATISTICS

	Kansas City	Denver
First downs	26	21
Rushes-yards	24-90	27-97
Passing	393	233
Punt returns-yards	3-17	4-31
Kickoff returns-yards	5-155	3-66
Interception returns-yards	0-0	1-(-3)
Comp.-att.-int.	34-54-1	18-29-0
Sacked-yards lost	0-0	6-30
Punts-average	4-46	7-40
Fumbles-lost	1-1	5-3
Penalties-yards	14-101	10-65
Time of possession	32:04	27:56

Attendance—75,151.

INDIVIDUAL STATISTICS

RUSHING—Kansas City, Allen 16-63, Hill 6-16, Anders 2-11. Denver, L. Russell 15-41, Elway 6-38, Milburn 3-17, Miller 1-3, Clark 2-(minus 2).

PASSING—Kansas City, Montana 34-54-1-393. Denver, Elway 18-29-0-263.

RECEIVING—Kansas City, Walker 8-98, Davis 7-88, Anders 6-56, Allen 5-49, Greene 3-43, Birden 2-31, Hill 2-24, Valerio 1-4. Denver, Miller 5-99, Sharpe 4-50, Milburn 3-56, L. Russell 3-10, Evans 2-34, Tillman 1-14.

MISSED FIELD GOAL ATTEMPTS—Kansas City, Elliott 27.

INTERCEPTIONS—Denver, D. Williams 1-(minus 3).

KICKOFF RETURNS—Kansas City, Dickerson 5-155. Denver, By'not'e 3-66.

PUNT RETURNS—Kansas City, Hughes 3-17. Denver, Milburn 4-31.

SACKS—Kansas City, N. Smith 2½, Thomas 1, Mickel 1, McDaniel 1, J. Williams ½.

WEEK 8

RESULTS

Minnesota 13, Green Bay 10 (OT)
Cleveland 37, Cincinnati 13
Dallas 28, Arizona 21
Denver 20, San Diego 15
Detroit 21, Chicago 16
Kansas City 38, Seattle 23
L.A. Raiders 30, Atlanta 17
New Orleans 37, L.A. Rams 34
Pittsburgh 10, N.Y. Giants 6
San Francisco 41, Tampa Bay 16
Washington 41, Indianapolis 27
Philadelphia 21, Houston 6
   Open date: Buffalo, Miami, New England,
N.Y. Jets

STANDINGS

AFC EAST	W	L	T	Pct.
Miami	5	2	0	.714
Buffalo	4	3	0	.571
N.Y. Jets	4	3	0	.571
New England	3	4	0	.429
Indianapolis	3	5	0	.375

AFC CENTRAL	W	L	T	Pct.
Cleveland	6	1	0	.857
Pittsburgh	5	2	0	.714
Houston	1	6	0	.143
Cincinnati	0	7	0	.000

AFC WEST	W	L	T	Pct.
San Diego	6	1	0	.857
Kansas City	5	2	0	.714
L.A. Raiders	3	4	0	.429
Seattle	3	4	0	.429
Denver	2	5	0	.286

NFC EAST	W	L	T	Pct.
Dallas	6	1	0	.857
Philadelphia	5	2	0	.714
N.Y. Giants	3	4	0	.429
Arizona	2	5	0	.286
Washington	2	6	0	.250

NFC CENTRAL	W	L	T	Pct.
Minnesota	5	2	0	.714
Chicago	4	3	0	.571
Detroit	3	4	0	.429
Green Bay	3	4	0	.429
Tampa Bay	2	5	0	.286

NFC WEST	W	L	T	Pct.
San Francisco	6	2	0	.750
Atlanta	4	4	0	.500
L.A. Rams	3	5	0	.375
New Orleans	3	5	0	.375

HIGHLIGHTS

Hero of the week: Tyrone Hughes of the New Orleans Saints, who was spectacular in his team's 37-34 victory over the Los Angeles Rams. He returned 10 kicks for an NFL-record 347 yards, and his 304 yards on kickoff returns set another league mark. Hughes tied a record by returning two kickoffs for touchdowns in one game, and he also intercepted a pass in his first career start at cornerback.

Goat(s) of the week: Houston safeties Marcus Robertson and Cris Dishman, who were burned for three catches of more than 50 yards by Philadelphia's Fred Barnett in the Monday night game. The Eagles won, 21-6, and Barnett finished with five catches for 187 yards and one touchdown.

Sub of the week: Dallas quarterback Rodney Peete, who threw two touchdown passes in the Cowboys' 28-21 victory over Arizona. Peete, who took over after Troy Aikman sustained a concussion on Dallas' first series of the game, completed 6-of-7 passes for 145 yards in the fourth quarter.

Comeback of the week: Minnesota beat Green Bay, 13-10, on Fuad Reveiz's 27-yard field goal at 4:26 of overtime. Reveiz sent the game into overtime on a 29-yard field goal with 17 seconds left after the Vikings had driven 55 yards in 14 plays; Warren Moon was 7-of-10 passing on the drive.

Blowout of the week: San Francisco whipped Tampa Bay, 41-16, behind Ricky Watters' two touchdowns and 103 yards rushing. The game marked the first NFL start for Buccaneers quarterback Trent Dilfer, who completed just seven of 23 passes for 45 yards before being replaced by Craig Erickson after the Bucs fell behind, 34-0.

Nail-biter of the week: Detroit beat Chicago, 21-16, in a game that wasn't decided until Lions cornerback Robert Massey broke up an Erik Kramer pass intended for Nate Lewis on fourth and 5 at Detroit's 20 with 41 seconds left.

Hit of the week: By Cardinals linebacker Wilber Marshall, whose hit to Aikman's chin forced the quarterback to leave the game on the Cowboys'

first possession. The game was scoreless at the time, but Peete came in to guide Dallas to victory.

Oddity of the week: On the same day Hughes set a record for kickoff-return yardage in one game, Detroit's Mel Gray became the NFL's career leader in that department. Gray's 174 kickoff-return yards against Chicago (including a 102-yard touchdown) moved him past Ron Smith (7,092-6,922) atop the all-time list.

Top rusher: Barry Sanders carried 23 times for 167 yards in Detroit's victory over Chicago.

Top passer: Randall Cunningham completed 13 of 24 passes for 310 yards and two touchdowns in Philadelphia's victory over Houston.

Top receiver: The Eagles' Barnett caught five passes for 187 yards and one touchdown.

Notes: Cleveland scored touchdowns on consecutive Cincinnati punts in its 37-13 victory. Travis Hill recovered a blocked punt in the end zone for one touchdown, and Eric Metcalf returned Lee Johnson's next punt 73 yards for another score. The loss was the Bengals' 20th in 22 AFC Central Division games since 1991.... Tampa Bay's loss at San Francisco dropped the Bucs' record in California since 1980 to 0-22.... The Saints and Rams combined for 797 all-purpose return yards (kickoffs, punts, fumbles and interceptions). Robert Bailey's 103-yard punt return for the Rams was the longest in NFL history. It was made possible when players on both teams thought the ball, punted into the end zone, was dead. It wasn't, and Bailey picked it up and took off.... Dennis Green won his 25th game faster than any coach in Vikings history. He did it in 39 games, five fewer than Bud Grant.... Gus Frerotte's 226 yards passing against Indianapolis were the most ever by a Redskins quarterback in his NFL debut, topping a 154-yard performance by Al Dorow in 1954. Frerotte became the second rookie to start at quarterback for Washington in 1994 (after Heath Shuler). Until '94, the Redskins had gone 33 years—since Norm Snead in 1961—without starting a rookie quarterback. . . . The Cowboys beat the Cards for the second time in three weeks and the ninth consecutive time overall. . . . Gale Gilbert's two completions for San Diego against Denver were his first in the NFL since 1990, when he played for Buffalo. . . . Kansas City beat Seattle for the seventh consecutive time. . . . Cincinnati's Dan Wilkinson, the first overall pick in the 1994 draft, recorded his first NFL sack. . . . San Diego's John Carney kicked five field goals for the second consecutive week and extended his string of successful field goals to 16.

Quote of the week: San Francisco center Bart Oates, on beating hapless Tampa Bay: "I think we have to look at this realistically, look at the level of competition. Let's look at it for what it's worth. It's a victory, but let's not get grandiose about it."

GAME SUMMARIES

VIKINGS 13, PACKERS 10
Thursday, October 20

Green Bay	0	10	0	0	0—10
Minnesota	7	0	0	3	3—13

First Quarter
Min—Parker 23 fumble return (Reveiz kick), 6:25.
Second Quarter
G.B.—FG Jacke 50, 9:32.
G.B.—Brunell 5 run (Jacke kick), 14:10.
Fourth Quarter
Min—FG Reveiz 29, 14:43.
Overtime
Min—FG Reveiz 27, 4:26.

TEAM STATISTICS

	Green Bay	Minnesota
First downs	12	16
Rushes-yards	26-71	19-22
Passing	87	230
Punt returns-yards	7-37	5-39
Kickoff returns-yards	3-57	4-81
Interception returns-yards	2-6	1-21
Comp.-att.-int.	17-34-1	31-50-2
Sacked-yards lost	3-24	4-41
Punts-average	10-46	10-40
Fumbles-lost	4-1	1-0
Penalties-yards	5-49	7-61
Time of possession	29:48	34:38
Attendance—63,041.		

INDIVIDUAL STATISTICS
RUSHING—Green Bay, Cobb 12-44, Bennett 8-13, Brunell 4-9, L. Johnson 1-5, Brooks 1-0. Minnesota, Allen 14-21, Moon 2-8, R. Smith 2-0, Lee 1-(minus 7).
PASSING—Green Bay, Favre 6-10-1-32, Brunell 11-24-0-79. Minnesota, Moon 31-50-2-271.
RECEIVING—Green Bay, Brooks 4-25, Sharpe 3-16, Bennett 3-7, West 2-33, Morgan 2-16, Cobb 2-8, L. Johnson 1-6. Minnesota, Carter 10-68, Reed 8-95, Lee 4-39, Cooper 3-15, Jordan 2-21, Ismail 2-17, R. Smith 2-16.
MISSED FIELD GOAL ATTEMPTS—None.
INTERCEPTIONS—Green Bay, Buckley 1-3, Willis 1-3. Minnesota, J. Harris 1-21.
KICKOFF RETURNS—Green Bay, C. Harris 1-25, J. Jurkovic 1-16, Levins 1-16. Minnesota, Ismail 4-81.
PUNT RETURNS—Green Bay, Brooks 4-17, Prior 3-20. Minnesota, Parker 3-31, Palmer 2-8.
SACKS—Green Bay, Jones 2, White 1, McMichael 1. Minnesota, Randle 2, J. Harris ½, McDaniel ½.

CHIEFS 38, SEAHAWKS 23
Sunday, October 23

Seattle	0	0	7	16—23
Kansas City	0	13	8	17—38

Second Quarter
K.C.—Anders 9 pass from Montana (Elliott kick), 7:12.
K.C.—FG Elliott 49, 8:33.
K.C.—FG Elliott 34, 14:40.
Third Quarter
Sea—Vaughn 3 run (Kasay kick), 6:26.
K.C.—Allen 36 run (Allen run), 12:17.
Fourth Quarter
K.C.—Dawson 21 pass from Montana (Elliott kick), :45.
K.C.—FG Elliott 27, 6:08.
Sea—Blades 1 pass from Mirer (Blades pass from Mirer), 9:10.
K.C.—E. Martin 32 pass from Bono (Elliott kick), 10:29.
Sea—Blades 9 pass from Mirer (Vaughn run), 12:48.

TEAM STATISTICS

	Seattle	Kansas City
First downs	16	24
Rushes-yards	29-167	37-172
Passing	96	305
Punt returns-yards	1-10	3-17
Kickoff returns-yards	7-186	2-40
Interception returns-yards	0-0	0-0
Comp.-att.-int.	15-30-0	23-33-0
Sacked-yards lost	3-30	1-6
Punts-average	5-46	2-39
Fumbles-lost	2-2	1-0
Penalties-yards	4-35	6-40
Time of possession	24:57	35:03
Attendance—78,847.		

INDIVIDUAL STATISTICS
RUSHING—Seattle, Warren 19-117, Vaughn 4-25, Mirer 3-16, Smith 3-9. Kansas City, Allen 14-77, Hill 17-74, Dawson 1-9, Bennett 3-7, Anders 1-6, Bono 1-(minus 1).
PASSING—Seattle, Mirer 15-30-0-126. Kansas City, Montana 21-31-0-270, Bono 2-2-0-41.
RECEIVING—Seattle, Blades 7-61, K. Martin 3-37, Warren 3-18, Edmunds 1-8, Green 1-2. Kansas City, Dawson 5-93, Anders 5-33, Davis 4-78, Walker 3-29, E. Martin 2-48, Birden 1-8, Hughes 1-5.
MISSED FIELD GOAL ATTEMPTS—Kansas City, Elliott 44.
INTERCEPTIONS—None.
KICKOFF RETURNS—Seattle, Bates 5-136, Vaughn 2-50. Kansas City, Dickerson 2-40.
PUNT RETURNS—Seattle, K. Martin 1-10. Kansas City, Hughes 3-17.
SACKS—Seattle, Nash 1. Kansas City, Mickell 1, Smith 1, Thomas 1.

BROWNS 37, BENGALS 13
Sunday, October 23

Cincinnati	10	3	0	0—13
Cleveland	3	7	17	10—37

First Quarter
Cle—FG Stover 45, 9:07.
Cin—FG Pelfrey 36, 12:45.
Cin—Ti. McGee 11 pass from Klingler (Pelfrey kick), 14:27.
Second Quarter
Cle—Hoard 11 pass from Testaverde (Stover kick), 5:31.
Cin—FG Pelfrey 49, 9:54.
Third Quarter
Cle—FG Stover 27, 11:40.
Cle—Hill recovered blocked punt in the end zone (Stover kick), 13:13.
Cle—Metcalf 73 punt return (Stover kick), 15:00.
Fourth Quarter
Cle—FG Stover 35, 9:26.
Cle—Hoard 1 run (Stover kick), 13:05.

TEAM STATISTICS

	Cincinnati	Cleveland
First downs	15	13
Rushes-yards	30-75	24-120
Passing	146	120
Punt returns-yards	4-17	3-83
Kickoff returns-yards	8-155	4-77
Interception returns-yards	1-19	0-0
Comp.-att.-int.	18-37-0	11-29-1
Sacked-yards lost	4-54	2-14
Punts-average	7-34	7-40
Fumbles-lost	2-1	0-0
Penalties-yards	5-30	3-46
Time of possession	34:19	25:41
Attendance—77,588.		

INDIVIDUAL STATISTICS

RUSHING—Cincinnati, Fenner 15-50, Green 6-15, Klingler 1-8, Broussard 5-1, Cothran 3-1. Cleveland, Hoard 9-58, Metcalf 12-57, Byner 1-3, Baldwin 1-1, Testaverde 1-1.

PASSING—Cincinnati, Klingler 18-34-0-200, Hollas 0-2-0-0, Blake 0-1-0-0. Cleveland, Testaverde 8-18-1-103, Rypien 3-11-0-31.

RECEIVING—Cincinnati, Ti. McGee 4-72, Scott 3-38, To. McGee 3-29, Green 2-37, Sadowski 2-13, Broussard 2-6, Fenner 1-4, Query 1-1. Cleveland, Hoard 5-22, Alexander 3-77, Carrier 2-28, Metcalf 1-7.

MISSED FIELD GOAL ATTEMPTS—Cincinnati, Pelfrey 50.

INTERCEPTIONS—Cincinnati, Oliver 1-19.

KICKOFF RETURNS—Cincinnati, Ball 5-101, Green 2-38, Stegall 1-16. Cleveland, Baldwin 2-40, Kinchen 1-15, Metcalf 1-22.

PUNT RETURNS—Cincinnati, Sawyer 3-13, D. Williams 1-4. Cleveland, Metcalf 3-83.

SACKS—Cincinnati, Tovar 1, Wilkinson 1. Cleveland, P. Johnson 1½, Footman 1, Stams 1, Pleasant ½.

SAINTS 37, RAMS 34

Sunday, October 23

L.A. Rams	0	17	3	14—34
New Orleans	14	13	10	0—37

First Quarter
N.O.—D. Brown 3 run (Andersen kick), 5:16.
N.O.—Walls 30 pass from Everett (Andersen kick), 12:56.
Second Quarter
L.A.—Bruce 19 pass from Miller (Zendejas kick), :05.
N.O.—FG Andersen 21, 5:04.
L.A.—Wright 98 fumble return (Zendejas kick), 6:52.
N.O.—Hughes 92 kickoff return (Andersen kick), 7:09.
L.A.—FG Zendejas 47, 10:16.
N.O.—FG Andersen 40, 14:56.
Third Quarter
N.O.—FG Andersen 37, 7:33.
L.A.—FG Zendejas 32, 14:42.
N.O.—Hughes 98 kickoff return (Andersen kick), 15:00.
Fourth Quarter
L.A.—J. Bailey 7 run (Zendejas kick), 6:42.
L.A.—R. Bailey 103 punt return (Zendejas kick), 10:52.

TEAM STATISTICS

	L.A. Rams	New Orleans
First downs	13	18
Rushes-yards	21-85	38-118
Passing	157	196
Punt returns-yards	4-144	3-43
Kickoff returns-yards	7-197	7-304
Interception returns-yards	0-0	3-11
Comp.-att.-int.	14-28-3	17-26-0
Sacked-yards lost	1-5	1-10
Punts-average	4-48	5-45
Fumbles-lost	1-0	2-1
Penalties-yards	9-84	5-45
Time of possession	23:40	36:20
Attendance—47,908.		

INDIVIDUAL STATISTICS

RUSHING—Los Angeles, Bettis 18-63, Miller 1-10, J. Bailey 1-7, Griffith 1-5. New Orleans, Brown 26-86, Bates 8-22, Haynes 1-12, Neal 2-(minus 1), Everett 1-(minus 1).

PASSING—Los Angeles, Miller 7-11-2-88, Chandler 7-17-1-74. New Orleans, Everett 17-26-0-206.

RECEIVING—Los Angeles, J. Bailey 4-36, Anderson 3-44, Bruce 3-44, Hester 1-11, Kinchen 1-11, Bettis 1-9, Griffith 1-7. New Orleans, Early 4-40, Haynes 4-36, Walls 1-30, Small 3-38, Smith 2-13, Brown 1-14.

MISSED FIELD GOAL ATTEMPTS—None.

INTERCEPTIONS—New Orleans, Spencer 2-11, Hughes 1-0.

KICKOFF RETURNS—Los Angeles, Kinchen 4-131, J. Bailey 2-52, Griffith 1-14. New Orleans, Hughes 7-304.

PUNT RETURNS—Los Angeles, J. Bailey 3-41, R. Bailey 1-103. New Orleans, Hughes 3-43.

SACKS—Los Angeles, Young 1. New Orleans, Martin 1.

REDSKINS 41, COLTS 27

Sunday, October 23

Washington	0	13	14	14—41
Indianapolis	3	14	0	10—27

First Quarter
Ind—FG Biasucci 50, 3:07.

Second Quarter
Ind—Dawkins 24 pass from Harbaugh (Biasucci kick), :46.
Was—FG Lohmiller 21, 3:27.
Ind—Faulk 85 pass from Harbaugh (Biasucci kick), 4:24.
Was—FG Lohmiller 27, 8:32.
Was—Jenkins 1 pass from Frerotte (Lohmiller kick), 14:53.
Third Quarter
Was—Ervins 1 run (Lohmiller kick), 7:21.
Was—Jenkins 5 pass from Frerotte (Lohmiller kick), 9:57.
Fourth Quarter
Ind—FG Biasucci 28, :48.
Was—Collins 21 interception return (Lohmiller kick), 5:26.
Was—Ervins 3 run (Lohmiller kick), 9:53.
Ind—Jackson 13 pass from Majkowski (Biasucci kick), 12:15.

TEAM STATISTICS

	Washington	Indianapolis
First downs	20	20
Rushes-yards	33-100	30-109
Passing	226	272
Punt returns-yards	1-17	4-15
Kickoff returns-yards	4-74	7-124
Interception returns-yards	3-79	0-0
Comp.-att.-int.	17-32-0	18-30-3
Sacked-yards lost	0-0	4-23
Punts-average	4-47	3-40
Fumbles-lost	1-0	1-0
Penalties-yards	6-50	8-68
Time of possession	29:08	30:52
Attendance—57,879.		

INDIVIDUAL STATISTICS

RUSHING—Washington, Ervins 27-90, C. Smith 1-5, Mitchell 2-4, Frerotte 3-1. Indianapolis, Faulk 22-86, Harbaugh 3-12, Potts 5-11.

PASSING—Washington, Frerotte 17-32-0-226. Indianapolis, Harbaugh 11-18-2-186, Majkowski 7-12-1-109.

RECEIVING—Washington, Ellard 6-108, Winans 2-66, Mitchell 2-16, Howard 2-12, Jenkins 2-6, Ervins 1-9, C. Smith 1-6, Horton 1-3. Indianapolis, Faulk 8-127, Turner 4-67, Dawkins 3-55, Jackson 2-22, Cash 1-24.

MISSED FIELD GOAL ATTEMPTS—None.

INTERCEPTIONS—Washington, Bayless 1-19, A. Collins 1-21, Hollinquest 1-39.

KICKOFF RETURNS—Washington, Mitchell 3-61, Wycheck 1-13. Indianapolis, Humphrey 5-99, Radecic 1-17, Toner 1-8.

PUNT RETURNS—Washington, Mitchell 1-17. Indianapolis, Brewer 4-15.

SACKS—Washington, Harvey 2, Marshall 1, Palmer 1.

STEELERS 10, GIANTS 6

Sunday, October 23

Pittsburgh	0	3	0	7—10
N.Y. Giants	3	3	0	0— 6

First Quarter
N.Y.—FG Treadwell 19, 10:14.
Second Quarter
N.Y.—FG Daluiso 49, 5:20.
Pit—FG Anderson 29, 11:22.
Fourth Quarter
Pit—Morris 6 run (Anderson kick), 6:43.

TEAM STATISTICS

	Pittsburgh	N.Y. Giants
First downs	16	8
Rushes-yards	36-175	24-53
Passing	121	162
Punt returns-yards	4-37	3-12
Kickoff returns-yards	2-43	3-46
Interception returns-yards	2-27	1-0
Comp.-att.-int.	16-29-1	13-25-2
Sacked-yards lost	2-17	5-44
Punts-average	8-37	9-40
Fumbles-lost	4-3	5-1
Penalties-yards	7-42	3-27
Time of possession	31:51	28:09
Attendance—71,819.		

INDIVIDUAL STATISTICS

RUSHING—Pittsburgh, Morris 29-146, J.L. Williams 4-29, Johnson 1-1, O'Donnell 2-(minus 1). New York, Hampton 18-34, Da. Brown 6-19.

PASSING—Pittsburgh, O'Donnell 16-29-1-138. New York, Da. Brown 13-25-2-206.

RECEIVING—Pittsburgh, Morris 4-27, Hastings 3-38, Green 3-27, J.L. Williams 3-26, Thigpen 3-20. New York, Sherrard 4-40, Calloway 3-93, Pierce 2-9, Marshall 1-31, Cross 1-20, Rasheed 1-10, Meggett 1-3.

MISSED FIELD GOAL ATTEMPTS—None.

INTERCEPTIONS—Pittsburgh, Perry 1-2, Woodson 1-25. New York, Sparks 1-0.

KICKOFF RETURNS—Pittsburgh, Thigpen 1-17, Woodson 1-26. New York, Meggett 2-43, Lewis 1-3.

PUNT RETURNS—Pittsburgh, Woodson 4-37. New York, Meggett 3-12.

SACKS—Pittsburgh, Buckner 1, Kirkland 1, Lake 1, Lloyd 1, Seals 1. New York, Armstead 1, Howard 1.

LIONS 21, BEARS 16

Sunday, October 23

Chicago	0	7	9	0—16
Detroit	0	14	7	0—21

Second Quarter

Det—Perriman 6 pass from Mitchell (Hanson kick), :51.
Det—Spielman 25 fumble return (Hanson kick), 1:09.
Chi—Lewis 5 pass from Kramer (Butler kick), 14:34.

Third Quarter

Chi—FG Butler 22, 10:58.
Det—Gray 102 kickoff return (Hanson kick), 11:17.
Chi—Graham 76 pass from Kramer (pass failed), 13:58.

TEAM STATISTICS

	Chicago	Detroit
First downs	22	8
Rushes-yards	28-117	31-183
Passing	285	49
Punt returns-yards	4-39	2-21
Kickoff returns-yards	1-14	4-174
Interception returns-yards	1-5	3-19
Comp.-att.-int.	29-48-3	6-17-1
Sacked-yards lost	3-24	1-10
Punts-average	6-45	7-45
Fumbles-lost	3-1	4-2
Penalties-yards	10-74	7-61
Time of possession	36:36	23:24
Attendance—73,574.		

INDIVIDUAL STATISTICS

RUSHING—Chicago, Harris 14-66, Green 4-31, Tillman 10-20. Detroit, Sanders 23-167, Perriman 1-10, Mitchell 5-3, Moore 2-3.

PASSING—Chicago, Kramer 29-48-3-309. Detroit, Mitchell 6-17-1-59.

RECEIVING—Chicago, Graham 7-136, Green 5-47, Cook 5-38, Conway 5-37, Harris 3-17, Gedney 2-18, Tillman 1-11, Lewis 1-5. Detroit, Hallock 1-21, H. Moore 1-14, Matthews 1-8, Holman 1-6, Perriman 1-6, Sanders 1-4.

MISSED FIELD GOAL ATTEMPTS—Chicago, Butler 46.

INTERCEPTIONS—Chicago, Woolford 1-5. Detroit, Mack 1-0, Massey 1-5, McNeil 1-14.

KICKOFF RETURNS—Chicago, Lewis 1-14. Detroit, Gray 4-174.

PUNT RETURNS—Chicago, Conway 4-39. Detroit, Gray 2-21.

SACKS—Chicago, Armstrong 1. Detroit, Porcher 1, Owens 1.

COWBOYS 28, CARDINALS 21

Sunday, October 23

Dallas	7	7	0	14—28
Arizona	0	14	0	7—21

First Quarter

Dal—Harper 15 pass from Aikman (Boniol kick), 4:33.

Second Quarter

Ari—Beuerlein 1 run (Peterson kick), :57.
Ari—Moore 4 run (Peterson kick), 13:04.
Dal—Irvin 5 pass from Peete (Boniol kick), 14:05.

Fourth Quarter

Ari—Proehl 9 pass from Beuerlein (Peterson kick), :08.
Dal—Irvin 65 pass from Peete (Boniol kick), 1:42.
Dal—E. Smith 6 run (Boniol kick), 9:47.

TEAM STATISTICS

	Dallas	Arizona
First downs	14	22
Rushes-yards	26-75	37-97
Passing	237	208
Punt returns-yards	4-35	3-13
Kickoff returns-yards	2-74	5-58
Interception returns-yards	0-0	0-0
Comp.-att.-int.	15-24-0	18-31-0

	Dallas	Arizona
Sacked-yards lost	0-0	1-5
Punts-average	5-43	7-45
Fumbles-lost	1-0	1-0
Penalties-yards	6-56	6-42
Time of possession	22:51	37:09
Attendance—71,023.		

INDIVIDUAL STATISTICS

RUSHING—Dallas, E. Smith 21-76, Johnston 1-3, Peete 4-(minus 4). Arizona, Moore 24-81, Centers 9-23, Hearst 2-2, Beuerlein 2-(minus 9).

PASSING—Dallas, Aikman 3-5-0-51, Peete 12-19-0-186. Arizona, Beuerlein 18-31-0-213.

RECEIVING—Dallas, Irvin 5-115, Harper 4-75, Novacek 3-31, E. Smith 2-10, Johnston 1-6. Arizona, Centers 7-52, Clark 3-65, Proehl 3-40, Ware 2-25, R. Hill 2-24, Hearst 1-7.

MISSED FIELD GOAL ATTEMPTS—Dallas, Boniol 43.

INTERCEPTIONS—None.

KICKOFF RETURNS—Dallas, K. Williams 2-74. Arizona, McAfee 4-45, Robinson 1-13.

PUNT RETURNS—Dallas, K. Williams 4-35. Arizona, Robinson 3-13.

SACKS—Dallas, Maryland 1.

RAIDERS 30, FALCONS 17

Sunday, October 23

Atlanta	10	0	0	7—17
L.A. Raiders	0	14	10	6—30

First Quarter

Atl—FG N. Johnson 23, 5:06.
Atl—Heyward 1 run (N. Johnson kick), 12:10.

Second Quarter

L.A.—H. Williams 1 run (Jaeger kick), 2:49.
L.A.—Brown 20 pass from Hostetler (Jaeger kick), 6:36.

Third Quarter

L.A.—Brown 31 pass from Hostetler (Jaeger kick), 4:05.
L.A.—FG Jaeger 46, 11:41.

Fourth Quarter

Atl—Mathis 3 pass from J. George (N. Johnson kick), :07.
L.A.—FG Jaeger 31, 6:21.
L.A.—FG Jaeger 24, 12:37.

TEAM STATISTICS

	Atlanta	L.A. Raiders
First downs	15	21
Rushes-yards	21-70	31-116
Passing	185	197
Punt returns-yards	1-9	2-20
Kickoff returns-yards	7-168	4-110
Interception returns-yards	0-0	2-34
Comp.-att.-int.	16-30-2	21-30-0
Sacked-yards lost	4-33	2-7
Punts-average	4-32	1-53
Fumbles-lost	1-0	1-1
Penalties-yards	8-70	7-31
Time of possession	27:28	32:32
Attendance—42,192.		

INDIVIDUAL STATISTICS

RUSHING—Atlanta, Heyward 19-71, Anderson 2-(minus 1). Los Angeles, H. Williams 27-107, Hostetler 4-9.

PASSING—Atlanta, J. George 16-29-1-218, Hebert 0-1-1-0. Los Angeles, Hostetler 21-30-0-204.

RECEIVING—Atlanta, Mathis 4-42, Lyons 4-25, Rison 2-56, Sanders 2-37, Heyward 2-35, Harris 2-23. Los Angeles, Brown 8-130, H. Williams 8-43, Rathman 3-13, Wright 1-10, Ismail 1-8.

MISSED FIELD GOAL ATTEMPTS—Los Angeles, Jaeger 38.

INTERCEPTIONS—Los Angeles, Washington 2-34.

KICKOFF RETURNS—Atlanta, Verdin 5-121, Harris 2-47. Los Angeles, Ismail 3-81, Wright 1-29.

PUNT RETURNS—Atlanta, Verdin 1-9. Los Angeles, Brown 2-20.

SACKS—Atlanta, Doleman 1, Harper 1. Los Angeles, Lewis 1, McGlockton 1, Trapp 1, Wallace 1.

49ERS 41, BUCCANEERS 16

Sunday, October 23

Tampa Bay	0	0	0	16—16
San Francisco	7	10	17	7—41

First Quarter

S.F.—Watters 13 run (Brien kick), 8:30.

Second Quarter
S.F.—FG Brien 23, :39.
S.F.—McCaffrey 7 pass from Young (Brien kick), 14:18.
Third Quarter
S.F.—Floyd 1 run (Brien kick), 6:34.
S.F.—FG Brien 35, 10:44.
S.F.—Watters 2 run (Brien kick), 12:52.
Fourth Quarter
T.B.—Rhett 1 run (Copeland pass from Erickson), 5:46.
S.F.—Logan 1 pass from Grbac (Brien kick), 11:18.
T.B.—Dawsey 34 pass from Erickson (Harris pass from Erickson), 13:36.

TEAM STATISTICS

	Tampa Bay	San Francisco
First downs	17	28
Rushes-yards	25-110	35-181
Passing	125	270
Punt returns-yards	1-3	1-(-1)
Kickoff returns-yards	7-148	1-17
Interception returns-yards	0-0	1-8
Comp.-att.-int.	13-32-1	23-29-0
Sacked-yards lost	1-8	2-13
Punts-average	6-35	2-35
Fumbles-lost	0-0	3-1
Penalties-yards	9-111	10-78
Time of possession	24:51	35:09
Attendance—62,741.		

INDIVIDUAL STATISTICS
RUSHING—Tampa Bay, Rhett 9-46, Workman 10-41, McDowell 5-23, Royster 1-0. San Francisco, Watters 14-103, Floyd 8-34, Young 2-31, Loville 6-11, Logan 3-4, Grbac 2-(minus 2).
PASSING—Tampa Bay, Dilfer 7-23-1-45, Erickson 5-8-0-67, Stryzinski 1-1-0-21. San Francisco, Young 20-26-0-255, Grbac 3-3-0-28.
RECEIVING—Tampa Bay, Dawsey 4-65, Harris 3-34, McDowell 3-10, Rhett 2-3, M. Carter 1-21. San Francisco, Jones 5-76, Watters 4-64, Rice 4-57, McCaffrey 3-34, Taylor 2-26, Singleton 2-7, D. Carter 1-10, Floyd 1-1, Logan 1-1.
MISSED FIELD GOAL ATTEMPTS—None.
INTERCEPTIONS—San Francisco, Davis 1-8.
KICKOFF RETURNS—Tampa Bay, Buckley 3-75, C. Wilson 3-73, M. Carter 1-0. San Francisco, D. Carter 1-17.
PUNT RETURNS—Tampa Bay, Hawkins 1-3. San Francisco, D. Carter 1-(minus 1).
SACKS—Tampa Bay, Culpepper 1, Dotson 1. San Francisco, Stublefield 1.

BRONCOS 20, CHARGERS 15
Sunday, October 23

Denver	0	7	7	6—20
San Diego	6	6	0	3—15

First Quarter
S.D.—FG Carney 22, 9:23.
S.D.—FG Carney 39, 11:27.
Second Quarter
S.D.—FG Carney 37, :53.
Den—L. Russell 3 run (Elam kick), 9:51.
S.D.—FG Carney 26, 15:00.
Third Quarter
Den—Sharpe 43 pass from Elway (Elam kick), 12:48.
Fourth Quarter
S.D.—FG Carney 44, 3:49.
Den—FG Elam 54, 4:58.
Den—FG Elam 25, 10:53.

TEAM STATISTICS

	Denver	San Diego
First downs	16	19
Rushes-yards	36-69	25-166
Passing	225	155
Punt returns-yards	4-70	2-9
Kickoff returns-yards	4-118	4-83
Interception returns-yards	3-5	1-32
Comp.-att.-int.	22-31-1	19-39-3
Sacked-yards lost	3-16	1-7
Punts-average	4-44	5-46
Fumbles-lost	2-2	1-0
Penalties-yards	7-70	9-81
Time of possession	34:09	25:51
Attendance—61,626.		

INDIVIDUAL STATISTICS
RUSHING—Denver, L. Russell 18-35, Elway 7-21, Milburn 5-8, Clark 2-5, Rivers 4-0. San Diego, Means 19-100, Bieniemy 2-39, Jefferson 1-22, Hendrickson 1-3, Harmon 2-2.
PASSING—Denver, Elway 22-31-1-241. San Diego, Humphries 17-33-3-142, Gilbert 2-6-0-20.
RECEIVING—Denver, Miller 7-51, Sharpe 6-121, L. Russell 4-33, Milburn 3-23, D. Russell 2-13. San Diego, Harmon 8-69, Means 6-41, Martin 3-39, Seay 1-8, Jefferson 1-5.
MISSED FIELD GOAL ATTEMPTS—Denver, Elam 49.
INTERCEPTIONS—Denver, Crockett 1-0, B. Smith 1-0, Washington 1-5. San Diego, Carrington 1-32.
KICKOFF RETURNS—Denver, By'not'e 4-118. San Diego, Coleman 3-71, Harmon 1-12.
PUNT RETURNS—Denver, Milburn 4-70. San Diego, Gordon 2-9.
SACKS—Denver, Dronett 1. San Diego, Mims 1, O'Neal 1, Seau 1.

EAGLES 21, OILERS 6
Monday, October 24

Houston	3	3	0	0— 6
Philadelphia	0	7	7	7—21

First Quarter
Hou—FG Del Greco 21, 8:32.
Second Quarter
Phi—Garner 1 run (Murray kick), 11:08.
Hou—FG Del Greco 24, 14:42.
Third Quarter
Phi—Barnett 53 pass from Cunningham (Murray kick), 10:36.
Fourth Quarter
Phi—Joseph 35 pass from Cunningham (Murray kick), 12:42.

TEAM STATISTICS

	Houston	Philadelphia
First downs	15	14
Rushes-yards	29-65	31-85
Passing	214	287
Punt returns-yards	5-6	4-52
Kickoff returns-yards	3-64	3-54
Interception returns-yards	1-13	1-17
Comp.-att.-int.	16-33-1	13-24-1
Sacked-yards lost	3-17	3-23
Punts-average	5-42	5-41
Fumbles-lost	4-3	2-1
Penalties-yards	1-5	9-65
Time of possession	31:06	28:54
Attendance—65,233.		

INDIVIDUAL STATISTICS
RUSHING—Houston, Brown 27-67, Carlson 1-1, Wellman 1-(minus 3). Philadelphia, Walker 9-37, Garner 13-24, Hebron 3-21, Cunningham 6-3.
PASSING—Houston, Carlson 11-22-1-164, Tolliver 5-11-0-67. Philadelphia, Cunningham 13-24-1-310.
RECEIVING—Houston, Givins 4-91, Jeffires 3-52, Brown 3-43, Slaughter 3-30, White 1-8, Carter 1-4, Wellman 1-3. Philadelphia, Barnett 5-187, Bavaro 3-38, Williams 2-43, Joseph 1-35, Garner 1-6, Alexander 1-1.
MISSED FIELD GOAL ATTEMPTS—None.
INTERCEPTIONS—Houston, D. Lewis 1-13. Philadelphia, Allen 1-17.
KICKOFF RETURNS—Houston, Mills 3-64. Philadelphia, Hebron 2-46, Sydner 1-8.
PUNT RETURNS—Houston, Givins 4-6, Dishman 1-0. Philadelphia, Sydner 4-52.
SACKS—Houston, Davidson 1, Steve Jackson 1, Lathon 1. Philadelphia, Thomas 2, Fuller 1.

WEEK 9

RESULTS

Arizona 20, Pittsburgh 17 (OT)
Buffalo 44, Kansas City 10
Dallas 23, Cincinnati 20
Denver 26, Cleveland 14
Detroit 28, N.Y. Giants 25 (OT)
Indianapolis 28, N.Y. Jets 25
L.A. Raiders 17, Houston 14
Miami 23, New England 3
Minnesota 36, Tampa Bay 13
Philadelphia 31, Washington 29
San Diego 35, Seattle 15
Green Bay 33, Chicago 6
   Open date: Atlanta, L.A. Rams, New
Orleans, San Francisco

STANDINGS

AFC EAST	W	L	T	Pct.
Miami	6	2	0	.750
Buffalo	5	3	0	.625
N.Y. Jets	4	4	0	.500
Indianapolis	4	5	0	.444
New England	3	5	0	.375

AFC CENTRAL	W	L	T	Pct.
Cleveland	6	2	0	.750
Pittsburgh	5	3	0	.625
Houston	1	7	0	.125
Cincinnati	0	8	0	.000

AFC WEST	W	L	T	Pct.
San Diego	7	1	0	.875
Kansas City	5	3	0	.625
L.A. Raiders	4	4	0	.500
Denver	3	5	0	.375
Seattle	3	5	0	.375

NFC EAST	W	L	T	Pct.
Dallas	7	1	0	.875
Philadelphia	6	2	0	.750
N.Y. Giants	3	5	0	.375
Arizona	3	5	0	.375
Washington	2	7	0	.222

NFC CENTRAL	W	L	T	Pct.
Minnesota	6	2	0	.750
Chicago	4	4	0	.500
Detroit	4	4	0	.500
Green Bay	4	4	0	.500
Tampa Bay	2	6	0	.250

NFC WEST	W	L	T	Pct.
San Francisco	6	2	0	.750
Atlanta	4	4	0	.500
L.A. Rams	3	5	0	.375
New Orleans	3	5	0	.375

HIGHLIGHTS

Hero of the week: Detroit's Barry Sanders, who rushed for 146 yards on 26 attempts in the Lions' 28-25 overtime victory against the New York Giants. Sanders caught only two passes, but he eluded two defenders to gain a first down on one of them to keep the Lions' game-winning drive alive.

Goat of the week: Pittsburgh rookie Charles Johnson, who fumbled the overtime kickoff to set up the game-winning points in the Steelers' 20-17 loss to Arizona. David Merritt recovered the ball at Pittsburgh's 32, and Greg Davis kicked a game-winning 51-yard field goal four plays later.

Sub of the week: San Diego quarterback Gale Gilbert, subbing for injured Stan Humphries, completed 11 of 14 passes for 125 yards and two touchdowns in a 35-15 victory over Seattle. The touchdown passes were the first in four seasons for Gilbert, a perennial clipboard holder who did not even get into a game in 1991 or '92.

Comeback of the week: Philadelphia edged Washington, 31-29, on Eddie Murray's 30-yard field goal with 19 seconds left. Randall Cunningham drove the Eagles 63 yards in 12 plays to set Murray's game-winner after Chip Lohmiller's 40-yard field goal with 3:58 left gave the Redskins a 29-28 lead.

Blowout of the week: Buffalo crushed Kansas City, 44-10, behind Jim Kelly's four touchdown passes and a defense that forced five turnovers. The Bills scored 17 points in 3:05 of the second quarter to take command en route to handing the Chiefs their worst defeat in a non-strike game since 1984.

Nail-biter of the week: The Los Angeles Raiders held on to beat Houston, 17-14, when a 52-yard field goal attempt by the Oilers' Al Del Greco hit the crossbar and bounced away as time expired. The Oilers had taken a 14-10 lead on Billy Joe Tolliver's 7-yard pass to Haywood Jeffires with 3:19 left. Jeff Hostetler completed four of five passes on the Raiders' ensuing 67-yard drive, which ended on his 11-yard touchdown pass to Tim Brown with 1:50 left.

Hit of the week: By Colts cornerback Eugene Daniel, who tackled Jets receiver Rob Moore just short of a first down after New York, trailing by three, had driven to the Colts' 38 in the final minute.

Oddity of the week: The Colts had no penalties in a game for the first time since 1976. In the '76 game, Ted Marchibroda was the Colts' coach and the opponent was the Jets.

Top rusher: Sanders' 146-yard effort against the Giants boosted him over the 1,000-yard mark for the sixth consecutive year.

Top passer: John Elway completed 30 of 41 passes for 349 yards and two touchdowns in Denver's 26-14 victory over Cleveland.

Top receiver: Darnay Scott caught four passes for 155 yards and two touchdowns in Cincinnati's 23-20 loss to Dallas.

Notes: Dallas tied a club record with its seventh consecutive road victory, but it didn't come easy. Cincinnati quarterback Jeff Blake, in his first NFL start, threw for 247 yards and two touchdowns, 67- and 55-yarders to Scott that stunned the Cowboys and gave the Bengals a short-lived 14-0 lead.... Detroit became the first NFL team to win three overtime games in one year.... Minnesota cornerback Anthony Parker scored a touchdown for the third consecutive game, the first Vikings defensive player to perform the feat.... Sanders became the second running back to rush for 1,000 yards in each of his first six seasons. Eric Dickerson had a seven-year streak from 1983-89.... Bernie Parmalee's 123 yards rushing against New England gave him 273 in his last two games, the best two-game total in Miami history. Mercury Morris had 258 yards in back-to-back games in 1973.... The Redskins used a different starting quarterback against the Eagles for the fifth consecutive game. Mark Rypien, Cary Conklin, Rich Gannon, Heath Shuler and Gus Frerotte made the starts, and Washington lost each time.... Natrone Means became the first Charger to rush for 100 yards in four consecutive games.... Tampa Bay lost its 200th regular-season game (in 284 contests) since entering the league in 1976. . . . Hall of Famers Dick Butkus (51) and Gale Sayers (40) had their uniform numbers retired at halftime of the Bears-Packers game on Monday night, but lousy weather resulted in a crowd of 47,381 at Soldier Field. A total of 66,941 tickets were sold.

Quote of the week: Buffalo's Bruce Smith, on the Bills-Chiefs matchup: "Before the game, in the locker room, I told the guys, 'This game is rated R—adult language and a lot of violence.' "

GAME SUMMARIES

BILLS 44, CHIEFS 10
Sunday, October 30

Kansas City	7	0	3	0—10
Buffalo	14	17	3	10—44

First Quarter
Buf—Metzelaars 11 pass from Kelly (Christie kick), 5:49.
K.C.—Allen 9 run (Elliott kick), 9:32.
Buf—Reed 23 pass from Kelly (Christie kick), 15:00.
Second Quarter
Buf—Thomas 2 run (Christie kick), 11:44.
Buf—FG Christie 49, 14:00.
Buf—Reed 6 pass from Kelly (Christie kick), 14:49.
Third Quarter
K.C.—FG Elliott 22, 4:26.
Buf—FG Christie 26, 9:15.
Fourth Quarter
Buf—Metzelaars 3 pass from Kelly (Christie kick), :06.
Buf—FG Christie 24, 5:27.

TEAM STATISTICS

	Kansas City	Buffalo
First downs	16	17
Rushes-yards	27-87	39-177
Passing	186	180
Punt returns-yards	2-5	3-20
Kickoff returns-yards	7-108	3-64
Interception returns-yards	0-0	3-51
Comp.-att.-int.	18-36-3	14-22-0
Sacked-yards lost	3-16	1-4
Punts-average	5-41	4-48
Fumbles-lost	2-2	1-0
Penalties-yards	10-75	3-20
Time of possession	30:17	29:43
Attendance—79,501.		

INDIVIDUAL STATISTICS
RUSHING—Kansas City, Hill 10-34, Allen 8-27, D. Bennett 4-14, Anders 3-13, Montana 2-(minus 1). Buffalo, K. Davis 11-83, Thomas 21-77, Reed 1-9, Reich 4-4, Turner 2-4.
PASSING—Kansas City, Montana 12-21-1-124, Bono 5-10-1-65, Blundin 1-5-1-13. Buffalo, Kelly 14-22-0-184.
RECEIVING—Kansas City, Dawson 6-74, Martin 4-43, Allen 3-18, W. Davis 2-29, D. Bennett 1-15, Greene 1-13, Anders 1-10. Buffalo, Reed 5-106, Metzelaars 4-33, Thomas 3-27, Beebe 1-9, Gardner 1-9.
MISSED FIELD GOAL ATTEMPTS—None.
INTERCEPTIONS—Buffalo, C. Bennett 1-6, Burris 1-0, Jones 1-45.
KICKOFF RETURNS—Kansas City, Dickerson 5-96, D. Bennett 1-12, Booker 1-0. Buffalo, Bu. Brooks 3-64.
PUNT RETURNS—Kansas City, Hughes 2-5. Buffalo, Burris 3-20.
SACKS—Kansas City, Mickell 1. Buffalo, Hansen 1, B. Smith 1, C. Bennett ½, Wright ½.

COWBOYS 23, BENGALS 20
Sunday, October 30

Dallas	0	14	6	3—23
Cincinnati	7	10	3	0—20

First Quarter
Cin—Scott 67 pass from Blake (Pelfrey kick), 6:02.
Second Quarter
Cin—Scott 55 pass from Blake (Pelfrey kick), :08.
Dal—Harper 27 pass from Aikman (Boniol kick), 3:04.
Cin—FG Pelfrey 22, 9:50.
Dal—Irvin 10 pass from Aikman (Boniol kick), 14:30.

Third Quarter
Dal—FG Boniol 37, 5:53.
Cin—FG Pelfrey 33, 7:58.
Dal—FG Boniol 43, 14:54.
Fourth Quarter
Dal—FG Boniol 38, 10:00.

TEAM STATISTICS

	Dallas	Cincinnati
First downs	20	13
Rushes-yards	32-96	23-77
Passing	272	243
Punt returns-yards	2-12	2-23
Kickoff returns-yards	4-122	6-117
Interception returns-yards	0-0	1-0
Comp.-att.-int.	20-33-1	14-32-0
Sacked-yards lost	0-0	1-4
Punts-average	3-44	6-42
Fumbles-lost	1-1	1-1
Penalties-yards	8-51	8-60
Time of possession	39:55	20:05
Attendance—57,096.		

INDIVIDUAL STATISTICS
RUSHING—Dallas, E. Smith 25-92, Johnston 3-13, Aikman 3-(minus 2), K. Williams 1-(minus 7). Cincinnati, Fenner 13-41, Broussard 5-14, Scott 1-13, Blake 3-9, Green 1-0.
PASSING—Dallas, Aikman 20-33-1-272. Cincinnati, Blake 14-32-0-247.
RECEIVING—Dallas, Harper 6-125, Johnston 6-30, Irvin 5-72, K. Williams 2-36, E. Smith 1-9. Cincinnati, Scott 4-155, Pickens 4-40, Green 2-26, To. McGee 2-17, Broussard 1-6, Sadowski 1-3.
MISSED FIELD GOAL ATTEMPTS—Dallas, Boniol 38.
INTERCEPTIONS—Cincinnati, Sawyer 1-0.
KICKOFF RETURNS—Dallas, K. Williams 4-122. Cincinnati, Ball 4-90, Green 1-23, To. McGee 1-4.
PUNT RETURNS—Dallas, K. Williams 2-12. Cincinnati, Sawyer 2-23.
SACKS—Dallas, Jeffcoat 1.

EAGLES 31, REDSKINS 29
Sunday, October 30

Philadelphia	0	7	7	17—31
Washington	7	10	3	9—29

First Quarter
Was—Howard 13 pass from Frerotte (Lohmiller kick), 10:37.
Second Quarter
Was—Horton 15 pass from Frerotte (Lohmiller kick), 3:56.
Phi—Walker 11 pass from Cunningham (Murray kick), 9:38.
Was—FG Lohmiller 54, 15:00.
Third Quarter
Phi—G. Jackson 55 interception return (Murray kick), 1:37.
Was—FG Lohmiller 23, 8:43.
Fourth Quarter
Phi—Walker 1 run (Murray kick), :03.
Phi—Hebron 6 run (Murray kick), 4:15.
Was—Jenkins 1 pass from Frerotte (run failed), 6:31.
Was—FG Lohmiller 40, 11:02.
Phi—FG Murray 30, 14:41.

TEAM STATISTICS

	Philadelphia	Washington
First downs	19	20
Rushes-yards	32-131	32-168
Passing	165	181
Punt returns-yards	2-(-3)	1-4
Kickoff returns-yards	6-144	6-138
Interception returns-yards	2-60	0-0
Comp.-att.-int.	18-31-0	13-30-2
Sacked-yards lost	1-8	1-8
Punts-average	5-41	3-39
Fumbles-lost	0-0	1-1
Penalties-yards	5-54	4-15
Time of possession	29:42	30:18
Attendance—53,530.		

INDIVIDUAL STATISTICS
RUSHING—Philadelphia, Hebron 8-47, Garner 12-38, Walker 5-16, Joseph 4-16, Cunningham 3-14. Washington, Mitchell 16-85, Ervins 16-83.
PASSING—Philadelphia, Cunningham 18-31-0-173. Washington, Frerotte 13-30-2-189.
RECEIVING—Philadelphia, Joseph 5-40, Walker 4-36, Barnett 2-32, Bavaro 2-11, Williams 1-14, Garner 1-12, Bailey 1-11, Hebron 1-9, M.

Johnson 1-8. Washington, Ellard 5-84, Howard 3-34, Smith 2-32, Winans 1-23, Horton 1-15, Jenkins 1-1.

MISSED FIELD GOAL ATTEMPTS—Philadelphia, Murray 49, 42.

INTERCEPTIONS—Philadelphia, G. Jackson 1-55, McMillian 1-5.

KICKOFF RETURNS—Philadelphia, Hebron 4-81, Walker 2-63. Washington, Mitchell 6-134, Tr. Johnson 0-4.

PUNT RETURNS—Philadelphia, Sydner 2-(minus 3). Washington, Mitchell 1-4.

SACKS—Philadelphia, Harmon 1. Washington, Ti. Johnson 1.

LIONS 28, GIANTS 25

Sunday, October 30

Detroit	2	6	10	7	3—28
N.Y. Giants	0	10	0	15	0—25

First Quarter
Det—Safety, Brown fumbled out of the end zone, 9:30.

Second Quarter
N.Y.—Hampton 4 run (Treadwell kick), 4:26.
N.Y.—FG Treadwell 25, 13:45.
Det—H. Moore 14 pass from Mitchell (pass failed), 14:35.

Third Quarter
Det—FG Hanson 31, 6:47.
Det—Johnson 48 interception return (Hanson kick), 11:16.

Fourth Quarter
N.Y.—Meggett 56 punt return (Hampton run), 3:53.
Det—H. Moore 1 pass from Mitchell (Hanson kick), 6:12.
N.Y.—Pierce 7 pass from Brown (Treadwell kick), 13:45.

Overtime
Det—FG Hanson 24, 6:43.

TEAM STATISTICS

	Detroit	N.Y. Giants
First downs	24	23
Rushes-yards	29-149	45-195
Passing	180	149
Punt returns-yards	2-20	2-64
Kickoff returns-yards	4-69	6-113
Interception returns-yards	1-48	3-12
Comp.-att.-int.	16-30-3	19-25-1
Sacked-yards lost	0-0	1-10
Punts-average	2-45	4-44
Fumbles-lost	1-0	3-0
Penalties-yards	6-44	14-120
Time of possession	28:26	38:17
Attendance—75,124.		

INDIVIDUAL STATISTICS

RUSHING—Detroit, Sanders 26-146, D. Moore 2-2, Mitchell 1-1. New York, Hampton 30-138, Meggett 4-35, Da. Brown 6-11, Downs 3-8, Rasheed 2-3.

PASSING—Detroit, Mitchell 16-30-3-180. New York, Da. Brown 19-25-1-159.

RECEIVING—Detroit, H. Moore 9-106, Perriman 3-40, Sanders 2-22, D. Moore 1-10, Hallock 1-2. New York, Pierce 5-49, Hampton 4-13, Marshall 3-47, Meggett 3-21, Calloway 2-16, Cross 1-8, Downs 1-5.

MISSED FIELD GOAL ATTEMPTS—New York, Treadwell 40.

INTERCEPTIONS—Detroit, Johnson 1-48. New York, Campbell 1-2, Raymond 1-0, J. Williams 1-10.

KICKOFF RETURNS—Detroit, Gray 3-69, Morton 1-0. New York, Lewis 5-90, Meggett 1-23.

PUNT RETURNS—Detroit, Gray 2-20. New York, Meggett 2-64.

SACKS—Detroit, Thomas 1.

VIKINGS 36, BUCCANEERS 13

Sunday, October 30

Minnesota	10	13	10	3—36	
Tampa Bay	0	7	0	6—13	

First Quarter
Min—FG Reveiz 36, 7:18.
Min—Parker 41 interception return (Reveiz kick), 8:24.

Second Quarter
Min—Allen 37 run (Reveiz kick), 1:27.
T.B.—Wilson 62 pass from Erickson (Husted kick), 3:04.
Min—FG Reveiz 21, 11:12.
Min—FG Reveiz 48, 14:03.

Third Quarter
Min—Lee 8 pass from Moon (Reveiz kick), 8:51.
Min—FG Reveiz 38, 13:50.

Fourth Quarter
Min—FG Reveiz 35, :25.
T.B.—Hawkins 3 pass from Dilfer (pass failed), 8:46.

TEAM STATISTICS

	Minnesota	Tampa Bay
First downs	19	14
Rushes-yards	32-149	14-49
Passing	212	185
Punt returns-yards	0-0	1-0
Kickoff returns-yards	2-31	9-265
Interception returns-yards	3-73	1-(-1)
Comp.-att.-int.	24-38-1	17-31-3
Sacked-yards lost	0-0	3-19
Punts-average	2-46	2-45
Fumbles-lost	1-1	4-2
Penalties-yards	5-30	4-35
Time of possession	37:12	22:48
Attendance—42,110.		

INDIVIDUAL STATISTICS

RUSHING—Minnesota, Allen 17-113, Evans 5-17, Moon 3-11, Graham 5-6, Smith 2-2. Tampa Bay, Rhett 9-22, Workman 3-21, McDowell 2-6.

PASSING—Minnesota, Moon 19-33-1-182, Johnson 5-5-0-30. Tampa Bay, Erickson 10-18-2-129, Dilfer 7-13-1-75.

RECEIVING—Minnesota, Carter 5-51, Jordan 5-49, Reed 4-41, Lee 4-28, Smith 2-15, Cooper 2-10, Allen 1-10, Ismail 1-8. Tampa Bay, Dawsey 5-73, J. Harris 3-28, Hawkins 3-18, Wilson 2-66, McDowell 2-8, Armstrong 1-8, Rhett 1-3.

MISSED FIELD GOAL ATTEMPTS—Tampa Bay, Husted 48, 44.

INTERCEPTIONS—Minnesota, Glenn 1-32, Parker 1-41, Washington 1-0. Tampa Bay, Nickerson 1-(minus 1).

KICKOFF RETURNS—Minnesota, Ismail 2-31. Tampa Bay, Turner 8-242, Buckley 1-26.

PUNT RETURNS—Tampa Bay, Turner 1-0.

SACKS—Minnesota, Barker 1, Randle 1, Thomas 1.

BRONCOS 26, BROWNS 14

Sunday, October 30

Cleveland	0	6	0	8—14	
Denver	7	7	6	6—26	

First Quarter
Den—Evans 1 pass from Elway (Elam kick), 14:43.

Second Quarter
Cle—FG Stover 43, 3:18.
Cle—FG Stover 45, 9:08.
Den—L. Russell 1 run (Elam kick), 13:16.

Third Quarter
Den—FG Elam 27, 4:54.
Den—FG Elam 32, 14:26.

Fourth Quarter
Cle—Carrier 6 pass from Rypien (Alexander pass from Rypien), 1:41.
Den—Milburn 17 pass from Elway (pass failed), 3:25.

TEAM STATISTICS

	Cleveland	Denver
First downs	17	29
Rushes-yards	17-41	37-114
Passing	276	343
Punt returns-yards	2-19	3-22
Kickoff returns-yards	4-71	4-61
Interception returns-yards	0-0	0-0
Comp.-att.-int.	23-45-0	30-41-0
Sacked-yards lost	1-8	1-6
Punts-average	5-45	4-41
Fumbles-lost	2-1	2-2
Penalties-yards	8-59	9-66
Time of possession	21:53	38:07
Attendance—73,190.		

INDIVIDUAL STATISTICS

RUSHING—Cleveland, Metcalf 11-32, Hoard 3-6, Rypien 2-3, D. Alexander 1-0. Denver, Milburn 8-38, L. Russell 16-26, Rivers 6-20, Clark 5-16, Elway 2-14.

PASSING—Cleveland, Testaverde 6-14-0-74, Rypien 17-30-0-210, Metcalf 0-1-0-0. Denver, Elway 30-41-0-349.

RECEIVING—Cleveland, Metcalf 8-62, D. Alexander 5-76, Hoard 5-57, Carrier 2-48, McCardell 2-35, Kinchen 1-6. Denver, Sharpe 9-85, Milburn 8-76, Miller 4-82, L. Russell 3-31, Rivers 3-27, D. Russell 2-47, Evans 1-1.

MISSED FIELD GOAL ATTEMPTS—None.

INTERCEPTIONS—None.

KICKOFF RETURNS—Cleveland, Baldwin 3-44, Metcalf 1-27. Denver, By'not'e 3-53, Campbell 1-8.

PUNT RETURNS—Cleveland, Metcalf 2-19. Denver, Milburn 3-22.

SACKS—Cleveland, Burnett 1. Denver, Fletcher 1.

CHARGERS 35, SEAHAWKS 15

Sunday, October 30

Seattle	0	7	0	8—15
San Diego	0	14	7	14—35

Second Quarter

Sea—C. Warren 9 run (Kasay kick), 2:19.

S.D.—FG Carney 25, 7:46.

S.D.—FG Carney 39, 13:15.

S.D.—Harmon 15 run (Harmon pass from Humphries), 13:45.

Third Quarter

S.D.—Means 5 run (Carney kick), 4:48.

Fourth Quarter

S.D.—Pupunu 8 pass from Gilbert (Carney kick), 3:17.

S.D.—T. Martin 16 pass from Gilbert (Carney kick), 13:14.

Sea—Vaughn 93 kickoff return (C. Warren run), 13:32.

TEAM STATISTICS

	Seattle	San Diego
First downs	14	25
Rushes-yards	24-112	41-161
Passing	171	187
Punt returns-yards	3-26	2-22
Kickoff returns-yards	6-196	2-60
Interception returns-yards	1-0	0-0
Comp.-att.-int.	15-30-0	18-31-1
Sacked-yards lost	3-6	2-24
Punts-average	8-44	6-48
Fumbles-lost	3-2	0-0
Penalties-yards	11-80	3-18
Time of possession	25:59	34:01
Attendance—59,001.		

INDIVIDUAL STATISTICS

RUSHING—Seattle, C. Warren 17-92, T. Warren 3-15, Mirer 3-7, S. Smith 1-(minus 2). San Diego, Means 26-104, Bieniemy 12-47, Harmon 1-15, Gilbert 2-(minus 5).

PASSING—Seattle, Mirer 15-30-0-177. San Diego, Humphries 7-17-0-86, Gilbert 11-14-1-125.

RECEIVING—Seattle, Blades 6-89, C. Warren 4-11, K. Martin 3-55, Johnson 2-22. San Diego, T. Martin 5-59, Harmon 3-60, Jefferson 2-29, Pupunu 2-23, Seay 2-18, Means 2-2, Young 1-14, Bieniemy 1-6.

MISSED FIELD GOAL ATTEMPTS—None.

INTERCEPTIONS—Seattle, Gray 1-0.

KICKOFF RETURNS—Seattle, Vaughn 6-196. San Diego, Coleman 2-60.

PUNT RETURNS—Seattle, McCloughan 3-26. San Diego, Gordon 2-22.

SACKS—Seattle, Spitulski 1, Wooden 1. San Diego, O'Neal 2, Mims 1.

DOLPHINS 23, PATRIOTS 3

Sunday, October 30

Miami	0	13	7	3—23
New England	3	0	0	0— 3

First Quarter

N.E.—FG Bahr 48, 8:20.

Second Quarter

Mia—FG Stoyanovich 44, 4:42.

Mia—FG Stoyanovich 50, 8:38.

Mia—Byars 1 run (Stoyanovich kick), 14:53.

Third Quarter

Mia—Byars 7 pass from Marino (Stoyanovich kick), 6:12.

Fourth Quarter

Mia—FG Stoyanovich 48, 2:04.

TEAM STATISTICS

	Miami	New England
First downs	20	11
Rushes-yards	34-140	20-46
Passing	198	142
Punt returns-yards	2-8	2-29
Kickoff returns-yards	2-39	6-110
Interception returns-yards	3-1	2-30
Comp.-att.-int.	21-36-2	21-41-3
Sacked-yards lost	0-0	2-11
Punts-average	4-40	4-38
Fumbles-lost	1-0	2-0
Penalties-yards	7-56	4-30
Time of possession	35:38	24:22
Attendance—59,167.		

INDIVIDUAL STATISTICS

RUSHING—Miami, Parmalee 25-123, Gary 4-8, Byars 2-5, Spikes 3-4. New England, Butts 6-23, Turner 6-18, Bledsoe 3-8, Thomas 3-(minus 1), Thompson 2-(minus 2).

PASSING—Miami, Marino 21-36-2-198. New England, Bledsoe 16-33-3-125, Zolak 5-8-0-28.

RECEIVING—Miami, Byars 8-77, Jackson 6-46, Parmalee 4-21, Fryar 2-33, Williams 1-21. New England, Thompson 8-45, Turner 6-36, Crittenden 3-29, Timpson 2-26, Coates 2-17.

MISSED FIELD GOAL ATTEMPTS—None.

INTERCEPTIONS—Miami, Atkins 1-1, Cross 1-0, Vincent 1-0. New England, H. Barnett 2-30.

KICKOFF RETURNS—Miami, McDuffie 2-39. New England, Thompson 4-83, Croom 1-18, Gash 1-9.

PUNT RETURNS—Miami, McDuffie 2-8. New England, T. Brown 2-29.

SACKS—Miami, Cross 1½, Veasey ½.

COLTS 28, JETS 25

Sunday, October 30

N.Y. Jets	0	10	8	7—25
Indianapolis	14	0	7	7—28

First Quarter

Ind—Turner 14 pass from Majkowski (Biasucci kick), 5:03.

Ind—Majkowski 3 run (Biasucci kick), 10:14.

Second Quarter

N.Y.—Monk 22 pass from Esiason (Lowery kick), 7:54.

N.Y.—FG Lowery 26, 15:00.

Third Quarter

Ind—Faulk 1 run (Biasucci kick), 7:12.

N.Y.—Lewis 18 interception return (Moore pass from Esiason), 11:27.

Fourth Quarter

Ind—Faulk 29 run (Biasucci kick), 6:33.

N.Y.—Moore 41 pass from Esiason (Lowery kick), 9:39.

TEAM STATISTICS

	N.Y. Jets	Indianapolis
First downs	14	22
Rushes-yards	21-57	39-179
Passing	199	151
Punt returns-yards	3-45	4-54
Kickoff returns-yards	5-106	4-70
Interception returns-yards	2-40	1-30
Comp.-att.-int.	22-41-1	14-22-2
Sacked-yards lost	1-2	1-8
Punts-average	7-42	3-44
Fumbles-lost	0-0	5-3
Penalties-yards	12-73	0-0
Time of possession	25:48	34:12
Attendance—44,350.		

INDIVIDUAL STATISTICS

RUSHING—New York, J. Johnson 12-44, A. Johnson 4-7, Baxter 2-6, Esiason 2-3, R. Moore 1-(minus 3). Indianapolis, Faulk 24-110, Humphrey 2-41, Majkowski 8-14, Potts 5-14.

PASSING—New York, Esiason 22-41-1-201. Indianapolis, Majkowski 14-22-2-159.

RECEIVING—New York, R. Moore 9-99, J. Johnson 4-21, Monk 3-34, Mitchell 3-26, A. Johnson 2-13, Thornton 1-8. Indianapolis, Turner 7-72, Potts 3-41, Faulk 2-21, Cash 1-18, Dawkins 1-7.

MISSED FIELD GOAL ATTEMPTS—None.

INTERCEPTIONS—New York, Hasty 1-22, Lewis 1-18. Indianapolis, Tate 1-30.

KICKOFF RETURNS—New York, Glenn 3-71, Prior 2-35. Indianapolis, Humphrey 3-56, Etheredge 1-14.

PUNT RETURNS—New York, Hicks 3-45. Indianapolis, Brewer 4-54.

SACKS—New York, Lageman 1. Indianapolis, Siragusa 1.

RAIDERS 17, OILERS 14

Sunday, October 30

Houston	0	7	0	7—14
L.A. Raiders	7	0	3	7—17

First Quarter

L.A.—H. Williams 2 run (Jaeger kick), 10:50.

Second Quarter

Hou—Tolliver 6 run (Del Greco kick), 14:34.

Third Quarter

L.A.—FG Jaeger 35, 11:39.

Fourth Quarter

Hou—Jeffires 7 pass from Tolliver (Del Greco kick), 11:41.

L.A.—T. Brown 11 pass from Hostetler (Jaeger kick), 13:10.

TEAM STATISTICS

	Houston	L.A. Raiders
First downs	21	16
Rushes-yards	25-99	33-134
Passing	203	144
Punt returns-yards	4-31	1-6
Kickoff returns-yards	4-79	3-54
Interception returns-yards	2-34	0-0
Comp.-att.-int.	19-43-0	15-29-2
Sacked-yards lost	3-23	1-7
Punts-average	7-40	5-46
Fumbles-lost	3-3	4-2
Penalties-yards	7-45	10-65
Time of possession	27:55	32:05

Attendance—40,473.

INDIVIDUAL STATISTICS

RUSHING—Houston, G. Brown 20-77, Tolliver 3-20, White 2-2. Los Angeles, H. Williams 29-128, Hostetler 4-6.

PASSING—Houston, Tolliver 19-43-0-226. Los Angeles, Hostetler 15-29-2-151.

RECEIVING—Houston, Slaughter 7-94, Jeffires 7-57, Wellman 2-35, G. Brown 2-33, Givins 1-7. Los Angeles, T. Brown 6-69, H. Williams 4-38, Wright 2-27, Glover 2-11, Ismail 1-6.

MISSED FIELD GOAL ATTEMPTS—Houston, Del Greco 52.

INTERCEPTIONS—Houston, D. Lewis 1-17, Robertson 1-17.

KICKOFF RETURNS—Houston, Jackson 4-79. Los Angeles, Ismail 2-54, J. Williams 1-0.

PUNT RETURNS—Houston, Givins 2-11, Hannah 1-0. Los Angeles, T. Brown 1-6.

SACKS—Houston, Childress 1. Los Angeles, McGlockton 2, Fredrickson 1.

CARDINALS 20, STEELERS 17

Sunday, October 30

Pittsburgh	0	14	0	3	0—17
Arizona	7	10	0	0	3—20

First Quarter
Ari—Centers 4 run (Davis kick), 11:10.
Second Quarter
Pit—Morris 11 run (Anderson kick), 2:02.
Ari—FG Davis 20, 11:47.
Pit—Thigpen 60 pass from O'Donnell (Anderson kick), 12:07.
Ari—Moore 1 run (Davis kick), 13:50.
Fourth Quarter
Pit—FG Anderson 23, 14:13.
Overtime
Ari—FG Davis 51, 1:40.

TEAM STATISTICS

	Pittsburgh	Arizona
First downs	13	17
Rushes-yards	20-85	37-99
Passing	232	236
Punt returns-yards	6-39	7-21
Kickoff returns-yards	4-86	4-73
Interception returns-yards	0-0	1-6
Comp.-att.-int.	18-31-1	13-27-0
Sacked-yards lost	4-28	2-15
Punts-average	6-41	7-43
Fumbles-lost	2-2	1-1
Penalties-yards	7-36	4-45
Time of possession	25:06	36:34

Attendance—73,400.

INDIVIDUAL STATISTICS

RUSHING—Pittsburgh, Morris 14-72, O'Donnell 3-13, Anderson 1-3, Williams 1-2, Johnson 1-(minus 5). Arizona, Moore 30-67, Beuerlein 1-19, Centers 6-13.

PASSING—Pittsburgh, O'Donnell 18-31-1-260. Arizona, Beuerlein 13-26-0-251, Moore 0-1-0-0.

RECEIVING—Pittsburgh, Williams 6-50, Green 5-97, Thigpen 3-95, Morris 2-12, Johnson 1-6, Hastings 1-0. Arizona, Proehl 3-94, Clark 3-38, R. Hill 2-88, Ware 2-22, Centers 2-6, Hearst 1-3.

MISSED FIELD GOAL ATTEMPTS—Arizona, Davis 26.

INTERCEPTIONS—Arizona, A. Williams 1-6.

KICKOFF RETURNS—Pittsburgh, Johnson 2-39, Thigpen 1-27, Woodson 1-20. Arizona, Henesey 4-73.

PUNT RETURNS—Pittsburgh, Woodson 3-29, Johnson 1-10. Arizona, Robinson 2-15.

SACKS—Pittsburgh, Lloyd 2. Arizona, Swann 1½, Joyner 1, Simmons 1, Bankston ½.

PACKERS 33, BEARS 6

Monday, October 31

Green Bay	0	14	7	12—33
Chicago	0	0	0	6— 6

Second Quarter
G.B.—Bennett 3 run (Jacke kick), 4:20.
G.B.—Favre 36 run (Jacke kick), 10:14.
Third Quarter
G.B.—Bennett 1 run (Jacke kick), 12:35.
Fourth Quarter
G.B.—Bennett 13 pass from Favre (run failed), 2:04.
Chi—Graham 5 pass from Walsh (pass failed), 9:05.
G.B.—Cobb 9 run (kick failed), 13:07.

TEAM STATISTICS

	Green Bay	Chicago
First downs	17	12
Rushes-yards	45-223	28-94
Passing	82	159
Punt returns-yards	1-0	1-0
Kickoff returns-yards	1-27	5-101
Interception returns-yards	3-37	0-0
Comp.-att.-int.	6-15-0	21-35-3
Sacked-yards lost	0-0	2-15
Punts-average	7-27	5-35
Fumbles-lost	1-0	4-2
Penalties-yards	3-15	3-10
Time of possession	31:18	28:42

Attendance—47,381.

INDIVIDUAL STATISTICS

RUSHING—Green Bay, Bennett 26-105, Favre 2-58, Cobb 16-54, L. Johnson 1-6. Chicago, Tillman 15-51, Green 5-30, R. Harris 7-13, Kramer 1-0.

PASSING—Green Bay, Favre 6-15-0-82. Chicago, Kramer 5-10-2-34, Walsh 16-25-1-140.

RECEIVING—Green Bay, Sharpe 3-43, Morgan 1-17, Bennett 1-13, Brooks 1-9. Chicago, Graham 4-26, Green 4-26, Waddle 4-24, Conway 3-49, Wetnight 2-23, Jennings 2-11, Christian 1-9, Cook 1-6.

MISSED FIELD GOAL ATTEMPTS—Green Bay, Jacke 30.

INTERCEPTIONS—Green Bay, Paup 2-37, Butler 1-0.

KICKOFF RETURNS—Green Bay, Jordan 1-27. Chicago, Green 3-40, Conway 1-33, Woolford 1-28.

PUNT RETURNS—Green Bay, Prior 1-0. Chicago, Conway 1-0.

SACKS—Green Bay, G. Brown 1, Paup 1.

RESULTS

Atlanta 10, San Diego 9
Chicago 20, Tampa Bay 6
Cincinnati 20, Seattle 17 (OT)
Cleveland 13, New England 6
Green Bay 38, Detroit 30
Kansas City 13, L.A. Raiders 3
L.A. Rams 27, Denver 21
Miami 22, Indianapolis 21
Minnesota 21, New Orleans 20
N.Y. Jets 22, Buffalo 17
Philadelphia 17, Arizona 7
Pittsburgh 12, Houston 9 (OT)
San Francisco 37, Washington 22
Dallas 38, N.Y. Giants 10

STANDINGS

AFC EAST

	W	L	T	Pct.
Miami	7	2	0	.778
Buffalo	5	4	0	.556
N.Y. Jets	5	4	0	.556
Indianapolis	4	6	0	.400
New England	3	6	0	.333

AFC CENTRAL

	W	L	T	Pct.
Cleveland	7	2	0	.778
Pittsburgh	6	3	0	.667
Cincinnati	1	8	0	.111
Houston	1	8	0	.111

AFC WEST

	W	L	T	Pct.
San Diego	7	2	0	.778
Kansas City	6	3	0	.667
L.A. Raiders	4	5	0	.444
Denver	3	6	0	.333
Seattle	3	6	0	.333

NFC EAST

	W	L	T	Pct.
Dallas	8	1	0	.889
Philadelphia	7	2	0	.778
Arizona	3	6	0	.333
N.Y. Giants	3	6	0	.333
Washington	2	8	0	.200

NFC CENTRAL

	W	L	T	Pct.
Minnesota	7	2	0	.778
Chicago	5	4	0	.556
Green Bay	5	4	0	.556
Detroit	4	5	0	.444
Tampa Bay	2	7	0	.222

NFC WEST

	W	L	T	Pct.
San Francisco	7	2	0	.778
Atlanta	5	4	0	.556
L.A. Rams	4	5	0	.444
New Orleans	3	6	0	.333

HIGHLIGHTS

Hero of the week: Minnesota quarterback Warren Moon, who threw for 420 yards and three touchdowns, including an 11-yard game-winner to Qadry Ismail with five seconds left, as the Vikings beat New Orleans, 21-20.

Goat of the week: Houston running back Gary Brown, whose fumble at the Oilers' 22 in overtime enabled the Steelers to win, 12-9. After Pittsburgh recovered the fumble and ran one play, Gary Anderson kicked the game-winning field goal with 3:36 left. Brown's fumble was the only turnover of the game.

Sub of the week: Detroit quarterback Dave Krieg, who came on to replace injured Scott Mitchell in the second quarter of a loss to Green Bay. Krieg threw for 275 yards and three touchdowns, but it wasn't enough as Detroit couldn't overcome a 24-point deficit, losing 38-30. The Lions' last chance ended when a Krieg pass was knocked down in the end zone with 42 seconds left.

Comeback of the week: Miami beat Indianapolis, 22-21, on a 34-yard field goal by Pete Stoyanovich with four seconds left. Miami, behind the passing of Dan Marino, scored 10 points in the final four minutes. It was the 28th fourth-quarter comeback of Marino's career.

Blowout of the week: Dallas rolled up 450 yards and held the New York Giants to 187 in winning 38-10. Dallas led 35-3 after three quarters.

Nail-biter of the week: Miami trailed 21-12 after Colts defensive back Ray Buchanan returned a Marino interception 28 yards for a touchdown with 7:32 left. But Marino—who moved into second place on the NFL's career passing list—connected with O.J. McDuffie on a 28-yard touchdown pass with 3:52 left to cap a 10-play, 83-yard drive. After the Colts ran three plays and punted, Miami took over on its 42 with 2:06 left. Marino then completed five consecutive passes to put the Dolphins on the Colts' 22. After Irving Spikes ran for five yards, Stoyanovich kicked the game-winning field goal.

Hit of the week: By Green Bay defensive lineman Reggie White, who crunched Mitchell midway through the second quarter. Mitchell, whose right hand was broken on the tackle, stayed in for one more play, then missed the rest of the season.

Oddity of the week: Four teams, including two winners, didn't score a touchdown. Pittsburgh kicked four field goals to beat Houston, 12-9, in a game in which all the points were scored by kickers. Cincinnati got six field goals and a safety to down Seattle, 20-17, for its first victory of the season. And Atlanta edged San Diego, 10-9; all of the Chargers' points came on field goals. Oddly enough, Atlanta drove 91 yards for a touchdown on its first possession of the game.

Top rusher: Dallas' Emmitt Smith rushed for 163 yards and two touchdowns on a team-record 35 carries in the rout of the Giants.

Top passer: Moon completed 33 of a personal-high 57 passes for 420 yards and three touchdowns in the victory. Moon became the seventh NFL passer to exceed 36,000 career yards.

Top receiver: Philadelphia's Fred Barnett had a career-high 11 receptions for 173 yards and two touchdowns in a 17-7 victory over Arizona.

Notes: San Francisco Coach George Seifert posted his 75th career victory. He reached the milestone faster (98 games) than any coach in NFL history .... Cincinnati's first victory came in the first game of the season in Seattle's Kingdome. The stadium had been closed since July 19 after roof tiles fell before a Mariners-Orioles baseball game. The victory also snapped the Bengals' road losing streak at 15.... The Jets' Boomer Esiason threw the 200th touchdown pass of his career (a four-yarder to Rob Moore in the third quarter) in a 22-17 victory over Buffalo.... The Eagles downed Arizona in Cardinals Coach Buddy Ryan's first game in Philadelphia since he was fired as Eagles coach after the 1990 season.... The Dolphins'

Don Shula coached in his 500th career game. . . . Four players—two from each team—were ejected for fighting in two separate incidents in the Bears-Bucs game. . . . Indianapolis had the ball for 11:14 of the first quarter against Miami. The Colts then had the ball for 11:15 total for the rest of the game. . . . San Francisco got touchdowns from its offense, defense and special teams in hammering Washington.

Quote of the week: Cincinnati quarterback Jeff Blake, on his team's first victory, which came in his second pro start: "I've always known what I can do. It just took someone to believe in me. I know what God has given me. This is my calling."

GAME SUMMARIES

DOLPHINS 22, COLTS 21

Sunday, November 6

Indianapolis	7	0	7	7—21
Miami	3	0	3	16—22

First Quarter
Mia—FG Stoyanovich 33, 9:17.
Ind—Majkowski 1 run (Biasucci kick), 13:27.

Third Quarter
Mia—FG Stoyanovich 20, 5:46.
Ind—Faulk 1 run (Biasucci kick), 11:36.

Fourth Quarter
Mia—Spikes 7 run (pass failed), 2:56.
Ind—Buchanan 28 interception return (Biasucci kick), 7:28.
Mia—McDuffie 28 pass from Marino (Stoyanovich kick), 11:08.
Mia—FG Stoyanovich 34, 14:56.

TEAM STATISTICS

	Indianapolis	Miami
First downs	17	25
Rushes-yards	24-105	32-118
Passing	108	254
Punt returns-yards	0-0	3-26
Kickoff returns-yards	4-81	4-87
Interception returns-yards	2-42	1-0
Comp.-att.-int.	11-21-1	30-41-2
Sacked-yards lost	2-3	1-7
Punts-average	4-51	1-38
Fumbles-lost	1-0	2-0
Penalties-yards	3-50	3-16
Time of possession	22:29	37:31
Attendance—67,863.		

INDIVIDUAL STATISTICS

RUSHING—Indianapolis, Faulk 14-69, Humphrey 3-14, Harbaugh 2-14, Potts 4-7, Majkowski 1-1. Miami, Parmalee 22-81, Spikes 9-37, Marino 1-0.
PASSING—Indianapolis, Majkowski 8-14-0-88, Harbaugh 3-7-1-23. Miami, Marino 30-41-2-261.
RECEIVING—Indianapolis, Faulk 5-43, Turner 4-49, Dawkins 1-10, M. Jackson 1-9. Miami, Saxon 8-34, McDuffie 7-108, Fryar 7-70, Ingram 2-14, Parmalee 2-11, Byars 2-9, Spikes 1-9, K. Jackson 1-6.
MISSED FIELD GOAL ATTEMPTS—Indianapolis, Biasucci 32. Miami, Stoyanovich 31.
INTERCEPTIONS—Indianapolis, Buchanan 1-28, Tate 1-14. Miami, Braxton 1-0.
KICKOFF RETURNS—Indianapolis, Humphrey 2-57, Brewer 1-15, Jackson 1-5, Mahlum 0-4. Miami, McDuffie 4-87.
PUNT RETURNS—Miami, McDuffie 3-26.
SACKS—Indianapolis, McDonald 1. Miami, Coleman 1, Veasey 1.

FALCONS 10, CHARGERS 9

Sunday, November 6

San Diego	0	3	3	3— 9
Atlanta	7	0	3	0—10

First Quarter
Atl—Mathis 9 pass from J. George (N. Johnson kick), 7:15.

Second Quarter
S.D.—FG Carney 50, 11:54.

Third Quarter
S.D.—FG Carney 33, 7:44.
Atl—FG N. Johnson 23, 9:49.

Fourth Quarter
S.D.—FG Carney 49, 1:08.

TEAM STATISTICS

	San Diego	Atlanta
First downs	21	11
Rushes-yards	29-117	17-43
Passing	179	176
Punt returns-yards	2-14	2-21
Kickoff returns-yards	3-55	4-121
Interception returns-yards	2-13	0-0
Comp.-att.-int.	22-38-0	19-31-2
Sacked-yards lost	4-28	1-4
Punts-average	5-43	6-46
Fumbles-lost	1-0	3-0
Penalties-yards	6-60	13-95
Time of possession	34:17	25:43
Attendance—59,217.		

INDIVIDUAL STATISTICS

RUSHING—San Diego, Means 25-102, Harmon 1-8, Gilbert 1-5, Bieniemy 2-2. Atlanta, Heyward 7-37, Pegram 4-12, J. George 6-(minus 6).
PASSING—San Diego, Gilbert 22-38-0-207. Atlanta, J. George 19-31-2-180.
RECEIVING—San Diego, Seay 6-65, Pupunu 4-28, Means 4-24, T. Martin 3-29, Harmon 2-33, Jefferson 1-16, Bieniemy 1-6, D. Young 1-6. Atlanta, Mathis 7-77, Sanders 7-53, Heyward 3-33, Emanuel 2-17.
MISSED FIELD GOAL ATTEMPTS—San Diego, Carney 47.
INTERCEPTIONS—San Diego, Harper 2-13.
KICKOFF RETURNS—San Diego, Coleman 3-55. Atlanta, Verdin 4-121.
PUNT RETURNS—San Diego, Gordon 2-14. Atlanta, Verdin 2-21.
SACKS—San Diego, O'Neal 1. Atlanta, Doleman 1½, Geathers 1½, C. Smith 1.

BEARS 20, BUCCANEERS 6

Sunday, November 6

Chicago	3	3	7	7—20
Tampa Bay	0	3	0	3— 6

First Quarter
Chi—FG Butler 18, 7:45.

Second Quarter
Chi—FG Butler 37, 2:09.
T.B.—FG Husted 33, 14:30.

Third Quarter
Chi—Jennings 1 pass from Walsh (Butler kick), 11:42.

Fourth Quarter
T.B.—FG Husted 38, 0:11.
Chi—R. Green 4 pass from Walsh (Butler kick), 4:11.

TEAM STATISTICS

	Chicago	Tampa Bay
First downs	23	9
Rushes-yards	45-178	14-38
Passing	205	150
Punt returns-yards	0-0	1-(-6)
Kickoff returns-yards	0-0	5-86
Interception returns-yards	1-7	1-0
Comp.-att.-int.	19-32-1	14-28-1
Sacked-yards lost	0-0	2-14
Punts-average	5-33	6-38
Fumbles-lost	0-0	1-0
Penalties-yards	1-15	4-40
Time of possession	39:28	20:32
Attendance—60,821.		

INDIVIDUAL STATISTICS

RUSHING—Chicago, R. Harris 19-79, Tillman 19-54, Christian 3-20, Conway 1-12, R. Green 2-11, Walsh 1-2. Tampa Bay, Rhett 12-20, Dilfer 1-15, McDowell 1-3.
PASSING—Chicago, Walsh 19-32-1-205. Tampa Bay, Dilfer 13-25-1-159, Weldon 1-3-0-5.
RECEIVING—Chicago, Waddle 4-49, Tillman 3-49, Graham 3-31, Wetnight 2-25, R. Harris 2-6, Conway 1-28, Lewis 1-8, Cook 1-4, R. Green 1-4, Jennings 1-1. Tampa Bay, Dawsey 5-85, McDowell 2-27, Copeland 2-17, Thomas 1-14, Workman 1-6, J. Harris 1-5, Hawkins 1-5, Rhett 1-5.
MISSED FIELD GOAL ATTEMPTS—Tampa Bay, Husted 48.
INTERCEPTIONS—Chicago, Carrier 1-7. Tampa Bay, Stargell 1-0.
KICKOFF RETURNS—Tampa Bay, Turner 3-63, Armstrong 1-6, Buckley 1-17.

PUNT RETURNS—Tampa Bay, Turner 1-(minus 6).
SACKS—Chicago, Douglass 1, A. Fontenot 1.

49ERS 37, REDSKINS 22

Sunday, November 6

San Francisco	10	7	13	7—37
Washington	0	3	3	16—22

First Quarter
S.F.—FG Brien 32, 5:04.
S.F.—Jones 69 pass from Young (Brien kick), 15:00.
Second Quarter
Wash—FG Lohmiller 22, 12:32.
S.F.—Young 1 run (Brien kick), 13:21.
Third Quarter
S.F.—McDonald 73 interception return (Brien kick), 9:27.
Wash—FG Lohmiller 23, 13:47.
S.F.—D. Carter 96 kickoff return (kick failed), 14:04.
Fourth Quarter
S.F.—Rice 28 run (Brien kick), :52.
Wash—Horton 4 pass from Friesz (Mitchell run), 7:50.
Wash—Morrison 32 fumble return (Winans pass from Friesz), 11:32.

TEAM STATISTICS

	San Francisco	Washington
First downs	17	20
Rushes-yards	28-117	26-76
Passing	304	206
Punt returns-yards	5-48	2-14
Kickoff returns-yards	4-148	6-154
Interception returns-yards	2-91	1-7
Comp.-att.-int.	18-28-1	23-44-2
Sacked-yards lost	2-3	3-18
Punts-average	4-43	7-50
Fumbles-lost	1-1	3-1
Penalties-yards	7-60	5-25
Time of possession	27:35	32:25
Attendance—54,335.		

INDIVIDUAL STATISTICS

RUSHING—San Francisco, Watters 11-46, Logan 7-39, Rice 1-28, Loville 3-9, Young 1-1, Floyd 4-(minus 1), D. Carter 1-(minus 5). Washington, Ervins 18-52, Mitchell 5-17, Winans 1-5, C. Smith 1-2, Frerotte 1-0.
PASSING—San Francisco, Young 15-25-1-291, Grbac 3-3-0-16. Washington, Frerotte 15-32-2-167, Friesz 8-12-0-57.
RECEIVING—San Francisco, Watters 6-66, Floyd 4-36, Rice 3-90, Singleton 2-37, Jones 1-69, D. Carter 1-4, Logan 1-4. Washington, Ellard 7-93, Ervins 7-41, Winans 4-52, Horton 2-17, Howard 1-12, Mitchell 1-6, C. Smith 1-3.
MISSED FIELD GOAL ATTEMPTS—None.
INTERCEPTIONS—San Francisco, Cook 1-18, McDonald 1-73. Washington, Gouveia 1-7.
KICKOFF RETURNS—San Francisco, D. Carter 4-148. Washington, Mitchell 5-136, Bell 1-18.
PUNT RETURNS—San Francisco, D. Carter 5-48. Washington, Mitchell 2-14.
SACKS—San Francisco, Mann 1, Stubblefield 1, B. Young 1. Washington, Harvey 2.

VIKINGS 21, SAINTS 20

Sunday, November 6

New Orleans	0	0	7	13—20
Minnesota	0	7	7	7—21

Second Quarter
Min—Lee 3 pass from Moon (Reveiz kick), 14:54.
Third Quarter
N.O.—Haynes 34 pass from Everett (Andersen kick), 2:27.
Min—Reed 13 pass from Moon (Reveiz kick), 11:30.
Fourth Quarter
N.O.—Walls 2 pass from Everett (Andersen kick), :03.
N.O.—FG Andersen 44, 10:48.
N.O.—FG Andersen 26, 12:16.
Min—Ismail 11 pass from Moon (Reveiz kick), 14:55.

TEAM STATISTICS

	New Orleans	Minnesota
First downs	17	28
Rushes-yards	21-72	20-84
Passing	241	410
Punt returns-yards	2-6	3-14

	New Orleans	Minnesota
Kickoff returns-yards	4-19	4-60
Interception returns-yards	1-3	1-0
Comp.-att.-int.	24-36-1	33-57-1
Sacked-yards lost	2-15	3-10
Punts-average	7-45	7-38
Fumbles-lost	1-0	3-2
Penalties-yards	3-15	11-90
Time of possession	28:33	31:27
Attendance—57,564.		

INDIVIDUAL STATISTICS

RUSHING—New Orleans, Bates 14-48, Everett 2-15, Hughes 1-7, Early 1-2, Brown 3-0. Minnesota, Allen 13-50, Lee 2-11, Graham 1-11, Moon 2-7, Smith 2-5.
PASSING—New Orleans, Everett 24-36-1-256. Minnesota, Moon 33-57-1-420.
RECEIVING—New Orleans, Early 8-69, Haynes 6-85, Walls 5-43, Bates 2-8, Brown 1-37, Small 1-9, Smith 1-5. Minnesota, Carter 12-151, Reed 8-157, Lee 7-59, Cooper 3-26, Ismail 2-22, Smith 1-5.
MISSED FIELD GOAL ATTEMPTS—None.
INTERCEPTIONS—New Orleans, Spencer 1-3. Minnesota, E. McDaniel 1-0.
KICKOFF RETURNS—New Orleans, Ned 2-0, Brown 1-3, Hughes 1-20, Neal 0-2, Bates 0-(minus 6). Minnesota, Ismail 4-60.
PUNT RETURNS—New Orleans, Hughes 2-6. Minnesota, Guilford 3-14.
SACKS—New Orleans, Turnbull 2, Tubbs 1. Minnesota, Barker 1, Sheppard 1.

STEELERS 12, OILERS 9

Sunday, November 6

Pittsburgh	0	6	0	3	3—12
Houston	3	3	0	3	0— 9

First Quarter
Hou—FG Del Greco 32, 6:35.
Second Quarter
Pit—FG Anderson 50, :48.
Pit—FG Anderson 39, 12:52.
Hou—FG Del Greco 49, 14:46.
Fourth Quarter
Pit—FG Anderson 37, 11:03.
Hou—FG Del Greco 38, 14:53.
Overtime
Pit—FG Anderson 40, 11:24.

TEAM STATISTICS

	Pittsburgh	Houston
First downs	17	17
Rushes-yards	34-111	25-84
Passing	155	160
Punt returns-yards	7-43	5-16
Kickoff returns-yards	4-56	3-64
Interception returns-yards	0-0	0-0
Comp.-att.-int.	17-29-0	22-48-0
Sacked-yards lost	4-29	6-45
Punts-average	11-39	11-46
Fumbles-lost	1-0	3-1
Penalties-yards	9-99	11-103
Time of possession	36:55	34:29
Attendance—47,822.		

INDIVIDUAL STATISTICS

RUSHING—Pittsburgh, Morris 28-74, O'Donnell 4-24, J. Williams 1-7, Tomczak 1-6. Houston, G. Brown 24-86, Carlson 1-(minus 2).
PASSING—Pittsburgh, O'Donnell 15-25-0-154, Tomczak 2-4-0-30. Houston, Carlson 22-48-0-205.
RECEIVING—Pittsburgh, E. Green 4-43, Thigpen 3-62, Hastings 2-20, Morris 2-14, C. Johnson 2-8, J. Williams 2-2, Stone 1-18, Hayes 1-17. Houston, Jeffires 7-53, Slaughter 5-52, Wellman 4-52, Givins 2-35, G. Brown 2-9, Coleman 1-8, McNair 1-(minus 4).
MISSED FIELD GOAL ATTEMPTS—None.
INTERCEPTIONS—None.
KICKOFF RETURNS—Pittsburgh, Stone 3-29, Johnson 1-27. Houston, Steve Jackson 3-64.
PUNT RETURNS—Pittsburgh, Woodson 4-29, Hastings 2-15, Johnson 1-(minus 1). Houston, Givins 3-3, Coleman 1-3, Hannah 1-10.
SACKS—Pittsburgh, Seals 3, Greene 1, Kirkland 1, Lloyd 1. Houston, A. Smith 1½, Barrow 1, Lathon 1, Bishop ½.

PACKERS 38, LIONS 30

Sunday, November 6

Detroit	0	7	7	16—30
Green Bay	10	21	7	0—38

G.B.—Paup 10 interception return (Jacke kick), 11:14.
G.B.—FG Jacke 30, 14:38.

Second Quarter
G.B.—Bennett 17 pass from Favre (Jacke kick), 8:32.
G.B.—Brooks 12 pass from Favre (Jacke kick), 12:30.
Det—Gray 91 kickoff return (Hanson kick), 12:46.
G.B.—Brooks 28 pass from Favre (Jacke kick), 13:34.

Third Quarter
Det—H. Moore 28 pass from Krieg (Hanson kick), 9:44.
G.B.—Cobb 10 run (Jacke kick), 14:56.

Fourth Quarter
Det—Matthews 15 pass from Krieg (Perriman pass from Krieg), 1:46.
Det—H. Moore 1 pass from Krieg (Perriman pass from Krieg), 6:29.

TEAM STATISTICS

	Detroit	Green Bay
First downs	20	21
Rushes-yards	19-49	28-117
Passing	317	230
Punt returns-yards	2-24	1-8
Kickoff returns-yards	7-157	4-53
Interception returns-yards	1-11	2-27
Comp.-att.-int.	28-48-2	24-36-1
Sacked-yards lost	3-21	1-7
Punts-average	3-41	4-50
Fumbles-lost	6-3	2-1
Penalties-yards	8-50	5-26
Time of possession	29:22	30:38
Attendance—54,995.		

INDIVIDUAL STATISTICS

RUSHING—Detroit, Sanders 15-47, D. Moore 2-3, Krieg 2-(minus 1). Green Bay, Cobb 13-66, Favre 3-17, L. Johnson 1-13, Bennett 8-11, Levens 3-10.

PASSING—Detroit, Mitchell 5-15-2-63, Krieg 23-33-0-275. Green Bay, Favre 24-36-1-237.

RECEIVING—Detroit, H. Moore 8-151, Sanders 8-51, Matthews 4-69, Perriman 3-39, Holman 3-14, Hall 2-14. Green Bay, Bennett 5-47, Sharpe 4-54, West 4-54, Brooks 3-45, Cobb 2-26, Morgan 2-25, L. Johnson 2-3, Mickens 1-10.

MISSED FIELD GOAL ATTEMPTS—Detroit, Hanson 51.

INTERCEPTIONS—Detroit, Colon 1-3, Clay 0-8. Green Bay, Butler 1-17, Paup 1-10.

KICKOFF RETURNS—Detroit, Lynch 3-37, D. Moore 2-23, Gray 1-91, Malone 1-6. Green Bay, Harris 2-36, Brooks 1-9, Wilson 1-0.

PUNT RETURNS—Detroit, Gray 2-24. Green Bay, Brooks 1-8.

SACKS—Detroit, Blades 1. Green Bay, Jones 1, McMichael 1, Paup 1.

BROWNS 13, PATRIOTS 6

Sunday, November 6

New England	0	0	3	3—	6
Cleveland	0	3	0	10—	13

Second Quarter
Cle—FG Stover 33, 14:38.

Third Quarter
N.E.—FG Bahr 20, 7:53.

Fourth Quarter
Cle—Hoard 1 pass from Rypien (Stover kick), 2:18.
Cle—FG Stover 41, 5:32.
N.E.—FG Bahr 39, 12:47.

TEAM STATISTICS

	New England	Cleveland
First downs	20	16
Rushes-yards	36-118	32-148
Passing	159	160
Punt returns-yards	3-8	1-(-10)
Kickoff returns-yards	3-42	1-20
Interception returns-yards	1-6	4-18
Comp.-att.-int.	20-43-4	14-28-1
Sacked-yards lost	2-7	1-4
Punts-average	5-43	5-35
Fumbles-lost	2-0	2-1
Penalties-yards	5-52	7-43
Time of possession	34:10	25:50
Attendance—73,878.		

INDIVIDUAL STATISTICS

RUSHING—New England, Butts 25-86, K. Turner 7-23, L. Thompson 3-9, Bledsoe 1-0. Cleveland, Hoard 21-123, Byner 6-19, Metcalf 3-5, Rypien 1-1, J. Jones 1-0.

PASSING—New England, Bledsoe 20-43-4-166. Cleveland, Rypien 14-28-1-164.

RECEIVING—New England, Timpson 7-69, Crittenden 3-31, Coates 3-24, L. Thompson 3-10, Hawkins 2-22, K. Turner 2-10. Cleveland, McCardell 4-80, Metcalf 3-32, Hoard 2-12, Kinchen 2-12, Alexander 1-20, Byner 1-7, J. Jones 1-1.

MISSED FIELD GOAL ATTEMPTS—None.

INTERCEPTIONS—New England, Hurst 1-6. Cleveland, Turner 2-10, Caldwell 1-0, Jacobs 1-8.

KICKOFF RETURNS—New England, Croom 2-28, T. Brown 1-14. Cleveland, Metcalf 1-20.

PUNT RETURNS—New England, T. Brown 3-8. Cleveland, Hill 1-(minus 10).

SACKS—New England, M. Jones 1. Cleveland, J. Jones 1, Burnett ½, Footman ½.

EAGLES 17, CARDINALS 7

Sunday, November 6

Arizona	0	0	0	7—	7
Philadelphia	0	3	14	0—	17

Second Quarter
Phi—FG Murray 36, 14:55.

Third Quarter
Phi—Barnett 47 pass from Cunningham (Murray kick), 3:41.
Phi—Barnett 50 pass from Cunningham (Murray kick), 9:48.

Fourth Quarter
Ari—Proehl 5 pass from Beuerlein (Davis kick), 13:09.

TEAM STATISTICS

	Arizona	Philadelphia
First downs	21	18
Rushes-yards	24-73	31-150
Passing	181	172
Punt returns-yards	3-9	1-11
Kickoff returns-yards	4-107	1-20
Interception returns-yards	0-0	0-0
Comp.-att.-int.	19-30-0	15-24-0
Sacked-yards lost	5-38	3-29
Punts-average	6-35	5-40
Fumbles-lost	4-2	2-1
Penalties-yards	12-82	10-79
Time of possession	30:26	29:34
Attendance—64,952.		

INDIVIDUAL STATISTICS

RUSHING—Arizona, Centers 10-33, R. Moore 9-21, Levy 2-17, Beuerlein 3-2. Philadelphia, Cunningham 8-63, Walker 9-42, Hebron 10-38, Garner 4-7.

PASSING—Arizona, Beuerlein 19-30-0-219. Philadelphia, Cunningham 15-24-0-201.

RECEIVING—Arizona, Proehl 5-36, Hill 4-66, Clark 3-50, Centers 3-33, Reeves 2-24, Ware 1-9, Samuels 1-1. Philadelphia, Barnett 11-173, C. Williams 2-16, M. Johnson 1-14, Walker 1-(minus 2).

MISSED FIELD GOAL ATTEMPTS—Arizona, Davis 52. Philadelphia, Murray 42.

INTERCEPTIONS—None.

KICKOFF RETURNS—Arizona, Henesey 2-35, Reeves 2-72. Philadelphia, Walker 1-20.

PUNT RETURNS—Arizona, Robinson 3-9. Philadelphia, Sydner 1-11.

SACKS—Arizona, Bankston 1, Hoage 1, Simmons 1. Philadelphia, Harmon 2, Grossman 1, Thomas 1, Zordich 1.

BENGALS 20, SEAHAWKS 17

Sunday, November 6

Cincinnati	5	3	3	6	3—20
Seattle	7	0	3	7	0—17

First Quarter
Sea—T. Johnson 1 run (Kasay kick), 4:09.
Cin—Safety, A. Williams sacked Mirer in the end zone, 8:52.
Cin—FG Pelfrey 36, 14:32.

Second Quarter
Cin—FG Pelfrey 44, 15:00.

Third Quarter
Cin—FG Pelfrey 36, 8:23.
Sea—FG Kasay 23, 12:22.

Fourth Quarter
Cin—FG Pelfrey 47, 1:48.
Sea—Smith 1 run (Kasay kick), 5:53.
Cin—FG Pelfrey 28, 10:33.

Overtime
Cin—FG Pelfrey 26, 8:14.

TEAM STATISTICS

	Cincinnati	Seattle
First downs	23	21
Rushes-yards	34-119	29-148
Passing	377	170
Punt returns-yards	2-32	1-4
Kickoff returns-yards	4-48	6-148
Interception returns-yards	0-0	1-0
Comp.-att.-int.	31-43-1	13-32-0
Sacked-yards lost	2-10	3-11
Punts-average	4-52	7-41
Fumbles-lost	3-1	1-1
Penalties-yards	11-69	3-30
Time of possession	39:48	28:26
Attendance—46,630.		

INDIVIDUAL STATISTICS
RUSHING—Cincinnati, Fenner 15-49, Broussard 9-32, Blake 5-23, H. Green 3-9, Scott 1-5, Ball 1-1. Seattle, C. Warren 24-92, Blades 1-40, Mirer 1-12, S. Smith 2-3, T. Johnson 1-1.

PASSING—Cincinnati, Blake 31-43-1-387. Seattle, Mirer 13-32-0-181.

RECEIVING—Cincinnati, Scott 7-157, Broussard 5-31, Pickens 4-90, To. McGee 4-34, H. Green 4-22, Sadowski 3-15, Ti. McGee 2-23, Fenner 2-15. Seattle, Blades 4-85, Martin 4-38, P. Green 2-32, Crumpler 1-12, S. Smith 1-8, C. Warren 1-6.

MISSED FIELD GOAL ATTEMPTS—None.

INTERCEPTIONS—Seattle, R. Robinson 1-0.

KICKOFF RETURNS—Cincinnati, Broussard 3-34, Sawyer 1-14. Seattle, T. Warren 1-28, Vaughn 1-20.

PUNT RETURNS—Cincinnati, Sawyer 2-32. Seattle, Martin 1-4.

SACKS—Cincinnati, Oliver 1, Wilkinson 1, A. Williams 1. Seattle, Adams 1, Team 1.

RAMS 27, BRONCOS 21
Sunday, November 6

Denver	0	3	3	15—21
L.A. Rams	7	10	7	3—27

First Quarter
L.A.—Bettis 1 run (Zendejas kick), 5:24.
Second Quarter
L.A.—Griffith 3 pass from Chandler (Zendejas kick), :04.
Den—FG Elam 42, 10:04.
L.A.—FG Zendejas 35, 14:29.
Third Quarter
L.A.—Anderson 30 pass from Chandler (Zendejas kick), 4:26.
Den—FG Elam 29, 8:47.
Fourth Quarter
Den—Milburn 20 pass from Elway (Sharpe pass from Elway), 1:04.
L.A.—FG Zendejas 18, 6:24.
Den—D. Russell 12 pass from Elway (Elam kick), 9:43.

TEAM STATISTICS

	Denver	L.A. Rams
First downs	14	23
Rushes-yards	14-48	38-141
Passing	236	244
Punt returns-yards	2-40	2-1
Kickoff returns-yards	6-105	4-79
Interception returns-yards	1-0	0-0
Comp.-att.-int.	24-45-0	22-29-1
Sacked-yards lost	1-5	0-0
Punts-average	4-42	3-45
Fumbles-lost	0-0	2-1
Penalties-yards	10-93	7-40
Time of possession	21:42	38:18
Attendance—48,103.		

INDIVIDUAL STATISTICS
RUSHING—Denver, Milburn 4-18, Elway 3-18, L. Russell 6-10, Rivers 1-2. Los Angeles, Bettis 33-91, Chandler 3-24, Hester 1-24, J. Bailey 1-2.

PASSING—Denver, Elway 24-45-0-241. Los Angeles, Chandler 19-25-1-223, Miller 3-4-0-21.

RECEIVING—Denver, Sharpe 7-69, Milburn 6-58, D. Russell 4-50, Tillman 3-40, Miller 3-29, L. Russell 1-(minus 5). Los Angeles, Bettis 6-21, Anderson 5-85, Drayton 3-37, Kinchen 2-50, Bruce 2-20, Hester 2-20, J. Bailey 1-8, Griffith 1-3.

MISSED FIELD GOAL ATTEMPTS—Denver, Elam 57.

INTERCEPTIONS—Denver, Hilliard 1-0.

KICKOFF RETURNS—Denver, Milburn 3-86, By'not'e 1-14, Campbell

1-5, Clark 1-0. Los Angeles, J. Bailey 3-61, Kinchen 1-18.

PUNT RETURNS—Denver, Milburn 2-40. Los Angeles, J. Bailey 2-1.

SACKS—Los Angeles, J. Jones 1.

JETS 22, BILLS 17
Sunday, November 6

Buffalo	0	14	0	3—17
N.Y. Jets	3	7	6	6—22

First Quarter
N.Y.—FG Lowery 26, 6:15.
Second Quarter
Buf—Thomas 2 run (Christie kick), 5:02.
Buf—Beebe 37 pass from Kelly (Christie kick), 8:23.
N.Y.—J. Johnson 5 pass from Esiason (Lowery kick), 13:45.
Third Quarter
N.Y.—Moore 4 pass from Esiason (kick failed), 13:58.
Fourth Quarter
N.Y.—FG Lowery 45, 3:45.
Buf—FG Christie 39, 7:08.
N.Y.—FG Lowery 41, 11:36.

TEAM STATISTICS

	Buffalo	N.Y. Jets
First downs	18	17
Rushes-yards	26-95	35-94
Passing	187	174
Punt returns-yards	0-0	4-43
Kickoff returns-yards	6-154	4-102
Interception returns-yards	1-11	1-21
Comp.-att.-int.	19-31-1	17-26-1
Sacked-yards lost	3-14	1-7
Punts-average	4-43	3-39
Fumbles-lost	2-1	0-0
Penalties-yards	5-39	5-30
Time of possession	26:34	33:26
Attendance—67,030.		

INDIVIDUAL STATISTICS
RUSHING—Buffalo, Thomas 18-59, K. Davis 4-25, Kelly 2-15, Gardner 1-3, Copeland 1-(minus 7). New York, Johnson 13-38, Anderson 7-35, Baxter 11-21, Esiason 4-0.

PASSING—Buffalo, Kelly 19-31-1-201. New York, Esiason 15-23-1-170, Trudeau 2-3-0-11.

RECEIVING—Buffalo, Beebe 4-62, Copeland 4-44, Metzelaars 3-36, Reed 2-22, Thomas 2-9, Brooks 2-7, Marrow 1-14, K. Davis 1-7. New York, Thornton 6-42, Moore 5-87, Monk 2-34, Johnson 2-3, Anderson 1-8, Baxter 1-7.

MISSED FIELD GOAL ATTEMPTS—None.

INTERCEPTIONS—Buffalo, Maddox 1-11. New York, Lewis 1-21.

KICKOFF RETURNS—Buffalo, Jourdain 3-97, Turner 3-57. New York, Glenn 2-71, Cadrez 1-10, Prior 1-5.

PUNT RETURNS—New York, Hicks 4-43.

SACKS—Buffalo, Hansen 1. New York, Casillas 1, Lewis 1, Lageman ½, M. Washington ½.

CHIEFS 13, RAIDERS 3
Sunday, November 6

L.A. Raiders	0	3	0	0—3
Kansas City	0	7	3	3—13

Second Quarter
K.C.—Walker 57 pass from Montana (Elliott kick), 5:38.
L.A.—FG Jaeger 50, 9:31.
Third Quarter
K.C.—FG Elliott 19, 12:14.
Fourth Quarter
K.C.—FG Elliott 27, 3:47.

TEAM STATISTICS

	L.A. Raiders	Kansas City
First downs	15	11
Rushes-yards	25-100	31-93
Passing	148	159
Punt returns-yards	5-88	3-5
Kickoff returns-yards	4-97	2-32
Interception returns-yards	0-0	2-13
Comp.-att.-int.	17-33-2	17-28-0
Sacked-yards lost	5-24	2-14
Punts-average	7-45	9-41
Fumbles-lost	2-1	0-0
Penalties-yards	15-115	6-40
Time of possession	29:41	30:19
Attendance—78,709.		

— 165 —

INDIVIDUAL STATISTICS

RUSHING—Los Angeles, H. Williams 24-93, Hostetler 1-7. Kansas City, Allen 15-62, Hill 10-16, Montana 4-9, Anders 2-6.

PASSING—Los Angeles, Hostetler 17-33-2-172. Kansas City, Montana 17-28-0-173.

RECEIVING—Los Angeles, T. Brown 6-84, H. Williams 5-38, Glover 3-26, Rathman 2-20, Jones 1-4. Kansas City, Allen 5-30, Walker 4-90, Anders 4-24, Davis 3-26, Dawson 1-3.

MISSED FIELD GOAL ATTEMPTS—Los Angeles, Jaeger 33, 44.

INTERCEPTIONS—Kansas City, Mincy 1-13, White 1-0.

KICKOFF RETURNS—Los Angeles, Ismail 4-97. Kansas City, Dickerson 2-32.

PUNT RETURNS—Los Angeles, T. Brown 5-88. Kansas City, Hughes 2-5, Carter 1-0.

SACKS—Los Angeles, McGlockton 1, A. Smith 1. Kansas City, N. Smith 2, Jamison 1, Mickell 1, Thomas 1.

COWBOYS 38, GIANTS 10

Monday, November 7

N.Y. Giants	0	3	0	7—10
Dallas	0	14	21	3—38

Second Quarter

Dal—Harper 22 pass from Aikman (Boniol kick), :05.

N.Y.—FG Treadwell 23, 5:06.

Dal—E. Smith 1 run (Boniol kick), 12:13.

Third Quarter

Dal—E. Smith 1 run (Boniol kick), 2:31.

Dal—Aikman 3 run (Boniol kick), 9:58.

Dal—Johnston 9 run (Boniol kick), 14:31.

Fourth Quarter

Dal—FG Boniol 45, 3:48.

N.Y.—Cross 9 pass from Graham (Treadwell kick), 9:14.

TEAM STATISTICS

	N.Y. Giants	Dallas
First downs	11	27
Rushes-yards	22-55	45-209
Passing	128	241
Punt returns-yards	0-0	4-5
Kickoff returns-yards	7-143	1-34
Interception returns-yards	0-0	1-2
Comp.-att.-int.	13-31-1	19-25-0
Sacked-yards lost	4-26	0-0
Punts-average	6-48	3-36
Fumbles-lost	2-2	2-2
Penalties-yards	3-19	6-40
Time of possession	23:40	36:20

Attendance—64,836.

INDIVIDUAL STATISTICS

RUSHING—New York, Downs 7-28, Hampton 11-14, Da. Brown 2-10, Meggett 2-3. Dallas, E. Smith 35-163, Coleman 6-23, Johnston 2-12, Aikman 2-11.

PASSING—New York, Da. Brown 4-17-0-56, Graham 9-14-1-98. Dallas, Aikman 19-24-0-241, Peete 0-1-0-0.

RECEIVING—New York, Cross 5-44, Sherrard 3-31, Calloway 2-39, Marshall 1-24, Meggett 1-11, Kozlowski 1-5. Dallas, Irvin 7-118, Johnston 5-57, E. Smith 3-13, Galbraith 2-9, Harper 1-22, K. Williams 1-22.

MISSED FIELD GOAL ATTEMPTS—None.

INTERCEPTIONS—Dallas, Washington 1-2.

KICKOFF RETURNS—New York, Meggett 4-74, Lewis 2-58, Marshall 1-11. Dallas, K. Williams 1-34.

PUNT RETURNS—Dallas, K. Williams 4-5.

SACKS—Dallas, Marion 1, Hennings 1, Lett 1, Tolbert 1.

WEEK 11

RESULTS

Arizona 10, N.Y. Giants 9
Chicago 17, Miami 14
Cincinnati 34, Houston 31
Cleveland 26, Philadelphia 7
Denver 17, Seattle 10
Detroit 14, Tampa Bay 9
Green Bay 17, N.Y. Jets 10
L.A. Raiders 20, L.A. Rams 17
New England 26, Minnesota 20 (OT)
New Orleans 33, Atlanta 32
San Diego 14, Kansas City 13
San Francisco 21, Dallas 14
Pittsburgh 23, Buffalo 10
    Open date: Indianapolis, Washington

STANDINGS

AFC EAST	W	L	T	Pct.
Miami	7	3	0	.700
Buffalo	5	5	0	.500
N.Y. Jets	5	5	0	.500
Indianapolis	4	6	0	.400
New England	4	6	0	.400

AFC CENTRAL	W	L	T	Pct.
Cleveland	8	2	0	.800
Pittsburgh	7	3	0	.700
Cincinnati	2	8	0	.200
Houston	1	9	0	.100

AFC WEST	W	L	T	Pct.
San Diego	8	2	0	.800
Kansas City	6	4	0	.600
L.A. Raiders	5	5	0	.500
Denver	4	6	0	.400
Seattle	3	7	0	.300

NFC EAST	W	L	T	Pct.
Dallas	8	2	0	.800
Philadelphia	7	3	0	.700
Arizona	4	6	0	.400
N.Y. Giants	3	7	0	.300
Washington	2	8	0	.200

NFC CENTRAL	W	L	T	Pct.
Minnesota	7	3	0	.700
Chicago	6	4	0	.600
Green Bay	6	4	0	.600
Detroit	5	5	0	.500
Tampa Bay	2	8	0	.200

NFC WEST	W	L	T	Pct.
San Francisco	8	2	0	.800
Atlanta	5	5	0	.500
L.A. Rams	4	6	0	.400
New Orleans	4	6	0	.400

HIGHLIGHTS

Hero of the week: New England quarterback Drew Bledsoe, who set NFL records for attempts and completions by going 45 of 70 for 426 yards and three touchdowns as the Patriots rallied past the Vikings in overtime, 26-20.

Goat of the week: Houston cornerback Cris Dishman, who was torched by Cincinnati wide receiver Carl Pickens. Pickens caught 11 passes for 188 yards and three touchdowns as the Bengals slipped past the Oilers, 34-31. Pickens caught the game-tying touchdown pass with 2:34 left, then caught a 50-yard pass to set up the Bengals' Doug Pelfrey for the game-winning field goal in the final seconds. Dishman also was called for a 26-yard pass interference penalty, which helped the Bengals on their first scoring drive.

Sub of the week: Green Bay wide receiver Anthony Morgan, who came in when Sterling Sharpe injured his hamstring in the third quarter against the Jets. Morgan caught three passes for 46 yards, including a 17-yard touchdown catch with 4:16 left in the third quarter to put the Packers ahead for good, 14-10, in a game they won 17-10.

Comeback of the week: New England rallied from a 20-3 halftime deficit to upend Minnesota. The Vikings scored on three of their first four possessions en route to the halftime lead. But Bledsoe threw for 354 yards in the second half against the league's fourth-ranked defense to rally the Patriots. Matt Bahr sent the game into overtime with a 23-yard field goal with 14 seconds left. Bledsoe hit fullback Kevin Turner with a 14-yard pass to win it with 4:10 left in overtime. The Patriots passed on 59 of their final 66 plays.

Blowout of the week: Cleveland started its first drive on Philadelphia's 18 and scored four plays later, setting the tone in its 26-7 victory over the Eagles. Philadelphia was 3 of 14 on third-down conversions and punted seven times.

Nail-biter of the week: Morten Andersen kicked a 39-yard field goal with eight seconds left as New Orleans downed Atlanta, 33-32. It was his fourth game-winning kick against the Falcons in the teams' past five meetings. Atlanta's Norm Johnson kicked a 30-yard field goal—his sixth of the game—to give Atlanta a 32-30 lead with 1:44 left. Jim Everett then drove the Saints 43 yards to Andersen's game-winning kick.

Hit of the week: By Kansas City special teams player Ron Dickerson, who ran into San Diego's John Kidd and was called for roughing the punter. The 15-yard penalty moved the ball to San Diego's 48. On the first play after the penalty, Chargers quarterback Stan Humphries hit Shawn Jefferson on a 52-yard touchdown pass to cut the Chiefs' lead to 13-7 with 30 seconds left in the third quarter. The Chargers won 14-13, holding Kansas City scoreless in the second half.

Oddity of the week: Broncos running back Leonard Russell went to a weird place for his honeymoon—Denver's Mile High Stadium. Russell got married on Saturday; on Sunday, he rushed for 109 yards and a touchdown to boost the Broncos past Seattle, 17-10.

Top rusher: Detroit's Barry Sanders rushed for 237 yards on 26 carries as the Lions beat the Bucs, 14-9. Sanders had 200 yards in the second half.

Top passer: New England's Bledsoe was 45 of 70 for 426 yards and three touchdowns in a victory.

Top receiver: Cincinnati's Pickens had 11 catches for 188 yards and three touchdowns in a victory.

Notes: Miami's Dan Marino set an NFL record for most seasons (11) with at least 20 touchdown passes.... The Rams rushed for just 22 yards against the Raiders, the second-lowest total in team history.... Police broke up 26 fights and arrested 25 people in the stands at the Los Angeles Coliseum during the Rams-Raiders game.... The Broncos' victory over Seattle was their sixth in a row over the Seahawks in Denver.... Eagles quarterback Randall Cunningham's 20-game home winning streak was snapped in the loss to the Browns.... San Diego's victory gave the Chargers a season sweep of the Chiefs; before the season, the Chargers had lost eight of the past nine regular-season games against Kansas City. . . . The Steelers had seven sacks in their victory over Buffalo. Both of the Steelers' touchdowns were scored by the defense.

Quote of the week: Detroit Coach Wayne Fontes, on Sanders: "God ain't made a better back in this lifetime. Maybe one will come along someday. But it hasn't happened yet."

GAME SUMMARIES

BEARS 17, DOLPHINS 14

Sunday, November 13

Chicago	7	0	0	10	17
Miami	3	3	0	8	14

First Quarter
Mia—FG Stoyanovich 29, 8:15.
Chi—Jennings 23 pass from Conway (Butler kick), 14:32.
Second Quarter
Mia—FG Stoyanovich 33, 5:34.
Fourth Quarter
Chi—Tillman 1 run (Butler kick), 3:47.
Mia—Jackson 11 pass from Marino (Craver run), 9:14.
Chi—FG Butler 40, 14:01.

TEAM STATISTICS

	Chicago	Miami
First downs	18	18
Rushes-yards	30-62	20-69
Passing	211	275
Punt returns-yards	1-4	3-18
Kickoff returns-yards	4-98	4-96
Interception returns-yards	1-25	0-0
Comp.-att.-int.	19-28-0	24-38-1
Sacked-yards lost	0-0	2-14
Punts-average	4-39	4-39
Fumbles-lost	2-2	2-1
Penalties-yards	3-15	10-59
Time of possession	30:13	29:47
Attendance—65,006.		

INDIVIDUAL STATISTICS
RUSHING—Chicago, Tillman 15-33, Harris 8-22, Conway 2-9, Walsh 5-(minus 2). Miami, Spikes 17-66, Gary 3-3.
PASSING—Chicago, Walsh 18-27-0-188, Conway 1-1-0-23. Miami, Marino 24-38-1-289.
RECEIVING—Chicago, Harris 7-51, Conway 3-59, Graham 3-32, Tillman 3-16, Jennings 2-29, McMurtry 1-24. Miami, Fryar 9-112, Jackson 5-58, McDuffie 2-43, Ingram 2-26, Craver 2-23, Gary 2-19, Spikes 2-8.
MISSED FIELD GOAL ATTEMPTS—Miami, Stoyanovich 45.
INTERCEPTIONS—Chicago, Woolford 1-25.
KICKOFF RETURNS—Chicago, Lewis 3-78, Carter 1-20. Miami, Spikes 3-78, McDuffie 1-18.
PUNT RETURNS—Chicago, Conway 1-4. Miami, McDuffie 3-18.
SACKS—Chicago, Epps 1, Spellman 1.

CHARGERS 14, CHIEFS 13

Sunday, November 13

San Diego	0	0	7	7	14
Kansas City	0	13	0	0	13

Second Quarter
K.C.—FG Elliott 27, 2:28.
K.C.—Anders 1 run (Elliott kick), 6:09.
K.C.—FG Elliott 34, 14:57.
Third Quarter
S.D.—Jefferson 52 pass from Humphries (Carney kick), 14:30.
Fourth Quarter
S.D.—Young 5 pass from Humphries (Carney kick), 8:19.

TEAM STATISTICS

	San Diego	Kansas City
First downs	13	15
Rushes-yards	26-48	27-84
Passing	187	165
Punt returns-yards	6-52	7-60
Kickoff returns-yards	4-57	3-51
Interception returns-yards	2-38	1-5
Comp.-att.-int.	21-36-1	20-46-2
Sacked-yards lost	2-19	2-13
Punts-average	10-44	11-42
Fumbles-lost	5-3	1-0
Penalties-yards	5-55	3-30
Time of possession	29:36	30:24
Attendance—76,997.		

INDIVIDUAL STATISTICS
RUSHING—San Diego, Means 21-55, Harmon 3-6, Humphries 1-0, T. Martin 1-(minus 13). Kansas City, Anders 13-40, Hill 12-38, Bennett 2-6.
PASSING—San Diego, Humphries 21-36-1-206. Kansas City, Montana 20-46-2-178.
RECEIVING—San Diego, Means 6-25, Seay 4-49, Harmon 4-33, Jefferson 2-60, Mitchell 2-14, T. Martin 1-14, Pupunu 1-6, Young 1-5. Kansas City, Anders 6-42, Hughes 4-53, Dawson 2-35, Dickerson 2-11, Hill 2-4, E. Martin 1-12, Walker 1-12, Greene 1-7, J. Johnson 1-2.
MISSED FIELD GOAL ATTEMPTS—None.
INTERCEPTIONS—San Diego, Carrington 1-19, Richard 1-19. Kansas City, Collins 1-5.
KICKOFF RETURNS—San Diego, Coleman 2-40, Harmon 1-16, Parker 1-1. Kansas City, Dickerson 2-34, Anders 1-17.
PUNT RETURNS—San Diego, Gordon 6-62. Kansas City, Carter 4-50, Hughes 3-10.
SACKS—San Diego, O'Neal 1, Parrella 1. Kansas City, Smith 2.

BROWNS 26, EAGLES 7

Sunday, November 13

Cleveland	10	3	6	7	26
Philadelphia	0	7	0	0	7

First Quarter
Cle—Carrier 3 pass from Rypien (Stover kick), 3:04.
Cle—FG Stover 35, 11:18.
Second Quarter
Phi—Hebron 15 run (Murray kick), 9:58.
Cle—FG Stover 41, 12:12.
Third Quarter
Cle—FG Stover 22, 2:57.
Cle—FG Stover 36, 9:40.
Fourth Quarter
Cle—Byner 4 run (Stover kick), 3:53.

TEAM STATISTICS

	Cleveland	Philadelphia
First downs	18	15
Rushes-yards	40-140	22-113
Passing	158	175
Punt returns-yards	4-26	4-28
Kickoff returns-yards	2-81	6-133
Interception returns-yards	1-7	1-14
Comp.-att.-int.	12-30-1	22-38-1
Sacked-yards lost	0-0	2-20
Punts-average	6-38	7-36
Fumbles-lost	1-0	4-1
Penalties-yards	7-97	9-84
Time of possession	32:24	27:36
Attendance—65,233.		

INDIVIDUAL STATISTICS
RUSHING—Cleveland, Hoard 21-86, Baldwin 6-36, Byner 9-26, Metcalf 4-(minus 8). Philadelphia, Cunningham 8-47, Hebron 12-39, Walker 2-27.
PASSING—Cleveland, Rypien 12-30-1-158. Philadelphia, Cunningham 22-38-1-195.
RECEIVING—Cleveland, Carrier 4-63, Hoard 2-37, Kinchen 2-21, Metcalf 2-7, Jackson 1-22, Hartley 1-8. Philadelphia, Barnett 7-56, Hebron 6-54, Williams 3-15, Walker 2-18, Bavaro 1-22, Johnson 1-19, Bailey 1-11, Alexander 1-0.
MISSED FIELD GOAL ATTEMPTS—None.
INTERCEPTIONS—Cleveland, Stams 1-7. Philadelphia, Zordich 1-14.
KICKOFF RETURNS—Cleveland, Baldwin 2-81. Philadelphia, Hebron 3-77, Walker 3-56.
PUNT RETURNS—Cleveland, Metcalf 4-26. Philadelphia, Sydner 4-28.
SACKS—Cleveland, Perry 1, Thompson 1.

CARDINALS 10, GIANTS 9

Sunday, November 13

Arizona	0	0	3	7	10
N.Y. Giants	7	2	0	0	9

First Quarter

N.Y.—Pierce 4 pass from Graham (Treadwell kick), 9:47.

Second Quarter

N.Y.—Safety, Cardinals were penalized for holding in the end zone, 11:45.

Third Quarter

Ari—FG Davis 45, 9:52.

Fourth Quarter

Ari—Reeves 9 pass from Beuerlein (Davis kick), 13:21.

TEAM STATISTICS

	Arizona	N.Y. Giants
First downs	18	17
Rushes-yards	28-66	33-150
Passing	173	81
Punt returns-yards	2-14	0-0
Kickoff returns-yards	1-23	4-90
Interception returns-yards	1-2	1-0
Comp.-att.-int.	17-33-1	9-26-1
Sacked-yards lost	2-7	1-11
Punts-average	4-39	5-37
Fumbles-lost	1-0	3-0
Penalties-yards	9-46	7-76
Time of possession	29:24	30:36

Attendance—71,719.

INDIVIDUAL STATISTICS

RUSHING—Arizona, Moore 13-44, Centers 6-16, Feagles 1-12, Beuerlein 7-(minus 2), Hearst 1-(minus 4). New York, Hampton 26-93, Calloway 2-37, Meggett 2-9, Rasheed 2-9, Graham 1-2.

PASSING—Arizona, Beuerlein 17-33-1-180. New York, Graham 9-26-1-92.

RECEIVING—Arizona, Proehl 4-39, Centers 4-38, Hill 2-36, Clark 2-25, Samuels 2-18, Ware 1-11, Reeves 1-9, Moore 1-4. New York, Calloway 4-33, Cross 2-36, Meggett 1-15, Pierce 1-4, Sherrard 1-4.

MISSED FIELD GOAL ATTEMPTS—New York, Treadwell 30.

INTERCEPTIONS—Arizona, Joyner 1-2. New York, Armstead 1-0.

KICKOFF RETURNS—Arizona, Levy 1-23. New York, Meggett 4-90.

PUNT RETURNS—Arizona, Robinson 2-14.

SACKS—Arizona, Joyner 1. New York, Hamilton 1, Howard 1.

SAINTS 33, FALCONS 32

Sunday, November 13

Atlanta	17	6	0	9—32
New Orleans	3	7	14	9—33

First Quarter

Atl—FG Johnson 23, 2:54.

Atl—Rison 4 pass from J. George (Johnson kick), 5:06.

Atl—Jack 27 fumble return (Johnson kick), 5:20.

N.O.—FG Andersen 34, 10:23.

Second Quarter

Atl—FG Johnson 33, 4:33.

N.O.—Smith 17 pass from Everett (Andersen kick), 8:38.

Atl—FG Johnson 33, 13:09.

Third Quarter

N.O.—Bates 9 run (Andersen kick), 4:13.

N.O.—Bates 4 run (Andersen kick), 11:55.

Fourth Quarter

Atl—FG Johnson 31, 5:06.

Atl—FG Johnson 48, 7:30.

N.O.—Walls 21 pass from Everett (pass failed), 10:42.

Atl—FG Johnson 30, 13:16.

N.O.—FG Andersen 39, 14:52.

TEAM STATISTICS

	Atlanta	New Orleans
First downs	21	30
Rushes-yards	16-72	26-153
Passing	317	276
Punt returns-yards	0-0	1-(-1)
Kickoff returns-yards	5-190	8-145
Interception returns-yards	3-34	1-31
Comp.-att.-int.	29-49-1	28-36-3
Sacked-yards lost	1-11	0-0
Punts-average	3-45	1-44
Fumbles-lost	2-0	2-2
Penalties-yards	6-71	3-15
Time of possession	28:29	31:31

Attendance—60,313.

INDIVIDUAL STATISTICS

RUSHING—Atlanta, Heyward 16-72. New Orleans, Bates 22-141, Dunbar 3-9, Brown 1-3.

PASSING—Atlanta, J. George 29-49-1-328. New Orleans, Everett 28-36-3-276.

RECEIVING—Atlanta, Mathis 10-125, Rison 8-118, Sanders 5-20, Heyward 3-34, Emanuel 3-31. New Orleans, Early 7-63, I. Smith 7-46, Haynes 3-55, Walls 3-36, Bates 3-28, Small 2-36, Ned 2-7, Neal 1-5.

MISSED FIELD GOAL ATTEMPTS—None.

INTERCEPTIONS—Atlanta, Case 1-12, Harper 1-22, Tuggle 1-0. New Orleans, Hughes 1-31.

KICKOFF RETURNS—Atlanta, Verdin 4-142, Heyward 1-7. New Orleans, Hughes 5-92, Dunbar 1-28, Neal 1-15, Smith 1-10.

PUNT RETURNS—New Orleans, Hughes 1-(minus 1).

SACKS—New Orleans, Conner 1.

BENGALS 34, OILERS 31

Sunday, November 13

Houston	10	7	7	7—31
Cincinnati	3	14	0	17—34

First Quarter

Cin—FG Pelfrey 50, 3:31.

Hou—Jeffires 11 pass from Tolliver (Del Greco kick), 9:51.

Hou—FG Del Greco 34, 11:44.

Second Quarter

Cin—Pickens 21 pass from Blake (Pelfrey kick), 1:32.

Hou—Brown 1 run (Del Greco kick), 8:58.

Cin—Fenner 14 pass from Blake (Pelfrey kick), 14:24.

Third Quarter

Hou—White 17 run (Del Greco kick), 8:46.

Fourth Quarter

Cin—Pickens 50 pass from Blake (Pelfrey kick), :51.

Hou—Slaughter 5 pass from Tolliver (Del Greco kick), 9:09.

Cin—Pickens 21 pass from Blake (Pelfrey kick), 12:26.

Cin—FG Pelfrey 40, 15:00.

TEAM STATISTICS

	Houston	Cincinnati
First downs	24	17
Rushes-yards	31-155	19-39
Passing	129	348
Punt returns-yards	4-21	3-5
Kickoff returns-yards	6-123	6-124
Interception returns-yards	0-0	0-0
Comp.-att.-int.	20-34-0	23-33-0
Sacked-yards lost	4-23	1-6
Punts-average	6-42	4-49
Fumbles-lost	0-0	2-2
Penalties-yards	2-36	8-45
Time of possession	36:34	23:26

Attendance—54,908.

INDIVIDUAL STATISTICS

RUSHING—Houston, White 16-95, Brown 12-50, Tolliver 3-10. Cincinnati, Fenner 7-24, Green 5-17, Blake 4-0, Broussard 3-(minus 2).

PASSING—Houston, Tolliver 20-34-0-152. Cincinnati, Blake 23-33-0-354.

RECEIVING—Houston, Jeffires 6-42, Slaughter 5-55, Givins 3-25, Brown 3-22, White 3-8. Cincinnati, Pickens 11-188, Fenner 4-58, To. McGee 4-55, Scott 2-15, Green 1-34, Ball 1-4.

MISSED FIELD GOAL ATTEMPTS—None.

INTERCEPTIONS—None.

KICKOFF RETURNS—Houston, Steve Jackson 6-123. Cincinnati, Broussard 4-81, Ball 2-43.

PUNT RETURNS—Houston, Givins 4-21. Cincinnati, Sawyer 3-5.

SACKS—Houston, Montgomery 1. Cincinnati, Wilkinson 1½, Krumrie 1, A. Williams 1, Francis ½.

PATRIOTS 26, VIKINGS 20

Sunday, November 13

Minnesota	10	10	0	0	0—20
New England	0	3	7	10	6—26

First Quarter

Min—Allen 2 run (Reveiz kick), 5:11.

Min—FG Reveiz 40, 12:27.

Second Quarter

Min—Ismail 65 pass from Moon (Reveiz kick), 3:35.

Min—FG Reveiz 33, 14:02.

N.E.—FG Bahr 38, 15:00.

Third Quarter

N.E.—Crittenden 31 pass from Bledsoe (Bahr kick), 1:38.

Fourth Quarter

N.E.—Thompson 5 pass from Bledsoe (Bahr kick), 12:33.

N.E.—FG Bahr 23, 14:46.

Overtime

N.E.—Turner 14 pass from Bledsoe, 4:10.

TEAM STATISTICS

	Minnesota	New England
First downs	22	27
Rushes-yards	31-101	12-42
Passing	339	426
Punt returns-yards	4-23	3-24
Kickoff returns-yards	3-63	6-117
Interception returns-yards	0-0	0-0
Comp.-att.-int.	26-42-0	45-70-0
Sacked-yards lost	1-10	0-0
Punts-average	7-43	8-41
Fumbles-lost	1-1	0-0
Penalties-yards	7-55	5-29
Time of possession	37:42	26:28

Attendance—58,382.

INDIVIDUAL STATISTICS

RUSHING—Minnesota, Allen 23-75, Moon 3-14, R. Smith 5- 12. New England, Butts 6-26, Thompson 4- 13, Bledsoe 2-3.

PASSING—Minnesota, Moon 26-42-0-349. New England, Bledsoe 45-70-0-426.

RECEIVING—Minnesota, Cooper 6-57, Jordan 5-57, Carter 5-33, Ismail 4-89, Reed 3-77, Lee 3-36. New England, Thompson 11-74, Timpson 10-113, Coates 10-74, Brisby 5-68, Turner 4-27, Crittenden 3-54, Burke 2-16.

MISSED FIELD GOAL ATTEMPTS—New England, Bahr 39.

INTERCEPTIONS—None.

KICKOFF RETURNS—Minnesota, Ismail 3-63. New England, Thompson 4-98, Burke 1-5, DeOssie 1-14.

PUNT RETURNS—Minnesota, Palmer 4-23. New England, T. Brown 3-24.

SACKS—New England, A. Jones 1.

BRONCOS 17, SEAHAWKS 10

Sunday, November 13

Seattle	0	0	3	7—10
Denver	0	7	3	7—17

Second Quarter

Den—Elway 12 run (Elam kick), 6:19.

Third Quarter

Den—FG Elam 42, 10:14.

Sea—FG Kasay 19, 13:02.

Fourth Quarter

Sea—C. Warren 23 run (Kasay kick), 3:21.

Den—L. Russell 11 run (Elam kick), 9:17.

TEAM STATISTICS

	Seattle	Denver
First downs	14	21
Rushes-yards	28-158	38-169
Passing	131	128
Punt returns-yards	2-15	3-25
Kickoff returns-yards	4-93	2-38
Interception returns-yards	2-13	0-0
Comp.-att.-int.	10-30-0	17-33-2
Sacked-yards lost	2-2	2-18
Punts-average	5-46	5-37
Fumbles-lost	2-1	1-0
Penalties-yards	12-79	1-23
Time of possession	27:06	32:54

Attendance—71,290.

INDIVIDUAL STATISTICS

RUSHING—Seattle, C. Warren 18-122, S. Smith 3- 14, Vaughn 3-14, Mirer 3-7, Johnson 1- 1. Denver, L. Russell 19- 109, Elway 9-36, Clark 4-19, D. Russell 1-6, Milburn 2-3, Campbell 1-0, Rivers 2- (minus 4).

PASSING—Seattle, Mirer 10-29-0-133, Tuten 0-1-0-0. Denver, Elway 17-32-2- 146, Rivers 0- 1-0-0.

RECEIVING—Seattle, Martin 5-49, C. Warren 4-78, Blades 1-6. Denver, Milburn 5-27, Sharpe 3-28, Rivers 3- 19, Miller 2-35, L. Russell 1-14, D. Russell 1- 13, Clark 1-5, Evans 1-5.

MISSED FIELD GOAL ATTEMPTS—Seattle, Kasay 56.

INTERCEPTIONS—Seattle, Watters 1-4, Wooden 1-9.

KICKOFF RETURNS—Seattle, Vaughn 4-93. Denver, By'not'e 1-24, Milburn 1-14.

PUNT RETURNS—Seattle, Martin 2- 15. Denver, Milburn 3-25.

SACKS—Seattle, Adams 1, Kennedy 1. Denver, Dronett 1, Fletcher 1.

49ERS 21, COWBOYS 14

Sunday, November 13

Dallas	7	0	0	7—14
San Francisco	0	7	7	7—21

First Quarter

Dal—E. Smith 4 run (Boniol kick), 13:00.

Second Quarter

S.F.—S. Young 1 run (Brien kick), 3:15.

Third Quarter

S.F.—Rice 57 pass from S. Young (Brien kick), 12:20.

Fourth Quarter

S.F.—Jones 13 pass from S. Young (Brien kick), 12:28.

Dal—E. Smith 2 run (Boniol kick), 13:40.

TEAM STATISTICS

	Dallas	San Francisco
First downs	19	19
Rushes-yards	29-87	32- 147
Passing	321	161
Punt returns-yards	3-2	4-30
Kickoff returns-yards	4-79	2-31
Interception returns-yards	0-0	3-22
Comp.-att.-int.	23-42-3	12-21-0
Sacked-yards lost	3-18	3-22
Punts-average	6-42	8-42
Fumbles-lost	0-0	0-0
Penalties-yards	7-48	5-35
Time of possession	31:57	28:03

Attendance—69,014.

INDIVIDUAL STATISTICS

RUSHING—Dallas, E. Smith 26-78, Aikman 2-9, Johnston 1-0. San Francisco, Watters 17-65, S. Young 8-60, Rice 1- 11, Floyd 6-11.

PASSING—Dallas, Aikman 23-42-3-339. San Francisco, S. Young 12-21-0- 183.

RECEIVING—Dallas, Irvin 8-94, Smith 6-32, Novacek 5-51, Harper 3- 136, Williams 1-26. San Francisco, Rice 5-93, Watters 4-32, Taylor 2-45, Jones 1- 13.

MISSED FIELD GOAL ATTEMPTS—Dallas, Boniol 43.

INTERCEPTIONS—San Francisco, Hanks 2- 19, Sanders 1-3.

KICKOFF RETURNS—Dallas, K. Williams 4-79. San Francisco, Carter 2-31.

PUNT RETURNS—Dallas, K. Williams 3-2. San Francisco, Carter 4-30.

SACKS—Dallas, Lett 2, Hennings 1. San Francisco, Jackson 1, Stublefield 1, B. Young 1.

RAIDERS 20, RAMS 17

Sunday, November 13

L.A. Raiders	7	7	0	6—20
L.A. Rams	7	0	0	10—17

First Quarter

Raiders—Glover 27 pass from Hostetler (Jaeger kick), 10:24.

Rams—Anderson 22 pass from Chandler (Zendejas kick), 14:43.

Second Quarter

Raiders—Ismail 10 pass from Hostetler (Jaeger kick), 5:53.

Fourth Quarter

Raiders—FG Jaeger 44, 2:25.

Rams—FG Zendejas 22, 7:20.

Raiders—FG Jaeger 47, 12:42.

Rams—Kinchen 4 pass from Miller (Zendejas kick), 13:33.

TEAM STATISTICS

	Raiders	Rams
First downs	18	21
Rushes-yards	36-95	11-22
Passing	208	268
Punt returns-yards	1-8	2-45
Kickoff returns-yards	3-64	5-96
Interception returns-yards	1-9	1-23
Comp.-att.-int.	17-26-1	23-37-1
Sacked-yards lost	3-10	4-34
Punts-average	2-45	3-48
Fumbles-lost	1-0	0-0
Penalties-yards	13-108	8-66
Time of possession	34:52	25:08

Attendance—65,208.

INDIVIDUAL STATISTICS

RUSHING—Raiders, H. Williams 21-44, Jones 6-32, Hostetler 3- 13, Rathman 3-9, Evans 3- (minus 3). Rams, Bettis 10- 13, Miller 1-9.

PASSING—Raiders, Hostetler 17-25-1-218, Evans 0- 1-0-0. Rams,

Miller 13-26-1-131, Chandler 10-11-0-171.

RECEIVING—Raiders, Brown 5-53, H. Williams 3-34, Glover 2-47, Jett 2-42, Ismail 2-17, Rathman 2-9, J. Williams 1-16. Rams, Drayton 6-36, Anderson 5-105, Bruce 4-48, Hester 3-54, Kinchen 3-33, Bettis 2-26.

MISSED FIELD GOAL ATTEMPTS—Rams, Zendejas 41.

INTERCEPTIONS—Raiders, McDaniel 1-9. Rams, Henley 1-23.

KICKOFF RETURNS—Raiders, Ismail 2-40, Wright 1-24. Rams, Lang 3-59, Kinchen 2-37.

PUNT RETURNS—Raiders, T. Brown 1-8. Rams, Kinchen 2-45.

SACKS—Raiders, McGlockton 1½, A. Smith 1, White 1, Harrison ½. Rams, J. Jones 1, Kelly 1, Robinson ½, Young ½.

PACKERS 17, JETS 10

Sunday, November 13

N.Y. Jets	0	10	0	0—10
Green Bay	7	0	7	3—17

First Quarter
G.B.—Brooks 11 pass from Favre (Jacke kick), 4:15.
Second Quarter
N.Y.—FG Lowery 20, 8:32.
N.Y.—Moore 11 pass from Esiason (Lowery kick), 13:57.
Third Quarter
G.B.—Morgan 17 pass from Favre (Jacke kick), 10:34.
Fourth Quarter
G.B.—FG Jacke 46, 7:49.

TEAM STATISTICS

	N.Y. Jets	Green Bay
First downs	16	14
Rushes-yards	23-116	23-62
Passing	199	172
Punt returns-yards	3-25	4-20
Kickoff returns-yards	4-68	2-52
Interception returns-yards	0-0	1-8
Comp.-att.-int.	24-43-1	20-28-0
Sacked-yards lost	2-15	1-11
Punts-average	7-42	6-55
Fumbles-lost	2-0	2-1
Penalties-yards	5-65	6-52
Time of possession	32:48	27:12
Attendance—58,307.		

INDIVIDUAL STATISTICS

RUSHING—New York, R. Anderson 9-74, J. Johnson 6-19, Baxter 5-16, Esiason 3-7. Green Bay, Cobb 11-21, Favre 7-21, Bennett 5-20.

PASSING—New York, Esiason 24-43-1-214. Green Bay, Favre 20-28-0-183.

RECEIVING—New York, Moore 7-72, Monk 5-48, Mitchell 4-50, Thornton 3-30, R. Anderson 3-11, Baxter 1-2, J. Johnson 1-1. Green Bay, Cobb 4-24, Morgan 3-46, Brooks 3-8, West 2-24, R. Johnson 2-19, Sharpe 1-13, Levens 1-9, Mickens 1-8.

MISSED FIELD GOAL ATTEMPTS—Green Bay, Jacke 51.

INTERCEPTIONS—Green Bay, Buckley 1-8.

KICKOFF RETURNS—New York, A. Prior 3-55, Clifton 1-13. Green Bay, Harris 1-28, Jordan 1-24.

PUNT RETURNS—New York, Hicks 3-25. Green Bay, Brooks 3-20, Jordan 1-0.

SACKS—New York, Green 1. Green Bay, Paup 2.

LIONS 14, BUCCANEERS 9

Sunday, November 13

Tampa Bay	3	0	3	3— 9
Detroit	0	0	14	0—14

First Quarter
T.B.—FG Husted 20, 2:22.
Third Quarter
Det—D. Moore 1 run (Hanson kick), 5:32.
T.B.—FG Husted 41, 11:27.
Det—H. Moore 9 pass from Krieg (Hanson kick), 12:29.
Fourth Quarter
T.B.—FG Husted 34, 3:45.

TEAM STATISTICS

	Tampa Bay	Detroit
First downs	18	16
Rushes-yards	32-125	33-243
Passing	218	99
Punt returns-yards	2-18	0-0
Kickoff returns-yards	2-32	4-50
Interception returns-yards	0-0	0-0
Comp.-att.-int.	16-23-0	5-13-0
Sacked-yards lost	3-25	0-0
Punts-average	2-41	4-49
Fumbles-lost	2-0	2-0
Penalties-yards	6-33	8-64
Time of possession	34:53	25:07
Attendance—50,814.		

INDIVIDUAL STATISTICS

RUSHING—Tampa Bay, Rhett 25-112, Erickson 3-6, Workman 3-5, McDowell 1-2. Detroit, Sanders 26-237, D. Moore 3-5, Krieg 4-1.

PASSING—Tampa Bay, Erickson 16-23-0-243. Detroit, Krieg 5-13-0-99.

RECEIVING—Tampa Bay, Dawsey 4-65, Copeland 3-98, Armstrong 3-30, Hawkins 2-29, Workman 2-9, McDowell 1-6, Rhett 1-6. Detroit, Perriman 1-37, Matthews 1-23, Sanders 1-16, Hall 1-14, H. Moore 1-9.

MISSED FIELD GOAL ATTEMPTS—Tampa Bay, Husted 49.

INTERCEPTIONS—None.

KICKOFF RETURNS—Tampa Bay, Turner 2-32. Detroit, Gray 2-25, Malone 1-12, D. Moore 1-0.

PUNT RETURNS—Tampa Bay, Turner 2-18.

SACKS—Detroit, Scroggins 1½, Owens 1, Johnson ½.

STEELERS 23, BILLS 10

Monday, November 14

Buffalo	0	3	7	0—10
Pittsburgh	10	6	7	0—23

First Quarter
Pit—FG Anderson 39, 6:59.
Pit—Woodson 37 interception return (Anderson kick), 14:04.
Second Quarter
Pit—FG Anderson 39, 10:11.
Buf—FG Christie 52, 13:53.
Pit—FG Anderson 30, 14:54.
Third Quarter
Buf—Reed 19 pass from Kelly (Christie kick), 3:04.
Pit—G. Williams recovered fumble in end zone (Anderson kick), 8:22.

TEAM STATISTICS

	Buffalo	Pittsburgh
First downs	24	10
Rushes-yards	31-128	26-86
Passing	198	140
Punt returns-yards	4-41	5-32
Kickoff returns-yards	6-109	3-85
Interception returns-yards	1-0	2-39
Comp.-att.-int.	27-53-2	14-27-1
Sacked-yards lost	7-60	1-8
Punts-average	7-43	9-45
Fumbles-lost	1-0	0-0
Penalties-yards	8-55	7-64
Time of possession	32:57	27:03
Attendance—59,019.		

INDIVIDUAL STATISTICS

RUSHING—Buffalo, Thomas 21-91, Reed 2-29, Jourdain 4-16, K. Davis 2-0, Kelly 2-(minus 8). Pittsburgh, Morris 15-61, Foster 8-32, Mills 1-(minus 1), J.L. Williams 2-(minus 6).

PASSING—Buffalo, Kelly 22-43-2-212, Reich 5-10-0-46. Pittsburgh, O'Donnell 14-27-1-148.

RECEIVING—Buffalo, Bl. Brooks 7-89, Reed 6-63, Copeland 4-47, Metzelaars 4-27, Thomas 2-14, Jourdain 2-5, Gardner 1-9, K. Davis 1-4. Pittsburgh, C. Johnson 4-40, Morris 2-41, Foster 2-19, Thigpen 2-8, J.L. Williams 2-0, Mills 1-26, Hastings 1-14.

MISSED FIELD GOAL ATTEMPTS—Buffalo, Christie 32.

INTERCEPTIONS—Buffalo, Jones 1-0. Pittsburgh, Woodson 1-37, Lake 1-2.

KICKOFF RETURNS—Buffalo, Jourdain 4-91, Turner 1-17, J. Patton 1-1. Pittsburgh, Thigpen 2-54, Stone 1-31.

PUNT RETURNS—Buffalo, Burris 4-41. Pittsburgh, Woodson 3-13, Johnson 2-19.

SACKS—Buffalo, Bennett 1. Pittsburgh, Greene 3, C. Brown 1, Woodson 1, Lloyd 1, Seals 1.

WEEK 12

RESULTS

Arizona 12, Philadelphia 6
Buffalo 29, Green Bay 20
Chicago 20, Detroit 10
Dallas 31, Washington 7
Denver 32, Atlanta 28
Indianapolis 17, Cincinnati 13
Kansas City 20, Cleveland 13
L.A. Raiders 24, New Orleans 19
N.Y. Jets 31, Minnesota 21
New England 23, San Diego 17
Pittsburgh 16, Miami 13 (OT)
San Francisco 31, L.A. Rams 27
Seattle 22, Tampa Bay 21
N.Y. Giants 13, Houston 10

STANDINGS

AFC EAST	W	L	T	Pct.
Miami	7	4	0	.636
Buffalo	6	5	0	.545
N.Y. Jets	6	5	0	.545
Indianapolis	5	6	0	.455
New England	5	6	0	.455

AFC CENTRAL	W	L	T	Pct.
Cleveland	8	3	0	.727
Pittsburgh	8	3	0	.727
Cincinnati	2	9	0	.182
Houston	1	10	0	.091

AFC WEST	W	L	T	Pct.
San Diego	8	3	0	.727
Kansas City	7	4	0	.636
L.A. Raiders	6	5	0	.545
Denver	5	6	0	.455
Seattle	4	7	0	.364

NFC EAST	W	L	T	Pct.
Dallas	9	2	0	.818
Philadelphia	7	4	0	.636
Arizona	5	6	0	.455
N.Y. Giants	4	7	0	.364
Washington	2	9	0	.182

NFC CENTRAL	W	L	T	Pct.
Chicago	7	4	0	.636
Minnesota	7	4	0	.636
Green Bay	6	5	0	.545
Detroit	5	6	0	.455
Tampa Bay	2	9	0	.182

NFC WEST	W	L	T	Pct.
San Francisco	9	2	0	.818
Atlanta	5	6	0	.455
L.A. Rams	4	7	0	.364
New Orleans	4	7	0	.364

HIGHLIGHTS

Hero of the week: New York Jets cornerback Marcus Turner, who tied a team record with three interceptions in a 31-21 upset of Minnesota. Turner, a career backup (two starts in six NFL seasons) who was playing in the Jets' nickel package, returned one of the interceptions 90 yards for a touchdown. Turner's other interceptions also came deep in Jets territory—one on the 17, the other in the end zone.

Goat of the week: Minnesota quarterback Warren Moon, who threw four interceptions in a loss to the Jets. Moon was 33 of 50 for 400 yards, but each of the interceptions came deep in Jets territory (on the 17, on the 10, on the 9 and in the end zone).

Sub of the week: Pittsburgh quarterback Mike Tomczak, who started in place of injured Neil O'Donnell. Tomczak was 26 of 42 for 343 yards in leading the Steelers past the Dolphins, 16-13, in overtime. Tomczak hit two key passes—a 23-yarder to fullback John L. Williams and a 13-yarder to tight end Eric Green—on a drive that ended with Gary Anderson kicking the game-winning field goal with 4:41 left.

Comeback of the week: Denver overcame a 28-17 fourth-quarter deficit to down Atlanta 32-28. The Falcons took the 11-point lead on a 49-yard pass from Jeff George to Terance Mathis with 14:11 left. But John Elway—who threw for 382 yards—then drove Denver 72 yards for a touchdown, passing 32 yards to Anthony Miller for a score and then hitting Miller on a two-point conversion pass to make it 28-25 with 10:19 remaining. The Broncos got another opportunity with six minutes left. Elway moved the team 57 yards for the clinching score. He completed a 13-yard pass to running back Reggie Rivers on third-and-13. On the next play, Elway scrambled 11 yards to the Falcons' 4. He then scored on a quarterback draw. It was the 34th fourth-quarter comeback of Elway's career.

Blowout of the week: Dallas built a 17-0 first-quarter lead and cruised past Washington, 31-7. The Redskins had five turnovers.

Nail-biter of the week: Seattle's Mack Strong scored on a seven-yard run with 42 seconds left as the Seahawks edged Tampa Bay, 22-21. Seattle led 15-10 entering the fourth quarter. After Tampa Bay's Michael Husted kicked a 35-yard field goal for a 21-15 lead, Seattle marched 77 yards in 12 plays to snap a six-game losing streak.

Hit of the week: By Buffalo nose tackle Jeff Wright, whose last-minute sack of Green Bay's Brett Favre helped the Bills hold off the Packers. With just over two minutes left, Wright sacked Favre on the Packers' 1. On the next play, the Packers' Joe Sims was called for holding in the end zone, which gave the Bills a safety and the final two points of a 29-20 victory.

Oddity of the week: Three Vikings receivers topped the 100-yard mark in receptions—in a loss. Jake Reed had five catches for 121 yards, Adrian Cooper seven for 101 and Cris Carter 11 for 100.

Top rusher: Houston's Lorenzo White ran for a career-high 156 yards on 27 carries in a loss to the New York Giants.

Top passer: Minnesota's Moon completed 33 of 50 passes for 400 yards and two touchdowns in a loss to the Jets.

Top receiver: Buffalo's Andre Reed had 15 catches for 191 yards and two touchdowns in a victory over Green Bay.

Notes: Six quarterbacks were used and seven players threw passes in the Cowboys' rout of the Redskins. . . . The Cardinals beat Philadelphia, 12-6, the Cards' first win without scoring a touchdown since 1966. . . . The 49ers beat the Rams for the ninth consecutive time; it was San Francisco's fourth consecutive season sweep of their California rival. . . . Dallas completed a season sweep of the Redskins for the first time since 1985. . . . Detroit had the ball for just 15:48 in its loss to Chicago. The Bears controlled the ball for 44:12. . . . Houston's Jeff Fisher became the eighth coach to make his debut on Monday Night Football. He was the fifth to lose. . . . Green Bay's Chris Jacke had an extra-point attempt blocked for the first time in his six-year career in a loss to Buffalo. . . . Tampa Bay and Seattle came into the league together as expansion brothers in 1976. The teams met once each in '76 and '77, then not again until this season. . . . The Oilers lost by three points for an NFL-record fourth consecutive time.

Quote of the week: Atlanta Coach June Jones, on Elway's heroics: "Elway did what he's supposed to do. He's good at winning games in the fourth quarter, and he did it again."

GAME SUMMARIES

BEARS 20, LIONS 10

Sunday, November 20

Detroit	0	10	0	0	—10
Chicago	0	10	3	7	—20

Second Quarter
Chi—Tillman 1 run (Butler kick), :45.
Det—H. Moore 9 pass from Krieg (Hanson kick), 5:54.
Chi—FG Butler 28, 13:50.
Det—FG Hanson 29, 14:54.
Third Quarter
Chi—FG Butler 23, 14:08.
Fourth Quarter
Chi—Graham 30 pass from Walsh (Butler kick), 2:10.

TEAM STATISTICS

	Detroit	Chicago
First downs	11	23
Rushes-yards	12-52	43-161
Passing	128	177
Punt returns-yards	0-0	2-11
Kickoff returns-yards	4-68	3-65
Interception returns-yards	1-0	0-0
Comp.-att.-int.	11-21-0	25-31-1
Sacked-yards lost	3-20	2-8
Punts-average	3-40	2-39
Fumbles-lost	0-0	0-0
Penalties-yards	4-24	8-79
Time of possession	15:48	44:12

Attendance—55,035.

INDIVIDUAL STATISTICS

RUSHING—Detroit, Sanders 11-42, Krieg 1-10. Chicago, Tillman 32-126, Green 3-17, Harris 5-14, Christian 2-5, Walsh 1-(minus 1).
PASSING—Detroit, Krieg 11-21-0-148. Chicago, Walsh 25-31-1-185.
RECEIVING—Detroit, Perriman 6-120, H. Moore 2-19, Sanders 2-6, Matthews 1-3. Chicago, Harris 7-53, Tillman 6-34, Graham 5-53, Wetnight 2-24, Jennings 2-7, Cook 1-5, Primus 1-5, Green 1-4.
MISSED FIELD GOALS ATTEMPTS—Detroit, Hanson 43.
INTERCEPTIONS—Detroit, Blades 1-0.
KICKOFF RETURNS—Detroit, Gray 2-37, Lynch 1-12, D. Moore 1-19. Chicago, Lewis 2-60, Green 1-5.
PUNT RETURNS—Chicago, Graham 2-11.
SACKS—Detroit, Scroggins 1, Thomas 1. Chicago, A. Fontenot 1, Spellman 1, Zorich 1.

COLTS 17, BENGALS 13

Sunday, November 20

Indianapolis	7	0	0	10	—17
Cincinnati	3	3	7	0	—13

First Quarter
Ind—Faulk 1 run (Biasucci kick), 9:34.
Cin—FG Pelfrey 29, 14:50.
Second Quarter
Cin—FG Pelfrey 46, 8:12.
Third Quarter
Cin—Scott 15 pass from Blake (Pelfrey kick), 12:43.
Fourth Quarter
Ind—FG Biasucci 35, 8:29.
Ind—Dawkins 8 pass from Majkowski (Biasucci kick), 13:06.

TEAM STATISTICS

	Indianapolis	Cincinnati
First downs	15	16
Rushes-yards	32-72	25-103
Passing	165	250
Punt returns-yards	3-22	1-5
Kickoff returns-yards	3-71	4-92
Interception returns-yards	1-0	0-0
Comp.-att.-int.	14-24-0	22-38-1
Sacked-yards lost	0-0	1-10
Punts-average	6-39	4-43
Fumbles-lost	2-0	3-1
Penalties-yards	4-25	5-33
Time of possession	29:03	30:57

Attendance—55,566.

INDIVIDUAL STATISTICS

RUSHING—Indianapolis, Potts 11-45, Faulk 16-28, Majkowski 5-(minus 1). Cincinnati, Fenner 13-46, Blake 4-27, Green 6-21, Cothran 2-9.
PASSING—Indianapolis, Majkowski 14-24-0-165. Cincinnati, Blake 21-37-1-207, Scott 1-1-0-53.
RECEIVING—Indianapolis, Turner 6-50, Dawkins 5-68, Warren 1-29, Jackson 1-11, Faulk 1-7. Cincinnati, Pickens 6-103, To. McGee 5-70, Fenner 5-36, Scott 3-32, Green 2-16, Sadowski 1-3.
MISSED FIELD GOAL ATTEMPTS—None.
INTERCEPTIONS—Indianapolis, Buchanan 1-0.
KICKOFF RETURNS—Indianapolis, Brewer 2-44, Humphrey 1-27. Cincinnati, Ball 4-92.
PUNT RETURNS—Indianapolis, Brewer 3-22. Cincinnati, Sawyer 1-5.
SACKS—Indianapolis, Nunn 1.

BILLS 29, PACKERS 20

Sunday, November 20

Green Bay	0	6	14	0	—20
Buffalo	14	13	0	2	—29

First Quarter
Buf—Thomas 5 run (Christie kick), 4:20.
Buf—Reed 15 pass from Kelly (Christie kick), 14:29.
Second Quarter
Buf—FG Christie 38, 7:25.
Buf—Reed 10 pass from Kelly (Christie kick), 12:48.
G.B.—Sharpe 29 pass from Favre (kick blocked), 13:57.
Buf—FG Christie 51, 15:00.
Third Quarter
G.B.—E. Bennett 5 pass from Favre (Jacke kick), 5:58.
G.B.—Sharpe 26 pass from Favre (Jacke kick), 12:45.
Fourth Quarter
Buf—Safety, Sims holding penalty in the end zone, 13:09.

TEAM STATISTICS

	Green Bay	Buffalo
First downs	18	27
Rushes-yards	12-61	40-108
Passing	205	347
Punt returns-yards	2-11	1-8
Kickoff returns-yards	5-99	4-66
Interception returns-yards	1-26	1-36
Comp.-att.-int.	22-40-1	32-44-1
Sacked-yards lost	1-9	2-18
Punts-average	5-43	3-40
Fumbles-lost	0-0	0-0
Penalties-yards	3-16	6-35
Time of possession	21:37	38:23

Attendance—79,029.

INDIVIDUAL STATISTICS

RUSHING—Green Bay, E. Bennett 8-45, Favre 1-9, Cobb 3-7. Buffalo, T. Thomas 31-80, Gardner 5-16, K. Davis 2-9, Reed 1-4, Kelly 1-(minus 1).
PASSING—Green Bay, Favre 22-40-1-214. Buffalo, Kelly 32-44-1-365.
RECEIVING—Green Bay, Sharpe 5-86, R. Brooks 5-40, E. Bennett 5-22, Cobb 4-37, R. Johnson 2-20, Morgan 1-9. Buffalo, Reed 15-191, Bl. Brooks 5-53, Metzelaars 5-35, T. Thomas 4-25, Copeland 2-44, D. Thomas 1-17.
MISSED FIELD GOAL ATTEMPTS—Buffalo, Christie 25.
INTERCEPTIONS—Green Bay, Buckley 1-26. Buffalo, Washington 1-36.
KICKOFF RETURNS—Green Bay, Harris 3-64, Thompson 2-35. Buffalo, Turner 2-28, Copeland 1-23, Jourdain 1-15.
PUNT RETURNS—Green Bay, R. Brooks 2-11. Buffalo, Burris 1-8.
SACKS—Green Bay, Gi. Brown 1, Jones 1. Buffalo, Wright 1.

STEELERS 16, DOLPHINS 13

Sunday, November 20

Miami	0	7	3	3	0—13
Pittsburgh	3	3	0	7	3—16

First Quarter
Pit—FG Anderson 19, 7:04.
Second Quarter
Mia—Jackson 2 pass from Marino (Stoyanovich kick), 13:46.
Pit—FG Anderson 48, 14:54.
Third Quarter
Mia—FG Stoyanovich 34, 4:32.
Fourth Quarter
Pit—Foster 10 run (Anderson kick), 6:25.
Mia—FG Stoyanovich 48, 15:00.
Overtime
Pit—FG Anderson 39, 10:19.

TEAM STATISTICS

	Miami	Pittsburgh
First downs	20	21
Rushes-yards	19-37	31-88
Passing	283	335
Punt returns-yards	1-1	2-9
Kickoff returns-yards	4-44	4-63
Interception returns-yards	0-0	1-0
Comp.-att.-int.	31-45-1	26-42-0
Sacked-yards lost	4-29	1-8
Punts-average	4-34	5-35
Fumbles-lost	3-1	1-0
Penalties-yards	5-35	8-63
Time of possession	32:46	37:33

Attendance—59,148.

INDIVIDUAL STATISTICS

RUSHING—Miami, Parmalee 16-29, Craver 1-13, Marino 2-(minus 5). Pittsburgh, Foster 31-88.
PASSING—Miami, Marino 31-45-1-312. Pittsburgh, Tomczak 26-42-0-343.
RECEIVING—Miami, Fryar 6-113, Jackson 6-45, Saxon 5-15, McDuffie 4-50, Craver 4-29, Parmalee 4-29, Miller 1-27, M. Williams 1-4. Pittsburgh, Johnson 7-84, J.L. Williams 7-62, Foster 4-29, Mills 3-98, Green 3-39, Stone 1-21, Hayes 1-10.
MISSED FIELD GOAL ATTEMPTS—Miami, Stoyanovich 36.
INTERCEPTIONS—Pittsburgh, Kirkland 1-0.
KICKOFF RETURNS—Miami, Baty 1-0, McDuffie 1-21, Spikes 1-13, R. Williams 1-0. Pittsburgh, Stone 3-63, Mills 1-0.
PUNT RETURNS—Miami, McDuffie 1-1. Pittsburgh, Woodson 2-9.
SACKS—Miami, Singleton 1. Pittsburgh, Brown 2, Gildon 1, Steed 1.

PATRIOTS 23, CHARGERS 17

Sunday, November 20

San Diego	0	0	10	7—17	
New England	7	3	3	10—23	

First Quarter
N.E.—Thompson 27 pass from Bledsoe (Bahr kick), 9:40.
Second Quarter
N.E.—FG Bahr 39, 2:32.
Third Quarter
S.D.—FG Carney 34, 4:14.
N.E.—FG Bahr 38, 14:22.
S.D.—Coleman 80 kickoff return (Carney kick), 14:36.
Fourth Quarter
N.E.—Butts 1 run (Bahr kick), 5:41.
N.E.—FG Bahr 23, 8:43.
S.D.—Martin 2 pass from Humphries (Carney kick), 14:05.

TEAM STATISTICS

	San Diego	New England
First downs	18	21
Rushes-yards	19-72	36-101
Passing	169	217
Punt returns-yards	0-0	2-10
Kickoff returns-yards	6-174	3-64
Interception returns-yards	2-(-7)	3-37
Comp.-att.-int.	20-37-3	21-36-2
Sacked-yards lost	5-50	1-7
Punts-average	4-37	3-34
Fumbles-lost	2-0	1-0
Penalties-yards	6-45	2-20
Time of possession	24:27	35:33

Attendance—59,690.

INDIVIDUAL STATISTICS

RUSHING—San Diego, Means 15-59, Harmon 1-8, Bi-eniemy 2-5, Humphries 1-0. New England, Butts 28-88, Thompson 2-7, Turner 1-4, Bledsoe 4-2, Coates 1-0.
PASSING—San Diego, Humphries 20-37-3-219. New England, Bledsoe 21-36-2-224.
RECEIVING—San Diego, Jefferson 6-64, Young 4-69, Seay 4-48, Mitchell 2-21, Means 2-5, Harmon 1-10, Martin 1-2. New England, Timpson 8-82, Thompson 3-45, Turner 3-25, Brisby 2-27, Coates 2-22, Gash 2-19, Butts 1-4.
MISSED FIELD GOAL ATTEMPTS—San Diego, Carney 48. New England, Bahr 44, 48.
INTERCEPTIONS—San Diego, Gordon 2-(minus 7). New England, Hurst 2-25, V. Brown 1-12.
KICKOFF RETURNS—San Diego, Coleman 4-137, Harmon 2-37. New England, Thompson 2-43, Crittenden 1-21.
PUNT RETURNS—New England, T. Brown 2-10.
SACKS—San Diego, Lee 1. New England, Slade 3½, Reynolds 1, M. Jones ½.

CHIEFS 20, BROWNS 13

Sunday, November 20

Cleveland	0	6	7	0—13	
Kansas City	0	7	3	10—20	

Second Quarter
K.C.—Greene 6 pass from Montana (Elliott kick), 3:51.
Cle—Metcalf 15 pass from Testaverde (run failed), 12:51.
Third Quarter
K.C.—FG Elliott 22, 9:42.
Cle—Jackson 15 pass from Rypien (Stover kick), 12:12.
Fourth Quarter
K.C.—FG Elliott 28, :53.
K.C.—Anders 1 run (Elliott kick), 7:14.

TEAM STATISTICS

	Cleveland	Kansas City
First downs	15	23
Rushes-yards	27-94	37-134
Passing	145	153
Punt returns-yards	7-93	3-8
Kickoff returns-yards	3-54	2-41
Interception returns-yards	0-0	1-0
Comp.-att.-int.	14-37-1	19-33-0
Sacked-yards lost	1-7	2-16
Punts-average	8-42	9-41
Fumbles-lost	4-3	3-1
Penalties-yards	15-142	9-72
Time of possession	25:17	34:43

Attendance—66,129.

INDIVIDUAL STATISTICS

RUSHING—Cleveland, Hoard 17-68, Byner 6-26, Rypien 2-2, Metcalf 2-(minus 2). Kansas City, Hill 12-66, Bennett 11-41, Anders 9-26, Dawson 1-2, Montana 4-(minus 1).
PASSING—Cleveland, Rypien 10-24-1-114, Testaverde 4-12-0-38, Jackson 0-1-0-0. Kansas City, Montana 19-33-0-169.
RECEIVING—Cleveland, Hoard 6-56, Jackson 3-51, Kinchen 3-24, Metcalf 1-15, Byner 1-6. Kansas City, Martin 4-54, Hill 3-26, Dawson 2-18, Anders 2-15, Birden 2-14, Walker 2-5, Hughes 1-13, Bennett 1-12, Greene 1-6, Penn 1-6.
MISSED FIELD GOAL ATTEMPTS—None.
INTERCEPTIONS—Kansas City, Carter 1-0.
KICKOFF RETURNS—Cleveland, Baldwin 2-35, Metcalf 1-19. Kansas City, Dickerson 1-19, Hughes 1-22.
PUNT RETURNS—Cleveland, Carrier 4-67, Metcalf 3-26. Kansas City, Carter 3-8.
SACKS—Cleveland, Burnett 1, B. Johnson 1. Kansas City, Thomas 1.

COWBOYS 31, REDSKINS 7

Sunday, November 20

Washington	0	7	0	0— 7	
Dallas	17	7	7	0—31	

First Quarter
Dal—E. Smith 8 run (Boniol kick), 5:53.
Dal—E. Smith 3 run (Boniol kick), 9:11.
Dal—FG Boniol 32, 11:36.
Second Quarter
Was—Howard 19 pass from Friesz (Lohmiller kick), 3:24.
Dal—Harper 15 pass from Peete (Boniol kick), 13:51.
Third Quarter
Dal—K. Williams 83 punt return (Boniol kick), 6:41.

TEAM STATISTICS

	Washington	Dallas
First downs	20	15
Rushes-yards	27-84	38-130
Passing	229	111
Punt returns-yards	5-32	3-96
Kickoff returns-yards	5-180	2-61
Interception returns-yards	0-0	4-37
Comp.-att.-int.	22-51-4	11-23-0
Sacked-yards lost	2-14	0-0
Punts-average	5-50	8-40
Fumbles-lost	1-1	1-1
Penalties-yards	6-52	8-61
Time of possession	29:25	30:35

Attendance—64,644.

INDIVIDUAL STATISTICS

RUSHING—Washington, Ervins 12-37, Brooks 10-33, C. Smith 3-8, Mitchell 2-6. Dallas, E. Smith 21-85, Coleman 9-21, Johnston 3-12, Aikman 2-12, Peete 1-2, Garrett 2-(minus 2).

PASSING—Washington, Frerotte 1-6-1-18, Friesz 16-35-2-193, Shuler 5-9-0-32, Mitchell 0-1-1-0. Dallas, Aikman 8-13-0-87, Peete 2-5-0-20, Garrett 1-5-0-4.

RECEIVING—Washington, Howard 7-107, Brooks 3-16, Wycheck 3-13, Winans 2-37, C. Smith 2-25, Mitchell 2-11, Horton 1-18, Truitt 1-12, Ervins 1-4. Dallas, Irvin 3-36, Novacek 2-34, Johnston 2-14, E. Smith 2-8, Harper 1-15, Coleman 1-4.

MISSED FIELD GOAL ATTEMPTS—Washington, Lohmiller 53. Dallas, Boniol 51.

INTERCEPTIONS—Dallas, K. Smith 2-11, Marion 1-11, Washington 1-15.

KICKOFF RETURNS—Washington, Mitchell 5-180. Dallas, K. Williams 2-61.

PUNT RETURNS—Washington, Mitchell 5-32. Dallas, K. Williams 3-96.

SACKS—Dallas, Haley 1, Tolbert 1.

BRONCOS 32, FALCONS 28

Sunday, November 20

Atlanta	0	14	7	7—28
Denver	10	0	7	15—32

First Quarter
Den—Rivers 1 run (Elam kick), 8:05.
Den—FG Elam 35, 13:31.
Second Quarter
Atl—Heyward 6 pass from J. George (Johnson kick), 4:36.
Atl—Emanuel 11 pass from J. George (Johnson kick), 7:00.
Third Quarter
Den—Campbell 22 pass from Elway (Elam kick), 11:36.
Atl—Mathis 47 pass from J. George (Johnson kick), 14:05.
Fourth Quarter
Atl—Mathis 49 pass from J. George (Johnson kick), :46.
Den—Miller 32 pass from Elway (Miller pass from Elway), 4:41.
Den—Elway 4 run (Elam kick), 13:04.

TEAM STATISTICS

	Atlanta	Denver
First downs	16	25
Rushes-yards	17-76	29-89
Passing	254	336
Punt returns-yards	1-8	1-0
Kickoff returns-yards	5-80	5-119
Interception returns-yards	1-2	0-0
Comp.-att.-int.	19-43-0	27-42-1
Sacked-yards lost	0-0	5-46
Punts-average	7-42	3-43
Fumbles-lost	1-0	1-1
Penalties-yards	8-62	5-40
Time of possession	25:02	34:58

Attendance—70,594.

INDIVIDUAL STATISTICS

RUSHING—Atlanta, Heyward 15-73, J. George 2-3. Denver, L. Russell 16-36, Milburn 5-31, Elway 6-17, Clark 1-4, Rivers 1-1.

PASSING—Atlanta, J. George 19-43-0-254. Denver, Elway 27-42-1-382.

RECEIVING—Atlanta, Mathis 8-163, Heyward 4-23, Emanuel 3-42, Harris 3-21, Sanders 1-5. Denver, Tillman 8-175, Miller 6-102, Milburn 6-14, Sharpe 4-44, Campbell 1-22, Rivers 1-13, Kimbrough 1-12.

MISSED FIELD GOAL ATTEMPTS—None.

INTERCEPTIONS—Atlanta, Doleman 1-2.

KICKOFF RETURNS—Atlanta, Verdin 4-69, Anderson 1-11. Denver, Milburn 3-73, By'not'e 2-46.

PUNT RETURNS—Atlanta, Verdin 1-8. Denver, Milburn 1-0.
SACKS—Atlanta, Geathers 3, Doleman 2.

JETS 31, VIKINGS 21

Sunday, November 20

N.Y. Jets	10	7	7	7—31
Minnesota	7	7	0	7—21

First Quarter
N.Y.—Turner 90 interception return (Lowery kick), 2:07.
Min—Graham 4 run (Reveiz kick), 5:04.
N.Y.—FG Lowery 38, 10:59.
Second Quarter
Min—Carter 6 pass from Moon (Reveiz kick), 9:30.
N.Y.—Yarborough 11 pass from Esiason (Lowery kick), 13:54.
Third Quarter
N.Y.—Moore 5 pass from Esiason (Lowery kick), 2:10.
Fourth Quarter
N.Y.—Monk 14 pass from Esiason (Lowery kick), :56.
Min—Ismail 2 pass from Moon (Reveiz kick), 6:36.

TEAM STATISTICS

	N.Y. Jets	Minnesota
First downs	17	26
Rushes-yards	26-62	18-87
Passing	220	374
Punt returns-yards	1-12	1-8
Kickoff returns-yards	2-64	6-170
Interception returns-yards	4-156	0-0
Comp.-att.-int.	22-29-0	33-51-4
Sacked-yards lost	1-10	3-26
Punts-average	5-38	2-39
Fumbles-lost	1-1	2-0
Penalties-yards	6-47	2-16
Time of possession	29:15	30:45

Attendance—60,687.

INDIVIDUAL STATISTICS

RUSHING—New York, J. Johnson 23-62, R. Anderson 1-1, Esiason 2-(minus 1). Minnesota, Allen 12-59, Lee 5-24, Graham 1-4.

PASSING—New York, Esiason 22-29-0-230. Minnesota, Moon 33-50-4-400, Saxon 0-1-0-0.

RECEIVING—New York, Mitchell 11-120, Thornton 3-37, Moore 3-36, Monk 2-19, Yarborough 1-11, B. Baxter 1-6, J. Johnson 1-1. Minnesota, Carter 11-100, Cooper 7-101, Reed 5-121, Lee 3-33, Jordan 3-23, Ismail 3-18, Allen 1-4.

MISSED FIELD GOAL ATTEMPTS—None.

INTERCEPTIONS—New York, Turner 3-116, Hasty 1-40.

KICKOFF RETURNS—New York, Glenn 2-64. Minnesota, Ismail 4-107, R. Smith 2-63.

PUNT RETURNS—New York, Hicks 1-12. Minnesota, Palmer 1-8.

SACKS—New York, Hasty 1, Lageman 1, Lewis 1. Minnesota, Jenkins 1.

SEAHAWKS 22, BUCCANEERS 21

Sunday, November 20

Tampa Bay	0	7	3	11—21
Seattle	7	8	0	7—22

First Quarter
Sea—Warren 3 pass from Mirer (Kasay kick), 4:51.
Second Quarter
Sea—Vaughn 5 pass from Mirer (Tuten run), 2:17.
T.B.—Hawkins 2 pass from Erickson (Husted kick), 14:27.
Third Quarter
T.B.—FG Husted 30, 4:59.
Fourth Quarter
T.B.—Hawkins 13 pass from Erickson (Rhett run), 2:40.
T.B.—FG Husted 35, 11:36.
Sea—Strong 7 run (Kasay kick), 14:18.

TEAM STATISTICS

	Tampa Bay	Seattle
First downs	23	18
Rushes-yards	32-120	34-177
Passing	212	117
Punt returns-yards	1-5	1-8
Kickoff returns-yards	4-75	3-56
Interception returns-yards	1-4	1-0
Comp.-att.-int.	22-32-1	13-25-1
Sacked-yards lost	0-0	1-10
Punts-average	4-37	3-49

	Tampa Bay	Seattle
Fumbles-lost	1-1	2-2
Penalties-yards	8-81	7-53
Time of possession	33:09	26:51
Attendance—37,466.		

INDIVIDUAL STATISTICS

RUSHING—Tampa Bay, Rhett 24-111, Royster 4-11, Erickson 1-1, McDowell 1-0, T. Armstrong 1-(minus 1), Turner 1-(minus 2), Seattle, C. Warren 16-116, Strong 9-37, Mirer 4-20, S. Smith 2-7, T. Johnson 1-2, Vaughn 2-(minus 5).

PASSING—Tampa Bay, Erickson 22-32-1-212. Seattle, Mirer 13-25-1-127.

RECEIVING—Tampa Bay, Dawsey 6-63, Hawkins 6-41, Copeland 3-35, Royster 3-24, Armstrong 1-26, C. Wilson 1-13, Rhett 1-7, McDowell 1-3. Seattle, Blades 5-58, Green 2-17, C. Warren 2-16, Martin 1-20, T. Johnson 1-6, Strong 1-5, Vaughn 1-5.

MISSED FIELD GOAL ATTEMPTS—None.

INTERCEPTIONS—Tampa Bay, Mayhew 1-4. Seattle, E. Robinson 1-0.

KICKOFF RETURNS—Tampa Bay, Turner 4-75. Seattle, Bates 3-56.

PUNT RETURNS—Tampa Bay, Turner 1-5. Seattle, Martin 1-8.

SACKS—Tampa Bay, Dotson 1.

CARDINALS 12, EAGLES 6

Sunday, November 20

Philadelphia	0	3	0	3—6
Arizona	3	3	3	3—12

First Quarter
Ari—FG Davis 24, 11:39.

Second Quarter
Ari—FG Davis 24, 13:08.
Phi—FG Murray 26, 14:50.

Third Quarter
Ari—FG Davis 24, 9:20.

Fourth Quarter
Phi—FG Murray 30, 3:19.
Ari—FG Davis 39, 9:44.

TEAM STATISTICS

	Philadelphia	Arizona
First downs	14	16
Rushes-yards	14-75	39-158
Passing	110	123
Punt returns-yards	2-16	3-15
Kickoff returns-yards	5-128	2-55
Interception returns-yards	0-0	1-0
Comp.-att.-int.	17-44-1	12-23-0
Sacked-yards lost	4-41	1-9
Punts-average	6-43	6-36
Fumbles-lost	1-1	1-1
Penalties-yards	7-55	12-85
Time of possession	23:37	36:23
Attendance—62,779.		

INDIVIDUAL STATISTICS

RUSHING—Philadelphia, Garner 7-42, Walker 4-18, Cunningham 1-18, Joseph 2-(minus 3). Arizona, Moore 16-65, Centers 10-40, Higgs 9-38, Schroeder 4-15.

PASSING—Philadelphia, Cunningham 17-44-1-151. Arizona, Schroeder 12-23-0-132.

RECEIVING—Philadelphia, C. Williams 6-56, Barnett 4-24, Joseph 3-19, Walker 2-31, Bailey 1-12, Johnson 1-9. Arizona, Centers 6-48, Clark 3-63, R. Hill 2-10, Reeves 1-11.

MISSED FIELD GOAL ATTEMPTS—None.

INTERCEPTIONS—Arizona, A. Williams 1-0.

KICKOFF RETURNS—Philadelphia, Walker 5-128. Arizona, Levy 2-55.

PUNT RETURNS—Philadelphia, Sydner 2-16. Arizona, Robinson 3-15.

SACKS—Philadelphia, Townsend 1. Arizona, Joyner 2, Simmons 1, Swann 1.

RAIDERS 24, SAINTS 19

Sunday, November 20

New Orleans	0	0	7	12—19
L.A. Raiders	7	3	7	7—24

First Quarter
L.A.—T. Brown 12 pass from Hostetler (Jaeger kick), 5:51.

Second Quarter
L.A.—FG Jaeger 51, 15:00.

Third Quarter
N.O.—Hughes 42 fumble return (Andersen kick), 4:19.
L.A.—Ismail 17 pass from Hostetler (Jaeger kick), 9:16.

Fourth Quarter
L.A.—T. Brown 30 pass from Hostetler (Jaeger kick), 9:09.
N.O.—Small 9 pass from Everett (pass failed), 11:11.
N.O.—Small 14 pass from Everett (pass failed), 13:09.

TEAM STATISTICS

	New Orleans	L.A. Raiders
First downs	16	22
Rushes-yards	11-16	34-121
Passing	230	307
Punt returns-yards	1-7	6-81
Kickoff returns-yards	4-112	2-41
Interception returns-yards	2-1	1-35
Comp.-att.-int.	28-44-1	22-28-2
Sacked-yards lost	4-32	2-3
Punts-average	7-41	3-46
Fumbles-lost	0-0	2-2
Penalties-yards	8-55	11-89
Time of possession	27:12	32:48
Attendance—41,722.		

INDIVIDUAL STATISTICS

RUSHING—New Orleans, Bates 10-17, Hughes 1-(minus 1). Los Angeles, H. Williams 24-88, C. Jones 6-20, Rathman 1-8, Hostetler 3-5.

PASSING—New Orleans, Everett 28-44-1-262. Los Angeles, Hostetler 22-28-2-310.

RECEIVING—New Orleans, Small 8-86, D. Brown 8-64, Early 5-62, Haynes 3-25, Smith 2-17, Walls 2-8. Los Angeles, T. Brown 8-132, Ismail 4-68, Glover 3-48, Jett 3-32, H. Williams 1-11, Rathman 1-8, Wright 1-7, J. Williams 1-4.

MISSED FIELD GOAL ATTEMPTS—New Orleans, Ander-sen 51. Los Angeles, Jaeger 46.

INTERCEPTIONS—New Orleans, Lumpkin 1-1, Tubbs 1-0. Los Angeles, McDaniel 1-35.

KICKOFF RETURNS—New Orleans, Hughes 3-93, Ned 1-19. Los Angeles, Ismail 2-41.

PUNT RETURNS—New Orleans, Hughes 1-7. Los Ang., T. Brown 6-81.

SACKS—New Orleans, Warren 1, Turnbull 1. Los Angeles, Harrison 1½, Fredrickson 1, Moss 1, Smith ½.

49ERS 31, RAMS 27

Sunday, November 20

L.A. Rams	3	3	13	8—27
San Francisco	14	7	3	7—31

First Quarter
S.F.—Taylor 7 pass from Young (Brien kick), 3:55.
L.A.—FG Zendejas 31, 7:20.
S.F.—Rice 7 pass from Young (Brien kick), 14:03.

Second Quarter
L.A.—FG Zendejas 27, 2:48.
S.F.—Rice 5 pass from Young (Brien kick), 14:22.

Third Quarter
L.A.—Kinchen 44 run (pass failed), 3:01.
S.F.—FG Brien 28, 8:35.
L.A.—Anderson 50 pass from Miller (Zendejas kick), 11:39.

Fourth Quarter
L.A.—Hester 22 pass from Miller (Bettis run), 1:55.
S.F.—Rice 18 pass from Young (Brien kick), 13:04.

TEAM STATISTICS

	L.A. Rams	San Francisco
First downs	17	32
Rushes-yards	18-86	37-134
Passing	272	325
Punt returns-yards	1-2	0-0
Kickoff returns-yards	6-122	6-98
Interception returns-yards	0-0	0-0
Comp.-att.-int.	19-37-0	30-44-0
Sacked-yards lost	2-11	0-0
Punts-average	3-38	2-38
Fumbles-lost	0-0	1-1
Penalties-yards	5-50	7-60
Time of possession	22:31	37:29
Attendance—62,774.		

INDIVIDUAL STATISTICS

RUSHING—Los Angeles, Kinchen 1-44, Bettis 15-29, Miller 1-8, Lang 1-5. San Francisco, Watters 20-81, Young 10-23, Carter 2-17, Floyd 4-10, Rice 1-3.

PASSING—Los Angeles, Miller 16-33-0-228, Maddox 3-4-0-55. San Francisco, Young 30-44-0-325.

RECEIVING—Los Angeles, Anderson 5-99, Hester 3-50, Bettis 3-43, Kinchen 2-51, Bruce 2-18, Lang 2-14, Drayton 1-6, Griffith 1-2. San Fran-

cisco, Rice 16-165, Watters 5-74, Taylor 5-49, Jones 3-31, Carter 1-6.
MISSED FIELD GOAL ATTEMPTS—San Francisco, Brien 41.
INTERCEPTIONS—None.
KICKOFF RETURNS—Los Angeles, Kinchen 3-56, Lang 2-45, Griffith 1-21. San Francisco, Carter 4-74, Walker 2-24.
PUNT RETURNS—Los Angeles, Kinchen 1-2.
SACKS—San Francisco, Stubblefield 1, B. Young 1.

GIANTS 13, OILERS 10
Monday, November 21

N.Y. Giants	0	0	7	6—13
Houston	0	0	7	3—10

Third Quarter
Hou—Tolliver 1 run (Del Greco kick), 10:16.
N.Y.—Sherrard 40 pass from Graham (Treadwell kick), 14:01.
Fourth Quarter
N.Y.—FG Treadwell 26, 6:41.
Hou—FG Del Greco 43, 10:52.
N.Y.—FG Treadwell 37, 14:58.

TEAM STATISTICS

	N.Y. Giants	Houston
First downs	18	13
Rushes-yards	43-163	29-166
Passing	124	112

	N.Y. Giants	Houston
Punt returns-yards	2-22	2-5
Kickoff returns-yards	3-44	3-37
Interception returns-yards	0-0	0-0
Comp.-att.-int.	10-21-0	10-15-0
Sacked-yards lost	0-0	1-7
Punts-average	4-47	4-39
Fumbles-lost	0-0	1-0
Penalties-yards	4-45	10-78
Time of possession	33:16	26:44
Attendance—53,201.		

INDIVIDUAL STATISTICS
RUSHING—New York, Hampton 34-122, Meggett 6-17, Calloway 1-14, Graham 1-9, Rasheed 1-1. Houston, L. White 27-156, Tillman 1-9, Tolliver 1-1.
PASSING—New York, Da. Brown 4-7-0-19, Graham 6-13-0-105, Meggett 0-1-0-0. Houston, Tolliver 10-15-0-119.
RECEIVING—New York, Sherrard 6-109, Hampton 1-6, Meggett 1-6, Calloway 1-3, Cross 1-0. Houston, L. White 2-49, Givins 2-23, Slaughter 2-17, Jeffires 1-21, Mills 1-4, McNair 1-3, Maston 1-2.
MISSED FIELD GOAL ATTEMPTS—None.
INTERCEPTIONS—None.
KICKOFF RETURNS—New York, Marshall 2-35, Meggett 1-9. Houston, Jackson 1-19, McNair 1-18, Teeter 1-0.
PUNT RETURNS—New York, Meggett 2-22. Houston, Givins 2-5.
SACKS—New York, Strahan 1.

WEEK 13

Dallas 42, Green Bay 31
Detroit 35, Buffalo 21
Atlanta 28, Philadelphia 21
Chicago 19, Arizona 16 (OT)
Cleveland 34, Houston 10
Denver 15, Cincinnati 13
Miami 28, N.Y. Jets 24
N.Y. Giants 21, Washington 19
New England 12, Indianapolis 10
Pittsburgh 21, L.A. Raiders 3
San Diego 31, L.A. Rams 17
Seattle 10, Kansas City 9
Tampa Bay 20, Minnesota 17 (OT)
San Francisco 35, New Orleans 14

STANDINGS

AFC EAST	W	L	T	Pct.
Miami	8	4	0	.667
N.Y. Jets	6	6	0	.500
Buffalo	6	6	0	.500
New England	6	6	0	.500
Indianapolis	5	7	0	.417

AFC CENTRAL	W	L	T	Pct.
Pittsburgh	9	3	0	.750
Cleveland	9	3	0	.750
Cincinnati	2	10	0	.167
Houston	1	11	0	.083

AFC WEST	W	L	T	Pct.
San Diego	9	3	0	.750
Kansas City	7	5	0	.583
Denver	6	6	0	.500
L.A. Raiders	6	6	0	.500
Seattle	5	7	0	.417

NFC EAST	W	L	T	Pct.
Dallas	10	2	0	.833
Philadelphia	7	5	0	.583
N.Y. Giants	5	7	0	.417
Arizona	5	7	0	.417
Washington	2	10	0	.167

NFC CENTRAL	W	L	T	Pct.
Chicago	8	4	0	.667
Minnesota	7	5	0	.583
Green Bay	6	6	0	.500
Detroit	6	6	0	.500
Tampa Bay	3	9	0	.250

NFC WEST	W	L	T	Pct.
San Francisco	10	2	0	.833
Atlanta	6	6	0	.500
L.A. Rams	4	8	0	.333
New Orleans	4	8	0	.333

HIGHLIGHTS

Hero of the week: Detroit cornerback Willie Clay, who had two interceptions in a 35-21 victory over Buffalo. The first came early in the fourth quarter, when he picked off a pass at Detroit's 3. The second came with 1:07 left and iced the victory. Clay stepped in front of a pass intended for Thurman Thomas and returned the interception 28 yards for a touchdown. The interceptions were the first two of Clay's three-year NFL career.

Goats of the week: New York Jets cornerbacks James Hasty and Aaron Glenn, who were burned repeatedly by Miami wide receiver Mark Ingram in a 28-24 loss. Ingram caught a team-record four touchdown passes, including two in the fourth quarter. The game-winner came with 22 seconds left when Glenn got faked out by Dan Marino, who fooled the rookie into thinking he would spike the ball to stop the clock. Ingram—who caught nine passes for 117 yards—was wide open when he caught the winning pass.

Sub of the week: Dallas quarterback Jason Garrett, who threw for 311 yards and two touchdowns against the league's fifth-ranked defense to lead the Cowboys past Green Bay, 42-31. Garrett, a third-stringer starting because of injuries to starter Troy Aikman and backup Rodney Peete, had not thrown a touchdown pass in his six NFL seasons before the game.

Comeback of the week: Miami rallied from deficits of 17-0 and 24-6 to stun the Jets. The winning touchdown came on a eight-yard touchdown pass from Marino to Ingram with 22 seconds left. It was the fifth time in his career that Marino engineered a fourth-quarter comeback against the Jets.

Blowout of the week: Cleveland took advantage of two Houston fumbles in Oilers territory to romp to a 34-10 victory. The Browns converted the fumbles into a field goal and a touchdown run to pull away from a 17-10 halftime lead. The final nine Oilers series ended with six punts, two fumbles and a fourth-down incompletion.

Nail-biter of the week: Chicago's Kevin Butler kicked a 27-yard field goal with 6:49 left in overtime to lift the Bears past Arizona, 19-16. Arizona's Greg Davis booted a 47-yard field goal to tie it at 16 with 58 seconds left in regulation. Arizona recovered the ensuing squib kick, but Chicago held and the game went into overtime.

Hit of the week: By Denver defensive tackle Ted Washington and safety Steve Atwater, who forced a fumble by Cincinnati's Harold Green with the Bengals threatening to score late in the game. Washington met Green head-on at the Broncos' 20 with 3:50 left, with Atwater coming in to jar the ball loose. Denver linebacker Elijah Alexander pounced on the fumble to preserve the victory.

Oddity of the week: The Jets recovered fumbles—three of them their own—on four consecutive plays in the fourth quarter in their loss.

Top rusher: Dallas' Emmitt Smith rushed for 133 yards and two touchdowns on 32 carries in a victory over Green Bay. He became the first back to gain 100 yards against the Packers in 1994.

Top passer: The Jets' Boomer Esiason completed 26 of 41 passes for 382 yards and two touchdowns in a loss to Miami.

Top receiver: Detroit's Herman Moore had seven receptions for 169 yards and a touchdown in a victory over Buffalo.

Notes: Kansas City's Joe Montana threw for 163 yards in a loss to Seattle to become just the fifth NFL passer to reach the 40,000-yard mark in a career. He joined Fran Tarkenton, Marino, Dan Fouts and Johnny Unitas. . . . The Cincinnati-Denver game marked the first time that sons of NFL head coaches faced each other. Bengals Coach Dave Shula is the son of Dolphins Coach Don Shula and Broncos Coach Wade Phillips is the son of former Oilers and Saints coach Bum Phillips. . . . Seattle's victory snapped its seven-game losing streak to Kansas City. . . . The Giants' victory over Washington was their 11th in the past 14 games against their NFC East rival. It was the fourth straight win and the sixth in the past seven games at the Redskins' RFK Stadium.... San Francisco became the first team to clinch a division title with the victory over New Orleans.... Denver QB John Elway reached two milestones. He became just the seventh NFL player to reach 40,000 career total yards, and also surpassed 3,000 yards passing for the ninth time in his career. Marino holds the NFL record (10).... New England's Ben Coates became the first NFL tight end to reach the 1,000-yard receiving mark since 1986.... Dallas scored a club-record 36 points in the second half to down Green Bay.... Philadelphia's Herschel Walker scored on a 91-yard run in a loss to Atlanta; it was the longest scoring run in the NFL since Bo Jackson went 92 yards in 1989.

Quote of the week: Dallas guard Nate Newton, on the performance by the heretofore-unknown Garrett: "If there is such a thing as fairy tales, then Jason I guess has a fairy god-daddy."

GAME SUMMARIES

LIONS 35, BILLS 21
Thursday, November 24

Buffalo	0	7	7	7—21
Detroit	7	14	0	14—35

First Quarter
Det—Moore 51 pass from Krieg (Hanson kick), :47.
Second Quarter
Det—Sanders 4 run (Hanson kick), 1:22.
Buf—Copeland 20 pass from Kelly (Christie kick), 5:07.
Det—Matthews 28 pass from Krieg (Hanson kick), 13:55.
Third Quarter
Buf—Metzelaars 27 pass from Kelly (Christie kick), 5:44.
Fourth Quarter
Det—Perriman 12 pass from Krieg (Hanson kick), 7:59.
Buf—Kelly 15 run (Christie kick), 10:56.
Det—Clay 28 interception return (Hanson kick), 13:53.

TEAM STATISTICS

	Buffalo	Detroit
First downs	25	20
Rushes-yards	29-121	21-47
Passing	246	341
Punt returns-yards	2-2	1-6
Kickoff returns-yards	5-110	3-67
Interception returns-yards	0-0	2-28
Comp.-att.-int.	29-35-2	20-25-0
Sacked-yards lost	3-27	2-10
Punts-average	3-38	4-46
Fumbles-lost	1-0	2-0
Penalties-yards	7-55	3-29
Time of possession	33:24	26:36
Attendance—75,672.		

INDIVIDUAL STATISTICS
RUSHING—Buffalo, T. Thomas 17-58, Jourdain 3-24, Kelly 3-23, Gardner 3-15, K. Davis 3-1. Detroit, Sanders 19-45, D. Moore 1-2, Krieg 1-0.
PASSING—Buffalo, Kelly 29-35-2-273. Detroit, Krieg 20-25-0-351.
RECEIVING—Buffalo, Reed 8-58, T. Thomas 8-58, Copeland 4-53, Metzelaars 3-43, Jourdain 3-28, Brooks 2-19, D. Thomas 1-14. Detroit, H. Moore 7-169, Perriman 5-65, Matthews 3-55, Hall 3-43, Lynch 1-12, Hallock 1-7.
MISSED FIELD GOAL ATTEMPTS—None.
INTERCEPTIONS—Detroit, Clay 2-28.
KICKOFF RETURNS—Buffalo, Jourdain 3-88, Copeland 1-13, Pike 1-9. Detroit, Gray 3-67.
PUNT RETURNS—Buffalo, Burris 2-2. Detroit, Gray 1-6.
SACKS—Buffalo, Hansen 1½, Wright ½. Detroit, Pritchett 3.

COWBOYS 42, PACKERS 31
Thursday, November 24

Green Bay	7	10	7	7—31
Dallas	0	6	19	17—42

First Quarter
G.B.—Sharpe 1 pass from Favre (Jacke kick), 10:40.
Second Quarter
G.B.—FG Jacke 28, 5:20.
Dal—FG Boniol 41, 8:44.
G.B.—Sharpe 36 pass from Favre (Jacke kick), 14:24.
Dal—FG Boniol 37, 15:00.
Third Quarter
Dal—E. Smith 5 run (Boniol kick), :23.
G.B.—Sharpe 30 pass from Favre (Jacke kick), 1:32.
Dal—Harper 45 pass from Garrett (run failed), 4:15.
Dal—Johnston 3 run (run failed), 9:26.
Fourth Quarter
Dal—E. Smith 18 run (Boniol kick), :05.
Dal—Irvin 35 pass from Garrett (Boniol kick), 3:40.
G.B.—Sharpe 5 pass from Favre (Jacke kick), 7:57.
Dal—FG Boniol 35, 14:13.

TEAM STATISTICS

	Green Bay	Dallas
First downs	17	23
Rushes-yards	18-29	37-138
Passing	248	298
Punt returns-yards	2-20	4-25
Kickoff returns-yards	8-173	6-177
Interception returns-yards	1-1	0-0
Comp.-att.-int.	27-40-0	15-26-1
Sacked-yards lost	2-9	2-13
Punts-average	6-46	4-44
Fumbles-lost	0-0	2-0
Penalties-yards	8-94	10-95
Time of possession	27:54	32:06
Attendance—64,597.		

INDIVIDUAL STATISTICS
RUSHING—Green Bay, Cobb 9-17, Bennett 7-12, Favre 2-0. Dallas, Smith 32-133, Johnston 3-4, Coleman 1-1, Garrett 1-0.
PASSING—Green Bay, Favre 27-40-0-257. Dallas, Garrett 15-26-1-311.
RECEIVING—Green Bay, Sharpe 9-122, West 5-36, Bennett 4-22, Brooks 3-29, Chmura 3-28, Morgan 1-14, Cobb 1-4, Mickens 1-2. Dallas, E. Smith 6-95, Harper 3-91, Irvin 3-64, Novacek 2-37, Johnston 1-24.
MISSED FIELD GOAL ATTEMPTS—None.
INTERCEPTIONS—Green Bay, Buckley 1-1.
KICKOFF RETURNS—Green Bay, Harris 5-135, Thompson 2-32, Davey 1-6. Dallas, K. Williams 5-169, R. Jones 1-8.
PUNT RETURNS—Green Bay, Brooks 2-20. Dallas, K. Williams 4-25.
SACKS—Green Bay, Koonce 1, White 1. Dallas, Hennings 1, Haley 1.

BROWNS 34, OILERS 10
Sunday, November 27

Houston	0	10	0	0—10
Cleveland	3	14	0	17—34

First Quarter
Cle—FG Stover 37, 5:14.
Second Quarter
Cle—Hartley 1 pass from Testaverde (Stover kick), 2:16.
Hou—White 1 run (Del Greco kick), 5:46.
Cle—Kinchen 11 pass from Testaverde (Stover kick), 8:46.
Hou—FG Del Greco 42, 12:23.
Fourth Quarter
Cle—Hoard 1 run (Stover kick), :52.
Cle—FG Stover 23, 5:31.
Cle—Hoard 5 run (Stover kick), 7:52.

TEAM STATISTICS

	Houston	Cleveland
First downs	11	23
Rushes-yards	19-80	38-144
Passing	102	199
Punt returns-yards	2-14	4-27
Kickoff returns-yards	7-163	2-28
Interception returns-yards	1-0	0-0
Comp.-att.-int.	16-33-0	15-28-1
Sacked-yards lost	4-22	1-0
Punts-average	7-43	2-41

	Houston	Cleveland
Fumbles-lost	3-2	3-2
Penalties-yards	9-99	6-43
Time of possession	24:47	35:13
Attendance—65,088.		

INDIVIDUAL STATISTICS

RUSHING—Houston, White 19-80. Cleveland, Hoard 23-103, Byner 7-23, Metcalf 3-14, Baldwin 2-7, Testaverde 3-(minus 3).

PASSING—Houston, Tolliver 16-33-0-124. Cleveland, Testaverde 15-28-1-199.

RECEIVING—Houston, Slaughter 5-55, White 4-19, Jeffires 3-34, Carter 2-9, Wellman 2-7. Cleveland, Kinchen 4-62, Jackson 3-50, Alexander 2-35, Hoard 2-20, Hartley 2-5, Byner 1-15, Metcalf 1-12.

MISSED FIELD GOAL ATTEMPTS—None.

INTERCEPTIONS—Houston, D. Lewis 1-0.

KICKOFF RETURNS—Houston, McNair 6-149, Tillman 1-14. Cleveland, Kinchen 1-8, Metcalf 1-20.

PUNT RETURNS—Houston, Givins 1-14, Robertson 1-0. Cleveland, Metcalf 4-27.

SACKS—Houston, Lathon 1. Cleveland, Burnett 1½, Dixon 1, J. Jones 1, Perry ½.

FALCONS 28, EAGLES 21

Sunday, November 27

Philadelphia	0	7	7	7—21
Atlanta	7	6	8	7—28

First Quarter
Atl—Mathis 9 pass from J. George (N. Johnson kick), 2:47.
Second Quarter
Phi—Cunningham 1 run (Murray kick), 11:39.
Atl—FG N. Johnson 50, 12:52.
Atl—FG N. Johnson 40, 15:00.
Third Quarter
Phi—H. Walker 91 run (Murray kick), 1:14.
Atl—Mathis 7 pass from J. George (Mathis pass from J. George), 6:30.
Fourth Quarter
Atl—Heyward 5 run (N. Johnson kick), 0:05.
Phi—H. Walker 2 run (Murray kick), 10:38.

TEAM STATISTICS

	Philadelphia	Atlanta
First downs	14	24
Rushes-yards	14-115	24-64
Passing	203	354
Punt returns-yards	2-15	5-13
Kickoff returns-yards	4-53	4-77
Interception returns-yards	3-33	1-0
Comp.-att.-int.	19-36-1	26-46-3
Sacked-yards lost	5-45	2-10
Punts-average	9-45	8-39
Fumbles-lost	1-1	0-0
Penalties-yards	10-75	14-95
Time of possession	23:32	36:28
Attendance—60,008.		

INDIVIDUAL STATISTICS

RUSHING—Philadelphia, H. Walker 3-98, Cunningham 4-14, Garner 4-2, Joseph 3-1. Atlanta, Heyward 16-66, Pegram 7-0, J. George 1-(minus 2).

PASSING—Philadelphia, Cunningham 19-36-1-248. Atlanta, J. George 26-46-3-364.

RECEIVING—Philadelphia, Joseph 6-45, Bailey 4-94, H. Walker 4-41, Barnett 3-47, C. Williams 1-14, M. Johnson 1-7. Atlanta, Mathis 10-124, Sanders 7-87, Rison 4-92, Harris 2-34, Heyward 2-13, Pegram 1-14.

MISSED FIELD GOAL ATTEMPTS—None.

INTERCEPTIONS—Philadelphia, Allen 1-33, G. Jackson 1-0, Romanowski 1-0. Atlanta, Phillips 1-0.

KICKOFF RETURNS—Philadelphia, H. Walker 3-39, Hebron 1-14. Atlanta, Verdin 4-77.

PUNT RETURNS—Philadelphia, Sydner 2-15. Atlanta, Verdin 5-13.

SACKS—Philadelphia, Harmon 1, O. Smith 1. Atlanta, C. Smith 3, Doleman 1, Ross 1.

DOLPHINS 28, JETS 24

Sunday, November 27

Miami	0	0	14	14—28
N.Y. Jets	3	7	14	0—24

First Quarter
N.Y.—FG Lowery 24, 11:14.
Second Quarter
N.Y.—Mitchell 30 pass from Esiason (Lowery kick), 8:12.
Third Quarter
N.Y.—B. Baxter 3 run (Lowery kick), 2:02.
Mia—Ingram 10 pass from Marino (pass failed), 6:19.
N.Y.—Mitchell 14 pass from Esiason (Lowery kick), 11:21.
Mia—Ingram 17 pass from Marino (Fryar pass from Marino), 14:18.
Fourth Quarter
Mia—Ingram 28 pass from Marino (Stoyanovich kick), 4:47.
Mia—Ingram 8 pass from Marino (Stoyanovich kick), 14:38.

TEAM STATISTICS

	Miami	N.Y. Jets
First downs	22	25
Rushes-yards	11-38	28-76
Passing	359	365
Punt returns-yards	2-3	3-13
Kickoff returns-yards	5-93	4-39
Interception returns-yards	2-34	2-22
Comp.-att.-int.	31-44-2	26-41-2
Sacked-yards lost	0-0	2-17
Punts-average	3-35	2-44
Fumbles-lost	2-2	4-0
Penalties-yards	3-32	4-35
Time of possession	23:19	36:41
Attendance—75,606.		

INDIVIDUAL STATISTICS

RUSHING—Miami, Parmalee 8-23, Spikes 2-14, Saxon 1-1. New York, B. Baxter 12-41, J. Johnson 13-27, Esiason 2-9, R. Anderson 1-(minus 1).

PASSING—Miami, Marino 31-44-2-359. New York, Esiason 26-41-2-382.

RECEIVING—Miami, Ingram 9-117, Parmalee 6-40, Fryar 5-103, Saxon 5-31, Jackson 3-29, Williams 2-28, McDuffie 1-11. New York, Moore 7-124, Monk 5-108, Mitchell 5-81, R. Anderson 4-27, Thornton 2-9, S. Anderson 1-17, J. Johnson 1-10, B. Baxter 1-6.

MISSED FIELD GOAL ATTEMPTS—None.

INTERCEPTIONS—Miami, Brown 1-12, Vincent 1-22. New York, Hasty 1-22, B. Washington 1-0.

KICKOFF RETURNS—Miami, McDuffie 4-74, Spikes 1-19. New York, Glenn 3-39, Thornton 1-0.

PUNT RETURNS—Miami, McDuffie 2-3. New York, Hicks 3-13.

SACKS—Miami, Bowens 1, Cox 1.

BUCCANEERS 20, VIKINGS 17

Sunday, November 27

Tampa Bay	7	7	0	3	3—20
Minnesota	0	9	0	8	0—17

First Quarter
T.B.—Rhett 1 run (Husted kick), 3:46.
Second Quarter
Min—FG Reveiz 23, 1:24.
Min—FG Reveiz 21, 6:44.
T.B.—Hawkins 14 pass from Erickson (Husted kick), 9:47.
Min—FG Reveiz 51, 14:27.
Fourth Quarter
T.B.—FG Husted 27, 9:36.
Min—Ismail 40 pass from Moon (Carter pass from Moon), 13:33.
Overtime
T.B.—FG Husted 22, 2:08.

TEAM STATISTICS

	Tampa Bay	Minnesota
First downs	20	19
Rushes-yards	31-72	22-85
Passing	254	246
Punt returns-yards	1-8	2-0
Kickoff returns-yards	6-147	3-73
Interception returns-yards	1-38	1-14
Comp.-att.-int.	20-38-1	24-46-1
Sacked-yards lost	0-0	5-40
Punts-average	6-37	6-48
Fumbles-lost	0-0	1-1
Penalties-yards	4-20	7-45
Time of possession	31:59	30:09
Attendance—47,259.		

INDIVIDUAL STATISTICS

RUSHING—Tampa Bay, Rhett 24-55, Workman 3-10, Erickson 2-4, McDowell 2-3. Minnesota, Allen 16-54, Lee 4-25, R. Smith 2-6.

PASSING—Tampa Bay, Erickson 20-38-1-254. Minnesota, Moon 24-46-1-286.

RECEIVING—Tampa Bay, Hawkins 6-80, Dawsey 4-41, C. Wilson 3-34, Armstrong 3-33, Copeland 1-43, Moore 1-13, Rhett 1-6, McDowell 1-4. Minnesota, Lee 7-71, Ismail 6-101, C. Carter 5-46, Reed 2-30, Jordan 2-16, R. Smith 1-12, Cooper 1-10.

MISSED FIELD GOAL ATTEMPTS—Tampa Bay, Husted 51, 45.

INTERCEPTIONS—Tampa Bay, Covington 1-38. Minnesota, Parker 1-14.

KICKOFF RETURNS—Tampa Bay, C. Wilson 4-109, Buckley 1-26, R. Harris 1-12. Minnesota, Ismail 2-52, R. Smith 1-21.

PUNT RETURNS—Tampa Bay, Hawkins 1-8. Minnesota, Guliford 2-0.

SACKS—Tampa Bay, M. Carter 1, Culpepper 1, Curry 1, Nickerson 1, Wheeler 1.

STEELERS 21, RAIDERS 3

Sunday, November 27

Pittsburgh	7	0	0	14—21
L.A. Raiders	0	3	0	0— 3

First Quarter
Pit—Thigpen 27 pass from Tomczak (Anderson kick), 10:30.

Second Quarter
L.A.—FG Jaeger 32, 3:37.

Fourth Quarter
Pit—Green 15 pass from Tomczak (Anderson kick), 5:38.
Pit—Morris 3 run (Anderson kick), 12:58.

TEAM STATISTICS

	Pittsburgh	L.A. Raiders
First downs	19	14
Rushes-yards	39-175	25-57
Passing	131	122
Punt returns-yards	4-45	2-28
Kickoff returns-yards	2-25	4-75
Interception returns-yards	0-0	0-0
Comp.-att.-int.	12-27-0	15-28-0
Sacked-yards lost	0-0	5-24
Punts-average	5-45	6-44
Fumbles-lost	1-0	2-2
Penalties-yards	8-57	2-10
Time of possession	32:44	27:16
Attendance—58,327.		

INDIVIDUAL STATISTICS

RUSHING—Pittsburgh, Foster 20-82, Morris 12-50, J.L. Williams 5-40, Tomczak 2-3. Los Angeles, H. Williams 18-42, Hostetler 3-12, Rathman 4-3.

PASSING—Pittsburgh, Tomczak 12-27-0-131. Los Angeles, Hostetler 8-17-0-85, Evans 7-11-0-61.

RECEIVING—Pittsburgh, Thigpen 4-57, Green 2-35, J.L. Williams 2-8, Johnson 1-14, Mills 1-10, Foster 1-6, Morris 1-1. Los Angeles, Jett 4-45, H. Williams 3-30, Brown 3-21, Glover 2-34, Wright 2-14, C. Jones 1-2.

MISSED FIELD GOAL ATTEMPTS—Pittsburgh, Anderson 49, 54, 27.

INTERCEPTIONS—None.

KICKOFF RETURNS—Pittsburgh, Stone 1-25, Los Angeles, Ismail 4-75.

PUNT RETURNS—Pittsburgh, Woodson 4-45. Los Angeles, T. Brown 2-28.

SACKS—Pittsburgh, Greene 2, C. Brown 1, Lloyd 1, Gildon 1.

BRONCOS 15, BENGALS 13

Sunday, November 27

Cincinnati	0	6	0	7—13
Denver	6	9	0	0—15

First Quarter
Den—FG Elam 34, 2:30.
Den—FG Elam 33, 10:47.

Second Quarter
Cin—FG Pelfrey 43, 7:41.
Den—Miller 16 pass from Elway (kick failed), 10:51.
Den—FG Elam 37, 12:03.
Cin—FG Pelfrey 32, 14:49.

Fourth Quarter
Cin—Pickens 70 pass from Blake (Pelfrey kick), :12.

TEAM STATISTICS

	Cincinnati	Denver
First downs	16	12
Rushes-yards	30-130	22-50
Passing	198	206
Punt returns-yards	3-13	4-40
Kickoff returns-yards	4-98	4-66

	Cincinnati	Denver
Interception returns-yards	0-0	1-6
Comp.-att.-int.	16-34-1	21-38-0
Sacked-yards lost	3-20	4-33
Punts-average	5-46	7-42
Fumbles-lost	3-3	1-0
Penalties-yards	6-40	3-25
Time of possession	30:03	29:57
Attendance—69,714.		

INDIVIDUAL STATISTICS

RUSHING—Cincinnati, Broussard 8-52, Blake 4-37, Fenner 10-30, Green 6-7, Cothran 2-4. Denver, L. Russell 13-30, Rivers 2-12, Elway 5-11, Clark 1-0, Milburn 1-(minus 3).

PASSING—Cincinnati, Blake 15-33-1-215, Klingler 1-1-0-3. Denver, Elway 21-38-0-239.

RECEIVING—Cincinnati, Pickens 6-132, To. McGee 5-38, Fenner 3-13, Scott 2-35. Denver, Milburn 6-31, Miller 5-116, Sharpe 3-42, L. Russell 3-13, Rivers 2-3, Tillman 1-26, D. Russell 1-8.

MISSED FIELD GOAL ATTEMPTS—Cincinnati, Pelfrey 51. Denver, Elam 45, 44.

INTERCEPTIONS—Denver, Crockett 1-6.

KICKOFF RETURNS—Cincinnati, Hall 3-76, Hardy 1-22. Denver, Milburn 3-66, Carswell 1-0.

PUNT RETURNS—Cincinnati, Pickens 2-5, Sawyer 1-8. Denver, Milburn 4-40.

SACKS—Cincinnati, A. Williams 1½, Rog. Jones 1½, Francis 1. Denver, Washington 1, Hasselbach 1, D. Smith 1.

BEARS 19, CARDINALS 16

Sunday, November 27

Chicago	7	3	6	0	3—19
Arizona	0	3	3	10	0—16

First Quarter
Chi—Wetnight 2 pass from Walsh (Butler kick), 14:24.

Second Quarter
Ari—FG Davis 49, 4:22.
Chi—FG Butler 35, 12:26.

Third Quarter
Chi—FG Butler 52, 4:18.
Ari—FG Davis 22, 9:42.
Chi—FG Butler 31, 12:34.

Fourth Quarter
Ari—McCants 46 interception return (Davis kick), 7:24.
Ari—FG Davis 47, 14:02.

Overtime
Chi—FG Butler 27, 8:11.

TEAM STATISTICS

	Chicago	Arizona
First downs	20	15
Rushes-yards	40-132	17-67
Passing	186	178
Punt returns-yards	2-22	2-14
Kickoff returns-yards	3-59	6-105
Interception returns-yards	1-0	2-59
Comp.-att.-int.	15-28-2	23-43-1
Sacked-yards lost	0-0	2-15
Punts-average	3-40	6-40
Fumbles-lost	0-0	1-0
Penalties-yards	3-30	8-71
Time of possession	38:12	29:59
Attendance—72,199.		

INDIVIDUAL STATISTICS

RUSHING—Chicago, Tillman 24-77, Harris 13-54, Walsh 2-1, Christian 1-0. Arizona, Moore 8-35, Centers 6-25, Schroeder 1-6, Higgs 1-2, Reeves 1-(minus 1).

PASSING—Chicago, Walsh 15-28-2-186. Arizona, Schroeder 23-43-1-192.

RECEIVING—Chicago, Graham 8-154, McMurtry 2-16, Wetnight 2-14, Harris 2-(minus 3), Jennings 1-5. Arizona, Centers 10-59, Fann 6-47, Proehl 4-38, Clark 3-48.

MISSED FIELD GOAL ATTEMPTS—None.

INTERCEPTIONS—Chicago, Woolford 1-0. Arizona, McCants 1-46, A. Williams 1-13.

KICKOFF RETURNS—Chicago, Lewis 2-38, Carter 1-21. Arizona, Levy 5-94, Reeves 1-11.

PUNT RETURNS—Chicago, Graham 2-22. Arizona, Robinson 2-14.

SACKS—Chicago, Zorich 1, Douglass ½, Mangum ½.

SEAHAWKS 10, CHIEFS 9
Sunday, November 27

Kansas City	3	3	0	3— 9
Seattle	0	0	0	10—10

First Quarter
K.C.—FG Elliott 32, 7:54.
Second Quarter
K.C.—FG Elliott 23, 6:17.
Fourth Quarter
Sea—S. Smith 2 run (Kasay kick), 1:58.
K.C.—FG Elliott 38, 7:33.
Sea—FG Kasay 32, 13:18.

TEAM STATISTICS
	Kansas City	Seattle
First downs	18	12
Rushes-yards	29- 115	26-59
Passing	197	207
Punt returns-yards	4-66	5-37
Kickoff returns-yards	3-81	3-66
Interception returns-yards	0-0	0-0
Comp.-att.-int.	26-47-0	18-35-0
Sacked-yards lost	1-5	2-11
Punts-average	7-39	10-44
Fumbles-lost	2-2	1-0
Penalties-yards	2- 15	5-40
Time of possession	32:04	27:56
Attendance—54, 120.		

INDIVIDUAL STATISTICS
RUSHING—Kansas City, Bennett 8-42, Hill 13-38, Anders 8-35. Seattle, C. Warren 22-53, Mirer 3-4, S. Smith 1-2.
PASSING—Kansas City, Montana 19-35-0- 163, Bono 7- 12-0-39. Seattle, Mirer 15-31-0- 195, McGwire 3-4-0-23.
RECEIVING—Kansas City, Dawson 8-66, Anders 5-43, Walker 4-25, E. Martin 3-33, Birden 3-28, Hill 2-(minus 1), Bennett 1-8. Seattle, Blades 7- 141, P. Green 5-38, C. Warren 3-14, K. Martin 2-20, Strong 1-5.
MISSED FIELD GOAL ATTEMPTS—Kansas City, Elliott 37.
INTERCEPTIONS—None.
KICKOFF RETURNS—Kansas City, Hughes 3-81. Seattle, Bates 3-66.
PUNT RETURNS—Kansas City, Carter 3-60, Hughes 1-6. Seattle, Martin 5-37.
SACKS—Kansas City, Thomas 1, McDaniels 1. Seattle, Sinclair 1.

GIANTS 21, REDSKINS 19
Sunday, November 27

N.Y. Giants	7	7	7	0—21
Washington	3	6	3	7— 19

First Quarter
Was—FG Lohmiller 43, 7:43.
N.Y.—Da. Brown 2 run (Treadwell kick), 12:52.
Second Quarter
Was—FG Lohmiller 29, 4:20.
N.Y.—Calloway 34 pass from Da. Brown (Treadwell kick), 13:08.
Was—FG Lohmiller 29, 14:39.
Third Quarter
N.Y.—Sherrard 6 pass from Da. Brown (Treadwell kick), 4:41.
Was—FG Lohmiller 46, 7:26.
Fourth Quarter
Was—Bayless 60 fumble return (Lohmiller kick), 10:16.

TEAM STATISTICS
	N.Y. Giants	Washington
First downs	20	14
Rushes-yards	45- 131	24- 152
Passing	160	161
Punt returns-yards	1-6	2-24
Kickoff returns-yards	6- 102	4-70
Interception returns-yards	1-25	0-0
Comp.-att.-int.	10-17-0	11-28-1
Sacked-yards lost	1-1	1-4
Punts-average	5-39	4-36
Fumbles-lost	2-1	0-0
Penalties-yards	2- 15	9-97
Time of possession	34:48	25:12
Attendance—43,384.		

INDIVIDUAL STATISTICS
RUSHING—New York, Hampton 34- 106, Meggett 3- 12, Da. Brown 5-10, Calloway 3-3. Washington, Ervins 14-92, Mitchell 5-36, Shuler 4-23, Brooks 1- 1.

PASSING—New York, Da. Brown 10- 17-0- 161. Washington, Shuler 11-28- 1- 165.
RECEIVING—New York, Hampton 3-24, Calloway 2-47, Pierce 2-21, Marshall 1-34, Cross 1-29, Sherrard 1-6. Washington, Ellard 4-81, Howard 3-59, Ervins 3- 12, Winans 1- 13.
MISSED FIELD GOAL ATTEMPTS—New York, Treadwell 43, 34.
INTERCEPTIONS—New York, Booty 1-25.
KICKOFF RETURNS—New York, Meggett 3-55, Marshall 2-33, Kozlowski 1- 14. Washington, Rush 2-37, Mitchell 2-33.
PUNT RETURNS—New York, Meggett 1-6. Washington, Mitchell 2-24.
SACKS—New York, Howard 1. Washington, Harvey ½, Hollinquest ½.

CHARGERS 31, RAMS 17
Sunday, November 27

L.A. Rams	0	14	0	3—17
San Diego	0	6	15	10—31

Second Quarter
L.A.—Hester 40 pass from C. Miller (Zendejas kick), :51.
S.D.—FG Carney 31, 8:02.
L.A.—Drayton 12 pass from C. Miller (Zendejas kick), 12:09.
S.D.—FG Carney 48, 14:01.
Third Quarter
S.D.—Gordon 75 punt return (Harmon run), 1:39.
S.D.—Harmon 11 pass from Humphries (Carney kick), 8:40.
Fourth Quarter
S.D.—FG Carney 37, 5:02.
L.A.—FG Zendejas 33, 11:12.
S.D.—Vanhorse 50 interception return (Carney kick), 14:09.

TEAM STATISTICS
	L.A. Rams	San Diego
First downs	17	16
Rushes-yards	13-48	30- 114
Passing	278	129
Punt returns-yards	4-40	6- 128
Kickoff returns-yards	7- 186	4- 104
Interception returns-yards	1- 14	4-84
Comp.-att.-int.	26-47-4	17-33-1
Sacked-yards lost	4-20	2- 18
Punts-average	6-46	7-41
Fumbles-lost	1-1	1-0
Penalties-yards	7-61	5-40
Time of possession	29:03	30:57
Attendance—59,579.		

INDIVIDUAL STATISTICS
RUSHING—Los Angeles, Bettis 10-38, Griffith 1-6, J. Bailey 1-2, Bruce 1-2. San Diego, Means 23-95, Harmon 2- 14, Bieniemy 4-7, Humphries 1-(minus 2).
PASSING—Los Angeles, C. Miller 26-47-4-298. San Diego, Humphries 17-33- 1- 147.
RECEIVING—Los Angeles, J. Bailey 8-77, Griffith 6-41, Hester 4-85, Drayton 2- 17, Anderson 1-23, Kinchen 1- 17, Bruce 1- 13, Lang 1- 12, Brantley 1- 10, Bettis 1-3. San Diego, Harmon 5-41, Seay 4-42, Jefferson 3-39, T. Martin 2- 11, Mitchell 2- 10, Means 1-4.
MISSED FIELD GOAL ATTEMPTS—None.
INTERCEPTIONS—Los Angeles, Lyght 1- 14. San Diego, Vanhorse 1-50, Richard 1-33, Gordon 1- 16, Harper 1- 15.
KICKOFF RETURNS—Los Angeles, Lang 5- 151, Farr 1- 16, Kinchen 1- 19. San Diego, Coleman 4- 104.
PUNT RETURNS—Los Angeles, Kinchen 4- 12, Lyght 0-27. San Diego, Gordon 6- 128.
SACKS—Los Angeles, Gilbert 1, J. Jones 1. San Diego, O'Neal 2, Parrella 1, R. Davis ½, L. Miller ½.

PATRIOTS 12, COLTS 10
Sunday, November 27

New England	3	0	3	6—12
Indianapolis	0	7	0	3—10

First Quarter
N.E.—FG Bahr 22, 8:58.
Second Quarter
Ind—Dawkins 23 pass from Majkowski (Biasucci kick), 14:26.
Third Quarter
N.E.—FG Bahr 37, 9:35.
Fourth Quarter
N.E.—FG Bahr 25, :47.
Ind—FG Biasucci 50, 4:38.
N.E.—FG Bahr 43, 10:59.

TEAM STATISTICS

	New England	Indianapolis
First downs	19	15
Rushes-yards	35-79	19-132
Passing	257	158
Punt returns-yards	3-19	2-13
Kickoff returns-yards	2-41	4-101
Interception returns-yards	0-0	1-20
Comp.-att.-int.	26-36-1	16-27-0
Sacked-yards lost	2-14	2-28
Punts-average	3-48	4-40
Fumbles-lost	0-0	3-2
Penalties-yards	5-35	4-35
Time of possession	38:05	21:55

Attendance—43,839.

INDIVIDUAL STATISTICS

RUSHING—New England, Butts 17-45, Thompson 9-29, Gash 4-6, K. Turner 1-3, Bledsoe 4-(minus 4). Indianapolis, Potts 6-74, Faulk 11-48, Majkowski 2-10.

PASSING—New England, Bledsoe 26-36-1-271. Indianapolis, Majkowski 16-27-0-186.

RECEIVING—New England, Coates 12-119, Timpson 4-71, Brisby 4-58, Thompson 4-7, K. Turner 1-14, Butts 1-2. Indianapolis, Dawkins 7-85, Faulk 5-42, F. Turner 3-51, Jackson 1-8.

MISSED FIELD GOAL ATTEMPTS—Indianapolis, Biasucci 41.

INTERCEPTIONS—Indianapolis, Buchanan 1-20.

KICKOFF RETURNS—New England, Crittenden 2-41. Indianapolis, Humphrey 4-101.

PUNT RETURNS—New England, T. Brown 3-19. Indianapolis, Brewer 2-13.

SACKS—New England, Hurst 1, McGinest 1. Indianapolis, McCoy 1, Alberts 1.

49ERS 35, SAINTS 14

Monday, November 28

San Francisco	10	10	8	7—35
New Orleans	0	14	0	0—14

First Quarter

S.F.—FG Brien 40, 9:06.
S.F.—B. Jones 4 pass from S. Young (Brien kick), 14:50.

Second Quarter

N.O.—Bates 3 run (Andersen kick), 8:39.
S.F.—Taylor 4 pass from S. Young (Brien kick), 11:50.
N.O.—Hughes 86 fumble return (Andersen kick), 14:26.
S.F.—FG Brien 48, 14:57.

Third Quarter

S.F.—B. Jones 6 pass from S. Young (Rice pass from S. Young), 9:02.

Fourth Quarter

S.F.—Singleton 43 pass from S. Young (Brien kick), 3:03.

TEAM STATISTICS

	San Francisco	New Orleans
First downs	28	13
Rushes-yards	42-191	17-83
Passing	270	139
Punt returns-yards	2-11	1(-4)
Kickoff returns-yards	3-71	7-115
Interception returns-yards	2-49	0-0
Comp.-att.-int.	24-30-0	13-25-2
Sacked-yards lost	2-11	1-8
Punts-average	1-38	3-37
Fumbles-lost	4-2	2-1
Penalties-yards	4-30	6-45
Time of possession	38:29	21:31

Attendance—61,304.

INDIVIDUAL STATISTICS

RUSHING—San Francisco, Watters 26-105, S. Young 7-43, Floyd 8-40, Carter 1-3. New Orleans, Bates 14-69, Neal 2-11, Derek Brown 1-3.

PASSING—San Francisco, S. Young 24-30-0-281. New Orleans, Everett 13-25-2-147.

RECEIVING—San Francisco, Rice 7-80, B. Jones 5-39, Taylor 4-35, Watters 2-37, Carter 2-25, Floyd 2-17, Singleton 1-43, Popson 1-5. New Orleans, Haynes 4-66, Small 4-34, Walls 2-17, Bates 2-16, Derek Brown 1-14.

MISSED FIELD GOAL ATTEMPTS—None.

INTERCEPTIONS—San Francisco, Sanders 1-43, McDonald 1-6.

KICKOFF RETURNS—San Francisco, Walker 2-26, D. Carter 1-45. New Orleans, Hughes 5-96, Ned 1-19, Smith 1-0.

PUNT RETURNS—San Francisco, D. Carter 2-11. New Orleans, Hughes 1-(minus 4).

SACKS—San Francisco, Harris 1. New Orleans, Warren 1, Johnson ½, Turnbull ½.

WEEK 14

RESULTS

Minnesota 33, Chicago 27 (OT)
Arizona 30, Houston 12
Buffalo 42, Miami 31
Dallas 31, Philadelphia 19
Denver 20, Kansas City 17 (OT)
Detroit 34, Green Bay 31
Indianapolis 31, Seattle 19
N.Y. Giants 16, Cleveland 13
New England 24, N.Y. Jets 13
New Orleans 31, L.A. Rams 15
Pittsburgh 38, Cincinnati 15
San Francisco 50, Atlanta 14
Tampa Bay 26, Washington 21
L.A. Raiders 24, San Diego 17

STANDINGS

AFC EAST	W	L	T	Pct.
Miami	8	5	0	.615
Buffalo	7	6	0	.538
New England	7	6	0	.538
N.Y. Jets	6	7	0	.462
Indianapolis	6	7	0	.462

AFC CENTRAL	W	L	T	Pct.
Pittsburgh	10	3	0	.769
Cleveland	9	4	0	.692
Cincinnati	2	11	0	.154
Houston	1	12	0	.077

AFC WEST	W	L	T	Pct.
San Diego	9	4	0	.692
Denver	7	6	0	.538
Kansas City	7	6	0	.538
L.A. Raiders	7	6	0	.538
Seattle	5	8	0	.385

NFC EAST	W	L	T	Pct.
Dallas	11	2	0	.846
Philadelphia	7	6	0	.538
N.Y. Giants	6	7	0	.462
Arizona	6	7	0	.462
Washington	2	11	0	.154

NFC CENTRAL	W	L	T	Pct.
Minnesota	8	5	0	.615
Chicago	8	5	0	.615
Detroit	7	6	0	.538
Green Bay	6	7	0	.462
Tampa Bay	4	9	0	.308

NFC WEST	W	L	T	Pct.
San Francisco	11	2	0	.846
Atlanta	6	7	0	.462
New Orleans	5	8	0	.385
L.A. Rams	4	9	0	.308

HIGHLIGHTS

Hero of the week: Denver kicker Jason Elam, who kicked a 34-yard field goal with 2:48 left in overtime to give the Broncos their fourth consecutive victory, 20-17 over Kansas City.

Goat of the week: Philadelphia quarterback Randall Cunningham, who threw an interception on Dallas' 8 with seven minutes left. With the Eagles trailing 24-19, Cunningham threw a pass to running back James Joseph. But Cowboys strong safety Darren Woodson picked off the aerial, jumped over Cunningham's diving attempt at a tackle and returned the interception 94 yards for a touchdown in Dallas' 31-19 victory. The win clinched a third consecutive NFC East title for the Cowboys.

Sub of the week: Dallas quarterback Rodney Peete, who threw for 172 yards and a touchdown against the Eagles. The Cowboys won despite starting their third different quarterback in as many weeks.

Comeback of the week: Tampa Bay downed Washington, 26-21, thanks to a last-minute touchdown drive. Trailing 21-20 with 2:57 left, the Bucs drove 80 yards in 11 plays, capped by quarterback Craig Erickson's one-yard sneak with 32 seconds left. Rookie Errict Rhett led Tampa Bay's charge, outrushing Washington 192-10. It was the third time in four games that Rhett topped 100 yards.

Blowout of the week: Steve Young passed for 294 yards and three touchdowns and ran for two more scores as San Francisco beat Atlanta, 50-14. The 49ers, who totaled 476 yards, outscored the Falcons 92-17 in their two meetings in 1994.

Nail-biter of the week: Minnesota's Cris Carter beat Chicago linebacker Joe Cain to catch a 65-yard touchdown pass from Warren Moon with 9:14 left in overtime as the Vikings beat the Bears, 33-27. Chicago's Kevin Butler, who kicked a game-tying 33-yard field goal with 1:55 left in regulation, missed a 40-yard field goal just before Moon's scoring strike to Carter.

Hit of the week: By Denver linebacker Karl Mecklenburg, who forced a Marcus Allen fumble that led to a Broncos victory. After recovering a Denver fumble at the Broncos' 35 in overtime, Kansas City looked to break a 17-17 tie and claim victory. But five plays later, Allen was stripped of the ball by Mecklenburg and safety Dennis Smith recovered. The Broncos subsequently drove 41 yards to set up Elam's game-winning field goal.

Oddity of the week: Despite being involved in a car accident on Thursday night that left defensive tackle Mike Frier paralyzed and rookie running back Lamar Smith with a fractured foot, Seattle running back Chris Warren played on Sunday against Indianapolis. Hampered by two broken ribs sustained when Smith's car crashed into a utility pole, Warren gained 81 yards on 23 carries in the Seahawks' 31-19 loss to the Colts.

Top rusher: Tampa Bay's Rhett ran 40 times for 192 yards and a touchdown in Tampa Bay's victory.

Top passer: Green Bay's Brett Favre completed 29 of 43 passes for 366 yards with three touchdowns and two interceptions in a 34-31 loss to Detroit.

Top receiver: Cleveland rookie Derrick Alexander had seven receptions for 171 yards in a 16-13 loss to the New York Giants.

Notes: Before losing to Minnesota, Chicago had been 7-0 in games Steve Walsh started.... The Jets' Art Monk tied the NFL record of 177 consecutive games with a reception with a seven-yard catch in the first quarter of New York's 24-13 loss to New England.... Indianapolis' Marshall Faulk ran 27 times for 129 yards—his fourth 100-yard effort of the season—in a victory over Seattle, giving him a franchise rookie-record 1,086 yards rushing. In the same game, Seahawks quarterback Rick Mirer broke his left thumb when trying to tackle Colts cornerback Ray Buchanan, who had intercepted a Mirer pass. Buchanan returned the second-quarter interception 37 yards for a touchdown, and Mirer was lost for the season.... Cincinnati's Carl Pickens caught four passes for 105 yards in the Bengals' 38-15 loss to Pittsburgh, the fourth consecutive week he surpassed the 100-yard barrier. Atlanta's Andre Rison was

the last player to accomplish the feat (1990)....
The Raiders tied a team record with 17 penalties in
a 24-17 victory over San Diego.... In the loss to
Tampa Bay, Washington rushed for no first downs
and just 10 yards in 12 attempts—the franchise's
lowest total since a 14-yard effort against Philadelphia in 1947.... There were eight interception
returns for touchdowns in 14 games, the most in a
week since 1984. In the first 13 weeks of the 1994
season (168 games), there were 29 interception
returns for touchdowns.... The Giants' Mike
Sherrard had 101 yards receiving against Cleveland, making him the first receiver or rusher to
gain 100 yards against the Browns this season.

Quote of the week: Saints quarterback Jim Everett,
who threw for 161 yards and a touchdown in guid-
ing his team to a victory over his old team, the Los
Angeles Rams: "It's very special to come back
here and get this one. Being 2-0 (against the
Rams since signing with the Saints in the off-
season) after going through all the stuff I went
through here, well, it's hard to describe how that
makes me feel."

GAME SUMMARIES

VIKINGS 33, BEARS 27
Thursday, December 1

Chicago	7	0	17	3	0—27
Minnesota	7	6	3	11	6—33

First Quarter
Min—Washington 54 interception return (Reveiz kick), 1:35.
Chi—Green 39 pass from S. Walsh (Butler kick), 5:55.

Second Quarter
Min—FG Reveiz 45, 10:22.
Min—FG Reveiz 41, 15:00.

Third Quarter
Chi—J. Graham 60 punt return (Butler kick), 2:05.
Min—FG Reveiz 29, 6:09.
Chi—FG Butler 29, 12:30.
Chi—McMurtry 15 pass from S. Walsh (Butler kick), 13:30.

Fourth Quarter
Min—FG Reveiz 38, 2:06.
Min—C. Carter 1 pass from Moon (A. Jordan pass from Moon), 10:48.
Chi—FG Butler 33, 13:05.

Overtime
Min—C. Carter 65 pass from Moon, 5:46.

TEAM STATISTICS

	Chicago	Minnesota
First downs	15	21
Rushes-yards	32-80	27-100
Passing	232	285
Punt returns-yards	3-73	1-0
Kickoff returns-yards	7-221	6-107
Interception returns-yards	1-0	1-54
Comp.-att.-int.	24-33-1	27-48-1
Sacked-yards lost	1-1	3-21
Punts-average	5-35	6-36
Fumbles-lost	2-2	2-1
Penalties-yards	2-15	4-39
Time of possession	33:21	32:25
Attendance—61,483.		

INDIVIDUAL STATISTICS

RUSHING—Chicago, Tillman 21-49, R. Harris 5-15, Green 3-15, S. Walsh 3-1. Minnesota, Allen 18-74, S. Graham 6-22, Moon 1-4, Lee 2-0.
PASSING—Chicago, S. Walsh 24-33-1-233. Minnesota, Moon 27-48-1-306.
RECEIVING—Chicago, Green 6-69, McMurtry 4-63, J. Graham 4-37, Cook 4-25, Primus 2-20, R. Harris 2-10, Tillman 1-6, Wetnight 1-3. Minnesota, C. Carter 9-124, Ismail 6-71, Reed 5-70, Lee 5-12, A. Jordan 1-19, S. Jordan 1-10.

MISSED FIELD GOAL ATTEMPTS—Chicago, Butler 40.
INTERCEPTIONS—Chicago, Woolford 1-0. Minnesota, Washington 1-54.
KICKOFF RETURNS—Chicago, Lewis 7-221. Minnesota, Ismail 5-99, A. Jordan 1-8.
PUNT RETURNS—Chicago, J. Graham 3-73. Minnesota, Palmer 1-0.
SACKS—Chicago, Zorich 1½, Armstrong 1, Spellman ½. Minnesota, Randle 1.

COWBOYS 31, EAGLES 19
Sunday, December 4

Dallas	7	7	7	10—31	
Philadelphia	0	6	7	6—19	

First Quarter
Dal—Irvin 19 pass from Peete (Boniol kick), 10:54.

Second Quarter
Phi—FG Murray 22, 8:34.
Dal—E. Smith 4 run (Boniol kick), 12:21.
Phi—FG Murray 19, 14:49.

Third Quarter
Dal—E. Smith 4 run (Boniol kick), 5:37.
Phi—Barnett 25 pass from Cunningham (Murray kick), 8:53.

Fourth Quarter
Dal—FG Boniol 19, :03.
Phi—Johnson 5 pass from Cunningham (pass failed), 4:45.
Dal—Woodson 94 interception return (Boniol kick), 8:17.

TEAM STATISTICS

	Dallas	Philadelphia
First downs	15	25
Rushes-yards	32-104	26-108
Passing	160	285
Punt returns-yards	3-14	3-57
Kickoff returns-yards	5-121	6-140
Interception returns-yards	1-94	1-7
Comp.-att.-int.	10-17-1	29-46-1
Sacked-yards lost	3-12	5-42
Punts-average	5-49	5-37
Fumbles-lost	1-0	0-0
Penalties-yards	4-30	6-41
Time of possession	26:25	33:35
Attendance—65,974.		

INDIVIDUAL STATISTICS

RUSHING—Dallas, E. Smith 25-91, K. Williams 1-7, Johnston 2-5, Coleman 2-1, Peete 2-0. Philadelphia, Walker 13-54, Joseph 11-43, Cunningham 2-11.
PASSING—Dallas, Peete 10-17-1-172. Philadelphia, Cunningham 29-46-1-327.
RECEIVING—Dallas, Irvin 4-117, E. Smith 4-39, Novacek 1-9, Johnston 1-7. Philadelphia, Barnett 7-99, C. Williams 6-75, Joseph 6-39, Walker 5-70, Bailey 3-29, M. Johnson 2-15.
MISSED FIELD GOAL ATTEMPTS—None.
INTERCEPTIONS—Dallas, Woodson 1-94. Philadelphia, Thomas 1-7.
KICKOFF RETURNS—Dallas, K. Williams 5-121. Philadelphia, He-bron 4-70, Walker 2-70.
PUNT RETURNS—Dallas, K. Williams 3-14. Philadelphia, Sydner 3-57.
SACKS—Dallas, Haley 3, Tolbert 2. Philadelphia, Fuller 1½, Harmon 1, Grossman ½.

STEELERS 38, BENGALS 15
Sunday, December 4

Pittsburgh	7	7	7	17—38	
Cincinnati	7	0	0	8—15	

First Quarter
Pit—Morris 1 run (Anderson kick), 3:40.
Cin—Pickens 7 pass from Blake (Pelfrey kick), 5:28.

Second Quarter
Pit—Green 5 pass from O'Donnell (Anderson kick), 6:46.

Third Quarter
Pit—Morris 8 run (Anderson kick), 14:22.

Fourth Quarter
Pit—FG Anderson 41, 3:33.
Pit—Woodson 27 interception return (Anderson kick), 3:52.
Cin—Blake 5 run (Blake run), 5:53.
Pit—Hayes 3 pass from O'Donnell (Anderson kick), 13:54.

— 185 —

TEAM STATISTICS

	Pittsburgh	Cincinnati
First downs	23	13
Rushes-yards	47- 185	20-76
Passing	123	119
Punt returns-yards	1- 10	1- 16
Kickoff returns-yards	3-87	6- 163
Interception returns-yards	2-35	0-0
Comp.-att.-int.	17-24-0	8-20-2
Sacked-yards lost	1-8	5-37
Punts-average	3-40	3-34
Fumbles-lost	0-0	1-1
Penalties-yards	10-94	3- 15
Time of possession	40:00	20:00

Attendance—59,997.

INDIVIDUAL STATISTICS

RUSHING—Pittsburgh, Morris 24- 108, J.L. Williams 15-60, McAfee 6- 18, O'Donnell 2- (minus 1). Cincinnati, Blake 3-23, Fenner 6- 19, Cothran 5- 19, Broussard 6- 15.

PASSING—Pittsburgh, O'Donnell 17-24-0- 131. Cincinnati, Blake 8- 19-2- 156, Broussard 0- 1-0-0.

RECEIVING—Pittsburgh, Morris 5-25, Green 4-37, Thigpen 3-38, Mills 1-29, J.L. Williams 2-9, Hayes 1-3. Cincinnati, Pickens 4- 105, Broussard 2-30, Scott 1- 12, Fenner 1-9.

MISSED FIELD GOAL ATTEMPTS—None.

INTERCEPTIONS—Pittsburgh, Lloyd 1-8, Woodson 1-27.

KICKOFF RETURNS—Pittsburgh, Johnson 2-79, Zgonina 1-8. Cincinnati, Ball 5- 125, Hardy 1-38.

PUNT RETURNS—Pittsburgh, Woodson 1- 10. Cincinnati, Pickens 1- 16.

SACKS—Pittsburgh, Greene 2, Brown 1, Lloyd 1, Woodson 1. Cincinnati, Rucker 1.

BUCCANEERS 26, REDSKINS 21

Sunday, December 4

Washington	7	14	0	0—21
Tampa Bay	3	14	0	9—26

First Quarter

Was—A. Collins 92 interception return (Lohmiller kick), 2:10.
T.B.—FG Husted 53, 11:55.

Second Quarter

T.B.—Rhett 2 run (Husted kick), 4:41.
Was—Howard 81 pass from Shuler (Lohmiller kick), 5:10.
T.B.—McDowell 13 pass from Erickson (Husted kick), 11:09.
Was—Truitt 77 pass from Shuler (Lohmiller kick), 14:32.

Fourth Quarter

T.B.—FG Husted 22, 7:04.
T.B.—Erickson 1 run (pass failed), 14:28.

TEAM STATISTICS

	Washington	Tampa Bay
First downs	7	29
Rushes-yards	12- 10	48-213
Passing	258	251
Punt returns-yards	3-7	2-8
Kickoff returns-yards	5- 103	1-21
Interception returns-yards	2-92	1-0
Comp.-att.-int.	13-25- 1	18-35-2
Sacked-yards lost	3-20	0-0
Punts-average	6-56	5-44
Fumbles-lost	2-2	0-0
Penalties-yards	3-30	5-35
Time of possession	17:46	42:14

Attendance—45,121.

INDIVIDUAL STATISTICS

RUSHING—Washington, Ervins 8- 14, Brooks 2-2, Mitchell 1- (minus 5), Shuler 1-(minus 1). Tampa Bay, Rhett 40- 192, Workman 4- 16, McDowell 1-3, Erickson 3-2.

PASSING—Washington, Shuler 13-25- 1-278. Tampa Bay, Erickson 18-35-2-251.

RECEIVING—Washington, Howard 5- 130, Ervins 2-6, Truitt 1-77, Mitchell 1-22, Ellard 1- 19, Horton 1- 13, Sheppherd 1-8, C. Smith 1-3. Tampa Bay, Dawsey 5-91, Hawkins 5-65, McDowell 3-28, Armstrong 2-26, Copeland 1- 19, Moore 1- 13, Workman 1-9.

MISSED FIELD GOAL ATTEMPTS—None.

INTERCEPTIONS—Washington, Bayless 1-0, A. Collins 1-92. Tampa Bay, McGruder 1-0.

KICKOFF RETURNS—Washington, Mitchell 4-95, Rush 1-8. Tampa Bay, C. Wilson 1-21.

PUNT RETURNS—Washington, Mitchell 3-7. Tampa Bay, Hawkins 2-8.

SACKS—Tampa Bay, Culpepper 1½, Curry 1, Wheeler ½.

PATRIOTS 24, JETS 13

Sunday, December 4

N.Y. Jets	0	10	3	0—13
New England	3	7	7	7—24

First Quarter

N.E.—FG Bahr 33, 7:55.

Second Quarter

N.Y.—Monk 15 pass from Esiason (Lowery kick), 1:31.
N.E.—Brisby 16 pass from Bledsoe (Bahr kick), 10:17.
N.Y.—FG Lowery 46, 14:56.

Third Quarter

N.Y.—FG Lowery 26, 6:17.
N.E.—Reynolds 11 interception return (Bahr kick), 11:09.

Fourth Quarter

N.E.—Thompson 2 run (Bahr kick), 11:17.

TEAM STATISTICS

	N.Y. Jets	New England
First downs	13	20
Rushes-yards	19-64	39- 135
Passing	155	191
Punt returns-yards	0-0	5-36
Kickoff returns-yards	5- 115	4-53
Interception returns-yards	1-6	1-11
Comp.-att.-int.	16-40- 1	19-34- 1
Sacked-yards lost	0-0	1-8
Punts-average	6-49	4-40
Fumbles-lost	1-0	1-1
Penalties-yards	5-40	8-52
Time of possession	23:40	36:20

Attendance—60,138.

INDIVIDUAL STATISTICS

RUSHING—New York, Johnson 12-32, Anderson 4-29, B. Baxter 2-2, Esiason 1-1. New England, Thompson 20-80, Butts 14-45, Gash 2-7, Bledsoe 3-3.

PASSING—New York, Esiason 16-40-1-155. New England, Bledsoe 19-34-1-199.

RECEIVING—New York, Moore 5-35, Monk 4-61, Mitchell 4-35, Johnson 1- 16, B. Baxter 1-5, Thornton 1-3. New England, Brisby 8-90, Timpson 4-44, Turner 2-22, Coates 2-21, Butts 2- 15, Thompson 1-7.

MISSED FIELD GOAL ATTEMPTS—None.

INTERCEPTIONS—New York, Hasty 1-6. New England, Reynolds 1- 11.

KICKOFF RETURNS—New York, Glenn 4-99, Prior 1- 16. New England, Thompson 3-53, Burke 1-0.

PUNT RETURNS—New England, T. Brown 5-36.

SACKS—New York, Evans ½, Houston ½.

GIANTS 16, BROWNS 13

Sunday, December 4

N.Y. Giants	7	0	3	6— 16
Cleveland	3	3	0	7— 13

First Quarter

Cle—FG Stover 41, 6:05.
N.Y.—Pierce 10 pass from Da. Brown (Treadwell kick), 12:18.

Second Quarter

Cle—FG Stover 23, 2:54.

Third Quarter

N.Y.—FG Daluiso 25, 11:36.

Fourth Quarter

N.Y.—FG Daluiso 30, 6:45.
Cle—Hoard 5 run (Stover kick), 10:36.
N.Y.—FG Daluiso 33, 14:41.

TEAM STATISTICS

	N.Y. Giants	Cleveland
First downs	18	13
Rushes-yards	32-99	17-77
Passing	199	229
Punt returns-yards	2- 10	3-2
Kickoff returns-yards	4-74	3-39
Interception returns-yards	2- 15	1-24
Comp.-att.-int.	17-33- 1	20-38-2
Sacked-yards lost	5-27	1-9
Punts-average	5-40	3-39
Fumbles-lost	1-0	3-3
Penalties-yards	10-74	11-88
Time of possession	33:15	26:45

Attendance—72,068.

INDIVIDUAL STATISTICS

RUSHING—New York, Hampton 23-77, Da. Brown 4-17, Rasheed 2-8, Meggett 3-(minus 3). Cleveland, Hoard 11-45, Metcalf 5-25, Testaverde 1-7.

PASSING—New York, Da. Brown 17-33-1-226. Cleveland, Testaverde 20-38-2-238.

RECEIVING—New York, Sherrard 5-101, Rasheed 3-27, Calloway 2-33, Cross 2-21, Meggett 2-12, Hampton 1-17, Pierce 1-10, Marshall 1-5. Cleveland, Alexander 7-171, Hoard 4-16, Metcalf 3-20, Byner 3-12, Kinchen 2-12, Carrier 1-7.

MISSED FIELD GOAL ATTEMPTS—New York, Treadwell 37.

INTERCEPTIONS—New York, Brooks 1-14, Campbell 1-1. Cleveland, Turner 1-24.

KICKOFF RETURNS—New York, Marshall 2-39, Meggett 2-35. Cleveland, Baldwin 3-39.

PUNT RETURNS—New York, Meggett 2-10. Cleveland, Metcalf 2-0, Caldwell 1-2.

SACKS—New York, Dillard 1. Cleveland, Griffin 2, Moore 1, Pleasant 1, Banks ½, Burnett ½.

CARDINALS 30, OILERS 12

Sunday, December 4

Arizona	0	10	0	20—30
Houston	9	3	0	0—12

First Quarter
Hou—Safety, Lathon tackled Schroeder in the end zone, 9:38.
Hou—Dishman 36 interception return (Del Greco kick), 11:49.
Second Quarter
Ari—Centers 1 run (Davis kick), 5:17.
Ari—FG Davis 25, 13:51.
Hou—FG Del Greco 34, 14:57.
Fourth Quarter
Ari—Clark 13 pass from Schroeder (Moore run), :05.
Ari—FG Davis 23, 1:58.
Ari—Centers 4 run (Davis kick), 4:58.
Ari—Safety, Swann tackled Tolliver in the end zone, 12:23.

TEAM STATISTICS

	Arizona	Houston
First downs	18	10
Rushes-yards	45-159	16-37
Passing	171	161
Punt returns-yards	3-17	3-3
Kickoff returns-yards	4-61	6-109
Interception returns-yards	5-88	1-36
Comp.-att.-int.	12-20-1	11-34-5
Sacked-yards lost	1-5	4-23
Punts-average	6-38	5-45
Fumbles-lost	2-0	2-1
Penalties-yards	3-25	2-10
Time of possession	39:55	20:05
Attendance—39,821.		

INDIVIDUAL STATISTICS

RUSHING—Arizona, Hearst 3-56, Higgs 15-37, Moore 11-36, Centers 14-30, Schroeder 2-0. Houston, White 13-40, Brown 1-1, Richardson 1-1, Givins 1-(minus 5).

PASSING—Arizona, Schroeder 12-20-1-176. Houston, Tolliver 11-31-4-184, Richardson 0-3-1-0.

RECEIVING—Arizona, Clark 6-120, Proehl 2-29, Centers 2-14, Reeves 1-11, Samuels 1-2. Houston, McNair 5-77, Jeffires 3-43, Slaughter 2-56, Givins 1-8.

MISSED FIELD GOAL ATTEMPTS—None.

INTERCEPTIONS—Arizona, Hoage 2-41, Lynch 1-12, A. Williams 1-6, J. Williams 1-29. Houston, Dishman 1-36.

KICKOFF RETURNS—Arizona, Higgs 1-17, Levy 1-20, Robinson 1-18, Samuels 1-6. Houston, McNair 4-71, Bishop 1-11, Givins 1-27.

PUNT RETURNS—Arizona, Robinson 3-17. Houston, Givins 3-(minus 2).

SACKS—Arizona, Swann 1½, Marshall 1, Simmons 1, Bankston ½. Houston, Lathon 1.

SAINTS 31, RAMS 15

Sunday, December 4

New Orleans	7	21	3	0—31
L.A. Rams	0	7	0	8—15

First Quarter
N.O.—Bates 26 run (Andersen kick), 11:19.
Second Quarter
N.O.—Bates 11 run (Andersen kick), :05.

L.A.—Kinchen 24 pass from Miller (Zendejas kick), 4:49.
N.O.—Bates 1 run (Andersen kick), 13:08.
N.O.—Haynes 30 pass from Everett (Andersen kick), 14:41.
Third Quarter
N.O.—FG Andersen 46, 14:47.
Fourth Quarter
L.A.—Bettis 5 pass from Miller (Bettis run), 3:31.

TEAM STATISTICS

	New Orleans	L.A. Rams
First downs	20	20
Rushes-yards	38-137	21-75
Passing	191	258
Punt returns-yards	2-5	3-1
Kickoff returns-yards	3-72	4-89
Interception returns-yards	0-0	1-3
Comp.-att.-int.	17-27-1	26-37-0
Sacked-yards lost	2-14	3-26
Punts-average	5-45	4-46
Fumbles-lost	0-0	5-4
Penalties-yards	10-65	10-94
Time of possession	33:07	26:53
Attendance—34,960.		

INDIVIDUAL STATISTICS

RUSHING—New Orleans, Bates 25-96, Brown 7-30, Neal 2-5, Haynes 1-3, Wilson 2-2, Everett 1-1. Los Angeles, Bettis 15-53, Miller 4-18, Lang 1-3, Chandler 1-1.

PASSING—New Orleans, Everett 13-22-1-161, Wilson 4-5-0-44. Los Angeles, Miller 17-24-0-198, Chandler 9-13-0-86.

RECEIVING—New Orleans, Haynes 5-80, Small 3-32, Early 3-30, Smith 3-30, Mitchell 1-13, Walls 1-11, Brown 1-9. Los Angeles, Bailey 11-116, Kinchen 5-76, Anderson 4-43, Bettis 3-13, Hester 2-25, Drayton 1-11.

MISSED FIELD GOAL ATTEMPTS—None.

INTERCEPTIONS—Los Angeles, Henley 1-3.

KICKOFF RETURNS—New Orleans, Mitchell 3-72. Los Angeles, Kinchen 4-89.

PUNT RETURNS—New Orleans, Mitchell 2-5. Los Angeles, Kinchen 3-1.

SACKS—New Orleans, Conner 1, Martin 1, Warren 1. Los Angeles, Ottis 1, Stokes 1.

49ERS 50, FALCONS 14

Sunday, December 4

Atlanta	7	7	0	0—14
San Francisco	3	24	7	16—50

First Quarter
S.F.—FG Brien 24, 5:23.
Atl—Emanuel 11 pass from J. George (N. Johnson kick), 12:25.
Second Quarter
S.F.—Taylor 12 pass from Young (Brien kick), :05.
S.F.—Young 1 run (Brien kick), 4:57.
Atl—Smith 36 interception return (N. Johnson kick), 6:57.
S.F.—Watters 2 pass from Young (Brien kick), 14:24.
S.F.—FG Brien 36, 15:00.
Third Quarter
S.F.—Young 7 run (Brien kick), 12:54.
Fourth Quarter
S.F.—Rice 9 pass from Young (run failed), 2:46.
S.F.—FG Brien 32, 5:20.
S.F.—Walker 2 run (Brien kick), 9:01.

TEAM STATISTICS

	Atlanta	San Francisco
First downs	12	28
Rushes-yards	12-43	39-161
Passing	206	315
Punt returns-yards	1-29	2-8
Kickoff returns-yards	9-134	3-53
Interception returns-yards	1-36	3-20
Comp.-att.-int.	19-40-3	25-38-1
Sacked-yards lost	3-22	2-6
Punts-average	7-32	2-41
Fumbles-lost	3-2	1-0
Penalties-yards	8-98	5-30
Time of possession	23:14	36:46
Attendance—60,549.		

INDIVIDUAL STATISTICS

RUSHING—Atlanta, Pegram 8-32, Heyward 4-11. San Francisco, Floyd 8-61, Watters 16-53, Walker 5-22, Young 3-16, Loville 4-11, Grbac 3-(minus 2).

PASSING—Atlanta, J. George 15-29-2-193, Hebert 4-11-1-34. San Francisco, Young 22-33-1-294, Grbac 3-5-0-27.

RECEIVING—Atlanta, Mathis 7-128, Sanders 5-53, Rison 2-16, Pegram 2-12, Heyward 2-7, Emanuel 1-11. San Francisco, Rice 7-92, Watters 6-73, Jones 4-81, Taylor 3-43, Singleton 2-20, Loville 1-7, Floyd 1-6, Popson 1-(minus 1).

MISSED FIELD GOAL ATTEMPTS—San Francisco, Brien 37.

INTERCEPTIONS—Atlanta, C. Smith 1-36. San Francisco, Hanks 2-14, Drakeford 1-6.

KICKOFF RETURNS—Atlanta, Verdin 7-119, Pegram 2-15. San Francisco, Walker 2-32, Carter 1-21.

PUNT RETURNS—Atlanta, Verdin 1-29. San Francisco, Carter 2-8.

SACKS—Atlanta, C. Smith 2. San Francisco, R. Hall 1, Kelly 1, Hanks ½, Stubblefield ½.

LIONS 34, PACKERS 31

Sunday, December 4

Green Bay	14	7	10	0—31
Detroit	3	21	3	7—34

First Quarter
G.B.—Morgan 26 pass from Favre (Jacke kick), 5:57.
Det—FG Hanson 27, 13:46.
G.B.—Brooks 96 kickoff return (Jacke kick), 14:06.

Second Quarter
Det—H. Moore 24 pass from Krieg (Hanson kick), 1:23.
Det—Sanders 13 run (Hanson kick), 6:38.
G.B.—Sharpe 22 pass from Favre (Jacke kick), 12:36.
Det—Conover 1 pass from Krieg (Hanson kick), 14:11.

Third Quarter
G.B.—FG Jacke 24, 5:03.
G.B.—Morgan 47 pass from Favre (Jacke kick), 8:15.
Det—FG Hanson 34, 13:55.

Fourth Quarter
Det—D. Moore 1 run (Hanson kick), 5:58.

TEAM STATISTICS

	Green Bay	Detroit
First downs	23	21
Rushes-yards	23-58	27-199
Passing	359	188
Punt returns-yards	2-23	1-3
Kickoff returns-yards	6-195	6-86
Interception returns-yards	0-0	2-35
Comp.-att.-int.	29-43-2	18-30-0
Sacked-yards lost	1-7	1-8
Punts-average	2-41	4-43
Fumbles-lost	2-0	0-0
Penalties-yards	6-55	7-60
Time of possession	31:59	28:01
Attendance—76,338.		

INDIVIDUAL STATISTICS

RUSHING—Green Bay, Bennett 11-25, Cobb 8-21, Favre 4-12. Detroit, Sanders 20-188, Krieg 5-17, D. Moore 1-1, Perriman 1-(minus 7).

PASSING—Green Bay, Favre 29-43-2-366. Detroit, Krieg 18-30-0-196.

RECEIVING—Green Bay, Sharpe 10-115, Morgan 6-103, Brooks 4-79, Bennett 3-27, Chmura 3-26, Cobb 2-7, Wilner 1-9. Detroit, Matthews 5-25, Perriman 4-63, H. Moore 3-55, Sanders 3-17, Holman 1-18, Morton 1-17, Conover 1-1.

MISSED FIELD GOAL ATTEMPTS—Green Bay, Jacke 42.

INTERCEPTIONS—Detroit, Clay 1-18, Massey 1-17.

KICKOFF RETURNS—Green Bay, Harris 3-79, Brooks 2-113, J. Jurkovic 1-13. Detroit, Gray 2-44, Lynch 2-25, D. Moore 2-17.

PUNT RETURNS—Green Bay, Prior 2-23. Detroit, Massey 1-3.

SACKS—Green Bay, White 1. Detroit, Team 1.

BRONCOS 20, CHIEFS 17

Sunday, December 4

Denver	7	0	7	3 3—20
Kansas City	0	3	6	8 0—17

First Quarter
Den—Rivers 1 run (Elam kick), 7:54.

Second Quarter
K.C.—FG Elliott 22, 9:59.

Third Quarter
Den—Sharpe 24 pass from Elway (Elam kick), 9:27.
K.C.—Allen 1 run (run failed), 11:46.

Fourth Quarter
Den—FG Elam 34, 7:34.
K.C.—Davis 62 pass from Bono (Davis pass from Bono), 7:52.

Overtime
Den—FG Elam 34, 12:12.

TEAM STATISTICS

	Denver	Kansas City
First downs	26	17
Rushes-yards	44-129	25-78
Passing	264	323
Punt returns-yards	5-37	3-9
Kickoff returns-yards	5-98	4-91
Interception returns-yards	0-0	0-0
Comp.-att.-int.	23-35-0	18-37-0
Sacked-yards lost	5-29	0-0
Punts-average	7-47	7-42
Fumbles-lost	1-1	2-1
Penalties-yards	9-70	8-66
Time of possession	46:01	26:11
Attendance—77,631.		

INDIVIDUAL STATISTICS

RUSHING—Denver, L. Russell 20-62, Rivers 7-25, Millen 1-21, Elway 7-20, Clark 6-4, Milburn 3-(minus 3). Kansas City, Allen 16-49, Hill 3-17, Bennett 4-10, Anders 1-3, Bono 1-(minus 1).

PASSING—Denver, Elway 18-22-0-256, Millen 5-13-0-37. Kansas City, Bono 18-37-0-323.

RECEIVING—Denver, Sharpe 10-95, Miller 6-153, Evans 2-20, D. Russell 2-12, Milburn 2-4, L. Russell 1-9. Kansas City, Birden 7-101, Davis 3-107, Martin 3-82, Allen 2-12, Penn 1-13, Johnson 1-5, Hill 1-3.

MISSED FIELD GOAL ATTEMPTS—Kansas City, Elliott 37.

INTERCEPTIONS—None.

KICKOFF RETURNS—Denver, Milburn 5-98. Kansas City, Vaughn 4-91.

PUNT RETURNS—Denver, Milburn 5-37. Kansas City, Carter 2-5, Hughes 1-4.

SACKS—Kansas City, Phillips 2, Collins 1, Mickell 1, Thomas 1.

COLTS 31, SEAHAWKS 19

Sunday, December 4

Indianapolis	7	7	7	10—31
Seattle	10	3	0	6—19

First Quarter
Sea—FG Kasay 37, 11:27.
Sea—Green 18 pass from Mirer (Kasay kick), 11:38.
Ind—Faulk 45 run (Biasucci kick), 14:18.

Second Quarter
Ind—Buchanan 37 interception return (Biasucci kick), 8:06.
Sea—FG Kasay 31, 14:17.

Third Quarter
Ind—Majkowski 1 run (Biasucci kick), 6:59.

Fourth Quarter
Ind—Dawkins 16 pass from Majkowski (Biasucci kick), 4:40.
Ind—FG Biasucci 21, 6:57.
Sea—S. Smith 1 pass from McGwire (pass failed), 13:16.

TEAM STATISTICS

	Indianapolis	Seattle
First downs	14	15
Rushes-yards	39-183	27-107
Passing	105	131
Punt returns-yards	5-5	3-24
Kickoff returns-yards	5-46	6-171
Interception returns-yards	2-79	2-18
Comp.-att.-int.	10-19-2	20-37-2
Sacked-yards lost	0-0	5-42
Punts-average	6-40	7-39
Fumbles-lost	3-2	3-3
Penalties-yards	2-10	13-124
Time of possession	28:15	31:45
Attendance—39,574.		

INDIVIDUAL STATISTICS

RUSHING—Indianapolis, Faulk 27-129, L. Warren 5-50, Potts 4-4, Majkowski 3-0. Seattle, C. Warren 23-81, Strong 2-17, Mirer 1-8, S. Smith 1-1.

PASSING—Indianapolis, Majkowski 10-19-2-105. Seattle, Mirer 5-13-1-28, McGwire 15-24-1-145.

RECEIVING—Indianapolis, Dawkins 3-42, Turner 3-29, Potts 2-16, Cash 1-9, Faulk 1-9. Seattle, Green 7-35, Blades 4-55, Thomas 3-55, Martin 3-27, S. Smith 2-8, Strong 1-(minus 7).

MISSED FIELD GOAL ATTEMPTS—None.

INTERCEPTIONS—Indianapolis, Ambrose 1-42, Buchanan 1-37. Seattle, Hunter 1-0, E. Robinson 1-18.

KICKOFF RETURNS—Indianapolis, Humphrey 3-25, Brewer 1-21. Seattle, T. Warren 4-121, Bates 2-50.

PUNT RETURNS—Indianapolis, Brewer 5-5. Seattle, Martin 3-24.
SACKS—Indianapolis, Siragusa 2, Bennett 1, Buchanan 1, McCoy 1.

BILLS 42, DOLPHINS 31
Sunday, December 4

Buffalo	7	0	21	14—42
Miami	0	17	0	14—31

First Quarter
Buf—Brooks 8 pass from Kelly (Christie kick), 10:35.
Second Quarter
Mia—Fryar 3 pass from Marino (Stoyanovich kick), :08.
Mia—FG Stoyanovich 23, 9:24.
Mia—Fryar 45 pass from Marino (Stoyanovich kick), 13:29.
Third Quarter
Buf—Beebe 72 pass from Kelly (Christie kick), :59.
Buf—Reed 21 pass from Kelly (Christie kick), 6:51.
Buf—Gardner 1 run (Christie kick), 13:58.
Fourth Quarter
Mia—K. Jackson 23 pass from Marino (pass failed), :48.
Buf—Gardner 1 run (Christie kick), 3:19.
Buf—Reed 83 pass from Kelly (Christie kick), 8:40.
Mia—S. Miller 1 pass from Kosar (Parmalee run), 14:50.

TEAM STATISTICS

	Buffalo	Miami
First downs	19	25
Rushes-yards	28-76	19-73
Passing	314	387
Punt returns-yards	2-28	2-17
Kickoff returns-yards	5-75	7-163
Interception returns-yards	4-52	1-0
Comp.-att.-int.	19-29-1	32-54-4
Sacked-yards lost	2-17	1-4
Punts-average	4-49	4-42
Fumbles-lost	7-1	1-0
Penalties-yards	5-42	9-87
Time of possession	26:56	33:04
Attendance—69,358.		

INDIVIDUAL STATISTICS

RUSHING—Buffalo, Thomas 16-63, Gardner 5-10, K. Davis 3-5, Beebe 1-5, Reed 1-3, Moore 1-(minus 9), Reich 1-(minus 1). Miami, Parmalee 13-40, Kosar 1-17, Spikes 3-15, McDuffie 1-3, Marino 1-(minus 2).

PASSING—Buffalo, Kelly 18-28-1-299, Reed 1-1-0-32. Miami, Marino 25-42-3-311, Kosar 7-12-1-80.

RECEIVING—Buffalo, Thomas 4-26, Reed 3-106, Beebe 3-89, Brooks 3-49, Johnson 3-42, Metzelaars 1-9, K. Davis 1-7, Gardner 1-3. Miami, Craver 7-67, Jackson 7-64, Fryar 5-110, McDuffie 4-47, Williams 3-62, Parmalee 2-18, Ingram 2-6, Saxon 1-6, Miller 1-1.

MISSED FIELD GOAL ATTEMPTS—None.

INTERCEPTIONS—Buffalo, Darby 2-20, Burris 1-24, M. Patton 1-8.

Miami, Vincent 1-0.
KICKOFF RETURNS—Buffalo, Jourdain 3-44, Copeland 1-31, K. Davis 1-0. Miami, Spikes 6-146, McDuffie 1-17.
PUNT RETURNS—Buffalo, Burris 2-28. Miami, McDuffie 2-17.
SACKS—Buffalo, B. Smith 1. Miami, Coleman 1, Cross 1.

RAIDERS 24, CHARGERS 17
Monday, December 5

L.A. Raiders	7	7	0	10—24
San Diego	7	7	0	3—17

First Quarter
L.A.—Wright 76 pass from Hostetler (Jaeger kick), 1:10.
S.D.—Jefferson 29 pass from Humphries (Carney kick), 3:51.
Second Quarter
L.A.—Ismail 6 pass from Evans (Jaeger kick), 4:33.
S.D.—Martin 16 pass from Gilbert (Carney kick), 14:53.
Fourth Quarter
L.A.—FG Jaeger 43, 2:05.
S.D.—FG Carney 24, 2:26.
L.A.—Ismail 6 pass from Hostetler (Jaeger kick), 7:37.

TEAM STATISTICS

	L.A. Raiders	San Diego
First downs	23	18
Rushes-yards	29-88	22-47
Passing	322	214
Punt returns-yards	1-3	2-26
Kickoff returns-yards	4-63	5-132
Interception returns-yards	0-0	1-11
Comp.-att.-int.	24-31-1	20-37-0
Sacked-yards lost	1-6	2-22
Punts-average	5-36	5-30
Fumbles-lost	0-0	2-1
Penalties-yards	17-146	9-63
Time of possession	33:53	26:07
Attendance—63,012.		

INDIVIDUAL STATISTICS

RUSHING—Los Angeles, H. Williams 20-41, C. Jones 5-21, Hostetler 3-13, Ismail 1-13. San Diego, Means 18-41, Harmon 4-6.

PASSING—Los Angeles, Hostetler 22-29-1-319, Evans 2-2-0-9. San Diego, Humphries 17-33-0-202, Gilbert 3-3-0-34, Means 0-1-0-0.

RECEIVING—Los Angeles, Brown 7-96, Rathman 4-34, Ismail 4-31, H. Williams 4-15, Bender 2-14, Wright 1-76, Jett 1-54, Glover 1-8. San Diego, Seay 4-61, Harmon 4-40, Jefferson 3-58, Martin 3-43, Mitchell 2-16, Means 2-8, D. Young 1-6, Pupunu 1-4.

MISSED FIELD GOAL ATTEMPTS—None.

INTERCEPTIONS—San Diego, Griggs 1-11.

KICKOFF RETURNS—Los Angeles, Ismail 3-46, Wright 1-17. San Diego, Coleman 4-111, Harmon 1-21.

PUNT RETURNS—Los Angeles, T. Brown 1-3. San Diego, Gordon 2-26.

SACKS—Los Angeles, Smith 1, Wallace 1. San Diego, Mims 1.

WEEK 15

RESULTS

Cleveland 19, Dallas 14
Detroit 18, N.Y. Jets 7
Arizona 17, Washington 15
Green Bay 40, Chicago 3
L.A. Raiders 23, Denver 13
Minnesota 21, Buffalo 17
N.Y. Giants 27, Cincinnati 20
New England 28, Indianapolis 13
New Orleans 29, Atlanta 20
Pittsburgh 14, Philadelphia 3
San Francisco 38, San Diego 15
Seattle 16, Houston 14
Tampa Bay 24, L.A. Rams 14
Miami 45, Kansas City 28

STANDINGS

AFC EAST	W	L	T	Pct.
Miami	9	5	0	.643
New England	8	6	0	.571
Buffalo	7	7	0	.500
N.Y. Jets	6	8	0	.429
Indianapolis	6	8	0	.429

AFC CENTRAL	W	L	T	Pct.
Pittsburgh	11	3	0	.786
Cleveland	10	4	0	.714
Cincinnati	2	12	0	.143
Houston	1	13	0	.071

AFC WEST	W	L	T	Pct.
San Diego	9	5	0	.643
L.A. Raiders	8	6	0	.571
Denver	7	7	0	.500
Kansas City	7	7	0	.500
Seattle	6	8	0	.429

NFC EAST	W	L	T	Pct.
Dallas	11	3	0	.786
N.Y. Giants	7	7	0	.500
Arizona	7	7	0	.500
Philadelphia	7	7	0	.500
Washington	2	12	0	.143

NFC CENTRAL	W	L	T	Pct.
Minnesota	9	5	0	.643
Detroit	8	6	0	.571
Chicago	8	6	0	.571
Green Bay	7	7	0	.500
Tampa Bay	5	9	0	.357

NFC WEST	W	L	T	Pct.
San Francisco	12	2	0	.857
New Orleans	6	8	0	.429
Atlanta	6	8	0	.429
L.A. Rams	4	10	0	.286

HIGHLIGHTS

Hero of the week: Minnesota linebacker Jack Del Rio, whose interception helped the Vikings beat Buffalo, 21-17. Buffalo was driving for another score with a 17-12 lead late in the third quarter. But Del Rio made a one-handed interception at the Vikings' 19 to thwart the drive. On the ensuing drive, Minnesota scored on a one-yard run by Terry Allen to take the lead for good.

Goat of the week: Philadelphia quarterback Randall Cunningham, who guided an offense that generated 105 yards in a 14-3 loss to Pittsburgh. Cunningham hit nine of 27 passes for 59 yards with an interception as the Eagles lost their fifth in a row. Cunningham: "Something's wrong. . . . Our offense just isn't working."

Sub of the week: Tampa Bay wide receiver Charles Wilson, who came on when Courtney Hawkins sprained a ligament in his left knee in the first quarter of a 24-14 victory over the Los Angeles Rams. Wilson teamed with Craig Erickson on a 71-yard scoring strike in the second quarter and a 44-yard touchdown pass with 1:34 left in the game. Wilson had four catches for 176 yards.

Comeback of the week: The New York Giants rallied to beat Cincinnati, 27-20. The Giants took possession on their 34 after Cincinnati's Doug Pelfrey kicked a game-tying 23-yard field goal with 1:47 left. Quarterback Dave Brown completed three passes to move the ball to the Bengals' 25. On first and 10, Brown caught Cincinnati in a blitz and threw down the left sideline to Mike Sherrard, who was covered by cornerback Corey Sawyer. The pass was incomplete, but pass interference was called. On the next play, Rodney Hampton ran three yards for the winning touchdown with 40 seconds left.

Blowout of the week: Edgar Bennett rushed for 106 yards and a touchdown as Green Bay ran for 257 yards, the club's best total in more than nine years, en route to a 40-3 rout of Chicago. The Packers finished with 516 total yards.

Nail-biter of the week: A 32-yard field goal by Matt Stover with 1:49 left in the fourth quarter gave Cleveland what looked like a safe 19-14 lead over Dallas. But Kevin Williams returned the ensuing kickoff 42 yards to Dallas' 49, and Troy Aikman proceeded to drive Dallas to the Browns' 6 with 10 seconds left. On what turned out to be the game's last play, Aikman passed to tight end Jay Novacek, who caught the ball over the middle at the 1 but slipped on the wet Texas Stadium turf. Cleveland safety Eric Turner instantly made contact with Novacek, who was inches from the goal line as time expired.

Hit of the week: By Seattle strong safety Robert Blackmon, whose tackle of Todd McNair saved a 16-14 victory over Houston. Blackmon tackled McNair on a two-point conversion pass from Billy Joe Tolliver with 2:53 left to deny the tying points.

Oddity of the week: In what turned out to be an accurate barometer of Super Bowl XXIX, San Francisco whipped San Diego, 38-15. The only thing different about this meeting and the Super Bowl encounter was the location. This game was in San Diego, and the Chargers' secondary was ripped for 298 yards and two touchdowns. In Miami on January 29, 1995, San Diego again had its secondary torched (316 yards and six touchdowns) in a 49-26 Super Bowl loss.

Top rusher: Chris Warren ran for 185 yards and a touchdown on 30 carries in Seattle's victory.

Top passer: San Diego's Stan Humphries completed 25 of 43 passes for 337 yards, one touchdown and two interceptions in the Chargers' loss.

Top receiver: Washington's Henry Ellard caught eight passes for 191 yards and a touchdown as the Redskins lost, 17-15, to Arizona.

Notes: Jets receiver Art Monk broke Steve Largent's all-time mark of 177 consecutive games with at least one reception when he caught a five-yard pass from quarterback Boomer Esiason on the first play from scrimmage in an 18-7 loss to

Detroit. . . . Kansas City's Jon Vaughn scored on a 91-yard kickoff return in a 45-28 loss to Miami, the first return for a touchdown against the Dolphins since 1975. . . . The Jets' loss to Detroit ensured the franchise of its sixth consecutive losing season. . . . Ernest Givins became the first Oiler to return a punt for a touchdown since 1977 when he ran one back 78 yards in the loss to Seattle. . . . Warren Moon threw for 261 yards against Buffalo, becoming the first Vikings quarterback to eclipse the 4,000-yard mark in a season. . . . Indianapolis cornerback Ray Buchanan returned an interception 90 yards for a touchdown in a 28-13 loss at New England, marking the third time in five games he turned the trick. . . . The Buccaneers' victory over the Rams was their third consecutive win, a feat they hadn't accomplished since they won their final three contests in 1982.

Quote of the week: New England quarterback Drew Bledsoe, who led New England to a victory over Indianapolis despite throwing four interceptions: "It's a great asset as a quarterback to know you have a coach that has confidence in you. He'll (Coach Bill Parcells) still let you throw the ball even if you're having an off day."

GAME SUMMARIES

LIONS 18, JETS 7
Saturday, December 10

Detroit	3	6	3	6— 18
N.Y. Jets	0	7	0	0— 7

First Quarter
Det—FG Hanson 37, 10:59.
Second Quarter
Det—Sanders 5 pass from Krieg (kick blocked), 6:09.
N.Y.—B. Baxter 1 run (Lowery kick), 14:40.
Third Quarter
Det—FG Hanson 49, 10:22.
Fourth Quarter
Det—FG Hanson 48, 3:00.
Det—FG Hanson 23, 11:58.

TEAM STATISTICS

	Detroit	N.Y. Jets
First downs	19	14
Rushes-yards	30-140	26-120
Passing	186	141
Punt returns-yards	1-9	0-0
Kickoff returns-yards	2-24	5-125
Interception returns-yards	0-0	1-0
Comp.-att.-int.	18-24-1	17-30-0
Sacked-yards lost	1-3	1-10
Punts-average	2-50	6-37
Fumbles-lost	0-0	2-1
Penalties-yards	4-20	8-50
Time of possession	32:16	27:44
Attendance—56,080.		

INDIVIDUAL STATISTICS
RUSHING—Detroit, Sanders 23-127, Krieg 5-9, D. Moore 2-4. New York, J. Johnson 15-64, R. Anderson 4-27, Esiason 2-21, B. Baxter 4-4, Murrell 1-4.
PASSING—Detroit, Krieg 18-24-1-189. New York, Esiason 17-30-0-151.
RECEIVING—Detroit, Perriman 6-79, H. Moore 6-70, Sanders 3-13, Holman 2-13, Carter 1-14. New York, J. Johnson 5-40, Mitchell 4-49, R. Moore 3-35, Monk 3-21, R. Anderson 2-6.
MISSED FIELD GOAL ATTEMPTS—None.
INTERCEPTIONS—New York, Hasty 1-0.
KICKOFF RETURNS—Detroit, Gray 1-14, D. Moore 1-10. New York, Glenn 4-105, F. Baxter 1-20.

PUNT RETURNS—Detroit, Gray 1-9.
SACKS—Detroit, Porcher 1. New York, Casillas ½, Lageman ½.

BROWNS 19, COWBOYS 14
Saturday, December 10

Cleveland	7	3	0	9— 19
Dallas	7	0	0	7— 14

First Quarter
Dal—E. Smith 7 pass from Aikman (Boniol kick), 10:49.
Cle—Jackson 2 pass from Testaverde (Stover kick), 15:00.
Second Quarter
Cle—FG Stover 34, 4:57.
Fourth Quarter
Cle—FG Stover 32, :46.
Cle—FG Stover 43, 2:16.
Dal—E. Smith 4 run (Boniol kick), 8:39.
Cle—FG Stover 32, 13:11.

TEAM STATISTICS

	Cleveland	Dallas
First downs	16	19
Rushes-yards	38-134	27-112
Passing	110	177
Punt returns-yards	1-3	1-13
Kickoff returns-yards	3-83	5-117
Interception returns-yards	2-2	1-7
Comp.-att.-int.	15-25-1	21-36-2
Sacked-yards lost	1-8	2-11
Punts-average	3-35	4-35
Fumbles-lost	1-1	2-2
Penalties-yards	3-15	4-70
Time of possession	32:36	27:24
Attendance—64,286.		

INDIVIDUAL STATISTICS
RUSHING—Cleveland, Hoard 25-99, Metcalf 3-19, Byner 4-8, Baldwin 4-6, Testaverde 2-2. Dallas, E. Smith 26-112, Aikman 1-0.
PASSING—Cleveland, Testaverde 15-25-1-118. Dallas, Aikman 21-36-2-188.
RECEIVING—Cleveland, Jackson 6-74, Kinchen 3-13, Metcalf 3-13, Hoard 1-9, Carrier 1-7, Baldwin 1-2. Dallas, Irvin 7-88, E. Smith 5-22, Johnston 3-15, K. Williams 2-26, Novacek 2-10, Harper 2-27.
MISSED FIELD GOAL ATTEMPTS—None.
INTERCEPTIONS—Cleveland, Griffin 1-2, Turner 1-0. Dallas, Brown 1-7.
KICKOFF RETURNS—Cleveland, Baldwin 2-51, Metcalf 1-32. Dallas, K. Williams 5-117.
PUNT RETURNS—Cleveland, Metcalf 1-3. Dallas, K. Williams 1-13.
SACKS—Cleveland, Griffin 1, Pleasant 1. Dallas, Haley 1.

STEELERS 14, EAGLES 3
Sunday, December 11

Philadelphia	3	0	0	0— 3
Pittsburgh	0	0	0	14— 14

First Quarter
Phi—FG Murray 21, 3:46.
Fourth Quarter
Pit—Hastings 18 pass from O'Donnell (Anderson kick), 4:56.
Pit—J. Williams 3 run (Anderson kick), 6:44.

TEAM STATISTICS

	Philadelphia	Pittsburgh
First downs	9	20
Rushes-yards	23-71	39-124
Passing	34	145
Punt returns-yards	5-15	7-33
Kickoff returns-yards	3-99	2-39
Interception returns-yards	1-0	1-38
Comp.-att.-int.	9-27-1	19-35-1
Sacked-yards lost	3-25	2-13
Punts-average	10-40	7-41
Fumbles-lost	1-0	1-1
Penalties-yards	10-67	6-57
Time of possession	23:57	36:03
Attendance—55,474.		

INDIVIDUAL STATISTICS
RUSHING—Philadelphia, Walker 15-52, Joseph 3-10, Cunningham 2-7, Garner 3-2. Pittsburgh, J. Williams 20-94, Morris 15-43, O'Donnell 3-0, Royals 1-(minus 13).
PASSING—Philadelphia, Cunningham 9-27-1-59. Pittsburgh,

O'Donnell 19-35-1-158.

RECEIVING—Philadelphia, Barnett 4-26, Walker 3-11, C. Williams 1-13, M. Johnson 1-9. Pittsburgh, Mills 4-35, J. Williams 4-17, Hastings 3-53, C. Johnson 2-23, Thigpen 2-16, Green 1-7, Morris 1-3, Avery 1-2, Keith 1-2.

MISSED FIELD GOAL ATTEMPTS—None.

INTERCEPTIONS—Philadelphia, Hager 1-0. Pittsburgh, Perry 1-38.

KICKOFF RETURNS—Philadelphia, Walker 2-80, Sydner 1-19. Pittsburgh, Johnson 2-39.

PUNT RETURNS—Philadelphia, Sydner 5-15. Pittsburgh, Johnson 6-37, Woodson 1-(minus 4).

SACKS—Philadelphia, Jeter 1, Thomas 1. Pittsburgh, Brown 1, Figures 1, Seals 1.

VIKINGS 21, BILLS 17

Sunday, December 11

Minnesota	3	6	3	9—21
Buffalo	7	3	7	0—17

First Quarter

Min—FG Reveiz 30, 6:31.
Buf—Metzelaars 35 pass from Kelly (Christie kick), 10:19.

Second Quarter

Buf—FG Christie 41, 4:40.
Min—FG Reveiz 38, 7:10.
Min—FG Reveiz 30, 14:36.

Third Quarter

Buf—Beebe 9 pass from Kelly (Christie kick), 5:18.
Min—FG Reveiz 25, 11:52.

Fourth Quarter

Min—Allen 1 run (pass failed), 5:16.
Min—FG Reveiz 22, 12:22.

TEAM STATISTICS

	Minnesota	Buffalo
First downs	20	19
Rushes-yards	32-116	27-85
Passing	261	183
Punt returns-yards	1-10	0-0
Kickoff returns-yards	4-61	7-134
Interception returns-yards	1-7	0-0
Comp.-att.-int.	21-34-0	19-32-1
Sacked-yards lost	0-0	4-31
Punts-average	1-64	2-42
Fumbles-lost	1-1	0-0
Penalties-yards	10-65	3-25
Time of possession	32:41	27:19
Attendance—66,501.		

INDIVIDUAL STATISTICS

RUSHING—Minnesota, Allen 25-90, Lee 4-23, Graham 3-3. Buffalo, Thomas 16-50, A. Reed 2-17, K. Davis 4-9, Beebe 1-6, Gardner 3-4, Kelly 1-(minus 1).

PASSING—Minnesota, Moon 21-34-0-261. Buffalo, Kelly 15-26-1-173, Reich 4-6-0-41.

RECEIVING—Minnesota, Carter 9-111, Allen 4-28, Ismail 3-63, J. Reed 3-45, Lee 2-14. Buffalo, Metzelaars 4-62, Beebe 3-30, Thomas 3-22, K. Davis 3-12, Bl. Brooks 2-28, A. Reed 2-19, Gardner 1-21, Copeland 1-20.

MISSED FIELD GOAL ATTEMPTS—None.

INTERCEPTIONS—Minnesota, Del Rio 1-0, Boyd 0-7.

KICKOFF RETURNS—Minnesota, R. Smith 3-61, Garnett 1-0. Buffalo, Jourdain 6-128, Gardner 1-6.

PUNT RETURNS—Minnesota, Palmer 1-10.

SACKS—Minnesota, Del Rio 1, J. Harris 1, Randle 1, Thomas 1.

PATRIOTS 28, COLTS 13

Sunday, December 11

Indianapolis	0	10	0	3—13
New England	0	7	14	7—28

Second Quarter

Ind—FG Biasucci 27, 7:51.
Ind—Buchanan 90 interception return (Biasucci kick), 12:12.
N.E.—Thompson 9 pass from Bledsoe (Bahr kick), 14:18.

Third Quarter

N.E.—Coates 6 pass from Bledsoe (Bahr kick), 10:39.
N.E.—Butts 1 run (Bahr kick), 14:44.

Fourth Quarter

Ind—FG Biasucci 47, 6:02.
N.E.—Thompson 6 run (Bahr kick), 13:06.

TEAM STATISTICS

	Indianapolis	New England
First downs	13	24
Rushes-yards	27-74	37-84
Passing	138	277
Punt returns-yards	2-17	4-62
Kickoff returns-yards	4-79	4-61
Interception returns-yards	4-126	2-23
Comp.-att.-int.	12-32-2	25-45-4
Sacked-yards lost	4-28	0-0
Punts-average	6-34	3-34
Fumbles-lost	3-2	2-1
Penalties-yards	9-70	6-35
Time of possession	27:03	32:57
Attendance—57,656.		

INDIVIDUAL STATISTICS

RUSHING—Indianapolis, Faulk 17-50, Potts 4-18, Maj-kowski 4-11, Warren 2-(minus 5). New England, Butts 20-39, Thompson 12-28, Bledsoe 1-7, Gash 2-5, Turner 2-5.

PASSING—Indianapolis, Majkowski 12-31-2-166, Warren 0-1-0-0. New England, Bledsoe 25-45-4-277.

RECEIVING—Indianapolis, Turner 3-61, Dawkins 2-22, Potts 2-22, Faulk 2-16, Cash 1-19, M. Jackson 1-13, Warren 1-13. New England, Coates 6-68, Timpson 5-54, Brisby 4-75, Thompson 4-30, Crittenden 3-31, Turner 2-14, Butts 1-5.

MISSED FIELD GOAL ATTEMPTS—New England, Bahr 36.

INTERCEPTIONS—Indianapolis, Buchanan 2-113, Daniel 1-6, Tate 1-7. New England, H. Barnett 1-21, Ray 1-2.

KICKOFF RETURNS—Indianapolis, Brewer 2-37, Humphrey 2-42. New England, Crittenden 2-19, Thompson 2-42.

PUNT RETURNS—Indianapolis, Brewer 2-17. New England, T. Brown 4-62.

SACKS—New England, M. Jones 1½, McGinest 1, Slade 1, Agnew ½.

BUCCANEERS 24, RAMS 14

Sunday, December 11

L.A. Rams	0	7	0	7—14
Tampa Bay	0	17	0	7—24

Second Quarter

T.B.—FG Husted 20, 3:47.
T.B.—C. Wilson 71 pass from Erickson (Husted kick), 5:56.
L.A.—Drayton 22 pass from Chandler (Zendejas kick), 10:08.
T.B.—Rhett 8 run (Husted kick), 14:10.

Fourth Quarter

L.A.—Hester 12 pass from Chandler (Zendejas kick), 2:18.
T.B.—C. Wilson 44 pass from Erickson (Husted kick), 13:26.

TEAM STATISTICS

	L.A. Rams	Tampa Bay
First downs	19	17
Rushes-yards	26-63	35-125
Passing	198	230
Punt returns-yards	2-42	3-11
Kickoff returns-yards	3-104	3-67
Interception returns-yards	0-0	0-0
Comp.-att.-int.	18-34-0	10-22-0
Sacked-yards lost	1-1	1-1
Punts-average	5-43	6-40
Fumbles-lost	2-2	0-0
Penalties-yards	9-83	10-80
Time of possession	27:20	32:40
Attendance—34,150.		

INDIVIDUAL STATISTICS

RUSHING—Los Angeles, Bettis 13-23, Lester 5-12, Chandler 5-13, Griffith 2-9, Bailey 1-6. Tampa Bay, Rhett 31-119, Workman 1-5, Erickson 2-4, Royster 1-(minus 3).

PASSING—Los Angeles, Chandler 18-34-0-199. Tampa Bay, Erickson 10-22-0-231.

RECEIVING—Los Angeles, Hester 6-82, Drayton 3-40, Anderson 3-36, Kinchen 3-19, Bettis 2-16, Bailey 1-6. Tampa Bay, C. Wilson 4-176, Dawsey 2-21, Copeland 1-18, Workman 1-7, Thomas 1-5, Rhett 1-4.

MISSED FIELD GOAL ATTEMPTS—Los Angeles, Zendejas 48. Tampa Bay, Husted 36.

INTERCEPTIONS—None.

KICKOFF RETURNS—Los Angeles, Lang 3-104. Tampa Bay, C. Wilson 2-48, Buckley 1-19.

PUNT RETURNS—Los Angeles, Kinchen 2-42. Tampa Bay, Everett 2-2, Hawkins 1-9.

SACKS—Los Angeles, J. Jones 1. Tampa Bay, Dotson 1.

GIANTS 27, BENGALS 20

Sunday, December 11

Cincinnati	0	7	3	10—20
N.Y. Giants	0	17	3	7—27

Second Quarter
N.Y.—Hampton 1 run (Daluiso kick), 3:14.
N.Y.—FG Daluiso 52, 10:26.
Cin—Pickens 5 pass from Blake (Pelfrey kick), 13:49.
N.Y.—Cross 8 pass from Da. Brown (Daluiso kick), 14:44.

Third Quarter
Cin—FG Pelfrey 38, 4:44.
N.Y.—FG Daluiso 33, 10:02.

Fourth Quarter
Cin—Pickens 3 pass from Blake (Pelfrey kick), 5:37.
Cin—FG Pelfrey 23, 13:13.
N.Y.—Hampton 3 run (Daluiso kick), 14:20.

TEAM STATISTICS

	Cincinnati	N.Y. Giants
First downs	20	18
Rushes-yards	37-121	30-89
Passing	205	215
Punt returns-yards	3-46	1-1
Kickoff returns-yards	5-135	5-77
Interception returns-yards	2-14	0-0
Comp.-att.-int.	18-38-0	16-26-2
Sacked-yards lost	1-3	1-7
Punts-average	5-34	6-31
Fumbles-lost	1-1	1-0
Penalties-yards	8-104	8-71
Time of possession	32:17	27:43

Attendance—67,530.

INDIVIDUAL STATISTICS

RUSHING—Cincinnati, Broussard 13-46, Blake 6-30, Fenner 11-24, Cothran 7-21. New York, Hampton 23-76, Da. Brown 3-7, Downs 1-4, Meggett 3-2.

PASSING—Cincinnati, Blake 17-37-0-200, Klingler 1-1-0-8. New York, Da. Brown 16-26-2-222.

RECEIVING—Cincinnati, Pickens 7-59, Scott 3-46, Broussard 3-32, To. McGee 2-42, Cothran 2-14, Fenner 1-15. New York, Sherrard 4-75, Calloway 3-48, Pierce 3-43, Hampton 3-22, Marshall 1-14, Meggett 1-12, Cross 1-8.

MISSED FIELD GOAL ATTEMPTS—Cincinnati, Pelfrey 33.

INTERCEPTIONS—Cincinnati, Sawyer 1-0, Tovar 1-14.

KICKOFF RETURNS—Cincinnati, Ball 3-85, Hardy 1-42, Tovar 1-8. New York, Meggett 2-49, De. Brown 1-1, Koz-Iowski 1-7, Marshall 1-20.

PUNT RETURNS—Cincinnati, Sawyer 3-46. New York, Marshall 1-1.

SACKS—Cincinnati, Francis 1. New York, Hamilton ½, Strahan ½.

PACKERS 40, BEARS 3

Sunday, December 11

Chicago	3	0	0	0— 3
Green Bay	7	17	10	6—40

First Quarter
Chi—FG Butler 25, 7:15.
G.B.—Brooks 12 pass from Favre (Jacke kick), 11:28.

Second Quarter
G.B.—FG Jacke 39, 4:04.
G.B.—Bennett 4 run (Jacke kick), 11:07.
G.B.—Sharpe 13 pass from Favre (Jacke kick), 14:32.

Third Quarter
G.B.—Sharpe 22 pass from Favre (Jacke kick), 4:57.
G.B.—FG Jacke 24, 12:17.

Fourth Quarter
G.B.—FG Jacke 20, 5:23.
G.B.—FG Jacke 29, 13:08.

TEAM STATISTICS

	Chicago	Green Bay
First downs	9	28
Rushes-yards	14-27	46-257
Passing	149	259
Punt returns-yards	0-0	2-27
Kickoff returns-yards	9-131	2-41
Interception returns-yards	1-0	2-54
Comp.-att.-int.	15-35-2	20-34-1
Sacked-yards lost	2-18	2-7
Punts-average	6-38	2-40
Fumbles-lost	2-0	2-0

	Chicago	Green Bay
Penalties-yards	1-5	2-40
Time of possession	21:00	39:00

Attendance—57,927.

INDIVIDUAL STATISTICS

RUSHING—Chicago, Tillman 5-15, Green 4-9, R. Harris 3-4, Walsh 2-(minus 1). Green Bay, Bennett 22-106, Cobb 11-78, L. Johnson 6-42, Favre 3-28, Levens 2-5, Brunell 2-(minus 2).

PASSING—Chicago, Walsh 13-26-1-143, Kramer 2-9-1-24. Green Bay, Favre 19-31-1-250, Brunell 1-3-0- 16.

RECEIVING—Chicago, Graham 3-22, Green 2-6, Cart-er 1-24, Conway 1-12, McMurtry 1-9, R. Harris 1-4. Green Bay, Sharpe 7-86, Brooks 6-105, R. Johnson 2-31, Cobb 1-15, Mickens 1-11, Mor-gan 1-11, Bennett 1-5, Chmura 1-2.

MISSED FIELD GOAL ATTEMPTS—None.

INTERCEPTIONS—Chicago, Gayle 1-0. Green Bay, Butler 1-51, K. Johnson 1-3.

KICKOFF RETURNS—Chicago, Lewis 5-83, Carter 3-32, Green 1-16. Green Bay, Brooks 2-41.

PUNT RETURNS—Green Bay, Brooks 2-27.

SACKS—Chicago, Armstrong 1, Spellman 1. Green Bay, Davey 1, Wilkins 1.

CARDINALS 17, REDSKINS 15

Sunday, December 11

Washington	3	3	0	9—15
Arizona	7	0	0	10—17

First Quarter
Ari—Proehl 48 pass from Schroeder (Davis kick), 7:59.
Was—FG Lohmiller 34, 13:29.

Second Quarter
Was—FG Lohmiller 31, 12:00.

Fourth Quarter
Ari—Moore 1 run (Davis kick), :50.
Was—Ellard 52 pass from Shuler (run failed), 2:30.
Was—FG Lohmiller 21, 12:06.
Ari—FG Davis 27, 15:00.

TEAM STATISTICS

	Washington	Arizona
First downs	19	14
Rushes-yards	28-123	28-84
Passing	283	194
Punt returns-yards	2-19	2-14
Kickoff returns-yards	3-55	5-86
Interception returns-yards	0-0	1-0
Comp.-att.-int.	16-27-1	16-25-0
Sacked-yards lost	1-3	3-22
Punts-average	4-33	7-40
Fumbles-lost	2-1	1-1
Penalties-yards	5-30	5-40
Time of possession	31:34	28:26

Attendance—53,790.

INDIVIDUAL STATISTICS

RUSHING—Washington, Mitchell 17-60, Shuler 2-38, Ervins 9-25. Arizona, Moore 10-43, Hearst 5-28, Centers 5- 10, Higgs 4-4, Schroe-der 4-(minus 4).

PASSING—Washington, Shuler 16-27-1-286. Arizona, Schroeder 16-25-0-216.

RECEIVING—Washington, Ellard 8-191, Howard 4-83, Ervins 1-6, Winans 1-4, Jenkins 1-1, Mitchell 1-1. Arizona, Centers 5-56, Proehl 4-89, Hearst 3-34, Fann 3-20, Samuels 1-17.

MISSED FIELD GOAL ATTEMPTS—Washington, Lohmiller 29.

INTERCEPTIONS—Arizona, A. Williams 1-0.

KICKOFF RETURNS—Washington, Mitchell 2-30, Bell 1-25. Arizona, Levy 4-78, Higgs 1-8.

PUNT RETURNS—Washington, Mitchell 2- 19. Arizona, Robinson 2-14.

SACKS—Washington, A. Collins 1½, Harvey 1, Coleman ½. Arizona, Swann ½, E. Hill ½.

SEAHAWKS 16, OILERS 14

Sunday, December 11

Seattle	3	7	6	0—16
Houston	0	0	0	14—14

First Quarter
Sea—FG Kasay 40, 1:37.

Second Quarter
Sea—C. Warren 33 run (Kasay kick), 2:26.

Third Quarter

Sea—Strong 13 run (kick blocked), 3:27.

Fourth Quarter

Hou—Slaughter 36 pass from Tolliver (Jeffires pass from Tolliver), 10:37.

Hou—Givins 78 punt return (pass failed), 12:07.

TEAM STATISTICS

	Seattle	Houston
First downs	21	14
Rushes-yards	50-266	20-63
Passing	64	145
Punt returns-yards	3-15	3-92
Kickoff returns-yards	2-29	4-71
Interception returns-yards	1-0	0-0
Comp.-att.-int.	8-17-0	16-29-1
Sacked-yards lost	4-31	6-39
Punts-average	6-41	6-42
Fumbles-lost	1-1	1-1
Penalties-yards	6-47	4-43
Time of possession	37:14	22:46

Attendance—31,453.

INDIVIDUAL STATISTICS

RUSHING—Seattle, C. Warren 30-185, Strong 10-44, Johnson 3-22, S. Smith 2-8, Bates 1-7, McGwire 4-0. Houston, White 17-53, Brown 1-9, Tolliver 2-1.

PASSING—Seattle, McGwire 8-17-0-95. Houston, Tolliver 16-29-1-184.

RECEIVING—Seattle, S. Smith 2-32, Blades 2-29, Johnson 2-16, Green 1-11, Crumpler 1-7. Houston, Slaughter 5-66, Givins 5-48, Carter 4-49, Jeffires 1-11, Maston 1-10.

MISSED FIELD GOAL ATTEMPTS—None.

INTERCEPTIONS—Seattle, Watters 1-0.

KICKOFF RETURNS—Seattle, Martin 1-16, T. Warren 1-13. Houston, McNair 4-71.

PUNT RETURNS—Seattle, Martin 3-15. Houston, Givins 3-92.

SACKS—Seattle, Kennedy 2, Adams 1, Spitulski 1, McCrary ½, Sinclair ½, Stephens ½, Wooden ½. Houston, Childress 2, Barrow 1½, Lathon ½.

RAIDERS 23, BRONCOS 13

Sunday, December 11

Denver	0	3	3	7—13
L.A. Raiders	0	6	3	14—23

Second Quarter

L.A.—FG Jaeger 44, 7:25.

L.A.—FG Jaeger 29, 11:49.

Den—FG Elam 20, 15:00.

Third Quarter

L.A.—FG Jaeger 47, 4:16.

Den—FG Elam 21, 12:03.

Fourth Quarter

L.A.—FG Jaeger 30, 2:11.

L.A.—H. Williams 5 pass from Hostetler (H. Williams run), 9:01.

L.A.—FG Jaeger 28, 12:39.

Den—Tillman 1 pass from Millen (Elam kick), 13:34.

TEAM STATISTICS

	Denver	L.A. Raiders
First downs	16	16
Rushes-yards	21-63	32-128
Passing	228	177
Punt returns-yards	3-10	5-58
Kickoff returns-yards	7-121	2-39
Interception returns-yards	0-0	0-0
Comp.-att.-int.	20-33-0	16-31-0
Sacked-yards lost	2-14	5-34
Punts-average	8-42	6-41
Fumbles-lost	3-2	0-0
Penalties-yards	4-35	12-81
Time of possession	25:47	34:13

Attendance—60,016.

INDIVIDUAL STATISTICS

RUSHING—Denver, Millen 1-24, Clark 6-21, Milburn 5-13, L. Russell 3-9, Rivers 6-(minus 4). Los Angeles, H. Williams 19-72, Hostetler 7-28, C. Jones 4-18, Rathman 2-10.

PASSING—Denver, Millen 20-33-0-242. Los Angeles, Hostetler 16-31-0-211.

RECEIVING—Denver, Sharpe 9-89, Tillman 4-37, Miller 3-73, Milburn 2-31, Rivers 1-7, L. Russell 1-5. Los Angeles, T. Brown 6-73, H.

Williams 3-38, Rathman 3-23, Ismail 2-65, Wright 2-12.

MISSED FIELD GOAL ATTEMPTS—None.

INTERCEPTIONS—None.

KICKOFF RETURNS—Denver, Milburn 7-121. Los Angeles, Ismail 1-23, Wright 1-16.

PUNT RETURNS—Denver, Milburn 3-10. Los Angeles, T. Brown 5-58.

SACKS—Denver, Dronett 3, Fletcher 2. Los Angeles, Ball 1, White 1.

49ERS 38, CHARGERS 15

Sunday, December 11

San Francisco	7	14	3	14—38
San Diego	0	3	6	6—15

First Quarter

S.F.—Jones 10 pass from S. Young (Brien kick), 13:29.

Second Quarter

S.F.—Taylor 4 pass from S. Young (Brien kick), 9:21.

S.F.—Watters 4 run (Brien kick), 13:09.

S.D.—FG Carney 50, 15:00.

Third Quarter

S.D.—Means 12 run (run failed), 5:45.

S.F.—FG Brien 22, 10:44.

Fourth Quarter

S.F.—Floyd 1 run (Brien kick), 6:40.

S.D.—Martin 2 pass from Humphries (run failed), 9:32.

S.F.—Sanders 90 interception return (Brien kick), 14:28.

TEAM STATISTICS

	San Francisco	San Diego
First downs	27	20
Rushes-yards	33-119	22-56
Passing	298	322
Punt returns-yards	3-32	1-11
Kickoff returns-yards	3-54	7-179
Interception returns-yards	2-90	0-0
Comp.-att.-int.	25-32-0	25-43-2
Sacked-yards lost	1-6	2-15
Punts-average	1-47	3-43
Fumbles-lost	3-1	1-0
Penalties-yards	6-31	5-49
Time of possession	32:06	27:54

Attendance—62,105.

INDIVIDUAL STATISTICS

RUSHING—San Francisco, Watters 17-53, Floyd 10-34, Rice 1-18, A. Walker 2-10, S. Young 2-4, Grbac 1-0. San Diego, Means 18-50, Humphries 2-4, Bieniemy 1-3, Harmon 1-(minus 1).

PASSING—San Francisco, S. Young 25-32-0-304. San Diego, Humphries 25-43-2-337.

RECEIVING—San Francisco, Rice 12-144, Taylor 5-53, Jones 3-48, Watters 2-12, McCaffrey 1-23, Popson 1-20, Floyd 1-4. San Diego, Martin 9-172, Harmon 5-42, Jefferson 4-53, Mitchell 3-44, Pupunu 2-10, Seay 1-10, Means 1-6.

MISSED FIELD GOAL ATTEMPTS—San Diego, Carney 42.

INTERCEPTIONS—San Francisco, Norton 1-0, Sanders 1-90.

KICKOFF RETURNS—San Francisco, Carter 3-54. San Diego, Coleman 7-179.

PUNT RETURNS—San Francisco, Carter 3-32. San Diego, Gordon 1-11.

SACKS—San Francisco, Harris 1, B. Young 1. San Diego, O'Neal 1.

SAINTS 29, FALCONS 20

Sunday, December 11

New Orleans	3	10	3	13—29
Atlanta	0	14	3	3—20

First Quarter

N.O.—FG Andersen 45, 14:14.

Second Quarter

Atl—Heyward 9 run (N. Johnson kick), 5:05.

N.O.—Haynes 78 pass from Everett (Andersen kick), 5:27.

Atl—Rison 1 pass from J. George (N. Johnson kick), 7:54.

N.O.—FG Andersen 33, 14:21.

Third Quarter

N.O.—FG Andersen 31, 6:55.

Atl—FG N. Johnson 42, 13:38.

Fourth Quarter

N.O.—FG Andersen 34, 3:49.

N.O.—Early 5 pass from Everett (Andersen kick), 11:02.

Atl—FG N. Johnson 21, 12:23.

N.O.—FG Andersen 35, 14:32.

TEAM STATISTICS

	New Orleans	Atlanta
First downs	19	23
Rushes-yards	32-138	20-92
Passing	264	284
Punt returns-yards	0-0	1-(-5)
Kickoff returns-yards	4-72	8-206
Interception returns-yards	1-10	0-0
Comp.-att.-int.	18-31-0	25-42-1
Sacked-yards lost	1-9	0-0
Punts-average	2-45	3-42
Fumbles-lost	1-0	1-0
Penalties-yards	7-50	4-29
Time of possession	31:26	28:34
Attendance—61,307.		

INDIVIDUAL STATISTICS

RUSHING—New Orleans, Bates 20-79, Brown 10-55, Everett 1-2, Neal 1-2. Atlanta, Heyward 10-72, Pegram 7-11, J. George 3-9.

PASSING—New Orleans, Everett 18-31-0-273. Atlanta, J. George 25-42-1-284.

RECEIVING—New Orleans, Early 6-72, Haynes 5-103, Small 4-72, Smith 2-13, Brown 1-13. Atlanta, Rison 9-98, Sanders 7-64, Mathis 6-83, Emanuel 2-39, Heyward 1-0.

MISSED FIELD GOAL ATTEMPTS—None.

INTERCEPTIONS—New Orleans, Mills 1-10.

KICKOFF RETURNS—New Orleans, Hughes 3-58, Ned 1-14. Atlanta, Verdin 7-198, Pegram 1-8.

PUNT RETURNS—Atlanta, Verdin 1-(minus 5).

SACKS—Atlanta, C. Smith 1.

DOLPHINS 45, CHIEFS 28

Monday, December 12

Kansas City	7	7	7	7—28
Miami	0	14	21	10—45

First Quarter
K.C.—Birden 22 pass from Bono (Elliott kick), 9:24.
Second Quarter
Mia—Parmalee 10 pass from Marino (Stoyanovich kick), :06.
K.C.—Allen 3 run (Elliott kick), 5:55.
Mia—Fryar 4 pass from Marino (Stoyanovich kick), 11:41.

Third Quarter
Mia—Marino 4 run (Stoyanovich kick), 9:03.
Mia—Vincent 58 lateral from Atkins (Stoyanovich kick), 11:04.
K.C.—Vaughn 91 kickoff return (Elliott kick), 11:21.
Mia—Parmalee 47 run (Stoyanovich kick), 14:24.
Fourth Quarter
Mia—FG Stoyanovich 21, 7:33.
K.C.—Davis 15 pass from Bono (Elliott kick), 11:34.
Mia—Spikes 1 run (Stoyanovich kick), 11:52.

TEAM STATISTICS

	Kansas City	Miami
First downs	26	23
Rushes-yards	16-84	31-144
Passing	314	241
Punt returns-yards	0-0	1-17
Kickoff returns-yards	8-251	5-110
Interception returns-yards	0-0	3-97
Comp.-att.-int.	33-55-3	21-30-0
Sacked-yards lost	0-0	0-0
Punts-average	3-45	2-56
Fumbles-lost	1-0	0-0
Penalties-yards	9-54	5-24
Time of possession	28:45	31:15
Attendance—71,578.		

INDIVIDUAL STATISTICS

RUSHING—Kansas City, Anders 3-22, Hill 2-22, Allen 7-19, Bennett 3-19, Bono 1-2. Miami, Parmalee 19-127, Spikes 5-7, Craver 2-6, McDuffie 1-5, Marino 4-(minus 1).

PASSING—Kansas City, Bono 33-55-3-314. Miami, Marino 21-30-0-241.

RECEIVING—Kansas City, Birden 10-131, Allen 5-49, Bennett 4-18, Davis 3-39, Anders 3-27, Dawson 3-25, Walker 2-12, Hill 2-8, Martin 1-5. Miami, McDuffie 5-66, Craver 5-55, Saxon 3-37, Jackson 3-18, Parmalee 2-32, Fryar 2-16, Williams 1-17.

MISSED FIELD GOAL ATTEMPTS—None.

INTERCEPTIONS—Miami, Oliver 1-0, Atkins 1-18, Vincent 1-79.

KICKOFF RETURNS—Kansas City, Vaughn 8-251. Miami, McDuffie 3-61, Braxton 1-34, Spikes 1-15.

PUNT RETURNS—Miami, McDuffie 1-17.

SACKS—None.

WEEK 16

RESULTS

Detroit 41, Minnesota 19
San Francisco 42, Denver 19
Arizona 28, Cincinnati 7
Chicago 27, L.A. Rams 13
Green Bay 21, Atlanta 17
Indianapolis 10, Miami 6
Kansas City 31, Houston 9
L.A. Raiders 17, Seattle 16
N.Y. Giants 16, Philadelphia 13
New England 41, Buffalo 17
Pittsburgh 17, Cleveland 7
San Diego 21, N.Y. Jets 6
Tampa Bay 17, Washington 14
Dallas 24, New Orleans 16

STANDINGS

AFC EAST	W	L	T	Pct.	AFC CENTRAL	W	L	T	Pct.	AFC WEST	W	L	T	Pct.
Miami	9	6	0	.600	Pittsburgh	12	3	0	.800	San Diego	10	5	0	.667
New England	9	6	0	.600	Cleveland	10	5	0	.667	L.A. Raiders	9	6	0	.600
Buffalo	7	8	0	.467	Cincinnati	2	13	0	.133	Kansas City	8	7	0	.533
Indianapolis	7	8	0	.467	Houston	1	14	0	.067	Denver	7	8	0	.467
N.Y. Jets	6	9	0	.400						Seattle	6	9	0	.400

NFC EAST	W	L	T	Pct.	NFC CENTRAL	W	L	T	Pct.	NFC WEST	W	L	T	Pct.
Dallas	12	3	0	.800	Minnesota	9	6	0	.600	San Francisco	13	2	0	.867
N.Y. Giants	8	7	0	.533	Detroit	9	6	0	.600	New Orleans	6	9	0	.400
Arizona	8	7	0	.533	Chicago	9	6	0	.600	Atlanta	6	9	0	.400
Philadelphia	7	8	0	.467	Green Bay	8	7	0	.533	L.A. Rams	4	11	0	.267
Washington	2	13	0	.133	Tampa Bay	6	9	0	.400					

HIGHLIGHTS

Hero of the week: Kansas City defensive end Neil Smith, who had two sacks, four tackles, one pass breakup, one forced fumble and one fumble recovery in the Chiefs' 31-9 trouncing of Houston.

Goat of the week: Seattle's John Kasay, who missed a game-winning field-goal attempt with nine seconds left against the Los Angeles Raiders. With Seattle trailing, 17-16, Kasay hooked the 43-yard attempt.

Sub of the week: Denver quarterback Hugh Millen, who came on when John Elway was forced to leave the Broncos' game in San Francisco in the third quarter after being sacked six times. Millen guided the Broncos to a pair of third-quarter touchdowns and extended his string of completions to 20 over two games before an incompletion in the fourth quarter. The incompletion left him two completions shy of Joe Montana's NFL record. But Millen's heroics were too little, too late, as the 49ers rolled, 42-19.

Comeback of the week: With Tampa Bay trailing Washington, 14-10, with 10 minutes remaining, the Bucs' Vernon Turner returned a punt 37 yards to the Redskins' 28. Four plays later, Errict Rhett scored his second touchdown of the game on a three-yard run. Washington got the ball back twice but couldn't manage a first down as the Buccaneers held on to win their fourth game in a row. The winning streak is Tampa Bay's longest since 1979 and gave the Redskins a 0-8 home record, the first time in franchise history Washington failed to win a home game.

Blowout of the week: Behind quarterback Drew Bledsoe, New England buried Buffalo, 41-17, for its sixth consecutive victory, which moved the Patriots closer to their first playoff berth in eight seasons and eliminated the Bills from playoff contention. Bledsoe completed 22 of 31 passes for 276 yards and three touchdowns to rally New England from a 17-3 deficit. It was the Patriots' first victory in Buffalo since 1987.

Nail-biter of the week: Brad Daluiso's 18-yard field goal with 54 seconds left gave the New York Giants a 16-13 victory over Philadelphia. It was the Giants' fifth victory in a row, including their third straight in the final minute, and kept them in the playoff hunt. Daluiso's decisive kick was set up when Philadelphia's Jeff Sydner fumbled a kickoff return after running into one of his blockers. After Daluiso's kick, Bubby Brister completed four passes to move the Eagles from their 42 to the Giants' 32. The last of those completions was a five-yard toss to Victor Bailey on the right sideline. With the Eagles out of timeouts, Bailey was unable to get out of bounds but attempted to push the ball to the sideline. Giants linebacker Jessie Armstead picked up the dead ball and headed in the other direction. But officials stopped play and allowed Philadelphia to run a play. Brister spiked the ball, which stopped the clock with two seconds left. That was enough time to give Eddie Murray a chance to kick a 44-yard field goal. His boot was long enough but wide left.

Hit of the week: By Chicago defenders Maurice Douglass and Chris Zorich, on Los Angeles Rams quarterback Chris Chandler. Chandler looked like he might score on a scramble from the Bears' 3 in the second quarter. But Zorich and Douglass tackled him at the 1. Los Angeles settled for a field goal. The hit on Chandler caused a knot in his back that forced him to miss the second half of a game Chicago won, 27-13.

Oddity of the week: Green Bay made its final game in Milwaukee's County Stadium memorable, beating Atlanta, 21-17, to finish with a 107-63-1 record in Brewtown. Brett Favre scrambled nine yards down the right sideline for the game-winning score with 14 seconds left.

Top rusher: Seattle's Chris Warren ran 24 times for 122 yards and a touchdown in the Seahawks' 17-16 loss to the Los Angeles Raiders. Warren became the Seahawks' all-time single-season rushing leader (1,484 yards).

Top passer: Steve Young completed 20 of 29 passes

for 350 yards with three touchdowns and an interception as San Francisco won its 10th in a row.

Top receiver: The 49ers' Jerry Rice caught nine passes for 121 yards and a touchdown in the victory over Denver.

Notes: Cris Carter caught eight passes for 80 yards in Minnesota's 41-19 loss to Detroit, giving him an NFL single-season-record 119 receptions. Detroit's Mel Gray ran back a kickoff 98 yards for a touchdown, which allowed him to tie NFL records for career kickoff returns for touchdowns (six) and career punt/kickoff returns for touchdowns (nine).... New England became the first team to have five players with 51 catches apiece in a season when Vincent Brisby made four receptions (giving him 51) in the Patriots' win. The other New England players with 51 receptions: Ben Coates, Michael Timpson, LeRoy Thompson and Kevin Turner.... San Diego beat the New York Jets, 21-6, to clinch the AFC West title. Natrone Means ran for 73 yards to become the Chargers' single-season rushing leader (1,265).... A 28-7 win over Cincinnati ensured Arizona of its first non-losing season since 1984.... Pittsburgh beat Cleveland, 17-7, making the Steelers 21-4 against the Browns at Three Rivers Stadium.

Quote of the week: Pittsburgh cornerback Tim McKyer, after the Steelers beat Cleveland to clinch the AFC Central title: "I've been around, and everywhere I go, we kick butt."

GAME SUMMARIES

LIONS 41, VIKINGS 19
Saturday, December 17

Minnesota	3	10	6	0—19
Detroit	10	10	14	7—41

First Quarter
Det—FG Hanson 39, 5:46.
Min—FG Reveiz 34, 10:36.
Det—Gray 98 kickoff return (Hanson kick), 10:57.
Second Quarter
Min—Reed 20 pass from Moon (Reveiz kick), 4:55.
Det—FG Hanson 41, 9:21.
Det—Morton 18 pass from Krieg (Hanson kick), 12:11.
Min—FG Reveiz 26, 14:48.
Third Quarter
Det—Sanders 18 run (Hanson kick), 5:43.
Min—FG Reveiz 37, 11:39.
Min—FG Reveiz 48, 13:27.
Det—Sanders 64 run (Hanson kick), 13:48.
Fourth Quarter
Det—A. Carter 4 pass from Krieg (Hanson kick), 3:46.

TEAM STATISTICS

	Minnesota	Detroit
First downs	18	17
Rushes-yards	23-64	25-124
Passing	273	160
Punt returns-yards	2-33	3-22
Kickoff returns-yards	7-216	6-199
Interception returns-yards	0-0	1-3
Comp.-att.-int.	29-51-1	15-20-0
Sacked-yards lost	2-17	0-0
Punts-average	4-47	3-43
Fumbles-lost	1-0	1-1
Penalties-yards	10-93	5-40
Time of possession	34:19	25:41
Attendance—73,881.		

INDIVIDUAL STATISTICS
RUSHING—Minnesota, Allen 15-35, R. Smith 2-12, Lee 3-10, Moon 2-6, Graham 1-1. Detroit, Sanders 17-110, Perriman 1-9, D. Moore 3-3, Krieg 4-2.
PASSING—Minnesota, Moon 15-22-1-186, Johnson 14-29-0-104. Detroit, Krieg 15-20-0-160.
RECEIVING—Minnesota, C. Carter 8-80, Reed 7-91, Ismail 4-43, A. Jordan 4-26, R. Smith 2-22, Lee 2-13, Palmer 1-12, Allen 1-3. Detroit, Sanders 4-27, H. Moore 2-62, Morton 2-22, Holman 2-20, Perriman 2-10, Hallock 1-9, Lynch 1-6, A. Carter 1-4.
MISSED FIELD GOAL ATTEMPTS—None.
INTERCEPTIONS—Detroit, Massey 1-3.
KICKOFF RETURNS—Minnesota, R. Smith 7-216. Detroit, Gray 4-172, Lynch 2-27.
PUNT RETURNS—Minnesota, Palmer 2-33. Detroit, Clay 2-8, Gray 1-14.
SACKS—Detroit, Swilling 1, Pritchett ½, Thomas ½.

49ERS 42, BRONCOS 19
Saturday, December 17

Denver	0	6	13	0—19
San Francisco	14	14	14	0—42

First Quarter
S.F.—Watters 12 pass from Young (Brien kick), 5:24.
S.F.—Rice 23 pass from Young (Brien kick), 5:46.
Second Quarter
S.F.—Floyd 11 run (Brien kick), :05.
Den—FG Elam 28, 5:41.
S.F.—Floyd 1 run (Brien kick), 12:56.
Den—FG Elam 45, 15:00.
Third Quarter
Den—Milburn 11 run (Elam kick), 6:26.
S.F.—Watters 9 run (Brien kick), 7:46.
Den—Clark 1 run (run failed), 8:45.
S.F.—Watters 65 pass from Young (Brien kick), 9:05.

TEAM STATISTICS

	Denver	San Francisco
First downs	20	25
Rushes-yards	15-48	30-102
Passing	286	386
Punt returns-yards	0-0	2-15
Kickoff returns-yards	7-148	4-85
Interception returns-yards	1-2	1-0
Comp.-att.-int.	29-41-1	23-33-1
Sacked-yards lost	7-37	1-8
Punts-average	4-40	3-37
Fumbles-lost	3-2	1-0
Penalties-yards	6-25	4-26
Time of possession	27:15	32:45
Attendance—64,884.		

INDIVIDUAL STATISTICS
RUSHING—Denver, Milburn 5-19, Clark 6-19, Rivers 2-6, Millen 2-4. San Francisco, Watters 13-40, Floyd 8-28, Loville 5-22, Young 1-11, Grbac 1-2, Walker 2-(minus 1).
PASSING—Denver, Elway 10-18-1-106, Millen 19-23-0-217. San Francisco, Young 20-29-1-350, Grbac 3-4-0-44.
RECEIVING—Denver, Sharpe 7-74, Milburn 5-19, Tillman 4-52, Miller 3-118, Russell 3-30, Evans 3-24, Rivers 2-5, Kimbrough 1-8, Clark 1-(minus 7). San Francisco, Rice 9-121, Watters 4-106, Floyd 3-15, Jones 2-38, Carter 1-44, Popson 1-24, Loville 1-19, Singleton 1-15, Taylor 1-12.
MISSED FIELD GOAL ATTEMPTS—None.
INTERCEPTIONS—Denver, Alexander 1-2. San Francisco, Sanders 1-0.
KICKOFF RETURNS—Denver, Milburn 5-123, Campbell 1-11, Clark 1-14. San Francisco, Carter 4-85.
PUNT RETURNS—San Francisco, Carter 2-15.
SACKS—Denver, Dronett 1. San Francisco, R. Hall 3, Brown 2, Jackson 1, Woodall 1.

PATRIOTS 41, BILLS 17
Sunday, December 18

New England	3	14	14	10—41
Buffalo	10	7	0	0—17

First Quarter
N.E.—FG Bahr 33, 3:15.
Buf—Turner 26 pass from Reich (Christie kick), 7:16.
Buf—FG Christie 24, 12:00.

Second Quarter
Buf—Gardner 3 run (Christie kick), 1:56.
N.E.—Coates 4 pass from Bledsoe (Bahr kick), 5:53.
N.E.—Brisby 7 pass from Bledsoe (Bahr kick), 13:48.
Third Quarter
N.E.—Reynolds 25 fumble return (Bahr kick), 1:00.
N.E.—Brisby 6 pass from Bledsoe (Bahr kick), 8:01.
Fourth Quarter
N.E.—Butts 1 run (Bahr kick), 1:32.
N.E.—FG Bahr 20, 8:35.

TEAM STATISTICS

	New England	Buffalo
First downs	23	16
Rushes-yards	34-101	26-135
Passing	276	191
Punt returns-yards	2-14	1-16
Kickoff returns-yards	4-67	5-78
Interception returns-yards	2-40	0-0
Comp.-att.-int.	22-31-0	19-29-2
Sacked-yards lost	0-0	2-16
Punts-average	3-48	3-36
Fumbles-lost	2-0	3-3
Penalties-yards	6-45	5-35
Time of possession	33:22	26:38

Attendance—56,784.

INDIVIDUAL STATISTICS

RUSHING—New England, Gash 15-56, Butts 13-34, Turner 1-11, Thompson 3-1, Bledsoe 1-0, Zolak 1-(minus 1). Buffalo, Thomas 12-77, K. Davis 9-43, Gardner 2-8, Jourdain 2-6, Reed 1-1.
PASSING—New England, Bledsoe 22-31-0-276, Zolak 0-0-0-0. Buffalo, Reich 19-29-2-207.
RECEIVING—New England, Coates 5-59, Burke 4-41, Brisby 4-38, Timpson 3-71, Crittenden 2-36, Turner 2-19, Gash 1-8, Thompson 1-4. Buffalo, Reed 6-112, Gardner 3-8, Jourdain 3-7, Beebe 2-22, Metzelaars 2-(minus 3), Turner 1-26, Thomas 1-22, Copeland 1-13.
MISSED FIELD GOAL ATTEMPTS—None.
INTERCEPTIONS—New England, Hurst 1-19, Whigham 1-21.
KICKOFF RETURNS—New England, Crittenden 2-30, Thompson 2-37. Buffalo, Jourdain 3-67, Copeland 1-11, Pike 1-0.
PUNT RETURNS—New England, T. Brown 2-14. Buffalo, Burris 1-16.
SACKS—New England, A. Jones 1, M. Jones 1.

BEARS 27, RAMS 13

Sunday, December 17

L.A. Rams	7	3	0	3—13
Chicago	3	14	3	7—27

First Quarter
L.A.—Chandler 1 run (Zendejas kick), 4:48.
Chi—FG Butler 41, 13:56.
Second Quarter
L.A.—FG Zendejas 18, 2:29.
Chi—Jennings 3 pass from Walsh (Butler kick), 7:39.
Chi—Harris 2 run (Butler kick), 14:39.
Third Quarter
Chi—FG Butler 30, 12:51.
Fourth Quarter
L.A.—FG Zendejas 21, 5:50.
Chi—Tillman 1 run (Butler kick), 11:24.

TEAM STATISTICS

	L.A. Rams	Chicago
First downs	13	19
Rushes-yards	19-37	42-163
Passing	206	135
Punt returns-yards	2-33	4-10
Kickoff returns-yards	6-134	4-116
Interception returns-yards	0-0	0-0
Comp.-att.-int.	17-35-0	12-25-0
Sacked-yards lost	2-8	0-0
Punts-average	5-46	5-45
Fumbles-lost	3-1	1-0
Penalties-yards	1-5	4-33
Time of possession	25:29	34:31

Attendance—56,276.

INDIVIDUAL STATISTICS

RUSHING—Los Angeles, J. Bailey 3-9, Bettis 8-7, Griffith 4-7, Miller 1-7, Chandler 2-4, Lester 1-3. Chicago, Harris 23-92, Tillman 14-69, Green 1-4, Conway 1-0, Walsh 3-(minus 2).
PASSING—Los Angeles, Chandler 8-13-0-145, Miller 9-22-0-69.

Chicago, Walsh 12-25-0-135.
RECEIVING—Los Angeles, J. Bailey 7-44, Hester 3-58, Anderson 2-69, Bettis 1-12, Kinchen 1-10, Drayton 1-8, Brantley 1-7, Griffith 1-6. Chicago, Graham 4-66, Conway 3-40, Harris 2-20, Waddle 1-7, Jennings 1-3, Green 1-(minus 1).
MISSED FIELD GOAL ATTEMPTS—Los Angeles, Zendejas 42.
INTERCEPTIONS—None.
KICKOFF RETURNS—Los Angeles, Lang 4-85, J. Bailey 1-28, Kinchen 1-21. Chicago, Lewis 2-74, Carter 1-26, Green 1-16.
PUNT RETURNS—Los Angeles, Kinchen 2-33. Chicago, Graham 4-10.
SACKS—Chicago, A. Fontenot 1, Armstrong ½, Spellman ½.

CHARGERS 21, JETS 6

Sunday, December 18

San Diego	0	7	7	7—21
N.Y. Jets	3	3	0	0— 6

First Quarter
N.Y.—FG Lowery 38, 14:23.
Second Quarter
N.Y.—FG Lowery 30, 11:05.
S.D.—Seay 2 pass from Humphries (Carney kick), 13:51.
Third Quarter
S.D.—Martin 44 pass from Humphries (Carney kick), 7:32.
Fourth Quarter
S.D.—Martin 60 pass from Humphries (Carney kick), 9:55.

TEAM STATISTICS

	San Diego	N.Y. Jets
First downs	24	14
Rushes-yards	38-152	21-76
Passing	251	167
Punt returns-yards	2-30	3-37
Kickoff returns-yards	3-58	4-58
Interception returns-yards	0-0	0-0
Comp.-att.-int.	19-26-0	20-32-0
Sacked-yards lost	3-29	5-28
Punts-average	5-40	7-43
Fumbles-lost	2-2	2-1
Penalties-yards	5-45	6-72
Time of possession	30:17	29:43

Attendance—48,213.

INDIVIDUAL STATISTICS

RUSHING—San Diego, Means 23-73, Culver 6-59, Bieniemy 6-22, Gilbert 3-(minus 2). New York, R. Anderson 6-23, J. Johnson 9-22, Murrell 3-18, Trudeau 3-13.
PASSING—San Diego, Humphries 19-26-0-280. New York, Esiason 9-12-0-96, Trudeau 11-20-0-99.
RECEIVING—San Diego, Seay 6-42, Jefferson 4-53, Martin 3-116, Pupunu 3-30, D. Young 2-26, Harmon 1-13. New York, R. Anderson 7-64, Moore 6-52, Mitchell 3-23, Murrell 2-21, Monk 1-20, Thornton 1-15.
MISSED FIELD GOAL ATTEMPTS—None.
INTERCEPTIONS—None.
KICKOFF RETURNS—San Diego, Coleman 3-58. New York, Glenn 4-58.
PUNT RETURNS—San Diego, Gordon 2-30. New York, Hicks 3-37.
SACKS—San Diego, Lee 2, White 1½, O'Neal 1, Parrella ½. New York, Frase 1, Hasty 1, Lageman ½, Lewis ½.

BUCCANEERS 17, REDSKINS 14

Sunday, December 18

Tampa Bay	0	10	0	7—17
Washington	0	14	0	0—14

Second Quarter
Was—Ervins 15 pass from Shuler (Lohmiller kick), :49.
T.B.—FG Husted 42, 5:29.
T.B.—Rhett 1 run (Husted kick), 9:18.
Was—Ellard 8 pass from Shuler (Lohmiller kick), 14:28.
Fourth Quarter
T.B.—Rhett 3 run (Husted kick), 7:58.

TEAM STATISTICS

	Tampa Bay	Washington
First downs	20	14
Rushes-yards	33-108	23-73
Passing	267	194
Punt returns-yards	3-50	1-19
Kickoff returns-yards	3-63	3-77
Interception returns-yards	0-0	2-2
Comp.-att.-int.	19-34-2	17-35-0
Sacked-yards lost	0-0	1-7

	Tampa Bay	Washington
Punts-average	4-32	6-41
Fumbles-lost	0-0	1-0
Penalties-yards	6-41	3-20
Time of possession	34:06	25:54
Attendance—47,315.		

INDIVIDUAL STATISTICS

RUSHING—Tampa Bay, Rhett 23-64, Workman 6-17, Wilson 2-15, Erickson 2-12. Washington, Ervins 17-57, Smith 1-7, Shuler 2-6, Howard 1-4, Brooks 2-(minus 1).

PASSING—Tampa Bay, Erickson 19-34-2-267. Washington, Shuler 17-35-0-201.

RECEIVING—Tampa Bay, Dawsey 7-116, Wilson 3-71, Rhett 3-26, McDowell 3-16, Armstrong 2-22, Thomas 1-16. Washington, Ellard 4-60, Howard 4-60, Ervins 3-18, Mitchell 3-12, Smith 2-21, Winans 1-30.

MISSED FIELD GOAL ATTEMPTS—Tampa Bay, Husted 46, 38. Washington, Lohmiller 44.

INTERCEPTIONS—Washington, Grant 1-0, Stowe 1-2.

KICKOFF RETURNS—Tampa Bay, Turner 2-47, Moore 1-16. Washington, Mitchell 3-77.

PUNT RETURNS—Tampa Bay, Turner 3-50. Washington, Mitchell 1-19.

SACKS—Tampa Bay, Bussey 1.

PACKERS 21, FALCONS 17

Sunday, December 18

Atlanta	3	6	0	8—	17
Green Bay	14	0	0	7—	21

First Quarter
G.B.—Sharpe 8 pass from Favre (Jacke kick), 5:40.
Atl—FG Johnson 20, 10:13.
G.B.—Morgan 15 pass from Favre (Jacke kick), 14:47.
Second Quarter
Atl—Heyward 2 run (pass failed), 8:22.
Fourth Quarter
Atl—Mathis 5 pass from Hebert (Rison pass from Hebert), 9:07.
G.B.—Favre 9 run (Jacke kick), 14:46.

TEAM STATISTICS

	Atlanta	Green Bay
First downs	22	23
Rushes-yards	22-97	21-74
Passing	236	310
Punt returns-yards	3-13	1-3
Kickoff returns-yards	4-46	4-74
Interception returns-yards	1-33	1-0
Comp.-att.-int.	21-45-1	29-44-1
Sacked-yards lost	0-0	2-11
Punts-average	5-32	4-45
Fumbles-lost	1-1	1-0
Penalties-yards	1-5	7-57
Time of possession	28:11	31:49
Attendance—54,885.		

INDIVIDUAL STATISTICS

RUSHING—Atlanta, Heyward 21-77, Hebert 1-20. Green Bay, Bennett 13-46, Favre 4-12, Cobb 3-11, Sharpe 1-5.

PASSING—Atlanta, J. George 1-3-0-15, Hebert 20-41-1-221, Klein 0-1-0-0. Green Bay, Favre 29-44-1-321.

RECEIVING—Atlanta, Sanders 7-46, Rison 6-95, Mathis 5-40, Emanuel 2-36, Heyward 1-19. Green Bay, Bennett 8-101, Brooks 8-74, Chmura 5-63, Morgan 4-50, Sharpe 3-33, Cobb 1-0.

MISSED FIELD GOAL ATTEMPTS—Green Bay, Jacke 51, 37.

INTERCEPTIONS—Atlanta, Walker 1-33. Green Bay, Evans 1-0.

KICKOFF RETURNS—Atlanta, Verdin 3-30, Pegram 1-16. Green Bay, Harris 3-54, Brooks 1-20.

PUNT RETURNS—Atlanta, Verdin 3-13. Green Bay, Brooks 1-3.

SACKS—Atlanta, Archambeau 1, Goathers 1.

COLTS 10, DOLPHINS 6

Sunday, December 18

Miami	3	0	3	0—	6
Indianapolis	7	0	0	3—	10

First Quarter
Mia—FG Stoyanovich 33, 11:26.
Ind—Brewer 75 punt return (Biasucci kick), 14:37.
Third Quarter
Mia—FG Stoyanovich 19, 4:56.
Fourth Quarter
Ind—FG Biasucci 19, 6:50.

TEAM STATISTICS

	Miami	Indianapolis
First downs	17	12
Rushes-yards	26-97	30-143
Passing	214	69
Punt returns-yards	1-6	4-107
Kickoff returns-yards	3-54	2-48
Interception returns-yards	0-0	0-0
Comp.-att.-int.	21-37-0	9-19-0
Sacked-yards lost	2-11	2-6
Punts-average	5-45	4-43
Fumbles-lost	1-0	0-0
Penalties-yards	4-30	2-15
Time of possession	33:30	26:30
Attendance—58,867.		

INDIVIDUAL STATISTICS

RUSHING—Miami, Spikes 7-59, Parmalee 16-33, Saxon 3-5. Indianapolis, Faulk 16-64, Harbaugh 7-33, Warren 3-28, Potts 2-10, Humphrey 1-4, Turner 1-4.

PASSING—Miami, Marino 21-37-0-225. Indianapolis, Harbaugh 9-19-0-75.

RECEIVING—Miami, Fryar 5-61, Parmalee 5-44, Jackson 4-64, McDuffie 3-50, Saxon 2-4, Ingram 1-6, Craver 1-(minus 4). Indianapolis, Dawkins 4-41, Faulk 2-15, Turner 1-8, Arbuckle 1-7, Humphrey 1-4.

MISSED FIELD GOAL ATTEMPTS—Indianapolis, Biasucci 40, 42.

INTERCEPTIONS—None.

KICKOFF RETURNS—Miami, McDuffie 1-21, Saxon 1-12, Spikes 1-21. Indianapolis, Humphrey 2-48.

PUNT RETURNS—Miami, McDuffie 1-6. Indianapolis, Brewer 4-107.

SACKS—Miami, Cross 1, Smith 1. Indianapolis, McCoy 2.

CARDINALS 28, BENGALS 7

Sunday, December 18

Cincinnati	0	0	7	0—	7
Arizona	14	7	0	7—	28

First Quarter
Ari—Hearst 1 run (Davis kick), 4:59.
Ari—Centers 10 pass from Hearst (Davis kick), 11:49.
Second Quarter
Ari—Proehl 15 pass from Schroeder (Davis kick), :09.
Third Quarter
Cin—Pickens 4 pass from Blake (Pelfrey kick), 7:21.
Fourth Quarter
Ari—Centers 10 run (Davis kick), 4:54.

TEAM STATISTICS

	Cincinnati	Arizona
First downs	12	24
Rushes-yards	14-64	39-152
Passing	125	223
Punt returns-yards	5-28	5-20
Kickoff returns-yards	3-69	2-54
Interception returns-yards	0-0	1-0
Comp.-att.-int.	10-28-1	21-34-0
Sacked-yards lost	4-24	1-7
Punts-average	8-50	7-44
Fumbles-lost	2-2	3-0
Penalties-yards	6-37	8-69
Time of possession	18:29	41:31
Attendance—50,110.		

INDIVIDUAL STATISTICS

RUSHING—Cincinnati, Green 7-24, Scott 1-23, Cothran 3-15, Blake 2-1, Fenner 1-1. Arizona, Hearst 13-62, Higgs 12-45, Moore 8-21, Centers 4-13, Schroeder 1-10, Samuels 1-1.

PASSING—Cincinnati, Blake 10-28-1-149. Arizona, Schroeder 12-20-0-122, Beuerlein 8-13-0-98, Hearst 1-1-0-10.

RECEIVING—Cincinnati, Pickens 5-59, To. McGee 2-65, Green 2-17, Scott 1-8. Arizona, Clark 7-101, R. Hill 4-40, Centers 4-28, Proehl 2-26, Samuels 2-13, Reeves 1-10, Fann 1-10.

MISSED FIELD GOAL ATTEMPTS—Arizona, Davis 51.

INTERCEPTIONS—Arizona, Joyner 1-0.

KICKOFF RETURNS—Cincinnati, Hardy 2-49, Ball 1-20. Arizona, Levy 2-54.

PUNT RETURNS—Cincinnati, Pickens 4-28, Rog. Jones 1-0. Arizona, Robinson 5-20.

SACKS—Cincinnati, Francis 1. Arizona, McCants 1, Swann 1, Wilson 1, Joyner ½, Lynch ½.

STEELERS 17, BROWNS 7
Sunday, December 18

Cleveland	0	7	0	0— 7
Pittsburgh	14	0	0	3—17

First Quarter
Pit—Thigpen 40 pass from O'Donnell (Anderson kick), 3:30.
Pit—Foster 1 run (Anderson kick), 10:39.
Second Quarter
Cle—Carrier 14 pass from Testaverde (Stover kick), 14:50.
Fourth Quarter
Pit—FG Anderson 49, 5:10.

TEAM STATISTICS

	Cleveland	Pittsburgh
First downs	21	18
Rushes-yards	24-86	41-123
Passing	245	153
Punt returns-yards	3-25	2-5
Kickoff returns-yards	4-85	2-26
Interception returns-yards	0-0	2-9
Comp.-att.-int.	21-42-2	10-18-0
Sacked-yards lost	1-5	2-22
Punts-average	6-39	7-38
Fumbles-lost	3-1	0-0
Penalties-yards	10-96	6-62
Time of possession	26:34	33:26
Attendance—60,808.		

INDIVIDUAL STATISTICS
RUSHING—Cleveland, Byner 7-26, Metcalf 8-26, Hoard 8-25, Testaverde 1-9. Pittsburgh, Foster 32-106, J.L. Williams 5-15, Mills 1-2, O'Donnell 3-0.
PASSING—Cleveland, Testaverde 21-42-2-250. Pittsburgh, O'Donnell 10-18-0-175.
RECEIVING—Cleveland, Alexander 5-74, Hoard 5-38, Metcalf 3-21, Carrier 2-40, Byner 2-32, Jackson 2-25, Kinchen 2-20. Pittsburgh, Thigpen 4-74, Green 2-44, Foster 2-13, Mills 1-42, J.L. Williams 1-2.
MISSED FIELD GOAL ATTEMPTS—Pittsburgh, Anderson 32.
INTERCEPTIONS—Pittsburgh, Brown 1-9, G. Jones 1-0.
KICKOFF RETURNS—Cleveland, Baldwin 3-59, Metcalf 1-26. Pittsburgh, Johnson 1-20, Mills 1-6.
PUNT RETURNS—Cleveland, Carrier 3-25. Pittsburgh, Johnson 2-5.
SACKS—Cleveland, Burnett 1, Perry 1. Pittsburgh, Woodson 1.

CHIEFS 31, OILERS 9
Sunday, December 18

Houston	3	0	0	6— 9
Kansas City	7	0	14	10—31

First Quarter
K.C.—Walker 10 pass from Montana (Elliott kick), 4:34.
Hou—FG Del Greco 48, 12:31.
Third Quarter
K.C.—Dawson 25 pass from Montana (Elliott kick), 3:22.
K.C.—Bennett 12 run (Elliott kick), 10:36.
Fourth Quarter
Hou—Jeffires 20 pass from Tolliver (pass failed), :05.
K.C.—FG Elliott 21, 2:07.
K.C.—Hill 8 run (Elliott kick), 10:50.

TEAM STATISTICS

	Houston	Kansas City
First downs	16	17
Rushes-yards	29-119	30-135
Passing	104	228
Punt returns-yards	3-12	1-3
Kickoff returns-yards	5-117	3-44
Interception returns-yards	0-0	1-5
Comp.-att.-int.	15-26-1	16-27-0
Sacked-yards lost	3-12	1-7
Punts-average	4-42	5-44
Fumbles-lost	4-4	0-0
Penalties-yards	4-35	8-45
Time of possession	30:03	29:57
Attendance—74,474.		

INDIVIDUAL STATISTICS
RUSHING—Houston, White 21-88, Brown 7-29, Tolliver 1-2. Kansas City, Hill 14-63, Allen 10-42, Bennett 5-23, Anders 1-7.
PASSING—Houston, Tolliver 15-26-1-116. Kansas City, Montana 16-27-0-235.
RECEIVING—Houston, Slaughter 5-34, Jeffires 4-57, P. Carter 2-9,

White 2-8, Lewis 1-6, McNair 1-2. Kansas City, Dawson 5-101, Anders 5-39, Birden 2-45, Walker 2-15, Davis 1-33, Allen 1-2.
MISSED FIELD GOAL ATTEMPTS—None.
INTERCEPTIONS—Kansas City, Mincy 1-5.
KICKOFF RETURNS—Houston, McNair 5-117. Kansas City, Vaughn 3-44.
PUNT RETURNS—Houston, Givins 3-12. Kansas City, Carter 1-3.
SACKS—Houston, Davidson 1. Kansas City, Smith 2, Mickel 1.

GIANTS 16, EAGLES 13
Sunday, December 18

N.Y. Giants	0	3	3	10—16
Philadelphia	7	3	3	0—13

First Quarter
Phi—Bavaro 27 pass from Brister (Murray kick), 12:15.
Second Quarter
Phi—FG Murray 32, 9:47.
N.Y.—FG Daluiso 47, 14:56.
Third Quarter
Phi—FG Murray 42, 4:55.
N.Y.—FG Daluiso 19, 13:04.
Fourth Quarter
N.Y.—Meggett 5 run (Daluiso kick), 11:06.
N.Y.—FG Daluiso 18, 14:06.

TEAM STATISTICS

	N.Y. Giants	Philadelphia
First downs	20	12
Rushes-yards	34-122	16-51
Passing	230	171
Punt returns-yards	4-25	2-29
Kickoff returns-yards	4-57	5-78
Interception returns-yards	1-0	1-7
Comp.-att.-int.	18-27-1	25-39-1
Sacked-yards lost	5-34	1-11
Punts-average	6-39	6-43
Fumbles-lost	3-1	1-1
Penalties-yards	5-78	11-98
Time of possession	32:21	27:39
Attendance—64,540.		

INDIVIDUAL STATISTICS
RUSHING—New York, Hampton 24-61, Da. Brown 6-47, Meggett 3-11, Rasheed 1-3. Philadelphia, Walker 4-23, Hebron 5-21, Brister 1-7, C. Williams 1-6, Garner 5-(minus 6).
PASSING—New York, Da. Brown 18-27-1-264. Philadelphia, Brister 25-39-1-182.
RECEIVING—New York, Sherrard 5-81, Calloway 5-73, Meggett 4-66, Pierce 1-17, Hampton 1-14, Cross 1-12, Rasheed 1-1. Philadelphia, Walker 7-37, Barnett 3-33, C. Williams 3-19, Garner 3-15, Hebron 3-14, Bavaro 2-45, Bailey 2-15, M. Johnson 1-2, Joseph 1-2.
MISSED FIELD GOAL ATTEMPTS—Philadelphia, Murray 44.
INTERCEPTIONS—New York, Randolph 1-0. Philadelphia, Zordich 1-7.
KICKOFF RETURNS—New York, Meggett 3-40, Marshall 1-17. Philadelphia, Sydner 2-48, M. Johnson 1-0, Joseph 1-11, Walker 1-19.
PUNT RETURNS—New York, Meggett 4-25. Philadelphia, Sydner 2-29.
SACKS—New York, Armstead 1. Philadelphia, Flores 2, Harmon 1, Thomas 1, Team 1.

RAIDERS 17, SEAHAWKS 16
Sunday, December 18

L.A. Raiders	0	10	0	7—17
Seattle	0	10	3	3—16

Second Quarter
L.A.—Williams 5 run (Jaeger kick), 1:22.
Sea—FG Kasay 41, 5:18.
L.A.—FG Jaeger 24, 9:40.
Sea—C. Warren 33 run (Kasay kick), 14:00.
Third Quarter
Sea—FG Kasay 50, 6:13.
Fourth Quarter
Sea—FG Kasay 33, 5:25.
L.A.—Brown 77 pass from Hostetler (Jaeger kick), 5:47.

TEAM STATISTICS

	L.A. Raiders	Seattle
First downs	16	15
Rushes-yards	27-116	30-125
Passing	206	155
Punt returns-yards	5-49	5-59

	L.A. Raiders	Seattle
Kickoff returns-yards	5-104	4-96
Interception returns-yards	0-0	0-0
Comp.-att.-int.	17-29-0	14-34-0
Sacked-yards lost	5-29	2-11
Punts-average	8-42	8-44
Fumbles-lost	0-0	4-0
Penalties-yards	7-50	9-50
Time of possession	29:36	30:24

Attendance—53,301.

INDIVIDUAL STATISTICS

RUSHING—Los Angeles, H. Williams 20-93, Rathman 2-12, Hostetler 4-9, Jones 1-2. Seattle, C. Warren 24-122, Strong 3-9, McGwire 3-(minus 6).

PASSING—Los Angeles, Hostetler 17-29-0-235. Seattle, McGwire 14-34-0-166.

RECEIVING—Los Angeles, Brown 4-107, Ismail 4-65, Rathman 3-26, Wright 2-17, Glover 2-9, H. Williams 1-6, J. Williams 1-5. Seattle, Blades 5-70, Green 4-32, Martin 3-47, C. Warren 2-17.

MISSED FIELD GOAL ATTEMPTS—Seattle, Kasay 43.

INTERCEPTIONS—None.

KICKOFF RETURNS—Los Angeles, Ismail 4-82, Wright 1-22. Seattle, Bryant 4-96.

PUNT RETURNS—Los Angeles, Brown 5-49. Seattle, Martin 5-59.

SACKS—Los Angeles, McGlockton 2. Seattle, Sinclair 2, Porter 1½, Edwards 1½.

COWBOYS 24, SAINTS 16

Monday, December 19

Dallas	7	3	7	7—24
New Orleans	0	6	3	7—16

First Quarter
Dal—Tolbert 54 interception return (Boniol kick), 4:36.
Second Quarter
N.O.—FG Andersen 21, 11:29.
N.O.—FG Andersen 32, 14:10.
Dal—FG Boniol 30, 15:00.

Third Quarter
Dal—E. Smith 1 run (Boniol kick), 8:33.
N.O.—FG Andersen 29, 13:31.
Fourth Quarter
Dal—D. Smith 13 interception return (Boniol kick), 5:43.
N.O.—D. Brown 4 run (Andersen kick), 9:23.

TEAM STATISTICS

	Dallas	New Orleans
First downs	23	19
Rushes-yards	34-105	25-90
Passing	175	147
Punt returns-yards	0-0	1-6
Kickoff returns-yards	5-101	4-90
Interception returns-yards	3-67	2-66
Comp.-att.-int.	21-28-2	18-32-3
Sacked-yards lost	0-0	2-15
Punts-average	2-46	1-48
Fumbles-lost	0-0	1-0
Penalties-yards	5-58	5-36
Time of possession	33:09	26:51

Attendance—67,323.

INDIVIDUAL STATISTICS

RUSHING—Dallas, E. Smith 19-74, Johnston 4-11, Thomas 6-7, K. Williams 1-7, Aikman 3-3, Agee 1-3. New Orleans, Bates 17-68, D. Brown 6-19, Neal 1-2, Everett 1-1.

PASSING—Dallas, Aikman 21-28-2-175. New Orleans, Everett 18-32-3-162.

RECEIVING—Dallas, Irvin 6-71, Novacek 5-50, E. Smith 5-21, Johnston 4-21, K. Williams 1-12. New Orleans, Haynes 7-59, Early 4-44, Small 3-32, D. Brown 2-15, Bates 1-10, Muster 1-2.

MISSED FIELD GOAL ATTEMPTS—Dallas, Boniol 20. New Orleans, Andersen 40.

INTERCEPTIONS—Dallas, D. Smith 2-13, Tolbert 1-54. New Orleans, Conner 1-56, Spencer 1-10.

KICKOFF RETURNS—Dallas, K. Williams 5-101. New Orleans, Hughes 3-74, Ned 1-16.

PUNT RETURNS—New Orleans, Hughes 1-6.

SACKS—Dallas, Edwards 1, Maryland 1.

WEEK 17

RESULTS

Atlanta 10, Arizona 6
Cincinnati 33, Philadelphia 30
Cleveland 35, Seattle 9
Green Bay 34, Tampa Bay 19
Houston 24, N.Y. Jets 10
Indianapolis 10, Buffalo 9
Kansas City 19, L.A. Raiders 9
N.Y. Giants 15, Dallas 10
New England 13, Chicago 3
New Orleans 30, Denver 28
San Diego 37, Pittsburgh 34
Washington 24, L.A. Rams 21
Miami 27, Detroit 20
Minnesota 21, San Francisco 14

STANDINGS

AFC EAST	W	L	T	Pct.
Miami	10	6	0	.625
New England	10	6	0	.625
Indianapolis	8	8	0	.500
Buffalo	7	9	0	.438
N.Y. Jets	6	10	0	.375

AFC CENTRAL	W	L	T	Pct.
Pittsburgh	12	4	0	.750
Cleveland	11	5	0	.688
Cincinnati	3	13	0	.188
Houston	2	14	0	.125

AFC WEST	W	L	T	Pct.
San Diego	11	5	0	.688
Kansas City	9	7	0	.563
L.A. Raiders	9	7	0	.563
Denver	7	9	0	.438
Seattle	6	10	0	.375

NFC EAST	W	L	T	Pct.
Dallas	12	4	0	.750
N.Y. Giants	9	7	0	.563
Arizona	8	8	0	.500
Philadelphia	7	9	0	.438
Washington	3	13	0	.188

NFC CENTRAL	W	L	T	Pct.
Minnesota	10	6	0	.625
Detroit	9	7	0	.563
Green Bay	9	7	0	.563
Chicago	9	7	0	.563
Tampa Bay	6	10	0	.375

NFC WEST	W	L	T	Pct.
San Francisco	13	3	0	.813
New Orleans	7	9	0	.438
Atlanta	7	9	0	.438
L.A. Rams	4	12	0	.250

HIGHLIGHTS

Hero of the week: Green Bay wide receiver Sterling Sharpe, who had seven receptions for 109 yards and three touchdowns in the first half of a 34-19 victory over Tampa Bay. But early in the second half, Sharpe sustained a neck injury that appeared to be career-threatening. Sharpe finished with nine catches for 132 yards and three touchdowns. His 18 touchdown catches in 1994 broke Don Hutson's club record of 17.

Goat of the week: Chicago's Kevin Butler, who missed two potential game-tying field goals (one was blocked, the other shanked) in the second half of the Bears' 13-3 loss to New England. Despite the loss, Chicago made the playoffs as the NFC's sixth seed. That meant an unprecedented four NFC Central teams would play in the postseason. The victory allowed the Patriots to qualify for the playoffs for the first time since 1986.

Sub of the week: Houston quarterback Bucky Richardson, who was making his first start since the team's sixth game. Richardson led Houston to a 24-10 victory over the New York Jets, ending the Oilers' 11-game losing streak. Richardson completed 17 of 29 passes for 220 yards and two inteceptions. He also rushed for 46 yards on six carries, including a one-yard touchdown run.

Comeback of the week: Trailing Philadelphia, 30-20, with 5:13 left, Cincinnati scored a touchdown and two field goals in the final 3:32 to register a 33-30 victory. The Bengals' Doug Pelfrey kicked a 22-yard field goal with three seconds left that tied it. Looking to run out the clock and go into overtime, Pelfrey squibbed the ensuing kickoff. But the Eagles fumbled the kick and Cincinnati recovered with one second left. Pelfrey kicked a game-winning 54-yard field goal as time expired.

Blowout of the week: Cleveland raced to a 35-3 lead before claiming a 35-9 victory over Seattle. The Browns scored a touchdown on their first possession and three of their first five, building a 21-0 halftime lead that never was threatened.

Nail-biter of the week: Trailing Indianapolis, 10-9, Buffalo had one last chance for victory. But Steve Christie's 46-yard field-goal attempt bounced off the right upright on the game's final play, allowing the Colts to post their first back-to-back victories of the season. Indianapolis didn't allow a touchdown in its final two games of 1994.

Hit of the week: By Atlanta linebackers Jessie Tuggle and Clay Matthews, who combined to stop Arizona's Ron Moore for no gain at the Falcons' 1 on the last play of the game as Atlanta won, 10-6.

Oddity of the week: It was business as usual for the Los Angeles Rams, who capped their fifth consecutive losing season with a 24-21 loss to Washington. It was the franchise's final game as a resident of Southern California, where the Rams have toiled since 1946. With attendance lagging and economic woes mounting, the Rams moved in the off-season to St. Louis. A crowd of 25,705, the smallest since the Rams moved to Anaheim from Los Angeles in 1980, turned out.

Top rusher: Kansas City's Marcus Allen ran 33 times for 132 yards in the Chiefs' 19-9 victory over the Los Angeles Raiders. Allen's effort pushed him over the 10,000-yard career plateau, making him just the ninth NFL player to accomplish the feat. The victory qualified Kansas City for a wild-card playoff berth.

Top passer: The Saints' Jim Everett completed 23 of 27 passes for 343 yards and three touchdowns in New Orleans' 30-28 victory over Denver.

Top receiver: Torrance Small caught six passes for a career-high 200 yards and two touchdowns in the Saints' triumph.

Notes: Washington finished 3-13, its worst record since going 1-12-1 in 1961.... The Jets-Oilers game drew 31,176, the smallest Oilers crowd at the Astrodome since 1987.... Steve Young completed 12 of 13 passes for 94 yards and a touchdown before leaving early in the second quarter of the 49ers' loss to Minnesota. That effort helped him surpass Joe Montana's NFL-record passing rating (112.4, set in 1989) with a 112.8. Young also eclipsed Ken Anderson's record for completion percentage (70.55, set in 1982) with a 70.7. The victory gave the Vikings their second NFC Central title in three seasons. . . . Barry Sanders' bid for 2,000 yards was smothered by Miami, which beat the Lions, 27-20, to win its second AFC East title in three seasons. Sanders needed 169 yards to become the third 2,000-yard rusher in NFL history but was held to 52 yards on 12 carries. . . . Dallas had its 14-game NFC East winning streak ended in a 15-10 loss to the New York Giants. . . . New England's Drew Bledsoe set an NFL record for pass attempts in a season with 691. Teammate Ben Coates caught three passes to set an NFL single-season record for receptions by a tight end (96). . . . Tampa Bay's loss to Green Bay was the Bucs' 10th of 1994, extending the franchise's NFL-record streak of consecutive seasons with double-digit losses to 12. . . . Jeff George started all 16 games, a first for an Atlanta quarterback since Steve Bartkowski did it in 1981. . . . The Colts' Marshall Faulk rushed for 82 yards to finish with a franchise rookie-record 1,282.

Quote of the week: San Diego linebacker Junior Seau, after the Chargers downed Pittsburgh, 37-34: "We've got to learn how to tackle again. If we learned how to tackle, we could limit plays to nine yards instead of 90."

GAME SUMMARIES

BROWNS 35, SEAHAWKS 9
Saturday, December 24

Seattle	0	0	3	6— 9
Cleveland	7	14	7	7—35

First Quarter
Cle—Metcalf 6 run (Stover kick), 6:22.
Second Quarter
Cle—Carrier 35 pass from Testaverde (Stover kick), 4:22.
Cle—Testaverde 1 run (Stover kick), 12:45.
Third Quarter
Sea—FG Kasay 30, 3:32.
Cle—Alexander 3 pass from Testaverde (Stover kick), 10:46.
Fourth Quarter
Cle—Carrier 14 run (Stover kick), 3:09.
Sea—McKnight 25 pass from Gelbaugh (pass failed), 13:38.

TEAM STATISTICS

	Seattle	Cleveland
First downs	18	23
Rushes-yards	23-84	38-106
Passing	217	245
Punt returns-yards	1-31	3-32
Kickoff returns-yards	6-64	2-74
Interception returns-yards	1-0	1-22
Comp.-att.-int.	18-37-1	19-26-1
Sacked-yards lost	2-12	0-0
Punts-average	3-47	2-34
Fumbles-lost	3-2	1-0
Penalties-yards	8-65	6-42
Time of possession	25:54	34:06
Attendance—54,180.		

INDIVIDUAL STATISTICS
RUSHING—Seattle, C. Warren 16-61, Gelbaugh 1-10, Strong 3-7, Bryant 1-6, McGwire 2-0. Cleveland, Hoard 24-74, Carrier 1-14, Metcalf 3-10, Testaverde 3-5, Baldwin 4-3, Alexander 1-2, Rypien 2-(minus 2).
PASSING—Seattle, McGwire 11-26-1-149, Gelbaugh 7-11-0-80. Cleveland, Testaverde 16-22-1-228, Rypien 3-4-0-17.
RECEIVING—Seattle, Blades 6-80, Martin 3-49, Smith 3-33, Green

2-12, McKnight 1-25, Thomas 1-15, Bates 1-10, T. Johnson 1-5. Cleveland, Carrier 5-98, Alexander 5-47, Metcalf 3-12, Kinchen 2-39, McCardell 2-36, Baldwin 2-13.
MISSED FIELD GOAL ATTEMPTS—Seattle, Kasay 47.
INTERCEPTIONS—Seattle, Taylor 1-0. Cleveland, Turner 1-22.
KICKOFF RETURNS—Seattle, Bates 3-24, B. Bryant 3-40. Cleveland, Baldwin 2-74.
PUNT RETURNS—Seattle, B. Bryant 1-31. Cleveland, Carrier 2-20, Metcalf 1-12.
SACKS—Cleveland, Pleasant 1, Burnett ½, Perry ½.

COLTS 10, BILLS 9
Saturday, December 24

Buffalo	0	6	0	3— 9
Indianapolis	0	0	10	0—10

Second Quarter
Buf—FG Christie 20, 5:12.
Buf—FG Christie 21, 11:29.
Third Quarter
Ind—Turner 13 pass from Harbaugh (Biasucci kick), 5:37.
Ind—FG Biasucci 22, 12:26.
Fourth Quarter
Buf—FG Christie 24, 4:27.

TEAM STATISTICS

	Buffalo	Indianapolis
First downs	20	13
Rushes-yards	25-57	27-145
Passing	243	100
Punt returns-yards	5-49	2-5
Kickoff returns-yards	3-56	4-102
Interception returns-yards	1-4	2-32
Comp.-att.-int.	26-46-2	12-28-1
Sacked-yards lost	2-15	2-18
Punts-average	5-41	6-41
Fumbles-lost	2-0	2-1
Penalties-yards	6-40	2-10
Time of possession	33:18	26:42
Attendance—38,458.		

INDIVIDUAL STATISTICS
RUSHING—Buffalo, Thomas 12-36, Jourdain 8-10, K. Davis 2-7, Gardner 2-4, Reich 1-0. Indianapolis, Faulk 17-82, Potts 7-42, Nagle 1-12, Harbaugh 2-9.
PASSING—Buffalo, Reich 26-46-2-258. Indianapolis, Nagle 8-21-1-69, Harbaugh 4-7-0-49.
RECEIVING—Buffalo, Beebe 8-111, Metzelaars 7-56, Reed 3-40, Thomas 3-1, Brooks 2-30, Jourdain 2-16, Copeland 1-4. Indianapolis, Turner 3-29, Faulk 3-20, Potts 2-3, Bailey 1-23, Jackson 1-22, Dawkins 1-15, Cash 1-6.
MISSED FIELD GOAL ATTEMPTS—Buffalo, Christie 49, 46. Indianapolis, Biasucci 31, 38.
INTERCEPTIONS—Buffalo, T. Smith 1-4. Indianapolis, Belser 1-31, Buchanan 1-1.
KICKOFF RETURNS—Buffalo, Jourdain 2-39, Copeland 1-17. Indianapolis, Brewer 2-46, Warren 2-56.
PUNT RETURNS—Buffalo, Burris 5-49. Indianapolis, Brewer 2-5.
SACKS—Buffalo, Hansen 1, Jones 1. Indianapolis, Alberts 1, T. Bennett 1.

FALCONS 10, CARDINALS 6
Saturday, December 24

Arizona	0	3	0	3— 6
Atlanta	7	0	3	0—10

First Quarter
Atl—Emanuel 85 pass from J. George (N. Johnson kick), 8:42.
Second Quarter
Ari—FG G. Davis 22, 5:55.
Third Quarter
Atl—FG N. Johnson 24, 13:58.
Fourth Quarter
Ari—FG G. Davis 49, 5:38.

TEAM STATISTICS

	Arizona	Atlanta
First downs	18	12
Rushes-yards	25-72	19-51
Passing	313	256
Punt returns-yards	4-31	3-5
Kickoff returns-yards	3-61	2-31

	Arizona	Atlanta
Interception returns-yards	1-0	0-0
Comp.-att.-int.	26-42-0	15-32-1
Sacked-yards lost	1-4	2-24
Punts-average	6-40	8-36
Fumbles-lost	3-2	1-0
Penalties-yards	8-45	8-43
Time of possession	33:00	27:00

Attendance—35,311.

INDIVIDUAL STATISTICS

RUSHING—Arizona, Moore 14-44, Hearst 7-18, Centers 1-9, Higgs 2-1, Schroeder 1-0. Atlanta, Heyward 16-33, Hebert 3-18.

PASSING—Arizona, Schroeder 26-42-0-317. Atlanta, J. George 5-10-0-125, Hebert 10-22-1-155.

RECEIVING—Arizona, Clark 6-96, Proehl 6-68, Centers 5-66, Reeves 2-26, Fann 2-19, Hill 2-13, Moore 1-18, Samuels 1-6, Hearst 1-5. Atlanta, Emanuel 4-136, Sanders 3-20, Mathis 3-18, Heyward 2-40, Spencer 1-40, Harris 1-18, Rison 1-8.

MISSED FIELD GOAL ATTEMPTS—None.

INTERCEPTIONS—Arizona, Swann 1-0.

KICKOFF RETURNS—Arizona, Levy 3-61. Atlanta, Pegram 2-31.

PUNT RETURNS—Arizona, Robinson 4-31. Atlanta, Verdin 3-5.

SACKS—Arizona, Miller 2. Atlanta, Archambeau 1.

GIANTS 15, COWBOYS 10

Saturday, December 24

Dallas	3	0	7	0—10
N.Y. Giants	0	10	2	3—15

First Quarter
Dal—FG Boniol 37, 10:18.

Second Quarter
N.Y.—Sherrard 49 pass from Da. Brown (Daluiso kick), :16.
N.Y.—FG Daluiso 38, 2:57.

Third Quarter
Dal—B. Thomas 1 run (Boniol kick), 3:59.
N.Y.—Safety, ball rolled through the end zone after Armstead sacked Peete, 10:23.

Fourth Quarter
N.Y.—FG Daluiso 30, 1:05.

TEAM STATISTICS

	Dallas	N.Y. Giants
First downs	11	15
Rushes-yards	24-90	37-127
Passing	93	122
Punt returns-yards	4-64	2-30
Kickoff returns-yards	1-29	4-49
Interception returns-yards	0-0	0-0
Comp.-att.-int.	15-19-0	11-19-0
Sacked-yards lost	3-19	4-19
Punts-average	4-39	6-43
Fumbles-lost	3-1	1-0
Penalties-yards	7-45	5-46
Time of possession	27:25	32:35

Attendance—66,943.

INDIVIDUAL STATISTICS

RUSHING—Dallas, B. Thomas 18-63, Aikman 2-13, K. Williams 1-8, Johnston 2-7, Peete 1-(minus 1). New York, Hampton 26-91, Meggett 4-14, Da. Brown 5-13, Rasheed 1-6, Calloway 1-3.

PASSING—Dallas, Aikman 9-11-0-62, Peete 6-8-0-50. New York, Brown 11-19-0-141.

RECEIVING—Dallas, Johnston 5-23, Novacek 4-38, Irvin 2-27, B. Thomas 2-1, Williams 1-21, Agee 1-12. New York, Sherrard 3-65, Calloway 2-30, Cross 2-18, Meggett 2-13, Marshall 1-12, Rasheed 1-3.

MISSED FIELD GOAL ATTEMPTS—Dallas, Boniol 37.

INTERCEPTIONS—None.

KICKOFF RETURNS—Dallas, K. Williams 1-29. New York, Marshall 3-29, Meggett 1-20.

PUNT RETURNS—Dallas, K. Williams 4-64. New York, Meggett 2-30.

SACKS—Dallas, Haley 1, Jeffcoat 1, Lett 1, Tolbert 1. New York, Armstead 1, Howard 1, Strahan 1.

PATRIOTS 13, BEARS 3

Saturday, December 24

New England	3	3	0	7—13
Chicago	3	0	0	0— 3

First Quarter
Chi—FG Butler 44, 3:01.
N.E.—FG Bahr 29, 10:52.

Second Quarter
N.E.—FG Bahr 22, 3:37.

Fourth Quarter
N.E.—Thompson 3 pass from Bledsoe (Bahr kick), 12:28.

TEAM STATISTICS

	New England	Chicago
First downs	19	14
Rushes-yards	31-80	21-65
Passing	263	183
Punt returns-yards	0-0	4-24
Kickoff returns-yards	2-43	4-89
Interception returns-yards	0-0	1-3
Comp.-att.-int.	23-38-1	17-38-0
Sacked-yards lost	2-14	1-3
Punts-average	5-41	6-34
Fumbles-lost	2-0	3-1
Penalties-yards	4-30	4-22
Time of possession	33:21	26:39

Attendance—60,178.

INDIVIDUAL STATISTICS

RUSHING—New England, Thompson 7-32, Butts 12-31, Timpson 1-10, Gash 6-9, Turner 1-1, Bledsoe 4-(minus 3). Chicago, Tillman 10-33, Harris 6-16, Walsh 3-12, Green 1-3, Conway 1-1.

PASSING—New England, Bledsoe 23-38-1-277. Chicago, Walsh 17-38-0-186.

RECEIVING—New England, Brisby 6-115, Thompson 5-44, Timpson 4-61, Burke 3-29, Coates 3-26, Gash 2-2. Chicago, Conway 4-56, Graham 3-38, Harris 3-31, Waddle 3-27, Jennings 2-19, Wetnight 2-15.

MISSED FIELD GOAL ATTEMPTS—New England, Bahr 46. Chicago, Butler 38, 36.

INTERCEPTIONS—Chicago, Carrier 1-3.

KICKOFF RETURNS—New England, Crittenden 1-23, Thompson 1-20. Chicago, Lewis 4-89.

PUNT RETURNS—Chicago, Graham 4-24.

SACKS—New England, McGinest 1. Chicago, Armstrong 1, Spellman 1.

PACKERS 34, BUCCANEERS 19

Saturday, December 24

Green Bay	14	14	6	0—34
Tampa Bay	0	6	6	7—19

First Quarter
G.B.—Bennett 39 run (Jacke kick), 2:58.
G.B.—Sharpe 6 pass from Favre (Jacke kick), 13:37.

Second Quarter
T.B.—FG Husted 38, 1:01.
T.B.—FG Husted 27, 7:29.
G.B.—Sharpe 22 pass from Favre (Jacke kick), 10:50.
G.B.—Sharpe 6 pass from Favre (Jacke kick), 14:33.

Third Quarter
T.B.—C. Wilson 17 pass from Erickson (pass failed), 3:55.
G.B.—FG Jacke 38, 7:57.
G.B.—FG Jacke 18, 11:20.

Fourth Quarter
T.B—Armstrong 1 pass from Erickson (Husted kick), 13:44.

TEAM STATISTICS

	Green Bay	Tampa Bay
First downs	25	14
Rushes-yards	38-143	16-62
Passing	290	152
Punt returns-yards	0-0	0-0
Kickoff returns-yards	4-83	6-95
Interception returns-yards	1-16	1-10
Comp.-att.-int.	24-36-1	16-32-1
Sacked-yards lost	1-1	1-9
Punts-average	2-27	5-42
Fumbles-lost	2-1	2-1
Penalties-yards	3-25	2-20
Time of possession	37:17	22:43

Attendance—65,076.

INDIVIDUAL STATISTICS

RUSHING—Green Bay, Bennett 21-100, Cobb 11-38, Favre 5-3, Sharpe 1-2. Tampa Bay, Rhett 15-54, McDowell 1-8.

PASSING—Green Bay, Favre 24-36-1-291. Tampa Bay, Erickson 16-32-1-161.

RECEIVING—Green Bay, Sharpe 9-132, Bennett 6-35, Chmura 2-46, Brooks 2-18, Cobb 1-15, L. Johnson 1-13, West 1-13, Morgan 1-10, R. Johnson 1-9. Tampa Bay, Dawsey 4-53, Armstrong 4-39, C. Wilson 4-37, McDowell 3-14, Moore 1-18.

MISSED FIELD GOAL ATTEMPTS—None.

INTERCEPTIONS—Green Bay, Teague 1-16. Tampa Bay, Nickerson 1-10.
KICKOFF RETURNS—Green Bay, Brooks 3-69, J. Jurkovic 1-14. Tampa Bay, Turner 6-95.
PUNT RETURNS—None.
SACKS—Green Bay, Jones 1. Tampa Bay, Ahanotu 1.

BENGALS 33, EAGLES 30

Saturday, December 24

Philadelphia	3	17	7	3—30
Cincinnati	7	3	10	13—33

First Quarter
Cin—Pickens 14 pass from Blake (Pelfrey kick), 3:06.
Phi—FG Murray 34, 12:01.
Second Quarter
Cin—FG Pelfrey 18, 2:22.
Phi—H. Walker 94 kickoff return (Murray kick), 2:39.
Phi—Joseph 7 pass from Brister (Murray kick), 9:58.
Phi—FG Murray 23, 14:56.
Third Quarter
Phi—Zordich 18 interception return (Murray kick), 3:41.
Cin—Green 5 run (Pelfrey kick), 9:28.
Cin—FG Pelfrey 36, 14:58.
Fourth Quarter
Phi—FG Murray 35, 9:47.
Cin—To. McGee 8 pass from Blake (Pelfrey kick), 11:28.
Cin—FG Pelfrey 22, 14:57.
Cin—FG Pelfrey 54, 15:00.

TEAM STATISTICS

	Philadelphia	Cincinnati
First downs	19	23
Rushes-yards	24-81	28-152
Passing	297	233
Punt returns-yards	1-4	2-13
Kickoff returns-yards	6-167	7-141
Interception returns-yards	3-26	0-0
Comp.-att.-int.	26-37-0	17-43-3
Sacked-yards lost	4-28	1-6
Punts-average	4-36	4-45
Fumbles-lost	5-3	2-1
Penalties-yards	6-39	2-10
Time of possession	31:26	28:34
Attendance—39,923.		

INDIVIDUAL STATISTICS

RUSHING—Philadelphia, Hebron 16-58, H. Walker 6-19, Joseph 2-4. Cincinnati, Green 16-70, Blake 6-54, Cothran 4-16, Scott 1-12, Fenner 1-0.
PASSING—Philadelphia, Brister 26-37-0-325. Cincinnati, Blake 17-43-3-239.
RECEIVING—Philadelphia, Barnett 7-90, C. Williams 6-122, Joseph 4-17, M. Johnson 3-50, Hebron 3-7, Bailey 1-31, Sydner 1-10, H. Walker 1-(minus 2). Cincinnati, Pickens 9-135, Green 3-57, Scott 3-36, To. McGee 1-8, Cothran 1-3.
MISSED FIELD GOAL ATTEMPTS—None.
INTERCEPTIONS—Philadelphia, G. Jackson 1-0, Romanowski 1-8, Zordich 1-18.
KICKOFF RETURNS—Philadelphia, Hebron 2-47, H. Walker 2-106, O'Neal 1-0. Cincinnati, Hill 4-97, Hardy 3-44.
PUNT RETURNS—Philadelphia, Sydner 1-4. Cincinnati, Pickens 2-13.
SACKS—Philadelphia, Fuller 1. Cincinnati, Wilkinson 2, Rucker 1, Tovar 1.

CHIEFS 19, RAIDERS 9

Saturday, December 24

Kansas City	7	7	3	2—19
L.A. Raiders	0	3	0	6—9

First Quarter
K.C.—W. Davis 47 pass from Montana (Elliott kick), 1:54.
Second Quarter
L.A.—FG Jaeger 30, 7:58.
K.C.—Collins 78 interception return (Elliott kick), 15:00.
Third Quarter
K.C.—FG Elliott 22, 9:57.
Fourth Quarter
K.C.—Safety, Mosebar penalized for tripping in the end zone, 3:03.
L.A.—Wright 65 pass from Evans (pass failed), 8:39.

TEAM STATISTICS

	Kansas City	L.A. Raiders
First downs	25	14
Rushes-yards	44-204	16-53
Passing	218	221
Punt returns-yards	1-2	1-8
Kickoff returns-yards	4-69	3-60
Interception returns-yards	1-78	0-0
Comp.-att.-int.	16-25-0	15-28-1
Sacked-yards lost	1-10	2-11
Punts-average	4-37	4-51
Fumbles-lost	1-1	1-0
Penalties-yards	11-73	9-49
Time of possession	38:12	21:48
Attendance—64,130.		

INDIVIDUAL STATISTICS

RUSHING—Kansas City, Allen 33-132, Hill 8-51, Dawson 1-13, Anders 1-9, Bono 1-(minus 1). Los Angeles, H. Williams 14-48, Ismail 1-5, Hostetler 1-0.
PASSING—Kansas City, Montana 15-24-0-214, Bono 1-1-0-14. Los Angeles, Hostetler 14-27-1-167, Evans 1-1-0-65.
RECEIVING—Kansas City, Anders 6-73, W. Davis 3-83, Martin 3-30, Birden 2-26, Walker 2-16. Los Angeles, Brown 6-85, Glover 3-46, H. Williams 3-17, Ismail 2-19, Wright 1-65.
MISSED FIELD GOAL ATTEMPTS—None.
INTERCEPTIONS—Kansas City, Collins 1-78.
KICKOFF RETURNS—Kansas City, Hughes 4-69. Los Angeles, Ismail 3-60.
PUNT RETURNS—Kansas City, Carter 1-(minus 2). Los Angeles, Brown 1-8.
SACKS—Kansas City, Mickell 1, Thomas 1. Los Angeles, Biekert 1.

OILERS 24, JETS 10

Saturday, December 24

N.Y. Jets	0	7	3	0—10
Houston	7	6	8	3—24

First Quarter
Hou—Richardson 1 run (Del Greco kick), 12:58.
Second Quarter
N.Y.—Johnson 1 run (Lowery kick), 4:57.
Hou—FG Del Greco 28, 8:03.
Hou—FG Del Greco 50, 15:00.
Third Quarter
Hou—White 3 run (Richardson pass to Jeffires), 4:34.
N.Y.—FG Lowery 49, 10:05.
Fourth Quarter
Hou—FG Del Greco 42, 13:54.

TEAM STATISTICS

	N.Y. Jets	Houston
First downs	14	25
Rushes-yards	23-89	40-176
Passing	127	206
Punt returns-yards	3-17	4-0
Kickoff returns-yards	5-75	3-55
Interception returns-yards	2-16	1-32
Comp.-att.-int.	15-31-1	17-30-2
Sacked-yards lost	0-0	3-14
Punts-average	5-48	4-44
Fumbles-lost	2-2	2-1
Penalties-yards	4-61	7-53
Time of possession	24:07	35:53
Attendance—31,176.		

INDIVIDUAL STATISTICS

RUSHING—New York, J. Johnson 15-75, R. Anderson 8-14. Houston, L. White 27-97, Richardson 6-46, Brown 7-33.
PASSING—New York, Esiason 10-23-0-82, Foley 5-8-1-45. Houston, Richardson 17-29-2-220, Tolliver 0-1-0-0.
RECEIVING—New York, R. Anderson 4-47, Moore 2-29, Yarborough 2-12, F. Baxter 2-10, J. Johnson 2-10, Mitchell 1-7, Parker 1-7, Monk 1-5. Houston, Slaughter 8-123, R. Lewis 3-42, Jeffires 3-31, Givins 2-9, Wellman 1-15.
MISSED FIELD GOAL ATTEMPTS—None.
INTERCEPTIONS—New York, Turner 1-9, M. Washington 1-7. Houston, Robertson 1-32.
KICKOFF RETURNS—New York, Glenn 5-75. Houston, McNair 3-55.
PUNT RETURNS—New York, Hicks 3-17. Houston, Givins 4-0.
SACKS—New York, Lewis 3.

SAINTS 30, BRONCOS 28

Saturday, December 24

New Orleans	0	17	7	6—30
Denver	0	6	8	14—28

Second Quarter

Den—FG Elam 32, :52.
N.O.—FG Andersen 26, 5:04.
N.O.—Haynes 8 pass from Everett (Andersen kick), 9:14.
Den—FG Elam 30, 13:15.
N.O.—Small 36 pass from Everett (Andersen kick), 14:31.

Third Quarter

Den—D. Clark 4 run (Sharpe pass from Millen), 12:14.
N.O.—Small 75 pass from Everett (Andersen kick), 12:40.

Fourth Quarter

Den—D. Clark 1 run (Elam kick), :46.
N.O.—FG Andersen 37, 9:15.
N.O.—FG Andersen 40, 13:04.
Den—Sharpe 5 pass from Millen (Elam kick), 14:16.

TEAM STATISTICS

	New Orleans	Denver
First downs	22	23
Rushes-yards	26-80	23-90
Passing	367	258
Punt returns-yards	4-13	4-27
Kickoff returns-yards	5-92	5-108
Interception returns-yards	3-33	0-0
Comp.-att.-int.	28-35-0	25-44-3
Sacked-yards lost	5-24	4-32
Punts-average	5-47	6-47
Fumbles-lost	2-1	1-1
Penalties-yards	7-63	4-56
Time of possession	33:15	26:45
Attendance—64,445.		

INDIVIDUAL STATISTICS

RUSHING—New Orleans, Brown 8-42, Bates 14-25, Wilson 4-13. Denver, D. Clark 15-55, Milburn 6-26, Millen 1-8, Rivers 1-1.
PASSING—New Orleans, Everett 23-27-0-343, Wilson 5-8-0-48. Denver, Millen 25-44-3-290.
RECEIVING—New Orleans, Early 8-56, Small 6-200, I. Smith 5-53, Brown 3-31, Muster 3-30, Haynes 3-21. Denver, Sharpe 5-39, Miller 4-87, Rivers 4-25, Milburn 4-18, Russell 3-65, D. Clark 3-19, Tillman 1-25, Evans 1-12.
MISSED FIELD GOAL ATTEMPTS—New Orleans, Ander-sen 44, 32.
INTERCEPTIONS—New Orleans, Lee 2-3, Clark 1-30.
KICKOFF RETURNS—New Orleans, Mitchell 3-57, Hughes 2-35. Denver, Milburn 5-108.
PUNT RETURNS—New Orleans, Hughes 3-9, Mitchell 1-4. Denver, Milburn 4-27.
SACKS—New Orleans, Martin 2, Turnbull 1, Conner ½, J. Johnson ½. Denver, Bradford 1, Fletcher 1, Hasselbach 1, Robinson 1, Washington 1.

REDSKINS 24, RAMS 21

Saturday, December 24

Washington	0	17	7	0—24
L.A. Rams	7	14	0	0—21

First Quarter

L.A.—Newman 22 interception return (Zendejas kick), 7:16.

Second Quarter

Was—Brooks 2 run (Lohmiller kick), 7:05.
L.A.—Kinchen 34 pass from Miller (Zendejas kick), 10:41.
Was—Mitchell 78 punt return (Lohmiller kick), 13:27.
Was—FG Lohmiller 37, 14:03.
L.A.—Ross 36 pass from Miller (Zendejas kick), 14:56.

Third Quarter

Was—Jenkins 1 pass from Shuler (Lohmiller kick), 14:11.

TEAM STATISTICS

	Washington	L.A. Rams
First downs	19	18
Rushes-yards	37-150	21-77
Passing	138	293
Punt returns-yards	2-90	2-17
Kickoff returns-yards	4-55	5-106
Interception returns-yards	1-19	1-22
Comp.-att.-int.	13-28-1	27-40-1
Sacked-yards lost	1-11	2-11
Punts-average	5-41	7-46
Fumbles-lost	0-0	1-0

	Washington	L.A. Rams
Penalties-yards	2-9	5-46
Time of possession	30:49	29:11
Attendance—25,705.		

INDIVIDUAL STATISTICS

RUSHING—Washington, Brooks 13-50, Mitchell 9-33, Ervins 8-33, Smith 3-24, Shuler 4-10. Los Angeles, Bettis 15-48, Miller 2-17, Bailey 2-5, Drayton 1-4, Griffith 1-3.
PASSING—Washington, Shuler 13-28-1-149. Los Angeles, Miller 27-40-1-304.
RECEIVING—Washington, Ellard 5-81, Smith 3-8, Howard 1-39, Winans 1-10, Ervins 1-9, Brooks 1-1, Jenkins 1-1. Los Angeles, Bailey 7-49, Hester 5-66, Bettis 3-26, Lang 3-17, Kinchen 2-50, Anderson 2-39, Griffith 2-12, Ross 1-36, Drayton 1-8, Lester 1-1.
MISSED FIELD GOAL ATTEMPTS—Washington, Lohmiller 42. Los Angeles, Zendejas 33.
INTERCEPTIONS—Washington, Bayless 1-19. Los Angeles, Newman 1-22.
KICKOFF RETURNS—Washington, Mitchell 2-51, A. Collins 1-0, Jenkins 1-4. Los Angeles, Lang 3-55, Kinchen 2-51.
PUNT RETURNS—Washington, Mitchell 2-90. Los Angeles, Kinchen 2-17.
SACKS—Washington, Harvey 1½, Woods ½. Los Angeles, Robinson 1.

CHARGERS 37, STEELERS 34

Saturday, December 24

Pittsburgh	0	13	6	15—34
San Diego	3	14	7	13—37

First Quarter

S.D.—FG Carney 37, 8:41.

Second Quarter

Pit—FG Anderson 28, 5:50.
S.D.—Coleman 90 kickoff return (Carney kick), 6:07.
Pit—FG Anderson 28, 11:53.
Pit—C. Johnson 19 pass from O'Donnell (Anderson kick), 14:00.
S.D.—Seay 2 pass from Humphries (Carney kick), 14:34.

Third Quarter

S.D.—Means 2 run (Carney kick), 7:48.
Pit—McAfee 6 run (pass failed), 11:55.

Fourth Quarter

Pit—C. Johnson 84 pass from Tomczak (Stone pass from Tomczak), :12.
S.D.—FG Carney 40, 4:31.
Pit—Hastings 11 pass from Tomczak (Anderson kick), 8:31.
S.D.—Means 20 run (Carney kick), 10:28.
S.D.—FG Carney 32, 14:57.

TEAM STATISTICS

	Pittsburgh	San Diego
First downs	22	21
Rushes-yards	29-136	27-87
Passing	300	263
Punt returns-yards	3-20	2-24
Kickoff returns-yards	6-88	7-206
Interception returns-yards	0-0	0-0
Comp.-att.-int.	18-29-0	24-41-0
Sacked-yards lost	2-21	1-10
Punts-average	4-39	4-42
Fumbles-lost	2-1	0-0
Penalties-yards	6-57	3-52
Time of possession	29:37	30:23
Attendance—58,379.		

INDIVIDUAL STATISTICS

RUSHING—Pittsburgh, Morris 9-56, McAfee 10-38, Foster 6-28, Tomczak 1-13, Stone 1-3, Avery 1-(minus 1), O'Donnell 1-(minus 1). San Diego, Means 22-85, Culver 2-4, Bieniemy 1-1, Gilbert 1-1, Harmon 1-(minus 4).
PASSING—Pittsburgh, O'Donnell 8-13-0-73, Tomczak 10-16-0-248. San Diego, Humphries 21-35-0-249, Gilbert 3-6-0-24.
RECEIVING—Pittsburgh, Hastings 5-52, C. Johnson 4-165, Stone 3-31, Mills 2-43, Thigpen 2-25, Morris 1-5, Foster 1-0. San Diego, Harmon 6-85, Martin 6-77, Seay 6-57, Jefferson 3-18, Pupunu 2-32, Bieniemy 1-4.
MISSED FIELD GOAL ATTEMPTS—None.
INTERCEPTIONS—None.
KICKOFF RETURNS—Pittsburgh, C. Johnson 6-88. San Diego, Coleman 6-195, Harmon 1-11.
PUNT RETURNS—Pittsburgh, C. Johnson 3-20. San Diego, Gordon 2-24.
SACKS—Pittsburgh, Brown 1. San Diego, Mims 2.

DOLPHINS 27, LIONS 20

Sunday, December 25

Detroit	3	7	3	7—20
Miami	7	20	0	0—27

First Quarter
Mia—Parmalee 1 run (Stoyanovich kick), 3:23.
Det—FG Hanson 32, 8:17.

Second Quarter
Mia—FG Stoyanovich 40, 2:04.
Mia—Parmalee 1 run (Stoyanovich kick), 9:41.
Mia—Parmalee 6 run (Stoyanovich kick), 13:45.
Det—Morton 93 kickoff return (Hanson kick), 13:59.
Mia—FG Stoyanovich 45, 14:58.

Third Quarter
Det—FG Hanson 40, 13:51.

Fourth Quarter
Det—A. Matthews 5 pass from Krieg (Hanson kick), 9:14.

TEAM STATISTICS

	Detroit	Miami
First downs	15	21
Rushes-yards	14-52	36-98
Passing	170	285
Punt returns-yards	0-0	1-16
Kickoff returns-yards	6-160	5-142
Interception returns-yards	0-0	2-36
Comp.-att.-int.	21-46-2	26-35-0
Sacked-yards lost	5-41	0-0
Punts-average	4-39	3-31
Fumbles-lost	1-0	5-3
Penalties-yards	3-20	7-58
Time of possession	23:28	36:32

Attendance—70,980.

INDIVIDUAL STATISTICS

RUSHING—Detroit, Sanders 12-52, Lynch 1-0, D. Moore 1-0. Miami, Parmalee 18-39, Spikes 10-35, Craver 3-24, McDuffie 1-4, Marino 4-(minus 4).

PASSING—Detroit, Krieg 21-46-2-211. Miami, Marino 26-35-0-285.

RECEIVING—Detroit, Sanders 7-58, H. Moore 5-55, A. Matthews 4-41, Perriman 4-40, Holman 1-17. Miami, Craver 5-67, Parmalee 5-47, McDuffie 4-23, Ingram 3-35, Saxon 3-24, Jackson 2-35, Fryar 1-38, R. Williams 1-9, M. Williams 1-8, Spikes 1-(minus 1).

MISSED FIELD GOAL ATTEMPTS—None.

INTERCEPTIONS—Miami, Hollier 1-36, Stewart 1-0.

KICKOFF RETURNS—Detroit, Morton 3-117, Gray 2-39, Lynch 1-4. Miami, Spikes 3-86, McDuffie 2-56.

PUNT RETURNS—Miami, McDuffie 1-16.

SACKS—Miami, Cross 2, Bowens 1, Cox 1, Veasey 1.

VIKINGS 21, 49ERS 14

Monday, December 26

San Francisco	0	7	0	7—14
Minnesota	7	3	11	0—21

First Quarter
Min—Washington 17 fumble return (Reveiz kick), 4:53.

Second Quarter
S.F.—Rice 6 pass from S. Young (Brien kick), :09.
Min—FG Reveiz 48, 15:00.

Third Quarter
Min—FG Reveiz 27, 8:08.
Min—Allen 1 run (Allen run), 14:51.

Fourth Quarter
S.F.—McCaffrey 1 pass from Grbac (Brien kick), 11:07.

TEAM STATISTICS

	San Francisco	Minnesota
First downs	18	14
Rushes-yards	19-49	32-102
Passing	246	150
Punt returns-yards	6-37	5-29
Kickoff returns-yards	4-71	2-51
Interception returns-yards	1-1	0-0
Comp.-att.-int.	30-36-1	16-34-1
Sacked-yards lost	3-32	1-6
Punts-average	6-40	7-43
Fumbles-lost	4-3	2-1
Penalties-yards	8-56	3-29
Time of possession	30:06	29:54

Attendance—63,326.

INDIVIDUAL STATISTICS

RUSHING—San Francisco, Walker 3-23, Watters 7-13, Floyd 3-7, Grbac 3-6, S. Young 1-6, D. Carter 2-(minus 6). Minnesota, Graham 17-70, Allen 9-21, R. Smith 1-6, Lee 2-3, Salisbury 3-2.

PASSING—San Francisco, S. Young 12-13-0-94, Grbac 18-23-1-184. Minnesota, Salisbury 16-34-1-156.

RECEIVING—San Francisco, Popson 8-80, Singleton 6-74, McCaffrey 5-59, Rice 4-33, Watters 3-4, Carolan 2-10, D. Carter 1-9, Floyd 1-9. Minnesota, Reed 5-44, Lee 3-28, C. Carter 3-24, S. Jordan 2-13, Ismail 1-38, Palmer 1-8, Graham 1-1.

MISSED FIELD GOAL ATTEMPTS—None.

INTERCEPTIONS—San Francisco, Plummer 1-1. Minnesota, Glenn 1-0.

KICKOFF RETURNS—San Francisco, D. Carter 4-71. Minnesota, Lee 1-26, R. Smith 1-25.

PUNT RETURNS—San Francisco, D. Carter 4-24, Singleton 2-13. Minnesota, Palmer 4-29, Parker 1-0.

SACKS—San Francisco, D. Brown ½, Kelly ½. Minnesota, Randle 2, Thomas 1.

WILD-CARD GAMES

AFC

MIAMI 27, KANSAS CITY 17

Why the Dolphins won: Dan Marino was splendid, completing 22 of 29 passes for 257 yards and two touchdowns. Behind his guidance, Miami converted nine of 15 third-/fourth-down conversions.

Why the Chiefs lost: Following a stellar first half that ended in a 17-17 tie, Kansas City's offense and defense faltered in the second half. Two fourth-quarter turnovers in Miami territory ruined scoring chances, and the Chiefs' defense couldn't stop Marino.

The turning points:

1. With Kansas City trailing, 27-17, in the fourth quarter, Joe Montana forced a pass to Eric Martin, which Miami cornerback J.B. Brown intercepted at the goal line with 10:15 remaining.

2. After holding Miami following the Montana interception, Kansas City again turned over the ball in Dolphins' territory. This time, Marcus Allen allowed Miami safety Michael Stewart to wrestle the ball away from him.

3. Following the Allen fumble, outside linebacker Derrick Thomas ended any remaining hope by being penalized for illegal use of the hands after the Chiefs had held Miami on third and 11 with 4:37 remaining. The penalty gave the Dolphins a first down at Kansas City's 46.

Notable: Marino has thrown a touchdown pass in an NFL-record 11 consecutive playoff games. . . . Miami linebacker Jesse Solomon, playing for injured Dwight Hollier, earned a game ball by making eight tackles. Entering the game, Solomon had just one all season.

Quotable: Dolphins Coach Don Shula, on the fact that Miami responded with scores after each of Kansas City's first three scoring drives in the opening half: "That really gave us great momentum going into the locker room and coming out for the third-quarter drive (which saw Miami score 10 points)."

DOLPHINS 27, CHIEFS 17

Saturday, December 31

Kansas City	14	3	0	0—17
Miami	7	10	10	0—27

First Quarter
K.C.—Walker 1 pass from Montana (Elliott kick), 6:28.
Mia—Parmalee 1 run (Stoyanovich kick), 12:40.
K.C.—Anders 57 pass from Montana (Elliott kick), 14:20.

Second Quarter
Mia—FG Stoyanovich 40, 2:45.
K.C.—FG Elliott 21, 8:48.
Mia—R. Williams 1 pass from Marino (Stoyanovich kick), 14:38.

Third Quarter
Mia—Fryar 7 pass from Marino (Stoyanovich kick), 3:02.
Mia—FG Stoyanovich 40, 14:48.

TEAM STATISTICS

	Kansas City	Miami
First downs	24	22
Rushes-yards	23-100	31-132
Passing	314	249
Punt returns-yards	1-7	0-0
Kickoff returns-yards	5-81	3-95
Interception returns-yards	0-0	1-24
Comp.-att.-int.	26-37-1	22-29-0
Sacked-yards lost	0-0	1-8
Punts-average	2-40	3-43
Fumbles-lost	3-1	0-0
Penalties-yards	4-15	6-50
Time of possession	27:30	32:30

Attendance—67,487.

INDIVIDUAL STATISTICS

RUSHING—Kansas City, Allen 14-64, Anders 5-17, Hill 2-14, Montana 2-5. Miami, Parmalee 18-57, Spikes 9-49, McDuffie 1-19, Marino 2-4, Craver 1-3.

PASSING—Kansas City, Montana 26-37-1-314. Miami, Marino 22-29-0-257.

RECEIVING—Kansas City, Anders 6-103, Allen 5-49, Birden 4-56, Cash 3-38, Walker 3-27, Dawson 3-21, Hill 1-11, Davis 1-9. Miami, Fryar 6-71, Craver 4-35, Parmalee 2-34, K. Jackson 2-29, M. Williams 2-28, McDuffie 2-25, Saxon 2-24, Miller 1-10, R. Williams 1-1.

MISSED FIELD GOAL ATTEMPTS—None.

INTERCEPTIONS—Miami, Brown 1-24.

KICKOFF RETURNS—Kansas City, Vaughn 4-67, Hughes 1-14. Miami, McDuffie 2-57, Spikes 1-38.

PUNT RETURNS—Kansas City, Carter 1-7.

SACKS—Kansas City, Thomas 1.

CLEVELAND 20, NEW ENGLAND 13

Why the Browns won: Avoiding the mistakes that had become his trademark since his days at the University of Miami, Cleveland quarterback Vinny Testaverde completed 20 of 30 passes for 268 yards and a touchdown. At one point, Testaverde, playing in his first playoff game, completed 11 consecutive attempts.

Why the Patriots lost: Drew Bledsoe was intercepted three times, including twice in the fourth quarter, en route to completing just 21 of 50 passes for 235 yards. The Browns intercepted Bledsoe four times in a 13-6 win over New England on November 6, the last time the Patriots had lost before this wild-card game.

The turning points

1. With the game tied at 10, Testaverde completed all four passes on a 79-yard drive that was capped by Leroy Hoard's 10-yard scoring run, which put Cleveland ahead to stay with 2:21 left in the third quarter.

2. New England, in the playoffs for the first time since 1986, had a chance to tie it after recovering an onside kick at its 36 with 1:28 left. But after leading the Patriots to one first down, Bledsoe threw four consecutive incompletions from his 48.

Notable: By running for 30 yards, Earnest Byner became Cleveland's all-time leading playoff rusher with 437 yards in five games. . . . This was the Browns' first postseason game since 1989. . . . Cleveland Coach Bill Belichick was a defensive assistant under New England Coach Bill Parcells for eight years with the New York Giants. . . . Patriots kicker Matt Bahr, who spent nine seasons (1981-89) with Cleveland, scored seven points to become the second-leading scorer in NFL postseason history. Bahr has 103 points, one more than Pittsburgh's Franco Harris. Only George Blanda, with 115, has scored more. Bahr also has 21 field goals in the playoffs, second to Blanda's 22.

Quotable: Testaverde: "This was the biggest game of my career, and next week (at Pittsburgh) will be even bigger. I am satisfied with the way I played and with the way the team played."

BROWNS 20, PATRIOTS 13

Sunday, January 1

New England	0	10	0	3—13
Cleveland	3	7	7	3—20

First Quarter

Cle—FG Stover 30, 7:20.

Second Quarter

N.E.—Thompson 13 pass from Bledsoe (Bahr kick), 4:12.
Cle—Carrier 5 pass from Testaverde (Stover kick), 7:57.
N.E.—FG Bahr 23, 14:30.

Third Quarter

Cle—Hoard 10 run (Stover kick), 12:39.

Fourth Quarter

Cle—FG Stover 21, 11:24.
N.E.—FG Bahr 33, 13:30.

TEAM STATISTICS

	New England	Cleveland
First downs	20	22
Rushes-yards	16-57	34-125
Passing	246	254
Punt returns-yards	2-5	1-1
Kickoff returns-yards	5-99	3-70
Interception returns-yards	0-0	3-47
Comp.-att.-int.	22-51-3	20-30-0
Sacked-yards lost	1-10	2-14
Punts-average	4-42	3-38
Fumbles-lost	0-0	2-1
Penalties-yards	3-21	4-25
Time of possession	24:18	35:42

Attendance—77,452.

INDIVIDUAL STATISTICS

RUSHING—New England, Croom 9-35, Thompson 4-16, K. Turner 1-4, Bledsoe 2-2. Cleveland, Hoard 17-66, Byner 10-30, Testaverde 5-19, Metcalf 2-10.

PASSING—New England, Bledsoe 21-50-3-235, O'Neill 1-1-0-21. Cleveland, Testaverde 20-30-0-268.

RECEIVING—New England, Brisby 6-83, Coates 6-79, Thompson 4-33, Timpson 2-20, C. Brown 1-21, Burke 1-8, K. Turner 1-7, Croom 1-5. Cleveland, Jackson 7-122, Alexander 5-69, Hartley 2-17, Byner 2-16, Carrier 2-13, Hoard 1-25, Kinchen 1-6.

MISSED FIELD GOAL ATTEMPTS—Cleveland, Stover 50, 49.

INTERCEPTIONS—Cleveland, E. Turner 1-28, Riddick 1-16, P. Johnson 1-3.

KICKOFF RETURNS—New England, Thompson 4-71, Crittenden 1-28. Cleveland, Metcalf 2-46, Kinchen 1-24.

PUNT RETURNS—New England, Brown 2-5. Cleveland, Metcalf 1-1.

SACKS—New England, McGinest 1, Pitts 1. Cleveland, P. Johnson 1.

GREEN BAY 16, DETROIT 12

Why the Packers won: Wide receiver Robert Brooks and tight end Mark Chmura stepped up. The Packers were without star receiver Sterling Sharpe, sidelined by a career-threatening neck injury sustained late in the season. Brooks made seven catches for 88 yards and Chmura five for 75 yards. **Why the Lions lost:** Detroit's Barry Sanders, who led the NFL with 1,883 yards rushing during the regular season, was held to a career-low minus-1 yard on 13 carries. As a team, the Lions rushed for minus-4 yards on 15 carries, which set an NFL playoff record.

The turning points:

1. Trailing, 16-10, Detroit faced a fourth and 14 from Green Bay's 17 with 1:51 left. Lions quarterback Dave Krieg threw to the back of the end zone to Herman Moore, who outleaped Packers safety George Teague to make the catch. But Moore landed out of bounds. Green Bay took over on downs, but its offense couldn't run out the clock and faced a fourth and five from its 22. Faced with the prospect of punting to Mel Gray, who had run back four kickoffs for 159 yards and one punt for 17 in the game, the Packers had punter Craig Hentrich kill the clock by running into the end zone and taking a safety.

2. Trailing, 10-0, in the third quarter, Detroit made things interesting with two big plays. First, a 36-yard pass from Krieg to Moore set up a 38-yard field goal by Jason Hanson. After a 32-yard field goal by Chris Jacke restored Green Bay's lead to 10 (13-3), Gray returned the ensuing kickoff 68 yards to the Packers' 18 on the last play of the third quarter. Five plays later, Krieg passed to Brett Perriman in the back left corner of the end zone for a three-yard touchdown pass with 13:35 remaining. That cut the lead to 13-10, but it was the last time the Detroit offense would score.

Notable: Jacke's 51-yard field goal in the second quarter was the longest in Packers postseason history. . . . The contest was the first non-strike playoff game at Lambeau Field since the "Ice Bowl" contest in 1967, when Green Bay beat Dallas, 21-17, to win its third consecutive NFL title.

Quotable: Green Bay defensive lineman Reggie White, on shutting down Sanders, who ran for 188 yards against Green Bay on December 4: "That is inconceivable. He does things that no other back does."

PACKERS 16, LIONS 12

Saturday, December 31

Detroit	0	0	3	9—12
Green Bay	7	3	3	3—16

First Quarter
G.B.—Levens 3 run (Jacke kick), 7:24.
Second Quarter
G.B.—FG Jacke 51, 12:04.
Third Quarter
Det—FG Hanson 38, 9:22.
G.B.—FG Jacke 32, 14:49.
Fourth Quarter
Det—Perriman 3 pass from Krieg (Hanson kick), 1:25.
G.B.—FG Jacke 28, 9:25.
Det—Safety, Hentrich ran out of the end zone from punt formation, 15:00.

TEAM STATISTICS

	Detroit	Green Bay
First downs	9	18
Rushes-yards	15-(-4)	35-81
Passing	175	255
Punt returns-yards	2-17	3-15
Kickoff returns-yards	5-186	3-45
Interception returns-yards	0-0	0-0
Comp.-att.-int.	17-35-0	23-38-0
Sacked-yards lost	4-24	1-7
Punts-average	8-37	5-39
Fumbles-lost	1-0	0-0
Penalties-yards	4-30	3-35
Time of possession	22:32	37:28

Attendance—58,125.

INDIVIDUAL STATISTICS

RUSHING—Detroit, Sanders 13-(minus 1), Krieg 1-1, Perriman 1-(minus 4). Green Bay, Bennett 22-70, Brooks 1-13, Cobb 8-12, Favre 2-5, Levens 1-3, Hentrich 1-(minus 22).

PASSING—Detroit, Krieg 17-35-0-199. Green Bay, Favre 23-38-0-262.

RECEIVING—Detroit, Perriman 4-62, Holman 4-30, Matthews 3-36, Sanders 3-4, Moore 2-52, Hallock 1-15. Green Bay, Brooks 7-88, Bennett 6-31, Chmura 5-75, Morgan 3-33, Cobb 1-18, Mickens 1-17.

MISSED FIELD GOAL ATTEMPTS—Detroit, Hanson 30. Green Bay, Jacke 37.

INTERCEPTIONS—None.

KICKOFF RETURNS—Detroit, Gray 4-159, Lynch 1-27. Green Bay, Harris 1-17, Jordan 1-15, Levens 1-13.

PUNT RETURNS—Detroit, Gray 1-17. Green Bay, Brooks 3-15.

SACKS—Detroit, Porcher ½, Scroggins ½. Green Bay, Paup 2, Jones 1, White 1.

CHICAGO 35, MINNESOTA 18

Why the Bears won: Steve Walsh, playing in his hometown area, completed 15 of 23 passes for 221 yards. It was his best game since he quarterbacked the Bears in a 33-27 overtime loss at the Metrodome on December 1. Walsh, a St. Paul native, started Chicago's last eight games in place of Erik Kramer, who signed a lucrative free-agent contract with the Bears in the off-season. Walsh won eight of 11 regular-season starts.

Why the Vikings lost: Warren Moon continued to be frustrated in the postseason. Hampered by a sprained left knee ligament that caused him to miss the regular-season finale, Moon hit 29 of 52 passes for 294 yards with two touchdowns and two interceptions in the defeat, his fourth consecutive playoff loss. Moon set Minnesota playoff records for attempts and completions.

Turning points:

1. Chicago was sloppy early. First, running back Lewis Tillman fumbled at Chicago's 6 on the Bears' first possession. On Chicago's next drive, Walsh hit a Bears lineman in the helmet with a pass that bounced into the air and was intercepted. But Minnesota didn't take advantage of the turnovers, managing only a 3-0 lead.

2. After the shaky start, Walsh engineered touchdown drives of 80 and 71 yards. He was 6 for 6 on the Bears' first touchdown drive, capped by Tillman's one-yard run. Walsh's 52-yard pass to Jeff Graham highlighted Chicago's next touchdown drive, which ended with a nine-yard scoring strike from Walsh to Keith Jennings as the Bears took a 14-9 halftime lead.

Notable: The loss made Moon 3-7 in the postseason. . . . Dennis Green, who took over as Minnesota coach in 1992, is 0-3 in the playoffs with the Vikings. . . . The victory was Chicago's first in the postseason since 1990, and its first as a wild-card team. . . . Raymont Harris' 29-yard touchdown run in the third quarter was the longest of the season for Chicago. It came against a Minnesota defense that entered the game first in the NFL against the run. . . . Vikings running back Amp Lee caught a team-playoff-record 11 passes.

Quotable: Bears receiver Curtis Conway: ''We've been underdogs all year. A lot of people said we couldn't beat the Vikings. We won when we needed to win.''

BEARS 35, VIKINGS 18

Sunday, January 1

Chicago	0	14	7	14—35
Minnesota	3	6	3	6—18

First Quarter
Min—FG Reveiz 29, 6:59.

Second Quarter
Chi—Tillman 1 run (Butler kick), 3:14.
Chi—Jennings 9 pass from S. Walsh (Butler kick), 6:57.
Min—C. Carter 4 pass from Moon (pass failed), 14:41.

Third Quarter
Chi—Ra. Harris 29 run (Butler kick), 2:03.
Min—FG Reveiz 48, 14:55.

Fourth Quarter
Chi—J. Graham 21 pass from S. Walsh (Butler kick), 2:18.
Min—Lee 11 pass from Moon (pass failed), 9:24.
Chi—Miniefield 48 fumble return (Butler kick), 11:55.

TEAM STATISTICS

	Chicago	Minnesota
First downs	18	22
Rushes-yards	30-94	19-49
Passing	214	342
Punt returns-yards	1-1	0-0
Kickoff returns-yards	3-65	6-132
Interception returns-yards	2-19	1-10
Comp.-att.-int.	15-23-1	33-61-2
Sacked-yards lost	1-7	2-11
Punts-average	3-39	4-33
Fumbles-lost	1-1	3-2
Penalties-yards	6-30	11-85
Time of possession	25:21	34:39

Attendance—60,347.

INDIVIDUAL STATISTICS

RUSHING—Chicago, Ra. Harris 13-67, Tillman 11-19, S. Walsh 5-5, J. Graham 1-3. Minnesota, Allen 12-27, S. Graham 4-13, Moon 2-9, R. Smith 1-0.

PASSING—Chicago, S. Walsh 15-23-1-221. Minnesota, Moon 29-52-2-294, Salisbury 4-9-0-59.

RECEIVING—Chicago, J. Graham 4-108, Conway 4-56, Ra. Harris 3-20, T. Carter 1-16, Jennings 1-9, Tillman 1-7, Green 1-5. Minnesota, Lee 11-161, C. Carter 8-61, A. Jordan 4-35, Reed 3-39, Ismail 3-29, S. Jordan 2-16, Palmer 1-11, Allen 1-1.

MISSED FIELD GOAL ATTEMPTS—None.

INTERCEPTIONS—Chicago, Lincoln 1-12, Minter 1-7. Minnesota, Parker 1-10.

KICKOFF RETURNS—Chicago, Lewis 2-47, Green 1-18. Minnesota, R. Smith 6-132.

PUNT RETURNS—Chicago, J. Graham 1-1.

SACKS—Chicago, Armstrong 2. Minnesota, Parker 1.

DIVISIONAL PLAYOFFS

AFC

PITTSBURGH 29, CLEVELAND 9

Why the Steelers won: Barry Foster was able to run wild, gaining 133 yards on 24 carries. That allowed Neil O'Donnell, who completed 16 of 23 passes for 186 yards and two touchdowns, to pick apart a frustrated Cleveland defense.

Why the Browns lost: After an excellent performance in a wild-card victory over New England the previous week, Vinny Testaverde reverted to his familiar mistake-prone ways by completing just 13 of 31 passes for 144 yards and two interceptions. He was forced into many bad throws by the Steelers' vaunted "Blitzburgh" defense.

The turning points:

1. Cleveland failed to score on its first three possessions, as Derrick Alexander and Earnest Byner dropped two passes apiece. Conversely, Pittsburgh scored on its first three drives en route to building a 17-0 lead.

2. The Steelers put the game away late in the second quarter. After Cleveland kicker Matt Stover booted a 22-yard field goal to cut the Steelers' lead to 17-3, the Browns got the ball back when Pittsburgh receiver Ernie Mills fumbled. But a Testaverde pass to Alexander, who was covered well, was intercepted by Tim McKyer. The Steelers promptly scored, as O'Donnell hooked up with Yancey Thigpen on a nine-yard scoring strike with 16 seconds left in the half. That gave Pittsburgh a 24-3 halftime lead.

Notable: The victory was the Steelers' third of the season over the Browns, an unprecedented feat in the teams' 45-year rivalry. This was the first time the two clubs had met in the postseason, and it was Pittsburgh's first home playoff victory since 1979.... The loss made Cleveland 4-22 all-time in Three Rivers Stadium.... Since a 1969 postseason victory at Dallas, the Browns have dropped eight consecutive road playoff games.

Quotable: Cleveland safety Eric Turner: "They dominated the whole game. It's hard for me to say it, but that's what they did. They were at a championship level. You can't let a team run on you like that in a game like this."

STEELERS 29, BROWNS 9

Saturday, January 7

Cleveland	0	3	0	6—	9
Pittsburgh	3	21	3	2—	29

First Quarter
Pit—FG Anderson 39, 9:38.
Second Quarter
Pit—Green 2 pass from O'Donnell (Anderson kick), :48.
Pit—J. Williams 26 run (Anderson kick), 5:57.
Cle—FG Stover 22, 12:23.
Pit—Thigpen 9 pass from O'Donnell (Anderson kick), 14:44.
Third Quarter
Pit—FG Anderson 40, 12:25.
Fourth Quarter
Cle—McCardell 20 pass from Testaverde (pass failed), 9:07.
Pit—Safety, Lake sacked Testaverde in the end zone, 12:15.

TEAM STATISTICS

	Cleveland	Pittsburgh
First downs	10	23
Rushes-yards	17-55	51-238
Passing	131	186
Punt returns-yards	3-40	1-0
Kickoff returns-yards	6-106	3-30
Interception returns-yards	0-0	2-21
Comp.-att.-int.	13-31-2	16-23-0
Sacked-yards lost	2-13	0-0
Punts-average	5-38	5-38
Fumbles-lost	0-0	2-1
Penalties-yards	2-17	4-50
Time of possession	17:33	42:27

Attendance—58,185.

INDIVIDUAL STATISTICS

RUSHING—Cleveland, Byner 9-43, Hoard 3-8, Metcalf 5-4. Pittsburgh, Foster 24-133, Morris 22-60, J. Williams 2-43, Tomczak 3-2.

PASSING—Cleveland, Testaverde 13-31-2-144. Pittsburgh, O'Donnell 16-23-0-186.

RECEIVING—Cleveland, Jackson 3-47, McCardell 3-47, Metcalf 2-18, Carrier 2-8, Byner 1-14, Hoard 1-5, Kinchen 1-5. Pittsburgh, Mills 5-117, J. Williams 4-20, Green 3-21, Hastings 2-18, Thigpen 2-10.

MISSED FIELD GOAL ATTEMPTS—None.

INTERCEPTIONS—Pittsburgh, McKyer 1-21, Perry 1-0.

KICKOFF RETURNS—Cleveland, Metcalf 4-69, Baldwin 1-32, J. Jones 1-5. Pittsburgh, Johnson 2-28, Woodson 1-2.

PUNT RETURNS—Cleveland, Carrier 3-40. Pittsburgh, Woodson 1-0.

SACKS—Pittsburgh, Buckner 1, Lake 1.

SAN DIEGO 22, MIAMI 21

Why the Chargers won: They were able to keep Miami quarterback Dan Marino on the sidelines for most of the second half. He shredded the blitzing San Diego defense for 206 yards and three touchdowns in the first half, as Miami built a 21-6 lead. But in the second half, the Dolphins ran only 17 plays and had the ball for just 7:22, thanks largely to a 202-yard Chargers rushing attack spearheaded by Natrone Means. Marino netted only 56 yards passing in the second half, when the Dolphins were shut out.

Why the Dolphins lost: After San Diego battled back from a 21-6 deficit to take a 22-21 lead with 35 seconds left, the Dolphins quickly got themselves in position to win the game. Miami, which started its final drive on its 38 after recovering a squib kickoff, was aided by a 32-yard pass interference penalty against safety Eric Castle. That helped put kicker Pete Stoyanovich in position to win the game with a 48-yard field goal. But his kick sailed wide right with one second left.

The turning points:

1. The Chargers' comeback got off to an ominous start. With Miami leading, 21-6, San Diego took the second-half kickoff and marched 71 yards to Miami's 1. But on fourth down, Means was stopped. But the Chargers' defense stepped up, as tackle Reuben Davis stopped Bernie Parmalee in the end zone for a safety with 6:54 left in the third quarter. The comeback had begun.

2. San Diego trailed, 21-15, but had the ball on Miami's 8 late in the fourth quarter. San Diego lined up tight in a running formation, then sent everybody left. After a slight delay, receiver Mark Seay went right and was wide open. Stan Humphries, who faked a handoff and rolled right, quickly found Seay and hit him with what proved to be the game-winning touchdown pass with 35 seconds left.

Notable: Marino extended his NFL record to 12 consecutive playoff games with at least one touchdown pass. . . . By winning, the Chargers advanced to their first AFC title game since the 1981 season. . . . Trailing, 21-15, with 4:37 left in the game, San Diego scored what appeared to be the go-ahead touchdown when Humphries hit Shawn Jefferson with a 37-yard scoring strike. But officials ruled Jefferson was out of bounds. TV replays showed Jefferson had both feet in bounds on the reception. On the next play, Humphries was intercepted by safety Michael Stewart.

Quotable: Seay on his game-winning catch: "When I looked up, it just seemed to take forever for the ball to get there. I was going to catch the ball no matter if there was a diesel truck in front of me."

CHARGERS 22, DOLPHINS 21

Sunday, January 8

Miami	7	14	0	0—21
San Diego	0	6	9	7—22

First Quarter
Mia—K. Jackson 8 pass from Marino (Stoyanovich kick), 12:36.
Second Quarter
S.D.—FG Carney 20, 4:24.
Mia—K. Jackson 9 pass from Marino (Stoyanovich kick), 7:39.
S.D.—FG Carney 21, 12:13.
Mia—M. Williams 16 pass from Marino (Stoyanovich kick), 14:33.
Third Quarter
S.D.—Safety, R. Davis tackled Parmalee in the end zone, 8:06.
S.D.—Means 24 run (Carney kick), 12:18.
Fourth Quarter
S.D.—Seay 8 pass from Humphries (Carney kick), 14:25.

TEAM STATISTICS

	Miami	San Diego
First downs	17	28
Rushes-yards	8-26	40-202
Passing	257	264
Punt returns-yards	1-14	2-14
Kickoff returns-yards	5-112	5-88
Interception returns-yards	2-14	0-0
Comp.-att.-int.	24-38-0	28-43-2
Sacked-yards lost	1-5	2-12
Punts-average	5-45	2-44
Fumbles-lost	1-0	2-1
Penalties-yards	7-47	5-67
Time of possession	20:40	39:20
Attendance—63,381.		

INDIVIDUAL STATISTICS

RUSHING—Miami, Parmalee 7-16, Craver 1-10. San Diego, Means 24-139, Bieniemy 4-33, Culver 6-14, Harmon 3-12, Jefferson 1-3, Humphries 2-1.

PASSING—Miami, Marino 24-38-0-262. San Diego, Humphries 28-43-2-276.

RECEIVING—Miami, K. Jackson 8-109, Fryar 5-70, McDuffie 5-46, Craver 2-8, Parmalee 2-8, M. Williams 1-16, Saxon 1-5. San Diego, Harmon 7-57, Seay 6-61, Martin 5-62, Jefferson 3-44, Means 3-16, Culver 2-23, Pupunu 2-13.

MISSED FIELD GOAL ATTEMPTS—Miami, Stoyanovich 48.

INTERCEPTIONS—Miami, Smith 1-14, Stewart 1-0.

KICKOFF RETURNS—Miami, McDuffie 3-87, Spikes 1-18, R. Williams 1-7. San Diego, A. Coleman 3-57, Bieniemy 1-13, Harmon 1-18.

PUNT RETURNS—Miami, McDuffie 1-14. San Diego, A. Coleman 1-14, Gordon 1-0.

SACKS—Miami, M. Coleman 2. San Diego, Team 1.

SAN FRANCISCO 44, CHICAGO 15

Why the 49ers won: San Francisco's offense couldn't be stopped, as it surpassed 30 points for the ninth time in 11 games. Steve Young completed 16 of 22 passes for 143 yards, and a host of runners combined for 145 yards. The 49ers raced to a 30-3 halftime lead and increased their edge to 37-3 late in the third quarter. By then, most of the starters had been pulled.

Why the Bears lost: The high-powered San Francisco offense doesn't need help getting started, but Chicago provided a boost. A pair of Steve Walsh interceptions and a botched fake punt, all in the first half, helped fuel a streak of 37 consecutive points by the 49ers.

Turning points:

1. San Francisco tight end Brent Jones fumbled after catching a pass and Chicago defensive end Alonzo Spellman recovered the ball at the 49ers' 36. But the Bears had to settle for Kevin Butler's 39-yard field goal and a 3-0 lead. From there, it was all San Francisco, which scored on its next five possessions.

2. Trailing, 23-3, and struggling to move the ball, the Bears tried a fake punt with 2:15 left in the first half. The ball was snapped to the upback, Tony Carter, but he dropped it as he began to run and Dedrick Dodge swooped in to make the tackle and prevent Chicago from getting a first down.

Notable: Chicago has been outscored, 150-32, in its past four games against San Francisco.... The defeat was the third-worst playoff beating in Chicago history.... After Young scored on a six-yard touchdown run with 1:17 left in the first half, he was leveled in the end zone by Chicago safety Shaun Gayle. Young got up and spiked the ball at Gayle's feet, while Jones and Jerry Rice confronted Gayle. A brief melee ensued.

Quotable: San Francisco Coach George Seifert: "I didn't see much of anything we did wrong. We're pleased with our first step. We know we have to crank it up."

49ERS 44, BEARS 15

Saturday, January 7

Chicago	3	0	0	12—15
San Francisco	7	23	7	7—44

First Quarter
Chi—FG Butler 39, 3:58.
S.F.—Floyd 2 run (Brien kick), 11:19.
Second Quarter
S.F.—Jones 8 pass from S. Young (kick failed), :44.
S.F.—Floyd 4 run (Brien kick), 8:56.
S.F.—FG Brien 36, 12:15.
S.F.—S. Young 6 run (Brien kick), 13:43.
Third Quarter
S.F.—Floyd 1 run (Brien kick), 8:01.
Fourth Quarter
Chi—Flanigan 2 pass from Kramer (pass failed), :49.
S.F.—Walker 1 run (Brien kick), 3:09.
Chi—Tillman 1 run (pass failed), 9:16.

TEAM STATISTICS

	Chicago	San Francisco
First downs	20	27
Rushes-yards	18-39	37-145
Passing	208	185
Punt returns-yards	0-0	2-6
Kickoff returns-yards	6-137	2-24
Interception returns-yards	0-0	2-31
Comp.-att.-int.	29-47-2	18-26-0
Sacked-yards lost	4-31	1-5
Punts-average	4-37	2-39
Fumbles-lost	2-0	3-1
Penalties-yards	4-32	3-16
Time of possession	29:40	30:20
Attendance—64,644.		

INDIVIDUAL STATISTICS

RUSHING—Chicago, Harris 8-26, Green 2-8, Tillman 6-5, Walsh 1-0, T. Carter 1-0. San Francisco, Watters 11-55, S. Young 5-32, Floyd 10-25, D. Carter 3-20, Taylor 1-15, Walker 3-3, Grbac 4-(minus 5).

PASSING—Chicago, Walsh 10-19-2-78, Kramer 19-28-0-161. San Francisco, S. Young 16-22-0-143.

RECEIVING—Chicago, Green 5-43, Wetnight 5-39, Harris 5-24, Graham 4-33, Waddle 3-49, Conway 3-25, Jennings 2-20, Tillman 1-4, Flanigan 1-2. San Francisco, Jones 5-26, Taylor 4-51, Rice 4-48, Watters 3-18, D. Carter 1-44, Popson 1-3.

MISSED FIELD GOAL ATTEMPTS—None.

INTERCEPTIONS—San Francisco, Davis 1-0, Hanks 1-31.

KICKOFF RETURNS—Chicago, Lewis 5-125, Green 1-12. San Francisco, D. Carter 1-10, Walker 1-14.

PUNT RETURNS—San Francisco, D. Carter 2-6.

SACKS—Chicago, Spellman 1. San Francisco, Harris 2, R. Hall 1, B. Young 1.

DALLAS 35, GREEN BAY 9

Why the Cowboys won: Troy Aikman, who had one touchdown pass and seven interceptions in his previous five games, registered the best postseason numbers of his career, completing 23 of 30 passes for 337 yards with two touchdown passes.

Why the Packers lost: Poor play in the secondary, particularly by cornerback Terrell Buckley, doomed Green Bay. The 5-foot-9 Buckley was overmatched by the big Dallas receivers. Also, the absence of star receiver Sterling Sharpe, who missed the game with a neck injury, hindered the Packers' attack.

Turning points:

1. Nursing a 7-3 lead in the first quarter, Dallas took control. Aikman, standing three yards deep in his end zone, launched a pass to Alvin Harper, who caught it at the 50. Harper proceeded to outrun Buckley before breaking safety George Teague's attempted arm tackle at the 10-yard line en route to scoring a 94-yard touchdown.

2. A one-yard touchdown run by Edgar Bennett with 4:31 left in the first half cut Dallas' lead to 21-9 and gave Green Bay life. But the Packers' comeback hopes were dashed on the Cowboys' ensuing possession, when Buckley dropped a potential interception in the end zone. Five plays later, Buckley, who was whistled for illegal contact in the third quarter, was called for pass interference. The Dallas drive culminated with Aikman's one-yard pass to tight end Scott Galbraith with 11 seconds left in the half. That gave the Cowboys a 28-9 halftime lead.

Notable: Harper's 94-yard touchdown catch was the longest in NFL postseason history. Of Harper's 23 career postseason receptions, nine have been for at least 35 yards. . . . Three Cowboys—tight end Jay Novacek (104) and wide receivers Michael Irvin (111) and Harper (108)—finished with 100 receiving yards, which equaled an NFL postseason record. . . . Aikman improved to 7-0 as a postseason starter. The victory also was Dallas' 28th all-time playoff triumph, the most in the NFL. . . . Emmitt Smith left the game in the final minutes of the first quarter after reinjuring his left hamstring, which he originally hurt three weeks ago. He finished the game with seven carries for 44 yards. Blair Thomas took his place, rushing for a game-high 70 yards on 23 carries.

Quotable: Green Bay Coach Mike Holmgren: "They have a lot of great weapons, and it seems like they always pop big plays whenever they play us. All the teams in the NFL are trying to catch the 49ers and the Cowboys. Next week will be a great game (Dallas-San Francisco in the NFC final). It's what the public wanted and now here it is."

COWBOYS 35, PACKERS 9

Sunday, January 8

Green Bay	3	6	0	0— 9
Dallas	14	14	0	7—35

First Quarter
Dal—E. Smith 5 run (Boniol kick), 3:53.
G.B.—FG Jacke 50, 7:28.
Dal—Harper 94 pass from Aikman (Boniol kick), 11:20.
Second Quarter
Dal—B. Thomas 1 run (Boniol kick), 8:15.
G.B.—Bennett 1 run (pass failed), 10:29.
Dal—Galbraith 1 pass from Aikman (Boniol kick), 14;49.
Fourth Quarter
Dal—B. Thomas 2 run (Boniol kick), 3:32.

TEAM STATISTICS

	Green Bay	Dallas
First downs	18	27
Rushes-yards	23-99	32-120
Passing	228	330
Punt returns-yards	2-23	0-0
Kickoff returns-yards	6-144	3-88
Interception returns-yards	1-34	1-2
Comp.-att.-int.	21-46-1	23-32-1
Sacked-yards lost	1-8	1-7
Punts-average	4-44	4-46
Fumbles-lost	0-0	1-1
Penalties-yards	8-43	7-46
Time of possession	26:52	33:08
Attendance—64,745.		

INDIVIDUAL STATISTICS

RUSHING—Green Bay, Bennett 11-34, Brunell 4-26, Brooks 2-23, Cobb 4-14, Favre 2-2. Dallas, B. Thomas 23-70, E. Smith 7-44, Johnston 1-4, Aikman 1-2.

PASSING—Green Bay, Favre 18-35-1-211, Brunell 3-11-0-25. Dallas, Aikman 23-30-1-337, Peete 0-2-0-0.

RECEIVING—Green Bay, Brooks 8-138, Morgan 5-52, Bennett 3-11, Chmura 2-13, Cobb 1-12, R. Johnson 1-9, Levens 1-1. Dallas, Novacek 11-104, Irvin 6-111, Harper 2-108, Johnston 1-8, E. Smith 1-3, B. Thomas 1-2, Galbraith 1-1.

MISSED FIELD GOAL ATTEMPTS—Green Bay, Jacke 37.

INTERCEPTIONS—Green Bay, Paup 1-34. Dallas, K. Smith 1-2.

KICKOFF RETURNS—Green Bay, Harris 5-132, Jordan 1-12. Dallas, K. Williams 3-88.

PUNT RETURNS—Green Bay, Brooks 2-23.

SACKS—Green Bay, Jones 1. Dallas, Jeffcoat 1.

CONFERENCE CHAMPIONSHIPS

SAN DIEGO 17, PITTSBURGH 13

Why the Chargers won: The San Diego offense made the big plays when needed. The Chargers ran just 16 plays and had the ball for a mere 7:49 in the first half but only trailed 10-3 because Pittsburgh's offense had trouble scoring despite racking up yardage. San Diego took command in the second half, when Stan Humphries tossed two 43-yard touchdown passes.

Why the Steelers lost: After finding it easy to throw on the Chargers early in the game, Pittsburgh all but abandoned its running attack and switched to a short- to medium-range passing game. Despite compiling gaudy statistics, the Steelers had trouble finishing drives, mainly because their rushing game never got on track.

Turning points:

1. Trailing, 13-10, late in the fourth quarter, the Chargers faced a third and 14 from the Steelers' 43. Humphries threw deep despite a blitz. His pass was caught for what proved to be the game-winning touchdown by Tony Martin, who beat veteran cornerback Tim McKyer.

2. Trailing, 17-13, Pittsburgh drove from its 17 to San Diego's 3 with 68 seconds left. On fourth down, Neil O'Donnell passed to Barry Foster, who was open briefly over the middle just inside the end zone. But linebacker Dennis Gibson reached in front of Foster and knocked down the low pass, clinching victory for the Chargers.

Notable: By winning, San Diego advanced to the Super Bowl for the first time. . . . O'Donnell set AFC title game marks for attempts (54) and completions (32). . . . It was the first time since the 1979 season that Pittsburgh hosted the AFC title game. . . . The Chargers improved their all-time record in Pittsburgh to 2-9. Ironically, San Diego's only other victory in the Steel City was in the postseason, when the Chargers beat the Steelers, 31-28, in 1982. Like this encounter, the '82 contest also featured San Diego rallying from a 10-point second-half deficit to win. . . . San Diego entered the game with the NFL's best road record (6-2). . . . Pittsburgh had the NFL's top rushing offense during the regular season. But the Steelers ran for only 66 yards on 26 carries against the Chargers. San Diego hasn't allowed a 100-yard rusher in 29 contests. The last to run for 100 against the Chargers was Foster on October 10, 1993.

Quotable: Pittsburgh linebacker Chad Brown: "This is an awful feeling. We're not going to the Super Bowl. We're not going to the show."

CHARGERS 17, STEELERS 13

Sunday, January 15

San Diego	0	3	7	7—17
Pittsburgh	7	3	3	0—13

First Quarter
Pit—J. Williams 16 pass from O'Donnell (Anderson kick), 7:32.

Second Quarter
S.D.—FG Carney 20, 11:19.
Pit—FG Anderson 39, 14:51.

Third Quarter
Pit—FG Anderson 23, 4:23.
S.D.—Pupunu 43 pass from Humphries (Carney kick), 6:57.

Fourth Quarter
S.D.—Martin 43 pass from Humphries (Carney kick), 9:47.

TEAM STATISTICS

	San Diego	Pittsburgh
First downs	13	22
Rushes-yards	24-66	26-66
Passing	160	349
Punt returns-yards	2-2	2-10
Kickoff returns-yards	3-72	4-73
Interception returns-yards	0-0	1-6
Comp.-att.-int.	11-22-1	32-54-0
Sacked-yards lost	1-5	0-0
Punts-average	5-38	5-44
Fumbles-lost	0-0	3-1
Penalties-yards	3-15	8-111
Time of possession	22:47	37:13

Attendance—61,545.

INDIVIDUAL STATISTICS

RUSHING—San Diego, Means 20-69, Humphries 4-(minus 3). Pittsburgh, Foster 20-47, J. Williams 3-16, Morris 2-2, O'Donnell 1-1.

PASSING—San Diego, Humphries 11-22-1-165. Pittsburgh, O'Donnell 32-54-0-349.

RECEIVING—San Diego, Pupunu 4-76, Means 2-19, Jefferson 2-16, Martin 1-43, Mitchell 1-19, Harmon 1-(minus 8). Pittsburgh, Mills 8-106, J. Williams 7-45, Hastings 5-55, Green 4-80, Thigpen 3-35, Foster 3-12, Hayes 1-16, Morris 1-0.

MISSED FIELD GOAL ATTEMPTS—None.

INTERCEPTIONS—Pittsburgh, Woodson 1-6.

KICKOFF RETURNS—San Diego, Coleman 2-49, Harmon 1-23. Pittsburgh, Johnson 4-73.

PUNT RETURNS—San Diego, Gordon 2-2. Pittsburgh, Woodson 2-10.

SACKS—Pittsburgh, Buckner 1.

SAN FRANCISCO 38, DALLAS 28

Why the 49ers won: San Francisco's defense, which was retooled in the off-season specifically to beat Dallas, scored the first touchdown of the game and set the tone for victory early.

Why the Cowboys lost: Turnovers doomed Dallas. Troy Aikman threw three interceptions and the Cowboys lost two fumbles. Dallas committed three of its miscues early in the first quarter, as San Francisco converted the turnovers into a 21-0 lead with 7:33 left in the quarter. The Cowboys never got closer than 10 points thereafter.

The turning points:

1. Three plays into the game, San Francisco cornerback Eric Davis switched off Michael Irvin at the last moment and stepped in front of Kevin Williams to pick off a pass and subsequently race untouched 44 yards for the first touchdown.

2. Dallas' second possession was as disastrous as its first. On the third play of the series, Davis forced a second turnover when he stripped Irvin of the ball. It took the 49ers just five plays to score, as Ricky Watters caught a 29-yard touchdown pass from Steve Young to cap the 39-yard drive.

3. After San Francisco took a 14-0 lead, Williams fumbled the ensuing kickoff after he was hit by Adam Walker. The 49ers recovered and proceeded to move 35 yards in seven plays en route to their third touchdown of the first quarter, as William Floyd scored on a one-yard run.

Notable: The loss was the first for Aikman in the postseason (7-1). . . . Irvin set an NFC championship game record with 192 yards receiving. His 12 catches tied an NFC title game mark. . . . Emmitt Smith, whose status was in doubt until game time because of a nagging hamstring pull in his left leg, gained 74 yards on 20 carries before injuring his right hamstring in the fourth quarter. . . . San Francisco had lost the previous two NFC title games to Dallas.

Quotable: Dallas Coach Barry Switzer: "You go out and play five minutes of the ball game and give San Francisco 21 points. . . . It's kind of like the Keystone Cops. It's a laugher."

49ERS 38, COWBOYS 28

Sunday, January 15

Dallas	7	7	7	7—28
San Francisco	21	10	7	0—38

First Quarter
S.F.—Davis 44 interception return (Brien kick), 1:02.
S.F.—Watters 29 pass from S. Young (Brien kick), 4:19.
S.F.—Floyd 1 run (Brien kick), 7:27.
Dal—Irvin 44 pass from Aikman (Boniol kick), 12:46.

Second Quarter
S.F.—FG Brien 34, 9:06.
Dal—E. Smith 4 run (Boniol kick), 13:04.
S.F.—Rice 28 pass from S. Young (Brien kick), 14:52.

Third Quarter
Dal—E. Smith 1 run (Boniol kick), 3:12.
S.F.—S. Young 3 run (Brien kick), 8:21.

Fourth Quarter
Dal—Irvin 10 pass from Aikman (Boniol kick), 6:31.

TEAM STATISTICS

	Dallas	San Francisco
First downs	29	19
Rushes-yards	24-99	31-139
Passing	352	155
Punt returns-yards	1-10	0-0
Kickoff returns-yards	7-144	5-90
Interception returns-yards	0-0	3-44
Comp.-att.-int.	30-53-3	13-29-0
Sacked-yards lost	4-28	0-0
Punts-average	1-23	5-36
Fumbles-lost	2-2	1-1
Penalties-yards	9-98	4-30
Time of possession	33:56	26:04

Attendance—69,125.

INDIVIDUAL STATISTICS

RUSHING—Dallas, E. Smith 20-74, K. Williams 2-12, Aikman 1-9, Johnston 1-4. San Francisco, Watters 14-72, S. Young 10-47, Floyd 7-20.

PASSING—Dallas, Aikman 30-53-3-380. San Francisco, S. Young 13-29-0-155.

RECEIVING—Dallas, Irvin 12-192, K. Williams 6-78, Novacek 5-72, Johnston 3-19, E. Smith 3-5, Harper 1-14. San Francisco, B. Jones 3-37, Floyd 3-16, Rice 2-36, Taylor 2-31, Popson 2-6, Watters 1-29.

MISSED FIELD GOAL ATTEMPTS—Dallas, Boniol 27.

INTERCEPTIONS—San Francisco, Davis 2-44, Sanders 1-0.

KICKOFF RETURNS—Dallas, K. Williams 6-130, Marion 1-14. San Francisco, D. Carter 3-65, Sanders 1-25, Walker 1-0.

PUNT RETURNS—Dallas, K. Williams 1-10.

SACKS—San Francisco, R. Hall 2, Harris 2.

SUPER BOWL XXIX

AT JOE ROBBIE STADIUM. MIAMI. JANUARY 29. 1995

SAN FRANCISCO 49, SAN DIEGO 26

Why the 49ers won: San Francisco's offense was unstoppable, scoring on six of its first eight possessions. The 49ers led, 28-10, at halftime and by as many as 32 points in the second half.

Why the Chargers lost: The San Diego defense, particularly its secondary, was beaten often and tackled poorly. Steve Young, the game's MVP, completed 24 of 36 passes for 325 yards and a Super Bowl-record six touchdowns. He also paced the 49ers with 49 yards rushing.

The turning points:

1. After receiving the opening kickoff, San Francisco needed just two plays to reach San Diego territory. On San Francisco's third play, Jerry Rice split safeties Stanley Richard and Darren Carrington and caught Young's 44-yard touchdown pass. Only 84 seconds had expired, making it the quickest touchdown in Super Bowl history.

2. After falling behind, 14-0, with 10:05 left in the first quarter, the Chargers tried to stay close. They orchestrated an impressive 13-play, 78-yard drive behind the running of Natrone Means, who capped the effort with a one-yard scoring run. But San Francisco responded on its next possession, driving 70 yards on 10 plays, with Young finishing off the drive with a five-yard touchdown pass to William Floyd for a 21-7 lead with 13:02 left in the first half.

Notable: It was a record fifth Super Bowl win—against no losses—for San Francisco.... Rice set Super Bowl career records for touchdowns (seven), points (42) and reception yards (512). ... In the third quarter, San Diego's Andre Coleman tied a Super Bowl record when he returned a kickoff 98 yards for a touchdown. It was just the third kickoff return for a score in Super Bowl history.... 49ers linebacker Ken Norton, who left Dallas in the off-season to sign a free-agent deal with San Francisco, became the first player to be a member of three consecutive Super Bowl champs.... The AFC has lost the past 11 Super Bowls.

Quotable: San Francisco tight end Brent Jones, on the 49ers' offense: "I don't think anybody can touch it. The statistics speak for themselves. The yards. The points. The weapons. I mean, every one of these guys is an All-Pro, all the time."

49ERS 49, CHARGERS 26

Sunday, January 29

San Diego	7	3	8	8—26
San Francisco	14	14	14	7—49

First Quarter
S.F.—Rice 44 pass from Young (Brien kick), 1:24.
S.F.—Watters 51 pass from Young (Brien kick), 4:55.
S.D.—Means 1 run (Carney kick), 12:16.

Second Quarter
S.F.—Floyd 5 pass from Young (Brien kick), 1:58.
S.F.—Watters 8 pass from Young (Brien kick), 10:16.
S.D.—FG Carney 31, 13:16.

Third Quarter
S.F.—Watters 9 run (Brien kick), 5:25.
S.F.—Rice 15 pass from Young (Brien kick), 11:42.
S.D.—Coleman 98 kickoff return (Seay pass from Humphries), 11:59.

Fourth Quarter
S.F.—Rice 7 pass from Young (Brien kick), 1:11.
S.D.—Martin 30 pass from Humphries (Pupunu pass from Humphries), 12:35.

TEAM STATISTICS

	San Diego	San Francisco
First downs	20	28
Rushes-yards	19-67	32-133
Passing	287	316
Punt returns-yards	3-1	2-12
Kickoff returns-yards	8-242	4-48
Interception returns-yards	0-0	3-16
Comp.-att.-int.	27-55-3	25-38-0
Sacked-yards lost	2-18	3-15
Punts-average	4-49	5-40
Fumbles-lost	1-0	2-0
Penalties-yards	6-63	3-18
Time of possession	28:29	31:31

Attendance—74,107.

INDIVIDUAL STATISTICS

RUSHING—San Diego, Means 13-33, Jefferson 1-10, Harmon 2-10, Gilbert 1-8, Bieniemy 1-3, Humphries 1-3. San Francisco, Young 5-49, Watters 15-47, Floyd 9-32, Rice 1-10, Carter 2-(minus 5).

PASSING—San Diego, Humphries 24-49-2-275, Gilbert 3-6-1-30. San Francisco, Young 24-36-0-325, Grbac 0-1-0-0, Musgrave 1-1-0-6.

RECEIVING—San Diego, Harmon 8-68, Seay 7-75, Pupunu 4-48, Martin 3-59, Jefferson 2-15, Bieniemy 1-33, Means 1-4, Young 1-3. San Francisco, Rice 10-149, Taylor 4-43, Floyd 4-26, Watters 3-61, Jones 2-41, Popson 1-6, McCaffrey 1-5.

MISSED FIELD GOAL ATTEMPTS—San Francisco, Brien 47.

INTERCEPTIONS—San Francisco, Sanders 1-15, Cook 1-1, Davis 1-0.

KICKOFF RETURNS—San Diego, Coleman 8-242. San Francisco, Carter 4-48.

PUNT RETURNS—San Diego, Gordon 3-1. San Francisco, Carter 2-12.

SACKS—San Diego, Johnson 2-11, Seau 1-4. San Francisco, Stublefield 1-9, Brown 0.5-4.5, Harris 0.5-4.5.

PRO BOWL

AFC 41, NFC 13

Why the AFC won: Its running game was terrific. The AFC piled up 400 yards on 40 attempts, and Marshall Faulk of the Indianapolis Colts, the only rookie in the game, set a Pro Bowl rushing record with 180 yards on 13 carries.

Why the NFC lost: Unlike the AFC, the NFC could muster little offense. Three quarterbacks combined to complete just 13 of 32 passes and the running game was held to just 41 yards. The NFC scored only three points in the final 50 minutes.

The turning point:

1. After the first quarter ended with the NFC leading, 10-0, the AFC scored its first points on Denver quarterback John Elway's 22-yard touchdown pass to Pittsburgh tight end Eric Green. The TD came after San Diego's Natrone Means ran 41 yards to the NFC 47-yard line and Elway completed a 5-yard pass to Tim Brown on 4th-and-2 to the NFC 34.

Notable: O.J. Simpson's 22-year-old Pro Bowl rushing record (112 yards) was broken twice in the game. Seattle's Chris Warren carried 14 times for 127 yards before being replaced late in the contest by Faulk, who ran 41 yards on the next play to surpass Warren. Faulk later ran 49 yards off a fake punt for the game's final touchdown. . . . Redskins linebacker Ken Harvey and Chargers linebacker Junior Seau each made a game-high seven tackles. . . . There were no fumbles. . . . The NFC leads the Pro Bowl series, 14-11.

Quotable: Faulk: "To have a big game here means a lot. I ran behind an All-Pro line, and it showed. We just blew them off the ball."

AFC 41, NFC 13
Sunday, February 5

AFC	0	17	3	21—41
NFC	10	0	3	0—13

First Quarter
NFC—FG Reveiz 28, 6:55.
NFC—Carter 51 pass from Young (Reveiz kick), 9:09.
Second Quarter
AFC—Green 22 pass from Elway (Carney kick), 0:43.
AFC—FG Carney 22, 7:28.
AFC—Hoard 4 run (Carney kick), 12:53.
Third Quarter
NFC—FG Reveiz 49, 4:58.
AFC—FG Carney 23, 13:24.
Fourth Quarter
AFC—Warren 11 run (Carney kick), 2:31.
AFC—Green 16 pass from Hostetler (Carney kick), 8:17.
AFC—Faulk 49 run (Carney kick), 12:31.

TEAM STATISTICS

	AFC	NFC
First downs	27	10
Rushes-yards	40-400	19-41
Passing	152	155
Punt returns-yards	7-105	2-47
Kickoff returns-yards	4-61	8-184
Interception returns-yards	0-0	1-10
Comp.-att.-int.	12-28-1	13-32-0
Sacked-yards lost	1-5	2-13
Punts-average	4-40.3	8-50.1
Fumbles-lost	0-0	0-0
Penalties-yards	6-35	7-45
Time of possession	33:53	26:07

Attendance—49,121.

INDIVIDUAL STATISTICS

RUSHING—AFC, Faulk 13-180, Warren 14-127, Means 5-61, Hoard 4-20, Hostetler 1-10, Bledsoe 2-3, Reed 1-(-1). NFC, Bettis 6-22, B. Sanders 8-17, Johnston 2-6, Watters 1-2, Aikman 1-0, D. Sanders 1-(-6).

PASSING—AFC, Elway 3-7-0-31, Bledsoe 5-13-1-43, Hostetler 4-8-0-83. NFC, Young 8-15-0-129, Aikman 2-9-0-17, Moon 3-8-0-22.

RECEIVING—AFC, Green 4-50, Faulk 2-27, Coates 2-12, Brown 2-9, Fryar 1-35, Hoard 1-24. NFC, Carter 4-81, Mathis 2-23, Johnston 2-17, Irvin 1-18, D. Sanders 1-15, H. Moore 1-13, B. Sanders 1-2, Bettis 1-(-1).

MISSED FIELD GOAL ATTEMPTS—None.

INTERCEPTIONS—AFC, none. NFC, D. Sanders 1-10.

KICKOFF RETURNS—AFC, Faulk 2-37, Metcalf 2-24. NFC, Gray 7-162, Mathis 1-22.

PUNT RETURNS—AFC, Metcalf 6-89, Brown 1-16. NFC, Gray 2-47.

SACKS—AFC, Burnett 1, O'Neal 1. NFC, Lett 1.

AFC SQUAD

OFFENSE

WR—Tim Brown, L.A. Raiders*
　　Andre Reed, Buffalo*
　　Irving Fryar, Miami
　　Rob Moore, N.Y. Jets
TE—Ben Coates, New England*
　　Shannon Sharpe, Denver
　T—Richmond Webb, Miami*
　　Bruce Armstrong, New England*
　　Gary Zimmerman, Denver
　G—Keith Sims, Miami*
　　Steve Wisniewski, L.A. Raiders*
　　Duval Love, Pittsburgh
　C—Dermontti Dawson, Pittsburgh*
　　Bruce Matthews, Houston
QB—Dan Marino, Miami*
　　John Elway, Denver
　　Drew Bledsoe, New England
RB—Marshall Faulk, Indianapolis*
　　Natrone Means, San Diego*
　　Chris Warren, Seattle
FB—Leroy Hoard, Cleveland

NOTE: TE Sharpe replaced due to injury by Eric Green, Pittsburgh; QB Marino replaced due to injury by Jeff Hostetler, L.A. Raiders.

DEFENSE

DE—Bruce Smith, Buffalo*
　　Leslie O'Neal, San Diego*
　　Neil Smith, Kansas City
DT—Michael Dean Perry, Cleveland*
　　Cortez Kennedy, Seattle*
　　Chester McGlockton, L.A. Raiders
OLB—Derrick Thomas, Kansas City*
　　Greg Lloyd, Pittsburgh*
　　Kevin Greene, Pittsburgh
ILB—Junior Seau, San Diego*
　　Bryan Cox, Miami
　　Pepper Johnson, Cleveland†
CB—Rod Woodson, Pittsburgh*
　　Terry McDaniel, L.A. Raiders*
　　Dale Carter, Kansas City
SS—Carnell Lake, Pittsburgh*
　　Steve Atwater, Denver
FS—Eric Turner, Cleveland*

NOTE: DE N. Smith replaced due to injury by Rob Burnett, Cleveland.

SPECIALISTS

P—Rick Tuten, Seattle
K—John Carney, San Diego
KR—Eric Metcalf, Cleveland
ST—Steve Tasker, Buffalo

NFC SQUAD

OFFENSE

WR—Jerry Rice, San Francisco*
　　Cris Carter, Minnesota*
　　Sterling Sharpe, Green Bay
　　Michael Irvin, Dallas
TE—Brent Jones, San Francisco*
　　Jay Novacek, Dallas
　T—William Roaf, New Orleans*
　　Lomas Brown, Detroit*
　　Mark Tuinei, Dallas
　G—Nate Newton, Dallas*
　　Randall McDaniel, Minnesota*
　　Jesse Sapolu, San Francisco
　C—Mark Stepnoski, Dallas*
　　Bart Oates, San Francisco
QB—Steve Young, San Francisco*
　　Troy Aikman, Dallas
　　Warren Moon, Minnesota
RB—Emmitt Smith, Dallas*
　　Barry Sanders, Detroit*
　　Jerome Bettis, L.A. Rams
FB—Daryl Johnston, Dallas

NOTE: WR Rice replaced due to injury by Herman Moore, Detroit; WR Sharpe replaced due to injury by Terance Mathis, Atlanta; RB Smith replaced due to injury by Ricky Watters, San Francisco.

DEFENSE

DE—Reggie White, Green Bay*
　　Charles Haley, Dallas*
　　William Fuller, Philadelphia
DT—John Randle, Minnesota*
　　Leon Lett, Dallas*
　　Dana Stubblefield, San Francisco
OLB—Ken Harvey, Washington*
　　Bryce Paup, Green Bay*
　　Seth Joyner, Arizona
ILB—Chris Spielman, Detroit*
　　Jessie Tuggle, Atlanta
　　Jack Del Rio, Minnesota†
CB—Deion Sanders, San Francisco*
　　Aeneas Williams, Arizona*
　　Eric Allen, Philadelphia
　S—Darren Woodson, Dallas*
　　Merton Hanks, San Francisco*
　　Tim McDonald, San Francisco

NOTE: DE White replaced due to injury by Wayne Martin, New Orleans.

SPECIALISTS

P—Reggie Roby, Washington
K—Fuad Reveiz, Minnesota
KR—Mel Gray, Detroit
ST—Elbert Shelley, Atlanta

*Elected starter.
†Selected as need player.

PLAYER PARTICIPATION

Player, Team	GP	GS	Player, Team	GP	GS	Player, Team	GP	GS
Abrams, Bobby, Minnesota	16	0	Barnes, Tomur, Houston	1	0	Bowens, Tim, Miami	16	15
Adams, Sam, Seattle	12	7	Barnett, Fred, Philadelphia	16	16	Boyd, Malik, Minnesota	16	1
Adams, Scott, New Orleans	11	0	Barnett, Harlon, New England	16	16	Boyer, Brant, Miami	14	0
Agee, Mel, Atlanta	16	6	Barnett, Oliver, Buffalo	16	2	Boykin, Deral, Washington	12	0
Agee, Tommie, Dallas	15	0	Barnett, Troy, New England	14	0	Brabham, Cary, L.A. Raiders	7	0
Agnew, Ray, New England	11	3	Barnhardt, Tommy, New Orleans	16	0	Bradford, Ronnie, Denver	12	0
Aguiar, Louie, Kansas City	16	0	Barrie, Sebastian, Arizona	10	0	Brady, Ed, Tampa Bay	16	0
Ahanotu, Chidi, Tampa Bay	16	16	Barrow, Micheal, Houston	16	16	Brady, Jeff, Tampa Bay	16	0
Aikman, Troy, Dallas	14	14	Barton, Harris, San Francisco	9	9	Brady, Rickey, L.A. Rams	1	0
Alberts, Trev, Indianapolis	5	0	Bates, Bill, Dallas	15	0	Braham, Rich, Cincinnati	3	0
Aldridge, Allen, Denver	16	2	Bates, Mario, New Orleans	11	7	Brandon, David, Seattle	13	0
Ale, Arnold, Kansas City	2	0	Bates, Michael, Seattle	15	0	Brandon, Michael, Arizona	1	0
Alexander, Brent, Arizona	16	7	Bates, Patrick, L.A. Raiders	16	9	Brantley, Chris, L.A. Rams	15	0
Alexander, David, Philadelphia	16	16	Baty, Greg, Miami	16	0	Bratzke, Chad, N.Y. Giants	2	0
Alexander, Derrick, Cleveland	14	12	Bavaro, David, New England	9	5	Braxton, David, Cincinnati	9	0
Alexander, Elijah, Denver	16	16	Bavaro, Mark, Philadelphia	12	11	Braxton, Tyrone, Miami	16	0
Alexander, Harold, Atlanta	15	0	Baxter, Brad, N.Y. Jets	15	9	Brewer, Dewell, Indianapolis	16	0
Alipate, Tuineau, N.Y. Jets	8	0	Baxter, Fred, N.Y. Jets	11	1	Brien, Doug, San Francisco	16	0
Allen, Eric, Philadelphia	16	16	Bayless, Martin, Washington	16	15	Brilz, Darrick, Cincinnati	15	15
Allen, Larry, Dallas	16	10	Beamon, Willie, N.Y. Giants	15	0	Brim, Mike, Cincinnati	16	16
Allen, Marcus, Kansas City	13	13	Beavers, Aubrey, Miami	16	10	Brisby, Vincent, New England	14	11
Allen, Terry, Minnesota	16	16	Beckles, Ian, Tampa Bay	16	16	Brister, Bubby, Philadelphia	7	2
Alt, John, Kansas City	13	13	Beebe, Don, Buffalo	13	11	Brock, Matt, Green Bay	5	0
Ambrose, Ashley, Indianapolis	16	4	Beer, Tom, Detroit	9	0	Brock, Stan, San Diego	16	16
Anders, Kimble, Kansas City	16	13	Belin, Chuck, L.A. Rams	14	6	Brooks, Bill, Buffalo	16	9
Andersen, Morten, New Orleans	16	0	Bell, Myron, Pittsburgh	15	0	Brooks, Bucky, Buffalo	3	0
Anderson, Darren, Kansas City	15	1	Bell, William, Washington	7	0	Brooks, Michael, N.Y. Giants	16	16
Anderson, Dunstan, Atlanta	1	0	Bellamy, Jay, Seattle	3	0	Brooks, Reggie, Washington	13	5
Anderson, Eddie, L.A. Raiders	14	14	Belser, Jason, Indianapolis	13	12	Brooks, Robert, Green Bay	16	16
Anderson, Erick, Washington	2	0	Bender, Wes, L.A. Raiders	9	0	Brostek, Bern, L.A. Rams	10	10
Anderson, Gary, Pittsburgh	16	0	Benfatti, Lou, N.Y. Jets	7	0	Broussard, Steve, Cincinnati	13	3
Anderson, Jamal, Atlanta	3	0	Bennett, Cornelius, Buffalo	16	16	Brown, Chad, Arizona	8	2
Anderson, Richie, N.Y. Jets	13	5	Bennett, Donnell, Kansas City	15	0	Brown, Chad, Pittsburgh	16	16
Anderson, Stevie, N.Y. Jets	10	0	Bennett, Edgar, Green Bay	16	15	Brown, Corwin, New England	16	0
Anderson, Willie, L.A. Rams	16	16	Bennett, Tony, Indianapolis	16	15	Brown, Dave, N.Y. Giants	15	15
Arbuckle, Charles, Indianapolis	7	1	Berger, Mitch, Philadelphia	5	0	Brown, Dennis, San Francisco	16	14
Archambeau, Lester, Atlanta	16	12	Bernstine, Rod, Denver	3	3	Brown, Derek, New Orleans	16	9
Armstead, Jessie, N.Y. Giants	16	0	Bettis, Jerome, L.A. Rams	16	16	Brown, Derek, N.Y. Giants	13	0
Armstrong, Bruce, New England	16	16	Beuerlein, Steve, Arizona	9	7	Brown, Gary, Green Bay	1	0
Armstrong, Trace, Chicago	15	15	Biasucci, Dean, Indianapolis	16	0	Brown, Gary, Houston	12	8
Armstrong, Tyji, Tampa Bay	16	9	Bickett, Duane, Seattle	7	1	Brown, Gilbert, Green Bay	13	1
Arnold, Jim, Miami	12	0	Biekert, Greg, L.A. Raiders	16	14	Brown, J. B., Miami	16	16
Arthur, Mike, New England	12	11	Bieniemy, Eric, San Diego	16	0	Brown, James, N.Y. Jets	16	6
Arvie, Herman, Cleveland	16	1	Binn, David, San Diego	16	0	Brown, Larry, Dallas	15	15
Ashmore, Darryl, L.A. Rams	11	3	Birden, J. J., Kansas City	13	13	Brown, Lomas, Detroit	16	16
Atkins, Gene, Miami	15	15	Bishop, Blaine, Houston	16	13	Brown, Monty, Buffalo	3	0
Atkins, James, Seattle	4	2	Bishop, Greg, N.Y. Giants	16	1	Brown, Orlando, Cleveland	14	8
Atwater, Steve, Denver	14	14	Bishop, Harold, Tampa Bay	6	0	Brown, Ray, Washington	16	16
Auzenne, Troy, Chicago	11	3	Blackmon, Robert, Seattle	15	15	Brown, Reggie, Houston	4	0
Avery, Steve, Pittsburgh	14	1	Blackshear, Jeff, Seattle	16	16	Brown, Richard, Minnesota	3	0
Bahr, Matt, New England	16	0	Blades, Bennie, Detroit	16	16	Brown, Tim, L.A. Raiders	16	16
Bailey, Aaron, Indianapolis	13	0	Blades, Brian, Seattle	16	16	Brown, Tony, Seattle	13	5
Bailey, Carlton, N.Y. Giants	16	11	Blake, Jeff, Cincinnati	10	9	Brown, Troy, New England	9	0
Bailey, Johnny, L.A. Rams	14	0	Bledsoe, Drew, New England	16	16	Brown, Vincent, New England	16	16
Bailey, Robert, L.A. Rams	16	2	Blundin, Matt, Kansas City	1	0	Brownlow, Darrick, Dallas	16	0
Bailey, Victor, Philadelphia	16	0	Boatswain, Harry, San Francisco	13	4	Bruce, Aundray, L.A. Raiders	16	0
Baker, Myron, Chicago	16	3	Bollinger, Brian, San Francisco	7	0	Bruce, Isaac, L.A. Rams	12	0
Baker, Shannon, Indianapolis	4	0	Bonham, Shane, Detroit	15	1	Brumfield, Scott, Cincinnati	2	0
Baldwin, Randy, Cleveland	16	0	Boniol, Chris, Dallas	16	0	Brunell, Mark, Green Bay	2	0
Ball, Eric, Cincinnati	16	0	Bono, Steve, Kansas City	7	2	Bryant, Beno, Seattle	2	0
Ball, Jerry, L.A. Raiders	16	14	Booker, Vaughn, Kansas City	13	0	Buchanan, Ray, Indianapolis	16	16
Ballard, Howard, Seattle	16	16	Booth, Issac, Cleveland	16	1	Buchanan, Richard, L.A. Rams	3	0
Banks, Carl, Cleveland	16	15	Booty, John, N.Y. Giants	16	9	Buck, Vince, New Orleans	16	16
Bankston, Michael, Arizona	16	16	Borgella, Jocelyn, Detroit	4	0	Buckley, Curtis, Tampa Bay	13	0
Banta, Bradford, Indianapolis	16	0	Bortz, Mark, Chicago	12	12	Buckley, Marcus, N.Y. Giants	16	1
Barber, Kurt, N.Y. Jets	15	0	Botkin, Kirk, New Orleans	3	0	Buckley, Terrell, Green Bay	16	16
Barker, Bryan, Philadelphia	11	0	Boutte, Marc, Washington	9	3	Buckner, Brentson, Pittsburgh	13	5
Barker, Roy, Minnesota	16	15	Bouwens, Shawn, Detroit	16	16	Bullough, Chuck, Miami	1	1
Barnes, Johnnie, San Diego	11	0	Bowden, Joe, Houston	14	1	Bunch, Jarrod, L.A. Raiders	3	0

Player, Team	GP	GS	Player, Team	GP	GS	Player, Team	GP	GS
Burger, Todd, Chicago	4	0	Collins, Mark, Kansas City	14	13	DeOssie, Steve, New England	16	0
Burke, John, New England	16	6	Collins, Shane, Washington	7	0	Devlin, Mike, Buffalo	16	0
Burnett, Rob, Cleveland	16	16	Collins, Todd, New England	7	7	Dickerson, Ron, Kansas City	9	0
Burns, Keith, Denver	11	1	Colon, Harry, Detroit	16	0	Dilfer, Trent, Tampa Bay	5	2
Burris, Jeff, Buffalo	16	0	Compton, Mike, Detroit	2	0	Dill, Scott, Tampa Bay	16	16
Burton, James, Chicago	13	1	Conlan, Shane, L.A. Rams	15	15	Dillard, Stacey, N.Y. Giants	16	0
Bush, Blair, L.A. Rams	16	0	Conner, Darion, New Orleans	16	13	Dimry, Charles, Tampa Bay	16	16
Bush, Lewis, San Diego	16	0	Conover, Scott, Detroit	11	0	Dishman, Cris, Houston	16	16
Bussey, Barney, Tampa Bay	16	15	Conway, Curtis, Chicago	13	12	Dixon, Cal, N.Y. Jets	15	0
Butcher, Paul, Indianapolis	13	0	Cook, Marv, Chicago	16	8	Dixon, David, Minnesota	1	0
Butler, Kevin, Chicago	15	0	Cook, Toi, San Francisco	16	2	Dixon, Ernest, New Orleans	15	1
Butler, LeRoy, Green Bay	13	13	Cooper, Adrian, Minnesota	12	11	Dixon, Gerald, Cleveland	16	0
Butts, Marion, New England	16	15	Cooper, Richard, New Orleans	14	14	Dixon, Randy, Indianapolis	14	14
Byars, Keith, Miami	9	9	Copeland, Horace, Tampa Bay	16	2	Dodge, Dedrick, San Francisco	15	0
Byner, Earnest, Cleveland	16	1	Copeland, John, Cincinnati	12	12	Doleman, Chris, Atlanta	14	7
By'not'e, Butler, Denver	9	0	Copeland, Russell, Buffalo	15	4	Dombrowski, Jim, New Orleans	16	16
Byrd, Israel, New Orleans	3	0	Cornish, Frank, Minnesota	7	0	Donahue, Mitch, Denver	3	0
Cadigan, Dave, Cincinnati	13	13	Coryatt, Quentin, Indianapolis	16	16	Donaldson, Ray, Seattle	16	16
Cadrez, Glenn, N.Y. Jets	16	0	Cothran, Jeff, Cincinnati	14	4	Donnalley, Kevin, Houston	13	11
Cain, Joe, Chicago	16	15	Covington, John, Indianapolis	3	0	Dotson, Earl, Green Bay	4	0
Caldwell, Mike, Cleveland	16	1	Covington, Tony, Tampa Bay	14	2	Dotson, Santana, Tampa Bay	16	9
Calloway, Chris, N.Y. Giants	16	14	Cox, Bryan, Miami	16	16	Douglas, Omar, N.Y. Giants	6	0
Camarillo, Rich, Houston	16	0	Cox, Ron, Chicago	15	3	Douglass, Maurice, Chicago	16	4
Campbell, Jeff, Denver	16	1	Crafts, Jerry, Buffalo	16	7	Downs, Gary, N.Y. Giants	14	0
Campbell, Jesse, N.Y. Giants	14	10	Craver, Aaron, Miami	8	0	Drakeford, Tyronne, S.F.	13	0
Carlson, Cody, Houston	5	5	Criswell, Jeff, N.Y. Jets	15	15	Drayton, Troy, L.A. Rams	16	16
Carney, John, San Diego	16	0	Crittenden, Ray, New England	16	2	Dronett, Shane, Denver	16	15
Carolan, Brett, San Francisco	4	0	Crockett, Ray, Denver	14	14	DuBose, Demetrius, Tampa Bay	16	1
Carpenter, Rob, N.Y. Jets	3	0	Croel, Mike, Denver	13	12	Duckett, Forey, Cin.-G.B.-Sea.	7	0
Carrier, Mark, Chicago	16	15	Croom, Corey, New England	16	0	Duff, John, L.A. Raiders	4	0
Carrier, Mark, Cleveland	16	6	Cross, Howard, N.Y. Giants	16	16	Duffy, Roger, N.Y. Jets	16	14
Carrington, Darren, San Diego	16	16	Cross, Jeff, Miami	13	10	Dukes, Jamie, Green Bay	6	6
Carroll, Herman, New Orleans	4	0	Crumpler, Carlester, Seattle	9	4	Dumas, Mike, Buffalo	14	0
Carswell, Dwayne, Denver	4	0	Culpepper, Brad, Tampa Bay	16	15	Dunbar, Karl, Arizona	4	0
Carter, Anthony, Detroit	4	1	Culver, Rodney, San Diego	3	0	Dunbar, Vaughn, New Orleans	8	0
Carter, Antonio, Chicago	14	0	Cunningham, Ed, Arizona	16	16	Dye, Ernest, Arizona	16	16
Carter, Cris, Minnesota	16	16	Cunningham, Randall, Phi.	14	14	Early, Quinn, New Orleans	16	13
Carter, Dale, Kansas City	16	16	Cunningham, Rick, Arizona	11	10	Eatman, Irv, Atlanta	4	0
Carter, Dexter, San Francisco	16	0	Currie, Herschel, Arizona	1	0	Edmunds, Ferrell, Seattle	7	7
Carter, Marty, Tampa Bay	16	14	Curry, Eric, Tampa Bay	15	14	Edwards, Antonio, Seattle	15	14
Carter, Pat, Houston	16	13	Cuthbert, Randy, Pittsburgh	1	0	Edwards, Brad, Atlanta	4	0
Carter, Tom, Washington	16	16	Dafney, Bernard, Minnesota	16	16	Edwards, Dixon, Dallas	16	15
Carthen, Jason, New England	1	0	Dahl, Bob, Cleveland	15	15	Eilers, Pat, Washington	16	0
Carver, Shante, Dallas	10	0	Daigle, Anthony, Pittsburgh	1	0	Elam, Jason, Denver	16	0
Case, Scott, Atlanta	15	3	Dalman, Chris, San Francisco	16	4	Elias, Keith, N.Y. Giants	2	0
Cash, Keith, Kansas City	6	5	Daluiso, Brad, N.Y. Giants	16	0	Ellard, Henry, Washington	16	16
Cash, Kerry, Indianapolis	16	16	Daniel, Eugene, Indianapolis	16	15	Elliott, John, N.Y. Giants	16	15
Casillas, Tony, N.Y. Jets	12	11	Darby, Matt, Buffalo	16	16	Elliott, Lin, Kansas City	16	0
Castle, Eric, San Diego	16	1	Davenport, Charles, Pittsburgh	7	0	Elway, John, Denver	14	14
Centers, Larry, Arizona	16	5	Davey, Don, Green Bay	16	2	Emanuel, Bert, Atlanta	16	16
Chandler, Chris, L.A. Rams	12	6	Davidson, Kenny, Houston	16	16	Emtman, Steve, Indianapolis	4	0
Childress, Ray, Houston	16	16	Davis, Anthony, Kansas City	5	0	England, Eric, Arizona	11	1
Chmura, Mark, Green Bay	14	4	Davis, Antone, Philadelphia	16	14	Epps, Tory, Chicago	5	0
Christian, Bob, Chicago	12	0	Davis, Brian, Minnesota	9	0	Erickson, Craig, Tampa Bay	15	15
Christie, Steve, Buffalo	16	0	Davis, Dexter, L.A. Rams	4	0	Ervins, Ricky, Washington	16	10
Christy, Jeff, Minnesota	16	16	Davis, Eric, San Francisco	16	16	Esiason, Boomer, N.Y. Jets	15	14
Chung, Eugene, New England	3	0	Davis, Greg, Arizona	14	0	Etheredge, Carlos, Indianapolis	9	0
Clark, Derrick, Denver	16	4	Davis, Isaac, San Diego	13	2	Evans, Byron, Philadelphia	10	10
Clark, Gary, Arizona	15	2	Davis, John, Buffalo	16	16	Evans, Chuck, Minnesota	14	0
Clark, Reggie, Pittsburgh	5	0	Davis, Kenneth, Buffalo	16	1	Evans, Donald, N.Y. Jets	16	0
Clark, Vinnie, Atl.-N.O.	16	15	Davis, Michael, Houston	16	0	Evans, Doug, Green Bay	16	15
Clark, Willie, San Diego	6	0	Davis, Reuben, San Diego	16	16	Evans, Jerry, Denver	16	11
Clay, Willie, Detroit	16	16	Davis, Scott, L.A. Raiders	14	1	Evans, Vince, L.A. Raiders	9	0
Clifton, Kyle, N.Y. Jets	16	5	Davis, Scott, N.Y. Giants	15	4	Everett, Jim, New Orleans	16	16
Coates, Ben, New England	16	16	Davis, Willie, Kansas City	14	13	Everett, Thomas, Tampa Bay	15	15
Cobb, Reggie, Green Bay	16	13	Dawkins, Sean, Indianapolis	16	16	Everitt, Steve, Cleveland	15	15
Cobb, Trevor, Chicago	1	0	Dawsey, Lawrence, Tampa Bay	10	5	Fann, Chad, Arizona	16	9
Cocozzo, Joe, San Diego	13	13	Dawson, Dermontti, Pittsburgh	16	16	Farr, D'Marco, L.A. Rams	10	3
Coleman, Andre, San Diego	13	0	Dawson, Doug, Cleveland	12	9	Faryniarz, Brett, Houston	16	0
Coleman, Ben, Arizona	15	13	Dawson, Lake, Kansas City	12	6	Faulk, Marshall, Indianapolis	16	16
Coleman, Lincoln, Dallas	11	0	Deese, Derrick, San Francisco	16	15	Faumui, Ta'ase, Pittsburgh	5	0
Coleman, Marco, Miami	16	16	Del Greco, Al, Houston	16	0	Favre, Brett, Green Bay	16	16
Coleman, Monte, Washington	16	0	Dellenbach, Jeff, Miami	16	16	Feagles, Jeff, Arizona	16	0
Coleman, Pat, Houston	10	2	Del Rio, Jack, Minnesota	16	16	Fenner, Derrick, Cincinnati	16	13
Collins, Andre, Washington	16	16	Dennis, Mark, Cincinnati	7	1	Fichtel, Brad, L.A. Rams	1	0
Collins, Brett, L.A. Rams	2	0	Dent, Richard, San Francisco	2	2	Fields, Jaime, Kansas City	11	2

Player, Team	GP	GS
Figures, Deon, Pittsburgh	16	15
Fina, John, Buffalo	12	12
Fishback, Joe, Dallas	12	0
Flanigan, Jim, Chicago	14	0
Flannery, John, Houston	16	16
Fleming, Cory, Dallas	2	0
Fletcher, Simon, Denver	16	16
Flores, Mike, Philadelphia	15	2
Floyd, William, San Francisco	16	11
Foggie, Fred, Pittsburgh	3	0
Foley, Glenn, N.Y. Jets	1	0
Folston, James, L.A. Raiders	7	0
Fontenot, Albert, Chicago	16	8
Fontenot, Jerry, Chicago	16	16
Footman, Dan, Cleveland	16	2
Ford, Darryl, Atlanta	15	0
Ford, Henry, Houston	11	0
Fortin, Roman, Atlanta	16	16
Foster, Barry, Pittsburgh	11	10
Fox, Mike, N.Y. Giants	16	16
Foxx, Dion, Miami	16	0
Francis, James, Cincinnati	16	16
Frank, Donald, L.A. Raiders	16	0
Frase, Paul, N.Y. Jets	16	5
Frazier, Derrick, Philadelphia	12	0
Fredrickson, Rob, L.A. Raiders	16	12
Freeman, Russell, Denver	13	8
Frerotte, Gus, Washington	4	4
Frier, Mike, Cin.-Sea.	4	0
Friesz, John, Washington	16	4
Frisch, David, Cincinnati	16	0
Fryar, Irving, Miami	16	16
Fuller, Randy, Denver	10	1
Fuller, William, Philadelphia	16	16
Gaines, William, Miami	7	0
Galbraith, Scott, Dallas	16	2
Galbreath, Harry, Green Bay	16	16
Gammon, Kendall, Pittsburgh	16	0
Gandy, Wayne, L.A. Rams	16	9
Gant, Kenneth, Dallas	16	0
Gardner, Carwell, Buffalo	17	7
Gardner, Moe, Atlanta	16	16
Gardocki, Chris, Chicago	16	0
Garner, Charlie, Philadelphia	10	8
Garnett, Dave, Minnesota	9	0
Garrett, Jason, Dallas	2	1
Gary, Cleveland, Miami	2	0
Gash, Sam, New England	13	6
Gay, Matt, Kansas City	2	0
Gayle, Shaun, Chicago	16	16
Geathers, Jumpy, Atlanta	16	1
Gedney, Chris, Chicago	7	7
Gelbaugh, Stan, Seattle	1	0
George, Jeff, Atlanta	16	16
George, Ron, Atlanta	16	9
Gerak, John, Minnesota	13	3
Gesek, John, Washington	15	12
Gibson, Dennis, San Diego	16	15
Gilbert, Gale, San Diego	15	1
Gilbert, Sean, L.A. Rams	14	14
Gildon, Jason, Pittsburgh	16	1
Gisler, Mike, New England	15	5
Givins, Ernest, Houston	16	16
Glenn, Aaron, N.Y. Jets	15	15
Glenn, Vencie, Minnesota	16	16
Glover, Andrew, L.A. Raiders	16	16
Glover, Kevin, Detroit	16	16
Goad, Tim, New England	13	13
Goeas, Leo, L.A. Rams	13	13
Goebel, Brad, Cleveland	1	0
Goff, Robert, New Orleans	16	0
Gogan, Kevin, L.A. Raiders	16	16
Goganious, Keith, Buffalo	16	1
Goldberg, Bill, Atlanta	5	0
Gordon, Darrien, San Diego	16	16
Gordon, Dwayne, Atlanta	16	0
Goss, Antonio, San Francisco	16	1
Gossett, Jeff, L.A. Raiders	16	0
Gouveia, Kurt, Washington	14	1
Graham, Derrick, Kansas City	16	11
Graham, Jeff, Chicago	16	15
Graham, Kent, N.Y. Giants	13	1
Graham, Scottie, Minnesota	16	0
Grant, Alan, Washington	13	0
Grant, Stephen, Indianapolis	16	12
Gray, Carlton, Seattle	11	11
Gray, Cecil, Indianapolis	16	5
Gray, Chris, Miami	16	2
Gray, Derwin, Indianapolis	16	2
Gray, Mel, Detroit	16	0
Grbac, Elvis, San Francisco	11	0
Green, Chris, Miami	16	1
Green, Darrell, Washington	16	16
Green, Eric, Pittsburgh	15	14
Green, Harold, Cincinnati	14	11
Green, Paul, Seattle	16	11
Green, Robert, Chicago	15	0
Green, Rogerick, Tampa Bay	11	0
Green, Victor, N.Y. Jets	16	0
Green, Willie, Tampa Bay	5	0
Greene, Kevin, Pittsburgh	16	16
Greene, Tracy, Kansas City	7	2
Griffin, Don, Cleveland	15	15
Griffith, Howard, L.A. Rams	16	10
Griffith, Robert, Minnesota	15	0
Griggs, David, San Diego	16	15
Grossman, Burt, Philadelphia	14	2
Grow, Monty, Kansas City	15	0
Gruber, Paul, Tampa Bay	16	16
Grunhard, Tim, Kansas City	16	16
Guliford, Eric, Minnesota	7	1
Gunn, Mark, N.Y. Jets	3	0
Guyton, Myron, New England	16	16
Habib, Brian, Denver	16	16
Hager, Britt, Philadelphia	16	5
Hairston, Stacey, Cleveland	15	0
Haley, Charles, Dallas	16	16
Hall, Courtney, San Diego	15	15
Hall, Dana, San Francisco	16	4
Hall, Darryl, Denver	16	3
Hall, Rhett, San Francisco	12	2
Hall, Ron, Detroit	13	10
Hallock, Ty, Detroit	15	10
Hamilton, Keith, N.Y. Giants	15	15
Hamilton, Rick, Was.-K.C.	3	0
Hamilton, Ruffin, Green Bay	5	0
Hampton, Rodney, N.Y. Giants	14	13
Hand, Jon, Indianapolis	5	3
Hanks, Merton, San Francisco	16	16
Hanna, Jim, New Orleans	7	0
Hannah, Travis, Houston	9	0
Hansen, Brian, N.Y. Jets	16	0
Hansen, Phil, Buffalo	16	16
Hanson, Jason, Detroit	16	0
Harbaugh, Jim, Indianapolis	12	9
Hardy, Adrian, S.F.-Cin.	16	0
Harlow, Pat, New England	16	16
Harmon, Andy, Philadelphia	16	16
Harmon, Ronnie, San Diego	16	0
Harper, Alvin, Dallas	16	14
Harper, Dwayne, San Diego	16	16
Harper, Roger, Atlanta	10	10
Harris, Corey, Green Bay	16	2
Harris, Jackie, Tampa Bay	9	9
Harris, James, Minnesota	16	16
Harris, Leonard, Atlanta	8	2
Harris, Odie, Arizona	13	0
Harris, Raymont, Chicago	16	11
Harris, Robert, Minnesota	11	1
Harris, Ronnie, N.E.-Sea.	2	0
Harris, Rudy, Tampa Bay	8	0
Harris, Tim, San Francisco	5	1
Harrison, Martin, Minnesota	13	0
Harrison, Nolan, L.A. Raiders	16	16
Harrison, Rodney, San Diego	15	0
Hartley, Frank, Cleveland	10	5
Harvey, Frank, Arizona	2	0
Harvey, Ken, Washington	16	16
Harvey, Richard, Denver	16	1
Hasselbach, Harald, Denver	16	9
Hastings, Andre, Pittsburgh	16	8
Hasty, James, N.Y. Jets	16	16
Hauck, Tim, Green Bay	13	3
Hawkins, Courtney, Tampa Bay	13	12
Hawkins, Steve, New England	7	0
Haws, Kurt, Washington	6	0
Hayes, Jonathan, Pittsburgh	16	6
Haynes, Michael, New Orleans	16	16
Hayworth, Tracy, Detroit	9	1
Hearst, Garrison, Arizona	8	0
Hebert, Bobby, Atlanta	8	0
Hebron, Vaughn, Philadelphia	16	2
Heck, Andy, Chicago	14	14
Hegamin, George, Dallas	2	0
Heller, Ron, Miami	16	16
Hellestrae, Dale, Dallas	16	0
Henderson, Jerome, Buffalo	12	0
Henderson, Othello, New Orleans	16	0
Henderson, Wymon, L.A. Rams	15	1
Hendrickson, Steve, San Diego	16	0
Henesey, Brian, Arizona	3	0
Henley, Darryl, L.A. Rams	15	14
Hennings, Chad, Dallas	16	0
Henry, Kevin, Pittsburgh	16	5
Hentrich, Craig, Green Bay	16	0
Herrod, Jeff, Indianapolis	15	15
Hester, Jessie, L.A. Rams	16	15
Heyward, Craig, Atlanta	16	11
Hicks, Clifford, N.Y. Jets	16	0
Higgs, Mark, Mia.-Ari.	11	1
Hill, Eric, Arizona	16	15
Hill, Greg, Kansas City	16	1
Hill, Jeff, Cincinnati	1	0
Hill, Randal, Arizona	14	14
Hill, Sean, Miami	16	1
Hill, Travis, Cleveland	14	0
Hilliard, Randy, Denver	15	6
Hinton, Chris, Minnesota	16	16
Hitchcock, Bill, Seattle	5	5
Hoage, Terry, Arizona	16	16
Hoard, Leroy, Cleveland	16	12
Hobbs, Daryl, L.A. Raiders	10	0
Hoge, Merril, Chicago	5	5
Hollas, Donald, Cincinnati	2	0
Hollier, Dwight, Miami	11	7
Hollinquest, Lamont, Washington	14	0
Holman, Rodney, Detroit	15	7
Holmberg, Rob, L.A. Raiders	16	0
Holmes, Clayton, Dallas	16	1
Holmes, Lester, Philadelphia	16	16
Holt, Pierce, Atlanta	12	12
Homco, Thomas, L.A. Rams	15	0
Hoover, Houston, Miami	3	0
Hope, Charles, Green Bay	6	0
Hopkins, Brad, Houston	16	15
Horan, Mike, N.Y. Giants	16	0
Horton, Ethan, Washington	16	15
Hoskins, Derrick, L.A. Raiders	15	9
Hostetler, Jeff, L.A. Raiders	16	16
Houston, Bobby, N.Y. Jets	16	16
Howard, Desmond, Washington	16	15
Howard, Erik, N.Y. Giants	16	16
Howe, Garry, Indianapolis	1	0
Hoyem, Steve, Buffalo	6	0
Hudson, John, Philadelphia	16	0
Hughes, Danan, Kansas City	16	0
Hughes, Tyrone, New Orleans	15	5
Hull, Kent, Buffalo	16	16

Player, Team	GP	GS
Humphrey, Ronald, Indianapolis	15	0
Humphries, Leonard, Ind.	13	0
Humphries, Stan, San Diego	15	15
Hunter, Jeff, Tampa Bay	1	0
Hunter, Patrick, Seattle	5	5
Hurst, Maurice, New England	16	16
Husted, Michael, Tampa Bay	16	0
Hutchins, Paul, Green Bay	16	2
Ingram, Mark, Miami	15	13
Ireland, Darwin, Chicago	2	0
Irvin, Michael, Dallas	16	16
Irving, Terry, Arizona	16	0
Irwin, Tim, T.B.-Mia.	13	6
Ismail, Qadry, Minnesota	16	3
Ismail, Raghib, L.A. Raiders	16	0
Israel, Steve, L.A. Rams	10	2
Jack, Eric, Atlanta	16	0
Jacke, Chris, Green Bay	16	0
Jackson, Al, Philadelphia	11	0
Jackson, Calvin, Miami	2	0
Jackson, Greg, Philadelphia	16	16
Jackson, John, Pittsburgh	16	16
Jackson, Keith, Miami	16	16
Jackson, Mark, NYG-Ind.	14	0
Jackson, Michael, Cleveland	9	7
Jackson, Rickey, San Francisco	16	14
Jackson, Steve, Houston	11	0
Jackson, Tyoka, Miami	1	0
Jacobs, Ray, Denver	16	0
Jacobs, Tim, Cleveland	9	1
Jaeger, Jeff, L.A. Raiders	16	0
Jamison, George, Kansas City	13	12
Jax, Garth, Arizona	16	0
Jeffcoat, Jim, Dallas	16	0
Jefferson, Kevin, Cincinnati	6	0
Jefferson, Shawn, San Diego	16	16
Jeffires, Haywood, Houston	16	16
Jeffries, Greg, Detroit	16	1
Jenkins, Carlos, Minnesota	16	16
Jenkins, James, Washington	16	3
Jenkins, Robert, L.A. Raiders	10	4
Jennings, Keith, Chicago	9	1
Jeter, Tommy, Philadelphia	14	0
Jett, James, L.A. Raiders	16	1
Jett, John, Dallas	16	0
Johnson, A.J., Washington	11	0
Johnson, Anthony, N.Y. Jets	15	0
Johnson, Bill, Cleveland	14	13
Johnson, Brad, Minnesota	4	0
Johnson, Charles, Pittsburgh	16	9
Johnson, D.J., Atlanta	16	16
Johnson, Jimmie, Kansas City	7	1
Johnson, Joe, New Orleans	15	14
Johnson, John, Cincinnati	5	0
Johnson, Johnny, N.Y. Jets	16	14
Johnson, Keshon, Chi.-G.B.	13	0
Johnson, Lee, Cincinnati	16	0
Johnson, LeShon, Green Bay	12	0
Johnson, Lonnie, Buffalo	10	1
Johnson, Maurice, Philadelphia	16	10
Johnson, Mike, Detroit	16	16
Johnson, Norm, Atlanta	16	0
Johnson, Pepper, Cleveland	16	16
Johnson, Raylee, San Diego	15	0
Johnson, Reggie, Green Bay	9	2
Johnson, Tim, Washington	14	13
Johnson, Tracy, Seattle	16	10
Johnson, Tre, Washington	14	1
Johnson, Tyrone, New Orleans	1	0
Johnson, Vaughan, Philadelphia	4	0
Johnston, Daryl, Dallas	16	16
Jonassen, Eric, San Diego	16	0
Jones, Aaron, New England	16	0
Jones, Brent, San Francisco	15	15
Jones, Calvin, L.A. Raiders	7	0
Jones, Clarence, L.A. Rams	16	16

Player, Team	GP	GS
Jones, Dan, Cincinnati	14	0
Jones, Dante, Chicago	15	11
Jones, Gary, Pittsburgh	14	0
Jones, Henry, Buffalo	16	16
Jones, James, Cleveland	16	5
Jones, Jimmie, L.A. Rams	14	14
Jones, Marvin, N.Y. Jets	15	11
Jones, Mike, L.A. Raiders	16	1
Jones, Mike, New England	16	16
Jones, Reginald, New Orleans	1	1
Jones, Robert, Dallas	16	16
Jones, Rod, Cincinnati	16	16
Jones, Roger, Cincinnati	16	0
Jones, Rondell, Denver	16	3
Jones, Sean, Green Bay	16	16
Jones, Selwyn, New Orleans	5	1
Jones, Tony, Cleveland	16	16
Jones, Victor, Pit.-K.C.	11	0
Jones, Victor, Detroit	16	0
Jordan, Andrew, Minnesota	16	12
Jordan, Charles, Green Bay	10	0
Jordan, Steve, Minnesota	4	1
Joseph, James, Philadelphia	14	5
Jourdain, Yonel, Buffalo	9	0
Joyner, Seth, Arizona	16	16
Junkin, Trey, Seattle	16	0
Jurkovic, John, Green Bay	16	15
Kalis, Todd, Pittsburgh	11	11
Kasay, John, Seattle	16	0
Keim, Mike, Seattle	16	0
Keith, Craig, Pittsburgh	16	1
Kelly, Jim, Buffalo	14	14
Kelly, Joe, L.A. Rams	16	14
Kelly, Todd, San Francisco	11	1
Kenn, Mike, Atlanta	15	15
Kennard, Derek, Dallas	16	16
Kennedy, Cortez, Seattle	16	16
Kennedy, Lincoln, Atlanta	16	2
Kidd, John, S.D.-Mia.	6	0
Kimbrough, Tony, Denver	12	0
Kinchen, Brian, Cleveland	16	11
Kinchen, Todd, L.A. Rams	13	0
Kirby, Terry, Miami	4	4
Kirk, Randy, Arizona	16	0
Kirkland, Levon, Pittsburgh	16	15
Klein, Perry, Atlanta	2	0
Klingbeil, Chuck, Miami	16	15
Klingler, David, Cincinnati	10	7
Knapp, Lindsay, Kansas City	2	0
Knox, Kevin, Arizona	2	0
Koonce, George, Green Bay	16	16
Kosar, Bernie, Miami	2	0
Kowalkowski, Scott, Detroit	16	0
Kozerski, Bruce, Cincinnati	16	16
Kozlowski, Brian, N.Y. Giants	16	2
Kragen, Greg, Kansas City	16	2
Kramer, Erik, Chicago	6	5
Kratch, Bob, New England	16	16
Krieg, Dave, Detroit	14	7
Krumrie, Tim, Cincinnati	16	4
Lachey, Jim, Washington	13	13
Lacina, Corbin, Buffalo	11	10
Lageman, Jeff, N.Y. Jets	16	16
Laing, Aaron, San Diego	5	1
Lake, Carnell, Pittsburgh	16	16
Lambert, Dion, Seattle	1	1
Land, Dan, L.A. Raiders	16	0
Landeta, Sean, L.A. Rams	16	0
Lane, Max, New England	14	0
Lang, David, L.A. Rams	13	0
Langham, Antonio, Cleveland	16	16
Lanier, Ken, Denver	4	0
Lathon, Lamar, Houston	16	15
LeBel, Harper, Atlanta	16	0
Lee, Amp, Minnesota	13	0
Lee, Carl, New Orleans	12	8

Player, Team	GP	GS
Lee, Shawn, San Diego	15	15
Leeuwenburg, Jay, Chicago	16	16
Legette, Burnie, New England	3	0
Legette, Tyrone, New Orleans	15	2
Lester, Tim, L.A. Rams	14	4
Lett, Leon, Dallas	16	16
Levens, Dorsey, Green Bay	14	0
Levy, Chuck, Arizona	11	0
Lewis, Albert, L.A. Raiders	14	9
Lewis, Darryll, Houston	16	15
Lewis, Mo, N.Y. Jets	16	16
Lewis, Nate, Chicago	13	0
Lewis, Rod, Houston	3	1
Lewis, Ron, Green Bay	6	1
Lewis, Thomas, N.Y. Giants	9	0
Lewis, Vernon, New England	11	0
Lincoln, Jeremy, Chicago	15	14
Lingner, Adam, Buffalo	16	0
Lloyd, Greg, Pittsburgh	15	15
Lodish, Mike, Buffalo	15	5
Logan, Marc, San Francisco	10	5
Lohmiller, Chip, Washington	16	0
London, Antonio, Detroit	16	0
Loneker, Keith, L.A. Rams	2	2
Lott, Ronnie, N.Y. Jets	15	15
Love, Duval, Pittsburgh	16	16
Love, Sean, Tampa Bay	6	0
Loville, Derek, San Francisco	14	0
Lowdermilk, Kirk, Indianapolis	16	16
Lowery, Nick, N.Y. Jets	16	0
Lumpkin, Sean, New Orleans	16	15
Lutz, Dave, Detroit	16	16
Lyght, Todd, L.A. Rams	16	16
Lyle, Keith, L.A. Rams	16	0
Lyle, Rick, Cleveland	3	0
Lynch, Eric, Detroit	12	3
Lynch, John, Tampa Bay	16	0
Lynch, Lorenzo, Arizona	15	15
Lyons, Mitch, Atlanta	7	2
Mack, Milton, Detroit	16	3
Maddox, Mark, Buffalo	15	14
Maddox, Tommy, L.A. Rams	5	0
Maggs, Don, Denver	9	1
Mahlum, Eric, Indianapolis	16	2
Majkowski, Don, Indianapolis	9	6
Malamala, Siupeli, N.Y. Jets	12	10
Malone, Darrell, Miami	5	2
Malone, Van, Detroit	16	0
Mangum, John, Chicago	16	3
Mann, Charles, San Francisco	14	0
Manusky, Greg, Kansas City	16	2
Marino, Dan, Miami	16	16
Marion, Brock, Dallas	14	1
Marrow, Vince, Buffalo	10	0
Marshall, Anthony, Chicago	3	0
Marshall, Arthur, N.Y. Giants	16	0
Marshall, Leonard, Washington	16	3
Marshall, Wilber, Arizona	15	15
Martin, Chris, L.A. Rams	14	0
Martin, Eric, Kansas City	10	1
Martin, Kelvin, Seattle	16	15
Martin, Tony, San Diego	16	1
Martin, Wayne, New Orleans	16	16
Marts, Lonnie, Tampa Bay	16	14
Maryland, Russell, Dallas	16	16
Massey, Robert, Detroit	16	15
Maston, Le'Shai, Houston	5	1
Mathews, Jason, Indianapolis	10	0
Mathis, Terance, Atlanta	16	16
Matich, Trevor, Washington	16	0
Matthews, Aubrey, Detroit	14	3
Matthews, Bruce, Houston	16	16
Matthews, Clay, Atlanta	15	15
Maumalanga, Chris, N.Y. Giants	7	0
Mawae, Kevin, Seattle	14	11
Maxie, Brett, Atlanta	4	2

Player, Team	GP	GS
May, Deems, San Diego	5	2
Mayberry, Tony, Tampa Bay	16	16
Mayhew, Martin, Tampa Bay	16	16
Mays, Alvoid, Washington	2	0
McAfee, Fred, Ari.-S.F.	13	0
McCaffrey, Ed, San Francisco	16	0
McCallum, Napoleon, L.A. Rai.	1	0
McCants, Keith, Hou.-Ari.	12	2
McCardell, Keenan, Cleveland	13	3
McCleskey, J. J., New Orleans	13	0
McCloughan, Dave, Seattle	13	2
McCormack, Hurvin, Dallas	4	0
McCoy, Tony, Indianapolis	15	15
McCrary, Michael, Seattle	16	0
McDaniel, Ed, Minnesota	16	16
McDaniel, Randall, Minnesota	16	16
McDaniel, Terry, L.A. Raiders	16	16
McDaniels, Pellom, Kansas City	12	3
McDonald, Devon, Indianapolis	16	3
McDonald, Ricardo, Cincinnati	13	13
McDonald, Tim, San Francisco	16	16
McDowell, Anthony, Tampa Bay	14	11
McDowell, Bubba, Houston	9	3
McDuffie, O. J., Miami	15	3
McElroy, Reggie, Minnesota	10	0
McGee, Tim, Cincinnati	14	1
McGee, Tony, Cincinnati	16	16
McGhee, Kanavis, Cincinnati	1	0
McGill, Lenny, Green Bay	6	0
McGinest, Willie, New England	16	7
McGlockton, Chester, L.A. Rai.	16	16
McGriggs, Lamar, Minnesota	16	1
McGruder, Mike, Tampa Bay	15	3
McGwire, Dan, Seattle	7	3
McHale, Tom, Philadelphia	13	2
McIntosh, Toddrick, Tampa Bay	4	0
McIntyre, Guy, Green Bay	10	10
McIver, Everett, N.Y. Jets	4	0
McKenzie, Raleigh, Washington	16	16
McKnight, James, Seattle	2	0
McKyer, Tim, Pittsburgh	16	2
McLemore, Tom, Cleveland	2	1
McMahon, Jim, Arizona	2	1
McMichael, Steve, Green Bay	16	14
McMillian, Mark, Philadelphia	16	16
McMurtry, Greg, Chicago	9	4
McNair, Todd, Houston	16	1
McNeil, Ryan, Detroit	14	13
McRae, Charles, Tampa Bay	15	10
Means, Natrone, San Diego	16	16
Mecklenburg, Karl, Denver	16	15
Meggett, Dave, N.Y. Giants	16	3
Melander, Jon, Denver	15	15
Merritt, David, Arizona	16	0
Metcalf, Eric, Cleveland	16	8
Metzelaars, Pete, Buffalo	16	16
Miano, Rich, Philadelphia	16	0
Mickell, Darren, Kansas City	16	13
Mickens, Terry, Green Bay	12	0
Middleton, Ron, L.A. Rams	16	3
Milburn, Glyn, Denver	16	3
Milinichik, Joe, San Diego	16	16
Millen, Hugh, Denver	5	2
Miller, Anthony, Denver	16	15
Miller, Chris, L.A. Rams	13	10
Miller, Corey, N.Y. Giants	15	13
Miller, Doug, San Diego	15	0
Miller, Jamir, Arizona	16	0
Miller, Les, N.O.-S.D.	12	5
Miller, Scott, Miami	9	0
Mills, Ernie, Pittsburgh	15	6
Mills, John Henry, Houston	16	1
Mills, Lamar, Washington	13	4
Mills, Sam, New Orleans	16	16
Milstead, Rod, San Francisco	5	0
Mims, Chris, San Diego	16	16
Mims, David, Atlanta	2	2
Mincy, Charles, Kansas City	16	7
Miniefield, Kevin, Chicago	12	0
Minter, Barry, Chicago	13	1
Mirer, Rick, Seattle	13	13
Mitchell, Brian, Washington	16	7
Mitchell, Derrell, New Orleans	14	0
Mitchell, Johnny, N.Y. Jets	16	14
Mitchell, Kevin, San Francisco	16	0
Mitchell, Roland, Green Bay	1	1
Mitchell, Scott, Detroit	9	9
Mitchell, Shannon, San Diego	16	6
Mohr, Chris, Buffalo	16	0
Monk, Art, N.Y. Jets	16	15
Montana, Joe, Kansas City	14	14
Montgomery, Alton, Atlanta	2	1
Montgomery, Glenn, Houston	14	14
Montgomery, Greg, Detroit	16	0
Montgomery, Tyrone, L.A. Rai.	6	6
Montoya, Max, L.A. Raiders	13	0
Moon, Warren, Minnesota	15	15
Moore, Brandon, New England	4	0
Moore, Dave, Tampa Bay	15	5
Moore, Derrick, Detroit	16	0
Moore, Eric, Cincinnati	6	6
Moore, Herman, Detroit	16	16
Moore, Marty, New England	16	4
Moore, Rob, N.Y. Jets	16	16
Moore, Ronald, Arizona	16	16
Moore, Stevon, Cleveland	16	16
Morgan, Anthony, Green Bay	16	0
Morris, Bam, Pittsburgh	15	6
Morris, Mike, Minnesota	16	0
Morrison, Darryl, Washington	16	16
Morton, Johnnie, Detroit	14	0
Mosebar, Don, L.A. Raiders	16	16
Moss, Winston, L.A. Raiders	16	15
Moss, Zefross, Indianapolis	11	11
Moyer, Ken, Cincinnati	16	14
Murray, Eddie, Philadelphia	16	0
Murrell, Adrian, N.Y. Jets	10	1
Muster, Brad, New Orleans	7	1
Myles, Godfrey, Dallas	15	0
Myslinski, Tom, Chicago	4	0
Nagle, Browning, Indianapolis	1	1
Nalen, Tom, Denver	7	1
Nash, Joe, Seattle	16	15
Neal, Lorenzo, New Orleans	16	7
Ned, Derrick, New Orleans	16	1
Newberry, Tom, L.A. Rams	15	14
Newman, Anthony, L.A. Rams	16	14
Newton, Nate, Dallas	16	16
Newman, Patrick, Cleveland	1	0
Nickerson, Hardy, Tampa Bay	14	14
Nix, Roosevelt, Minnesota	2	0
Noga, Al, Indianapolis	4	0
Norgard, Erik, Houston	16	7
Norton, Ken, San Francisco	16	16
Nottage, Dexter, Washington	15	1
Novacek, Jay, Dallas	16	14
Novak, Jeff, Miami	6	0
Novitsky, Craig, New Orleans	9	1
Novoselsky, Brent, Minnesota	12	0
Nunley, Jeremy, Houston	12	0
Nunn, Freddie Joe, Indianapolis	11	6
Oates, Bart, San Francisco	16	15
Oden, Derrick, Philadelphia	11	0
O'Donnell, Neil, Pittsburgh	14	14
Oglesby, Alfred, N.Y. Jets	15	1
Oldham, Chris, Arizona	11	1
Oliver, Louis, Cincinnati	12	12
Oliver, Muhammad, Miami	13	2
Olsavsky, Jerry, Pittsburgh	1	0
O'Neal, Brian, Philadelphia	14	0
O'Neal, Leslie, San Diego	16	16
O'Neal, Robert, Indianapolis	2	0
O'Neill, Pat, New England	16	0
Orlando, Bo, Houston	16	0
Oshodin, Willie, Denver	13	0
Ostroski, Jerry, Buffalo	4	3
Ottis, Brad, L.A. Rams	13	0
Owens, Dan, Detroit	16	8
Palmer, David, Minnesota	13	1
Palmer, Sterling, Washington	16	16
Panos, Joe, Philadelphia	16	2
Parker, Anthony, Minnesota	15	15
Parker, Glenn, Buffalo	16	16
Parker, Orlando, N.Y. Jets	2	0
Parker, Vaughn, San Diego	6	0
Parmalee, Bernie, Miami	15	10
Parrella, John, San Diego	13	1
Parten, Ty, Cincinnati	14	4
Patton, James, Buffalo	11	0
Patton, Joe, Washington	2	0
Patton, Marvcus, Buffalo	16	16
Paup, Bryce, Green Bay	16	16
Peete, Rodney, Dallas	7	1
Pegram, Erric, Atlanta	13	5
Pelfrey, Doug, Cincinnati	16	0
Penn, Chris, Kansas City	8	0
Perriman, Brett, Detroit	16	14
Perry, Darren, Pittsburgh	16	16
Perry, Gerald, L.A. Raiders	12	12
Perry, Marlo, Buffalo	2	0
Perry, Michael Dean, Cleveland	15	14
Perry, Todd, Chicago	15	4
Perry, William, Philadelphia	16	16
Peterson, Todd, Arizona	2	0
Peterson, Tony, San Francisco	15	0
Phifer, Roman, L.A. Rams	16	15
Philion, Ed, Buffalo	4	0
Phillips, Anthony, Atlanta	5	0
Phillips, Joe, Kansas City	16	16
Pickel, Bill, N.Y. Jets	11	0
Pickens, Carl, Cincinnati	15	15
Pierce, Aaron, N.Y. Giants	16	11
Pike, Mark, Buffalo	16	0
Pitts, Mike, New England	16	16
Pleasant, Anthony, Cleveland	14	14
Plummer, Gary, San Francisco	16	16
Pollack, Frank, San Francisco	12	4
Pollard, Trent, Cincinnati	8	0
Pool, David, Miami	1	0
Pope, Marquez, L.A. Rams	16	16
Popson, Ted, San Francisco	16	1
Porcher, Robert, Detroit	15	15
Port, Chris, New Orleans	16	16
Porter, Rufus, Seattle	16	15
Potts, Roosevelt, Indianapolis	16	15
Powe, Keith, Tampa Bay	5	0
Powell, Andre, N.Y. Giants	1	0
Price, Shawn, Tampa Bay	6	0
Primus, Greg, Chicago	3	1
Prior, Anthony, N.Y. Jets	13	0
Prior, Mike, Green Bay	16	0
Pritchard, Mike, Denver	3	0
Pritchett, Kelvin, Detroit	16	15
Proehl, Ricky, Arizona	16	16
Pupunu, Alfred, San Diego	13	10
Query, Jeff, Cincinnati	10	4
Radecic, Scott, Indianapolis	16	1
Randle, John, Minnesota	16	16
Randolph, Thomas, N.Y. Giants	16	10
Rasby, Walter, Pittsburgh	2	0
Rasheed, Kenyon, N.Y. Giants	16	7
Rathman, Tom, L.A. Raiders	16	16
Ratigan, Brian, Indianapolis	14	0
Ravotti, Eric, Pittsburgh	2	0
Ray, Terry, New England	16	0
Raymond, Corey, N.Y. Giants	16	12
Redmon, Anthony, Arizona	6	5
Reed, Andre, Buffalo	16	16

Player, Team	GP	GS
Reed, Jake, Minnesota	16	16
Reeves, Bryan, Arizona	14	0
Reeves, Walter, Cleveland	5	5
Reich, Frank, Buffalo	16	2
Reid, Mike, Philadelphia	3	0
Renfro, Leonard, Philadelphia	9	0
Reveiz, Fuad, Minnesota	16	0
Reynolds, Ricky, New England	15	10
Rhem, Steve, New Orleans	7	0
Rhett, Errict, Tampa Bay	16	8
Rice, Jerry, San Francisco	16	16
Richard, Stanley, San Diego	16	16
Richards, David, Atlanta	15	15
Richardson, Bucky, Houston	7	4
Riddick, Louis, Cleveland	16	0
Riesenberg, Doug, N.Y. Giants	16	16
Rison, Andre, Atlanta	15	14
Ritcher, Jim, Atlanta	2	0
Rivers, Reggie, Denver	16	1
Roaf, Willie, New Orleans	16	16
Robbins, Austin, L.A. Raiders	2	0
Roberts, Ray, Seattle	14	14
Roberts, Tim, Houston	12	2
Roberts, William, N.Y. Giants	16	15
Robertson, Marcus, Houston	16	16
Robinson, Ed, Pittsburgh	16	0
Robinson, Eddie, Houston	15	15
Robinson, Eugene, Seattle	14	14
Robinson, Gerald, L.A. Rams	13	0
Robinson, Jeff, Denver	16	0
Robinson, Patrick, Arizona	15	0
Robinson, Rafael, Seattle	16	1
Roby, Reggie, Washington	16	0
Rocker, David, L.A. Rams	11	1
Rodenhauser, Mark, Detroit	16	0
Rodgers, Tyrone, Seattle	5	0
Rogers, Sam, Buffalo	14	0
Rogers, Tracy, Kansas City	14	3
Rolling, Henry, L.A. Rams	9	2
Romanowski, Bill, Philadelphia	16	15
Rose, Ken, Philadelphia	16	0
Ross, Jermaine, L.A. Rams	4	0
Ross, Kevin, Atlanta	16	16
Rouen, Tom, Denver	16	0
Royals, Mark, Pittsburgh	16	0
Royster, Mazio, Tampa Bay	14	1
Rucci, Todd, New England	13	10
Rucker, Keith, Cincinnati	16	14
Ruddy, Tim, Miami	16	0
Rudolph, Coleman, N.Y. Giants	12	2
Ruettgers, Ken, Green Bay	16	16
Rush, Tyrone, Washington	5	0
Russell, Derek, Denver	12	12
Russell, Leonard, Denver	14	13
Rypien, Mark, Cleveland	6	3
Sabb, Dwayne, New England	16	8
Sadowski, Troy, Cincinnati	15	1
Sagapolutele, Pio, Cleveland	11	0
Saleaumua, Dan, Kansas City	14	14
Salisbury, Sean, Minnesota	1	1
Samuels, Terry, Arizona	16	6
Sanders, Barry, Detroit	16	16
Sanders, Deion, San Francisco	14	12
Sanders, Glenell, Denver	1	0
Sanders, Ricky, Atlanta	14	12
Sapolu, Jesse, San Francisco	13	13
Sargent, Kevin, Cincinnati	15	15
Savage, Sebastian, Washington	1	0
Sawyer, Corey, Cincinnati	15	0
Saxon, James, Miami	16	7
Saxon, Mike, Minnesota	16	0
Schlereth, Mark, Washington	16	6
Schreiber, Adam, N.Y. Giants	16	2
Schroeder, Jay, Arizona	9	8
Schulz, Kurt, Buffalo	16	0
Schwantz, Jim, Dallas	7	0
Scott, Darnay, Cincinnati	16	12
Scott, Todd, Minnesota	15	15
Scrafford, Kirk, Denver	16	7
Scroggins, Tracy, Detroit	16	9
Seabron, Malcolm, Houston	13	0
Seals, Ray, Pittsburgh	13	11
Searcy, Leon, Pittsburgh	16	16
Seau, Junior, San Diego	16	16
Seay, Mark, San Diego	16	14
Sehorn, Jason, N.Y. Giants	8	0
Selby, Rob, Philadelphia	2	0
Sharpe, Luis, Arizona	11	11
Sharpe, Shannon, Denver	15	13
Sharpe, Sterling, Green Bay	16	16
Shaw, Eric, Cincinnati	3	0
Shelley, Elbert, Atlanta	16	0
Shepherd, Leslie, Washington	3	0
Sheppard, Ashley, Minnesota	7	0
Sherrard, Mike, N.Y. Giants	16	14
Shields, Will, Kansas City	16	16
Shufelt, Pete, N.Y. Giants	5	0
Shuler, Heath, Washington	11	8
Siglar, Ricky, Kansas City	16	8
Simien, Tracy, Kansas City	15	15
Simmons, Clyde, Arizona	16	16
Simmons, Ed, Washington	16	16
Simmons, Wayne, Green Bay	12	1
Simpson, Carl, Chicago	15	8
Simpson, Tim, Pittsburgh	4	0
Sims, Joe, Green Bay	15	14
Sims, Keith, Miami	16	16
Sims, Tom, Indianapolis	16	1
Sims, William, Minnesota	8	0
Sinclair, Michael, Seattle	12	2
Singleton, Chris, Miami	11	11
Singleton, Nate, San Francisco	16	1
Siragusa, Tony, Indianapolis	16	16
Skene, Doug, New England	6	6
Skrepenak, Greg, L.A. Raiders	12	10
Slade, Chris, New England	16	16
Slater, Jackie, L.A. Rams	12	7
Slaughter, Webster, Houston	16	12
Small, Torrance, New Orleans	16	0
Smeenge, Joel, New Orleans	16	2
Smith, Al, Houston	16	16
Smith, Anthony, L.A. Raiders	16	16
Smith, Artie, S.F.-Cin.	9	0
Smith, Ben, Denver	14	14
Smith, Bruce, Buffalo	15	15
Smith, Cedric, Washington	14	8
Smith, Chuck, Atlanta	15	10
Smith, Darrin, Dallas	16	16
Smith, Dennis, Denver	12	12
Smith, Emmitt, Dallas	15	15
Smith, Fernando, Minnesota	7	0
Smith, Frankie, Miami	13	2
Smith, Irv, New Orleans	16	16
Smith, Kevin, L.A. Raiders	3	0
Smith, Kevin, Dallas	16	16
Smith, Lamar, Seattle	2	0
Smith, Lance, N.Y. Giants	13	13
Smith, Neil, Kansas City	14	13
Smith, Otis, Philadelphia	16	2
Smith, Rico, Cleveland	5	4
Smith, Robert, Minnesota	14	0
Smith, Rod, New England	16	7
Smith, Steve, Seattle	16	0
Smith, Thomas, Buffalo	16	16
Smith, Tony, Atlanta	4	0
Smith, Vernice, Washington	4	0
Smith, Vinson, Chicago	12	10
Solomon, Ariel, Pittsburgh	16	0
Solomon, Jesse, Miami	6	0
Sparks, Phillippi, N.Y. Giants	11	11
Speer, Del, Cle.-Sea.	9	0
Spellman, Alonzo, Chicago	16	16
Spencer, Darryl, Atlanta	8	0
Spencer, Jimmy, New Orleans	16	16
Spielman, Chris, Detroit	16	16
Spikes, Irving, Miami	12	1
Spindler, Marc, Detroit	9	8
Spitulski, Bob, Seattle	16	1
Stallings, Ramondo, Cincinnati	6	0
Stams, Frank, Cleveland	16	15
Stanley, Buster, New England	7	0
Stargell, Tony, Tampa Bay	10	2
Stark, Rohn, Indianapolis	16	0
Staysniak, Joe, Indianapolis	16	16
Steed, Joel, Pittsburgh	16	16
Stegall, Milt, Cincinnati	1	0
Stephens, Rod, Seattle	16	16
Stephens, Santo, Cincinnati	14	3
Stepnoski, Mark, Dallas	16	16
Steussie, Todd, Minnesota	16	16
Stewart, Michael, Miami	16	16
Stokes, Fred, L.A. Rams	16	15
Stone, Dwight, Pittsburgh	15	1
Stone, Ron, Dallas	16	0
Stonebreaker, Mike, New Orleans	2	0
Stover, Matt, Cleveland	16	0
Stowe, Tyronne, Washington	16	15
Stowers, Tommie, Kansas City	1	0
Stoyanovich, Pete, Miami	16	0
Strahan, Michael, N.Y. Giants	15	15
Strickland, Fred, Green Bay	16	14
Strong, Mack, Seattle	8	1
Strother, Deon, Denver	2	0
Stryzinski, Dan, Tampa Bay	16	0
Strzelczyk, Justin, Pittsburgh	16	5
Stubblefield, Dana, S.F.	14	14
Studstill, Darren, Dallas	1	0
Sullivan, Mike, Tampa Bay	16	1
Sutter, Eddie, Cleveland	16	0
Swann, Charles, Denver	13	0
Swann, Eric, Arizona	16	16
Swayne, Harry, San Diego	16	16
Sweeney, Jim, N.Y. Jets	16	16
Swilling, Pat, Detroit	16	7
Sydner, Jeff, Philadelphia	16	0
Szott, David, Kansas City	16	16
Talley, Darryl, Buffalo	16	16
Tamm, Ralph, San Francisco	1	1
Tasker, Steve, Buffalo	14	0
Tate, David, Indianapolis	16	8
Taylor, Jay, Kansas City	16	4
Taylor, John, San Francisco	15	15
Taylor, Keith, Washington	1	1
Taylor, Terry, Seattle	5	3
Teague, George, Green Bay	16	16
Teeter, Mike, Houston	14	0
Teichelman, Lance, Indianapolis	1	0
Terrell, Pat, N.Y. Jets	16	2
Terry, Doug, Kansas City	10	1
Testaverde, Vinny, Cleveland	14	13
Thierry, John, Chicago	16	1
Thigpen, Yancey, Pittsburgh	15	6
Thomas, Blair, N.E.-Dal.	6	1
Thomas, Broderick, Detroit	16	16
Thomas, Damon, Buffalo	3	0
Thomas, Dave, Dallas	16	0
Thomas, Derrick, Kansas City	16	15
Thomas, Eric, N.Y. Jets	16	0
Thomas, Henry, Minnesota	16	16
Thomas, Johnny, Washington	16	0
Thomas, Lamar, Tampa Bay	11	0
Thomas, Mark, San Francisco	9	0
Thomas, Robb, Seattle	16	1
Thomas, Stan, Houston	16	0
Thomas, Thurman, Buffalo	15	15
Thomas, William, Philadelphia	16	16
Thompson, Bennie, Cleveland	16	0
Thompson, Broderick, Phi.	14	14

Player, Team	GP	GS	Player, Team	GP	GS	Player, Team	GP	GS
Thompson, Darrell, Green Bay ...	8	0	Warren, Chris, Seattle	16	15	Williams, Jarvis, N.Y. Giants	13	12
Thompson, Leroy, New England	16	1	Warren, Frank, New Orleans	16	11	Williams, Jerrol, Kansas City	6	0
Thornton, James, N.Y. Jets	15	5	Warren, Lamont, Indianapolis	11	0	Williams, John L., Pittsburgh	15	12
Tillman, Cedric, Denver	16	4	Warren, Terrence, Seattle	14	0	Williams, Kevin, Dallas	15	2
Tillman, Lewis, Chicago	16	15	Washington, Brian, N.Y. Jets	15	15	Williams, Mark, Green Bay	16	0
Tillman, Spencer, Houston	16	0	Washington, Charles, Atlanta	16	1	Williams, Mike, Miami	15	0
Timpson, Michael, New England	15	14	Washington, Dewayne, Min.	16	16	Williams, Ronnie, Miami	14	0
Tippins, Ken, Atlanta	16	7	Washington, James, Dallas	16	16	Williams, Wally, Cleveland	11	7
Tobeck, Robbie, Atlanta	5	0	Washington, Lionel, L.A. Raiders	11	7	Williams, Willie, New Orleans	16	5
Tofflemire, Joe, Seattle	1	0	Washington, Marvin, N.Y. Jets	15	15	Williams, Willie, Pittsburgh	16	1
Tolbert, Tony, Dallas	16	16	Washington, Mickey, Buffalo	16	16	Willig, Matt, N.Y. Jets	16	3
Tolliver, Billy Joe, Houston	10	7	Washington, Ted, Denver	15	15	Willis, James, Green Bay	12	0
Tomczak, Mike, Pittsburgh	6	2	Waters, Andre, Arizona	12	4	Wilmsmeyer, Klaus, S.F.	16	0
Toner, Ed, Indianapolis	9	0	Watson, Tim, Kansas City	1	0	Wilner, Jeff, Green Bay	11	1
Tovar, Steve, Cincinnati	16	16	Watters, Orlando, Seattle	16	8	Wilson, Bernard, T.B.-Ari.	14	12
Townsend, Greg, Philadelphia ...	16	12	Watters, Ricky, San Francisco ..	16	16	Wilson, Bobby, Washington	9	9
Trapp, James, L.A. Raiders	16	2	Watts, Damon, Indianapolis	16	8	Wilson, Charles, Tampa Bay	14	7
Treadwell, David, N.Y. Giants	13	0	Webb, Richmond, Miami	16	16	Wilson, Karl, Tampa Bay	14	2
Trudeau, Jack, N.Y. Jets	5	2	Webster, Larry, Miami	16	7	Wilson, Marcus, Green Bay	12	0
Truitt, Greg, Cincinnati	16	0	Weidner, Bert, Miami	14	14	Wilson, Ray, N.O.-G.B.	6	0
Truitt, Olanda, Washington	9	0	Weldon, Casey, Tampa Bay	2	0	Wilson, Robert, Dal.-Mia.	4	0
Tuaolo, Esera, Minnesota	16	0	Wellman, Gary, Houston	8	0	Wilson, Troy, San Francisco	11	0
Tubbs, Winfred, New Orleans	13	7	Wells, Dean, Seattle	15	0	Wilson, Wade, New Orleans	4	0
Tucker, Mark, Arizona	16	3	Wells, Mike, Detroit	4	0	Winans, Tydus, Washington	15	0
Tuggle, Jessie, Atlanta	16	16	West, Ed, Green Bay	14	12	Winston, DeMond, New Orleans	3	0
Tuinei, Mark, Dallas	15	15	Wetnight, Ryan, Chicago	11	0	Winter, Blaise, San Diego	2	0
Tupa, Tom, Cleveland	16	0	Wheeler, Mark, Tampa Bay	15	8	Winters, Frank, Green Bay	16	16
Turk, Dan, L.A. Raiders	16	0	Whigham, Larry, New England	12	0	Wisniewski, Steve, L.A. Raiders....	16	16
Turnbull, Renaldo, New Orleans.	16	16	White, Alberto, L.A. Raiders	8	0	Wolf, Joe, Arizona	7	6
Turner, Eric, Cleveland	16	16	White, Dwayne, N.Y. Jets	16	16	Wolford, Will, Indianapolis	16	16
Turner, Floyd, Indianapolis	16	16	White, Lorenzo, Houston	15	8	Woodall, Lee, San Francisco	15	13
Turner, Marcus, N.Y. Jets	16	1	White, Reggie, San Diego	11	0	Woodard, Marc, Philadelphia	16	0
Turner, Nate, Buffalo	13	0	White, Reggie, Green Bay	16	15	Wooden, Terry, Seattle	16	15
Turner, Kevin, New England	16	9	White, William, Kansas City	15	14	Woods, Tony, Washington	15	15
Turner, Vernon, Tampa Bay	12	1	Whitfield, Bob, Atlanta	16	16	Woodson, Darren, Dallas	16	16
Tuten, Rick, Seattle	16	0	Whitley, Curtis, San Diego	12	2	Woodson, Rod, Pittsburgh	15	15
Tyner, Scott, Atlanta	6	0	Whitmore, David, Kansas City ...	12	10	Woolford, Donnell, Chicago	16	16
Uhlenhake, Jeff, New Orleans ...	16	15	Whittington, Bernard, Ind.	13	8	Wooten, Tito, N.Y. Giants	16	2
Valerio, Joe, Kansas City	16	1	Widell, Dave, Denver	16	16	Word, Barry, Arizona	1	0
Vanderbeek, Matt, Dallas	12	0	Widell, Doug, Detroit	16	16	Workman, Vince, Tampa Bay	15	8
Vanhorse, Sean, San Diego	16	1	Widmer, Corey, N.Y. Giants	16	5	Worley, Tim, Chicago	5	0
Vardell, Tommy, Cleveland	5	5	Wilhelm, Erik, Cincinnati	1	0	Wortham, Barron, Houston	16	1
Vaughn, Jon, Sea.-K.C.	13	0	Wilkerson, Bruce, L.A. Raiders ..	11	6	Wren, Darryl, New England	8	0
Veasey, Craig, Miami	12	1	Wilkins, Gabe, Green Bay	15	0	Wright, Alexander, L.A. Raiders	16	15
Verdin, Clarence, Atlanta	12	0	Wilkins, Jeff, Philadelphia	6	0	Wright, Jeff, Buffalo	12	11
Villa, Danny, Kansas City	14	0	Wilkinson, Dan, Cincinnati	16	14	Wright, Toby, L.A. Rams	16	2
Vincent, Troy, Miami	13	12	Williams, Aeneas, Arizona	16	16	Wycheck, Frank, Washington ...	9	1
Vinson, Fernandus, Cincinnati...	16	4	Williams, Alfred, Cincinnati	16	16	Wyman, David, Denver	4	0
von Oelhoffen, Kimo, Cincinnati.	7	0	Williams, Bernard, Philadelphia.	16	16	Yarborough, Ryan, N.Y. Jets	13	0
Waddle, Tom, Chicago	9	1	Williams, Brent, Seattle	10	9	Young, Bryant, San Francisco ...	16	16
Wagner, Bryan, San Diego	14	0	Williams, Brian, N.Y. Giants	14	14	Young, Duane, San Diego	14	14
Waldrop, Rob, Kansas City	3	0	Williams, Calvin, Philadelphia ...	16	14	Young, Lonnie, San Diego	12	0
Walker, Adam, San Francisco ...	8	0	Williams, Dan, Denver	12	7	Young, Mike, Kansas City	2	0
Walker, Bracey, K.C.-Cin.	9	0	Williams, Darryl, Cincinnati	16	16	Young, Robert, L.A. Rams	16	16
Walker, Darnell, Atlanta	16	5	Williams, David, Houston	16	16	Young, Steve, San Francisco	16	16
Walker, Derrick, Kansas City	15	11	Williams, Erik, Dallas	7	7	Zandofsky, Mike, Atlanta	16	16
Walker, Herschel, Philadelphia..	16	14	Williams, Gene, Cleveland	15	9	Zendejas, Tony, L.A. Rams	16	0
Wallace, Aaron, L.A. Raiders	16	5	Williams, Gerald, Pittsburgh	11	11	Zgonina, Jeff, Pittsburgh	16	0
Wallace, Steve, San Francisco ..	15	15	Williams, Harvey, L.A. Raiders ..	16	10	Zimmerman, Gary, Denver	16	16
Wallerstedt, Brett, Cincinnati	10	0	Williams, James, Arizona	15	7	Zolak, Scott, New England	16	0
Walls, Wesley, New Orleans	15	7	Williams, James, Chicago	16	15	Zomalt, Eric, Philadelphia	12	0
Walsh, Chris, Minnesota	10	0	Williams, James, New Orleans ...	16	7	Zordich, Michael, Philadelphia ...	16	16
Walsh, Steve, Chicago	12	11	Williams, Jamie, L.A. Raiders	16	0	Zorich, Chris, Chicago	16	16
Ware, Derek, Arizona	15	12						

PLAYERS WITH TWO OR MORE CLUBS

Player, Team	GP	GS
Clark, Vinnie, Atlanta	11	11
Clark, Vinnie, New Orleans	5	4
Duckett, Forey, Cincinnati	2	0
Duckett, Forey, Green Bay	3	0
Duckett, Forey, Seattle	2	0
Frier, Mike, Cincinnati	1	0
Frier, Mike, Seattle	3	0
Hamilton, Rick, Washington	1	0
Hamilton, Rick, Kansas City	2	0
Hardy, Adrian, San Francisco	2	0
Hardy, Adrian, Cincinnati	14	0
Harris, Ronnie, New England	1	0
Harris, Ronnie, Seattle	1	0
Higgs, Mark, Miami	5	1
Higgs, Mark, Arizona	6	0
Irwin, Tim, Tampa Bay	8	6

Player, Team	GP	GS
Irwin, Tim, Miami	5	0
Jackson, Mark, N.Y. Giants	2	0
Jackson, Mark, Indianapolis	12	0
Johnson, Keshon, Chicago	6	0
Johnson, Keshon, Green Bay	7	0
Jones, Victor, Pittsburgh	10	0
Jones, Victor, Kansas City	1	0
Kidd, John, San Diego	2	0
Kidd, John, Miami	4	0
McAfee, Fred, Arizona	7	0
McAfee, Fred, Pittsburgh	6	0
McCants, Keith, Houston	4	1
McCants, Keith, Arizona	8	1
Miller, Les, New Orleans	8	5
Miller, Les, San Diego	4	0
Smith, Artie, San Francisco	2	0

Player, Team	GP	GS
Smith, Artie, Cincinnati	7	0
Speer, Del, Cleveland	8	0
Speer, Del, Seattle	1	0
Thomas, Blair, New England	4	0
Thomas, Blair, Dallas	2	1
Vaughn, Jon, Seattle	9	0
Vaughn, Jon, Kansas City	3	0
Walker, Bracey, Kansas City	2	0
Walker, Bracey, Cincinnati	7	0
Wilson, Bernard, Tampa Bay	1	0
Wilson, Bernard, Arizona	13	12
Wilson, Ray, New Orleans	3	0
Wilson, Ray, Green Bay	3	0
Wilson, Robert, Dallas	2	0
Wilson, Robert, Miami	2	0

ATTENDANCE

REGULAR SEASON

Team	Home Attendance	Average	NFL Rank	Road Attendance	Average	NFL Rank
Arizona	511,317	63,915	12	422,127	52,766	27
Atlanta	458,509	57,314	19	437,110	54,639	25
Buffalo	595,543	74,443	2	487,641	60,955	13
Chicago	468,015	58,502	17	526,706	65,838	3
Cincinnati	421,964	52,746	21	464,395	58,049	19
Cleveland	559,582	69,948	5	488,609	61,076	12
Dallas	516,088	64,511	11	512,923	64,115	7
Denver	574,180	71,773	4	524,941	65,618	4
Detroit	547,977	68,497	7	471,677	58,960	17
Green Bay	458,074	57,259	20	516,906	64,613	6
Houston	353,514	44,189	27	469,224	58,653	18
Indianapolis	396,462	49,558	25	456,978	57,122	20
Kansas City	610,878	76,360	1	544,122	68,015	1
L.A. Raiders	409,564	51,196	24	533,295	66,662	2
L.A. Rams	338,497	42,312	28	453,160	56,645	22
Miami	551,970	68,996	6	506,381	63,298	10
Minnesota	474,744	59,343	14	506,678	63,335	9
New England	472,718	59,090	15	481,673	60,209	14
New Orleans	469,900	58,738	16	433,313	54,164	26
N.Y. Giants	583,857	72,982	3	453,645	56,706	21
N.Y. Jets	528,538	66,067	8	478,498	59,812	15
Philadelphia	518,691	64,836	9	477,318	59,665	16
Pittsburgh	461,272	57,659	18	507,155	63,394	8
San Diego	479,842	59,980	13	489,635	61,204	11
San Francisco	516,736	64,592	10	522,094	65,262	5
Seattle	420,136	52,517	22	448,420	56,053	23
Tampa Bay	367,443	45,930	26	418,623	52,328	28
Washington	413,669	51,709	23	446,433	55,804	24
NFL total	13,479,680	60,177		13,479,680	60,177	

HISTORICAL

TOP REGULAR-SEASON HOME CROWDS

Team	Attendance	Date	Site	Opponent
Arizona	73,400	October 30, 1994	Sun Devil Stadium	Pittsburgh
Atlanta	71,253	November 21, 1993	Georgia Dome	Dallas
Buffalo	80,368	October 4, 1992	Rich Stadium	Miami
Chicago	66,900	September 5, 1993	Soldier Field	N.Y. Giants
Cincinnati	60,284	October 17, 1971	Riverfront Stadium	Cleveland
Cleveland	85,703	September 21, 1970	Cleveland Stadium	New York Jets
Dallas	80,259	November 24, 1966	Cotton Bowl	Cleveland
Denver	76,089	October 26, 1986	Mile High Stadium	Seattle
Detroit	80,444	December 20, 1981	Pontiac Silverdome	Tampa Bay
Green Bay	59,487	September 4, 1994	Lambeau Field	Minnesota
Houston	63,713	September 6, 1992	Astrodome	Pittsburgh
Indianapolis	60,544	October 31, 1988	Hoosier Dome	Denver
Kansas City	82,094	November 5, 1972	Arrowhead Stadium	Oakland
Los Angeles Raiders	92,496	November 2, 1986	Los Angeles Memorial Coliseum	Denver
Los Angeles Rams	102,368	November 10, 1957	Los Angeles Memorial Coliseum	San Francisco
Miami	78,914	November 19, 1972	Orange Bowl	New York Jets
Minnesota	64,035	September 25, 1994	Metrodome	Miami
New England	61,457	December 5, 1971	Schaefer Stadium*	Miami
New Orleans	83,437	November 12, 1967	Tulane Stadium	Dallas
		November 26, 1967	Tulane Stadium	Atlanta
New York Giants	77,356	January 2, 1994	Giants Stadium	Dallas
New York Jets	75,606	November 27, 1994	Giants Stadium	Miami
Philadelphia	72,111	November 1, 1981	Veterans Stadium	Dallas
Pittsburgh	60,808	December 18, 1994	Three Rivers Stadium	Cleveland
San Diego	63,012	December 5, 1994	San Diego Jack Murphy Stadium	L.A. Raiders
San Francisco	69,014	November 13, 1994	Candlestick Park	Dallas
Seattle	65,902	December 13, 1992	Kingdome	Philadelphia
Tampa Bay	72,077	October 8, 1989	Tampa Stadium	Chicago
Washington	56,454	September 4, 1994	Robert F. Kennedy Memorial Stadium	Seattle

*Now known as Foxboro Stadium.

NATIONAL FOOTBALL LEAGUE

Year	Regular season*		Average	Postseason†	
1934	492,684	(60)	8,211	35,059	(1)
1935	638,178	(53)	12,041	15,000	(1)
1936	816,007	(54)	15,111	29,545	(1)
1937	963,039	(55)	17,510	15,878	(1)
1938	937,197	(55)	17,040	48,120	(1)
1939	1,071,200	(55)	19,476	32,279	(1)
1940	1,063,025	(55)	19,328	36,034	(1)
1941	1,108,615	(55)	20,157	55,870	(2)
1942	887,920	(55)	16,144	36,006	(1)
1943	969,128	(50)	19,383	71,315	(2)
1944	1,019,649	(50)	20,393	46,016	(1)
1945	1,270,401	(50)	25,408	32,178	(1)
1946	1,732,135	(55)	31,493	58,346	(1)
1947	1,837,437	(60)	30,624	66,268	(2)
1948	1,525,243	(60)	25,421	36,309	(1)
1949	1,391,735	(60)	23,196	27,980	(1)
1950	1,977,753	(78)	25,356	136,647	(3)
1951	1,913,019	(72)	26,570	57,522	(1)
1952	2,052,126	(72)	28,502	97,507	(2)
1953	2,164,585	(72)	30,064	54,577	(1)
1954	2,190,571	(72)	30,425	43,827	(1)
1955	2,521,836	(72)	35,026	85,693	(1)
1956	2,551,263	(72)	35,434	56,836	(1)
1957	2,836,318	(72)	39,393	119,579	(2)
1958	3,006,124	(72)	41,752	123,659	(2)
1959	3,140,000	(72)	43,617	57,545	(1)
1960	3,128,296	(78)	40,106	67,325	(1)
1961	3,986,159	(98)	40,675	39,029	(1)
1962	4,003,421	(98)	40,851	64,892	(1)
1963	4,163,643	(98)	42,486	45,801	(1)
1964	4,563,049	(98)	46,562	79,544	(1)
1965	4,634,021	(98)	47,296	100,304	(2)
1966	5,337,044	(105)	50,829	135,098	(2)
1967	5,938,924	(112)	53,026	241,754	(4)
1968	5,882,313	(112)	52,521	291,279	(4)
1969	6,096,127	(112)	54,430	242,841	(4)
1970	9,533,333	(182)	52,381	410,371	(7)
1971	10,076,035	(182)	55,363	430,244	(7)
1972	10,445,827	(182)	57,395	435,466	(7)
1973	10,730,933	(182)	58,961	458,515	(7)
1974	10,236,322	(182)	56,224	412,180	(7)
1975	10,213,193	(182)	56,116	443,811	(7)
1976	11,070,543	(196)	56,482	428,733	(7)
1977	11,018,632	(196)	56,218	483,588	(7)
1978	12,771,800	(224)	57,017	578,107	(9)
1979	13,182,039	(224)	58,848	582,266	(9)
1980	13,392,230	(224)	59,787	577,186	(9)
1981	13,606,990	(224)	60,745	587,361	(9)
1982‡	7,367,438	(126)	58,472	985,952	(15)
1983	13,277,222	(224)	59,273	625,068	(9)
1984	13,398,112	(224)	59,813	614,809	(9)
1985	13,345,047	(224)	59,567	660,667	(9)
1986	13,588,551	(224)	60,663	683,901	(9)
1987§	10,032,493	(168)	59,717	606,864	(9)
1988	13,539,848	(224)	60,446	608,204	(9)
1989	13,625,662	(224)	60,829	635,326	(9)
1990	14,266,240	(224)	63,689	797,198	(11)
1991	13,187,478	(224)	58,873	758,186	(11)
1992	13,159,387	(224)	58,747	756,005	(11)
1993	13,328,760	(224)	59,503	755,625	(11)
1994	13,479,680	(224)	60,177	719,143	(11)

*Number of tickets sold, including no-shows; number of regular-season games in parentheses.

†Includes conference, league championship and Super Bowl games, but not Pro Bowl; number of postseason games in parentheses.

‡A 57-day players strike reduced 224-game schedule to 126 games.

§A 24-day players strike reduced 224-game schedule to 168 non-strike games.

AMERICAN FOOTBALL LEAGUE

Year	Regular season*		Average	AFL Champ. Game
1960	926,156	(56)	16,538	32,183
1961	1,002,657	(56)	17,904	29,556
1962	1,147,302	(56)	20,487	37,981
1963	1,241,741	(56)	22,174	30,127
1964	1,447,875	(56)	25,855	40,242
1965	1,782,384	(56)	31,828	30,361
1966	2,160,369	(63)	34,291	42,080
1967	2,295,697	(63)	36,439	53,330
1968	2,635,004	(70)	37,643	62,627
1969	2,843,373	(70)	40,620	53,564

*Number of regular-season games in parentheses.

TRADES

1994-95 TRADES

(Covering June 1994 through May 1995)

JUNE 17

Arizona traded LB Tyronne Stowe to Washington for a 1995 sixth-round draft choice. Arizona selected WR Billy Williams (Tennessee).

JULY 13

Detroit traded S William White to Kansas City for a conditional 1995 draft choice.

AUGUST 10

Pittsburgh traded RB Leroy Thompson to New England for a 1995 fourth-round draft choice. Pittsburgh selected DL Oliver Gibson (Notre Dame).

AUGUST 23

Tampa Bay traded CB Darren Anderson to Kansas City for a 1995 seventh-round draft choice. Tampa Bay selected DE Jeffrey Rodgers (Texas A&M-Kingsville).

AUGUST 27

Denver traded QB Tommy Maddox to L.A. Rams for a 1995 fourth-round draft pick. Denver selected LB Ken Brown (Virginia Tech).

AUGUST 28

Chicago traded LB Jim Schwantz to Dallas for an undisclosed 1996 draft choice.

L.A. Raiders traded WR Charles Jordan to Green Bay for a 1995 draft pick. The Raiders later traded the choice to Washington.

Washington traded G Darryl Moore to Green Bay for a 1995 fifth-round draft choice. Washington later traded fifth-round choice to L.A. Raiders.

OCTOBER 11

New Orleans traded CB Reginald Jones to Cleveland for an undisclosed draft choice.

MARCH 2

Atlanta traded P Harold Alexander to Detroit for an undisclosed draft choice.

MARCH 21

Miami traded WR Mark Ingram to Green Bay for a 1995 fourth-round draft choice. Miami later traded the fourth-round choice back to Green Bay.

MARCH 25

Cleveland traded RB/KR Eric Metcalf and a 1995 first-round draft choice to Atlanta for a 1995 first-round draft choice. Cleveland later traded its first-round choice to San Francisco. Atlanta selected DB Devin Bush (Florida State).

MARCH 29

Miami traded TE Keith Jackson and a 1995 fourth-round draft choice to Green Bay for a 1995 second-round draft choice. Miami selected G Andrew Greene (Indiana). Green Bay later traded its fourth-round choice back to Miami.

APRIL 3

Arizona traded WR Ricky Proehl to Seattle for a 1995 fourth-round draft choice. Arizona later traded the fourth-round choice to the N.Y. Jets.

Green Bay traded CB Terrell Buckley to Miami for past considerations.

APRIL 4

Chicago traded DE Trace Armstrong to Miami for 1995 second- and third-round draft choices. Chicago selected P Todd Sauerbrun and G Evan Pilgrim.

APRIL 17

Detroit traded RB Derrick Moore to San Francisco for a 1995 fifth-round draft choice. Detroit selected T Ronald Cherry (McNeese State).

APRIL 21

Green Bay traded QB Mark Brunell to Jacksonville for 1995 third- and fifth-round draft choices. Green Bay selected FB William Henderson (North Carolina) and RB Travis Jervey (The Citadel).

Arizona traded RB Ronald Moore and 1995 first- and fourth-round draft choices to N.Y. Jets for WR Rob Moore. The Jets selected DE Hugh Douglas (Central State, O.) and T Melvin Hayes (Mississippi State).

APRIL 22

Carolina traded a 1995 first-round draft choice to Cincinnati for 1995 first- and second-round draft choices. Cincinnati selected RB Ki-Jana Carter (Penn State). Carolina selected QB Kerry Collins (Penn State) and DE Shawn King (Northeast Louisiana).

Tampa Bay traded 1995 first- and third-round draft choices to Philadelphia for a 1995 first- and two second-round draft choices. Philadelphia selected DE Mike Mamula (Boston College) and DE Greg Jefferson (Central Florida). Tampa Bay selected DT Warren Sapp (Miami, Fla.); DB Melvin Johnson (Kentucky) and later traded the second second-round choice to Dallas.

Cleveland traded a 1995 first-round draft choice to San Francisco for 1995 first-, third-, fourth- and 1996 fifth-round draft choices. San Francisco selected WR J.J. Stokes, (UCLA). Cleveland selected LB Craig Powell (Ohio State), DE Mike Frederick (Virginia), and traded the fourth-round choice to Philadelphia.

Kansas City traded a 1995 first-round draft choice to Jacksonville for 1995 first-, third-, fourth- and 1996 fourth-round draft choices. Jacksonville selected RB James Stewart (Tennessee). Kansas City selected T Trezelle Jenkins (Michigan), LB Troy Dumas (Nebraska) and QB Steve Stenstrom (Stanford).

Green Bay traded 1995 first- and sixth-round draft choices to Carolina for 1995 first-, third- and sixth-round draft choices. Carolina selected DB Tyrone Poole (Fort Valley State) and DT Steve Strahan (Baylor). Green Bay selected DB Craig Newsome (Arizona State), DT Darius Holland (Colorado) and WR Charlie Simmons (Georgia Tech).

Dallas traded a 1995 first-round draft choice to Tampa Bay for two 1995 second-round draft choices. Tampa Bay selected LB Derrick Brooks (Florida State). Dallas traded the first second-round choice to Atlanta and selected G Shane Hannah (Michigan State).

San Diego traded a 1995 first-round draft choice to Carolina for 1995 second-, third- and fourth-round draft choices. Carolina selected T Blake Brockermeyer (Texas). San Diego selected DB Terrance Shaw (Stephen F. Austin State), LB Preston Harrison (Ohio State) and LB Chris Cowart (Florida State).

Jacksonville traded a 1995 second-round draft choice to N.Y. Jets for 1995 second- and third-round draft choices. The Jets selected G Matt O'Dwyer (Northwestern). Jacksonville selected T Brian DeMarco (Michigan State) and DB Chris Hudson (Colorado).

Dallas traded a 1995 second-round draft choice to Atlanta for 1995 second- and fourth-round draft choices. Atlanta selected DB Ronald Davis (Tennessee). Dallas selected RB Sherman Williams (Alabama) and WR Eric Bjornson (Washington).

Kansas City traded a 1995 second-round draft choice to Philadelphia for WR Victor Bailey and a 1995 fourth-round draft choice. Philadelphia selected DB Bobby Taylor (Notre Dame). Kansas City traded the fourth-round choice to New England.

Detroit traded a 1995 second-round draft choice to San Diego for a 1996 first-round draft choice. San Diego selected RB Terrell Fletcher (Wisconsin).

APRIL 23

St. Louis traded a 1995 third-round draft choice to Detroit for 1995 third- and fourth-round draft choices. Detroit selected TE David Sloan (New Mexico). St. Louis selected K Steve McLaughlin (Arizona) and TE Lovell Pinkney (Texas).

Green Bay traded a 1995 third-round draft choice to Cleveland for 1995 third- and fifth-round draft choices. Cleveland selected QB Eric Zeier (Georgia). Green Bay selected WR Antonio Freeman (Virginia Tech) and QB Jay Barker (Alabama).

N.Y. Giants traded a 1995 sixth-round draft choice to Minnesota for DB Vencie Glenn. Minnesota selected LB John Sollomon (Sam Houston State).

Denver traded a 1995 fourth-round draft choice to Minnesota for 1995 fourth- and sixth-round draft choices. Minnesota selected QB Chad May (Kansas State). Denver selected T Jamie Brown (Florida A&M) and RB Terrell Davis (Georgia).

Kansas City traded a 1995 fourth-round draft choice to New England for a 1996 third-round draft choice. New England selected C Dave Wohlabaugh (Syracuse).

Cleveland traded a 1995 fourth-round draft choice to Jacksonville for a 1995 fifth-round draft choice and a 1996 sixth-round draft choice. Jacksonville selected DT Mike Thompson (Wisconsin). Cleveland selected DL Tau Pupua (Weber State).

Cleveland traded a 1995 fourth-round draft choice to Philadelphia for 1995 and 1996 fifth-round draft choices. Philadelphia selected QB Dave Barr (California). Cleveland selected WR/KR Mike Miller (Notre Dame).

Washington traded a 1995 fifth-round draft choice to Los Angeles for 1995 fifth- and seventh-round draft choices. Los Angeles selected LB Matt Dyson (Michigan). Washington selected DE Rich Owens (Lehigh) and DB Scott Turner (Illinois).

Philadelphia traded 1995 fifth- and seventh-round draft choices to Jacksonville for 1995 sixth- and two seventh-round draft choices. Jacksonville selected FB Ryan Christopherson (Wyoming) and WR Curtis Marsh (Utah). Philadelphia selected RB Kevin Bouie (Mississippi State) and T Howard Smothers (Bethune-Cookman).

Kansas City traded a 1995 sixth-round draft choice to Carolina for a 1996 sixth-round draft choice. Carolina selected QB Jerry Colquitt (Tennessee).

New England traded a 1995 seventh-round draft choice to Cleveland for a 1995 seventh-round choice. Cleveland selected WR A.C. Tellison (Miami, Fla.). New England selected DB Carlos Yancy (Georgia).

APRIL 26

Tampa Bay traded QB Craig Erickson to Indianapolis for a 1996 first- and a conditional fourth-round draft choice.

MAY 19

Tampa Bay traded TE Harold Bishop to Cleveland for an undisclosed draft choice.

MAY 30

Pittsburgh traded RB Barry Foster to Carolina for a 1996 sixth-round draft choice and a 1997 conditional fourth-round draft choice.

Jacksonville traded CB Corey Raymond to Detroit for TE Ty Hallock.

NFL EXPANSION DRAFT OF FEBRUARY 15, 1995

JACKSONVILLE JAGUARS

1. Steve Beuerlein, QB, Arizona
3. Corey Raymond, DB, N.Y. Giants
5. Jeff Novak, T, Miami
7. John Duff, DE, L.A. Raiders
9. Keith Goganious, LB, Buffalo
11. Mark Williams, LB, Green Bay
13. Al Jackson, DB, Philadelphia
15. Mark Tucker, C, Arizona
17. Paul Frase, DE, N.Y. Jets
19. Tom Myslinski, G, Chicago
21. Willie Jackson, WR, Dallas
23. Othello Henderson, DB, New Orleans
25. Santo Stephens, LB, Cincinnati
27. Darren Carrington, S, San Diego
29. Michael Davis, DB, Houston
31. Dave Thomas, DB, Dallas
33. Mazio Royster, RB, Tampa Bay
35. Le'Shai Maston, LB, Houston
37. Charles Davenport, WR, Pittsburgh
39. Monty Grow, DB, Kansas City
41. Marcus Wilson, RB, Green Bay
43. Brant Boyer, LB, Miami
45. Harry Colon, DB, Detroit
47. Derek Brown, TE, N.Y. Giants
49. James Williams, LB, New Orleans
51. Eugene Chung, G, New England
53. Reggie Cobb, RB, Green Bay
55. Desmond Howard, WR, Washington
57. Kelvin Martin, WR, Seattle
59. Cedric Tillman, WR, Denver
61. Rogerick Green, CB, Tampa Bay

NOTE: The Jaguars passed on the 63rd, 65th, 67th, 69th and 71st picks.

CAROLINA PANTHERS

2. Rod Smith, DB, New England
4. Harry Boatswain, T, San Francisco
6. Kurt Haws, TE, Washington
8. Tyrone Rodgers, DE, Seattle
10. Mark Thomas, DE, San Francisco
12. Tim McKyer, DB, Pittsburgh
14. Curtis Whitley, OL, San Diego
16. Howard Griffith, RB, L.A. Rams
18. Greg Kragen, NT, Kansas City
20. Cary Brabham, DB, L.A. Raiders
22. Dave Garnett, LB, Minnesota
24. Andre Powell, LB, N.Y. Giants
26. Dewell Brewer, RB, Indianapolis
28. Bob Christian, RB, Chicago
30. Fred Foggie, DB, Pittsburgh
32. Mark Carrier, RB, Tampa Bay
34. Mark Rodenhauser, C, Detroit
36. Steve Hawkins, WR, New England
38. Brian O'Neal, FB, Philadelphia
40. Derrick Lassic, RB, Dallas
42. Richard Buchanan, WR, L.A. Rams
44. Doug Pederson, QB, Miami
46. Vince Marrow, TE, Buffalo
48. Larry Ryans, WR, Detroit
50. Baron Rollins, G, New Orleans
52. William Sims, LB, Minnesota
54. Paul Butcher, LB, Indianapolis
56. Jack Trudeau, QB, N.Y. Jets
58. Charles Swann, WR, Denver
60. David Mims, WR, Atlanta
62. Shawn Price, DE, Tampa Bay
64. Eric Guilford, WR, Minnesota
66. Bill Goldberg, DL, Atlanta
68. Eric Ball, RB, Cincinnati
70. Mike Teeter, DT, Houston

NOTE: The Panthers passed on the 72nd pick, ending the draft.

1994 STATISTICS

Rushing

Passing

Receiving

Scoring

Interceptions

Sacks

Fumbles

Field goals

Punting

Punt returns

Kickoff returns

Miscellaneous

RUSHING

TEAM

AFC

Team	Att.	Yds.	Avg.	Long	TD
Pittsburgh	546	2180	4.0	29t	15
Seattle	480	2084	4.3	41	16
Indianapolis	495	2060	4.2	52	15
San Diego	482	1852	3.8	36	13
Buffalo	483	1831	3.8	60	14
Kansas City	464	1732	3.7	36t	12
Houston	417	1682	4.0	33	10
Miami	433	1658	3.8	47t	13
Cleveland	449	1657	3.7	39	12
N.Y. Jets	416	1566	3.8	90	8
Cincinnati	404	1556	3.9	37t	5
L.A. Raiders	428	1512	3.5	28	7
Denver	431	1470	3.4	24	19
New England	478	1332	2.8	26	12
AFC total	6406	24172	3.8	90	171
AFC average	457.6	1726.6	3.8	....	12.2

t—touchdown.

NFC

Team	Att.	Yds.	Avg.	Long	TD
Detroit	406	2080	5.1	85	12
Dallas	550	1953	3.6	46	26
San Francisco	491	1897	3.9	28t	23
Philadelphia	432	1761	4.1	91t	14
N.Y. Giants	525	1754	3.3	27t	12
Chicago	487	1588	3.3	25t	10
Arizona	480	1560	3.3	36	12
Green Bay	417	1543	3.7	43	11
Minnesota	419	1524	3.6	45	11
Tampa Bay	430	1489	3.5	27	8
Washington	407	1415	3.5	49	5
L.A. Rams	397	1389	3.5	44t	6
New Orleans	373	1336	3.6	40	11
Atlanta	330	1249	3.8	25	8
NFC total	6144	22538	3.7	91t	169
NFC average	438.9	1609.9	3.7	....	12.1
NFL total	12550	46710	....	91t	340
NFL average	448.2	1668.2	3.7	....	12.1

INDIVIDUAL

BESTS OF THE SEASON

Yards, season
NFC: 1883—Barry Sanders, Detroit.
AFC: 1545—Chris Warren, Seattle.

Yards, game
NFC: 237—Barry Sanders, Detroit vs. Tampa Bay, Nov. 13 (26 attempts, 0 TD).
AFC: 185—Chris Warren, Seattle at Houston, Dec. 11 (30 attempts, 1 TD).

Longest gain
NFC: 91—Herschel Walker, Philadelphia at Atlanta, Nov. 27 (TD).
AFC: 90—Johnny Johnson, N.Y. Jets vs. Chicago, Sept. 25.

Attempts, season
NFC: 368—Emmitt Smith, Dallas.
AFC: 343—Natrone Means, San Diego.

Attempts, game
NFC: 40—Barry Sanders, Detroit at Dallas, Sept. 15 (194 yards); Errict Rhett, Tampa Bay vs. Washington, Dec. 4 (192 yards).
AFC: 33—Marcus Allen, Kansas City at L.A. Raiders, Dec. 24 (132 yards).

Yards per attempt, season
NFC: 5.7—Barry Sanders, Detroit.
AFC: 4.6—Chris Warren, Seattle.

Touchdowns, season
NFC: 21—Emmitt Smith, Dallas.
AFC: 12—Natrone Means, San Diego.

Team leaders, yards
AFC:

Buffalo	1093	Thurman Thomas
Cincinnati	468	Derrick Fenner
Cleveland	890	Leroy Hoard
Denver	620	Leonard Russell
Houston	757	Lorenzo White
Indianapolis	1282	Marshall Faulk
Kansas City	709	Marcus Allen
L.A. Raiders	983	Harvey Williams
Miami	868	Bernie Parmalee
New England	703	Marion Butts
N.Y. Jets	931	Johnny Johnson
Pittsburgh	851	Barry Foster
San Diego	1350	Natrone Means
Seattle	1545	Chris Warren

NFC:

Arizona	780	Ron Moore
Atlanta	779	Craig Heyward
Chicago	899	Lewis Tillman
Dallas	1484	Emmitt Smith
Detroit	1883	Barry Sanders
Green Bay	623	Edgar Bennett
L.A. Rams	1025	Jerome Bettis
Minnesota	1031	Terry Allen
New Orleans	579	Mario Bates
N.Y. Giants	1075	Rodney Hampton
Philadelphia	528	Herschel Walker
San Francisco	877	Ricky Watters
Tampa Bay	1011	Errict Rhett
Washington	650	Ricky Ervins

NFL LEADERS

Player, Team	Att.	Yds.	Avg.	Long	TD
Sanders, Barry, Detroit	331	1883	5.7	85	7
Warren, Chris, Seattle*	333	1545	4.6	41	9
Smith, Emmitt, Dallas	368	1484	4.0	46	21
Means, Natrone, San Diego*	343	1350	3.9	25	12
Faulk, Marshall, Indianapolis*	314	1282	4.1	52	11
Thomas, Thurman, Buffalo*	287	1093	3.8	29	7
Hampton, Rodney, N.Y. Giants*	327	1075	3.3	t27	6
Allen, Terry, Minnesota	255	1031	4.0	45	8
Bettis, Jerome, L.A. Rams	319	1025	3.2	19	3
Rhett, Errict, Tampa Bay	284	1011	3.6	27	7
Williams, Harvey, L.A. Raiders*	282	983	3.5	28	4
Johnson, Johnny, N.Y. Jets*	240	931	3.9	90	3
Tillman, Lewis, Chicago	275	899	3.3	t25	7
Hoard, Leroy, Cleveland*	209	890	4.3	39	5
Watters, Ricky, San Francisco*	239	877	3.7	23	6
Parmalee, Bernie, Miami*	216	868	4.0	t47	6
Foster, Barry, Pittsburgh*	216	851	3.9	t29	5
Morris, Bam, Pittsburgh*	198	836	4.2	20	7
Moore, Ron, Arizona	232	780	3.4	24	4
Heyward, Craig, Atlanta	183	779	4.3	17	7
White, Lorenzo, Houston*	191	757	4.0	33	3

Player, Team	Att.	Yds.	Avg.	Long	TD
Allen, Marcus, Kansas City*	189	709	3.8	t36	7
Butts, Marion, New England*	243	703	2.9	26	8
Ervins, Ricky, Washington	185	650	3.5	49	3
Brown, Gary, Houston*	169	648	3.8	18	4
Bennett, Edgar, Green Bay	178	623	3.5	t39	5
Russell, Leonard, Denver*	190	620	3.3	t22	9
Bates, Mario, New Orleans	151	579	3.8	40	6
Cobb, Reggie, Green Bay	153	579	3.8	30	3
Hill, Greg, Kansas City*	141	574	4.1	20	1

*AFC.
t—touchdown.
Leader based on yards gained.

AFC

Player, Team	Att.	Yds.	Avg.	Long	TD
Alexander, Derrick, Cleveland	4	38	9.5	25	0
Allen, Marcus, Kansas City	189	709	3.8	t36	7
Anders, Kimble, Kansas City	62	231	3.7	19	2
Anderson, Gary, Pittsburgh	1	3	3.0	3	0
Anderson, Richie, N.Y. Jets	43	207	4.8	55	1
Avery, Steve, Pittsburgh	2	4	2.0	5	0
Baldwin, Randy, Cleveland	23	78	3.4	16	0
Ball, Eric, Cincinnati	2	0	0.0	1	0
Bates, Michael, Seattle	2	-4	-2.0	7	0
Baxter, Brad, N.Y. Jets	60	170	2.8	13	4
Beebe, Don, Buffalo	2	11	5.5	6	0
Bennett, Donnell, Kansas City	46	178	3.9	17	2
Bernstine, Rod, Denver	17	91	5.4	24	0
Bieniemy, Eric, San Diego	73	295	4.0	36	0
Blades, Brian, Seattle	2	32	16.0	40	0
Blake, Jeff, Cincinnati	37	204	5.5	16	1
Bledsoe, Drew, New England	44	40	0.9	7	0
Bono, Steve, Kansas City	4	-1	-.2	2	0
Broussard, Steve, Cincinnati	94	403	4.3	t37	2
Brown, Gary, Houston	169	648	3.8	18	4
Bryant, Beno, Seattle	1	6	6.0	6	0
Butts, Marion, New England	243	703	2.9	26	8
Byars, Keith, Miami	19	64	3.4	12	2
Byner, Earnest, Cleveland	75	219	2.9	15	2
Campbell, Jeff, Denver	2	6	3.0	6	0
Carlson, Cody, Houston	10	17	1.7	6	0
Carrier, Mark, Cleveland	1	14	14.0	t14	1
Clark, Derrick, Denver	56	168	3.0	12	3
Coates, Ben, New England	1	0	0.0	0	0
Coleman, Pat, Houston	1	2	2.0	2	0
Copeland, Russell, Buffalo	1	-7	-7.0	-7	0
Cothran, Jeff, Cincinnati	26	85	3.3	13	0
Craver, Aaron, Miami	6	43	7.2	19	0
Culver, Rodney, San Diego	8	63	7.9	22	0
Davis, Kenneth, Buffalo	91	381	4.2	60	2
Dawson, Lake, Kansas City	3	24	8.0	13	0
Dickerson, Ron, Kansas City	1	0	0.0	0	0
Elway, John, Denver	58	235	4.1	22	4
Esiason, Boomer, N.Y. Jets	28	59	2.1	15	0
Evans, Vince, L.A. Raiders	6	24	4.0	23	0
Faulk, Marshall, Indianapolis	314	1282	4.1	52	11
Fenner, Derrick, Cincinnati	141	468	3.3	21	1
Foster, Barry, Pittsburgh	216	851	3.9	t29	5
Gardner, Carwell, Buffalo	41	135	3.3	13	4
Gary, Cleveland, Miami	7	11	1.6	4	0
Gash, Sam, New England	30	86	2.9	10	0
Gelbaugh, Stan, Seattle	1	10	10.0	10	0
Gilbert, Gale, San Diego	8	-3	-.4	5	0
Givins, Ernest, Houston	1	-5	-5.0	-5	0
Green, Harold, Cincinnati	76	223	2.9	22	1
Harbaugh, Jim, Indianapolis	39	223	5.7	41	0
Harmon, Ronnie, San Diego	25	94	3.8	t15	1
Hendrickson, Steve, San Diego	1	3	3.0	3	0
Hill, Greg, Kansas City	141	574	4.1	20	1
Hoard, Leroy, Cleveland	209	890	4.3	39	5
Hostetler, Jeff, L.A. Raiders	46	159	3.5	14	2
Humphrey, Ronald, Indianapolis	18	85	4.7	27	0
Humphries, Stan, San Diego	19	19	1.0	8	0
Ismail, Raghib, L.A. Raiders	4	31	7.8	13	0
Jefferson, Shawn, San Diego	3	40	13.3	22	0
Johnson, Anthony, N.Y. Jets	5	12	2.4	5	0
Johnson, Charles, Pittsburgh	4	-1	-.2	7	0
Johnson, Johnny, N.Y. Jets	240	931	3.9	90	3
Johnson, Tracy, Seattle	12	44	3.7	14	2
Jones, Calvin, L.A. Raiders	22	93	4.2	10	0
Jones, James, Cleveland	1	0	0.0	0	0
Jourdain, Yonel, Buffalo	17	56	3.3	16	0
Kelly, Jim, Buffalo	25	77	3.1	18	1
Kirby, Terry, Miami	60	233	3.9	30	2
Klingler, David, Cincinnati	17	85	5.0	15	0
Kosar, Bernie, Miami	1	17	17.0	17	0
Majkowski, Don, Indianapolis	24	34	1.4	10	3
Marino, Dan, Miami	22	-6	-.3	10	1
Martin, Tony, San Diego	2	-9	-4.5	4	0
McAfee, Fred, Ari.-Pit.*	18	51	2.8	13	2
McCallum, Napoleon, Raiders	3	5	1.7	3	1
McDuffie, O. J., Miami	5	32	6.4	12	0
McGee, Tim, Cincinnati	1	-18	-18.0	-18	0
McGwire, Dan, Seattle	10	-6	-.6	2	0
Means, Natrone, San Diego	343	1350	3.9	25	12
Metcalf, Eric, Cleveland	93	329	3.5	t37	2
Milburn, Glyn, Denver	58	201	3.5	20	1
Millen, Hugh, Denver	5	57	11.4	24	0
Miller, Anthony, Denver	1	3	3.0	3	0
Mills, Ernie, Pittsburgh	3	18	6.0	17	0
Mirer, Rick, Seattle	34	153	4.5	14	0
Mohr, Chris, Buffalo	1	-9	-9.0	-9	0
Montana, Joe, Kansas City	18	17	0.9	13	0
Montgomery, Tyrone, Raiders	36	97	2.7	15	0
Moore, Rob, N.Y. Jets	1	-3	-3.0	-3	0
Morris, Bam, Pittsburgh	198	836	4.2	20	7
Murrell, Adrian, N.Y. Jets	33	160	4.8	19	0
Nagle, Browning, Indianapolis	1	12	12.0	12	0
O'Donnell, Neil, Pittsburgh	31	80	2.6	18	1
Parmalee, Bernie, Miami	216	868	4.0	t47	6
Potts, Roosevelt, Indianapolis	77	336	4.4	52	1
Rathman, Tom, L.A. Raiders	28	118	4.2	14	0
Reed, Andre, Buffalo	10	87	8.7	20	0
Reich, Frank, Buffalo	6	3	0.5	5	0
Richardson, Bucky, Houston	30	217	7.2	18	1
Rivers, Reggie, Denver	43	83	1.9	11	2
Royals, Mark, Pittsburgh	1	-13	-13.0	-13	0
Russell, Derek, Denver	1	6	6.0	6	0
Russell, Leonard, Denver	190	620	3.3	t22	9
Rypien, Mark, Cleveland	7	4	0.6	2	0
Saxon, James, Miami	8	16	2.0	7	0
Scott, Darnay, Cincinnati	10	106	10.6	23	0
Smith, Kevin, L.A. Raiders	1	2	2.0	2	0
Smith, Lamar, Seattle	2	-1	-.5	0	0
Smith, Steve, Seattle	26	80	3.1	12	2
Spikes, Irving, Miami	70	312	4.5	40	2
Stone, Dwight, Pittsburgh	2	7	3.5	4	0
Strong, Mack, Seattle	27	114	4.2	14	2
Testaverde, Vinny, Cleveland	21	37	1.8	12	2
Thomas, Thurman, Buffalo	287	1093	3.8	29	7
Thompson, Leroy, New England	102	312	3.1	13	2
Tillman, Spencer, Houston	2	12	6.0	9	0
Timpson, Michael, New England	2	14	7.0	10	0
Tolliver, Billy Joe, Houston	12	37	3.1	10	2
Tomczak, Mike, Pittsburgh	4	22	5.5	13	0
Toner, Ed, Indianapolis	1	11	11.0	11	0
Trudeau, Jack, N.Y. Jets	6	30	5.0	15	0
Turner, Floyd, Indianapolis	3	-3	-1.0	5	0
Turner, Kevin, New England	36	111	3.1	13	1
Turner, Nate, Buffalo	2	4	2.0	4	0
Vardell, Tommy, Cleveland	15	48	3.2	9	0
Vaughn, Jon, Seattle	27	96	3.6	16	1
Warren, Chris, Seattle	333	1545	4.6	41	9
Warren, Lamont, Indianapolis	18	80	4.4	34	0
Warren, Terrence, Seattle	3	15	5.0	11	0
Wellman, Gary, Houston	1	-3	-3.0	-3	0
White, Lorenzo, Houston	191	757	4.0	33	3
Williams, Harvey, L.A. Raiders	282	983	3.5	28	4
Williams, John L., Pittsburgh	68	317	4.7	23	1
Zolak, Scott, New England	1	-1	-1.0	-1	0

*Includes both NFC and AFC statistics.
t—touchdown.

NFC

Player, Team	Att.	Yds.	Avg.	Long	TD
Agee, Tommie, Dallas	5	4	0.8	3	0
Aikman, Troy, Dallas	30	62	2.1	13	1
Alexander, Harold, Atlanta	1	0	0.0	0	0
Allen, Terry, Minnesota	255	1031	4.0	45	8
Anderson, Jamal, Atlanta	2	-1	-.5	0	0
Anderson, Willie, L.A. Rams	1	11	11.0	11	0
Armstrong, Tyji, Tampa Bay	1	-1	-1.0	-1	0
Bailey, Johnny, L.A. Rams	11	35	3.2	9	1
Barnhardt, Tommy, New Orleans	1	21	21.0	21	0
Bates, Mario, New Orleans	151	579	3.8	40	6
Bennett, Edgar, Green Bay	178	623	3.5	t39	5
Bettis, Jerome, L.A. Rams	319	1025	3.2	19	3
Beuerlein, Steve, Arizona	22	39	1.8	19	1
Brister, Bubby, Philadelphia	1	7	7.0	7	0
Brooks, Reggie, Washington	100	297	3.0	15	2
Brooks, Robert, Green Bay	1	0	0.0	0	0
Brown, Dave, N.Y. Giants	60	196	3.3	21	2
Brown, Derek, New Orleans	146	489	3.3	16	3
Bruce, Isaac, L.A. Rams	1	2	2.0	2	0
Brunell, Mark, Green Bay	6	7	1.2	t5	1
Calloway, Chris, N.Y. Giants	8	77	9.6	20	0
Carter, Dexter, San Francisco	8	34	4.3	18	0
Centers, Larry, Arizona	115	336	2.9	17	5
Chandler, Chris, L.A. Rams	18	61	3.4	22	1
Christian, Bob, Chicago	7	29	4.1	8	0
Cobb, Reggie, Green Bay	153	579	3.8	30	3
Coleman, Lincoln, Dallas	64	180	2.8	13	1
Conway, Curtis, Chicago	6	31	5.2	12	0
Cunningham, Randall, Phi.	65	288	4.4	22	3
Dilfer, Trent, Tampa Bay	2	27	13.5	15	0
Downs, Gary, N.Y. Giants	15	51	3.4	8	0
Drayton, Troy, L.A. Rams	1	4	4.0	4	0
Dunbar, Vaughn, New Orleans	3	9	3.0	3	0
Early, Quinn, New Orleans	2	10	5.0	8	0
Elias, Keith, N.Y. Giants	2	4	2.0	5	0
Ellard, Henry, Washington	1	-5	-5.0	-5	0
Emanuel, Bert, Atlanta	2	4	2.0	2	0
Erickson, Craig, Tampa Bay	26	68	2.6	17	1
Ervins, Ricky, Washington	185	650	3.5	49	3
Evans, Chuck, Minnesota	6	20	3.3	8	0
Everett, Jim, New Orleans	15	35	2.3	14	0
Favre, Brett, Green Bay	42	202	4.8	t36	2
Feagles, Jeff, Arizona	2	8	4.0	12	0
Floyd, William, San Francisco	87	305	3.5	26	6
Frerotte, Gus, Washington	4	1	0.3	2	0
Friesz, John, Washington	1	1	1.0	1	0
Garner, Charlie, Philadelphia	109	399	3.7	t28	3
Garrett, Jason, Dallas	3	-2	-.7	0	0
George, Jeff, Atlanta	30	66	2.2	10	0
Graham, Kent, N.Y. Giants	2	11	5.5	9	0
Graham, Scottie, Minnesota	64	207	3.2	11	2
Grbac, Elvis, San Francisco	13	1	0.1	6	0
Green, Robert, Chicago	25	122	4.9	14	0
Griffith, Howard, L.A. Rams	9	30	3.3	7	0
Hampton, Rodney, N.Y. Giants	327	1075	3.3	t27	6
Harris, Raymont, Chicago	123	464	3.8	13	1
Harris, Rudy, Tampa Bay	2	0	0.0	3	0
Haynes, Michael, New Orleans	4	43	10.8	15	0
Hearst, Garrison, Arizona	37	169	4.6	36	1
Hebert, Bobby, Atlanta	9	43	4.8	20	0
Hebron, Vaughn, Philadelphia	82	325	4.0	19	2
Hester, Jessie, L.A. Rams	2	28	14.0	24	0
Heyward, Craig, Atlanta	183	779	4.3	17	7
Higgs, Mark, Mia.-Ari.*	62	195	3.1	21	0
Hoge, Merril, Chicago	6	24	4.0	8	0
Howard, Desmond, Washington	1	4	4.0	4	0
Hughes, Tyrone, New Orleans	2	6	3.0	7	0
Johnson, Brad, Minnesota	2	-2	-1.0	-1	0
Johnson, LeShon, Green Bay	26	99	3.8	43	0
Johnston, Daryl, Dallas	40	138	3.5	t9	2
Jordan, Charles, Green Bay	1	5	5.0	5	0

Player, Team	Att.	Yds.	Avg.	Long	TD
Joseph, James, Philadelphia	60	203	3.4	t34	1
Kinchen, Todd, L.A. Rams	1	44	44.0	t44	1
Kramer, Erik, Chicago	6	-2	-.3	2	0
Krieg, Dave, Detroit	23	35	1.5	15	0
Lang, David, L.A. Rams	6	34	5.7	17	0
Lee, Amp, Minnesota	29	104	3.6	16	0
Lester, Tim, L.A. Rams	7	14	2.0	8	0
Levens, Dorsey, Green Bay	5	15	3.0	5	0
Levy, Chuck, Arizona	3	15	5.0	22	0
Logan, Marc, San Francisco	33	143	4.3	22	1
Loville, Derek, San Francisco	31	99	3.2	13	0
Lynch, Eric, Detroit	1	0	0.0	0	0
Maddox, Tommy, L.A. Rams	1	1	1.0	1	0
Marshall, Arthur, N.Y. Giants	2	8	4.0	6	0
McDowell, Anthony, Tampa Bay	21	58	2.8	8	0
McMahon, Jim, Arizona	6	32	5.3	17	0
Meggett, Dave, N.Y. Giants	91	298	3.3	t26	4
Miller, Chris, L.A. Rams	20	100	5.0	16	0
Mitchell, Brian, Washington	78	311	4.0	33	0
Mitchell, Scott, Detroit	15	24	1.6	7	1
Moon, Warren, Minnesota	27	55	2.0	12	0
Moore, Derrick, Detroit	27	52	1.9	12	4
Moore, Ronald, Arizona	232	780	3.4	24	4
Muster, Brad, New Orleans	1	3	3.0	t3	1
Neal, Lorenzo, New Orleans	30	90	3.0	12	1
Ned, Derrick, New Orleans	11	36	3.3	15	0
Palmer, David, Minnesota	1	1	1.0	1	0
Peete, Rodney, Dallas	9	-2	-.2	2	0
Pegram, Erric, Atlanta	103	358	3.5	25	1
Perriman, Brett, Detroit	9	86	9.6	25	0
Rasheed, Kenyon, N.Y. Giants	17	44	2.6	6	0
Reeves, Bryan, Arizona	1	-1	-1.0	-1	0
Rhett, Errict, Tampa Bay	284	1011	3.6	27	7
Rice, Jerry, San Francisco	7	93	13.3	t28	2
Royster, Mazio, Tampa Bay	9	7	0.8	6	0
Salisbury, Sean, Minnesota	3	2	0.7	5	0
Samuels, Terry, Arizona	1	1	1.0	1	0
Sanders, Barry, Detroit	331	1883	5.7	85	7
Saxon, Mike, Minnesota	1	0	0.0	0	0
Schroeder, Jay, Arizona	16	59	3.7	16	0
Sharpe, Sterling, Green Bay	3	15	5.0	8	0
Sherrard, Mike, N.Y. Giants	1	-10	-10.0	-10	0
Shuler, Heath, Washington	26	103	4.0	26	0
Smith, Cedric, Washington	10	48	4.8	13	0
Smith, Emmitt, Dallas	368	1484	4.0	46	21
Smith, Robert, Minnesota	31	106	3.4	t14	1
Taylor, John, San Francisco	2	-2	-1.0	1	0
Thomas, Blair, N.E.-Dal.*	43	137	3.2	13	2
Thompson, Darrell, Green Bay	2	-2	-1.0	2	0
Tillman, Lewis, Chicago	275	899	3.3	t25	7
Turner, Vernon, Tampa Bay	4	13	3.3	9	0
Walker, Adam, San Francisco	13	54	4.2	14	1
Walker, Herschel, Philadelphia	113	528	4.7	t91	5
Walsh, Steve, Chicago	30	4	0.1	12	1
Watters, Ricky, San Francisco	239	877	3.7	23	6
Williams, Calvin, Philadelphia	2	11	5.5	6	0
Williams, Kevin, Dallas	6	20	3.3	8	0
Wilson, Charles, Tampa Bay	2	15	7.5	11	0
Wilson, Robert, Dallas	1	-1	-1.0	-1	0
Wilson, Wade, New Orleans	7	15	2.1	9	0
Winans, Tydus, Washington	1	5	5.0	5	0
Workman, Vince, Tampa Bay	79	291	3.7	18	0
Worley, Tim, Chicago	9	17	1.9	4	1
Young, Steve, San Francisco	58	293	5.1	27	7

*Includes both NFC and AFC statistics.
t—touchdown.

PLAYERS WITH TWO CLUBS

Player, Team	Att.	Yds.	Avg.	Long	TD
Higgs, Mark, Miami	19	68	3.6	21	0
Higgs, Mark, Arizona	43	127	3.0	16	0
McAfee, Fred, Arizona	2	-5	-2.5	2	1
McAfee, Fred, Pittsburgh	16	56	3.5	13	1
Thomas, Blair, New England	19	67	3.5	13	1
Thomas, Blair, Dallas	24	70	2.9	11	1

PASSING

TEAM

AFC

Team	Att.	Comp.	Pct. Comp.	Gross Yds.	Sack	Yds. Lost	Net Yds.	Yds./ Att.	Yds./ Comp.	TD	Pct. TD	Long	Had Int.	Pct. Int.
New England	699	405	57.9	4583	22	139	4444	6.56	11.32	25	3.58	t62	27	3.9
Miami	627	392	62.5	4533	18	113	4420	7.23	11.56	31	4.94	t64	18	2.9
Denver	626	388	62.0	4383	55	366	4017	7.00	11.30	18	2.88	76	13	2.1
Kansas City	615	366	59.5	4092	19	132	3960	6.65	11.18	20	3.25	t62	14	2.3
Buffalo	542	342	63.1	3714	41	301	3413	6.85	10.86	23	4.24	t83	21	3.9
San Diego	522	305	58.4	3619	29	251	3368	6.93	11.87	20	3.83	t99	14	2.7
L.A. Raiders	488	281	57.6	3556	50	289	3267	7.29	12.65	22	4.51	t77	16	3.3
Cincinnati	542	289	53.3	3541	44	305	3236	6.53	12.25	21	3.87	76	19	3.5
N.Y. Jets	539	310	57.5	3323	28	186	3137	6.17	10.72	18	3.34	69	18	3.3
Cleveland	507	266	52.5	3269	14	94	3175	6.45	12.29	20	3.94	t81	21	4.1
Pittsburgh	463	266	57.5	3247	39	283	2964	7.01	12.21	17	3.67	t84	9	1.9
Houston	554	274	49.5	3216	65	417	2799	5.81	11.74	13	2.35	81	17	3.1
Seattle	498	253	50.8	2809	40	241	2568	5.64	11.10	13	2.61	51	9	1.8
Indianapolis	376	217	57.7	2519	28	166	2353	6.70	11.61	15	3.99	t85	14	3.7
AFC total	7598	4354	....	50404	492	3283	47121	....	....	276	....	t99	230	....
AFC average	542.7	311.0	57.3	3600.3	35.1	234.5	3365.8	6.63	11.58	19.7	3.6	....	16.4	3.0

t—touchdown.
Leader based on net yards.

NFC

Team	Att.	Comp.	Pct. Comp.	Gross Yds.	Sack	Yds. Lost	Net Yds.	Yds./ Att.	Yds./ Comp.	TD	Pct. TD	Long	Had Int.	Pct. Int.
Minnesota	673	409	60.8	4570	31	246	4324	6.79	11.17	18	2.67	t65	20	3.0
San Francisco	511	359	70.3	4362	35	199	4163	8.54	12.15	37	7.24	t69	11	2.2
Atlanta	629	374	59.5	4344	37	232	4112	6.91	11.61	25	3.97	t85	25	4.0
New Orleans	569	366	64.3	4027	24	181	3846	7.08	11.00	22	3.87	t78	18	3.2
Green Bay	609	375	61.6	3977	33	204	3773	6.53	10.61	33	5.42	49	14	2.3
Philadelphia	566	316	55.8	3736	48	372	3364	6.60	11.82	18	3.18	93	14	2.5
L.A. Rams	512	291	56.8	3597	35	239	3358	7.03	12.36	23	4.49	t72	18	3.5
Washington	546	271	49.6	3524	21	146	3378	6.45	13.00	25	4.58	t81	27	4.9
Dallas	448	282	62.9	3461	20	93	3368	7.73	12.27	19	4.24	90	14	3.1
Tampa Bay	491	271	55.2	3436	30	171	3265	7.00	12.68	17	3.46	t71	16	3.3
Arizona	538	287	53.3	3284	34	237	3047	6.10	11.44	11	2.04	63	19	3.5
Chicago	502	308	61.4	3230	25	139	3091	6.43	10.49	19	3.78	t85	16	3.2
Detroit	459	250	54.5	3085	26	163	2922	6.72	12.34	24	5.23	t51	14	3.1
N.Y. Giants	405	226	55.8	2847	46	285	2562	6.33	12.60	16	3.95	55	18	4.4
NFC total	7458	4385	....	51480	445	2907	48573	....	....	307	....	93	244	....
NFC average	532.7	313.2	58.8	3677.1	31.8	207.6	3469.5	6.90	11.74	21.9	4.1	....	17.4	3.3
NFL total	15056	8739	....	101884	937	6190	95694	....	....	583	....	t99	474	....
NFL average	537.7	312.1	58.0	3638.7	33.5	221.1	3417.6	6.77	11.66	20.8	3.9	....	16.9	3.1

INDIVIDUAL

BESTS OF THE SEASON

Highest rating, season
NFC: 112.8—Steve Young, San Francisco.
AFC: 89.2—Dan Marino, Miami.

Completion percentage, season
NFC: 70.3—Steve Young, San Francisco.
AFC: 63.6—Jim Kelly, Buffalo.

Attempts, season
AFC: 691—Drew Bledsoe, New England.
NFC: 601—Warren Moon, Minnesota.

Completions, season
AFC: 400—Drew Bledsoe, New England.
NFC: 371—Warren Moon, Minnesota.

Yards, season
AFC: 4555—Drew Bledsoe, New England.
NFC: 4264—Warren Moon, Minnesota.

Yards, game
AFC: 473—Dan Marino, Miami vs. New England, Sept. 4 (23-42, 5 TDs).
NFC: 420—Warren Moon, Minnesota vs. New Orleans, Nov. 6 (33-57, 3 TDs).

Longest
AFC: 99—Stan Humphries (to Tony Martin), San Diego at Seattle, Sept. 18 (TD).
NFC: 93—Randall Cunningham (to Herschel Walker), Philadelphia at N.Y. Giants, Sept. 4.

Yards per attempt, season
NFC: 8.61—Steve Young, San Francisco.
AFC: 7.33—Jeff Hostetler, L.A. Raiders.

Touchdown passes, season
NFC: 35—Steve Young, San Francisco.
AFC: 30—Dan Marino, Miami.

Touchdown passes, game
AFC: 5—Dan Marino, Miami vs. New England, Sept. 4 (23-42, 456 yards).

NFC: 4—Steve Young, San Francisco vs. L.A. Raiders, Sept. 5 (19-32, 292 yards); John Friesz, Washington at New Orleans, Sept. 11 (15-22, 190 yards); Steve Young, San Francisco at Atlanta, Oct. 16 (15-16, 138 yards); Jeff George, Atlanta at Denver, Nov. 20 (19-43, 254 yards); Steve Young, San Francisco vs. L.A. Rams, Nov. 20 (30-44, 325 yards); Brett Favre, Green Bay at Dallas, Nov. 24 (27-40, 248 yards); Steve Young, San Francisco at New Orleans, Nov. 28 (24-30, 270 yards).

Lowest interception percentage, season
AFC: 1.8—Joe Montana, Kansas City.
NFC: 2.2—Steve Young, San Francisco.

NFL LEADERS

Player, Team	Att.	Comp.	Pct. Comp.	Yds.	Avg. Gain	TD	Pct. TD	Long	Int.	Pct. Int.	Sack	Yds. Lost	Rat. Pts.
Young, Steve, San Francisco	461	324	70.3	3969	8.61	35	7.6	t69	10	2.2	31	163	112.8
Favre, Brett, Green Bay	582	363	62.4	3882	6.67	33	5.7	49	14	2.4	31	188	90.7
Marino, Dan, Miami*	615	385	62.6	4453	7.24	30	4.9	t64	17	2.8	18	113	89.2
Elway, John, Denver*	494	307	62.1	3490	7.06	16	3.2	63	10	2.0	46	303	85.7
Everett, Jim, New Orleans	540	346	64.1	3855	7.14	22	4.1	t78	18	3.3	21	164	84.9
Aikman, Troy, Dallas	361	233	64.5	2676	7.41	13	3.6	90	12	3.3	14	59	84.9
Kelly, Jim, Buffalo*	448	285	63.6	3114	6.95	22	4.9	t83	17	3.8	34	244	84.6
Montana, Joe, Kansas City*	493	299	60.6	3283	6.66	16	3.2	t57	9	1.8	19	132	83.6
George, Jeff, Atlanta	524	322	61.5	3734	7.13	23	4.4	t85	18	3.4	32	206	83.3
Erickson, Craig, Tampa Bay	399	225	56.4	2919	7.32	16	4.0	t71	10	2.5	22	129	82.5
Humphries, Stan, San Diego*	453	264	58.3	3209	7.08	17	3.8	t99	12	2.6	25	223	81.6
Hostetler, Jeff, L.A. Raiders*	455	263	57.8	3334	7.33	20	4.4	t77	16	3.5	41	232	80.8
Moon, Warren, Minnesota	601	371	61.7	4264	7.09	18	3.0	t65	19	3.2	29	235	79.9
O'Donnell, Neil, Pittsburgh*	370	212	57.3	2443	6.60	13	3.5	t60	9	2.4	35	250	78.9
Walsh, Steve, Chicago	343	208	60.6	2078	6.06	10	2.9	50	8	2.3	11	52	77.9
Esiason, Boomer, N.Y. Jets*	440	255	58.0	2782	6.32	17	3.9	69	13	3.0	19	134	77.3
Blake, Jeff, Cincinnati*	306	156	51.0	2154	7.04	14	4.6	76	9	2.9	19	120	76.9
Cunningham, Randall, Philadelphia	490	265	54.1	3229	6.59	16	3.3	93	13	2.7	43	333	74.4
Bledsoe, Drew, New England*	691	400	57.9	4555	6.59	25	3.6	t62	27	3.9	22	139	73.6
Miller, Chris, L.A. Rams	317	173	54.6	2104	6.64	16	5.0	54	14	4.4	28	193	73.6
Brown, Dave, N.Y. Giants	350	201	57.4	2536	7.25	12	3.4	53	16	4.6	42	248	72.5
Testaverde, Vinny, Cleveland*	376	207	55.1	2575	6.85	16	4.3	t81	18	4.8	12	83	70.7
Mirer, Rick, Seattle*	381	195	51.2	2151	5.65	11	2.9	51	7	1.8	27	145	70.2
Schroeder, Jay, Arizona	238	133	55.9	1510	6.34	4	1.7	t48	7	2.9	11	85	68.4
Klingler, David, Cincinnati*	231	131	56.7	1327	5.74	6	2.6	56	9	3.9	24	165	65.7
Tolliver, Billy Joe, Houston*	240	121	50.4	1287	5.36	6	2.5	44	7	2.9	27	166	62.6
Mitchell, Scott, Detroit	246	119	48.4	1456	5.92	10	4.1	34	11	4.5	12	63	62.0
Beuerlein, Steve, Arizona	255	130	51.0	1545	6.06	5	2.0	63	9	3.5	20	129	61.6
Shuler, Heath, Washington	265	120	45.3	1658	6.26	10	3.8	t81	12	4.5	12	83	59.6

*AFC.
t—touchdown.
Leader based on rating points, minimum 224 attempts.

AFC

Player, Team	Att.	Comp.	Pct. Comp.	Yds.	Avg. Gain	TD	Pct. TD	Long	Int.	Pct. Int.	Sack	Yds. Lost	Rat. Pts.
Blake, Jeff, Cincinnati	306	156	51.0	2154	7.04	14	4.6	76	9	2.9	19	120	76.9
Bledsoe, Drew, New England	691	400	57.9	4555	6.59	25	3.6	t62	27	3.9	22	139	73.6
Blundin, Matt, Kansas City	5	1	20.0	13	2.60	0	0.0	13	1	20.0	0	0	0.0
Bono, Steve, Kansas City	117	66	56.4	796	6.80	4	3.4	t62	4	3.4	0	0	74.6
Broussard, Steve, Cincinnati	1	0	0.0	0	0.00	0	0.0	0	0	0.0	0	0	39.6
Camarillo, Rich, Houston	1	0	0.0	0	0.00	0	0.0	0	0	0.0	0	0	39.6
Carlson, Cody, Houston	132	59	44.7	727	5.51	1	0.8	81	4	3.0	15	115	52.2
Elway, John, Denver	494	307	62.1	3490	7.06	16	3.2	63	10	2.0	46	303	85.7
Esiason, Boomer, N.Y. Jets	440	255	58.0	2782	6.32	17	3.9	69	13	3.0	19	134	77.3
Evans, Vince, L.A. Raiders	33	18	54.5	222	6.73	2	6.1	t65	0	0.0	9	57	95.8
Foley, Glenn, N.Y. Jets	8	5	62.5	45	5.63	0	0.0	16	1	12.5	0	0	38.0
Gelbaugh, Stan, Seattle	11	7	63.6	80	7.27	1	9.1	t25	0	0.0	0	0	115.7
Gilbert, Gale, San Diego	67	41	61.2	410	6.12	3	4.5	26	1	1.5	4	28	87.3
Harbaugh, Jim, Indianapolis	202	125	61.9	1440	7.13	9	4.5	t85	6	3.0	17	72	85.8

Player, Team	Att.	Comp.	Pct. Comp.	Yds.	Avg. Gain	TD	Pct. TD	Long	Int.	Pct. Int.	Sack	Yds. Lost	Rat. Pts.
Hollas, Donald, Cincinnati	2	0	0.0	0	0.00	0	0.0	0	1	50.0	1	20	0.0
Hostetler, Jeff, L.A. Raiders	455	263	57.8	3334	7.33	20	4.4	t77	16	3.5	41	232	80.8
Humphries, Stan, San Diego	453	264	58.3	3209	7.08	17	3.8	t99	12	2.6	25	223	81.6
Jackson, Michael, Cleveland	2	0	0.0	0	0.00	0	0.0	0	0	0.0	0	0	39.6
Johnson, Lee, Cincinnati	1	1	100.0	7	7.00	1	100.0	t7	0	0.0	0	0	135.4
Kelly, Jim, Buffalo	448	285	63.6	3114	6.95	22	4.9	t83	17	3.8	34	244	84.6
Klingler, David, Cincinnati	231	131	56.7	1327	5.74	6	2.6	56	9	3.9	24	165	65.7
Kosar, Bernie, Miami	12	7	58.3	80	6.67	1	8.3	22	1	8.3	0	0	71.5
Majkowski, Don, Indianapolis	152	84	55.3	1010	6.64	6	3.9	29	7	4.6	9	76	69.8
Marino, Dan, Miami	615	385	62.6	4453	7.24	30	4.9	t64	17	2.8	18	113	89.2
Martin, Tony, San Diego	1	0	0.0	0	0.00	0	0.0	0	1	100.0	0	0	0.0
McGwire, Dan, Seattle	105	51	48.6	578	5.50	1	1.0	36	2	1.9	13	96	60.7
Means, Natrone, San Diego	1	0	0.0	0	0.00	0	0.0	0	0	0.0	0	0	39.6
Metcalf, Eric, Cleveland	1	0	0.0	0	0.00	0	0.0	0	0	0.0	0	0	39.6
Millen, Hugh, Denver	131	81	61.8	893	6.82	2	1.5	76	3	2.3	9	63	77.6
Mirer, Rick, Seattle	381	195	51.2	2151	5.65	11	2.9	51	7	1.8	27	145	70.2
Montana, Joe, Kansas City	493	299	60.6	3283	6.66	16	3.2	t57	9	1.8	19	132	83.6
Nagle, Browning, Indianapolis	21	8	38.1	69	3.29	0	0.0	23	1	4.8	2	18	27.7
O'Donnell, Neil, Pittsburgh	370	212	57.3	2443	6.60	13	3.5	t60	9	2.4	35	250	78.9
Reed, Andre, Buffalo	1	1	100.0	32	32.00	0	0.0	32	0	0.0	0	0	118.8
Reich, Frank, Buffalo	93	56	60.2	568	6.11	1	1.1	47	4	4.3	7	57	63.4
Richardson, Bucky, Houston	181	94	51.9	1202	6.64	6	3.3	t76	6	3.3	23	136	70.3
Rivers, Reggie, Denver	1	0	0.0	0	0.00	0	0.0	0	0	0.0	0	0	39.6
Rypien, Mark, Cleveland	128	59	46.1	694	5.42	4	3.1	43	3	2.3	2	11	63.7
Scott, Darnay, Cincinnati	1	1	100.0	53	53.00	0	0.0	53	0	0.0	0	0	118.8
Testaverde, Vinny, Cleveland	376	207	55.1	2575	6.85	16	4.3	t81	18	4.8	12	83	70.7
Tolliver, Billy Joe, Houston	240	121	50.4	1287	5.36	6	2.5	44	7	2.9	27	166	62.6
Tomczak, Mike, Pittsburgh	93	54	58.1	804	8.65	4	4.3	t84	0	0.0	4	33	100.8
Trudeau, Jack, N.Y. Jets	91	50	54.9	496	5.45	1	1.1	t24	4	4.4	9	52	55.9
Tuten, Rick, Seattle	1	0	0.0	0	0.00	0	0.0	0	0	0.0	0	0	39.6
Warren, Lamont, Indianapolis	1	0	0.0	0	0.00	0	0.0	0	0	0.0	0	0	39.6
Zolak, Scott, New England	8	5	62.5	28	3.50	0	0.0	13	0	0.0	0	0	68.8

t—touchdown.

NFC

Player, Team	Att.	Comp.	Pct. Comp.	Yds.	Avg. Gain	TD	Pct. TD	Long	Int.	Pct. Int.	Sack	Yds. Lost	Rat. Pts.
Aikman, Troy, Dallas	361	233	64.5	2676	7.41	13	3.6	90	12	3.3	14	59	84.9
Barnhardt, Tommy, New Orleans	1	0	0.0	0	0.00	0	0.0	0	0	0.0	0	0	39.6
Beuerlein, Steve, Arizona	255	130	51.0	1545	6.06	5	2.0	63	9	3.5	20	129	61.6
Brister, Bubby, Philadelphia	76	51	67.1	507	6.67	2	2.6	53	1	1.3	5	39	89.1
Brown, Dave, N.Y. Giants	350	201	57.4	2536	7.25	12	3.4	53	16	4.6	42	248	72.5
Brunell, Mark, Green Bay	27	12	44.4	95	3.52	0	0.0	25	0	0.0	2	16	53.8
Chandler, Chris, L.A. Rams	176	108	61.4	1352	7.68	7	4.0	t72	2	1.1	7	46	93.8
Conway, Curtis, Chicago	1	1	100.0	23	23.00	1	100.0	t23	0	0.0	0	0	158.3
Cunningham, Randall, Philadelphia	490	265	54.1	3229	6.59	16	3.3	93	13	2.7	43	333	74.4
Dilfer, Trent, Tampa Bay	82	38	46.3	433	5.28	1	1.2	42	6	7.3	8	42	36.3
Emanuel, Bert, Atlanta	1	0	0.0	0	0.00	0	0.0	0	1	100.0	0	0	0.0
Erickson, Craig, Tampa Bay	399	225	56.4	2919	7.32	16	4.0	t71	10	2.5	22	129	82.5
Everett, Jim, New Orleans	540	346	64.1	3855	7.14	22	4.1	t78	18	3.3	21	164	84.9
Favre, Brett, Green Bay	582	363	62.4	3882	6.67	33	5.7	49	14	2.4	31	188	90.7
Frerotte, Gus, Washington	100	46	46.0	600	6.00	5	5.0	51	5	5.0	3	18	61.3
Friesz, John, Washington	180	105	58.3	1266	7.03	10	5.6	t73	9	5.0	6	45	77.7
Garrett, Jason, Dallas	31	16	51.6	315	10.16	2	6.5	68	1	3.2	2	13	95.5
George, Jeff, Atlanta	524	322	61.5	3734	7.13	23	4.4	t85	18	3.4	32	206	83.3
Graham, Kent, N.Y. Giants	53	24	45.3	295	5.57	3	5.7	55	2	3.8	2	22	66.2
Grbac, Elvis, San Francisco	50	35	70.0	393	7.86	2	4.0	42	1	2.0	4	36	98.2
Hearst, Garrison, Arizona	1	1	100.0	10	10.00	1	100.0	t10	0	0.0	0	0	147.9
Hebert, Bobby, Atlanta	103	52	50.5	610	5.92	2	1.9	40	6	5.8	3	17	51.0
Johnson, Brad, Minnesota	37	22	59.5	150	4.05	0	0.0	15	0	0.0	1	5	68.5
Klein, Perry, Atlanta	1	0	0.0	0	0.00	0	0.0	0	0	0.0	2	9	39.6
Kramer, Erik, Chicago	158	99	62.7	1129	7.15	8	5.1	t85	8	5.1	14	87	79.9
Krieg, Dave, Detroit	212	131	61.8	1629	7.68	14	6.6	t51	3	1.4	14	100	101.7
Maddox, Tommy, L.A. Rams	19	10	52.6	141	7.42	0	0.0	39	2	10.5	0	0	37.3
Marshall, Arthur, N.Y. Giants	0	0	....	0	....	0	....	0	0	....	1	8	-1.0
McMahon, Jim, Arizona	43	23	53.5	219	5.09	1	2.3	33	3	7.0	3	23	46.6
Meggett, David, N.Y. Giants	2	1	50.0	16	8.00	1	50.0	t16	0	0.0	1	7	116.7
Miller, Chris, L.A. Rams	317	173	54.6	2104	6.64	16	5.0	54	14	4.4	28	193	73.6

Player, Team	Att.	Comp.	Pct. Comp.	Yds.	Avg. Gain	TD	Pct. TD	Long	Int.	Pct. Int.	Sack	Yds. Lost	Rat. Pts.
Mitchell, Brian, Washington	1	0	0.0	0	0.00	0	0.0	0	1	100.0	0	0	0.0
Mitchell, Scott, Detroit	246	119	48.4	1456	5.92	10	4.1	34	11	4.5	12	63	62.0
Moon, Warren, Minnesota	601	371	61.7	4264	7.09	18	3.0	t65	19	3.2	29	235	79.9
Moore, Ron, Arizona	1	0	0.0	0	0.00	0	0.0	0	0	0.0	0	0	39.6
Peete, Rodney, Dallas	56	33	58.9	470	8.39	4	7.1	t65	1	1.8	4	21	102.5
Perriman, Brett, Detroit	1	0	0.0	0	0.00	0	0.0	0	0	0.0	0	0	39.6
Salisbury, Sean, Minnesota	34	16	47.1	156	4.59	0	0.0	38	1	2.9	1	6	48.2
Saxon, Mike, Minnesota	1	0	0.0	0	0.00	0	0.0	0	0	0.0	0	0	39.6
Schroeder, Jay, Arizona	238	133	55.9	1510	6.34	4	1.7	t48	7	2.9	11	85	68.4
Shuler, Heath, Washington	265	120	45.3	1658	6.26	10	3.8	t81	12	4.5	12	83	59.6
Stryzinski, Dan, Tampa Bay	1	1	100.0	21	21.00	0	0.0	21	0	0.0	0	0	118.8
Walsh, Steve, Chicago	343	208	60.6	2078	6.06	10	2.9	50	8	2.3	11	52	77.9
Weldon, Casey, Tampa Bay	9	7	77.8	63	7.00	0	0.0	27	0	0.0	0	0	95.8
Wilson, Wade, New Orleans	28	20	71.4	172	6.14	0	0.0	16	0	0.0	3	17	87.2
Young, Steve, San Francisco	461	324	70.3	3969	8.61	35	7.6	t69	10	2.2	31	163	112.8

t—touchdown.

RECEIVING

INDIVIDUAL

BESTS OF THE SEASON

Receptions, season
NFC: 122—Cris Carter, Minnesota.
AFC: 96—Ben Coates, New England.

Receptions, game
NFC: 16—Jerry Rice, San Francisco vs. L.A. Rams, Nov. 20 (165 yards) (3 TDs).
AFC: 15—Andre Reed, Buffalo vs. Green Bay, Nov. 20 (191 yards) (2 TDs).

Yards, season
NFC: 1499—Jerry Rice, San Francisco.
AFC: 1309—Tim Brown, L.A. Raiders.

Yards, game
AFC: 211—Irving Fryar, Miami vs. New England, Sept. 4 (5 receptions, 3 TDs)
NFC: 200—Torrance Small, New Orleans at Denver, Dec. 24 (6 receptions, 2 TDs).

Longest
AFC: 99—Tony Martin (from Stan Humphries), San Diego at Seattle, Sept. 18 (TD).
NFC: 93—Herschel Walker (from Randall Cunningham), Philadelphia at N.Y. Giants, Sept. 4.

Yards per reception, season
NFC: 24.9—Alvin Harper, Dallas.
AFC: 18.8—Darnay Scott, Cincinnati.

Touchdowns, season
NFC: 18—Sterling Sharpe, Green Bay.
AFC: 11—Carl Pickens, Cincinnati.

Team leaders, receptions

AFC:

Buffalo	90	Andre Reed
Cincinnati	71	Carl Pickens
Cleveland	48	Derrick Alexander
Denver	87	Shannon Sharpe
Houston	68	Haywood Jeffires
		Webster Slaughter
Indianapolis	52	Marshall Faulk
		Floyd Turner
Kansas City	67	Kimble Anders
L.A. Raiders	89	Tim Brown
Miami	73	Irving Fryar
New England	96	Ben Coates
N.Y. Jets	78	Rob Moore
Pittsburgh	51	John L. Williams
San Diego	58	Ronnie Harmon
		Mark Seay
Seattle	81	Brian Blades

NFC:

Arizona	77	Larry Centers
Atlanta	111	Terance Mathis
Chicago	68	Jeff Graham
Dallas	79	Michael Irvin
Detroit	72	Herman Moore
Green Bay	94	Sterling Sharpe
L.A. Rams	58	Johnny Bailey
Minnesota	122	Cris Carter
New Orleans	82	Quinn Early
N.Y. Giants	53	Mike Sherrard
Philadelphia	78	Fred Barnett
San Francisco	112	Jerry Rice
Tampa Bay	46	Lawrence Dawsey
Washington	74	Henry Ellard

NFL LEADERS

Player, Team	No.	Yds.	Avg.	Long	TD
Carter, Cris, Minnesota	122	1256	10.3	t65	7
Rice, Jerry, San Francisco	112	1499	13.4	t69	13
Mathis, Terance, Atlanta	111	1342	12.1	81	11
Coates, Ben, New England*	96	1174	12.2	t62	7
Sharpe, Sterling, Green Bay	94	1119	11.9	49	18
Reed, Andre, Buffalo*	90	1303	14.5	t83	8
Brown, Tim, L.A. Raiders*	89	1309	14.7	t77	9
Sharpe, Shannon, Denver*	87	1010	11.6	44	4
Reed, Jake, Minnesota	85	1175	13.8	59	4
Early, Quinn, New Orleans	82	894	10.9	33	4
Rison, Andre, Atlanta	81	1088	13.4	t69	8
Blades, Brian, Seattle*	81	1086	13.4	45	4
Irvin, Michael, Dallas	79	1241	15.7	t65	6
Barnett, Fred, Philadelphia	78	1127	14.4	54	5
Moore, Rob, N.Y. Jets*	78	1010	12.9	t41	6
Bennett, Edgar, Green Bay	78	546	7.0	40	4
Haynes, Michael, New Orleans	77	985	12.8	t78	5
Centers, Larry, Arizona	77	647	8.4	36	2
Milburn, Glyn, Denver*	77	549	7.1	33	3
Ellard, Henry, Washington	74	1397	18.9	t73	6
Timpson, Michael, New England*...	74	941	12.7	37	3
Fryar, Irving, Miami*	73	1270	17.4	t54	7
Moore, Herman, Detroit	72	1173	16.3	t51	11
Pickens, Carl, Cincinnati*	71	1127	15.9	t70	11
Graham, Jeffrey, Chicago	68	944	13.9	t76	4
Slaughter, Webster, Houston*	68	846	12.4	57	2
Jeffires, Haywood, Houston*	68	783	11.5	50	6
Sanders, Ricky, Atlanta	67	599	8.9	28	1
Anders, Kimble, Kansas City*	67	525	7.8	30	1
Watters, Ricky, San Francisco	66	719	10.9	t65	5

t—touchdown.
Leader based on most passes caught.

AFC

Player, Team	No.	Yds.	Avg.	Long	TD
Alexander, Derrick, Cleveland	48	828	17.3	t81	2
Allen, Marcus, Kansas City	42	349	8.3	38	0
Anders, Kimble, Kansas City	67	525	7.8	30	1
Anderson, Richie, N.Y. Jets	25	212	8.5	t27	1
Anderson, Stevie, N.Y. Jets	9	90	10.0	17	0
Arbuckle, Charles, Indianapolis	1	7	7.0	7	0
Avery, Steve, Pittsburgh	1	2	2.0	2	0
Bailey, Aaron, Indianapolis	2	30	15.0	23	0
Baker, Shannon, Indianapolis	2	15	7.5	10	0
Baldwin, Randy, Cleveland	3	15	5.0	15	0
Ball, Eric, Cincinnati	1	4	4.0	4	0
Barnes, Johnnie, San Diego	1	6	6.0	6	0
Bates, Michael, Seattle	5	112	22.4	t40	1
Baty, Greg, Miami	2	11	5.5	8	0
Baxter, Brad, N.Y. Jets	10	40	4.0	7	0
Baxter, Fred, N.Y. Jets	3	11	3.7	6	1
Beebe, Don, Buffalo	40	527	13.2	t72	4
Bender, Wes, L.A. Raiders	2	14	7.0	7	0
Bennett, Donnell, Kansas City	7	53	7.6	15	0
Bernstine, Rod, Denver	9	70	7.8	16	0
Bieniemy, Eric, San Diego	5	48	9.6	25	0
Birden, J.J., Kansas City	48	637	13.3	44	4
Blades, Brian, Seattle	81	1086	13.4	45	4
Brisby, Vincent, New England	58	904	15.6	43	5
Brooks, Bill, Buffalo	42	482	11.5	32	2
Broussard, Steve, Cincinnati	34	218	6.4	25	0
Brown, Gary, Houston	18	194	10.8	24	1
Brown, Reggie, Houston	4	34	8.5	11	0
Brown, Tim, L.A. Raiders	89	1309	14.7	t77	9
Burke, John, New England	9	86	9.6	17	0

Player, Team	No.	Yds.	Avg.	Long	TD
Butts, Marion, New England	9	54	6.0	15	0
Byars, Keith, Miami	49	418	8.5	34	5
Byner, Earnest, Cleveland	11	102	9.3	30	0
Campbell, Jeff, Denver	1	22	22.0	t22	1
Carrier, Mark, Cleveland	29	452	15.6	43	5
Carter, Pat, Houston	11	74	6.7	19	1
Cash, Keith, Kansas City	19	192	10.1	31	2
Cash, Kerry, Indianapolis	16	190	11.9	24	1
Clark, Derrick, Denver	9	47	5.2	10	0
Coates, Ben, New England	96	1174	12.2	t62	7
Coleman, Pat, Houston	20	298	14.9	81	1
Copeland, Russell, Buffalo	21	255	12.1	35	1
Cothran, Jeff, Cincinnati	4	24	6.0	8	1
Craver, Aaron, Miami	24	237	9.9	28	0
Crittenden, Ray, New England	28	379	13.5	32	3
Crumpler, Carlester, Seattle	2	19	9.5	12	0
Davis, Kenneth, Buffalo	18	82	4.6	12	0
Davis, Willie, Kansas City	51	822	16.1	t62	5
Dawkins, Sean, Indianapolis	51	742	14.5	49	5
Dawson, Lake, Kansas City	37	537	14.5	50	2
Dickerson, Ron, Kansas City	2	11	5.5	6	0
Edmunds, Ferrell, Seattle	7	43	6.1	8	0
Etheredge, Carlos, Indianapolis	1	6	6.0	6	0
Evans, Jerry, Denver	13	127	9.8	t20	2
Faulk, Marshall, Indianapolis	52	522	10.0	t85	1
Fenner, Derrick, Cincinnati	36	276	7.7	29	1
Foster, Barry, Pittsburgh	20	124	6.2	27	0
Fryar, Irving, Miami	73	1270	17.4	t54	7
Gardner, Carwell, Buffalo	11	89	8.1	21	0
Gary, Cleveland, Miami	2	19	9.5	11	0
Gash, Sam, New England	9	61	6.8	19	0
Givins, Ernest, Houston	36	521	14.5	t76	1
Glover, Andrew, L.A. Raiders	33	371	11.2	t27	2
Green, Eric, Pittsburgh	46	618	13.4	46	4
Green, Harold, Cincinnati	27	267	9.9	34	1
Green, Paul, Seattle	30	208	6.9	20	1
Greene, Tracy, Kansas City	6	69	11.5	20	1
Hannah, Travis, Houston	3	24	8.0	11	0
Harmon, Ronnie, San Diego	58	615	10.6	35	1
Harris, Ronnie, New England	1	11	11.0	11	0
Hartley, Frank, Cleveland	3	13	4.3	8	1
Hastings, Andre, Pittsburgh	20	281	14.1	46	2
Hawkins, Steve, New England	2	22	11.0	14	0
Hayes, Jonathan, Pittsburgh	5	50	10.0	17	1
Hill, Greg, Kansas City	16	92	5.8	21	0
Hoard, Leroy, Cleveland	45	445	9.9	t65	4
Hobbs, Daryl, L.A. Raiders	5	52	10.4	14	0
Hughes, Danan, Kansas City	7	80	11.4	22	0
Humphrey, Ronald, Indianapolis	3	19	6.3	12	0
Ingram, Mark, Miami	44	506	11.5	t64	6
Ismail, Raghib, L.A. Raiders	34	513	15.1	42	5
Jackson, Keith, Miami	59	673	11.4	35	7
Jackson, Mark, Indianapolis	8	97	12.1	22	1
Jackson, Michael, Cleveland	21	304	14.5	30	2
Jefferson, Shawn, San Diego	43	627	14.6	t52	3
Jeffires, Haywood, Houston	68	783	11.5	50	6
Jett, James, L.A. Raiders	15	253	16.9	54	0
Johnson, Anthony, N.Y. Jets	5	31	6.2	9	0
Johnson, Charles, Pittsburgh	38	577	15.2	t84	3
Johnson, Jimmy, Kansas City	2	7	3.5	5	0
Johnson, Johnny, N.Y. Jets	42	303	7.2	24	2
Johnson, Lonnie, Buffalo	3	42	14.0	21	0
Johnson, Tracy, Seattle	10	91	9.1	17	0
Jones, Calvin, L.A. Raiders	2	6	3.0	4	0
Jones, James, Cleveland	1	1	1.0	1	0
Jourdain, Yonel, Buffalo	10	56	5.6	18	0
Junkin, Trey, Seattle	1	1	1.0	t1	1
Keith, Craig, Pittsburgh	1	2	2.0	2	0
Kimbrough, Tony, Denver	2	20	10.0	12	0
Kinchen, Brian, Cleveland	24	232	9.7	38	1
Kirby, Terry, Miami	14	154	11.0	26	0
Klingler, David, Cincinnati	1	-6	-6.0	-6	0
Lewis, Rod, Houston	4	48	12.0	19	0
Marrow, Vince, Buffalo	5	44	8.8	14	0
Martin, Eric, Kansas City	21	307	14.6	61	1
Martin, Kelvin, Seattle	56	681	12.2	32	1
Martin, Tony, San Diego	50	885	17.7	t99	7
Maston, Le'Shai, Houston	2	12	6.0	10	0
May, Deems, San Diego	2	22	11.0	18	0
McCardell, Keenan, Cleveland	10	182	18.2	34	0
McDuffie, O.J., Miami	37	488	13.2	30	3
McGee, Tim, Cincinnati	13	175	13.5	25	1
McGee, Tony, Cincinnati	40	492	12.3	54	1
McKnight, James, Seattle	1	25	25.0	t25	1
McNair, Todd, Houston	8	78	9.8	21	0
Means, Natrone, San Diego	39	235	6.0	22	0
Metcalf, Eric, Cleveland	47	436	9.3	t57	3
Metzelaars, Pete, Buffalo	49	428	8.7	t35	5
Milburn, Glyn, Denver	77	549	7.1	33	3
Miller, Anthony, Denver	60	1107	18.5	76	5
Miller, Scott, Miami	6	94	15.7	27	1
Mills, Ernie, Pittsburgh	19	384	20.2	43	1
Mills, John Henry, Houston	1	4	4.0	4	0
Mitchell, Johnny, N.Y. Jets	58	749	12.9	55	4
Mitchell, Shannon, San Diego	11	105	9.5	36	0
Monk, Art, N.Y. Jets	46	581	12.6	69	3
Montgomery, Tyrone, L.A. Raiders	8	126	15.8	t65	1
Moore, Rob, N.Y. Jets	78	1010	12.9	t41	6
Morris, Bam, Pittsburgh	22	204	9.3	49	0
Murrell, Adrian, N.Y. Jets	7	76	10.9	20	0
Parker, Orlando, N.Y. Jets	1	7	7.0	7	0
Parmalee, Bernie, Miami	34	249	7.3	22	1
Penn, Chris, Kansas City	3	24	8.0	13	0
Pickens, Carl, Cincinnati	71	1127	15.9	t70	11
Potts, Roosevelt, Indianapolis	26	251	9.7	30	1
Pritchard, Mike, Denver	19	271	14.3	t50	1
Pupunu, Alfred, San Diego	21	214	10.2	25	2
Query, Jeff, Cincinnati	5	44	8.8	14	0
Rathman, Tom, L.A. Raiders	26	194	7.5	18	0
Reed, Andre, Buffalo	90	1303	14.5	t83	8
Reeves, Walter, Cleveland	6	61	10.2	22	1
Rivers, Reggie, Denver	20	136	6.8	25	0
Russell, Derek, Denver	25	342	13.7	43	1
Russell, Leonard, Denver	38	227	6.0	19	0
Sadowski, Troy, Cincinnati	11	54	4.9	11	0
Saxon, James, Miami	27	151	5.6	25	0
Scott, Darnay, Cincinnati	46	866	18.8	76	5
Seay, Mark, San Diego	58	645	11.1	t49	6
Sharpe, Shannon, Denver	87	1010	11.6	44	4
Slaughter, Webster, Houston	68	846	12.4	57	2
Smith, Kevin, L.A. Raiders	1	8	8.0	8	0
Smith, Rico, Cleveland	2	61	30.5	50	0
Smith, Steve, Seattle	11	142	12.9	25	1
Spikes, Irving, Miami	4	16	4.0	9	0
Stone, Dwight, Pittsburgh	7	81	11.6	25	0
Strong, Mack, Seattle	3	3	1.0	5	0
Thigpen, Yancey, Pittsburgh	36	546	15.2	t60	4
Thomas, Damon, Buffalo	2	31	15.5	17	0
Thomas, Robb, Seattle	4	70	17.5	35	0
Thomas, Thurman, Buffalo	50	349	7.0	28	2
Thompson, Leroy, New England	65	465	7.2	t27	5
Thornton, James, N.Y. Jets	20	171	8.6	25	0
Tillman, Cedric, Denver	28	455	16.3	63	1
Timpson, Michael, New England	74	941	12.7	37	3
Turner, Floyd, Indianapolis	52	593	11.4	28	6
Turner, Kevin, New England	52	471	9.1	32	2
Turner, Nate, Buffalo	1	26	26.0	t26	1
Valerio, Joe, Kansas City	2	5	2.5	t4	2
Vardell, Tommy, Cleveland	16	137	8.6	19	1
Vaughn, Jon, Seattle	1	5	5.0	t5	1
Walker, Derrick, Kansas City	36	382	10.6	t57	2
Warren, Chris, Seattle	41	323	7.9	51	2
Warren, Lamont, Indianapolis	3	47	15.7	29	0
Wellman, Gary, Houston	10	112	11.2	25	0
White, Lorenzo, Houston	21	188	9.0	41	1
Williams, Harvey, L.A. Raiders	47	391	8.3	t27	3
Williams, Jamie, L.A. Raiders	3	25	8.3	16	0
Williams, John L., Pittsburgh	51	378	7.4	23	2
Williams, Mike, Miami	15	221	14.7	29	0
Williams, Ronnie, Miami	2	26	13.0	17	0
Wright, Alexander, L.A. Raiders	16	294	18.4	t76	2
Yarborough, Ryan, N.Y. Jets	6	42	7.0	12	1

Player, Team	No.	Yds.	Avg.	Long	TD
Young, Duane, San Diego	17	217	12.8	31	1

t—touchdown.

NFC

Player, Team	No.	Yds.	Avg.	Long	TD
Agee, Tommie, Dallas	1	2	2.0	2	0
Alexander, David, Philadelphia	2	1	0.5	1	0
Allen, Terry, Minnesota	17	148	8.7	31	0
Anderson, Willie, L.A. Rams	46	945	20.5	t72	5
Armstrong, Tyji, Tampa Bay	22	265	12.0	29	1
Bailey, Johnny, L.A. Rams	58	516	8.9	28	0
Bailey, Victor, Philadelphia	20	311	15.6	61	1
Barnett, Fred, Philadelphia	78	1127	14.4	54	5
Bates, Mario, New Orleans	8	62	7.8	14	0
Bavaro, Mark, Philadelphia	17	215	12.6	t27	3
Bennett, Edgar, Green Bay	78	546	7.0	40	4
Bettis, Jerome, L.A. Rams	31	293	9.5	34	1
Brantley, Chris, L.A. Rams	4	29	7.3	10	0
Brooks, Reggie, Washington	13	68	5.2	16	0
Brooks, Robert, Green Bay	58	648	11.2	35	4
Brown, Derek, New Orleans	44	428	9.7	37	1
Bruce, Isaac, L.A. Rams	21	272	13.0	t34	3
Buchanan, Richard, L.A. Rams	5	60	12.0	18	0
Calloway, Chris, N.Y. Giants	43	666	15.5	t51	2
Carolan, Brett, San Francisco	2	10	5.0	6	0
Carter, Anthony, Detroit	8	97	12.1	18	3
Carter, Antonio, Chicago	1	24	24.0	24	0
Carter, Cris, Minnesota	122	1256	10.3	t65	7
Carter, Dexter, San Francisco	7	99	14.1	44	0
Carter, Marty, Tampa Bay	1	21	21.0	21	0
Centers, Larry, Arizona	77	647	8.4	36	2
Chmura, Mark, Green Bay	14	165	11.8	27	0
Christian, Bob, Chicago	2	30	15.0	21	0
Clark, Gary, Arizona	50	771	15.4	45	1
Cobb, Reggie, Green Bay	35	299	8.5	t37	1
Coleman, Lincoln, Dallas	8	46	5.8	14	0
Conover, Scott, Detroit	1	1	1.0	t1	1
Conway, Curtis, Chicago	39	546	14.0	t85	2
Cook, Marv, Chicago	21	212	10.1	34	1
Cooper, Adrian, Minnesota	32	363	11.3	34	0
Copeland, Horace, Tampa Bay	17	308	18.1	65	0
Cross, Howard, N.Y. Giants	31	364	11.7	40	4
Dawsey, Lawrence, Tampa Bay	46	673	14.6	46	1
Downs, Gary, N.Y. Giants	2	15	7.5	10	0
Drayton, Troy, L.A. Rams	32	276	8.6	t22	6
Early, Quinn, New Orleans	82	894	10.9	34	4
Ellard, Henry, Washington	74	1397	18.9	t73	6
Emanuel, Bert, Atlanta	46	649	14.1	t85	4
Ervins, Ricky, Washington	51	293	5.7	21	1
Evans, Chuck, Minnesota	1	2	2.0	2	0
Fann, Chad, Arizona	12	96	8.0	16	0
Floyd, William, San Francisco	19	145	7.6	15	0
Galbraith, Scott, Dallas	4	31	7.8	15	0
Garner, Charlie, Philadelphia	8	74	9.3	28	0
Gedney, Chris, Chicago	13	157	12.1	t37	3
Graham, Jeff, Chicago	68	944	13.9	t76	4
Graham, Scottie, Minnesota	1	1	1.0	1	0
Green, Robert, Chicago	24	199	8.3	t39	2
Green, Willie, Tampa Bay	9	150	16.7	28	0
Griffith, Howard, L.A. Rams	16	113	7.1	13	1
Hall, Ron, Detroit	10	106	10.6	18	0
Hallock, Ty, Detroit	7	75	10.7	21	0
Hampton, Rodney, N.Y. Giants	14	103	7.4	17	0
Harper, Alvin, Dallas	33	821	24.9	90	8
Harris, Jackie, Tampa Bay	26	337	13.0	t48	3
Harris, Leonard, Atlanta	9	113	12.6	26	0
Harris, Raymont, Chicago	39	236	6.1	18	0
Harris, Rudy, Tampa Bay	2	11	5.5	8	0
Hawkins, Courtney, Tampa Bay	37	438	11.8	32	5
Haynes, Michael, New Orleans	77	985	12.8	t78	5
Hearst, Garrison, Arizona	6	49	8.2	29	0
Hebron, Vaughn, Philadelphia	18	137	7.6	29	0
Hester, Jessie, L.A. Rams	45	644	14.3	41	3
Heyward, Craig, Atlanta	32	335	10.5	34	1
Hill, Randal, Arizona	38	544	14.3	51	0
Hoge, Merril, Chicago	13	79	6.1	11	0
Holman, Rodney, Detroit	17	163	9.6	18	0
Horton, Ethan, Washington	15	157	10.5	20	3
Howard, Desmond, Washington	40	727	18.2	t81	5
Irvin, Michael, Dallas	79	1241	15.7	t65	6
Ismail, Qadry, Minnesota	45	696	15.5	t65	5
Jenkins, James, Washington	8	32	4.0	9	4
Jennings, Keith, Chicago	11	75	6.8	t23	3
Johnson, LeShon, Green Bay	13	168	12.9	33	0
Johnson, Maurice, Philadelphia	21	204	9.7	22	2
Johnson, Reggie, Green Bay	7	79	11.3	24	0
Johnston, Daryl, Dallas	44	325	7.4	24	2
Jones, Brent, San Francisco	49	670	13.7	t69	9
Jordan, Andrew, Minnesota	35	336	9.6	25	0
Jordan, Steve, Minnesota	3	23	7.7	10	0
Joseph, James, Philadelphia	43	344	8.0	t35	2
Kennard, Derek, Dallas	1	-3	-3.0	-3	0
Kinchen, Todd, L.A. Rams	23	352	15.3	43	3
Kozlowski, Brian, N.Y. Giants	1	5	5.0	5	0
Lang, David, L.A. Rams	8	60	7.5	12	0
Lee, Amp, Minnesota	45	368	8.2	35	2
Lester, Tim, L.A. Rams	1	1	1.0	1	0
Levens, Dorsey, Green Bay	1	9	9.0	9	0
Levy, Chuck, Arizona	4	35	8.8	15	0
Lewis, Nate, Chicago	2	13	6.5	8	1
Lewis, Ron, Green Bay	7	108	15.4	38	0
Lewis, Thomas, N.Y. Giants	4	46	11.5	23	0
Logan, Marc, San Francisco	16	97	6.1	15	1
Loville, Derek, San Francisco	2	26	13.0	19	0
Lynch, Eric, Detroit	2	18	9.0	12	0
Lyons, Mitch, Atlanta	7	54	7.7	10	0
Marshall, Arthur, N.Y. Giants	16	219	13.7	34	0
Mathis, Terance, Atlanta	111	1342	12.1	81	11
Matthews, Aubrey, Detroit	29	359	12.4	33	3
McAfee, Fred, Arizona	1	4	4.0	4	0
McCaffrey, Ed, San Francisco	11	131	11.9	32	2
McDowell, Anthony, Tampa Bay	29	193	6.7	19	1
McMurtry, Greg, Chicago	8	112	14.0	30	1
Meggett, Dave, N.Y. Giants	32	293	9.2	34	0
Mickens, Terry, Green Bay	4	31	7.8	11	0
Mims, David, Atlanta	3	14	4.7	6	0
Mitchell, Brian, Washington	26	236	9.1	t46	0
Mitchell, Derrell, New Orleans	1	13	13.0	13	0
Moore, Dave, Tampa Bay	4	57	14.3	18	0
Moore, Derrick, Detroit	1	10	10.0	10	0
Moore, Herman, Detroit	72	1173	16.3	t51	11
Moore, Ronald, Arizona	8	52	6.5	18	1
Morgan, Anthony, Green Bay	28	397	14.2	t47	4
Morton, Johnnie, Detroit	3	39	13.0	t18	1
Muster, Brad, New Orleans	10	88	8.8	21	0
Neal, Lorenzo, New Orleans	2	9	4.5	5	0
Ned, Derrick, New Orleans	13	86	6.6	19	0
Novacek, Jay, Dallas	47	475	10.1	27	2
Novoselsky, Brent, Minnesota	2	7	3.5	4	0
Palmer, David, Minnesota	6	90	15.0	39	0
Pegram, Erric, Atlanta	16	99	6.2	28	0
Perriman, Brett, Detroit	56	761	13.6	39	4
Pierce, Aaron, N.Y. Giants	20	214	10.7	29	4
Popson, Ted, San Francisco	13	141	10.8	24	0
Primus, Greg, Chicago	3	25	8.3	12	0
Proehl, Ricky, Arizona	51	651	12.8	63	5
Rasheed, Kenyon, N.Y. Giants	10	97	9.7	22	0
Reed, Jake, Minnesota	85	1175	13.8	59	4
Reeves, Bryan, Arizona	14	202	14.4	33	1
Rhett, Errict, Tampa Bay	22	119	5.4	12	0
Rice, Jerry, San Francisco	112	1499	13.4	t69	13
Rison, Andre, Atlanta	81	1088	13.4	t69	8
Robinson, Patrick, Arizona	1	5	5.0	5	0
Ross, Jermaine, L.A. Rams	1	36	36.0	t36	1
Royster, Mazio, Tampa Bay	7	36	5.1	12	0
Samuels, Terry, Arizona	8	57	7.1	17	0
Sanders, Barry, Detroit	44	283	6.4	22	1
Sanders, Ricky, Atlanta	67	599	8.9	28	1
Sharpe, Sterling, Green Bay	94	1119	11.9	49	18

— 243 —

Player, Team	No.	Yds.	Avg.	Long	TD
Shepherd, Leslie, Washington	1	8	8.0	8	0
Sherrard, Mike, N.Y. Giants	53	825	15.6	55	6
Singleton, Nate, San Francisco	21	294	14.0	t43	2
Small, Torrance, New Orleans	49	719	14.7	t75	5
Smith, Cedric, Washington	15	118	7.9	28	1
Smith, Emmitt, Dallas	50	341	6.8	68	1
Smith, Irv, New Orleans	41	330	8.0	19	3
Smith, Robert, Minnesota	15	105	7.0	15	0
Spencer, Darryl, Atlanta	2	51	25.5	40	0
Sydner, Jeff, Philadelphia	1	10	10.0	10	0
Taylor, John, San Francisco	41	531	13.0	35	5
Thomas, Blair, N.E.-Dal.*	4	16	4.0	9	0
Thomas, Lamar, Tampa Bay	7	94	13.4	27	0
Tillman, Lewis, Chicago	27	222	8.2	39	0
Truitt, Olanda, Washington	2	89	44.5	t77	1
Waddle, Tom, Chicago	25	244	9.8	22	1
Walker, Herschel, Philadelphia	50	500	10.0	93	2
Walls, Wesley, New Orleans	38	406	10.7	31	4
Ware, Derek, Arizona	17	171	10.1	33	1
Watters, Ricky, San Francisco	66	719	10.9	t65	5

Player, Team	No.	Yds.	Avg.	Long	TD
West, Ed, Green Bay	31	377	12.2	26	2
Wetnight, Ryan, Chicago	11	104	9.5	19	1
Williams, Calvin, Philadelphia	58	813	14.0	53	3
Williams, Kevin, Dallas	13	181	13.9	29	0
Williams, Willie, New Orleans	1	7	7.0	7	0
Wilner, Jeff, Green Bay	5	31	6.2	9	0
Wilson, Charles, Tampa Bay	31	652	21.0	t71	6
Winans, Tydus, Washington	19	344	18.1	51	2
Workman, Vince, Tampa Bay	11	82	7.5	23	0
Worley, Tim, Chicago	1	8	8.0	8	0
Wycheck, Frank, Washington	7	55	7.9	20	1

*Includes both AFC and NFC statistics.
t—touchdown.

PLAYERS WITH TWO CLUBS

Player, Team	No.	Yds.	Avg.	Long	TD
Thomas, Blair, New England	2	15	7.5	9	0
Thomas, Blair, Dallas	2	1	0.5	5	0

SCORING

AFC

Team	Total TD	TD Rush	TD Pass	TD Misc.	XP	2Pt.	XPA	FG	FGA	Safeties	Total Pts.
Miami	45	13	31	1	35	6	45	24	31	0	389
San Diego	40	13	20	7	33	3	40	34	38	0	381
New England	39	12	25	2	36	0	38	27	35	0	351
Denver	37	19	18	0	29	3	37	30	37	0	347
Cleveland	37	12	20	5	32	4	37	26	28	0	340
Buffalo	38	14	23	1	38	0	38	24	28	1	340
Kansas City	34	12	20	2	30	3	34	25	30	2	319
Pittsburgh	35	15	17	3	32	1	35	24	29	0	316
Indianapolis	37	15	15	7	37	0	37	16	24	0	307
L.A. Raiders	34	7	22	5	31	1	34	22	28	0	303
Seattle	32	16	13	3	25	4	32	20	24	1	287
Cincinnati	27	5	21	1	24	2	27	28	33	1	276
N.Y. Jets	29	8	18	3	26	2	29	20	23	0	264
Houston	25	10	13	2	18	4	25	16	20	1	226
AFC Total	489	171	276	42	426	33	488	336	408	6	4446
AFC Average	34.9	12.2	19.7	3.0	30.4	2.4	34.9	24.0	29.1	0.4	317.6

NFC

Team	Total TD	TD Rush	TD Pass	TD Misc.	XP	2Pt.	XPA	FG	FGA	Safeties	Total Pts.
San Francisco	66	23	37	6	60	2	66	15	20	0	505
Dallas	50	26	19	5	48	0	50	22	29	0	414
Green Bay	47	11	33	3	41	1	47	19	26	0	382
Detroit	43	12	24	7	39	2	43	18	27	1	357
Minnesota	36	11	18	7	30	4	35	34	39	0	356
New Orleans	38	11	22	5	32	2	38	28	39	0	348
Washington	37	5	25	7	30	3	37	20	28	1	320
Atlanta	36	8	25	3	32	3	36	21	25	0	317
Philadelphia	35	14	18	3	33	0	35	21	25	1	308
L.A. Rams	33	6	23	4	28	2	33	18	23	1	286
N.Y. Giants	30	12	16	2	27	1	30	22	28	2	279
Chicago	30	10	19	1	24	2	30	21	29	0	271
Tampa Bay	26	8	17	1	20	3	26	23	35	0	251
Arizona	24	12	11	1	21	1	24	22	30	1	235
NFC Total	531	169	307	55	465	26	530	304	403	7	4629
NFC Average	37.9	12.1	21.9	3.9	33.2	1.9	37.9	21.7	28.8	0.5	330.6
NFL Total	1020	340	583	97	891	59	1018	640	811	13	9075
NFL Average	36.4	12.1	20.8	3.5	31.8	2.1	36.4	22.9	29.0	0.5	324.1

INDIVIDUAL

BESTS OF THE SEASON

Points, season
AFC: 135—John Carney, San Diego.
NFC: 132—Fuad Reveiz, Minnesota.

Touchdowns, season
NFC: 22—Emmitt Smith, Dallas.
AFC: 12—Marshall Faulk, Indianapolis; Natrone Means, San Diego.

Extra points, season
NFC: 60—Doug Brien, San Francisco.
AFC: 38—Steve Christie, Buffalo.

Field goals, season
AFC: 34—John Carney, San Diego.
NFC: 34—Fuad Reveiz, Minnesota.

Field-goal attempts, season
NFC: 39—Morten Andersen, New Orleans; Fuad Reveiz, Minnesota.
AFC: 38—John Carney, San Diego.

Longest field goal
AFC: 54—Jason Elam, Denver at San Diego, Oct. 23; Doug Pelfrey, Cincinnati vs. Philadelphia, Dec. 24.
NFC: 54—Chip Lohmiller, Washington vs. Philadelphia, Oct. 3.

Most points, game
AFC: 24—Mark Ingram, Miami at N.Y. Jets, Nov. 27 (4 TDs).
NFC: 24—Sterling Sharpe, Green Bay at Dallas, Nov. 24 (4 TDs).

Team leaders, points
AFC:
Buffalo 110   Steve Christie
Cincinnati 108   Doug Pelfrey

Cleveland	110	Matt Stover
Denver	119	Jason Elam
Houston	66	Al Del Greco
Indianapolis	85	Dean Biasucci
Kansas City	105	Lin Elliott
L.A. Raiders	97	Jeff Jaeger
Miami	107	Pete Stoyanovich
New England	117	Matt Bahr
N.Y. Jets	86	Nick Lowery
Pittsburgh	104	Gary Anderson
San Diego	135	John Carney
Seattle	85	John Kasay

NFC:

Arizona	77	Greg Davis
Atlanta	95	Norm Johnson
Chicago	87	Kevin Butler
Dallas	132	Emmitt Smith
Detroit	93	Jason Hanson
Green Bay	108	Sterling Sharpe
L.A. Rams	82	Tony Zendejas
Minnesota	132	Fuad Reveiz
New Orleans	116	Morten Andersen
N.Y. Giants	55	David Treadwell
Philadelphia	96	Eddie Murray
San Francisco	105	Doug Brien
Tampa Bay	89	Michael Husted
Washington	90	Chip Lohmiller

NFL LEADERS

KICKERS

Player, Team	XP Made	XP Att	FG Made	FG Att	Tot. Pts.
Carney, John, San Diego*	33	33	34	38	135
Reveiz, Fuad, Minnesota	30	30	34	39	132
Elam, Jason, Denver*	29	29	30	37	119
Bahr, Matt, New England*	36	36	27	34	117
Andersen, Morten, New Orleans	32	32	24	39	116
Boniol, Chris, Dallas	48	48	22	29	114
Stover, Matt, Cleveland*	32	32	26	28	110
Christie, Steve, Buffalo*	38	38	24	28	110
Pelfrey, Doug, Cincinnati*	24	25	28	33	108
Stoyanovich, Pete, Miami*	35	35	24	31	107
Elliott, Lin, Kansas City*	30	30	25	30	105
Brien, Doug, San Francisco	60	62	15	20	105
Anderson, Gary, Pittsburgh*	32	32	24	29	104
Jacke, Chris, Green Bay	41	43	19	26	98
Jaeger, Jeff, L.A. Raiders*	31	31	22	28	97
Murray, Eddie, Philadelphia	33	33	21	25	96
Johnson, Norm, Atlanta	32	32	21	25	95
Hanson, Jason, Detroit	39	40	18	27	93
Lohmiller, Chip, Washington	30	32	20	28	90
Husted, Michael, Tampa Bay	20	20	23	35	89

*AFC.

NON-KICKERS

Player, Team	Tot. TD	Rush TD	Pass TD	Misc. TD	2Pt.	Tot. Pts.
Smith, Emmitt, Dallas	22	21	1	0	0	132
Sharpe, Sterling, Green Bay	18	0	18	0	0	108
Rice, Jerry, S.F.	15	2	13	0	1	92
Means, Natrone, S.D.*	12	12	0	0	0	72
Faulk, Marshall, Ind.*	12	11	1	0	0	72
Mathis, Terance, Atlanta	11	0	11	0	2	70
Warren, Chris, Seattle*	11	9	2	0	1	68
Moore, Herman, Detroit	11	0	11	0	0	66
Pickens, Carl, Cincinnati*	11	0	11	0	0	66
Watters, Ricky, S.F.	11	6	5	0	0	66
Jones, Brent, S.F.	9	0	9	0	1	56
Bennett, Edgar, Green Bay	9	5	4	0	0	54
Brown, Tim, Raiders*	9	0	9	0	0	54
Hoard, Leroy, Cleveland*	9	5	4	0	0	54
Russell, Leonard, Denver*	9	9	0	0	0	54

Player, Team	Tot. TD	Rush TD	Pass TD	Misc. TD	2Pt.	Tot. Pts.
Thomas, Thurman, Buffalo*	9	7	2	0	0	54
Allen, Terry, Minnesota	8	8	0	0	1	50
Rison, Andre, Atlanta	8	0	8	0	1	50
Butts, Marion, N.E.*	8	8	0	0	0	48
Harper, Alvin, Dallas	8	0	8	0	0	48
Heyward, Craig, Atlanta	8	7	1	0	0	48
Reed, Andre, Buffalo*	8	0	8	0	0	48
Sanders, Barry, Detroit	8	7	1	0	0	48
Walker, Herschel, Phi.	8	5	2	1	0	48
Carter, Cris, Minnesota	7	0	7	0	2	46
Fryar, Irving, Miami*	7	0	7	0	2	46

*AFC.

AFC

KICKERS

Player, Team	XP Made	XP Att	FG Made	FG Att	Tot. Pts.
Anderson, Gary, Pittsburgh	32	32	24	29	104
Bahr, Matt, New England	36	36	27	34	117
Biasucci, Dean, Indianapolis	37	37	16	24	85
Carney, John, San Diego	33	33	34	38	135
Christie, Steve, Buffalo	38	38	24	28	110
Del Greco, Al, Houston	18	18	16	20	66
Elam, Jason, Denver	29	29	30	37	119
Elliott, Lin, Kansas City	30	30	25	30	105
Jaeger, Jeff, L.A. Raiders	31	31	22	28	97
Kasay, John, Seattle	25	26	20	24	85
Lowery, Nick, N.Y. Jets	26	27	20	23	86
O'Neill, Pat, New England	0	0	0	1	0
Pelfrey, Doug, Cincinnati	24	25	28	33	108
Stover, Matt, Cleveland	32	32	26	28	110
Stoyanovich, Pete, Miami	35	35	24	31	107

NON-KICKERS

Player, Team	Tot. TD	Rush TD	Pass TD	Misc. TD	2Pt.	Tot. Pts.
Alexander, Derrick, Cle.	2	0	2	0	1	14
Allen, Marcus, Kansas City	7	7	0	0	1	44
Anders, Kimble, K.C.	3	2	1	0	0	18
Anderson, Richie, N.Y. Jets	2	1	1	0	0	12
Baldwin, Randy, Cleveland	1	0	0	1	0	6
Bates, Michael, Seattle	1	0	1	0	0	6
Baty, Greg, Miami	1	0	1	0	0	6
Baxter, Brad, N.Y. Jets	4	4	0	0	0	24
Baxter, Fred, N.Y. Jets	1	0	1	0	0	6
Beebe, Don, Buffalo	4	0	4	0	0	24
Bennett, Donnell, K.C.	2	2	0	0	0	12
Bennett, Tony, Ind.	1	0	0	1	0	6
Birden, J.J., Kansas City	4	0	4	0	1	26
Blades, Brian, Seattle	4	0	4	0	1	26
Blake, Jeff, Cincinnati	1	1	0	0	0	8
Brewer, Dewell, Ind.	1	0	0	1	0	6
Brisby, Vincent, N.E.	5	0	5	0	0	30
Brooks, Bill, Buffalo	2	0	2	0	0	12
Broussard, Steve, Cin.	2	2	0	0	1	14
Brown, Gary, Houston	5	4	1	0	0	30
Brown, Reggie, Houston	0	0	0	0	1	2
Brown, Tim, Raiders	9	0	9	0	0	54
Buchanan, Ray, Ind.	3	0	0	3	0	18
Butts, Marion, New England	8	8	0	0	0	48
Byars, Keith, Miami	7	2	5	0	0	42
Byner, Earnest, Cleveland	2	2	0	0	0	12
Campbell, Jeff, Denver	1	0	1	0	0	6
Carrier, Mark, Cleveland	6	1	5	0	0	36
Carter, Pat, Houston	1	0	1	0	0	6
Cash, Keith, Kansas City	2	0	2	0	0	12
Cash, Kerry, Ind.	1	0	1	0	0	6
Clark, Derrick, Denver	3	3	0	0	0	18
Coates, Ben, New England	7	0	7	0	0	42
Coleman, Andre, San Diego	2	0	0	2	0	12
Coleman, Pat, Houston	1	0	1	0	0	6

Player, Team	Tot. TD	Rush TD	Pass TD	Misc. TD	2Pt.	Tot. Pts.
Collins, Mark, Kansas City..	1	0	0	1	0	6
Copeland, Russell, Buffalo..	1	0	1	0	0	6
Coryatt, Quentin, Ind.	1	0	0	1	0	6
Cothran, Jeff, Cincinnati.....	1	0	1	0	0	6
Craver, Aaron, Miami	0	0	0	0	1	2
Crittenden, Ray, N.E.	3	0	3	0	0	18
Davis, Kenneth, Buffalo	2	2	0	0	0	12
Davis, Willie, Kansas City ...	5	0	5	0	1	32
Dawkins, Sean, Ind.............	5	0	5	0	0	30
Dawson, Lake, Kansas City .	2	0	2	0	0	12
Dishman, Cris, Houston	1	0	0	1	0	6
Elway, John, Denver	4	4	0	0	0	24
Evans, Jerry, Denver..........	2	0	2	0	0	12
Faulk, Marshall, Ind.	12	11	1	0	0	72
Fenner, Derrick, Cincinnati..	2	1	1	0	0	12
Foster, Barry, Pittsburgh.....	5	5	0	0	0	30
Fryar, Irving, Miami	7	0	7	0	2	46
Gardner, Carwell, Buffalo....	4	4	0	0	0	24
Givins, Ernest, Houston	2	0	1	1	0	12
Glover, Andrew, Raiders	2	0	2	0	0	12
Gordon, Darrien, San Diego .	2	0	0	2	0	12
Green, Eric, Pittsburgh.......	4	0	4	0	0	24
Green, Harold, Cincinnati.....	2	1	1	0	0	12
Green, Paul, Seattle	1	0	1	0	0	6
Greene, Tracy, Kansas City .	1	0	1	0	0	6
Harmon, Ronnie, San Diego .	2	1	1	0	3	18
Hartley, Frank, Cleveland ...	1	0	1	0	0	6
Hastings, Andre, Pittsburgh	2	0	2	0	0	12
Hayes, Jonathan, Pit.	1	0	1	0	0	6
Hill, Greg, Kansas City	1	1	0	0	0	6
Hill, Travis, Cleveland	1	0	0	1	0	6
Hoard, Leroy, Cleveland......	9	5	4	0	0	54
Hostetler, Jeff, Raiders.......	2	2	0	0	0	12
Humphrey, Ronald, Ind.........	1	0	0	1	0	6
Ingram, Mark, Miami	6	0	6	0	0	36
Ismail, Raghib, Raiders	5	0	5	0	0	30
Jackson, Keith, Miami.........	7	0	7	0	1	44
Jackson, Mark, Ind.	1	0	1	0	0	6
Jackson, Michael, Cle.	2	0	2	0	0	12
Jefferson, Shawn, S.D.........	3	0	3	0	0	18
Jeffires, Haywood, Houston .	6	0	6	0	3	42
Johnson, Charles, Pit.	3	0	3	0	0	18
Johnson, Johnny, N.Y. Jets .	5	3	2	0	0	30
Johnson, Tracy, Seattle.......	2	2	0	0	0	12
Junkin, Trey, Seattle	1	0	1	0	0	6
Kelly, Jim, Buffalo	1	1	0	0	0	6
Kinchen, Brian, Cleveland....	1	0	1	0	0	6
Kirby, Terry, Miami	2	2	0	0	1	14
Lathon, Lamar, Houston	0	0	0	0	0	*2
Lewis, Mo, N.Y. Jets	2	0	0	2	0	12
Lodish, Mike, Buffalo..........	1	0	0	1	0	6
Majkowski, Don, Ind............	3	3	0	0	0	18
Marino, Dan, Miami	1	1	0	0	0	6
Martin, Eric, Kansas City	1	0	1	0	0	6
Martin, Kelvin, Seattle.........	1	0	1	0	0	6
Martin, Tony, San Diego	7	0	7	0	0	42
McAfee, Fred, Ari.-Pit.*	2	2	0	0	0	12
McCallum, Napoleon, Raiders	1	1	0	0	0	6
McDaniel, Terry, Raiders	3	0	0	3	0	18
McDuffie, O.J., Miami	3	0	3	0	0	18
McGee, Tim, Cincinnati	1	0	1	0	0	6
McGee, Tony, Cincinnati......	1	0	1	0	0	6
McKnight, James, Seattle	1	0	1	0	0	6
Means, Natrone, San Diego..	12	12	0	0	0	72
Metcalf, Eric, Cleveland	7	2	3	2	0	42
Metzelaars, Pete, Buffalo....	5	0	5	0	0	30
Milburn, Glyn, Denver	4	1	3	0	0	24
Miller, Anthony, Denver	5	0	5	0	1	32
Miller, Scott, Miami	1	0	1	0	0	6
Mills, Ernie, Pittsburgh	1	0	1	0	0	6
Mitchell, Johnny, N.Y. Jets ..	4	0	4	0	0	24
Monk, Art, N.Y. Jets	3	0	3	0	0	18
Montgomery, Tyrone, Raiders	1	0	1	0	0	6
Moore, Rob, N.Y. Jets	6	0	6	0	2	40
Morris, Bam, Pittsburgh......	7	7	0	0	0	42

Player, Team	Tot. TD	Rush TD	Pass TD	Misc. TD	2Pt.	Tot. Pts.
O'Donnell, Neil, Pittsburgh..	1	1	0	0	0	6
Parmalee, Bernie, Miami	7	6	1	0	1	44
Pickens, Carl, Cincinnati.....	11	0	11	0	0	66
Potts, Roosevelt, Ind.	2	1	1	0	0	12
Pritchard, Mike, Denver	1	0	1	0	0	6
Pupunu, Alfred, San Diego ..	2	0	2	0	0	12
Reed, Andre, Buffalo	8	0	8	0	0	48
Reeves, Walter, Cleveland ..	1	0	1	0	0	6
Reynolds, Ricky, N.E.	2	0	0	2	0	12
Richard, Stanley, San Diego	2	0	0	2	0	12
Richardson, Bucky, Hou.	1	1	0	0	0	6
Rivers, Reggie, Denver	2	2	0	0	0	12
Russell, Derek, Denver	1	0	1	0	0	6
Russell, Leonard, Denver	9	9	0	0	0	54
Sawyer, Corey, Cincinnati ..	1	0	0	1	0	6
Scott, Darnay, Cincinnati	5	0	5	0	0	30
Seay, Mark, San Diego	6	0	6	0	0	36
Sharpe, Shannon, Denver ...	4	0	4	0	2	28
Slaughter, Webster, Hou.....	2	0	2	0	0	12
Smith, Anthony, Raiders	1	0	0	1	0	6
Smith, Steve, Seattle	3	2	1	0	0	18
Spikes, Irving, Miami...........	2	2	0	0	0	12
Stone, Dwight, Pittsburgh....	0	0	0	0	1	2
Strong, Mack, Seattle..........	2	2	0	0	0	12
Testaverde, Vinny, Cle.	2	2	0	0	0	12
Thigpen, Yancey, Pit.	4	0	4	0	0	24
Thomas, Derrick, K.C.	0	0	0	0	0	*2
Thomas, Thurman, Buffalo..	9	7	2	0	0	54
Thompson, Leroy, N.E.........	7	2	5	0	0	42
Tillman, Cedric, Denver.......	1	0	1	0	0	6
Timpson, Michael, N.E.	3	0	3	0	0	18
Tolliver, Billy Joe, Hou.	2	2	0	0	0	12
Tupa, Tom, Cleveland	0	0	0	0	3	6
Turner, Eric, Cleveland	1	0	0	1	0	6
Turner, Floyd, Ind...............	6	0	6	0	0	36
Turner, Kevin, N.E.	3	1	2	0	0	18
Turner, Marcus, N.Y. Jets...	1	0	0	1	0	6
Turner, Nate, Buffalo	1	0	1	0	0	6
Tuten, Rick, Seattle	0	0	0	0	1	2
Valerio, Joe, Kansas City	2	0	2	0	0	12
Vanhorse, Sean, San Diego..	1	0	0	1	0	6
Vardell, Tommy, Cleveland..	1	0	1	0	0	6
Vaughn, Jon, Sea.-K.C........	4	1	1	2	1	26
Vincent, Troy, Miami	1	0	0	1	0	6
Walker, Derrick, K.C...........	2	0	2	0	0	12
Warren, Chris, Seattle.........	11	9	2	0	1	68
Washington, Lionel, Raiders	1	0	0	1	0	6
Watters, Orlando, Seattle.....	1	0	0	1	0	6
White, Lorenzo, Houston.....	4	3	1	0	0	24
Williams, Alfred, Cincinnati..	0	0	0	0	0	*2
Williams, Gerald, Pittsburgh	1	0	0	1	0	6
Williams, Harvey, Raiders...	7	4	3	0	1	44
Williams, John L., Pit.	3	1	2	0	0	18
Wooden, Terry, Seattle	1	0	0	1	0	6
Woodson, Rod, Pittsburgh ..	2	0	0	2	0	12
Wright, Alexander, Raiders .	2	0	2	0	0	12
Yarborough, Ryan, NYJ	1	0	1	0	0	6
Young, Duane, San Diego....	1	0	1	0	0	6

*Includes safety.

NOTE: Team safeties credited to Buffalo, Kansas City and and Seattle.

NFC

KICKERS

Player, Team	XP Made	XP Att.	FG Made	FG Att.	Tot. Pts.
Andersen, Morten, New Orleans	32	32	28	39	116
Boniol, Chris, Dallas	48	48	22	29	114
Brien, Doug, San Francisco	60	62	15	20	105
Butler, Kevin, Chicago....................	24	24	21	29	87
Daluiso, Brad, N.Y. Giants	5	5	11	11	38
Davis, Greg, Arizona	17	17	20	26	77

Player, Team	XP Made	XP Att	FG Made	FG Att	Tot. Pts.
Hanson, Jason, Detroit	39	40	18	27	93
Husted, Michael, Tampa Bay	20	20	23	35	89
Jacke, Chris, Green Bay	41	43	19	26	98
Johnson, Norm, Atlanta	32	32	21	25	95
Lohmiller, Chip, Washington	30	32	20	28	90
Murray, Eddie, Philadelphia	33	33	21	25	96
Peterson, Todd, Arizona	4	4	2	4	10
Reveiz, Fuad, Minnesota	30	30	34	39	132
Treadwell, David, N.Y. Giants	22	23	11	17	55
Zendejas, Tony, L.A. Rams	28	28	18	23	82

NON-KICKERS

Player, Team	Tot. TD	Rush TD	Pass TD	Misc. TD	2Pt.	Tot. Pts.
Aikman, Troy, Dallas	1	1	0	0	0	6
Allen, Terry, Minnesota	8	8	0	0	1	50
Anderson, Willie, L.A. Rams	5	0	5	0	0	30
Armstrong, Tyji, T.B.	1	0	1	0	0	6
Bailey, Johnny, L.A. Rams	1	1	0	0	0	6
Bailey, Robert, L.A. Rams	1	0	0	1	0	6
Bailey, Victor, Phi.	1	0	1	0	0	6
Barnett, Fred, Phi.	5	0	5	0	0	30
Bates, Mario, New Orleans	6	6	0	0	0	36
Bavaro, Mark, Phi.	3	0	3	0	0	18
Bayless, Martin, Was.	1	0	0	1	0	6
Bennett, Edgar, Green Bay	9	5	4	0	0	54
Bettis, Jerome, L.A. Rams	4	3	1	0	2	28
Beuerlein, Steve, Arizona	1	1	0	0	0	6
Brooks, Reggie, Was.	2	2	0	0	0	12
Brooks, Robert, Green Bay	6	0	4	2	0	36
Brown, Dave, N.Y. Giants	2	2	0	0	0	12
Brown, Derek, New Orleans	4	3	1	0	0	24
Bruce, Isaac, L.A. Rams	3	0	3	0	0	18
Brunell, Mark, Green Bay	1	1	0	0	0	6
Calloway, Chris, N.Y. Giants	2	0	2	0	0	12
Carter, Anthony, Detroit	3	0	3	0	0	18
Carter, Cris, Minnesota	7	0	7	0	2	46
Carter, Dexter, S.F.	1	0	0	1	0	6
Centers, Larry, Arizona	7	5	2	0	0	42
Chandler, Chris, L.A. Rams	1	1	0	0	0	6
Clark, Gary, Arizona	1	0	1	0	0	6
Clay, Willie, Detroit	1	0	0	1	0	6
Cobb, Reggie, Green Bay	4	3	1	0	0	24
Coleman, Lincoln, Dallas	1	1	0	0	0	6
Collins, Andre, Was.	2	0	0	2	0	12
Conover, Scott, Detroit	1	0	1	0	0	6
Conway, Curtis, Chicago	2	0	2	0	1	14
Cook, Marv, Chicago	1	0	1	0	0	6
Copeland, Horace, T.B.	0	0	0	0	1	*2
Cross, Howard, N.Y. Giants	4	0	4	0	0	24
Cunningham, Randall, Phi.	3	3	0	0	0	18
Dawsey, Lawrence, T.B.	1	0	1	0	0	6
Drayton, Troy, L.A. Rams	6	0	6	0	0	36
Early, Quinn, New Orleans	4	0	4	0	0	24
Ellard, Henry, Was.	6	0	6	0	0	36
Emanuel, Bert, Atlanta	4	0	4	0	0	24
Erickson, Craig, T.B.	1	1	0	0	0	6
Ervins, Ricky, Was.	4	3	1	0	0	24
Favre, Brett, Green Bay	2	2	0	0	0	12
Floyd, William, S.F.	6	6	0	0	0	36
Fuller, William, Phi.	0	0	0	0	0	*2
Garner, Charlie, Phi.	3	3	0	0	0	18
Gedney, Chris, Chicago	3	0	3	0	0	18
Gilbert, Sean, L.A. Rams	0	0	0	0	0	*2
Graham, Jeff, Chicago	5	0	4	1	1	32
Graham, Scottie, Minnesota	2	2	0	0	0	12
Gray, Mel, Detroit	3	0	0	3	0	18
Green, Darrell, Was.	1	0	0	1	0	6
Green, Robert, Chicago	2	0	2	0	0	12
Griffith, Howard, L.A. Rams	1	0	1	0	0	6
Hampton, Rodney, NYG	6	6	0	0	1	38
Harper, Alvin, Dallas	8	0	8	0	0	48
Harris, Jackie, T.B.	3	0	3	0	1	20
Harris, James, Minnesota	1	0	0	1	0	6

Player, Team	Tot. TD	Rush TD	Pass TD	Misc. TD	2Pt.	Tot. Pts.
Harris, Raymont, Chicago	1	1	0	0	0	6
Hawkins, Courtney, T.B.	5	0	5	0	0	30
Haynes, Michael, N.O.	5	0	5	0	0	30
Hearst, Garrison, Arizona	1	1	0	0	0	6
Hebron, Vaughn, Phi.	2	2	0	0	0	12
Hester, Jessie, L.A. Rams	3	0	3	0	0	18
Heyward, Craig, Atlanta	8	7	1	0	0	48
Horton, Ethan, Was.	3	0	3	0	0	18
Howard, Desmond, Was.	5	0	5	0	1	32
Hughes, Tyrone, N.O.	4	0	0	4	0	24
Irvin, Michael, Dallas	6	0	6	0	0	36
Ismail, Qadry, Minnesota	5	0	5	0	0	30
Jack, Eric, Atlanta	1	0	0	1	0	6
Jackson, Greg, Phi.	1	0	0	1	0	6
Jenkins, James, Was.	4	0	4	0	0	24
Jennings, Keith, Chicago	3	0	3	0	0	18
Johnson, Maurice, Phi.	2	0	2	0	0	12
Johnson, Mike, Detroit	1	0	0	1	0	6
Johnston, Daryl, Dallas	4	2	2	0	0	24
Jones, Brent, S.F.	9	0	9	0	1	56
Jordan, Andrew, Minnesota	0	0	0	0	1	2
Joseph, James, Phi.	3	1	2	0	0	18
Kinchen, Todd, L.A. Rams	4	1	3	0	0	24
Lee, Amp, Minnesota	2	0	2	0	0	12
Lewis, Nate, Chicago	1	0	1	0	0	6
Logan, Marc, S.F.	2	1	1	0	0	12
Lyght, Todd, L.A. Rams	1	0	0	1	0	6
Mathis, Terance, Atlanta	11	0	11	0	2	70
Matthews, Aubrey, Detroit	3	0	3	0	0	18
McCaffrey, Ed, S.F.	2	0	2	0	0	12
McCants, Keith, Arizona	1	0	0	1	0	6
McDonald, Tim, S.F.	2	0	0	2	0	12
McDowell, Anthony, T.B.	1	0	1	0	0	6
McMurtry, Greg, Chicago	1	0	1	0	0	6
Meggett, Dave, N.Y. Giants	6	4	0	2	0	36
Mitchell, Brian, Was.	3	0	1	2	1	20
Mitchell, Scott, Detroit	1	1	0	0	0	6
Moore, Derrick, Detroit	4	4	0	0	0	24
Moore, Herman, Detroit	11	0	11	0	0	66
Moore, Ronald, Arizona	5	4	1	0	1	32
Morgan, Anthony, G.B.	4	0	4	0	0	24
Morrison, Darryl, Was.	1	0	0	1	0	6
Morton, Johnnie, Detroit	2	0	1	1	0	12
Muster, Brad, New Orleans	1	1	0	0	0	6
Neal, Lorenzo, New Orleans	1	1	0	0	0	6
Newman, Anthony, L.A. Rams	1	0	0	1	0	6
Novacek, Jay, Dallas	2	0	2	0	0	12
Parker, Anthony, Minnesota	3	0	0	3	0	18
Paup, Bryce, Green Bay	1	0	0	1	0	6
Pegram, Erric, Atlanta	1	1	0	0	0	6
Perriman, Brett, Detroit	4	0	4	0	2	28
Pierce, Aaron, N.Y. Giants	4	0	4	0	0	24
Proehl, Ricky, Arizona	5	0	5	0	0	30
Reed, Jake, Minnesota	4	0	4	0	0	24
Reeves, Bryan, Arizona	1	0	1	0	0	6
Rhett, Errict, T.B.	7	7	0	0	1	44
Rice, Jerry, S.F.	15	2	13	0	1	92
Rison, Andre, Atlanta	8	0	8	0	1	50
Ross, Jermaine, L.A. Rams	1	0	1	0	0	6
Sanders, Barry, Detroit	8	7	1	0	0	48
Sanders, Deion, S.F.	3	0	0	3	0	18
Sanders, Ricky, Atlanta	1	0	1	0	0	6
Sharpe, Sterling, G.B.	18	0	18	0	0	108
Sherrard, Mike, N.Y. Giants	6	0	6	0	0	36
Singleton, Nate, S.F.	2	0	2	0	0	12
Small, Torrance, N.O.	5	0	5	0	1	32
Smith, Cedric, Was.	1	0	1	0	0	6
Smith, Chuck, Atlanta	1	0	0	1	0	6
Smith, Darrin, Dallas	1	0	0	1	0	6
Smith, Emmitt, Dallas	22	21	1	0	0	132
Smith, Irv, New Orleans	3	0	3	0	0	18
Smith, Robert, Minnesota	1	1	0	0	0	6
Spielman, Chris, Detroit	1	0	0	1	0	6
Swann, Eric, Arizona	0	0	0	0	0	*2
Taylor, John, S.F.	5	0	5	0	0	30

Player, Team	Tot. TD	Rush TD	Pass TD	Misc. TD	2Pt.	Tot. Pts.
Thomas, Blair, N.E.-Dal.*	2	2	0	0	0	12
Tillman, Lewis, Chicago	7	7	0	0	0	42
Tolbert, Tony, Dallas	1	0	0	1	0	6
Truitt, Olanda, Was.	1	0	1	0	0	6
Turner, Vernon, T.B.	1	0	0	1	0	6
Waddle, Tom, Chicago	1	0	1	0	0	6
Walker, Adam, S.F.	1	1	0	0	0	6
Walker, Darnell, Atlanta	1	0	0	1	0	6
Walker, Herschel, Phi.	8	5	2	1	0	48
Walls, Wesley, New Orleans	4	0	4	0	1	26
Walsh, Steve, Chicago	1	1	0	0	0	6
Ware, Derek, Arizona	1	0	1	0	0	6
Washington, Dewayne, Min.	3	0	0	3	0	18
Watters, Ricky, S.F.	11	6	5	0	0	66
West, Ed, Green Bay	2	0	2	0	1	14
Wetnight, Ryan, Chicago	1	0	1	0	0	6
Williams, Calvin, Phi.	3	0	3	0	0	18
Williams, James, N.O.	1	0	0	1	0	6
Williams, Kevin, Dallas	2	0	0	2	0	12
Wilson, Charles, T.B.	6	0	6	0	0	36
Winans, Tydus, Was.	2	0	2	0	1	14
Woodson, Darren, Dallas	1	0	0	1	0	6

Player, Team	Tot. TD	Rush TD	Pass TD	Misc. TD	2Pt.	Tot. Pts.
Worley, Tim, Chicago	1	1	0	0	0	6
Wright, Toby, L.A. Rams	1	0	0	1	0	6
Wycheck, Frank, Was.	1	0	1	0	0	6
Young, Steve, S.F.	7	7	0	0	0	42
Zordich, Mike, Phi.	1	0	0	1	0	6

*Includes safety.

NOTE: Team safeties credited to N.Y. Giants (2), Detroit and Washington.

PLAYERS WITH TWO CLUBS
NON-KICKERS

Player, Team	Tot. TD	Rush TD	Pass TD	Misc. TD	2Pt.	Tot. Pts.
McAfee, Fred, Arizona	1	1	0	0	0	6
McAfee, Fred, Pittsburgh	1	1	0	0	0	6
Thomas, Blair, New England	1	1	0	0	0	6
Thomas, Blair, Dallas	1	1	0	0	0	6
Vaughn, Jon, Seattle	3	1	1	1	1	20
Vaughn, Jon, Kansas City	1	0	0	1	0	6

INTERCEPTIONS

TEAM

AFC

Team	No.	Yds.	Avg.	Long	TD
Miami	23	276	12.0	t76	1
New England	22	209	9.5	24	1
Seattle	19	284	14.9	t69	2
Cleveland	18	223	12.4	t93	1
Indianapolis	18	360	20.0	t90	3
N.Y. Jets	17	355	20.9	t90	3
San Diego	17	402	23.6	t99	3
Pittsburgh	17	240	14.1	42	2
Buffalo	16	175	10.9	45	0
Houston	14	242	17.3	41	1
L.A Raiders	12	187	15.6	35	3
Kansas City	12	218	18.2	t78	1
Denver	12	55	4.6	24	0
Cincinnati	10	167	16.7	49	0
AFC total	227	3393	14.9	t99	21
AFC average	16.2	242.4	14.9	....	1.5

t—touchdown.

NFC

Team	No.	Yds.	Avg.	Long	TD
Arizona	23	297	12.9	t46	1
San Francisco	23	508	22.1	t93	4
Atlanta	22	322	14.6	74	2
Dallas	22	297	13.5	t94	3
Philadelphia	21	209	10.0	t55	2
Green Bay	21	232	11.0	51	1
Minnesota	18	338	18.8	t81	4
New Orleans	17	197	11.6	56	1
Washington	17	326	19.2	t92	3
N.Y. Giants	16	128	8.0	36	0
L.A. Rams	14	211	15.1	51	1
Chicago	12	127	10.6	33	0
Detroit	12	144	12.0	t48	2
Tampa Bay	9	77	8.6	38	0
NFC total	247	3413	13.8	t94	24
NFC average	17.6	243.8	13.8	....	1.7
NFL total	474	6806	....	t99	45
NFL average	16.9	243.1	14.4	....	1.6

INDIVIDUAL

BESTS OF THE SEASON

Interceptions, season
AFC: 9—Eric Turner, Cleveland.
NFC: 9—Aeneas Williams, Arizona.

Interceptions, game
AFC: 3—Darren Perry, Pittsburgh at Cleveland, Sept. 11;
Terry McDaniel, L.A. Raiders at New England, Oct.
9; Marcus Turner, N.Y. Jets at Minnesota, Nov. 20.
NFC: 2—Held by many players.

Yards, season
NFC: 303—Deion Sanders, San Francisco.
AFC: 224—Stanley Richard, San Diego.

Longest
AFC: 99—Stanley Richard, San Diego at Denver, Sept. 4
(TD).
NFC: 94—Darren Woodson, Dallas at Philadelphia, Dec. 4
(TD).

Touchdowns, season
NFC: 3—Deion Sanders, San Francisco.
AFC: 3—Ray Buchanan, Indianapolis.

Team leaders, Interceptions
AFC:

Buffalo	4	Matt Darby
Cincinnati	3	Louis Oliver
Cleveland	9	Eric Turner
Denver	2	Ray Crockett
		Randy Hilliard
		Rondell Jones
Houston	5	Darryll Lewis
Indianapolis	8	Ray Buchanan
Kansas City	3	Charles Mincy
L.A. Raiders	5	Terry McDaniel
Miami	5	Troy Vincent
New England	7	Maurice Hurst
N.Y. Jets	5	James Hasty
		Marcus Turner
Pittsburgh	7	Darren Perry

San Diego	4	Darrien Gordon
		Stanley Richard
Seattle	3	Patrick Hunter
		Orlando Watters
		Terry Wooden

NFC:

Arizona	9	Aeneas Williams
Atlanta	5	D.J. Johnson
Chicago	5	Donnell Woolford
Dallas	5	James Washington
		Darren Woodson
Detroit	4	Robert Massey
Green Bay	5	Terrell Buckley
L.A. Rams	3	Darryl Henley
		Marquez Pope
Minnesota	4	Vencie Glenn
		Anthony Parker
New Orleans	5	Jimmy Spencer
N.Y. Giants	3	John Booty
		Phillippi Sparks
Philadelphia	6	Greg Jackson
San Francisco	7	Merton Hanks
Tampa Bay	2	Martin Mayhew
		Hardy Nickerson
Washington	4	Andre Collins

NFL LEADERS

Player, Team	No.	Yds.	Avg.	Long	TD
Turner, Eric, Cleveland*	9	199	22.1	t93	1
Williams, Aeneas, Arizona	9	89	9.9	43	0
Buchanan, Ray, Indianapolis*	8	221	27.6	t90	3
Hanks, Merton, San Francisco	7	93	13.3	38	0
Hurst, Maurice, New England*	7	68	9.7	24	0
McDaniel, Terry, L.A. Raiders*	7	103	14.7	35	2
Perry, Darren, Pittsburgh*	7	112	16.0	42	0
Jackson, Greg, Philadelphia	6	86	14.3	t55	1
Sanders, Deion, San Francisco*	6	303	50.5	t93	3
Turner, Marcus, N.Y. Jets*	5	155	31.0	t90	1
Clark, Vinnie, Atl.-N.O	5	149	29.8	74	0
Woodson, Darren, Dallas	5	140	28.0	t94	1
Vincent, Troy, Miami*	5	113	22.6	t58	1
Hasty, James, N.Y. Jets*	5	90	18.0	40	0

Player, Team	No.	Yds.	Avg.	Long	TD
Lewis, Darryll, Houston*	5	57	11.4	20	0
Washington, James, Dallas	5	43	8.6	25	0
Buckley, Terrell, Green Bay	5	38	7.6	26	0
Woolford, Donnell, Chicago	5	30	6.0	25	0
Spencer, Jimmy, New Orleans	5	24	4.8	11	0
Johnson, D.J., Atlanta	5	0	0.0	0	0

*AFC.
t—touchdown.
Leader based on most interceptions.

AFC

Player, Team	No.	Yds.	Avg.	Long	TD
Alexander, Elijah, Denver	1	2	2.0	2	0
Ambrose, Ashley, Indianapolis	2	50	25.0	42	0
Atkins, Gene, Miami	3	24	8.0	18	0
Atwater, Steve, Denver	1	24	24.0	24	0
Barnett, Harlon, New England	3	51	17.0	24	0
Beavers, Aubrey, Miami	2	0	0.0	0	0
Belser, Jason, Indianapolis	1	31	31.0	31	0
Biekert, Greg, L.A. Raiders	1	11	11.0	11	0
Bishop, Blaine, Houston	1	21	21.0	21	0
Blackmon, Robert, Seattle	1	24	24.0	24	0
Booth, Issac, Cleveland	1	4	4.0	4	0
Braxton, Tyrone, Miami	2	3	1.5	3	0
Brim, Mike, Cincinnati	2	72	36.0	49	0
Brown, Chad, Pittsburgh	1	9	9.0	9	0
Brown, J.B., Miami	3	82	27.3	38	0
Brown, Vincent, New England	3	22	7.3	12	0
Buchanan, Ray, Indianapolis	8	221	27.6	t90	3
Burris, Jeff, Buffalo	2	24	12.0	24	0
Caldwell, Mike, Cleveland	1	0	0.0	0	0
Carrington, Darren, San Diego	3	51	17.0	32	0
Carter, Dale, Kansas City	2	24	12.0	24	0
Collins, Mark, Kansas City	2	83	41.5	t78	1
Crockett, Ray, Denver	2	6	3.0	6	0
Cross, Jeff, Miami	1	0	0.0	0	0
Daniel, Eugene, Indianapolis	2	6	3.0	6	0
Darby, Matt, Buffalo	4	20	5.0	20	0
Dishman, Cris, Houston	4	74	18.5	38	1
Fletcher, Simon, Denver	1	4	4.0	4	0
Frank, Donald, L.A. Raiders	1	8	8.0	8	0
Gordon, Darrien, San Diego	4	32	8.0	23	0
Gray, Carlton, Seattle	2	0	0.0	0	0
Griffin, Don, Cleveland	2	2	1.0	2	0
Griggs, David, San Diego	1	11	11.0	11	0
Grow, Monty, Kansas City	1	21	21.0	21	0
Guyton, Myron, New England	2	18	9.0	15	0
Harper, Dwayne, San Diego	3	28	9.3	15	0
Hasty, James, N.Y. Jets	5	90	18.0	40	0
Hilliard, Randy, Denver	2	8	4.0	8	0
Hollier, Dwight, Miami	1	36	36.0	36	0
Humphries, Leonard, Indianapolis	1	1	1.0	1	0
Hunter, Patrick, Seattle	3	85	28.3	51	0
Hurst, Maurice, New England	7	68	9.7	24	0
Jackson, Steve, Houston	1	0	0.0	0	0
Jacobs, Tim, Cleveland	2	9	4.5	8	0
Jones, Gary, Pittsburgh	1	0	0.0	0	0
Jones, Henry, Buffalo	2	45	22.5	45	0
Jones, Rondell, Denver	2	9	4.5	9	0
Kirkland, Levon, Pittsburgh	2	0	0.0	0	0
Lake, Carnell, Pittsburgh	1	2	2.0	2	0
Langham, Antonio, Cleveland	2	2	1.0	2	0
Lewis, Darryll, Houston	5	57	11.4	20	0
Lewis, Mo, N.Y. Jets	4	106	26.5	t67	2
Lloyd, Greg, Pittsburgh	1	8	8.0	8	0
Maddox, Mark, Buffalo	1	11	11.0	11	0
Malone, Darrell, Miami	1	0	0.0	0	0
McDaniel, Terry, L.A. Raiders	7	103	14.7	35	2
Mincy, Charles, Kansas City	3	49	16.3	31	0
Oliver, Louis, Cincinnati	3	36	12.0	19	0
Oliver, Muhammad, Miami	1	0	0.0	0	0
Patton, Marvcus, Buffalo	2	8	4.0	8	0
Perry, Darren, Pittsburgh	7	112	16.0	42	0

Player, Team	No.	Yds.	Avg.	Long	TD
Porter, Rufus, Seattle	1	33	33.0	33	0
Ray, Terry, New England	1	2	2.0	2	0
Reynolds, Ricky, New England	1	11	11.0	t11	1
Richard, Stanley, San Diego	4	224	56.0	t99	2
Robertson, Marcus, Houston	3	90	30.0	41	0
Robinson, Eugene, Seattle	3	18	6.0	18	0
Robinson, Rafael, Seattle	1	0	0.0	0	0
Sabb, Dwayne, New England	2	6	3.0	5	0
Sawyer, Corey, Cincinnati	2	0	0.0	0	0
Smith, Ben, Denver	1	0	0.0	0	0
Smith, Bruce, Buffalo	1	0	0.0	0	0
Smith, Neil, Kansas City	1	41	41.0	41	0
Smith, Rod, New England	2	10	5.0	10	0
Smith, Thomas, Buffalo	1	4	4.0	4	0
Spitulski, Bob, Seattle	1	7	7.0	7	0
Stams, Frank, Cleveland	1	7	7.0	7	0
Stewart, Michael, Miami	3	11	3.7	11	0
Tate, David, Indianapolis	3	51	17.0	30	0
Taylor, Jay, Kansas City	1	0	0.0	0	0
Taylor, Terry, Seattle	1	0	0.0	0	0
Tovar, Steve, Cincinnati	1	14	14.0	14	0
Turner, Eric, Cleveland	9	199	22.1	t93	1
Turner, Marcus, N.Y. Jets	5	155	31.0	t90	1
Vanhorse, Sean, San Diego	2	56	28.0	t50	1
Veasey, Craig, Miami	1	7	7.0	7	0
Vincent, Troy, Miami	5	113	22.6	t58	1
Washington, Brian, N.Y. Jets	2	-3	-1.5	0	0
Washington, Lionel, L.A. Raiders	3	65	21.7	t31	1
Washington, Marvin, N.Y. Jets	1	7	7.0	7	0
Washington, Mickey, Buffalo	3	63	21.0	36	0
Washington, Ted, Denver	1	5	5.0	5	0
Watters, Orlando, Seattle	3	39	13.0	t35	1
Watts, Damon, Indianapolis	1	0	0.0	0	0
Whigham, Larry, New England	1	21	21.0	21	0
White, William, Kansas City	2	0	0.0	0	0
Williams, Dan, Denver	1	-3	-3.0	-3	0
Williams, Darryl, Cincinnati	2	45	22.5	33	0
Wooden, Terry, Seattle	3	78	26.0	t69	1
Woodson, Rod, Pittsburgh	4	109	27.3	t37	2

t—touchdown.

NFC

Player, Team	No.	Yds.	Avg.	Long	TD
Allen, Eric, Philadelphia	3	61	20.3	33	0
Armstead, Jessie, N.Y. Giants	1	0	0.0	0	0
Bayless, Martin, Washington	3	38	12.7	19	0
Blades, Bennie, Detroit	1	0	0.0	0	0
Booty, John, N.Y. Giants	3	95	31.7	36	0
Boyd, Malik, Minnesota	1	22	22.0	15	0
Brooks, Michael, N.Y. Giants	1	10	10.0	10	0
Brown, Dennis, San Francisco	1	0	0.0	0	0
Brown, Larry, Dallas	4	21	5.3	14	0
Buck, Vince, New Orleans	1	0	0.0	0	0
Buckley, Terrell, Green Bay	5	38	7.6	26	0
Butler, LeRoy, Green Bay	3	68	22.7	51	0
Campbell, Jesse, N.Y. Giants	2	3	1.5	2	0
Carrier, Mark, Chicago	2	10	5.0	7	0
Carter, Tom, Washington	3	58	19.3	40	0
Case, Scott, Atlanta	2	12	6.0	12	0
Clark, Vinnie, Atl.-N.O.	5	149	29.8	74	0
Clay, Willie, Detroit	3	54	18.0	t28	1
Collins, Andre, Washington	4	150	37.5	t92	2
Colon, Harry, Detroit	1	3	3.0	3	0
Conner, Darion, New Orleans	1	56	56.0	56	0
Cook, Toi, San Francisco	1	18	18.0	18	0
Covington, Tony, Tampa Bay	1	38	38.0	38	0
Davis, Eric, San Francisco	1	8	8.0	8	0
Del Rio, Jack, Minnesota	3	5	1.7	5	0
Dimry, Charles, Tampa Bay	1	0	0.0	0	0
Doleman, Chris, Atlanta	1	2	2.0	2	0
Douglass, Maurice, Chicago	1	18	18.0	18	0
Drakeford, Tyronne, San Francisco	1	6	6.0	6	0
Evans, Byron, Philadelphia	1	6	6.0	6	0

Player, Team	No.	Yds.	Avg.	Long	TD
Evans, Doug, Green Bay	1	0	0.0	0	0
Everett, Thomas, Tampa Bay	1	26	26.0	26	0
Gant, Kenneth, Dallas	1	0	0.0	0	0
Gayle, Shaun, Chicago	2	33	16.5	33	0
Glenn, Vencie, Minnesota	4	55	13.8	32	0
Gouveia, Kurt, Washington	1	7	7.0	7	0
Grant, Alan, Washington	1	0	0.0	0	0
Green, Darrell, Washington	3	32	10.7	t27	1
Hager, Britt, Philadelphia	1	0	0.0	0	0
Haley, Charles, Dallas	1	1	1.0	1	0
Hall, Dana, San Francisco	2	0	0.0	0	0
Hanks, Merton, San Francisco	7	93	13.3	38	0
Harmon, Andy, Philadelphia	1	0	0.0	0	0
Harper, Roger, Atlanta	1	22	22.0	22	0
Harris, James, Minnesota	1	21	21.0	21	0
Henley, Darryl, L.A. Rams	3	46	15.3	23	0
Hoage, Terry, Arizona	3	64	21.3	41	0
Hollinquest, Lamont, Washington	1	39	39.0	39	0
Holmes, Clayton, Dallas	0	3	....	3	0
Hughes, Tyrone, New Orleans	2	31	15.5	31	0
Jackson, Greg, Philadelphia	6	86	14.3	t55	1
Johnson, D.J., Atlanta	5	0	0.0	0	0
Johnson, Keshon, Green Bay	1	3	3.0	3	0
Johnson, Mike, Detroit	1	48	48.0	t48	1
Joyner, Seth, Arizona	3	2	0.7	2	0
Kelly, Joe, L.A. Rams	1	31	31.0	31	0
Lee, Carl, New Orleans	2	3	1.5	3	0
Lincoln, Jeremy, Chicago	1	5	5.0	5	0
Lumpkin, Sean, New Orleans	1	1	1.0	1	0
Lyght, Todd, L.A. Rams	1	14	14.0	14	0
Lyle, Keith, L.A. Rams	2	1	0.5	1	0
Lynch, Lorenzo, Arizona	2	35	17.5	23	0
Mack, Milton, Detroit	1	0	0.0	0	0
Marion, Brock, Dallas	1	11	11.0	11	0
Marshall, Wilber, Arizona	0	13	....	13	0
Massey, Robert, Detroit	4	25	6.3	17	0
Mayhew, Martin, Tampa Bay	2	4	2.0	4	0
McCants, Keith, Arizona	1	46	46.0	t46	1
McDaniel, Ed, Minnesota	0	0	0.0	0	0
McDonald, Tim, San Francisco	2	79	39.5	t73	1
McGill, Lenny, Green Bay	2	16	8.0	16	0
McGriggs, Lamar, Minnesota	1	1	1.0	1	0
McGruder, Mike, Tampa Bay	1	0	0.0	0	0
McMillian, Mark, Philadelphia	2	2	1.0	5	0
McNeil, Ryan, Detroit	1	14	14.0	14	0
Miller, Corey, N.Y. Giants	2	6	3.0	6	0
Mills, Sam, New Orleans	1	10	10.0	10	0
Newman, Anthony, L.A. Rams	2	46	23.0	24	1
Nickerson, Hardy, Tampa Bay	2	9	4.5	10	0
Norton, Ken, San Francisco	1	0	0.0	0	0
Parker, Anthony, Minnesota	4	99	24.8	t44	2
Paup, Bryce, Green Bay	3	47	15.7	30	0
Phifer, Roman, L.A. Rams	2	7	3.5	7	0
Phillips, Anthony, Atlanta	1	0	0.0	0	0
Plummer, Gary, San Francisco	1	1	1.0	1	0
Pope, Marquez, L.A. Rams	3	66	22.0	51	0
Randolph, Thomas, N.Y. Giants	1	0	0.0	0	0
Raymond, Corey, N.Y. Giants	1	0	0.0	0	0
Romanowski, Bill, Philadelphia	2	8	4.0	8	0
Ross, Kevin, Atlanta	3	26	8.7	16	0
Sanders, Deion, San Francisco	6	303	50.5	t93	3
Smith, Chuck, Atlanta	1	36	36.0	t36	1
Smith, Darrin, Dallas	2	13	6.5	t13	1
Smith, Kevin, Dallas	2	11	5.5	11	0
Sparks, Phillippi, N.Y. Giants	3	4	1.3	4	0
Spellman, Alonzo, Chicago	1	31	31.0	31	0
Spencer, Jimmy, New Orleans	5	24	4.8	11	0
Stargell, Tony, Tampa Bay	1	0	0.0	0	0
Stowe, Tyronne, Washington	1	2	2.0	2	0
Strickland, Fred, Green Bay	1	7	7.0	7	0
Swann, Eric, Arizona	1	0	0.0	0	0
Teague, George, Green Bay	3	33	11.0	16	0
Thomas, William, Philadelphia	1	7	7.0	7	0
Tolbert, Tony, Dallas	1	54	54.0	t54	1
Tubbs, Winfred, New Orleans	1	0	0.0	0	0
Tuggle, Jessie, Atlanta	1	0	0.0	0	0
Walker, Darnell, Atlanta	3	105	35.0	t44	1
Washington, Dewayne, Minnesota	3	135	45.0	t81	2
Washington, James, Dallas	5	43	8.6	25	0
Williams, Aeneas, Arizona	9	89	9.9	43	0
Williams, James, Arizona	4	48	12.0	29	0
Williams, James, New Orleans	2	42	21.0	t33	1
Williams, Jarvis, N.Y. Giants	2	10	5.0	10	0
Willis, James, Green Bay	2	20	10.0	17	0
Woodson, Darren, Dallas	5	140	28.0	t94	1
Woolford, Donnell, Chicago	5	30	6.0	25	0
Zordich, Mike, Philadelphia	4	39	9.8	t18	1

t—touchdown.

PLAYERS WITH TWO CLUBS

Player, Team	No.	Yds.	Avg.	Long	TD
Clark, Vinnie, Atlanta	4	119	29.8	74	0
Clark, Vinnie, New Orleans	1	30	30.0	30	0

SACKS

TEAM

AFC

Team	Sacks	Yards
Pittsburgh	55	382
San Diego	43	253
New England	39	290
Kansas City	39	234
L.A. Raiders	38	284
Cleveland	38	268
Cincinnati	31	210
Houston	31	168
Miami	29	160
N.Y. Jets	29	201
Indianapolis	29	218
Seattle	29	206
Buffalo	25	152
Denver	23	141
AFC total	478	3167
AFC average	34.1	226.2

NFC

Team	Sacks	Yards
Dallas	47	299
Philadelphia	42	265
San Francisco	38	255
Green Bay	37	276
New Orleans	36	196
Minnesota	36	250
Arizona	35	272
Atlanta	32	229
Detroit	28	199
Washington	28	165
Chicago	28	175
N.Y. Giants	26	169
L.A. Rams	26	159
Tampa Bay	20	114
NFC total	459	3023
NFC average	32.8	215.9
NFL total	937	6190
NFL average	33.5	221.1

INDIVIDUAL

BESTS OF THE SEASON

Sacks, season
AFC: 14.0—Kevin Greene, Pittsburgh.
NFC: 13.5—Ken Harvey, Washington; John Randle, Minnesota.

Sacks, game
AFC: 4.0—Bruce Smith, Buffalo at Houston, Sept. 18; Alfred Williams, Cincinnati at Pittsburgh, Oct. 16.
NFC: 4.0—Charles Haley, Dallas at Pittsburgh, Sept. 4.

NFL LEADERS

Player, Team	No.
Greene, Kevin, Pittsburgh*	14.0
Harvey, Ken, Washington	13.5
Randle, John, Minnesota	13.5
Haley, Charles, Dallas	12.5
O'Neal, Leslie, San Diego*	12.5
Smith, Neil, Kansas City*	11.5
Mims, Chris, San Diego*	11.0
Smith, Chuck, Atlanta	11.0
Thomas, Derrick, Kansas City*	11.0
Conner, Darion, New Orleans	10.5
Jones, Sean, Green Bay	10.5
*AFC.	

AFC

Player, Team	No.
Adams, Sam, Seattle	4.0
Agnew, Ray, New England	0.5
Alberts, Trev, Indianapolis	2.0
Alexander, Elijah, Denver	1.0
Anderson, Eddie, L.A. Raiders	2.0
Atkins, Gene, Miami	1.0
Ball, Jerry, L.A. Raiders	3.0
Banks, Carl, Cleveland	1.5
Barber, Kurt, N.Y. Jets	1.0
Barnett, Oliver, Buffalo	1.0
Barnett, Troy, New England	1.0

Player, Team	No.
Barrow, Micheal, Houston	2.5
Bennett, Cornelius, Buffalo	5.0
Bennett, Tony, Indianapolis	9.0
Biekert, Greg, L.A. Raiders	1.5
Bishop, Blaine, Houston	1.5
Bowens, Tim, Miami	3.0
Bradford, Ronnie, Denver	1.0
Brown, Chad, Pittsburgh	8.5
Brown, Vincent, New England	1.5
Buchanan, Ray, Indianapolis	1.0
Buckner, Brentson, Pittsburgh	2.0
Burnett, Rob, Cleveland	10.0
Casillas, Tony, N.Y. Jets	1.5
Childress, Ray, Houston	6.0
Coleman, Marco, Miami	6.0
Collins, Mark, Kansas City	2.0
Copeland, John, Cincinnati	1.0
Coryatt, Quentin, Indianapolis	1.0
Cox, Bryan, Miami	3.0
Cross, Jeff, Miami	9.5
Davidson, Kenny, Houston	6.0
Davis, Reuben, San Diego	0.5
Dixon, Gerald, Cleveland	1.0
Dronett, Shane, Denver	6.0
Edwards, Antonio, Seattle	2.5
Emtman, Steve, Indianapolis	1.0
Evans, Donald, N.Y. Jets	0.5
Figures, Deon, Pittsburgh	1.0
Fletcher, Simon, Denver	7.0
Footman, Dan, Cleveland	2.5
Francis, James, Cincinnati	4.5
Frase, Paul, N.Y. Jets	1.0
Fredrickson, Rob, L.A. Raiders	3.0
Gildon, Jason, Pittsburgh	2.0
Goad, Tim, New England	3.0
Green, Victor, N.Y. Jets	1.0
Greene, Kevin, Pittsburgh	14.0
Griffin, Don, Cleveland	4.0
Hansen, Phil, Buffalo	5.5
Harrison, Nolan, L.A. Raiders	5.0
Hasselbach, Harald, Denver	2.0
Hasty, James, N.Y. Jets	3.0
Herrod, Jeff, Indianapolis	1.0
Houston, Bobby, N.Y. Jets	3.5

— 253 —

Player, Team	No.
Hurst, Maurice, New England	2.0
Jackson, Steve, Houston	1.0
Jamison, George, Kansas City	1.0
Johnson, Bill, Cleveland	1.0
Johnson, Pepper, Cleveland	2.5
Johnson, Raylee, San Diego	1.5
Jones, Aaron, New England	4.0
Jones, Henry, Buffalo	1.0
Jones, James, Cleveland	3.0
Jones, Marvin, N.Y. Jets	0.5
Jones, Mike, New England	6.0
Jones, Roger, Cincinnati	1.5
Kennedy, Cortez, Seattle	4.0
Kirkland, Levon, Pittsburgh	3.0
Krumrie, Tim, Cincinnati	1.0
Lageman, Jeff, N.Y. Jets	6.5
Lake, Carnell, Pittsburgh	1.0
Lathon, Lamar, Houston	8.5
Lee, Shawn, San Diego	6.5
Lewis, Albert, L.A. Raiders	1.0
Lewis, Mo, N.Y. Jets	6.0
Lloyd, Greg, Pittsburgh	10.0
Lott, Ronnie, N.Y. Jets	1.0
McCoy, Tony, Indianapolis	6.0
McCrary, Michael, Seattle	1.5
McDaniels, Pellom, Kansas City	2.0
McDonald, Devon, Indianapolis	1.0
McDonald, Ricardo, Cincinnati	1.0
McGinest, Willie, New England	4.5
McGlockton, Chester, L.A. Raiders	9.5
Mecklenburg, Karl, Denver	1.5
Mickell, Darren, Kansas City	7.0
Miller, Les, San Diego	0.5
Mims, Chris, San Diego	11.0
Montgomery, Glenn, Houston	3.0
Moss, Winston, L.A. Raiders	2.0
Nash, Joe, Seattle	2.0
Noga, Al, Indianapolis	1.0
Nunn, Freddie Joe, Indianapolis	1.0
Oglesby, Alfred, N.Y. Jets	0.5
Oliver, Louis, Cincinnati	1.0
O'Neal, Leslie, San Diego	12.5
Parrella, John, San Diego	1.0
Perry, Michael Dean, Cleveland	4.0
Phillips, Joe, Kansas City	3.0
Pitts, Mike, New England	1.0
Pleasant, Anthony, Cleveland	4.5
Porter, Rufus, Seattle	1.5
Reynolds, Ricky, New England	2.0
Robinson, Eugene, Seattle	1.0
Robinson, Jeff, Denver	1.0
Rucker, Keith, Cincinnati	2.0
Sabb, Dwayne, New England	3.5
Saleaumua, Dan, Kansas City	1.0
Seals, Ray, Pittsburgh	7.0
Seau, Junior, San Diego	5.5
Sinclair, Michael, Seattle	4.5
Singleton, Chris, Miami	2.0
Siragusa, Tony, Indianapolis	5.0
Slade, Chris, New England	9.5
Smith, Al, Houston	2.5
Smith, Anthony, L.A. Raiders	6.0
Smith, Bruce, Buffalo	10.0
Smith, Dennis, Denver	1.0
Smith, Frankie, Miami	1.0
Smith, Neil, Kansas City	11.5
Smith, Rod, New England	0.5
Spitulski, Bob, Seattle	3.0
Stams, Frank, Cleveland	2.0
Steed, Joel, Pittsburgh	2.0
Stephens, Rod, Seattle	2.5
Thomas, Derrick, Kansas City	11.0
Thompson, Bennie, Cleveland	1.0
Tovar, Steve, Cincinnati	3.0
Trapp, James, L.A. Raiders	1.0
Turner, Eric, Cleveland	1.0

Player, Team	No.
Veasey, Craig, Miami	2.5
Wallace, Aaron, L.A. Raiders	2.0
Washington, Marvin, N.Y. Jets	3.0
Washington, Mickey, Buffalo	0.5
Washington, Ted, Denver	2.5
White, Alberto, L.A. Raiders	2.0
White, Reggie, San Diego	2.0
Wilkinson, Dan, Cincinnati	5.5
Williams, Alfred, Cincinnati	9.5
Williams, Brent, Seattle	1.0
Williams, Darryl, Cincinnati	1.0
Williams, Gerald, Pittsburgh	1.5
Williams, Jerrol, Kansas City	0.5
Wooden, Terry, Seattle	1.5
Woodson, Rod, Pittsburgh	3.0
Wright, Jeff, Buffalo	2.0
Young, Lonnie, San Diego	1.0

NOTE: Miami and San Diego were awarded one team sack each.

NFC

Player, Team	No.
Ahanotu, Chidi, Tampa Bay	1.0
Archambeau, Lester, Atlanta	2.0
Armstead, Jessie, N.Y. Giants	3.0
Armstrong, Trace, Chicago	7.5
Bankston, Michael, Arizona	7.0
Barker, Roy, Minnesota	3.5
Bates, Bill, Dallas	1.0
Beamon, Willie, N.Y. Giants	1.0
Blades, Bennie, Detroit	1.0
Brooks, Michael, N.Y. Giants	1.0
Brown, Dennis, San Francisco	3.0
Brown, Gilbert, Green Bay	3.0
Buck, Vince, New Orleans	1.0
Bussey, Barney, Tampa Bay	1.5
Butler, LeRoy, Green Bay	1.0
Carter, Marty, Tampa Bay	1.0
Coleman, Monte, Washington	0.5
Collins, Andre, Washington	1.5
Conlan, Shane, L.A. Rams	1.0
Conner, Darion, New Orleans	10.5
Culpepper, Brad, Tampa Bay	4.0
Curry, Eric, Tampa Bay	3.0
Davey, Don, Green Bay	1.5
Del Rio, Jack, Minnesota	2.0
Dent, Richard, San Francisco	2.0
Dillard, Stacey, N.Y. Giants	1.5
Doleman, Chris, Atlanta	7.0
Dotson, Santana, Tampa Bay	3.0
Douglass, Maurice, Chicago	1.5
Edwards, Dixon, Dallas	1.0
Epps, Tory, Chicago	1.0
Evans, Byron, Philadelphia	0.5
Evans, Doug, Green Bay	1.0
Farr, D'Marco, L.A. Rams	1.0
Flores, Mike, Philadelphia	3.0
Fontenot, Albert, Chicago	4.0
Fox, Mike, N.Y. Giants	1.0
Fuller, William, Philadelphia	9.5
Geathers, Jumpy, Atlanta	8.0
Gilbert, Sean, L.A. Rams	3.0
Glenn, Vencie, Minnesota	1.0
Grossman, Burt, Philadelphia	5.5
Hager, Britt, Philadelphia	1.0
Haley, Charles, Dallas	12.5
Hall, Rhett, San Francisco	4.0
Hamilton, Keith, N.Y. Giants	6.5
Hanks, Merton, San Francisco	0.5
Harmon, Andy, Philadelphia	9.0
Harper, Roger, Atlanta	1.0
Harris, James, Minnesota	3.0
Harris, Robert, Minnesota	2.0
Harris, Tim, San Francisco	2.0

Player, Team	No.	Player, Team	No.
Harvey, Ken, Washington	13.5	Pritchett, Kelvin, Detroit	5.5
Hayworth, Tracy, Detroit	1.0	Randle, John, Minnesota	13.5
Hennings, Chad, Dallas	7.0	Robinson, Gerald, L.A. Rams	2.5
Hill, Eric, Arizona	1.5	Rocker, David, L.A. Rams	0.5
Hoage, Terry, Arizona	1.0	Romanowski, Bill, Philadelphia	2.5
Hollinquest, Lamont, Washington	0.5	Ross, Kevin, Atlanta	1.0
Howard, Erik, N.Y. Giants	6.5	Scroggins, Tracy, Detroit	2.5
Jackson, Rickey, San Francisco	3.5	Sheppard, Ashley, Minnesota	0.5
Jeffcoat, Jim, Dallas	8.0	Simmons, Clyde, Arizona	6.0
Jenkins, Carlos, Minnesota	1.0	Smith, Chuck, Atlanta	11.0
Jeter, Tommy, Philadelphia	1.0	Smith, Darrin, Dallas	4.0
Johnson, Joe, New Orleans	1.0	Smith, Otis, Philadelphia	1.0
Johnson, Mike, Detroit	1.5	Smith, Vinson, Chicago	1.0
Johnson, Tim, Washington	1.0	Spellman, Alonzo, Chicago	7.0
Jones, Jimmie, L.A. Rams	5.0	Stokes, Fred, L.A. Rams	2.0
Jones, Sean, Green Bay	10.5	Strahan, Michael, N.Y. Giants	4.5
Joyner, Seth, Arizona	6.0	Stubblefield, Dana, San Francisco	8.5
Kelly, Joe, L.A. Rams	2.0	Swann, Eric, Arizona	7.0
Kelly, Todd, San Francisco	3.5	Swilling, Pat, Detroit	3.5
Koonce, George, Green Bay	1.0	Thomas, Broderick, Detroit	7.0
Legette, Tyrone, New Orleans	1.0	Thomas, Henry, Minnesota	7.0
Lett, Leon, Dallas	4.0	Thomas, Mark, San Francisco	1.0
Lynch, Lorenzo, Arizona	0.5	Thomas, William, Philadelphia	6.0
Mangum, John, Chicago	0.5	Tolbert, Tony, Dallas	5.5
Mann, Charles, San Francisco	1.0	Townsend, Greg, Philadelphia	2.0
Marion, Brock, Dallas	1.0	Tubbs, Winfred, New Orleans	1.0
Marshall, Leonard, Washington	2.0	Turnbull, Renaldo, New Orleans	6.5
Marshall, Wilber, Arizona	1.0	Walker, Darnell, Atlanta	1.0
Martin, Wayne, New Orleans	10.0	Warren, Frank, New Orleans	4.0
Maryland, Russell, Dallas	3.0	Wheeler, Mark, Tampa Bay	3.0
Matthews, Clay, Atlanta	1.0	White, Reggie, Green Bay	8.0
McCants, Keith, Arizona	1.0	Widmer, Corey, N.Y. Giants	1.0
McDaniel, Ed, Minnesota	1.5	Wilkins, Gabe, Green Bay	1.0
McMichael, Steve, Green Bay	2.5	Wilson, Bernard, Arizona	1.0
Miller, Jamir, Arizona	3.0	Wilson, Bobby, Washington	2.5
Mills, Sam, New Orleans	1.0	Wilson, Karl, Tampa Bay	2.5
Nickerson, Hardy, Tampa Bay	1.0	Wilson, Troy, San Francisco	2.0
Nottage, Dexter, Washington	1.0	Woodall, Lee, San Francisco	1.0
Ottis, Brad, L.A. Rams	1.0	Woods, Tony, Washington	4.5
Owens, Dan, Detroit	3.0	Young, Bryant, San Francisco	6.0
Palmer, Sterling, Washington	1.0	Young, Robert, L.A. Rams	6.5
Paup, Bryce, Green Bay	7.5	Zordich, Mike, Philadelphia	1.0
Phifer, Roman, L.A. Rams	1.5	Zorich, Chris, Chicago	5.5
Porcher, Robert, Detroit	3.0		

NOTE: Minnesota was awarded one team sack.

FUMBLES

TEAM

AFC

Team	Fum.	Own Fum. Rec.	Own Fum *O.B.	Own Fum. Lost	TD	Opp. Fum. Rec.	TD	†Yards	Total Rec.
Pittsburgh	18	8	2	8	0	14	1	- 1	22
San Diego	19	8	2	9	0	15	0	6	23
Kansas City	21	8	1	12	0	26	0	51	34
L.A. Raiders	22	7	1	14	0	13	2	109	20
Cleveland	26	9	3	14	0	13	0	29	22
Denver	27	8	1	18	0	14	0	63	22
New England	28	14	3	11	0	18	1	105	32
Miami	28	12	2	14	0	9	0	14	21
N.Y. Jets	28	15	3	10	0	21	0	3	36
Buffalo	30	13	4	13	0	12	1	18	25
Indianapolis	30	12	1	17	0	10	2	119	22
Seattle	31	11	1	19	0	11	0	3	22
Cincinnati	31	8	1	22	0	8	0	-4	16
Houston	42	15	2	25	0	12	0	12	27
AFC total	381	148	27	206	0	196	7	527	344
AFC average	27.2	10.6	1.9	14.7	0.0	14.0	0.5	37.6	24.6

*Fumbled out of bounds.
†Includes all fumble yardage (aborted plays and recoveries of own and opponents' fumbles).

NFC

Team	Fum.	Own Fum. Rec.	Own Fum *O.B.	Own Fum. Lost	TD	Opp. Fum. Rec.	TD	†Yards	Total Rec.
Tampa Bay	18	10	1	7	0	12	0	1	22
Washington	21	6	2	13	0	6	2	95	12
Chicago	21	11	0	10	0	10	0	-9	21
Dallas	22	9	3	10	0	9	0	28	18
New Orleans	22	7	1	14	0	14	2	120	21
Philadelphia	23	11	0	12	0	14	0	47	25
San Francisco	25	11	1	13	0	12	1	45	23
Arizona	25	14	1	10	0	13	0	25	27
Green Bay	25	12	5	8	0	12	0	-3	24
L.A. Rams	26	13	0	13	0	6	2	164	19
Detroit	26	13	3	10	0	11	1	44	24
Atlanta	28	17	0	11	0	11	1	22	28
N.Y. Giants	28	18	3	7	0	16	0	-38	34
Minnesota	32	13	5	14	1	16	2	58	29
NFC total	342	165	25	152	1	162	11	599	327
NFC average	24.4	11.8	1.8	10.9	0.1	11.6	0.8	42.8	23.4
NFL total	723	313	52	358	1	358	18	1126	671
NFL average	25.8	11.2	1.9	12.8	0.0	12.8	0.6	40.2	24.0

INDIVIDUAL

BESTS OF THE SEASON

Fumbles, season
NFC: 12—Jeff George, Atlanta.
AFC: 11—John Elway, Denver; Boomer Esiason, N.Y. Jets; Jim Kelly, Buffalo.

Fumbles, game
AFC: 4—Dan McGwire, Seattle vs. L.A. Raiders, Dec. 18.
NFC: 4—Steve Beuerlein, Arizona at Philadelphia, Nov. 6; Randall Cunningham, Philadelphia vs. Cleveland, Nov. 13.

Own fumbles recovered, season
NFC: 6—Jeff George, Atlanta.
AFC: 3—Drew Bledsoe, New England; Boomer Esiason, N.Y. Jets; Ernest Givins, Houston; Dan Marino, Miami; Dan McGwire, Seattle, Bucky Richardson, Houston.

Own fumbles recovered, game
NFC: 3—Jeff George, Atlanta vs. San Diego, Nov. 6.
AFC: 2—Jim Kelly, Buffalo at New England, Sept. 11; Clifford Hicks, N.Y. Jets vs. New England, Oct. 16; Dan McGwire, Seattle vs. L.A. Raiders, Dec. 18.

Opponents' fumbles recovered, season
NFC: 3—Michael Brooks, N.Y. Giants; James Harris, Minnesota; Sean Jones, Green Bay; Chris Spielman, Detroit; Mike Zordich, Philadelphia.
AFC: 3—Held by many players.

Opponents' fumbles recovered, game
NFC: 2—Othello Henderson, New Orleans at L.A. Rams, Dec. 4; Chris Spielman, Detroit at Miami, Dec. 25.
AFC: 2—Held by many players.

Yards returning fumbles
NFC: 128—Tyrone Hughes, New Orleans.
AFC: 78—Quentin Coryatt, Indianapolis.

Longest fumble return
NFC: 98—Toby Wright, L.A. Rams at New Orleans, Oct. 23 (TD).
AFC: 78—Quentin Coryatt, Indianapolis at Pittsburgh, Sept. 18 (TD).

| | | AFC | | | | |

Player, Team	Fum.	Own Rec.	Opp. Rec.	Yds.	Tot. Rec.	TD
Alexander, Derrick, Cle.	2	0	0	0	0	0
Alexander, Elijah, Denver	0	0	1	9	1	0
Alipate, Tuineau, N.Y. Jets	0	0	1	0	1	0
Allen, Marcus, Kansas City	3	0	0	0	0	0
Ambrose, Ashley, Ind.	0	0	1	0	1	0
Anders, Kimble, Kansas City	1	2	0	0	2	0
Anderson, Darren, K.C.	0	0	1	0	1	0
Anderson, Eddie, Raiders	0	0	1	0	1	0
Anderson, Richie, N.Y. Jets	1	1	0	0	1	0
Arthur, Mike, New England	1	1	0	-2	1	0
Atwater, Steve, Denver	0	0	2	17	2	0
Baldwin, Randy, Cleveland	1	1	0	0	1	0
Ball, Eric, Cincinnati	1	1	0	0	1	0
Ball, Jerry, Raiders	0	0	1	0	1	0
Barnett, Harlon, N.E.	0	0	2	7	2	0
Bates, Michael, Seattle	3	0	0	0	0	0
Bates, Patrick, Raiders	0	0	2	0	2	0
Baty, Greg, Miami	1	0	0	0	0	0
Baxter, Fred, N.Y. Jets	0	0	1	0	1	0
Beebe, Don, Buffalo	3	0	0	0	0	0
Bennett, Cornelius, Buffalo	0	0	3	14	3	0
Bennett, Donnell, K.C.	2	1	0	0	1	0
Bennett, Tony, Indianapolis	0	0	1	75	1	1
Bieniemy, Eric, San Diego	1	1	0	0	1	0
Birden, J.J., Kansas City	1	1	0	0	1	0
Bishop, Blaine, Houston	0	0	1	0	1	0
Blackmon, Robert, Seattle	0	0	3	18	3	0
Blades, Brian, Seattle	1	2	0	0	2	0
Blake, Jeff, Cincinnati	6	0	0	-5	0	0
Bledsoe, Drew, New England	9	3	0	-5	3	0
Booker, Vaughn, K.C.	0	0	2	6	2	0
Bowens, Tim, Miami	0	0	1	0	1	0
Bradford, Ronnie, Denver	0	1	1	0	2	0
Brewer, Dewell, Indianapolis	3	0	0	0	0	0
Brilz, Darrick, Cincinnati	0	1	0	0	1	0
Brim, Mike, Cincinnati	0	0	1	1	1	0
Brisby, Vincent, N.E.	1	0	0	0	0	0
Brooks, Bucky, Buffalo	1	0	1	0	1	0
Brooks, Bill, Buffalo	1	0	0	0	0	0
Broussard, Steve, Cincinnati	5	1	0	0	1	0
Brown, Gary, Houston	6	0	0	0	0	0
Brown, James, N.Y. Jets	0	1	0	0	1	0
Brown, Tim, Raiders	3	0	0	0	0	0
Brown, Troy, New England	2	2	0	0	2	0
Brown, Vincent, N.E.	0	0	1	5	1	0
Buchanan, Ray, Indianapolis	0	0	1	0	1	0
Buckner, Brentson, Pit.	0	0	1	0	1	0
Burnett, Rob, Cleveland	0	0	1	0	1	0
Burris, Jeff, Buffalo	2	1	0	0	1	0
Bush, Lewis, San Diego	0	0	1	0	1	0
Butts, Marion, New England	1	1	0	0	1	0
Cadrez, Glenn, N.Y. Jets	0	1	0	0	1	0
Camarillo, Rich, Houston	1	1	0	0	1	0
Campbell, Jeff, Denver	0	1	0	0	1	0
Carlson, Cody, Houston	6	1	0	0	1	0
Carrier, Mark, Cleveland	1	1	0	0	1	0
Carrington, Darren, S.D.	0	0	2	0	2	0
Carswell, Dwayne, Denver	0	1	0	0	1	0
Carter, Dale, Kansas City	1	0	0	0	1	0
Cash, Kerry, Indianapolis	1	1	0	0	1	0
Christie, Steve, Buffalo	0	0	1	0	1	0
Clark, Derrick, Denver	1	0	0	0	0	0

Player, Team	Fum.	Own Rec.	Opp. Rec.	Yds.	Tot. Rec.	TD
Clark, Reggie, Pittsburgh	0	0	1	0	1	0
Clifton, Kyle, N.Y. Jets	0	0	1	0	1	0
Coates, Ben, New England	2	2	0	0	2	0
Coleman, Andre, San Diego	3	1	0	0	1	0
Coleman, Marco, Miami	0	0	1	0	1	0
Collins, Mark, Kansas City	0	0	2	0	2	0
Coryatt, Quentin, Ind.	0	0	1	78	1	1
Crafts, Jerry, Buffalo	0	2	0	0	2	0
Craver, Aaron, Miami	1	1	0	0	1	0
Criswell, Jeff, N.Y. Jets	0	1	0	0	1	0
Crittenden, Ray, N.E.	1	1	0	0	1	0
Crockett, Ray, Denver	0	0	2	43	2	0
Croom, Corey, New England	1	0	0	0	0	0
Cross, Jeff, Miami	0	0	1	0	1	0
Davis, Kenneth, Buffalo	3	0	0	0	0	0
Davis, Reuben, Miami	0	0	1	0	1	0
Davis, Willie, Kansas City	1	0	0	0	0	0
Dawkins, Sean, Indianapolis	1	0	0	0	0	0
Dawson, Doug, Cleveland	0	1	0	0	1	0
Dawson, Lake, Kansas City	1	0	0	0	0	0
Dellenbach, Jeff, Miami	1	0	0	-11	0	0
Dickerson, Ron, Kansas City	1	0	0	0	0	0
Dishman, Cris, Houston	0	0	1	29	1	0
Donaldson, Ray, Seattle	2	0	0	-3	0	0
Dumas, Mike, Buffalo	0	2	0	40	2	0
Edmunds, Ferrell, Seattle	1	0	0	0	0	0
Elliott, Lin, Kansas City	0	0	1	0	1	0
Elway, John, Denver	11	2	0	-5	2	0
Emtman, Steve, Ind.	0	0	1	0	1	0
Esiason, Boomer, NYJ	11	3	0	-11	3	0
Evans, Donald, N.Y. Jets	0	0	1	0	1	0
Evans, Vince, Raiders	2	1	0	0	1	0
Faulk, Marshall, Ind.	5	1	0	0	1	0
Fenner, Derrick, Cin.	6	1	0	0	1	0
Fields, Jaime, Kansas City	0	0	1	0	1	0
Figures, Deon, Pittsburgh	0	1	0	0	1	0
Flannery, John, Houston	0	2	0	0	2	0
Fletcher, Simon, Denver	0	0	2	0	2	0
Frank, Donald, Raiders	0	0	1	30	1	0
Frase, Paul, N.Y. Jets	0	0	1	0	1	0
Fryar, Irving, Miami	0	1	0	7	1	0
Gardner, Carwell, Buffalo	1	0	0	0	0	0
Gary, Cleveland, Miami	1	0	0	0	0	0
Gash, Sam, New England	1	1	0	0	1	0
Givins, Ernest, Houston	3	3	0	0	3	0
Glenn, Aaron, N.Y. Jets	2	1	0	0	1	0
Goad, Tim, New England	0	0	1	8	1	0
Gordon, Darrien, S.D.	2	1	2	15	3	0
Grant, Stephen, Indianapolis	0	0	1	2	1	0
Gray, Chris, Miami	0	1	0	0	1	0
Green, Eric, Pittsburgh	2	0	0	0	0	0
Green, Harold, Cincinnati	1	1	0	0	1	0
Green, Paul, Seattle	1	1	0	0	1	0
Green, Victor, N.Y. Jets	0	0	1	0	1	0
Greene, Kevin, Pittsburgh	0	0	3	0	3	0
Griffin, Don, Cleveland	1	0	3	15	3	0
Grow, Monty, Kansas City	1	0	0	0	0	0
Guyton, Myron, N.E.	0	0	3	34	3	0
Habib, Brian, Denver	0	1	0	0	1	0
Hannah, Travis, Houston	1	0	0	0	0	0
Harbaugh, Jim, Indianapolis	0	0	0	0	0	0
Hardy, Adrian, Cincinnati	0	0	1	0	1	0
Harmon, Ronnie, San Diego	0	1	0	0	1	0
Harris, Ronnie, New England	1	0	0	0	0	0
Harrison, Nolan, Raiders	0	0	2	0	2	0
Harrison, Rodney, San Diego	0	1	0	0	1	0
Harvey, Richard, Denver	0	0	1	0	1	0
Hasty, James, N.Y. Jets	0	0	2	0	2	0
Hayes, Jonathan, Pittsburgh	1	0	0	0	0	0
Hendrickson, Steve, S.D.	0	0	1	0	1	0
Henry, Kevin, Pittsburgh	0	0	1	0	1	0
Hicks, Clifford, N.Y. Jets	5	2	0	0	2	0
Higgs, Mark, Miami	1	0	0	0	0	0
Hill, Greg, Kansas City	1	0	0	0	0	0
Hoard, Leroy, Cleveland	8	0	0	0	0	0

FUMBLES

Player, Team	Fum.	Own Rec.	Opp. Rec.	Yds.	Tot. Rec.	TD
Hopkins, Brad, Houston	0	1	0	0	1	0
Hoskins, Derrick, Raiders	0	0	1	0	1	0
Hostetler, Jeff, Raiders	10	0	0	-9	0	0
Houston, Bobby, N.Y. Jets	0	0	1	0	1	0
Hull, Kent, Buffalo	1	0	0	-19	0	0
Humphrey, Ronald, Ind.	4	1	0	0	1	0
Humphries, Leonard, Ind.	0	1	0	0	1	0
Humphries, Stan, San Diego	6	2	0	-9	2	0
Ingram, Mark, Miami	1	1	0	0	1	0
Jackson, John, Pittsburgh	0	2	0	0	2	0
Jackson, Keith, Miami	2	1	0	0	1	0
Jackson, Tyoka, Miami	0	0	1	0	1	0
Jamison, George, K.C.	0	0	3	22	3	0
Jett, James, Raiders	0	2	0	15	2	0
Johnson, Charles, Pit.	2	0	0	0	0	0
Johnson, Johnny, N.Y. Jets	4	0	0	0	0	0
Johnson, Pepper, Cleveland	0	0	1	10	1	0
Johnson, Tracy, Seattle	1	0	0	0	0	0
Johnson, Bill, Cleveland	0	0	1	0	1	0
Jones, Aaron, New England	1	0	3	28	3	0
Jones, Gary, Pittsburgh	0	0	1	0	1	0
Jones, Henry, Buffalo	0	0	1	0	1	0
Jones, James, Cleveland	0	0	2	0	2	0
Jones, Mike, New England	0	0	1	0	1	0
Jones, Roger, Cincinnati	1	0	0	0	0	0
Jones, Rondell, Denver	0	0	1	0	1	0
Jones, Tony, Cleveland	0	1	0	0	1	0
Jourdain, Yonel, Buffalo	1	0	0	0	0	0
Kelly, Jim, Buffalo	11	2	0	-19	2	0
Kennedy, Cortez, Seattle	0	0	1	0	1	0
Kinchen, Brian, Cleveland	1	0	0	0	0	0
Kirby, Terry, Miami	2	0	0	0	0	0
Klingler, David, Cin.	7	1	0	0	1	0
Lageman, Jeff, N.Y. Jets	0	0	3	0	3	0
Lake, Carnell, Pittsburgh	0	0	1	0	1	0
Langham, Antonio, Cle.	1	0	0	0	0	0
Lathon, Lamar, Houston	0	0	1	0	1	0
Lee, Shawn, San Diego	0	0	1	0	1	0
Lewis, Mo, N.Y. Jets	0	0	1	11	1	0
Lloyd, Greg, Pittsburgh	0	0	1	0	1	0
Lodish, Mike, Buffalo	0	0	1	0	1	1
Lott, Ronnie, N.Y. Jets	0	0	1	0	1	0
Lowdermilk, Kirk, Ind.	1	0	0	-4	0	0
Maddox, Mark, Buffalo	0	0	1	0	1	0
Majkowski, Don, Ind.	5	2	0	-14	2	0
Manusky, Greg, K.C.	0	1	1	0	2	0
Marino, Dan, Miami	9	3	0	-4	3	0
Martin, Kelvin, Seattle	2	1	0	0	1	0
Martin, Tony, San Diego	2	0	0	0	0	0
Matthews, Bruce, Houston	2	0	0	-9	0	0
Mawae, Kevin, Seattle	0	1	0	0	1	0
McCoy, Tony, Indianapolis	0	0	1	0	1	0
McDaniel, Terry, Raiders	0	0	3	48	3	1
McDaniels, Pellom, K.C.	0	0	1	0	1	0
McDonald, Devon, Ind.	0	1	0	0	1	0
McDowell, Bubba, Houston	0	0	1	0	1	0
McDuffie, O.J., Miami	3	1	0	0	1	0
McGinest, Willie, N.E.	0	0	2	0	2	0
McGlockton, Chester, Raiders	0	0	1	0	1	0
McGwire, Dan, Seattle	9	3	0	-7	3	0
McNair, Todd, Houston	0	0	1	0	1	0
Means, Natrone, San Diego	5	0	0	0	0	0
Mecklenburg, Karl, Denver	0	0	2	0	2	0
Metcalf, Eric, Cleveland	6	0	0	0	0	0
Mickell, Darren, K.C.	0	0	1	0	1	0
Milburn, Glyn, Denver	4	1	0	0	1	0
Millen, Hugh, Denver	2	0	0	0	0	0
Mills, Ernie, Pittsburgh	1	0	0	0	0	0
Mills, John Henry, Hou.	1	0	0	0	0	0
Mims, Chris, San Diego	0	0	2	0	2	0
Mirer, Rick, Seattle	2	1	0	-7	1	0
Mitchell, Johnny, N.Y. Jets	1	1	0	4	1	0
Montana, Joe, Kansas City	7	1	0	-6	1	0
Montgomery, Glenn, Hou.	0	0	3	-2	3	0
Montgomery, Tyrone, Raiders	2	0	0	0	0	0
Moore, Rob, N.Y. Jets	0	1	0	0	1	0
Moore, Stevon, Cleveland	0	2	3	3	5	0
Morris, Bam, Pittsburgh	3	1	0	0	1	0
Murrell, Adrian, N.Y. Jets	1	0	0	0	0	0
Nagle, Browning, Ind.	2	0	0	0	0	0
O'Donnell, Neil, Pit.	4	1	0	0	1	0
Oliver, Louis, Cincinnati	1	0	0	0	0	0
O'Neal, Leslie, San Diego	0	0	1	0	1	0
Parmalee, Bernie, Miami	5	2	1	20	3	0
Patton, Marvcus, Buffalo	1	1	0	0	1	0
Perry, Darren, Pittsburgh	0	0	2	0	2	0
Phillips, Joe, Kansas City	0	0	1	0	1	0
Pickens, Carl, Cincinnati	1	1	0	0	1	0
Pitts, Mike, New England	0	0	2	8	2	0
Potts, Roosevelt, Ind.	5	1	0	0	1	0
Pritchard, Mike, Denver	1	0	0	0	0	0
Reed, Andre, Buffalo	3	2	0	0	2	0
Reich, Frank, Buffalo	1	1	0	0	1	0
Reynolds, Ricky, N.E.	0	1	2	25	3	1
Richardson, Bucky, Houston	7	3	0	-2	3	0
Rivers, Reggie, Denver	1	0	1	0	1	0
Robertson, Marcus, Houston	1	1	0	0	1	0
Robinson, Ed, Pittsburgh	0	1	0	0	1	0
Robinson, Eugene, Seattle	0	0	1	0	1	0
Robinson, Rafael, Seattle	0	0	1	0	1	0
Russell, Leonard, Denver	4	0	0	0	0	0
Rypien, Mark, Cleveland	2	0	0	-1	0	0
Sadowski, Troy, Cincinnati	0	1	0	0	1	0
Saleaumua, Dan, K.C.	0	0	1	0	1	0
Sawyer, Corey, Cincinnati	2	0	1	0	1	0
Scrafford, Kirk, Denver	0	1	0	0	1	0
Seals, Ray, Pittsburgh	0	0	2	0	2	0
Seau, Junior, San Diego	0	0	3	0	3	0
Sharpe, Shannon, Denver	1	0	0	0	0	0
Shields, Will, Kansas City	0	1	0	0	1	0
Simien, Tracy, Kansas City	0	0	2	0	2	0
Sims, Keith, Miami	0	1	1	0	2	0
Singleton, Chris, Miami	0	0	2	2	2	0
Siragusa, Tony, Indianapolis	0	0	1	0	1	0
Slaughter, Webster, Houston	2	1	0	0	1	0
Smith, Al, Houston	0	0	1	0	1	0
Smith, Anthony, Raiders	0	0	1	25	1	1
Smith, Bruce, Buffalo	0	0	2	0	2	0
Smith, Dennis, Denver	0	0	1	0	1	0
Smith, Neil, Kansas City	0	0	1	6	1	0
Spikes, Irving, Miami	1	0	0	0	0	0
Staysniak, Joe, Ind.	1	2	0	-18	2	0
Stephens, Rod, Seattle	0	0	2	0	2	0
Stewart, Michael, Miami	0	0	1	0	1	0
Strong, Mack, Seattle	1	0	0	0	0	0
Sweeney, Jim, N.Y. Jets	0	1	0	0	1	0
Talley, Darryl, Buffalo	0	0	1	2	1	0
Taylor, Jay, Kansas City	0	0	1	0	1	0
Teeter, Mike, Houston	1	0	0	0	0	0
Terry, Doug, Kansas City	0	0	3	12	3	0
Testaverde, Vinny, Cle.	3	2	0	2	2	0
Thomas, Derrick, K.C.	0	0	3	11	3	0
Thomas, Thurman, Buffalo	1	2	0	0	2	0
Thompson, Bennie, Cle.	0	0	1	0	1	0
Thompson, Leroy, N.E.	2	1	0	0	1	0
Thornton, James, N.Y. Jets	0	0	2	0	2	0
Tillman, Cedric, Denver	1	0	0	0	0	0
Tillman, Spencer, Houston	1	1	1	0	2	0
Tolliver, Billy Joe, Hou.	7	0	0	-3	0	0
Tomczak, Mike, Pittsburgh	2	0	0	-1	0	0
Toner, Ed, Indianapolis	0	0	1	0	1	0
Tovar, Steve, Cincinnati	0	0	2	0	2	0
Trudeau, Jack, N.Y. Jets	2	1	0	-1	1	0
Turner, Eric, Cleveland	0	0	1	0	1	0
Turner, Floyd, Indianapolis	1	1	0	0	1	0
Turner, Marcus, N.Y. Jets	0	0	1	0	1	0
Turner, Kevin, New England	4	1	1	-3	2	0
Vaughn, Jon, Seattle	3	0	0	0	0	0
Walker, Derrick, K.C.	1	0	0	0	0	0
Warren, Chris, Seattle	5	2	0	0	2	0

Player, Team	Fum.	Own Rec.	Opp. Rec.	Yds.	Tot. Rec.	TD
Warren, Terrence, Seattle	0	0	1	0	1	0
Washington, Brian, NYJ	0	0	3	0	3	0
Washington, Marvin, NYJ	1	0	1	0	1	0
Washington, Mickey, Buf.	0	0	1	0	1	0
Wellman, Gary, Houston	1	0	0	0	0	0
Whigham, Larry, N.E.	1	0	0	0	0	0
White, Dwayne, N.Y. Jets	0	1	0	0	1	0
White, Lorenzo, Houston	2	0	1	-1	1	0
Whitley, Curtis, San Diego	0	1	0	0	1	0
Whitmore, David, K.C.	0	0	1	0	1	0
Widell, Dave, Denver	1	0	0	-1	0	0
Wilkerson, Bruce, Raiders	0	1	0	0	1	0
Williams, Alfred, Cincinnati	0	0	1	0	1	0
Williams, Darryl, Cincinnati	0	0	2	0	2	0
Williams, David W., Houston	0	1	0	0	1	0
Williams, Gerald, Pittsburgh	0	0	1	0	1	1
Williams, Harvey, Raiders	4	2	0	0	2	0
Williams, Jamie, Raiders	1	0	0	0	1	0
Williams, Wally, Cleveland	0	1	0	0	1	0
Winter, Blaise, San Diego	0	0	1	0	1	0
Wolford, Will, Indianapolis	0	0	1	0	1	0
Wooden, Terry, Seattle	0	0	2	2	2	0
Woodson, Rod, Pittsburgh	2	1	0	0	1	0
Wortham, Barron, Houston	0	0	1	0	1	0
Wright, Alexander, Raiders	0	1	0	0	1	0
Zgonina, Jeff, Pittsburgh	1	1	0	0	1	0

NFC

Player, Team	Fum.	Own Rec.	Opp. Rec.	Yds.	Tot. Rec.	TD
Adams, Scott, New Orleans	0	1	0	0	1	0
Aikman, Troy, Dallas	2	2	0	0	2	0
Alexander, David, Phi.	0	1	0	0	1	0
Alexander, Harold, Atlanta	0	1	0	0	1	0
Allen, Eric, Philadelphia	0	0	1	30	1	0
Allen, Terry, Minnesota	3	2	0	4	2	0
Anderson, Willie, L.A. Rams	0	1	0	7	1	0
Armstrong, Tyji, Tampa Bay	2	1	0	0	1	0
Bailey, Carlton, N.Y. Giants	0	0	1	2	1	0
Bailey, Johnny, L.A. Rams	2	0	0	0	0	0
Bailey, Robert, L.A. Rams	0	1	0	0	1	0
Bankston, Michael, Arizona	0	0	1	2	1	0
Barker, Roy, Minnesota	0	0	1	0	1	0
Barnett, Fred, Philadelphia	1	0	0	0	0	0
Bates, Mario, New Orleans	3	1	0	0	1	0
Bayless, Martin, Was.	0	0	1	60	1	1
Beamon, Willie, N.Y. Giants	0	0	2	0	2	0
Beckles, Ian, Tampa Bay	0	1	1	0	2	0
Belin, Chuck, L.A. Rams	0	1	0	0	1	0
Bennett, Edgar, Green Bay	1	1	0	0	1	0
Bettis, Jerome, L.A. Rams	5	3	0	0	3	0
Beuerlein, Steve, Arizona	8	3	0	-13	3	0
Bishop, Greg, N.Y. Giants	0	1	1	0	2	0
Blades, Bennie, Detroit	0	1	1	0	2	0
Booty, John, N.Y. Giants	0	1	1	5	2	0
Bouwens, Shawn, Detroit	1	3	0	0	3	0
Brady, Ed, Tampa Bay	0	0	1	0	1	0
Brooks, Michael, NYG	1	0	3	0	3	0
Brooks, Reggie, Washington	3	0	0	0	0	0
Brooks, Robert, Green Bay	4	1	0	0	1	0
Brown, Dave, N.Y. Giants	11	4	0	-15	4	0
Brown, Derek, New Orleans	4	2	0	0	2	0
Brown, Derek, N.Y. Giants	0	0	1	0	1	0
Brown, Richard, Minnesota	0	1	0	0	1	0
Brunell, Mark, Green Bay	1	0	0	-2	0	0
Buck, Vince, New Orleans	0	0	1	0	1	0
Buckley, Curtis, Tampa Bay	1	1	1	0	2	0
Buckley, Terrell, Green Bay	0	0	1	0	1	0
Bussey, Barney, Tampa Bay	0	0	1	0	1	0
Cain, Joe, Chicago	0	0	1	0	1	0
Calloway, Chris, N.Y. Giants	1	0	0	0	0	0
Campbell, Jesse, N.Y. Giants	0	0	2	3	2	0
Carter, Cris, Minnesota	4	0	0	0	0	0

Player, Team	Fum.	Own Rec.	Opp. Rec.	Yds.	Tot. Rec.	TD
Carter, Dexter, S.F.	2	2	0	0	2	0
Centers, Larry, Arizona	2	2	0	27	2	0
Chandler, Chris, L.A. Rams	3	0	0	-10	0	0
Cobb, Reggie, Green Bay	1	0	0	0	0	0
Coleman, Lincoln, Dallas	2	0	0	0	0	0
Collins, Andre, Washington	0	0	1	16	1	0
Conner, Darion, New Orleans	0	0	1	0	1	0
Conway, Curtis, Chicago	2	1	0	0	1	0
Cook, Marv, Chicago	0	1	0	0	1	0
Cooper, Adrian, Minnesota	2	1	0	0	1	0
Cross, Howard, N.Y. Giants	0	1	0	1	1	0
Culpepper, Brad, Tampa Bay	0	0	1	0	1	0
Cunningham, Randall, Phi.	10	2	0	-15	2	0
Dafney, Bernard, Minnesota	0	1	0	0	1	0
Dalman, Chris, S.F.	1	0	0	-3	0	0
Davis, Dexter, L.A. Rams	0	1	0	0	1	0
Davis, Eric, San Francisco	1	0	2	0	2	0
Del Rio, Jack, Minnesota	0	0	2	0	2	0
Dilfer, Trent, Tampa Bay	2	0	0	0	0	0
Dimry, Charles, Tampa Bay	0	0	1	0	1	0
Douglass, Maurice, Chicago	0	0	1	0	1	0
Downs, Gary, N.Y. Giants	1	0	0	0	0	0
Dye, Ernest, Arizona	0	1	0	0	1	0
Edwards, Dixon, Dallas	0	0	1	21	1	0
Ellard, Henry, Washington	1	0	0	0	0	0
Erickson, Craig, Tampa Bay	6	1	0	-1	1	0
Ervins, Ricky, Washington	1	0	0	0	0	0
Evans, Byron, Philadelphia	0	0	1	0	1	0
Evans, Doug, Green Bay	0	0	1	3	1	0
Everett, Jim, New Orleans	3	0	0	-2	0	0
Everett, Thomas, T.B.	0	0	1	0	1	0
Fann, Chad, Arizona	1	0	0	0	0	0
Favre, Brett, Green Bay	7	1	0	-2	1	0
Flores, Mike, Philadelphia	0	0	1	0	1	0
Frazier, Derrick, Phi.	0	0	1	3	1	0
Frerotte, Gus, Washington	4	2	0	-4	2	0
Friesz, John, Washington	2	1	0	0	1	0
Fuller, William, Phi.	0	0	1	0	1	0
Gardner, Moe, Atlanta	0	0	1	0	1	0
Garner, Charlie, Phi.	3	0	0	0	0	0
Garnett, Dave, Minnesota	0	0	2	0	2	0
Garrett, Jason, Dallas	0	1	0	0	1	0
Gayle, Shaun, Chicago	0	0	1	9	1	0
Gedney, Chris, Chicago	1	0	0	0	0	0
George, Jeff, Atlanta	12	6	0	-12	6	0
George, Ron, Atlanta	0	0	1	0	1	0
Gesek, John, Washington	0	1	0	0	1	0
Goeas, Leo, L.A. Rams	0	1	0	0	1	0
Graham, Jeff, Chicago	1	1	0	0	1	0
Graham, Kent, N.Y. Giants	2	1	0	0	1	0
Gray, Mel, Detroit	3	2	0	13	2	0
Grbac, Elvis, San Francisco	5	0	0	-2	0	0
Green, Robert, Chicago	1	0	1	0	1	0
Gruber, Paul, Tampa Bay	0	1	0	0	1	0
Guliford, Eric, Minnesota	1	0	0	0	0	0
Hager, Britt, Philadelphia	0	0	1	0	1	0
Hall, Rhett, San Francisco	0	0	1	0	1	0
Hall, Ron, Detroit	1	0	0	0	0	0
Hamilton, Keith, NYG	0	1	2	0	3	0
Hampton, Rodney, NYG	0	1	0	0	1	0
Hanks, Merton, S.F.	1	1	1	0	2	0
Harmon, Andy, Philadelphia	0	0	2	0	2	0
Harper, Alvin, Dallas	2	0	0	0	0	0
Harris, Corey, Green Bay	1	1	0	0	1	0
Harris, James, Minnesota	2	0	3	18	3	1
Harris, Odie, Arizona	0	0	1	0	1	0
Harris, Rudy, Tampa Bay	1	0	0	0	0	0
Harris, Raymont, Chicago	1	2	1	0	3	0
Harvey, Ken, Washington	0	0	1	0	1	0
Haynes, Michael, N.O.	1	0	0	0	0	0
Hebert, Bobby, Atlanta	2	0	0	-5	0	0
Henderson, Othello, N.O.	0	0	2	0	2	0
Hennings, Chad, Dallas	0	0	1	0	1	0
Hester, Jessie, L.A. Rams	1	0	0	0	0	0
Heyward, Craig, Atlanta	5	2	0	0	2	0

Player, Team	Fum.	Own Rec.	Opp. Rec.	Yds.	Tot. Rec.	TD
Hoage, Terry, Arizona	0	0	2	4	2	0
Hollinquest, Lamont, Was.	0	0	1	0	1	0
Holman, Rodney, Detroit	1	2	0	-4	2	0
Holmes, Clayton, Dallas	1	0	0	0	0	0
Holmes, Lester, Phi.	0	3	0	0	3	0
Holt, Pierce, Atlanta	0	0	1	0	1	0
Howard, Erik, N.Y. Giants	0	0	1	0	1	0
Hughes, Tyrone, N.O.	7	1	2	128	3	2
Irving, Terry, Arizona	0	0	1	0	1	0
Ismail, Qadry, Minnesota	2	0	1	1	1	0
Jack, Eric, Atlanta	0	0	1	27	1	1
Jackson, Rickey, S.F.	0	0	2	5	2	0
Jenkins, Carlos, Minnesota ..	0	0	2	0	2	0
Johnson, D.J., Atlanta	0	0	2	15	2	0
Johnson, Joe, New Orleans	0	0	1	0	1	0
Johnson, Keshon, Green Bay	0	0	1	0	1	0
Johnson, Maurice, Phi.	1	1	0	0	1	0
Johnson, Mike, Detroit	0	0	1	0	1	0
Johnston, Daryl, Dallas	2	0	0	0	0	0
Jones, Brent, San Francisco.	1	1	0	0	1	0
Jones, Dante, Chicago	0	0	2	0	2	0
Jones, Sean, Green Bay	0	0	3	0	3	0
Jones, Jimmie, L.A. Rams	0	0	1	0	1	0
Jones, Robert, Dallas	0	0	1	0	1	0
Jordan, Andrew, Minnesota..	1	1	0	0	1	0
Jordan, Charles, Green Bay ..	1	0	0	0	0	0
Joseph, James, Philadelphia	1	1	0	0	1	0
Kelly, Joe, L.A. Rams	0	0	1	0	1	0
Kennard, Derek, Dallas	1	0	0	0	0	0
Kennedy, Lincoln, Atlanta	0	1	0	0	1	0
Kinchen, Todd, L.A. Rams	5	0	0	0	0	0
Koonce, George, Green Bay	0	0	2	0	2	0
Kramer, Erik, Chicago	3	2	0	-5	2	0
Krieg, Dave, Detroit	4	2	0	-1	2	0
Lang, David, L.A. Rams	2	0	0	0	0	0
LeBel, Harper, Atlanta	1	0	0	-5	0	0
Lee, Amp, Minnesota	1	1	0	0	1	0
Lee, Carl, New Orleans	0	0	1	0	1	0
Legette, Tyrone, N.O.	1	0	0	0	0	0
Lester, Tim, L.A. Rams	1	1	0	0	1	0
Levy, Chuck, Arizona	0	1	0	0	1	0
Lewis, Nate, Chicago	1	0	0	0	0	0
Lewis, Thomas, N.Y. Giants..	2	2	0	0	2	0
Lumpkin, Sean, New Orleans	0	0	1	0	1	0
Lyght, Todd, L.A. Rams	0	0	1	74	1	1
Malone, Van, Detroit	1	0	0	0	0	0
Mann, Charles, S.F.	0	0	1	0	1	0
Marshall, Arthur, NYG	1	0	0	0	0	0
Marshall, Wilber, Arizona	0	0	1	0	1	0
Marts, Lonnie, Tampa Bay	0	0	2	0	2	0
Maryland, Russell, Dallas	0	0	1	0	1	0
Massey, Robert, Detroit	1	0	0	0	0	0
Mathis, Terance, Atlanta	0	1	0	0	1	0
Matthews, Aubrey, Detroit..	1	0	0	0	0	0
Mayberry, Tony, Tampa Bay	0	1	0	0	1	0
Mayhew, Martin, T.B.	0	0	1	0	1	0
McAfee, Fred, Arizona	1	0	0	0	0	0
McCants, Keith, Arizona	0	0	1	0	1	0
McCleskey, J.J., N.O.	0	0	1	0	1	0
McDaniel, Randall, Min.	0	1	0	0	1	0
McDonald, Tim, S.F.	0	0	1	49	1	1
McDowell, Anthony, T.B.	0	1	0	0	1	0
McKenzie, Raleigh, Was.	0	1	0	0	1	0
McMahon, Jim, Arizona	1	0	0	0	0	0
McMichael, Steve, G.B.	0	0	1	0	1	0
McMillian, Mark, Phi.	0	0	1	0	1	0
Meggett, David, NYG	6	4	1	0	5	0
Merritt, David, Arizona	0	0	1	0	1	0
Miller, Chris, L.A. Rams	7	3	0	-5	3	0
Miller, Corey, N.Y. Giants..	0	0	1	0	1	0
Mills, Sam, New Orleans	0	0	1	0	1	0
Miniefield, Kevin, Chi.	0	0	1	-5	1	0
Minter, Barry, Chicago	0	0	1	0	1	0
Mitchell, Brian, Was.	4	0	0	0	0	0
Mitchell, Derrell, N.O.	0	0	1	0	1	0
Mitchell, Scott, Detroit	8	2	0	-5	2	0
Moon, Warren, Minnesota	9	2	0	-5	2	0
Moore, Derrick, Detroit	2	0	0	0	0	0
Moore, Herman, Detroit	1	0	0	0	0	0
Moore, Ron, Arizona	2	1	0	0	1	0
Morgan, Anthony, G.B.	1	0	0	0	0	0
Morrison, Darryl, Was.	0	0	2	32	2	1
Morton, Johnnie, Detroit	1	1	0	0	1	0
Neal, Lorenzo, N.O.	1	0	0	0	0	0
Ned, Derrick, New Orleans	1	0	0	0	0	0
Newberry, Tom, L.A. Rams	0	1	0	0	1	0
Newman, Anthony, L.A. Rams .	0	0	1	0	1	0
O'Neal, Brian, Philadelphia	1	0	0	0	0	0
Palmer, David, Minnesota	2	0	0	0	0	0
Parker, Anthony, Min.	1	1	0	23	1	1
Paup, Bryce, Green Bay	0	1	1	0	2	0
Peete, Rodney, Dallas	3	2	0	-1	2	0
Pegram, Erric, Atlanta	2	1	0	2	1	0
Perriman, Brett, Detroit	1	0	0	0	0	0
Plummer, Gary, S.F.	0	0	1	0	1	0
Porcher, Robert, Detroit	0	0	1	0	1	0
Prior, Mike, Green Bay	3	2	0	0	2	0
Pritchett, Kelvin, Detroit	0	0	1	0	1	0
Proehl, Ricky, Arizona	2	2	0	0	2	0
Randle, John, Minnesota	0	0	2	0	2	0
Rasheed, Kenyon, NYG	1	0	0	0	0	0
Reed, Jake, Minnesota	3	0	0	0	0	0
Reeves, Bryan, Arizona	1	1	1	0	2	0
Rhett, Errict, Tampa Bay	2	1	0	0	1	0
Rice, Jerry, San Francisco	1	0	0	0	0	0
Richards, Dave, Atlanta	0	1	0	0	1	0
Riesenberg, Doug, NYG	0	1	0	0	1	0
Rison, Andre, Atlanta	1	0	0	0	0	0
Roaf, Willie, New Orleans	0	0	1	0	1	0
Robinson, Gerald, L.A. Rams	0	0	1	0	1	0
Robinson, Patrick, Arizona	1	1	0	0	1	0
Roby, Reggie, Washington	1	1	0	0	1	0
Romanowski, Bill, Phi.	0	0	1	0	1	0
Royster, Mazio, Tampa Bay..	1	0	0	0	0	0
Ruettgers, Ken, Green Bay	0	1	0	0	1	0
Sanders, Deion, S.F.	0	1	0	0	1	0
Sanders, Ricky, Atlanta	0	0	1	0	1	0
Sapolu, Jesse, S.F.	0	1	0	0	1	0
Saxon, Mike, Minnesota	1	0	0	0	0	0
Schroeder, Jay, Arizona	5	1	0	-5	1	0
Scroggins, Tracy, Detroit	0	0	1	0	1	0
Sharpe, Sterling, G.B.	1	0	0	0	0	0
Shelley, Elbert, Atlanta	0	1	0	0	1	0
Sheppard, Ashley, Min.	0	0	1	0	1	0
Shuler, Heath, Washington...	3	0	0	-9	0	0
Sims, Joe, Green Bay	0	1	0	0	1	0
Small, Torrance, N.O.	0	0	1	1	1	0
Smith, Cedric, Washington	1	0	0	0	0	0
Smith, Chuck, Atlanta	0	0	2	0	2	0
Smith, Darrin, Dallas	0	0	2	11	2	0
Smith, Emmitt, Dallas	1	0	0	0	0	0
Smith, Tony, Atlanta	1	0	0	0	0	0
Spencer, Jimmy, N.O.	0	0	1	0	1	0
Spielman, Chris, Detroit	0	0	3	25	3	1
Stargell, Tony, Tampa Bay	0	0	1	2	1	0
Stepnoski, Mark, Dallas	4	0	0	-3	0	0
Steussie, Todd, Minnesota...	0	1	0	0	1	0
Stone, Ron, Dallas	0	1	0	0	1	0
Stowe, Tyronne, Was.	1	0	0	0	0	0
Strickland, Fred, G.B.	0	0	1	0	1	0
Swann, Eric, Arizona	0	0	1	10	1	0
Swilling, Pat, Detroit	0	0	1	5	1	0
Sydner, Jeff, Philadelphia	2	0	0	0	0	0
Taylor, John, San Francisco.	1	0	0	0	0	0
Thomas, Broderick, Detroit...	0	0	2	11	2	0
Thomas, Henry, Minnesota	0	0	1	0	1	0
Thompson, Broderick, Phi...	0	1	0	0	1	0
Tillman, Lewis, Chicago	1	0	0	0	0	0
Tippins, Ken, Atlanta	0	0	1	0	1	0
Tolbert, Tony, Dallas	0	0	1	0	1	0

Player, Team	Fum.	Own Rec.	Opp. Rec.	Yds.	Tot. Rec.	TD
Townsend, Greg, Phi.	0	0	1	24	1	0
Tuggle, Jessie, Atlanta	1	0	1	0	1	0
Turner, Vernon, Tampa Bay .	1	1	0	0	1	0
Verdin, Clarence, Atlanta......	3	2	0	0	2	0
Waddle, Tom, Chicago	1	1	0	0	1	0
Walker, Adam, S.F................	0	0	1	0	1	0
Walker, Herschel, Phi...........	4	1	0	0	1	0
Wallace, Steve, S.F...............	0	2	0	0	2	0
Walsh, Steve, Chicago	7	3	0	-8	3	0
Ware, Derek, Arizona	1	1	0	0	1	0
Warren, Frank, New Orleans	0	0	1	0	1	0
Washington, Charles, Atl......	0	1	0	0	1	0
Washington, Dewayne, Min..	0	1	1	17	2	1
Washington, James, Dallas..	0	0	1	0	1	0
Watters, Ricky, S.F.	8	2	0	0	2	0
West, Ed, Green Bay..............	1	0	0	0	0	0
White, Reggie, Green Bay......	0	0	1	0	1	0
Williams, Aeneas, Arizona	0	0	1	0	1	0
Williams, Brian, NYG	2	1	0	-34	1	0

Player, Team	Fum.	Own Rec.	Opp. Rec.	Yds.	Tot. Rec.	TD
Williams, Calvin, Phi.	0	1	0	0	1	0
Williams, James, Arizona	0	0	2	0	2	0
Williams, Kevin, Dallas	4	3	0	0	3	0
Williams, Mark, Green Bay ...	0	1	0	0	1	0
Willis, James, Green Bay	1	1	0	0	1	0
Wilson, Wade, New Orleans..	1	0	0	-7	0	0
Wilson, Marcus, Green Bay ..	1	0	0	0	0	0
Wilson, Karl, Tampa Bay	0	0	1	0	1	0
Winters, Frank, G.B...............	1	1	0	-2	1	0
Woodall, Lee, S.F.................	0	0	1	0	1	0
Woodson, Darren, Dallas......	0	0	1	0	1	0
Woolford, Donnell, Chicago ..	1	0	0	0	0	0
Workman, Vince, T.B.	2	1	0	0	1	0
Worley, Tim, Chicago............	1	0	0	0	0	0
Wright, Toby, L.A. Rams.......	0	0	1	98	1	1
Young, Bryant, S.F................	0	0	1	0	1	0
Young, Steve, S.F.	4	1	0	-4	1	0
Zordich, Mike, Phi.................	0	0	3	5	3	0
Zorich, Chris, Chicago...........	0	0	1	0	1	0

FIELD GOALS

TEAM

AFC

Team	Made	Att.	Pct.	Long
Cleveland	26	28	.929	45
San Diego	34	38	.895	50
N.Y. Jets	20	23	.870	49
Buffalo	24	28	.857	52
Cincinnati	28	33	.848	54
Seattle	20	24	.833	50
Kansas City	25	30	.833	49
Pittsburgh	24	29	.828	50
Denver	30	37	.811	54
Houston	16	20	.800	50
L.A Raiders	22	28	.786	51
Miami	24	31	.774	50
New England	27	35	.771	48
Indianapolis	16	24	.667	50
AFC total	336	408	....	54
AFC average	24.0	29.1	.824	....

Leader based on percentage.

NFC

Team	Made	Att.	Pct.	Long
Minnesota	34	39	.872	51
Atlanta	21	25	.840	50
Philadelphia	21	25	.840	42
N.Y. Giants	22	28	.786	52
L.A. Rams	18	23	.783	47
Dallas	22	29	.759	47
San Francisco	15	20	.750	48
Arizona	22	30	.733	51
Green Bay	19	26	.731	50
Chicago	21	29	.724	52
New Orleans	28	39	.718	48
Washington	20	28	.714	54
Detroit	18	27	.667	49
Tampa Bay	23	35	.657	53
NFC total	304	403	....	54
NFC average	21.7	28.8	.754	....
NFL total	640	811	....	54
NFL average	22.9	29.0	.789	....

INDIVIDUAL

BESTS OF THE SEASON

Field-goal percentage, season
AFC: .929—Matt Stover, Cleveland.
NFC: .872—Fuad Reveiz, Minnesota.

Field goals, season
AFC: 34—John Carney, San Diego.
NFC: 34—Fuad Reveiz, Minnesota.

Field-goal attempts, season
NFC: 39—Morten Andersen, New Orleans; Fuad Reveiz, Minnesota.
AFC: 38—John Carney, San Diego.

Longest field goal
AFC: 54—Jason Elam, Denver at San Diego, Oct. 23; Doug Pelfrey, Cincinnati vs. Philadelphia, Dec. 24.
NFC: 54—Chip Lohmiller, Washington vs. Philadelphia, Oct. 3.

Average yards made, season
AFC: 37.4—Al Del Greco, Houston.
NFC: 34.3—Jason Hanson, Detroit.

NFL LEADERS

Player, Team	Made	Att.	Pct.	Long
Stover, Matt, Cleveland*	26	28	.929	45
Carney, John, San Diego*	34	38	.895	50
Reveiz, Fuad, Minnesota	34	39	.872	51
Lowery, Nick, N.Y. Jets*	20	23	.870	49
Christie, Steve, Buffalo*	24	28	.857	52
Pelfrey, Doug, Cincinnati*	28	33	.848	54
Johnson, Norm, Atlanta	21	25	.840	50
Murray, Eddie, Philadelphia	21	25	.840	42
Elliott, Lin, Kansas City*	25	30	.833	49
Kasay, John, Seattle*	20	24	.833	50

*AFC.
Leader based on percentage, minimum 16 attempts.

AFC

Player, Team	1-19	20-29	30-39	40-49	50 & Over	Totals	Avg. Yds. Att.	Avg. Yds. Made	Avg. Yds. Miss	Long
Anderson, Gary	1-1	7-8	8-9	7-9	1-2	24-29	36.4	35.3	41.6	50
Pittsburgh	1.000	.875	.889	.778	.500	.828				
Bahr, Matt	0-0	14-14	9-12	4-8	0-0	27-34	32.9	30.6	41.9	48
New England	....	1.000	.750	.500	....	.794				
Biasucci, Dean	1-1	5-5	3-7	5-9	2-2	16-24	36.5	35.6	38.3	50
Indianapolis	1.000	1.000	.429	.556	1.000	.667				
Carney, John	0-0	12-12	15-15	5-9	2-2	34-38	35.4	34.1	46.3	50
San Diego	....	1.000	1.000	.556	1.000	.895				
Christie, Steve	0-0	11-12	6-7	5-7	2-2	24-28	34.6	34.0	38.0	52
Buffalo	....	.917	.857	.714	1.000	.857				
Del Greco, Al	0-0	4-5	4-4	7-8	1-3	16-20	39.2	37.4	46.0	50
Houston	....	.800	1.000	.875	.333	.800				
Elam, Jason	0-0	11-11	11-11	7-12	1-3	30-37	36.0	33.4	47.0	54
Denver	....	1.000	1.000	.583	.333	.811				
Elliott, Lin	3-3	15-17	4-6	3-4	0-0	25-30	29.1	28.0	34.2	49
Kansas City	1.000	.882	.667	.750	....	.833				
Jaeger, Jeff	1-1	5-5	6-9	8-11	2-2	22-28	37.1	36.3	40.2	51
L.A. Raiders	1.000	1.000	.667	.727	1.000	.786				

Player, Team	1-19	20-29	30-39	40-49	50 & Over	Totals	Avg. Yds. Att.	Avg. Yds. Made	Avg. Yds. Miss	Long
Kasay, John	1-1	1-1	11-11	6-9	1-2	20-24	37.5	35.6	47.3	50
Seattle	1.000	1.000	1.000	.667	.500	.833				
Lowery, Nick	0-0	8-8	6-7	6-8	0-0	20-23	34.9	34.1	40.0	49
N.Y. Jets	....	1.000	.857	.750	....	.870				
O'Neill, Pat	0-0	0-0	0-0	0-1	0-0	0-1	47.0	....	47.0	0
New England	....	....	....	.000	....	.000				
Pelfrey, Doug	1-1	8-8	8-10	9-10	2-4	28-33	37.5	36.5	43.0	54
Cincinnati	1.000	1.000	.800	.900	.500	.848				
Stover, Matt	1-1	7-7	10-11	8-8	0-1	26-28	33.9	33.3	41.0	45
Cleveland	1.000	1.000	.909	1.000	.000	.929				
Stoyanovich, Pete	1-1	8-8	6-10	8-10	1-2	24-31	35.8	34.2	41.3	50
Miami	1.000	1.000	.600	.800	.500	.774				
AFC totals	10-10	116-121	107-129	88-123	15-25	336-408	35.4	34.0	41.8	54
	1.000	.959	.829	.715	.600	.824				

NFC

Player, Team	1-19	20-29	30-39	40-49	50 & Over	Totals	Avg. Yds. Att.	Avg. Yds. Made	Avg. Yds. Miss	Long
Andersen, Morten	0-0	9-9	11-14	8-10	0-6	28-39	37.3	34.0	45.5	48
New Orleans	....	1.000	.786	.800	.000	.718				
Boniol, Chris	3-3	3-4	10-12	6-9	0-1	22-29	35.0	33.7	39.0	47
Dallas	1.000	.750	.833	.667	.000	.759				
Brien, Doug	1-1	4-4	5-6	5-8	0-1	15-20	36.1	33.7	43.2	48
San Francisco	1.000	1.000	.833	.625	.000	.750				
Butler, Kevin	1-1	7-7	6-9	5-8	2-4	21-29	36.1	33.6	42.9	52
Chicago	1.000	1.000	.667	.625	.500	.724				
Daluiso, Brad	2-2	1-1	5-5	2-2	1-1	11-11	34.0	34.0	....	52
N.Y. Giants	1.000	1.000	1.000	1.000	1.000	1.000				
Davis, Greg	0-0	10-11	3-4	6-7	1-4	20-26	36.4	33.6	45.8	51
Arizona	....	.909	.750	.857	.250	.769				
Hanson, Jason	0-0	6-7	7-7	5-8	0-5	18-27	38.4	34.3	46.6	49
Detroit	....	.857	1.000	.625	.000	.667				
Husted, Michael	0-0	8-8	10-12	4-10	1-5	23-35	37.9	33.0	47.3	53
Tampa Bay	....	1.000	.833	.400	.200	.657				
Jacke, Chris	1-1	11-11	4-6	2-5	1-3	19-26	33.8	30.2	43.7	50
Green Bay	1.000	1.000	.667	.400	.333	.731				
Johnson, Norm	0-0	9-9	7-7	4-4	1-5	21-25	34.7	31.5	51.5	50
Atlanta	....	1.000	1.000	1.000	.200	.840				
Lohmiller, Chip	0-0	9-11	5-6	5-8	1-3	20-28	35.1	33.0	40.4	54
Washington	....	.818	.833	.625	.333	.714				
Murray, Eddie	1-1	8-8	10-10	2-6	0-0	21-25	32.6	30.4	44.3	42
Philadelphia	1.000	1.000	1.000	.333	....	.840				
Peterson, Todd	0-0	1-1	1-1	0-2	0-0	2-4	38.0	32.0	44.0	35
Arizona	....	1.000	1.000	.000	....	.500				
Reveiz, Fuad	0-0	13-13	12-13	8-10	1-3	34-39	35.5	34.0	45.8	51
Minnesota	....	1.000	.923	.800	.333	.872				
Treadwell, David	1-1	5-5	4-7	1-4	0-0	11-17	32.4	28.9	38.7	41
N.Y. Giants	1.000	1.000	.571	.250	....	.647				
Zendejas, Tony	2-2	9-9	6-7	1-5	0-0	18-23	31.2	28.4	41.4	47
L.A. Rams	1.000	1.000	.857	.200	....	.783				
NFC totals	12-12	113-118	106-126	64-106	9-41	304-403	35.4	32.6	44.1	54
	1.000	.958	.841	.604	.220	.754				
NFL totals	22-22	229-239	213-255	152-229	24-66	640-811	35.4	33.3	43.1	54
	1.000	.958	.835	.664	.364	.789				

PUNTING

TEAM

AFC

Team	Total Punts	Yards	Long	Avg.	TB	Blocked	Opp. Ret.	Ret. Yards	Inside 20	Net Avg.
L.A. Raiders	77	3377	65	43.9	15	0	38	366	19	35.2
Cincinnati	80	3461	64	43.3	9	1	43	459	19	35.3
Seattle	91	3905	64	42.9	7	0	43	426	33	36.7
Denver	76	3258	59	42.9	8	0	39	275	23	37.1
Houston	96	4115	58	42.9	9	0	50	438	35	36.4
Kansas City	85	3582	61	42.1	7	0	50	506	15	34.5
N.Y. Jets	84	3534	64	42.1	12	0	38	260	25	36.1
Indianapolis	74	3092	60	41.8	10	1	40	366	22	34.1
Buffalo	67	2799	71	41.8	3	0	38	324	13	36.0
New England	69	2841	67	41.2	6	0	34	260	25	35.7
San Diego	72	2951	59	41.0	4	0	38	348	21	35.0
Miami	60	2412	58	40.2	7	0	32	324	16	32.5
Cleveland	80	3211	65	40.1	8	0	38	220	27	35.4
Pittsburgh	97	3849	64	39.7	6	0	39	263	35	35.7
AFC total	1108	46387	71	....	111	2	560	4835	328	....
AFC average	79.1	3313.4	....	41.9	7.9	0.1	40.0	345.4	23.4	35.5

Leader based on average.

NFC

Team	Total Punts	Yards	Long	Avg.	TB	Blocked	Opp. Ret.	Ret. Yards	Inside 20	Net Avg.
L.A. Rams	78	3494	62	44.8	9	0	47	637	23	34.3
Washington	82	3639	65	44.4	12	0	45	441	21	36.1
New Orleans	67	2920	57	43.6	9	0	40	495	14	33.5
Detroit	64	2782	64	43.5	8	1	36	431	19	34.2
Minnesota	77	3301	67	42.9	5	0	44	410	28	36.2
Dallas	70	2935	58	41.9	4	0	36	378	26	35.4
San Francisco	54	2235	60	41.4	3	0	28	242	18	35.4
Green Bay	81	3351	70	41.4	10	0	36	272	24	35.5
Arizona	98	3997	54	40.8	10	0	40	270	33	36.0
Philadelphia	92	3727	80	40.5	9	0	47	286	29	35.4
N.Y. Giants	89	3578	63	40.2	8	2	39	307	26	35.0
Atlanta	79	3121	61	39.5	6	0	31	273	14	34.5
Tampa Bay	74	2853	53	38.6	6	0	19	103	22	35.5
Chicago	76	2871	57	37.8	9	0	26	225	23	32.4
NFC total	1081	44804	80	....	108	3	514	4770	320	....
NFC average	77.2	3200.3	....	41.4	7.7	0.2	36.7	340.7	22.9	35.0
NFL total	2189	91191	80	....	219	5	1074	9605	648	....
NFL average	78.2	3256.8	....	41.7	7.8	0.2	38.4	343.0	23.1	35.3

INDIVIDUAL

BESTS OF THE SEASON

Average yards per punt, season
NFC: 44.8—Sean Landeta, L.A. Rams.
AFC: 43.9—Jeff Gossett, L.A. Raiders.

Net average yards per punt, season
AFC: 37.1—Tom Rouen, Denver.
NFC: 36.3—Bryan Barker, Philadelphia.

Longest
NFC: 80—Randall Cunningham, Philadelphia at Dallas, Oct. 16.
AFC: 71—Chris Mohr, Buffalo at Indianapolis, Dec. 24.

Punts, season
NFC: 98—Jeff Feagles, Arizona.
AFC: 97—Mark Royals, Pittsburgh.

Punts, game
AFC: 11—Rich Camarillo, Houston vs. Pittsburgh, Nov. 6 (OT) (502 yards); Mark Royals, Pittsburgh at Houston, Nov. 6 (OT) (432 yards); Louie Aguiar, Kansas City vs. San Diego, Nov. 13 (460 yards).
NFC: 10—Reggie Roby, Washington vs. Arizona, Oct. 16 (OT) (448 yards); Craig Hentrich, Green Bay at Minnesota, Oct. 20 (OT) (460 yards); Mike Saxon, Minnesota vs. Green Bay, Oct. 20 (OT) (396 yards); Bryan Barker, Philadelphia at Pittsburgh, Dec. 11 (401 yards).

NFL LEADERS

Player, Team	Net Punts	Yards	Long	Avg.	Total Punts	TB	Blk.	Opp. Ret.	Ret. Yds.	In 20	Net Avg.
Landeta, Sean, L.A. Rams	78	3494	62	44.8	78	9	0	47	637	23	34.3
Roby, Reggie, Washington	82	3639	65	44.4	82	12	0	45	441	21	36.1

Player, Team	Net Punts	Yards	Long	Avg.	Total Punts	TB	Blk.	Opp. Ret.	Ret. Yds.	In 20	Net Avg.
Montgomery, Greg, Detroit	63	2782	64	44.2	64	8	1	36	431	19	34.2
Gossett, Jeff, L.A. Raiders*	77	3377	65	43.9	77	15	0	38	366	19	35.2
Johnson, Lee, Cincinnati*	79	3461	64	43.8	80	9	1	43	459	19	35.3
Barnhardt, Tommy, New Orleans	67	2920	57	43.6	67	9	0	40	495	14	33.5
Tuten, Rick, Seattle*	91	3905	64	42.9	91	7	0	43	426	33	36.7
Saxon, Mike, Minnesota	77	3301	67	42.9	77	5	0	44	410	28	36.2
Rouen, Tom, Denver*	76	3258	59	42.9	76	8	0	39	275	23	37.1
Camarillo, Rich, Houston*	96	4115	58	42.9	96	9	0	50	438	35	36.4

*AFC.
Leader based on average, minimum 40 punts.

AFC

Player, Team	Net Punts	Yards	Long	Avg.	Total Punts	TB	Blk.	Opp. Ret.	Ret. Yds.	In 20	Net Avg.
Aguiar, Louie, Kansas City	85	3582	61	42.1	85	7	0	50	506	15	34.5
Arnold, Jim, Miami	46	1810	53	39.3	46	4	0	26	189	14	33.5
Camarillo, Rich, Houston	96	4115	58	42.9	96	9	0	50	438	35	36.4
Gossett, Jeff, L.A. Raiders	77	3377	65	43.9	77	15	0	38	366	19	35.2
Hansen, Brian, N.Y. Jets	84	3534	64	42.1	84	12	0	38	260	25	36.1
Johnson, Lee, Cincinnati	79	3461	64	43.8	80	9	1	43	459	19	35.3
Kidd, John, San Diego-Miami	21	848	58	40.4	21	4	0	6	135	3	30.1
Mohr, Chris, Buffalo	67	2799	71	41.8	67	3	0	38	324	13	36.0
O'Neill, Pat, New England	69	2841	67	41.2	69	6	0	34	260	25	35.7
Rouen, Tom, Denver	76	3258	59	42.9	76	8	0	39	275	23	37.1
Royals, Mark, Pittsburgh	97	3849	64	39.7	97	6	0	39	263	35	35.7
Stark, Rohn, Indianapolis	73	3092	60	42.4	74	10	1	40	366	22	34.1
Tupa, Tom, Cleveland	80	3211	65	40.1	80	8	0	38	220	27	35.4
Tuten, Rick, Seattle	91	3905	64	42.9	91	7	0	43	426	33	36.7
Wagner, Bryan, San Diego	65	2705	59	41.6	65	3	0	38	348	20	35.3

NFC

Player, Team	Net Punts	Yards	Long	Avg.	Total Punts	TB	Blk.	Opp. Ret.	Ret. Yds.	In 20	Net Avg.
Alexander, Harold, Atlanta	71	2836	61	39.9	71	6	0	27	242	12	34.8
Barker, Bryan, Philadelphia	66	2696	67	40.8	66	7	0	37	158	20	36.3
Barnhardt, Tommy, New Orleans	67	2920	57	43.6	67	9	0	40	495	14	33.5
Berger, Mitch, Philadelphia	25	951	57	38.0	25	2	0	10	128	8	31.3
Brown, Dave, N.Y. Giants	2	57	33	28.5	2	1	0	0	0	1	18.5
Cunningham, Randall, Philadelphia	1	80	80	80.0	1	0	0	0	0	1	80.0
Feagles, Jeff, Arizona	98	3997	54	40.8	98	10	0	40	270	33	36.0
Gardocki, Chris, Chicago	76	2871	57	37.8	76	9	0	26	225	23	32.4
Hentrich, Craig, Green Bay	81	3351	70	41.4	81	10	0	36	272	24	35.5
Horan, Mike, N.Y. Giants	85	3521	63	41.4	87	7	2	39	307	25	35.3
Husted, Michael, Tampa Bay	2	53	32	26.5	2	0	0	1	9	2	22.0
Jett, John, Dallas	70	2935	58	41.9	70	4	0	36	378	26	35.4
Landeta, Sean, L.A. Rams	78	3494	62	44.8	78	9	0	47	637	23	34.3
Montgomery, Greg, Detroit	63	2782	64	44.2	64	8	1	36	431	19	34.2
Roby, Reggie, Washington	82	3639	65	44.4	82	12	0	45	441	21	36.1
Saxon, Mike, Minnesota	77	3301	67	42.9	77	5	0	44	410	28	36.2
Stryzinski, Dan, Tampa Bay	72	2800	53	38.9	72	6	0	18	94	20	35.9
Tyner, Scott, Atlanta	8	285	46	35.6	8	0	0	4	31	2	31.8
Wilmsmeyer, Klaus, San Francisco	54	2235	60	41.4	54	3	0	28	242	18	35.8

PLAYERS WITH TWO CLUBS

Player, Team	Net Punts	Yards	Long	Avg.	Total Punts	TB	Blk.	Opp. Ret.	Ret. Yds.	In 20	Net Avg.
Kidd, John, San Diego	7	246	53	35.1	7	1	0	0	0	1	32.3
Kidd, John, Miami	14	602	58	43.0	14	3	0	6	135	2	29.1

PUNT RETURNS

TEAM

AFC

Team	No.	FC	Yds.	Avg.	Long	TD
San Diego	36	19	475	13.2	t90	2
L.A Raiders	40	14	487	12.2	48	0
Buffalo	33	8	343	10.4	57	0
Cincinnati	37	18	373	10.1	t82	1
Cleveland	46	7	462	10.0	t92	2
Denver	41	4	379	9.2	44	0
Seattle	37	23	337	9.1	31	0
N.Y. Jets	39	5	345	8.8	26	0
New England	46	16	383	8.3	38	0
Indianapolis	42	8	339	8.1	t75	1
Pittsburgh	56	16	424	7.6	42	0
Kansas City	43	13	316	7.3	43	0
Miami	33	17	241	7.3	26	0
Houston	50	12	281	5.6	t78	1
AFC total	579	180	5185	9.0	t92	7
AFC average	41.4	12.9	370.4	9.0	....	0.5

t—touchdown.

NFC

Team	No.	FC	Yds.	Avg.	Long	TD
Washington	32	24	452	14.1	t78	2
N.Y. Giants	32	17	388	12.1	t68	2
L.A. Rams	40	10	461	11.5	t103	1
Detroit	25	12	256	10.2	24	0
Philadelphia	41	18	381	9.3	49	0
Dallas	44	14	404	9.2	t83	1
Tampa Bay	28	8	248	8.9	t80	1
Green Bay	49	18	414	8.4	t85	1
San Francisco	40	13	334	8.4	26	0
Chicago	27	20	218	8.1	t61	1
Arizona	42	13	286	6.8	23	0
Minnesota	39	16	238	6.1	25	0
New Orleans	25	10	152	6.1	35	0
Atlanta	31	16	188	6.1	29	0
NFC total	495	209	4420	8.9	t103	9
NFC average	35.4	14.9	315.7	8.9	....	0.6
NFL total	1074	389	9605	....	t103	16
NFL average	38.4	13.9	343.0	8.9	....	0.6

INDIVIDUAL

BESTS OF THE SEASON

Yards per return, season
NFC: 14.1—Brian Mitchell, Washington.
AFC: 13.2—Darrien Gordon, San Diego.

Yards, season
AFC: 487—Tim Brown, L.A. Raiders.
NFC: 452—Brian Mitchell, Washington.

Yards, game
AFC: 128—Darrien Gordon, San Diego vs. L.A. Rams, Nov. 27 (6 returns, 1 TD).
NFC: 122—Robert Brooks, Green Bay vs. L.A. Rams, Oct. 9 (4 returns, 1 TD).

Longest
NFC: 103—Robert Bailey, L.A. Rams at New Orleans, Oct. 23 (TD).
AFC: 92—Eric Metcalf, Cleveland at Cincinnati, Sept. 4 (TD).

Returns, season
AFC: 42—Dewell Brewer, Indianapolis.
NFC: 41—Patrick Robinson, Arizona.

Returns, game
AFC: 7—Ray Crittenden, New England vs. Green Bay, Oct. 2 (63 yards).
NFC: 7—Robert Brooks, Green Bay at New England, Oct. 2 (34 yards).

Fair catches, season
NFC: 24—Brian Mitchell, Washington.
AFC: 20—Kelvin Martin, Seattle.

Touchdowns, season
AFC: 2—Darrien Gordon, San Diego; Eric Metcalf, Cleveland.
NFC: 2—David Meggett, N.Y. Giants; Brian Mitchell, Washington.

NFL LEADERS

Player, Team	No.	FC	Yds.	Avg.	Long	TD
Mitchell, Brian, Washington	32	24	452	14.1	t78	2
Gordon, Darrien, San Diego*	36	19	475	13.2	t90	2
Meggett, David, N.Y. Giants	26	14	323	12.4	t68	2

Player, Team	No.	FC	Yds.	Avg.	Long	TD
Brown, Tim, L.A. Raiders*	40	14	487	12.2	48	0
Sawyer, Corey, Cincinnati*	26	16	307	11.8	t82	1
Gray, Mel, Detroit	21	12	233	11.1	24	0
Turner, Vernon, Tampa Bay	21	4	218	10.4	t80	1
Burris, Jeff, Buffalo*	32	6	332	10.4	57	0
Metcalf, Eric, Cleveland*	35	6	348	9.9	t92	2
Sydner, Jeff, Philadelphia	40	17	381	9.5	49	0

*AFC.
t—touchdown.
Leader based on average return, minimum 20.

AFC

Player, Team	No.	FC	Yds.	Avg.	Long	TD
Brewer, Dewell, Indianapolis	42	8	339	8.1	t75	1
Brown, Tim, L.A. Raiders	40	14	487	12.2	48	0
Brown, Troy, New England	24	10	202	8.4	38	0
Bryant, Beno, Seattle	1	0	31	31.0	31	0
Burris, Jeff, Buffalo	32	6	332	10.4	57	0
Caldwell, Mike, Cleveland	1	0	2	2.0	2	0
Carrier, Mark, Cleveland	9	1	112	12.4	60	0
Carter, Dale, Kansas City	16	4	124	7.8	42	0
Coleman, Pat, Houston	2	2	13	6.5	10	0
Copeland, Russell, Buffalo	1	2	11	11.0	11	0
Crittenden, Ray, New England	19	6	155	8.2	26	0
Dishman, Cris, Houston	1	0	0	0.0	0	0
Givins, Ernest, Houston	37	9	210	5.7	t78	1
Gordon, Darrien, San Diego	36	19	475	13.2	t90	2
Hannah, Travis, Houston	9	0	58	6.4	13	0
Harris, Ronnie, New England	3	0	26	8.7	12	0
Hastings, Andre, Pittsburgh	2	0	15	7.5	12	0
Hicks, Clifford, N.Y. Jets	38	5	342	9.0	26	0
Hughes, Danan, Kansas City	27	9	192	7.1	43	0
Johnson, Anthony, N.Y. Jets	1	0	3	3.0	3	0
Johnson, Charles, Pittsburgh	15	7	90	6.0	15	0
Jones, Roger, Cincinnati	1	0	0	0.0	0	0
Martin, Kelvin, Seattle	33	20	280	8.5	23	0
McCloughan, Dave, Seattle	3	3	26	8.7	16	0
McDuffie, O.J., Miami	32	15	228	7.1	26	0
Metcalf, Eric, Cleveland	35	6	348	9.9	t92	2
Milburn, Glyn, Denver	41	4	379	9.2	44	0
Miller, Scott, Miami	1	2	13	13.0	13	0
Pickens, Carl, Cincinnati	9	2	62	6.9	16	0
Robertson, Marcus, Houston	1	1	0	0.0	0	0

Player, Team	No.	FC	Yds.	Avg.	Long	TD
Sawyer, Corey, Cincinnati	26	16	307	11.8	t82	1
Turner, Eric, Cleveland	1	0	0	0.0	0	0
Williams, Darryl, Cincinnati..	1	0	4	4.0	4	0
Woodson, Rod, Pittsburgh	39	9	319	8.2	42	0

t—touchdown.

NFC

Player, Team	No.	FC	Yds.	Avg.	Long	TD
Bailey, Johnny, L.A. Rams....	19	4	153	8.1	24	0
Bailey, Robert, L.A. Rams.....	1	0	103	103.0	t103	1
Bailey, Victor, Philadelphia...	0	1	0	....	....	0
Brantley, Chris, L.A. Rams....	3	1	18	6.0	7	0
Brooks, Robert, Green Bay....	40	13	352	8.8	t85	1
Carter, Dexter, San Francisco.	38	12	321	8.4	26	0
Clay, Willie, Detroit..............	3	0	20	6.7	12	0
Conway, Curtis, Chicago.......	8	9	63	7.9	24	0
Everett, Thomas, Tampa Bay..	2	2	2	1.0	1	0
Graham, Jeff, Chicago..........	15	5	140	9.3	t61	1
Gray, Mel, Detroit	21	12	233	11.1	24	0
Guliford, Eric, Minnesota	5	6	14	2.8	12	0
Hawkins, Courtney, T.B.	5	2	28	5.6	9	0
Holmes, Clayton, Dallas	5	1	55	11.0	19	0
Hughes, Tyrone, New Orleans	21	8	143	6.8	35	0
Jordan, Charles, Green Bay ..	1	1	0	0.0	0	0
Kinchen, Todd, L.A. Rams.....	16	5	158	9.9	40	0
Legette, Tyrone, New Orleans.	1	0	0	0.0	0	0
Lewis, Nate, Chicago............	1	3	7	7.0	7	0
Lewis, Thomas, N.Y. Giants..	5	2	64	12.8	35	0
Lyght, Todd, L.A. Rams.........	1	0	29	29.0	27	0
Marshall, Arthur, N.Y. Giants..	1	1	1	1.0	1	0
Massey, Robert, Detroit	1	0	3	3.0	3	0
Meggett, David, N.Y. Giants..	26	14	323	12.4	t68	2
Mitchell, Brian, Washington .	32	24	452	14.1	t78	2
Mitchell, Derrell, New Orleans.	3	2	9	3.0	5	0
O'Neal, Brian, Philadelphia ...	1	0	0	0.0	0	0
Palmer, David, Minnesota.....	30	9	193	6.4	20	0
Parker, Anthony, Minnesota.	4	1	31	7.8	25	0
Prior, Mike, Green Bay	8	4	62	7.8	16	0
Reeves, Bryan, Arizona.........	1	1	1	1.0	1	0
Robinson, Patrick, Arizona ...	41	12	285	7.0	23	0
Singleton, Nate, San Francisco	2	1	13	6.5	8	0
Smith, Tony, Atlanta	8	3	75	9.4	20	0
Sydner, Jeff, Philadelphia	40	17	381	9.5	49	0
Turner, Vernon, Tampa Bay .	21	4	218	10.4	t80	1
Verdin, Clarence, Atlanta......	23	13	113	4.9	29	0
Waddle, Tom, Chicago	3	3	8	2.7	6	0
Williams, Kevin, Dallas	39	13	349	8.9	t83	1

t—touchdown.

KICKOFF RETURNS

TEAM

AFC

Team	No.	Yds.	Avg.	Long	TD
Cleveland	42	1031	24.5	t85	1
San Diego	68	1636	24.1	t90	2
Kansas City	59	1300	22.0	t91	1
L.A Raiders	62	1358	21.9	55	0
Seattle	67	1467	21.9	t93	1
Cincinnati	86	1810	21.0	43	0
Indianapolis	60	1254	20.9	t95	1
Pittsburgh	55	1141	20.7	71	0
Denver	75	1523	20.3	41	0
Miami	66	1294	19.6	46	0
N.Y. Jets	66	1282	19.4	45	0
Houston	74	1436	19.4	44	0
Buffalo	72	1345	18.7	42	0
New England	63	1123	17.8	36	0
AFC total	915	19000	20.8	t95	6
AFC average	65.4	1357.1	20.8	....	0.4

t—touchdown.
Leader based on average.

NFC

Team	No.	Yds.	Avg.	Long	TD
Dallas	50	1284	25.7	t87	1
Washington	71	1685	23.7	86	0
Detroit	71	1675	23.6	t102	4
L.A. Rams	71	1605	22.6	57	0
New Orleans	82	1840	22.4	t98	2
Atlanta	75	1627	21.7	69	0
Minnesota	60	1296	21.6	61	0
Philadelphia	67	1441	21.5	t94	1
San Francisco	58	1244	21.4	t96	1
Chicago	66	1402	21.2	55	0
Green Bay	56	1168	20.9	t96	1
Tampa Bay	70	1422	20.3	77	0
Arizona	57	1079	18.9	53	0
N.Y. Giants	73	1328	18.2	36	0
NFC total	927	20096	21.7	t102	10
NFC average	66.2	1435.4	21.7	....	0.7
NFL total	1842	39096	....	t102	16
NFL average	65.8	1396.3	21.2	....	0.6

INDIVIDUAL

BESTS OF THE SEASON

Yards per return, season
NFC: 28.4—Mel Gray, Detroit.
AFC: 26.9—Randy Baldwin, Cleveland.

Yards, season
NFC: 1556—Tyrone Hughes, New Orleans.
AFC: 1293—Andre Coleman, San Diego.

Yards, game
NFC: 304—Tyrone Hughes, New Orleans vs. L.A. Rams, Oct. 23 (7 returns, 2 TDs).
AFC: 251—Jon Vaughn, Kansas City at Miami, Dec. 12 (4 returns, 1 TD).

Longest
NFC: 102—Mel Gray, Detroit vs. Chicago, Oct. 23 (TD).
AFC: 95—Ronald Humphrey, Indianapolis at Pittsburgh, Sept. 18 (TD).

Returns, season
NFC: 63—Tyrone Hughes, New Orleans.
AFC: 49—Andre Coleman, San Diego.

Returns, game
NFC: 8—Tyrone Hughes, New Orleans vs. San Diego, Oct. 16 (196 yards); Vernon Turner, Tampa Bay vs. Minnesota, Oct. 30 (242 yards).
AFC: 8—Jon Vaughn, Kansas City at Miami, Dec. 12 (251 yards, 1 TD).

Touchdowns, season
NFC: 3—Mel Gray, Detroit.
AFC: 2—Andre Coleman, San Diego; Jon Vaughn, Seattle-Kansas City.

NFL LEADERS

Player, Team	No.	Yds.	Avg.	Long	TD
Gray, Mel, Detroit	45	1276	28.4	t102	3
Walker, Herschel, Philadelphia	21	581	27.7	t94	1

Player, Team	No.	Yds.	Avg.	Long	TD
Baldwin, Randy, Cleveland*	28	753	26.9	t85	1
Williams, Kevin, Dallas	43	1148	26.7	t87	1
Coleman, Andre, San Diego*	49	1293	26.4	t90	2
Mitchell, Brian, Washington	58	1478	25.5	86	0
Vaughn, Jon, Sea.*-K.C.*	33	829	25.1	t93	2
Lewis, Nate, Chicago	35	874	25.0	55	0
Hughes, Tyrone, New Orleans	63	1556	24.7	t98	2
Kinchen, Todd, L.A. Rams	21	510	24.3	46	0

*AFC.
t—touchdown.
Leader based on average return, minimum 20.

AFC

Player, Team	No.	Yds.	Avg.	Long	TD
Anders, Kimble, Kansas City	2	36	18.0	19	0
Anderson, Richie, N.Y. Jets	3	43	14.3	18	0
Baldwin, Randy, Cleveland	28	753	26.9	t85	1
Ball, Eric, Cincinnati	42	915	21.8	43	0
Bates, Michael, Seattle	26	508	19.5	38	0
Baty, Greg, Miami	1	0	0.0	0	0
Baxter, Fred, N.Y. Jets	1	20	20.0	20	0
Beebe, Don, Buffalo	12	230	19.2	35	0
Bennett, Donnell, Kansas City	1	12	12.0	12	0
Bishop, Blaine, Houston	2	18	9.0	11	0
Booker, Vaughn, Kansas City	2	10	5.0	10	0
Braxton, Tyrone, Miami	1	34	34.0	34	0
Brewer, Dewell, Indianapolis	18	358	19.9	34	0
Brooks, Bucky, Buffalo	9	162	18.0	25	0
Broussard, Steve, Cincinnati	7	115	16.4	24	0
Brown, Troy, New England	1	14	14.0	14	0
Bryant, Beno, Seattle	7	136	19.4	38	0
Burke, John, New England	3	11	3.7	6	0
By'not'e, Butler, Denver	24	545	22.7	41	0
Cadrez, Glenn, N.Y. Jets	1	10	10.0	10	0
Campbell, Jeff, Denver	f3	24	8.0	11	0
Carswell, Dwayne, Denver	1	0	0.0	0	0
Clark, Derrick, Denver	3	34	11.3	20	0
Clifton, Kyle, N.Y. Jets	1	13	13.0	13	0
Coleman, Andre, San Diego	49	1293	26.4	t90	2
Copeland, Russell, Buffalo	12	232	19.3	32	0
Crittenden, Ray, New England	24	460	19.2	36	0
Croom, Corey, New England	10	172	17.2	24	0

Player, Team	No.	Yds.	Avg.	Long	TD
Davis, Kenneth, Buffalo	1	0	0.0	0	0
DeOssie, Steve, New England	1	14	14.0	14	0
Dickerson, Ron, Kansas City	21	472	22.5	62	0
Etheredge, Carlos, Indianapolis	2	23	11.5	14	0
Evans, Jerry, Denver	1	6	6.0	6	0
Gardner, Carwell, Buffalo	1	6	6.0	6	0
Gash, Sam, New England	1	9	9.0	9	0
Givins, Ernest, Houston	1	27	27.0	27	0
Glenn, Aaron, N.Y. Jets	27	582	21.6	45	0
Gray, Derwin, Indianapolis	0	4	....	4	0
Green, Harold, Cincinnati	5	113	22.6	31	0
Guyton, Myron, New England	1	-1	-1.0	-1	0
Hannah, Travis, Houston	5	116	23.2	39	0
Hardy, Adrian, Cincinnati	8	185	23.1	42	0
Harmon, Ronnie, San Diego	9	157	17.4	25	0
Hicks, Clifford, N.Y. Jets	2	30	15.0	16	0
Hill, Jeff, Cincinnati	4	97	24.3	40	0
Hoard, Leroy, Cleveland	f2	30	15.0	20	0
Hughes, Danan, Kansas City	9	190	21.1	32	0
Humphrey, Ronald, Indianapolis	35	783	22.4	t95	1
Ingram, Mark, Miami	1	0	0.0	0	0
Ismail, Raghib, L.A. Raiders	43	923	21.5	51	0
Jackson, Mark, Indianapolis	1	5	5.0	5	0
Jackson, Steve, Houston	14	285	20.4	40	0
Johnson, Charles, Pittsburgh	16	345	21.6	71	0
Jourdain, Yonel, Buffalo	27	601	22.3	42	0
Kinchen, Brian, Cleveland	3	38	12.7	15	0
Martin, Kelvin, Seattle	2	30	15.0	16	0
Martin, Tony, San Diego	8	167	20.9	29	0
McDuffie, O.J., Miami	36	767	21.3	46	0
McGee, Tony, Cincinnati	1	4	4.0	4	0
McNair, Todd, Houston	23	481	20.9	44	0
Metcalf, Eric, Cleveland	9	210	23.3	32	0
Milburn, Glyn, Denver	37	793	21.4	40	0
Miller, Scott, Miami	1	13	13.0	13	0
Mills, Ernie, Pittsburgh	2	6	3.0	6	0
Mills, John Henry, Houston	15	282	18.8	34	0
Mitchell, Shannon, San Diego	1	18	18.0	18	0
Morris, Bam, Pittsburgh	4	114	28.5	45	0
Murrell, Adrian, N.Y. Jets	14	268	19.1	37	0
Parker, Vaughn, San Diego	1	1	1.0	1	0
Parmalee, Bernie, Miami	2	0	0.0	0	0
Patton, James, Buffalo	1	1	1.0	1	0
Penn, Chris, Kansas City	9	194	21.6	34	0
Pike, Mark, Buffalo	2	9	4.5	9	0
Prior, Anthony, N.Y. Jets	16	316	19.8	27	0
Radecic, Scott, Indianapolis	1	17	17.0	17	0
Russell, Derek, Denver	5	105	21.0	34	0
Sawyer, Corey, Cincinnati	1	14	14.0	14	0
Saxon, James, Miami	1	12	12.0	12	0
Scott, Darnay, Cincinnati	15	342	22.8	34	0
Shaw, Eric, Cincinnati	1	1	1.0	1	0
Spikes, Irving, Miami	19	434	22.8	34	0
Stegall, Milt, Cincinnati	1	16	16.0	16	0
Stone, Dwight, Pittsburgh	11	182	16.5	31	0
Swann, Charles, Denver	1	16	16.0	16	0
Tasker, Steve, Buffalo	1	2	2.0	2	0
Teeter, Mike, Houston	f2	9	4.5	9	0
Thigpen, Yancey, Pittsburgh	f5	121	24.2	31	0
Thomas, Blair, New England	3	40	13.3	16	0
Thompson, Leroy, New England	18	376	20.9	30	0
Thornton, James, N.Y. Jets	1	0	0.0	0	0
Tillman, Spencer, Houston	4	51	12.8	19	0
Timpson, Michael, New England	1	28	28.0	28	0
Toner, Ed, Indianapolis	1	8	8.0	8	0
Tovar, Steve, Cincinnati	1	8	8.0	8	0
Turner, Nate, Buffalo	6	102	17.0	23	0
Vaughn, Jon, Sea.-K.C.	33	829	25.1	t93	2
Warren, Lamont, Indianapolis	2	56	28.0	38	0
Warren, Terrence, Seattle	14	350	25.0	47	0
White, Lorenzo, Houston	8	167	20.9	28	0
Williams, Harvey, L.A. Raiders	8	153	19.1	24	0
Williams, Jamie, L.A. Raiders	1	0	0.0	0	0
Williams, Mike, Miami	2	9	4.5	9	0
Williams, Ronnie, Miami	2	25	12.5	15	0
Woodson, Rod, Pittsburgh	15	365	24.3	54	0

Player, Team	No.	Yds.	Avg.	Long	TD
Wright, Alexander, L.A. Raiders	10	282	28.2	55	0
Zgonina, Jeff, Pittsburgh	2	8	4.0	8	0

t—touchdown.
f—includes at least one fair catch.

NFC

Player, Team	No.	Yds.	Avg.	Long	TD
Anderson, Jamal, Atlanta	1	11	11.0	11	0
Armstrong, Tyji, Tampa Bay	1	6	6.0	6	0
Bailey, Johnny, L.A. Rams	12	260	21.7	32	0
Bates, Mario, New Orleans	1	20	20.0	26	0
Bell, William, Washington	2	43	21.5	25	0
Brantley, Chris, L.A. Rams	7	150	21.4	33	0
Brooks, Robert, Green Bay	9	260	28.9	t96	1
Brown, Derek, N.Y. Giants	1	1	1.0	1	0
Brown, Derek, New Orleans	1	3	3.0	3	0
Buckley, Curtis, Tampa Bay	8	177	22.1	35	0
Carter, Antonio, Chicago	6	99	16.5	26	0
Carter, Dexter, San Francisco	48	1105	23.0	t96	1
Carter, Marty, Tampa Bay	1	0	0.0	0	0
Collins, Andre, Washington	1	0	0.0	0	0
Conway, Curtis, Chicago	10	228	22.8	34	0
Culpepper, Brad, Tampa Bay	2	30	15.0	18	0
Davey, Don, Green Bay	1	6	6.0	6	0
Dunbar, Vaughn, New Orleans	1	28	28.0	28	0
Ervins, Ricky, Washington	1	17	17.0	17	0
Evans, Chuck, Minnesota	1	4	4.0	4	0
Farr, D'Marco, L.A. Rams	1	16	16.0	16	0
Flanigan, Jim, Chicago	f2	26	13.0	14	0
Garnett, Dave, Minnesota	1	0	0.0	0	0
Gray, Mel, Detroit	45	1276	28.4	t102	3
Green, Robert, Chicago	6	77	12.8	16	0
Green, Rogerick, Tampa Bay	2	33	16.5	18	0
Griffith, Howard, L.A. Rams	2	35	17.5	21	0
Harris, Corey, Green Bay	29	618	21.3	59	0
Harris, Leonard, Atlanta	2	47	23.5	30	0
Harris, Raymont, Chicago	1	18	18.0	18	0
Harris, Rudy, Tampa Bay	1	12	12.0	12	0
Haws, Kurt, Washington	1	10	10.0	10	0
Hebron, Vaughn, Philadelphia	21	443	21.1	33	0
Henesey, Brian, Arizona	6	108	18.0	25	0
Heyward, Craig, Atlanta	1	7	7.0	7	0
Higgs, Mark, Arizona	2	25	12.5	17	0
Holmes, Clayton, Dallas	4	89	22.3	32	0
Hughes, Tyrone, New Orleans	63	1556	24.7	t98	2
Ismail, Qadry, Minnesota	35	807	23.1	61	0
Jenkins, James, Washington	1	4	4.0	4	0
Johnson, Maurice, Philadelphia	1	0	0.0	0	0
Johnson, Tre, Washington	0	4	....	4	0
Jones, Robert, Dallas	1	8	8.0	8	0
Jordan, Andrew, Minnesota	1	8	8.0	8	0
Jordan, Charles, Green Bay	5	115	23.0	33	0
Joseph, James, Philadelphia	1	11	11.0	11	0
Jurkovic, John, Green Bay	4	57	14.3	16	0
Kinchen, Todd, L.A. Rams	21	510	24.3	46	0
Kozlowski, Brian, N.Y. Giants	2	21	10.5	14	0
Lang, David, L.A. Rams	27	626	23.2	57	0
Lee, Amp, Minnesota	3	42	14.0	26	0
Lester, Tim, L.A. Rams	1	8	8.0	8	0
Levens, Dorsey, Green Bay	2	31	15.5	16	0
Levy, Chuck, Arizona	26	513	19.7	31	0
Lewis, Nate, Chicago	35	874	25.0	55	0
Lewis, Thomas, N.Y. Giants	26	509	19.6	36	0
Loville, Derek, San Francisco	2	34	17.0	19	0
Lynch, Eric, Detroit	9	105	11.7	16	0
Malone, Van, Detroit	3	38	12.7	20	0
Marion, Brock, Dallas	2	39	19.5	21	0
Marshall, Arthur, N.Y. Giants	15	249	16.6	30	0
McAfee, Fred, Arizona	7	113	16.1	19	0
Meggett, David, N.Y. Giants	29	548	18.9	30	0
Mitchell, Brian, Washington	58	1478	25.5	86	0
Mitchell, Derrell, New Orleans	6	129	21.5	30	0
Montgomery, Alton, Atlanta	2	58	29.0	37	0
Moore, Dave, Tampa Bay	2	27	13.5	16	0

Player, Team	No.	Yds.	Avg.	Long	TD
Moore, Derrick, Detroit	10	113	11.3	19	0
Morton, Johnnie, Detroit	4	143	35.8	t93	1
Neal, Lorenzo, New Orleans	1	17	17.0	15	0
Ned, Derrick, New Orleans	7	77	11.0	19	0
Novoselsky, Brent, Minnesota	2	10	5.0	10	0
O'Neal, Brian, Philadelphia	1	0	0.0	0	0
Pegram, Erric, Atlanta	9	145	16.1	35	0
Reeves, Bryan, Arizona	3	83	27.7	53	0
Robinson, Patrick, Arizona	12	231	19.3	33	0
Rush, Tyrone, Washington	3	45	15.0	25	0
Samuels, Terry, Arizona	1	6	6.0	6	0
Singleton, Nate, San Francisco	2	23	11.5	17	0
Smith, Irv, New Orleans	2	10	5.0	10	0
Smith, Otis, Philadelphia	1	14	14.0	14	0
Smith, Robert, Minnesota	16	419	26.2	45	0
Smith, Tony, Atlanta	16	333	20.8	31	0
Sydner, Jeff, Philadelphia	20	392	19.6	34	0
Thierry, John, Chicago	1	0	0.0	0	0
Thompson, Darrell, Green Bay	4	67	16.8	19	0
Turner, Vernon, Tampa Bay	43	886	20.6	77	0

Player, Team	No.	Yds.	Avg.	Long	TD
Verdin, Clarence, Atlanta	44	1026	23.3	69	0
Walker, Adam, San Francisco	6	82	13.7	19	0
Walker, Herschel, Philadelphia	21	581	27.7	t94	1
Walsh, Chris, Minnesota	1	6	6.0	6	0
Williams, Kevin, Dallas	43	1148	26.7	t87	1
Wilson, Charles, Tampa Bay	10	251	25.1	41	0
Wilson, Marcus, Green Bay	2	14	7.0	14	0
Woolford, Donnell, Chicago	1	28	28.0	28	0
Worley, Tim, Chicago	4	52	13.0	25	0
Wycheck, Frank, Washington	4	84	21.0	43	0
Zordich, Mike, Philadelphia	1	0	0.0	0	0

t—touchdown.
f—includes at least one fair catch.

PLAYERS WITH TWO CLUBS

Player, Team	No.	Yds.	Avg.	Long	TD
Vaughn, Jon, Seattle	18	443	24.6	t93	1
Vaughn, Jon, Kansas City	15	386	25.7	t91	1

MISCELLANEOUS

CLUB RANKINGS BY YARDS

	OFFENSE			DEFENSE		
Team	Total	Rush	Pass	Total	Rush	Pass
Arizona.............	25	17	22	3	4	4
Atlanta	7	28	5	27	14	27
Buffalo	10	8	10	17	8	23
Chicago.............	23	15	21	13	24	5
Cincinnati	18	18	18	15	23	9
Cleveland	16	14	19	7	13	7
Dallas................	8	5	†12	*1	10	*1
Denver...............	6	23	6	28	17	28
Detroit...............	15	3	24	24	22	19
Green Bay	9	19	9	6	3	15
Houston.............	26	12	25	9	28	2
Indianapolis.......	27	4	28	20	12	24
Kansas City	5	11	7	12	16	10
L.A. Raiders.......	19	21	16	10	9	14
L.A. Rams	21	25	15	16	20	12
Miami	*1	13	2	19	6	25
Minnesota	3	20	3	5	*1	21
New England.......	4	27	*1	18	19	16
New Orleans.......	12	26	8	25	18	26
N.Y. Giants........	28	10	27	11	15	8
N.Y. Jets............	22	16	20	22	21	18
Philadelphia.......	14	9	14	4	11	6
Pittsburgh..........	13	*1	23	2	7	3
San Diego..........	11	7	†12	14	5	22
San Francisco ...	2	6	4	8	2	17
Seattle...............	24	2	26	23	25	13
Tampa Bay	20	22	17	21	26	11
Washington	17	24	11	26	27	20

*NFL leader.
†Tied for position.

TAKEAWAYS/GIVEAWAYS

AFC

	TAKEAWAYS			GIVEAWAYS			Net.
	Int.	Fum.	Tot.	Int.	Fum.	Tot.	Diff.
Pittsburgh............	17	14	31	9	8	17	14
Kansas City	12	26	38	14	12	26	12
N.Y. Jets.............	17	21	38	18	10	28	10
San Diego............	17	15	32	14	9	23	9
New England........	22	18	40	27	11	38	2
Seattle................	19	11	30	9	19	28	2
Miami	23	9	32	18	14	32	0
Indianapolis........	18	10	28	14	17	31	-3
Cleveland	18	13	31	21	14	35	-4
Denver................	12	14	26	13	18	31	-5
L.A. Raiders	12	13	25	16	14	30	-5
Buffalo	16	12	28	21	13	34	-6
Houston...............	14	12	26	17	25	42	-16
Cincinnati	10	8	18	19	22	41	-23

NFC

	TAKEAWAYS			GIVEAWAYS			Net.
	Int.	Fum.	Tot.	Int.	Fum.	Tot.	Diff.
San Francisco	23	12	35	11	13	24	11
Green Bay	21	12	33	14	8	22	11
Philadelphia	21	14	35	14	12	26	9
N.Y. Giants...........	16	16	32	18	7	25	7
Arizona................	23	13	36	19	10	29	7
Dallas.................	22	9	31	14	10	24	7
Minnesota	18	16	34	20	14	34	0
New Orleans.........	17	14	31	18	14	32	-1
Detroit.................	12	11	23	14	10	24	-1
Tampa Bay	9	12	21	16	7	23	-2
Atlanta................	22	11	33	25	11	36	-3
Chicago...............	12	10	22	16	10	26	-4
L.A. Rams	14	6	20	18	13	31	-11
Washington	17	6	23	27	13	40	-17

CLUB LEADERS

	Offense	Defense
First downs..........................	S.F. 362	Arizona 245
Rushing........................	Pit. 138	Minnesota 65
Passing........................	N.E. 243	Houston 132
Penalty........................	Denver 43	Chicago 12
Rushes..............................	Dallas 550	Minnesota 355
Net yards gained	Pit. 2180	Minnesota 1090
Average gain	Detroit 5.1	Minnesota 3.1
Passes attempted..................	N.E. 699	Houston 400
Completed	Minnesota 409	Houston 221
Percent completed	S.F. 70.3	Arizona 50.3
Total yards gained	N.E. 4583	Houston 2963
Times sacked.................	Cleveland 14	Pittsburgh 55
Yards lost	Dallas 93	Pittsburgh 382
Net yards gained	N.E. 4444	Dallas 2752
Net yards per pass play .	S.F. 7.62	Dallas 4.84
Yds. gained per comp.....	Was. 13.00	Detroit 10.12
Combined net yards gained	Miami 6078	Dallas 4313
Pct. total yards rushing .	Ind. 46.7	Minnesota 23.0
Pct. total yards passing .	N.E. 76.9	Houston 56.9
Ball-control plays	N.E. 1199	Arizona 909
Average yards per play ..	S.F. 5.80	Dallas 4.29
Avg. time of possession .	Arizona 32:37	—
Third-down efficiency	S.F. 51.0	Arizona 27.8
Interceptions..........................	—	3 tied with 23
Yards returned	—	S.F. 508
Returned for TD	—	Min., S.F. 4
Punts	Arizona 98	—
Yards punted	Houston 4115	—
Average yards per punt .	Rams 44.8	—
Punt returns	Pit. 56	Tampa Bay 19
Yards returned	Raiders 487	Tampa Bay 103
Average yds. per return .	Was. 14.1	Tampa Bay 5.4
Returned for TD	4 tied with 2	—
Kickoff returns	Cin. 86	NYG, T.B. 44
Yards returned	N.O. 1840	Houston 832
Average yds. per return .	Dallas 25.7	Houston 17.3
Returned for TD	Detroit 4	—
Total points scored	S.F. 505	Cleveland 204
Total TDs	S.F. 66	Cleveland 22
TDs rushing	Dallas 26	Ari., Pit. 7
TDs passing	S.F. 37	Pittsburgh 12
TDs on ret. and recov.....	5 with 7	Cle., Dal. 0
Extra points	S.F. 62	Cleveland 20
Safeties	K.C., NYG 2	—
Field goals made............	Min., S.D. 34	Miami 11
Field goals attempted.....	Min., N.O. 39	Miami 18
Percent successful.........	Cleveland 92.9	Washington 60.7

TEAM-BY-TEAM SUMMARIES

AFC

OFFENSE

	Buff.	Cin.	Clev.	Den.	Hou.	Ind.	K.C.	Raid.	Mia.	N.E.	N.Y.J.	Pitt.	S.D.	Sea.
First downs	319	267	273	346	278	252	322	267	344	348	265	307	311	285
Rushing	107	84	80	101	97	108	97	87	109	83	90	138	102	114
Passing	181	158	161	202	158	126	211	158	220	243	164	148	181	143
Penalty	31	25	32	43	23	18	14	22	15	22	11	21	28	28
Rushes	483	404	449	431	417	495	464	428	433	478	416	546	482	480
Net yards gained	1831	1556	1657	1470	1682	2060	1732	1512	1658	1332	1566	2180	1852	2084
Average gain	3.8	3.9	3.7	3.4	4.0	4.2	3.7	3.5	3.8	2.8	3.8	4.0	3.8	4.3
Average yards per game	114.4	97.3	103.6	91.9	105.1	128.8	108.3	94.5	103.6	83.3	97.9	136.3	115.8	130.3
Passes attempted	542	542	507	626	554	376	615	488	627	699	539	463	522	498
Completed	342	289	266	388	274	217	366	281	392	405	310	266	305	253
Percent completed	63.1	53.3	52.5	62.0	49.5	57.7	59.5	57.6	62.5	57.9	57.5	57.5	58.4	50.8
Total yards gained	3714	3541	3269	4383	3216	2519	4092	3556	4533	4583	3323	3247	3619	2809
Times sacked	41	44	14	55	65	28	19	50	18	22	28	39	29	40
Yards lost	301	305	94	366	417	166	132	289	113	139	186	283	251	241
Net yards gained	3413	3236	3175	4017	2799	2353	3960	3267	4420	4444	3137	2964	3368	2568
Average yards per game	213.3	202.3	198.4	251.1	174.9	147.1	247.5	204.2	276.3	277.8	196.1	185.3	210.5	160.5
Net yards per pass play	5.85	5.52	6.09	5.90	4.52	5.82	6.25	6.07	6.85	6.16	5.53	5.90	6.11	4.77
Yards gained per completion	10.86	12.25	12.29	11.30	11.74	11.61	11.18	12.65	11.56	11.32	10.72	12.21	11.87	11.10
Combined net yards gained	5244	4792	4832	5487	4481	4413	5692	4779	6078	5776	4703	5144	5220	4652
Percent total yards rushing	34.9	32.5	34.3	26.8	37.5	46.7	30.4	31.6	27.3	23.1	33.3	42.4	35.5	44.8
Percent total yards passing	65.1	67.5	65.7	73.2	62.5	53.3	69.6	68.4	72.7	76.9	66.7	57.6	64.5	55.2
Average yards per game	327.8	299.5	302.0	342.9	280.1	275.8	355.8	298.7	379.9	361.0	293.9	321.5	326.3	290.8
Ball-control plays	1066	990	970	1112	1036	899	1098	966	1078	1199	983	1048	1033	1018
Average yards per play	4.9	4.8	5.0	4.9	4.3	4.9	5.2	4.9	5.6	4.8	4.8	4.9	5.1	4.6
Average time of possession	29:21	27:11	28:44	30:58	29:06	28:31	30:55	29:30	31:46	32:08	29:54	31:58	30:19	28:43
Third-down efficiency	43.2	31.0	33.8	37.7	34.8	35.4	39.5	39.4	46.1	41.2	34.7	39.0	39.5	37.9
Had intercepted	21	19	21	13	17	14	14	16	18	27	18	9	14	9
Yards opponents returned	262	176	225	288	188	174	217	202	190	252	232	106	233	210
Returned by opponents for TD	2	2	0	3	0	2	1	1	1	2	1	1	2	2
Punts	67	80	80	76	96	74	85	77	60	69	84	97	72	91
Yards punted	2799	3461	3211	3258	4115	3092	3582	3377	2412	2841	3534	3849	2951	3905
Average yards per punt	41.8	43.3	40.1	42.9	42.9	41.8	42.1	43.9	40.2	41.2	42.1	39.7	41.0	42.9
Punt returns	33	37	46	41	50	42	43	40	33	46	39	56	36	37
Yards returned	343	373	462	379	281	339	316	487	241	383	345	424	475	337
Average yards per return	10.4	10.1	10.0	9.2	5.6	8.1	7.3	12.2	7.3	8.3	8.8	7.6	13.2	9.1
Returned for TD	0	1	2	0	1	1	0	0	0	0	0	0	2	0
Kickoff returns	72	86	42	75	74	60	59	62	66	63	66	55	68	67
Yards returned	1345	1810	1031	1523	1436	1254	1300	1358	1294	1123	1282	1141	1636	1467
Average yards per return	18.7	21.0	24.5	20.3	19.4	20.9	22.0	21.9	19.6	17.8	19.4	20.7	24.1	21.9
Returned for TD	0	0	1	0	0	1	1	0	0	0	0	0	2	1
Fumbles	30	31	26	27	42	30	21	22	28	28	28	18	19	31
Lost	13	22	14	18	25	17	12	14	14	11	10	8	9	19
Out of bounds	4	1	3	1	2	1	1	1	2	3	3	2	2	1
Recovered for TD	0	0	0	0	0	0	0	0	0	0	0	0	0	0
Penalties	92	90	113	101	115	82	127	156	92	78	95	119	96	114
Yards penalized	631	618	969	865	959	658	911	1186	747	597	754	974	875	898
Total points scored	340	276	340	347	226	307	319	303	389	351	264	316	381	287
Total TDs	38	27	37	37	25	37	34	34	45	39	29	35	40	32
TDs rushing	14	5	12	19	10	15	12	7	13	12	8	15	13	16
TDs passing	23	20	20	18	13	15	20	22	31	25	18	17	20	13
TDs on returns and recoveries	1	1	5	0	2	7	2	5	1	2	3	3	7	3
Extra points	38	26	36	32	22	37	33	32	41	36	28	33	36	29
2-Pt. conversions	0	2	4	3	4	0	3	1	6	0	2	1	3	4

DEFENSE

	Buff.	Cin.	Clev.	Den.	Hou.	Ind.	K.C.	Raid.	Mia.	N.E.	N.Y.J.	Pitt.	S.D.	Sea.
First downs	294	310	304	303	275	311	289	303	305	280	315	262	308	318
Rushing	82	126	98	103	112	98	93	94	85	86	105	76	89	122
Passing	199	168	173	182	132	192	164	176	195	173	189	156	191	178
Penalty	13	16	33	18	31	21	32	33	25	21	21	30	28	18
Rushes	447	517	465	432	540	463	446	444	394	422	463	421	385	511
Net yards gained	1515	1906	1669	1752	2120	1646	1734	1543	1430	1760	1809	1452	1404	1952
Average gain	3.4	3.7	3.6	4.1	3.9	3.6	3.9	3.5	3.6	4.2	3.9	3.4	3.6	3.8
Average yards per game	94.7	119.1	104.3	109.5	132.5	102.9	108.4	96.4	89.4	110.0	113.1	90.8	87.8	122.0
Passes attempted	535	505	587	568	400	598	504	564	577	545	522	532	577	537
Completed	314	294	325	322	221	354	300	306	334	298	333	280	363	313
Percent completed	58.7	58.2	55.4	56.7	55.3	59.2	59.5	54.3	57.9	54.7	63.8	52.6	62.9	58.3
Total yards gained	3812	3458	3425	4296	2963	3897	3500	3684	3954	3737	3730	3256	3911	3603
Times sacked	25	31	38	23	31	29	39	38	29	39	29	55	43	29
Yards lost	152	210	268	141	168	218	234	284	160	290	201	382	253	206
Net yards gained	3660	3248	3157	4155	2795	3679	3266	3400	3794	3447	3529	2874	3658	3397
Average yards per game	228.8	203.0	197.3	259.7	174.7	229.9	204.1	212.5	237.1	215.4	220.6	179.6	228.6	212.3
Net yards per pass play	6.54	6.06	5.05	7.03	6.48	5.87	6.01	5.65	6.26	5.90	6.40	4.90	5.90	6.00
Yards gained per completion	12.14	11.76	10.54	13.34	13.41	11.01	11.67	12.04	11.84	12.54	11.20	11.63	10.77	11.51
Comb net yards gained	5175	5154	4826	5907	4915	5325	5000	4943	5224	5207	5338	4326	5062	5349
Percent total yards rushing	29.3	37.0	34.6	29.7	43.1	30.9	34.7	31.2	27.4	33.8	33.9	33.6	27.7	36.5
Percent total yards passing	70.7	63.0	65.4	70.3	56.9	69.1	65.3	68.8	72.6	66.2	66.1	66.4	72.3	63.5
Average yards per game	323.4	322.1	301.6	369.2	307.2	332.8	312.5	308.9	326.5	325.4	333.6	270.4	316.4	334.3
Ball-control plays	1007	1053	1090	1023	971	1090	989	1046	1000	1006	1014	1008	1005	1077
Average yards per play	5.1	4.9	4.4	5.8	5.1	4.9	5.1	4.7	5.2	5.2	5.3	4.3	5.0	5.0
Average time of possession	30:39	32:49	31:16	29:02	30:54	31:29	29:05	30:30	28:14	27:52	30:06	28:02	29:41	31:17
Third-down efficiency	41.9	39.8	34.3	39.6	36.5	45.8	37.7	38.6	38.6	33.5	39.9	32.0	36.7	37.1
Intercepted by	16	10	18	12	14	18	12	12	23	22	17	17	17	19
Yards returned by	175	167	223	55	242	360	218	187	276	209	355	240	402	284
Returned for TD	0	0	1	0	1	3	1	3	1	1	3	2	3	2
Punts	69	87	97	76	82	72	85	84	68	83	62	97	76	78
Yards punted	2916	3528	3880	3303	3443	3039	3822	3414	2834	3333	2675	4096	3290	3188
Average yards per punt	42.3	40.6	40.0	43.5	42.0	42.2	45.0	40.6	41.7	40.2	43.1	42.2	43.3	40.9
Punt returns	38	43	38	39	50	40	50	38	32	34	38	39	38	43
Yards returned	324	459	220	275	438	366	506	366	324	260	260	263	348	426
Average yards per return	8.5	10.7	5.8	7.1	8.8	9.2	10.1	9.6	10.1	7.6	6.8	6.7	9.2	9.9
Returned for TD	0	2	0	0	1	0	0	1	1	0	0	0	0	0
Kickoff returns	72	61	71	70	48	65	66	65	74	63	61	68	79	61
Yards returned	1455	1408	1372	1396	832	1316	1447	1406	1549	1375	1195	1530	1740	1229
Average yards per return	20.2	23.1	19.3	19.9	17.3	20.2	21.9	21.6	20.9	21.8	19.6	22.5	22.0	20.1
Returned for TD	0	2	0	0	0	0	0	0	2	1	0	2	1	0
Fumbles	23	26	26	24	20	21	36	26	29	34	30	31	29	21
Recovered	13	22	14	18	25	17	12	14	14	11	10	8	9	19
Out of bounds	1	2	1	1	1	1	1	1	5	1	2	3	0	2
Recovered for TD	2	0	0	0	1	0	0	1	1	1	0	1	0	1
Penalties	101	99	129	134	102	110	119	113	82	110	63	91	109	103
Yards penalized	770	861	1139	1031	807	824	925	823	653	795	489	763	989	773
Total points scored	356	406	204	396	352	320	298	327	327	312	320	234	306	323
Total TDs	40	45	22	43	37	34	35	38	42	36	37	23	34	34
TDs rushing	10	16	9	12	17	8	11	11	14	11	17	7	11	15
TDs passing	26	22	13	28	18	24	23	24	23	21	19	12	20	15
TDs on returns and recoveries	4	7	0	3	2	2	1	3	5	4	1	4	3	4
Extra points	36	42	20	40	36	31	32	34	41	34	33	23	33	32
Safeties	0	0	0	0	1	1	0	1	0	0	0	0	0	1
Field goals made	26	31	17	31	30	27	18	21	11	20	21	24	22	27
Field goals attempted	30	35	26	37	31	34	23	29	18	25	27	29	27	33
Percent successful	86.7	88.6	65.4	83.8	96.8	79.4	78.3	72.4	61.1	80.0	77.8	82.8	81.5	81.8
2-Pt. conversions	2	1	1	5	2	2	2	0	1	2	2	1	3	4

OFFENSE

	Ariz.	Atl.	Chi.	Dall.	Det.	G.B.	Rams	Minn.	N.O.	N.Y.G.	Phil.	S.F.	T.B.	Wash.
First downs	287	302	274	322	280	314	274	325	308	263	293	362	276	269
Rushing	90	63	88	136	94	88	80	92	78	103	103	122	104	79
Passing	169	218	165	160	164	205	163	215	203	136	168	210	149	166
Penalty	28	21	21	26	22	21	31	18	27	24	22	30	23	24
Rushes	480	330	487	550	406	417	397	419	373	525	432	491	430	407
Net yards gained	1560	1249	1588	1953	2080	1543	1389	1524	1336	1754	1761	1897	1489	1415
Average gain	3.3	3.8	3.3	3.6	5.1	3.7	3.5	3.6	3.6	3.3	4.1	3.9	3.5	3.5
Average yards per game	97.5	78.1	99.3	122.1	130.0	96.4	86.8	95.3	83.5	109.6	110.1	118.6	93.1	88.4
Passes attempted	538	629	502	448	459	609	512	673	569	405	566	511	491	546
Completed	287	374	308	282	250	375	291	409	366	226	316	359	271	271
Percent completed	53.3	59.5	61.4	62.9	54.5	61.6	56.8	60.8	64.3	55.8	55.8	70.3	55.2	49.6
Total yards gained	3284	4344	3230	3461	3085	3977	3597	4570	4027	2847	3736	4362	3436	3524
Times sacked	34	37	25	20	26	33	35	31	24	46	48	35	30	21
Yards lost	237	232	139	93	163	204	239	246	181	285	372	199	171	146
Net yards gained	3047	4112	3091	3368	2922	3773	3358	4324	3846	2562	3364	4163	3265	3378
Average yards per game	190.4	257.0	193.2	210.5	182.6	235.8	209.9	270.3	240.4	160.1	210.3	260.2	204.1	211.1
Net yards per pass play	5.33	6.17	5.87	7.20	6.02	5.88	6.14	6.14	6.49	5.68	5.48	7.62	6.27	5.96
Yards gained per completion	11.44	11.61	10.49	12.27	12.34	10.61	12.36	11.17	11.00	12.60	11.82	12.15	12.68	13.00
Combined net yards gained	4607	5361	4679	5321	5002	5316	4747	5848	5182	4316	5125	6060	4754	4793
Percent total yards rushing	33.9	23.3	33.9	36.7	41.6	29.0	29.3	26.1	25.8	40.6	34.4	31.3	31.3	29.5
Percent total yards passing	66.1	76.7	66.1	63.3	58.4	71.0	70.7	73.9	74.2	59.4	65.6	68.7	68.7	70.5
Average yards per game	287.9	335.1	292.4	332.6	312.6	332.3	296.7	365.5	323.9	269.8	320.3	378.8	297.1	299.6
Ball-control plays	1052	996	1014	1018	891	1059	944	1123	966	976	1046	1037	951	974
Average yards per play	4.4	5.4	4.6	5.2	5.6	5.0	5.0	5.2	5.4	4.4	4.9	5.8	5.0	4.9
Average time of possession	32:37	29:10	31:37	31:35	26:06	30:56	27:59	32:06	29:04	30:28	30:47	31:38	29:55	26:55
Third-down efficiency	32.9	37.3	41.8	44.5	39.9	43.1	39.2	41.1	35.7	34.5	41.6	51.0	36.7	35.9
Had intercepted	19	25	16	14	14	14	18	20	18	18	14	11	16	27
Yards opponents returned	262	419	335	180	154	193	213	292	386	299	206	107	323	482
Returned by opponents for TD	3	1	3	0	1	0	2	1	3	3	1	1	2	4
Punts	98	79	76	70	64	81	78	77	67	89	92	54	74	82
Yards punted	3997	3121	2871	2935	2782	3351	3494	3301	2920	3578	3727	2235	2853	3639
Average yards per punt	40.8	39.5	37.8	41.9	43.5	41.4	44.8	42.9	43.6	40.2	40.5	41.4	38.6	44.4
Punt returns	42	31	27	44	25	49	40	39	25	32	41	40	28	32
Yards returned	286	188	218	404	256	414	461	238	152	388	381	334	248	452
Average yards per return	6.8	6.1	8.1	9.2	10.2	8.4	11.5	6.1	6.1	12.1	9.3	8.4	8.9	14.1
Returned for TD	0	0	1	1	0	1	1	0	0	2	0	0	1	2
Kickoff returns	57	75	66	50	71	56	71	60	82	73	67	58	70	71
Yards returned	1079	1627	1402	1284	1675	1168	1605	1296	1840	1328	1441	1244	1422	1685
Average yards per return	18.9	21.7	21.2	25.7	23.6	20.9	22.6	21.6	22.4	18.2	21.5	21.4	20.3	23.7
Returned for TD	0	0	0	1	4	1	0	0	2	0	1	1	0	0
Fumbles	25	28	21	22	26	25	26	32	22	28	23	25	18	21
Lost	10	11	10	10	10	8	13	14	14	7	12	13	7	13
Out of bounds	1	0	0	3	3	5	0	5	1	3	0	1	1	2
Recovered for TD	0	1	0	0	1	0	2	2	2	0	0	1	0	2
Penalties	128	119	65	100	109	85	112	112	88	92	138	109	93	88
Yards penalized	1090	934	503	895	781	760	922	880	678	818	1107	890	805	730
Total points scored	235	317	271	414	357	382	286	356	348	279	308	505	251	320
Total TDs	24	36	30	50	43	47	33	36	38	30	35	66	26	37
TDs rushing	12	8	10	26	12	11	6	11	11	12	14	23	8	5
TDs passing	11	25	19	19	24	33	23	18	22	16	18	37	17	25
TDs on returns and recoveries	1	3	1	5	7	3	4	7	5	2	3	6	1	7
Extra points	22	35	26	48	41	42	30	34	34	28	33	62	23	33
Safeties	1	0	0	0	1	0	1	0	0	2	1	0	0	1
Field goals made	22	21	21	22	18	19	18	34	28	22	21	15	23	20
Field goals attempted	30	25	29	29	27	26	23	39	39	28	25	20	35	28
Percent successful	73.3	84.0	72.4	75.9	66.7	73.1	78.3	87.2	71.8	78.6	84.0	75.0	65.7	71.4
2-Pt. conversions	1	3	2	0	2	1	2	4	2	1	0	2	3	3

DEFENSE

	Ariz.	Atl.	Chi.	Dall.	Det.	G.B.	Rams	Minn.	N.O.	N.Y.G.	Phil.	S.F.	T.B.	Wash.
First downs	245	330	275	273	326	281	333	287	337	280	275	285	298	331
Rushing	71	107	100	86	131	82	103	65	106	92	94	82	100	129
Passing	144	201	163	157	169	182	198	195	208	166	151	182	179	182
Penalty	30	22	12	30	26	17	32	27	23	22	30	21	19	20
Rushes	409	426	432	437	511	381	496	355	458	447	449	375	468	556
Net yards gained	1370	1693	1922	1561	1859	1363	1781	1090	1758	1728	1616	1338	1964	1975
Average gain	3.3	4.0	4.4	3.6	3.6	3.6	3.6	3.1	3.8	3.9	3.6	3.6	4.2	3.6
Average yards per game	85.6	105.8	120.1	97.6	116.2	85.2	111.3	68.1	109.9	108.0	101.0	83.6	122.8	123.4
Passes attempted	465	580	522	522	547	605	541	597	559	500	490	583	498	496
Completed	234	364	295	269	370	337	320	368	353	289	251	329	303	300
Percent completed	50.3	62.8	56.5	51.5	67.6	55.7	59.1	61.6	63.1	57.8	51.2	56.4	60.8	60.5
Total yards gained	3310	4365	3262	3051	3745	3677	3548	3902	4007	3391	3359	3756	3486	3799
Times sacked	35	32	28	47	28	37	26	36	36	26	42	38	20	28
Yards lost	272	229	175	299	199	276	159	250	196	169	265	255	114	165
Net yards gained	3038	4136	3087	2752	3546	3401	3389	3652	3811	3222	3094	3501	3372	3634
Average yards per game	189.9	258.5	192.9	172.0	221.6	212.6	211.8	228.3	238.2	201.4	193.4	218.8	210.8	227.1
Net yards per pass play	6.08	6.76	5.61	4.84	6.17	5.30	5.98	5.77	6.41	6.13	5.82	5.64	6.51	6.94
Yards gained per completion	14.15	11.99	11.06	11.34	10.12	10.91	11.09	10.60	11.35	11.73	13.38	11.42	11.50	12.66
Combined net yards gained	4408	5829	5009	4313	5405	4764	5170	4742	5569	4950	4710	4839	5336	5609
Percent total yards rushing	31.1	29.0	38.4	36.2	34.4	28.6	34.4	23.0	31.6	34.9	34.3	27.7	36.8	35.2
Percent total yards passing	68.9	71.0	61.6	63.8	65.6	71.4	65.6	77.0	68.4	65.1	65.7	72.3	63.2	64.8
Average yards per game	275.5	364.3	313.1	269.6	337.8	297.8	323.1	296.4	348.1	309.4	294.4	302.4	333.5	350.6
Ball-control plays	909	1038	982	1006	1086	1023	1063	988	1053	973	981	996	986	1080
Average yards per play	4.8	5.6	5.1	4.3	5.0	4.7	4.9	4.8	5.3	5.1	4.8	4.9	5.4	5.2
Average time of possession	27:23	30:50	28:23	28:25	33:54	29:04	32:01	27:54	30:56	29:32	29:13	28:22	30:05	33:05
Third-down efficiency	27.8	41.0	37.2	39.7	48.5	35.6	45.7	36.3	43.3	41.1	36.4	39.4	43.9	39.0
Intercepted by	23	22	12	22	12	21	14	18	17	16	21	23	9	17
Yards returned by	297	322	127	297	144	232	211	338	197	128	209	508	77	326
Returned for TD	1	2	0	3	2	1	1	4	1	0	2	4	0	3
Punts	90	62	72	84	66	88	74	86	60	69	90	77	68	87
Yards punted	3677	2661	2808	3637	2963	3491	3106	3485	2558	2792	3570	3274	2902	3506
Average yards per punt	40.9	42.9	39.0	43.3	44.9	39.7	42.0	40.5	42.6	40.5	39.7	42.5	42.7	40.3
Punt returns	40	31	26	36	36	36	47	44	40	39	47	28	19	45
Yards returned	270	273	225	378	431	272	637	410	495	307	286	242	103	441
Average yards per return	6.8	8.8	8.7	10.5	12.0	7.6	13.6	9.3	12.4	7.9	6.1	8.6	5.4	9.8
Returned for TD	0	0	0	0	2	0	3	1	2	0	1	0	0	1
Kickoff returns	53	66	65	82	65	75	63	83	63	44	64	89	44	62
Yards returned	1214	1328	1271	1709	1572	1380	1446	1843	1493	923	1425	1912	941	1389
Average yards per return	22.9	20.1	19.6	20.8	24.2	18.4	23.0	22.2	23.7	21.0	22.3	21.5	21.4	22.4
Returned for TD	1	0	1	0	1	1	2	1	0	0	0	0	0	1
Fumbles	28	20	29	15	34	32	15	25	28	25	29	25	21	21
Recovered	10	11	10	10	10	8	13	14	14	7	12	13	7	13
Out of bounds	2	1	4	2	7	6	0	1	0	2	1	0	3	1
Recovered for TD	1	1	1	0	0	1	0	0	2	1	0	3	0	0
Penalties	108	111	80	102	130	82	114	83	105	130	98	108	94	98
Yards penalized	800	853	645	826	1036	675	1015	614	922	1122	844	912	690	839
Total points scored	267	385	307	248	342	287	365	314	407	305	308	296	351	412
Total TDs	31	44	31	27	40	32	42	37	45	31	33	35	40	52
TDs rushing	7	16	10	8	15	9	12	9	10	11	11	16	13	24
TDs passing	19	26	16	19	21	20	23	25	28	16	20	15	25	22
TDs on returns and recoveries	5	2	5	0	4	3	7	3	7	4	2	4	2	6
Extra points	29	40	28	24	38	27	41	33	44	30	31	30	40	48
Safeties	3	1	0	1	0	1	0	0	0	1	0	2	0	0
Field goals made	15	26	30	20	21	21	23	19	30	29	25	15	23	17
Field goals attempted	24	33	41	25	28	25	29	30	37	34	26	21	26	28
Percent successful	62.5	78.8	73.2	80.0	75.0	84.0	79.3	63.3	81.1	85.3	96.2	71.4	88.5	60.7
2-Pt. conversions	1	1	3	0	1	3	3	2	3	0	4	7	2	1

AFC, NFC AND NFL SUMMARIES

	AFC Offense Total	AFC Offense Average	AFC Defense Total	AFC Defense Average	NFC Offense Total	NFC Offense Average	NFC Defense Total	NFC Defense Average	NFL Total	NFL Average
First downs	4184	298.9	4177	298.4	4149	296.4	4156	296.9	8333	297.6
Rushing	1397	99.8	1369	97.8	1320	94.3	1348	96.3	2717	97.0
Passing	2454	175.3	2468	176.3	2491	177.9	2477	176.9	4945	176.6
Penalty	333	23.8	340	24.3	338	24.1	331	23.6	671	24.0
Rushes	6406	457.6	6350	453.6	6144	438.9	6200	442.9	12550	448.2
Net yards gained	24172	1726.6	23692	1692.3	22538	1609.9	23018	1644.1	46710	1668.2
Average gain	....	3.8	....	3.7	....	3.7	....	3.7	....	3.7
Average yards per game	....	107.9	....	105.8	....	100.6	....	102.8	....	104.3
Passes attempted	7598	542.7	7551	539.4	7458	532.7	7505	536.1	15056	537.7
Completed	4354	311.0	4357	311.2	4385	313.2	4382	313.0	8739	312.1
Percent completed	....	57.3	....	57.7	....	58.8	....	58.4	....	58.0
Total yards gained	50404	3600.3	51226	3659.0	51480	3677.1	50658	3618.4	101884	3638.7
Times sacked	492	35.1	478	34.1	445	31.8	459	32.8	937	33.5
Yards lost	3283	234.5	3167	226.2	2907	207.6	3023	215.9	6190	221.1
Net yards gained	47121	3365.8	48059	3432.8	48573	3469.5	47635	3402.5	95694	3417.6
Average yards per game	....	210.4	....	214.5	....	216.8	....	212.7	....	213.6
Net yards per pass play	....	5.82	....	5.99	....	6.15	....	5.98	....	5.98
Yards gained per completion	....	11.58	....	11.76	....	11.74	....	11.56	....	11.66
Combined net yards gained	71293	5092.4	71751	5125.1	71111	5079.4	70653	5046.6	142404	5085.9
Percent total yards rushing	....	33.9	....	33.0	....	31.7	....	32.6	....	32.8
Percent total yards passing	....	66.1	....	67.0	....	68.3	....	67.4	....	67.2
Average yards per game	....	318.3	....	320.3	....	317.5	....	315.4	....	317.9
Ball-control plays	14496	1035.4	14379	1027.1	14047	1003.4	14164	1011.7	28543	1019.0
Average yards per play	....	4.9	....	5.0	....	5.1	....	5.0	....	5.0
Third-down efficiency	....	38.2	....	38.1	....	39.7	....	39.8	....	38.9
Interceptions	230	16.4	227	16.2	244	17.4	247	17.6	474	16.9
Yards returned	2955	211.1	3393	242.4	3851	275.1	3413	243.8	6806	243.1
Returned for TD	20	1.4	21	1.5	25	1.8	24	1.7	45	1.6
Punts	1108	79.1	1116	79.7	1081	77.2	1073	76.6	2189	78.2
Yards punted	46387	3313.4	46761	3340.1	44804	3200.3	44430	3173.6	91191	3256.8
Average yards per punt	....	41.9	....	41.9	....	41.4	....	41.4	....	41.7
Punt Returns	579	41.4	560	40.0	495	35.4	514	36.7	1074	38.4
Yards returned	5185	370.4	4835	345.4	4420	315.7	4770	340.7	9605	343.0
Average yards per return	....	9.0	....	8.6	....	8.9	....	9.3	....	8.9
Returned for TD	7	0.5	6	0.4	9	0.6	10	0.7	16	0.6
Kickoff Returns	915	65.4	924	66.0	927	66.2	918	65.6	1842	65.8
Yards returned	19000	1357.1	19250	1375.0	20096	1435.4	19846	1417.6	39096	1396.3
Average yards per return	....	20.8	....	20.8	....	21.7	....	21.6	....	21.2
Returned for TD	6	0.4	8	0.6	10	0.7	8	0.6	16	0.6
Fumbles	381	27.2	376	26.9	342	24.4	347	24.8	723	25.8
Lost	206	14.7	196	14.0	152	10.9	162	11.6	358	12.8
Out of bounds	27	1.9	22	1.6	25	1.8	30	2.1	52	1.9
Own recovered for TD	0	0.0	0	0.0	1	0.1	1	0.1	1	0.0
Opponents recovered by	196	14.0	206	14.7	162	11.6	152	10.9	358	12.8
Opponents recovered for TD	7	0.5	8	0.6	11	0.8	10	0.7	18	0.6
Penalties	1470	105.0	1465	104.6	1438	102.7	1443	103.1	2908	103.9
Yards penalized	11642	831.6	11642	831.6	11793	842.4	11793	842.4	23435	837.0
Total points scored	4446	317.6	4481	320.1	4629	330.6	4594	328.1	9075	324.1
Total TDs	489	34.9	500	35.7	531	37.9	520	37.1	1020	36.4
TDs rushing	171	12.2	169	12.1	169	12.1	171	12.2	340	12.1
TDs passing	276	19.7	288	20.6	307	21.9	295	21.1	583	20.8
TDs on returns and receptions	42	3.0	43	3.1	55	3.9	54	3.9	97	3.5
Extra points	459	32.8	467	33.4	491	35.1	483	34.5	950	33.9
Safeties	6	0.4	4	0.3	7	0.5	9	0.6	13	0.5
Field goals made	336	24.0	326	23.3	304	21.7	314	22.4	640	22.9
Field goals attempted	408	29.1	404	28.9	403	28.8	407	29.1	811	29.0
Percent successful	....	82.4	....	80.7	....	75.4	....	77.1	....	78.9
2-Pt. conversions	33	2.4	28	2.0	26	1.9	31	2.2	59	2.1

RUSHING

Player, Team	Opponent	Date	Att.	Yds.	TD
Barry Sanders, Detroit	vs. Tampa Bay	November 13	26	237	0
Barry Sanders, Detroit	at Dallas	September 19*	40	194	0
Errict Rhett, Tampa Bay	vs. Washington	December 4	40	192	1
Barry Sanders, Detroit	vs. Green Bay	December 4	20	188	1
Chris Warren, Seattle	at Houston	December 11	30	185	1
Barry Foster, Pittsburgh	vs. Indianapolis	September 18	31	179	1
Emmitt Smith, Dallas	at Pittsburgh	September 4	31	171	1
Barry Sanders, Detroit	vs. Chicago	October 23	23	167	0
Barry Sanders, Detroit	at Tampa Bay	October 2	20	166	0
Emmitt Smith, Dallas	vs. N.Y. Giants	November 7	35	163	2
Terry Allen, Minnesota	at Chicago	September 18	22	159	2
Lorenzo White, Houston	vs. N.Y. Giants	November 21	27	156	0
Bernie Parmalee, Miami	vs. L.A. Raiders	October 16*	30	150	0
Bam Morris, Pittsburgh	at N.Y. Giants	October 23	29	146	1
Barry Sanders, Detroit	at N.Y. Giants	October 30	26	146	0
Marshall Faulk, Indianapolis	vs. Houston	September 4	23	143	3
Emmitt Smith, Dallas	vs. Detroit	September 19*	29	143	1
Mario Bates, New Orleans	vs. Atlanta	November 13	22	141	2
Rodney Hampton, N.Y. Giants	vs. Detroit	October 30*	30	138	1
Emmitt Smith, Dallas	vs. Green Bay	November 24	32	133	2
Jerome Bettis, L.A. Rams	at Kansas City	September 25	35	132	0
Marcus Allen, Kansas City	at L.A. Raiders	December 24	33	132	0
Barry Sanders, Detroit	vs. New England	September 25	18	131	2
Marshall Faulk, Indianapolis	at Seattle	December 4	27	129	1
Harvey Williams, L.A. Raiders	vs. Houston	October 30	29	128	1
Barry Sanders, Detroit	at N.Y. Jets	December 10	23	127	0
Bernie Parmalee, Miami	vs. Kansas City	December 11	19	127	1
Chris Warren, Seattle	vs. Pittsburgh	September 25	26	126	1
Johnny Johnson, N.Y. Jets	vs. Chicago	September 25	12	126	1
Lewis Tillman, Chicago	vs. Detroit	November 20	32	126	1
Thurman Thomas, Buffalo	vs. Miami	October 9	31	125	2
Natrone Means, San Diego	vs. Kansas City	October 9	19	125	1
Bernie Parmalee, Miami	at New England	October 30	25	123	0
Leroy Hoard, Cleveland	vs. New England	November 6	21	123	0
Charlie Garner, Philadelphia	vs. Washington	October 9	28	122	0
Johnny Johnson, N.Y. Jets	vs. New England	October 16	21	122	0
Chris Warren, Seattle	at Denver	November 13	18	122	1
Rodney Hampton, N.Y. Giants	at Houston	November 21	34	122	0
Chris Warren, Seattle	vs. L.A. Raiders	December 18	24	122	1
Barry Sanders, Detroit	vs. Atlanta	September 4*	27	120	0
Natrone Means, San Diego	at New Orleans	October 16	26	120	3
Errict Rhett, Tampa Bay	vs. L.A. Rams	December 11	31	119	1
Ron Moore, Arizona	at Washington	October 16*	28	118	1
Jerome Bettis, L.A. Rams	vs. Atlanta	October 2	29	117	0
Chris Warren, Seattle	at Kansas City	October 23	19	117	0
Chris Warren, Seattle	vs. Tampa Bay	November 20	16	116	0
Barry Foster, Pittsburgh	vs. Houston	October 3	21	115	1
Terry Allen, Minnesota	vs. Miami	September 25	15	113	1
Terry Allen, Minnesota	at Tampa Bay	October 30	17	113	1
Thurman Thomas, Buffalo	at Houston	September 18	28	112	0
Rodney Hampton, N.Y. Giants	at L.A. Rams	October 16	27	112	1
Errict Rhett, Tampa Bay	at Detroit	November 13	25	112	0
Emmitt Smith, Dallas	vs. Cleveland	December 10	26	112	1
Charlie Garner, Philadelphia	at San Francisco	October 2	16	111	2
Errict Rhett, Tampa Bay	at Seattle	November 20	24	111	0
Marshall Faulk, Indianapolis	vs. N.Y. Jets	October 30	24	110	2
Barry Sanders, Detroit	vs. Minnesota	December 17	17	110	2
Leonard Russell, Denver	vs. Seattle	November 13	19	109	1
Bam Morris, Pittsburgh	at Cincinnati	December 4	24	108	1
Natrone Means, San Diego	vs. Cincinnati	September 11	21	107	1
Harvey Williams, L.A. Raiders	vs. Atlanta	October 23	27	107	1
Thurman Thomas, Buffalo	at New England	September 11	26	106	0
Emmitt Smith, Dallas	vs. Philadelphia	October 16	26	106	1
Rodney Hampton, N.Y. Giants	at Washington	November 27	34	106	0
Edgar Bennett, Green Bay	vs. Chicago	December 11	22	106	1
Barry Foster, Pittsburgh	vs. Cleveland	December 18	32	106	1
Edgar Bennett, Green Bay	vs. Chicago	October 31	26	105	2
Ricky Watters, San Francisco	at New Orleans	November 28	26	105	0
Marshall Faulk, Indianapolis	at Tampa Bay	September 11	18	104	0
Jerome Bettis, L.A. Rams	vs. San Francisco	September 18	21	104	1
Natrone Means, San Diego	vs. Seattle	October 30	26	104	1

Player, Team	Opponent	Date	Att.	Yds.	TD
Thurman Thomas, Buffalo	vs. Denver	September 26	17	103	2
Leonard Russell, Denver	at Seattle	October 9	24	103	0
Ricky Watters, San Francisco	vs. Tampa Bay	October 23	14	103	2
Leroy Hoard, Cleveland	vs. Houston	November 27	23	103	2
Jerome Bettis, L.A. Rams	at Atlanta	September 11	24	102	0
Natrone Means, San Diego	at Atlanta	November 6	26	102	0
Chris Warren, Seattle	at Washington	September 4	22	100	2
Terry Kirby, Miami	vs. N.Y. Jets	September 18	15	100	1
Lewis Tillman, Chicago	vs. New Orleans	October 9	23	100	1
Natrone Means, San Diego	vs. Denver	October 23	19	100	1
Edgar Bennett, Green Bay	at Tampa Bay	December 24	21	100	1

*Overtime game.

PASSING

Team, Player	Opponent	Date	Att.	Comp.	Yds.	TD	Int.
Dan Marino, Miami	vs. New England	September 4	42	23	473	5	1
Dan Marino, Miami	at Minnesota	September 25	54	29	431	3	3
Drew Bledsoe, New England	vs. Minnesota	November 13*	70	45	426	3	3
Drew Bledsoe, New England	at Miami	September 4	51	32	421	4	2
Warren Moon, Minnesota	vs. New Orleans	November 6	57	33	420	3	1
Warren Moon, Minnesota	vs. N.Y. Jets	November 20	50	33	400	2	4
Joe Montana, Kansas City	at Denver	October 17	54	34	393	3	1
Jeff Blake, Cincinnati	at Seattle	November 6	43	31	387	0	1
John Elway, Denver	vs. Atlanta	November 20	42	27	382	2	1
Boomer Esiason, N.Y. Jets	vs. Miami	November 27	41	26	382	2	2
John Friesz, Washington	at N.Y. Giants	September 18	50	32	381	2	2
Drew Bledsoe, New England	vs. Buffalo	September 11	42	26	380	3	2
Jim Everett, New Orleans	vs. Washington	September 11	46	31	376	2	1
John Elway, Denver	vs. San Diego	September 4	46	36	371	3	2
Brett Favre, Green Bay	at Detroit	December 4	43	29	366	3	2
Drew Bledsoe, New England	at Cincinnati	September 18	50	30	365	1	2
Jim Kelly, Buffalo	vs. Green Bay	November 20	44	32	365	2	1
Jeff George, Atlanta	vs. Philadelphia	November 27	46	26	364	2	3
Brett Favre, Green Bay	vs. Miami	September 11	51	31	362	2	1
Joe Montana, Kansas City	at Atlanta	September 18	39	28	361	2	2
Dan Marino, Miami	at N.Y. Jets	November 27	44	31	359	4	2
Steve Young, San Francisco	at L.A. Rams	September 18	39	31	355	2	0
Warren Moon, Minnesota	at Arizona	October 2	47	29	355	1	2
Jeff Blake, Cincinnati	vs. Houston	November 13	33	23	354	4	0
Dave Krieg, Detroit	vs. Buffalo	November 24	25	20	351	3	0
Steve Young, San Francisco	vs. Denver	December 17	29	20	350	3	1
John Elway, Denver	vs. Cleveland	October 30	41	30	349	2	0
Warren Moon, Minnesota	at New England	November 13*	42	26	349	1	0
Randall Cunningham, Philadelphia	at N.Y. Giants	September 4	39	20	344	2	0
Mike Tomczak, Pittsburgh	vs. Miami	November 20*	42	26	343	0	0
Jim Everett, New Orleans	at Denver	December 24	27	23	343	3	0
Troy Aikman, Dallas	at San Francisco	November 13	42	23	339	0	3
Jeff Hostetler, L.A. Raiders	at Denver	September 18	33	21	338	4	0
Stan Humphries, San Diego	vs. San Francisco	December 11	43	25	337	1	1
Drew Bledsoe, New England	vs. Green Bay	October 2	53	29	334	2	1
Jim Kelly, Buffalo	at New England	September 11	41	25	328	4	3
Jeff George, Atlanta	at New Orleans	November 13	49	29	328	1	1
Randall Cunningham, Philadelphia	vs. Dallas	December 4	46	29	327	2	1
Warren Moon, Minnesota	vs. Miami	September 25	37	26	326	3	0
Steve Young, San Francisco	vs. L.A. Rams	November 20	44	30	325	4	0
Bubby Brister, Philadelphia	at Cincinnati	December 24	37	26	325	1	0
Steve Bono, Kansas City	vs. Denver	December 4*	37	18	323	1	0
Drew Bledsoe, New England	vs. L.A. Raiders	October 9	55	23	321	2	3
Brett Favre, Green Bay	vs. Atlanta at Milw.	December 18	44	29	321	2	1
John Elway, Denver	at N.Y. Jets	September 11*	42	29	319	1	1
Jeff Hostetler, L.A. Raiders	at San Diego	December 5	29	22	319	2	1
Jay Schroeder, Arizona	at Atlanta	December 24	42	26	317	0	0
Joe Montana, Kansas City	at New Orleans	September 4	33	24	315	2	0
Steve Bono, Kansas City	at Miami	December 12	55	33	314	2	3
Craig Erickson, Tampa Bay	vs. Indianapolis	September 11	24	19	313	3	0
Dan Marino, Miami	at Pittsburgh	November 20*	45	31	312	1	1
Randall Cunningham, Philadelphia	vs. Chicago	September 12	36	24	311	3	0
Jason Garrett, Dallas	vs. Green Bay	November 24	26	15	311	2	1
Dan Marino, Miami	vs. Buffalo	December 4	42	25	311	3	3
Joe Montana, Kansas City	at San Diego	October 9	55	37	310	0	1
Randall Cunningham, Philadelphia	vs. Houston	October 24	24	13	310	2	1
Jeff Hostetler, L.A. Raiders	vs. New Orleans	November 20	28	22	310	3	2
Erik Kramer, Chicago	at Detroit	October 23	48	29	309	2	3
Steve Young, San Francisco	vs. L.A. Raiders	September 5	32	19	308	4	1

Team, Player	Opponent	Date	Att.	Comp.	Yds.	TD	Int.
Brett Favre, Green Bay	vs. Tampa Bay	September 25	39	30	306	3	0
Warren Moon, Minnesota	vs. Chicago	December 1*	48	27	306	2	1
Steve Young, San Francisco	at San Diego	December 11	32	25	304	2	0
Chris Miller, L.A. Rams	vs. Washington	December 24	40	27	304	2	1

*Overtime game.

RECEIVING

Team, Player	Opponent	Date	Rec.	Yds.	TD
Irving Fryar, Miami	vs. New England	September 4	5	211	3
Torrance Small, New Orleans	at Denver	December 24	6	200	2
Henry Ellard, Washington	at N.Y. Giants	September 18	10	197	1
Andre Rison, Atlanta	at Detroit	September 4*	14	193	2
Andre Reed, Buffalo	vs. Green Bay	November 20	15	191	2
Henry Ellard, Washington	at Arizona	December 11	8	191	1
Carl Pickens, Cincinnati	vs. Houston	November 13	11	188	3
Fred Barnett, Philadelphia	vs. Houston	October 24	5	187	1
Charles Wilson, Tampa Bay	vs. L.A. Rams	December 11	4	176	2
Cedric Tillman, Denver	vs. Atlanta	November 20	8	175	0
Fred Barnett, Philadelphia	vs. Arizona	November 6	11	173	2
Derrick Alexander, Cleveland	vs. N.Y. Giants	December 4	7	171	0
Jerry Rice, San Francisco	vs. L.A. Raiders	September 5	7	169	2
Herman Moore, Detroit	vs. Buffalo	November 24	7	169	1
Cris Carter, Minnesota	at Arizona	October 2	14	167	0
Jerry Rice, San Francisco	vs. L.A. Rams	November 20	16	165	3
Charles Johnson, Pittsburgh	at San Diego	December 24	4	165	2
Terance Mathis, Atlanta	at Denver	November 20	8	163	2
Henry Ellard, Washington	vs. Atlanta	September 25	6	162	1
Ben Coates, New England	at Miami	September 4	8	161	2
Irving Fryar, Miami	at Minnesota	September 25	6	160	0
Jake Reed, Minnesota	vs. New Orleans	November 6	8	157	1
Darnay Scott, Cincinnati	at Seattle	November 6*	7	157	0
Darnay Scott, Cincinnati	vs. Dallas	October 30	4	155	2
Willie Anderson, L.A. Rams	at Atlanta	September 11	5	154	1
Jeff Graham, Chicago	at Arizona	November 27*	8	154	0
Anthony Miller, Denver	at Kansas City	December 4*	6	153	0
Tony Martin, San Diego	at Seattle	September 18	6	152	1
Cris Carter, Minnesota	vs. New Orleans	November 6	12	151	0
Herman Moore, Detroit	vs. Green Bay at Milw.	November 6	8	151	2
Curtis Conway, Chicago	at Philadelphia	September 12	7	148	2
Rob Moore, N.Y. Jets	vs. Denver	September 11*	9	147	1
Jerry Rice, San Francisco	at L.A. Rams	September 18	11	147	1
Jerry Rice, San Francisco	at San Diego	December 11	12	144	1
Andre Reed, Buffalo	at New England	September 11	7	142	1
Brian Blades, Seattle	vs. Kansas City	November 27	7	141	0
Michael Irvin, Dallas	at Pittsburgh	September 4	8	139	1
Derrick Alexander, Cleveland	vs. Arizona	September 18	6	136	1
Tim Brown, L.A. Raiders	at Denver	September 18	7	136	1
Michael Irvin, Dallas	vs. Arizona	October 9	8	136	1
Jeff Graham, Chicago	at Detroit	October 23	7	136	1
Alvin Harper, Dallas	at San Francisco	November 13	3	136	0
Bert Emanuel, Atlanta	vs. Arizona	December 24	4	136	1
Carl Pickens, Cincinnati	vs. Philadelphia	December 24	9	135	1
Sterling Sharpe, Green Bay	at New England	October 2	9	132	1
Tim Brown, L.A. Raiders	vs. New Orleans	November 20	8	132	2
Carl Pickens, Cincinnati	at Denver	November 27	6	132	1
Sterling Sharpe, Green Bay	at Tampa Bay	December 24	9	132	3
J.J. Birden, Kansas City	at Miami	December 12	10	131	1
Tim Brown, L.A. Raiders	vs. Atlanta	October 23	8	130	2
Desmond Howard, Washington	at Tampa Bay	December 4	5	130	1
Terance Mathis, Atlanta	at San Francisco	December 4	7	128	0
Jake Reed, Minnesota	vs. Miami	September 25	9	127	0
Marshall Faulk, Indianapolis	vs. Washington	October 23	8	127	1
Michael Timpson, New England	at Cincinnati	September 18	10	125	1
Alvin Harper, Dallas	at Cincinnati	October 30	6	125	1
Terance Mathis, Atlanta	at New Orleans	November 13	10	125	0
Ben Coates, New England	vs. Buffalo	September 11	9	124	2
Terance Mathis, Atlanta	vs. Philadelphia	November 27	10	124	2
Rob Moore, N.Y. Jets	vs. Miami	November 27	7	124	0
Cris Carter, Minnesota	vs. Chicago	December 1*	9	124	2
Andre Rison, Atlanta	vs. L.A. Rams	September 11	12	123	2
Terance Mathis, Atlanta	vs. Kansas City	September 18	13	123	0
Ben Coates, New England	vs. L.A. Raiders	October 9	9	123	0
Webster Slaughter, Houston	vs. N.Y. Jets	December 24	8	123	0
Calvin Williams, Philadelphia	at San Francisco	October 2	9	122	0
Sterling Sharpe, Green Bay	at Dallas	November 24	9	122	4

Team, Player	Opponent	Date	Rec.	Yds.	TD
Calvin Williams, Philadelphia	at Cincinnati	December 24	6	122	0
Shannon Sharpe, Denver	at San Diego	October 23	6	121	1
Jake Reed, Minnesota	vs. N.Y. Jets	November 20	5	121	0
Jerry Rice, San Francisco	vs. Denver	December 17	9	121	1
Brett Perriman, Detroit	at Chicago	November 20	6	120	0
Johnny Mitchell, N.Y. Jets	at Minnesota	November 20	11	120	0
Gary Clark, Arizona	at Houston	December 4	6	120	1
Mike Pritchard, Denver	vs. San Diego	September 4	5	119	1
Mark Seay, San Diego	vs. Cincinnati	September 11	8	119	2
Ben Coates, New England	at Indianapolis	November 27	12	119	0
Michael Irvin, Dallas	vs. N.Y. Giants	November 7	7	118	0
Andre Rison, Atlanta	at New Orleans	November 13	8	118	1
Vincent Brisby, New England	vs. Green Bay	October 2	6	117	2
Qadry Ismail, Minnesota	at N.Y. Giants	October 10	7	117	0
Mark Ingram, Miami	at N.Y. Jets	November 27	9	117	4
Michael Irvin, Dallas	at Philadelphia	December 4	4	117	1
Anthony Miller, Denver	vs. Cincinnati	November 27	5	116	1
Johnny Bailey, L.A. Rams	vs. New Orleans	December 4	11	116	0
Tony Martin, San Diego	at N.Y. Jets	December 18	3	116	2
Lawrence Dawsey, Tampa Bay	at Washington	December 18	7	116	0
Michael Irvin, Dallas	at Arizona	October 23	5	115	2
Sterling Sharpe, Green Bay	at Detroit	December 4	10	115	1
Vincent Brisby, New England	at Chicago	December 24	6	115	0
Michael Timpson, New England	vs. Minnesota	November 13*	10	113	0
Irving Fryar, Miami	at Pittsburgh	November 20*	6	113	0
Pat Coleman, Houston	vs. Cincinnati	September 25	4	112	0
Irving Fryar, Miami	vs. Chicago	November 13	9	112	0
Andre Reed, Buffalo	vs. New England	December 18	6	112	0
Cris Carter, Minnesota	at Buffalo	December 11	9	111	0
Don Beebe, Buffalo	at Indianapolis	December 24	8	111	0
Webster Slaughter, Houston	vs. Buffalo	September 18	4	110	0
Irving Fryar, Miami	vs. Buffalo	December 4	5	110	2
Willie Davis, Kansas City	at New Orleans	September 4	7	109	1
Alvin Harper, Dallas	vs. Houston	September 11	3	109	1
Mike Sherrard, N.Y. Giants	at Houston	November 21	6	109	1
Sterling Sharpe, Green Bay	at Philadelphia	September 18	6	108	1
Ben Coates, New England	at Cincinnati	September 18	8	108	0
Henry Ellard, Washington	at Indianapolis	October 23	6	108	0
O.J. McDuffie, Miami	vs. Indianapolis	November 6	7	108	1
Art Monk, N.Y. Jets	vs. Miami	November 27	5	108	0
Desmond Howard, Washington	at Dallas	November 20	7	107	1
Willie Davis, Kansas City	vs. Denver	December 4*	3	107	1
Tim Brown, L.A. Raiders	at Seattle	December 18	4	107	1
Andre Reed, Buffalo	vs. Kansas City	October 30	5	106	2
Herman Moore, Detroit	at N.Y. Giants	October 30*	9	106	2
Andre Reed, Buffalo	at Miami	December 4	3	106	2
Ricky Watters, San Francisco	vs. Denver	December 17	4	106	2
Henry Ellard, Washington	vs. Seattle	September 4	7	105	0
Anthony Miller, Denver	at N.Y. Jets	September 11*	6	105	1
Derrick Alexander, Cleveland	vs. N.Y. Jets	October 2	7	105	0
Sean Dawkins, Indianapolis	at Buffalo	October 16	6	105	0
Willie Anderson, L.A. Rams	vs. L.A. Raiders	November 13	5	105	1
Carl Pickens, Cincinnati	vs. Pittsburgh	December 4	4	105	1
Robert Brooks, Green Bay	vs. Chicago	December 11	6	105	1
Kelvin Martin, Seattle	at Indianapolis	October 2	8	104	1
Haywood Jeffires, Houston	at Dallas	September 11	6	103	0
John Taylor, San Francisco	at L.A. Rams	September 18	7	103	1
Carl Pickens, Cincinnati	vs. Indianapolis	November 20	6	103	0
Irving Fryar, Miami	at N.Y. Jets	November 27	5	103	0
Anthony Morgan, Green Bay	at Detroit	December 4	6	103	2
Michael Haynes, New Orleans	at Atlanta	December 11	5	103	1
Fred Barnett, Philadelphia	vs. Chicago	September 12	8	102	0
Anthony Miller, Denver	vs. Atlanta	November 20	6	102	1
Quinn Early, New Orleans	vs. Kansas City	September 4	8	101	0
Michael Timpson, New England	vs. Buffalo	September 11	5	101	1
Adrian Cooper, Minnesota	vs. N.Y. Jets	November 20	7	101	0
Qadry Ismail, Minnesota	vs. Tampa Bay	November 27*	6	101	1
Mike Sherrard, N.Y. Giants	at Cleveland	December 4	5	101	0
J.J. Birden, Kansas City	vs. Denver	December 4*	7	101	0
Edgar Bennett, Green Bay	vs. Atlanta at Milw.	December 18	8	101	0
Gary Clark, Arizona	vs. Cincinnati	December 18	7	101	0
Lake Dawson, Kansas City	vs. Houston	December 18	5	101	1
Mike Pritchard, Denver	at N.Y. Jets	September 11*	9	100	0
Cris Carter, Minnesota	vs. N.Y. Jets	November 20	11	100	1

*Overtime game.

HISTORY

Championship games

Year-by-year standings

Super Bowls

Pro Bowls

Records

Statistical leaders

Coaching records

Hall of Fame

The Sporting News awards

Team histories

CHAMPIONSHIP GAMES

NFL (1933-1969); NFC (1970-1994)

RESULTS

Sea.	Date	Winner (Share)	Loser (Share)	Score	Site	Attendance
1933	Dec. 17	Chicago Bears ($210.34)	N.Y. Giants ($140.22)	23-21	Chicago	26,000
1934	Dec. 9	N.Y. Giants ($621)	Chicago Bears ($414.02)	30-13	N.Y. Giants	35,059
1935	Dec. 15	Detroit ($313.35)	N.Y. Giants ($200.20)	26-7	Detroit	15,000
1936	Dec. 13	Green Bay ($250)	Boston Redskins ($180)	21-6	N.Y. Giants	29,545
1937	Dec. 12	Washington ($225.90)	Chicago Bears ($127.78)	28-21	Chicago	15,870
1938	Dec. 11	N.Y. Giants ($504.45)	Green Bay ($368.81)	23-17	N.Y. Giants	48,120
1939	Dec. 10	Green Bay ($703.97)	N.Y. Giants ($455.57)	27-0	Milwaukee	32,279
1940	Dec. 8	Chicago Bears ($873)	Washington ($606)	73-0	Washington	36,034
1941	Dec. 21	Chicago Bears ($430)	N.Y. Giants ($288)	37-9	Chicago	13,341
1942	Dec. 13	Washington ($965)	Chicago Bears ($637)	14-6	Washington	36,006
1943	Dec. 26	Chicago Bears ($1,146)	Washington ($765)	41-21	Chicago	34,320
1944	Dec. 17	Green Bay ($1,449)	N.Y. Giants ($814)	14-7	N.Y. Giants	46,016
1945	Dec. 16	Cleveland Rams ($1,469)	Washington ($902)	15-14	Cleveland	32,178
1946	Dec. 15	Chicago Bears ($1,975)	N.Y. Giants ($1,295)	24-14	N.Y. Giants	58,346
1947	Dec. 28	Chi. Cardinals ($1,132)	Philadelphia ($754)	28-21	Chicago	30,759
1948	Dec. 19	Philadelphia ($1,540)	Chi. Cardinals ($874)	7-0	Philadelphia	36,309
1949	Dec. 18	Philadelphia ($1,094)	L.A. Rams ($739)	14-0	L.A. Rams	27,980
1950	Dec. 24	Cleve. Browns ($1,113)	L.A. Rams ($686)	30-28	Cleveland	29,751
1951	Dec. 23	L. A. Rams ($2,108)	Cleve. Browns ($1,483)	24-17	L.A. Rams	57,522
1952	Dec. 28	Detroit ($2,274)	Cleveland Browns ($1,712)	17-7	Cleveland	50,934
1953	Dec. 27	Detroit ($2,424)	Cleveland Browns ($1,654)	17-16	Detroit	54,577
1954	Dec. 26	Cleve. Browns ($2,478)	Detroit ($1,585)	56-10	Cleveland	43,827
1955	Dec. 26	Cleve. Browns ($3,508)	L.A. Rams ($2,316)	38-14	L.A. Rams	85,693
1956	Dec. 30	N.Y. Giants ($3,779)	Chicago Bears ($2,485)	47-7	N.Y. Giants	56,836
1957	Dec. 29	Detroit ($4,295)	Cleveland Browns ($2,750)	59-14	Detroit	55,263
1958	Dec. 28	Baltimore ($4,718)	N.Y. Giants ($3,111)	23-17*	N.Y. Giants	64,185
1959	Dec. 27	Baltimore ($4,674)	N.Y. Giants ($3,083)	31-16	Baltimore	57,545
1960	Dec. 26	Philadelphia ($5,116)	Green Bay ($3,105)	17-13	Philadelphia	67,325
1961	Dec. 31	Green Bay ($5,195)	N.Y. Giants ($3,339)	37-0	Green Bay	39,029
1962	Dec. 30	Green Bay ($5,888)	N.Y. Giants ($4,166)	16-7	N.Y. Giants	64,892
1963	Dec. 29	Chicago Bears ($5,899)	N.Y. Giants ($4,218)	14-10	Chicago	45,801
1964	Dec. 27	Cleve. Browns ($8,052)	Baltimore ($5,571)	27-0	Cleveland	79,544
1965	Jan. 2	Green Bay ($7,819)	Cleveland Browns ($5,288)	23-12	Green Bay	50,777
1966	Jan. 1	Green Bay ($9,813)	Dallas ($6,527)	34-27	Dallas	74,152
1967	Dec. 31	Green Bay ($7,950)	Dallas ($5,299)	21-17	Green Bay	50,861
1968	Dec. 29	Baltimore ($9,306)	Cleveland Browns ($5,963)	34-0	Cleveland	78,410
1969	Jan. 4	Minnesota ($7,930)	Cleveland Browns ($5,118)	27-7	Minnesota	46,503
1970	Jan. 3	Dallas ($8,500)	San Francisco ($5,500)	17-10	San Francisco	59,364
1971	Jan. 2	Dallas ($8,500)	San Francisco ($5,500)	14-3	Dallas	63,409
1972	Dec. 31	Washington ($8,500)	Dallas ($5,500)	26-3	Washington	53,129
1973	Dec. 30	Minnesota ($8,500)	Dallas ($5,500)	27-10	Dallas	64,422
1974	Dec. 29	Minnesota ($8,500)	L.A. Rams ($5,500)	14-10	Minnesota	48,444
1975	Jan. 4	Dallas ($8,500)	L.A. Rams ($5,500)	37-7	L.A. Rams	88,919
1976	Dec. 26	Minnesota ($8,500)	L.A. Rams ($5,500)	24-13	Minnesota	48,379
1977	Jan. 1	Dallas ($9,000)	Minnesota ($9,000)	23-6	Dallas	64,293
1978	Jan. 7	Dallas ($9,000)	L.A. Rams ($9,000)	28-0	L.A. Rams	71,086
1979	Jan. 6	L.A. Rams ($9,000)	Tampa Bay ($9,000)	9-0	Tampa Bay	72,033
1980	Jan. 11	Philadelphia ($9,000)	Dallas ($9,000)	20-7	Philadelphia	70,696
1981	Jan. 10	San Francisco ($9,000)	Dallas ($9,000)	28-27	San Francisco	60,525
1982	Jan. 22	Washington ($18,000)	Dallas ($18,000)	31-17	Washington	55,045
1983	Jan. 8	Washington ($18,000)	San Francisco ($18,000)	24-21	Washington	55,363
1984	Jan. 6	San Francisco ($18,000)	Chicago Bears ($18,000)	23-0	San Francisco	61,040
1985	Jan. 12	Chicago Bears ($18,000)	L.A. Rams ($18,000)	24-0	Chicago	63,522
1986	Jan. 11	N. Y. Giants ($18,000)	Washington ($18,000)	17-0	N.Y. Giants	76,633
1987	Jan. 17	Washington ($18,000)	Minnesota ($18,000)	17-10	Washington	55,212
1988	Jan. 8	San Francisco ($18,000)	Chicago Bears ($18,000)	28-3	Chicago	64,830
1989	Jan. 14	San Francisco ($18,000)	L.A. Rams ($18,000)	30-3	San Francisco	64,769
1990	Jan. 20	N. Y. Giants ($18,000)	San Francisco ($18,000)	15-13	San Francisco	65,750
1991	Jan. 12	Washington ($18,000)	Detroit ($18,000)	41-10	Washington	55,585
1992	Jan. 17	Dallas ($18,000)	San Francisco ($18,000)	30-20	San Francisco	64,920
1993	Jan. 23	Dallas ($18,000)	San Francisco ($18,000)	38-21	Dallas	64,902
1994	Jan. 15	San Francisco ($18,000)	Dallas ($18,000)	38-28	San Francisco	69,125

*Sudden-death overtime.

COMPOSITE STANDINGS

	W	L	Pct.	PF	PA		W	L	Pct.	PF	PA
Green Bay Packers	8	2	.800	223	116	Phoenix Cardinals*	1	1	.500	28	28
Philadelphia Eagles	4	1	.800	79	48	Dallas Cowboys	7	8	.467	323	292
Baltimore Colts	3	1	.750	88	60	San Francisco 49ers	5	6	.455	235	199
Detroit Lions	4	2	.667	139	141	Cleveland Browns	4	7	.364	224	253
Minnesota Vikings	4	2	.667	108	80	New York Giants	5	11	.313	240	322
Washington Redskins†	7	5	.583	222	255	Los Angeles Rams‡	3	9	.250	123	270
Chicago Bears	7	6	.538	286	245	Tampa Bay Buccaneers	0	1	.000	0	9

*Both games played when franchise was in Chicago; won 28-21, lost 7-0.
†One game played when franchise was in Boston; lost 21-6.
‡One game played when franchise was in Cleveland; won 15-14.

AFL (1960-1969); AFC (1970-1994)

RESULTS

Sea.	Date	Winner (Share)	Loser (Share)	Score	Site	Attendance
1960	Jan. 1	Houston ($1,025)	L.A. Chargers ($718)	24-16	Houston	32,183
1961	Dec. 24	Houston ($1,792)	San Diego ($1,111)	10-3	San Diego	29,556
1962	Dec. 23	Dallas Texans ($2,206)	Houston ($1,471)	20-17*	Houston	37,981
1963	Jan. 5	San Diego ($2,498)	Boston Patriots ($1,596)	51-10	San Diego	30,127
1964	Dec. 26	Buffalo ($2,668)	San Diego ($1,738)	20-7	Buffalo	40,242
1965	Dec. 26	Buffalo ($5,189)	San Diego ($3,447)	23-0	Buffalo	30,361
1966	Jan. 1	Kansas City ($5,309)	Buffalo ($3,799)	31-7	Buffalo	42,080
1967	Dec. 31	Oakland ($6,321)	Houston ($4,996)	40-7	Oakland	53,330
1968	Dec. 29	N.Y. Jets ($7,007)	Oakland ($5,349)	27-23	New York	62,627
1969	Jan. 4	Kansas City ($7,755)	Oakland ($6,252)	17-7	Oakland	53,564
1970	Jan. 3	Baltimore ($8,500)	Oakland ($5,500)	27-17	Baltimore	54,799
1971	Jan. 2	Miami ($8,500)	Baltimore ($5,500)	21-0	Miami	76,622
1972	Dec. 31	Miami ($8,500)	Pittsburgh ($5,500)	21-17	Pittsburgh	50,845
1973	Dec. 30	Miami ($8,500)	Oakland ($5,500)	27-10	Miami	79,325
1974	Dec. 29	Pittsburgh ($8,500)	Oakland ($5,500)	24-13	Oakland	53,800
1975	Jan. 4	Pittsburgh ($8,500)	Oakland ($5,500)	16-10	Pittsburgh	50,609
1976	Dec. 28	Oakland ($8,500)	Pittsburgh ($5,500)	24-7	Oakland	53,821
1977	Jan. 1	Denver ($9,000)	Oakland ($9,000)	20-17	Denver	75,044
1978	Jan. 7	Pittsburgh ($9,000)	Houston ($9,000)	34-5	Pittsburgh	50,725
1979	Jan. 6	Pittsburgh ($9,000)	Houston ($9,000)	27-13	Pittsburgh	50,475
1980	Jan. 11	Oakland ($9,000)	San Diego ($9,000)	34-27	San Diego	52,428
1981	Jan. 10	Cincinnati ($9,000)	San Diego ($9,000)	27-7	Cincinnati	46,302
1982	Jan. 23	Miami ($18,000)	N.Y. Jets ($18,000)	14-0	Miami	67,396
1983	Jan. 8	L.A. Raiders ($18,000)	Seattle ($18,000)	30-14	Los Angeles	88,734
1984	Jan. 6	Miami ($18,000)	Pittsburgh ($18,000)	45-28	Miami	76,029
1985	Jan. 12	New England ($18,000)	Miami ($18,000)	31-14	Miami	74,978
1986	Jan. 11	Denver ($18,000)	Cleveland ($18,000)	23-20*	Cleveland	79,915
1987	Jan. 17	Denver ($18,000)	Cleveland ($18,000)	38-33	Denver	75,993
1988	Jan. 8	Cincinnati ($18,000)	Buffalo ($18,000)	21-10	Cincinnati	59,747
1989	Jan. 14	Denver ($18,000)	Cleveland ($18,000)	37-21	Denver	76,046
1990	Jan. 20	Buffalo ($18,000)	L.A. Raiders ($18,000)	51-3	Buffalo	80,234
1991	Jan. 12	Buffalo ($18,000)	Denver ($18,000)	10-7	Buffalo	80,272
1992	Jan. 17	Buffalo ($18,000)	Miami ($18,000)	29-10	Miami	72,703
1993	Jan. 23	Buffalo ($18,000)	Kansas City ($18,000)	30-13	Buffalo	76,642
1994	Jan. 15	San Diego ($18,000)	Pittsburgh ($18,000)	17-13	Pittsburgh	61,545

*Sudden-death overtime.

COMPOSITE STANDINGS

	W	L	Pct.	PF	PA		W	L	Pct.	PF	PA
Cincinnati Bengals	2	0	1.000	48	17	New York Jets	1	1	.500	27	37
Denver Broncos	4	1	.800	125	101	Pittsburgh Steelers	4	4	.500	166	148
Buffalo Bills	6	2	.750	180	92	Los Angeles Raiders§	4	8	.333	228	264
Kansas City Chiefs†	3	1	.750	81	61	Houston Oilers	2	4	.333	76	140
Miami Dolphins	5	2	.714	152	115	San Diego Chargers*	2	6	.250	128	161
Baltimore Colts	1	1	.500	27	38	Seattle Seahawks	0	1	.000	14	30
New England Patriots‡	1	1	.500	41	65	Cleveland Browns	0	3	.000	74	98

*One game played when franchise was in Los Angeles; lost 24-16.
†One game played when franchise was in Dallas (Texans); won 20-17.
‡One game played when franchise was in Boston; lost 51-10.
§10 games played when franchise was in Oakland; record of 3-7.

	W	L	Pct.	PF	PA		W	L	Pct.	PF	PA
Green Bay Packers	15	7	.682	486	357	New York Jets	5	6	.455	216	200
San Francisco 49ers	21	11	.656	843	605	New York Giants	14	18	.438	529	593
Dallas Cowboys	28	18	.609	1102	836	Seattle Seahawks	3	4	.429	128	139
Washington Redskins‡	21	14	.600	738	625	Minnesota Vikings	13	18	.419	553	646
Pittsburgh Steelers	17	12	.586	651	571	Cincinnati Bengals	5	7	.417	246	257
Los Angeles Raiders◆	21	15	.583	855	659	San Diego Chargers•	7	10	.412	312	393
Miami Dolphins	17	13	.567	675	596	Houston Oilers	9	13	.409	371	533
Buffalo Bills	13	11	.542	563	520	Los Angeles Rams†	13	20	.394	501	697
Chicago Bears	14	14	.500	579	552	Cleveland Browns	11	19	.367	596	702
Detroit Lions	7	7	.500	305	299	New England Patriots§	4	7	.363	218	278
Indianapolis Colts■	8	8	.500	285	300	Atlanta Falcons	2	4	.333	119	144
Denver Broncos	9	10	.474	380	502	Tampa Bay Buccaneers	1	3	.250	41	94
Kansas City Chiefs*	8	9	.471	284	360	Arizona Cardinals★	1	4	.200	81	134
Philadelphia Eagles	8	9	.471	287	288	New Orleans Saints	0	4	.000	56	123

*One game played when franchise was in Dallas (Texans); won 20-17.
†One game played when franchise was in Cleveland; won 15-14.
‡One game played when franchise was in Boston; lost 21-6.
§Two games played when franchise was in Boston; won 26-8, lost 51-10.
★Two games played when franchise was in Chicago; won 28-21, lost 7-0. Three games played when franchise was in St. Louis; lost 35-23, lost 30-14, lost 41-16.
•††One game played when franchise was in Los Angeles; lost 24-16.
◆24 games played when franchise was in Oakland; record of 15-9.
■15 games played when franchise was in Baltimore; record of 8-7.

1920

Team	W	L	T	Pct.
Akron Pros*	8	0	3	1.000
Decatur Staleys	10	1	2	.909
Buffalo All-Americans	9	1	1	.900
Chicago Cardinals	6	2	2	.750
Rock Island Independents	6	2	2	.750
Dayton Triangles	5	2	2	.714
Rochester Jeffersons	6	3	2	.667
Canton Bulldogs	7	4	2	.636
Detroit Heralds	2	3	3	.400
Cleveland Tigers	2	4	2	.333
Chicago Tigers	2	5	1	.286
Hammond Pros	2	5	0	.286
Columbus Panhandles	2	6	2	.250
Muncie Flyers	0	1	0	.000

*No official standings were maintained for the 1920 season, and the championship was awarded to the Akron Pros in a League meeting on April 30, 1921. Clubs played schedules which included games against non-league opponents. Records of clubs against all opponents are listed above.

1921

Team	W	L	T	Pct.
Chicago Staleys	9	1	1	.900
Buffalo All-Americans	9	1	2	.900
Akron Pros	8	3	1	.727
Canton Bulldogs	5	2	3	.714
Rock Island Independents	4	2	1	.667
Evansville Crimson Giants	3	2	0	.600
Green Bay Packers	3	2	1	.600
Dayton Triangles	4	4	1	.500
Chicago Cardinals	3	3	2	.500
Rochester Jeffersons	2	3	0	.400
Cleveland Indians	3	5	0	.375
Washington Senators	1	2	0	.333
Cincinnati Celts	1	3	0	.250
Hammond Pros	1	3	1	.250
Minneapolis Marines	1	3	1	.250
Detroit Heralds	1	5	1	.167
Columbus Panhandles	1	8	0	.111
Tonawanda Kardex	0	1	0	.000
Muncie Flyers	0	2	0	.000
Louisville Brecks	0	2	0	.000
New York Giants	0	2	0	.000

1922

Team	W	L	T	Pct.
Canton Bulldogs	10	0	2	1.000
Chicago Bears	9	3	0	.750
Chicago Cardinals	8	3	0	.727
Toledo Maroons	5	2	2	.714
Rock Island Independents	4	2	1	.667
Racine Legion	6	4	1	.600
Dayton Triangles	4	3	1	.571
Green Bay Packers	4	3	3	.571
Buffalo All-Americans	5	4	1	.556
Akron Pros	3	5	2	.375
Milwaukee Badgers	2	4	3	.333
Oorang Indians	2	6	0	.250
Minneapolis Marines	1	3	0	.250
Louisville Brecks	1	3	0	.250
Evansville Crimson Giants	0	3	0	.000
Rochester Jeffersons	0	4	1	.000
Hammond Pros	0	5	1	.000
Columbus Panhandles	0	7	0	.000

1923

Team	W	L	T	Pct.
Canton Bulldogs	11	0	1	1.000
Chicago Bears	9	2	1	.818
Green Bay Packers	7	2	1	.778
Milwaukee Badgers	7	2	3	.778
Cleveland Indians	3	1	3	.750
Chicago Cardinals	8	4	0	.667
Duluth Kelleys	4	3	0	.571
Columbus Tigers	5	4	1	.556
Buffalo All-Americans	4	4	3	.500
Racine Legion	4	4	2	.500
Toledo Maroons	2	3	2	.400
Rock Island Independents	2	3	3	.400
Minneapolis Marines	2	5	2	.286
St. Louis All-Stars	1	4	2	.200
Hammond Pros	1	5	1	.167
Dayton Triangles	1	6	1	.143
Akron Indians	1	6	0	.143
Oorang Indians	1	10	0	.091
Rochester Jeffersons	0	2	0	.000
Louisville Brecks	0	3	0	.000

1924

Team	W	L	T	Pct.
Cleveland Bulldogs	7	1	1	.875
Chicago Bears	6	1	4	.857
Frankford Yellow Jackets	11	2	1	.846
Duluth Kelleys	5	1	0	.833
Rock Island Independents	6	2	2	.750
Green Bay Packers	7	4	0	.636
Racine Legion	4	3	3	.571
Chicago Cardinals	5	4	1	.556
Buffalo Bisons	6	5	0	.545
Columbus Tigers	4	4	0	.500
Hammond Pros	2	2	1	.500
Milwaukee Badgers	5	8	0	.385
Akron Indians	2	6	0	.250
Dayton Triangles	2	6	0	.250
Kansas City Blues	2	7	0	.222
Kenosha Maroons	0	5	1	.000
Minneapolis Marines	0	6	0	.000
Rochester Jeffersons	0	7	0	.000

1925

Team	W	L	T	Pct.
Chicago Cardinals	11	2	1	.846
Pottsville Maroons	10	2	0	.833
Detroit Panthers	8	2	2	.800
New York Giants	8	4	0	.667
Akron Indians	4	2	2	.667
Frankford Yellow Jackets	13	7	0	.650
Chicago Bears	9	5	3	.643
Rock Island Independents	5	3	3	.625
Green Bay Packers	8	5	0	.615
Providence Steam Roller	6	5	1	.545
Canton Bulldogs	4	4	0	.500
Cleveland Bulldogs	5	8	1	.385
Kansas City Cowboys	2	5	1	.286
Hammond Pros	1	4	0	.200
Buffalo Bisons	1	6	2	.143
Duluth Kelleys	0	3	0	.000
Rochester Jeffersons	0	6	1	.000
Milwaukee Badgers	0	6	0	.000
Dayton Triangles	0	7	1	.000
Columbus Tigers	0	9	0	.000

1926

Team	W	L	T	Pct.
Frankford Yellow Jackets	14	1	1	.933
Chicago Bears	12	1	3	.923
Pottsville Maroons	10	2	1	.833
Kansas City Cowboys	8	3	0	.727
Green Bay Packers	7	3	3	.700
Los Angeles Buccaneers	6	3	1	.667
New York Giants	8	4	1	.667

Team	W	L	T	Pct.
Duluth Eskimos	6	5	3	.545
Buffalo Rangers	4	4	2	.500
Chicago Cardinals	5	6	1	.455
Providence Steam Roller	5	7	1	.417
Detroit Panthers	4	6	2	.400
Hartford Blues	3	7	0	.300
Brooklyn Lions	3	8	0	.273
Milwaukee Badgers	2	7	0	.222
Akron Pros	1	4	3	.200
Dayton Triangles	1	4	1	.200
Racine Tornadoes	1	4	0	.200
Columbus Tigers	1	6	0	.143
Canton Bulldogs	1	9	3	.100
Hammond Pros	0	4	0	.000
Louisville Colonels	0	4	0	.000

1927

Team	W	L	T	Pct.
New York Giants	11	1	1	.917
Green Bay Packers	7	2	1	.778
Chicago Bears	9	3	2	.750
Cleveland Bulldogs	8	4	1	.667
Providence Steam Roller	8	5	1	.615
New York Yankees	7	8	1	.467
Frankford Yellow Jackets	6	9	3	.400
Pottsville Maroons	5	8	0	.385
Chicago Cardinals	3	7	1	.300
Dayton Triangles	1	6	1	.143
Duluth Eskimos	1	8	0	.111
Buffalo Bisons	0	5	0	.000

1928

Team	W	L	T	Pct.
Providence Steam Roller	8	1	2	.889
Frankford Yellow Jackets	11	3	2	.786
Detroit Wolverines	7	2	1	.778
Green Bay Packers	6	4	3	.600
Chicago Bears	7	5	1	.583
New York Giants	4	7	2	.364
New York Yankees	4	8	1	.333
Pottsville Maroons	2	8	0	.200
Chicago Cardinals	1	5	0	.167
Dayton Triangles	0	7	0	.000

1929

Team	W	L	T	Pct.
Green Bay Packers	12	0	1	1.000
New York Giants	13	1	1	.929
Frankford Yellow Jackets	9	4	5	.692
Chicago Cardinals	6	6	1	.500

Team	W	L	T	Pct.
Boston Bulldogs	4	4	0	.500
Orange Tornadoes	3	4	4	.429
Staten Island Stapletons	3	4	3	.429
Providence Steam Roller	4	6	2	.400
Chicago Bears	4	9	2	.308
Buffalo Bisons	1	7	1	.125
Minneapolis Red Jackets	1	9	0	.100
Dayton Triangles	0	6	0	.000

1930

Team	W	L	T	Pct.
Green Bay Packers	10	3	1	.769
New York Giants	13	4	0	.765
Chicago Bears	9	4	1	.692
Brooklyn Dodgers	7	4	1	.636
Providence Steam Roller	6	4	1	.600
Staten Island Stapletons	5	5	2	.500
Chicago Cardinals	5	6	2	.455
Portsmouth Spartans	5	6	3	.455
Frankford Yellow Jackets	4	13	1	.222
Minneapolis Red Jackets	1	7	1	.125
Newark Tornadoes	1	10	1	.091

1931

Team	W	L	T	Pct.
Green Bay Packers	12	2	0	.857
Portsmouth Spartans	11	3	0	.786
Chicago Bears	8	5	0	.615
Chicago Cardinals	5	4	0	.556
New York Giants	7	6	1	.538
Providence Steam Roller	4	4	3	.500
Staten Island Stapletons	4	6	1	.400
Cleveland Indians	2	8	0	.200
Brooklyn Dodgers	2	12	0	.143
Frankford Yellow Jackets	1	6	1	.143

1932

Team	W	L	T	Pct.
Chicago Bears	7	1	6	.875
Green Bay Packers	10	3	1	.769
Portsmouth Spartans	6	2	4	.750
Boston Braves	4	4	2	.500
New York Giants	4	6	2	.400
Brooklyn Dodgers	3	9	0	.250
Chicago Cardinals	2	6	2	.250
Staten Island Stapletons	2	7	3	.222

NOTE: Chicago Bears and Portsmouth finished regularly scheduled games tied for first place. Bears won playoff game, which counted in standings, 9-0.

1933

EASTERN DIVISION

Team	W	L	T	Pct.	PF	PA
N.Y. Giants	11	3	0	.786	244	101
Brooklyn	5	4	1	.556	93	54
Boston	5	5	2	.500	103	97
Philadelphia	3	5	1	.375	77	158
Pittsburgh	3	6	2	.333	67	208

WESTERN DIVISION

Team	W	L	T	Pct.	PF	PA
Chicago Bears	10	2	1	.833	133	82
Portsmouth	6	5	0	.545	128	87
Green Bay	5	7	1	.417	170	107
Cincinnati	3	6	1	.333	38	110
Chi. Cardinals	1	9	1	.100	52	101

PLAYOFFS

NFL championship

Chicago Bears 23 vs. N.Y. Giants 21

1934

EASTERN DIVISION

Team	W	L	T	Pct.	PF	PA
N.Y. Giants	8	5	0	.615	147	107
Boston	6	6	0	.500	107	94
Brooklyn	4	7	0	.364	61	153
Philadelphia	4	7	0	.364	127	85
Pittsburgh	2	10	0	.167	51	206

WESTERN DIVISION

Team	W	L	T	Pct.	PF	PA
Chicago Bears	13	0	0	1.000	286	86
Detroit	10	3	0	.769	238	59
Green Bay	7	6	0	.538	156	112
Chi. Cardinals	5	6	0	.455	80	84
St. Louis	1	2	0	.333	27	61
Cincinnati	0	8	0	.000	10	243

PLAYOFFS

NFL championship

N.Y. Giants 30 vs. Chicago Bears 13

EASTERN DIVISION

Team	W	L	T	Pct.	PF	PA
N.Y. Giants	9	3	0	.750	180	96
Brooklyn	5	6	1	.455	90	141
Pittsburgh	4	8	0	.333	100	209
Boston	2	8	1	.200	65	123
Philadelphia	2	9	0	.182	60	179

NOTE: One game between Boston and Philadelphia was cancelled.

WESTERN DIVISION

Team	W	L	T	Pct.	PF	PA
Detroit	7	3	2	.700	191	111
Green Bay	8	4	0	.667	181	96
Chicago Bears	6	4	2	.600	192	106
Chi. Cardinals	6	4	2	.600	99	97

PLAYOFFS

NFL championship
Detroit 26 vs. N.Y. Giants 7

EASTERN DIVISION

Team	W	L	T	Pct.	PF	PA
Boston	7	5	0	.583	149	110
Pittsburgh	6	6	0	.500	98	187
N.Y. Giants	5	6	1	.455	115	163
Brooklyn	3	8	1	.273	92	161
Philadelphia	1	11	0	.083	51	206

WESTERN DIVISION

Team	W	L	T	Pct.	PF	PA
Green Bay	10	1	1	.909	248	118
Chicago Bears	9	3	0	.750	222	94
Detroit	8	4	0	.667	235	102
Chi. Cardinals	3	8	1	.273	74	143

PLAYOFFS

NFL championship
Green Bay 21, Boston 6, at New York.

EASTERN DIVISION

Team	W	L	T	Pct.	PF	PA
Washington	8	3	0	.727	195	120
N.Y. Giants	6	3	2	.667	128	109
Pittsburgh	4	7	0	.364	122	145
Brooklyn	3	7	1	.300	82	174
Philadelphia	2	8	1	.200	86	177

WESTERN DIVISION

Team	W	L	T	Pct.	PF	PA
Chicago Bears	9	1	1	.900	201	100
Green Bay	7	4	0	.636	220	122
Detroit	7	4	0	.636	180	105
Chi. Cardinals	5	5	1	.500	135	165
Cleveland	1	10	0	.091	75	207

PLAYOFFS

NFL championship
Washington 28 at Chicago Bears 21

EASTERN DIVISION

Team	W	L	T	Pct.	PF	PA
N.Y. Giants	8	2	1	.800	194	79
Washington	6	3	2	.667	148	154
Brooklyn	4	4	3	.500	131	161
Philadelphia	5	6	0	.455	154	164
Pittsburgh	2	9	0	.182	79	169

WESTERN DIVISION

Team	W	L	T	Pct.	PF	PA
Green Bay	8	3	0	.727	223	118
Detroit	7	4	0	.636	119	108
Chicago Bears	6	5	0	.545	194	148
Cleveland	4	7	0	.364	131	215
Chi. Cardinals	2	9	0	.182	111	168

PLAYOFFS

NFL championship
N.Y. Giants 23 vs. Green Bay 17

EASTERN DIVISION

Team	W	L	T	Pct.	PF	PA
N.Y. Giants	9	1	1	.900	168	85
Washington	8	2	1	.800	242	94
Brooklyn	4	6	1	.400	108	219
Philadelphia	1	9	1	.100	105	200
Pittsburgh	1	9	1	.100	114	216

WESTERN DIVISION

Team	W	L	T	Pct.	PF	PA
Green Bay	9	2	0	.818	233	153
Chicago Bears	8	3	0	.727	298	157
Detroit	6	5	0	.545	145	150
Cleveland	5	5	1	.500	195	164
Chi. Cardinals	1	10	0	.091	84	254

PLAYOFFS

NFL championship
Green Bay 27 vs. N.Y. Giants 0

EASTERN DIVISION

Team	W	L	T	Pct.	PF	PA
Washington	9	2	0	.818	245	142
Brooklyn	8	3	0	.727	186	120
N.Y. Giants	6	4	1	.600	131	133
Pittsburgh	2	7	2	.222	60	178
Philadelphia	1	10	0	.091	111	211

WESTERN DIVISION

Team	W	L	T	Pct.	PF	PA
Chicago Bears	8	3	0	.727	238	152
Green Bay	6	4	1	.600	238	155
Detroit	5	5	1	.500	138	153
Cleveland	4	6	1	.400	171	191
Chi. Cardinals	2	7	2	.222	139	222

PLAYOFFS

NFL championship
Chicago Bears 73 at Washington 0

1941

EASTERN DIVISION

Team	W	L	T	Pct.	PF	PA
N.Y. Giants	8	3	0	.727	238	114
Brooklyn	7	4	0	.636	158	127
Washington	6	5	0	.545	176	174
Philadelphia	2	8	1	.200	119	218
Pittsburgh	1	9	1	.100	103	276

WESTERN DIVISION

Team	W	L	T	Pct.	PF	PA
Chicago Bears	10	1	0	.909	396	147
Green Bay	10	1	0	.909	258	120
Detroit	4	6	1	.400	121	195
Chi. Cardinals	3	7	1	.300	127	197
Cleveland	2	9	0	.182	116	244

PLAYOFFS

Western Division playoff
Chicago Bears 33 vs. Green Bay 14

NFL championship
Chicago Bears 37 vs. N.Y. Giants 9

1942

EASTERN DIVISION

Team	W	L	T	Pct.	PF	PA
Washington	10	1	0	.909	227	102
Pittsburgh	7	4	0	.636	167	119
N.Y. Giants	5	5	1	.500	155	139
Brooklyn	3	8	0	.273	100	168
Philadelphia	2	9	0	.182	134	239

WESTERN DIVISION

Team	W	L	T	Pct.	PF	PA
Chicago Bears	11	0	0	1.000	376	84
Green Bay	8	2	1	.800	300	215
Cleveland	5	6	0	.455	150	207
Chi. Cardinals	3	8	0	.273	98	209
Detroit	0	11	0	.000	38	263

PLAYOFFS

NFL championship
Washington 14 vs. Chicago Bears 6

1943

EASTERN DIVISION

Team	W	L	T	Pct.	PF	PA
Washington	6	3	1	.667	229	137
N.Y. Giants	6	3	1	.667	197	170
Phil.-Pitt.	5	4	1	.556	225	230
Brooklyn	2	8	0	.200	65	234

NOTE: Cleveland Rams did not play in 1943.

WESTERN DIVISION

Team	W	L	T	Pct.	PF	PA
Chicago Bears	8	1	1	.889	303	157
Green Bay	7	2	1	.778	264	172
Detroit	3	6	1	.333	178	218
Chi. Cardinals	0	10	0	.000	95	238

PLAYOFFS

Eastern Division playoff
Washington 28 at N.Y. Giants 0

NFL championship
Chicago Bears 41 vs. Washington 21

1944

EASTERN DIVISION

Team	W	L	T	Pct.	PF	PA
N.Y. Giants	8	1	1	.889	206	75
Philadelphia	7	1	2	.875	267	131
Washington	6	3	1	.667	169	180
Boston	2	8	0	.200	82	233
Brooklyn	0	10	0	.000	69	166

WESTERN DIVISION

Team	W	L	T	Pct.	PF	PA
Green Bay	8	2	0	.800	238	141
Chicago Bears	6	3	1	.667	258	172
Detroit	6	3	1	.667	216	151
Cleveland	4	6	0	.400	188	224
Card-Pitt	0	10	0	.000	108	328

PLAYOFFS

NFL championship
Green Bay 14 at N.Y. Giants 7

1945

EASTERN DIVISION

Team	W	L	T	Pct.	PF	PA
Washington	8	2	0	.800	209	121
Philadelphia	7	3	0	.700	272	133
N.Y. Giants	3	6	1	.333	179	198
Boston	3	6	1	.333	123	211
Pittsburgh	2	8	0	.200	79	220

WESTERN DIVISION

Team	W	L	T	Pct.	PF	PA
Cleveland	9	1	0	.900	244	136
Detroit	7	3	0	.700	195	194
Green Bay	6	4	0	.600	258	173
Chicago Bears	3	7	0	.300	192	235
Chi. Cardinals	1	9	0	.100	98	228

PLAYOFFS

NFL championship
Cleveland 15 vs. Washington 14

1946

AAFC

EASTERN DIVISION

Team	W	L	T	Pct.	PF	PA
New York	10	3	1	.769	270	192
Brooklyn	3	10	1	.231	226	339
Buffalo	3	10	1	.231	249	370
Miami	3	11	0	.154	167	378

WESTERN DIVISION

Team	W	L	T	Pct.	PF	PA
Cleveland	12	2	0	.857	423	137
San Francisco	9	5	0	.643	307	189
Los Angeles	7	5	2	.583	305	290
Chicago	5	6	3	.455	263	315

PLAYOFFS

AAFC championship
Cleveland 14 vs. New York 9

NFL

EASTERN DIVISION

Team	W	L	T	Pct.	PF	PA
N.Y. Giants	7	3	1	.700	236	162
Philadelphia	6	5	0	.545	231	220
Washington	5	5	1	.500	171	191
Pittsburgh	5	5	1	.500	136	117
Boston	2	8	1	.200	189	273

WESTERN DIVISION

Team	W	L	T	Pct.	PF	PA
Chicago Bears	8	2	1	.800	289	193
Los Angeles	6	4	1	.600	277	257
Green Bay	6	5	0	.545	148	158
Chi. Cardinals	6	5	0	.545	260	198
Detroit	1	10	0	.091	142	310

PLAYOFFS

NFL championship
Chicago Bears 24 at N.Y. Giants 14

1947

AAFC

EASTERN DIVISION

Team	W	L	T	Pct.	PF	PA
New York	11	2	1	.846	378	239
Buffalo	8	4	2	.667	320	288
Brooklyn	3	10	1	.231	181	340
Baltimore	2	11	1	.154	167	377

WESTERN DIVISION

Team	W	L	T	Pct.	PF	PA
Cleveland	12	1	1	.923	410	185
San Francisco	8	4	2	.667	327	264
Los Angeles	7	7	0	.500	328	256
Chicago	1	13	0	.071	263	425

PLAYOFFS

AAFC championship
Cleveland 14 at New York 3

NFL

EASTERN DIVISION

Team	W	L	T	Pct.	PF	PA
Philadelphia	8	4	0	.667	308	242
Pittsburgh	8	4	0	.667	240	259
Boston	4	7	1	.364	168	256
Washington	4	8	0	.333	295	367
N.Y. Giants	2	8	2	.200	190	309

WESTERN DIVISION

Team	W	L	T	Pct.	PF	PA
Chi. Cardinals	9	3	0	.750	306	231
Chicago Bears	8	4	0	.667	363	241
Green Bay	6	5	1	.545	274	210
Los Angeles	6	6	0	.500	259	214
Detroit	3	9	0	.250	231	305

PLAYOFFS

Eastern Division playoff
Philadelphia 21 at Pittsburgh 0

NFL championship
Chi. Cardinals 28 vs. Philadelphia 21

1948

AAFC

EASTERN DIVISION

Team	W	L	T	Pct.	PF	PA
Buffalo	7	7	0	.500	360	358
Baltimore	7	7	0	.500	333	327
New York	6	8	0	.429	265	301
Brooklyn	2	12	0	.143	253	387

WESTERN DIVISION

Team	W	L	T	Pct.	PF	PA
Cleveland	14	0	0	1.000	389	190
San Francisco	12	2	0	.857	495	248
Los Angeles	7	7	0	.500	258	305
Chicago	1	13	0	.071	202	439

PLAYOFFS

Eastern Division playoff
Buffalo 28 vs. Baltimore 17

AAFC championship
Cleveland 49 vs. Buffalo 7

NFL

EASTERN DIVISION

Team	W	L	T	Pct.	PF	PA
Philadelphia	9	2	1	.818	376	156
Washington	7	5	0	.583	291	287
N.Y. Giants	4	8	0	.333	297	388
Pittsburgh	4	8	0	.333	200	243
Boston	3	9	0	.250	174	372

WESTERN DIVISION

Team	W	L	T	Pct.	PF	PA
Chi. Cardinals	11	1	0	.917	395	226
Chicago Bears	10	2	0	.833	375	151
Los Angeles	6	5	1	.545	327	269
Green Bay	3	9	0	.250	154	290
Detroit	2	10	0	.167	200	407

PLAYOFFS

NFL championship
Philadelphia 7 vs. Chi. Cardinals 0

1949

AAFC

Team	W	L	T	Pct.	PF	PA
Cleveland	9	1	2	.900	339	171
San Francisco	9	3	0	.750	416	227
Brooklyn-N.Y.	8	4	0	.667	196	206
Buffalo	5	5	2	.500	236	256
Chicago	4	8	0	.333	179	268
Los Angeles	4	8	0	.333	253	322
Baltimore	1	11	0	.083	172	341

PLAYOFFS

AFC Semifinals
Cleveland 31 vs. Buffalo 21
San Francisco 17 vs. Bkn-N.Y. 7

AAFC championship
Cleveland 21 vs. San Francisco 7

NFL

EASTERN DIVISION

Team	W	L	T	Pct.	PF	PA
Philadelphia	11	1	0	.917	364	134
Pittsburgh	6	5	1	.545	224	214
N.Y. Giants	6	6	0	.500	287	298
Washington	4	7	1	.364	268	339
N.Y. Bulldogs	1	10	1	.091	153	365

WESTERN DIVISION

Team	W	L	T	Pct.	PF	PA
Los Angeles	8	2	2	.800	360	239
Chicago Bears	9	3	0	.750	332	218
Chi. Cardinals	6	5	1	.545	360	301
Detroit	4	8	0	.333	237	259
Green Bay	2	10	0	.167	114	329

PLAYOFFS

NFL championship
Philadelphia 14 at Los Angeles 0

1950

AMERICAN CONFERENCE

Team	W	L	T	Pct.	PF	PA
Cleveland	10	2	0	.833	310	144
N.Y. Giants	10	2	0	.833	268	150
Philadelphia	6	6	0	.500	254	141
Pittsburgh	6	6	0	.500	180	195
Chi. Cardinals	5	7	0	.417	233	287
Washington	3	9	0	.250	232	326

NATIONAL CONFERENCE

Team	W	L	T	Pct.	PF	PA
Los Angeles	9	3	0	.750	466	309
Chicago Bears	9	3	0	.750	279	207
N.Y. Yanks	7	5	0	.583	366	367
Detroit	6	6	0	.500	321	285
Green Bay	3	9	0	.250	244	406
San Francisco	3	9	0	.250	213	300
Baltimore	1	11	0	.083	213	462

PLAYOFFS

American Conference playoff
Cleveland 8 vs. N.Y. Giants 3

National Conference playoff
Los Angeles 24 vs. Chicago Bears 14

NFL championship
Cleveland 30 vs. Los Angeles 28

1951

AMERICAN CONFERENCE

Team	W	L	T	Pct.	PF	PA
Cleveland	11	1	0	.917	331	152
N.Y. Giants	9	2	1	.818	254	161
Washington	5	7	0	.417	183	296
Pittsburgh	4	7	1	.364	183	235
Philadelphia	4	8	0	.333	234	264
Chi. Cardinals	3	9	0	.250	210	287

NATIONAL CONFERENCE

Team	W	L	T	Pct.	PF	PA
Los Angeles	8	4	0	.667	392	261
Detroit	7	4	1	.636	336	259
San Francisco	7	4	1	.636	255	205
Chicago Bears	7	5	0	.583	286	282
Green Bay	3	9	0	.250	254	375
N.Y. Yanks	1	9	2	.100	241	382

PLAYOFFS

NFL championship
Los Angeles 24 vs. Cleveland 17

1952

AMERICAN CONFERENCE

Team	W	L	T	Pct.	PF	PA
Cleveland	8	4	0	.667	310	213
N.Y. Giants	7	5	0	.583	234	231
Philadelphia	7	5	0	.583	252	271
Pittsburgh	5	7	0	.417	300	273
Chi. Cardinals	4	8	0	.333	172	221
Washington	4	8	0	.333	240	287

NATIONAL CONFERENCE

Team	W	L	T	Pct.	PF	PA
Detroit	9	3	0	.750	344	192
Los Angeles	9	3	0	.750	349	234
San Francisco	7	5	0	.583	285	221
Green Bay	6	6	0	.500	295	312
Chicago Bears	5	7	0	.417	245	326
Dallas Texans	1	11	0	.083	182	427

PLAYOFFS

National Conference playoff
Detroit 31 vs. Los Angeles 21

NFL championship
Detroit 17 at Cleveland 7

1953

EASTERN CONFERENCE

Team	W	L	T	Pct.	PF	PA
Cleveland	11	1	0	.917	348	162
Philadelphia	7	4	1	.636	352	215
Washington	6	5	1	.545	208	215
Pittsburgh	6	6	0	.500	211	263
N.Y. Giants	3	9	0	.250	179	277
Chi. Cardinals	1	10	1	.091	190	337

WESTERN CONFERENCE

Team	W	L	T	Pct.	PF	PA
Detroit	10	2	0	.833	271	205
San Francisco	9	3	0	.750	372	237
Los Angeles	8	3	1	.727	366	236
Chicago Bears	3	8	1	.273	218	262
Baltimore	3	9	0	.250	182	350
Green Bay	2	9	1	.182	200	338

PLAYOFFS

NFL championship
Detroit 17 vs. Cleveland 16

1954

EASTERN CONFERENCE

Team	W	L	T	Pct.	PF	PA
Cleveland	9	3	0	.750	336	162
Philadelphia	7	4	1	.636	284	230
N.Y. Giants	7	5	0	.583	293	184
Pittsburgh	5	7	0	.417	219	263
Washington	3	9	0	.250	207	432
Chi. Cardinals	2	10	0	.167	183	347

WESTERN CONFERENCE

Team	W	L	T	Pct.	PF	PA
Detroit	9	2	1	.818	337	189
Chicago Bears	8	4	0	.667	301	279
San Francisco	7	4	1	.636	313	251
Los Angeles	6	5	1	.545	314	285
Green Bay	4	8	0	.333	234	251
Baltimore	3	9	0	.250	131	279

PLAYOFFS

NFL championship
Cleveland 56 vs. Detroit 10

1955

EASTERN CONFERENCE

Team	W	L	T	Pct.	PF	PA
Cleveland	9	2	1	.818	349	218
Washington	8	4	0	.667	246	222
N.Y. Giants	6	5	1	.545	267	223
Chi. Cardinals	4	7	1	.364	224	252
Philadelphia	4	7	1	.364	248	231
Pittsburgh	4	8	0	.333	195	285

WESTERN CONFERENCE

Team	W	L	T	Pct.	PF	PA
Los Angeles	8	3	1	.727	260	231
Chicago Bears	8	4	0	.667	294	251
Green Bay	6	6	0	.500	258	276
Baltimore	5	6	1	.455	214	239
San Francisco	4	8	0	.333	216	298
Detroit	3	9	0	.250	230	275

PLAYOFFS

NFL championship
Cleveland 38 at Los Angeles 14

1956

EASTERN CONFERENCE

Team	W	L	T	Pct.	PF	PA
N.Y. Giants	8	3	1	.727	264	197
Chi. Cardinals	7	5	0	.583	240	182
Washington	6	6	0	.500	183	225
Cleveland	5	7	0	.417	167	177
Pittsburgh	5	7	0	.417	217	250
Philadelphia	3	8	1	.273	143	215

WESTERN CONFERENCE

Team	W	L	T	Pct.	PF	PA
Chicago Bears	9	2	1	.818	363	246
Detroit	9	3	0	.750	300	188
San Francisco	5	6	1	.455	233	284
Baltimore	5	7	0	.417	270	322
Green Bay	4	8	0	.333	264	342
Los Angeles	4	8	0	.333	291	307

PLAYOFFS

NFL championship

N.Y. Giants 47 vs. Chicago Bears 7

1957

EASTERN CONFERENCE

Team	W	L	T	Pct.	PF	PA
Cleveland	9	2	1	.818	269	172
N.Y. Giants	7	5	0	.583	254	211
Pittsburgh	6	6	0	.500	161	178
Washington	5	6	1	.455	251	230
Philadelphia	4	8	0	.333	173	230
Chi. Cardinals	3	9	0	.250	200	299

WESTERN CONFERENCE

Team	W	L	T	Pct.	PF	PA
Detroit	8	4	0	.667	251	231
San Francisco	8	4	0	.667	260	264
Baltimore	7	5	0	.583	303	235
Los Angeles	6	6	0	.500	307	278
Chicago Bears	5	7	0	.417	203	211
Green Bay	3	9	0	.250	218	311

PLAYOFFS

Western Conference playoff

Detroit 31 at San Francisco 27

NFL championship

Detroit 59 vs. Cleveland 14

1958

EASTERN CONFERENCE

Team	W	L	T	Pct.	PF	PA
N.Y. Giants	9	3	0	.750	246	183
Cleveland	9	3	0	.750	302	217
Pittsburgh	7	4	1	.636	261	230
Washington	4	7	1	.364	214	268
Chi. Cardinals	2	9	1	.182	261	356
Philadelphia	2	9	1	.182	235	306

WESTERN CONFERENCE

Team	W	L	T	Pct.	PF	PA
Baltimore	9	3	0	.750	381	203
Chicago Bears	8	4	0	.667	298	230
Los Angeles	8	4	0	.667	344	278
San Francisco	6	6	0	.500	257	324
Detroit	4	7	1	.364	261	276
Green Bay	1	10	1	.091	193	382

PLAYOFFS

Eastern Conference playoff

N.Y. Giants 10 vs. Cleveland 0

NFL championship

Baltimore 23 at N.Y. Giants 17 (OT)

1959

EASTERN CONFERENCE

Team	W	L	T	Pct.	PF	PA
N.Y. Giants	10	2	0	.833	284	170
Cleveland	7	5	0	.583	270	214
Philadelphia	7	5	0	.583	268	278
Pittsburgh	6	5	1	.545	257	216
Washington	3	9	0	.250	185	350
Chi. Cardinals	2	10	0	.167	234	324

WESTERN CONFERENCE

Team	W	L	T	Pct.	PF	PA
Baltimore	9	3	0	.750	374	251
Chicago Bears	8	4	0	.667	252	196
Green Bay	7	5	0	.583	248	246
San Francisco	7	5	0	.583	255	237
Detroit	3	8	1	.273	203	275
Los Angeles	2	10	0	.167	242	315

PLAYOFFS

NFL championship

Baltimore 31 vs. N.Y. Giants 16

1960

AFL

EASTERN DIVISION

Team	W	L	T	Pct.	PF	PA
Houston	10	4	0	.714	379	285
N.Y. Titans	7	7	0	.500	382	399
Buffalo	5	8	1	.385	296	303
Boston Patriots	5	9	0	.357	286	349

WESTERN DIVISION

Team	W	L	T	Pct.	PF	PA
L.A. Chargers	10	4	0	.714	373	336
Dallas Texans	8	6	0	.571	362	253
Oakland	6	8	0	.429	319	388
Denver	4	9	1	.308	309	393

PLAYOFFS

AFL championship

Houston 24 vs. L.A. Chargers 16

NFL

EASTERN CONFERENCE

Team	W	L	T	Pct.	PF	PA
Philadelphia	10	2	0	.833	321	246
Cleveland	8	3	1	.727	362	217
N.Y. Giants	6	4	2	.600	271	261
St. Louis	6	5	1	.545	288	230
Pittsburgh	5	6	1	.455	240	275
Washington	1	9	2	.100	178	309

WESTERN CONFERENCE

Team	W	L	T	Pct.	PF	PA
Green Bay	8	4	0	.667	332	209
Detroit	7	5	0	.583	239	212
San Francisco	7	5	0	.583	208	205
Baltimore	6	6	0	.500	288	234
Chicago	5	6	1	.455	194	299
L.A. Rams	4	7	1	.364	265	297
Dallas Cowboys	0	11	1	.000	177	369

PLAYOFFS

NFL championship

Philadelphia 17 vs. Green Bay 13

1961

AFL

EASTERN DIVISION							WESTERN DIVISION							PLAYOFFS
Team	W	L	T	Pct.	PF	PA	Team	W	L	T	Pct.	PF	PA	AFL championship
Houston	10	3	1	.769	513	242	San Diego	12	2	0	.857	396	219	Houston 10 at San Diego 3
Boston Patriots	9	4	1	.692	413	313	Dallas Texans	6	8	0	.429	334	343	
N.Y. Titans	7	7	0	.500	301	390	Denver	3	11	0	.214	251	432	
Buffalo	6	8	0	.429	294	342	Oakland	2	12	0	.143	237	458	

NFL

EASTERN CONFERENCE							WESTERN CONFERENCE							PLAYOFFS
Team	W	L	T	Pct.	PF	PA	Team	W	L	T	Pct.	PF	PA	NFL championship
N.Y. Giants	10	3	1	.769	368	220	Green Bay	11	3	0	.786	391	223	Green Bay 37 vs. N.Y. Giants 0
Philadelphia	10	4	0	.714	361	297	Detroit	8	5	1	.615	270	258	
Cleveland	8	5	1	.615	319	270	Baltimore	8	6	0	.571	302	307	
St. Louis	7	7	0	.500	279	267	Chicago	8	6	0	.571	326	302	
Pittsburgh	6	8	0	.429	295	287	San Francisco	7	6	1	.538	346	272	
Dallas Cowboys	4	9	1	.308	236	380	Los Angeles	4	10	0	.286	263	333	
Washington	1	12	1	.077	174	392	Minnesota	3	11	0	.214	285	407	

1962

AFL

EASTERN DIVISION							WESTERN DIVISION							PLAYOFFS
Team	W	L	T	Pct.	PF	PA	Team	W	L	T	Pct.	PF	PA	AFL championship
Houston	11	3	0	.786	387	270	Dallas Texans	11	3	0	.786	389	233	Dallas Texans 20 at Houston 17 (OT)
Boston Patriots	9	4	1	.692	346	295	Denver	7	7	0	.500	353	334	
Buffalo	7	6	1	.538	309	272	San Diego	4	10	0	.286	314	392	
N.Y. Titans	5	9	0	.357	278	423	Oakland	1	13	0	.071	213	370	

NFL

EASTERN CONFERENCE							WESTERN CONFERENCE							PLAYOFFS
Team	W	L	T	Pct.	PF	PA	Team	W	L	T	Pct.	PF	PA	NFL championship
N.Y. Giants	12	2	0	.857	398	283	Green Bay	13	1	0	.929	415	148	Green Bay 16 at N.Y. Giants 7
Pittsburgh	9	5	0	.643	312	363	Detroit	11	3	0	.786	315	177	
Cleveland	7	6	1	.538	291	257	Chicago	9	5	0	.643	321	287	
Washington	5	7	2	.417	305	376	Baltimore	7	7	0	.500	293	288	
Dallas Cowboys	5	8	1	.385	398	402	San Francisco	6	8	0	.429	282	331	
St. Louis	4	9	1	.308	287	361	Minnesota	2	11	1	.154	254	410	
Philadelphia	3	10	1	.231	282	356	Los Angeles	1	12	1	.077	220	334	

1963

AFL

EASTERN DIVISION							WESTERN DIVISION							PLAYOFFS
Team	W	L	T	Pct.	PF	PA	Team	W	L	T	Pct.	PF	PA	Eastern Division playoff
Boston Patriots	7	6	1	.538	327	257	San Diego	11	3	0	.786	399	256	Boston 26 at Buffalo 8
Buffalo	7	6	1	.538	304	291	Oakland	10	4	0	.714	363	288	AFL championship
Houston	6	8	0	.429	302	372	Kansas City	5	7	2	.417	347	263	San Diego 51 vs. Boston 10
N.Y. Jets	5	8	1	.385	249	399	Denver	2	11	1	.154	301	473	

NFL

EASTERN CONFERENCE							WESTERN CONFERENCE							PLAYOFFS
Team	W	L	T	Pct.	PF	PA	Team	W	L	T	Pct.	PF	PA	NFL championship
N.Y. Giants	11	3	0	.786	448	280	Chicago	11	1	2	.917	301	144	Chicago 14 vs. N.Y. Giants 10
Cleveland	10	4	0	.714	343	262	Green Bay	11	2	1	.846	369	206	
St. Louis	9	5	0	.643	341	283	Baltimore	8	6	0	.571	316	285	
Pittsburgh	7	4	3	.636	321	295	Detroit	5	8	1	.385	326	265	
Dallas	4	10	0	.286	305	378	Minnesota	5	8	1	.385	309	390	
Washington	3	11	0	.214	279	398	Los Angeles	5	9	0	.357	210	350	
Philadelphia	2	10	2	.167	242	381	San Francisco	2	12	0	.143	198	391	

1964

AFL

EASTERN DIVISION

Team	W	L	T	Pct.	PF	PA
Buffalo	12	2	0	.857	400	242
Boston Patriots	10	3	1	.769	365	297
N.Y. Jets	5	8	1	.385	278	315
Houston	4	10	0	.286	310	355

WESTERN DIVISION

Team	W	L	T	Pct.	PF	PA
San Diego	8	5	1	.615	341	300
Kansas City	7	7	0	.500	366	306
Oakland	5	7	2	.417	303	350
Denver	2	11	1	.154	240	438

PLAYOFFS

AFL championship
Buffalo 20 vs. San Diego 7

NFL

EASTERN CONFERENCE

Team	W	L	T	Pct.	PF	PA
Cleveland	10	3	1	.769	415	293
St. Louis	9	3	2	.750	357	331
Philadelphia	6	8	0	.429	312	313
Washington	6	8	0	.429	307	305
Dallas	5	8	1	.385	250	289
Pittsburgh	5	9	0	.357	253	315
N.Y. Giants	2	10	2	.167	241	399

WESTERN CONFERENCE

Team	W	L	T	Pct.	PF	PA
Baltimore	12	2	0	.857	428	225
Green Bay	8	5	1	.615	342	245
Minnesota	8	5	1	.615	355	296
Detroit	7	5	2	.583	280	260
Los Angeles	5	7	2	.417	283	339
Chicago	5	9	0	.357	260	379
San Francisco	4	10	0	.286	236	330

PLAYOFFS

NFL championship
Cleveland 27 vs. Baltimore 0

1965

AFL

EASTERN DIVISION

Team	W	L	T	Pct.	PF	PA
Buffalo	10	3	1	.769	313	226
N.Y. Jets	5	8	1	.385	285	303
Boston Patriots	4	8	2	.333	244	302
Houston	4	10	0	.286	298	429

WESTERN DIVISION

Team	W	L	T	Pct.	PF	PA
San Diego	9	2	3	.818	340	227
Oakland	8	5	1	.615	298	239
Kansas City	7	5	2	.583	322	285
Denver	4	10	0	.286	303	392

PLAYOFFS

AFL championship
Buffalo 23 at San Diego 0

NFL

EASTERN CONFERENCE

Team	W	L	T	Pct.	PF	PA
Cleveland	11	3	0	.786	363	325
Dallas	7	7	0	.500	325	280
N.Y. Giants	7	7	0	.500	270	338
Washington	6	8	0	.429	257	301
Philadelphia	5	9	0	.357	363	359
St. Louis	5	9	0	.357	296	309
Pittsburgh	2	12	0	.143	202	397

WESTERN CONFERENCE

Team	W	L	T	Pct.	PF	PA
Green Bay	10	3	1	.769	316	224
Baltimore	10	3	1	.769	389	284
Chicago	9	5	0	.643	409	275
San Francisco	7	6	1	.538	421	402
Minnesota	7	7	0	.500	383	403
Detroit	6	7	1	.462	257	295
Los Angeles	4	10	0	.286	269	328

PLAYOFFS

Western Conference playoff
Green Bay 13 vs. Baltimore 10 (OT)
NFL championship
Green Bay 23 vs. Cleveland 12

1966

AFL

EASTERN DIVISION

Team	W	L	T	Pct.	PF	PA
Buffalo	9	4	1	.692	358	255
Boston Patriots	8	4	2	.667	315	283
N.Y. Jets	6	6	2	.500	322	312
Houston	3	11	0	.214	335	396
Miami	3	11	0	.214	213	362

WESTERN DIVISION

Team	W	L	T	Pct.	PF	PA
Kansas City	11	2	1	.846	448	276
Oakland	8	5	1	.615	315	288
San Diego	7	6	1	.538	335	284
Denver	4	10	0	.286	196	381

PLAYOFFS

AFL championship
Kansas City 31 at Buffalo 7

NFL

EASTERN CONFERENCE

Team	W	L	T	Pct.	PF	PA
Dallas	10	3	1	.769	445	239
Cleveland	9	5	0	.643	403	259
Philadelphia	9	5	0	.643	326	340
St. Louis	8	5	1	.615	264	265
Washington	7	7	0	.500	351	355
Pittsburgh	5	8	1	.385	316	347
Atlanta	3	11	0	.214	204	437
N.Y. Giants	1	12	1	.077	263	501

WESTERN CONFERENCE

Team	W	L	T	Pct.	PF	PA
Green Bay	12	2	0	.857	335	163
Baltimore	9	5	0	.643	314	226
Los Angeles	8	6	0	.571	289	212
San Francisco	6	6	2	.500	320	325
Chicago	5	7	2	.417	234	272
Detroit	4	9	1	.308	206	317
Minnesota	4	9	1	.308	292	304

PLAYOFFS

NFL championship
Green Bay 34 at Dallas 27
Super Bowl I
Green Bay 35, Kansas City 10, at Los Angeles.

— 293 —

1967

AFL

EASTERN DIVISION

Team	W	L	T	Pct.	PF	PA
Houston	9	4	1	.692	258	199
N.Y. Jets	8	5	1	.615	371	329
Buffalo	4	10	0	.286	237	285
Miami	4	10	0	.286	219	407
Boston Patriots	3	10	1	.231	280	389

WESTERN DIVISION

Team	W	L	T	Pct.	PF	PA
Oakland	13	1	0	.929	468	233
Kansas City	9	5	0	.643	408	254
San Diego	8	5	1	.615	360	352
Denver	3	11	0	.214	256	409

PLAYOFFS

AFL championship
Oakland 40 vs. Houston 7

NFL

EASTERN CONFERENCE

Capitol Division

Team	W	L	T	Pct.	PF	PA
Dallas	9	5	0	.643	342	268
Philadelphia	6	7	1	.462	351	409
Washington	5	6	3	.455	347	353
New Orleans	3	11	0	.214	233	379

Century Division

Team	W	L	T	Pct.	PF	PA
Cleveland	9	5	0	.643	334	297
N.Y. Giants	7	7	0	.500	369	379
St. Louis	6	7	1	.462	333	356
Pittsburgh	4	9	1	.308	281	320

WESTERN CONFERENCE

Coastal Division

Team	W	L	T	Pct.	PF	PA
Los Angeles	11	1	2	.917	398	196
Baltimore	11	1	2	.917	394	198
San Francisco	7	7	0	.500	273	337
Atlanta	1	12	1	.077	175	422

Central Division

Team	W	L	T	Pct.	PF	PA
Green Bay	9	4	1	.692	332	209
Chicago	7	6	1	.538	239	218
Detroit	5	7	2	.417	260	259
Minnesota	3	8	3	.273	233	294

PLAYOFFS

Conference championships
Dallas 52 vs. Cleveland 14
Green Bay 28 vs. Los Angeles 7

NFL championship
Green Bay 21 vs. Dallas 17

Super Bowl II
Green Bay 33, Oakland 14, at Miami.

1968

AFL

EASTERN DIVISION

Team	W	L	T	Pct.	PF	PA
N.Y. Jets	11	3	0	.786	419	280
Houston	7	7	0	.500	303	248
Miami	5	8	1	.385	276	355
Boston Patriots	4	10	0	.286	229	406
Buffalo	1	12	1	.077	199	367

WESTERN DIVISION

Team	W	L	T	Pct.	PF	PA
Oakland	12	2	0	.857	453	233
Kansas City	12	2	0	.857	371	170
San Diego	9	5	0	.643	382	310
Denver	5	9	0	.357	255	404
Cincinnati	3	11	0	.214	215	329

PLAYOFFS

Western Division playoff
Oakland 41 vs. Kansas City 6

AFL championship
N.Y. Jets 27 vs. Oakland 23

NFL

EASTERN CONFERENCE

Capitol Division

Team	W	L	T	Pct.	PF	PA
Dallas	12	2	0	.857	431	186
N.Y. Giants	7	7	0	.500	294	325
Washington	5	9	0	.357	249	358
Philadelphia	2	12	0	.143	202	351

Century Division

Team	W	L	T	Pct.	PF	PA
Cleveland	10	4	0	.714	394	273
St. Louis	9	4	1	.692	325	289
New Orleans	4	9	1	.308	246	327
Pittsburgh	2	11	1	.154	244	397

WESTERN CONFERENCE

Coastal Division

Team	W	L	T	Pct.	PF	PA
Baltimore	13	1	0	.929	402	144
Los Angeles	10	3	1	.769	312	200
San Francisco	7	6	1	.538	303	310
Atlanta	2	12	0	.143	170	389

Central Division

Team	W	L	T	Pct.	PF	PA
Minnesota	8	6	0	.571	282	242
Chicago	7	7	0	.500	250	333
Green Bay	6	7	1	.462	281	227
Detroit	4	8	2	.333	207	241

PLAYOFFS

Conference championships
Cleveland 31 vs. Dallas 20
Baltimore 24 vs. Minnesota 14

NFL championship
Baltimore 34 at Cleveland 0

Super Bowl III
N.Y. Jets 16, Baltimore 7, at Miami.

1969

AFL

EASTERN DIVISION

Team	W	L	T	Pct.	PF	PA
N.Y. Jets	10	4	0	.714	353	269
Houston	6	6	2	.500	278	279
Boston Patriots	4	10	0	.286	266	316
Buffalo	4	10	0	.286	230	359
Miami	3	10	1	.231	233	332

WESTERN DIVISION

Team	W	L	T	Pct.	PF	PA
Oakland	12	1	1	.923	377	242
Kansas City	11	3	0	.786	359	177
San Diego	8	6	0	.571	288	276
Denver	5	8	1	.385	297	344
Cincinnati	4	9	1	.308	280	367

PLAYOFFS

Divisional games
Kansas City 13 at N.Y. Jets 6
Oakland 56 vs. Houston 7

AFL championship
Kansas City 17 at Oakland 7

NFL

EASTERN CONFERENCE

Capitol Division

Team	W	L	T	Pct.	PF	PA
Dallas	11	2	1	.846	369	223
Washington	7	5	2	.583	307	319
New Orleans	5	9	0	.357	311	393
Philadelphia	4	9	1	.308	279	377

Century Division

Team	W	L	T	Pct.	PF	PA
Cleveland	10	3	1	.769	351	300
N.Y. Giants	6	8	0	.429	264	298
St. Louis	4	9	1	.308	314	389
Pittsburgh	1	13	0	.071	218	404

WESTERN CONFERENCE

Coastal Division

Team	W	L	T	Pct.	PF	PA
Los Angeles	11	3	0	.786	320	243
Baltimore	8	5	1	.615	279	268
Atlanta	6	8	0	.429	276	268
San Francisco	4	8	2	.333	277	319

Central Division

Team	W	L	T	Pct.	PF	PA
Minnesota	12	2	0	.857	379	133
Detroit	9	4	1	.692	259	188
Green Bay	8	6	0	.571	269	221
Chicago	1	13	0	.071	210	339

PLAYOFFS

Conference championships
Cleveland 38 at Dallas 14
Minnesota 23 vs. Los Angeles 20

NFL championship
Minnesota 27 vs. Cleveland 7

Super Bowl IV
Kansas City 23, Minnesota 7, at New Orleans.

1970

AMERICAN CONFERENCE

Eastern Division

Team	W	L	T	Pct.	PF	PA
Baltimore*	11	2	1	.846	321	234
Miami†	10	4	0	.714	297	228
N.Y. Jets	4	10	0	.286	255	286
Buffalo	3	10	1	.231	204	337
Boston Patriots	2	12	0	.143	149	361

Central Division

Team	W	L	T	Pct.	PF	PA
Cincinnati*	8	6	0	.571	312	255
Cleveland	7	7	0	.500	286	265
Pittsburgh	5	9	0	.357	210	272
Houston	3	10	1	.231	217	352

Western Division

Team	W	L	T	Pct.	PF	PA
Oakland*	8	4	2	.667	300	293
Kansas City	7	5	2	.583	272	244
San Diego	5	6	3	.455	282	278
Denver	5	8	1	.385	253	264

NATIONAL CONFERENCE

Eastern Division

Team	W	L	T	Pct.	PF	PA
Dallas*	10	4	0	.714	299	221
N.Y. Giants	9	5	0	.643	301	270
St. Louis	8	5	1	.615	325	228
Washington	6	8	0	.429	297	314
Philadelphia	3	10	1	.231	241	332

Central Division

Team	W	L	T	Pct.	PF	PA
Minnesota*	12	2	0	.857	335	143
Detroit†	10	4	0	.714	347	202
Chicago	6	8	0	.429	256	261
Green Bay	6	8	0	.429	196	293

Western Division

Team	W	L	T	Pct.	PF	PA
San Francisco*	10	3	1	.769	352	267
Los Angeles	9	4	1	.692	325	202
Atlanta	4	8	2	.333	206	261
New Orleans	2	11	1	.154	172	347

PLAYOFFS

AFC divisional games
Baltimore 17 vs. Cincinnati 0
Oakland 21 vs. Miami 14

AFC championship
Baltimore 27 vs. Oakland 17

NFC divisional games
Dallas 5 vs. Detroit 0
San Francisco 17 at Minnesota 14

NFC championship
Dallas 17 at San Francisco 10

Super Bowl V
Baltimore 16, Dallas 13, at Miami.

*Division champion.
†Wild-card team.

1971

AMERICAN CONFERENCE

Eastern Division

Team	W	L	T	Pct.	PF	PA
Miami*	10	3	1	.769	315	174
Baltimore†	10	4	0	.714	313	140
New England	6	8	0	.429	238	325
N.Y. Jets	6	8	0	.429	212	299
Buffalo	1	13	0	.071	184	394

Central Division

Team	W	L	T	Pct.	PF	PA
Cleveland*	9	5	0	.643	285	273
Pittsburgh	6	8	0	.429	246	292
Houston	4	9	1	.308	251	330
Cincinnati	4	10	0	.286	284	265

Western Division

Team	W	L	T	Pct.	PF	PA
Kansas City*	10	3	1	.769	302	208
Oakland	8	4	2	.667	344	278
San Diego	6	8	0	.429	311	341
Denver	4	9	1	.308	203	275

NATIONAL CONFERENCE

Eastern Division

Team	W	L	T	Pct.	PF	PA
Dallas*	11	3	0	.786	406	222
Washington†	9	4	1	.692	276	190
Philadelphia	6	7	1	.462	221	302
St. Louis	4	9	1	.308	231	279
N.Y. Giants	4	10	0	.286	228	362

Central Division

Team	W	L	T	Pct.	PF	PA
Minnesota*	11	3	0	.786	245	139
Detroit	7	6	1	.538	341	286
Chicago	6	8	0	.429	185	276
Green Bay	4	8	2	.333	274	298

Western Division

Team	W	L	T	Pct.	PF	PA
San Francisco*	9	5	0	.643	300	216
Los Angeles	8	5	1	.615	313	260
Atlanta	7	6	1	.538	274	277
New Orleans	4	8	2	.333	266	347

PLAYOFFS

AFC divisional games
Miami 27 at Kansas City 24 (OT)
Baltimore 20 at Cleveland 3

AFC championship
Miami 21 vs. Baltimore 0

NFC divisional games
Dallas 20 at Minnesota 12
San Francisco 24 vs. Washington 20

NFC championship
Dallas 14 vs. San Francisco 3

Super Bowl VI
Dallas 24, Miami 3, at New Orleans.

*Division champion.
†Wild-card team.

1972

AMERICAN CONFERENCE

Eastern Division

Team	W	L	T	Pct.	PF	PA
Miami*	14	0	0	1.000	385	171
N.Y. Jets	7	7	0	.500	367	324
Baltimore	5	9	0	.357	235	252
Buffalo	4	9	1	.321	257	377
New England	3	11	0	.214	192	446

Central Division

Team	W	L	T	Pct.	PF	PA
Pittsburgh*	11	3	0	.786	343	175
Cleveland†	10	4	0	.714	268	249
Cincinnati	8	6	0	.571	299	229
Houston	1	13	0	.071	164	380

Western Division

Team	W	L	T	Pct.	PF	PA
Oakland*	10	3	1	.750	365	248
Kansas City	8	6	0	.571	287	254
Denver	5	9	0	.357	325	350
San Diego	4	9	1	.321	264	344

*Division champion.
†Wild-card team.

NATIONAL CONFERENCE

Eastern Division

Team	W	L	T	Pct.	PF	PA
Washington*	11	3	0	.786	336	218
Dallas†	10	4	0	.714	319	240
N.Y. Giants	8	6	0	.571	331	247
St. Louis	4	9	1	.321	193	303
Philadelphia	2	11	1	.179	145	352

Central Division

Team	W	L	T	Pct.	PF	PA
Green Bay*	10	4	0	.714	304	226
Detroit	8	5	1	.607	339	290
Minnesota	7	7	0	.500	301	252
Chicago	4	9	1	.321	225	275

Western Division

Team	W	L	T	Pct.	PF	PA
San Francisco*	8	5	1	.607	353	249
Atlanta	7	7	0	.500	269	274
Los Angeles	6	7	1	.464	291	286
New Orleans	2	11	1	.179	215	361

PLAYOFFS

AFC divisional games
Pittsburgh 13 vs. Oakland 7
Miami 20 vs. Cleveland 14

AFC championship
Miami 21 at Pittsburgh 17

NFC divisional games
Dallas 30 at San Francisco 28
Washington 16 vs. Green Bay 3

NFC championship
Washington 26 vs. Dallas 3

Super Bowl VII
Miami 14, Washington 7, at
Los Angeles.

1973

AMERICAN CONFERENCE

Eastern Division

Team	W	L	T	Pct.	PF	PA
Miami*	12	2	0	.857	343	150
Buffalo	9	5	0	.643	259	230
New England	5	9	0	.357	258	300
Baltimore	4	10	0	.286	226	341
N.Y. Jets	4	10	0	.286	240	306

Central Division

Team	W	L	T	Pct.	PF	PA
Cincinnati*	10	4	0	.714	286	231
Pittsburgh†	10	4	0	.714	347	210
Cleveland	7	5	2	.571	234	255
Houston	1	13	0	.071	199	447

Western Division

Team	W	L	T	Pct.	PF	PA
Oakland*	9	4	1	.679	292	175
Denver	7	5	2	.571	354	296
Kansas City	7	5	2	.571	231	192
San Diego	2	11	1	.179	188	386

*Division champion.
†Wild-card team.

NATIONAL CONFERENCE

Eastern Division

Team	W	L	T	Pct.	PF	PA
Dallas*	10	4	0	.714	382	203
Washington†	10	4	0	.714	325	198
Philadelphia	5	8	1	.393	310	393
St. Louis	4	9	1	.321	286	365
N.Y. Giants	2	11	1	.179	226	362

Central Division

Team	W	L	T	Pct.	PF	PA
Minnesota*	12	2	0	.857	296	168
Detroit	6	7	1	.464	271	247
Green Bay	5	7	2	.429	202	259
Chicago	3	11	0	.214	195	334

Western Division

Team	W	L	T	Pct.	PF	PA
Los Angeles*	12	2	0	.857	388	178
Atlanta	9	5	0	.643	318	224
New Orleans	5	9	0	.357	163	312
San Francisco	5	9	0	.357	262	319

PLAYOFFS

AFC divisional games
Oakland 33 vs. Pittsburgh 14
Miami 34 vs. Cincinnati 16

AFC championship
Miami 27 vs. Oakland 10

NFC divisional games
Minnesota 27 vs. Washington 20
Dallas 27 vs. Los Angeles 16

NFC championship
Minnesota 27 at Dallas 10

Super Bowl VIII
Miami 24, Minnesota 7, at Houston.

DOLPHINS CAN'T BE BEAT

In 1972, the Miami Dolphins became the first team in modern NFL history to finish a season unbeaten and untied as they won all 17 of their games and beat Washington, 14-7, in Super Bowl VII. The Dolphins paced the league in both points for and points against in regular-season play. Miami's ground-oriented offense was led by running backs Larry Csonka, Jim Kiick and Mercury Morris, while tackle Manny Fernandez, linebacker Nick Buoniconti and safeties Dick Anderson and Jake Scott led the team's "No-Name Defense."

1974

AMERICAN CONFERENCE
Eastern Division

Team	W	L	T	Pct.	PF	PA
Miami*	11	3	0	.786	327	216
Buffalo†	9	5	0	.643	264	244
New England	7	7	0	.500	348	289
N.Y. Jets	7	7	0	.500	279	300
Baltimore	2	12	0	.143	190	329

Central Division

Team	W	L	T	Pct.	PF	PA
Pittsburgh*	10	3	1	.750	305	189
Cincinnati	7	7	0	.500	283	259
Houston	7	7	0	.500	236	282
Cleveland	4	10	0	.286	251	344

Western Division

Team	W	L	T	Pct.	PF	PA
Oakland*	12	2	0	.857	355	228
Denver	7	6	1	.536	302	294
Kansas City	5	9	0	.357	233	293
San Diego	5	9	0	.357	212	285

*Division champion.
†Wild-card team.

NATIONAL CONFERENCE
Eastern Division

Team	W	L	T	Pct.	PF	PA
St. Louis*	10	4	0	.714	285	218
Washington†	10	4	0	.714	320	196
Dallas	8	6	0	.571	297	235
Philadelphia	7	7	0	.500	242	217
N.Y. Giants	2	12	0	.143	195	299

Central Division

Team	W	L	T	Pct.	PF	PA
Minnesota*	10	4	0	.714	310	195
Detroit	7	7	0	.500	256	270
Green Bay	6	8	0	.429	210	206
Chicago	4	10	0	.286	152	279

Western Division

Team	W	L	T	Pct.	PF	PA
Los Angeles*	10	4	0	.714	263	181
San Francisco	6	8	0	.429	226	236
New Orleans	5	9	0	.357	166	263
Atlanta	3	11	0	.214	111	271

PLAYOFFS
AFC divisional games
Oakland 28 vs. Miami 26
Pittsburgh 32 vs. Buffalo 14
AFC championship
Pittsburgh 24 at Oakland 13
NFC divisional games
Minnesota 30 vs. St. Louis 14
Los Angeles 19 vs. Washington 10
NFC championship
Minnesota 14 vs. Los Angeles 10
Super Bowl IX
Pittsburgh 16, Minnesota 6, at New Orleans.

1975

AMERICAN CONFERENCE
Eastern Division

Team	W	L	T	Pct.	PF	PA
Baltimore*	10	4	0	.714	395	269
Miami	10	4	0	.714	357	222
Buffalo	8	6	0	.571	420	355
New England	3	11	0	.214	258	358
N.Y. Jets	3	11	0	.214	258	433

Central Division

Team	W	L	T	Pct.	PF	PA
Pittsburgh*	12	2	0	.857	373	162
Cincinnati†	11	3	0	.786	340	246
Houston	10	4	0	.714	293	226
Cleveland	3	11	0	.214	218	372

Western Division

Team	W	L	T	Pct.	PF	PA
Oakland*	11	3	0	.786	375	255
Denver	6	8	0	.429	254	307
Kansas City	5	9	0	.357	282	341
San Diego	2	12	0	.143	189	345

*Division champion.
†Wild-card team.

NATIONAL CONFERENCE
Eastern Division

Team	W	L	T	Pct.	PF	PA
St. Louis*	11	3	0	.786	356	276
Dallas†	10	4	0	.714	350	268
Washington	8	6	0	.571	325	276
N.Y. Giants	5	9	0	.357	216	306
Philadelphia	4	10	0	.286	225	302

Central Division

Team	W	L	T	Pct.	PF	PA
Minnesota*	12	2	0	.857	377	180
Detroit	7	7	0	.500	245	262
Chicago	4	10	0	.286	191	379
Green Bay	4	10	0	.286	226	285

Western Division

Team	W	L	T	Pct.	PF	PA
Los Angeles*	12	2	0	.857	312	135
San Francisco	5	9	0	.357	255	286
Atlanta	4	10	0	.286	240	289
New Orleans	2	12	0	.143	165	360

PLAYOFFS
AFC divisional games
Pittsburgh 28 vs. Baltimore 10
Oakland 31 vs. Cincinnati 28
AFC championship
Pittsburgh 16 vs. Oakland 10
NFC divisional games
Los Angeles 35 vs. St. Louis 23
Dallas 17 at Minnesota 14
NFC championship
Dallas 37 at Los Angeles 7
Super Bowl X
Pittsburgh 21, Dallas 17, at Miami.

A LONG WAIT ENDS

The Pittsburgh Steelers won their first NFL title with a 16-6 victory over Minnesota in Super Bowl IX. Franco Harris carried 34 times for a Super Bowl-record 158 yards to help Steelers founder Art Rooney visualize his dream of an NFL championship after 42 years of ownership. Before winning the AFC Central Division title in 1972 (their first championship of any kind; their second came in 1974), Rooney's Steelers had finished last 11 times, fourth 10 times and second six times since entering the NFL in 1933.

1976

AMERICAN CONFERENCE

Eastern Division

Team	W	L	T	Pct.	PF	PA
Baltimore*	11	3	0	.786	417	246
New England†	11	3	0	.786	376	236
Miami	6	8	0	.429	263	264
N.Y. Jets	3	11	0	.214	169	383
Buffalo	2	12	0	.143	245	363

Central Division

Team	W	L	T	Pct.	PF	PA
Pittsburgh*	10	4	0	.714	342	138
Cincinnati	10	4	0	.714	335	210
Cleveland	9	5	0	.643	267	287
Houston	5	9	0	.357	222	273

Western Division

Team	W	L	T	Pct.	PF	PA
Oakland*	13	1	0	.929	350	237
Denver	9	5	0	.643	315	206
San Diego	6	8	0	.429	248	285
Kansas City	5	9	0	.357	290	376
Tampa Bay	0	14	0	.000	125	412

*Division champion.
†Wild-card team.

NATIONAL CONFERENCE

Eastern Division

Team	W	L	T	Pct.	PF	PA
Dallas*	11	3	0	.786	296	194
Washington†	10	4	0	.714	291	217
St. Louis	10	4	0	.714	309	267
Philadelphia	4	10	0	.286	165	286
N.Y. Giants	3	11	0	.214	170	250

Central Division

Team	W	L	T	Pct.	PF	PA
Minnesota*	11	2	1	.821	305	176
Chicago	7	7	0	.500	253	216
Detroit	6	8	0	.429	262	220
Green Bay	5	9	0	.357	218	299

Western Division

Team	W	L	T	Pct.	PF	PA
Los Angeles*	10	3	1	.750	351	190
San Francisco	8	6	0	.571	270	190
Atlanta	4	10	0	.286	172	312
New Orleans	4	10	0	.286	253	346
Seattle	2	12	0	.143	229	429

PLAYOFFS

AFC divisional games

Oakland 24 vs. New England 21
Pittsburgh 40 at Baltimore 14

AFC championship

Oakland 24 vs. Pittsburgh 7

NFC divisional games

Minnesota 35 vs. Washington 20
Los Angeles 14 at Dallas 12

NFC championship

Minnesota 24 vs. Los Angeles 13

Super Bowl XI

Oakland 32, Minnesota 14, at Pasadena, Calif.

1977

AMERICAN CONFERENCE

Eastern Division

Team	W	L	T	Pct.	PF	PA
Baltimore*	10	4	0	.714	295	221
Miami	10	4	0	.714	313	197
New England	9	5	0	.643	278	217
N.Y. Jets	3	11	0	.214	191	300
Buffalo	3	11	0	.214	160	313

Central Division

Team	W	L	T	Pct.	PF	PA
Pittsburgh*	9	5	0	.643	283	243
Houston	8	6	0	.571	299	230
Cincinnati	8	6	0	.571	238	235
Cleveland	6	8	0	.429	269	267

Western Division

Team	W	L	T	Pct.	PF	PA
Denver*	12	2	0	.857	274	148
Oakland†	11	3	0	.786	351	230
San Diego	7	7	0	.500	222	205
Seattle	5	9	0	.357	282	373
Kansas City	2	12	0	.143	225	349

*Division champion.
†Wild-card team.

NATIONAL CONFERENCE

Eastern Division

Team	W	L	T	Pct.	PF	PA
Dallas*	12	2	0	.857	345	212
Washington	9	5	0	.643	196	189
St. Louis	7	7	0	.500	272	287
Philadelphia	5	9	0	.357	220	207
N.Y. Giants	5	9	0	.357	181	265

Central Division

Team	W	L	T	Pct.	PF	PA
Minnesota*	9	5	0	.643	231	227
Chicago†	9	5	0	.643	255	253
Detroit	6	8	0	.429	183	252
Green Bay	4	10	0	.286	134	219
Tampa Bay	2	12	0	.143	103	223

Western Division

Team	W	L	T	Pct.	PF	PA
Los Angeles*	10	4	0	.714	302	146
Atlanta	7	7	0	.500	179	129
San Francisco	5	9	0	.357	220	260
New Orleans	3	11	0	.214	232	336

PLAYOFFS

AFC divisional games

Denver 34 vs. Pittsburgh 21
Oakland 37 at Baltimore 31 (OT)

AFC championship

Denver 20 vs. Oakland 17

NFC divisional games

Dallas 37 vs. Chicago 7
Minnesota 14 at Los Angeles 7

NFC championship

Dallas 23 vs. Minnesota 6

Super Bowl XII

Dallas 27, Denver 10, at New Orleans.

A SUPER SLUMP

The Minnesota Vikings' knack for losing Super Bowls continued in January 1977 as the Vikings lost in the NFL's big game for the fourth time in eight years, including three of the past four seasons. Minnesota's latest setback was a 32-14 loss to the Oakland Raiders, who jumped out to a 16-0 halftime lead and never looked back. The Raiders rolled up 429 total yards in offense and held Chuck Foreman, the Vikings' star running back, to 44 yards on 17 attempts.

AMERICAN CONFERENCE

Eastern Division

Team	W	L	T	Pct.	PF	PA
New England*	11	5	0	.688	358	286
Miami†	11	5	0	.688	372	254
N.Y. Jets	8	8	0	.500	359	364
Buffalo	5	11	0	.313	302	354
Baltimore	5	11	0	.313	239	421

Central Division

Team	W	L	T	Pct.	PF	PA
Pittsburgh*	14	2	0	.875	356	195
Houston†	10	6	0	.625	283	298
Cleveland	8	8	0	.500	334	356
Cincinnati	4	12	0	.250	252	284

Western Division

Team	W	L	T	Pct.	PF	PA
Denver*	10	6	0	.625	282	198
Oakland	9	7	0	.563	311	283
Seattle	9	7	0	.563	345	358
San Diego	9	7	0	.563	355	309
Kansas City	4	12	0	.250	243	327

*Division champion.
†Wild-card team.

NATIONAL CONFERENCE

Eastern Division

Team	W	L	T	Pct.	PF	PA
Dallas*	12	4	0	.750	384	208
Philadelphia†	9	7	0	.563	270	250
Washington	8	8	0	.500	273	283
St. Louis	6	10	0	.375	248	296
N.Y. Giants	6	10	0	.375	264	298

Central Division

Team	W	L	T	Pct.	PF	PA
Minnesota*	8	7	1	.531	294	306
Green Bay	8	7	1	.531	249	269
Detroit	7	9	0	.438	290	300
Chicago	7	9	0	.438	253	274
Tampa Bay	5	11	0	.313	241	259

Western Division

Team	W	L	T	Pct.	PF	PA
Los Angeles*	12	4	0	.750	316	245
Atlanta†	9	7	0	.563	240	290
New Orleans	7	9	0	.438	281	298
San Francisco	2	14	0	.125	219	350

PLAYOFFS

AFC wild-card game
Houston 17 at Miami 9

AFC divisional games
Houston 31 at New England 14
Pittsburgh 33 vs. Denver 10

AFC championship
Pittsburgh 34 vs. Houston 5

NFC wild-card game
Atlanta 14 vs. Philadelphia 13

NFC divisional games
Dallas 27 vs. Atlanta 20
Los Angeles 34 vs. Minnesota 10

NFC championship
Dallas 28 at Los Angeles 0

Super Bowl XIII
Pittsburgh 35, Dallas 31, at Miami.

AMERICAN CONFERENCE

Eastern Division

Team	W	L	T	Pct.	PF	PA
Miami*	10	6	0	.625	341	257
New England	9	7	0	.563	411	326
N.Y. Jets	8	8	0	.500	337	383
Buffalo	7	9	0	.438	268	279
Baltimore	5	11	0	.313	271	351

Central Division

Team	W	L	T	Pct.	PF	PA
Pittsburgh*	12	4	0	.750	416	262
Houston†	11	5	0	.688	362	331
Cleveland	9	7	0	.563	359	352
Cincinnati	4	12	0	.250	337	421

Western Division

Team	W	L	T	Pct.	PF	PA
San Diego*	12	4	0	.750	411	246
Denver†	10	6	0	.625	289	262
Seattle	9	7	0	.563	378	372
Oakland	9	7	0	.563	365	337
Kansas City	7	9	0	.438	238	262

*Division champion.
†Wild-card team.

NATIONAL CONFERENCE

Eastern Division

Team	W	L	T	Pct.	PF	PA
Dallas*	11	5	0	.688	371	313
Philadelphia†	11	5	0	.688	339	282
Washington	10	6	0	.625	348	295
N.Y. Giants	6	10	0	.375	237	323
St. Louis	5	11	0	.313	307	358

Central Division

Team	W	L	T	Pct.	PF	PA
Tampa Bay*	10	6	0	.625	273	237
Chicago†	10	6	0	.625	306	249
Minnesota	7	9	0	.438	259	337
Green Bay	5	11	0	.313	246	316
Detroit	2	14	0	.125	219	365

Western Division

Team	W	L	T	Pct.	PF	PA
Los Angeles*	9	7	0	.563	323	309
New Orleans	8	8	0	.500	370	360
Atlanta	6	10	0	.375	300	388
San Francisco	2	14	0	.125	308	416

PLAYOFFS

AFC wild-card game
Houston 13 vs. Denver 7

AFC divisional games
Houston 17 at San Diego 14
Pittsburgh 34 vs. Miami 14

AFC championship
Pittsburgh 27 vs. Houston 13

NFC wild-card game
Philadelphia 27 vs. Chicago 17

NFC divisional games
Tampa Bay 24 vs. Philadelphia 17
Los Angeles 21 at Dallas 19

NFC championship
Los Angeles 9 at Tampa Bay 0

Super Bowl XIV
Pittsburgh 31, Los Angeles 19, at Pasadena, Calif.

THE BEST EVER?

Such things are subjective, but the 1978 Pittsburgh Steelers could make a legitimate claim for being the best team in NFL history. With Terry Bradshaw at quarterback, Franco Harris at running back and Lynn Swann and John Stallworth at wide receiver, the '78 Steelers steamrolled the rest of the league. Of their 17 victories (including playoffs), 11 were by 10 points or more. The club's two defeats totaled 10 points. Pittsburgh's "Steel Curtain" defense of Joe Greene, Jack Ham, Jack Lambert and Mel Blount (all Hall of Famers) yielded a league-low 195 points during the regular season. When the Steelers edged Dallas, 35-31, in Super Bowl XIII, it marked their third league championship in five years.

1980

AMERICAN CONFERENCE

Eastern Division

Team	W	L	T	Pct.	PF	PA
Buffalo*	11	5	0	.688	320	260
New England	10	6	0	.625	441	325
Miami	8	8	0	.500	266	305
Baltimore	7	9	0	.438	355	387
N.Y. Jets	4	12	0	.250	302	395

Central Division

Team	W	L	T	Pct.	PF	PA
Cleveland*	11	5	0	.688	357	310
Houston†	11	5	0	.688	295	251
Pittsburgh	9	7	0	.563	352	313
Cincinnati	6	10	0	.375	244	312

Western Division

Team	W	L	T	Pct.	PF	PA
San Diego*	11	5	0	.688	418	327
Oakland†	11	5	0	.688	364	306
Kansas City	8	8	0	.500	319	336
Denver	8	8	0	.500	310	323
Seattle	4	12	0	.250	291	408

NATIONAL CONFERENCE

Eastern Division

Team	W	L	T	Pct.	PF	PA
Philadelphia*	12	4	0	.750	384	222
Dallas†	12	4	0	.750	454	311
Washington	6	10	0	.375	261	293
St. Louis	5	11	0	.313	299	350
N.Y. Giants	4	12	0	.250	249	425

Central Division

Team	W	L	T	Pct.	PF	PA
Minnesota*	9	7	0	.563	317	308
Detroit	9	7	0	.563	334	272
Chicago	7	9	0	.438	304	264
Tampa Bay	5	10	1	.344	271	341
Green Bay	5	10	1	.344	231	371

Western Division

Team	W	L	T	Pct.	PF	PA
Atlanta*	12	4	0	.750	405	272
Los Angeles†	11	5	0	.688	424	289
San Francisco	6	10	0	.375	320	415
New Orleans	1	15	0	.063	291	487

*Division champion.
†Wild-card team.

PLAYOFFS

AFC wild-card game
Oakland 27 vs. Houston 7

AFC divisional games
San Diego 20 vs. Buffalo 14
Oakland 14 at Cleveland 12

AFC championship
Oakland 34 at San Diego 27

NFC wild-card game
Dallas 34 vs. Los Angeles 13

NFC divisional games
Philadelphia 31 vs. Minnesota 16
Dallas 30 at Atlanta 27

NFC championship
Philadelphia 20 vs. Dallas 7

Super Bowl XV
Oakland 27, Philadelphia 10, at New Orleans.

1981

AMERICAN CONFERENCE

Eastern Division

Team	W	L	T	Pct.	PF	PA
Miami*	11	4	1	.719	345	275
N.Y. Jets†	10	5	1	.656	355	287
Buffalo†	10	6	0	.625	311	276
Baltimore	2	14	0	.125	259	533
New England	2	14	0	.125	322	370

Central Division

Team	W	L	T	Pct.	PF	PA
Cincinnati*	12	4	0	.750	421	304
Pittsburgh	8	8	0	.500	356	297
Houston	7	9	0	.438	281	355
Cleveland	5	11	0	.313	276	375

Western Division

Team	W	L	T	Pct.	PF	PA
San Diego*	10	6	0	.625	478	390
Denver	10	6	0	.625	321	289
Kansas City	9	7	0	.563	343	290
Oakland	7	9	0	.438	273	343
Seattle	6	10	0	.375	322	388

NATIONAL CONFERENCE

Eastern Division

Team	W	L	T	Pct.	PF	PA
Dallas*	12	4	0	.750	367	277
Philadelphia†	10	6	0	.625	368	221
N.Y. Giants†	9	7	0	.563	295	257
Washington	8	8	0	.500	347	349
St. Louis	7	9	0	.438	315	408

Central Division

Team	W	L	T	Pct.	PF	PA
Tampa Bay*	9	7	0	.563	315	268
Detroit	8	8	0	.500	397	322
Green Bay	8	8	0	.500	324	361
Minnesota	7	9	0	.438	325	369
Chicago	6	10	0	.375	253	324

Western Division

Team	W	L	T	Pct.	PF	PA
San Francisco*	13	3	0	.813	357	250
Atlanta	7	9	0	.438	426	355
Los Angeles	6	10	0	.375	303	351
New Orleans	4	12	0	.250	207	378

*Division champion.
†Wild-card team.

PLAYOFFS

AFC wild-card game
Buffalo 31 at New York Jets 27

AFC divisional games
San Diego 41 at Miami 38 (OT)
Cincinnati 28 vs. Buffalo 21

AFC championship
Cincinnati 27 vs. San Diego 7

NFC wild-card game
N.Y. Giants 27 at Philadelphia 21

NFC divisional games
Dallas 38 vs. Tampa Bay 0
San Francisco 38 vs. N.Y. Giants 24

NFC championship
San Francisco 28 vs. Dallas 27

Super Bowl XVI
San Francisco 26, Cincinnati 21, at Pontiac, Mich.

BEGINNING OF A DYNASTY

NFL fans got a peek of things to come in 1981 as the San Francisco 49ers won the first of what would become five Super Bowl championships for the franchise. Although their running game scared few opponents, the 49ers' passing game certainly did. Joe Montana completed a league-high 64 percent of his passes and Dwight Clark caught 85 passes, tops in the NFC. Defensively, San Francisco allowed the second-fewest points in the league after finishing 26th in that department the year before. The 49ers thrived despite starting three rookies in the secondary. One of them, Ronnie Lott, was voted to the Pro Bowl.

1982

AMERICAN CONFERENCE

Team	W	L	T	Pct.	PF	PA
L.A. Raiders	8	1	0	.889	260	200
Miami	7	2	0	.778	198	131
Cincinnati	7	2	0	.778	232	177
Pittsburgh	6	3	0	.667	204	146
San Diego	6	3	0	.667	288	221
N.Y. Jets	6	3	0	.667	245	166
New England	5	4	0	.556	143	157
Cleveland	4	5	0	.444	140	182
Buffalo	4	5	0	.444	150	154
Seattle	4	5	0	.444	127	147
Kansas City	3	6	0	.333	176	184
Denver	2	7	0	.222	148	226
Houston	1	8	0	.111	136	245
Baltimore	0	8	1	.056	113	236

NATIONAL CONFERENCE

Team	W	L	T	Pct.	PF	PA
Washington	8	1	0	.889	190	128
Dallas	6	3	0	.667	226	145
Green Bay	5	3	1	.611	226	169
Minnesota	5	4	0	.556	187	198
Atlanta	5	4	0	.556	183	199
St. Louis	5	4	0	.556	135	170
Tampa Bay	5	4	0	.556	158	178
Detroit	4	5	0	.444	181	176
New Orleans	4	5	0	.444	129	160
N.Y. Giants	4	5	0	.444	164	160
San Francisco	3	6	0	.333	209	206
Chicago	3	6	0	.333	141	174
Philadelphia	3	6	0	.333	191	195
L.A. Rams	2	7	0	.222	200	250

PLAYOFFS

AFC first round

Miami 28 vs. New England 13
L.A. Raiders 27 vs. Cleveland 10
New York Jets 44 at Cincinnati 17
San Diego 31 at Pittsburgh 28

AFC second round

N.Y. Jets 17 at L.A. Raiders 14
Miami 34 vs. San Diego 13

AFC championship

Miami 14 vs. New York Jets 0

NFC first round

Washington 31 vs. Detroit 7
Green Bay 41 vs. St. Louis 16
Minnesota 30 vs. Atlanta 24
Dallas 30 vs. Tampa Bay 17

NFC second round

Washington 21 vs. Minnesota 7
Dallas 37 vs. Green Bay 26

NFC championship

Washington 31 vs. Dallas 17

Super Bowl XVII

Washington 27, Miami 17, at Pasadena, Calif.

As a result of a 57-day players' strike, the 1982 NFL regular season schedule was reduced from 16 weeks to 9. At the conclusion of the regular season, a 16-team Super Bowl Tournament was held. Eight teams from each conference were seeded 1 through 8 based on their records during regular season play.

Miami finished ahead of Cincinnati based on a better conference record. Pittsburgh won common games tiebreaker with San Diego after New York Jets were eliminated from three-way tie based on conference record. Cleveland finished ahead of Buffalo and Seattle based on better conference record. Minnesota, Atlanta, St. Louis and Tampa Bay seeds were determined by best won-lost record in conference games. Detroit finished ahead of New Orleans and the New York Giants based on a better conference record.

1983

AMERICAN CONFERENCE

Eastern Division

Team	W	L	T	Pct.	PF	PA
Miami*	12	4	0	.750	389	250
New England	8	8	0	.500	274	289
Buffalo	8	8	0	.500	283	351
Baltimore	7	9	0	.438	264	354
N.Y. Jets	7	9	0	.438	313	331

Central Division

Team	W	L	T	Pct.	PF	PA
Pittsburgh*	10	6	0	.625	355	303
Cleveland	9	7	0	.563	356	342
Cincinnati	7	9	0	.438	346	302
Houston	2	14	0	.125	288	460

Western Division

Team	W	L	T	Pct.	PF	PA
L.A. Raiders*	12	4	0	.750	442	338
Seattle†	9	7	0	.563	403	397
Denver†	9	7	0	.563	302	327
San Diego	6	10	0	.375	358	462
Kansas City	6	10	0	.375	386	367

NATIONAL CONFERENCE

Eastern Division

Team	W	L	T	Pct.	PF	PA
Washington*	14	2	0	.875	541	332
Dallas†	12	4	0	.750	479	360
St. Louis	8	7	1	.531	374	428
Philadelphia	5	11	0	.313	233	322
N.Y. Giants	3	12	1	.219	267	347

Central Division

Team	W	L	T	Pct.	PF	PA
Detroit*	9	7	0	.563	347	286
Green Bay	8	8	0	.500	429	439
Chicago	8	8	0	.500	311	301
Minnesota	8	8	0	.500	316	348
Tampa Bay	2	14	0	.125	241	380

Western Division

Team	W	L	T	Pct.	PF	PA
San Francisco*	10	6	0	.625	432	293
L.A. Rams†	9	7	0	.563	361	344
New Orleans	8	8	0	.500	319	337
Atlanta	7	9	0	.438	370	389

*Division champion.
†Wild-card team.

PLAYOFFS

AFC wild-card game

Seattle 31 vs. Denver 7

AFC divisional games

Seattle 27 at Miami 20
L.A. Raiders 38 vs. Pittsburgh 10

AFC championship game

L.A. Raiders 30 vs. Seattle 14

NFC wild-card game

Los Angeles Rams 24 at Dallas 17

NFC divisional games

San Francisco 24 vs. Detroit 23
Washington 51 vs. L.A. Rams 7

NFC championship

Washington 24 vs. San Francisco 21

Super Bowl XVIII

L.A. Raiders 38, Washington 9, at Tampa, Fla.

PRO FOOTBALL STRIKES OUT

The NFL was hit by its first in-season work stoppage in history on September 20, 1982, when the players union, unhappy that an impasse had been reached on a new collective bargaining agreement with management, called a strike. When play resumed November 21, the two-month layoff seemed to have had a varying effect. Tampa Bay, for example, may have been helped. After an 0-2 start, the Buccaneers righted themselves to win five of their last six games and qualify for the playoffs. Defending league-champion San Francisco, however, was hurt. The 49ers began the year 0-2 and didn't regain their footing when the season resumed. The Dallas Cowboys, losers of the previous two NFC title games, weren't affected much at all. They went on to lose their third consecutive conference championship game.

1984

AMERICAN CONFERENCE

Eastern Division

Team	W	L	T	Pct.	PF	PA
Miami*	14	2	0	.875	513	298
New England	9	7	0	.563	362	352
N.Y. Jets	7	9	0	.438	332	364
Indianapolis	4	12	0	.250	239	414
Buffalo	2	14	0	.125	250	454

Central Division

Team	W	L	T	Pct.	PF	PA
Pittsburgh*	9	7	0	.563	387	310
Cincinnati	8	8	0	.500	339	339
Cleveland	5	11	0	.313	250	297
Houston	3	13	0	.188	240	437

Western Division

Team	W	L	T	Pct.	PF	PA
Denver*	13	3	0	.813	353	241
Seattle†	12	4	0	.750	418	282
L.A. Raiders†	11	5	0	.688	368	278
Kansas City	8	8	0	.500	314	324
San Diego	7	9	0	.438	394	413

*Division champion.
†Wild-card team.

NATIONAL CONFERENCE

Eastern Division

Team	W	L	T	Pct.	PF	PA
Washington*	11	5	0	.688	426	310
N.Y. Giants†	9	7	0	.563	299	301
St. Louis	9	7	0	.563	423	345
Dallas	9	7	0	.563	308	308
Philadelphia	6	9	1	.406	278	320

Central Division

Team	W	L	T	Pct.	PF	PA
Chicago*	10	6	0	.625	325	248
Green Bay	8	8	0	.500	390	309
Tampa Bay	6	10	0	.375	335	380
Detroit	4	11	1	.281	283	408
Minnesota	3	13	0	.188	276	484

Western Division

Team	W	L	T	Pct.	PF	PA
San Francisco*	15	1	0	.938	475	227
L.A. Rams†	10	6	0	.625	346	316
New Orleans	7	9	0	.438	298	361
Atlanta	4	12	0	.250	281	382

PLAYOFFS

AFC wild-card game

Seattle 13 vs. Los Angeles Raiders 7

AFC divisional games

Miami 31 vs. Seattle 10
Pittsburgh 24 at Denver 17

AFC championship

Miami 45 vs. Pittsburgh 28

NFC wild-card game

N.Y. Giants 16 at L.A. Rams 13

NFC divisional games

San Francisco 21 vs. N.Y. Giants 10
Chicago 23 at Washington 19

NFC championship

San Francisco 23 vs. Chicago 0

Super Bowl XIX

San Francisco 38, Miami 16, at
Palo Alto, Calif.

1985

AMERICAN CONFERENCE

Eastern Division

Team	W	L	T	Pct.	PF	PA
Miami*	12	4	0	.750	428	320
N.Y. Jets†	11	5	0	.688	393	264
New England†	11	5	0	.688	362	290
Indianapolis	5	11	0	.313	320	386
Buffalo	2	14	0	.125	200	381

Central Division

Team	W	L	T	Pct.	PF	PA
Cleveland*	8	8	0	.500	287	294
Cincinnati	7	9	0	.438	441	437
Pittsburgh	7	9	0	.438	379	355
Houston	5	11	0	.313	284	412

Western Division

Team	W	L	T	Pct.	PF	PA
L.A. Raiders*	12	4	0	.750	354	308
Denver	11	5	0	.688	380	329
Seattle	8	8	0	.500	349	303
San Diego	8	8	0	.500	467	435
Kansas City	6	10	0	.375	317	360

*Division champion.
†Wild-card team.

NATIONAL CONFERENCE

Eastern Division

Team	W	L	T	Pct.	PF	PA
Dallas*	10	6	0	.625	357	333
N.Y. Giants†	10	6	0	.625	399	283
Washington	10	6	0	.625	297	312
Philadelphia	7	9	0	.438	286	310
St. Louis	5	11	0	.313	278	414

Central Division

Team	W	L	T	Pct.	PF	PA
Chicago*	15	1	0	.938	456	198
Green Bay	8	8	0	.500	337	355
Minnesota	7	9	0	.438	346	359
Detroit	7	9	0	.438	307	366
Tampa Bay	2	14	0	.125	294	448

Western Division

Team	W	L	T	Pct.	PF	PA
L.A. Rams*	11	5	0	.688	340	277
San Francisco†	10	6	0	.625	411	263
New Orleans	5	11	0	.313	294	401
Atlanta	4	12	0	.250	282	452

PLAYOFFS

AFC wild-card game

New England 26 at N.Y. Jets 14

AFC divisional games

Miami 24 vs. Cleveland 21
New England 27 at L.A. Raiders 20

AFC championship

New England 31 at Miami 14

NFC wild-card game

N.Y. Giants 17 vs. San Francisco 3

NFC divisional games

Los Angeles Rams 20 vs. Dallas 0
Chicago 21 vs. New York Giants 0

NFC championship

Chicago 24 vs. Los Angeles Rams 0

Super Bowl XX

Chicago 46, New England 10, at
New Orleans.

BIG BAD BEARS

The Chicago Bears dominated pro football in 1985 like few teams in NFL history, winning all but one game during the regular season and outscoring three opponents, 91-10, in the playoffs (two by shutout). The Bears, in fact, were so confident of their eventual Super Bowl triumph that a number of them recorded a video, The Super Bowl Shuffle, weeks before the playoffs even began. As it turned out, the players were right. The Bears' 46-10 victory over New England was the most lopsided in Super Bowl history. Chicago's defense allowed the fewest points in the league, its offense scored the second-most, and a league-high nine Bears made the Pro Bowl.

1986

AMERICAN CONFERENCE

Eastern Division

Team	W	L	T	Pct.	PF	PA
New England*	11	5	0	.688	412	307
N.Y. Jets†	10	6	0	.625	364	386
Miami	8	8	0	.500	430	405
Buffalo	4	12	0	.250	287	348
Indianapolis	3	13	0	.188	229	400

Central Division

Team	W	L	T	Pct.	PF	PA
Cleveland*	12	4	0	.750	391	310
Cincinnati	10	6	0	.625	409	394
Pittsburgh	6	10	0	.375	307	336
Houston	5	11	0	.313	274	329

Western Division

Team	W	L	T	Pct.	PF	PA
Denver*	11	5	0	.688	378	327
Kansas City†	10	6	0	.625	358	326
Seattle	10	6	0	.625	366	293
L.A. Raiders	8	8	0	.500	323	346
San Diego	4	12	0	.250	335	396

*Division champion.
†Wild-card team.

NATIONAL CONFERENCE

Eastern Division

Team	W	L	T	Pct.	PF	PA
N.Y. Giants*	14	2	0	.875	371	236
Washington†	12	4	0	.750	368	296
Dallas	7	9	0	.438	346	337
Philadelphia	5	10	1	.344	256	312
St. Louis	4	11	1	.281	218	351

Central Division

Team	W	L	T	Pct.	PF	PA
Chicago*	14	2	0	.875	352	187
Minnesota	9	7	0	.563	398	273
Detroit	5	11	0	.313	277	326
Green Bay	4	12	0	.250	254	418
Tampa Bay	2	14	0	.125	239	473

Western Division

Team	W	L	T	Pct.	PF	PA
San Francisco*	10	5	1	.656	374	247
L.A. Rams†	10	6	0	.625	309	267
Atlanta	7	8	1	.469	280	280
New Orleans	7	9	0	.438	288	287

PLAYOFFS

AFC wild-card game
N.Y. Jets 35 vs. Kansas City 15

AFC divisional games
Cleveland 23 vs. N.Y. Jets 20 (OT)
Denver 22 vs. New England 17

AFC championship
Denver 23 at Cleveland 20 (OT)

NFC wild-card game
Washington 19 vs. L.A. Rams 7

NFC divisional games
Washington 27 at Chicago 13
N.Y. Giants 49 vs. San Francisco 3

NFC championship
N.Y. Giants 17 vs. Washington 0

Super Bowl XXI
New York Giants 39, Denver 20, at Pasadena, Calif.

1987

AMERICAN CONFERENCE

Eastern Division

Team	W	L	T	Pct.	PF	PA
Indianapolis*	9	6	0	.600	300	238
New England	8	7	0	.533	320	293
Miami	8	7	0	.533	362	335
Buffalo	7	8	0	.467	270	305
N.Y. Jets	6	9	0	.400	334	360

Central Division

Team	W	L	T	Pct.	PF	PA
Cleveland*	10	5	0	.667	390	239
Houston†	9	6	0	.600	345	349
Pittsburgh	8	7	0	.533	285	299
Cincinnati	4	11	0	.267	285	370

Western Division

Team	W	L	T	Pct.	PF	PA
Denver*	10	4	1	.700	379	288
Seattle†	9	6	0	.600	371	314
San Diego	8	7	0	.533	253	317
L.A. Raiders	5	10	0	.333	301	289
Kansas City	4	11	0	.267	273	388

*Division champion.
†Wild-card team.

Note: The 1987 NFL regular season was reduced from 224 games to 210 (16 to 15 for each team) due to players' strike.

NATIONAL CONFERENCE

Eastern Division

Team	W	L	T	Pct.	PF	PA
Washington*	11	4	0	.733	379	285
Dallas	7	8	0	.467	340	348
St. Louis	7	8	0	.467	362	368
Philadelphia	7	8	0	.467	337	380
N.Y. Giants	6	9	0	.400	280	312

Central Division

Team	W	L	T	Pct.	PF	PA
Chicago*	11	4	0	.733	356	282
Minnesota†	8	7	0	.533	336	335
Green Bay	5	9	1	.367	255	300
Tampa Bay	4	11	0	.267	286	360
Detroit	4	11	0	.267	269	384

Western Division

Team	W	L	T	Pct.	PF	PA
San Francisco*	13	2	0	.867	459	253
New Orleans†	12	3	0	.800	422	283
L.A. Rams	6	9	0	.400	317	361
Atlanta	3	12	0	.200	205	436

PLAYOFFS

AFC wild-card game
Houston 23 vs. Seattle 20 (OT)

AFC divisional games
Cleveland 38 vs. Indianapolis 21
Denver 34 vs. Houston 10

AFC championship
Denver 38 vs. Cleveland 33

NFC wild-card game
Minnesota 44 at New Orleans 10

NFC divisional games
Minnesota 36 at San Francisco 24
Washington 21 at Chicago 17

NFC championship
Washington 17 vs. Minnesota 10

Super Bowl XXII
Washington 42, Denver 10, at San Diego.

COWBOYS' STREAK ENDS

In 1986, sports fans witnessed something they hadn't seen in a generation—a losing season by the Dallas Cowboys. Beginning with their 10-3-1 record in 1966, the Cowboys compiled a string of 20 consecutive winning seasons, the longest of any NFL team and the third-longest such streak in pro sports history. Only the New York Yankees, who had a 39-year streak from 1926-64, and the Montreal Canadiens, who had a 32-year streak from 1952-83, put together longer streaks of consecutive winning seasons.

1988

AMERICAN CONFERENCE

Eastern Division

Team	W	L	T	Pct.	PF	PA
Buffalo*	12	4	0	.750	329	237
Indianapolis	9	7	0	.563	354	315
New England	9	7	0	.563	250	284
N.Y. Jets	8	7	1	.531	372	354
Miami	6	10	0	.375	319	380

Central Division

Team	W	L	T	Pct.	PF	PA
Cincinnati*	12	4	0	.750	448	329
Cleveland†	10	6	0	.625	304	288
Houston†	10	6	0	.625	424	365
Pittsburgh	5	11	0	.313	336	421

Western Division

Team	W	L	T	Pct.	PF	PA
Seattle*	9	7	0	.563	339	329
Denver	8	8	0	.500	327	352
L.A. Raiders	7	9	0	.438	325	369
San Diego	6	10	0	.375	231	332
Kansas City	4	11	1	.281	254	320

*Division champion.
†Wild-card team.

NATIONAL CONFERENCE

Eastern Division

Team	W	L	T	Pct.	PF	PA
Philadelphia*	10	6	0	.625	379	319
N.Y. Giants	10	6	0	.625	359	304
Washington	7	9	0	.438	345	387
Phoenix	7	9	0	.438	344	398
Dallas	3	13	0	.188	265	381

Central Division

Team	W	L	T	Pct.	PF	PA
Chicago*	12	4	0	.750	312	215
Minnesota†	11	5	0	.688	406	233
Tampa Bay	5	11	0	.313	261	350
Detroit	4	12	0	.250	220	313
Green Bay	4	12	0	.250	240	315

Western Division

Team	W	L	T	Pct.	PF	PA
San Francisco*	10	6	0	.625	369	294
L.A. Rams†	10	6	0	.625	407	293
New Orleans	10	6	0	.625	312	283
Atlanta	5	11	0	.313	244	315

PLAYOFFS

AFC wild-card game
Houston 24 at Cleveland 23

AFC divisional games
Cincinnati 21 vs. Seattle 13
Buffalo 17 vs. Houston 10

AFC championship
Cincinnati 21 vs. Buffalo 10

NFC wild-card game
Minnesota 28 vs. L.A. Rams 17

NFC divisional games
Chicago 20 vs. Philadelphia 12
San Francisco 34 vs. Minnesota 9

NFC championship
San Francisco 28 at Chicago 3

Super Bowl XXIII
San Francisco 20, Cincinnati 16, at Miami.

1989

AMERICAN CONFERENCE

Eastern Division

Team	W	L	T	Pct.	PF	PA
Buffalo*	9	7	0	.563	409	317
Indianapolis	8	8	0	.500	298	301
Miami	8	8	0	.500	331	379
New England	5	11	0	.313	297	391
N.Y. Jets	4	12	0	.250	253	411

Central Division

Team	W	L	T	Pct.	PF	PA
Cleveland*	9	6	1	.594	334	254
Houston†	9	7	0	.563	365	412
Pittsburgh†	9	7	0	.563	265	326
Cincinnati	8	8	0	.500	404	285

Western Division

Team	W	L	T	Pct.	PF	PA
Denver*	11	5	0	.688	362	226
Kansas City	8	7	1	.531	318	286
L.A. Raiders	8	8	0	.500	315	297
Seattle	7	9	0	.438	241	327
San Diego	6	10	0	.375	266	290

*Division champion.
†Wild-card team.

NATIONAL CONFERENCE

Eastern Division

Team	W	L	T	Pct.	PF	PA
N.Y. Giants*	12	4	0	.750	348	252
Philadelphia†	11	5	0	.688	342	274
Washington	10	6	0	.625	386	308
Phoenix	5	11	0	.313	258	377
Dallas	1	15	0	.063	204	393

Central Division

Team	W	L	T	Pct.	PF	PA
Minnesota*	10	6	0	.625	351	275
Green Bay	10	6	0	.625	362	356
Detroit	7	9	0	.438	312	364
Chicago	6	10	0	.375	358	377
Tampa Bay	5	11	0	.313	320	419

Western Division

Team	W	L	T	Pct.	PF	PA
San Francisco*	14	2	0	.875	442	253
L.A. Rams†	11	5	0	.688	426	344
New Orleans	9	7	0	.563	386	301
Atlanta	3	13	0	.188	279	437

PLAYOFFS

AFC wild-card game
Pittsburgh 26 at Houston 23 (OT)

AFC divisional games
Cleveland 34 vs. Buffalo 30
Denver 24 vs. Pittsburgh 23

AFC championship
Denver 37 vs. Cleveland 21

NFC wild-card game
L.A. Rams 21 at Philadelphia 7

NFC divisional games
L.A. Rams 19 at N.Y. Giants 13 (OT)
San Francisco 41 vs. Minnesota 13

NFC championship
San Francisco 30 vs. L.A. Rams 3

Super Bowl XXIV
San Francisco 55, Denver 10, at New Orleans.

NINERS ARE FINER

In 1988 and '89, the San Francisco 49ers became the first team since the Pittsburgh Steelers a decade earlier to win back-to-back Super Bowl titles. San Francisco's latest two Super Bowl victories, however, were as dissimilar as night and day. The 49ers' 20-16 victory over Cincinnati in January 1989 was one of the most dramatic in Super Bowl history, undecided until Joe Montana hit John Taylor with a 10-yard scoring pass with 34 seconds left. A year later, San Francisco beat Denver, 55-10, as Montana threw five TD passes in one of the worst thrashings in Super Bowl history.

AMERICAN CONFERENCE

Eastern Division

Team	W	L	T	Pct.	PF	PA
Buffalo*	13	3	0	.813	428	263
Miami†	12	4	0	.750	336	242
Indianapolis	7	9	0	.438	281	353
N.Y. Jets	6	10	0	.375	295	345
New England	1	15	0	.063	181	446

Central Division

Team	W	L	T	Pct.	PF	PA
Cincinnati*	9	7	0	.563	360	352
Houston†	9	7	0	.563	405	307
Pittsburgh	9	7	0	.563	292	240
Cleveland	3	13	0	.188	228	462

Western Division

Team	W	L	T	Pct.	PF	PA
L.A. Raiders*	12	4	0	.750	337	268
Kansas City†	11	5	0	.688	369	257
Seattle	9	7	0	.563	306	286
San Diego	6	10	0	.375	315	281
Denver	5	11	0	.313	331	374

NATIONAL CONFERENCE

Eastern Division

Team	W	L	T	Pct.	PF	PA
N.Y. Giants*	13	3	0	.813	335	211
Philadelphia†	10	6	0	.625	396	299
Washington†	10	6	0	.625	381	301
Dallas	7	9	0	.438	244	308
Phoenix	5	11	0	.313	268	396

Central Division

Team	W	L	T	Pct.	PF	PA
Chicago*	11	5	0	.688	348	280
Tampa Bay	6	10	0	.375	264	367
Detroit	6	10	0	.375	373	413
Green Bay	6	10	0	.375	271	347
Minnesota	6	10	0	.375	351	326

Western Division

Team	W	L	T	Pct.	PF	PA
San Francisco*	14	2	0	.875	353	239
New Orleans†	8	8	0	.500	274	275
L.A. Rams	5	11	0	.313	345	412
Atlanta	5	11	0	.313	348	365

*Division champion.
†Wild-card team.

PLAYOFFS

AFC wild-card playoffs
Miami 17 vs. Kansas City 16
Cincinnati 41 vs. Houston 14

AFC divisional playoffs
Buffalo 44 vs. Miami 34
L.A. Raiders 20 vs. Cincinnati 10

AFC championship
Buffalo 51 vs. L.A. Raiders 3

NFC wild-card playoffs
Washington 20 at Philadelphia 6
Chicago 16 vs. New Orleans 6

NFC divisional playoffs
San Francisco 28 vs. Washington 10
N.Y. Giants 31 vs. Chicago 3

NFC championship
N.Y. Giants 15 at San Francisco 13

Super Bowl XXV
N.Y. Giants 20 vs. Buffalo 19, at Tampa, Fla.

AMERICAN CONFERENCE

Eastern Division

Team	W	L	T	Pct.	PF	PA
Buffalo*	13	3	0	.813	458	318
N.Y. Jets†	8	8	0	.500	314	293
Miami	8	8	0	.500	343	349
New England	6	10	0	.375	211	305
Indianapolis	1	15	0	.063	143	381

Central Division

Team	W	L	T	Pct.	PF	PA
Houston*	11	5	0	.688	386	251
Pittsburgh	7	9	0	.438	292	344
Cleveland	6	10	0	.375	293	298
Cincinnati	3	13	0	.188	263	435

Western Division

Team	W	L	T	Pct.	PF	PA
Denver*	12	4	0	.750	304	235
Kansas City†	10	6	0	.625	322	252
L.A. Raiders†	9	7	0	.563	298	297
Seattle	7	9	0	.438	276	261
San Diego	4	12	0	.250	274	342

NATIONAL CONFERENCE

Eastern Division

Team	W	L	T	Pct.	PF	PA
Washington*	14	2	0	.875	485	224
Dallas†	11	5	0	.688	342	310
Philadelphia	10	6	0	.625	285	244
N.Y. Giants	8	8	0	.500	281	297
Phoenix	4	12	0	.250	196	344

Central Division

Team	W	L	T	Pct.	PF	PA
Detroit*	12	4	0	.750	339	295
Chicago†	11	5	0	.688	299	269
Minnesota	8	8	0	.500	301	306
Green Bay	4	12	0	.250	273	313
Tampa Bay	3	13	0	.188	199	365

Western Division

Team	W	L	T	Pct.	PF	PA
New Orleans*	11	5	0	.688	341	211
Atlanta†	10	6	0	.625	361	338
San Francisco	10	6	0	.625	393	239
L.A. Rams	3	13	0	.188	234	390

*Division champion.
†Wild-card team.

PLAYOFFS

AFC wild-card playoffs
Kansas City 10 vs. L.A. Raiders 6
Houston 17 vs. N.Y. Jets 10

AFC divisional playoffs
Denver 26 vs. Houston 24
Buffalo 37 vs. Kansas City 14

AFC championship
Buffalo 10 vs. Denver 7

NFC wild-card playoffs
Atlanta 27 at New Orleans 20
Dallas 17 at Chicago 13

NFC divisional playoffs
Washington 24 vs. Atlanta 7
Detroit 38 vs. Dallas 6

NFC championship
Washington 41 vs. Detroit 10

Super Bowl XXVI
Washington 37 vs. Buffalo 24, at Minneapolis.

BILLS BUFFALOED

Symmetry-wise, the 1990 NFL season was a strange one. In the AFC, all three division races were close, with the Buffalo Bills and Los Angeles Raiders winning their divisions by one game and the Central Division winding up in a three-way tie for first. In the NFC, the races looked more like runaways as the Giants, Bears and 49ers dominated. So what happened in the two conference title games? The Bills blew out the Raiders and the Giants edged the 49ers, setting the stage for one of the most memorable Super Bowls ever. The Giants nipped the Bills, 20-19, when Buffalo's Scott Norwood misfired on a 47-yard field goal attempt with eight seconds left.

1992

AMERICAN CONFERENCE

Eastern Division

Team	W	L	T	Pct.	PF	PA
Miami*	11	5	0	.688	340	281
Buffalo†	11	5	0	.688	381	283
Indianapolis	9	7	0	.563	216	302
N.Y. Jets	4	12	0	.250	220	315
New England	2	14	0	.125	205	363

Central Division

Team	W	L	T	Pct.	PF	PA
Pittsburgh*	11	5	0	.688	299	225
Houston†	10	6	0	.625	352	258
Cleveland	7	9	0	.438	272	275
Cincinnati	5	11	0	.313	274	364

Western Division

Team	W	L	T	Pct.	PF	PA
San Diego*	11	5	0	.688	335	241
Kansas City†	10	6	0	.625	348	282
Denver	8	8	0	.500	262	329
L.A. Raiders	7	9	0	.438	249	281
Seattle	2	14	0	.125	140	312

*Division champion.
†Wild-card team.

NATIONAL CONFERENCE

Eastern Division

Team	W	L	T	Pct.	PF	PA
Dallas*	13	3	0	.813	409	243
Philadelphia†	11	5	0	.688	354	245
Washington†	9	7	0	.563	300	255
N.Y. Giants	6	10	0	.375	306	367
Phoenix	4	12	0	.250	243	332

Central Division

Team	W	L	T	Pct.	PF	PA
Minnesota*	11	5	0	.688	374	249
Green Bay	9	7	0	.563	276	296
Tampa Bay	5	11	0	.313	267	365
Chicago	5	11	0	.313	295	361
Detroit	5	11	0	.313	273	332

Western Division

Team	W	L	T	Pct.	PF	PA
San Francisco*	14	2	0	.875	431	236
New Orleans†	12	4	0	.750	330	202
Atlanta	6	10	0	.375	327	414
L.A. Rams	6	10	0	.375	313	383

PLAYOFFS

AFC wild-card playoffs

San Diego 17 vs. Kansas City 0
Buffalo 41 vs. Houston 38 (OT)

AFC divisional playoffs

Buffalo 24 at Pittsburgh 3
Miami 31 vs. San Diego 0

AFC championship

Buffalo 29 at Miami 10

NFC wild-card playoffs

Washington 24 at Minnesota 7
Philadelphia 36 at New Orleans 20

NFC divisional playoffs

San Francisco 20 vs. Washington 13
Dallas 34 vs. Philadelphia 10

NFC championship

Dallas 30 at San Francisco 20

Super Bowl XXVII

Dallas 52 vs. Buffalo 17, at Pasadena, Calif.

1993

AMERICAN CONFERENCE

Eastern Division

Team	W	L	T	Pct.	PF	PA
Buffalo*	12	4	0	.750	329	242
Miami	9	7	0	.563	349	351
N.Y. Jets	8	8	0	.500	270	247
New England	5	11	0	.313	238	286
Indianapolis	4	12	0	.250	189	378

Central Division

Team	W	L	T	Pct.	PF	PA
Houston*	12	4	0	.750	368	238
Pittsburgh†	9	7	0	.563	308	281
Cleveland	7	9	0	.438	304	307
Cincinnati	3	13	0	.188	187	319

Western Division

Team	W	L	T	Pct.	PF	PA
Kansas City*	11	5	0	.688	328	291
L.A. Raiders†	10	6	0	.625	306	326
Denver†	9	7	0	.563	373	284
San Diego	8	8	0	.500	322	290
Seattle	6	10	0	.375	280	314

*Division champion.
†Wild-card team.

NATIONAL CONFERENCE

Eastern Division

Team	W	L	T	Pct.	PF	PA
Dallas*	12	4	0	.750	376	229
N.Y. Giants†	11	5	0	.688	288	205
Philadelphia	8	8	0	.500	293	315
Phoenix	7	9	0	.438	326	269
Washington	4	12	0	.250	230	345

Central Division

Team	W	L	T	Pct.	PF	PA
Detroit*	10	6	0	.625	298	292
Minnesota†	9	7	0	.563	277	290
Green Bay†	9	7	0	.563	340	282
Chicago	7	9	0	.438	234	230
Tampa Bay	5	11	0	.313	237	376

Western Division

Team	W	L	T	Pct.	PF	PA
San Francisco*	10	6	0	.625	473	295
New Orleans	8	8	0	.500	317	343
Atlanta	6	10	0	.375	316	385
L.A. Rams	5	11	0	.313	221	367

PLAYOFFS

AFC wild-card playoffs

Kansas City 27 vs. Pit. 24 (OT)
L.A. Raiders 42 vs. Denver 24

AFC divisional playoffs

Buffalo 29 vs. L.A. Raiders 23
Kansas City 28 at Houston 20

AFC championship

Buffalo 30 vs. Kansas City 13

NFC wild-card playoffs

Green Bay 28 at Detroit 24
N.Y. Giants 17 vs. Minnesota 10

NFC divisional playoffs

San Francisco 44 vs. N.Y. Giants 3
Dallas 27 vs. Green Bay 17

NFC championship

Dallas 38 vs. San Francisco 21

Super Bowl XXVIII

Dallas 30 vs. Buffalo 13, at Atlanta.

COACHING CAROUSEL

The biggest coaching turnover in 14 years occurred in 1992 as nine coaches debuted with new teams. Two of them—Chuck Knox of the Rams and Ted Marchibroda of the Colts—were returning to clubs they had coached previously, while two others (Seattle's Tom Flores and Tampa Bay's Sam Wyche) had prior NFL head-coaching experience. Of the five first-time coaches, three led their teams to division championships: Pittsburgh's Bill Cowher, Minnesota's Dennis Green and San Diego's Bobby Ross.

SUPER BOWLS

SUPER BOWL I

January 15, 1967, at Los Angeles

Kansas City (AFL)	0	10	0	0 —	10
Green Bay (NFL)	7	7	14	7 —	35

Winning coach—Vince Lombardi.
Most Valuable Player—Bart Starr.
Attendance—61,946.

SUPER BOWL II

January 14, 1968, at Miami

Green Bay (NFL)	3	13	10	7 —	33
Oakland (AFL)	0	7	0	7 —	14

Winning coach—Vince Lombardi.
Most Valuable Player—Bart Starr.
Attendance—75,546.

SUPER BOWL III

January 12, 1969, at Miami

New York (AFL)	0	7	6	3 —	16
Baltimore (NFL)	0	0	0	7 —	7

Winning coach—Weeb Ewbank.
Most Valuable Player—Joe Namath.
Attendance—75,389.

SUPER BOWL IV

January 11, 1970, at New Orleans

Minnesota (NFL)	0	0	7	0 —	7
Kansas City (AFL)	3	13	7	0 —	23

Winning coach—Hank Stram.
Most Valuable Player—Len Dawson.
Attendance—80,562.

SUPER BOWL V

January 17, 1971, at Miami

Baltimore (AFC)	0	6	0	10 —	16
Dallas (NFC)	3	10	0	0 —	13

Winning coach—Don McCafferty.
Most Valuable Player—Chuck Howley.
Attendance—79,204.

SUPER BOWL VI

January 16, 1972, at New Orleans

Dallas (NFC)	3	7	7	7 —	24
Miami (AFC)	0	3	0	0 —	3

Winning coach—Tom Landry.
Most Valuable Player—Roger Staubach.
Attendance—81,023.

SUPER BOWL VII

January 14, 1973, at Los Angeles

Miami (AFC)	7	7	0	0 —	14
Washington (NFC)	0	0	0	7 —	7

Winning coach—Don Shula.
Most Valuable Player—Jake Scott.
Attendance—90,182.

SUPER BOWL VIII

January 13, 1974, at Houston

Minnesota (NFC)	0	0	0	7 —	7
Miami (AFC)	14	3	7	0 —	24

Winning coach—Don Shula.
Most Valuable Player—Larry Csonka.
Attendance—71,882.

SUPER BOWL IX

January 12, 1975, at New Orleans

Pittsburgh (AFC)	0	2	7	7 —	16
Minnesota (NFC)	0	0	0	6 —	6

Winning coach—Chuck Noll.
Most Valuable Player—Franco Harris.
Attendance—80,997.

SUPER BOWL X

January 18, 1976, at Miami

Dallas (NFC)	7	3	0	7 —	17
Pittsburgh (AFC)	7	0	0	14 —	21

Winning coach—Chuck Noll.
Most Valuable Player—Lynn Swann.
Attendance—80,187.

SUPER BOWL XI

January 9, 1977, at Pasadena, Calif.

Oakland (AFC)	0	16	3	13 —	32
Minnesota (NFC)	0	0	7	7 —	14

Winning coach—John Madden.
Most Valuable Player—Fred Biletnikoff.
Attendance—103,428.

SUPER BOWL XII

January 15, 1978, at New Orleans

Dallas (NFC)	10	3	7	7 —	27
Denver (AFC)	0	0	10	0 —	10

Winning coach—Tom Landry.
Most Valuable Players—Harvey Martin and Randy White.
Attendance—75,804.

SUPER BOWL XIII

January 21, 1979, at Miami

Pittsburgh (AFC)	7	14	0	14 —	35
Dallas (NFC)	7	7	3	14 —	31

Winning coach—Chuck Noll.
Most Valuable Player—Terry Bradshaw.
Attendance—78,656.

SUPER BOWL XIV

January 20, 1980, Pasadena, Calif.

Los Angeles (NFC)	7	6	6	0 —	19
Pittsburgh (AFC)	3	7	7	14 —	31

Winning coach—Chuck Noll.
Most Valuable Player—Terry Bradshaw.
Attendance—103,985.

SUPER BOWL XV

January 25, 1981, at New Orleans

Oakland (AFC)	14	0	10	3	—	27
Philadelphia (NFC)	0	3	0	7	—	10

Winning coach—Tom Flores.
Most Valuable Player—Jim Plunkett.
Attendance—75,500.

SUPER BOWL XVI

January 24, 1982, at Pontiac, Mich.

San Fran. (NFC)	7	13	0	6	—	26
Cincinnati (AFC)	0	0	7	14	—	21

Winning coach—Bill Walsh.
Most Valuable Player—Joe Montana.
Attendance—81,270.

SUPER BOWL XVII

January 30, 1983, at Pasadena, Calif.

Miami (AFC)	7	10	0	0	—	17
Washington (NFC)	0	10	3	14	—	27

Winning coach—Joe Gibbs.
Most Valuable Player—John Riggins.
Attendance—103,667.

SUPER BOWL XVIII

January 22, 1984, at Tampa

Washington (NFC)	0	3	6	0	—	9
Los Angeles (AFC)	7	14	14	3	—	38

Winning coach—Tom Flores.
Most Valuable Player—Marcus Allen.
Attendance—72,920.

SUPER BOWL XIX

January 20, 1985, at Palo Alto, Calif.

Miami (AFC)	10	6	0	0	—	16
San Fran. (NFC)	7	21	10	0	—	38

Winning coach—Bill Walsh.
Most Valuable Player—Joe Montana.
Attendance—84,059.

SUPER BOWL XX

January 26, 1986, at New Orleans

Chicago (NFC)	13	10	21	2	—	46
New England (AFC)	3	0	0	7	—	10

Winning coach—Mlke Ditka.
Most Valuable Player—Richard Dent.
Attendance—73,818.

SUPER BOWL XXI

January 25, 1987, at Pasadena, Calif.

Denver (AFC)	10	0	0	10	—	20
N.Y. Giants (NFC)	7	2	17	13	—	39

Winning coach—Bill Parcells.
Most Valuable Player—Phil Simms.
Attendance—101,063.

SUPER BOWL XXII

January 31, 1988, at San Diego

Washington (NFC)	0	35	0	7	—	42
Denver (AFC)	10	0	0	0	—	10

Winning coach—Joe Gibbs.
Most Valuable Player—Doug Williams.
Attendance—73,302.

SUPER BOWL XXIII

January 22, 1989, at Miami

Cincinnati (AFC)	0	3	10	3	—	16
San Fran. (NFC)	3	0	3	14	—	20

Winning coach—Bill Walsh.
Most Valuable Player—Jerry Rice.
Attendance—75,179.

SUPER BOWL XXIV

January 28, 1990, at New Orleans

San Fran. (NFC)	13	14	14	14	—	55
Denver (AFC)	3	0	7	0	—	10

Winning coach—George Seifert.
Most Valuable Player—Joe Montana.
Attendance—72,919.

SUPER BOWL XXV

January 27, 1991, at Tampa

Buffalo (AFC)	3	9	0	7	—	19
New York (NFC)	3	7	7	3	—	20

Winning coach—Bill Parcells.
Most Valuable Player—Ottis Anderson.
Attendance—73,813.

SUPER BOWL XXVI

January 26, 1992, at Minneapolis

Washington (NFC)	0	17	14	6	—	37
Buffalo (AFC)	0	0	10	14	—	24

Winning coach—Joe Gibbs.
Most Valuable Player—Mark Rypien.
Attendance—63,130.

SUPER BOWL XXVII

January 31, 1993, at Pasadena, Calif.

Buffalo (AFC)	7	3	7	0	—	17
Dallas (NFC)	14	14	3	21	—	52

Winning coach—Jimmy Johnson.
Most Valuable Player—Troy Aikman.
Attendance—98,374.

SUPER BOWL XXVIII

January 30, 1994, at Atlanta, Ga.

Dallas (NFC)	6	0	14	10	—	30
Buffalo (AFC)	3	10	0	0	—	13

Winning coach—Jimmy Johnson.
Most Valuable Player—Emmitt Smith.
Attendance—72,817.

SUPER BOWL XXIX

January 29, 1995, at Miami, Fla.

San Diego (AFC)	7	3	8	8	—	26
San Francisco (NFC)	14	14	14	7	—	49

Winning coach—George Seifert.
Most Valuable Player—Steve Young.
Attendance—74,107.

PRO BOWLS

Date	Site	Winning team, score	Losing team, score	Att.
1-15-39	Wrigley Field, Los Angeles	New York Giants, 13	Pro All-Stars, 10	†20,000
1-14-40	Gilmore Stadium, Los Angeles	Green Bay Packers, 16	NFL All-Stars, 7	†18,000
12-29-40	Gilmore Stadium, Los Angeles	Chicago Bears, 28	NFL All-Stars, 14	21,624
1-4-42	Polo Grounds, New York	Chicago Bears, 35	NFL All-Stars, 24	17,725
12-27-42	Shibe Park, Philadelphia	NFL All-Stars, 17	Washington Redskins, 14	18,671
1943-50	No games played.			
1-14-51	Los Angeles Memorial Coliseum	American Conference, 28	National Conference, 27	53,676
1-12-52	Los Angeles Memorial Coliseum	National Conference, 30	American Conference, 13	19,400
1-10-53	Los Angeles Memorial Coliseum	National Conference, 27	American Conference, 7	34,208
1-17-54	Los Angeles Memorial Coliseum	East, 20	West, 9	44,214
1-16-55	Los Angeles Memorial Coliseum	West, 26	East, 19	43,972
1-15-56	Los Angeles Memorial Coliseum	East, 31	West, 30	37,867
1-13-57	Los Angeles Memorial Coliseum	West, 19	East, 10	44,177
1-12-58	Los Angeles Memorial Coliseum	West, 26	East, 7	66,634
1-11-59	Los Angeles Memorial Coliseum	East, 28	West, 21	72,250
1-17-60	Los Angeles Memorial Coliseum	West, 38	East, 21	56,876
1-15-61	Los Angeles Memorial Coliseum	West, 35	East, 31	62,971
1-7-62*	Balboa Stadium, San Diego	West, 47	East, 27	20,973
1-14-62	Los Angeles Memorial Coliseum	West, 31	East, 30	57,409
1-13-63*	Balboa Stadium, San Diego	West, 21	East, 14	27,641
1-13-63	Los Angeles Memorial Coliseum	East, 30	West, 20	61,374
1-12-64	Los Angeles Memorial Coliseum	West, 31	East, 17	67,242
1-19-64*	Balboa Stadium, San Diego	West, 27	East, 24	20,016
1-10-65	Los Angeles Memorial Coliseum	West, 34	East, 14	60,598
1-16-65*	Jeppesen Stadium, Houston	West, 38	East, 14	15,446
1-15-66*	Rice Stadium, Houston	AFL All-Stars, 30	Buffalo Bills, 19	35,572
1-15-66	Los Angeles Memorial Coliseum	East, 36	West, 7	60,124
1-21-67*	Oakland-Alameda County Coliseum	East, 30	West, 23	18,876
1-22-67	Los Angeles Memorial Coliseum	East, 20	West, 10	15,062
1-21-68*	Gator Bowl, Jacksonville, Fla.	East, 25	West, 24	40,103
1-21-68	Los Angeles Memorial Coliseum	West, 38	East, 20	53,289
1-19-69*	Gator Bowl, Jacksonville, Fla.	West, 38	East, 25	41,058
1-19-69	Los Angeles Memorial Coliseum	West, 10	East, 7	32,050
1-17-70*	Astrodome, Houston	West, 26	East, 3	30,170
1-18-70	Los Angeles Memorial Coliseum	West, 16	East, 13	57,786
1-24-71	Los Angeles Memorial Coliseum	NFC, 27	AFC, 6	48,222
1-23-72	Los Angeles Memorial Coliseum	AFC, 26	NFC, 13	53,647
1-21-73	Texas Stadium, Irving	AFC, 33	NFC, 28	37,091
1-20-74	Arrowhead Stadium, Kansas City	AFC, 15	NFC, 13	66,918
1-20-75	Orange Bowl, Miami	NFC, 17	AFC, 10	26,484
1-26-76	Louisiana Superdome, New Orleans	NFC, 23	AFC, 20	30,546
1-17-77	Kingdome, Seattle	AFC, 24	NFC, 14	64,752
1-23-78	Tampa Stadium	NFC, 14	AFC, 13	51,337
1-29-79	Los Angeles Memorial Coliseum	NFC, 13	AFC, 7	46,281
1-27-80	Aloha Stadium, Honolulu	NFC, 37	AFC, 27	49,800
2-1-81	Aloha Stadium, Honolulu	NFC, 21	AFC, 7	50,360
1-31-82	Aloha Stadium, Honolulu	AFC, 16	NFC, 13	50,402
2-6-83	Aloha Stadium, Honolulu	NFC, 20	AFC, 19	49,883
1-29-84	Aloha Stadium, Honolulu	NFC, 45	AFC, 3	50,445
1-27-85	Aloha Stadium, Honolulu	AFC, 22	NFC, 14	50,385
2-2-86	Aloha Stadium, Honolulu	NFC, 28	AFC, 24	50,101
2-1-87	Aloha Stadium, Honolulu	AFC, 10	NFC, 6	50,101
2-7-88	Aloha Stadium, Honolulu	AFC, 15	NFC, 6	50,113
1-29-89	Aloha Stadium, Honolulu	NFC, 34	AFC, 3	50,113
2-4-90	Aloha Stadium, Honolulu	NFC, 27	AFC, 21	50,445
2-3-91	Aloha Stadium, Honolulu	AFC, 23	NFC, 21	50,345
2-2-92	Aloha Stadium, Honolulu	NFC, 21	AFC, 15	50,209
2-7-93	Aloha Stadium, Honolulu	AFC, 23 (OT)	NFC, 20	50,007
2-6-94	Aloha Stadium, Honolulu	NFC, 17	AFC, 3	50,026
2-5-95	Aloha Stadium, Honolulu	AFC, 41	NFC, 13	49,121

*AFL game.
†Estimated figure.

Year—Name, team

1951—Otto Graham, Cleveland Browns
1952—Dan Towler, Los Angeles Rams
1953—Dan Doll, Detroit Lions
1954—Chuck Bednarik, Philadelphia Eagles
1955—Billy Wilson, San Francisco 49ers
1956—Ollie Matson, Chicago Cardinals
1957—Bert Rechichar, Baltimore Colts (back)
    Ernie Stautner, Pittsburgh Steelers (lineman)
1958—Hugh McElhenny, San Francisco 49ers (back)
    Gene Brito, Washington Redskins (lineman)
1959—Frank Gifford, New York Giants (back)
    Doug Atkins, Chicago Bears (lineman)
1960—Johnny Unitas, Baltimore Colts (back)
    Gene Lipscomb, Baltimore Colts (lineman)
1961—Johnny Unitas, Baltimore Colts (back)
    Sam Huff, New York Giants (lineman)
1962—Cotton Davidson, Dallas Texans*
    Jim Brown, Cleveland Browns (back)
    Henry Jordan, Green Bay Packers (lineman)
1963—Curtis McClinton, Dallas Texans* (offense)
    Earl Faison, San Diego Chargers* (defense)
    Jim Brown, Cleveland Browns (back)
    Gene Lipscomb, Pittsburgh Steelers (lineman)
1964—Keith Lincoln, San Diego Chargers* (offense)
    Archie Matsos, Oakland Raiders* (defense)
    Johnny Unitas, Baltimore Colts (back)
    Gino Marchetti, Baltimore Colts (lineman)
1965—Keith Lincoln, San Diego Chargers* (offense)
    Willie Brown, Denver Broncos* (defense)
    Fran Tarkenton, Minnesota Vikings (back)
    Terry Barr, Detroit Lions (lineman)
1966—Joe Namath, New York Jets* (offense)
    Frank Buncom, San Diego Chargers* (defense)
    Jim Brown, Cleveland Browns (back)
    Dale Meinert, St. Louis Cardinals (lineman)
1967—Babe Parilli, Boston Patriots* (offense)
    Verlon Biggs, New York Jets* (defense)
    Gale Sayers, Chicago Bears (back)
    Floyd Peters, Philadelphia Eagles (lineman)
1968—Joe Namath, New York Jets* (offense)
    Don Maynard, New York Jets* (offense)
    Speedy Duncan, San Diego Chargers (defense)
    Gale Sayers, Chicago Bears (back)
    Dave Robinson, Green Bay Packers (lineman)

Year—Name, team

1969—Len Dawson, Kansas City Chiefs* (offense)
    George Webster, Houston* (defense)
    Roman Gabriel, Los Angeles Rams (back)
    Merlin Olsen, Los Angeles Rams (lineman)
1970—John Hadl, San Diego Chargers*
    Gale Sayers, Chicago Bears (back)
    George Andrie, Dallas Cowboys (lineman)
1971—Mel Renfro, Dallas Cowboys (back)
    Fred Carr, Green Bay Packers (lineman)
1972—Jan Stenerud, Kansas City Chiefs (offense)
    Willie Lanier, Kansas City Chiefs (defense)
1973—O.J. Simpson, Buffalo Bills
1974—Garo Yepremian, Miami Dolphins
1975—James Harris, Los Angeles Rams
1976—Billy Johnson, Houston Oilers
1977—Mel Blount, Pittsburgh Steelers
1978—Walter Payton, Chicago Bears
1979—Ahmad Rashad, Minnesota Vikings
1980—Chuck Muncie, New Orleans Saints
1981—Eddie Murray, Detroit Lions
1982—Kellen Winslow, San Diego Chargers
    Lee Roy Selmon, Tampa Bay Buccaneers
1983—Dan Fouts, San Diego Chargers
    John Jefferson, Green Bay Packers
1984—Joe Theismann, Washington Redskins
1985—Mark Gastineau, New York Jets
1986—Phil Simms, New York Giants
1987—Reggie White, Philadelphia Eagles
1988—Bruce Smith, Buffalo Bills
1989—Randall Cunningham, Philadelphia Eagles
1990—Jerry Gray, Los Angeles Rams
1991—Jim Kelly, Buffalo Bills
1992—Michael Irvin, Dallas Cowboys
1993—Steve Tasker, Buffalo Bills
1994—Andre Rison, Atlanta Falcons
1995—Marshall Faulk, Indianapolis Colts

   *AFL game.

RECORDS

INDIVIDUAL SERVICE

PLAYERS

Most years played

26—George Blanda, Chicago Bears, Baltimore, Houston, Oakland, 1949 through 1975, except 1959.

Most years with one club

19—Jim Marshall, Minnesota, 1961 through 1979.
Jackie Slater, L.A. Rams, 1976 through 1994.

Most games played, career

340—George Blanda, Chicago Bears, Baltimore, Houston, Oakland, 1949 through 1975, except 1959.

Most consecutive games played, career

282—Jim Marshall, Cleveland, Minnesota, September 25, 1960 through December 16, 1979.

COACHES

Most years as head coach

40—George Halas, Chicago Bears, 1920 through 1929, 1933 through 1942, 1946 through 1955 and 1958 through 1967.

Most games won as head coach

319—Don Shula, Baltimore, 1963 through 1969; Miami, 1970 through 1994.

Most games lost as head coach

162—Tom Landry, Dallas, 1960 through 1988.

INDIVIDUAL OFFENSE

RUSHING

YARDS

Most yards, career

16,726—Walter Payton, Chicago, 1975 through 1987.

Most yards, season

2,105—Eric Dickerson, Los Angeles Rams, 1984.

Most years leading league in yards

8—Jim Brown, Cleveland, 1957 through 1965, except 1962.

Most consecutive years leading league in yards

5—Jim Brown, Cleveland, 1957 through 1961.

Most years with 1,000 or more yards

10—Walter Payton, Chicago, 1976 through 1986, except 1982.

Most consecutive years with 1,000 or more yards

7—Eric Dickerson, Los Angeles Rams, Indianapolis, 1983 through 1989.

Most yards, game

275—Walter Payton, Chicago vs. Minnesota, November 20, 1977.

Most games with 200 or more yards, career

6—O.J. Simpson, Buffalo, San Francisco, 1969 through 1979.

Most games with 200 or more yards, season

4—Earl Campbell, Houston, 1980.

Most consecutive games with 200 or more yards, season

2—O.J. Simpson, Buffalo, December 9 through 16, 1973.
O.J. Simpson, Buffalo, November 25 through December 5, 1976.
Earl Campbell, Houston, October 19 through 26, 1980.

Most games with 100 or more yards, career

77—Walter Payton, Chicago, 1975 through 1987.

Most games with 100 or more yards, season

12—Eric Dickerson, Los Angeles Rams, 1984.
Barry Foster, Pittsburgh, 1992.

Most consecutive games with 100 or more yards, career

11—Marcus Allen, Los Angeles Raiders, October 28, 1985 through September 14, 1986.

Most consecutive games with 100 or more yards, season

9—Walter Payton, Chicago, October 13 through December 8, 1985.
Marcus Allen, Los Angeles Raiders, October 28 through December 23, 1985.

Longest run from scrimmage

99 yards—Tony Dorsett, Dallas at Minnesota, January 3, 1983 (touchdown).

ATTEMPTS

Most attempts, career

3,838—Walter Payton, Chicago, 1975 through 1987.

Most attempts, season

407—James Wilder, Tampa Bay, 1984.

Most attempts, game

45—Jamie Morris, Washington at Cincinnati, December 17, 1988, overtime.

43—Butch Woolfolk, New York Giants at Philadelphia, November 20, 1983.
James Wilder, Tampa Bay vs. Green Bay, September 30, 1984, overtime.

Most years leading league in attempts

6—Jim Brown, Cleveland, 1958 through 1965, except 1960 and 1962.

Most consecutive years leading league in attempts

4—Steve Van Buren, Philadelphia, 1947 through 1950.
Walter Payton, Chicago, 1976 through 1979.

TOUCHDOWNS

Most touchdowns, career

110—Walter Payton, Chicago, 1975 through 1987.

Most touchdowns, season

24—John Riggins, Washington, 1983.

Most years leading league in touchdowns

5—Jim Brown, Cleveland, 1957 through 1959, 1963, 1965.

Most consecutive years leading league in touchdowns

3—Steve Van Buren, Philadelphia, 1947 through 1949.
Jim Brown, Cleveland, 1957 through 1959.
Abner Haynes, Dallas Texans, 1960 through 1962.
Cookie Gilchrist, Buffalo, 1962 through 1964.
Leroy Kelly, Cleveland, 1966 through 1968.

Most touchdowns, game

6—Ernie Nevers, Chicago Cardinals vs. Chicago Bears, November 28, 1929.

Most consecutive games with one or more touchdowns, career

13—John Riggins, Washington, December 26, 1982 through November 27, 1983.
George Rogers, Washington, November 24, 1985 through November 2, 1986.

Most consecutive games with one or more touchdowns, season

12—John Riggins, Washington, September 5 through November 27, 1983.

PASSING

PASSER RATING

Highest rating, career (1,500 or more attempts)

96.8—Steve Young, Tampa Bay, San Francisco, 1985

through 1994.

Highest rating, season (qualifiers)

112.8—Steve Young, San Francisco, 1994.

ATTEMPTS

Most attempts, career

6,467—Fran Tarkenton, Minnesota, New York Giants, 1961 through 1978.

Most attempts, season

691—Drew Bledsoe, New England, 1994.

Most years leading league in attempts

4—Sammy Baugh, Washington, 1937, 1943, 1947, 1948.
Johnny Unitas, Baltimore, 1957, 1959 through 1961.
George Blanda, Chicago Bears, Houston, 1953, 1963 through 1965.
Dan Marino, Miami, 1984, 1986, 1988, 1992.

Most consecutive years leading league in attempts

3—Johnny Unitas, Baltimore, 1959 through 1961.
George Blanda, Houston, 1963 through 1965.

Most attempts, game

70—Drew Bledsoe, New England vs. Minnesota, November 13, 1994 (overtime).
68—George Blanda, Houston vs. Buffalo, November 1, 1964.

COMPLETIONS

Most completions, career

3,686—Fran Tarkenton, Minnesota, New York Giants, 1961 through 1978.

Most completions, season

404—Warren Moon, Houston, 1991.

Most years leading league in completions

5—Sammy Baugh, Washington, 1937, 1943, 1945, 1947, 1948.
Dan Marino, Miami, 1984, 1985, 1986, 1988, 1992.

Most consecutive years leading league in completions

3—George Blanda, Houston, 1963 through 1965.
Dan Marino, Miami, 1984 through 1986.

Most completions, game

45—Drew Bledsoe, New England vs. Minnesota, November 13, 1994 (overtime).
42—Richard Todd, New York Jets vs. San Francisco, September 21, 1980.

YARDS

Most yards, career

47,003—Fran Tarkenton, Minnesota, New York Giants, 1961 through 1978.

Most yards, season

5,084—Dan Marino, Miami, 1984.

Most years leading league in yards

5—Sonny Jurgensen, Philadelphia, Washington, 1961, 1962, 1966, 1967, 1969.
Dan Marino, Miami, 1984 through 1986, 1988, 1992.

Most consecutive years leading league in yards

4—Dan Fouts, San Diego, 1979 through 1982.

Most years with 3,000 or more yards

10—Dan Marino, Miami, 1984 through 1994, except 1993.

Most yards, game

554—Norm Van Brocklin, Los Angeles at New York Yanks, September 28, 1951.

Most games with 400 or more yards, career

12—Dan Marino, Miami, 1983 through 1994.

Most games with 400 or more yards, season

4—Dan Marino, Miami, 1984.

Most consecutive games with 400 or more yards, season

2—Dan Fouts, San Diego, December 11 through 20, 1982.

Dan Marino, Miami, December 2 through 9, 1984.
Phil Simms, New York Giants, October 6 through 13, 1985.

Most games with 300 or more yards, career

51—Dan Fouts, San Diego, 1973 through 1987.

Most games with 300 or more yards, season

9—Dan Marino, Miami, 1984.
Warren Moon, Houston, 1990.

Most consecutive games with 300 or more yards, season

5—Joe Montana, San Francisco, September 19 through December 11, 1982.

Longest pass completion

99 yards—Frank Filchock, Washington vs. Pittsburgh, October 15, 1939 (touchdown).
George Izo, Washington at Cleveland, September 15, 1963 (touchdown).
Karl Sweetan, Detroit at Baltimore, October 16, 1966 (touchdown).
Sonny Jurgensen, Washington at Chicago, September 15, 1968 (touchdown).
Jim Plunkett, Los Angeles Raiders vs. Washington, October 2, 1983 (touchdown).
Ron Jaworski, Philadelphia vs. Atlanta, November 10, 1985 (touchdown).
Stan Humphries, San Diego at Seattle, September 18, 1994 (touchdown).

YARDS PER ATTEMPT

Most yards per attempt, career (1,500 or more attempts)

8.63—Otto Graham, Cleveland, 1950 through 1955 (13,499 yards, 1,565 attempts).

Most yards per attempt, season (qualifiers)

11.17—Tommy O'Connell, Cleveland, 1957 (1,229 yards, 110 attempts).

Most years leading league in yards per attempt

7—Sid Luckman, Chicago Bears, 1939 through 1943, 1946, 1947.

Most consecutive years leading league in yards per attempt

5—Sid Luckman, Chicago Bears, 1939 through 1943.

Most yards per attempt, game (20 or more attempts)

18.58—Sammy Baugh, Washington vs. Boston, October 31, 1948 (446 yards, 24 attempts).

TOUCHDOWNS

Most touchdowns, career

342—Fran Tarkenton, Minnesota, New York Giants, 1961 through 1978.

Most touchdowns, season

48—Dan Marino, Miami, 1984.

Most years leading league in touchdowns

4—Johnny Unitas, Baltimore, 1957 through 1960.
Len Dawson, Dallas Texans, Kansas City, 1962 through 1966, except 1964.

Most consecutive years leading league in touchdowns

4—Johnny Unitas, Baltimore, 1957 through 1960.

Most touchdowns, game

7—Sid Luckman, Chicago Bears at New York Giants, November 14, 1943.
Adrian Burk, Philadelphia at Washington, October 17, 1954.
George Blanda, Houston vs. New York Titans, November 19, 1961.
Y.A. Tittle, New York Giants vs. Washington, October 28, 1962.
Joe Kapp, Minnesota vs. Baltimore, September 28, 1969.

INTERCEPTIONS

Most interceptions, career

277—George Blanda, Chicago Bears, Baltimore, Houston, Oakland, 1949 through 1975, except 1959.

Most interceptions, season

42—George Blanda, Houston, 1962.

Most interceptions, game

8—Jim Hardy, Chicago Cardinals vs. Philadelphia, September 24, 1950.

Most attempts with no interceptions, game

70—Drew Bledsoe, New England vs. Minnesota, November 13, 1994 (overtime).

63—Rich Gannon, Minnesota at New England, October 20, 1991 (overtime).

60—Davey O'Brien, Philadelphia at Washington, December 1, 1940.

INTERCEPTION PERCENTAGE

Lowest interception percentage, career (1,500 or more attempts)

2.54—Bernie Kosar, Cleveland, Dallas, Miami, 1985 through 1994 (3,225 attempts, 82 interceptions).

Lowest interception percentage, season (qualifiers)

0.66—Joe Ferguson, Buffalo, 1976 (151 attempts, one interception).

Most years leading league in lowest interception percentage

5—Sammy Baugh, Washington, 1940, 1942, 1944, 1945, 1947.

SACKS (SINCE 1963)

Most sacks, career

483—Fran Tarkenton, Minnesota, New York Giants, 1961 through 1978.

Most sacks, season

72—Randall Cunningham, Philadelphia, 1986.

Most sacks, game

12—Bert Jones, Baltimore vs. St. Louis, October 26, 1980.
Warren Moon, Houston vs. Dallas, September 29, 1985.

RECEIVING

RECEPTIONS

Most receptions, career

934—Art Monk, Washington, New York Jets, 1980 through 1994.

Most receptions, season

122—Cris Carter, Minnesota, 1994.

Most years leading league in receptions

8—Don Hutson, Green Bay, 1936 through 1945, except 1938 and 1940.

Most consecutive years leading league in receptions

5—Don Hutson, Green Bay, 1941 through 1945.

Most receptions, game

18—Tom Fears, Los Angeles vs. Green Bay, December 3, 1950.

Most consecutive games with one or more receptions

180—Art Monk, Washington, N.Y. Jets, January 2, 1983 through December 24, 1994.

YARDS

Most yards, career

14,004—James Lofton, Green Bay, Los Angeles Raiders, Buffalo, Los Angeles Rams, Philadelphia, 1978 through 1993.

Most yards, season

1,746—Charley Hennigan, Houston, 1961.

Most years leading league in yards

7—Don Hutson, Green Bay, 1936 through 1944, except 1937 and 1940.

Most consecutive years leading league in yards

4—Don Hutson, Green Bay, 1941 through 1944.

Most years with 1,000 or more yards

9—Jerry Rice, San Francisco, 1986 through 1994.

Most yards, game

336—Willie Anderson, Los Angeles Rams at New Orleans, November 26, 1989 (overtime).

309—Stephone Paige, Kansas City vs. San Diego, December 22, 1985.

Most games with 200 or more yards, career

5—Lance Alworth, San Diego, Dallas, 1962 through 1972.

Most games with 200 or more yards, season

3—Charley Hennigan, Houston, 1961.

Most games with 100 or more yards, career

50—Don Maynard, New York Giants, New York Jets, St. Louis, 1958 through 1973, except 1959.

Most games with 100 or more yards, season

10—Charley Hennigan, Houston, 1961.

Most consecutive games with 100 or more yards, season

7—Charley Hennigan, Houston, 1961.
Bill Groman, Houston, 1961.

Longest reception

99 yards—Andy Farkas, Washington vs. Pittsburgh, October 15, 1939 (touchdown).
Bobby Mitchell, Washington at Cleveland, September 15, 1963 (touchdown).
Pat Studstill, Detroit at Baltimore, October 16, 1966 (touchdown).
Gerry Allen, Washington at Chicago, September 15, 1968 (touchdown).
Cliff Branch, Los Angeles Raiders vs. Washington, October 2, 1983 (touchdown).
Mike Quick, Philadelphia vs. Atlanta, November 10, 1985 (touchdown).
Tony Martin, San Diego at Seattle, September 18, 1994 (touchdown).

TOUCHDOWNS

Most touchdowns, career

131—Jerry Rice, San Francisco, 1985 through 1994.

Most touchdowns, season

22—Jerry Rice, San Francisco, 1987.

Most years leading league in touchdowns

9—Don Hutson, Green Bay, 1935 through 1944, except 1939.

Most consecutive years leading league in touchdowns

5—Don Hutson, Green Bay, 1940 through 1944.

Most touchdowns, game

5—Bob Shaw, Chicago Cardinals vs. Baltimore, October 2, 1950.
Kellen Winslow, San Diego at Oakland, November 22, 1981.
Jerry Rice, San Francisco at Atlanta, October 14, 1990.

Most consecutive games with one or more touchdowns

13—Jerry Rice, San Francisco, December 19, 1986 through December 27, 1987.

COMBINED NET YARDS

(Rushing, receiving, interception returns, punt returns, kickoff returns and fumble returns)

ATTEMPTS

Most attempts, career

4,368—Walter Payton, Chicago, 1975 through 1987.

Most attempts, season

496—James Wilder, Tampa Bay, 1984.

Most attempts, game

48—James Wilder, Tampa Bay at Pittsburgh, October 30, 1983.

YARDS

Most yards, career

21,803—Walter Payton, Chicago, 1975 through 1987.

Most yards, season

2,535—Lionel James, San Diego, 1985.

Most years leading league in yards

5—Jim Brown, Cleveland, 1958 through 1961, 1964.

Most consecutive years leading league in yards

4—Jim Brown, Cleveland, 1958 through 1961.

Most yards, game

373—Billy Cannon, Houston at New York Titans, December 10, 1961.

SCORING
POINTS

Most points, career

2,002—George Blanda, Chicago Bears, Baltimore, Houston, Oakland, 1949 through 1975, except 1959.

Most points, season

176—Paul Hornung, Green Bay, 1960.

Most years leading league in points

5—Don Hutson, Green Bay, 1940 through 1944.
Gino Cappelletti, Boston, 1961 through 1966, except 1962.

Most consecutive years leading league in points

5—Don Hutson, Green Bay, 1940 through 1944.

Most years with 100 or more points

11—Nick Lowery, Kansas City, 1981 through 1993, except 1982 and 1987.

Most points, game

40—Ernie Nevers, Chicago Cardinals vs. Chicago Bears, November 28, 1929.

Most consecutive games with one or more points

186—Jim Breech, Oakland, Cincinnati, September 2, 1979 through October 11, 1992.

TOUCHDOWNS

Most touchdowns, career

139—Jerry Rice, San Francisco, 1985 through 1994.

Most touchdowns, season

24—John Riggins, Washington, 1983.

Most years leading league in touchdowns

8—Don Hutson, Green Bay, 1935 through 1938 and 1941 through 1944.

Most consecutive years leading league in touchdowns

4—Don Hutson, Green Bay, 1935 through 1938 and 1941 through 1944.

Most touchdowns, game

6—Ernie Nevers, Chicago Cardinals vs. Chicago Bears, November 28, 1929.
Dub Jones, Cleveland vs. Chicago Bears, November 25, 1951.
Gale Sayers, Chicago vs. San Francisco, December 12, 1965.

Most consecutive games with one or more touchdowns

18—Lenny Moore, Baltimore, October 27, 1963 through September 19, 1965.

EXTRA POINTS

Most extra points attempted, career

959—George Blanda, Chicago Bears, Baltimore, Houston, Oakland, 1949 through 1975, except 1959.

Most extra points made, career

943—George Blanda, Chicago Bears, Baltimore, Houston, Oakland, 1949 through 1975, except 1959.

Most extra points attempted, season

70—Uwe von Schamann, Miami, 1984.

Most extra points made, season

66—Uwe von Schamann, Miami, 1984.

Most extra points attempted, game

10—Charlie Gogolak, Washington vs. New York Giants, November 27, 1966.

Most extra points made, game

9—Pat Harder, Chicago Cardinals at New York Giants, October 17, 1948.
Bob Waterfield, Los Angeles vs. Baltimore, October 22, 1950.
Charlie Gogolak, Washington vs. New York Giants, November 27, 1966.

FIELD GOALS AND FIELD-GOAL PERCENTAGE

Most field goals attempted, career

638—George Blanda, Chicago Bears, Baltimore, Houston, Oakland, 1949 through 1975, except 1959.

Most field goals made, career

373—Jan Stenerud, Kansas City, Green Bay, Minnesota, 1967 through 1985.

Most field goals attempted, season

49—Bruce Gossett, Los Angeles, 1966.
Curt Knight, Washington, 1971.

Most field goals made, season

35—Ali Haji-Sheikh, New York Giants, 1983.
Jeff Jaeger, Los Angeles Raiders, 1993.

Most field goals attempted, game

9—Jim Bakken, St. Louis at Pittsburgh, September 24, 1967.

Most field goals made, game

7—Jim Bakken, St. Louis at Pittsburgh, September 24, 1967.
Rich Karlis, Minnesota vs. Los Angeles Rams, November 5, 1989 (overtime).

Most field goals made, one quarter

4—Garo Yepremian, Detroit vs. Minnesota, November 13, 1966, second quarter.
Curt Knight, Washington at New York Giants, November 15, 1970, second quarter.
Roger Ruzek, Dallas vs. New York Giants, November 2, 1987, fourth quarter.

Most consecutive games with one or more field goals made, career

31—Fred Cox, Minnesota, November 17, 1968 through December 5, 1970.

Most consecutive field goals made, career

29—John Carney, San Diego, November 22, 1992 through September 19, 1993.

Most field goals of 50 or more yards, career

22—Morten Andersen, New Orleans, 1982 through 1994.

Most field goals of 50 or more yards, season

6—Dean Biasucci, Indianapolis, 1988.
Chris Jacke, Green Bay, 1993.
Tony Zendejas, Los Angeles Rams, 1993.

Most field goals of 50 or more yards, game

2—Held by many players.

Longest field goal made

63 yards—Tom Dempsey, New Orleans vs. Detroit, November 8, 1970.

Highest field-goal percentage, career (100 or more made)

80.41—Nick Lowery, New England, Kansas City, New York Jets, 1978 through 1994, except 1979 (434 attempted, 349 made).

Highest field-goal percentage, season (qualifiers)

100.00—Tony Zendejas, Los Angeles Rams, 1991 (17 attempted, 17 made).

SAFETIES

Most safeties, career

4—Ted Hendricks, Baltimore, Green Bay, Oakland, Los Angeles Raiders, 1969 through 1983.
Doug English, Detroit, 1975 through 1985, except 1980.

Most safeties, season
2—Held by many players.
Most safeties, game
2—Fred Dryer, Los Angeles vs. Green Bay, October 21, 1973.

PUNTING

Most punts, career
1,154—Dave Jennings, New York Giants, New York Jets, 1974 through 1987.
Most punts, season
114—Bob Parsons, Chicago, 1981.
Most seasons leading league in punting
4—Sammy Baugh, Washington, 1940 through 1943.
Jerrel Wilson, Kansas City, 1965, 1968, 1972, 1973.
Most consecutive seasons leading league in punting
4—Sammy Baugh, Washington, 1940 through 1943.
Most punts, game
15—John Teltschik, Philadelphia at New York Giants, December 6, 1987 (overtime).
14—Dick Nesbitt, Chicago Cardinals at Chicago Bears, November 30, 1933.
Keith Molesworth, Chicago Bears vs. Green Bay, December 10, 1933.
Sammy Baugh, Washington vs. Philadelphia, November 5, 1939.
Carl Kinscherf, New York Giants at Detroit, November 7, 1943.
George Taliaferro, New York Yanks vs. Los Angeles, September 28, 1951.
Longest punt
98 yards—Steve O'Neal, New York Jets at Denver, September 21, 1969.

FUMBLES

Most fumbles, career
128—Dave Krieg, Seattle, Kansas City, Detroit, 1980 through 1994.
Most fumbles, season
18—Dave Krieg, Seattle, 1989.
Warren Moon, Houston, 1990.
Most fumbles, game
7—Len Dawson, Kansas City vs. San Diego, November 15, 1964.

PUNT RETURNS

Most punt returns, career
292—Vai Sikahema, St. Louis, Phoenix, Green Bay, Philadelphia, 1986 through 1993.
Most punt returns, season
70—Danny Reece, Tampa Bay, 1979.
Most years leading league in punt returns
3—Les "Speedy" Duncan, San Diego, Washington, 1965, 1966, 1971.
Rick Upchurch, Denver, 1976, 1978, 1982.
Most punt returns, game
11—Eddie Brown, Washington at Tampa Bay, October 9, 1977.

YARDS

Most yards, career
3,317—Billy "White Shoes" Johnson, Houston, Atlanta, Washington, 1974 through 1988, except 1981.
Most yards, season
692—Fulton Walker, Miami, Los Angeles Raiders, 1985.

Most yards, game
207—LeRoy Irvin, Los Angeles at Atlanta, October 11, 1981.
Longest punt return
103 yards—Robert Bailey, Los Angeles Rams at New Orleans, October 23, 1994 (touchdown).

FAIR CATCHES

Most fair catches, career
102—Willie Wood, Green Bay, 1960 through 1971.
Most fair catches, season
27—Leo Lewis, Minnesota, 1989.
Most fair catches, game
7—Lem Barney, Detroit vs. Chicago, November 21, 1976.
Bobby Morse, Philadelphia vs. Buffalo, December 27, 1987.

TOUCHDOWNS

Most touchdowns, career
8—Jack Christiansen, Detroit, 1951 through 1958.
Rick Upchurch, Denver, 1975 through 1983.
Most touchdowns, season
4—Jack Christiansen, Detroit, 1951.
Rick Upchurch, Denver, 1976.
Most touchdowns, game
2—Jack Christiansen, Detroit vs. Los Angeles, October 14, 1951.
Jack Christiansen, Detroit vs. Green Bay, November 22, 1951.
Dick Christy, New York Titans vs. Denver, September 24, 1961.
Rick Upchurch, Denver vs. Cleveland, September 26, 1976.
LeRoy Irvin, Los Angeles at Atlanta, October 11, 1981.
Vai Sikahema, St. Louis vs. Tampa Bay, December 21, 1986.
Todd Kinchen, Los Angeles Rams vs. Atlanta, December 27, 1992.

KICKOFF RETURNS

Most kickoff returns, career
309—Mel Gray, New Orleans, Detroit, 1986 through 1994.
Most kickoff returns, season
63—Tyrone Hughes, New Orleans, 1994.
Most years leading league in kickoff returns
3—Abe Woodson, San Francisco, 1959, 1962, 1963.
Most kickoff returns, game
9—Noland Smith, Kansas City vs. Oakland, November 23, 1967.
Dino Hall, Cleveland vs. Pittsburgh, October 7, 1979.
Paul Palmer, Kansas City at Seattle, September 20, 1987.

YARDS

Most yards, career
7,650—Mel Gray, New Orleans, Detroit, 1986 through 1994.
Most yards, season
1,556—Tyrone Hughes, New Orleans, 1994.
Most years leading league in yards
3—Bruce Harper, New York Jets, 1977 through 1979.
Most yards, game
304—Tyrone Hughes, New Orleans vs. Los Angeles Rams, October 23, 1994.
Longest kickoff return
106 yards—Al Carmichael, Green Bay vs. Chicago Bears, October 7, 1956 (touchdown).
Noland Smith, Kansas City at Denver, December 17, 1967.
Roy Green, St. Louis at Dallas, October 21, 1979.

TOUCHDOWNS

Most touchdowns, career

6—Ollie Matson, Chicago Cardinals, Los Angeles Rams, Detroit, Philadelphia, 1952 through 1964, except 1953.
Gale Sayers, Chicago, 1965 through 1971.
Travis Williams, Green Bay, Los Angeles, 1967 through 1971.
Mel Gray, New Orleans, Detroit, 1986 through 1994.

Most touchdowns, season

4—Travis Williams, Green Bay, 1967.
Cecil Turner, Chicago, 1970.

Most touchdowns, game

2—Timmy Brown, Philadelphia vs. Dallas, November 6, 1966.
Travis Williams, Green Bay vs. Cleveland, November 12, 1967.
Ron Brown, Los Angeles Rams vs. Green Bay, November 24, 1985.
Tyrone Hughes, New Orleans vs. Los Angeles Rams, October 23, 1994.

☐ COMBINED KICK RETURNS (KICKOFFS AND PUNTS) ☐

Most kick returns, career

527—Vai Sikahema, St. Louis, Phoenix, Green Bay, Philadelphia, 1986 through 1993.

Most kick returns, season

100—Larry Jones, Washington, 1975.

Most kick returns, game

13—Stump Mitchell, St. Louis at Atlanta, October 18, 1981.
Ron Harris, New England at Pittsburgh, December 5, 1993.

YARDS

Most yards, career

9,735—Mel Gray, New Orleans, Detroit, 1986 through 1994.

Most yards, season

1,930—Brian Mitchell, Washington, 1994.

Most yards, game

347—Tyrone Hughes, New Orleans vs. Los Angeles Rams, October 23, 1994.

TOUCHDOWNS

Most touchdowns, career

9—Ollie Matson, Chicago Cardinals, Los Angeles Rams, Detroit, Philadelphia, 1952 through 1966, except 1953.
Mel Gray, New Orleans, Detroit, 1986 through 1994.

Most touchdowns, season

4—Jack Christiansen, Detroit, 1951.
Emlen Tunnell, New York Giants, 1951.
Gale Sayers, Chicago, 1967.
Travis Williams, Green Bay, 1967.
Cecil Turner, Chicago, 1970.
Billy "White Shoes" Johnson, Houston, 1975.
Rick Upchurch, Denver, 1976.

Most touchdowns, game

2—Held by many players.

INDIVIDUAL DEFENSE

☐ INTERCEPTIONS ☐

Most interceptions, career

81—Paul Krause, Washington, Minnesota, 1964 through 1979.

Most interceptions, season

14—Dick "Night Train" Lane, Los Angeles, 1952.

Most interceptions, game

4—Held by many players.

Most consecutive games with one or more interceptions

8—Tom Morrow, Oakland, 1962 through 1963.

Most yards on interceptions, career

1,282—Emlen Tunnell, New York Giants, Green Bay, 1948 through 1961.

Most yards on interceptions, season

349—Charlie McNeil, San Diego, 1961.

Most yards on interceptions, game

177—Charlie McNeil, San Diego vs. Houston, September 24, 1961.

Longest interception return

103—Vencie Glenn, San Diego vs. Denver, November 29, 1987.
Louis Oliver, Miami vs. Buffalo, October 4, 1992.

TOUCHDOWNS

Most touchdowns, career

9—Ken Houston, Houston, Washington, 1967 through 1980.

Most touchdowns, season

4—Ken Houston, Houston, 1971.
Jim Kearney, Kansas City, 1972.
Eric Allen, Philadelphia, 1993.

Most touchdowns, game

2—Held by many players.

☐ FUMBLES RECOVERED ☐

Most fumbles recovered (own and opponents'), career

43—Fran Tarkenton, Minnesota, New York Giants, 1961 through 1978.

Most fumbles recovered (own), career

43—Fran Tarkenton, Minnesota, New York Giants, 1961 through 1978.

Most opponents' fumbles recovered, career

29—Jim Marshall, Cleveland, Minnesota, 1960 through 1979.

Most fumbles recovered (own and opponents'), season

9—Don Hultz, Minnesota, 1963.
Dave Krieg, Seattle, 1989.

Most fumbles recovered (own), season

9—Dave Krieg, Seattle, 1989.

Most opponents' fumbles recovered, season

9—Don Hultz, Minnesota, 1963.

Most fumbles recovered (own and opponents'), game

4—Otto Graham, Cleveland at New York Giants, October 25, 1953.
Sam Etcheverry, St. Louis at New York Giants, September 17, 1961.
Roman Gabriel, Los Angeles at San Francisco, October 12, 1969.
Joe Ferguson, Buffalo vs. Miami, September 18, 1977.
Randall Cunningham, Philadelphia at Los Angeles Raiders, November 30, 1986 (overtime).

Most fumbles recovered (own), game

4—Otto Graham, Cleveland at New York Giants, October 25, 1953.
Sam Etcheverry, St. Louis at New York Giants, September 17, 1961.
Roman Gabriel, Los Angeles at San Francisco, October 12, 1969.
Joe Ferguson, Buffalo vs. Miami, September 18, 1977.
Randall Cunningham, Philadelphia at Los Angeles Raiders, November 30, 1986 (overtime).

Most opponents' fumbles recovered, game

3—Held by many players.

Longest fumble return

104 yards—Jack Tatum, Oakland at Green Bay, September 24, 1972 (touchdown).

TOUCHDOWNS

Most touchdowns (own and opponents' recovered), career

4—Bill Thompson, Denver, 1969 through 1981.
  Jessie Tuggle, Atlanta, 1987 through 1992.

Most touchdowns (own recovered), career

2—Held by many players.

Most touchdowns (opponents' recovered), career

4—Jessie Tuggle, Atlanta, 1987 through 1992.

Most touchdowns, season

2—Held by many players.

Most touchdowns, game

2—Fred "Dippy" Evans, Chicago Bears vs. Washington, November 28, 1948.

SACKS (SINCE 1982)

Most sacks, career

145—Reggie White, Philadelphia, Green Bay, 1985 through 1994.

Most sacks, season

22—Mark Gastineau, New York Jets, 1984.

Most sacks, game

7—Derrick Thomas, Kansas City vs. Seattle, November 11, 1990.

TEAM MISCELLANEOUS

CHAMPIONSHIPS

Most league championships won

11—Green Bay, 1929, 1930, 1931, 1936, 1939, 1944, 1961, 1962, 1965, 1966, 1967.

Most consecutive league championships won

3—Green Bay, 1929 through 1931.
  Green Bay, 1965 through 1967.

Most first-place finishes during regular season (since 1933)

18—Cleveland Browns, 1950 through 1955, 1957, 1964, 1965, 1967, 1968, 1969, 1971, 1980, 1985, 1986, 1987, 1989.

Most consecutive first-place finishes during regular season (since 1933)

7—Los Angeles, 1973 through 1979.

GAMES WON

Most games won, season

15—San Francisco, 1984.
  Chicago, 1985.

Most consecutive games won, season

14—Miami, September 17 through December 16, 1972.

Most consecutive games won from start of season

14—Miami, September 17 through December 16, 1972 (entire season).

Most consecutive games won at end of season

14—Miami, September 17 through December 16, 1972 (entire season).

Most consecutive undefeated games, season

14—Miami, September 17 through December 16, 1972 (entire season).

Most consecutive games won

17—Chicago Bears, November 26, 1933 through December 2, 1934.

Most consecutive undefeated games

25—Canton, 1921 through 1923 (won 22, tied three).

Most consecutive home games won

27—Miami, October 17, 1971 through December 15, 1974.

Most consecutive undefeated home games

30—Green Bay, 1928 through 1933 (won 27, tied three).

Most consecutive road games won

18—San Francisco, November 27, 1988 through December 30, 1990.

Most consecutive undefeated road games

18—San Francisco, November 27, 1988 through December 30, 1990 (won 18).

GAMES LOST

Most games lost, season

15—New Orleans, 1980.
  Dallas, 1989.
  New England, 1990.
  Indianapolis, 1991.

Most consecutive games lost

26—Tampa Bay, September 12, 1976 through December 4, 1977.

Most consecutive winless games

26—Tampa Bay, September 12, 1976 through December 4, 1977 (lost 26).

Most consecutive games lost, season

14—Tampa Bay, September 12 through December 12, 1976.
  New Orleans, September 7 through December 7, 1980.
  Baltimore, September 13 through December 13, 1981.
  New England, September 23 through December 30, 1990.

Most consecutive games lost from start of season

14—Tampa Bay, September 12 through December 12, 1976 (entire season).
  New Orleans, September 7 through December 7, 1980.

Most consecutive games lost at end of season

14—Tampa Bay, September 12 through December 12, 1976 (entire season).
  New England, September 23 through December 30, 1990.

Most consecutive winless games, season

14—Tampa Bay, September 12 through December 12, 1976 (lost 14; entire season).
  New Orleans, September 7 through December 7, 1980 (lost 14).
  Baltimore, September 13 through December 13, 1981 (lost 14).
  New England, September 23 through December 30, 1990 (lost 14).

Most consecutive home games lost

14—Dallas, October 9, 1988 through December 24, 1989.

Most consecutive winless home games

14—Dallas, October 9, 1988 through December 24, 1989 (lost 14).

Most consecutive road games lost

23—Houston, September 27, 1981 through November 4, 1984.

Most consecutive winless road games

23—Houston, September 27, 1981 through November 4, 1984 (lost 23).

TIE GAMES

Most tie games, season

6—Chicago Bears, 1932.

Most consecutive tie games

3—Chicago Bears, September 25 through October 9, 1932.

TEAM OFFENSE

RUSHING

Most years leading league in rushing

16—Chicago Bears, 1932, 1934, 1935, 1939, 1940, 1941, 1942, 1951, 1955, 1956, 1968, 1977, 1983, 1984, 1985, 1986.

Most consecutive years leading league in rushing

4—Chicago Bears, 1939 through 1942.
Chicago Bears, 1983 through 1986.

ATTEMPTS

Most attempts, season

681—Oakland, 1977.

Most attempts, game

72—Chicago Bears vs. Brooklyn, October 20, 1935.

Most attempts by both teams, game

108—Chicago Cardinals 70, Green Bay 38, December 5, 1948.

Fewest attempts, game

6—Chicago Cardinals at Boston, October 29, 1933.

Fewest attempts by both teams, game

35—New Orleans 20, Seattle 15, September 1, 1991.

YARDS

Most yards, season

3,165—New England, 1978.

Fewest yards, season

298—Philadelphia, 1940.

Most yards, game

426—Detroit vs. Pittsburgh, November 4, 1934.

Most yards by both teams, game

595—Los Angeles 371, New York Yanks 224, November 18, 1951.

Fewest yards, game

-53—Detroit at Chicago Cardinals, October 17, 1943.

Fewest yards by both teams, game

-15—Detroit -53, Chicago Cardinals 38, October 17, 1943.

TOUCHDOWNS

Most touchdowns, season

36—Green Bay, 1962.

Fewest touchdowns, season

1—Brooklyn, 1934.

Most touchdowns, game

7—Los Angeles vs. Atlanta, December 4, 1976.

Most touchdowns by both teams, game

8—Los Angeles 6, New York Yanks 2, November 18, 1951.
Chicago Bears 5, Green Bay 3, November 6, 1955.
Cleveland 6, Los Angeles 2, November 24, 1957.

PASSING

ATTEMPTS

Most attempts, season

709—Minnesota, 1981.

Fewest attempts, season

102—Cincinnati, 1933.

Most attempts, game

70—New England vs. Minnesota, November 13, 1994 (overtime).
68—Houston at Buffalo, November 1, 1964.

Most attempts by both teams, game

112—New England 70, Minnesota 42, November 13, 1994 (overtime).

104—Miami 55, New York Jets 49, October 18, 1987 (overtime).
102—San Francisco 57, Atlanta 45, October 6, 1985.

Fewest attempts, game

0—Green Bay vs. Portsmouth, October 8, 1933.
Detroit at Cleveland, September 10, 1937.
Pittsburgh vs. Brooklyn, November 16, 1941.
Pittsburgh vs. Los Angeles, November 13, 1949.
Cleveland vs. Philadelphia, December 3, 1950.

Fewest attempts by both teams, game

4—Detroit 3, Chicago Cardinals 1, November 3, 1935.
Cleveland 4, Detroit 0, September 10, 1937.

COMPLETIONS

Most completions, season

411—Houston, 1991.

Fewest completions, season

25—Cincinnati, 1933.

Most completions, game

45—New England vs. Minnesota, November 13, 1994 (overtime).
42—New York Jets vs. San Francisco, September 21, 1980.

Most completions by both teams, game

71—New England 45, Minnesota 26, November 13, 1994 (overtime).
68—San Francisco 37, Atlanta 31, October 6, 1985.

Fewest completions, game

0—Held by many teams. Last team: Buffalo vs. New York Jets, September 29, 1974.

Fewest completions by both teams, game

1—Philadelphia 1, Chicago Cardinals 0, November 8, 1936.
Cleveland 1, Detroit 0, September 10, 1937.
Detroit 1, Chicago Cardinals 0, September 15, 1940.
Pittsburgh 1, Brooklyn 0, November 29, 1942.

YARDS

Most yards, season

5,018—Miami, 1984.

Most years leading league in yards

10—San Diego, 1965, 1968, 1971, 1978 through 1983, 1985.

Most consecutive years leading league in yards

6—San Diego, 1978 through 1983.

Fewest yards, season

302—Chicago Cardinals, 1934.

Most yards, game

554—Los Angeles at New York Yanks, September 28, 1951.

Most yards by both teams, game

884—New York Jets 449, Miami 435, September 21, 1986 (overtime).
883—San Diego 486, Cincinnati 397, December 20, 1982.

Fewest yards, game

-53—Denver at Oakland, September 10, 1967.

Fewest yards by both teams, game

-11—Green Bay -10, Dallas -1, October 24, 1965.

TOUCHDOWNS

Most touchdowns, season

49—Miami, 1984.

Fewest touchdowns, season

0—Cincinnati, 1933.
Pittsburgh, 1945.

Most touchdowns, game

7—Chicago Bears at New York Giants, November 14, 1943.
Philadelphia at Washington, October 17, 1954.
Houston vs. New York Titans, November 19, 1961.
Houston vs. New York Titans, October 14, 1962.
New York Giants vs. Washington, October 28, 1962.

Minnesota vs. Baltimore, September 28, 1969.
San Diego at Oakland, November 22, 1981.

Most touchdowns by both teams, game

12—New Orleans 6, St. Louis 6, November 2, 1969.

INTERCEPTIONS

Most interceptions, season

48—Houston, 1962.

Fewest interceptions, season

5—Cleveland, 1960.
Green Bay, 1966.
Kansas City, 1990.
New York Giants, 1990.

Most interceptions, game

9—Detroit vs. Green Bay, October 24, 1943.
Pittsburgh vs. Philadelphia, December 12, 1965.

Most interceptions by both teams, game

13—Denver 8, Houston 5, December 2, 1962.

SACKS

Most sacks allowed, season

104—Philadelphia, 1986.

Most years leading league in fewest sacks allowed

10—Miami, 1973 and 1982 through 1990.

Most consecutive years leading league in fewest sacks allowed

9—Miami, 1982 through 1990.

Fewest sacks allowed, season

7—Miami, 1988.

Most sacks allowed, game

12—Pittsburgh at Dallas, November 20, 1966.
Baltimore vs. St. Louis, October 26, 1980.
Detroit vs. Chicago, December 16, 1984.
Houston vs. Dallas, September 29, 1985.

Most sacks allowed by both teams, game

18—Green Bay 10, San Diego 8, September 24, 1978.

SCORING

POINTS

Most points, season

541—Washington, 1983.

Most points, game

72—Washington vs. New York Giants, November 27, 1966.

Most points by both teams, game

113—Washington 72, New York Giants 41, November 27, 1966.

Fewest points by both teams, game

0—Occurred many times. Last time: New York Giants 0, Detroit 0, November 7, 1943.

Most points in a shutout victory

64—Philadelphia vs. Cincinnati, November 6, 1934.

Fewest points in a shutout victory

2—Green Bay at Chicago Bears, October 16, 1932.
Chicago Bears at Green Bay, September 18, 1938.

Most points in first half of game

49—Green Bay vs. Tampa Bay, October 2, 1983.

Most points in first half of game by both teams

70—Houston 35, Oakland 35, December 22, 1963.

Most points in second half of game

49—Chicago Bears at Philadelphia, November 30, 1941.

Most points in second half of game by both teams

65—Washington 38, New York Giants 27, November 27, 1966.

Most points in one quarter

41—Green Bay vs. Detroit, October 7, 1945, second quarter.
Los Angeles vs. Detroit, October 29, 1950, third quarter.

Most points in one quarter by both teams

49—Oakland 28, Houston 21, December 22, 1963, second quarter.

Most points in first quarter

35—Green Bay vs. Cleveland, November 12, 1967.

Most points in first quarter by both teams

42—Green Bay 35, Cleveland 7, November 12, 1967.

Most points in second quarter

41—Green Bay vs. Detroit, October 7, 1945.

Most points in second quarter by both teams

49—Oakland 28, Houston 21, December 22, 1963.

Most points in third quarter

41—Los Angeles vs. Detroit, October 29, 1950.

Most points in third quarter by both teams

48—Los Angeles 41, Detroit 7, October 29, 1950.

Most points in fourth quarter

31—Oakland vs. Denver, December 17, 1960.
Oakland vs. San Diego, December 8, 1963.
Atlanta at Green Bay, September 13, 1981.

Most points in fourth quarter by both teams

42—Chicago Cardinals 28, Philadelphia 14, December 7, 1947.
Green Bay 28, Chicago Bears 14, November 6, 1955.
New York Jets 28, Boston 14, October 27, 1968.
Pittsburgh 21, Cleveland 21, October 18, 1969.

Most consecutive games without being shut out

274—Cleveland, October 7, 1950 through October 17, 1971.
San Francisco, October 16, 1977 through December 26, 1994.

TIMES SHUT OUT

Most times shut out, season

8—Frankford, 1927 (lost six, tied two).
Brooklyn, 1931 (lost eight).

Most consecutive times shut out

8—Rochester, 1922 through 1924 (lost eight).

TOUCHDOWNS

Most touchdowns, season

70—Miami, 1984.

Most years leading league in touchdowns

13—Chicago Bears, 1932, 1934, 1935, 1939, 1941, 1942, 1943, 1944, 1946, 1947, 1948, 1956, 1965.

Most consecutive years leading league in touchdowns

4—Chicago Bears, 1941 through 1944.
Los Angeles, 1949 through 1952.

Most touchdowns, game

10—Philadelphia vs. Cincinnati, November 6, 1934.
Los Angeles vs. Baltimore, October 22, 1950.
Washington vs. New York Giants, November 27, 1966.

Most touchdowns by both teams, game

16—Washington 10, New York Giants 6, November 27, 1966.

Most consecutive games with one or more touchdowns

166—Cleveland, 1957 through 1969.

EXTRA POINTS

Most extra points, season

66—Miami, 1984.

Fewest extra points, season

2—Chicago Cardinals, 1933.

Most extra points, game

10—Los Angeles vs. Baltimore, October 22, 1950.

Most extra points by both teams, game

14—Chicago Cardinals 9, New York Giants 5, October 17, 1948.
Houston 7, Oakland 7, December 22, 1963.
Washington 9, New York Giants 5, November 27, 1966.

— 319 —

FIELD GOALS

Most field goals attempted, season

49—Los Angeles, 1966.
Washington, 1971.

Most field goals made, season

35—New York Giants, 1983.
Los Angeles Raiders, 1993.

Most field goals attempted, game

9—St. Louis at Pittsburgh, September 24, 1967.

Most field goals made, game

7—St. Louis at Pittsburgh, September 24, 1967.
Minnesota vs. Los Angeles Rams, November 5, 1989 (overtime).

Most field goals attempted by both teams, game

11—St. Louis 6, Pittsburgh 5, November 13, 1966.
Washington 6, Chicago 5, November 14, 1971.
Green Bay 6, Detroit 5, September 29, 1974.
Washington 6, New York Giants 5, November 14, 1976.

Most field goals made by both teams, game

8—Cleveland 4, St. Louis 4, September 20, 1964.
Chicago 5, Philadelphia 3, October 20, 1968.
Washington 5, Chicago 3, November 14, 1971.
Kansas City 5, Buffalo 3, December 19, 1971.
Detroit 4, Green Bay 4, September 29, 1974.
Cleveland 5, Denver 3, October 19, 1975.
New England 4, San Diego 4, November 9, 1975.
San Francisco 6, New Orleans 2, October 16, 1983.
Seattle 5, Los Angeles Raiders 3, December 18, 1988.

Most consecutive games with one or more field goals made

31—Minnesota, November 17, 1968 through December 5, 1970.

SAFETIES

Most safeties, season

4—Cleveland, 1927.
Detroit, 1962.
Seattle, 1993.

Most safeties, game

3—Los Angeles Rams vs. New York Giants, September 30, 1984.

Most safeties by both teams, game

3—Los Angeles Rams 3, New York Giants 0, September 30, 1984.

FIRST DOWNS

Most first downs, season

387—Miami, 1984.

Most first downs, game

39—New York Jets vs. Miami, November 27, 1988.
Washington at Detroit, November 4, 1990 (overtime).

Most first downs by both teams, game

62—San Diego 32, Seattle 30, September 15, 1985.

PUNTING

Most punts, season

114—Chicago, 1981.

Fewest punts, season

23—San Diego, 1982.

Most punts, game

17—Chicago Bears vs. Green Bay, October 22, 1933.
Cincinnati vs. Pittsburgh, October 22, 1933.

Most punts by both teams, game

31—Chicago Bears 17, Green Bay 14, October 22, 1933.
Cincinnati 17, Pittsburgh 14, October 22, 1933.

Fewest punts, game

0—Held by many teams.

Fewest punts by both teams, game

0—Buffalo 0, San Francisco 0, September 13, 1992.

FUMBLES

Most fumbles, season

56—Chicago Bears, 1938.
San Francisco, 1978.

Fewest fumbles, season

8—Cleveland, 1959.

Most fumbles, game

10—Philadelphia/Pittsburgh vs. New York, October 9, 1943.
Detroit at Minnesota, November 12, 1967.
Kansas City vs. Houston, October 12, 1969.
San Francisco at Detroit, December 17, 1978.

Most fumbles by both teams, game

14—Washington 8, Pittsburgh 6, November 14, 1937.
Chicago Bears 7, Cleveland 7, November 24, 1940.
St. Louis 8, New York Giants 6, September 17, 1961.
Kansas City 10, Houston 4, October 12, 1969.

LOST

Most fumbles lost, season

36—Chicago Cardinals, 1959.

Fewest fumbles lost, season

3—Philadelphia, 1938.
Minnesota, 1980.

Most fumbles lost, game

8—St. Louis at Washington, October 25, 1976.
Cleveland at Pittsburgh, December 23, 1990.

RECOVERED

Most fumbles recovered (own and opponents'), season

58—Minnesota, 1963.

Fewest fumbles recovered (own and opponents'), season

9—San Francisco, 1982.

Most fumbles recovered (own and opponents'), game

10—Denver vs. Buffalo, December 13, 1964.
Pittsburgh vs. Houston, December 9, 1973.
Washington vs. St. Louis, October 25, 1976.

Most fumbles recovered (own), season

37—Chicago Bears, 1938.

Fewest fumbles recovered (own), season

2—Washington, 1958.

TOUCHDOWNS

Most touchdowns on fumbles recovered (own and opponents'), season

5—Chicago Bears, 1942.
Los Angeles, 1952.
San Francisco, 1965.
Oakland, 1978.

Most touchdowns on own fumbles recovered, season

2—Held by many teams. Last team: Green Bay, 1989.

Most touchdowns on fumbles recovered (own and opponents'), game

2—Held by many teams.

Most touchdowns on fumbles recovered (own and opponents'), game

3—Detroit 2, Minnesota 1, December 9, 1962.
Green Bay 2, Dallas 1, November 29, 1964.
Oakland 2, Buffalo 1, December 24, 1967.

Most touchdowns on own fumbles recovered, game

1—Held by many teams.

Most touchdowns on opponents' fumbles recovered by both teams, game

3—Green Bay 2, Dallas 1, November 29, 1964.
Oakland 2, Buffalo 1, December 24, 1967.

TURNOVERS

Most turnovers, season

63—San Francisco, 1978.

Fewest turnovers, season

12—Kansas City, 1982.

Most turnovers, game

12—Detroit vs. Chicago Bears, November 22, 1942.
   Chicago Cardinals vs. Philadelphia, September 24, 1950.
   Pittsburgh vs. Philadelphia, December 12, 1965.

Most turnovers by both teams, game

17—Detroit 12, Chicago Bears 5, November 22, 1942.
   Boston 9, Philadelphia 8, December 8, 1946.

PUNT RETURNS

Most punt returns, season

71—Pittsburgh, 1976.
   Tampa Bay, 1979.
   Los Angeles Raiders, 1985.

Fewest punt returns, season

12—Baltimore, 1981.
   San Diego, 1982.

Most punt returns, game

12—Philadelphia at Cleveland, December 3, 1950.

Most punt returns by both teams, game

17—Philadelphia 12, Cleveland 5, December 3, 1950.

YARDS

Most yards, season

785—Los Angeles Raiders, 1985.

Fewest yards, season

27—St. Louis, 1965.

Most yards, game

231—Detroit vs. San Francisco, October 6, 1963.

Most yards by both teams, game

282—Los Angeles 219, Atlanta 63, October 11, 1981.

TOUCHDOWNS

Most touchdowns, season

5—Chicago Cardinals, 1959.

Most touchdowns, game

2—Held by many teams. Last team: Cleveland vs. Pittsburgh,
   October 24, 1993.

Most touchdowns by both teams, game

2—Occurred many times. Last time: Cleveland 2, Pittsburgh
   0, October 24, 1993.

KICKOFF RETURNS

Most kickoff returns, season

88—New Orleans, 1980.

Fewest kickoff returns, season

17—New York Giants, 1944.

Most kickoff returns, game

12—New York Giants at Washington, November 27, 1966.

Most kickoff returns by both teams, game

19—New York Giants 12, Washington 7, November 27, 1966.

YARDS

Most yards, season

1,973—New Orleans, 1980.

Fewest yards, season

282—New York Giants, 1940.

Most yards, game

362—Detroit at Los Angeles, October 29, 1950.

Most yards by both teams, game

560—Detroit 362, Los Angeles 198, October 29, 1950.

TOUCHDOWNS

Most touchdowns, season

4—Green Bay, 1967.
   Chicago, 1970.
   Detroit, 1994.

Most touchdowns, game

2—Chicago Bears at Green Bay, September 22, 1940.
   Chicago Bears vs. Green Bay, November 9, 1952.
   Philadelphia vs. Dallas, November 6, 1966.
   Green Bay vs. Cleveland, November 12, 1967.
   Los Angeles Rams vs. Green Bay, November 24, 1985.
   New Orleans vs. Los Angeles Rams, October 23, 1994.

Most touchdowns by both teams, game (each team scoring)

2—Occurred many times. Last time: Houston 1, Pittsburgh 1,
   December 4, 1988.

PENALTIES

Most penalties, season

156—L.A. Raiders, 1994.

Fewest penalties, season

19—Detroit, 1937.

Most penalties, game

22—Brooklyn at Green Bay, September 17, 1944.
   Chicago Bears at Philadelphia, November 26, 1944.

Most penalties by both teams, game

37—Cleveland 21, Chicago Bears 16, November 25, 1951.

Fewest penalties, game

0—Held by many teams. Last team: San Francisco vs. Philadelphia, November 29, 1992.

Fewest penalties by both teams, game

0—Brooklyn 0, Pittsburgh 0, October 28, 1934.
   Brooklyn 0, Boston 0, September 28, 1936.
   Cleveland 0, Chicago Bears 0, October 9, 1938.
   Pittsburgh 0, Philadelphia 0, November 10, 1940.

YARDS PENALIZED

Most yards penalized, season

1,274—Oakland, 1969.

Fewest yards penalized, season

139—Detroit, 1937.

Most yards penalized, game

209—Cleveland vs. Chicago Bears, November 25, 1951.

Most yards penalized by both teams, game

374—Cleveland 209, Chicago Bears 165, November 25, 1951.

Fewest yards penalized, game

0—Held by many teams. Last team: San Francisco vs. Philadelphia, November 29, 1992.

Fewest yards penalized by both teams, game

0—Brooklyn 0, Pittsburgh 0, October 28, 1934.
   Brooklyn 0, Boston 0, September 28, 1936.
   Cleveland 0, Chicago Bears 0, October 9, 1938.
   Pittsburgh 0, Philadelphia 0, November 10, 1940.

TEAM DEFENSE

RUSHING

YARDS ALLOWED

Most yards allowed, season

3,228—Buffalo, 1978.

Fewest yards allowed, season

519—Chicago Bears, 1942.

TOUCHDOWNS ALLOWED

Most touchdowns allowed, season

36—Oakland, 1961.

Fewest touchdowns allowed, season

2—Detroit, 1934.
   Dallas, 1968.
   Minnesota, 1971.

PASSING

YARDS ALLOWED

Most yards allowed, season

4,389—New York Jets, 1986.

Fewest yards allowed, season

545—Philadelphia, 1934.

TOUCHDOWNS ALLOWED

Most touchdowns allowed, season

40—Denver, 1963.

Fewest touchdowns allowed, season

1—Portsmouth, 1932.
   Philadelphia, 1934.

YARDS ALLOWED (RUSHING AND PASSING)

Most yards allowed rushing and passing, season

6,793—Baltimore, 1981.

Fewest yards allowed rushing and passing, season

1,539—Chicago Cardinals, 1934.

SCORING

POINTS ALLOWED

Most points allowed, season

533—Baltimore, 1981.

Fewest points allowed, season (since 1932)

44—Chicago Bears, 1932.

SHUTOUTS

Most shutouts, season

10—Pottsville, 1926 (won nine, tied one).
   New York Giants, 1927 (won nine, tied one).

Most consecutive shutouts

13—Akron, 1920 through 1921 (won 10, tied three).

TOUCHDOWNS ALLOWED

Most touchdowns allowed, season

68—Baltimore, 1981.

Fewest touchdowns allowed, season (since 1932)

6—Chicago Bears, 1932.
   Brooklyn, 1933.

FIRST DOWNS ALLOWED

Most first downs allowed, season

406—Baltimore, 1981.

Fewest first downs allowed, season

77—Detroit, 1935.

Most first downs allowed by rushing, season

179—Detroit, 1985.

Fewest first downs allowed by rushing, season

35—Chicago Bears, 1942.

Most first downs allowed by passing, season

218—San Diego, 1985.

Fewest first downs allowed by passing, season

33—Chicago Bears, 1943.

Most first downs allowed by penalties, season

48—Houston, 1985.

Fewest first downs allowed by penalties, season

1—Boston, 1944.

INTERCEPTIONS

Most interceptions, season

49—San Diego, 1961.

Fewest interceptions, season

3—Houston, 1982.

Most interceptions, game

9—Green Bay at Detroit, October 24, 1943.
   Philadelphia at Pittsburgh, December 12, 1965.

Most yards returning interceptions, season

929—San Diego, 1961.

Fewest yards returning interceptions, season

5—Los Angeles, 1959.

Most yards returning interceptions, game

325—Seattle vs. Kansas City, November 4, 1984.

Most touchdowns returning interceptions, season

9—San Diego, 1961.

Most touchdowns returning interceptions, game

4—Seattle vs. Kansas City, November 4, 1984.

Most touchdowns returning interceptions by both teams, game

4—Philadelphia 3, Pittsburgh 1, December 12, 1965.
   Seattle 4, Kansas City 0, November 4, 1984.

FUMBLES

Most opponents' fumbles forced, season

50—Minnesota, 1963.
   San Francisco, 1978.

Fewest opponents' fumbles forced, season

11—Cleveland, 1956.
   Baltimore, 1982.

RECOVERED

Most opponents' fumbles recovered, season

31—Minnesota, 1963.

Fewest opponents' fumbles recovered, season

3—Los Angeles, 1974.

Most opponents' fumbles recovered, game

8—Washington vs. St. Louis, October 25, 1976.
   Pittsburgh vs. Cleveland, December 23, 1990.

TOUCHDOWNS

Most touchdowns on opponents' fumbles recovered, season

4—Held by many teams. Last team: Atlanta, 1991.

Most touchdowns on opponents' fumbles recovered, game

2—Held by many teams. Last team: Cincinnati at Seattle,
   September 6, 1992.

TURNOVERS

Most opponents' turnovers, season

66—San Diego, 1961.

Fewest opponents' turnovers, season

11—Baltimore, 1982.

Most opponents' turnovers, game

12—Chicago Bears at Detroit, November 22, 1942.
   Philadelphia at Chicago Cardinals, September 24, 1950.
   Philadelphia at Pittsburgh, December 12, 1965.

SACKS

Most sacks, season
72—Chicago, 1984.

Fewest sacks, season
11—Baltimore, 1982.

Most sacks, game
12—Dallas at Pittsburgh, November 20, 1966.
   St. Louis at Baltimore, October 26, 1980.
   Chicago at Detroit, December 16, 1984.
   Dallas at Houston, September 29, 1985.

PUNTS RETURNED

Most punts returned by opponents, season
71—Tampa Bay, 1976.
   Tampa Bay, 1977.

Fewest punts returned by opponents, season
7—Washington, 1962.
   San Diego, 1982.

Most yards allowed on punts returned by opponents, season
932—Green Bay, 1949.

Fewest yards allowed on punts returned by opponents, season
22—Green Bay, 1967.

Most touchdowns allowed on punts returned by opponents, season
4—New York, 1959.
   Atlanta, 1992.

KICKOFFS RETURNED

Most kickoffs returned by opponents, season
91—Washington, 1983.

Fewest kickoffs returned by opponents, season
10—Brooklyn, 1943.

Most yards allowed on kickoffs returned by opponents, season
2,045—Kansas City, 1966.

Fewest yards allowed on kickoffs returned by opponents, season
225—Brooklyn, 1943.

Most touchdowns allowed on kickoffs returned by opponents, season
3—Minnesota, 1963.
   Dallas, 1966.
   Minnesota, 1970.
   Detroit, 1980.
   Pittsburgh, 1986.

STATISTICAL LEADERS

CAREER MILESTONES

TOP 20 RUSHERS

Player	League	Years	Att.	Yds.	Avg.	Long	TD
Walter Payton	NFL	13	3838	16726	4.4	76	110
Eric Dickerson	NFL	11	2996	13259	4.4	85	90
Tony Dorsett	NFL	12	2936	12739	4.3	99	77
Jim Brown	NFL	9	2359	12312	5.2	80	106
Franco Harris	NFL	13	2949	12120	4.1	75	91
John Riggins	NFL	14	2916	11352	3.9	66	104
O.J. Simpson	AFL-NFL	11	2404	11236	4.7	94	61
Ottis Anderson	NFL	14	2562	10273	4.0	76	81
Marcus Allen*	NFL	13	2485	10018	4.0	61	98
Joe Perry	AAFC-NFL	16	1929	9723	5.0	78	71
Earl Campbell	NFL	8	2187	9407	4.3	81	74
Thurman Thomas*	NFL	7	2018	8724	4.3	80	48
Barry Sanders*	NFL	6	1763	8672	4.9	85	62
Jim Taylor	NFL	10	1941	8597	4.4	84	83
Roger Craig	NFL	11	1991	8189	4.1	71	56
Gerald Riggs	NFL	10	1989	8188	4.1	58	69
Larry Csonka	AFL-NFL	11	1891	8081	4.3	54	64
Freeman McNeil	NFL	12	1798	8074	4.5	69	38
Herschel Walker*	NFL	9	1907	7996	4.2	91	60
James Brooks	NFL	12	1685	7962	4.7	65	49

*Active through 1994 season.

TOP 20 PASSERS

Player	League	Years	Att.	Comp.	Yds.	TD	Int.	Rating Pts.
Steve Young*	NFL	10	2429	1546	19869	140	68	96.8
Joe Montana*	NFL	15	5391	3409	40551	273	139	92.3
Dan Marino*	NFL	12	6049	3604	45173	328	185	88.2
Otto Graham	AAFC-NFL	10	2626	1464	23584	174	135	86.6
Jim Kelly*	NFL	9	3942	2397	29527	201	143	85.8
Roger Staubach	NFL	11	2958	1685	22700	153	109	83.4
Dave Krieg*	NFL	15	4390	2562	32114	231	166	83.0
Neil Lomax	NFL	8	3153	1817	22771	136	90	82.7
Sonny Jurgensen	NFL	18	4262	2433	32224	255	189	82.625
Len Dawson	NFL-AFL	19	3741	2136	28711	239	183	82.555
Brett Favre*	NFL	4	1580	983	10412	70	53	82.2
Ken Anderson	NFL	16	4475	2654	32838	197	160	81.9
Bernie Kosar*	NFL	10	3225	1896	22394	120	82	81.817
Jeff Hostetler*	NFL	9	1505	864	10985	54	38	81.776
Danny White	NFL	13	2950	1761	21959	155	132	81.7
Boomer Esiason*	NFL	11	4291	2440	31874	207	153	81.643
Troy Aikman*	NFL	6	2281	1424	16303	82	78	81.623
Bart Starr	NFL	16	3149	1808	24718	152	138	80.5
Ken O'Brien	NFL	11	3602	2110	25094	128	98	80.436
Fran Tarkenton	NFL	18	6467	3686	47003	342	266	80.354

*Active through 1994 season.

TOP 20 RECEIVERS

Player	League	Years	No.	Yds.	Avg.	Long	TD
Art Monk*	NFL	15	934	12607	13.5	79	68
Jerry Rice*	NFL	10	820	13275	16.2	96	131
Steve Largent	NFL	14	819	13089	16.0	74	100
James Lofton	NFL	16	764	14004	18.3	80	75
Charlie Joiner	AFL-NFL	18	750	12146	16.2	87	65
Andre Reed*	NFL	10	676	9536	14.1	83	66
Henry Ellard*	NFL	12	667	11158	16.7	81	54
Gary Clark*	NFL	10	662	10331	15.6	84	63
Ozzie Newsome	NFL	13	662	7980	12.1	74	47
Charley Taylor	NFL	13	649	9110	14.0	88	79
Drew Hill	NFL	15	634	9831	15.5	81	60
Don Maynard	NFL-AFL	15	633	11834	18.7	87	88
Raymond Berry	NFL	13	631	9275	14.7	70	68
Sterling Sharpe*	NFL	7	595	8134	13.7	79	65
Harold Carmichael	NFL	14	590	8985	15.2	85	79
Fred Biletnikoff	AFL-NFL	14	589	8974	15.2	82	76

Player	League	Years	No.	Yds.	Avg.	Long	TD
Mark Clayton	NFL	11	582	8974	15.4	78	84
Harold Jackson	NFL	16	579	10372	17.9	79	76
Lionel Taylor	NFL	10	567	7195	12.7	80	45
Roger Craig	NFL	11	566	4911	8.7	73	17

*Active through 1994 season.

TOP 20 SCORERS

Player	League	Years	TD	XP Made	FG Made	Total
George Blanda	NFL-AFL	26	9	943	335	2002
Jan Stenerud	AFL-NFL	19	0	580	373	1699
Lou Groza	AAFC-NFL	21	1	810	264	1608
Nick Lowery*	NFL	16	0	512	349	1559
Pat Leahy	NFL	18	0	558	304	1470
Jim Turner	AFL-NFL	16	1	521	304	1439
Mark Moseley	NFL	16	0	482	300	1382
Jim Bakken	NFL	17	0	534	282	1380
Fred Cox	NFL	15	0	519	282	1365
Eddie Murray*	NFL	15	0	465	298	1359
Gary Anderson*	NFL	13	0	416	309	1343
Matt Bahr*	NFL	16	0	495	277	1326
Morten Andersen*	NFL	13	0	412	302	1318
Jim Breech	NFL	14	0	517	243	1246
Chris Bahr	NFL	14	0	490	241	1213
Norm Johnson*	NFL	13	0	476	243	1205
Gino Cappelletti	AFL-NFL	11	42	350	†176	†1130
Ray Wersching	NFL	15	0	456	222	1122
Don Cockroft	NFL	13	0	432	216	1080
Garo Yepremian	NFL-AFL	14	0	444	210	1074

*Active through 1994 season.
†Includes four two-point conversions.

YEAR BY YEAR

AFC

RUSHING
(Based on most net yards)

	Net Yds.	Att.	TD
1960—Abner Haynes, Dallas	875	156	9
1961—Billy Cannon, Houston	948	200	6
1962—Cookie Gilchrist, Buffalo	1096	214	13
1963—Clem Daniels, Oakland	1099	215	3
1964—Cookie Gilchrist, Buffalo	981	230	6
1965—Paul Lowe, San Diego	1121	222	7
1966—Jim Nance, Boston	1458	299	11
1967—Jim Nance, Boston	1216	269	7
1968—Paul Robinson, Cincinnati	1023	238	8
1969—Dick Post, San Diego	873	182	6
1970—Floyd Little, Denver	901	209	3
1971—Floyd Little, Denver	1133	284	6
1972—O.J. Simpson, Buffalo	1251	292	6
1973—O.J. Simpson, Buffalo	2003	332	12
1974—Otis Armstrong, Denver	1407	263	9
1975—O.J. Simpson, Buffalo	1817	329	16
1976—O.J. Simpson, Buffalo	1503	290	8
1977—Mark van Eeghen, Oakland	1273	324	7
1978—Earl Campbell, Houston	1450	302	13
1979—Earl Campbell, Houston	1697	368	19
1980—Earl Campbell, Houston	1934	373	13
1981—Earl Campbell, Houston	1376	361	10
1982—Freeman McNeil, N.Y. Jets	786	151	6
1983—Curt Warner, Seattle	1449	335	13
1984—Earnest Jackson, San Diego	1179	296	8
1985—Marcus Allen, L.A. Raiders	1759	380	11
1986—Curt Warner, Seattle	1481	319	13
1987—Eric Dickerson, Indianapolis	1288	283	6
1988—Eric Dickerson, Indianapolis	1659	388	14
1989—Christian Okoye, Kansas City	1480	370	12
1990—Thurman Thomas, Buffalo	1297	271	11
1991—Thurman Thomas, Buffalo	1407	288	7
1992—Barry Foster, Pittsburgh	1690	390	11
1993—Thurman Thomas, Buffalo	1315	355	6
1994—Chris Warren, Seattle	1545	333	9

PASSING
(Based on highest passer rating among qualifiers*)

	Att.	Com.	Yds.	TD	Int.	Rat.
1960—Jack Kemp, Chargers	406	211	3018	20	25	67.1
1961—George Blanda, Hou..	362	187	3330	36	22	91.3
1962—Len Dawson, Dal. ...	310	189	2759	29	17	98.3
1963—Tobin Rote, S.D.	286	170	2510	20	17	86.7
1964—Cookie Gilchrist, Buffalo	354	199	2879	30	18	89.9
1965—John Hadl, S.D.	348	174	2798	20	21	71.3
1966—Len Dawson, K.C.	284	159	2527	26	10	101.7
1967—Daryle Lamonica, Oak.	425	220	3228	30	20	80.8
1968—Len Dawson, K.C.	224	131	2109	17	9	98.6
1969—Greg Cook, Cin.	197	106	1854	15	11	88.3
1970—Daryle Lamonica, Oak.	356	179	2516	22	15	76.5
1971—Bob Griese, Mia.	263	145	2089	19	9	90.9
1972—Earl Morrall, Mia.	150	83	1360	11	7	91.0
1973—Ken Stabler, Oak.	260	163	1997	14	10	88.5
1974—Ken Anderson, Cin.	328	213	2667	18	10	95.9
1975—Ken Anderson, Cin.	377	228	3169	21	11	94.1
1976—Ken Stabler, Oak.	291	194	2737	27	17	103.7
1977—Bob Griese, Mia.	307	180	2252	22	13	88.0
1978—Terry Bradshaw, Pit.	368	207	2915	28	20	84.8
1979—Dan Fouts, S.D.	530	332	4082	24	24	82.6
1980—Brian Sipe, Cle.	554	337	4132	30	14	91.4
1981—Ken Anderson, Cin.	479	300	3754	29	10	98.5
1982—Ken Anderson, Cin.	309	218	2495	12	9	95.5
1983—Dan Marino, Mia.	296	173	2210	20	6	96.0
1984—Dan Marino, Mia.	564	362	5084	48	17	108.9
1985—Ken O'Brien, NYJ	488	297	3888	25	8	96.2
1986—Dan Marino, Mia.	623	378	4746	44	23	92.5
1987—Bernie Kosar, Cle.	389	241	3033	22	9	95.4

	Att.	Com.	Yds.	TD	Int.	Rat.
1988—Boomer Esiason, Cin.	388	223	3572	28	14	97.4
1989—Boomer Esiason, Cin.	455	258	3525	28	11	92.1
1990—Jim Kelly, Buf.	346	219	2829	24	9	101.2
1991—Jim Kelly, Buf.	474	304	3844	33	17	97.6
1992—Warren Moon, Hou.	346	224	2521	18	12	89.3
1993—John Elway, Den.	551	348	4030	25	10	92.8
1994—Dan Marino, Mia.	615	385	4453	30	17	89.2

*This chart includes passer rating points for all leaders, although the same rating system was not used for determining leading quarterbacks prior to 1973. The old system was less equitable, yet similar to the new in that the rating was based on percentage of completions, touchdown passes, percentage of interceptions and average gain in yards.

RECEIVING
(Based on most receptions)

	No.	Yds.	TD
1960—Lionel Taylor, Denver	92	1235	12
1961—Lionel Taylor, Denver	100	1176	4
1962—Lionel Taylor, Denver	77	908	4
1963—Lionel Taylor, Denver	78	1101	10
1964—Charley Hennigan, Houston	101	1546	8
1965—Lionel Taylor, Denver	85	1131	6
1966—Lance Alworth, San Diego	73	1383	13
1967—George Sauer, N.Y. Jets	75	1189	6
1968—Lance Alworth, San Diego	68	1312	10
1969—Lance Alworth, San Diego	64	1003	4
1970—Marlin Briscoe, Buffalo	57	1036	8
1971—Fred Biletnikoff, Oakland	61	929	9
1972—Fred Biletnikoff, Oakland	58	802	7
1973—Fred Willis, Houston	57	371	1
1974—Lydell Mitchell, Baltimore	72	544	2
1975—Reggie Rucker, Cleveland	60	770	3
Lydell Mitchell, Baltimore	60	544	4
1976—MacArthur Lane, Kansas City	66	686	1
1977—Lydell Mitchell, Baltimore	71	620	4
1978—Steve Largent, Seattle	71	1168	8
1979—Joe Washington, Baltimore	82	750	3
1980—Kellen Winslow, San Diego	89	1290	9
1981—Kellen Winslow, San Diego	88	1075	10
1982—Kellen Winslow, San Diego	54	721	6
1983—Todd Christensen, L.A. Raiders	92	1247	12
1984—Ozzie Newsome, Cleveland	89	1001	5
1985—Lionel James, San Diego	86	1027	6
1986—Todd Christensen, L.A. Raiders	95	1153	8
1987—Al Toon, N.Y. Jets	68	976	5
1988—Al Toon, N.Y. Jets	93	1067	5
1989—Andre Reed, Buffalo	88	1312	9
1990—Haywood Jeffires, Houston	74	1048	8
Drew Hill, Houston	74	1019	5
1991—Haywood Jeffires, Houston	100	1181	7
1992—Haywood Jeffires, Houston	90	913	9
1993—Reggie Langhorne, Indianapolis	85	1038	3
1994—Ben Coates, New England	96	1174	7

SCORING
(Based on most total points)

	TD	PAT	FG	Tot.
1960—Gene Mingo, Denver	6	33	18	123
1961—Gino Cappelletti, Boston	8	48	17	147
1962—Gene Mingo, Denver	4	32	27	137
1963—Gino Cappelletti, Boston	2	35	22	113
1964—Gino Cappelletti, Boston	7	36	25	155
1965—Gino Cappelletti, Boston	9	27	17	132
1966—Gino Cappelletti, Boston	6	35	16	119
1967—George Blanda, Oakland	0	56	20	116
1968—Jim Turner, N.Y. Jets	0	43	34	145
1969—Jim Turner, N.Y. Jets	0	33	32	129
1970—Jan Stenerud, Kansas City	0	26	30	116
1971—Garo Yepremian, Miami	0	33	28	117
1972—Bobby Howfield, N.Y. Jets	0	40	27	121
1973—Roy Gerela, Pittsburgh	0	36	29	123

	TD	PAT	FG	Tot.
1974—Roy Gerela, Pittsburgh	0	33	20	93
1975—O.J. Simpson, Buffalo	23	0	0	138
1976—Toni Linhart, Baltimore	0	49	20	109
1977—Errol Mann, Oakland	0	39	20	99
1978—Pat Leahy, N.Y. Jets	0	41	22	107
1979—John Smith, New England	0	46	23	115
1980—John Smith, New England	0	51	26	129
1981—Jim Breech, Cincinnati	0	49	22	115
Nick Lowery, Kansas City	0	37	26	115
1982—Marcus Allen, L.A. Raiders	14	0	0	84
1983—Gary Anderson, Pittsburgh	0	38	27	119
1984—Gary Anderson, Pittsburgh	0	45	24	117
1985—Gary Anderson, Pittsburgh	0	40	33	139
1986—Tony Franklin, New England	0	44	32	140
1987—Jim Breech, Cincinnati	0	25	24	97
1988—Scott Norwood, Buffalo	0	33	32	129
1989—David Treadwell, Denver	0	39	27	120
1990—Nick Lowery, Kansas City	0	37	34	139
1991—Pete Stoyanovich, Miami	0	28	31	121
1992—Pete Stoyanovich, Miami	0	34	30	124
1993—Jeff Jaeger, L.A. Raiders	0	27	35	132
1994—John Carney, San Diego	0	33	34	135

FIELD GOALS

	No.
1960—Gene Mingo, Denver	18
1961—Gino Cappelletti, Boston	17
1962—Gene Mingo, Denver	27
1963—Gino Cappelletti, Boston	22
1964—Gino Cappelletti, Boston	25
1965—Pete Gogolak, Buffalo	28
1966—Mike Mercer, Oakland-Kansas City	21
1967—Jan Stenerud, Kansas City	21
1968—Jim Turner, N.Y. Jets	34
1969—Jim Turner, N.Y. Jets	32
1970—Jan Stenerud, Kansas City	30
1971—Garo Yepremian, Miami	28
1972—Roy Gerela, Pittsburgh	28
1973—Roy Gerela, Pittsburgh	29
1974—Roy Gerela, Pittsburgh	20
1975—Jan Stenerud, Kansas City	22
1976—Jan Stenerud, Kansas City	21
1977—Errol Mann, Oakland	20
1978—Pat Leahy, N.Y. Jets	22
1979—John Smith, New England	23
1980—John Smith, New England	26
Fred Steinfort, Denver	26
1981—Nick Lowery, Kansas City	26
1982—Nick Lowery, Kansas City	19
1983—Raul Allegre, Baltimore	30
1984—Gary Anderson, Pittsburgh	24
Matt Bahr, Cleveland	24
1985—Gary Anderson, Pittsburgh	33
1986—Tony Franklin, New England	32
1987—Dean Biasucci, Indianapolis	24
Jim Breech, Cincinnati	24
1988—Scott Norwood, Buffalo	32
1989—David Treadwell, Denver	27
1990—Nick Lowery, Kansas City	34
1991—Pete Stoyanovich, Miami	31
1992—Pete Stoyanovich, Miami	30
1993—Jeff Jaeger, L.A. Raiders	35
1994—John Carney, San Diego	34

INTERCEPTIONS

	No.	Yds.
1960—Austin Gonsoulin, Denver	11	98
1961—Bill Atkins, Buffalo	10	158
1962—Lee Riley, N.Y. Jets	11	122
1963—Fred Glick, Houston	12	180
1964—Dainard Paulson, N.Y. Jets	12	157
1965—W.K. Hicks, Houston	9	156

		No.	Yds.
1966—	Johnny Robinson, Kansas City	10	136
	Bobby Hunt, Kansas City	10	113
1967—	Miller Farr, Houston	10	264
	Tom Janik, Buffalo	10	222
	Dick Westmoreland, Miami	10	127
1968—	Dave Grayson, Oakland	10	195
1969—	Emmitt Thomas, Kansas City	9	146
1970—	Johnny Robinson, Kansas City	10	155
1971—	Ken Houston, Houston	9	220
1972—	Mike Sensibaugh, Kansas City	8	65
1973—	Dick Anderson, Miami	8	136
	Mike Wagner, Pittsburgh	8	134
1974—	Emmitt Thomas, Kansas City	12	214
1975—	Mel Blount, Pittsburgh	11	121
1976—	Ken Riley, Cincinnati	9	141
1977—	Lyle Blackwood, Baltimore	10	163
1978—	Thom Darden, Cleveland	10	200
1979—	Mike Reinfeldt, Houston	12	205
1980—	Lester Hayes, Oakland	13	273
1981—	John Harris, Seattle	10	155
1982—	Ken Riley, Cincinnati	5	88
	Bobby Jackson, N.Y. Jets	5	84
	Dwayne Woodruff, Pittsburgh	5	53
	Donnie Shell, Pittsburgh	5	27
1983—	Ken Riley, Cincinnati	8	89
	Vann McElroy, Los Angeles	8	68
1984—	Kenny Easley, Seattle	10	126
1985—	Eugene Daniel, Indianapolis	8	53
	Albert Lewis, Kansas City	8	59
1986—	Deron Cherry, Kansas City	9	150
1987—	Mike Prior, Indianapolis	6	57
	Mark Kelso, Buffalo	6	25
	Keith Bostic, Houston	6	- 14
1988—	Erik McMillan, N.Y. Jets	8	168
1989—	Felix Wright, Cleveland	9	91
1990—	Richard Johnson, Houston	8	100
1991—	Ronnie Lott, L.A. Raiders	8	52
1992—	Henry Jones, Buffalo	8	263
1993—	Nate Odomes, Buffalo	9	65
	Eugene Robinson, Seattle	9	80
1994—	Eric Turner, Cleveland	9	199

PUNTING
(Based on highest average yardage per punt by qualifiers)

		No.	Avg.
1960—	Paul Maguire, L.A. Chargers	43	40.5
1961—	Bill Atkins, Buffalo	85	44.5
1962—	Jim Fraser, Denver	55	43.6
1963—	Jim Fraser, Denver	81	44.4
1964—	Jim Fraser, Denver	73	44.2
1965—	Jerrel Wilson, Kansas City	69	45.4
1966—	Bob Scarpitto, Denver	76	45.8
1967—	Bob Scarpitto, Denver	105	44.9
1968—	Jerrel Wilson, Kansas City	63	45.1
1969—	Dennis Partee, San Diego	71	44.6
1970—	Dave Lewis, Cincinnati	79	46.2
1971—	Dave Lewis, Cincinnati	72	44.8
1972—	Jerrel Wilson, Kansas City	66	44.8
1973—	Jerrel Wilson, Kansas City	80	45.5
1974—	Ray Guy, Oakland	74	42.2
1975—	Ray Guy, Oakland	68	43.8
1976—	Marv Bateman, Buffalo	86	42.8
1977—	Ray Guy, Oakland	59	43.4
1978—	Pat McInally, Cincinnati	91	43.1
1979—	Bob Grupp, Kansas City	89	43.6
1980—	Luke Prestridge, Denver	70	43.9
1981—	Pat McInally, Cincinnati	72	45.4
1982—	Luke Prestridge, Denver	45	45.0
1983—	Rohn Stark, Baltimore	91	45.3
1984—	Jim Arnold, Kansas City	98	44.9
1985—	Rohn Stark, Indianapolis	78	45.9
1986—	Rohn Stark, Indianapolis	76	45.2
1987—	Ralf Mojsiejenko, San Diego	67	42.9
1988—	Harry Newsome, Pittsburgh	65	45.4

		No.	Avg.
1989—	Greg Montgomery, Houston	56	43.3
1990—	Mike Horan, Denver	58	44.4
1991—	Reggie Roby, Miami	54	45.7
1992—	Greg Montgomery, Houston	53	46.9
1993—	Greg Montgomery, Houston	54	45.6
1994—	Jeff Gossett, L.A. Raiders	77	43.9

PUNT RETURNS
(Based on most total yards)

		No.	Yds.	Avg.
1960—	Abner Haynes, Dallas	14	215	15.4
1961—	Dick Christy, N.Y. Jets	18	383	21.3
1962—	Dick Christy, N.Y. Jets	15	250	16.7
1963—	Claude Gibson, Oakland	26	307	11.8
1964—	Bobby Jancik, Houston	12	220	18.3
1965—	Leslie Duncan, San Diego	30	464	15.5
1966—	Leslie Duncan, San Diego	18	238	13.2
1967—	Floyd Little, Denver	16	270	16.9
1968—	Noland Smith, Kansas City	18	270	15.0
1969—	Bill Thompson, Denver	25	288	11.5
1970—	Ed Podolak, Kansas City	23	311	13.5
1971—	Leroy Kelly, Cleveland	30	292	9.7
1972—	Chris Farasopolous, N.Y. Jets	17	179	10.5
1973—	Ron Smith, San Diego	27	352	15.0
1974—	Lemar Parrish, Cincinnati	18	338	18.8
1975—	Billy Johnson, Houston	40	612	15.3
1976—	Rick Upchurch, Denver	39	536	13.7
1977—	Billy Johnson, Houston	30	539	15.4
1978—	Rick Upchurch, Denver	36	493	13.7
1979—	Tony Nathan, Miami	28	306	10.9
1980—	J. T. Smith, Kansas City	40	581	14.5
1981—	James Brooks, San Diego	22	290	13.2
1982—	Rick Upchurch, Denver	15	242	16.1
1983—	Kirk Springs, N.Y. Jets	23	287	12.5
1984—	Mike Martin, Cincinnati	24	376	15.7
1985—	Irving Fryar, New England	37	520	14.1
1986—	Bobby Joe Edmonds, Seattle	34	419	12.3
1987—	Bobby Joe Edmonds, Seattle	20	251	12.6
1988—	Jojo Townsell, N.Y. Jets	35	409	11.7
1989—	Clarence Verdin, Indianapolis	23	296	12.9
1990—	Clarence Verdin, Indianapolis	31	396	12.8
1991—	Rod Woodson, Pittsburgh	28	320	11.4
1992—	Rod Woodson, Pittsburgh	32	364	11.4
1993—	Tim Brown, L.A. Raiders	40	465	11.6
1994—	Tim Brown, L.A. Raiders	40	487	12.2

KICKOFF RETURNS
(Based on most total yards)

		No.	Yds.	Avg.
1960—	Ken Hall, Houston	19	594	31.3
1961—	Dave Grayson, Dallas	16	453	28.3
1962—	Bobby Jancik, Houston	24	726	30.3
1963—	Bobby Jancik, Houston	45	1317	29.3
1964—	Bo Roberson, Oakland	36	975	27.1
1965—	Abner Haynes, Denver	34	901	26.5
1966—	Goldie Sellers, Denver	19	541	28.5
1967—	Zeke Moore, Houston	14	405	28.9
1968—	George Atkinson, Oakland	32	802	25.1
1969—	Bill Thompson, Denver	19	594	31.3
1970—	Jim Duncan, Baltimore	20	707	35.4
1971—	Mercury Morris, Miami	15	423	28.2
1972—	Bruce Laird, Baltimore	29	843	29.1
1973—	Wallace Francis, Buffalo	23	687	29.9
1974—	Greg Pruitt, Cleveland	22	606	27.5
1975—	Harold Hart, Oakland	17	518	30.5
1976—	Duriel Harris, Miami	17	559	32.9
1977—	Raymond Clayborn, New England	20	869	31.0
1978—	Keith Wright, Cleveland	30	789	26.3
1979—	Larry Brunson, Oakland	17	441	25.9
1980—	Horace Ivory, New England	36	992	27.6
1981—	Carl Roaches, Houston	28	769	27.5
1982—	Mike Mosley, Buffalo	18	487	27.1

	No.	Yds.	Avg.
1983—Fulton Walker, Miami	36	962	26.7
1984—Bobby Humphrey, N.Y. Jets	22	675	30.7
1985—Glen Young, Cleveland	35	898	25.7
1986—Lupe Sanchez, Pittsburgh	25	591	23.6
1987—Paul Palmer, Kansas City	38	923	24.3
1988—Tim Brown, L.A. Raiders	41	1098	26.8
1989—Rod Woodson, Pittsburgh	36	982	27.3
1990—Kevin Clark, Denver	20	505	25.3
1991—Nate Lewis, San Diego	23	578	25.1
1992—Jon Vaughn, New England	20	564	28.2
1993—Clarence Verdin, Indianapolis	50	1050	21.0
1994—Andre Coleman, San Diego	49	1293	26.4

SACKS

	No.
1982—Jesse Baker, Houston	7.5
1983—Mark Gastineau, N.Y. Jets	19.0
1984—Mark Gastineau, N.Y. Jets	22.0
1985—Andre Tippett, New England	16.5
1986—Sean Jones, L.A. Raiders	15.5
1987—Andre Tippett, New England	12.5
1988—Greg Townsend, L.A. Raiders	11.5
1989—Lee Williams, San Diego	14.0
1990—Derrick Thomas, Kansas City	20.0
1991—William Fuller, Houston	15.0
1992—Leslie O'Neal, San Diego	17.0
1993—Neil Smith, Kansas City	15.0
1994—Kevin Greene, Pittsburgh	14.0

NFC

RUSHING
(Based on most net yards)

	Net Yds.	Att.	TD
1960—Jim Brown, Cleveland	1257	215	9
1961—Jim Brown, Cleveland	1408	305	8
1962—Jim Taylor, Green Bay	1474	272	19
1963—Jim Brown, Cleveland	1863	291	12
1964—Jim Brown, Cleveland	1446	280	7
1965—Jim Brown, Cleveland	1544	289	17
1966—Gale Sayers, Chicago	1231	229	8
1967—Leroy Kelly, Cleveland	1205	235	11
1968—Leroy Kelly, Cleveland	1239	248	16
1969—Gale Sayers, Chicago	1032	236	8
1970—Larry Brown, Washington	1125	237	5
1971—John Brockington, Green Bay	1105	216	4
1972—Larry Brown, Washington	1216	285	8
1973—John Brockington, Green Bay	1144	265	3
1974—Lawrence McCutcheon, L.A. Rams	1109	236	3
1975—Jim Otis, St. Louis	1076	269	5
1976—Walter Payton, Chicago	1390	311	13
1977—Walter Payton, Chicago	1852	339	14
1978—Walter Payton, Chicago	1395	333	11
1979—Walter Payton, Chicago	1610	369	14
1980—Walter Payton, Chicago	1460	317	6
1981—George Rogers, New Orleans	1674	378	13
1982—Tony Dorsett, Dallas	745	177	5
1983—Eric Dickerson, L.A. Rams	1808	390	18
1984—Eric Dickerson, L.A. Rams	2105	379	14
1985—Gerald Riggs, Atlanta	1719	397	10
1986—Eric Dickerson, L.A. Rams	1821	404	11
1987—Charles White, L.A. Rams	1374	324	11
1988—Herschel Walker, Dallas	1514	361	5
1989—Barry Sanders, Detroit	1470	280	14
1990—Barry Sanders, Detroit	1304	255	13
1991—Emmitt Smith, Dallas	1563	365	12
1992—Emmitt Smith, Dallas	1713	373	18
1993—Emmitt Smith, Dallas	1486	283	9
1994—Barry Sanders, Detroit	1883	331	7

PASSING
(Based on highest passer rating among qualifiers*)

	Att.	Com.	Yds.	TD	Int.	Rat.
1960—Milt Plum, Cle.	250	151	2297	21	5	110.4
1961—Milt Plum, Cle.	302	177	2416	18	10	90.3
1962—Bart Starr, G.B.	285	178	2438	12	9	90.7
1963—Y.A. Tittle, NYG	367	221	3145	36	14	104.8
1964—Bart Starr, G.B.	272	163	2144	15	4	97.1
1965—Rudy Bukich, Chi.	312	176	2641	20	9	93.7
1966—Bart Starr, G.B.	251	156	2257	14	3	105.0
1967—Sonny Jurgensen, Was.	508	288	3747	31	16	87.3
1968—Earl Morrall, Bal.	317	182	2909	26	17	93.2
1969—Sonny Jurgensen, Was.	442	274	3102	22	15	85.4
1970—John Brodie, S.F.	378	223	2941	24	10	93.8
1971—Roger Staubach, Dal.	211	126	1882	15	4	104.8
1972—Norm Snead, NYG	325	196	2307	17	12	84.0

	Att.	Com.	Yds.	TD	Int.	Rat.
1973—Roger Staubach, Dal.	286	179	2428	23	15	94.6
1974—Sonny Jurgensen, Was.	167	107	1185	11	5	94.6
1975—Fran Tarkenton, Min.	425	273	2994	25	13	91.7
1976—James Harris, L.A.	158	91	1460	8	6	89.8
1977—Roger Staubach, Dal.	361	210	2620	18	9	87.1
1978—Roger Staubach, Dal.	413	231	3190	25	16	84.9
1979—Roger Staubach, Dal.	461	267	3586	27	11	92.4
1980—Ron Jaworski, Phi.	451	257	3529	27	12	90.0
1981—Joe Montana, S.F.	488	311	3565	19	12	88.4
1982—Joe Theismann, Was.	252	161	2033	13	9	91.3
1983—Steve Bartkowski, Atl.	432	274	3167	22	5	97.6
1984—Joe Montana, S.F.	432	279	3630	28	10	102.9
1985—Joe Montana, S.F.	494	303	3653	27	13	91.3
1986—Tommy Kramer, Min.	372	208	3000	24	10	92.6
1987—Joe Montana, S.F.	398	266	3054	31	13	102.1
1988—Wade Wilson, Min.	332	204	2746	15	9	91.5
1989—Joe Montana, S.F.	386	271	3521	26	8	112.4
1990—Phil Simms, NYG	311	184	2284	15	4	92.7
1991—Steve Young, S.F.	279	180	2517	17	8	101.8
1992—Steve Young, S.F.	402	268	3465	25	7	107.0
1993—Steve Young, S.F.	462	314	4023	29	16	101.5
1994—Steve Young, S.F.	461	324	3969	35	10	112.8

*This chart includes passer rating points for all leaders, although the same rating system was not used for determining leading quarterbacks prior to 1973. The old system was less equitable, yet similar to the new in that the rating was based on percentage of completions, touchdown passes, percentage of interceptions and average gain in yards.

RECEIVING
(Based on most receptions)

	No.	Yds.	TD
1960—Raymond Berry, Baltimore	74	1298	10
1961—Jim Phillips, L.A. Rams	78	1092	5
1962—Bobby Mitchell, Washington	72	1384	11
1963—Bobby Joe Conrad, St. Louis	73	967	10
1964—Johnny Morris, Chicago	93	1200	10
1965—Dave Parks, San Francisco	80	1344	12
1966—Charley Taylor, Washington	72	1119	12
1967—Charley Taylor, Washington	70	990	9
1968—Clifton McNeil, San Francisco	71	994	7
1969—Dan Abramowicz, New Orleans	73	1015	7
1970—Dick Gordon, Chicago	71	1026	13
1971—Bob Tucker, N.Y. Giants	59	791	4
1972—Harold Jackson, Philadelphia	62	1048	4
1973—Harold Carmichael, Philadelphia	67	1116	9
1974—Charles Young, Philadelphia	63	696	3
1975—Chuck Foreman, Minnesota	73	691	9
1976—Drew Pearson, Dallas	58	806	6
1977—Ahmad Rashad, Minnesota	51	681	2
1978—Rickey Young, Minnesota	88	704	5
1979—Ahmad Rashad, Minnesota	80	1156	9
1980—Earl Cooper, San Francisco	83	567	4
1981—Dwight Clark, San Francisco	85	1105	4

		No.	Yds.	Avg.
1982—Dwight Clark, San Francisco		60	913	5
1983—Roy Green, St. Louis		78	1227	14
	Charlie Brown, Washington	78	1225	8
	Earnest Gray, N.Y. Giants	78	1139	5
1984—Art Monk, Washington		106	1372	7
1985—Roger Craig, San Francisco		92	1016	6
1986—Jerry Rice, San Francisco		86	1570	15
1987—J.T. Smith, St. Louis		91	1117	8
1988—Henry Ellard, L.A. Rams		86	1414	10
1989—Sterling Sharpe, Green Bay		90	1423	12
1990—Jerry Rice, San Francisco		100	1502	13
1991—Michael Irvin, Dallas		93	1523	8
1992—Sterling Sharpe, Green Bay		108	1461	13
1993—Sterling Sharpe, Green Bay		112	1274	11
1994—Cris Carter, Minnesota		122	1256	7

SCORING
(Based on most total points)

	TD	PAT	FG	Tot.
1960—Paul Hornung, Green Bay	15	41	15	176
1961—Paul Hornung, Green Bay	10	41	15	146
1962—Jim Taylor, Green Bay	19	0	0	114
1963—Don Chandler, N.Y. Giants	0	52	18	106
1964—Lenny Moore, Baltimore	20	0	0	120
1965—Gale Sayers, Chicago	22	0	0	132
1966—Bruce Gossett, L.A. Rams	0	29	28	113
1967—Jim Bakken, St. Louis	0	36	27	117
1968—Leroy Kelly, Cleveland	20	0	0	120
1969—Fred Cox, Minnesota	0	43	26	121
1970—Fred Cox, Minnesota	0	35	30	125
1971—Curt Knight, Washington	0	27	29	114
1972—Chester Marcol, Green Bay	0	29	33	128
1973—David Ray, L.A. Rams	0	40	30	130
1974—Chester Marcol, Green Bay	0	19	25	94
1975—Chuck Foreman, Minnesota	22	0	0	132
1976—Mark Moseley, Washington	0	31	22	97
1977—Walter Payton, Chicago	16	0	0	96
1978—Frank Corral, L.A. Rams	0	31	29	118
1979—Mark Moseley, Washington	0	39	25	114
1980—Ed Murray, Detroit	0	35	27	116
1981—Ed Murray, Detroit	0	46	25	121
	Rafael Septien, Dallas	0	40	27	121
1982—Wendell Tyler, L.A. Rams	13	0	0	78
1983—Mark Moseley, Washington	0	62	33	161
1984—Ray Wersching, S.F.	0	56	25	131
1985—Kevin Butler, Chicago	0	51	31	144
1986—Kevin Butler, Chicago	0	36	28	120
1987—Jerry Rice, San Francisco	23	0	0	138
1988—Mike Cofer, San Francisco	0	40	27	121
1989—Mike Cofer, San Francisco	0	49	29	136
1990—Chip Lohmiller, Washington	0	41	30	131
1991—Chip Lohmiller, Washington	0	56	31	149
1992—Morten Andersen, New Orleans	0	33	29	120
	Chip Lohmiller, Washington	0	30	30	120
1993—Jason Hanson, Detroit	0	28	34	130
1994—Fuad Reveiz, Minnesota	0	30	34	132

FIELD GOALS

	No.
1960—Tommy Davis, San Francisco	19
1961—Steve Myhra, Baltimore	21
1962—Lou Michaels, Pittsburgh	26
1963—Jim Martin, Baltimore	24
1964—Jim Bakken, St. Louis	25
1965—Fred Cox, Minnesota	23
1966—Bruce Gossett, L.A. Rams	28
1967—Jim Bakken, St. Louis	27
1968—Mac Percival, Chicago	25
1969—Fred Cox, Minnesota	26
1970—Fred Cox, Minnesota	30
1971—Curt Knight, Washington	29
1972—Chester Marcol, Green Bay	33

	No.
1973—David Ray, L.A. Rams	30
1974—Chester Marcol, Green Bay	25
1975—Toni Fritsch, Dallas	22
1976—Mark Moseley, Washington	22
1977—Mark Moseley, Washington	21
1978—Frank Corral, L.A. Rams	29
1979—Mark Moseley, Washington	25
1980—Eddie Murray, Detroit	27
1981—Rafael Septien, Dallas	27
1982—Mark Moseley, Washington	20
1983—Ali Haji-Sheikh, N.Y. Giants	35
1984—Paul McFadden, Philadelphia	30
1985—Morten Andersen, New Orleans	31
	Kevin Butler, Chicago	31
1986—Kevin Butler, Chicago	28
1987—Morten Andersen, New Orleans	28
1988—Mike Cofer, San Francisco	27
1989—Rich Karlis, Minnesota	31
1990—Chip Lohmiller, Washington	30
1991—Chip Lohmiller, Washington	31
1992—Chip Lohmiller, Washington	30
1993—Jason Hanson, Detroit	34
1994—Fuad Reveiz, Minnesota	34

INTERCEPTIONS

	No.	Yds.
1960—Dave Baker, San Francisco	10	96
	Jerry Norton, St. Louis	10	96
1961—Dick Lynch, N.Y. Giants	9	60
1962—Willie Wood, Green Bay	9	132
1963—Dick Lynch, N.Y. Giants	9	251
	Rosie Taylor, Chicago	9	172
1964—Paul Krause, Washington	12	140
1965—Bobby Boyd, Baltimore	9	78
1966—Larry Wilson, St. Louis	10	180
1967—Lem Barney, Detroit	10	232
	Dave Whitsell, New Orleans	10	178
1968—Willie Williams, N.Y. Giants	10	103
1969—Mel Renfro, Dallas	10	118
1970—Dick Le Beau, Detroit	9	96
1971—Bill Bradley, Philadelphia	11	248
1972—Bill Bradley, Philadelphia	9	73
1973—Bob Bryant, Minnesota	7	105
1974—Ray Brown, Atlanta	8	164
1975—Paul Krause, Minnesota	10	201
1976—Monte Jackson, L.A. Rams	10	173
1977—Rolland Lawrence, Atlanta	7	138
1978—Ken Stone, St. Louis	9	139
	Willie Buchanon, Green Bay	9	93
1979—Lemar Parrish, Washington	9	65
1980—Nolan Cromwell, L.A. Rams	8	140
1981—Everson Walls, Dallas	11	133
1982—Everson Walls, Dallas	7	61
1983—Mark Murphy, Washington	9	127
1984—Tom Flynn, Green Bay	9	106
1985—Everson Walls, Dallas	9	31
1986—Ronnie Lott, San Francisco	10	134
1987—Barry Wilburn, Washington	9	135
1988—Scott Case, Atlanta	10	47
1989—Eric Allen, Philadelphia	8	38
1990—Mark Carrier, Chicago	10	39
1991—Ray Crockett, Detroit	6	141
	Tim McKyer, Atlanta	6	24
	Deion Sanders, Atlanta	6	119
	Aeneas Williams, Phoenix	6	60
1992—Aubray McMillian, Minnesota	8	157
1993—Deion Sanders, Atlanta	7	91
1994—Aeneas Williams, Arizona	9	89

PUNTING
(Based on highest average yardage per punt by qualifiers)

	No.	Avg.
1960—Jerry Norton, St. Louis	39	45.6
1961—Yale Lary, Detroit	52	48.4

Year		No.	Avg.
1962	Tommy Davis, San Francisco	48	45.8
1963	Yale Lary, Detroit	35	48.9
1964	Bobby Walden, Minnesota	72	46.4
1965	Gary Collins, Cleveland	65	46.7
1966	David Lee, Baltimore	49	45.6
1967	Billy Lothridge, Atlanta	87	43.7
1968	Billy Lothridge, Atlanta	75	44.3
1969	David Lee, Baltimore	50	45.3
1970	Julian Fagan, New Orleans	77	42.5
1971	Tom McNeill, Philadelphia	73	42.0
1972	Dave Chapple, L.A. Rams	53	44.2
1973	Tom Wittum, San Francisco	79	43.7
1974	Tom Blanchard, New Orleans	88	42.1
1975	Herman Weaver, Detroit	80	42.0
1976	John James, Atlanta	101	42.1
1977	Tom Blanchard, New Orleans	82	42.4
1978	Tom Skladany, Detroit	86	42.5
1979	Dave Jennings, N.Y. Giants	104	42.7
1980	Dave Jennings, N.Y. Giants	94	44.8
1981	Tom Skladany, Detroit	64	43.5
1982	Carl Birdsong, St. Louis	54	43.8
1983	Frank Garcia, Tampa Bay	95	42.2
1984	Brian Hansen, New Orleans	69	43.8
1985	Rick Donnelly, Atlanta	59	43.6
1986	Sean Landeta, N.Y. Giants	79	44.8
1987	Rick Donnelly, Atlanta	61	44.0
1988	Jim Arnold, Detroit	97	42.4
1989	Rich Camarillo, Phoenix	76	43.4
1990	Sean Landeta, N.Y. Giants	75	44.1
1991	Harry Newsome, Minnesota	68	45.5
1992	Harry Newsome, Minnesota	72	45.0
1993	Jim Arnold, Detroit	72	44.5
1994	Sean Landeta, L.A. Rams	78	44.8

PUNT RETURNS
(Based on most total yards)

Year		No.	Yds.	Avg.
1960	Abe Woodson, San Francisco	13	174	13.4
1961	Willie Wood, Green Bay	14	225	16.1
1962	Pat Studstill, Detroit	29	457	15.8
1963	Dick James, Washington	16	214	13.4
1964	Tommy Watkins, Detroit	16	238	14.9
1965	Leroy Kelly, Cleveland	17	265	15.6
1966	Johnny Roland, St. Louis	20	221	11.1
1967	Ben Davis, Cleveland	18	229	12.7
1968	Bob Hayes, Dallas	15	312	20.8
1969	Alvin Haymond, L.A. Rams	33	435	13.2
1970	Bruce Taylor, San Francisco	43	516	12.0
1971	Les Duncan, Washington	22	233	10.6
1972	Ken Ellis, Green Bay	14	215	15.4
1973	Bruce Taylor, San Francisco	15	207	13.8
1974	Dick Jauron, Detroit	17	286	16.8
1975	Terry Metcalf, St. Louis	23	285	12.4
1976	Eddie Brown, Washington	48	646	13.5
1977	Larry Marshall, Philadelphia	46	489	10.6
1978	Jackie Wallace, L.A. Rams	52	618	11.9
1979	John Sciarra, Philadelphia	16	182	11.4
1980	Kenny Johnson, Atlanta	23	281	12.2
1981	LeRoy Irvin, L.A. Rams	46	615	13.4
1982	Billy Johnson, Atlanta	24	273	11.4
1983	Henry Ellard, L.A. Rams	16	217	13.6
1984	Henry Ellard, L.A. Rams	30	403	13.4
1985	Henry Ellard, L.A. Rams	37	501	13.5
1986	Vai Sikahema, St. Louis	43	522	12.1
1987	Mel Gray, New Orleans	24	352	14.7

Year		No.	Yds.	Avg.
1988	John Taylor, San Francisco	44	556	12.6
1989	Walter Stanley, Detroit	36	496	13.8
1990	Johnny Bailey, Chicago	36	399	11.1
1991	Mel Gray, Detroit	25	385	15.4
1992	Johnny Bailey, Phoenix	20	263	13.2
1993	Tyrone Hughes, New Orleans	37	503	13.6
1994	Brian Mitchell, Washington	32	452	14.1

KICKOFF RETURNS
(Based on most total yards)

Year		No.	Yds.	Avg.
1960	Tom Moore, Green Bay	12	397	33.1
1961	Dick Bass, L.A. Rams	23	698	30.3
1962	Abe Woodson, San Francisco	37	1157	31.3
1963	Abe Woodson, San Francisco	29	935	32.3
1964	Clarence Childs, N.Y. Giants	34	987	29.0
1965	Tommy Watkins, Detroit	17	584	34.4
1966	Gale Sayers, Chicago	23	718	31.2
1967	Travis Williams, Green Bay	18	739	41.1
1968	Preston Pearson, Baltimore	15	527	35.1
1969	Bobby Williams, Detroit	17	563	33.1
1970	Cecil Turner, Chicago	23	752	32.7
1971	Travis Williams, L.A. Rams	25	743	29.7
1972	Ron Smith, Chicago	30	924	30.8
1973	Carl Garrett, Chicago	16	486	30.4
1974	Terry Metcalf, St. Louis	20	623	31.2
1975	Walter Payton, Chicago	14	444	31.7
1976	Cullen Bryant, L.A. Rams	16	459	28.7
1977	Wilbert Montgomery, Phila.	23	619	26.9
1978	Steve Odom, Green Bay	25	677	27.1
1979	Jimmy Edwards, Minnesota	44	1103	25.1
1980	Rich Mauti, New Orleans	31	798	27.6
1981	Mike Nelms, Washington	37	1099	29.7
1982	Alvin Hall, Detroit	16	426	26.6
1983	Darrin Nelson, Minnesota	18	445	24.7
1984	Barry Redden, L.A. Rams	23	530	23.0
1985	Ron Brown, L.A. Rams	28	918	32.8
1986	Dennis Gentry, Chicago	20	576	28.8
1987	Sylvester Stamps, Atlanta	24	660	27.5
1988	Donnie Elder, Tampa Bay	34	772	22.7
1989	Mel Gray, Detroit	24	640	26.7
1990	Dave Meggett, N.Y. Giants	21	492	23.4
1991	Mel Gray, Detroit	36	929	25.8
1992	Deion Sanders, Atlanta	40	1067	26.7
1993	Tony Smith, Atlanta	38	948	24.9
1994	Tyrone Hughes, New Orleans	63	1556	24.7

SACKS

Year		No.
1982	Doug Martin, Minnesota	11.5
1983	Fred Dean, San Francisco	17.5
1984	Richard Dent, Chicago	17.5
1985	Richard Dent, Chicago	17.0
1986	Lawrence Taylor, N.Y. Giants	20.5
1987	Reggie White, Philadelphia	21.0
1988	Reggie White, Philadelphia	18.0
1989	Chris Doleman, Minnesota	21.0
1990	Charles Haley, San Francisco	16.0
1991	Pat Swilling, New Orleans	17.0
1992	Clyde Simmons, Philadelphia	19.0
1993	Renaldo Turnbull, New Orleans	13.0
	Reggie White, Green Bay	13.0
1994	Ken Harvey, Washington	13.5
	John Randle, Minnesota	13.5

COACHING RECORDS

(Ranked according to career wins)

		REGULAR SEASON				POSTSEASON			CAREER			
	Yrs.	Won	Lost	Tied	Pct.	Won	Lost	Pct.	Won	Lost	Tied	Pct.
*Don Shula	32	319	149	6	.679	19	16	.543	338	165	6	.670
George Halas	40	318	148	31	.671	6	3	.667	324	151	31	.671
Tom Landry	29	250	162	6	.605	20	16	.556	270	178	6	.601
Curly Lambeau	33	226	132	22	.624	3	2	.600	229	134	22	.623
Chuck Noll	23	193	148	1	.566	16	8	.667	209	156	1	.572
*Chuck Knox	22	186	147	1	.558	7	11	.389	193	158	1	.550
Paul Brown	21	166	100	6	.621	4	9	.308	170	109	6	.607
Bud Grant	18	158	96	5	.620	10	13	.435	168	109	5	.605
Steve Owen	23	151	100	17	.595	3	8	.273	154	108	17	.582
Joe Gibbs	12	124	60	0	.674	16	5	.762	140	65	0	.683
*Dan Reeves	14	130	85	1	.604	8	7	.533	138	92	1	.600
Hank Stram	17	131	97	10	.571	5	3	.625	136	100	10	.573
Weeb Ewbank	20	130	129	7	.502	4	1	.800	134	130	7	.507
*Marv Levy	14	117	90	0	.565	10	6	.625	127	96	0	.570
Sid Gillman	18	122	99	7	.550	1	5	.167	123	104	7	.541
George Allen	12	116	47	5	.705	4	7	.364	120	54	5	.684
Don Coryell	14	111	83	1	.572	3	6	.333	114	89	1	.561
Mike Ditka	11	106	62	0	.631	6	6	.500	112	68	0	.622
John Madden	10	103	32	7	.750	9	7	.563	112	39	7	.731
*Marty Schottenheimer	11	103	63	1	.620	5	9	.357	108	72	1	.599
Buddy Parker	15	104	75	9	.577	3	2	.600	107	77	9	.578
Vince Lombardi	10	96	34	6	.728	8	2	.800	104	36	6	.733
Bill Walsh	10	92	59	1	.609	10	4	.714	102	63	1	.617
*Bill Parcells	10	92	66	1	.582	8	4	.667	100	70	1	.588

*Active NFL coaches in 1994.

(Ranked according to career NFL percentages)

		REGULAR SEASON				POSTSEASON			CAREER			
	Yrs.	Won	Lost	Tied	Pct.	Won	Lost	Pct.	Won	Lost	Tied	Pct.
George Seifert	6	75	21	0	.781	9	3	.750	84	24	0	.778
Barry Switzer	1	12	4	0	.750	1	1	.500	13	5	0	.722
Don Shula	32	319	149	6	.679	19	16	.543	338	165	6	.670
Bill Cowher	3	32	16	0	.667	1	3	.250	33	19	0	.635
Bobby Ross	3	30	18	0	.625	3	2	.600	33	20	0	.623
Dan Reeves	14	130	85	1	.604	8	7	.533	138	92	1	.600
Marty Schottenheimer	11	103	63	1	.620	5	9	.357	108	72	1	.599
Dennis Green	3	30	18	0	.625	0	3	.000	30	21	0	.588
Bill Parcells	10	92	66	1	.582	8	4	.667	100	70	1	.588
Jim Mora	9	84	59	0	.587	0	4	.000	84	63	0	.571
USFL totals	3	41	12	1	.769	7	1	.875	48	13	1	.782
Marv Levy	14	117	90	0	.565	10	6	.625	127	96	0	.570
CFL totals	5	43	31	4	.577	7	3	.700	50	34	4	.591
USFL totals	1	5	13	0	.278	0	0	.000	5	13	0	.278
Rich Kotite	4	36	28	0	.563	1	1	.500	37	29	0	.561
Mike Holmgren	3	27	21	0	.563	2	2	.500	29	23	0	.558
Buddy Ryan	6	51	43	1	.542	0	3	.000	51	46	1	.526
Dave Wannstedt	2	16	16	0	.500	1	1	.500	17	17	0	.500
Ted Marchibroda	8	62	60	0	.508	0	3	.000	62	63	0	.496
Wayne Fontes	7	51	50	0	.505	1	3	.250	52	53	0	.495
Bill Belichick	4	31	33	0	.484	1	1	.500	32	34	0	.485
Sam Wyche	11	77	98	0	.440	3	2	.600	80	100	0	.444
June Jones	1	7	9	0	.438	0	0	.000	7	9	0	.438
Mike Shanahan	2	8	12	0	.400	0	0	.000	8	12	0	.400
David Shula	3	11	37	0	.229	0	0	.000	11	37	0	.229
Norv Turner	1	3	13	0	.188	0	0	.000	3	13	0	.188
Jeff Fisher	1	1	5	0	.167	0	0	.000	1	5	0	.167
Rich Brooks	0	0	0	0	.000	0	0	.000	0	0	0	.000
Dom Capers	0	0	0	0	.000	0	0	.000	0	0	0	.000
Tom Coughlin	0	0	0	0	.000	0	0	.000	0	0	0	.000
Dennis Erickson	0	0	0	0	.000	0	0	.000	0	0	0	.000
Ray Rhodes	0	0	0	0	.000	0	0	.000	0	0	0	.000
Mike White	0	0	0	0	.000	0	0	.000	0	0	0	.000

HALL OF FAME

ROSTER OF MEMBERS

FIVE NEW INDUCTEES IN 1995

Jim Finks, Henry Jordan, Steve Largent, Lee Roy Selmon and Kellen Winslow were inducted into Pro Football's Hall of Fame in 1995, expanding the list of former stars honored at Canton, Ohio, to 180.

HERB ADDERLEY (Michigan State), 1980, cornerback, Green Bay Packers (1961-69), Dallas Cowboys (1970-72).

LANCE ALWORTH (Arkansas), 1978, wide receiver, San Diego Chargers (1962-70), Dallas Cowboys (1971-72).

DOUG ATKINS (Tennessee), 1982, defensive end, Cleveland Browns (1953-54), Chicago Bears (1955-66), New Orleans Saints (1967-69).

MORRIS (RED) BADGRO (Southern California), 1981, end, New York Yankees (1926), New York Giants (1930-35).

LEM BARNEY (Jackson State), 1992, cornerback, Detroit Lions (1967-77).

CLIFF BATTLES (West Virginia Wesleyan), 1968, halfback/quarterback, Boston Braves, Boston Redskins, Washington Redskins (1932-37); coach, Brooklyn Dodgers (1946-47).

SAMMY BAUGH (Texas Christian), Charter 1963, quarterback, Washington Redskins (1937-52); coach, New York Titans (1960-61); Houston Oilers (1964).

CHUCK BEDNARIK (Pennsylvania), 1967, center/linebacker, Philadelphia Eagles (1949-62).

BERT BELL (Pennsylvania), Charter 1963, NFL Commissioner (1946-59).

BOBBY BELL (Minnesota), 1983, linebacker, Kansas City Chiefs (1963-74).

RAYMOND BERRY (Southern Methodist), 1973, end, Baltimore Colts (1955-67), coach, New England Patriots, (1984-89).

CHARLES W. BIDWILL (Loyola), 1967, owner, Chicago Cardinals (1933-47).

FRED BILETNIKOFF (Florida State), 1988, wide receiver, Oakland Raiders (1965-78).

GEORGE BLANDA (Kentucky), 1981, quarterback/placekicker, Chicago Bears (1949-58), Baltimore Colts (1950), Houston Oilers (1960-66), Oakland Raiders (1967-75).

MEL BLOUNT (Southern), 1989, cornerback, Pittsburgh Steelers (1970-83).

TERRY BRADSHAW (Louisiana Tech), 1989, quarterback, Pittsburgh Steelers (1970-83).

JIM BROWN (Syracuse), 1971, fullback, Cleveland Browns (1957-65).

PAUL BROWN (Miami of Ohio), 1967, coach, Cleveland Browns (1946-62), Cincinnati Bengals (1968-75).

ROOSEVELT BROWN (Morgan State), 1975, tackle, New York Giants (1953-66).

WILLIE BROWN (Grambling), 1984, defensive back, Denver Broncos (1963-66), Oakland Raiders (1967-78).

BUCK BUCHANAN (Grambling), 1990, defensive tackle, Kansas City Chiefs (1963-75).

DICK BUTKUS (Illinois), 1979, linebacker, Chicago Bears (1965-73).

EARL CAMPBELL (Texas), 1991, running back, Houston Oilers (1978-84), New Orleans Saints (1984-85).

TONY CANADEO (Gonzaga), 1974, halfback, Green Bay Packers (1941-44, 46-52).

JOE CARR Charter 1963, NFL President (1921-39).

GUY CHAMBERLIN (Nebraska), 1965, player/coach, Canton Bulldogs, Cleveland, Frankford Yellowjackets, Chicago Bears, Chicago Cardinals (1919-28).

JACK CHRISTIANSEN (Colorado A&M), 1970, defensive back, Detroit Lions (1951-58); coach, San Francisco 49ers (1963-67).

DUTCH CLARK (Colorado College), Charter 1963, quarterback, Portsmouth Spartans, Detroit Lions (1931-38).

GEORGE CONNOR (Notre Dame), 1975, tackle/linebacker, Chicago Bears (1948-55).

JIMMY CONZELMAN (Washington, Mo.), 1964, halfback, coach, executive, Decatur, Rock Island, Milwaukee, Detroit, Providence, Chicago Cardinals (1920-48).

LARRY CSONKA (Syracuse), 1987, running back, Miami Dolphins (1968-74, 79), New York Giants (1976-78).

AL DAVIS (Syracuse), 1992, coach/general manager/president, Oakland-Los Angeles Raiders (1963-present).

WILLIE DAVIS (Grambling), 1981, defensive end, Cleveland Browns (1958-59), Green Bay Packers (1960-69).

LEN DAWSON (Purdue), 1987, quarterback, Pittsburgh Steelers (1957-58), Cleveland Browns (1960-61), Dallas Texans (1962), Kansas City Chiefs (1963-75).

MIKE DITKA (Pittsburgh), 1988, tight end, Chicago Bears (1961-66), Philadelphia Eagles (1967-68), Dallas Cowboys (1969-72), coach, Chicago Bears (1982-92).

ART DONOVAN (Boston College), 1968, defensive tackle, Baltimore Colts, New York Yanks, Dallas Texans, Baltimore Colts (1950-61).

TONY DORSETT (Pittsburgh), 1994, running back, Dallas Cowboys (1977-87), Denver Broncos (1988).

PADDY DRISCOLL (Northwestern), 1965, player/coach, Chicago Cardinals, Chicago Bears (1919-31, 41-68).

BILL DUDLEY (Virginia), 1966, halfback, Pittsburgh Steelers, Detroit Lions Washington Redskins (1942-53).

TURK EDWARDS (Washington State), 1969, tackle, Boston Braves, Boston Redskins, Washington Redskins (1932-40).

WEEB EWBANK (Miami of Ohio), 1978, coach, Baltimore Colts (1954-62), New York Jets (1963-73).

TOM FEARS (Santa Clara, UCLA), 1970, end, Los Angeles Rams (1948-56), coach, New Orleans Saints (1967-70).

JIM FINKS (Tulsa), 1995, quarterback, Pittsburgh Steelers (1949-55); administrator, Minnesota Vikings (1964-73), Chicago Bears (1974-86), New Orleans Saints (1987-93).

RAY FLAHERTY (Gonzaga), 1976, player/coach, Los Angeles Wildcats, New York Yankees (AFL), New York Giants, Boston Redskins, Washington Redskins, New York Yankees (AAFC), Chicago Hornets (1926-49).

LEN FORD (Michigan), 1976, end, Los Angeles Dons, Cleveland Browns (1948-58).

DANNY FORTMANN (Colgate), 1965, guard, Chicago Bears (1936-43).

DAN FOUTS (Oregon), 1993, quarterback, San Diego Chargers (1973-87).

FRANK GATSKI (Marshall), 1985, center, Cleveland Browns (1946-56), Detroit Lions (1957).

BILL GEORGE (Wake Forest), 1974, linebacker, Chicago Bears, Los Angeles Rams (1952-66).

FRANK GIFFORD (Southern California), 1977, halfback/end, New York Giants (1952-60, 62-64).

SID GILLMAN (Ohio State), 1983, end, Cleveland Rams (1936); coach, Los Angeles Rams (1955-59), Los Angeles Chargers (1960), San Diego Chargers (1961-69, 71), Houston Oilers (1973-74).

OTTO GRAHAM (Northwestern), 1965, quarterback, Cleveland Browns (1946-55); coach, Washington Redskins (1966-68).

RED GRANGE (Illinois), Charter 1963, halfback, Chicago Bears (1925, 29-34), New York Yankees (1926-27).

BUD GRANT (Minnesota), 1994, wide receiver, Philadelphia Eagles (1951-52), coach, Minnesota Vikings (1967-83, 1985).

JOE GREENE (North Texas State), 1987, defensive tackle, Pittsburgh Steelers (1969-81).

FORREST GREGG (Southern Methodist), 1977, tackle, Green Bay Packers, Dallas Cowboys (1956, 58-71); coach, Cleveland Browns (1975-77), Cincinnati Bengals (1980-83), Green Bay Packers (1984-87).

BOB GRIESE (Purdue), 1990, quarterback, Miami Dolphins (1967-80).

LOU GROZA (Ohio State), 1974, tackle-placekicker, Cleveland Browns (1946-59, 61-67).

JOE GUYON (Carlisle, Georgia Tech), 1966, halfback, Canton Bulldogs, Cleveland Indians, Oorang Indians, Rock Island Independents, Kansas City Cowboys, New York Giants (1918-27).

GEORGE HALAS (Illinois), Charter 1963, player/coach/founder, Chicago Bears (1920-83).

JACK HAM (Penn State), 1988, linebacker, Pittsburgh Steelers (1971-82).

JOHN HANNAH (Alabama), 1991, guard, New England Patriots (1973-85).

FRANCO HARRIS (Penn State), 1990, running back, Pittsburgh Steelers (1972-83), Seattle Seahawks (1984).

ED HEALEY (Dartmouth), 1964, tackle, Rock Island, Chicago Bears (1920-27).

MEL HEIN (Washington State), Charter 1963, center, New York Giants (1931-45).

TED HENDRICKS (Miami, Fla.), 1990, linebacker, Baltimore Colts (1969-73), Green Bay Packers (1974), Oakland/Los Angeles Raiders (1975-83).

WILBUR HENRY (Washington & Jefferson), Charter 1963, tackle, Canton Bulldogs, Akron Indians, New York Giants, Pottsville Maroons, Pittsburgh Steelers (1920-30).

ARNIE HERBER (Regis), 1966, halfback, Green Bay Packers, New York Giants (1930-45).

BILL HEWITT (Michigan), 1971, end, Chicago Bears (1932-36), Philadelphia Eagles (1937-39), Philadelphia/ Pittsburgh (1943).

CLARKE HINKLE (Bucknell), 1964, fullback, Green Bay Packers (1932-41).

ELROY (CRAZYLEGS) HIRSCH (Wisconsin), 1968, end/halfback, Chicago Rockets, Los Angeles Rams (1946-57).

PAUL HORNUNG (Notre Dame), 1986, running back, Green Bay Packers (1957-62, 64-66).

KEN HOUSTON (Prairie View), 1986, defensive back, Houston Oilers (1967-72), Washington Redskins (1973-80).

CAL HUBBARD (Centenary, Geneva), Charter 1963, tackle/end, New York Giants, Green Bay Packers, Pittsburgh Steelers (1927-36).

SAM HUFF (West Virginia), 1982, linebacker, New York Giants (1956-63), Washington Redskins (1964-67, 69).

LAMAR HUNT (Southern Methodist), 1972, founder, American Football League, 1959; president, Dallas Texas (1960-62), Kansas City Chiefs (1963-present).

DON HUTSON (Alabama), Charter 1963, end, Green Bay Packers (1935-45).

JIMMY JOHNSON (UCLA), 1994, defensive back, San Francisco 49ers (1961-76).

JOHN HENRY JOHNSON (Arizona State), 1987, fullback, San Francisco 49ers (1954-56), Detroit Lions (1957-59), Pittsburgh Steelers (1960-65), Houston Oilers (1966).

DEACON JONES (South Carolina State), 1980, defensive end, Los Angeles Rams (1961-71), San Diego Chargers (1972-73), Washington Redskins (1974).

STAN JONES (Maryland), 1991, guard/defensive tackle, Chicago Bears (1954-65), Washington Redskins (1966).

HENRY JORDAN (Virginia), 1995, defensive tackle, Cleveland Browns (1957-58), Green Bay Packers (1959-69).

SONNY JURGENSEN (Duke), 1983, quarterback, Philadelphia Eagles (1957-63), Washington Redskins (1964-74).

LEROY KELLY (Morgan State), 1994, running back, Cleveland Browns (1964-73).

WALTER KIESLING (St. Thomas), 1966, player/coach, Duluth Eskimos, Pottsville Maroons, Boston Braves, Chicago Cardinals, Chicago Bears, Green Bay Packers, Pittsburgh Steelers (1926-56).

FRANK (BRUISER) KINARD (Mississippi), 1971, tackle, Brooklyn Dodgers (1938-45), New York Yankees (1946-47).

CURLY LAMBEAU (Notre Dame), Charter 1963, founder, player, coach, Green Bay Packers (1919-49).

JACK LAMBERT (Kent State), 1990, linebacker, Pittsburgh Steelers (1974-84).

TOM LANDRY (Texas), 1990, coach, Dallas Cowboys (1960-88).

DICK (NIGHT TRAIN) LANE (Scottsbluff JC), 1974, defensive back, Los Angeles Rams, Chicago Cardinals, Detroit Lions (1952-65).

JIM LANGER (South Dakota State), 1987, center, Miami Dolphins (1970-79), Minnesota Vikings (1980-81).

WILLIE LANIER (Morgan State), 1986, linebacker, Kansas City Chiefs (1967-77).

STEVE LARGENT (Tulsa), 1995, wide receiver, Seattle Seahawks (1976-89).

YALE LARY (Texas A&M), 1979, defensive back, Detroit Lions (1952-53, 56-64).

DANTE LAVELLI (Ohio State), 1975, end, Cleveland Browns (1946-56).

BOBBY LAYNE (Texas), 1967, quarterback, Chicago Bears, New York Bulldogs, Detroit Lions, Pittsburgh Steelers (1948-62).

TUFFY LEEMANS (George Washington), 1978, fullback, New York Giants (1936-43).

BOB LILLY (Texas Christian), 1980, defensive tackle, Dallas Cowboys (1961-74).

LARRY LITTLE (Bethune Cookman), 1993, guard, San Diego Chargers (1967-68), Miami Dolphins (1969-80).

VINCE LOMBARDI (Fordham), 1971, coach, Green Bay Packers (1959-67), Washington Redskins (1969).

SID LUCKMAN (Columbia), 1965, quarterback, Chicago Bears (1939-50).

ROY (LINK) LYMAN 1964, tackle, Canton Bulldogs, Cleveland, Chicago Bears (1922-34).

JOHN MACKEY (Syracuse), 1992, tight end, Baltimore Colts (1963-71), San Diego Chargers (1972).

TIM MARA Charter 1963, founder, New York Giants (1925-65).

GINO MARCHETTI (San Francisco), 1972, defensive end, Dallas Texans (1952), Baltimore Colts (1953-66).

GEORGE PRESTON MARSHALL Charter 1963, founder, Washington Redskins (1932-65).

OLLIE MATSON (San Francisco), 1972, halfback, Chicago Cardinals (1952, 54-58), Los Angeles Rams (1959-62), Detroit Lions (1963), Philadelphia Eagles (1964-66).

DON MAYNARD (Texas Western College), 1987, wide receiver, New York Giants (1958), New York Jets (1960-72), St. Louis Cardinals (1973).

GEORGE McAFEE (Duke), 1966, halfback, Chicago Bears (1940-41, 45-50).

MIKE McCORMACK (Kansas), 1984, tackle, New York Yanks (1951), Cleveland Browns (1954-62).

HUGH McELHENNY (Washington), 1970, San Francisco 49ers, Minnesota Vikings, New York Giants, Detroit Lions (1952-64).

JOHNNY BLOOD (McNALLY) (St. John's, Minn.), Charter 1963, halfback, Milwaukee Badgers, Duluth Eskimos, Pottsville Maroons, Green Bay Packers, Pittsburgh Steelers (1925-39).

AUGUST (MIKE) MICHALSKE (Penn State), 1964, guard, New York Yankees, Green Bay Packers (1927-37).

WAYNE MILLNER (Notre Dame), 1968, end, Boston Redskins, Washington Redskins (1936-41, 45).

BOBBY MITCHELL (Illinois), 1983, running back/receiver, Cleveland Browns (1958-61), Washington Redskins (1962-68).

RON MIX (Southern California), 1979, offensive tackle, Los Angeles Chargers (1960), San Diego Chargers (1961-69), Oakland Raiders (1971).

LENNY MOORE (Penn State), 1975, halfback, Baltimore Colts

(1956-67).

MARION MOTLEY (Nevada), 1968, fullback/linebacker, Cleveland Browns, Pittsburgh Steelers (1946-55).

GEORGE MUSSO (Millikin), 1982, guard/defensive tackle, Chicago Bears (1933-44).

BRONKO NAGURSKI (Minnesota), Charter 1963, fullback/tackle, Chicago Bears (1930-37, 43).

JOE NAMATH (Alabama), 1985, quarterback, New York Jets (1965-76), Los Angeles Rams (1977).

EARLE (GREASY) NEALE (West Virginia Wesleyan), 1969, coach, Philadelphia Eagles (1941-50).

ERNIE NEVERS (Stanford), Charter 1963, fullback, Duluth Eskimos, Chicago Cardinals (1926-37).

RAY NITSCHKE (Illinois), 1978, linebacker, Green Bay Packers (1958-72).

CHUCK NOLL (Dayton), 1993, coach, Pittsburgh Steelers (1969-91).

LEO NOMELLINI (Minnesota), 1969, defensive tackle, San Francisco 49ers (1953-63).

MERLIN OLSEN (Utah State), 1982, defensive tackle, Los Angeles Rams (1962-76).

JIM OTTO (Miami, Fla.), 1980, center, Oakland Raiders (1960-74).

STEVE OWEN (Phillips), 1966, player/coach, Kansas City Cowboys, New York Giants (1924-53).

ALAN PAGE (Notre Dame), 1988, defensive tackle, Minnesota Vikings (1967-78), Chicago Bears (1978-81).

CLARENCE (ACE) PARKER (Duke), 1972, halfback, Brooklyn Dodgers (1937-41), Boston Yanks (1945), New York Yankees (1946).

JIM PARKER (Ohio State), 1973, guard, Baltimore Colts (1957-67).

WALTER PAYTON (Jackson State), 1993, running back, Chicago Bears (1975-87).

JOE PERRY (Compton JC), 1969, fullback, San Francisco 49ers, Baltimore Colts (1948-63).

PETE PIHOS (Indiana), 1970, end, Philadelphia Eagles (1947-55).

HUGH (SHORTY) RAY (Illinois), 1966, NFL technical adviser and supervisor of officials (1938-56).

DANIEL F. REEVES (Georgetown), 1967, founder, Los Angeles Rams (1941-71).

JOHN RIGGINS (Kansas), 1992, fullback, New York Jets (1971-75), Washington Redskins (1976-85).

JIM RINGO (Syracuse), 1981, center, Green Bay Packers (1953-63), Philadelphia Eagles (1964-67).

ANDY ROBUSTELLI (Arnold), 1971, defensive end, Los Angeles Rams (1951-55), New York Giants (1956-64).

ARTHUR J. ROONEY (Georgetown), 1964, founder, Pittsburgh Steelers (1933-82).

PETE ROZELLE (San Francisco), 1985, NFL Commissioner (1960-89).

BOB ST. CLAIR (Tulsa), 1990, tackle, San Francisco 49ers (1953-63).

GALE SAYERS (Kansas), 1977, running back, Chicago Bears (1965-71).

JOE SCHMIDT (Pittsburgh), 1973, linebacker, Detroit Lions (1953-65); coach, Detroit Lions (1967-72).

TEX SCHRAMM (Texas), 1991, president/general manager, Dallas Cowboys (1960-88).

LEE ROY SELMON (Oklahoma), 1995, defensive end, Tampa Bay Buccaneers (1976-84).

ART SHELL (Maryland-Eastern Shore), 1989, tackle, Oakland/Los Angeles Raiders (1968-82), coach, Los Angeles Raiders (1989-94).

O.J. SIMPSON (Southern California), 1985, running back, Buffalo Bills (1969-77), San Francisco 49ers (1978).

JACKIE SMITH (Northwestern Louisiana), 1994, tight end, St.

Louis Cardinals (1963-77), Dallas Cowboys (1978).

BART STARR (Alabama), 1977, quarterback, Green Bay Packers (1956-71); coach, Green Bay Packers (1975-83).

ROGER STAUBACH (Navy), 1985, quarterback, Dallas Cowboys (1969-79).

ERNIE STAUTNER (West Virginia), 1969, defensive tackle, Pittsburgh Steelers (1950-63).

JAN STENERUD (Montana State), 1991, placekicker, Kansas City Chiefs (1967-79), Green Bay Packers (1980-83), Minnesota Vikings (1984-85).

KEN STRONG (New York U.), 1967, halfback/placekicker, Staten Island Stapletons, New York Yankees, New York Giants (1929-39, 44-47).

JOE STYDAHAR (West Virginia), 1967, tackle, Chicago Bears (1936-42, 45-46).

FRAN TARKENTON (Georgia), 1986, quarterback, Minnesota Vikings (1961-66, 72-78), New York Giants (1967-71).

CHARLEY TAYLOR (Arizona State), 1984, wide receiver, Washington Redskins (1964-75, 77).

JIM TAYLOR (Louisiana State), 1976, fullback, Green Bay Packers (1958-66), New Orleans Saints (1967).

JIM THORPE (Carlisle), Charter 1963, halfback, Canton Bulldogs, Oorang Indians, Cleveland Indians, Toledo Maroons, Rock Island Independents, New York Giants (1915-26, 29).

Y.A. TITTLE (Louisiana State), 1971, quarterback, Baltimore Colts (1948-50), San Francisco 49ers (1951-60), New York Giants (1961-64).

GEORGE TRAFTON (Notre Dame), 1964, center, Chicago Bears (1920-32).

CHARLIE TRIPPI (Georgia), 1968, halfback, Chicago Cardinals (1947-55).

EMLEN TUNNELL (Iowa), 1967, defensive back, New York Giants, Green Bay Packers (1948-61).

CLYDE (BULLDOG) TURNER (Hardin-Simmons), 1966, center/linebacker, Chicago Bears (1940-52); coach, New York Titans (1962).

JOHN UNITAS (Louisville), 1979, quarterback, Baltimore Colts (1956-72), San Diego Chargers (1973).

GENE UPSHAW (Texas A&I), 1987, guard, Oakland Raiders (1967-81).

NORM VAN BROCKLIN (Oregon), 1971, quarterback, Los Angeles Rams (1949-57), Philadelphia Eagles (1958-60), coach, Minnesota Vikings (1961-66), Atlanta Falcons (1968-74).

STEVE VAN BUREN (Louisiana State), 1965, halfback, Philadelphia Eagles (1944-51).

DOAK WALKER (Southern Methodist), 1986, running back, Detroit Lions (1950-55).

BILL WALSH (San Jose State), 1993, coach, San Francisco 49ers (1979-88).

PAUL WARFIELD (Ohio State), 1983, receiver, Cleveland Browns (1964-69, 76-77), Miami Dolphins (1970-74).

BOB WATERFIELD (UCLA), 1965, quarterback, Cleveland Rams, Los Angeles Rams (1945-52); coach, Los Angeles Rams (1960-62).

ARNIE WEINMEISTER (Washington), 1984, tackle, New York Yankees (1948-49), New York Giants (1950-53).

RANDY WHITE (Maryland), 1994, defensive tackle, Dallas Cowboys (1975-88).

BILL WILLIS (Ohio State), 1977, guard, Cleveland Browns (1946-53).

LARRY WILSON (Utah), 1978, defensive back, St. Louis Cardinals (1960-72).

KELLEN WINSLOW (Missouri), 1995, tight end, San Diego Chargers (1979-87).

ALEX WOJCIECHOWICZ (Fordham), 1968, center/linebacker, Detroit Lions, Philadelphia Eagles (1938-50).

WILLIE WOOD (Southern California), 1989, safety, Green Bay Packers (1960-71).

The Sporting News® AWARDS

NFL EXECUTIVE OF THE YEAR

1955—Dan Reeves, L.A. Rams	1983—Bobby Beathard, Washington
1956—George Halas, Chicago	1984—George Young, N.Y. Giants
1972—Dan Rooney, Pittsburgh	1985—Mike McCaskey, Chicago
1973—Jim Finks, Minnesota	1986—George Young, N.Y. Giants
1974—Art Rooney, Pittsburgh	1987—Jim Finks, New Orleans
1975—Joe Thomas, Baltimore	1988—Bill Polian, Buffalo
1976—Al Davis, Oakland	1989—John McVay, San Francisco
1977—Tex Schramm, Dallas	1990—George Young, N.Y. Giants
1978—John Thompson, Seattle	1991—Bill Polian, Buffalo
1979—John Sanders, San Diego	1992—Ron Wolf, Green Bay
1980—Eddie LeBaron, Atlanta	1993—George Young, N.Y. Giants
1981—Paul Brown, Cincinnati	1994—Carmen Policy, San Francisco
1982—Bobby Beathard, Washington	

NOTE: The Executive of the Year Award was not given from 1957-71.

NFL COACH OF THE YEAR

1947—Jimmy Conzelman, Chi. Cardinals	1971—George Allen, Washington
1948—Earle (Greasy) Neale, Philadelphia	1972—Don Shula, Miami
1949—Paul Brown, Cleveland (AAFC)	1973—Chuck Knox, L.A. Rams
1950—Steve Owen, N.Y. Giants	1974—Don Coryell, St. Louis
1951—Paul Brown, Cleveland	1975—Ted Marchibroda, Baltimore
1952—J. Hampton Pool, L.A. Rams	1976—Chuck Fairbanks, New England
1953—Paul Brown, Cleveland	1977—Red Miller, Denver
1954—None	1978—Jack Patera, Seattle
1955—Joe Kuharich, Washington	1979—Dick Vermeil, Philadelphia
1956—Jim Lee Howell, N.Y. Giants	1980—Chuck Knox, Buffalo
1957—None	1981—Bill Walsh, San Francisco
1958—None	1982—Joe Gibbs, Washington
1959—None	1983—Joe Gibbs, Washington
1960—None	1984—Chuck Knox, Seattle
1961—Vince Lombardi, Green Bay	1985—Mike Ditka, Chicago
1962—None	1986—Bill Parcells, N.Y. Giants
1963—George Halas, Chicago	1987—Jim Mora, New Orleans
1964—Don Shula, Baltimore	1988—Marv Levy, Buffalo
1965—George Halas, Chicago	1989—Lindy Infante, Green Bay
1966—Tom Landry, Dallas	1990—George Seifert, San Francisco
1967—George Allen, L.A. Rams	1991—Joe Gibbs, Washington
1968—Don Shula, Baltimore	1992—Bill Cowher, Pittsburgh
1969—Bud Grant, Minnesota	1993—Dan Reeves, N.Y. Giants
1970—Don Shula, Miami	1994—George Seifert, San Francisco

ROOKIE OF THE YEAR

1955—Alan Ameche, FB, Baltimore	1975—NFC: Steve Bartkowski, QB, Atlanta
1956—J.C. Caroline, HB, Chicago	AFC: Robert Brazile, LB, Houston
1957—Jim Brown, FB, Cleveland	1976—NFC: Sammy White, WR, Minnesota
1958—Bobby Mitchell, HB, Cleveland	AFC: Mike Haynes, CB, New England
1959—Nick Pietrosante, FB, Detroit	1977—NFC: Tony Dorsett, RB, Dallas
1960—Gail Cogdill, E, Detroit	AFC: A.J. Duhe, DT, Miami
1961—Mike Ditka, E, Chicago	1978—NFC: Al Baker, DE, Detroit
1962—Ronnie Bull, HB, Chicago	AFC: Earl Campbell, RB, Houston
1963—Paul Flatley, WR, Minnesota	1979—NFC: Ottis Anderson, RB, St. Louis
1964—Charley Taylor, HB, Washington	AFC: Jerry Butler, WR, Buffalo
1965—Gale Sayers, RB, Chicago	1980—Billy Sims, RB, Detroit
1966—Tommy Nobis, LB, Atlanta	1981—George Rogers, RB, New Orleans
1967—Mel Farr, RB, Detroit	1982—Marcus Allen, RB, L.A. Raiders
1968—Earl McCullouch, WR, Detroit	1983—Dan Marino, QB, Miami
1969—Calvin Hill, RB, Dallas	1984—Louis Lipps, WR, Pittsburgh
1970—NFC: Bruce Taylor, CB, San Francisco	1985—Eddie Brown, WR, Cincinnati
AFC: Dennis Shaw, QB, Buffalo	1986—Rueben Mayes, RB, New Orleans
1971—NFC: John Brockington, RB, Green Bay	1987—Robert Awalt, TE, St. Louis
AFC: Jim Plunkett, QB, New England	1988—Keith Jackson, TE, Philadelphia
1972—NFC: Chester Marcol, PK, Green Bay	1989—Barry Sanders, RB, Detroit
AFC: Franco Harris, RB, Pittsburgh	1990—Richmond Webb, T, Miami
1973—NFC: Chuck Foreman, RB, Minnesota	1991—Mike Croel, LB, Denver
AFC: Boobie Clark, RB, Cincinnati	1992—Santana Dotson, DL, Tampa Bay
1974—NFC: Wilbur Jackson, RB, San Francisco	1993—Jerome Bettis, RB, L.A. Rams
AFC: Don Woods, RB, San Diego	1994—Marshall Faulk, RB, Indianapolis

NOTE: In 1980, The Sporting News began selecting one rookie as Rookie of the Year for the entire NFL.

PLAYER OF THE YEAR

1954—Lou Groza, OT/K, Cleveland
1955—Otto Graham, QB, Cleveland
1956—Frank Gifford, HB, N.Y. Giants
1957—Jim Brown, RB, Cleveland
1958—Jim Brown, RB, Cleveland
1959—Johnny Unitas, QB, Baltimore
1960—Norm Van Brocklin, QB, Philadelphia
1961—Paul Hornung, HB, Green Bay
1962—Y.A. Tittle, QB, N.Y. Giants
1963—Y.A. Tittle, QB, N.Y. Giants
1964—Johnny Unitas, QB, Baltimore
1965—Jim Brown, RB, Cleveland
1966—Bart Starr, QB, Green Bay
1967—Johnny Unitas, QB, Baltimore
1968—Earl Morrall, QB, Baltimore
1969—Roman Gabriel, QB, L.A. Rams
1970—NFC: John Brodie, QB, San Francisco
     AFC: George Blanda, QB/PK, Oakland
1971—NFC: Roger Staubach, QB, Dallas
     AFC: Bob Griese, QB, Miami
1972—NFC: Larry Brown, RB, Washington
     AFC: Earl Morrall, QB, Miami
1973—NFC: John Hadl, QB, L.A. Rams
     AFC: O.J. Simpson, RB, Buffalo
1974—NFC: Chuck Foreman, RB, Minnesota
     AFC: Ken Stabler, QB, Oakland

1975—NFC: Fran Tarkenton, QB, Minnesota
     AFC: O.J. Simpson, RB, Buffalo
1976—NFC: Walter Payton, RB, Chicago
     AFC: Ken Stabler, QB, Oakland
1977—NFC: Walter Payton, RB, Chicago
     AFC: Craig Morton, QB, Denver
1978—NFC: Archie Manning, QB, New Orleans
     AFC: Earl Campbell, RB, Houston
1979—NFC: Ottis Anderson, RB, St. Louis
     AFC: Dan Fouts, QB, San Diego
1980—Brian Sipe, QB, Cleveland
1981—Ken Anderson, QB, Cincinnati
1982—Mark Moseley, PK, Washington
1983—Eric Dickerson, RB, L.A. Rams
1984—Dan Marino, QB, Miami
1985—Marcus Allen, RB, L.A. Raiders
1986—Lawrence Taylor, LB, N.Y. Giants
1987—Jerry Rice, WR, San Francisco
1988—Boomer Esiason, QB, Cincinnati
1989—Joe Montana, QB, San Francisco
1990—Jerry Rice, WR, San Francisco
1991—Thurman Thomas, RB, Buffalo
1992—Steve Young, QB, San Francisco
1993—Emmitt Smith, RB, Dallas
1994—Steve Young, QB, San Francisco

NOTE: From 1970-79, a player was selected as Player of the Year for both the NFC and AFC. In 1980 The Sporting News reinstated the selection of one player as Player of the Year for the entire NFL.

1994 NFL ALL-PRO TEAM

OFFENSE

WR—Jerry Rice, San Francisco
    Cris Carter, Minnesota
TE—Ben Coates, New England
T—William Roaf, New Orleans
    Richmond Webb, Miami
C—Dermontti Dawson, Pittsburgh
G—Randall McDaniel, Minnesota
    Steve Wisniewski, L.A. Raiders
QB—Steve Young, San Francisco
RB—Barry Sanders, Detroit
    Emmitt Smith, Dallas

DEFENSE

DE—Charles Haley, Dallas
    Bruce Smith, Buffalo
DT—Chester McGlockton, L.A. Raiders
    John Randle, Minnesota
OLB—Kevin Greene, Pittsburgh
    Greg Lloyd, Pittsburgh
ILB—Junior Seau, San Diego
    Chris Spielman, Detroit
CB—Deion Sanders, San Francisco
    Rod Woodson, Pittsburgh
SS—Darren Woodson, Dallas
FS—Merton Hanks, San Francisco

SPECIALISTS

PR—Eric Metcalf, Cleveland
KR—Mel Gray, Detroit
K—John Carney, San Diego
P—Reggie Roby, Washington

TEAM HISTORIES

YEAR-BY-YEAR RECORDS

			REGULAR SEASON					PLAYOFFS		
Year	W	L	T	Pct.	PF	PA	Finish	W	L	Highest round	Coach
1920*	6	2	2	.750	...	...	T4th				Paddy Driscoll
1921*	3	3	2	.500	...	...	T8th				Paddy Driscoll
1922*	8	3	0	.727	...	...	3rd				Paddy Driscoll
1923*	8	4	0	.667	...	...	6th				Arnold Horween
1924*	5	4	1	.556	...	...	8th				Arnold Horween
1925*	11	2	1	.846	...	...	1st				Norman Barry
1926*	5	6	1	.455	...	...	10th				Norman Barry
1927*	3	7	1	.300	...	...	9th				Guy Chamberlin
1928*	1	5	0	.167	...	...	9th				Fred Gillies
1929*	6	6	1	.500	...	...	T4th				Dewey Scanlon
1930*	5	6	2	.455	...	...	T7th				Ernie Nevers
1931*	5	4	0	.556	...	...	4th				LeRoy Andrews, Ernie Nevers
1932*	2	6	2	.250	...	...	7th				Jack Chevigny
1933*	1	9	1	.100	52	101	5th/Western Div.	—	—		Paul Schissler
1934*	5	6	0	.455	80	84	4th/Western Div.	—	—		Paul Schissler
1935*	6	4	2	.600	99	97	T3rd/Western Div.	—	—		Milan Creighton
1936*	3	8	1	.273	74	143	4th/Western Div.	—	—		Milan Creighton
1937*	5	5	1	.500	135	165	4th/Western Div.	—	—		Milan Creighton
1938*	2	9	0	.182	111	168	5th/Western Div.	—	—		Milan Creighton
1939*	1	10	0	.091	84	254	5th/Western Div.	—	—		Ernie Nevers
1940*	2	7	2	.222	139	222	5th/Western Div.	—	—		Jimmy Conzelman
1941*	3	7	1	.300	127	197	4th/Western Div.	—	—		Jimmy Conzelman
1942*	3	8	0	.273	98	209	4th/Western Div.	—	—		Jimmy Conzelman
1943*	0	10	0	.000	95	238	4th/Western Div.	—	—		Phil Handler
1944†	0	10	0	.000	108	328	5th/Western Div.	—	—		Phil Handler-Walt Kiesling
1945*	1	9	0	.100	98	228	5th/Western Div.	—	—		Phil Handler
1946*	6	5	0	.545	260	198	T3rd/Western Div.	—	—		Jimmy Conzelman
1947*	9	3	0	.750	306	231	1st/Western Div.	1	0	NFL champ	Jimmy Conzelman
1948*	11	1	0	.917	395	226	1st/Western Div.	0	1	NFL championship game	Jimmy Conzelman
1949*	6	5	1	.545	360	301	3rd/Western Div.	—	—		Phil Handler-Buddy Parker
1950*	5	7	0	.417	233	287	5th/American Conf.	—	—		Curly Lambeau
1951*	3	9	0	.250	210	287	6th/American Conf.	—	—		Curly Lambeau, Phil Handler-Cecil Isbell
1952*	4	8	0	.333	172	221	T5th/American Conf.	—	—		Joe Kuharich
1953*	1	10	1	.091	190	337	6th/Eastern Conf.	—	—		Joe Stydahar
1954*	2	10	0	.167	183	347	6th/Eastern Conf.	—	—		Joe Stydahar
1955*	4	7	1	.364	224	252	T4th/Eastern Conf.	—	—		Ray Richards
1956*	7	5	0	.583	240	182	2nd/Eastern Conf.	—	—		Ray Richards
1957*	3	9	0	.250	200	299	6th/Eastern Conf.	—	—		Ray Richards
1958*	2	9	1	.182	261	356	T5th/Eastern Conf.	—	—		Pop Ivy
1959*	2	10	0	.167	234	324	6th/Eastern Conf.	—	—		Pop Ivy
1960‡	6	5	1	.545	288	230	4th/Eastern Conf.	—	—		Pop Ivy
1961‡	7	7	0	.500	279	267	4th/Eastern Conf.	—	—		Pop Ivy
1962‡	4	9	1	.308	287	361	6th/Eastern Conf.	—	—		Wally Lemm
1963‡	9	5	0	.643	341	283	3rd/Eastern Conf.	—	—		Wally Lemm
1964‡	9	3	2	.750	357	331	2nd/Eastern Conf.	—	—		Wally Lemm
1965‡	5	9	0	.357	296	309	T5th/Eastern Conf.	—	—		Wally Lemm
1966‡	8	5	1	.615	264	265	4th/Eastern Conf.	—	—		Charley Winner
1967‡	6	7	1	.462	333	356	3rd/Century Div.	—	—		Charley Winner
1968‡	9	4	1	.692	325	289	2nd/Century Div.	—	—		Charley Winner
1969‡	4	9	1	.308	314	389	3rd/Century Div.	—	—		Charley Winner
1970‡	8	5	1	.615	325	228	3rd/NFC Eastern Div.	—	—		Charley Winner
1971‡	4	9	1	.308	231	279	4th/NFC Eastern Div.	—	—		Bob Hollway
1972‡	4	9	1	.308	193	303	4th/NFC Eastern Div.	—	—		Bob Hollway
1973‡	4	9	1	.308	286	365	4th/NFC Eastern Div.	—	—		Don Coryell
1974‡	10	4	0	.714	285	218	1st/NFC Eastern Div.	0	1	NFC div. playoff game	Don Coryell
1975‡	11	3	0	.786	356	276	1st/NFC Eastern Div.	0	1	NFC div. playoff game	Don Coryell
1976‡	10	4	0	.714	309	267	3rd/NFC Eastern Div.	—	—		Don Coryell
1977‡	7	7	0	.500	272	287	3rd/NFC Eastern Div.	—	—		Don Coryell
1978‡	6	10	0	.375	248	296	T4th/NFC Eastern Div.	—	—		Bud Wilkinson
1979‡	5	11	0	.313	307	358	5th/NFC Eastern Div.	—	—		Bud Wilkinson, Larry Wilson
1980‡	5	11	0	.313	299	350	4th/NFC Eastern Div.	—	—		Jim Hanifan
1981‡	7	9	0	.438	315	408	5th/NFC Eastern Div.	—	—		Jim Hanifan
1982‡	5	4	0	.556	135	170	T4th/NFC	0	1	NFC first-round pl. game	Jim Hanifan
1983‡	8	7	1	.531	374	428	3rd/NFC Eastern Div.	—	—		Jim Hanifan

Year	W	L	T	Pct.	PF	PA	Finish	W	L	Highest round	Coach
							REGULAR SEASON			**PLAYOFFS**	
1984‡	9	7	0	.563	423	345	T3rd/NFC Eastern Div.	—	—		Jim Hanifan
1985‡	5	11	0	.313	278	414	5th/NFC Eastern Div.	—	—		Jim Hanifan
1986‡	4	11	1	.281	218	351	5th/NFC Eastern Div.	—	—		Gene Stallings
1987‡	7	8	0	.467	362	368	T2nd/NFC Eastern Div.	—	—		Gene Stallings
1988§	7	9	0	.438	344	398	T3rd/NFC Eastern Div.	—	—		Gene Stallings
1989§	5	11	0	.313	258	377	4th/NFC Eastern Div.	—	—		G. Stallings, Hank Kuhlmann
1990§	5	11	0	.313	268	396	5th/NFC Eastern Div.	—	—		Joe Bugel
1991§	4	12	0	.250	196	344	5th/NFC Eastern Div.	—	—		Joe Bugel
1992§	4	12	0	.250	243	332	5th/NFC Eastern Div.	—	—		Joe Bugel
1993§	7	9	0	.438	326	366	4th/NFC Eastern Div.	—	—		Joe Bugel
1994	8	8	0	.500	235	267	3rd/NFC Eastern Div.	—	—		Buddy Ryan

*Chicago Cardinals.
†Card-Pitt, a combined squad of Chicago Cardinals and Pittsburgh Steelers.
‡St. Louis Cardinals.
§Phoenix Cardinals.

FIRST-ROUND DRAFT PICKS

1936—Jim Lawrence, B, Texas Christian
1937—Ray Buivid, B, Marquette
1938—Jack Robbins, B, Arkansas
1939—Charles Aldrich, C, Texas Christian*
1940—George Cafego, B, Tennessee*
1941—John Kimbrough, B, Texas A&M
1942—Steve Lach, B, Duke
1943—Glenn Dobbs, B, Tulsa
1944—Pat Harder, B, Wisconsin
1945—Charley Trippi, B, Georgia*
1946—Dub Jones, B, Louisiana State
1947—DeWitt (Tex) Coulter, T, Army
1948—Jim Spavital, B, Oklahoma A&M
1949—Bill Fischer, G, Notre Dame
1950—None
1951—Jerry Groom, C, Notre Dame
1952—Ollie Matson, B, San Francisco
1953—Johnny Olszewski, QB, California
1954—Lamar McHan, B, Arkansas
1955—Max Boydston, E, Oklahoma
1956—Joe Childress, B, Auburn
1957—Jerry Tubbs, C, Oklahoma
1958—King Hill, B, Rice*
1959—Billy Stacy, B, Mississippi State
1960—George Izo, QB, Notre Dame
1961—Ken Rice, T, Auburn
1962—Fate Echols, DT, Northwestern
      Irv Goode, C, Kentucky
1963—Jerry Stovall, DB, Louisiana State
      Don Brumm, E, Purdue
1964—Ken Kortas, DT, Louisville
1965—Joe Namath, QB, Alabama
1966—Carl McAdams, LB, Oklahoma
1967—Dave Williams, WR, Washington

1968—MacArthur Lane, RB, Utah State
1969—Roger Wehrli, DB, Missouri
1970—Larry Stegent, RB, Texas A&M
1971—Norm Thompson, DB, Utah
1972—Bobby Moore, RB, Oregon
1973—Dave Butz, DT, Purdue
1974—J.V. Cain, TE, Colorado
1975—Tim Gray, DB, Texas A&M
1976—Mike Dawson, DT, Arizona
1977—Steve Pisarkiewicz, QB, Missouri
1978—Steve Little, K, Arkansas
      Ken Greene, DB, Washington St.
1979—Ottis Anderson, RB, Miami (Fla.)
1980—Curtis Greer, DE, Michigan
1981—E.J. Junior, LB, Alabama
1982—Luis Sharpe, T, UCLA
1983—Leonard Smith, DB, McNeese State
1984—Clyde Duncan, WR, Tennessee
1985—Freddie Joe Nunn, LB, Miss.
1986—Anthony Bell, LB, Michigan St.
1987—Kelly Stouffer, QB, Colorado St.
1988—Ken Harvey, LB, California
1989—Eric Hill, LB, Louisiana State
      Joe Wolf, G, Boston College
1990—None
1991—Eric Swann, DL, None
1992—None
1993—Garrison Hearst, RB, Georgia
      Ernest Dye, T, South Carolina
1994—Jamir Miller, LB, UCLA
1995—None
      *First player chosen in draft.

FRANCHISE RECORDS

Most rushing yards, career
7,999—Ottis Anderson

Most rushing yards, season
1,605—Ottis Anderson, 1979

Most rushing yards, game
203—John David Crow vs. Pit., Dec. 18, 1960

Most rushing touchdowns, season
14—John David Crow, 1962

Most passing attempts, season
560—Neil Lomax, 1984

Most passing attempts, game
61—Neil Lomax at S.D., Sept. 20, 1987

Most passes completed, season
345—Neil Lomax, 1984

Most passes completed, game
37—Neil Lomax at Was., Dec. 16, 1984

Most passing yards, career
34,639—Jim Hart

Most passing yards, season
4,614—Neil Lomax, 1984

Most passing yards, game
468—Neil Lomax at Was., Dec. 16, 1984

Most touchdown passes, season
28—Charley Johnson, 1963
   Neil Lomax, 1984

Most pass receptions, career
522—Roy Green

Most pass receptions, season
91—J.T. Smith, 1987

Most pass receptions, game
16—Sonny Randle at NYG, Nov. 4, 1962

Most receiving yards, career
8,497—Roy Green

Most receiving yards, season
1,555—Roy Green, 1984

Most receiving yards, game
256—Sonny Randle vs. NYG, Nov. 4, 1962

Most receiving touchdowns, season
16—Sonny Randle, 1960
Most touchdowns, career
66—Roy Green
Most field goals, season
27—Jim Bakken, 1967

Longest field goal
55 yards—Greg Davis at Sea., Dec. 19, 1993
Most interceptions, career
52—Larry Wilson

Most interceptions, season
12—Bob Nussbaumer, 1949

SERIES RECORDS

Arizona vs.: Atlanta 11-6; Buffalo 3-3; Chicago 25-54-6; Cincinnati 2-3; Cleveland 10-32-3; Dallas 22-42-1; Denver 0-3-1; Detroit 14-28-3; Green Bay 21-41-4; Houston 4-2; Indianapolis 6-5; Kansas City 1-3-1; L.A. Raiders 1-2; L.A. Rams 12-16-2; Miami 0-6; Minnesota 8-4; New England 6-2; New Orleans 10-9; N.Y. Giants 36-67-2; N.Y. Jets 2-1; Philadelphia 45-45-5; Pittsburgh 22-29-3; San Diego 1-5; San Francisco 9-10; Seattle 4-0; Tampa Bay 6-6; Washington 36-58-1.

NOTE: Includes records for entire franchise, from 1920 to present.

RETIRED UNIFORM NUMBERS

No.	Player
8	Larry Wilson
77	Stan Mauldin
88	J.V. Cain
99	Marshall Goldberg

ATLANTA FALCONS

YEAR-BY-YEAR RECORDS

			REGULAR SEASON					PLAYOFFS		
Year	W	L	T	Pct.	PF	PA	Finish	W	L	Highest round	Coach
1966	3	11	0	.214	204	437	7th/Eastern Conf.	—	—		Norb Hecker
1967	1	12	1	.077	175	422	4th/Coastal Div.	—	—		Norb Hecker
1968	2	12	0	.143	170	389	4th/Coastal Div.	—	—		N. Hecker, N. Van Brocklin
1969	6	8	0	.429	276	268	3rd/Coastal Div.	—	—		Norm Van Brocklin
1970	4	8	2	.333	206	261	3rd/NFC Western Div.	—	—		Norm Van Brocklin
1971	7	6	1	.538	274	277	3rd/NFC Western Div.	—	—		Norm Van Brocklin
1972	7	7	0	.500	269	274	2nd/NFC Western Div.	—	—		Norm Van Brocklin
1973	9	5	0	.643	318	224	2nd/NFC Western Div.	—	—		Norm Van Brocklin
1974	3	11	0	.214	111	271	4th/NFC Western Div.	—	—		N. Van Brocklin, M. Campbell
1975	4	10	0	.286	240	289	3rd/NFC Western Div.	—	—		Marion Campbell
1976	4	10	0	.286	172	312	T3rd/NFC Western Div.	—	—		M. Campbell, Pat Peppler
1977	7	7	0	.500	179	129	2nd/NFC Western Div.	—	—		Leeman Bennett
1978	9	7	0	.563	240	290	2nd/NFC Western Div.	1	1	NFC div. playoff game	Leeman Bennett
1979	6	10	0	.375	300	388	3rd/NFC Western Div.	—	—		Leeman Bennett
1980	12	4	0	.750	405	272	1st/NFC Western Div.	0	1	NFC div. playoff game	Leeman Bennett
1981	7	9	0	.438	426	355	2nd/NFC Western Div.	—	—		Leeman Bennett
1982	5	4	0	.556	183	199	T4th/NFC	0	1	NFC first-round pl. game	Leeman Bennett
1983	7	9	0	.438	370	389	4th/NFC Western Div.	—	—		Dan Henning
1984	4	12	0	.250	281	382	4th/NFC Western Div.	—	—		Dan Henning
1985	4	12	0	.250	282	452	4th/NFC Western Div.	—	—		Dan Henning
1986	7	8	1	.469	280	280	3rd/NFC Western Div.	—	—		Dan Henning
1987	3	12	0	.200	205	436	4th/NFC Western Div.	—	—		Marion Campbell
1988	5	11	0	.313	244	315	4th/NFC Western Div.	—	—		Marion Campbell
1989	3	13	0	.188	279	437	4th/NFC Western Div.	—	—		M. Campbell, Jim Hanifan
1990	5	11	0	.313	348	365	T3rd/NFC Western Div.	—	—		Jerry Glanville
1991	10	6	0	.625	361	338	2nd/NFC Western Div.	1	1	NFC div. playoff game	Jerry Glanville
1992	6	10	0	.375	327	414	T3rd/NFC Western Div.	—	—		Jerry Glanville
1993	6	10	0	.375	316	385	3rd/NFC Western Div.	—	—		Jerry Glanville
1994	7	9	0	.438	313	389	T2nd/NFC Western Div.	—	—		June Jones

FIRST-ROUND DRAFT PICKS

1966—Tommy Nobis, LB, Texas*
      Randy Johnson, QB, Texas A&I
1967—None
1968—Claude Humphrey, DE, Tennessee State
1969—George Kunz, T, Notre Dame
1970—John Small, LB, Citadel
1971—Joe Profit, RB, Northeast Louisiana State
1972—Clarence Ellis, DB, Notre Dame
1973—None
1974—None
1975—Steve Bartkowski, QB, California*
1976—Bubba Bean, RB, Texas A&M
1977—Warren Bryant, T, Kentucky
      Wilson Faumuina, DT, San Jose State
1978—Mike Kenn, T, Michigan
1979—Don Smith, DE, Miami (Fla.)

1980—Junior Miller, TE, Nebraska
1981—Bobby Butler, DB, Florida State
1982—Gerald Riggs, RB, Arizona State
1983—Mike Pitts, DE, Alabama
1984—Rick Bryan, DT, Oklahoma
1985—Bill Fralic, T, Pittsburgh
1986—Tony Casillas, DT, Oklahoma
      Tim Green, LB, Syracuse
1987—Chris Miller, QB, Oregon
1988—Aundray Bruce, LB, Auburn*
1989—Deion Sanders, DB, Florida State
      Shawn Collins, WR, Northern Arizona
1990—Steve Broussard, RB, Washington State
1991—Bruce Pickens, CB, Nebraska
      Mike Pritchard, WR, Colorado

1992—Bob Whitfield, T, Stanford
      Tony Smith, RB, Southern Mississippi
1993—Lincoln Kennedy, T, Washington

1994—None
1995—Devin Bush, DB, Florida State
   *First player chosen in draft.

FRANCHISE RECORDS

Most rushing yards, career
6,631—Gerald Riggs
Most rushing yards, season
1,719—Gerald Riggs, 1985
Most rushing yards, game
202—Gerald Riggs at N.O., Sept. 2, 1984
Most rushing touchdowns, season
13—Gerald Riggs, 1984
Most passing attempts, season
533—Steve Bartkowski, 1981
Most passing attempts, game
66—Chris Miller vs. Det., Dec. 24, 1989
Most passes completed, season
322—Jeff George, 1994
Most passes completed, game
37—Chris Miller vs. Det., Dec. 24, 1989
Most passing yards, career
23,468—Steve Bartkowski
Most passing yards, season
3,830—Steve Bartkowski, 1981
Most passing yards, game
416—Steve Bartkowski vs. Pit., Nov. 15, 1981

Most touchdown passes, season
31—Steve Bartkowski, 1980
Most pass receptions, career
423—Andre Rison
Most pass receptions, season
111—Terance Mathis, 1994
Most pass receptions, game
15—William Andrews vs. Pit., Nov. 15, 1981
Most receiving yards, career
6,257—Alfred Jenkins
Most receiving yards, season
1,358—Alfred Jenkins, 1981
Most receiving yards, game
193—Alfred Jackson vs. S.F., Dec. 2, 1984
      Andre Rison at Det., Sept. 4, 1994
Most receiving touchdowns, season
15—Andre Rison, 1993
Most touchdowns, career
56—Andre Rison

Most field goals, season
26—Nick Mike-Mayer, 1973
      Norm Johnson, 1991
Longest field goal
54 yards—Paul McFadden at Buf., Nov. 5, 1989
      Norm Johnson vs. NYJ, Sept. 6, 1992
      Norm Johnson vs. N.E., Nov. 29, 1992
      Norm Johnson at Det., Sept. 5, 1993
Most interceptions, career
39—Rolland Lawrence
Most interceptions, season
10—Scott Case, 1988
Most sacks, career
62.5—Claude Humphrey
Most sacks, season
16—Joel Williams, 1980

SERIES RECORDS

Atlanta vs.: Arizona 6-11; Buffalo 3-3; Chicago 9-9; Cincinnati 2-6; Cleveland 2-8; Dallas 6-9; Denver 3-5; Detroit 5-18; Green Bay 9-10; Houston 5-3; Indianapolis 0-10; Kansas City 0-4; L.A. Raiders 3-5; L.A. Rams 18-36-1; Miami 1-5; Minnesota 6-12; New England 4-3; New Orleans 27-24; N.Y. Giants 6-6; N.Y. Jets 3-3; Philadelphia 7-8-1; Pittsburgh 1-9; San Diego 4-1; San Francisco 21-34-1; Seattle 1-4; Tampa Bay 7-6; Washington 4-13-1.

RETIRED UNIFORM NUMBERS

No.	Player
10	Steve Bartkowski
31	William Andrews
57	Jeff Van Note
60	Tommy Nobis

BUFFALO BILLS

YEAR-BY-YEAR RECORDS

| | | REGULAR SEASON | | | | | | PLAYOFFS | | |
Year	W	L	T	Pct.	PF	PA	Finish	W	L	Highest round	Coach
1960*	5	8	1	.385	296	303	3rd/Eastern Div.	—	—		Buster Ramsey
1961*	6	8	0	.429	294	342	4th/Eastern Div.	—	—		Buster Ramsey
1962*	7	6	1	.538	309	272	3rd/Eastern Div.	—	—		Lou Saban
1963*	7	6	1	.538	304	291	2nd/Eastern Div.	0	1	E. Div. championship game	Lou Saban
1964*	12	2	0	.857	400	242	1st/Eastern Div.	1	0	AFL champ	Lou Saban
1965*	10	3	1	.769	313	226	1st/Eastern Div.	1	0	AFL champ	Lou Saban
1966*	9	4	1	.692	358	255	1st/Eastern Div.	0	1	AFL championship game	Joe Collier
1967*	4	10	0	.286	237	285	T3rd/Eastern Div.	—	—		Joe Collier
1968*	1	12	1	.077	199	367	5th/Eastern Div.	—	—		Joe Collier, Harvey Johnson
1969*	4	10	0	.286	230	359	T3rd/Eastern Div.	—	—		John Rauch
1970	3	10	1	.231	204	337	4th/AFC Eastern Div.	—	—		John Rauch
1971	1	13	0	.071	184	394	5th/AFC Eastern Div.	—	—		Harvey Johnson
1972	4	9	1	.321	257	377	4th/AFC Eastern Div.	—	—		Lou Saban
1973	9	5	0	.643	259	230	2nd/AFC Eastern Div.	—	—		Lou Saban
1974	9	5	0	.643	264	244	2nd/AFC Eastern Div.	0	1	AFC div. playoff game	Lou Saban
1975	8	6	0	.571	420	355	3rd/AFC Eastern Div.	—	—		Lou Saban
1976	2	12	0	.143	245	363	5th/AFC Eastern Div.	—	—		Lou Saban, Jim Ringo
1977	3	11	0	.214	160	313	T4th/AFC Eastern Div.	—	—		Jim Ringo
1978	5	11	0	.313	302	354	T4th/AFC Eastern Div.	—	—		Chuck Knox
1979	7	9	0	.438	268	279	4th/AFC Eastern Div.	—	—		Chuck Knox
1980	11	5	0	.688	320	260	1st/AFC Eastern Div.	0	1	AFC div. playoff game	Chuck Knox
1981	10	6	0	.625	311	276	3rd/AFC Eastern Div.	1	1	AFC div. playoff game	Chuck Knox

Year	W	L	T	Pct.	PF	PA	Finish	W	L	Highest round	Coach
1982	4	5	0	.444	150	154	T8th/AFC	—	—		Chuck Knox
1983	8	8	0	.500	283	351	T2nd/AFC Eastern Div.	—	—		Kay Stephenson
1984	2	14	0	.125	250	454	5th/AFC Eastern Div.	—	—		Kay Stephenson
1985	2	14	0	.125	200	381	5th/AFC Eastern Div.	—	—		Hank Bullough
1986	4	12	0	.250	287	348	4th/AFC Eastern Div.	—	—		Hank Bullough, Marv Levy
1987	7	8	0	.467	270	305	4th/AFC Eastern Div.	—	—		Marv Levy
1988	12	4	0	.750	329	237	1st/AFC Eastern Div.	1	1	AFC championship game	Marv Levy
1989	9	7	0	.563	409	317	1st/AFC Eastern Div.	0	1	AFC div. playoff game	Marv Levy
1990	13	3	0	.813	428	263	1st/AFC Eastern Div.	2	1	Super Bowl	Marv Levy
1991	13	3	0	.813	458	318	1st/AFC Eastern Div.	2	1	Super Bowl	Marv Levy
1992	11	5	0	.688	381	283	2nd/AFC Eastern Div.	3	1	Super Bowl	Marv Levy
1993	12	4	0	.750	329	242	1st/AFC Eastern Div.	2	1	Super Bowl	Marv Levy
1994	7	9	0	.438	340	356	4th/AFC Eastern Div.	—	—		Marv Levy

*American Football League.

FIRST-ROUND DRAFT PICKS

1960—Richie Lucas, QB, Penn State
1961—Ken Rice, T, Auburn* (AFL)
1962—Ernie Davis, RB, Syracuse
1963—Dave Behrman, C, Michigan State
1964—Carl Eller, DE, Minnesota
1965—Jim Davidson, T, Ohio State
1966—Mike Dennis, RB, Mississippi
1967—John Pitts, DB, Arizona State
1968—Haven Moses, WR, San Diego St.
1969—O.J. Simpson, RB, Southern California*
1970—Al Cowlings, DE, Southern California
1971—J.D. Hill, WR, Arizona State
1972—Walt Patulski, DE, Notre Dame*
1973—Paul Seymour, T, Michigan
      Joe DeLamielleure, G, Michigan State
1974—Reuben Gant, TE, Oklahoma State
1975—Tom Ruud, LB, Nebraska
1976—Mario Clark, DB, Oregon
1977—Phil Dokes, DT, Oklahoma State
1978—Terry Miller, RB, Oklahoma State
1979—Tom Cousineau, LB, Ohio State*
      Jerry Butler, WR, Clemson

1980—Jim Ritcher, C, North Carolina State
1981—Booker Moore, RB, Penn State
1982—Perry Tuttle, WR, Clemson
1983—Tony Hunter, TE, Notre Dame
      Jim Kelly, QB, Miami (Fla.)
1984—Greg Bell, RB, Notre Dame
1985—Bruce Smith, DT, Virginia Tech*
      Derrick Burroughs, DB, Memphis State
1986—Ronnie Harmon, RB, Iowa
      Will Wolford, T, Vanderbilt
1987—Shane Conlan, LB, Penn State
1988—None
1989—None
1990—James Williams, DB, Fresno State
1991—Henry Jones, S, Illinois
1992—John Fina, T, Arizona
1993—Thomas Smith, DB, North Carolina
1994—Jeff Burris, DB, Notre Dame
1995—Ruben Brown, G, Pittsburgh

   *First player chosen in draft.

FRANCHISE RECORDS

Most rushing yards, career
10,183—O.J. Simpson

Most rushing yards, season
2,003—O.J. Simpson, 1973

Most rushing yards, game
273—O.J. Simpson at Det., Nov. 25, 1976

Most rushing touchdowns, season
16—O.J. Simpson, 1975

Most passing attempts, season
508—Joe Ferguson, 1983

Most passing attempts, game
55—Joe Ferguson at Mia., Oct. 9, 1983

Most passes completed, season
304—Jim Kelly, 1991

Most passes completed, game
38—Joe Ferguson at Mia., Oct. 9, 1983

Most passing yards, career
29,527—Jim Kelly

Most passing yards, season
3,844—Jim Kelly, 1991

Most passing yards, game
419—Joe Ferguson at Mia., Oct. 9, 1983

Most touchdown passes, season
33—Jim Kelly, 1991

Most pass receptions, career
676—Andre Reed

Most pass receptions, season
90—Andre Reed, 1994

Most pass receptions, game
15—Andre Reed vs. G.B., Nov. 20, 1994

Most receiving yards, career
9,536—Andre Reed

Most receiving yards, season
1,312—Andre Reed, 1989

Most receiving yards, game
255—Jerry Butler vs. NYJ, Sept. 23, 1979

Most receiving touchdowns, season
10—Elbert Dubenion, 1964
     Bob Chandler, 1976
     Andre Reed, 1991

Most touchdowns, career
70—O.J. Simpson

Most field goals, season
32—Scott Norwood, 1988

Longest field goal
59 yards—Steve Christie vs. Mia., Sept. 26, 1993

Most interceptions, career
40—George Byrd

Most interceptions, season
10—Billy Atkins, 1961
     Tom Janik, 1967

Most sacks, career
116—Bruce Smith

Most sacks, season
19—Bruce Smith, 1990

Buffalo vs.: Arizona 3-3; Atlanta 3-3; Chicago 2-4; Cincinnati 7-10; Cleveland 3-7; Dallas 2-3; Denver 17-10-1; Detroit 1-3-1; Green Bay 5-1; Houston 13-20; Indianapolis 26-22-1; Kansas City 16-13-1; L.A. Raiders 14-15; L.A. Rams 3-3; Miami 20-37-1; Minnesota 2-5; New England 34-35-1; New Orleans 3-2; N.Y. Giants 4-2; N.Y. Jets 38-31; Philadelphia 3-4; Pittsburgh 7-7; San Diego 7-16-2; San Francisco 3-2; Seattle 1-3; Tampa Bay 2-4; Washington 3-4.

No. Player
None

CHICAGO BEARS

YEAR-BY-YEAR RECORDS

			REGULAR SEASON						PLAYOFFS		
Year	W	L	T	Pct.	PF	PA	Finish	W	L	Highest round	Coach
1920*	10	1	2	.909	...	...	2nd				George Halas
1921†	9	1	1	.900	...	...	1st				George Halas
1922	9	3	0	.750	...	...	2nd				George Halas
1923	9	2	1	.818	...	...	2nd				George Halas
1924	6	1	4	.857	...	...	2nd				George Halas
1925	9	5	3	.643	...	...	7th				George Halas
1926	12	1	3	.923	...	...	2nd				George Halas
1927	9	3	2	.750	...	...	3rd				George Halas
1928	7	5	1	.583	...	...	5th				George Halas
1929	4	9	2	.308	...	...	9th				George Halas
1930	9	4	1	.692	...	...	3rd				Ralph Jones
1931	8	5	0	.615	...	...	3rd				Ralph Jones
1932	7	1	6	.875	...	...	1st				Ralph Jones
1933	10	2	1	.833	133	82	1st/Western Div.	1	0	NFL champ	George Halas
1934	13	0	0	1.000	286	86	1st/Western Div.	0	1	NFL championship game	George Halas
1935	6	4	2	.600	192	106	T3rd/Western Div.	—	—		George Halas
1936	9	3	0	.750	222	94	2nd/Western Div.	—	—		George Halas
1937	9	1	1	.900	201	100	1st/Western Div.	0	1	NFL championship game	George Halas
1938	6	5	0	.545	194	148	3rd/Western Div.	—	—		George Halas
1939	8	3	0	.727	298	157	2nd/Western Div.	—	—		George Halas
1940	8	3	0	.727	238	152	1st/Western Div.	1	0	NFL champ	George Halas
1941	10	1	0	.909	396	147	1st/Western Div.	2	0	NFL champ	George Halas
1942	11	0	0	1.000	376	84	1st/Western Div.	0	1	NFL championship game	George Halas, Hunk Anderson-Luke Johnsos
1943	8	1	1	.889	303	157	1st/Western Div.	0	1	NFL champ	H. Anderson-Luke Johnsos
1944	6	3	1	.667	258	172	T2nd/Western Div.	—	—		H. Anderson-Luke Johnsos
1945	3	7	0	.300	192	235	4th/Western Div.	—	—		H. Anderson-Luke Johnsos
1946	8	2	1	.800	289	193	1st/Western Div.	1	0	NFL champ	George Halas
1947	8	4	0	.667	363	241	2nd/Western Div.	—	—		George Halas
1948	10	2	0	.833	375	151	2nd/Western Div.	—	—		George Halas
1949	9	3	0	.750	332	218	2nd/Western Div.	—	—		George Halas
1950	9	3	0	.750	279	207	2nd/National Conf.	0	1	Nat. Conf. champ. game	George Halas
1951	7	5	0	.583	286	282	4th/National Conf.	—	—		George Halas
1952	5	7	0	.417	245	326	5th/National Conf.	—	—		George Halas
1953	3	8	1	.273	218	262	T4th/Western Conf.	—	—		George Halas
1954	8	4	0	.667	301	279	2nd/Western Conf.	—	—		George Halas
1955	8	4	0	.667	294	251	2nd/Western Conf.	—	—		George Halas
1956	9	2	1	.818	363	246	1st/Western Conf.	0	1	NFL championship game	Paddy Driscoll
1957	5	7	0	.417	203	211	5th/Western Conf.	—	—		Paddy Driscoll
1958	8	4	0	.667	298	230	T2nd/Western Conf.	—	—		George Halas
1959	8	4	0	.667	252	196	2nd/Western Conf.	—	—		George Halas
1960	5	6	1	.455	194	299	5th/Western Conf.	—	—		George Halas
1961	8	6	0	.571	326	302	T3rd/Western Conf.	—	—		George Halas
1962	9	5	0	.643	321	287	3rd/Western Conf.	—	—		George Halas
1963	11	1	2	.917	301	144	1st/Western Conf.	1	0	NFL champ	George Halas
1964	5	9	0	.357	260	379	6th/Western Conf.	—	—		George Halas
1965	9	5	0	.643	409	275	3rd/Western Conf.	—	—		George Halas
1966	5	7	2	.417	234	272	5th/Western Conf.	—	—		George Halas
1967	7	6	1	.538	239	218	2nd/Central Div.	—	—		George Halas
1968	7	7	0	.500	250	333	2nd/Central Div.	—	—		Jim Dooley
1969	1	13	0	.071	210	339	4th/Central Div.	—	—		Jim Dooley
1970	6	8	0	.429	256	261	T3rd/NFC Central Div.	—	—		Jim Dooley
1971	6	8	0	.429	185	276	3rd/NFC Central Div.	—	—		Jim Dooley
1972	4	9	1	.321	225	275	4th/NFC Central Div.	—	—		Abe Gibron
1973	3	11	0	.214	195	334	4th/NFC Central Div.	—	—		Abe Gibron
1974	4	10	0	.286	152	279	4th/NFC Central Div.	—	—		Abe Gibron
1975	4	10	0	.286	191	379	T3rd/NFC Central Div.	—	—		Jack Pardee
1976	7	7	0	.500	253	216	2nd/NFC Central Div.	—	—		Jack Pardee
1977	9	5	0	.643	255	253	2nd/NFC Central Div.	0	1	NFC div. playoff game	Jack Pardee
1978	7	9	0	.438	253	274	T3rd/NFC Central Div.	—	—		Neill Armstrong

				REGULAR SEASON					PLAYOFFS		
Year	W	L	T	Pct.	PF	PA	Finish	W	L	Highest round	Coach
1979	10	6	0	.625	306	249	2nd/NFC Central Div.	0	1	AFC wild-card game	Neill Armstrong
1980	7	9	0	.438	304	264	3rd/NFC Central Div.	—	—		Neill Armstrong
1981	6	10	0	.375	253	324	5th/NFC Central Div.	—	—		Neill Armstrong
1982	3	6	0	.333	141	174	T11th/NFC	—	—		Mike Ditka
1983	8	8	0	.500	311	301	T2nd/NFC Central Div.	—	—		Mike Ditka
1984	10	6	0	.625	325	248	1st/NFC Central Div.	1	1	NFC championship game	Mike Ditka
1985	15	1	0	.938	456	198	1st/NFC Central Div.	3	0	Super Bowl champ	Mike Ditka
1986	14	2	0	.875	352	187	1st/NFC Central Div.	0	1	NFC div. playoff game	Mike Ditka
1987	11	4	0	.733	356	282	1st/NFC Central Div.	0	1	NFC div. playoff game	Mike Ditka
1988	12	4	0	.750	312	215	1st/NFC Central Div.	1	1	NFC championship game	Mike Ditka
1989	6	10	0	.375	358	377	4th/NFC Central Div.	—	—		Mike Ditka
1990	11	5	0	.688	348	280	1st/NFC Central Div.	1	1	NFC div. playoff game	Mike Ditka
1991	11	5	0	.688	299	269	2nd/NFC Central Div.	0	1	NFC wild-card game	Mike Ditka
1992	5	11	0	.313	295	361	T3rd/NFC Central Div.	—	—		Mike Ditka
1993	7	9	0	.438	234	230	4th/NFC Central Div.	—	—		Dave Wannstedt
1994	9	7	0	.563	271	307	T2nd/NFC Central Div.	1	1	NFC div. playoff game	Dave Wannstedt

*Decatur Staleys.
†Chicago Staleys.

FIRST-ROUND DRAFT PICKS

1936 — Joe Stydahar, T, West Virginia
1937 — Les McDonald, E, Nebraska
1938 — Joe Gray, B, Oregon State
1939 — Sid Luckman, B, Columbia
        Bill Osmanski, B, Holy Cross
1940 — C. Turner, C, Hardin-Simmons
1941 — Tom Harmon, B, Michigan*
        Norm Standlee, B, Stanford
        Don Scott, B, Ohio State
1942 — Frankie Albert, B, Stanford
1943 — Bob Steuber, B, Missouri
1944 — Ray Evans, B, Kansas
1945 — Don Lund, B, Michigan
1946 — Johnny Lujack, QB, Notre Dame
1947 — Bob Fenimore, B, Oklahoma A&M*
1948 — Bobby Layne, QB, Texas
        Max Baumgardner, E, Texas
1949 — Dick Harris, C, Texas
1950 — Chuck Hunsinger, B, Florida
1951 — Bob Williams, B, Notre Dame
        Billy Stone, B, Bradley
        Gene Schroeder, E, Virginia
1952 — Jim Dooley, B, Miami
1953 — Billy Anderson, B, Compton (Ca.) J.C.
1954 — Stan Wallace, B, Illinois
1955 — Ron Drzewiecki, B, Marquette
1956 — Menan (Tex) Schriewer, E, Texas
1957 — Earl Leggett, DT, Louisiana State
1958 — Chuck Howley, LB, West Virginia
1959 — Don Clark, B, Ohio State
1960 — Roger Davis, G, Syracuse
1961 — Mike Ditka, E, Pittsburgh
1962 — Ron Bull, RB, Baylor
1963 — Dave Behrman, C, Michigan State
1964 — Dick Evey, DT, Tennessee
1965 — Dick Butkus, LB, Illinois
        Gale Sayers, RB, Kansas
        Steve DeLong, DE, Tennessee

1966 — George Rice, DT, Louisiana State
1967 — Loyd Phillips, DE, Arkansas
1968 — Mike Hull, RB, Southern California
1969 — Rufus Mayes, T, Ohio State
1970 — None
1971 — Joe Moore, RB, Missouri
1972 — Lionel Antoine, T, Southern Illinois
        Craig Clemons, DB, Iowa
1973 — Wally Chambers, DE, Eastern Kentucky
1974 — Waymond Bryant, LB, Tennessee State
        Dave Gallagher, DE, Michigan
1975 — Walter Payton, RB, Jackson State
1976 — Dennis Lick, T, Wisconsin
1977 — Ted Albrecht, T, California
1978 — None
1979 — Dan Hampton, DT, Arkansas
        Al Harris, DE, Arizona State
1980 — Otis Wilson, LB, Louisville
1981 — Keith Van Horne, T, Southern California
1982 — Jim McMahon, QB, Brigham Young
1983 — Jimbo Covert, T, Pittsburgh
        Willie Gault, WR, Tennessee
1984 — Wilber Marshall, LB, Florida
1985 — William Perry, DT, Clemson
1986 — Neal Anderson, RB, Florida
1987 — Jim Harbaugh, QB, Michigan
1988 — Brad Muster, RB, Stanford
        Wendell Davis, WR, Louisiana State
1989 — Donnell Woolford, DB, Clemson
        Trace Armstrong, DE, Florida
1990 — Mark Carrier, DB, Southern California
1991 — Stan Thomas, T, Texas
1992 — Alonzo Spellman, DE, Ohio State
1993 — Curtis Conway, WR, Southern California
1994 — John Thierry, LB, Alcorn State
1995 — Rashaan Salaam, RB, Colorado
    *First player chosen in draft.

FRANCHISE RECORDS

Most rushing yards, career
16,726 — Walter Payton
Most rushing yards, season
1,852 — Walter Payton, 1977
Most rushing yards, game
275 — Walter Payton vs. Min., Nov. 20, 1977
Most rushing touchdowns, season
14 — Gale Sayers, 1965

Walter Payton, 1977
Walter Payton, 1979

Most passing attempts, season
478 — Jim Harbaugh, 1991
Most passing attempts, game
57 — Bill Wade at Was., Oct. 25, 1964
Most passes completed, season
275 — Jim Harbaugh, 1991

Most passes completed, game
33 — Bill Wade at Was., Oct. 25, 1964
Most passing yards, career
14,686 — Sid Luckman
Most passing yards, season
3,172 — Bill Wade, 1962
Most passing yards, game
468 — Johnny Lujack vs. Chi. Cards, Dec. 11, 1949

Most touchdown passes, season
28—Sid Luckman, 1943

Most pass receptions, career
492—Walter Payton

Most pass receptions, season
93—Johnny Morris, 1964

Most pass receptions, game
14—Jim Keane at NYG, Oct. 23, 1949

Most receiving yards, career
5,059—Johnny Morris

Most receiving yards, season
1,200—Johnny Morris, 1964

Most receiving yards, game
214—Harlon Hill at S.F., Oct. 31, 1954

Most receiving touchdowns, season
13—Ken Kavanaugh, 1947
Dick Gordon, 1970

Most touchdowns, career
125—Walter Payton

Most field goals, season
31—Kevin Butler, 1985

Longest field goal
55 yards—Bob Thomas at L.A. Rams, Nov. 23, 1975

Kevin Butler vs. Min., Oct. 25, 1993
Kevin Butler at T.B., Dec. 12, 1993

Most interceptions, career
38—Gary Fencik

Most interceptions, season
10—Mark Carrier, 1990

Most sacks, career
124.5—Richard Dent

Most sacks, season
17.5—Richard Dent, 1984

SERIES RECORDS

Chicago vs.: Arizona 54-25-6; Atlanta 9-9; Buffalo 4-2; Cincinnati 2-3; Cleveland 3-8; Dallas 6-8; Denver 5-5; Detroit 70-48-3; Green Bay 82-61-6; Houston 2-4; Indianapolis 16-21; Kansas City 4-2; L.A. Raiders 3-5; L.A. Rams 34-24-3; Miami 2-5; Minnesota 29-36-2; New England 2-4; New Orleans 10-5; N.Y. Giants 24-16-2; N.Y. Jets 4-1; Philadelphia 24-4-1; Pittsburgh 19-4-1; San Diego 2-4; San Francisco 25-25-1; Seattle 2-4; Tampa Bay 26-8; Washington 14-11.

NOTE: Includes records as Decatur Staleys in 1920 and Chicago Staleys in 1921.

RETIRED UNIFORM NUMBERS

No.	Player
3	Bronko Nagurski
5	George McAfee
7	George Halas
28	Willie Galimore
34	Walter Payton
40	Gale Sayers
41	Brian Piccolo
42	Sid Luckman
51	Dick Butkus
56	Bill Hewitt
61	Bill George
66	Bulldog Turner
77	Red Grange

CINCINNATI BENGALS

YEAR-BY-YEAR RECORDS

				REGULAR SEASON					PLAYOFFS		
Year	W	L	T	Pct.	PF	PA	Finish	W	L	Highest round	Coach
1968*	3	11	0	.214	215	329	5th/Western Div.	—	—		Paul Brown
1969*	4	9	1	.308	280	367	5th/Western Div.	—	—		Paul Brown
1970	8	6	0	.571	312	255	1st/AFC Central Div.	0	1	AFC div. playoff game	Paul Brown
1971	4	10	0	.286	284	265	4th/AFC Central Div.	—	—		Paul Brown
1972	8	6	0	.571	299	229	3rd/AFC Central Div.	—	—		Paul Brown
1973	10	4	0	.714	286	231	1st/AFC Central Div.	0	1	AFC div. playoff game	Paul Brown
1974	7	7	0	.500	283	259	T2nd/AFC Central Div.	—	—		Paul Brown
1975	11	3	0	.786	340	246	2nd/AFC Central Div.	0	1	AFC div. playoff game	Paul Brown
1976	10	4	0	.714	335	210	2nd/AFC Central Div.	—	—		Bill Johnson
1977	8	6	0	.571	238	235	T2nd/AFC Central Div.	—	—		Bill Johnson
1978	4	12	0	.250	252	284	4th/AFC Central Div.	—	—		Bill Johnson, Homer Rice
1979	4	12	0	.250	337	421	4th/AFC Central Div.	—	—		Homer Rice
1980	6	10	0	.375	244	312	4th/AFC Central Div.	—	—		Forrest Gregg
1981	12	4	0	.750	421	304	1st/AFC Central Div.	2	1	Super Bowl	Forrest Gregg
1982	7	2	0	.778	232	177	T2nd/AFC	0	1	AFC first-round pl. game	Forrest Gregg
1983	7	9	0	.438	346	302	3rd/AFC Central Div.	—	—		Forrest Gregg
1984	8	8	0	.500	339	339	2nd/AFC Central Div.	—	—		Sam Wyche
1985	7	9	0	.438	441	437	T2nd/AFC Central Div.	—	—		Sam Wyche
1986	10	6	0	.625	409	394	2nd/AFC Central Div.	—	—		Sam Wyche
1987	4	11	0	.267	285	370	4th/AFC Central Div.	—	—		Sam Wyche
1988	12	4	0	.750	448	329	1st/AFC Central Div.	2	1	Super Bowl	Sam Wyche
1989	8	8	0	.500	404	285	4th/AFC Central Div.	—	—		Sam Wyche
1990	9	7	0	.563	360	352	1st/AFC Central Div.	1	1	AFC div. playoff game	Sam Wyche
1991	3	13	0	.188	263	435	4th/AFC Central Div.	—	—		Sam Wyche
1992	5	11	0	.313	274	364	4th/AFC Central Div.	—	—		David Shula
1993	3	13	0	.188	187	319	4th/AFC Central Div.	—	—		David Shula
1994	3	13	0	.188	276	406	3rd/AFC Central Div.	—	—		David Shula

*American Football League.

FIRST-ROUND DRAFT PICKS

1968—Bob Johnson, C, Tennessee
1969—Greg Cook, QB, Cincinnati
1970—Mike Reid, DT, Penn State
1971—Vernon Holland, T, Tennessee State

1972—Sherman White, DE, California
1973—Issac Curtis, WR, San Diego State
1974—Bill Kollar, DT, Montana State
1975—Glenn Cameron, LB, Florida

1976—Billy Brooks, WR, Oklahoma
    Archie Griffin, RB, Ohio State
1977—Eddie Edwards, DT, Miami (Fla.)
    Wilson Whitley, DT, Houston
    Mike Cobb, TE, Michigan State
1978—Ross Browner, DE, Notre Dame
    Blair Bush, C, Washington
1979—Jack Thompson, QB, Washington State
    Charles Alexander, RB, Louisiana State
1980—Anthony Munoz, T, Southern California
1981—David Verser, WR, Kansas
1982—Glen Collins, DE, Mississippi State
1983—Dave Rimington, C, Nebraska
1984—Ricky Hunley, LB, Arizona
    Pete Koch, DE, Maryland
    Brian Blados, T, North Carolina

1985—Eddie Brown, WR, Miami (Fla.)
    Emanuel King, LB, Alabama
1986—Joe Kelly, LB, Washington
    Tim McGee, WR, Tennessee
1987—Jason Buck, DT, Brigham Young
1988—Rickey Dixon, S, Oklahoma
1989—None
1990—James Francis, LB, Baylor
1991—Alfred Williams, LB, Colorado
1992—David Klingler, QB, Houston
    Darryl Williams, DB, Miami (Fla.)
1993—John Copeland, DE, Alabama
1994—Dan Wilkinson, DT, Ohio State*
1995—Ki-Jana Carter, RB, Penn State*
*First player chosen in draft.

FRANCHISE RECORDS

Most rushing yards, career
6,447—James Brooks

Most rushing yards, season
1,239—James Brooks, 1989

Most rushing yards, game
201—James Brooks vs. Hou., Dec. 23, 1990

Most rushing touchdowns, season
15—Ickey Woods, 1988

Most passing attempts, season
479—Ken Anderson, 1981

Most passing attempts, game
56—Ken Anderson at S.D., Dec. 20, 1982

Most passes completed, season
300—Ken Anderson, 1981

Most passes completed, game
40—Ken Anderson at S.D., Dec. 20, 1982

Most passing yards, career
32,838—Ken Anderson

Most passing yards, season
3,959—Boomer Esiason, 1986

Most passing yards, game
490—Boomer Esiason at L.A. Rams, Oct. 7, 1990

Most touchdown passes, season
29—Ken Anderson, 1981

Most pass receptions, career
420—Isaac Curtis

Most pass receptions, season
71—Dan Ross, 1981
    Carl Pickens, 1994

Most pass receptions, game
12—James Brooks at Min., Dec. 25, 1989

Most receiving yards, career
7,106—Isaac Curtis

Most receiving yards, season
1,273—Eddie Brown, 1988

Most receiving yards, game
216—Eddie Brown vs. Pit., Nov. 16, 1988

Most receiving touchdowns, season
11—Carl Pickens, 1994

Most touchdowns, career
70—Pete Johnson

Most field goals, season
28—Doug Pelfrey, 1994

Longest field goal
55 yards—Chris Bahr vs. Hou., Sept. 23, 1979

Most interceptions, career
65—Ken Riley

Most interceptions, season
9—Ken Riley, 1976

Most sacks, career
84.5—Eddie Edwards

Most sacks, season
21.5—Coy Bacon, 1976

SERIES RECORDS

Cincinnati vs.: Arizona 3-2; Atlanta 6-2; Buffalo 10-7; Chicago 3-2; Cleveland 24-25; Dallas 2-4; Denver 6-11; Detroit 3-3; Green Bay 4-3; Houston 25-26-1; Indianapolis 5-10; Kansas City 9-11; L.A. Raiders 7-14; L.A. Rams 5-2; Miami 3-11; Minnesota 3-4; New England 7-9; New Orleans 3-5; N.Y. Giants 4-1; N.Y. Jets 6-9; Philadelphia 6-1; Pittsburgh 21-28; San Diego 8-13; San Francisco 1-6; Seattle 7-6; Tampa Bay 3-1; Washington 2-4.

RETIRED UNIFORM NUMBERS

No.	Player
54	Bob Johnson

CLEVELAND BROWNS

YEAR-BY-YEAR RECORDS

| | | | REGULAR SEASON | | | | PLAYOFFS | | | |
Year	W	L	T	Pct.	PF	PA	Finish	W	L	Highest round	Coach
1946*	12	2	0	.857	423	137	1st/Western Div.	—	—		Paul Brown
1947*	12	1	1	.923	410	185	1st/Western Div.	—	—		Paul Brown
1948*	14	0	0	1.000	389	190	1st/Western Div.	—	—		Paul Brown
1949*	9	1	2	.900	339	171	1st	—	—		Paul Brown
1950	10	2	0	.833	310	144	1st/American Conf.	2	0	NFL champ	Paul Brown
1951	11	1	0	.917	331	152	1st/American Conf.	0	1	NFL championship game	Paul Brown
1952	8	4	0	.667	310	213	1st/American Conf.	0	1	NFL championship game	Paul Brown
1953	11	1	0	.917	348	162	1st/Eastern Conf.	0	1	NFL championship game	Paul Brown
1954	9	3	0	.750	336	162	1st/Eastern Conf.	1	0	NFL champ	Paul Brown
1955	9	2	1	.818	349	218	1st/Eastern Conf.	1	0	NFL champ	Paul Brown
1956	5	7	0	.417	167	177	4th/Eastern Conf.	—	—		Paul Brown
1957	9	2	1	.818	269	172	1st/Eastern Conf.	0	1	NFL championship game	Paul Brown

	REGULAR SEASON							PLAYOFFS			
Year	W	L	T	Pct.	PF	PA	Finish	W	L	Highest round	Coach
1958	9	3	0	.750	302	217	2nd/Eastern Conf.	0	1	E. Conf. championship game	Paul Brown
1959	7	5	0	.583	270	214	T2nd/Eastern Conf.	—	—		Paul Brown
1960	8	3	1	.727	362	217	2nd/Eastern Conf.	—	—		Paul Brown
1961	8	5	1	.615	319	270	3rd/Eastern Conf.	—	—		Paul Brown
1962	7	6	1	.538	291	257	3rd/Eastern Conf.	—	—		Paul Brown
1963	10	4	0	.714	343	262	2nd/Eastern Conf.	—	—		Blanton Collier
1964	10	3	1	.769	415	293	1st/Eastern Conf.	1	0	NFL champ	Blanton Collier
1965	11	3	0	.786	363	325	1st/Eastern Conf.	0	1	NFL championship game	Blanton Collier
1966	9	5	0	.643	403	259	T2nd/Eastern Conf.	—	—		Blanton Collier
1967	9	5	0	.643	334	297	1st/Century Div.	0	1	E. Conf. championship game	Blanton Collier
1968	10	4	0	.714	394	273	1st/Century Div.	1	1	NFL championship game	Blanton Collier
1969	10	3	1	.769	351	300	1st/Century Div.	1	1	NFL championship game	Blanton Collier
1970	7	7	0	.500	286	265	2nd/AFC Central Div.	—	—		Blanton Collier
1971	9	5	0	.643	285	273	1st/AFC Central Div.	0	1	AFC div. playoff game	Nick Skorich
1972	10	4	0	.714	268	249	2nd/AFC Central Div.	0	1	AFC div. playoff game	Nick Skorich
1973	7	5	2	.571	234	255	3rd/AFC Central Div.	—	—		Nick Skorich
1974	4	10	0	.286	251	344	4th/AFC Central Div.	—	—		Nick Skorich
1975	3	11	0	.214	218	372	4th/AFC Central Div.	—	—		Forrest Gregg
1976	9	5	0	.643	267	287	3rd/AFC Central Div.	—	—		Forrest Gregg
1977	6	8	0	.429	269	267	4th/AFC Central Div.	—	—		F. Gregg, Dick Modzelewski
1978	8	8	0	.500	334	356	3rd/AFC Central Div.	—	—		Sam Rutigliano
1979	9	7	0	.563	359	352	3rd/AFC Central Div.	—	—		Sam Rutigliano
1980	11	5	0	.688	357	310	1st/AFC Central Div.	0	1	AFC div. playoff game	Sam Rutigliano
1981	5	11	0	.313	276	375	4th/AFC Central Div.	—	—		Sam Rutigliano
1982	4	5	0	.444	140	182	T8th/AFC	0	1	AFC first-round pl. game	Sam Rutigliano
1983	9	7	0	.563	356	342	2nd/AFC Central Div.	—	—		Sam Rutigliano
1984	5	11	0	.313	250	297	3rd/AFC Central Div.	—	—		Rutigliano, Schottenheimer
1985	8	8	0	.500	287	294	1st/AFC Central Div.	0	1	AFC div. playoff game	Marty Schottenheimer
1986	12	4	0	.750	391	310	1st/AFC Central Div.	1	1	AFC championship game	Marty Schottenheimer
1987	10	5	0	.667	390	239	1st/AFC Central Div.	1	1	AFC championship game	Marty Schottenheimer
1988	10	6	0	.625	304	288	T2nd/AFC Central Div.	0	1	AFC wild-card game	Marty Schottenheimer
1989	9	6	1	.594	334	254	1st/AFC Central Div.	1	1	AFC championship game	Bud Carson
1990	3	13	0	.188	228	462	4th/AFC Central Div.	—	—		Bud Carson, Jim Shofner
1991	6	10	0	.375	293	298	3rd/AFC Central Div.	—	—		Bill Belichick
1992	7	9	0	.438	272	275	3rd/AFC Central Div.	—	—		Bill Belichick
1993	7	9	0	.438	304	307	3rd/AFC Central Div.	—	—		Bill Belichick
1994	11	5	0	.688	340	204	2nd/AFC Central Div.	1	1	AFC div. playoff game	Bill Belichick

*All-America Football Conference.

FIRST-ROUND DRAFT PICKS

1950—Ken Carpenter, B, Oregon State
1951—Ken Konz, B, Louisiana State
1952—Bert Rechichar, DB, Tennessee
 Harry Agganis, QB, Boston University
1953—Doug Atkins, DT, Tennessee
1954—Bobby Garrett, QB, Stanford*
 John Bauer, G, Illinois
1955—Kent Burris, C, Oklahoma
1956—Preston Carpenter, B, Arkansas
1957—Jim Brown, B, Syracuse
1958—Jim Shofner, DB, Texas Christian
1959—Rich Kreitling, DE, Illinois
1960—Jim Houston, DE, Ohio State
1961—None
1962—Gary Collins, WR, Maryland
 Leroy Jackson, B, Western Illinois
1963—Tom Hutchinson, TE, Kentucky
1964—Paul Warfield, WR, Ohio State
1965—None
1966—Milt Morin, TE, Massachusetts
1967—Bob Matheson, LB, Duke
1968—M. Upshaw, DE, Trinity (Tex.)
1969—Ron Johnson, RB, Michigan
1970—Mike Phipps, QB, Purdue
 Bob McKay, T, Texas
1971—Clarence Scott, DB, Kansas State
1972—Thom Darden, DB, Michigan
1973—Steve Holden, WR, Arizona State
 Pete Adams, G, Southern California

1974—None
1975—Mack Mitchell, DE, Houston
1976—Mike Pruitt, RB, Purdue
1977—Robert Jackson, LB, Texas A&M
1978—Clay Matthews, LB, Southern California
 Ozzie Newsome, WR, Alabama
1979—Willis Adams, WR, Houston
1980—Charles White, RB, Southern California
1981—Hanford Dixon, CB, Southern Mississippi
1982—Chip Banks, LB, Southern California
1983—None
1984—Don Rogers, DB, UCLA
1985—None
1986—None
1987—Mike Junkin, LB, Duke
1988—Clifford Charlton, LB, Florida
1989—Eric Metcalf, RB, Texas
1990—None
1991—Eric Turner, S, UCLA
1992—Tommy Vardell, FB, Stanford
1993—Steve Everitt, C, Michigan
1994—Antonio Langham, DB, Alabama
 Derrick Alexander, WR, Michigan
1995—Craig Powell, LB, Ohio State

*First player chosen in draft.

Most rushing yards, career
12,312—Jim Brown
Most rushing yards, season
1,863—Jim Brown, 1963
Most rushing yards, game
237—Jim Brown vs. L.A., Nov. 24, 1957
  Jim Brown vs. Phi., Nov. 19, 1961
Most rushing touchdowns, season
17—Jim Brown, 1958
  Jim Brown, 1965
Most passing attempts, season
567—Brian Sipe, 1981
Most passing attempts, game
57—Brian Sipe vs. S.D., Sept. 7, 1981
Most passes completed, season
337—Brian Sipe, 1980
Most passes completed, game
33—Brian Sipe vs. S.D., Dec. 5, 1982
Most passing yards, career
23,713—Brian Sipe

Most passing yards, season
4,132—Brian Sipe, 1980
Most passing yards, game
444—Brian Sipe vs. Bal., Oct. 25, 1981
Most touchdown passes, season
30—Brian Sipe, 1980
Most pass receptions, career
662—Ozzie Newsome
Most pass receptions, season
89—Ozzie Newsome, 1983
  Ozzie Newsome, 1984
Most pass receptions, game
14—Ozzie Newsome vs. NYJ, Oct. 14, 1984
Most receiving yards, career
7,980—Ozzie Newsome
Most receiving yards, season
1,236—Webster Slaughter, 1989
Most receiving yards, game
191—Ozzie Newsome vs. NYJ, Oct. 14, 1984

Most receiving touchdowns, season
13—Gary Collins, 1963
Most touchdowns, career
126—Jim Brown
Most field goals, season
26—Matt Stover, 1994
Longest field goal
60 yards—Steve Cox at Cin., Oct. 21, 1984
Most interceptions, career
45—Thom Darden
Most interceptions, season
10—Thom Darden, 1978
Most sacks, career
71—Clay Matthews
Most sacks, season
14.5—Bill Glass, 1965

SERIES RECORDS

Cleveland vs.: Arizona 32-10-3; Atlanta 8-2; Buffalo 7-3; Chicago 8-3; Cincinnati 25-24; Dallas 15-9; Denver 5-13; Detroit 3-11; Green Bay 6-7; Houston 29-20; Indianapolis 13-7; Kansas City 7-7-2; L.A. Raiders 3-9; L.A. Rams 8-7; Miami 4-6; Minnesota 3-7; New England 10-3; New Orleans 9-3; N.Y. Giants 25-17-2; N.Y. Jets 9-6; Philadelphia 31-12-1; Pittsburgh 52-38; San Diego 6-8-1; San Francisco 9-6; Seattle 4-9; Tampa Bay 4-0; Washington 32-9-1.

RETIRED UNIFORM NUMBERS

No.	Player
14	Otto Graham
32	Jim Brown
45	Ernie Davis
46	Don Fleming
76	Lou Groza

DALLAS COWBOYS

YEAR-BY-YEAR RECORDS

Year	W	L	T	Pct.	PF	PA	Finish	W	L	Highest round	Coach
1960	0	11	1	.000	177	369	7th/Western Conf.	—	—		Tom Landry
1961	4	9	1	.308	236	380	6th/Eastern Conf.	—	—		Tom Landry
1962	5	8	1	.385	398	402	5th/Eastern Conf.	—	—		Tom Landry
1963	4	10	0	.286	305	378	5th/Eastern Conf.	—	—		Tom Landry
1964	5	8	1	.385	250	289	5th/Eastern Conf.	—	—		Tom Landry
1965	7	7	0	.500	325	280	T2nd/Eastern Conf.	—	—		Tom Landry
1966	10	3	1	.769	445	239	1st/Eastern Conf.	0	1	NFL championship game	Tom Landry
1967	9	5	0	.643	342	268	1st/Capitol Div.	1	1	NFL championship game	Tom Landry
1968	12	2	0	.857	431	186	1st/Capitol Div.	0	1	E. Conf. championship game	Tom Landry
1969	11	2	1	.846	369	223	1st/Capitol Div.	0	1	E. Conf. championship game	Tom Landry
1970	10	4	0	.714	299	221	1st/NFC Eastern Div.	2	1	Super Bowl	Tom Landry
1971	11	3	0	.786	406	222	1st/NFC Eastern Div.	3	0	Super Bowl champ	Tom Landry
1972	10	4	0	.714	319	240	2nd/NFC Eastern Div.	1	1	NFC championship game	Tom Landry
1973	10	4	0	.714	382	203	1st/NFC Eastern Div.	1	1	NFC championship game	Tom Landry
1974	8	6	0	.571	297	235	3rd/NFC Eastern Div.	—	—		Tom Landry
1975	10	4	0	.714	350	268	2nd/NFC Eastern Div.	2	1	Super Bowl	Tom Landry
1976	11	3	0	.786	296	194	1st/NFC Eastern Div.	0	1	NFC div. playoff game	Tom Landry
1977	12	2	0	.857	345	212	1st/NFC Eastern Div.	3	0	Super Bowl champ	Tom Landry
1978	12	4	0	.750	384	208	1st/NFC Eastern Div.	2	1	Super Bowl	Tom Landry
1979	11	5	0	.688	371	313	1st/NFC Eastern Div.	0	1	NFC div. playoff game	Tom Landry
1980	12	4	0	.750	454	311	2nd/NFC Eastern Div.	2	1	NFC championship game	Tom Landry
1981	12	4	0	.750	367	277	1st/NFC Eastern Div.	1	1	NFC championship game	Tom Landry
1982	6	3	0	.667	226	145	2nd/NFC	2	1	NFC championship game	Tom Landry
1983	12	4	0	.750	479	360	2nd/NFC Eastern Div.	0	1	NFC wild-card game	Tom Landry
1984	9	7	0	.563	308	308	T3rd/NFC Eastern Div.	—	—		Tom Landry
1985	10	6	0	.625	357	333	1st/NFC Eastern Div.	0	1	NFC div. playoff game	Tom Landry
1986	7	9	0	.438	346	337	3rd/NFC Eastern Div.	—	—		Tom Landry
1987	7	8	0	.467	340	348	T2nd/NFC Eastern Div.	—	—		Tom Landry
1988	3	13	0	.188	265	381	5th/NFC Eastern Div.	—	—		Tom Landry
1989	1	15	0	.063	204	393	5th/NFC Eastern Div.	—	—		Jimmy Johnson
1990	7	9	0	.438	244	308	4th/NFC Eastern Div.	—	—		Jimmy Johnson

		REGULAR SEASON							PLAYOFFS		
Year	W	L	T	Pct.	PF	PA	Finish	W	L	Highest round	Coach
1991	11	5	0	.688	342	310	2nd/NFC Eastern Div.	1	1	NFC div. playoff game	Jimmy Johnson
1992	13	3	0	.813	409	243	1st/NFC Eastern Div.	3	0	Super Bowl champ	Jimmy Johnson
1993	12	4	0	.750	376	229	1st/NFC Eastern Div.	3	0	Super Bowl champ	Jimmy Johnson
1994	12	4	0	.750	414	248	1st/NFC Eastern Div.	1	1	NFC championship game	Barry Switzer

FIRST-ROUND DRAFT PICKS

1961—Bob Lilly, DT, Texas Christian
1962—None
1963—Lee Roy Jordan, LB, Alabama
1964—Scott Appleton, DT, Texas
1965—Craig Morton, QB, California
1966—John Niland, G, Iowa
1967—None
1968—Dennis Homan, WR, Alabama
1969—Calvin Hill, RB, Yale
1970—Duane Thomas, RB, West Texas State
1971—Tody Smith, DE, Southern California
1972—Bill Thomas, RB, Boston College
1973—Billy Joe DuPree, TE, Michigan State
1974—Ed Jones, DE, Tennessee State*
    Charles Young, RB, North Carolina State
1975—Randy White, LB, Maryland
    Thomas Henderson, LB, Langston
1976—Aaron Kyle, DB, Wyoming
1977—Tony Dorsett, RB, Pittsburgh
1978—Larry Bethea, DE, Michigan State
1979—Robert Shaw, C, Tennessee

1980—None
1981—Howard Richards, T, Missouri
1982—Rod Hill, DB, Kentucky State
1983—Jim Jeffcoat, DE, Arizona State
1984—Billy Cannon Jr., LB, Texas A&M
1985—Kevin Brooks, DE, Michigan
1986—Mike Sherrard, WR, UCLA
1987—Danny Noonan, DT, Nebraska
1988—Michael Irvin, WR, Miami (Fla.)
1989—Troy Aikman, QB, UCLA*
1990—Emmitt Smith, RB, Florida
1991—Russell Maryland, DL, Miami (Fla.)*
    Alvin Harper, WR, Tennessee
    Kelvin Pritchett, DT, Mississippi
1992—Kevin Smith, DB, Texas A&M
    Robert Jones, LB, East Carolina
1993—None
1994—Shante Carver, DE, Arizona State
1995—None

*First player chosen in draft.

FRANCHISE RECORDS

Most rushing yards, career
12,036—Tony Dorsett
Most rushing yards, season
1,713—Emmitt Smith, 1990
Most rushing yards, game
237—Emmitt Smith at Phi., Oct. 31, 1993
Most rushing touchdowns, season
21—Emmitt Smith, 1994
Most passing attempts, season
533—Danny White, 1983
Most passing attempts, game
49—Roger Staubach at Phi., Oct. 26, 1975
    Gary Hogeboom at S.F., Dec. 22, 1985
    Danny White at Was., Oct. 13, 1987
    Steve Walsh vs. Pho., Oct. 29, 1989
Most passes completed, season
334—Danny White, 1983
Most passes completed, game
33—Gary Hogeboom at L.A. Rams, Sept. 3, 1984
Most passing yards, career
22,700—Roger Staubach

Most passing yards, season
3,980—Danny White, 1983
Most passing yards, game
460—Don Meredith at S.F., Nov. 10, 1963
Most touchdown passes, season
29—Danny White, 1983
Most pass receptions, career
489—Drew Pearson
Most pass receptions, season
93—Michael Irvin, 1991
Most pass receptions, game
13—Lance Rentzel vs. Was., Nov. 19, 1967
Most receiving yards, career
7,988—Tony Hill
Most receiving yards, season
1,523—Michael Irvin, 1991
Most receiving yards, game
246—Bob Hayes at Was., Nov. 13, 1966

Most receiving touchdowns, season
14—Frank Clarke, 1962
Most touchdowns, career
86—Tony Dorsett
Most field goals, season
28—Eddie Murray, 1993
Longest field goal
54 yards—Toni Fritsch at NYG, Sept. 24, 1972
    Ken Willis at Cle., Sept. 1, 1991
Most interceptions, career
52—Mel Renfro
Most interceptions, season
11—Everson Walls, 1981
Most sacks, career
113—Harvey Martin
Most sacks, season
20—Harvey Martin, 1977

SERIES RECORDS

Dallas vs.: Arizona 42-22-1; Atlanta 9-6; Buffalo 3-2; Chicago 8-6; Cincinnati 4-2; Cleveland 9-15; Denver 3-2; Detroit 7-6; Green Bay 6-9; Houston 5-3; Indianapolis 7-2; Kansas City 3-2; L.A. Raiders 2-3; L.A. Rams 8-9; Miami 1-6; Minnesota 8-6; New England 6-0; New Orleans 14-3; N.Y. Giants 41-22-2; N.Y. Jets 5-1; Philadelphia 42-26; Pittsburgh 13-11; San Diego 4-1; San Francisco 6-10-1; Seattle 4-1; Tampa Bay 6-0; Washington 39-27-2.

RETIRED UNIFORM NUMBERS

No.	Player
	None

DENVER BRONCOS

YEAR-BY-YEAR RECORDS

Year	W	L	T	Pct.	PF	PA	Finish	W	L	Highest round	Coach
1960*	4	9	1	.308	309	393	4th/Western Div.	—	—		Frank Filchock
1961*	3	11	0	.214	251	432	3rd/Western Div.	—	—		Frank Filchock
1962*	7	7	0	.500	353	334	2nd/Western Div.	—	—		Jack Faulkner
1963*	2	11	1	.154	301	473	4th/Western Div.	—	—		Jack Faulkner
1964*	2	11	1	.154	240	438	4th/Western Div.	—	—		Jack Faulkner, Mac Speedie
1965*	4	10	0	.286	303	392	4th/Western Div.	—	—		Mac Speedie
1966*	4	10	0	.286	196	381	4th/Western Div.	—	—		Mac Speedie, Ray Malavasi
1967*	3	11	0	.214	256	409	4th/Western Div.	—	—		Lou Saban
1968*	5	9	0	.357	255	404	4th/Western Div.	—	—		Lou Saban
1969*	5	8	1	.385	297	344	4th/Western Div.	—	—		Lou Saban
1970	5	8	1	.385	253	264	4th/AFC Western Div.	—	—		Lou Saban
1971	4	9	1	.308	203	275	4th/AFC Western Div.	—	—		Lou Saban, Jerry Smith
1972	5	9	0	.357	325	350	3rd/AFC Western Div.	—	—		John Ralston
1973	7	5	2	.571	354	296	T2nd/AFC Western Div.	—	—		John Ralston
1974	7	6	1	.536	302	294	2nd/AFC Western Div.	—	—		John Ralston
1975	6	8	0	.429	254	307	2nd/AFC Western Div.	—	—		John Ralston
1976	9	5	0	.643	315	206	2nd/AFC Western Div.	—	—		John Ralston
1977	12	2	0	.857	274	148	1st/AFC Western Div.	2	1	Super Bowl	Red Miller
1978	10	6	0	.625	282	198	1st/AFC Western Div.	0	1	AFC div. playoff game	Red Miller
1979	10	6	0	.625	289	262	2nd/AFC Western Div.	0	1	AFC wild-card game	Red Miller
1980	8	8	0	.500	310	323	T3rd/AFC Western Div.	—	—		Red Miller
1981	10	6	0	.625	321	289	2nd/AFC Western Div.	—	—		Dan Reeves
1982	2	7	0	.222	148	226	12th/AFC	—	—		Dan Reeves
1983	9	7	0	.563	302	327	T2nd/AFC Western Div.	0	1	AFC wild-card game	Dan Reeves
1984	13	3	0	.813	353	241	1st/AFC Western Div.	0	1	AFC div. playoff game	Dan Reeves
1985	11	5	0	.688	380	329	2nd/AFC Western Div.	—	—		Dan Reeves
1986	11	5	0	.688	378	327	1st/AFC Western Div.	2	1	Super Bowl	Dan Reeves
1987	10	4	1	.700	379	288	1st/AFC Western Div.	2	1	Super Bowl	Dan Reeves
1988	8	8	0	.500	327	352	2nd/AFC Western Div.	—	—		Dan Reeves
1989	11	5	0	.688	362	226	1st/AFC Western Div.	2	1	Super Bowl	Dan Reeves
1990	5	11	0	.313	331	374	5th/AFC Western Div.	—	—		Dan Reeves
1991	12	4	0	.750	304	235	1st/AFC Western Div.	1	1	AFC championship game	Dan Reeves
1992	8	8	0	.500	262	329	3rd/AFC Western Div.	—	—		Dan Reeves
1993	9	7	0	.563	373	284	3rd/AFC Western Div.	0	1	AFC wild-card game	Wade Phillips
1994	7	9	0	.438	347	396	4th/AFC Western Div.	—	—		Wade Phillips

*American Football League.

FIRST-ROUND DRAFT PICKS

1960—Roger Leclerc, C, Trinity (Conn.)
1961—Bob Gaiters, RB, New Mexico State
1962—Merlin Olsen, DT, Utah State
1963—Kermit Alexander, DB, UCLA
1964—Bob Brown, T, Nebraska
1965—None
1966—Jerry Shay, DT, Purdue
1967—Floyd Little, RB, Syracuse
1968—None
1969—None
1970—Bob Anderson, RB, Colorado
1971—Marv Montgomery, T, Southern California
1972—Riley Odoms, TE, Houston
1973—Otis Armstrong, RB, Purdue
1974—Randy Gradishar, LB, Ohio State
1975—Louis Wright, DB, San Jose State
1976—Tom Glassic, G, Virginia
1977—Steve Schindler, G, Boston College

1978—Don Latimer, DT, Miami (Fla.)
1979—Kevin Clark, T, Nebraska
1980—None
1981—Dennis Smith, DB, Southern California
1982—Gerald Willhite, RB, San Jose State
1983—Chris Hinton, G, Northwestern
1984—None
1985—Steve Sewell, RB, Oklahoma
1986—None
1987—Ricky Nattiel, WR, Florida
1988—Ted Gregory, DT, Syracuse
1989—Steve Atwater, DB, Arkansas
1990—None
1991—Mike Croel, LB, Nebraska
1992—Tommy Maddox, QB, UCLA
1993—Dan Williams, DE, Toledo
1994—None
1995—None

FRANCHISE RECORDS

Most rushing yards, career
6,323—Floyd Little

Most rushing yards, season
1,407—Otis Armstrong, 1974

Most rushing yards, game
183—Otis Armstrong vs. Hou., Dec. 8, 1974

Most rushing touchdowns, season
12—Floyd Little, 1973

Most passing attempts, season
605—John Elway, 1985

Most passing attempts, game
59—John Elway at G.B., Oct. 10, 1993

Most passes completed, season
348—John Elway, 1993

Most passes completed, game
36—John Elway vs. S.D., Sept. 4, 1994

Most passing yards, career
37,736—John Elway

Most passing yards, season
4,030—John Elway, 1993
Most passing yards, game
447—Frank Tripucka at Buf., Sept. 15, 1962
Most touchdown passes, season
25—John Elway, 1993
Most pass receptions, career
543—Lionel Taylor
Most pass receptions, season
100—Lionel Taylor, 1961
Most pass receptions, game
13—Lionel Taylor vs. Oak., Nov. 29, 1964

Robert Anderson vs. Chi., Sept. 30, 1973
Most receiving yards, career
6,872—Lionel Taylor
Most receiving yards, season
1,244—Steve Watson, 1981
Most receiving yards, game
199—Lionel Taylor vs. Buf., Nov. 27, 1960
Most receiving touchdowns, season
13—Steve Watson, 1981
Most touchdowns, career
54—Floyd Little

Most field goals, season
30—Jason Elam, 1994
Longest field goal
57 yards—Fred Steinfort vs. Was., Oct. 13, 1980
Most interceptions, career
44—Steve Foley
Most interceptions, season
11—Goose Gonsoulin, 1960
Most sacks, career
92.5—Simon Fletcher
Most sacks, season
16—Simon Fletcher, 1992

SERIES RECORDS

Denver vs.: Arizona 3-0-1; Atlanta 5-3; Buffalo 10-17-1; Chicago 5-5; Cincinnati 11-6; Cleveland 13-5; Dallas 2-3; Detroit 4-3; Green Bay 4-2-1; Houston 11-19-1; Indianapolis 9-2; Kansas City 30-39; L.A. Raiders 19-48-2; L.A. Rams 3-4; Miami 2-5-1; Minnesota 3-5; New England 16-12; New Orleans 4-2; N.Y. Giants 3-3; N.Y. Jets 12-12-1; Philadelphia 2-5; Pittsburgh 10-5-1; San Diego 36-33-1; San Francisco 4-3; Seattle 22-13; Tampa Bay 2-1; Washington 3-3.

RETIRED UNIFORM NUMBERS

No.	Player
18	Frank Tripucka
44	Floyd Little

DETROIT LIONS

YEAR-BY-YEAR RECORDS

			REGULAR SEASON					PLAYOFFS		
Year	W	L	T	Pct.	PF	PA	Finish	W	L	Highest round	Coach
1930*	5	6	3	.455	...	...	T7th				Tubby Griffen
1931*	11	3	0	.786	...	...	2nd				Potsy Clark
1932*	6	2	4	.750	...	...	3rd				Potsy Clark
1933*	6	5	0	.545	128	87	2nd/Western Div.	—	—		Potsy Clark
1934	10	3	0	.769	238	59	2nd/Western Div.	—	—		Potsy Clark
1935	7	3	2	.700	191	111	1st/Western Div.	1	0	NFL champ	Potsy Clark
1936	8	4	0	.667	235	102	3rd/Western Div.	—	—		Potsy Clark
1937	7	4	0	.636	180	105	T2nd/Western Div.	—	—		Dutch Clark
1938	7	4	0	.636	119	108	2nd/Western Div.	—	—		Dutch Clark
1939	6	5	0	.545	145	150	3rd/Western Div.	—	—		Gus Henderson
1940	5	5	1	.500	138	153	3rd/Western Div.	—	—		Potsy Clark
1941	4	6	1	.400	121	195	3rd/Western Div.	—	—		Bill Edwards
1942	0	11	0	.000	38	263	5th/Western Div.	—	—		Bill Edwards, John Karcis
1943	3	6	1	.333	178	218	3rd/Western Div.	—	—		Gus Dorais
1944	6	3	1	.667	216	151	T2nd/Western Div.	—	—		Gus Dorais
1945	7	3	0	.700	195	194	2nd/Western Div.	—	—		Gus Dorais
1946	1	10	0	.091	142	310	2nd/Western Div.	—	—		Gus Dorais
1947	3	9	0	.250	231	305	5th/Western Div.	—	—		Gus Dorais
1948	2	10	0	.167	200	407	5th/Western Div.	—	—		Bo McMillin
1949	4	8	0	.333	237	259	4th/Western Div.	—	—		Bo McMillin
1950	6	6	0	.500	321	285	4th/National Conf.	—	—		Bo McMillin
1951	7	4	1	.636	336	259	T2nd/National Conf.	—	—		Buddy Parker
1952	9	3	0	.750	344	192	1st/National Conf.	2	0	NFL champ	Buddy Parker
1953	10	2	0	.833	271	205	1st/Western Conf.	1	0	NFL champ	Buddy Parker
1954	9	2	1	.818	337	189	1st/Western Conf.	0	1	NFL championship game	Buddy Parker
1955	3	9	0	.250	230	275	6th/Western Conf.	—	—		Buddy Parker
1956	9	3	0	.750	300	188	2nd/Western Conf.	—	—		Buddy Parker
1957	8	4	0	.667	251	231	1st/Western Conf.	2	0	NFL champ	George Wilson
1958	4	7	1	.364	261	276	5th/Western Conf.	—	—		George Wilson
1959	3	8	1	.273	203	275	5th/Western Conf.	—	—		George Wilson
1960	7	5	0	.583	239	212	T2nd/Western Conf.	—	—		George Wilson
1961	8	5	1	.615	270	258	2nd/Western Conf.	—	—		George Wilson
1962	11	3	0	.786	315	177	2nd/Western Conf.	—	—		George Wilson
1963	5	8	1	.385	326	265	T4th/Western Conf.	—	—		George Wilson
1964	7	5	2	.583	280	260	4th/Western Conf.	—	—		George Wilson
1965	6	7	1	.462	257	295	6th/Western Conf.	—	—		Harry Gilmer
1966	4	9	1	.308	206	317	T6th/Western Conf.	—	—		Harry Gilmer
1967	5	7	2	.417	260	259	3rd/Central Div.	—	—		Joe Schmidt
1968	4	8	2	.333	207	241	4th/Central Div.	—	—		Joe Schmidt
1969	9	4	1	.692	259	188	2nd/Central Div.	—	—		Joe Schmidt
1970	10	4	0	.714	347	202	2nd/NFC Central Div.	0	1	NFC div. playoff game	Joe Schmidt
1971	7	6	1	.538	341	286	2nd/NFC Central Div.	—	—		Joe Schmidt

Year	W	L	T	Pct.	PF	PA	Finish	W	L	Highest round	Coach
1972	8	5	1	.607	339	290	2nd/NFC Central Div.	—	—		Joe Schmidt
1973	6	7	1	.464	271	247	2nd/NFC Central Div.	—	—		Don McCafferty
1974	7	7	0	.500	256	270	2nd/NFC Central Div.	—	—		Rick Forzano
1975	7	7	0	.500	245	262	2nd/NFC Central Div.	—	—		Rick Forzano
1976	6	8	0	.429	262	220	3rd/NFC Central Div.	—	—		R. Forzano, T. Hudspeth
1977	6	8	0	.429	183	252	3rd/NFC Central Div.	—	—		Tommy Hudspeth
1978	7	9	0	.438	290	300	T3rd/NFC Central Div.	—	—		Monte Clark
1979	2	14	0	.125	219	365	5th/NFC Central Div.	—	—		Monte Clark
1980	9	7	0	.563	334	272	2nd/NFC Central Div.	—	—		Monte Clark
1981	8	8	0	.500	397	322	2nd/NFC Central Div.	—	—		Monte Clark
1982	4	5	0	.444	181	176	T8th/NFC	0	1	NFC first-round pl. game	Monte Clark
1983	9	7	0	.563	347	286	1st/NFC Central Div.	0	1	NFC div. playoff game	Monte Clark
1984	4	11	1	.281	283	408	4th/NFC Central Div.	—	—		Monte Clark
1985	7	9	0	.438	307	366	T3rd/NFC Central Div.	—	—		Darryl Rogers
1986	5	11	0	.313	277	326	3rd/NFC Central Div.	—	—		Darryl Rogers
1987	4	11	0	.267	269	384	T4th/NFC Central Div.	—	—		Darryl Rogers
1988	4	12	0	.250	220	313	T4th/NFC Central Div.	—	—		Darryl Rogers
1989	7	9	0	.438	312	364	3rd/NFC Central Div.	—	—		Wayne Fontes
1990	6	10	0	.375	373	413	T2nd/NFC Central Div.	—	—		Wayne Fontes
1991	12	4	0	.750	339	295	1st/NFC Central Div.	1	1	NFC championship game	Wayne Fontes
1992	5	11	0	.313	273	332	T3rd/NFC Central Div.	—	—		Wayne Fontes
1993	10	6	0	.625	298	292	1st/NFC Central Div.	0	1	NFC wild-card game	Wayne Fontes
1994	9	7	0	.563	357	342	T2nd/NFC Central Div.	0	1	NFC wild-card game	Wayne Fontes

*Portsmouth Spartans.

FIRST-ROUND DRAFT PICKS

1936—Sid Wagner, G, Michigan State
1937—Lloyd Cardwell, B, Nebraska
1938—Alex Wojciechowicz, C, Fordham
1939—John Pingel, B, Michigan State
1940—Doyle Nave, B, Southern California
1941—Jim Thomason, B, Texas A&M
1942—Bob Westfall, B, Michigan
1943—Frank Sinkwich, B, Georgia*
1944—Otto Graham, B, Northwestern
1945—Frank Szymanski, B, Notre Dame
1946—Bill Dellastatious, B, Missouri
1947—Glenn Davis, B, Army
1948—Y.A. Tittle, B, Louisiana State
1949—John Rauch, B, Georgia
1950—Leon Hart, E, Notre Dame*
      Joe Watson, C, Rice
1951—None
1952—None
1953—Harley Sewell, G, Texas
1954—Dick Chapman, T, Rice
1955—Dave Middleton, B, Auburn
1956—Howard Cassidy, B, Ohio State
1957—Bill Glass, G, Baylor
1958—Alex Karras, DT, Iowa
1959—Nick Pietrosante, B, Notre Dame
1960—John Robinson, DB, Louisiana State
1961—None
1962—John Hadl, QB, Kansas
1963—Daryl Sanders, T, Ohio State
1964—Pete Beathard, QB, Southern California
1965—Tom Nowatzke, RB, Indiana
1966—None
1967—Mel Farr, RB, UCLA

1968—Greg Landry, QB, Massachusetts
      Earl McCullouch, E, Southern California
1969—None
1970—Steve Owens, RB, Oklahoma
1971—Bob Bell, DT, Cincinnati
1972—Herb Orvis, DE, Colorado
1973—Ernie Price, DE, Texas A&I
1974—Ed O'Neil, LB, Penn State
1975—Lynn Boden, G, South Dakota State
1976—James Hunter, DB, Grambling State
      Lawrence Gaines, FB, Wyoming
1977—None
1978—Luther Bradley, DB, Notre Dame
1979—Keith Dorney, T, Penn State
1980—Billy Sims, RB, Oklahoma*
1981—Mark Nichols, WR, San Jose State
1982—Jimmy Williams, LB, Nebraska
1983—James Jones, RB, Florida
1984—David Lewis, TE, California
1985—Lomas Brown, T, Florida
1986—Chuck Long, QB, Iowa
1987—Reggie Rogers, DE, Washington
1988—Bennie Blades, S, Miami (Fla.)
1989—Barry Sanders, RB, Oklahoma State
1990—Andre Ware, QB, Houston
1991—Herman Moore, WR, Virginia
1992—Robert Porcher, DE, South Carolina State
1993—None
1994—Johnnie Morton, WR, Southern California
1995—Luther Elliss, DT, Utah

*First player chosen in draft.

FRANCHISE RECORDS

Most rushing yards, career
8,672—Barry Sanders
Most rushing yards, season
1,883—Barry Sanders, 1994
Most rushing yards, game
237—Barry Sanders vs. T.B., Nov. 13, 1994
Most rushing touchdowns, season
16—Barry Sanders, 1991

Most passing attempts, season
417—Gary Danielson, 1980
Most passing attempts, game
50—Eric Hipple at L.A. Rams, Oct. 19, 1986
Most passes completed, season
252—Gary Danielson, 1984
Most passes completed, game
33—Eric Hipple at Cle., Sept. 28, 1986

Chuck Long vs. G.B., Oct. 25, 1987
Most passing yards, career
15,710—Bobby Layne
Most passing yards, season
3,223—Gary Danielson, 1980
Most passing yards, game
374—Bobby Layne vs. Chi. Bears, Nov. 5, 1950

Most receiving touchdowns, season
15—Cloyce Box, 1952
Most touchdowns, career
68—Barry Sanders
Most field goals, season
34—Jason Hanson, 1993
Longest field goal
54 yards—Glenn Presnell at G.B., Oct. 7, 1934
Eddie Murray at Cin., Dec. 11, 1983

Most interceptions, career
62—Dick LeBeau
Most interceptions, season
12—Don Doll, 1950
Jack Christiansen, 1953
Most sacks, season
23—Al Baker, 1978
Most touchdown passes, season
26—Bobby Layne, 1951
Most pass receptions, career
336—Charlie Sanders

Most pass receptions, season
77—James Jones, 1984
Most pass receptions, game
12—Cloyce Box at Bal., Dec. 3, 1950
James Jones at Cle., Sept. 28, 1986
Most receiving yards, career
5,220—Gail Cogdill
Most receiving yards, season
1,266—Pat Studstill, 1966
Most receiving yards, game
302—Cloyce Box vs. Bal., Dec. 3, 1950

SERIES RECORDS

Detroit vs.: Arizona 28-14-3; Atlanta 18-5; Buffalo 3-1-1; Chicago 48-70-3; Cincinnati 3-3; Cleveland 11-3; Dallas 6-7; Denver 3-4; Green Bay 55-62-6; Houston 2-4; Indianapolis 18-17-2; Kansas City 3-4; L.A. Raiders 2-5; L.A. Rams 27-32-1; Miami 2-3; Minnesota 24-41-2; New England 3-3; New Orleans 6-7-1; N.Y. Giants 14-12-1; N.Y. Jets 4-3; Philadelphia 11-9-2; Pittsburgh 13-11-1; San Diego 3-2; San Francisco 25-27-1; Seattle 2-4; Tampa Bay 17-17; Washington 3-22.

NOTE: Includes records only from 1934 to present.

RETIRED UNIFORM NUMBERS

No.	Player
7	Dutch Clark
22	Bobby Layne
37	Doak Walker
56	Joe Schmidt
85	Chuck Hughes
88	Charlie Sanders

GREEN BAY PACKERS

YEAR-BY-YEAR RECORDS

				REGULAR SEASON					PLAYOFFS		
Year	W	L	T	Pct.	PF	PA	Finish	W	L	Highest round	Coach
1921	3	2	1	.600	...	...	T6th				Curly Lambeau
1922	4	3	3	.571	...	...	T7th				Curly Lambeau
1923	7	2	1	.778	...	...	3rd				Curly Lambeau
1924	7	4	0	.636	...	...	6th				Curly Lambeau
1925	8	5	0	.615	...	...	9th				Curly Lambeau
1926	7	3	3	.700	...	...	5th				Curly Lambeau
1927	7	2	1	.778	...	...	2nd				Curly Lambeau
1928	6	4	3	.600	...	...	4th				Curly Lambeau
1929	12	0	1	1.000	...	...	1st				Curly Lambeau
1930	10	3	1	.769	...	...	1st				Curly Lambeau
1931	12	2	0	.857	...	...	1st				Curly Lambeau
1932	10	3	1	.769	...	...	2nd				Curly Lambeau
1933	5	7	1	.417	170	107	3rd/Western Div.	—	—		Curly Lambeau
1934	7	6	0	.538	156	112	3rd/Western Div.	—	—		Curly Lambeau
1935	8	4	0	.667	181	96	2nd/Western Div.	—	—		Curly Lambeau
1936	10	1	1	.909	248	118	1st/Western Div.	1	0	NFL champ	Curly Lambeau
1937	7	4	0	.636	220	122	T2nd/Western Div.	—	—		Curly Lambeau
1938	8	3	0	.727	223	118	1st/Western Div.	0	1	NFL championship game	Curly Lambeau
1939	9	2	0	.818	233	153	1st/Western Div.	1	0	NFL champ	Curly Lambeau
1940	6	4	1	.600	238	155	2nd/Western Div.	—	—		Curly Lambeau
1941	10	1	0	.909	258	120	2nd/Western Div.	0	1	W. Div. championship game	Curly Lambeau
1942	8	2	1	.800	300	215	2nd/Western Div.	—	—		Curly Lambeau
1943	7	2	1	.778	264	172	2nd/Western Div.	—	—		Curly Lambeau
1944	8	2	0	.800	238	141	1st/Western Div.	1	0	NFL champ	Curly Lambeau
1945	6	4	0	.600	258	173	3rd/Western Div.	—	—		Curly Lambeau
1946	6	5	0	.545	148	158	T3rd/Western Div.	—	—		Curly Lambeau
1947	6	5	1	.545	274	210	3rd/Western Div.	—	—		Curly Lambeau
1948	3	9	0	.250	154	290	4th/Western Div.	—	—		Curly Lambeau
1949	2	10	0	.167	114	329	5th/Western Div.	—	—		Curly Lambeau
1950	3	9	0	.250	244	406	T5th/National Conf.	—	—		Gene Ronzani
1951	3	9	0	.250	254	375	5th/National Conf.	—	—		Gene Ronzani
1952	6	6	0	.500	295	312	4th/National Conf.	—	—		Gene Ronzani
1953	2	9	1	.182	200	338	6th/Western Conf.	—	—		Gene Ronzani, Hugh Devore-Scooter McLean
1954	4	8	0	.333	234	251	5th/Western Conf.	—	—		Lisle Blackbourn
1955	6	6	0	.500	258	276	3rd/Western Conf.	—	—		Lisle Blackbourn
1956	4	8	0	.333	264	342	5th/Western Conf.	—	—		Lisle Blackbourn
1957	3	9	0	.250	218	311	6th/Western Conf.	—	—		Lisle Blackbourn
1958	1	10	1	.091	193	382	6th/Western Conf.	—	—		Scooter McLean
1959	7	5	0	.583	248	246	T3rd/Western Conf.	—	—		Vince Lombardi
1960	8	4	0	.667	332	209	1st/Western Conf.	0	1	NFL championship game	Vince Lombardi
1961	11	3	0	.786	391	223	1st/Western Conf.	1	0	NFL champ	Vince Lombardi
1962	13	1	0	.929	415	148	1st/Western Conf.	1	0	NFL champ	Vince Lombardi
1963	11	2	1	.846	369	206	2nd/Western Conf.	—	—		Vince Lombardi

Year	W	L	T	Pct.	PF	PA	Finish	W	L	Highest round	Coach
							REGULAR SEASON			PLAYOFFS	
1964	8	5	1	.615	342	245	T2nd/Western Conf.	—	—		Vince Lombardi
1965	10	3	1	.769	316	224	1st/Western Conf.	2	0	NFL champ	Vince Lombardi
1966	12	2	0	.857	335	163	1st/Western Conf.	2	0	Super Bowl champ	Vince Lombardi
1967	9	4	1	.692	332	209	1st/Central Div.	3	0	Super Bowl champ	Vince Lombardi
1968	6	7	1	.462	281	227	3rd/Central Div.	—	—		Phil Bengtson
1969	8	6	0	.571	269	221	3rd/Central Div.	—	—		Phil Bengtson
1970	6	8	0	.429	196	293	T3rd/NFC Central Div.	—	—		Phil Bengtson
1971	4	8	2	.333	274	298	4th/NFC Central Div.	—	—		Dan Devine
1972	10	4	0	.714	304	226	1st/NFC Central Div.	0	1	NFC div. playoff game	Dan Devine
1973	5	7	2	.429	202	259	3rd/NFC Central Div.	—	—		Dan Devine
1974	6	8	0	.429	210	206	3rd/NFC Central Div.	—	—		Dan Devine
1975	4	10	0	.286	226	285	T3rd/NFC Central Div.	—	—		Bart Starr
1976	5	9	0	.357	218	299	4th/NFC Central Div.	—	—		Bart Starr
1977	4	10	0	.286	134	219	4th/NFC Central Div.	—	—		Bart Starr
1978	8	7	1	.531	249	269	2nd/NFC Central Div.	—	—		Bart Starr
1979	5	11	0	.313	246	316	4th/NFC Central Div.	—	—		Bart Starr
1980	5	10	1	.344	231	371	T4th/NFC Central Div.	—	—		Bart Starr
1981	8	8	0	.500	324	361	3rd/NFC Central Div.	—	—		Bart Starr
1982	5	3	1	.611	226	169	3rd/NFC	1	1	NFC second-round pl. game	Bart Starr
1983	8	8	0	.500	429	439	T2nd/NFC Central Div.	—	—		Bart Starr
1984	8	8	0	.500	390	309	2nd/NFC Central Div.	—	—		Forrest Gregg
1985	8	8	0	.500	337	355	2nd/NFC Central Div.	—	—		Forrest Gregg
1986	4	12	0	.250	254	418	4th/NFC Central Div.	—	—		Forrest Gregg
1987	5	9	1	.367	255	300	3rd/NFC Central Div.	—	—		Forrest Gregg
1988	4	12	0	.250	240	315	T4th/NFC Central Div.	—	—		Lindy Infante
1989	10	6	0	.625	362	356	2nd/NFC Central Div.	—	—		Lindy Infante
1990	6	10	0	.375	271	347	T2nd/NFC Central Div.	—	—		Lindy Infante
1991	4	12	0	.250	273	313	4th/NFC Central Div.	—	—		Lindy Infante
1992	9	7	0	.563	276	296	2nd/NFC Central Div.	—	—		Mike Holmgren
1993	9	7	0	.563	340	282	T2nd/NFC Central Div.	1	1	NFC div. playoff game	Mike Holmgren
1994	9	7	0	.563	382	287	T2nd/NFC Central Div.	1	1	NFC div. playoff game	Mike Holmgren

FIRST-ROUND DRAFT PICKS

1936—Russ Letlow, G, San Francisco
1937—Ed Jankowski, B, Wisconsin
1938—Cecil Isbell, B, Purdue
1939—Larry Buhler, B, Minnesota
1940—Hal Van Every, B, Marquette
1941—George Paskvan, B, Wisconsin
1942—Urban Odson, T, Minnesota
1943—Dick Wildung, T, Minnesota
1944—Merv Pregulman, G, Michigan
1945—Walt Schlinkman, G, Texas Tech
1946—Johnny Strzykalski, B, Marquette
1947—Ernie Case, B, UCLA
1948—Earl Girard, B, Wisconsin
1949—Stan Heath, B, Nevada
1950—Clayton Tonnemaker, G, Minnesota
1951—Bob Gain, T, Kentucky
1952—Babe Parilli, QB, Kentucky
1953—Al Carmichael, B, Southern California
1954—Art Hunter, T, Notre Dame
    Veryl Switzer, B, Kansas State
1955—Tom Bettis, G, Purdue
1956—Jack Losch, B, Miami
1957—Paul Hornung, B, Notre Dame*
    Ron Kramer, E, Michigan
1958—Dan Currie, C, Michigan State
1959—Randy Duncan, B, Iowa*
1960—Tom Moore, RB, Vanderbilt
1961—Herb Adderley, DB, Michigan State
1962—Earl Gros, RB, Louisiana State
1963—Dave Robinson, LB, Penn State
1964—Lloyd Voss, DT, Nebraska
1965—Donny Anderson, RB, Texas Tech
    Larry Elkins, E, Baylor
1966—Jim Grabowski, RB, Illinois
    Gale Gillingham, G, Minnesota
1967—Bob Hyland, C, Boston College
    Don Horn, QB, San Diego State
1968—Fred Carr, LB, Texas-El Paso
    Bill Lueck, G, Arizona

1969—Rich Moore, DT, Villanova
1970—Mike McCoy, DT, Notre Dame
    Rich McGeorge, TE, Elon
1971—John Brockington, RB, Ohio State
1972—Willie Buchanon, DB, San Diego State
    Jerry Tagge, QB, Nebraska
1973—Barry Smith, WR, Florida State
1974—Barty Smith, RB, Richmond
1975—None
1976—Mark Koncar, T, Colorado
1977—Mike Butler, DE, Kansas
    Ezra Johnson, DE, Morris Brown
1978—James Lofton, WR, Stanford
    John Anderson, LB, Michigan
1979—Eddie Lee Ivery, RB, Georgia Tech
1980—Bruce Clark, DT, Penn State
    George Cumby, LB, Oklahoma
1981—Rich Campbell, QB, California
1982—Ron Hallstrom, G, Iowa
1983—Tim Lewis, DB, Pittsburgh
1984—Alphonso Carreker, DT, Florida State
1985—Ken Ruettgers, T, Southern California
1986—None
1987—Brent Fullwood, RB, Auburn
1988—Sterling Sharpe, WR, South Carolina
1989—Tony Mandarich, T, Michigan State
1990—Tony Bennett, LB, Mississippi
    Darrell Thompson, RB, Minnesota
1991—Vincent Clark, DB, Ohio State
1992—Terrell Buckley, DB, Florida State
1993—Wayne Simmons, LB, Clemson
    George Teague, DB, Alabama
1994—Aaron Taylor, T, Notre Dame
1995—Craig Newsome, DB, Arizona State
    *First player chosen in draft.

FRANCHISE RECORDS

Most rushing yards, career
8,207—Jim Taylor

Most rushing yards, season
1,474—Jim Taylor, 1962

Most rushing yards, game
186—Jim Taylor vs. NYG, Dec. 3, 1961

Most rushing touchdowns, season
19—Jim Taylor, 1962

Most passing attempts, season
599—Don Majkowski, 1989

Most passing attempts, game
59—Don Majkowski at Det., Nov. 12, 1989

Most passes completed, season
363—Brett Favre, 1994

Most passes completed, game
36—Brett Favre at Chi., Dec. 5, 1993

Most passing yards, career
23,718—Bart Starr

Most passing yards, season
4,458—Lynn Dickey, 1983

Most passing yards, game
418—Lynn Dickey at T.B., Oct. 12, 1980

Most touchdown passes, season
33—Brett Favre, 1994

Most pass receptions, career
595—Sterling Sharpe

Most pass receptions, season
112—Sterling Sharpe, 1993

Most pass receptions, game
14—Don Hutson at NYG, Nov. 22, 1942

Most receiving yards, career
9,656—James Lofton

Most receiving yards, season
1,461—Sterling Sharpe, 1992

Most receiving yards, game
257—Bill Howton vs. L.A. Rams, Oct. 21, 1956

Most receiving touchdowns, season
18—Sterling Sharpe, 1994

Most touchdowns, career
105—Don Hutson

Most field goals, season
33—Chester Marcol, 1972

Longest field goal
54 yards—Chris Jacke at Det., Jan. 2, 1994

Most interceptions, career
52—Bobby Dillon

Most interceptions, season
10—Irv Comp, 1943

Most sacks, career
84—Ezra Johnson

Most sacks, season
20.5—Ezra Johnson, 1978

SERIES RECORDS

Green Bay vs.: Arizona 41-21-4; Atlanta 10-9; Buffalo 1-5; Chicago 61-82-6; Cincinnati 3-4; Cleveland 7-6; Dallas 9-6; Denver 2-4-1; Detroit 62-55-6; Houston 3-3; Indianapolis 18-18-1; Kansas City 1-4-1; L.A. Raiders 2-5; L.A. Rams 25-39-1; Miami 0-8; Minnesota 32-34-1; New England 2-3; New Orleans 12-4; N.Y. Giants 21-20-2; N.Y. Jets 2-5; Philadelphia 19-8; Pittsburgh 20-11; San Diego 4-1; San Francisco 21-25-1; Seattle 3-3; Tampa Bay 19-12-1; Washington 9-11.

RETIRED UNIFORM NUMBERS

No.	Player
3	Tony Canadeo
14	Don Hutson
15	Bart Starr
66	Ray Nitschke

HOUSTON OILERS

YEAR-BY-YEAR RECORDS

| | | | REGULAR SEASON | | | | | | PLAYOFFS | | |
Year	W	L	T	Pct.	PF	PA	Finish	W	L	Highest round	Coach
1960*	10	4	0	.714	379	285	1st/Eastern Div.	1	0	AFL champ	Lou Rymkus
1961*	10	3	1	.769	513	242	1st/Eastern Div.	1	0	AFL champ	Lou Rymkus, Wally Lemm
1962*	11	3	0	.786	387	270	1st/Eastern Div.	0	1	AFL championship game	Pop Ivy
1963*	6	8	0	.429	302	372	3rd/Eastern Div.	—	—		Pop Ivy
1964*	4	10	0	.286	310	355	4th/Eastern Div.	—	—		Sammy Baugh
1965*	4	10	0	.286	298	429	4th/Eastern Div.	—	—		Hugh Taylor
1966*	3	11	0	.214	335	396	T4th/Eastern Div.	—	—		Wally Lemm
1967*	9	4	1	.692	258	199	1st/Eastern Div.	0	1	AFL championship game	Wally Lemm
1968*	7	7	0	.500	303	248	2nd/Eastern Div.	—	—		Wally Lemm
1969*	6	6	2	.500	278	279	2nd/Eastern Div.	0	1	Div. playoff game	Wally Lemm
1970	3	10	1	.231	217	352	4th/AFC Central Div.	—	—		Wally Lemm
1971	4	9	1	.308	251	330	3rd/AFC Central Div.	—	—		Ed Hughes
1972	1	13	0	.071	164	380	4th/AFC Central Div.	—	—		Bill Peterson
1973	1	13	0	.071	199	447	4th/AFC Central Div.	—	—		Bill Peterson, Sid Gillman
1974	7	7	0	.500	236	282	T2nd/AFC Central Div.	—	—		Sid Gillman
1975	10	4	0	.714	293	226	3rd/AFC Central Div.	—	—		Bum Phillips
1976	5	9	0	.357	222	273	4th/AFC Central Div.	—	—		Bum Phillips
1977	8	6	0	.571	299	230	T2nd/AFC Central Div.	—	—		Bum Phillips
1978	10	6	0	.625	283	298	2nd/AFC Central Div.	2	1	AFC championship game	Bum Phillips
1979	11	5	0	.688	362	331	2nd/AFC Central Div.	2	1	AFC championship game	Bum Phillips
1980	11	5	0	.688	295	251	2nd/AFC Central Div.	0	1	AFC wild-card game	Bum Phillips
1981	7	9	0	.438	281	355	3rd/AFC Central Div.	—	—		Ed Biles
1982	1	8	0	.111	136	245	13th/AFC	—	—		Ed Biles
1983	2	14	0	.125	288	460	4th/AFC Central Div.	—	—		Ed Biles, Chuck Studley
1984	3	13	0	.188	240	437	4th/AFC Central Div.	—	—		Hugh Campbell
1985	5	11	0	.313	284	412	4th/AFC Central Div.	—	—		H. Campbell, J. Glanville
1986	5	11	0	.313	274	329	4th/AFC Central Div.	—	—		Jerry Glanville
1987	9	6	0	.600	345	349	2nd/AFC Central Div.	1	1	AFC div. playoff game	Jerry Glanville
1988	10	6	0	.625	424	365	T2nd/AFC Central Div.	1	1	AFC div. playoff game	Jerry Glanville
1989	9	7	0	.563	365	412	T2nd/AFC Central Div.	0	1	AFC wild-card game	Jerry Glanville
1990	9	7	0	.563	405	307	2nd/AFC Central Div.	0	1	AFC wild-card game	Jack Pardee
1991	11	5	0	.688	386	251	1st/AFC Central Div.	1	1	AFC div. playoff game	Jack Pardee

				REGULAR SEASON						PLAYOFFS		
Year	W	L	T	Pct.	PF	PA	Finish	W	L	Highest round	Coach
1992	10	6	0	.625	352	258	2nd/AFC Central Div.	0	1	AFC wild-card game	Jack Pardee
1993	12	4	0	.750	368	238	1st/AFC Central Div.	0	1	AFC div. playoff game	Jack Pardee
1994	2	14	0	.125	226	352	4th/AFC Central Div.	—	—		Jack Pardee, Jeff Fisher

*American Football League.

FIRST-ROUND DRAFT PICKS

1960—Billy Cannon, RB, Louisiana State
1961—Mike Ditka, E, Pittsburgh
1962—Ray Jacobs, DT, Howard Payne
1963—Danny Brabham, LB, Arkansas
1964—Scott Appleton, DT, Texas
1965—Lawrence Elkins, WR, Baylor* (AFL)
1966—Tommy Nobis, LB, Texas
1967—George Webster, LB, Michigan State
      Tom Regner, G, Notre Dame
1968—None
1969—Ron Pritchard, LB, Arizona State
1970—Doug Wilkerson, G, North Carolina Central
1971—Dan Pastorini, QB, Santa Clara
1972—Greg Sampson, DE, Stanford
1973—John Matuszak, DE, Tampa*
      George Amundson, RB, Iowa State
1974—None
1975—Robert Brazile, LB, Jackson State
      Don Hardeman, RB, Texas A&I
1976—None
1977—Morris Towns, T, Missouri
1978—Earl Campbell, RB, Texas*

1979—None
1980—None
1981—None
1982—Mike Munchak, G, Penn State
1983—Bruce Matthews, G, Southern California
1984—Dean Steinkuhler, G, Nebraska
1985—Ray Childress, DE, Texas A&M
      Richard Johnson, DB, Wisconsin
1986—Jim Everett, QB, Purdue
1987—Alonzo Highsmith, FB, Miami (Fla.)
      Haywood Jeffires, WR, North Carolina State
1988—Lorenzo White, RB, Michigan State
1989—David Williams, T, Florida
1990—Lamar Lathon, LB, Houston
1991—None
1992—None
1993—Brad Hopkins, G, Illinois
1994—Henry Ford, DE, Arkansas
1995—Steve McNair, QB, Alcorn State
*First player chosen in draft.

FRANCHISE RECORDS

Most rushing yards, career
8,574—Earl Campbell
Most rushing yards, season
1,934—Earl Campbell, 1980
Most rushing yards, game
216—Billy Cannon at N.Y. Titans, Dec. 10, 1961
Most rushing touchdowns, season
19—Earl Campbell, 1979
Most passing attempts, season
655—Warren Moon, 1991
Most passing attempts, game
68—George Blanda at Buf., Nov. 1, 1964
Most passes completed, season
404—Warren Moon, 1991
Most passes completed, game
41—Warren Moon vs. Dal., Nov. 10, 1991
Most passing yards, career
33,685—Warren Moon

Most passing yards, season
4,690—Warren Moon, 1991
Most passing yards, game
527—Warren Moon at K.C., Dec. 16, 1990
Most touchdown passes, season
36—George Blanda, 1961
Most pass receptions, career
542—Ernest Givins
Most pass receptions, season
101—Charley Hennigan, 1964
Most pass receptions, game
13—Charley Hennigan at Boston, Oct. 13, 1961
    Haywood Jeffires at NYJ, Oct. 13, 1991
Most receiving yards, career
7,935—Ernest Givins
Most receiving yards, season
1,746—Charley Hennigan, 1961

Most receiving yards, game
272—Charley Hennigan at Boston, Oct. 13, 1961
Most receiving touchdowns, season
17—Bill Groman, 1961
Most touchdowns, career
73—Earl Campbell
Most field goals, season
29—Al Del Greco, 1993
Longest field goal
55 yards—George Blanda vs. S.D., Dec. 3, 1961
Most interceptions, career
45—Jim Norton
Most interceptions, season
12—Freddy Glick, 1963
    Mike Reinfeldt, 1979
Most sacks, season
15.5—Jesse Baker, 1979

SERIES RECORDS

Houston vs.: Arizona 2-4; Atlanta 3-5; Buffalo 20-13; Chicago 4-2; Cincinnati 26-25-1; Cleveland 20-29; Dallas 3-5; Denver 19-11-1; Detroit 4-2; Green Bay 3-3; Indianapolis 7-7; Kansas City 17-22; L.A. Raiders 13-20; L.A. Rams 2-5; Miami 11-11; Minnesota 3-3; New England 14-17-1; New Orleans 3-4-1; N.Y. Giants 0-5; N.Y. Jets 18-12-1; Philadelphia 0-6; Pittsburgh 18-31; San Diego 13-18-1; San Francisco 3-5; Seattle 4-4; Tampa Bay 3-1; Washington 3-3.

RETIRED UNIFORM NUMBERS

No.	Player
34	Earl Campbell
43	Jim Norton
63	Mike Munchak
65	Elvin Bethea

INDIANAPOLIS COLTS

YEAR-BY-YEAR RECORDS

				REGULAR SEASON				PLAYOFFS			
Year	W	L	T	Pct.	PF	PA	Finish	W	L	Highest round	Coach
1953*	3	9	0	.250	182	350	5th/Western Conf.	—	—		Keith Molesworth
1954*	3	9	0	.250	131	279	6th/Western Conf.	—	—		Weeb Ewbank
1955*	5	6	1	.455	214	239	4th/Western Conf.	—	—		Weeb Ewbank
1956*	5	7	0	.417	270	322	4th/Western Conf.	—	—		Weeb Ewbank
1957*	7	5	0	.583	303	235	3rd/Western Conf.	—	—		Weeb Ewbank
1958*	9	3	0	.750	381	203	1st/Western Conf.	1	0	NFL champ	Weeb Ewbank
1959*	9	3	0	.750	374	251	1st/Western Conf.	1	0	NFL champ	Weeb Ewbank
1960*	6	6	0	.500	288	234	4th/Western Conf.	—	—		Weeb Ewbank
1961*	8	6	0	.571	302	307	T3rd/Western Conf.	—	—		Weeb Ewbank
1962*	7	7	0	.500	293	288	4th/Western Conf.	—	—		Weeb Ewbank
1963*	8	6	0	.571	316	285	3rd/Western Conf.	—	—		Don Shula
1964*	12	2	0	.857	428	225	1st/Western Conf.	0	1	NFL championship game	Don Shula
1965*	10	3	1	.769	389	284	2nd/Western Conf.	0	1	W. Conf. champ. game	Don Shula
1966*	9	5	0	.643	314	226	2nd/Western Conf.	—	—		Don Shula
1967*	11	1	2	.917	394	198	2nd/Coastal Div.	—	—		Don Shula
1968*	13	1	0	.929	402	144	1st/Coastal Div.	2	1	Super Bowl	Don Shula
1969*	8	5	1	.615	279	268	2nd/Coastal Div.	—	—		Don Shula
1970*	11	2	1	.846	321	234	1st/AFC Eastern Div.	3	0	Super Bowl champ	Don McCafferty
1971*	10	4	0	.714	313	140	2nd/AFC Eastern Div.	1	1	AFC championship game	Don McCafferty
1972*	5	9	0	.357	235	252	3rd/AFC Eastern Div.	—	—		McCafferty, John Sandusky
1973*	4	10	0	.286	226	341	T4th/AFC Eastern Div.	—	—		Howard Schnellenberger
1974*	2	12	0	.143	190	329	5th/AFC Eastern Div.	—	—		Schnellenberger, Joe Thomas
1975*	10	4	0	.714	395	269	1st/AFC Eastern Div.	0	1	AFC div. playoff game	Ted Marchibroda
1976*	11	3	0	.786	417	246	1st/AFC Eastern Div.	0	1	AFC div. playoff game	Ted Marchibroda
1977*	10	4	0	.714	295	221	1st/AFC Eastern Div.	0	1	AFC div. playoff game	Ted Marchibroda
1978*	5	11	0	.313	239	421	T4th/AFC Eastern Div.	—	—		Ted Marchibroda
1979*	5	11	0	.313	271	351	5th/AFC Eastern Div.	—	—		Ted Marchibroda
1980*	7	9	0	.438	355	387	4th/AFC Eastern Div.	—	—		Mike McCormack
1981*	2	14	0	.125	259	533	4th/AFC Eastern Div.	—	—		Mike McCormack
1982*	0	8	1	.056	113	236	14th/AFC	—	—		Frank Kush
1983*	7	9	0	.438	264	354	T4th/AFC Eastern Div.	—	—		Frank Kush
1984	4	12	0	.250	239	414	4th/AFC Eastern Div.	—	—		Frank Kush, Hal Hunter
1985	5	11	0	.313	320	386	4th/AFC Eastern Div.	—	—		Rod Dowhower
1986	3	13	0	.188	229	400	5th/AFC Eastern Div.	—	—		Rod Dowhower, Ron Meyer
1987	9	6	0	.600	300	238	1st/AFC Eastern Div.	0	1	AFC div. playoff game	Ron Meyer
1988	9	7	0	.563	354	315	T2nd/AFC Eastern Div.	—	—		Ron Meyer
1989	8	8	0	.500	298	301	T2nd/AFC Eastern Div.	—	—		Ron Meyer
1990	7	9	0	.438	281	353	3rd/AFC Eastern Div.	—	—		Ron Meyer
1991	1	15	0	.063	143	381	5th/AFC Eastern Div.	—	—		Ron Meyer, Rick Venturi
1992	9	7	0	.563	216	302	3rd/AFC Eastern Div.	—	—		Ted Marchibroda
1993	4	12	0	.250	189	378	5th/AFC Eastern Div.	—	—		Ted Marchibroda
1994	8	8	0	.500	307	320	3rd/AFC Eastern Div.	—	—		Ted Marchibroda

*Baltimore Colts.

FIRST-ROUND DRAFT PICKS

1953—Billy Vessels, B, Oklahoma
1954—Cotton Davidson, B, Baylor
1955—George Shaw, B, Oregon*
    Alan Ameche, B, Wisconsin
1956—Lenny Moore, B, Penn State
1957—Jim Parker, T, Ohio State
1958—Lenny Lyles, B, Louisville
1959—Jackie Burkett, C, Auburn
1960—Ron Mix, T, Southern California
1961—Tom Matte, RB, Ohio State
1962—Wendell Harris, DB, Louisiana State
1963—Bob Vogel, T, Ohio State
1964—Marv Woodson, DB, Indiana
1965—Mike Curtis, LB, Duke
1966—Sam Ball, T, Kentucky
1967—Bubba Smith, DT, Michigan State*
    Jim Detwiler, RB, Michigan
1968—John Williams, G, Minnesota
1969—Eddie Hinton, WR, Oklahoma
1970—Norm Bulaich, RB, Texas Christian
1971—Don McCauley, RB, North Carolina
    Leonard Dunlap, DB, North Texas State

1972—Tom Drougas, T, Oregon
1973—Bert Jones, QB, Louisiana State
    Joe Ehrmann, DT, Syracuse
1974—John Dutton, DE, Nebraska
    Roger Carr, WR, Louisiana Tech
1975—Ken Huff, G, North Carolina
1976—Ken Novak, DT, Purdue
1977—Randy Burke, WR, Kentucky
1978—Reese McCall, TE, Auburn
1979—Barry Krauss, LB, Alabama
1980—Curtis Dickey, RB, Texas A&M
    Derrick Hatchett, DB, Texas
1981—Randy McMillan, RB, Pittsburgh
    Donnell Thompson, DT, North Carolina
1982—Johnie Cooks, LB, Mississippi State
    Art Schlichter, QB, Ohio State
1983—John Elway, QB, Stanford*
1984—L. Coleman, DB, Vanderbilt
    Ron Solt, G, Maryland
1985—Duane Bickett, LB, Southern California
1986—Jon Hand, DT, Alabama
1987—Cornelius Bennett, LB, Alabama

1988—None
1989—Andre Rison, WR, Michigan State
1990—Jeff George, QB, Illinois*
1991—None
1992—Steve Emtman, DE, Washington*
     Quentin Coryatt, LB, Texas A&M

1993—Sean Dawkins, WR, California
1994—Marshall Faulk, RB, San Diego State
     Trev Alberts, LB, Nebraska
1995—Ellis Johnson, DT, Florida
   *First player chosen in draft.

FRANCHISE RECORDS

Most rushing yards, career
5,487—Lydell Mitchell
Most rushing yards, season
1,659—Eric Dickerson, 1988
Most rushing yards, game
198—Norm Bulaich vs. NYJ, Sept. 19, 1971
Most rushing touchdowns, season
16—Lenny Moore, 1964
Most passing attempts, season
485—Jeff George, 1991
Most passing attempts, game
59—Jeff George at Was., Nov. 7, 1993
Most passes completed, season
292—Jeff George, 1991
Most passes completed, game
37—Jeff George at Was., Nov. 7, 1993
Most passing yards, career
39,768—Johnny Unitas
Most passing yards, season
3,481—Johnny Unitas, 1963

Most passing yards, game
401—Johnny Unitas vs. Atl., Sept. 17, 1967
Most touchdown passes, season
32—Johnny Unitas, 1959
Most pass receptions, career
631—Raymond Berry
Most pass receptions, season
85—Reggie Langhorne, 1993
Most pass receptions, game
13—Lydell Mitchell vs. NYJ, Dec. 15, 1974
    Joe Washington at K.C., Sept. 2, 1979
Most receiving yards, career
9,275—Raymond Berry
Most receiving yards, season
1,298—Raymond Berry, 1960
Most receiving yards, game
224—Raymond Berry at Was., Nov. 10, 1957

Most receiving touchdowns, season
14—Raymond Berry, 1959
Most touchdowns, career
113—Lenny Moore
Most field goals, season
30—Raul Allegre, 1983
Longest field goal
58 yards—Dan Miller at S.D., Dec. 26, 1982
Most interceptions, career
57—Bob Boyd
Most interceptions, season
11—Tom Keane, 1953
Most sacks, career
56.5—Fred Cook
Most sacks, season
17—John Dutton, 1975

SERIES RECORDS

Indianapolis vs.: Arizona 5-6; Atlanta 10-0; Buffalo 22-26-1; Chicago 21-16; Cincinnati 10-5; Cleveland 7-13; Dallas 2-7; Denver 2-9; Detroit 17-18-2; Green Bay 18-18-1; Houston 7-7; Kansas City 4-6; L.A. Raiders 2-4; L.A. Rams 20-17-2; Miami 15-35; Minnesota 11-6-1; New England 20-29; New Orleans 3-2; N.Y. Giants 5-5; N.Y. Jets 28-21; Philadelphia 6-6; Pittsburgh 4-12; San Diego 6-8; San Francisco 21-16; Seattle 4-1; Tampa Bay 5-3; Washington 16-8.

   NOTE: Includes records as Baltimore Colts from 1953 through 1983.

RETIRED UNIFORM NUMBERS

No.	Player
19	Johnny Unitas
22	Buddy Young
24	Lenny Moore
70	Art Donovan
77	Jim Parker
82	Raymond Berry
89	Gino Marchetti

KANSAS CITY CHIEFS

YEAR-BY-YEAR RECORDS

			REGULAR SEASON				PLAYOFFS			
Year	W	L	T	Pct.	PF	PA	Finish	W	L	Highest round	Coach
1960*†	8	6	0	.571	362	253	2nd/Western Div.	—	—		Hank Stram
1961*†	6	8	0	.429	334	343	2nd/Western Div.	—	—		Hank Stram
1962*†	11	3	0	.786	389	233	1st/Western Div.	1	0	AFL champ	Hank Stram
1963*	5	7	2	.417	347	263	3rd/Western Div.	—	—		Hank Stram
1964*	7	7	0	.500	366	306	2nd/Western Div.	—	—		Hank Stram
1965*	7	5	2	.583	322	285	3rd/Western Div.	—	—		Hank Stram
1966*	11	2	1	.846	448	276	1st/Western Div.	1	1	Super Bowl	Hank Stram
1967*	9	5	0	.643	408	254	2nd/Western Div.	—	—		Hank Stram
1968*	12	2	0	.857	371	170	2nd/Western Div.	0	1	W. Div. champ. game	Hank Stram
1969*	11	3	0	.786	359	177	2nd/Western Div.	3	0	Super Bowl champ	Hank Stram
1970	7	5	2	.583	272	244	2nd/AFC Western Div.	—	—		Hank Stram
1971	10	3	1	.769	302	208	1st/AFC Western Div.	0	1	AFC div. playoff game	Hank Stram
1972	8	6	0	.571	287	254	2nd/AFC Western Div.	—	—		Hank Stram
1973	7	5	2	.571	231	192	T2nd/AFC Western Div.	—	—		Hank Stram
1974	5	9	0	.357	233	293	T3rd/AFC Western Div.	—	—		Hank Stram
1975	5	9	0	.357	282	341	3rd/AFC Western Div.	—	—		Paul Wiggin
1976	5	9	0	.357	290	376	4th/AFC Western Div.	—	—		Paul Wiggin
1977	2	12	0	.143	225	349	5th/AFC Western Div.	—	—		Paul Wiggin, Tom Bettis
1978	4	12	0	.250	243	327	5th/AFC Western Div.	—	—		Marv Levy

Year	W	L	T	Pct.	PF	PA	Finish	W	L	Highest round	Coach
1979	7	9	0	.438	238	262	5th/AFC Western Div.	—	—		Marv Levy
1980	8	8	0	.500	319	336	T3rd/AFC Western Div.	—	—		Marv Levy
1981	9	7	0	.563	343	290	3rd/AFC Western Div.	—	—		Marv Levy
1982	3	6	0	.333	176	184	11th/AFC	—	—		Marv Levy
1983	6	10	0	.375	386	367	T4th/AFC Western Div.	—	—		John Mackovic
1984	8	8	0	.500	314	324	4th/AFC Western Div.	—	—		John Mackovic
1985	6	10	0	.375	317	360	5th/AFC Western Div.	—	—		John Mackovic
1986	10	6	0	.625	358	326	2nd/AFC Western Div.	0	1	AFC wild-card game	John Mackovic
1987	4	11	0	.267	273	388	5th/AFC Western Div.	—	—		Frank Gansz
1988	4	11	1	.281	254	320	5th/AFC Western Div.	—	—		Frank Gansz
1989	8	7	1	.531	318	286	2nd/AFC Western Div.	—	—		Marty Schottenheimer
1990	11	5	0	.688	369	257	2nd/AFC Western Div.	0	1	AFC wild-card game	Marty Schottenheimer
1991	10	6	0	.625	322	252	2nd/AFC Western Div.	1	1	AFC div. playoff game	Marty Schottenheimer
1992	10	6	0	.625	348	282	2nd/AFC Western Div.	0	1	AFC wild-card game	Marty Schottenheimer
1993	11	5	0	.688	328	291	1st/AFC Western Div.	2	1	AFC championship game	Marty Schottenheimer
1994	9	7	0	.563	319	298	2nd/AFC Western Div.	0	1	AFC wild-card game	Marty Schottenheimer

*American Football League.
†Dallas Texans.

FIRST-ROUND DRAFT PICKS

1960—Don Meredith, QB, Southern Methodist
1961—E.J. Holub, C, Texas Tech
1962—Ronnie Bull, RB, Baylor
1963—Buck Buchanan, DT, Grambling* (AFL)
      Ed Budde, G, Michigan State
1964—Pete Beathard, QB, Southern California
1965—Gale Sayers, RB, Kansas
1966—Aaron Brown, DE, Minnesota
1967—Gene Trosch, DE, Miami
1968—Mo Moorman, G, Texas A&M
      George Daney, G, Texas-El Paso
1969—Jim Marsalis, DB, Tennessee State
1970—Sid Smith, T, Southern California
1971—Elmo Wright, WR, Houston
1972—Jeff Kinney, RB, Nebraska
1973—None
1974—Woody Green, RB, Arizona State
1975—None
1976—Rod Walters, G, Iowa
1977—Gary Green, DB, Baylor
1978—Art Still, DE, Kentucky

1979—Mike Bell, DE, Colorado State
      Steve Fuller, QB, Clemson
1980—Brad Budde, G, Southern California
1981—Willie Scott, TE, South Carolina
1982—Anthony Hancock, WR, Tennessee
1983—Todd Blackledge, QB, Penn State
1984—Bill Maas, DT, Pittsburgh
      John Alt, T, Iowa
1985—Ethan Horton, RB, North Carolina
1986—Brian Jozwiak, T, West Virginia
1987—Paul Palmer, RB, Temple
1988—Neil Smith, DE, Nebraska
1989—Derrick Thomas, LB, Alabama
1990—Percy Snow, LB, Michigan State
1991—Harvey Williams, RB, Louisiana State
1992—Dale Carter, DB, Tennessee
1993—None
1994—Greg Hill, RB, Texas A&M
1995—Trezelle Jenkins, T, Michigan
   *First player chosen in draft.

FRANCHISE RECORDS

Most rushing yards, career
4,897—Christian Okoye

Most rushing yards, season
1,480—Christian Okoye, 1989

Most rushing yards, game
200—Barry Word vs. Det., Oct. 14, 1990

Most rushing touchdowns, season
13—Abner Haynes, 1962

Most passing attempts, season
603—Bill Kenney, 1983

Most passing attempts, game
55—Joe Montana at S.D., Oct. 9, 1994
     Steve Bono at Mia., Dec. 12, 1994

Most passes completed, season
346—Bill Kenney, 1983

Most passes completed, game
37—Joe Montana at S.D., Oct. 9, 1994

Most passing yards, career
28,507—Len Dawson

Most passing yards, season
4,348—Bill Kenney, 1983

Most passing yards, game
435—Len Dawson vs. Den., Nov. 1, 1964

Most touchdown passes, season
30—Len Dawson, 1964

Most pass receptions, career
416—Henry Marshall

Most pass receptions, season
80—Carlos Carson, 1983

Most pass receptions, game
12—Ed Podolak vs. Den., Oct. 7, 1973

Most receiving yards, career
7,306—Otis Taylor

Most receiving yards, season
1,351—Carlos Carson, 1983

Most receiving yards, game
309—Stephone Paige vs. S.D., Dec. 22, 1985

Most receiving touchdowns, season
12—Chris Burford, 1962

Most touchdowns, career
57—Otis Taylor

Most field goals, season
34—Nick Lowery, 1990

Longest field goal
58 yards—Nick Lowery at Was., Sept. 18, 1983
     Nick Lowery vs. L.A. Raiders, Sept. 12, 1985

Most interceptions, career
58—Emmitt Thomas

Most interceptions, season
12—Emmitt Thomas, 1974

Most sacks, career
72.5—Art Still

Most sacks, season
20—Derrick Thomas, 1990

LOS ANGELES RAIDERS

YEAR-BY-YEAR RECORDS

		REGULAR SEASON						PLAYOFFS			
Year	W	L	T	Pct.	PF	PA	Finish	W	L	Highest round	Coach
1960*†	6	8	0	.429	319	388	3rd/Western Div.	—	—		Eddie Erdelatz
1961*†	2	12	0	.143	237	458	4th/Western Div.	—	—		E. Erdelatz, Marty Feldman
1962*†	1	13	0	.071	213	370	4th/Western Div.	—	—		M. Feldman, Red Conkright
1963*†	10	4	0	.714	363	288	2nd/Western Div.	—	—		Al Davis
1964*†	5	7	2	.417	303	350	3rd/Western Div.	—	—		Al Davis
1965*†	8	5	1	.615	298	239	2nd/Western Div.	—	—		Al Davis
1966*†	8	5	1	.615	315	288	2nd/Western Div.	—	—		John Rauch
1967*†	13	1	0	.929	468	233	1st/Western Div.	1	1	Super Bowl	John Rauch
1968*†	12	2	0	.857	453	233	1st/Western Div.	1	1	AFL championship game	John Rauch
1969*†	12	1	1	.923	377	242	1st/Western Div.	1	1	AFL championship game	John Madden
1970†	8	4	2	.667	300	293	1st/AFC Western Div.	1	1	AFC championship game	John Madden
1971†	8	4	2	.667	344	278	2nd/AFC Western Div.	—	—		John Madden
1972†	10	3	1	.750	365	248	1st/AFC Western Div.	0	1	AFC div. playoff game	John Madden
1973†	9	4	1	.679	292	175	1st/AFC Western Div.	1	1	AFC championship game	John Madden
1974†	12	2	0	.857	355	228	1st/AFC Western Div.	1	1	AFC championship game	John Madden
1975†	11	3	0	.786	375	255	1st/AFC Western Div.	1	1	AFC championship game	John Madden
1976†	13	1	0	.929	350	237	1st/AFC Western Div.	3	0	Super Bowl champ	John Madden
1977†	11	3	0	.786	351	230	2nd/AFC Western Div.	1	1	AFC championship game	John Madden
1978†	9	7	0	.563	311	283	T2nd/AFC Western Div.	—	—		John Madden
1979†	9	7	0	.563	365	337	T3rd/AFC Western Div.	—	—		Tom Flores
1980†	11	5	0	.688	364	306	2nd/AFC Western Div.	4	0	Super Bowl champ	Tom Flores
1981†	7	9	0	.438	273	343	4th/AFC Western Div.	—	—		Tom Flores
1982	8	1	0	.889	260	200	1st/AFC	1	1	AFC second-round pl. game	Tom Flores
1983	12	4	0	.750	442	338	1st/AFC Western Div.	3	0	Super Bowl champ	Tom Flores
1984	11	5	0	.688	368	278	3rd/AFC Western Div.	0	1	AFC wild-card game	Tom Flores
1985	12	4	0	.750	354	308	1st/AFC Western Div.	0	1	AFC div. playoff game	Tom Flores
1986	8	8	0	.500	323	346	4th/AFC Western Div.	—	—		Tom Flores
1987	5	10	0	.333	301	289	4th/AFC Western Div.	—	—		Tom Flores
1988	7	9	0	.438	325	369	3rd/AFC Western Div.	—	—		Mike Shanahan
1989	8	8	0	.500	315	297	3rd/AFC Western Div.	—	—		Mike Shanahan, Art Shell
1990	12	4	0	.750	337	268	1st/AFC Western Div.	1	1	AFC championship game	Art Shell
1991	9	7	0	.563	298	297	3rd/AFC Western Div.	0	1	AFC wild-card game	Art Shell
1992	7	9	0	.438	249	281	4th/AFC Western Div.	—	—		Art Shell
1993	10	6	0	.625	306	326	2nd/AFC Western Div.	1	1	AFC div. playoff game	Art Shell
1994	9	7	0	.563	303	327	3rd/AFC Western Div.	—	—		Art Shell

*American Football League.
†Oakland Raiders.

FIRST-ROUND DRAFT PICKS

1960—Dale Hackbart, DB, Wisconsin
1961—Joe Rutgens, DT, Illinois
1962—Roman Gabriel, QB, North Carolina State* (AFL)
1963—None
1964—Tony Lorick, RB, Arizona State
1965—Harry Schuh, T, Memphis State
1966—Rodger Bird, DB, Kentucky
1967—Gene Upshaw, G, Texas A&I
1968—Eldridge Dickey, QB, Tenn. State
1969—Art Thoms, DT, Syracuse
1970—Raymond Chester, TE, Morgan State
1971—Jack Tatum, DB, Ohio State
1972—Mike Siani, WR, Villanova
1973—Ray Guy, P, So. Mississippi
1974—Henry Lawrence, T, Florida A&M

1975—Neal Colzie, DB, Ohio State
1976—None
1977—None
1978—None
1979—None
1980—Marc Wilson, QB, Brigham Young
1981—Ted Watts, DB, Texas Tech
        Curt Marsh, G, Washington
1982—Marcus Allen, RB, Southern California
1983—Don Mosebar, T, Southern California
1984—None
1985—Jessie Hester, WR, Florida State
1986—Bob Buczkowski, DT, Pittsburgh
1987—John Clay, T, Missouri

1988—Tim Brown, WR, Notre Dame
      Terry McDaniel, CB, Tennessee
      Scott Davis, DE, Illinois
1989—None
1990—Anthony Smith, DE, Arizona
1991—Todd Marinovich, QB, Southern California

1992—Chester McGlockton, DT, Clemson
1993—Patrick Bates, DB, Texas A&M
1994—Rob Fredrickson, LB, Michigan State
1995—Napoleon Kaufman, RB, Washington
    *First player chosen in draft.

FRANCHISE RECORDS

Most rushing yards, career
8,545—Marcus Allen
Most rushing yards, season
1,759—Marcus Allen, 1985
Most rushing yards, game
221—Bo Jackson at Sea., Nov. 30, 1987
Most rushing touchdowns, season
16—Pete Banaszak, 1975
Most passing attempts, season
498—Ken Stabler, 1979
Most passing attempts, game
59—Todd Marinovich vs. Cle., Sept. 20, 1992
Most passes completed, season
304—Ken Stabler, 1979
Most passes completed, game
34—Jim Plunkett at K.C., Sept. 12, 1985
Most passing yards, career
19,078—Ken Stabler

Most passing yards, season
3,615—Ken Stabler, 1979
Most passing yards, game
424—Jeff Hostetler vs. S.D., Oct. 18, 1993
Most touchdown passes, season
34—Daryle Lamonica, 1969
Most pass receptions, career
589—Fred Biletnikoff
Most pass receptions, season
95—Todd Christensen, 1986
Most pass receptions, game
12—Dave Casper at N.E., Oct. 3, 1976
Most receiving yards, career
8,974—Fred Biletnikoff
Most receiving yards, season
1,361—Art Powell, 1964
Most receiving yards, game
247—Art Powell vs. Hou., Dec. 22, 1963

Most receiving touchdowns, season
16—Art Powell, 1964
Most touchdowns, career
76—Fred Biletnikoff
Most field goals, season
35—Jeff Jaeger, 1993
Longest field goal
54 yards—George Fleming vs. Den., Oct. 2, 1961
Most interceptions, career
39—Willie Brown
    Lester Hayes
Most interceptions, season
13—Lester Hayes, 1980
Most sacks, career
107.5—Greg Townsend
Most sacks, season
17.5—Tony Cline, 1970

SERIES RECORDS

L.A. Raiders vs.: Arizona 2-1; Atlanta 5-3; Buffalo 15-14; Chicago 5-3; Cincinnati 14-7; Cleveland 9-3; Dallas 3-2; Denver 48-19-2; Detroit 5-2; Green Bay 5-2; Houston 20-13; Indianapolis 4-2; Kansas City 35-32-2; L.A. Rams 6-2; Miami 14-5-1; Minnesota 6-2; New England 13-12-1; New Orleans 4-2-1; N.Y. Giants 4-2; N.Y. Jets 14-9-2; Philadelphia 2-4; Pittsburgh 7-4; San Diego 42-26-2; San Francisco 5-3; Seattle 19-15; Tampa Bay 3-0; Washington 5-2.

NOTE: Includes records as Oakland Raiders from 1960 through 1981.

RETIRED UNIFORM NUMBERS

No.   **Player**
    None

LOS ANGELES RAMS

YEAR-BY-YEAR RECORDS

		REGULAR SEASON						PLAYOFFS			
Year	W	L	T	Pct.	PF	PA	Finish	W	L	Highest round	Coach
1937*	1	10	0	.091	75	207	5th/Western Div.	—	—		Hugo Bezdek
1938*	4	7	0	.364	131	215	4th/Western Div.	—	—		Hugo Bezdek, Art Lewis
1939*	5	5	1	.500	195	164	4th/Western Div.	—	—		Dutch Clark
1940*	4	6	1	.400	171	191	4th/Western Div.	—	—		Dutch Clark
1941*	2	9	0	.182	116	244	5th/Western Div.	—	—		Dutch Clark
1942*	5	6	0	.455	150	207	3rd/Western Div.	—	—		Dutch Clark
1943*							Rams did not play in 1943.				
1944*	4	6	0	.400	188	224	4th/Western Div.	—	—		Buff Donelli
1945*	9	1	0	.900	244	136	1st/Western Div.	1	0	NFL champ	Adam Walsh
1946	6	4	1	.600	277	257	2nd/Western Div.	—	—		Adam Walsh
1947	6	6	0	.500	259	214	4th/Western Div.	—	—		Bob Snyder
1948	6	5	1	.545	327	269	3rd/Western Div.	—	—		Clark Shaughnessy
1949	8	2	2	.800	360	239	1st/Western Div.	0	1	NFL championship game	Clark Shaughnessy
1950	9	3	0	.750	466	309	1st/National Conf.	1	1	NFL championship game	Joe Stydahar
1951	8	4	0	.667	392	261	1st/National Conf.	1	0	NFL champ	Joe Stydahar
1952	9	3	0	.750	349	234	2nd/National Conf.	0	1	Nat. Conf. champ. game	Joe Stydahar, Hamp Pool
1953	8	3	1	.727	366	236	3rd/Western Conf.	—	—		Hamp Pool
1954	6	5	1	.545	314	285	4th/Western Conf.	—	—		Hamp Pool
1955	8	3	1	.727	260	231	1st/Western Conf.	0	1	NFL championship game	Sid Gillman
1956	4	8	0	.333	291	307	6th/Western Conf.	—	—		Sid Gillman
1957	6	6	0	.500	307	278	4th/Western Conf.	—	—		Sid Gillman
1958	8	4	0	.667	344	278	T2nd/Western Conf.	—	—		Sid Gillman
1959	2	10	0	.167	242	315	6th/Western Conf.	—	—		Sid Gillman

			REGULAR SEASON					PLAYOFFS		
Year	W	L	T	Pct.	PF	PA	Finish	W	L	Highest round	Coach
1960	4	7	1	.364	265	297	6th/Western Conf.	—	—		Bob Waterfield
1961	4	10	0	.286	263	333	6th/Western Conf.	—	—		Bob Waterfield
1962	1	12	1	.077	220	334	7th/Western Conf.	—	—		B. Waterfield, H. Svare
1963	5	9	0	.357	210	350	6th/Western Conf.	—	—		Harland Svare
1964	5	7	2	.417	283	339	5th/Western Conf.	—	—		Harland Svare
1965	4	10	0	.286	269	328	7th/Western Conf.	—	—		Harland Svare
1966	8	6	0	.571	289	212	3rd/Western Conf.	—	—		George Allen
1967	11	1	2	.917	398	196	1st/Coastal Div.	0	1	W. Conf. champ. game	George Allen
1968	10	3	1	.769	312	200	2nd/Coastal Div.	—	—		George Allen
1969	11	3	0	.786	320	243	1st/Coastal Div.	0	1	W. Conf. champ. game	George Allen
1970	9	4	1	.692	325	202	2nd/NFC Western Div.	—	—		George Allen
1971	8	5	1	.615	313	260	2nd/NFC Western Div.	—	—		Tommy Prothro
1972	6	7	1	.464	291	286	3rd/NFC Western Div.	—	—		Tommy Prothro
1973	12	2	0	.857	388	178	1st/NFC Western Div.	0	1	NFC div. playoff game	Chuck Knox
1974	10	4	0	.714	263	181	1st/NFC Western Div.	1	1	NFC championship game	Chuck Knox
1975	12	2	0	.857	312	135	1st/NFC Western Div.	1	1	NFC championship game	Chuck Knox
1976	10	3	1	.750	351	190	1st/NFC Western Div.	1	1	NFC championship game	Chuck Knox
1977	10	4	0	.714	302	146	1st/NFC Western Div.	0	1	NFC div. playoff game	Chuck Knox
1978	12	4	0	.750	316	245	1st/NFC Western Div.	1	1	NFC championship game	Ray Malavasi
1979	9	7	0	.563	323	309	1st/NFC Western Div.	2	1	Super Bowl	Ray Malavasi
1980	11	5	0	.688	424	289	2nd/NFC Western Div.	0	1	NFC wild-card game	Ray Malavasi
1981	6	10	0	.375	303	351	3rd/NFC Western Div.	—	—		Ray Malavasi
1982	2	7	0	.222	200	250	14th/NFC	—	—		Ray Malavasi
1983	9	7	0	.563	361	344	2nd/NFC Western Div.	1	1	NFC div. playoff game	John Robinson
1984	10	6	0	.625	346	316	2nd/NFC Western Div.	0	1	NFC wild-card game	John Robinson
1985	11	5	0	.688	340	277	1st/NFC Western Div.	1	1	NFC championship game	John Robinson
1986	10	6	0	.625	309	267	2nd/NFC Western Div.	0	1	NFC wild-card game	John Robinson
1987	6	9	0	.400	317	361	3rd/NFC Western Div.	—	—		John Robinson
1988	10	6	0	.625	407	293	2nd/NFC Western Div.	0	1	NFC wild-card game	John Robinson
1989	11	5	0	.688	426	344	2nd/NFC Western Div.	2	1	NFC championship game	John Robinson
1990	5	11	0	.313	345	412	T3rd/NFC Western Div.	—	—		John Robinson
1991	3	13	0	.188	234	390	4th/NFC Western Div.	—	—		John Robinson
1992	6	10	0	.375	313	383	T3rd/NFC Western Div.	—	—		Chuck Knox
1993	5	11	0	.313	221	367	4th/NFC Western Div.	—	—		Chuck Knox
1994	4	12	0	.250	286	365	4th/NFC Western Div.	—	—		Chuck Knox

*Cleveland Rams.

FIRST-ROUND DRAFT PICKS

1937—Johnny Drake, B, Purdue
1938—Corbett Davis, B, Indiana*
1939—Parker Hall, B, Mississippi
1940—Ollie Cordill, B, Rice
1941—Rudy Mucha, C, Washington
1942—Jack Wilson, B, Baylor
1943—Mike Holovak, B, Boston College
1944—Tony Butkovich, B, Illinois
1945—Elroy Hirsch, B, Wisconsin
1946—Emil Sitko, B, Notre Dame
1947—Herman Wedemeyer, B, St. Mary's (Cal.)
1948—None
1949—Bobby Thomason, B, Virginia Military
1950—Ralph Pasquariello, B, Villanova
       Stan West, G, Oklahoma
1951—Bud McFadin, G, Texas
1952—Bill Wade, B, Vanderbilt*
       Bob Carey, E, Michigan State
1953—Donn Moomaw, C, UCLA
       Ed Barker, E, Washington State
1954—Ed Beatty, C, Cincinnati
1955—Larry Morris, C, Georgia Tech
1956—Joe Marconi, B, West Virginia
       Charlie Horton, B, Vanderbilt
1957—Jon Arnett, B, Southern California
       Del Shofner, B, Baylor
1958—Lou Michaels, T, Kentucky
       Jim Phillips, E, Auburn
1959—Dick Bass, B, Pacific
       Paul Dickson, G, Baylor
1960—Billy Cannon, RB, Louisiana State*
1961—Marlin McKeever, LB, Southern California
1962—Roman Gabriel, QB, North Carolina State
       Merlin Olsen, DT, Utah State

1963—Terry Baker, QB, Oregon State*
       Rufus Guthrie, G, Georgia Tech
1964—Bill Munson, QB, Utah State
1965—Clancy Williams, DB, Washington State
1966—Tom Mack, G, Michigan
1967—None
1968—None
1969—Larry Smith, RB, Florida
       Jim Seymour, E, Notre Dame
       Bob Klein, TE, Southern California
1970—Jack Reynolds, LB, Tennessee
1971—Isiah Robertson, LB, Southern
       Jack Youngblood, DE, Florida
1972—None
1973—None
1974—John Cappelletti, RB, Penn State
1975—Mike Fanning, DT, Notre Dame
       Dennis Harrah, G, Miami (Fla.)
       Doug France, T, Ohio State
1976—Kevin McLain, LB, Colorado State
1977—Bob Brudzinski, LB, Ohio State
1978—Elvis Peacock, RB, Oklahoma
1979—George Andrews, LB, Nebraska
       Kent Hill, G, Georgia Tech
1980—Johnnie Johnson, DB, Texas
1981—Mel Owens, LB, Michigan
1982—Barry Redden, RB, Richmond
1983—Eric Dickerson, RB, Southern Methodist
1984—None
1985—Jerry Gray, DB, Texas
1986—Mike Schad, T, Queens College (Ont.)
1987—None
1988—Gaston Green, RB, UCLA
       Aaron Cox, WR, Arizona State

1989—Bill Hawkins, DE, Miami (Fla.)
Cleveland Gary, RB, Miami (Fla.)
1990—Bern Brostek, C, Washington
1991—Todd Lyght, CB, Notre Dame
1992—Sean Gilbert, DE, Pittsburgh

1993—Jerome Bettis, RB, Notre Dame
1994—Wayne Gandy, T, Auburn
1995—Kevin Carter, DE, Florida
*First player chosen in draft.

FRANCHISE RECORDS

Most rushing yards, career
7,245—Eric Dickerson

Most rushing yards, season
2,105—Eric Dickerson, 1984

Most rushing yards, game
247—Willie Ellison vs. N.O., Dec. 5, 1971

Most rushing touchdowns, season
18—Eric Dickerson, 1983

Most passing attempts, season
554—Jim Everett, 1990

Most passing attempts, game
53—Jim Hardy vs. Chi. Cardinals, Oct. 31, 1948

Most passes completed, season
308—Jim Everett, 1988

Most passes completed, game
35—Dieter Brock vs. S.F., Oct. 27, 1985

Most passing yards, career
23,758—Jim Everett

Most passing yards, season
4,310—Jim Everett, 1989

Most passing yards, game
554—Norm Van Brocklin at N.Y. Yanks, Sept. 28, 1951

Most touchdown passes, season
31—Jim Everett, 1988

Most pass receptions, career
593—Henry Ellard

Most pass receptions, season
86—Henry Ellard, 1988

Most pass receptions, game
18—Tom Fears vs. G.B., Dec. 3, 1950

Most receiving yards, career
9,761—Henry Ellard

Most receiving yards, season
1,495—Elroy Hirsch, 1951

Most receiving yards, game
336—Willie Anderson at N.O., Nov. 26, 1989

Most receiving touchdowns, season
17—Elroy Hirsch, 1951

Most touchdowns, career
58—Eric Dickerson

Most field goals, season
30—David Ray, 1973

Longest field goal
54 yards—Tony Zendejas vs. Pit., Sept. 12, 1993

Most interceptions, career
46—Ed Meador

Most interceptions, season
14—Night Train Lane, 1952

Most sacks, career
151.5—Deacon Jones

Most sacks, season
22—Deacon Jones, 1964
Deacon Jones, 1968

SERIES RECORDS

L.A. Rams vs.: Arizona 16-12-2; Atlanta 36-18-2; Buffalo 3-3; Chicago 24-34-3; Cincinnati 2-5; Cleveland 7-8; Dallas 9-8; Denver 4-3; Detroit 32-27-1; Green Bay 39-25-1; Houston 5-2; Indianapolis 17-20-2; Kansas City 4-1; L.A. Raiders 2-6; Miami 1-5; Minnesota 11-15-2; New England 3-3; New Orleans 27-23; N.Y. Giants 19-7; N.Y. Jets 5-2; Philadelphia 14-11-1; Pittsburgh 17-5-2; San Diego 3-3; San Francisco 47-39-2; Seattle 4-1; Tampa Bay 8-3; Washington 6-14-1.

NOTE: Includes records only from 1946 to present.

RETIRED UNIFORM NUMBERS

No.	Player
7	Bob Waterfield
74	Merlin Olsen

MIAMI DOLPHINS

YEAR-BY-YEAR RECORDS

		REGULAR SEASON						PLAYOFFS			
Year	W	L	T	Pct.	PF	PA	Finish	W	L	Highest round	Coach
1966*	3	11	0	.214	213	362	T4th/Eastern Div.	—	—		George Wilson
1967*	4	10	0	.286	219	407	T3rd/Eastern Div.	—	—		George Wilson
1968*	5	8	1	.385	276	355	3rd/Eastern Div.	—	—		George Wilson
1969*	3	10	1	.231	233	332	5th/Eastern Div.	—	—		George Wilson
1970	10	4	0	.714	297	228	2nd/AFC Eastern Div.	0	1	AFC div. playoff game	Don Shula
1971	10	3	1	.769	315	174	1st/AFC Eastern Div.	2	1	Super Bowl	Don Shula
1972	14	0	0	1.000	385	171	1st/AFC Eastern Div.	3	0	Super Bowl champ	Don Shula
1973	12	2	0	.857	343	150	1st/AFC Eastern Div.	3	0	Super Bowl champ	Don Shula
1974	11	3	0	.786	327	216	1st/AFC Eastern Div.	0	1	AFC div. playoff game	Don Shula
1975	10	4	0	.714	357	222	2nd/AFC Eastern Div.	—	—		Don Shula
1976	6	8	0	.429	263	264	3rd/AFC Eastern Div.	—	—		Don Shula
1977	10	4	0	.714	313	197	2nd/AFC Eastern Div.	—	—		Don Shula
1978	11	5	0	.688	372	254	2nd/AFC Eastern Div.	0	1	AFC wild-card game	Don Shula
1979	10	6	0	.625	341	257	1st/AFC Eastern Div.	0	1	AFC div. playoff game	Don Shula
1980	8	8	0	.500	266	305	3rd/AFC Eastern Div.	—	—		Don Shula
1981	11	4	1	.719	345	275	1st/AFC Eastern Div.	0	1	AFC div. playoff game	Don Shula
1982	7	2	0	.778	198	131	T2nd/AFC	3	1	Super Bowl	Don Shula
1983	12	4	0	.750	389	250	1st/AFC Eastern Div.	0	1	AFC div. playoff game	Don Shula
1984	14	2	0	.875	513	298	1st/AFC Eastern Div.	2	1	Super Bowl	Don Shula
1985	12	4	0	.750	428	320	1st/AFC Eastern Div.	1	1	AFC championship game	Don Shula
1986	8	8	0	.500	430	405	3rd/AFC Eastern Div.	—	—		Don Shula
1987	8	7	0	.533	362	335	T2nd/AFC Eastern Div.	—	—		Don Shula
1988	6	10	0	.375	319	380	5th/AFC Eastern Div.	—	—		Don Shula

				REGULAR SEASON					PLAYOFFS			
Year	W	L	T	Pct.	PF	PA	Finish	W	L	Highest round	Coach
1989	8	8	0	.500	331	379	T2nd/AFC Eastern Div.	—	—		Don Shula
1990	12	4	0	.750	336	242	2nd/AFC Eastern Div.	1	1	AFC div. playoff game	Don Shula
1991	8	8	0	.500	343	349	3rd/AFC Eastern Div.	—	—		Don Shula
1992	11	5	0	.688	340	281	1st/AFC Eastern Div.	1	1	AFC championship game	Don Shula
1993	9	7	0	.563	349	351	2nd/AFC Eastern Div.	—	—		Don Shula
1994	10	6	0	.625	389	327	1st/AFC Eastern Div.	1	1	AFC div. playoff game	Don Shula

*American Football League.

FIRST-ROUND DRAFT PICKS

1966—Jim Grabowski, RB, Illinois*
Rick Norton, QB, Kentucky
1967—Bob Griese, QB, Purdue
1968—Larry Csonka, RB, Syracuse
Doug Crusan, T, Indiana
1969—Bill Stanfill, DE, Georgia
1970—None
1971—None
1972—Mike Kadish, DT, Notre Dame
1973—None
1974—Don Reese, DE, Jackson State
1975—Darryl Carlton, T, Tampa
1976—Larry Gordon, LB, Arizona State
Kim Bokamper, LB, San Jose State
1977—A.J. Duhe, DE, Louisiana State
1978—None
1979—Jon Giesler, T, Michigan
1980—Don McNeal, DB, Alabama
1981—David Overstreet, RB, Oklahoma

1982—Roy Foster, G, Southern California
1983—Dan Marino, QB, Pittsburgh
1984—Jackie Shipp, LB, Oklahoma
1985—Lorenzo Hampton, RB, Florida
1986—None
1987—John Bosa, DE, Boston College
1988—Eric Kumerow, DE, Ohio State
1989—Sammie Smith, RB, Florida State
Louis Oliver, DB, Florida
1990—Richmond Webb, T, Texas A&M
1991—Randal Hill, WR, Miami (Fla.)
1992—Troy Vincent, DB, Wisconsin
Marco Coleman, LB, Georgia Tech
1993—O.J. McDuffie, WR, Penn State
1994—Tim Bowens, DT, Mississippi
1995—Billy Milner, T, Houston
*First player chosen in draft.

FRANCHISE RECORDS

Most rushing yards, career
6,737—Larry Csonka
Most rushing yards, season
1,258—Delvin Williams, 1978
Most rushing yards, game
197—Mercury Morris vs. N.E., Sept. 30, 1973
Most rushing touchdowns, season
12—Mercury Morris, 1972
Don Nottingham, 1975
Larry Csonka, 1979
Most passing attempts, season
623—Dan Marino, 1986
Most passing attempts, game
60—Dan Marino vs. NYJ, Oct. 23, 1988
Most passes completed, season
385—Dan Marino, 1994
Most passes completed, game
39—Dan Marino at Buf., Nov. 16, 1986
Most passing yards, career
45,173—Dan Marino

Most passing yards, season
5,084—Dan Marino, 1984
Most passing yards, game
521—Dan Marino vs. NYJ, Oct. 23, 1988
Most touchdown passes, season
48—Dan Marino, 1984
Most pass receptions, career
550—Mark Clayton
Most pass receptions, season
86—Mark Clayton, 1988
Most pass receptions, game
12—Jim Jensen at N.E., Nov. 6, 1988
Most receiving yards, career
8,869—Mark Duper
Most receiving yards, season
1,389—Mark Clayton, 1984
Most receiving yards, game
217—Mark Duper vs. NYJ, Nov. 10, 1985

Most receiving touchdowns, season
18—Mark Clayton, 1984
Most touchdowns, career
82—Mark Clayton
Most field goals, season
31—Pete Stoyanovich, 1991
Longest field goal
59 yards—Pete Stoyanovich at NYJ, Nov. 12, 1989
Most interceptions, career
35—Jake Scott
Most interceptions, season
10—Dick Westmoreland, 1967
Most sacks, career
67.5—Bill Stanfill
Most sacks, season
18.5—Bill Stanfill, 1973

SERIES RECORDS

Miami vs.: Arizona 6-0; Atlanta 5-1; Buffalo 37-20-1; Chicago 5-2; Cincinnati 11-3; Cleveland 6-4; Dallas 6-1; Denver 5-2-1; Detroit 3-2; Green Bay 8-0; Houston 11-11; Indianapolis 35-15; Kansas City 8-10; L.A. Raiders 5-14-1; L.A. Rams 5-1; Minnesota 4-2; New England 35-21; New Orleans 5-3; N.Y. Giants 1-2; N.Y. Jets 28-27-1; Philadelphia 6-2; Pittsburgh 7-6; San Diego 5-10; San Francisco 4-2; Seattle 4-1; Tampa Bay 4-1; Washington 5-2.

RETIRED UNIFORM NUMBERS

No.	Player
12	Bob Griese

MINNESOTA VIKINGS

YEAR-BY-YEAR RECORDS

		REGULAR SEASON						PLAYOFFS			
Year	W	L	T	Pct.	PF	PA	Finish	W	L	Highest round	Coach
1961	3	11	0	.214	285	407	7th/Western Conf.	—	—		Norm Van Brocklin
1962	2	11	1	.154	254	410	6th/Western Conf.	—	—		Norm Van Brocklin
1963	5	8	1	.385	309	390	T4th/Western Conf.	—	—		Norm Van Brocklin
1964	8	5	1	.615	355	296	T2nd/Western Conf.	—	—		Norm Van Brocklin
1965	7	7	0	.500	383	403	5th/Western Conf.	—	—		Norm Van Brocklin
1966	4	9	1	.308	292	304	T6th/Western Conf.	—	—		Norm Van Brocklin
1967	3	8	3	.273	233	294	4th/Central Div.	—	—		Bud Grant
1968	8	6	0	.571	282	242	1st/Central Div.	0	1	W. Conf. champ. game	Bud Grant
1969	12	2	0	.857	379	133	1st/Central Div.	2	1	Super Bowl	Bud Grant
1970	12	2	0	.857	335	143	1st/NFC Central Div.	0	1	NFC div. playoff game	Bud Grant
1971	11	3	0	.786	245	139	1st/NFC Central Div.	0	1	NFC div. playoff game	Bud Grant
1972	7	7	0	.500	301	252	3rd/NFC Central Div.	—	—		Bud Grant
1973	12	2	0	.857	296	168	1st/NFC Central Div.	2	1	Super Bowl	Bud Grant
1974	10	4	0	.714	310	195	1st/NFC Central Div.	2	1	Super Bowl	Bud Grant
1975	12	2	0	.857	377	180	1st/NFC Central Div.	0	1	NFC div. playoff game	Bud Grant
1976	11	2	1	.821	305	176	1st/NFC Central Div.	2	1	Super Bowl	Bud Grant
1977	9	5	0	.643	231	227	1st/NFC Central Div.	1	1	NFC championship game	Bud Grant
1978	8	7	1	.531	294	306	1st/NFC Central Div.	0	1	NFC div. playoff game	Bud Grant
1979	7	9	0	.438	259	337	3rd/NFC Central Div.	—	—		Bud Grant
1980	9	7	0	.563	317	308	1st/NFC Central Div.	0	1	NFC div. playoff game	Bud Grant
1981	7	9	0	.438	325	369	4th/NFC Central Div.	—	—		Bud Grant
1982	5	4	0	.556	187	198	T4th/NFC	1	1	NFC second-round pl. game	Bud Grant
1983	8	8	0	.500	316	348	T2nd/NFC Central Div.	—	—		Bud Grant
1984	3	13	0	.188	276	484	5th/NFC Central Div.	—	—		Les Steckel
1985	7	9	0	.438	346	359	T3rd/NFC Central Div.	—	—		Bud Grant
1986	9	7	0	.563	398	273	2nd/NFC Central Div.	—	—		Jerry Burns
1987	8	7	0	.533	336	335	2nd/NFC Central Div.	2	1	NFC championship game	Jerry Burns
1988	11	5	0	.688	406	233	2nd/NFC Central Div.	1	1	NFC div. playoff game	Jerry Burns
1989	10	6	0	.625	351	275	1st/NFC Central Div.	0	1	NFC div. playoff game	Jerry Burns
1990	6	10	0	.375	351	326	T2nd/NFC Central Div.	—	—		Jerry Burns
1991	8	8	0	.500	301	306	3rd/NFC Central Div.	—	—		Jerry Burns
1992	11	5	0	.688	374	249	1st/NFC Central Div.	0	1	NFC wild-card game	Dennis Green
1993	9	7	0	.563	277	290	T2nd/NFC Central Div.	0	1	NFC wild-card game	Dennis Green
1994	10	6	0	.625	356	314	1st/NFC Central Div.	0	1	NFC wild-card game	Dennis Green

FIRST-ROUND DRAFT PICKS

1961—Tommy Mason, RB, Tulane*
1962—None
1963—Jim Dunaway, T, Mississippi
1964—Carl Eller, DE, Minnesota
1965—Jack Snow, WR, Notre Dame
1966—Jerry Shay, DT, Purdue
1967—Clint Jones, RB, Michigan State
      Gene Washington, WR, Michigan State
      Alan Page, DT, Notre Dame
1968—Ron Yary, T, Southern California*
1969—None
1970—John Ward, DT, Oklahoma State
1971—Leo Hayden, RB, Ohio State
1972—Jeff Siemon, LB, Stanford
1973—Chuck Foreman, RB, Miami (Fla.)
1974—Fred McNeill, LB, UCLA
      Steve Riley, T, Southern California
1975—Mark Mullaney, DE, Colorado State
1976—James White, DT, Oklahoma State
1977—Tommy Kramer, QB, Rice
1978—Randy Holloway, DE, Pittsburgh

1979—Ted Brown, RB, North Carolina State
1980—Doug Martin, DT, Washington
1981—None
1982—Darrin Nelson, RB, Stanford
1983—Joey Browner, DB, Southern California
1984—Keith Millard, DE, Washington State
1985—Chris Doleman, LB, Pittsburgh
1986—Gerald Robinson, DE, Auburn
1987—D.J. Dozier, RB, Penn State
1988—Randall McDaniel, G, Arizona State
1989—None
1990—None
1991—None
1992—None
1993—Robert Smith, RB, Ohio State
1994—DeWayne Washington, CB, North Carolina State
      Todd Steussie, T, California
1995—Derrick Alexander, DE, Florida State
      Korey Stringer, T, Ohio State
   *First player chosen in draft.

FRANCHISE RECORDS

Most rushing yards, career
5,879—Chuck Foreman
Most rushing yards, season
1,201—Terry Allen, 1992

Most rushing yards, game
200—Chuck Foreman at Phi., Oct. 24, 1976

Most rushing touchdowns, season
13—Chuck Foreman, 1975
      Chuck Foreman, 1976
      Terry Allen, 1992

Most passing attempts, season
593—Tommy Kramer, 1981
Most passing attempts, game
63—Rich Gannon at N.E., Oct. 20, 1991
Most passes completed, season
371—Warren Moon, 1994
Most passes completed, game
38—Tommy Kramer vs. Cle., Dec. 14, 1980
Tommy Kramer vs. G.B., Nov. 29, 1981
Most passing yards, career
33,098—Fran Tarkenton
Most passing yards, season
4,264—Warren Moon, 1994
Most passing yards, game
490—Tommy Kramer at Was., Nov. 2, 1986

Most touchdown passes, season
26—Tommy Kramer, 1981
Most pass receptions, career
498—Steve Jordan
Most pass receptions, season
122—Cris Carter, 1994
Most pass receptions, game
15—Rickey Young at N.E., Dec. 16, 1979
Most receiving yards, career
7,636—Anthony Carter
Most receiving yards, season
1,256—Cris Carter, 1994
Most receiving yards, game
210—Sammy White vs. Det., Nov. 7, 1976
Most receiving touchdowns, season
11—Jerry Reichow, 1961

Most touchdowns, career
76—Bill Brown
Most field goals, season
46—Fred Cox, 1970
Longest field goal
54 yards—Jan Stenerud vs. Atl., Sept. 16, 1984
Most interceptions, career
53—Paul Krause
Most interceptions, season
10—Paul Krause, 1975
Most sacks, career
130—Carl Eller
Most sacks, season
21—Chris Doleman, 1989

SERIES RECORDS

Minnesota vs.: Arizona 4-8; Atlanta 12-6; Buffalo 5-2; Chicago 36-29-2; Cincinnati 4-3; Cleveland 7-3; Dallas 6-8; Denver 5-3; Detroit 41-24-2; Green Bay 34-32-1; Houston 3-3; Indianapolis 6-11-1; Kansas City 3-2; L.A. Raiders 2-6; L.A. Rams 15-11-2; Miami 2-4; New England 2-4; New Orleans 12-6; N.Y. Giants 7-4; N.Y. Jets 1-4; Philadelphia 10-6; Pittsburgh 7-4; San Diego 3-4; San Francisco 16-15-1; Seattle 2-3; Tampa Bay 24-10; Washington 4-6.

RETIRED UNIFORM NUMBERS

No.	Player
10	Fran Tarkenton
88	Alan Page

NEW ENGLAND PATRIOTS

YEAR-BY-YEAR RECORDS

		REGULAR SEASON					PLAYOFFS			
Year	W	L	T	Pct.	PF	PA	Finish	W	L	Highest round	Coach
1960*†	5	9	0	.357	286	349	4th/Eastern Div.	—	—		Lou Saban
1961*†	9	4	1	.692	413	313	2nd/Eastern Div.	—	—		Lou Saban, Mike Holovak
1962*†	9	4	1	.692	346	295	2nd/Eastern Div.	—	—		Mike Holovak
1963*†	7	6	1	.538	327	257	1st/Eastern Div.	1	1	AFL championship game	Mike Holovak
1964*†	10	3	1	.769	365	297	2nd/Eastern Div.	—	—		Mike Holovak
1965*†	4	8	2	.333	244	302	3rd/Eastern Div.	—	—		Mike Holovak
1966*†	8	4	2	.667	315	283	2nd/Eastern Div.	—	—		Mike Holovak
1967*†	3	10	1	.231	280	389	5th/Eastern Div.	—	—		Mike Holovak
1968*†	4	10	0	.286	229	406	4th/Eastern Div.	—	—		Mike Holovak
1969*†	4	10	0	.286	266	316	T3rd/Eastern Div.	—	—		Clive Rush
1970†	2	12	0	.143	149	361	5th/AFC Eastern Div.	—	—		Clive Rush, John Mazur
1971	6	8	0	.429	238	325	T3rd/AFC Eastern Div.	—	—		John Mazur
1972	3	11	0	.214	192	446	5th/AFC Eastern Div.	—	—		John Mazur, Phil Bengtson
1973	5	9	0	.357	258	300	3rd/AFC Eastern Div.	—	—		Chuck Fairbanks
1974	7	7	0	.500	348	289	T3rd/AFC Eastern Div.	—	—		Chuck Fairbanks
1975	3	11	0	.214	258	358	T4th/AFC Eastern Div.	—	—		Chuck Fairbanks
1976	11	3	0	.786	376	236	2nd/Eastern Div.	0	1	AFC div. playoff game	Chuck Fairbanks
1977	9	5	0	.643	278	217	3rd/AFC Eastern Div.	—	—		Chuck Fairbanks
1978	11	5	0	.688	358	286	1st/AFC Eastern Div.	0	1	AFC div. playoff game	Chuck Fairbanks, Hank Bullough-Ron Erhardt
1979	9	7	0	.563	411	326	2nd/AFC Eastern Div.	—	—		Ron Erhardt
1980	10	6	0	.625	441	325	2nd/AFC Eastern Div.	—	—		Ron Erhardt
1981	2	14	0	.125	322	370	T4th/AFC Eastern Div.	—	—		Ron Erhardt
1982	5	4	0	.556	143	157	7th/AFC	0	1	AFC first-round pl. game	Ron Meyer
1983	8	8	0	.500	274	289	T2nd/AFC Eastern Div.	—	—		Ron Meyer
1984	9	7	0	.563	362	352	2nd/AFC Eastern Div.	—	—		Ron Meyer, Raymond Berry
1985	11	5	0	.688	362	290	T2nd/AFC Eastern Div.	3	1	Super Bowl	Raymond Berry
1986	11	5	0	.688	412	307	1st/AFC Eastern Div.	0	1	AFC div. playoff game	Raymond Berry
1987	8	7	0	.533	320	293	T2nd/AFC Eastern Div.	—	—		Raymond Berry
1988	9	7	0	.563	250	284	T2nd/AFC Eastern Div.	—	—		Raymond Berry
1989	5	11	0	.313	297	391	4th/AFC Eastern Div.	—	—		Raymond Berry
1990	1	15	0	.063	181	446	5th/AFC Eastern Div.	—	—		Rod Rust
1991	6	10	0	.375	211	305	4th/AFC Eastern Div.	—	—		Dick MacPherson
1992	2	14	0	.125	205	363	5th/AFC Eastern Div.	—	—		Dick MacPherson
1993	5	11	0	.313	238	286	4th/AFC Eastern Div.	—	—		Bill Parcells
1994	10	6	0	.625	351	312	2nd/AFC Eastern Div.	0	1	AFC wild-card game	Bill Parcells

*American Football League.
†Boston Patriots.

FIRST-ROUND DRAFT PICKS

1960—Ron Burton, RB, Northwestern
1961—Tommy Mason, RB, Tulane
1962—Gary Collins, WR, Maryland
1963—Art Graham, E, Boston College
1964—Jack Concannon, QB, Boston College* (AFL)
1965—Jerry Rush, DE, Michigan State
　　　Dave McCormick, T, Louisiana State
1966—Karl Singer, T, Purdue
　　　Willie Townes, T, Tulsa
1967—John Charles, DB, Purdue
1968—Dennis Byrd, DE, North Carolina State
1969—Ron Sellers, WR, Florida State
1970—Phil Olsen, DT, Utah State
1971—Jim Plunkett, QB, Stanford*
1972—None
1973—John Hannah, G, Alabama
　　　Sam Cunningham, RB, Southern California
　　　Darryl Stingley, WR, Purdue
1974—None
1975—Russ Francis, TE, Oregon
1976—Mike Haynes, DB, Arizona State
　　　Pete Brock, C, Colorado
　　　Tim Fox, DB, Ohio State
1977—Raymond Clayborn, DB, Texas
　　　Stanley Morgan, WR, Tennessee

1978—Bob Cryder, G, Alabama
1979—Rick Sanford, DB, South Carolina
1980—Roland James, DB, Tennessee
　　　Vagas Ferguson, RB, Notre Dame
1981—Brian Holloway, T, Stanford
1982—Kenneth Sims, DT, Texas*
　　　Lester Williams, DT, Nebraska
1983—Tony Eason, QB, Illinois
1984—Irving Fryar, WR, Nebraska*
1985—Trevor Matich, C, Brigham Young
1986—Reggie Dupard, RB, Southern Methodist
1987—Bruce Armstrong, G, Louisville
1988—J. Stephens, RB, Northwestern Louisiana State
1989—Hart Lee Dykes, WR, Oklahoma State
1990—Chris Singleton, LB, Arizona
　　　Ray Agnew, DL, North Carolina State
1991—Pat Harlow, T, Southern California
　　　Leonard Russell, RB, Arizona State
1992—Eugene Chung, T, Virginia Tech
1993—Drew Bledsoe, QB, Washington State*
1994—Willie McGinest, DE, Southern California
1995—Ty Law, DB, Michigan
　　　*First player chosen in draft.

FRANCHISE RECORDS

Most rushing yards, career
5,453—Sam Cunningham

Most rushing yards, season
1,458—Jim Nance, 1966

Most rushing yards, game
212—Tony Collins vs. NYJ, Sept. 18, 1983

Most rushing touchdowns, season
12—Steve Grogan, 1976

Most passing attempts, season
691—Drew Bledsoe, 1994

Most passing attempts, game
70—Drew Bledsoe vs. Min., Nov. 13, 1994 (OT)
59—Steve Grogan vs. N.O., Nov. 12, 1989

Most passes completed, season
400—Drew Bledsoe, 1994

Most passes completed, game
45—Drew Bledsoe vs. Min., Nov. 13, 1994 (OT)
36—Tony Eason at L.A. Rams, Nov. 16, 1986

Most passing yards, career
26,886—Steve Grogan

Most passing yards, season
4,555—Drew Bledsoe, 1994

Most passing yards, game
426—Drew Bledsoe vs. Min., Nov. 13, 1994 (OT)
421—Drew Bledsoe at Mia., Sept. 5, 1994

Most touchdown passes, season
31—Babe Parilli, 1964

Most pass receptions, career
534—Stanley Morgan

Most pass receptions, season
96—Ben Coates, 1994

Most pass receptions, game
12—Ben Coates at Ind., Nov. 27, 1994

Most receiving yards, career
10,352—Stanley Morgan

Most receiving yards, season
1,491—Stanley Morgan, 1986

Most receiving yards, game
182—Stanley Morgan vs. Mia., Nov. 8, 1981

Most receiving touchdowns, season
12—Stanley Morgan, 1979

Most touchdowns, career
68—Stanley Morgan

Most field goals, season
32—Tony Franklin, 1986

Longest field goal
53 yards—Gino Cappelletti vs. NYJ, Nov. 28, 1965
　　　Jason Staurovsky vs. Sea., Oct. 7, 1990

Most interceptions, career
36—Raymond Clayborn

Most interceptions, season
11—Ron Hall, 1964

Most sacks, career
100—Andre Tippett

Most sacks, season
18.5—Andre Tippett, 1984

SERIES RECORDS

New England vs.: Arizona 2-6; Atlanta 3-4; Buffalo 35-34-1; Chicago 4-2; Cincinnati 9-7; Cleveland 3-10; Dallas 0-6; Denver 12-16; Detroit 3-3; Green Bay 3-2; Houston 17-14-1; Indianapolis 29-20; Kansas City 7-13-3; L.A. Raiders 12-13-1; L.A. Rams 3-3; Miami 21-35; Minnesota 4-2; New Orleans 5-2; N.Y. Giants 1-3; N.Y. Jets 29-39-1; Philadelphia 2-5; Pittsburgh 3-9; San Diego 14-11-2; San Francisco 1-6; Seattle 6-7; Tampa Bay 3-0; Washington 1-4.

　　　NOTE: Includes records as Boston Patriots from 1960 through 1970.

RETIRED UNIFORM NUMBERS

No.	Player
20	Gino Cappelletti
57	Steve Nelson
73	John Hannah
79	Jim Hunt
89	Bob Dee

NEW ORLEANS SAINTS

YEAR-BY-YEAR RECORDS

							REGULAR SEASON			PLAYOFFS	
Year	W	L	T	Pct.	PF	PA	Finish	W	L	Highest round	Coach
1967	3	11	0	.214	233	379	4th/Capitol Div.	—	—		Tom Fears
1968	4	9	1	.308	246	327	3rd/Century Div.	—	—		Tom Fears
1969	5	9	0	.357	311	393	3rd/Capitol Div.	—	—		Tom Fears
1970	2	11	1	.154	172	347	4th/NFC Western Div.	—	—		Tom Fears, J.D. Roberts
1971	4	8	2	.333	266	347	4th/NFC Western Div.	—	—		J.D. Roberts
1972	2	11	1	.179	215	361	4th/NFC Western Div.	—	—		J.D. Roberts
1973	5	9	0	.357	163	312	T3rd/NFC Western Div.	—	—		John North
1974	5	9	0	.357	166	263	3rd/NFC Western Div.	—	—		John North
1975	2	12	0	.143	165	360	4th/NFC Western Div.	—	—		John North, Ernie Hefferle
1976	4	10	0	.286	253	346	T3rd/NFC Western Div.	—	—		Hank Stram
1977	3	11	0	.214	232	336	4th/NFC Western Div.	—	—		Hank Stram
1978	7	9	0	.438	281	298	3rd/NFC Western Div.	—	—		Dick Nolan
1979	8	8	0	.500	370	360	2nd/NFC Western Div.	—	—		Dick Nolan
1980	1	15	0	.063	291	487	4th/NFC Western Div.	—	—		Dick Nolan, Dick Stanfel
1981	4	12	0	.250	207	378	4th/NFC Western Div.	—	—		Bum Phillips
1982	4	5	0	.444	129	160	T8th/NFC	—	—		Bum Phillips
1983	8	8	0	.500	319	337	3rd/NFC Western Div.	—	—		Bum Phillips
1984	7	9	0	.438	298	361	3rd/NFC Western Div.	—	—		Bum Phillips
1985	5	11	0	.313	294	401	3rd/NFC Western Div.	—	—		Bum Phillips, Wade Phillips
1986	7	9	0	.438	288	287	4th/NFC Western Div.	—	—		Jim Mora
1987	12	3	0	.800	422	283	2nd/NFC Western Div.	0	1	NFC wild-card game	Jim Mora
1988	10	6	0	.625	312	283	3rd/NFC Western Div.	—	—		Jim Mora
1989	9	7	0	.563	386	301	3rd/NFC Western Div.	—	—		Jim Mora
1990	8	8	0	.500	274	275	2nd/NFC Western Div.	0	1	NFC wild-card game	Jim Mora
1991	11	5	0	.688	341	211	1st/NFC Western Div.	0	1	NFC wild-card game	Jim Mora
1992	12	4	0	.750	330	202	2nd/NFC Western Div.	0	1	NFC wild-card game	Jim Mora
1993	8	8	0	.500	317	343	2nd/NFC Western Div.	—	—		Jim Mora
1994	7	9	0	.438	348	407	T2nd/NFC Western Div.	—	—		Jim Mora

FIRST-ROUND DRAFT PICKS

1967—Les Kelley, RB, Alabama
1968—Kevin Hardy, DE, Notre Dame
1969—John Shinners, G, Xavier (Ohio)
1970—Ken Burrough, WR, Texas Southern
1971—Archie Manning, QB, Mississippi
1972—Royce Smith, G, Georgia
1973—None
1974—Rick Middleton, LB, Ohio State
1975—Larry Burton, WR, Purdue
　　　Kurt Schumacher, G, Ohio State
1976—Chuck Muncie, RB, California
1977—Joe Campbell, DE, Maryland
1978—Wes Chandler, WR, Florida
1979—Russell Erxleben, P, Texas
1980—Stan Brock, T, Colorado
1981—George Rogers, RB, Southern Carolina*
1982—Lindsay Scott, WR, Georgia

1983—None
1984—None
1985—Alvin Toles, LB, Tennessee
1986—Jim Dombrowski, T, Virginia
1987—Shawn Knight, DE, Brigham Young
1988—Craig Heyward, RB, Pittsburgh
1989—Wayne Martin, DE, Arkansas
1990—Renaldo Turnbull, DE, West Virginia
1991—None
1992—Vaughn Dunbar, RB, Indiana
1993—Willie Roaf, T, Louisiana Tech
　　　Irv Smith, TE, Notre Dame
1994—Joe Johnson, DE, Louisville
1995—Mark Fields, LB, Washington State

*First player chosen in draft.

FRANCHISE RECORDS

Most rushing yards, career
4,267—George Rogers

Most rushing yards, season
1,674—George Rogers, 1981

Most rushing yards, game
206—George Rogers vs. St.L., Sept. 4, 1983

Most rushing touchdowns, season
13—George Rogers, 1981
　　　Dalton Hilliard, 1989

Most passing attempts, season
540—Jim Everett, 1994

Most passing attempts, game
55—Jim Everett at S.F., Sept. 25, 1994

Most passes completed, season
346—Jim Everett, 1994

Most passes completed, game
33—Archie Manning at G.B., Sept. 10, 1978

Most passing yards, career
21,734—Archie Manning

Most passing yards, season
3,855—Jim Everett, 1994

Most passing yards, game
377—Archie Manning at S.F., Dec. 7, 1980

Most touchdown passes, season
23—Archie Manning, 1980

Most pass receptions, career
532—Eric Martin

Most pass receptions, season
85—Eric Martin, 1988

Most pass receptions, game
14—Tony Galbreath at G.B., Sept. 10, 1978

Most receiving yards, career
7,854—Eric Martin

Most receiving yards, season
1,090—Eric Martin, 1989

Most receiving yards, game
205—Wes Chandler vs. Atl., Sept. 2, 1979

Most receiving touchdowns, season
9—Henry Childs, 1977
Most touchdowns, career
53—Dalton Hilliard
Most field goals, season
31—Morten Andersen, 1985

Longest field goal
63 yards—Tom Dempsey vs. Det., Nov. 8, 1970
Most interceptions, career
37—Dave Waymer

Most interceptions, season
10—Dave Whitsell, 1967
Most sacks, career
123—Rickey Jackson
Most sacks, season
17—Pat Swilling, 1991

SERIES RECORDS

New Orleans vs.: Arizona 9-10; Atlanta 24-27; Buffalo 2-3; Chicago 5-10; Cincinnati 5-3; Cleveland 3-9; Dallas 3-14; Denver 2-4; Detroit 7-6-1; Green Bay 4-12; Houston 4-3-1; Indianapolis 2-3; Kansas City 3-3; L.A. Raiders 2-4-1; L.A. Rams 23-27; Miami 3-5; Minnesota 6-12; New England 2-5; N.Y. Giants 7-9; N.Y. Jets 3-4; Philadelphia 8-11; Pittsburgh 5-6; San Diego 1-5; San Francisco 14-35-2; Seattle 3-2; Tampa Bay 12-4; Washington 5-12.

☐ RETIRED UNIFORM NUMBERS ☐

No.	Player
31	Jim Taylor
81	Doug Atkins

NEW YORK GIANTS

YEAR-BY-YEAR RECORDS

			REGULAR SEASON					PLAYOFFS		
Year	W	L	T	Pct.	PF	PA	Finish	W	L	Highest round	Coach
1925	8	4	0	.667	122	67	T4th				Bob Folwell
1926	8	4	1	.667	147	51	T6th				Joe Alexander
1927	11	1	1	.917	197	20	1st				Earl Potteiger
1928	4	7	2	.364	79	136	6th				Earl Potteiger
1929	13	1	1	.929	312	86	2nd				LeRoy Andrews
1930	13	4	0	.765	308	98	2nd				LeRoy Andrews, Benny Friedman-Steve Owen
1931	7	6	1	.538	154	100	5th				Steve Owen
1932	4	6	2	.400	93	113	5th				Steve Owen
1933	11	3	0	.786	244	101	1st/Eastern Div.	0	1	NFL championship game	Steve Owen
1934	8	5	0	.615	147	107	1st/Eastern Div.	1	0	NFL champ	Steve Owen
1935	9	3	0	.750	180	96	1st/Eastern Div.	0	1	NFL championship game	Steve Owen
1936	5	6	1	.455	115	163	3rd/Eastern Div.	—	—		Steve Owen
1937	6	3	2	.667	128	109	2nd/Eastern Div.	—	—		Steve Owen
1938	8	2	1	.800	194	79	1st/Eastern Div.	1	0	NFL champ	Steve Owen
1939	9	1	1	.900	168	85	1st/Eastern Div.	0	1	NFL championship game	Steve Owen
1940	6	4	1	.600	131	133	3rd/Eastern Div.	—	—		Steve Owen
1941	8	3	0	.727	238	114	1st/Eastern Div.	0	1	NFL championship game	Steve Owen
1942	5	5	1	.500	155	139	3rd/Eastern Div.	—	—		Steve Owen
1943	6	3	1	.667	197	170	2nd/Eastern Div.	0	1	E. Div. champ. game	Steve Owen
1944	8	1	1	.889	206	75	1st/Eastern Div.	0	1	NFL championship game	Steve Owen
1945	3	6	1	.333	179	198	T3rd/Eastern Div.	—	—		Steve Owen
1946	7	3	1	.700	236	162	1st/Eastern Div.	0	1	NFL championship game	Steve Owen
1947	2	8	2	.200	190	309	5th/Eastern Div.	—	—		Steve Owen
1948	4	8	0	.333	297	388	T3rd/Eastern Div.	—	—		Steve Owen
1949	6	6	0	.500	287	298	3rd/Eastern Div.	—	—		Steve Owen
1950	10	2	0	.833	268	150	2nd/American Conf.	0	1	Am. Conf. champ. game	Steve Owen
1951	9	2	1	.818	254	161	2nd/American Conf.	—	—		Steve Owen
1952	7	5	0	.583	234	231	T2nd/American Conf.	—	—		Steve Owen
1953	3	9	0	.250	179	277	5th/Eastern Conf.	—	—		Steve Owen
1954	7	5	0	.583	293	184	3rd/Eastern Conf.	—	—		Jim Lee Howell
1955	6	5	1	.545	267	223	3rd/Eastern Conf.	—	—		Jim Lee Howell
1956	8	3	1	.727	264	197	1st/Eastern Conf.	1	0	NFL champ	Jim Lee Howell
1957	7	5	0	.583	254	211	2nd/Eastern Conf.	—	—		Jim Lee Howell
1958	9	3	0	.750	246	183	1st/Eastern Conf.	1	1	NFL championship game	Jim Lee Howell
1959	10	2	0	.833	284	170	1st/Eastern Conf.	0	1	NFL championship game	Jim Lee Howell
1960	6	4	2	.600	271	261	3rd/Eastern Conf.	—	—		Jim Lee Howell
1961	10	3	1	.769	368	220	1st/Eastern Conf.	0	1	NFL championship game	Allie Sherman
1962	12	2	0	.857	398	283	1st/Eastern Conf.	0	1	NFL championship game	Allie Sherman
1963	11	3	0	.786	448	280	1st/Eastern Conf.	0	1	NFL championship game	Allie Sherman
1964	2	10	2	.167	241	399	7th/Eastern Conf.	—	—		Allie Sherman
1965	7	7	0	.500	270	338	T2nd/Eastern Conf.	—	—		Allie Sherman
1966	1	12	1	.077	263	501	8th/Eastern Conf.	—	—		Allie Sherman
1967	7	7	0	.500	369	379	2nd/Century Div.	—	—		Allie Sherman
1968	7	7	0	.500	294	325	2nd/Capitol Div.	—	—		Allie Sherman
1969	6	8	0	.429	264	298	2nd/Century Div.	—	—		Alex Webster
1970	9	5	0	.643	301	270	2nd/NFC Eastern Div.	—	—		Alex Webster
1971	4	10	0	.286	228	362	5th/NFC Eastern Div.	—	—		Alex Webster
1972	8	6	0	.571	331	247	3rd/NFC Eastern Div.	—	—		Alex Webster
1973	2	11	1	.179	226	362	5th/NFC Eastern Div.	—	—		Alex Webster
1974	2	12	0	.143	195	299	5th/NFC Eastern Div.	—	—		Bill Arnsparger

	REGULAR SEASON							PLAYOFFS			
Year	W	L	T	Pct.	PF	PA	Finish	W	L	Highest round	Coach
1975	5	9	0	.357	216	306	4th/NFC Eastern Div.	—	—		Bill Arnsparger
1976	3	11	0	.214	170	250	5th/NFC Eastern Div.	—	—		Bill Arnsparger, John McVay
1977	5	9	0	.357	181	265	T4th/NFC Eastern Div.	—	—		John McVay
1978	6	10	0	.375	264	298	T4th/NFC Eastern Div.	—	—		John McVay
1979	6	10	0	.375	237	323	4th/NFC Eastern Div.	—	—		Ray Perkins
1980	4	12	0	.250	249	425	5th/NFC Eastern Div.	—	—		Ray Perkins
1981	9	7	0	.563	295	257	3rd/NFC Eastern Div.	1	1	NFC div. playoff game	Ray Perkins
1982	4	5	0	.444	164	160	T8th/NFC	—	—		Ray Perkins
1983	3	12	1	.219	267	347	5th/NFC Eastern Div.	—	—		Bill Parcells
1984	9	7	0	.563	299	301	2nd/NFC Eastern Div.	1	1	NFC div. playoff game	Bill Parcells
1985	10	6	0	.625	399	283	2nd/NFC Eastern Div.	1	1	NFC div. playoff game	Bill Parcells
1986	14	2	0	.875	371	236	1st/NFC Eastern Div.	3	0	Super Bowl champ	Bill Parcells
1987	6	9	0	.400	280	312	5th/NFC Eastern Div.	—	—		Bill Parcells
1988	10	6	0	.625	359	304	2nd/NFC Eastern Div.	—	—		Bill Parcells
1989	12	4	0	.750	348	252	1st/NFC Eastern Div.	0	1	NFC div. playoff game	Bill Parcells
1990	13	3	0	.813	335	211	1st/NFC Eastern Div.	3	0	Super Bowl champ	Bill Parcells
1991	8	8	0	.500	281	297	4th/NFC Eastern Div.	—	—		Ray Handley
1992	6	10	0	.375	306	367	4th/NFC Eastern Div.	—	—		Ray Handley
1993	11	5	0	.688	288	205	2nd/NFC Eastern Div.	1	1	NFC div. playoff game	Dan Reeves
1994	9	7	0	.563	279	305	2nd/NFC Eastern Div.	—	—		Dan Reeves

FIRST-ROUND DRAFT PICKS

1936—Art Lewis, T, Ohio
1937—Ed Widseth, T, Minnesota
1938—George Karamatic, B, Gonzaga
1939—Walt Nielson, B, Arizona
1940—Grenville Lansdell, B, Southern California
1941—George Franck, B, Minnesota
1942—Merle Hapes, B, Mississippi
1943—Steve Filipowicz, B, Fordham
1944—Billy Hillenbrand, B, Indiana
1945—Elmer Barbour, B, Wake Forest
1946—George Connor, T, Notre Dame
1947—Vic Schwall, B, Northwestern
1948—Tony Minisi, B, Pennsylvania
1949—Paul Page, B, Southern Methodist
1950—Travis Tidwell, B, Auburn
1951—Kyle Rote, B, Southern Methodist*
    Kim Spavital, B, Oklahoma A&M
1952—Frank Gifford, B, Southern California
1953—Bobby Marlow, B, Alabama
1954—None
1955—Joe Heap, B, Notre Dame
1956—Henry Moore, B, Arkansas
1957—None
1958—Phil King, B, Vanderbilt
1959—Lee Grosscup, B, Utah
1960—Lou Cordileone, G, Clemson
1961—None
1962—Jerry Hillebrand, LB, Colorado
1963—None
1964—Joe Don Looney, RB, Oklahoma
1965—T. Frederickson, RB, Auburn*
1966—Francis Peay, T, Missouri
1967—None

1968—None
1969—Fred Dryer, DE, San Diego State
1970—Jim Files, LB, Oklahoma
1971—Rocky Thompson, RB, West Texas State
1972—Eldridge Small, DB, Texas A&I
    Larry Jacobson, DT, Nebraska
1973—None
1974—John Hicks, G, Ohio State
1975—None
1976—Troy Archer, DE, Colorado
1977—Gary Jeter, DT, Southern Cal
1978—Gordon King, T, Stanford
1979—Phil Simms, QB, Morehead State
1980—Mark Haynes, DB, Colorado
1981—Lawrence Taylor, LB, North Carolina
1982—Butch Woolfolk, RB, Michigan
1983—Terry Kinard, DB, Clemson
1984—Carl Banks, LB, Michigan State
    Bill Roberts, T, Ohio State
1985—George Adams, RB, Kentucky
1986—Eric Dorsey, DT, Notre Dame
1987—Mark Ingram, WR, Michigan State
1988—Eric Moore, T, Indiana
1989—Brian Williams, G, Minnesota
1990—Rodney Hampton, RB, Georgia
1991—Jarrod Bunch, FB, Michigan
1992—Derek Brown, TE, Notre Dame
1993—None
1994—Thomas Lewis, WR, Indiana
1995—Tyrone Wheatley, RB, Michigan
    *First player chosen in draft.

FRANCHISE RECORDS

Most rushing yards, career
5,296—Joe Morris

Most rushing yards, season
1,516—Joe Morris, 1986

Most rushing yards, game
218—Gene Roberts vs. Chi. Cardinals, Nov. 12, 1950

Most rushing touchdowns, season
21—Joe Morris, 1985

Most passing attempts, season
533—Phil Simms, 1984

Most passing attempts, game
62—Phil Simms at Cin., Oct. 13, 1985

Most passes completed, season
286—Phil Simms, 1984

Most passes completed, game
40—Phil Simms at Cin., Oct. 13, 1985

Most passing yards, career
33,462—Phil Simms

Most passing yards, season
4,044—Phil Simms, 1984

Most passing yards, game
513—Phil Simms at Cin., Oct. 13, 1985

Most touchdown passes, season
36—Y.A. Tittle, 1963

Most pass receptions, career
395—Joe Morrison

Most pass receptions, season
78—Earnest Gray, 1983

Most pass receptions, game
12—Mark Bavaro at Cin., Oct. 13, 1985

Most receiving yards, career
5,434—Frank Gifford
Most receiving yards, season
1,209—Homer Jones
Most receiving yards, game
269—Del Shofner vs. Was., Oct. 28, 1962
Most receiving touchdowns, season
13—Homer Jones, 1967

Most touchdowns, career
48—Kyle Rote
Most field goals, season
35—Ali Haji-Sheikh, 1983
Longest field goal
56 yards—Ali Haji-Sheikh at Det., Nov. 7, 1983
Most interceptions, career
74—Emlen Tunnell

Most interceptions, season
11—Otto Schellbacher, 1951
Jimmy Patton, 1958
Most sacks, career
132.5—Lawrence Taylor
Most sacks, season
20.5—Lawrence Taylor, 1986

SERIES RECORDS

N.Y. Giants vs.: Arizona 67-36-2; Atlanta 6-6; Buffalo 2-4; Chicago 16-24-2; Cincinnati 1-4; Cleveland 17-25-2; Dallas 22-41-2; Denver 3-3; Detroit 12-14-1; Green Bay 20-21-3; Houston 5-0; Indianapolis 5-5; Kansas City 6-1; L.A. Raiders 2-4; L.A. Rams 7-19; Miami 2-1; Minnesota 4-7; New England 3-1; New Orleans 9-7; N.Y. Jets 3-4; Philadelphia 63-55-2; Pittsburgh 44-28-3; San Diego 4-2; San Francisco 11-10; Seattle 5-2; Tampa Bay 8-3; Washington 64-48-2.

☐ RETIRED UNIFORM NUMBERS ☐

No.	Player
1	Ray Flaherty
7	Mel Hein
14	Y.A. Tittle
32	Al Blozis
40	Joe Morrison
42	Charlie Conerly
50	Ken Strong
56	Lawrence Taylor

NEW YORK JETS

YEAR-BY-YEAR RECORDS

				REGULAR SEASON						PLAYOFFS		
Year	W	L	T	Pct.	PF	PA	Finish	W	L	Highest round		Coach
1960*†	7	7	0	.500	382	399	2nd/Eastern Div.	—	—			Sammy Baugh
1961*†	7	7	0	.500	301	390	3rd/Eastern Div.	—	—			Sammy Baugh
1962*†	5	9	0	.357	278	423	4th/Eastern Div.	—	—			Bulldog Turner
1963*	5	8	1	.385	249	399	4th/Eastern Div.	—	—			Weeb Ewbank
1964*	5	8	1	.385	278	315	3rd/Eastern Div.	—	—			Weeb Ewbank
1965*	5	8	1	.385	285	303	2nd/Eastern Div.	—	—			Weeb Ewbank
1966*	6	6	2	.500	322	312	3rd/Eastern Div.	—	—			Weeb Ewbank
1967*	8	5	1	.615	371	329	2nd/Eastern Div.	—	—			Weeb Ewbank
1968*	11	3	0	.786	419	280	1st/Eastern Div.	2	0	Super Bowl champ		Weeb Ewbank
1969*	10	4	0	.714	353	269	1st/Eastern Div.	0	1	Div. playoff game		Weeb Ewbank
1970	4	10	0	.286	255	286	3rd/AFC Eastern Div.	—	—			Weeb Ewbank
1971	6	8	0	.429	212	299	T3rd/AFC Eastern Div.	—	—			Weeb Ewbank
1972	7	7	0	.500	367	324	2nd/AFC Eastern Div.	—	—			Weeb Ewbank
1973	4	10	0	.286	240	306	T4th/AFC Eastern Div.	—	—			Weeb Ewbank
1974	7	7	0	.500	279	300	T3rd/AFC Eastern Div.	—	—			Charley Winner
1975	3	11	0	.214	258	433	T4th/AFC Eastern Div.	—	—			Charley Winner, Ken Shipp
1976	3	11	0	.214	169	383	4th/AFC Eastern Div.	—	—			Lou Holtz, Mike Holovak
1977	3	11	0	.214	191	300	T4th/AFC Eastern Div.	—	—			Walt Michaels
1978	8	8	0	.500	359	364	3rd/AFC Eastern Div.	—	—			Walt Michaels
1979	8	8	0	.500	337	383	3rd/AFC Eastern Div.	—	—			Walt Michaels
1980	4	12	0	.250	302	395	5th/AFC Eastern Div.	—	—			Walt Michaels
1981	10	5	1	.656	355	287	2nd/AFC Eastern Div.	0	1	AFC wild-card game		Walt Michaels
1982	6	3	0	.667	245	166	T4th/AFC	2	1	AFC championship game		Walt Michaels
1983	7	9	0	.438	313	331	T4th/AFC Eastern Div.	—	—			Joe Walton
1984	7	9	0	.438	332	364	3rd/AFC Eastern Div.	—	—			Joe Walton
1985	11	5	0	.688	393	264	T2nd/AFC Eastern Div.	0	1	AFC wild-card game		Joe Walton
1986	10	6	0	.625	364	386	2nd/AFC Eastern Div.	1	1	AFC div. playoff game		Joe Walton
1987	6	9	0	.400	334	360	5th/AFC Eastern Div.	—	—			Joe Walton
1988	8	7	1	.531	372	354	4th/AFC Eastern Div.	—	—			Joe Walton
1989	4	12	0	.250	253	411	5th/AFC Eastern Div.	—	—			Joe Walton
1990	6	10	0	.375	295	345	4th/AFC Eastern Div.	—	—			Bruce Coslet
1991	8	8	0	.500	314	293	2nd/AFC Eastern Div.	0	1	AFC wild-card game		Bruce Coslet
1992	4	12	0	.250	220	315	4th/AFC Eastern Div.	—	—			Bruce Coslet
1993	8	8	0	.500	270	247	3rd/AFC Eastern Div.	—	—			Bruce Coslet
1994	6	10	0	.375	264	320	5th/AFC Eastern Div.	—	—			Pete Carroll

*American Football League.
†New York Titans.

FIRST-ROUND DRAFT PICKS

1960—George Izo, QB, Notre Dame
1961—Tom Brown, G, Minnesota
1962—Sandy Stephens, QB, Minnesota

1963—Jerry Stovall, RB, Louisiana State
1964—Matt Snell, RB, Ohio State

1965—Joe Namath, QB, Alabama
      Tom Nowatzke, RB, Indiana
1966—Bill Yearby, DT, Michigan
1967—Paul Seiler, G, Notre Dame
1968—Lee White, RB, Weber State
1969—Dave Foley, T, Ohio State
1970—Steve Tannen, DB, Florida
1971—John Riggins, RB, Kansas
1972—Jerome Barkum, WR, Jackson State
      Mike Taylor, LB, Michigan
1973—Burgess Owens, DB, Miami
1974—Carl Barzilauskas, DT, Indiana
1975—None
1976—Richard Todd, QB, Alabama
1977—Marvin Powell, T, Southern California
1978—Chris Ward, T, Ohio State
1979—Marty Lyons, DT, Alabama
1980—Lam Jones, WR, Texas

1981—Freeman McNeil, RB, UCLA
1982—Bob Crable, LB, Notre Dame
1983—Ken O'Brien, QB, California-Davis
1984—Russell Carter, DB, Southern Methodist
      Ron Faurot, DE, Arkansas
1985—Al Toon, WR, Wisconsin
1986—Mike Haight, T, Iowa
1987—Roger Vick, FB, Texas A&M
1988—Dave Cadigan, T, Southern California
1989—Jeff Lageman, LB, Virginia
1990—Blair Thomas, RB, Penn State
1991—None
1992—Johnny Mitchell, TE, Nebraska
1993—Marvin Jones, LB, Florida State
1994—Aaron Glenn, DB, Texas A&M
1995—Kyle Brady, TE, Penn State
      Hugh Douglas, DE, Central State (O.)

FRANCHISE RECORDS

Most rushing yards, career
8,074—Freeman McNeil

Most rushing yards, season
1,131—Freeman McNeil, 1985

Most rushing yards, game
192—Freeman McNeil vs. Buffalo, Sept. 15, 1985

Most rushing touchdowns, season
11—Emerson Boozer, 1972
    Johnny Hector, 1987
    Brad Baxter, 1991

Most passing attempts, season
518—Richard Todd, 1983

Most passing attempts, game
62—Joe Namath vs. Bal., Oct. 18, 1970

Most passes completed, season
308—Richard Todd, 1983

Most passes completed, game
42—Richard Todd vs. S.F., Sept. 21, 1980

Most passing yards, career
27,057—Joe Namath

Most passing yards, season
4,007—Joe Namath, 1967

Most passing yards, game
496—Joe Namath at Bal., Sept. 24, 1972

Most touchdown passes, season
26—Al Dorow, 1960
    Joe Namath, 1967

Most pass receptions, career
627—Don Maynard

Most pass receptions, season
93—Al Toon, 1988

Most pass receptions, game
17—Clark Gaines vs. S.F., Sept. 21, 1980

Most receiving yards, career
11,732—Don Maynard

Most receiving yards, season
1,434—Don Maynard, 1967

Most receiving yards, game
228—Don Maynard at Oak., Nov. 17, 1968

Most receiving touchdowns, season
14—Art Powell, 1960
    Don Maynard, 1965

Most touchdowns, career
88—Don Maynard

Most field goals, season
34—Jim Turner, 1968

Longest field goal
55 yards—Pat Leahy vs. Chi., Dec. 14, 1985

Most interceptions, career
34—Bill Baird

Most interceptions, season
12—Dainard Paulson, 1964

Most sacks, career
107.5—Mark Gastineau

Most sacks, season
22—Mark Gastineau, 1984

SERIES RECORDS

N.Y. Jets vs.: Arizona 1-2; Atlanta 3-3; Buffalo 31-38; Chicago 1-4; Cincinnati 9-6; Cleveland 6-9; Dallas 1-5; Denver 12-12-1; Detroit 3-4; Green Bay 5-2; Houston 12-18-1; Indianapolis 21-28; Kansas City 12-14-1; L.A. Raiders 9-14-2; L.A. Rams 2-5; Miami 27-28-1; Minnesota 4-1; New England 38-28-1; New Orleans 4-3; N.Y. Giants 4-3; Philadelphia 0-5; Pittsburgh 1-12; San Diego 9-17-1; San Francisco 1-6; Seattle 3-8; Tampa Bay 5-1; Washington 1-4.

NOTE: Includes records as New York Titans from 1960 through 1962.

RETIRED UNIFORM NUMBERS

No.	Player
12	Joe Namath
13	Don Maynard

PHILADELPHIA EAGLES

YEAR-BY-YEAR RECORDS

		REGULAR SEASON					PLAYOFFS			
Year	W	L	T	Pct.	PF	PA	Finish	W	L	Highest round	Coach
1933	3	5	1	.375	77	158	4th/Eastern Div.	—	—		Lud Wray
1934	4	7	0	.364	127	85	T3rd/Eastern Div.	—	—		Lud Wray
1935	2	9	0	.182	60	179	5th/Eastern Div.	—	—		Lud Wray
1936	1	11	0	.083	51	206	5th/Eastern Div.	—	—		Bert Bell
1937	2	8	1	.200	86	177	5th/Eastern Div.	—	—		Bert Bell
1938	5	6	0	.455	154	164	4th/Eastern Div.	—	—		Bert Bell
1939	1	9	1	.100	105	200	T4th/Eastern Div.	—	—		Bert Bell
1940	1	10	0	.091	111	211	5th/Eastern Div.	—	—		Bert Bell
1941	2	8	1	.200	119	218	4th/Eastern Div.	—	—		Greasy Neale
1942	2	9	0	.182	134	239	5th/Eastern Div.	—	—		Greasy Neale
1943*	5	4	1	.556	225	230	3rd/Eastern Div.	—	—		Greasy Neale-Walt Kiesling

		REGULAR SEASON						PLAYOFFS			
Year	W	L	T	Pct.	PF	PA	Finish	W	L	Highest round	Coach
1944	7	1	2	.875	267	131	2nd/Eastern Div.	—	—		Greasy Neale
1945	7	3	0	.700	272	133	2nd/Eastern Div.	—	—		Greasy Neale
1946	6	5	0	.545	231	220	2nd/Eastern Div.	—	—		Greasy Neale
1947	8	4	0	.667	308	242	1st/Eastern Div.	1	1	NFL championship game	Greasy Neale
1948	9	2	1	.818	376	156	1st/Eastern Div.	1	0	NFL champ	Greasy Neale
1949	11	1	0	.917	364	134	1st/Eastern Div.	1	0	NFL champ	Greasy Neale
1950	6	6	0	.500	254	141	T3rd/American Conf.	—	—		Greasy Neale
1951	4	8	0	.333	234	264	5th/American Conf.	—	—		Bo McMillin, Wayne Millner
1952	7	5	0	.583	252	271	T2nd/American Conf.	—	—		Jim Trimble
1953	7	4	1	.636	352	215	2nd/Eastern Conf.	—	—		Jim Trimble
1954	7	4	1	.636	284	230	2nd/Eastern Conf.	—	—		Jim Trimble
1955	4	7	1	.364	248	231	T4th/Eastern Conf.	—	—		Jim Trimble
1956	3	8	1	.273	143	215	6th/Eastern Conf.	—	—		Hugh Devore
1957	4	8	0	.333	173	230	5th/Eastern Conf.	—	—		Hugh Devore
1958	2	9	1	.182	235	306	T5th/Eastern Conf.	—	—		Buck Shaw
1959	7	5	0	.583	268	278	T2nd/Eastern Conf.	—	—		Buck Shaw
1960	10	2	0	.833	321	246	1st/Eastern Conf.	1	0	NFL champ	Buck Shaw
1961	10	4	0	.714	361	297	2nd/Eastern Conf.	—	—		Nick Skorich
1962	3	10	1	.231	282	356	7th/Eastern Conf.	—	—		Nick Skorich
1963	2	10	2	.167	242	381	7th/Western Conf.	—	—		Nick Skorich
1964	6	8	0	.429	312	313	T3rd/Eastern Conf.	—	—		Joe Kuharich
1965	5	9	0	.357	363	359	T5th/Eastern Conf.	—	—		Joe Kuharich
1966	9	5	0	.643	326	340	T2nd/Eastern Conf.	—	—		Joe Kuharich
1967	6	7	1	.462	351	409	2nd/Capitol Div.	—	—		Joe Kuharich
1968	2	12	0	.143	202	351	4th/Capitol Div.	—	—		Joe Kuharich
1969	4	9	1	.308	279	377	4th/Capitol Div.	—	—		Jerry Williams
1970	3	10	1	.231	241	332	5th/NFC Eastern Div.	—	—		Jerry Williams
1971	6	7	1	.462	221	302	3rd/NFC Eastern Div.	—	—		Jerry Williams, Ed Khayat
1972	2	11	1	.179	145	352	5th/NFC Eastern Div.	—	—		Ed Khayat
1973	5	8	1	.393	310	393	3rd/NFC Eastern Div.	—	—		Mike McCormack
1974	7	7	0	.500	242	217	4th/NFC Eastern Div.	—	—		Mike McCormack
1975	4	10	0	.286	225	302	5th/NFC Eastern Div.	—	—		Mike McCormack
1976	4	10	0	.286	165	286	4th/NFC Eastern Div.	—	—		Dick Vermeil
1977	5	9	0	.357	220	207	T4th/NFC Eastern Div.	—	—		Dick Vermeil
1978	9	7	0	.563	270	250	2nd/NFC Eastern Div.	0	1	NFC wild-card game	Dick Vermeil
1979	11	5	0	.688	339	282	2nd/NFC Eastern Div.	1	1	NFC div. playoff game	Dick Vermeil
1980	12	4	0	.750	384	222	1st/NFC Eastern Div.	2	1	Super Bowl	Dick Vermeil
1981	10	6	0	.625	368	221	2nd/NFC Eastern Div.	0	1	NFC wild-card game	Dick Vermeil
1982	3	6	0	.333	191	195	T11th/NFC	—	—		Dick Vermeil
1983	5	11	0	.313	233	322	4th/NFC Eastern Div.	—	—		Marion Campbell
1984	6	9	1	.406	278	320	5th/NFC Eastern Div.	—	—		Marion Campbell
1985	7	9	0	.438	286	310	4th/NFC Eastern Div.	—	—		M. Campbell, Fred Bruney
1986	5	10	1	.344	256	312	4th/NFC Eastern Div.	—	—		Buddy Ryan
1987	7	8	0	.467	337	380	T2nd/NFC Eastern Div.	—	—		Buddy Ryan
1988	10	6	0	.625	379	319	1st/NFC Eastern Div.	0	1	NFC div. playoff game	Buddy Ryan
1989	11	5	0	.688	342	274	2nd/NFC Eastern Div.	0	1	NFC wild-card game	Buddy Ryan
1990	10	6	0	.625	396	299	T2nd/NFC Eastern Div.	0	1	NFC wild-card game	Buddy Ryan
1991	10	6	0	.625	285	244	3rd/NFC Eastern Div.	—	—		Rich Kotite
1992	11	5	0	.688	354	245	2nd/NFC Eastern Div.	1	1	NFC div. playoff game	Rich Kotite
1993	8	8	0	.500	293	315	3rd/NFC Eastern Div.	—	—		Rich Kotite
1994	7	9	0	.438	308	308	4th/NFC Eastern Div.	—	—		Rich Kotite

*Phil-Pitt "Steagles," a combined squad of Philadelphia Eagles and Pittsburgh Steelers.

FIRST-ROUND DRAFT PICKS

1936—Jay Berwanger, B, Chicago*
1937—Sam Francis, B, Nebraska*
1938—John McDonald, B, Nebraska
1939—Davey O'Brien, QB, Texas Christian
1940—Wes McAfee, B, Duke
1941—None
1942—Pete Kmetovic, B, Stanford
1943—Joe Muha, B, Virginia Military
1944—Steve Van Buren, B, Louisiana State
1945—John Yonaker, E, Notre Dame
1946—Leo Riggs, B, Southern California
1947—Neil Armstrong, E, Oklahoma A&M
1948—Clyde Scott, B, Arkansas
1949—Chuck Bednarik, C, Pennsylvania*
      Frank Tripucka, QB, Notre Dame
1950—Bud Grant, E, Minnesota
1951—Ebert Van Buren, B, Louisiana State
      Chet Mutryn, B, Xavier

1952—John Bright, B, Drake
1953—None
1954—Neil Worden, B, Notre Dame
1955—Dick Bielski, B, Maryland
1956—Bob Pellegrini, C, Maryland
1957—Clarence Peaks, B, Michigan State
1958—Walter Kowalczyk, B, Michigan State
1959—None
1960—Ron Burton, B, Northwestern
1961—Art Baker, B, Syracuse
1962—None
1963—Ed Budde, T, Michigan State
1964—Bob Brown, T, Nebraska
1965—None
1966—Randy Beisler, T, Indiana
1967—Harry Jones, RB, Arkansas
1968—Tim Rossovich, DE, Southern California
1969—Leroy Keyes, RB, Purdue

1970—Steve Zabel, E, Oklahoma
1971—Richard Harris, DE, Grambling State
1972—John Reaves, QB, Florida
1973—Jerry Sisemore, T, Texas
    Charle Young, TE, Southern California
1974—None
1975—None
1976—None
1977—None
1978—None
1979—Jerry Robinson, LB, UCLA
1980—Roynell Young, DB, Alcorn State
1981—Leonard Mitchell, DE, Houston
1982—Mike Quick, WR, North Carolina State
1983—Michael Haddix, RB, Mississippi State

1984—Kenny Jackson, WR, Penn State
1985—Kevin Allen, T, Indiana
1986—Keith Byars, RB, Ohio State
1987—Jerome Brown, DT, Miami (Fla.)
1988—Keith Jackson, TE, Oklahoma
1989—None
1990—Ben Smith, DB, Georgia
1991—Antone Davis, T, Tennessee
1992—None
1993—Lester Holmes, T, Jackson State
    Leonard Renfro, DT, Colorado
1994—Bernard Williams, T, Georgia
1995—Mike Mamula, DE, Boston College
*First player chosen in draft.

FRANCHISE RECORDS

Most rushing yards, career
6,538—Wilbert Montgomery

Most rushing yards, season
1,512—Wilbert Montgomery, 1979

Most rushing yards, game
205—Steve Van Buren vs. Pit., Nov. 27, 1949

Most rushing touchdowns, season
15—Steve Van Buren, 1945

Most passing attempts, season
560—Randall Cunningham, 1988

Most passing attempts, game
62—Randall Cunningham at Chi., Oct. 2, 1989

Most passes completed, season
301—Randall Cunningham, 1988

Most passes completed, game
34—Randall Cunningham at Was., Sept. 17, 1989

Most passing yards, career
26,963—Ron Jaworski

Most passing yards, season
3,808—Randall Cunningham, 1988

Most passing yards, game
447—Randall Cunningham at Was., Sept. 17, 1989

Most touchdown passes, season
32—Sonny Jurgensen, 1961

Most pass receptions, career
589—Harold Carmichael

Most pass receptions, season
81—Keith Jackson, 1988
    Keith Byars, 1990

Most pass receptions, game
14—Don Looney at Was., Dec. 1, 1940

Most receiving yards, career
8,978—Harold Carmichael

Most receiving yards, season
1,409—Mike Quick, 1983

Most receiving yards, game
237—Tommy McDonald vs. NYG, Dec. 10, 1961

Most receiving touchdowns, season
13—Tommy McDonald, 1960
    Tommy McDonald, 1961
    Mike Quick, 1983

Most touchdowns, career
79—Harold Carmichael

Most field goals, season
30—Paul McFadden, 1984

Longest field goal
59 yards—Tony Franklin at Dal., Nov. 12, 1979

Most interceptions, career
34—Bill Bradley

Most interceptions, season
11—Bill Bradley, 1971

Most sacks, career
124—Reggie White

Most sacks, season
21—Reggie White, 1987

SERIES RECORDS

Philadelphia vs.: Arizona 45-45-5; Atlanta 8-7-1; Buffalo 4-3; Chicago 4-24-1; Cincinnati 1-6; Cleveland 12-31-1; Dallas 26-42; Denver 5-2; Detroit 9-11-2; Green Bay 8-19; Houston 6-0; Indianapolis 6-6; Kansas City 1-1; L.A. Raiders 4-2; L.A. Rams 11-14-1; Miami 2-6; Minnesota 6-10; New England 5-2; New Orleans 11-8; N.Y. Giants 55-63-2; N.Y. Jets 5-0; Pittsburgh 43-26-3; San Diego 2-3; San Francisco 6-13-1; Seattle 4-1; Tampa Bay 3-1; Washington 50-62-6.

NOTE: Includes records when team combined with Pittsburgh squad and was known as Phil-Pitt in 1943.

RETIRED UNIFORM NUMBERS

No.	Player
15	Steve Van Buren
40	Tom Brookshier
44	Pete Retzlaff
60	Chuck Bednarik
70	Al Wistert
99	Jerome Brown

PITTSBURGH STEELERS

YEAR-BY-YEAR RECORDS

		REGULAR SEASON						PLAYOFFS		
Year	W	L	T	Pct.	PF	PA	Finish	W	L	Highest round	Coach
1933*	3	6	2	.333	67	208	5th/Eastern Div.	—	—		Jap Douds
1934*	2	10	0	.167	51	206	5th/Eastern Div.	—	—		Luby DiMello
1935*	4	8	0	.333	100	209	3rd/Eastern Div.	—	—		Joe Bach
1936*	6	6	0	.500	98	187	2nd/Eastern Div.	—	—		Joe Bach
1937*	4	7	0	.364	122	145	3rd/Eastern Div.	—	—		Johnny Blood
1938*	2	9	0	.182	79	169	5th/Eastern Div.	—	—		Johnny Blood
1939*	1	9	1	.100	114	216	T4th/Eastern Div.	—	—		Johnny Blood-Walt Kiesling
1940*	2	7	2	.222	60	178	4th/Eastern Div.	—	—		Walt Kiesling
1941	1	9	1	.100	103	276	5th/Eastern Div.	—	—		Bert Bell-Buff Donelli-Walt Kiesling
1942	7	4	0	.636	167	119	2nd/Eastern Div.	—	—		Walt Kiesling
1943†	5	4	1	.556	225	230	3rd/Eastern Div.	—	—		Walt Kiesling-Greasy Neale

		REGULAR SEASON							PLAYOFFS		
Year	W	L	T	Pct.	PF	PA	Finish	W	L	Highest round	Coach
1944‡	0	10	0	.000	108	328	5th/Western Div.	—	—		Walt Kiesling-Phil Handler
1945	2	8	0	.200	79	220	5th/Eastern Div.	—	—		Jim Leonard
1946	5	5	1	.500	136	117	T3rd/Eastern Div.	—	—		Jock Sutherland
1947	8	4	0	.667	240	259	2nd/Eastern Div.	0	1	E. Div. champ. game	Jock Sutherland
1948	4	8	0	.333	200	243	T3rd/Eastern Div.	—	—		John Michelosen
1949	6	5	1	.545	224	214	2nd/Eastern Div.	—	—		John Michelosen
1950	6	6	0	.500	180	195	T3rd/American Conf.	—	—		John Michelosen
1951	4	7	1	.364	183	235	4th/American Conf.	—	—		John Michelosen
1952	5	7	0	.417	300	273	3rd/American Conf.	—	—		Joe Bach
1953	6	6	0	.500	211	263	4th/Eastern Conf.	—	—		Joe Bach
1954	5	7	0	.417	219	263	4th/Eastern Conf.	—	—		Walt Kiesling
1955	4	8	0	.333	195	285	6th/Eastern Conf.	—	—		Walt Kiesling
1956	5	7	0	.417	217	250	5th/Eastern Conf.	—	—		Walt Kiesling
1957	6	6	0	.500	161	178	3rd/Eastern Conf.	—	—		Buddy Parker
1958	7	4	1	.636	261	230	3rd/Eastern Conf.	—	—		Buddy Parker
1959	6	5	1	.545	257	216	4th/Eastern Conf.	—	—		Buddy Parker
1960	5	6	1	.455	240	275	5th/Eastern Conf.	—	—		Buddy Parker
1961	6	8	0	.429	295	287	5th/Eastern Conf.	—	—		Buddy Parker
1962	9	5	0	.643	312	363	2nd/Eastern Conf.	—	—		Buddy Parker
1963	7	4	3	.636	321	295	4th/Eastern Conf.	—	—		Buddy Parker
1964	5	9	0	.357	253	315	6th/Eastern Conf.	—	—		Buddy Parker
1965	2	12	0	.143	202	397	7th/Eastern Conf.	—	—		Mike Nixon
1966	5	8	1	.385	316	347	6th/Eastern Conf.	—	—		Bill Austin
1967	4	9	1	.308	281	320	4th/Century Div.	—	—		Bill Austin
1968	2	11	1	.154	244	397	4th/Century Div.	—	—		Bill Austin
1969	1	13	0	.071	218	404	4th/Century Div.	—	—		Chuck Noll
1970	5	9	0	.357	210	272	3rd/AFC Central Div.	—	—		Chuck Noll
1971	6	8	0	.429	246	292	2nd/AFC Central Div.	—	—		Chuck Noll
1972	11	3	0	.786	343	175	1st/AFC Central Div.	1	1	AFC championship game	Chuck Noll
1973	10	4	0	.714	347	210	2nd/AFC Central Div.	0	1	AFC div. playoff game	Chuck Noll
1974	10	3	1	.750	305	189	1st/AFC Central Div.	3	0	Super Bowl champ	Chuck Noll
1975	12	2	0	.857	373	162	1st/AFC Central Div.	3	0	Super Bowl champ	Chuck Noll
1976	10	4	0	.714	342	138	1st/AFC Central Div.	1	1	AFC championship game	Chuck Noll
1977	9	5	0	.643	283	243	1st/AFC Central Div.	0	1	AFC div. playoff game	Chuck Noll
1978	14	2	0	.875	356	195	1st/AFC Central Div.	3	0	Super Bowl champ	Chuck Noll
1979	12	4	0	.750	416	262	1st/AFC Central Div.	3	0	Super Bowl champ	Chuck Noll
1980	9	7	0	.563	352	313	3rd/AFC Central Div.	—	—		Chuck Noll
1981	8	8	0	.500	356	297	2nd/AFC Central Div.	—	—		Chuck Noll
1982	6	3	0	.667	204	146	T4th/AFC	0	1	AFC first-round pl. game	Chuck Noll
1983	10	6	0	.625	355	303	1st/AFC Central Div.	0	1	AFC div. playoff game	Chuck Noll
1984	9	7	0	.563	387	310	1st/AFC Central Div.	1	1	AFC championship game	Chuck Noll
1985	7	9	0	.438	379	355	T2nd/AFC Central Div.	—	—		Chuck Noll
1986	6	10	0	.375	307	336	3rd/AFC Central Div.	—	—		Chuck Noll
1987	8	7	0	.533	285	299	3rd/AFC Central Div.	—	—		Chuck Noll
1988	5	11	0	.313	336	421	4th/AFC Central Div.	—	—		Chuck Noll
1989	9	7	0	.563	265	326	T2nd/AFC Central Div.	1	1	AFC div. playoff game	Chuck Noll
1990	9	7	0	.563	292	240	3rd/AFC Central Div.	—	—		Chuck Noll
1991	7	9	0	.438	292	344	2nd/AFC Central Div.	—	—		Chuck Noll
1992	11	5	0	.688	299	225	1st/AFC Central Div.	0	1	AFC div. playoff game	Bill Cowher
1993	9	7	0	.563	308	281	2nd/AFC Central Div.	0	1	AFC wild-card game	Bill Cowher
1994	12	4	0	.750	316	234	1st/AFC Central Div.	1	1	AFC championship game	Bill Cowher

*Pittsburgh Pirates.
†Phil-Pitt "Steagles," a combined squad of Philadelphia Eagles and Pittsburgh Steelers.
‡Card-Pitt, a combined squad of Chicago Cardinals and Pittsburgh Steelers.

FIRST-ROUND DRAFT PICKS

1936—Bill Shakespeare, B, Notre Dame
1937—Mike Basrak, C, Duquesne
1938—Byron White, B, Colorado
    Frank Filchock, B, Indiana
1939—None
1940—Kay Eakin, B, Arkansas
1941—Chet Gladchuk, C, Boston College
1942—Bill Dudley, B, Virginia*
1943—Bill Daley, B, Minnesota
1944—Johnny Podesto, B, St. Mary's (Calif.)
1945—Paul Duhart, B, Florida
1946—Doc Blanchard, B, Army
1947—Hub Bechtol, E, Texas
1948—Dan Edwards, E, Georgia
1949—Bobby Gage, B, Clemson
1950—Lynn Chandnois, B, Michigan State

1951—Clarence Avinger, B, Alabama
1952—Ed Modzelewski, B, Maryland
1953—Ted Marchibroda, QB, St. Bonaventure
1954—John Lattner, B, Notre Dame
1955—Frank Varrichione, T, Notre Dame
1956—Gary Glick, B, Colorado State*
    Art Davis, B, Mississippi State
1957—Len Dawson, QB, Purdue
1958—None
1959—None
1960—Jack Spikes, B, Texas Christian
1961—None
1962—Bob Ferguson, RB, Ohio State
1963—None
1964—Paul Martha, RB, Pittsburgh
1965—None

1966—Dick Leftridge, RB, West Virginia
1967—None
1968—Mike Taylor, T, Southern California
1969—Joe Greene, DT, North Texas State
1970—Terry Bradshaw, QB, Louisiana Tech*
1971—Frank Lewis, WR, Grambling State
1972—Franco Harris, RB, Penn State
1973—James Thomas, DB, Florida State
1974—Lynn Swann, WR, Southern California
1975—Dave Brown, DB, Michigan
1976—Bennie Cunningham, TE, Clemson
1977—Robin Cole, LB, New Mexico
1978—Ron Johnson, DB, Eastern Michigan
1979—Greg Hawthorne, RB, Baylor
1980—Mark Malone, QB, Arizona State
1981—Keith Gary, DE, Oklahoma

1982—Walter Abercrombie, RB, Baylor
1983—Gabriel Rivera, DT, Texas Tech
1984—Louis Lipps, WR, Southern Mississippi
1985—Darryl Sims, DT, Wisconsin
1986—John Rienstra, G, Temple
1987—Rod Woodson, DB, Purdue
1988—Aaron Jones, DE, Eastern Kentucky
1989—Tim Worley, RB, Georgia
   Tom Ricketts, T, Pittsburgh
1990—Eric Green, TE, Liberty (Va.)
1991—Huey Richardson, LB, Florida
1992—Leon Searcy, T, Miami (Fla.)
1993—Deon Figures, DB, Colorado
1994—Charles Johnson, WR, Colorado
1995—Mark Bruener, TE, Washington
   *First player chosen in draft.

FRANCHISE RECORDS

Most rushing yards, career
11,950—Franco Harris
Most rushing yards, season
1,690—Barry Foster, 1992
Most rushing yards, game
218—John Fuqua at Phi., Dec. 20, 1970
Most rushing touchdowns, season
14—Franco Harris, 1976
Most passing attempts, season
486—Neil O'Donnell, 1993
Most passing attempts, game
50—Joe Gilliam at Den., Sept. 22, 1974 (OT)
49—Jim Finks at Chi. Cardinals, Nov. 5, 1955
   Bobby Layne vs. Chi. Cardinals, Dec. 13, 1958
Most passes completed, season
270—Neil O'Donnell, 1993
Most passes completed, game
31—Joe Gilliam at Den., Sept. 22, 1974 (OT)
30—Terry Bradshaw vs. Cle., Nov. 25, 1979 (OT)
29—Terry Bradshaw vs. Cin., Sept. 19, 1982 (OT)
28—Kent Nix vs. Dal., Oct. 22, 1967

Most passing yards, career
27,989—Terry Bradshaw
Most passing yards, season
3,724—Terry Bradshaw, 1979
Most passing yards, game
409—Bobby Layne vs. Chi. Cardinals, Dec. 13, 1958
Most touchdown passes, season
28—Terry Bradshaw, 1978
Most pass receptions, career
537—John Stallworth
Most pass receptions, season
80—John Stallworth, 1984
Most pass receptions, game
12—J.R. Wilburn vs. Dal., Oct. 22, 1967
Most receiving yards, career
8,723—John Stallworth
Most receiving yards, season
1,395—John Stallworth, 1984
Most receiving yards, game
235—Buddy Dial vs. Cle., Oct. 22, 1961
Most receiving touchdowns, season
12—Buddy Dial, 1961
   Louis Lipps, 1985

Most touchdowns, career
100—Franco Harris
Most field goals, season
33—Gary Anderson, 1985
Longest field goal
55 yards—Gary Anderson vs. S.D., Nov. 25, 1984
Most interceptions, career
57—Mel Blount
Most interceptions, season
11—Mel Blount, 1975
Most sacks, career
73.5—L.C. Greenwood
Most sacks, season
15—Mike Merriweather, 1984

SERIES RECORDS

Pittsburgh vs.: Arizona 29-21-3; Atlanta 9-1; Buffalo 7-7; Chicago 4-19-1; Cincinnati 28-21; Cleveland 38-52; Dallas 11-13; Denver 5-10-1; Detroit 11-13-1; Green Bay 11-20; Houston 31-18; Indianapolis 12-4; Kansas City 13-5; L.A. Raiders 4-7; L.A. Rams 5-17-2; Miami 6-7; Minnesota 4-7; New England 9-3; New Orleans 6-5; N.Y. Giants 28-44-3; N.Y. Jets 12-1; Philadelphia 26-43-3; San Diego 14-5; San Francisco 7-8; Seattle 5-6; Tampa Bay 4-0; Washington 24-39-4.

   NOTE: Includes records as Pittsburgh Pirates from 1933 through 1940; also includes records when team combined with Philadelphia squad and was known as Phil-Pitt in 1943 and when team combined with Chicago Cardinals squad and was known as Card-Pitt in 1944.

RETIRED UNIFORM NUMBERS

No.   Player
   None

SAN DIEGO CHARGERS

YEAR-BY-YEAR RECORDS

		REGULAR SEASON						PLAYOFFS			
Year	W	L	T	Pct.	PF	PA	Finish	W	L	Highest round	Coach
1960*†	10	4	0	.714	373	336	1st/Western Div.	0	1	AFL championship game	Sid Gillman
1961*	12	2	0	.857	396	219	1st/Western Div.	0	1	AFL championship game	Sid Gillman
1962*	4	10	0	.286	314	392	3rd/Western Div.	—	—		Sid Gillman

Year	W	L	T	Pct.	PF	PA	Finish	W	L	Highest round	Coach
1963*	11	3	0	.786	399	256	1st/Western Div.	1	0	AFL champ	Sid Gillman
1964*	8	5	1	.615	341	300	1st/Western Div.	0	1	AFL championship game	Sid Gillman
1965*	9	2	3	.818	340	227	1st/Western Div.	0	1	AFL championship game	Sid Gillman
1966*	7	6	1	.538	335	284	3rd/Western Div.	—	—		Sid Gillman
1967*	8	5	1	.615	360	352	3rd/Western Div.	—	—		Sid Gillman
1968*	9	5	0	.643	382	310	3rd/Western Div.	—	—		Sid Gillman
1969*	8	6	0	.571	288	276	3rd/Western Div.	—	—		Sid Gillman, Charlie Waller
1970	5	6	3	.455	282	278	3rd/AFC Western Div.	—	—		Charlie Waller
1971	6	8	0	.429	311	341	3rd/AFC Western Div.	—	—		Harland Svare
1972	4	9	1	.308	264	344	4th/AFC Western Div.	—	—		Harland Svare
1973	2	11	1	.179	188	386	4th/AFC Western Div.	—	—		Harland Svare, Ron Waller
1974	5	9	0	.357	212	285	T3rd/AFC Western Div.	—	—		Tommy Prothro
1975	2	12	0	.143	189	345	4th/AFC Western Div.	—	—		Tommy Prothro
1976	6	8	0	.429	248	285	3rd/AFC Western Div.	—	—		Tommy Prothro
1977	7	7	0	.500	222	205	3rd/AFC Western Div.	—	—		Tommy Prothro
1978	9	7	0	.563	355	309	T2nd/AFC Western Div.	—	—		Tommy Prothro, Don Coryell
1979	12	4	0	.750	411	246	1st/AFC Western Div.	0	1	AFC div. playoff game	Don Coryell
1980	11	5	0	.688	418	327	1st/AFC Western Div.	1	1	AFC championship game	Don Coryell
1981	10	6	0	.625	478	390	1st/AFC Western Div.	1	1	AFC championship game	Don Coryell
1982	6	3	0	.667	288	221	T4th/AFC	1	1	AFC second-round pl. game	Don Coryell
1983	6	10	0	.375	358	462	T4th/AFC Western Div.	—	—		Don Coryell
1984	7	9	0	.438	394	413	5th/AFC Western Div.	—	—		Don Coryell
1985	8	8	0	.500	467	435	T3rd/AFC Western Div.	—	—		Don Coryell
1986	4	12	0	.250	335	396	5th/AFC Western Div.	—	—		Don Coryell, Al Saunders
1987	8	7	0	.533	253	317	3rd/AFC Western Div.	—	—		Al Saunders
1988	6	10	0	.375	231	332	4th/AFC Western Div.	—	—		Al Saunders
1989	6	10	0	.375	266	290	5th/AFC Western Div.	—	—		Dan Henning
1990	6	10	0	.375	315	281	4th/AFC Western Div.	—	—		Dan Henning
1991	4	12	0	.250	274	342	5th/AFC Western Div.	—	—		Dan Henning
1992	11	5	0	.688	335	241	1st/AFC Western Div.	1	1	AFC div. playoff game	Bobby Ross
1993	8	8	0	.500	322	290	4th/AFC Western Div.	—	—		Bobby Ross
1994	11	5	0	.688	381	306	1st/AFC Western Div.	2	1	Super Bowl	Bobby Ross

*American Football League.
†Los Angeles Chargers.

FIRST-ROUND DRAFT PICKS

1960—Monty Stickles, E, Notre Dame
1961—Earl Faison, E, Indiana
1962—Bob Ferguson, RB, Ohio State
1963—Walt Sweeney, E, Syracuse
1964—Ted Davis, E, Georgia Tech
1965—Steve DeLong, DE, Tennessee
1966—Don Davis, T, Los Angeles State
1967—Ron Billingsley, DT, Wyoming
1968—Russ Washington, T, Missouri
     Jim Hill, DB, Texas A&I
1969—Marty Domres, QB, Columbia
     Bob Babich, LB, Miami of Ohio
1970—Walker Gillette, WR, Richmond
1971—Leon Burns, RB, Long Beach State
1972—None
1973—Johnny Rodgers, WR, Nebraska
1974—Bo Matthews, RB, Colorado
     Don Goode, LB, Kansas
1975—Gary Johnson, DT, Grambling State
     Mike Williams, DB, Louisiana State
1976—Joe Washington, RB, Oklahoma
1977—Bob Rush, C, Memphis State

1978—John Jefferson, WR, Arizona State
1979—Kellen Winslow, TE, Missouri
1980—None
1981—James Brooks, RB, Auburn
1982—None
1983—Billy Ray Smith, LB, Arkansas
     Gary Anderson, WR, Arkansas
     Gill Byrd, DB, San Jose State
1984—Mossy Cade, DB, Texas
1985—Jim Lachey, G, Ohio State
1986—Leslie O'Neal, DE, Oklahoma State
     Jim FitzPatrick, T, Southern California
1987—Rod Bernstine, TE, Texas A&M
1988—Anthony Miller, WR, Tennessee
1989—Burt Grossman, DE, Pittsburgh
1990—Junior Seau, LB, Southern California
1991—Stanley Richard, CB, Texas
1992—Chris Mims, DT, Tennessee
1993—Darrien Gordon, DB, Stanford
1994—None
1995—None

FRANCHISE RECORDS

Most rushing yards, career
4,963—Paul Lowe

Most rushing yards, season
1,350—Natrone Means, 1994

Most rushing yards, game
217—Gary Anderson vs. K.C., Dec. 18,
    1988

Most rushing touchdowns, season
19—Chuck Muncie, 1981

Most passing attempts, season
609—Dan Fouts, 1981

Most passing attempts, game
58—Mark Herrmann at K.C., Dec. 22, 1985

Most passes completed, season
360—Dan Fouts, 1981

Most passes completed, game
37—Dan Fouts vs. Mia., Nov. 18, 1984
    (OT)

    Mark Herrmann at K.C., Dec. 22,
    1985

Most passing yards, career
43,040—Dan Fouts

Most passing yards, season
4,802—Dan Fouts, 1981

Most passing yards, game
444—Dan Fouts vs. NYG, Oct. 19, 1980
    Dan Fouts at S.F., Dec. 11, 1982

Most touchdown passes, season
33—Dan Fouts, 1981

Most pass receptions, career
586—Charlie Joiner

Most pass receptions, season
89—Kellen Winslow, 1980

Most pass receptions, game
15—Kellen Winslow at G.B., Oct. 7, 1984

Most receiving yards, career
9,585—Lance Alworth

Most receiving yards, season
1,602—Lance Alworth, 1965

Most receiving yards, game
260—Wes Chandler vs. Cin., Dec. 20, 1982

Most receiving touchdowns, season
14—Lance Alworth, 1965

Most touchdowns, career
83—Lance Alworth

Most field goals, season
34—John Carney, 1994

Longest field goal
54 yards—John Carney vs. Sea., Nov. 10, 1991

Most interceptions, career
42—Gill Byrd

Most interceptions, season
9—Charlie McNeil, 1961

Most sacks, career
93—Leslie O'Neal

Most sacks, season
17.5—Gary Johnson, 1980

SERIES RECORDS

San Diego vs.: Arizona 5-1; Atlanta 1-4; Buffalo 16-7-2; Chicago 4-2; Cincinnati 13-8; Cleveland 8-6-1; Dallas 1-4; Denver 33-36-1; Detroit 2-3; Green Bay 1-4; Houston 18-13-1; Indianapolis 8-6; Kansas City 33-35-1; L.A. Raiders 26-42-2; L.A. Rams 3-3; Miami 10-5; Minnesota 4-3; New England 11-14-2; New Orleans 5-1; N.Y. Giants 2-4; N.Y. Jets 17-9-1; Philadelphia 3-2; Pittsburgh 5-14; San Francisco 3-4; Seattle 17-15; Tampa Bay 6-0; Washington 0-5.
NOTE: Includes records as Los Angeles Chargers in 1960.

RETIRED UNIFORM NUMBERS

No.	Player
14	Dan Fouts

SAN FRANCISCO 49ERS

YEAR-BY-YEAR RECORDS

		REGULAR SEASON						PLAYOFFS			
Year	W	L	T	Pct.	PF	PA	Finish	W	L	Highest round	Coach
1946*	9	5	0	.643	307	189	2nd/Western Div.	—	—		Buck Shaw
1947*	8	4	2	.667	327	264	2nd/Western Div.	—	—		Buck Shaw
1948*	12	2	0	.857	495	248	2nd/Western Div.	—	—		Buck Shaw
1949*	9	3	0	.750	416	227	2nd	—	—		Buck Shaw
1950	3	9	0	.250	213	300	T5th/National Conf.	—	—		Buck Shaw
1951	7	4	1	.636	255	205	T2nd/National Conf.	—	—		Buck Shaw
1952	7	5	0	.583	285	221	3rd/National Conf.	—	—		Buck Shaw
1953	9	3	0	.750	372	237	2nd/Western Conf.	—	—		Buck Shaw
1954	7	4	1	.636	313	251	3rd/Western Conf.	—	—		Buck Shaw
1955	4	8	0	.333	216	298	5th/Western Conf.	—	—		Red Strader
1956	5	6	1	.455	233	284	3rd/Western Conf.	—	—		Frankie Albert
1957	8	4	0	.667	260	264	2nd/Western Conf.	0	1	W. Conf. champ. game	Frankie Albert
1958	6	6	0	.500	257	324	4th/Western Conf.	—	—		Frankie Albert
1959	7	5	0	.583	255	237	T3rd/Western Conf.	—	—		Red Hickey
1960	7	5	0	.583	208	205	T2nd/Western Conf.	—	—		Red Hickey
1961	7	6	1	.538	346	272	5th/Western Conf.	—	—		Red Hickey
1962	6	8	0	.429	282	331	5th/Western Conf.	—	—		Red Hickey
1963	2	12	0	.143	198	391	7th/Western Conf.	—	—		R. Hickey, J. Christiansen
1964	4	10	0	.286	236	330	7th/Western Conf.	—	—		Jack Christiansen
1965	7	6	1	.538	421	402	4th/Western Conf.	—	—		Jack Christiansen
1966	6	6	2	.500	320	325	4th/Western Conf.	—	—		Jack Christiansen
1967	7	7	0	.500	273	337	3rd/Coastal Div.	—	—		Jack Christiansen
1968	7	6	1	.538	303	310	3rd/Coastal Div.	—	—		Dick Nolan
1969	4	8	2	.333	277	319	4th/Coastal Div.	—	—		Dick Nolan
1970	10	3	1	.769	352	267	1st/NFC Western Div.	1	1	NFC championship game	Dick Nolan
1971	9	5	0	.643	300	216	1st/NFC Western Div.	1	1	NFC championship game	Dick Nolan
1972	8	5	1	.607	353	249	1st/NFC Western Div.	0	1	NFC div. playoff game	Dick Nolan
1973	5	9	0	.357	262	319	T3rd/NFC Western Div.	—	—		Dick Nolan
1974	6	8	0	.429	226	236	2nd/NFC Western Div.	—	—		Dick Nolan
1975	5	9	0	.357	255	286	2nd/NFC Western Div.	—	—		Dick Nolan
1976	8	6	0	.571	270	190	2nd/NFC Western Div.	—	—		Monte Clark
1977	5	9	0	.357	220	260	3rd/NFC Western Div.	—	—		Ken Meyer
1978	2	14	0	.125	219	350	4th/NFC Western Div.	—	—		Pete McCulley, Fred O'Connor
1979	2	14	0	.125	308	416	4th/NFC Western Div.	—	—		Bill Walsh
1980	6	10	0	.375	320	415	3rd/NFC Western Div.	—	—		Bill Walsh
1981	13	3	0	.813	357	250	1st/NFC Western Div.	3	0	Super Bowl champ	Bill Walsh
1982	3	6	0	.333	209	206	T11th/NFC	—	—		Bill Walsh
1983	10	6	0	.625	432	293	1st/NFC Western Div.	1	1	NFC championship game	Bill Walsh
1984	15	1	0	.938	475	227	1st/NFC Western Div.	3	0	Super Bowl champ	Bill Walsh
1985	10	6	0	.625	411	263	2nd/NFC Western Div.	0	1	NFC wild-card game	Bill Walsh
1986	10	5	1	.656	374	247	1st/NFC Western Div.	0	1	NFC div. playoff game	Bill Walsh
1987	13	2	0	.867	459	253	1st/NFC Western Div.	0	1	NFC div. playoff game	Bill Walsh
1988	10	6	0	.625	369	294	1st/NFC Western Div.	3	0	Super Bowl champ	Bill Walsh

Year	W	L	T	Pct.	PF	PA	Finish	W	L	Highest round	Coach
1989	14	2	0	.875	442	253	1st/NFC Western Div.	3	0	Super Bowl champ	George Seifert
1990	14	2	0	.875	353	239	1st/NFC Western Div.	1	1	NFC championship game	George Seifert
1991	10	6	0	.625	393	239	3rd/NFC Western Div.	—	—		George Seifert
1992	14	2	0	.875	431	236	1st/NFC Western Div.	1	1	NFC championship game	George Seifert
1993	10	6	0	.625	473	295	1st/NFC Western Div.	1	1	NFC championship game	George Seifert
1994	13	3	0	.813	505	296	1st/NFC Western Div.	3	0	Super Bowl champ	George Seifert

*All-America Football Conference.

FIRST-ROUND DRAFT PICKS

1950—Leo Nomellini, T, Minnesota
1951—Y.A. Tittle, QB, Louisiana State
1952—Hugh McElhenny, RB, Washington
1953—Harry Babcock, E, Georgia*
      Tom Stolhandske, E, Texas
1954—Bernie Faloney, QB, Maryland
1955—Dick Moegel, HB, Rice
1956—Earl Morrall QB, Michigan State
1957—John Brodie, QB, Stanford
1958—Jim Pace, RB, Michigan
      Charles Krueger, T, Texas A&M
1959—Dave Baker, RB, Oklahoma
      Dan James, C, Ohio State
1960—Monty Stickles, E, Notre Dame
1961—Jim Johnson, RB, UCLA
      Bernie Casey, RB, Bowling Green State
      Billy Kilmer, QB, UCLA
1962—Lance Alworth, RB, Arkansas
1963—Kermit Alexander, RB, UCLA
1964—Dave Parks, E, Texas Tech*
1965—Ken Willard, RB, North Carolina
      George Donnelly, DB, Illinois
1966—Stan Hindman, DE, Mississippi
1967—Steve Spurrier, QB, Florida
      Cas Banaszek, LB, Northwestern
1968—Forrest Blue, C, Auburn
1969—Ted Kwalick, TE, Penn State
      Gene Washington, WR, Stanford
1970—Cedrick Hardman, DE, North Texas State
      Bruce Taylor, DB, Boston University
1971—Tim Anderson, DB, Ohio State
1972—Terry Beasley, WR, Auburn

1973—Mike Holmes, DB, Tex. Southern
1974—Wilbur Jackson, RB, Alabama
      Bill Sandifer, DT, UCLA
1975—Jimmy Webb, DT, Mississippi State
1976—None
1977—None
1978—Ken McAfee, TE, Notre Dame
      Dan Bunz, LB, Long Beach State
1979—None
1980—Earl Cooper, RB, Rice
      Jim Stuckey, DE, Clemson
1981—Ronnie Lott, DB, Southern California
1982—None
1983—None
1984—Todd Shell, LB, Brigham Young
1985—Jerry Rice, WR, Mississippi Valley State
1986—None
1987—Harris Barton, T, North Carolina
      Terrence Flager, RB, Clemson
1988—None
1989—Keith DeLong, LB, Tennessee
1990—Dexter Carter, RB, Florida State
1991—Ted Washington, DL, Louisville
1992—Dana Hall, DB, Washington
1993—Dana Stubblefield, DT, Kansas
      Todd Kelly, DE, Tennessee
1994—Bryant Young, DT, Notre Dame
      William Floyd, RB, Florida State
1995—J.J. Stokes, WR, UCLA
   *First player chosen in draft.

FRANCHISE RECORDS

Most rushing yards, career
7,344—Joe Perry
Most rushing yards, season
1,502—Roger Craig, 1988
Most rushing yards, game
194—Delvin Williams at St.L., Dec. 31, 1976
Most rushing touchdowns, season
10—Joe Perry, 1953
     J.D. Smith, 1959
     Billy Kilmer, 1961
     Ricky Watters, 1993
Most passing attempts, season
578—Steve DeBerg, 1979
Most passing attempts, game
60—Joe Montana at Was., Nov. 17, 1986
Most passes completed, season
347—Steve DeBerg, 1979
Most passes completed, game
37—Joe Montana at Atl., Nov. 6, 1985
Most passing yards, career
35,142—Joe Montana

Most passing yards, season
4,023—Steve Young, 1993
Most passing yards, game
476—Joe Montana at Atl., Oct. 14, 1990
Most touchdown passes, season
35—Steve Young, 1994
Most pass receptions, career
820—Jerry Rice
Most pass receptions, season
112—Jerry Rice, 1994
Most pass receptions, game
16—Jerry Rice at L.A. Rams, Nov. 20, 1994
Most receiving yards, career
13,275—Jerry Rice
Most receiving yards, season
1,570—Jerry Rice, 1986
Most receiving yards, game
286—John Taylor at L.A. Rams, Dec. 11, 1989

Most receiving touchdowns, season
22—Jerry Rice, 1987
Most touchdowns, career
139—Jerry Rice
Most field goals, season
29—Mike Cofer, 1989
Longest field goal
56 yards—Mike Cofer at Atl., Oct. 14, 1990
Most interceptions, career
51—Ronnie Lott
Most interceptions, season
10—Dave Baker, 1960
     Ronnie Lott, 1986
Most sacks, career
111.5—Cedrick Hardman
Most sacks, season
18—Cedrick Hardman

SERIES RECORDS

San Francisco vs.: Arizona 10-9; Atlanta 34-21-1; Buffalo 2-3; Chicago 25-25-1; Cincinnati 6-1; Cleveland 6-9; Dallas 10-6-1; Denver 3-4; Detroit 27-25-1; Green Bay 25-21-1; Houston 5-3; Indianapolis 16-21; Kansas City 4-2; L.A. Raiders 3-5; L.A. Rams 39-47-2; Miami 2-4; Minnesota 15-16-1; New England 6-1; New Orleans 35-14-2; N.Y. Giants 10-11; N.Y. Jets 6-1; Philadelphia 13-6-1; Pittsburgh 8-7; San Diego 4-3; Seattle 4-1; Tampa Bay 12-1; Washington 10-6-1.

NOTE: Includes records only from 1950 to present.

RETIRED UNIFORM NUMBERS

No.	Player
12	John Brodie
34	Joe Perry
37	Jimmy Johnson
39	Hugh McElhenny
70	Charlie Krueger
73	Leo Nomellini
87	Dwight Clark

SEATTLE SEAHAWKS

YEAR-BY-YEAR RECORDS

	REGULAR SEASON							PLAYOFFS			
Year	W	L	T	Pct.	PF	PA	Finish	W	L	Highest round	Coach
1976	2	12	0	.143	229	429	5th/NFC Western Div.	—	—		Jack Patera
1977	5	9	0	.357	282	373	4th/AFC Western Div.	—	—		Jack Patera
1978	9	7	0	.563	345	358	T2nd/AFC Western Div.	—	—		Jack Patera
1979	9	7	0	.563	378	372	T3rd	—	—		Jack Patera
1980	4	12	0	.250	291	408	5th/AFC Western Div.	—	—		Jack Patera
1981	6	10	0	.375	322	388	5th/AFC Western Div.	—	—		Jack Patera
1982	4	5	0	.444	127	147	T8th/AFC	—	—		J. Patera, Mike McCormack
1983	9	7	0	.562	403	397	T2nd/AFC Western Div.	2	1	AFC championship game	Chuck Knox
1984	12	4	0	.750	418	282	2nd/AFC Western Div.	1	1	AFC div. playoff game	Chuck Knox
1985	8	8	0	.500	349	303	T3rd/AFC Western Div.	—	—		Chuck Knox
1986	10	6	0	.625	366	293	T2nd/AFC Western Div.	—	—		Chuck Knox
1987	9	6	0	.600	371	314	2nd/AFC Western Div.	0	1	AFC wild-card game	Chuck Knox
1988	9	7	0	.563	339	329	1st/AFC Western Div.	0	1	AFC div. playoff game	Chuck Knox
1989	7	9	0	.438	241	327	4th/AFC Western Div.	—	—		Chuck Knox
1990	9	7	0	.563	306	286	3rd/AFC Western Div.	—	—		Chuck Knox
1991	7	9	0	.438	276	261	4th/AFC Western Div.	—	—		Chuck Knox
1992	2	14	0	.125	140	312	5th/AFC Western Div.	—	—		Tom Flores
1993	6	10	0	.375	280	314	5th/AFC Western Div.	—	—		Tom Flores
1994	6	10	0	.375	287	323	5th/AFC Western Div.	—	—		Tom Flores

FIRST-ROUND DRAFT PICKS

1976—Steve Niehaus, DT, Notre Dame
1977—Steve August, G, Tulsa
1978—Keith Simpson, DB, Memphis State
1979—Manu Tuiasosopo, DT, UCLA
1980—Jacob Green, DE, Texas A&M
1981—Kenny Easley, DB, UCLA
1982—Jeff Bryant, DE, Clemson
1983—Curt Warner, RB, Penn State
1984—Terry Taylor, DB, Southern Illinois
1985—None

1986—John L. Williams, RB, Florida
1987—Tony Woods, LB, Pittsburgh
1988—None
1989—Andy Heck, T, Notre Dame
1990—Cortez Kennedy, DT, Miami (Fla.)
1991—Dan McGwire, QB, San Diego State
1992—Ray Roberts, T, Virginia
1993—Rick Mirer, QB, Notre Dame
1994—Sam Adams, DE, Texas A&M
1995—Joey Galloway, WR, Ohio State

FRANCHISE RECORDS

Most rushing yards, career
6,705—Curt Warner

Most rushing yards, season
1,545—Chris Warren, 1994

Most rushing yards, game
207—Curt Warner vs. K.C., Nov. 27, 1983 (OT)
192—Curt Warner vs. Den., Dec. 20, 1986

Most rushing touchdowns, season
14—David Sims, 1978
Derrick Fenner, 1990

Most passing attempts, season
532—Dave Krieg, 1985

Most passing attempts, game
51—Dave Krieg vs. Atl., Oct. 13, 1985

Most passes completed, season
286—Dave Krieg, 1989

Most passes completed, game
33—Dave Krieg vs. Atl., Oct. 13, 1985

Most passing yards, career
26,132—Dave Krieg

Most passing yards, season
3,671—Dave Krieg, 1984

Most passing yards, game
418—Dave Krieg vs. Den., Nov. 20, 1983

Most touchdown passes, season
32—Dave Krieg, 1984

Most pass receptions, career
819—Steve Largent

Most pass receptions, season
81—Brian Blades, 1994

Most pass receptions, game
15—Steve Largent vs. Det., Oct. 18, 1987

Most receiving yards, career
13,089—Steve Largent

Most receiving yards, season
1,287—Steve Largent, 1985

Most receiving yards, game
261—Steve Largent vs. Det., Oct. 18, 1987

Most receiving touchdowns, season
13—Daryl Turner, 1985

Most touchdowns, career
101—Steve Largent

Most field goals, season
25—John Kasay, 1991

Longest field goal
55 yards—John Kasay vs. K.C., Jan. 2, 1994

Most interceptions, career
50—Dave Brown
Most interceptions, season
10—John Harris, 1981

Kenny Easley, 1984
Most sacks, career
116.0—Jacob Green

Most sacks, season
16.0—Jacob Green, 1983

SERIES RECORDS

Seattle vs.: Arizona 0-4; Atlanta 4-1; Buffalo 3-1; Chicago 4-2; Cincinnati 6-7; Cleveland 9-4; Dallas 1-4; Denver 13-22; Detroit 4-2; Green Bay 3-3; Houston 4-4; Indianapolis 1-4; Kansas City 12-20; L.A. Raiders 15-19; L.A. Rams 1-4; Miami 1-4; Minnesota 3-2; New England 7-6; New Orleans 2-3; N.Y. Giants 2-5; N.Y. Jets 8-3; Philadelphia 1-4; Pittsburgh 6-5; San Diego 15-17; San Francisco 1-4; Tampa Bay 3-0; Washington 2-5.

RETIRED UNIFORM NUMBERS

No.   Player
None

TAMPA BAY BUCCANEERS

YEAR-BY-YEAR RECORDS

							REGULAR SEASON			PLAYOFFS	
Year	W	L	T	Pct.	PF	PA	Finish	W	L	Highest round	Coach
1976	0	14	0	.000	125	412	5th/AFC Western Div.	—	—		John McKay
1977	2	12	0	.143	103	223	5th/NFC Central Div.	—	—		John McKay
1978	5	11	0	.313	241	259	5th/NFC Central Div.	—	—		John McKay
1979	10	6	0	.625	273	237	1st/NFC Central Div.	1	1	NFC championship game	John McKay
1980	5	10	1	.344	271	341	T4th/NFC Central Div.	—	—		John McKay
1981	9	7	0	.563	315	268	1st/NFC Central Div.	0	1	NFC div. playoff game	John McKay
1982	5	4	0	.556	158	178	T4th/NFC	0	1	NFC first-round pl. game	John McKay
1983	2	14	0	.125	241	380	5th/NFC Central Div.	—	—		John McKay
1984	6	10	0	.375	335	380	3rd/NFC Central Div.	—	—		John McKay
1985	2	14	0	.125	294	448	5th/NFC Central Div.	—	—		Leeman Bennett
1986	2	14	0	.125	239	473	5th/NFC Central Div.	—	—		Leeman Bennett
1987	4	11	0	.267	286	360	T4th/NFC Central Div.	—	—		Ray Perkins
1988	5	11	0	.313	261	350	3rd/NFC Central Div.	—	—		Ray Perkins
1989	5	11	0	.313	320	419	5th/NFC Central Div.	—	—		Ray Perkins
1990	6	10	0	.375	264	367	T2nd/NFC Central Div.	—	—		R. Perkins, R. Williamson
1991	3	13	0	.188	199	365	5th/NFC Central Div.	—	—		Richard Williamson
1992	5	11	0	.313	267	365	T3rd/NFC Central Div.	—	—		Sam Wyche
1993	5	11	0	.313	237	376	5th/NFC Central Div.	—	—		Sam Wyche
1994	6	10	0	.375	251	351	5th/NFC Central Div.	—	—		Sam Wyche

FIRST-ROUND DRAFT PICKS

1976—Lee Roy Selmon, DE, Oklahoma*
1977—Ricky Bell, RB, Southern California*
1978—Doug Williams, QB, Grambling State
1979—None
1980—Ray Snell, T, Wisconsin
1981—Hugh Green, LB, Pittsburgh
1982—Sean Farrell, G, Penn State
1983—None
1984—None
1985—Ron Holmes, DE, Washington
1986—Bo Jackson, RB, Auburn*
         Rod Jones, DB, Southern Methodist

1987—Vinny Testaverde, QB, Miami (Fla.)*
1988—Paul Gruber, T, Wisconsin
1989—Broderick Thomas, LB, Nebraska
1990—Keith McCants, LB, Alabama
1991—Charles McRae, T, Tennessee
1992—None
1993—Eric Curry, DE, Alabama
1994—Trent Dilfer, QB, Fresno State
1995—Warren Sapp, DT, Miami (Fla.)
         Derrick Brooks, LB, Florida State
    *First player chosen in draft.

FRANCHISE RECORDS

Most rushing yards, career
5,957—James Wilder
Most rushing yards, season
1,544—James Wilder, 1984
Most rushing yards, game
219—James Wilder at Min., Nov. 6, 1983
Most rushing touchdowns, season
13—James Wilder, 1984
Most passing attempts, season
521—Doug Williams, 1980
Most passing attempts, game
56—Doug Williams vs. Cle., Sept. 28, 1980

Most passes completed, season
308—Steve DeBerg, 1984
Most passes completed, game
31—Vinny Testaverde at Hou., Dec. 10, 1989
Most passing yards, career
14,820—Vinny Testaverde
Most passing yards, season
3,563—Doug Williams, 1981
Most passing yards, game
486—Doug Williams at Min., Nov. 16, 1980

Most touchdown passes, season
20—Doug Williams, 1980
         Vinny Testaverde, 1989
Most pass receptions, career
430—James Wilder
Most pass receptions, season
86—Mark Carrier, 1989
Most pass receptions, game
13—James Wilder vs. Min., Sept. 15, 1985
Most receiving yards, career
5,018—Mark Carrier

Most receiving yards, season
1,422—Mark Carrier, 1989

Most receiving yards, game
212—Mark Carrier at N.O., Dec. 6, 1987

Most receiving touchdowns, season
9—Kevin House, 1981
  Bruce Hill, 1988
  Mark Carrier, 1989

Most touchdowns, career
46—James Wilder

Most field goals, season
23—Steve Christie, 1990
  Michael Husted, 1994

Longest field goal
57 yards—Michael Husted at L.A.
  Raiders, Dec. 19, 1993

Most interceptions, career
29—Cedric Brown

Most interceptions, season
9—Cedric Brown, 1981

Most sacks, career
78.5—Lee Roy Selmon

Most sacks, season
13—Lee Roy Selmon, 1977

SERIES RECORDS

Tampa Bay vs.: Arizona 6-6; Atlanta 6-7; Buffalo 4-2; Chicago 8-26; Cincinnati 1-3; Cleveland 0-4; Dallas 0-6; Denver 1-2; Detroit 17-17; Green Bay 12-19-1; Houston 1-3; Indianapolis 3-5; Kansas City 2-5; L.A. Raiders 0-3; L.A. Rams 3-8; Miami 1-4; Minnesota 10-24; New England 0-3; New Orleans 4-12; N.Y. Giants 3-8; N.Y. Jets 1-5; Philadelphia 1-3; Pittsburgh 0-4; San Diego 0-6; San Francisco 1-12; Seattle 0-3; Washington 2-4.

RETIRED UNIFORM NUMBERS

No. Player
63   Lee Roy Selmon

WASHINGTON REDSKINS

YEAR-BY-YEAR RECORDS

			REGULAR SEASON					PLAYOFFS			
Year	W	L	T	Pct.	PF	PA	Finish	W	L	Highest round	Coach
1932*	4	4	2	.500	55	79	4th	—	—		Lud Wray
1933†	5	5	2	.500	103	97	3rd/Eastern Div.	—	—		Lone Star Dietz
1934†	6	6	0	.500	107	94	2nd/Eastern Div.	—	—		Lone Star Dietz
1935†	2	8	1	.200	65	123	4th/Eastern Div.	—	—		Eddie Casey
1936†	7	5	0	.583	149	110	1st/Eastern Div.	0	1	NFL championship game	Ray Flaherty
1937	8	3	0	.727	195	120	1st/Eastern Div.	1	0	NFL champ	Ray Flaherty
1938	6	3	2	.667	148	154	2nd/Eastern Div.	—	—		Ray Flaherty
1939	8	2	1	.800	242	94	2nd/Eastern Div.	—	—		Ray Flaherty
1940	9	2	0	.818	245	142	1st/Eastern Div.	0	1	NFL championship game	Ray Flaherty
1941	6	5	0	.545	176	174	3rd/Eastern Div.	—	—		Ray Flaherty
1942	10	1	0	.909	227	102	1st/Eastern Div.	1	0	NFL champ	Ray Flaherty
1943	6	3	1	.667	229	137	1st/Eastern Div.	1	1	NFL championship game	Dutch Bergman
1944	6	3	1	.667	169	180	3rd/Eastern Div.	—	—		Dudley DeGroot
1945	8	2	0	.800	209	121	1st/Eastern Div.	0	1	NFL championship game	Dudley DeGroot
1946	5	5	1	.500	171	191	T3rd/Eastern Div.	—	—		Turk Edwards
1947	4	8	0	.333	295	367	4th/Eastern Div.	—	—		Turk Edwards
1948	7	5	0	.583	291	287	2nd/Eastern Div.	—	—		Turk Edwards
1949	4	7	1	.364	268	339	4th/Eastern Div.	—	—		John Whelchel, Herman Ball
1950	3	9	0	.250	232	326	6th/American Conf.	—	—		Herman Ball
1951	5	7	0	.417	183	296	3rd/American Conf.	—	—		Herman Ball, Dick Todd
1952	4	8	0	.333	240	287	T5th/American Conf.	—	—		Curly Lambeau
1953	6	5	1	.545	208	215	3rd/Eastern Conf.	—	—		Curly Lambeau
1954	3	9	0	.250	207	432	5th/Eastern Conf.	—	—		Joe Kuharich
1955	8	4	0	.667	246	222	2nd/Eastern Conf.	—	—		Joe Kuharich
1956	6	6	0	.500	183	225	3rd/Eastern Conf.	—	—		Joe Kuharich
1957	5	6	1	.455	251	230	4th/Eastern Conf.	—	—		Joe Kuharich
1958	4	7	1	.364	214	268	4th/Eastern Conf.	—	—		Joe Kuharich
1959	3	9	0	.250	185	350	5th/Eastern Conf.	—	—		Mike Nixon
1960	1	9	2	.100	178	309	6th/Eastern Conf.	—	—		Mike Nixon
1961	1	12	1	.077	174	392	7th/Eastern Conf.	—	—		Bill McPeak
1962	5	7	2	.417	305	376	4th/Eastern Conf.	—	—		Bill McPeak
1963	3	11	0	.214	279	398	6th/Eastern Conf.	—	—		Bill McPeak
1964	6	8	0	.429	307	305	T3rd/Eastern Conf.	—	—		Bill McPeak
1965	6	8	0	.429	257	301	4th/Eastern Conf.	—	—		Bill McPeak
1966	7	7	0	.500	351	355	5th/Eastern Conf.	—	—		Otto Graham
1967	5	6	3	.455	347	353	3rd/Capitol Div.	—	—		Otto Graham
1968	5	9	0	.357	249	358	3rd/Capitol Div.	—	—		Otto Graham
1969	7	5	2	.583	307	319	2nd/Capitol Div.	—	—		Vince Lombardi
1970	6	8	0	.429	297	314	4th/NFC Eastern Div.	—	—		Bill Austin
1971	9	4	1	.692	276	190	2nd/NFC Eastern Div.	0	1	NFC div. playoff game	George Allen
1972	11	3	0	.786	336	218	1st/NFC Eastern Div.	2	1	Super Bowl	George Allen
1973	10	4	0	.714	325	198	2nd/NFC Eastern Div.	0	1	NFC div. playoff game	George Allen
1974	10	4	0	.714	320	196	2nd/NFC Eastern Div.	0	1	NFC div. playoff game	George Allen
1975	8	6	0	.571	325	276	3rd/NFC Eastern Div.	—	—		George Allen
1976	10	4	0	.714	291	217	2nd/NFC Eastern Div.	0	1	NFC div. playoff game	George Allen
1977	9	5	0	.643	196	189	2nd/NFC Eastern Div.	—	—		George Allen
1978	8	8	0	.500	273	283	3rd/NFC Eastern Div.	—	—		Jack Pardee
1979	10	6	0	.625	348	295	3rd/NFC Eastern Div.	—	—		Jack Pardee
1980	6	10	0	.375	261	293	3rd/NFC Eastern Div.	—	—		Jack Pardee

Year	W	L	T	Pct.	PF	PA	Finish	W	L	Highest round	Coach
1981	8	8	0	.500	347	349	4th/NFC Eastern Div.	—	—		Joe Gibbs
1982	8	1	0	.889	190	128	1st/NFC	4	0	Super Bowl champ	Joe Gibbs
1983	14	2	0	.875	541	332	1st/NFC Eastern Div.	2	1	Super Bowl	Joe Gibbs
1984	11	5	0	.688	426	310	1st/NFC Eastern Div.	0	1	NFC div. playoff game	Joe Gibbs
1985	10	6	0	.625	297	312	3rd/NFC Eastern Div.	—	—		Joe Gibbs
1986	12	4	0	.750	368	296	2nd/NFC Eastern Div.	2	1	NFC championship game	Joe Gibbs
1987	11	4	0	.733	379	285	1st/NFC Eastern Div.	3	0	Super Bowl champ	Joe Gibbs
1988	7	9	0	.438	345	387	T3rd/NFC Eastern Div.	—	—		Joe Gibbs
1989	10	6	0	.625	386	308	3rd/NFC Eastern Div.	—	—		Joe Gibbs
1990	10	6	0	.625	381	301	T2nd/NFC Eastern Div.	1	1	NFC div. playoff game	Joe Gibbs
1991	14	2	0	.875	485	224	1st/NFC Eastern Div.	3	0	Super Bowl champ	Joe Gibbs
1992	9	7	0	.563	300	255	3rd/NFC Eastern Div.	1	1	NFC div. playoff game	Joe Gibbs
1993	4	12	0	.250	230	345	5th/NFC Eastern Div.	—	—		Richie Petitbon
1994	3	13	0	.188	320	412	5th/NFC Eastern Div.	—	—		Norv Turner

*Boston Braves.
†Boston Redskins.

FIRST-ROUND DRAFT PICKS

1936—Riley Smith, QB, Alabama
1937—Sammy Baugh, QB, Texas Christian
1938—Andy Farkas, B, Detroit
1939—I.B. Hale, T, Texas Christian
1940—Ed Boell, B, New York University
1941—Forrest Evashevski, B, Michigan
1942—Orban Sanders, B, Texas
1943—Jack Jenkins, B, Missouri
1944—Mike Micka, B, Colgate
1945—Jim Hardy, B, Southern California
1946—Cal Rossi, B, UCLA
1947—Cal Rossi, B, UCLA
1948—Harry Gilmer, QB, Alabama*
1949—Rob Goode, RB, Texas A&M
1950—George Thomas, RB, Oklahoma
1951—Leon Heath, RB, Oklahoma
1952—Larry Isbell, QB, Baylor
1953—Jack Scarbath, QB, Maryland
1954—Steve Meilinger, TE, Kentucky
1955—Ralph Guglielmi, QB, Notre Dame
1956—Ed Vereb, RB, Maryland
1957—Don Bosseler, RB, Miami (Fla.)
1958—None
1959—Don Allard, QB, Boston College
1960—Richie Lucas, QB, Penn State
1961—Joe Rutgens, T, Illinois
　　　Norm Snead, QB, Wake Forest
1962—Ernie Davis, RB, Syracuse*
　　　Leroy Jackson, RB, Illinois Central
1963—Pat Richter, TE, Wisconsin
1964—Charley Taylor, RB, Arizona State
1965—None

1966—Charlie Gogolak, K, Princeton
1967—Ray McDonald, RB, Idaho
1968—Jim Smith, DB, Oregon
1969—None
1970—None
1971—None
1972—None
1973—None
1974—None
1975—None
1976—None
1977—None
1978—None
1979—None
1980—Art Monk, WR, Syracuse
1981—Mark May, T, Pittsburgh
1982—None
1983—Darrell Green, DB, Texas A&I
1984—None
1985—None
1986—None
1987—None
1988—None
1989—None
1990—None
1991—Bobby Wilson, DT, Michigan State
1992—Desmond Howard, WR, Michigan
1993—Tom Carter, DB, Notre Dame
1994—Heath Shuler, QB, Tennessee
1995—Michael Westbrook, WR, Colorado
　　　*First player chosen in draft.

FRANCHISE RECORDS

Most rushing yards, career
7,472—John Riggins
Most rushing yards, season
1,347—John Riggins, 1983
Most rushing yards, game
221—Gerald Riggs vs. Phi., Sept. 17, 1989
Most rushing touchdowns, season
24—John Riggins, 1983
Most passing attempts, season
541—Jay Schroeder, 1986
Most passing attempts, game
58—Jay Schroeder vs. S.F., Dec. 1, 1985
Most passes completed, season
293—Joe Theismann, 1981

Most passes completed, game
32—Sonny Jurgensen at Cle., Nov. 26, 1967
　　　John Friesz at NYG, Sept. 18, 1994
Most passing yards, career
25,206—Joe Theismann
Most passing yards, season
4,109—Jay Schroeder, 1986
Most passing yards, game
446—Sammy Baugh vs. N.Y. Yanks, Oct. 31, 1948
Most touchdown passes, season
31—Sonny Jurgensen, 1967
Most pass receptions, career
888—Art Monk

Most pass receptions, season
106—Art Monk, 1984
Most pass receptions, game
13—Art Monk vs. NYG, Dec. 15, 1985
　　　Kelvin Bryant vs. NYG, Dec. 7, 1986
　　　Art Monk at Det., Nov. 4, 1990
Most receiving yards, career
13,026—Art Monk
Most receiving yards, season
1,436—Bobby Mitchell, 1963
Most receiving yards, game
255—Anthony Allen vs. St.L., Oct. 4, 1987
Most receiving touchdowns, season
12—Hugh Taylor, 1952
　　　Charley Taylor, 1966

Jerry Smith, 1967
Ricky Sanders, 1988

Most touchdowns, career
90—Charley Taylor

Most field goals, season
33—Mark Moseley, 1983

Longest field goal
57 yards—Steve Cox vs. Sea., Sept. 28, 1986

Most interceptions, career
37—Darrell Green

Most interceptions, season
13—Dan Sandifer, 1948

Most sacks, career
97.5—Dexter Manley

Most sacks, season
18.0—Dexter Manley, 1986

SERIES RECORDS

Washington vs.: Arizona 58-36-1; Atlanta 13-4-1; Buffalo 4-3; Chicago 11-14; Cincinnati 4-2; Cleveland 9-32-1; Dallas 27-39-2; Denver 3-3; Detroit 22-3; Green Bay 11-9; Houston 3-3; Indianapolis 8-16; Kansas City 1-3; L.A. Raiders 2-5; L.A. Rams 14-6-1; Miami 2-5; Minnesota 6-4; New England 4-1; New Orleans 12-5; N.Y. Giants 48-64-2; N.Y. Jets 4-1; Philadelphia 62-50-6; Pittsburgh 39-24-4; San Diego 5-0; San Francisco 6-10-1; Seattle 5-2; Tampa Bay 4-2.

NOTE: Includes records only from 1937 to present.

RETIRED UNIFORM NUMBERS

No. **Player**
33   Sammy Baugh

OTHER BOOKS AVAILABLE
FROM THE SPORTING NEWS LIBRARY